MSWiM'17

Proceedings of the 20th ACM International Conference on

Modeling, Analysis and Simulation of Wireless and Mobile Systems

Sponsored by:

ACM SIGSIM

Advancing Computing as a Science & Profession

The Association for Computing Machinery
2 Penn Plaza, Suite 701
New York, New York 10121-0701

ISBN: 978-1-4503-5162-1 (Digital)

ISBN: 978-1-4503-5721-0 (Print)

Additional copies may be ordered prepaid from:

ACM Order Department
PO Box 30777
New York, NY 10087-0777, USA

Phone: 1-800-342-6626 (USA and Canada)
+1-212-626-0500 (Global)
Fax: +1-212-944-1318
E-mail: acmhelp@acm.org
Hours of Operation: 8:30 am – 4:30 pm ET

Welcome Message from General Chair

Welcome to the 20th ACM International Conference on Modelling, Analysis and Simulation of Wireless and Mobile Systems (MSWiM), held this year in beautiful Miami Beach, FL, USA. Besides being filled with wonderful landscapes, warm beaches, and eye-catching sites, Miami is very diverse; with expressive multi-culturalism, it contains more than 150 ethnicities as well as over 60 different languages spoken. Miami now presents the largest collection of Art Deco Architecture, having more than 800 buildings featuring this type of architecture. The warm climate and geography favors on biodiversity, which enables to have the only Everglades eco-system in the world. Also, Miami has regularly been one of America's preeminent beach resorts since the early 20th century.

MSWiM has established itself over the years as a leading venue where some of the best research in the area of performance evaluation of wireless and mobile systems is presented, and this is no exception. This can be testified once we reach its twentieth edition. Putting together a high-quality conference like MSWiM is an enormous undertaking that requires a great team effort. We thank Richard Yu and Hsiao-Chun Wu for putting together the technical program, from the Call for Papers to the final program selection and its schedule. We also acknowledge the volunteer efforts of TPC members and external reviewers whose expertise and hard work culminated in selecting excellent papers. This year, MSWiM presents strong poster and demonstration sessions, managed by Robson E. De Grande and Tomoaki Ohtsuki, the Poster Sessions Co-Chairs, and Raquel Mini, the Demo Session Chair. Finally, the technical program includes three distinguished keynotes addresses by the following outstanding experts, Prof. Albert Y. Zomaya from University of Sydney, Australia, Prof. Sotiris Nikoletseas from University of Patras and CTI, Greece, and Prof. Stephan Olariu from Old Dominion University, USA.

To recognize excellence in research work in the field of Wireless Communications and Mobile Networking from academia and industry, the ***ACM MSWiM Reginald G. Fessenden Award*** has been established three years ago, and it is granted to a distinguished researcher for the remarkable contributions that he/she has achieved in the area. In 2016, the award was presented to Professor Jean-Pierre Hubaux from Ecole Polytechnique Federale de Lausanne, Switzerland in recognition of "*his outstanding contributions to security and privacy protection in wireless networks*". The winner for this year will be announced at the ACM MSWiM 2017 banquet dinner.

Four symposia and two tutorials will be held this year along with the main conference program, covering several specializations within mobile and wireless systems. The four symposia are: *MobiWAC, PE-WASUN, DIVANET* and *Q2SWinet*. Over the years, these symposia have become successful and quite competitive in their own right.

We also wish to express our gratitude to those who have managed the many practical details of the event. These individuals include Mirela Notare and Salil Kanhere as the Publicity Co-Chairs; and Pan Li and Costas Busch for organizing the tutorials in the Conference. We also express our appreciation to the MSWiM Steering Committee for their guidance and support, which helped us to bring together an exceptional conference program this year. Last but not least, we wish to thank our main sponsor, ACM SIGSIM.

We are very pleased to welcome you to MSWiM 2017 and fascinating Miami Beach. We are certain that you will find this year's event full of stimulating ideas and discussions.

Antonio Loureiro, *General Chair*

Federal University of Minas Gerais, Brazil

Technical Program Chairs' Welcome

The technical program of the 20th ACM International Conference on Modeling, Analysis and Simulation of Wireless and Mobile Systems (MSWiM), held in Miami Beach, USA in 2017 continues to build upon the high standards set by previous editions of the conference.

In 2017, the call for papers attracted 142 registered papers in all areas of mobile and wireless systems. The submitted papers came from 36 countries. Members of the Technical Program Committee are affiliated to universities and industry in 15 countries spread over five continents, reflecting the truly international profile of MSWiM. The five most commonly listed topics for submissions to MSWiM'17 were:

- Performance evaluation and modeling
- Wireless network algorithms and protocols
- Wireless mesh networks, mobile ad hoc networks, Vehicular networks
- Algorithms and protocols for energy efficiency and power control
- Analytical models

The submissions included a large number of papers of very high quality making the selection process difficult and competitive. In the end, we selected 29 regular papers, which correspond to an acceptance rate of approximately 20%. An additional 12 short papers were recommended for the program owing to their quality and contribution.

Among the regular papers, the following three papers were shortlisted as candidates for the best paper award:

- "*Experimental Study of Packet Loss in a UWB Sensor Network for Aircraft,*" Naveen Kolar Daniel Neuhold (Alpen Adria Universität, Austria); Jorge F. Schmidt (Alpen-Adria-Universität Klagenfurt, Austria); Jirka Klaue (Airbus Group Innovations, Germany); Dominic A. Schupke (Airbus & Innovation, Germany); Christian Bettstetter (University of Klagenfurt, Austria);

- "*Carrier-Sense Multiple Access with Collision Avoidance and Detection,*" JJ Garcia-Luna-Aceves (University of California at Santa Cruz & Palo Alto Research Center, USA);

- "*Cost-Effective Processing in Fog-Integrated Internet of Things Ecosystems,*" Wei Bao and Wei Li (The University of Sydney, Australia); Flávia Coimbra Delicato and Paulo F. Pires (Federal University of Rio de Janeiro, Brazil); Dong Yuan, Bing Bing Zhou, and Albert Zomaya (University of Sydney, Australia).

The winner among these three papers will be announced at the conference banquet, and will be reported in the proceedings of MSWiM 2017. At this point, we take the opportunity to congratulate the winners of the best paper award for MSWiM 2016:

- "*Theoretical Interference Analysis of Inter-vehicular Communication at Intersection with Power Control,*" Tatsuaki Kimura (NTT Corporation, Japan) and Hiroshi Saito (NTT Corporation, Japan).

Richard Yu
TPC Co-Chairs
Carleton University, Canada

Hsiao-Chun Wu
TPC Co-Chairs
Louisiana State University, USA

Table of Contents

Session: Mobile Cloud/Fog/Edge Computing

Session: Wireless Sensor Networks

Session: 4G/5G Wireless Network

Session: Indoor Localization and Location Privacy

Session: User Mobility and Data Integration

Session: Scheduling and Prediction

Session: Performance Modeling and Measurement

Session: Traffic and Simulation Modeling

20th ACM MSWiM 2017 Conference Organization

General Chair: Antonio Loureiro *(Federal University of Minas Gerais, Brazil)*

Program Co-Chairs: Hsiao-Chun Wu *(Louisiana State University, USA)*
Richard Yu *(Carleton University, Canada)*

Workshop Chair: Paolo Bellavista *(University of Bologna, Italy)*

Poster Co-Chairs: Robson E. De Grande *(Brock University, Canada)*
Tomoaki Ohtsuki *(Keio University of Japan, Japan)*

Demo/Tools Chair: Raquel Mini *(PUC-Minas, Brazil)*

Tutorials Co-Chairs: Thomas Begin *(University Claude Bernard Lyon, France)*
Jalel Ben-Othman *(University Paris 13, France)*

Publicity Co-Chairs: Salil Kanhere *(University of New South Wales, Australia)*
Mirela. A. M. Notare *(Sao Jose Municipal University, Brazil)*

PhD Forum Chair: Bjorn Landfeldt *(Lund University, Sweden)*

Finance Chair: Azzedine Boukerche *(University of Ottawa, Canada)*

Steering Committee: Azzedine Boukerche *(University of Ottawa, Canada)*
Sajal K. Das *(University of Texas at Arlington, USA)*
Albert Zomaya *(University of Sydney, Australia)*
Lorenzo Donatiello *(Università di Bologna, Bologna, Italy)*
Jason Yi-Bing Lin *(National Chiao-Tung University, Taiwan)*
William C.Y.Lee *(AirTouch Inc., USA)*
Simon Taylor *(Brunel University, UK)*
Robson E. De Grande *(Brock University, Canada)*

Program Committee: Antonio A.F. Loureiro *(Federal University of Minas Gerais, Brazil)*
Adam Wolisz *(Technische Universität Berlin, Germany)*
Andrea Passarella *(IIT-CNR, Italy)*
Andreas Willig *(University of Canterbury, New Zealand)*
Angel Cuevas *(Universidad Carlos III de Madri, Spain)*
Azzedine Boukerche *(University of Ottawa, Canada)*
Bjorn Landfeldt *(Lund University)*
Brahim Bensaou *(The Hong Kong University of Science and Technology, Hong Kong)*
Carla-Fabiana Chiasserini *(Politecnico di Torino, Italy)*
Cheng Li *(Memorial University of Newfoundland, Canada)*
David Eckhoff *(University of Erlangen, Germany)*
Dirk Staehle *(Docomo Euro-Labs, Germany)*

Program Committee (Cont.): Ehab Elmallah *(University of Alberta, Canada)*
Enzo Mingozzi *(University of Pisa, Italy)*
Falko Dressler *(University of Innsbruck, Austria)*
Francesco Lo Presti *(Universita' di Roma Tor Vergata, Italy)*
Giovanni Giambene *(University of Siena, Italy)*
Harald Kosch *(University Passau, Germany)*
Holger Karl *(University of Paderborn, Germany)*
Hongyi Wu *(University of Louisiana at Lafayette, USA)*
Hossam Hassanein *(Queen's University, Canada)*
Isabel Wagner *(University of Hull, UK)*
Isabelle Guérin Lassous *(Université Claude Bernard Lyon 1 - LIP, France)*
Jalel Ben-Othman *(University of Paris 13, France)*
James Gross *(Royal Institute of Technology (KTH)*, Sweden)
JJ Garcia-Luna-Aceves *(University of California at Santa Cruz, USA)*
Juan-Carlos Cano *(Universidad Politecnica de Valencia, Spain)*
Klaus Wehrle *(RWTH Aachen University, Germany)*
Lorenzo Donatiello *(Università di Bologna, Italy)*
Luciano Bononi *(University of Bologna, Italy)*
Marco Di Renzo *(Supelec, France)*
Maria G. Martini *(Kingston College, UK)*
Martina Zitterbart *(Karlsruhe Institute of Technology, Germany)*
Matthias Wählisch *(Freie Universität Berlin)*
Mineo Takai *(University of California, Los Angeles, USA)*
Mónica Aguilar Igartua *(Universitat Politècnica de Catalunya, Spain)*
Olga Zlydareva *(Dublin City University, Ireland)*
Raffaele Bruno *(IIT-CNR, Italy)*
Ravi Prakash *(University of Texas at Dallas)*
Renato Lo Cigno *(University of Trento, Italy)*
Roberto Beraldi *(Università di Roma, Italy)*
Robson De Grande *(Brock University, Canada)*
Sotiris Nikoletseas *(University of Patras, Greece)*
Stephan Eidenbenz *(Los Alamos National Laboratory, USA)*
Terence D. Todd *(McMaster University, Canada)*
Thomas Begin (*University Claude Bernard, Lyon 1, France*)
Torsten Braun *(University of Bern, Switzerland)*
Violet Syrotiuk *(Arizona State University, USA)*
Xu Zhu *(University of Liverpool, UK)*
Zhengguo Sheng *(Sussex University, UK)*
Zygmunt Haas *(Cornell University, USA)*

Reviewers:

Aditya Mvs
Alex Vieira
AnAquino
Andrea Bonfante
Andreas Pressas
Andreas Reinhardt
André Riker
Antonio Uribe
Carlo Puliafito
Carlo Vallati
Carlos Figueiredo
Carlos Kamienski
Chaoyang Li
Christian Esteve Rothenberg
Cristian Lumezanu
Daeki Cho
Dimitrios Pliatsios
Eduardo Cerqueira
Eftychia Datsika
Emma Fitzgerald
Eryk Schiller
F. Richard Yu
Felipe Modesto
Frances Santos
Francesco Malandrino
Francesco Restuccia
Giacomo Tanganelli
Guilherme Maia
Guoqi Luo
Haitham Afifi
Haleh Amintoosi
Hosein Soleimani
Hussein Al-Zubaidy
Ioannis Manolopoulos
Ivan Martins
Joao Duarte
Jobish John
João Kleinschmidt
Kai Li
Kelvin Dias
Khalil Ibrahimi
Konstantia Barbatsalou
LeanVillas
Leticcia Lemux
Limeng Pu
Makoto Misumi
Marcio Correia
Masaki Suzuki
Mehdi Tavakoli Garrosi
Michelle Wangham
Nely Lopez
Nicolò Facchi
Nikolaos Giatsoglou
Nikos Dimitriou
Paulo Silva
Philipp Andelfinger
Rodolfo Coutinho
Rodolfo Meneguette
Roger Immich
Rossana Andrade
Sami Akin
Sarang Kahvazadeh
Sergio Correia
Shaoming Hu
Shintaro Mori
Tales Paiva Nogueira
Thomas Begin
Vaibhav Gupta
Vitor Souza
Vu Vu
Xin Zhang
Xiuhua Li
Zehua Guo

Sponsor: SIGSIM

Provisioning and Management of Internet of Things Applications: Open Issues and Insights

Albert Y. Zomaya
University of Sydney
School of Information Technologies
Australia
albert.zomaya@sydney.edu.au

ABSTRACT

Recent technological trends such as Industry 4.0 introduced new challenges that push the limit of current computer and networking architectures. It demands the connection of thousands, if not millions, of sensors and mobile devices coupled with optimized operations to automate various operations inside factories. This led to the new era of Internet of Things (IoTs) where lightweight (possibly mobile) devices are envisaged to send vital information to cloud data centres (mobile and fixed infrastructure) for further processing and decision making [1].

Current cloud computing systems, however, are not able to efficiently digest and process collected information from IoT devices with strict response requests for two main reasons: (1) the round trip delay between IoT devices to the processing engines of cloud could exceed an application's threshold, and (2) network links to cloud resources could be clogged when IoT devices flush data in an uncoordinated fashion. *Fog* and *Edge* Computing are two solutions to address both of the previous problems. Though designed to alleviate the same problem, they have fundamental differences that make adopting one more applicable than the other [2].

This talk will overview the practical concerns of today's IoT implementations through tackling the most important obstacles that hinder their adoption. First, production of applicable network (fixed and mobile) latency models to capture all elements of IoT platforms. Second, building a holistic platform to orchestrate various inter-related layers of IoT platforms, including connectivity, big-data analytics, and workload optimization. Third, proposing viable solutions that can be actually implemented in IoT-based applications. More details will be provided about the above issues during the talk.

MSWiM '17, November 21–25, 2017, Miami, FL, USA.

ACM ISBN 978-1-4503-5162-1/17/11.
DOI: https://doi.org/10.1145/3127540.3134269

CCS Concepts/ACM Classifiers

Mobile information processing systems; Mobile networks; Modeling and simulation; Network mobility

Author Keywords

Edge Computing; Fog Computing; Internet of Things; Resource Management

BIOGRAPHY

Dr. Albert Y. Zomaya is the *Chair Professor of High Performance Computing & Networking* and served as *Australian Research Council Professorial Fellow* (2010-2014) in the School of Information Technologies, Sydney University. He is also the *Director of the Centre for Distributed and High Performance Computing* which was established in late 2009.

Dr. Zomaya published more than 500 scientific papers and articles and is author, co-author or editor of more than 20 books. He served as the Editor in Chief of the *IEEE Transactions on Computers* (2011-2014) and was elected recently as a Founding Editor in Chief for the newly established *IEEE Transactions on Sustainable Computing*. Also, Dr. Zomaya serves as a Co-Founding Editor-in-Chief of *IET Cyber-Physical Systems,* Founding Editor-in-Chief of the *Journal of Scalable Computing and Communications* (Springer), and Associate Editor-in-Chief (Special Issues) of the *Journal of Parallel and Distributed Computing*. He also serves as an associate editor for 22 leading journals, such as, the *ACM Computing Surveys*, *ACM Transactions on Internet Technology*, *IEEE Transactions on Cloud Computing*, and *IEEE Transactions on Computational Social Systems*. Dr. Zomaya is the Founding Editor of several book series, such as, the *Wiley Book Series on Parallel and Distributed Computing*, *Springer Scalable Computing and Communications*, and *IET Book Series on Big Data*.

Dr. Zomaya has delivered more than 180 keynote addresses and invited seminars, and delivered many media briefings and has been actively involved, in a variety of capacities, in the organization of more than 700 conferences. Dr. Zomaya is the recipient of the *IEEE Technical Committee on*

Parallel Processing Outstanding Service Award (2011), the *IEEE Technical Committee on Scalable Computing Medal for Excellence in Scalable Computing* (2011), and the *IEEE Computer Society Technical Achievement Award* (2014). He is a Chartered Engineer, a Fellow of AAAS, IEEE, and IET. Dr. Zomaya's research interests are in the areas of parallel, distributed, and mobile computing, networking, and complex systems.

REFERENCES

1. Y. Nan, W. Li, W. Bao, F.C. Delicato, P.F. Pires, A.Y. Zomaya. Cost-Effective Processing for Delay-Sensitive Applications in Cloud of Things Systems. Proceedings of the 15th IEEE International Symposium on Network Computing and Applications: 162-169, Boston, 2016.
2. S.G. Deng, L. Huang, H. Wu, W. Tan, J. Taheri, A.Y. Zomaya, Z. Wu. Toward Mobile Service Computing: Opportunities and Challenges. *IEEE Cloud Computing*, 3(4):32-41, 2016.

Fundamental Concepts, Problems and Algorithms for Wireless Power Transfer in Adhoc Communication Networks

Sotiris Nikoletseas
University of Patras and CTI
Greece
nikole@cti.gr

ABSTRACT

A Wireless Power Transfer (WPT) system consists of chargers which transmit power wirelessly and receivers which harvest the radio frequency energy from the chargers. WPT has evolved to a very active research subject, as well as a topic of rapid technological progress and emerging practical development and commercial applications. However, a solid foundational and algorithmic framework seems still necessary for WPT to achieve its full potential.

In this respect, the talk aims to discuss different characteristic abstract WPT models (scalar, vector, peer to peer) and present key optimization problems (power maximization, coverage, placement, radiation control). Relevant algorithmic design and analysis methods and performance properties (and their trade-offs) are also provided, as well as interesting WPT notions and concepts (such as super-additive and cancellation phenomena in the received power, notions of electromagnetic radiation control in dense, strong WPT fields and energy-aware distributed network formation in large populations of very weak mobile nodes).

Author Keywords

Wireless Power Transfer; Algorithms; Ad Hoc Networks

BIOGRAPHY

Sotiris Nikoletseas is a Full Professor at the Computer Engineering and Informatics Department of Patras University, Greece and Director of the SensorsLab at the Computer Technology Institute (CTI).

He has been a visiting professor at the Universities of Geneva, Ottawa and Southern California (USC). His research interests include algorithms for sensor networks, IoT systems and testbeds, wireless energy transfer protocols, probabilistic methods and random graphs, and algorithmic engineering. He has edited 3 Books (on probabilistic methods, sensor networks, wireless power) and over 200 publications, while he has delivered several invited talks and tutorials. He has initiated international conferences on sensor networking. He has coordinated several externally funded European Union R&D Projects related to fundamental aspects of modern networks.

MSWiM '17, November 21–25, 2017, Miami, FL, USA.

ACM ISBN 978-1-4503-5162-1/17/11.
DOI: https://doi.org/10.1145/3127540.3134598

Data Collection in Underwater Wireless Sensor Networks: Research Challenges and Potential Approaches

Rodolfo W. L. Coutinho and Azzedine Boukerche
School of Electrical Engineering and Computer Science (EECS), University of Ottawa
800 King Edward Avenue, Ottawa, Ontario, K1N 6N5, Canada
rodolfo.coutinho@uottawa.ca,boukerch@site.uottawa.ca

ABSTRACT

Underwater wireless sensor networks (UWSNs) emerge as an enabling technology for the monitoring of vast areas of aquatic environments. This technology will pave the way for future large-scale applications of ocean monitoring, which will help to change the worryingly current reality where oceans are completely unknown. However, due to the harsh nature of aquatic environments and the underwater wireless communication features, efficient data collection in UWSN is still a daunting task. This tutorial will provide a comprehensive review of the research challenges and potential approaches for efficient data collection in UWSNs. It will highlight the characteristics of UWSNs and of the underwater acoustic channel, which diminish the performance of networking protocols. It will analyze the benefits of geographic and opportunistic routing for reliable data delivery and the potentials of duty-cycling for energy conservation in UWSN. Finally, based on an in-deep literature review, this tutorial will provide useful insights for the further design of networking protocols for data routing in UWSNs.

CCS CONCEPTS

• Networks → Network protocol design; Network layer protocols; Network reliability; Mobile networks;

KEYWORDS

Underwater sensor networks, reliable data collection, routing, energy-efficiency

1 INTRODUCTION

Seventy percent of the Earth's surface is covered by ocean. The ocean plays important roles for all living organisms on the earth. For instance, it absorbed more the 1/4 of CO_2 produced by human activity since 1800, and 90% of heat from global warming. For human beings, the ocean has served as a medium for transportation and as an important source of primary resources. More important facts about the role of the ocean can be find at the Ocean Explorer web page [15] of the National Oceanic and Atmospheric Administration (NOAA).

MSWiM '17, November 21–25, 2017, Miami, FL, USA

ACM ISBN 978-1-4503-5162-1/17/11...$15.00
https://doi.org/10.1145/3127540.3134267

Despite the notably influence of the ocean on Earth's living organisms, it is estimated that 95% of its volume remains unseen by human eyes [16]. The extensive and solid knowledge about the ocean and marine life that lies beneath it is fundamental for the sustainable exploration and protection of this great unknown. The adequate monitoring of aquatic environments is essential for the discovery of natural resources and understanding of the marine ecosystems. In addition, it is needed the monitoring of human activities in the ocean to avoid catastrophes resembling the oil spill occurred on April 20, 2010, in the Gulf of Mexico, United States [17].

Unfavorably, the current underwater monitoring technologies are costly and might not be enough scalable for the monitoring of vast areas in the ocean. Moreover, some underwater monitoring instruments (e.g., RAFOS [19]) are incapable of communicate with each other when in underwater. The lack of underwater wireless communication does not only affect the collaboration between the instruments but, more critically, the impossibility of instrument's reconfiguration, tracking, failure detection and maintenance, and data collection during the ongoing monitoring mission [1].

In this context, underwater wireless sensor networks (UWSNs) have been arising as an enabling technology for the autonomous monitoring and exploration of vast areas of aquatic environments. UWSNs are a special kind of wireless ad hoc networks [2, 3], composed of underwater sensor nodes and underwater autonomous vehicles (UAVs) equipped with underwater acoustic modems. In this sensor network, the underwater nodes wirelessly communicate with each other through underwater acoustic links, to collaborate in the process of data gathering and delivery for sinks (sonobuoys) deployed at the sea surface.

The use of underwater acoustic modems makes underwater nodes able to receive commands from and send collected data to a monitoring center. However, this technology severely impacts the performance of data collection in UWSNs. Underwater acoustic links suffer from low bandwidth, high path loss, high noise, high and variable delay, multipath propagation and shadow zones [20]. Moreover, underwater acoustic communication is expensive in terms of energy. These characteristics render challenging the task of data collection in UWSNs.

This tutorial will enable the attendees to gain a better understanding of challenging issues, which diminish the performance of data collection in UWSNs, and the state-of-the-art proposed towards efficient data collection in UWSNs. It will provide a comprehensive overview of the challenging facing by the solutions destined to efficiently collect data from UWSNs. It will highlight the characteristics of UWSNs and the underwater acoustic channels, which render impractical the direct use of networking protocols designed for wireless sensor networks (WSNs). It will discuss the potentials of the geographic routing paradigm for efficient data routing from underwater sensor nodes to sonobuoys at the sea surface. It will examine the communication void region problem and state-of-the-art solutions destined to overcome this critical problem. Moreover, this tutorial will explore the potentials of opportunistic routing to tackle the low reliability of the underwater acoustic channel and improve data delivery. It will discuss the challenges for the use of duty-cycling aimed to prolong the UWSN lifetime.

2 CHALLENGES FOR DATA COLLECTION

Efficient data collection in UWSNs is challenging and daunting. This is because the several characteristics of underwater sensor networks and the acoustic channel. In the following, we discuss some of the characteristics that will be covered in this tutorial.

First, UWSNs have highly dynamic topologies. In a UWSNs, frequent changes in the network topology happen because the involuntary mobility of underwater sensor nodes, occasioned by the sea currents, and the variability on the quality of underwater acoustic links. Therefore, traditional proactive and reactive routing protocols render impractical for data delivery in UWSNs [6]. This is because the excessive overhead for the discovery, establishment, and maintenance of end-to-end routing paths.

Second, underwater acoustic links are strongly affected by the aquatic environment. The acoustic signal is increasingly absorbed as the used frequency increases. It is also highly impaired by natural (waves and thermal) and human-made (turbulence and shipping) noises. Moreover, it presents a multipath propagation effect due to the signal reflection at the seabed and surface.

Third, data delivery in UWSN is performed through highly unreliable acoustic links. The quality of the underwater acoustic channel varies with time. It will depend on the weather condition, temperature, and salinity of the water, as well as the pressure level. It will experience temporal and spatial uncertainty in the communication range [18]. Moreover, the acoustic link can be completely down and incapable of successfully delivery data because the shadow zones and multipath propagation effects.

Fourth, UWSNs are energy hungry. By using underwater acoustic modems, the energy cost for data transmission in underwater is of the order of dozens of watts [12]. This is critical for this energy-constrained sensor network because (i) UWSN entails on low-density node deployments where each single node is fundamental for network connectivity and (ii) ship missions for UWSN maintenance and battery replacements are expensive. Therefore, energy-efficient solutions should be proposed towards long-lived green underwater sensor networks [10].

Finally, energy consumption among underwater sensor nodes will occur in an unbalanced manner. In a UWSNs, a few number of nodes will be central for the routing task [9], that is, they will be responsible for forwarding significant amount of the network traffic load. Therefore, these central nodes will be excessively demanded as relays by leaf nodes. This aspect is critical due to the high energy cost for transmissions. The central nodes will deplete their batteries sooner. Since UWSN relies on low-density deployments, the battery depletion of central nodes will result in network partitions and, consequently, in the incapability of data delivery for the application. Therefore, not only energy-efficient networking protocols are required but they need also to lead to a balanced energy consumption among underwater sensor nodes.

3 POTENTIAL APPROACHES

This tutorial covers recent works proposed to overcome the challenges highlighted in the previous section. It discusses how the geographic routing paradigm suits for data routing in the dynamic topologies of UWSNs. It examines current methodologies used for designing void-handling algorithms in UWSNs. It advocates for the use of opportunistic routing to handle the low-reliability problem of the underwater acoustic channel. Finally, it discusses the advantages and disadvantages of using duty-cycling for energy conservation in UWSNs. More details of the covered topics in this tutorial are given in the following subsections.

3.1 Geographic Routing

Geographic routing has been proposed for wireless ad hoc and sensor networks. It is simple and scalable. Geographic routing does not entail on the discovery, establishment and maintenance of end-to-end routing paths. This routing paradigm solely uses the location information of one-hop neighboring nodes for deciding the next-hop node that will continue forwarding data packets towards the destination. It works as follows. Every node obtains the one-hop neighboring nodes' location through periodic beaconing. Whenever a node has a data packet to send, it greedily selects its neighboring node closest to the destination.

However, geographic routing protocols suffer from a serious drawback called of communication void region. This problem occurs whenever a current forwarder node cannot find a neighboring node closest to the destination, that is, it is the closest node. The node located in a communication void region is called void node. Whenever a packet gets stuck in a void node, the routing protocol should attempt to route the packet using some recovery method or discard it [4].

3.2 Void-Handling Algorithms

Void-handling algorithms are used to route data packets from void nodes (see Section 3.1). These procedures have been implemented in the majority of geographic routing protocols designed for UWSNs [13]. In the literature, three main paradigms have been used for designing void-handling algorithms for UWSNs [11]: (i) bypassing void region methodology, (ii) power control-based methodology and, more recently, (iii) mobility assisted methodology.

Bypass void region-based void-handling protocols try to route data packets by circumventing the void region. To do so, a routing path from the void node to a node that can resume the greedy forwarding must be discovered and maintained. The main advantage of this approach is that it does not change the network topology and location of the nodes. However, it may increase the network energy consumption, especially in mobile UWSNs, because the overhead for path discovery and maintenance.

Power control-based void-handling protocols are simple and scalable. Using this approach, a void node just increases its communication range to find a novel neighboring node closest to the destination. The main advantage of this approach is that it does not rely on the transmission of control messages for route discovery. However, it might increase the network energy consumption as high transmission power will be used by void nodes.

Mobility assisted-based void-handling protocols leverage the mobility of underwater nodes to overcome the communication void region problem. In this approach, void nodes are moved to new locations outside of the communication void region. Thus, they can find neighboring nodes that can continue forwarding the data packet to the destination. The main advantage of this approach is that it does not produce long routing paths, which can increase the energy consumption. However, the displacement of void nodes for new locations can diminish sensing coverage.

3.3 Opportunistic Routing

Opportunistic routing has been shown effective to improve data delivery reliability in underwater sensor networks [7]. In this routing paradigm, the current sender node selects a set of next-hop candidate forwarder nodes to continue forwarding the data packet towards the destination. Next, it includes the data packet head either the unique identification of candidate nodes or a given information that will indicate which neighbors are forwarding candidates. Finally, it broadcasts the data packet.

At the candidate nodes, data packets are forwarded in a prioritized way. During the candidate set selection process, to each candidate node is assigned a transmission priority level. Whenever a candidate node successfully receives a data packet, based on the candidate's priority level, it schedules the further forwarding of the received packet. The packet is forwarded if the node, during its packet holding time, does not hear the transmission of the same packet, from a high priority level candidate.

When using the opportunistic routing paradigm, packet retransmissions will occur only if none of the candidate nodes receive it. This reduces the UWSN energy consumption as fewer transmissions will take place. In addition, the reduction of packet transmissions will reduce packet collisions, which will increase the packet delivery ratio.

3.4 Duty-Cycling

Duty cycling is a common approach for energy conservation in energy-constrained wireless sensor networks. In a duty-cycled network, each node periodically alternates the state of its wireless interface between active and sleep mode. Therefore, a prolonged network lifetime is achieved by avoiding the waste of energy due to the idle listening operation of sensor nodes, which is a dominant task in low traffic load UWSN.

In UWSNs, the use of duty cycling is still controversial. Indeed, this approach conserves energy by putting the nodes in the sleep mode, whenever it is possible. However, it is necessary to guarantee that a transmitter and receiver nodes are awake at the same time for the communication. Usually, the sender node transmits preambles to ensure that the intended receiver node will stay awake to receive the further data packet transmission [14]. The energy consumption for preamble transmissions before the sending of the data packet will overcome the energy conservation of using duty cycling.

Therefore, efficient mechanisms to guarantee that, in an asynchronous duty-cycled UWSNs, a pair of communicating nodes will awake at the same time should be further investigated [5]. Moreover, given the low-density deployments of UWSNs, a balanced energy consumption is preferable to avoid network partitions. In a duty-cycled UWSNs, balanced energy consumption can be achieved through the control of the sleep interval of the nodes [8].

4 PRESENTERS' BIOGRAPHY

The short biography of the presenters is described in the following.

Rodolfo W. L. Coutinho is currently a Research Associate at the University of Ottawa, Canada. He received a Joint PhD Degree in computer science from the University of Ottawa (uOttawa), Canada, and Federal University of Minas Gerais (UFMG), Brazil. He has received his Bachelor's Degree in 2009 and his Master's Degree in 2010, both at the Federal University of Para (UFPA), Brazil. He is conducting research in the area of underwater sensor networks, content distribution in vehicular information-centric networking, wireless networking and mobile computing.

Azzedine Boukerche *(FIEEE, FEiC, FCAE, FAAAS)* is a Distinguished University Professor and holds a Canada Research Chair Tier-1 position at the University of Ottawa. He is founding director of the PARADISE Research Laboratory and the DIVA Strategic Research Centre at the University of Ottawa. He has received the C. Gotlieb Computer Medal Award, Ontario Distinguished Researcher Award, Premier of Ontario Research Excellence Award, G. S. Glinski Award for Excellence in Research, IEEE Computer Society Golden Core Award, IEEE CS-Meritorious Award, IEEE TCPP Leaderships Award, IEEE ComSoc ASHN Leaderships and Contribution Award, and University of Ottawa Award for Excellence in Research. He serves as an Associate Editor for several IEEE transactions and ACM journals, and is also a Steering Committee Chair for several IEEE and ACM international conferences. His current research interests include wireless ad hoc and sensor networks, wireless networking and mobile computing, wireless multimedia, QoS service provisioning, performance evaluation and modeling of large-scale distributed and mobile systems, and large scale distributed and parallel discrete event simulation. He has published extensively in these areas and received several best research paper awards for his work. He is a Fellow of the Engineering Institute of Canada, a Fellow of the Canadian Academy of Engineering, and a Fellow of the American Association for the Advancement of Science.

REFERENCES

[1] I. F. Akyildiz, D. Pompili, and T. Melodia. 2005. Underwater acoustic sensor networks: research challenges. *Ad Hoc Networks* 3, 3 (2005), 257–279.

[2] A. Boukerche. 2008. *Algorithms and Protocols for Wireless, Mobile Ad Hoc Networks*. Vol. 77. Wiley-IEEE Press.

[3] A. Boukerche. 2008. *Algorithms and Protocols for Wireless Sensor Networks*. Vol. 62. Wiley-IEEE Press.

[4] D. Chen and P. K. Varshney. 2007. A survey of void handling techniques for geographic routing in wireless networks. *IEEE Communications Surveys Tutorials* 9, 1 (First 2007), 50–67.

[5] R. W. L. Coutinho, A. Boukerche, L. F. M. Vieira, and A. A.F. Loureiro. 2015. Modeling and Analysis of Opportunistic Routing in Low Duty-Cycle Underwater Sensor Networks. In *Proc. of the 18th ACM International Conference on Modeling, Analysis and Simulation of Wireless and Mobile Systems (MSWiM)*. 125–132.

[6] R. W. L. Coutinho, A. Boukerche, L. F. M. Vieira, and A. A.F. Loureiro. 2015. A novel void node recovery paradigm for long-term underwater sensor networks. *Ad Hoc Networks* 34 (2015), 144 – 156.

[7] R. W. L. Coutinho, A. Boukerche, L. F. M. Vieira, and A. A.F. Loureiro. 2016. Design guidelines for opportunistic routing in underwater networks. *IEEE Commun. Mag.* 54, 2 (Feb. 2016), 40–48.

[8] R. W. L. Coutinho, A. Boukerche, L. F. M. Vieira, and A. A.F. Loureiro. 2016. Modeling the sleep interval effects in duty-cycled underwater sensor networks. In *Proc. of the IEEE International Conference on Communications (ICC)*. 1–6.

[9] R. W. L. Coutinho, A. Boukerche, L. F. M. Vieira, and A. A.F. Loureiro. 2016. A Novel Centrality Metric for Topology Control in Underwater Sensor Networks. In *Proc. of the 19th ACM International Conference on Modeling, Analysis and Simulation of Wireless and Mobile Systems (MSWiM)*. 205–212.

[10] R. W. L. Coutinho, A. Boukerche, L. F. M. Vieira, and A. A.F. Loureiro. 2016. On the design of green protocols for underwater sensor networks. *IEEE Communications Magazine* 54, 10 (October 2016), 67–73.

[11] R. W. L. Coutinho, A. Boukerche, L. F. M. Vieira, and A. A.F. Loureiro. 2017. Performance modeling and analysis of void-handling methodologies in underwater wireless sensor networks. *Computer Networks* 126 (2017), 1 – 14.

[12] Eric Gallimore, Jim Partan, Ian Vaughn, Sandipa Singh, Jon Shusta, and Lee Freitag. 2010. The WHOI micromodem-2: A scalable system for acoustic communications and networking. In *Proceedings of the MTS/IEEE OCEANS - SEATTLE*. 1–7. https://doi.org/10.1109/OCEANS.2010.5664354

[13] S. M. Ghoreyshi, A. Shahrabi, and T. Boutaleb. 2017. Void-Handling Techniques for Routing Protocols in Underwater Sensor Networks: Survey and Challenges. *IEEE Communications Surveys Tutorials* 19, 2 (Secondquarter 2017), 800–827.

[14] Zhenjiang Li, Mo Li, and Yunhao Liu. 2014. Towards Energy-Fairness in Asynchronous Duty-Cycling Sensor Networks. *ACM Trans. Sen. Netw.* 10, 3, Article 38 (May 2014), 26 pages.

[15] National Oceanic and Atmospheric Administration. 2015. Discover: Ocean Exploration Facts. (March 2015). Retrieved August, 2017 from http://oceanexplorer.noaa.gov/facts/facts.html

[16] National Oceanic and Atmospheric Administration. 2017. How much of the ocean have we explored? (July 2017). Retrieved August, 2017 from http://oceanservice.noaa.gov/facts/exploration.html

[17] National Oceanic, Atmospheric Administration (Office of Response, and Restoration). 2017. Deepwater Horizon Oil Spill. (Aug. 2017). Retrieved August, 2017 from http://response.restoration.noaa.gov/deepwater-horizon-oil-spill

[18] Lina Pu, Yu Luo, Haining Mo, Son Le, Zheng Peng, Jun-Hong Cui, and Zaihan Jiang. 2015. Comparing underwater {MAC} protocols in real sea experiments. *Computer Communications* 56 (2015), 47 – 59.

[19] T. Rossby, D. Dorson, and J. Fontaine. 1986. The RAFOS system. *Journal of atmospheric and oceanic technology* 3 (1986), 672–680.

[20] M. Stojanovic and J. Preisig. 2009. Underwater acoustic communication channels: Propagation models and statistical characterization. *IEEE Communications Magazine* 47, 1 (January 2009), 84–89.

Optimal Mapping of Stations to Access Points in Enterprise Wireless Local Area Networks

Suzan Bayhan and Anatolij Zubow
Telecommunication Networks Group, Technische Universität Berlin, Germany
{bayhan,zubow}@tkn.tu-berlin.de

ABSTRACT

Efficient resource allocation in enterprise wireless local area networks (WLAN) has become more paramount with the shift of traffic toward WLANs and increasing share of the video traffic. Unfortunately, current practise of client-driven association to APs has several shortcomings, e.g., *sticky client problem.* As a remedy, we propose to move the AP association decision to a periodically-running central controller which aims to maximize the proportionally-fair network throughput. After formulating the optimal mapping problem, we devise several heuristics requiring various degrees of knowledge, e.g., pairwise user-AP link rates, throughput demand of each user. Our analysis via simulations on realistic scenarios (conference, office, and shopping mall) shows the superior performance of our proposals in terms of aggregate logarithmic throughput. While the utility gain over the conventional client-driven approach is modest, up to 18%, the resulting increase in the weakest user's throughput is significant (71-120%) as well as that of AP load balance and fairness of user throughputs. Moreover, our evaluations reveal a very small optimality gap (between 0.1-5%). The highest gain is observed in the conference setting where the users are unevenly distributed in the network and hence there is a huge load imbalance among the APs. While schemes requiring more knowledge, i.e., on handover-cost and traffic demands, perform the best, a naive approach which runs periodically and assigns each user to the AP providing the highest signal level to that user maintains up to 41% gain in the weakest user's throughput over the client-driven handover approach.

KEYWORDS

AP association, enterprise WLAN, handover

1 INTRODUCTION

IEEE 802.11 wireless local area networks (WLANs) have recently become the predominant access networks due to a variety of reasons: ease of deployment, the maturity of the WiFi standard, operating on the licence-exempt spectrum compared to the costly cellular bands, offloading strategy for network operators, to name possibly the most important ones. With this increasing shift to WLANs, managing the WiFi resources has gained more importance to provide a pleasant user experience. Enterprise WLANs, in contrast to its residential counterparts, are amenable to centralized resource management owing to the infrastructure with common management and control authority. For example, in an enterprise network, a controller can decide user-access point (AP) associations and trigger user handovers to improve the network performance, e.g., balancing the network loads on APs [4, 10, 16], managing user mobility [17] or interference by hidden nodes.

MSWiM '17, November 21–25, 2017, Miami, FL, USA

ACM ISBN 978-1-4503-5162-1/17/11...$15.00
https://doi.org/10.1145/3127540.3127556

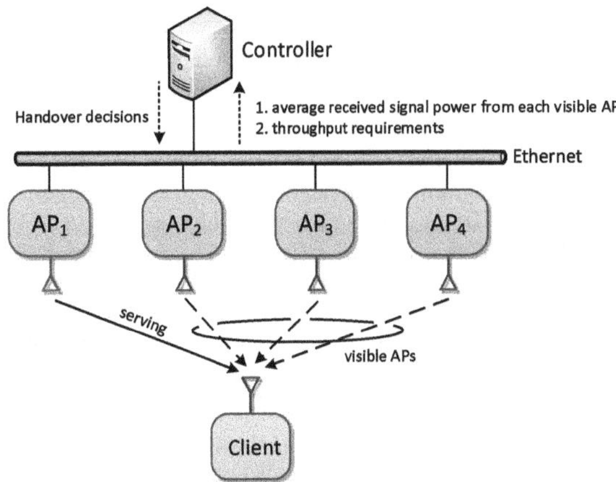

Figure 1: Dense enterprise WLAN setting. The controller collects channel state information and client throughput requirements from the APs for the optimal user-AP association.

Conventionally, a WiFi station[1] connects to the AP providing the highest signal strength and sticks to this AP until the received signal level is below some threshold received signal strength indicator (RSSI), e.g., -80 dBm [11]. When the signal level is low, the user scans for other APs and selects the AP having the strongest signal towards the user without considering the AP's load or the interference situation at the APs. However, as user's knowledge of the network state is much limited and local compared to that of an AP or the network, infrastructure-driven handover proposes to control or assist the handovers using a broader knowledge or even a global view of the network. Different than client-driven handovers which are triggered mostly as a result of decreasing RSSI of a mobile user, infrastructure-driven handovers can be triggered also to improve the network performance. On the other hand, since users experience some outage during a handover—around 4 s with today's hardware [17], frequent handovers will degrade the user experience. Therefore, it is not straightforward to decide how often a controller should manage user-AP associations and how

[1]We use the terms *user*, *client*, and *station* interchangeably.

much such a control would improve network performance over the conventional client-driven handover scheme.

An efficient user-AP association scheme must ensure high user throughput as well as fairness among users. Client-driven approach obviously falls short of meeting these requirements as it is not responsive to changes in the link quality unless the received signal drops below some threshold RSSI value. Moreover, selecting the link with the highest SNR does not guarantee a pleasant user experience as WiFi is a shared access medium and airtime must be shared with other users. Given that video traffic is becoming more predominant, ensuring high SNR and high airtime may not still provide user satisfaction unless minimum throughput requirement of an application is fulfilled. Hence, an efficient scheme should be aware of the application's throughput requirements. Finally, as aforementioned, handover-cost awareness is another desirable aspect.

Contributions: Our contributions in this paper are threefold:

- Based on the above-listed requirements, we first formulate optimal mapping of users to APs as a proportionally-fair network throughput maximization problem. Due to the hardness of this problem, we design efficient algorithms that are only slightly sub-optimal. Different than the existing solutions which are executed only when a user joins the network or leaves the coverage of an AP, we investigate the benefits of periodic management of user-AP associations.
- Different than existing solutions, we consider the entailed overhead of handover in terms of time lost for handover during which the user cannot get service from its AP. Moreover, with the increasing shift to video traffic, user-AP association without considering the throughput requirement of applications may fall short of providing a pleasant user experience. To represent this fact, we consider minimum rate requirements of users while deciding on user-AP associations.
- Our simulations of realistic scenarios—conference, office, and shopping mall settings, show the superior performance of our proposals under increasing controller period, number of users, and handover latency. We observe the highest gain (e.g., up to 120% increase in the weakest user's throughput) in the conference setting where there is a significant density imbalance in the network.

The rest of the paper is organized as follows. Section 2 describes the considered enterprise WLAN setting while Section 3 introduces the optimal user-AP association problem by modelling the airtime and expected throughput of each user under a particular AP association. Next, Section 4 presents lower-complexity user-AP association schemes as the formulated optimization problem is computationally hard. Section 5 assesses the performance of our proposals along with the traditional client-driven handover approach. Section 6 overviews the related work while Section 7 concludes the paper.

2 SYSTEM MODEL

We consider an enterprise WLAN with a central controller operating in a time-slotted manner. The controller collects statistics from APs at the beginning of each time slot after which it may trigger the APs to handover their users to the selected APs. Fig.1 shows the considered setting and Table 1 lists the used notations.

Let $\mathcal{A} = \{AP_j, \cdots, AP_K\}$ represent the set of APs with K APs and $C = \{1, \cdots, F\}$ the set of channels these APs can operate on. As enterprise networks are planned with the goal of ensuring high service continuity and high capacity for mobile users, AP coverage areas are mostly overlapping [6]. Each AP covers a circular region of radius r meters. We can represent the network topology by a connectivity graph $G = (\mathcal{A}, \mathcal{E})$ where APs are abstracted as the vertices and an edge between two APs, e.g., AP_j and AP_k, means that the two APs have some overlapping coverage region. We represent the channel allocation with $\mathcal{F} = [a_j^f]$ where a_j^f yields 1 if AP_j is assigned channel f for its operation. Denote the set of APs which are assigned to f by $\mathcal{A}_f$ and we refer to the APs in this set as *co-channel APs*. Note that an efficient channel assignment scheme should guarantee minimal interference among co-channel APs [5]. We assume that two APs which are in the interference range are assigned orthogonal channels.

Let $\mathcal{U} = \{u_i, \cdots u_n\}$ denote the set of n users in this network. As users might have different traffic types, e.g., voice vs. video, their throughput requirements may also vary. We denote by r_i^{min} the minimum required rate for user u_i. We assume that uplink traffic is negligible and focus only on the saturated downlink traffic.

As a result of overlapping cells, a user u_i may be receiving signals from a number of APs with varying signal strength. Let $d_{i,j}$ denote the distance between u_i and AP_j. We call the set of APs a user overhears as *visible APs* for this user, i.e., received signal power from the AP is above the receiver sensitivity of the station. We denote the visibility of AP_j at u_i by a binary variable $v_{i,j}$, which yields value 1 if AP_j is a visible AP for u_i. We consider mobile users which are moving with speed values uniformly distributed in interval $[v_{min}, v_{max}]$ m/s. We assume a Random-Waypoint mobility with some probability of pausing. After a user pauses or hits the borders, it changes its direction of movement with an angle $\sim$U$(0, 2\pi)$.

The controller maps users to APs periodically —every T time units, and we call the number of time slots elapsed between the two consecutive mapping as *controller period*. The collected statistics may include average SNR to each visible AP for each user and user's traffic requirements. Based on the collected statistics, the controller may trigger one or a subset of APs for switching their users from one to another. Note that in IEEE 802.11ac, users have already such SNR information for each primary and secondary channels. More specifically, users measure their links in each channel to APs which operate on the whole spectrum using multiple channels as secondary channels in addition to the primary channel. We assume such a system in our paper.

We call the users whose visible AP set has more than one AP as *handover candidates* denoted by $\mathcal{U}^{ho}$. The rest of the users, i.e., $u_k \in \mathcal{U} - \mathcal{U}^{ho}$, are either under outage or have only one visible AP. For the former, there is nothing a controller could do, and in fact, this case should rarely occur under a careful coverage planning, i.e., sufficiently dense AP deployment. For the latter, the controller assigns the user to its only option.

In the next section, we present several ways the controller can decide on these handover events and discuss how to set the controller period T. The controller sends the new user-AP association decision to the APs after which users with change in their AP associations are switched to the new APs. During handover, a user

Table 1: Summary of Key Parameters

Symbol	Description
$\mathcal{A} = \{AP_j\}, K$	Set of access points, number of APs
$\mathcal{U} = \{u_i\}, n$	Set of users, number of users
$\mathcal{U}_j, n_j$	Set and number of users associated to AP_j
B	Bandwidth available at each AP
a_j^f	Binary variable yielding 1 if AP_j uses channel f
P_j	Transmission power of AP_j
C, F	Set and number of channels
$x_{i,j}$	Binary decision variable showing if user i is assigned to AP j
$v_{i,j}$	Binary state variable showing whether u_i is in AP_j's service region
σ	Path loss coefficient of the environment
$\gamma_{i,j}$	Received signal strength of AP_j at u_i
$d_{i,j}$	Distance of u_i from AP_j
$r_{i,j}$	Capacity of the channel between u_i and AP_j
$R_{i,j}$	Throughput of u_i if associated to AP_j
$\mathcal{R}_{i,j}$	Utility of u_i if associated to AP_j
r_i^{min}	Min. rate required for u_i's application
$\alpha_{i,j}^{min}$	Needed min. airtime for u_i if served by AP_j
$\beta_{i,j}$	Acquired airtime for u_i if served by AP_j
$\alpha_{i,j}^{sw}$	Airtime for a switching u_i if served by AP_j
$\alpha_{i,j}$	Airtime for u_i who is already associated to AP_j
T	Controller period
t_{sw}	Handover cost in terms of outage time
ϕ_i	Binary variable showing if u_i switches from one AP to another AP at the current association period

experiences some outage period which may disrupt its communications. We represent the handover cost t_{sw} in terms of total time to complete association to a new AP. When controller is not active, conventional *client-driven handover scheme* (CD) is in effect, i.e., when the user-AP link becomes weak such that the signal level is below the handover threshold SNR, the user associates to the AP with the highest SNR regardless of the AP load.

3 OPTIMAL MAPPING OF STATIONS TO APS

3.1 Airtime share under handover latency

Assume that u_i is connected to AP_s. If the user or the controller has decided that the user connects to a destination AP denoted by AP_j, the user needs to perform association steps for $AP_j \neq AP_s$. To denote the handover status of u_i, we define a binary variable ϕ_i which yields 1 if $AP_j \neq AP_s$. We assume that handover operations are performed at the beginning of a time slot.

During handover period, a user which is being switched to AP_j is in outage and hence cannot be served by AP_j. As a result, the channel (medium) will be shared only among the users who are already associated to AP_j. Let $\mathcal{U}_j$ be the set of users including the switching users served by AP_j and n_j be the number of these users, i.e., $|\mathcal{U}_j| = n_j$. Moreover, denote the number of users who are being switched to AP_j by n_j^{sw}. We assume each AP targets fairness in airtime share in the downlink, e.g., IEEE 802.11e. As a result, each user gets an equal share of the medium for the downlink.

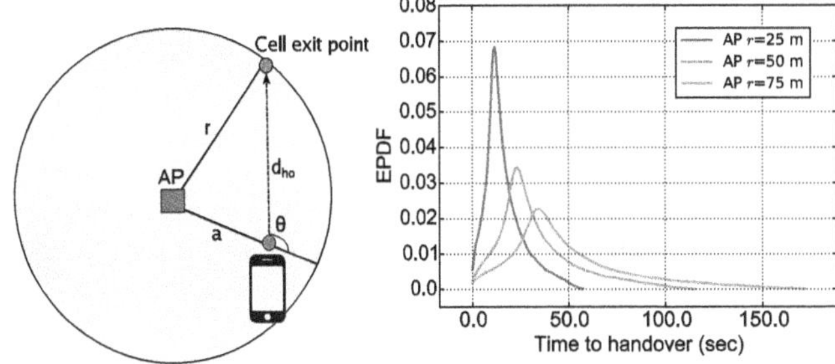

(a) Expected distance d_{ho} from the cell exit point.

(b) EPDF of time to handover calculated from Monte Carlo simulations, $v \sim U(1,5)$ m/sec.

Figure 2: Cell geometry to model expected time to handover and calculate controller period using Monte Carlo runs.

Assuming that T is set considering the expected time the population of an AP service set would not change drastically, we calculate the expected channel airtime a switching user gets from AP_j for its downlink traffic as:

$$\alpha_{i,j}^{sw} = \frac{T - t_{sw}}{T} \cdot \frac{1}{n_j}. \tag{1}$$

On the other hand, airtime a user which is already associated to AP_j gets is:

$$\alpha_{i,j} = \frac{t_{sw}}{T} \cdot \frac{1}{n_j - n_j^{sw}} + \frac{T - t_{sw}}{T} \cdot \frac{1}{n_j}. \tag{2}$$

In (2), the first term of the summation shows the airtime share of each user in the handover period and the second term represents the airtime each user gets after all switching users are associated to AP_j. Notice that the second term in (2) equals to $\alpha_{i,j}^{sw}$ in (1) showing that users which are already connected to this AP gets more airtime.

3.2 Controller period T

Since users are mobile, their signal qualities evolve with time. A controller needs to track such changes and to trigger handovers promptly to maintain high user satisfaction in the network. That means, controller period T should be short enough to react to degrading user-AP links. On the other hand, we need to set T sufficiently long to avoid a large fraction of airtime, i.e., t_{sw}/T, be lost to handover overhead.

Assume that a user's distance from its AP is $a \sim U(0, r)$ and it moves with a speed $v \sim U(v_{min}, v_{max})$ toward the cell edge with an angle $\theta \sim U(0, 2\pi)$ (cf. to Fig.2a). We need to find the expected time for a randomly-picked user to reach the cell edge where the user-to-AP link quality is poor and hence a handover needs to be performed. A similar problem is investigated in the context of handovers from WLANs to 3G networks, e.g., in [15]. We can derive the expected distance from the cell exit point, the point on the cell edge where this user leaves the AP coverage, denoted by d_{ho}, using the cosine theorem: $a^2 + d_{ho}^2 - 2 \cdot a \cdot d_{ho} \cdot \cos(\pi - \theta) = r^2$. We reorganize the above equation as a quadratic univariate equation where the only unknown is d_{ho}. Then, we can find the root of the above equation as: $d_{ho} = -a \cdot \cos\theta \pm \sqrt{(a \cdot \cos\theta)^2 + (r^2 - a^2)}$. Given this distance d_{ho}, we can derive $T_{ho} = d_{ho}/v$ which denotes the expected time to span d_{ho} with speed v. We can set T using T_{ho}. In Fig.2b, we plot experimental pdf of T_{ho} values driven from Monte Carlo simulations for a cell under various coverage radius values. The user speed is uniformly distributed with (1, 5) m/sec.

Unsurprisingly, we observe in the figure that the time to handover is longer for APs with larger footprints. Consequently, we can set controller period longer for such settings. Moreover, Fig.2b shows that there can be very short duration to next handover for users who are already close to the edge of an AP's coverage. As a result, we must set controller period small to detect these handovers. However, this analysis does not provide us how much performance loss a network will experience with longer controller periods. In Section 5, we address this question by the help of simulations.

3.3 Throughput for a given user-AP mapping

We can calculate the capacity of the downlink channel between AP_j and u_i, denoted by $r_{i,j}$, as a function of the signal-to-noise-plus-interference ratio (SINR) of AP_j's signal received by u_i. More formally, SINR of an AP signal operating at channel f with bandwidth B equals to:

$$\gamma_{i,j} = \frac{P_j d_{i,j}^{-\sigma}}{B\eta_0 + \sum_{k \in \mathcal{A}_f} P_k d_{i,k}^{-\sigma}}, \tag{3}$$

where P_j denotes the transmission power of AP_j, σ is the path loss coefficient, and η_0 is noise power per unitary bandwidth. SNIR of a link is a function of the channel assignment decision which is reflected in $\mathcal{A}_f$—the set of APs assigned to channel f. Corresponding capacity of the channel with bandwidth B units is then:

$$r_{i,j} = B \log(1 + \gamma_{i,j}) \text{ bits per second.} \tag{4}$$

If u_i is associated to AP_j, its downlink throughput is a function of $\gamma_{i,j}$ and the airtime it will get from AP_j.[2] As we assumed orthogonal channel assignment, there is only one AP operating at a particular WiFi channel in a collision domain. In other words, co-channel APs are outside their carrier sensing range and resulting interference is insignificant, i.e. below noise floor. Hence, each AP utilizes all the airtime itself without sharing it with other APs.

We set ϕ_i to 1 if u_i handovers. Then, we can calculate the expected throughput of u_i from AP_j, denoted by $R_{i,j}$, as:

$$R_{i,j} = r_{i,j}(\alpha_{i,j}^{sw}\phi_i + \alpha_{i,j}(1 - \phi_i)) \text{ bits,} \tag{5}$$

where the term $(\alpha_{i,j}^{sw}\phi_i + \alpha_{i,j}(1 - \phi_i))$ represents the airtime a user gets depending on whether it is switched to AP_j or not.

Although an AP allocates its airtime equally among its users, the actual airtime a user needs may differ across users. For instance, a user browsing the web would need less airtime compared to another having a video conference. We denote the airtime need of a user as $\alpha_{i,j}^{min}$ and airtime acquired by it as $\beta_{i,j}$. We calculate the minimum needed airtime for u_i from AP_j with rate requirement r_i^{min} as:

$$\alpha_{i,j}^{min} = \frac{r_i^{min}}{r_{i,j}}. \tag{6}$$

Note that satisfying $\beta_{i,j} \geqslant \alpha_{i,j}^{min}$ inequality is essential for some applications such as video communications whereas for best-effort traffic it is not a stringent requirement. In fact, we set $r^{min} = 0$ for best-effort traffic. If the throughput a user gets from its AP is at least equal to the requested minimum throughput, we call such user a *satisfied user* and define its utility as a function of its throughput. For unsatisfied users, the utility is zero as the user cannot get the bare minimum for a pleasant user experience. To reflect the two goals of our controller, i.e., high throughput efficiency and fairness among users, we define the utility of a user as its logarithmic throughput. More formally, utility of a user u_i connected to AP_j is defined as:

$$\mathcal{R}_{i,j} = \begin{cases} \log(1 + R_{i,j}), & \text{if } \beta_{i,j} \geqslant \alpha_{i,j}^{min} \\ 0, & \text{otherwise.} \end{cases} \tag{7}$$

3.4 Problem formulation

Let $x_{i,j}$ denote the binary decision variable yielding value 1 if the controller assigns user u_i to AP_j. We formulate centralized optimal user-AP assignment problem as follows:

$$\mathbf{P1}: \max_{X=[x_{i,j}]} \sum_{AP_j \in \mathcal{A}} \sum_{u_i \in \mathcal{U}} \log\left(1 + x_{i,j} r_{i,j}(\alpha_{i,j}^{sw}\phi_i + \alpha_{i,j}(1-\phi_i))\right) \tag{8}$$

$$\sum_{AP_j \in \mathcal{A}} x_{i,j} \leqslant 1 \qquad \forall u_i \in \mathcal{U} \tag{9}$$

$$x_{i,j} \leqslant v_{i,j} \qquad \forall u_i \in \mathcal{U}, \forall \mathrm{AP}_j \in \mathcal{A} \tag{10}$$

$$\sum_{u_i \in \mathcal{U}} x_{i,j}\alpha_{i,j}^{min} \leqslant 1 \qquad \forall \mathrm{AP}_j \in \mathcal{A} \tag{11}$$

$$x_{i,j}\alpha_{i,j}^{min} \leqslant \alpha_{i,j}^{sw}\phi_i + \alpha_{i,j}(1 - \phi_i), \forall u_i \in \mathcal{U}, \forall \mathrm{AP}_j \in \mathcal{A} \tag{12}$$

$$\alpha_{i,j}^{sw} = \frac{T - t_{sw}}{T \cdot \sum_{u_i \in \mathcal{U}} x_{i,j}} \tag{13}$$

$$\alpha_{i,j} = \frac{t_{sw}}{T \cdot \sum_{u_i \in \mathcal{U}} x_{i,j}(1 - \phi_i)} + \frac{T - t_{sw}}{T \cdot \sum_{u_i \in \mathcal{U}} x_{i,j}} \tag{14}$$

$$x_{i,j} \in \{0, 1\} \qquad \forall u_i \in \mathcal{U}, \forall \mathrm{AP}_j \in \mathcal{A}. \tag{15}$$

The objective function in (8) states that users must be associated to the APs that result in the highest network utility which is a function of logarithmic throughput maintained by each user. Const. (9) signifies that each user can be mapped to at most one AP, whereas Const. (10) is necessary for a feasible assignment, i.e., a user can only be associated to a visible AP. Const. (11) states that the minimum airtime demand of associated users cannot exceed the capacity of an AP, i.e., 100% airtime, whereas Const. (12) ensures that the airtime share this user will get from an AP is higher than its minimum bandwidth requirement. Eqns. (13) and (14) formally state the airtime a user gets if it is a switching user or otherwise, respectively. Finally, Const. (15) denotes that each assignment variable is a binary variable.

Note that the controller solves **P1** every T time units and sends to all APs only the changes in user-AP associations; entries of $X = [x_{i,j}]$ where $x_{i,j} = 1$ and different from the previous assignment. Complexity of **P1** depends on the number of users in the cell edges

[2] We user Shannon's capacity formula to calculate the rate of this user-AP link. However, in reality the actual rate depends also on the selected modulation and coding scheme (MCS) according to the channel quality.

with overlapping AP coverages and the number of APs visible to each such user. More particularly, it increases exponentially with number of such users: given that the number of users in these cell regions is n in the worst case and the number of APs each user can get service is K in the worst case, complexity is $O(K^n)$. The high computational complexity of **P1** renders it impractical for practical operation. Hence, we design lower complexity heuristics in the next section.

4 LOW-COMPLEXITY USER-AP ASSOCIATION SCHEMES

Two design goals for our heuristics are as follows: (i) minimum throughput requirements of the users must be satisfied, and if not, the utility of an unsatisfied user is zero, and (ii) a heuristic should have polynomial complexity in number of users and number of APs. For all schemes, the controller first identifies handover candidates ($\mathcal{U}^{ho}$) and assigns the rest to their only visible AP, if any.

4.1 Highest-SNR AP association (h-SNR)

A simple yet efficient handover scheme a controller can implement is to assign each user to the AP providing the highest signal strength. Note that the conventional *client-driven handover* (CD) has the same approach but with a difference that handover is triggered only after the user's AP can not provide the minimum required signal level for a reliable link. In h-SNR, the user does not stick to its AP but instead switches to the AP with the highest signal level. With h-SNR, we can assess the benefit of periodic handover management in comparison to client-driven handovers. Note that h-SNR is handover-cost oblivious and does not consider minimum rate requirements.

4.2 Airtime-aware AP association (AIR)

While a high SNR value ensures high link rate, it overlooks the time-sharing nature of WiFi. A user's throughput is a multiplication of its link rate and how much airtime it receives. Hence, to account for both parameters, we design airtime-aware AP association (AIR). More specifically, this scheme first calculates rates for each user-AP link as in (4). To have some notion of fairness, AIR starts with a randomly-picked user and assigns this user the AP which promises highest (air-time × rate). After each assignment, we update the airtime a user can get from each AP by considering the new number of associated users for each AP. Note that AIR is handover-cost aware, but it does not consider the minimum rate requirements.

4.3 Demand-aware AP association (DAW)

While airtime-aware AP association calculates expected throughput, it does not consider how a new association affects the performance of existing users of the AP. Given that some users require minimum rate to have a satisfactory quality of experience, demand-aware AP association (DAW) avoids violating the minimum rate requirements.

Similar to airtime-aware scheme, DAW first calculates (air-time× rate) for each user-AP pair as in (4). Different than the previous scheme, DAW checks if an AP has *spare* airtime. Given that an AP allocates its airtime equally among its users, the number of users it can serve is limited by the minimum rate requirements. Let $\mathcal{U}_j$ denote the set of users served by AP_j and total airtime demand from users of this AP as $\alpha_j^{min} = \sum_{u_i \in \mathcal{U}_j} \alpha_{i,j}^{min}$. While an AP with $\alpha_j^{min} = 0$ can in theory serve unlimited number of users, an AP with $\alpha_j^{min} > 0$ can serve at most n_j^{max} users where n_j^{max} is:

$$n_j^{max} = \lfloor \frac{1}{\max\limits_{u_i \in \mathcal{U}_j} \{\alpha_{i,j}^{min}\}} \rfloor. \tag{16}$$

Then, spare airtime s_j of this AP that can be allocated to a newly-joining user equals to:

$$s_j = \begin{cases} \frac{T-t_{sw}}{T(n_j+1)}, & \text{if } n_j < n_j^{max} \\ 0, & \text{otherwise.} \end{cases} \tag{17}$$

Let $\mathcal{A}^+$ be the set of APs that can accommodate newly joining users without violating the minimum rate requirements of the existing users, i.e., $\mathcal{A}^+ := \bigcup AP_j$ where $s_j > 0$ for $AP_j \in \mathcal{A}$. Our aim is to switch handover candidates to such APs in $\mathcal{A}^+$.

For a candidate AP, e.g., AP_j, we need to also consider the decrease in aggregate throughput of users in $\mathcal{U}_j$ after a new user joins. Since the number of users increases by 1 in AP_j's service region, users of AP_j will have less airtime and therefore will sustain lower throughput. The decrease in throughput results in a decrease in utility. Since our aim is to maximize the utility in (8), we consider the decrease in utility as follows:

$$\Delta u_{i,+j}^- = \sum_{u_k \in \mathcal{U}_j} \log\left(1 + \frac{r_{k,j}}{n_j}\right) - \sum_{u_k \in \mathcal{U}_j \setminus u_i} \log\left(1 + r_{k,j}\left(\frac{t_{sw}}{Tn_j} + \frac{T - t_{sw}}{T(n_j+1)}\right)\right). \tag{18}$$

In (18), the first term represents the aggregate utility of AP_j before u_i associates to this AP whereas the second term is the updated utility (excluding u_i) after u_i joins. Then, considering u_i's expected utility, we calculate the net utility of assigning user i to AP_j as:

$$\Delta u_{i,j} = \log\left(1 + \frac{r_{i,j}(T - t_{sw})}{T(n_j+1)}\right) - \Delta u_{i,+j}^-$$

Then, we take the pair user i^* and AP j^* achieving the highest net utility: $i^*, j^* = \arg\max \Delta u_{i,j}$. We update $\mathcal{U}^{ho}$ by removing the assigned user u_{i*} from the set of handover candidates. To avoid violation of minimum rate requirements, we update the spare capacity of each AP in $\mathcal{A}^+$ using (16) and (17). Next, we remove those APs with zero spare capacity from $\mathcal{A}^+$. DAW terminates when $\mathcal{A}^+$ or $\mathcal{U}^{ho}$ equals to empty set.

4.4 Comparison of heuristics

In Table 2, we compare the proposed heuristics and CD, according to their awareness in terms of AP load, handover cost (`HO cost` column), and traffic demands (`demand` column). We also denote if these schemes can be implemented in a distributed manner (`distributed` column). For CD and h-SNR, each client can decide by itself as these algorithms need only the user-received SNR from each AP which is already available at each user. On the contrary, more information on the whole network is required for AIR and DAW. For AIR, a controller needs to know the number of users at each AP and their handover status to calculate the airtime the user will get. In addition to this information, DAW requires the user-AP link rates for all users to make mapping decisions. The complexity of h-SNR, CD, and AIR equals to $O(nK)$ as for each client these algorithms iterate over all APs to find the AP with the highest utility, i.e., signal level or airtime×rate. DAW is of complexity $O(n^2K)$ as it iterates over all user-AP pairs to find the best mapping in each step.

Table 2: Comparison of Heuristics

Heuristic	AP load	HO cost	Demand	Distributed
CD	-	-	-	✓
h-SNR	-	-	-	✓
AIR	✓	✓	-	-
DAW	✓	✓	✓	-

5 PERFORMANCE EVALUATION

5.1 Performance metrics

We use the following performance metrics in our analysis.

- *Utility* is the objective function defined in (8).
- *Fraction of satisfied users* is the ratio of the users whose minimum required rate is satisfied over all users.
- *Fairness of user throughputs* is the Jain's fairness index considering the throughput distribution over all users.
- *Load balance across APs* is the Jain's fairness index considering the number of users served by each AP.
- *Probability of handover* is calculated as the ratio of total number of handovers over all connected users at a time slot.
- *Gain in weakest user's throughput* is the improvement achieved by a heuristic in the minimum user throughput over CD.

5.2 Parameters and scenarios

Our scenarios are similar to indoor scenario defined in IMT guidelines [12], e.g., indoor environments isolated from external interference and consisting of stationary or low-mobility pedestrians. More specifically, we define the following three scenarios (cf. to Table 3). For all scenarios, we set $n = 80$ and $K = 10$.

- **Conference scenario:** In this scenario, we model a conference environment in which a room with three APs hosts a large number of users. For the initial placement of users, 90% of the users are located in this room. Outside the conference hall, there are 7 APs deployed in a grid-like topology to serve the remaining 10% of the users.
- **Office scenario:** In this scenario, we model an office setting with a grid-like topology, e.g., we deploy APs on a grid and change the AP locations in a small radius to account for building imperfections. Users are deployed based on a skewed Pareto distribution which diverges from uniform deployment depending on the skewness parameter. Only a small fraction of users are mobile.
- **Shopping mall scenario**: In this scenario, we model WiFi usage in a shopping mall. APs are deployed in a grid topology and users are uniformly placed in the area. A large fraction of users are mobile while only a small fraction has minimum bandwidth requirements.

Table 3: Scenarios

Scenario	Fraction of mobile users	Fraction of users with throughput demand
Conference	0.5	0.3
Office	0.3	0.5
Shopping mall	0.9	0.3

Notice that although all scenarios have the same number of APs and users, AP deployment and user deployment differ across scenarios. To quantify the resulting imbalance in user distribution in the considered area, we define a metric called *density balance* which reflects the homogeneity in user distribution. More specifically, on each time slot, for each AP, we record the number of users for whom this AP is the nearest AP and is expected to provide the highest SNR. Then, we calculate the Jain's fairness index considering the number of users of each AP. Intuitively, for a grid AP topology and uniform deployment of users, the density balance is close to 1. Unless otherwise stated, we will use the settings listed in Table 3.

For a fair comparison across different settings, we assume that the total available bandwidth is the same in all settings, i.e., B_{tot} = 100 MHz. Based on the network topology, we first find the minimum number of channels needed for an orthogonal frequency assignment by solving a graph coloring problem on our AP topology. Then, we find the bandwidth per AP by dividing the available bandwidth to the required number of channels, i.e., $B = B_{tot}/\chi$ where χ is the chromatic number of the AP graph.

We set $t_{sw} = 0.2$ s while a time slot = 1 s, minimum rate requirements $\approx [5, 15]$ Mbps considering the video rates reported by Skype and Netflix.[3] All scenarios are assumed to cover an area of [150 m, 100 m]. For the conference case, the conference hall is located at the centre of the area and its size is [50 m, 30 m]. Mobility model is random-waypoint mobility with 0.2 pausing probability at each time slot and user speed $\approx [1, 5]$ m/s. [4] We model the user-AP links using Keenan-Motley model. While we calculate fairness of user throughputs, we consider the throughput accumulated in a time window of 5 slots, rather than instantaneous throughput value in that particular time slot. We report the average results of 100 repetitions for each scenario and a simulation time of 100 time slots.

5.3 Optimality gap

To understand the performance gap between our heuristics and the optimal solution, we find the optimal user-AP association by running A* search [13] considering utility in (8). Due to the high computation time, we show the performance for a smaller conference setting; 6 APs and 15 users in an area of 120m x 80m. Note that we expect a wider optimality gap for a larger scenario with many more users and APs. Fig. 3 depicts the utility, aggregate throughput, and load balance of the network. Regarding utility in Fig. 3a, the optimality gap of DAW is 0.1%, i.e., it achieves 0.1 percent less utility

[3]https://support.skype.com/en/faq/FA1417/how-much-bandwidth-does-skype-need, and https://help.netflix.com/en/node/306.

[4]Note that this interval covers also higher speeds than typical walking speeds. However, we chose these values for practical purpose of having more handover events in the given simulation period.

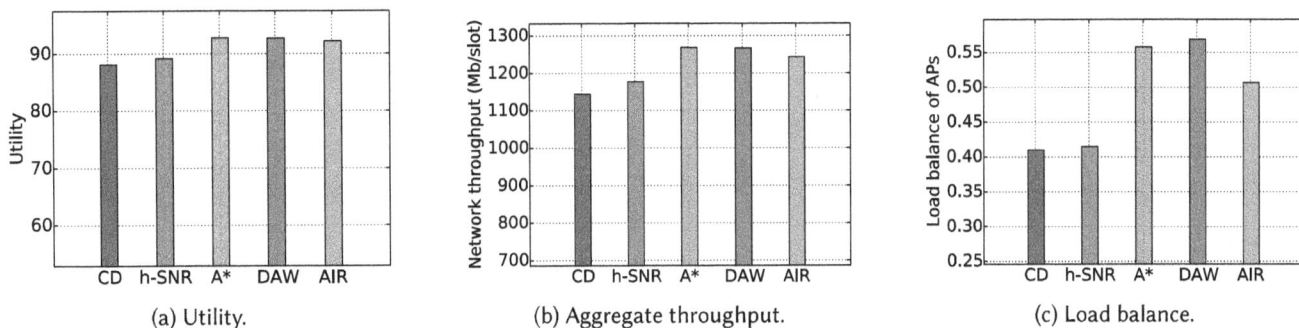

(a) Utility.

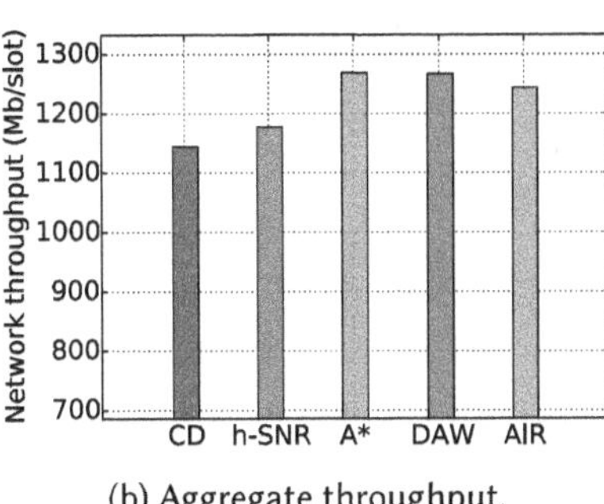

(b) Aggregate throughput.

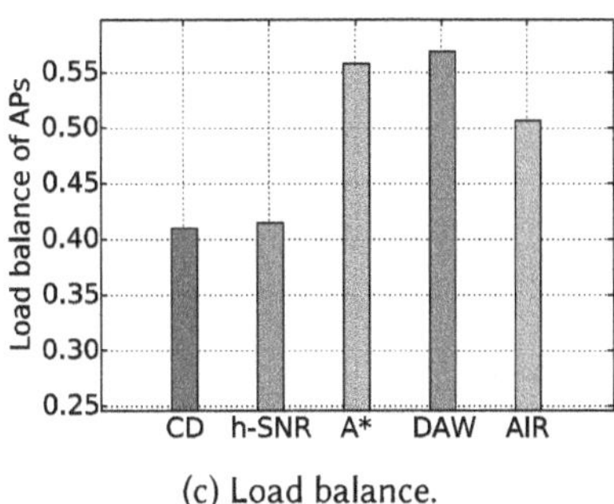

(c) Load balance.

Figure 3: Comparison of heuristics with the optimal solution A* for the conference setting with $n = 15$ and $K = 6$.

than the optimal solution. To give a perspective, CD has optimality gap of 5% while h-SNR and AIR has 3.9% and 0.6% lower utility than the optimal scheme, respectively. Similarly, Fig. 3b compares the network throughput. CD maintains 9.9% lower throughput than A* while those of h-SNR and AIR are 7.2% and 2% lower, respectively. DAW's performance approaches to that of optimal (0.2% lower) in terms of achieved aggregate throughput. Finally, as Fig. 3c shows, DAW outperforms A* solution only slightly (0.2%) while CD and h-SNR has around 26% and AIR 9% worse performance than A*.

5.4 Impact of controller period

First, we analyze the impact of controller period across different scenarios by setting $T = \{1, 2, 4, 10, 20\}$ time slots. Figs. 4, 5, and 6 show the impact of increasing controller period for conference, office, and mall scenarios, respectively.

Let us first focus on the case when $T = 1$. In this case, the highest gain in utility over CD is achieved in the conference scenario where we have the lowest density balance. The average density balance for each scenario is 0.33 (conference), 0.76 (office), and 0.95 (mall) while the corresponding gain in utility is up to 18%, 5%, and 2%. Note that while utility improvement values are moderate to low, the resulting gain on the minimum rate of the stations is up to 120%, 73%, and 71%. Regarding h-SNR, while it achieves the highest total network throughput (not plotted), its lack of fairness notion results in a much lower utility. Thus, DAW and AIR both outperform h-SNR in terms of utility, throughput fairness, and thereby gain in the weakest user's throughput. In addition, h-SNR is oblivious to handover cost and to traffic demands, which results in lower fraction of satisfied users around 0.92 (figure not depicted) compared to DAW and h-SNR around 0.98. However, since conference setting has only a small number of users with minimum rate requirements, we do not observe a significant difference in terms of satisfied users, e.g., satisfaction ratio is 0.91 for CD. DAW and AIR perform very similarly despite the fact that AIR neglects the traffic requirements. We attribute this behaviour to the available network resources, e.g., the capacity is not tight. However, with increasing user density with video traffic, we expect to see the superior performance of DAW over AIR.

With increasing T, the impact of controller decisions become less significant and eventually performance of all heuristics are expected to approach that of CD. Please recall that when controller is not active, the legacy CD approach at each client is in charge of AP association. Moreover, with longer T, the expected throughput calculated using (1) and (2) deviates from the actual user throughput due to variations in user location and channel states. We observe a steeper decrease in performance for the conference scenario comparing Figs.4a, 5a, and 6a. Primary reason for this trend is again the imbalance of AP loads. Note that although mall scenario has the highest mobility, the observed decrease in utility with increasing T is less pronounced due to the high density balance of the network. The average number of visible APs of a user is 3.47 APs for conference, 4.20 APs for office, and 3.89 APs for the mall setting. When controller period is longer, opportunities of more efficient user-AP association are lost. On the other hand, for the office and mall scenarios, almost all APs have the same number of users and they are deployed on a grid, there is less room for optimizations. Notice almost perfect AP load balance and throughput fairness in these scenarios depicted in Figs.5b, 6b, 5c, and 6c.

To understand whether our heuristics result in frequent handovers, we plot the probability of handover for each scenario in Fig.7. While our heuristics result in higher switching probability compared to CD and h-SNR, the handovers are yet very low —less than 0.10 probability. We attribute this behaviour to the low mobility of the considered settings. After a closer look to CD curves, we can observe the sticky user problem, e.g., very low probability of handover if clients decide on AP association.

In short, the controller should consider the expected density balance to set the period appropriately without sacrificing from the performance significantly. Another observation is that even a naïve heuristic like h-SNR which does not require any global knowledge can improve utility significantly if performed periodically rather than only when the station is about to lose its connectivity. In fact, h-SNR could be a good option as it can run in a distributed manner as opposed to AIR and DAW (as shown in Table 2).

5.5 Impact of handover cost

To see the impact of handover cost more clearly, we set the fraction of mobile users to 1 for the conference setting. Fig. 8 depicts the impact of increasing handover cost on each user-AP association scheme. As we consider scenarios with low mobility, the impact of handover on the overall utility is only marginal for all schemes. Moreover, this slight impact is due to the increased airtime for users

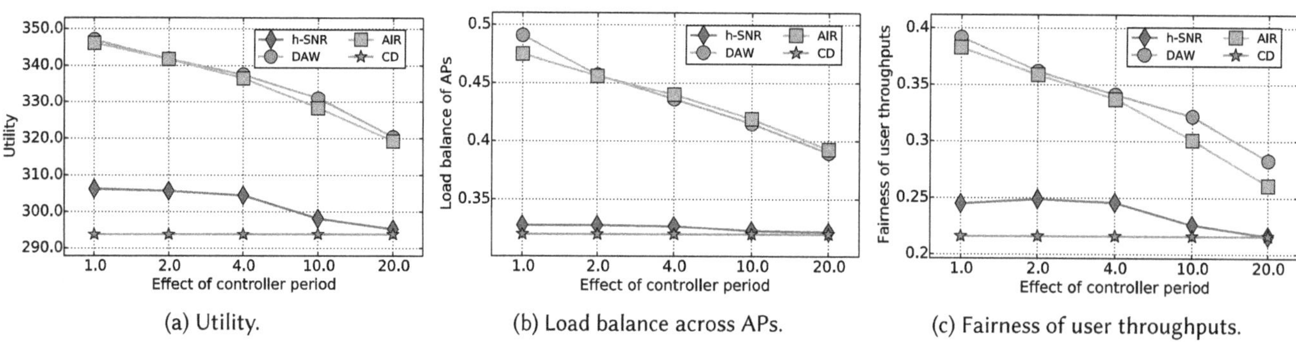

(a) Utility. (b) Load balance across APs. (c) Fairness of user throughputs.

Figure 4: Impact of controller period for conference scenario where the mean density balance is 0.33.

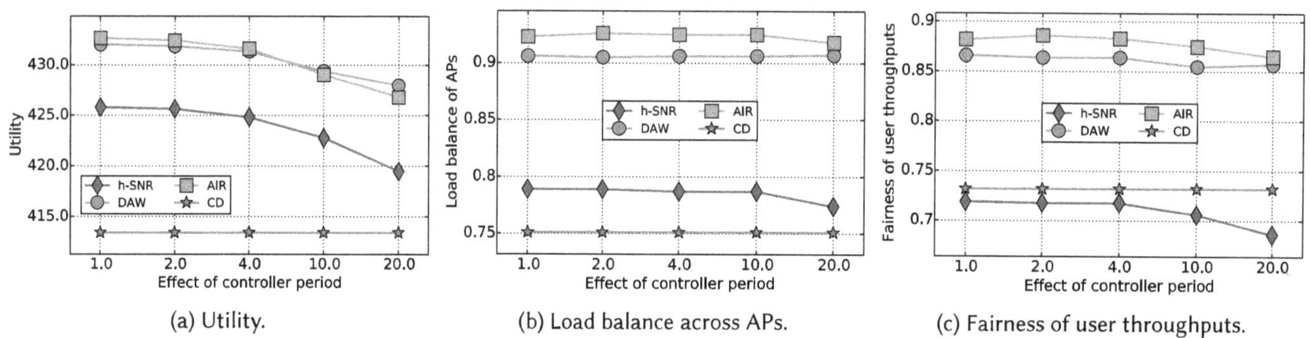

(a) Utility. (b) Load balance across APs. (c) Fairness of user throughputs.

Figure 5: Impact of controller period for office scenario where the mean density balance is 0.76.

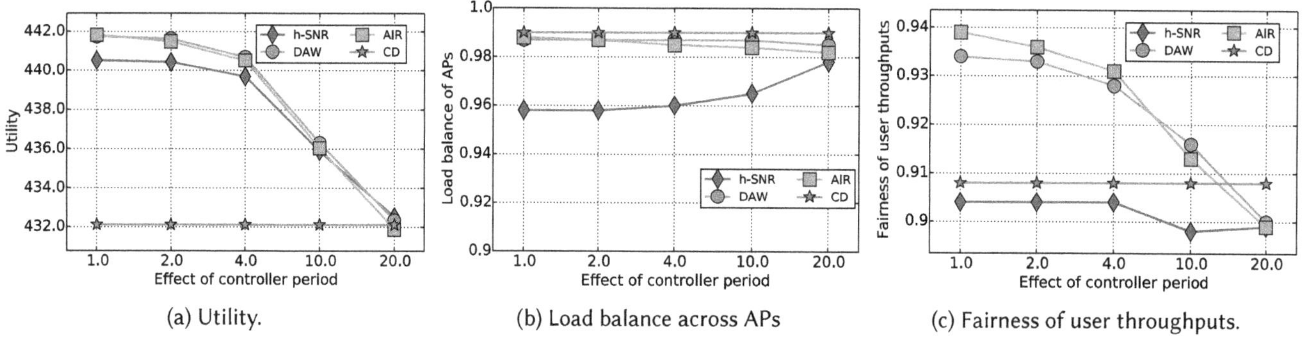

(a) Utility. (b) Load balance across APs (c) Fairness of user throughputs.

Figure 6: Impact of controller period for mall scenario where the mean density balance is 0.95.

who are already associated to their APs. Recall that as shown in (2), airtime lost by switching stations are used for stations that are already connected. In that respect, airtime of the AP is conserved. On the other hand, decrease in the gain of the weakest user's throughput in Fig.8b becomes more visible with increasing handover latency. For example, for h-SNR, the gain drops from 48% to 26% while that of AIR is from 140% to 114% in the considered cost range. Additionally, switching users may experience low satisfaction if their allocated airtime is insufficient to provide the required throughput for their applications. Fig. 8c shows that handover-cost aware schemes avoid changes in user-AP mappings with increasing handover cost.

5.6 Impact of user density

Fig. 9 shows the impact of increasing user density for the conference scenario. For low user density, all schemes including CD can meet the users' expectations as reflected by 100% satisfaction in Fig.9b. However, with increasing number of users, we observe how naive approaches fall short of providing user satisfaction while DAW and AIR can still maintain a high fraction of satisfied users. For example, for $n = 130$, satisfaction ratio is 0.78 for CD and 0.80 for h-SNR whereas it is 0.86 and 0.85 for DAW and AIR, respectively. Hence, we argue that for dense networks with many users implementing smart controller schemes becomes more paramount compared to

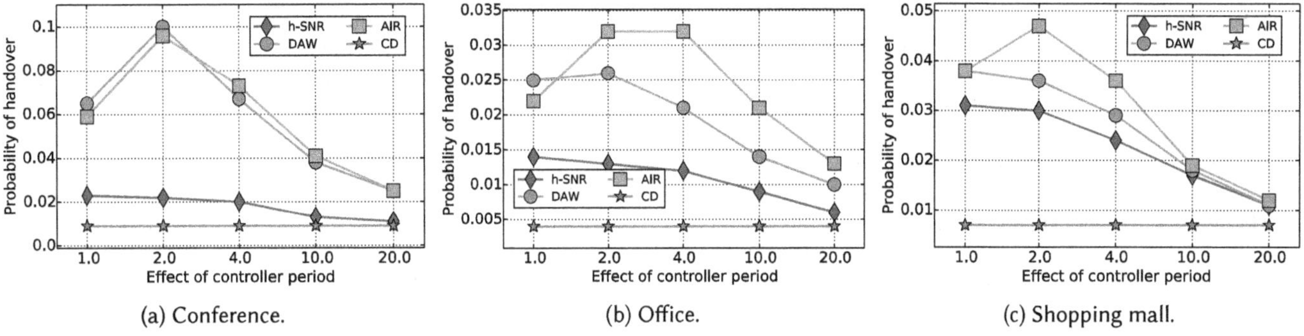

(a) Conference. (b) Office. (c) Shopping mall.

Figure 7: Probability of user handover with increasing controller period for n = 80.

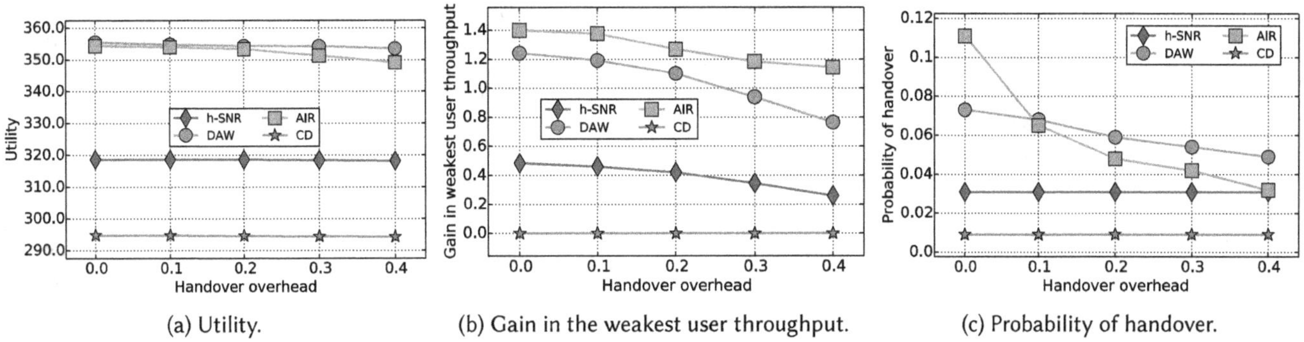

(a) Utility. (b) Gain in the weakest user throughput. (c) Probability of handover.

Figure 8: Impact of increasing handover latency for conference scenario.

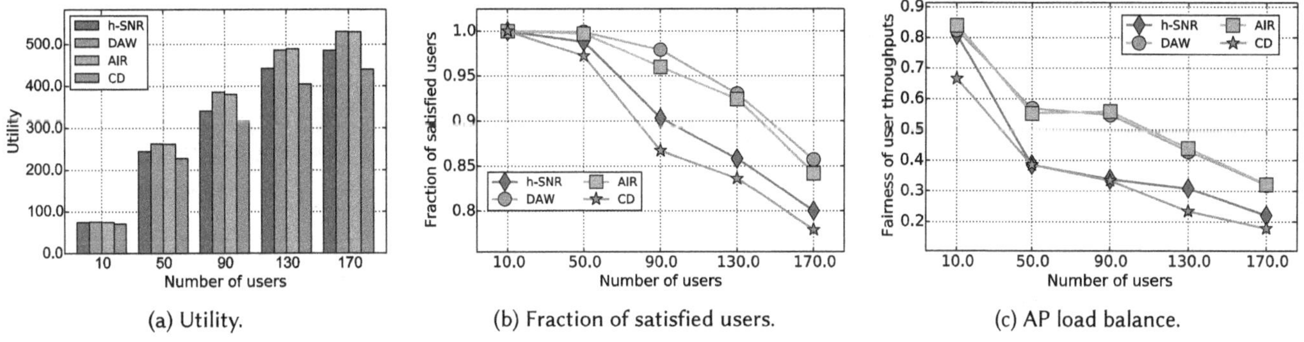

(a) Utility. (b) Fraction of satisfied users. (c) AP load balance.

Figure 9: Impact of increasing number of users for conference scenario.

sparse networks. Recall that only a small fraction, i.e., 0.3, has minimum rate requirements. For scenarios where there are more users with minimum rate requirements, we expect the performance gap between smart and naive schemes as well as between DAW and AIR to be more visible. For scenarios with only a few high-demand users, AIR provides a good balance between complexity and performance as it requires less knowledge compared to DAW.

6 RELATED WORK

Several works [2, 7, 9] have designed various optimal user-AP association schemes using different objectives and under different assumptions. For example, Amer et al. [2] assume that all users associate to an AP will get the same throughput due to the packet-level fairness of 802.11 WLAN and they all have the same traffic demands, whereas Karimi et al. [9] consider a scenario where a user might have explicit time limitations for using an AP's resources. Both [2] and [9] take the logarithmic network-wide downlink throughput as maximization objective to achieve a tradeoff between aggregated throughput and fairness among users. Authors of [8] define a MAC efficiency metric to account for both uplink and downlink throughput of a user and focus on the heterogeneity of the clients, i.e., IEEE 802.11a/b/g/n, while deciding on the optimal users-AP associations in an IEEE 802.11n network. For multiple WiFi deployments, [3] argues that cooperation among different WiFi networks can increase the throughput of the weakest user by alleviating the inter-network interference.

Although optimal user-AP association has been widely studied in the literature [1, 8, 9], when to trigger association control other than upon a new user joining the network is yet to be understood. A user-AP association decision which is optimal at the time of a user joining the network might later become suboptimal due to several reasons, e.g., mobility of the user or new traffic arrival to the user's AP. Amer et al. [2] propose to solve the formulated optimization problem periodically without discussing how long this period should be, whether there is a need for such periodic changes in the user-AP association, and most importantly, how a handover as a result of new association decision affects ongoing communications. Similarly, Karimi et al. [9] envisage that users may change deployment parameters, which then triggers the controller, i.e., the upstream WLAN provider in [9], to run its optimal association algorithm. Different than these works, we provide a thorough analysis of how a range of WLAN scenarios can be affected by the increase in the period of user-AP mapping algorithm.

The key reason for avoiding the periodic or frequent changes in user-AP association is the long duration of switching period due to the set of control messages between the user and the old and new APs for connection breakdown and re-association. To decrease the overhead, [10] virtualizes the wireless NIC as if the user is connected to multiple APs simultaneously. BigAP proposed in [17] exploits the Dynamic Frequency Selection functionality of IEEE 802.11n/ac cards, as if a radar signal is detected, to trigger the handover of some clients on congested/highly-loaded APs to less-loaded APs. Handover is seamless in BigAP as all APs are assigned the same BSSID. Our work can be considered as a complementary solution to [17] in that user-AP mapping decisions are applied by such a mechanism in [17] with very smooth handover.

Another line of related research is on load balancing among APs [4, 10, 14, 16]. In cases where a group of WLAN clients are compactly packed in the coverage of an AP, clients all connect to the same nearby AP. To tackle with the a potential load imbalance, [4] proposes to dynamically adjust the signal power of AP beacons in a way similar to cell breathing in cellular networks. While our proposals do not directly optimize load balance, schemes with AP-load awareness achieve a drastic improvement in load balance compared with the client-driven AP association scheme.

As a WLAN's load balance changes with incoming and leaving users, understanding the nature of these events is crucial. Analysis in [14] on the traces of a campus WLAN shows a high correlation between some users in their AP association history and uplink/downlink traffic volume. Exploiting the social relation among these users, [14] proposes to map such users to different APs to avoid sudden changes in AP loads and overloading of some APs. We plan to extend our analysis with more realistic group mobility models considering the results of [14].

7 CONCLUSION

Motivated by the need for more efficient enterprise WLANs, we have formulated optimal user-AP association as proportionally-fair sum throughput maximization problem solved by a central controller periodically. Different than the existing user-AP association proposals, our proposal is handover-cost aware and considers the minimum throughput requirements (e.g., video or best-effort traffic) of each user while assigning users to APs. Due to the hardness of the optimal solution, we provide several sub-optimal yet efficient heuristics whose achieved utility is slightly lower than the optimal solution. Via simulations, we assess the performance of our proposals for realistic scenarios, e.g., a conference environment. Our results prove the superiority of periodic user-AP association control over the conventional client-driven AP association which is only triggered when the user joins a network or is about to lose connectivity to its serving AP due to user mobility. Generally speaking, our proposals achieve the highest gain for scenarios where users are unevenly distributed in the network.

As future work, we plan to consider also the uplink traffic which has been increasing with wide usage of cloud storage as well as video streaming applications. Another possible direction is to explore how mobility affects the performance of each scheme.

REFERENCES

[1] Murad Abusubaih and Adam Wolisz. 2007. An optimal station association policy for multi-rate IEEE 802.11 wireless LANs. In ACM MsWiM. ACM, 117–123.

[2] Mohammed Amer, Anthony Busson, and Isabelle Guérin Lassous. 2016. Association Optimization in WiFi Networks: Use of an Access-based Fairness. In ACM MsWiM. 119–126.

[3] Akash Baid, Michael Schapira, Ivan Seskar, Jennifer Rexford, and Dipankar Raychaudhuri. 2012. Network cooperation for client-AP association optimization. In IEEE WiOpt. 431–436.

[4] Yigal Bejerano and Seung-Jae Han. 2009. Cell breathing techniques for load balancing in wireless LANs. IEEE Trans. on Mobile Comp. 8, 6 (2009), 735–49.

[5] Surachai Chieochan, Ekram Hossain, and Jeffrey Diamond. 2010. Channel assignment schemes for infrastructure-based 802.11 WLANs: A survey. IEEE Communications Surveys & Tutorials 12, 1 (2010), 124–136.

[6] Cisco. 2017. Channel Planning Best Practices. https://documentation.meraki.com/MR/WiFi_Basics_and_Best_Practices/Channel_Planning_Best_Practices. (2017).

[7] Sourav Kumar Dandapat, Bivas Mitra, Romit Roy Choudhury, and Niloy Ganguly. 2012. Smart association control in wireless mobile environment using max-flow. IEEE Trans. on Network and Service Management 9, 1 (2012), 73–86.

[8] Dawei Gong and Yuanyuan Yang. 2014. On-line AP association algorithms for 802.11n WLANs with heterogeneous clients. *IEEE Trans. Comput.* 63, 11 (2014), 2772–86.

[9] O. B. Karimi, J. Liu, and J. Rexford. 2014. Optimal collaborative AP association in wireless networks. In IEEE INFOCOM.

[10] Masahiro Kawada, Morihiko Tamai, and Keiichi Yasumoto. 2013. A trigger-based dynamic load balancing method for WLANs using virtualized network interfaces. In IEEE Wireless Comms. and Netw. Conference (WCNC). 1091–96.

[11] Nicolas Montavont, Alberto Blanc, Renzo Navas, Tanguy Kerdoncuff, and German Castignani. 2015. Handover triggering in IEEE 802.11 Networks. In IEEE Symp. on a World of Wireless, Mobile and Multimedia Netws. (WoWMoM).

[12] ITUR Resolution. 2009. Guidelines for evaluation of radio interface technologies for IMT-Advanced. (2009).

[13] Thomas Weise. 2009. Global Optimization Algorithms- Theory and Application.

[14] Guangtao Xue, Qi He, Hongzi Zhu, Tian He, and Yunhuai Liu. 2013. Sociality-aware access point selection in enterprise wireless LANs. IEEE Trans. on Parallel and Distributed Systems 24, 10 (2013), 2069–78.

[15] Xiaohuan Yan, Nallasamy Mani, and Y Ahmet Sekercioglu. 2008. A traveling distance prediction based method to minimize unnecessary handovers from cellular networks to WLANs. IEEE Communications Letters 12, 1 (2008), 14–16.

[16] Li-Hsing Yen, Tse-Tsung Yeh, and Kuang-Hui Chi. 2009. Load balancing in IEEE 802.11 networks. IEEE Internet Computing 13, 1 (2009), 56–64.

[17] Anatolij Zubow, Sven Zehl, and Adam Wolisz. 2016. BigAP–Seamless Handover in High Performance Enterprise IEEE 802.11 Networks. In IEEE/IFIP Network Operations and Management Symposium (IEEE NOMS).

Semi-Blind Interference Prediction in Wireless Networks

Mahin K. Atiq, Udo Schilcher, Jorge F. Schmidt, and Christian Bettstetter
Institute of Networked and Embedded Systems, University of Klagenfurt, Austria
Email: firstname.lastname@aau.at

ABSTRACT

Our research investigates the concept of interference prediction as an unprecedented approach for interference management and medium access in wireless networks. This paper is a first step in this direction: it proposes and evaluates a simple interference prediction technique that is based on low-complexity learning. Nodes predict the interference situation they expect to experience in the near future and select the most favorable time slot to start the transmission of a multislot message. The performance gain is evaluated in a small-scale fading environment in terms of link outage and delay against random slot selection. Simulation results show that interference prediction is a promising building block for wireless systems. Additional studies are needed to explore advanced techniques and assess their feasibility.

KEYWORDS

Wireless networks; Interference prediction; Interference modeling

ACM Reference format:
Mahin K. Atiq, Udo Schilcher, Jorge F. Schmidt, and Christian Bettstetter. 2017. Semi-Blind Interference Prediction in Wireless Networks. In *Proceedings of MSWiM '17, Miami, FL, USA, November 21–25, 2017,* 5 pages. https://doi.org/10.1145/3127540.3127579

1 INTRODUCTION

Interference is a stochastic signal that disturbs the reception of an intended signal at a node in a network. Despite advances in understanding the space-time dynamics of interference in wireless networks [4, 6, 13, 16], researchers have not progressed from modeling to designing so far. In other words, an open issue is: How can knowledge about interference dynamics be harnessed to improve communication – maybe in a similar way as we harness knowledge about channel dynamics (e.g., coherence time, decorrelation distances) in today's technologies? Addressing this question may open a new field with potentially high impact: the science of *interference prediction.* This paper is our first step in this direction. We propose a simple interference predictor and analyze its potential, thus going beyond using interference dynamics as a sole analysis tool.

We focus on interference dynamics arising from nodes' traffic patterns. Different nodes send, in general, at different time instances and with different sending durations. Such traffic patterns can be acquired in practice by monitoring the activity of nodes. Three contributions are made: First, we design an interference predictor based on learning the transmission behavior of interfering nodes. Second, we propose a transmission slot selection technique based on interference prediction for slotted medium access. Third, we assess the gains in outage and delay resulting from using such slot selection in a Poisson network with small-scale fading.

Based on the fact that interference is dominated by the closest interferers [3], we develop a predictor that adaptively learns interference patterns. Our design requires only an initial reception of pilot symbols used as input in a setup phase. This pilot scheme has been inspired by *semi-blind* channel estimation techniques [2], where a certain number of known pilot symbols are transmitted periodically for channel estimation and synchronization [11, 15, 17]. The pilot symbols help to estimate the expected reception power from the closest nodes. This power is used to construct a set of binary words, called *transcodes.* This set indicates the possible combinations of active interferers. In a learning phase, expected interference values accounting for contributions from nonclosest nodes are associated to each transcode. Finally, prediction is performed by combining these estimated transcode-interference pairs with the learning of the message durations of closest nodes. Using the current active interferers and the learnt traffic statistics, we predict the nodes that will remain active in future slots and thus the interference level to be expected. This interference prediction is used in the context of slot selection. Nodes attempt to select the most favorable starting slot for the transmission of a multislot message, from a set of slots, given an outage constraint. The performance is evaluated in terms of outage rate and delay; it is compared to a baseline scenario that selects slots uniformly at random.

Some related work is available: A cooperative interference prediction is used for link adaptation in [10]. Call admission control for DS-CDMA systems is done using intercell interference prediction in [7], and power control is achieved with interference prediction using a Kalman filter in [9]. A dynamical interference model is used in [1], where a mobility model is proposed to predict interference.

2 NETWORK MODEL

The nodes of a wireless network are distributed according to a Poisson point process (PPP) Φ with intensity λ without mobility. A specific transmitter-receiver pair (s, r) is considered for interference analysis (Fig. 1). Time is divided into slots. Medium access follows a slotted ALOHA-like scheme: every node i generates messages of length L_i slots by a Poisson arrival process with intensity p and stores them in a queue. If the queue is not empty at the beginning of a new slot, the first message in the queue is transmitted within the next τ slots. The first slot of this message is determined by slot selection. The number of slots until this first slot is called delay W. A transmitting node is called active node. The message length L_i of node i is chosen from an exponential distribution with parameter η rounded up to the next integer and remains at this value for this node. This yields a mean message length of $\mathbb{E}[L] = \frac{e^{\eta}}{e^{\eta}-1}$. The

MSWiM '17, November 21–25, 2017, Miami, FL, USA

ACM ISBN 978-1-4503-5162-1/17/11.
https://doi.org/10.1145/3127540.3127579

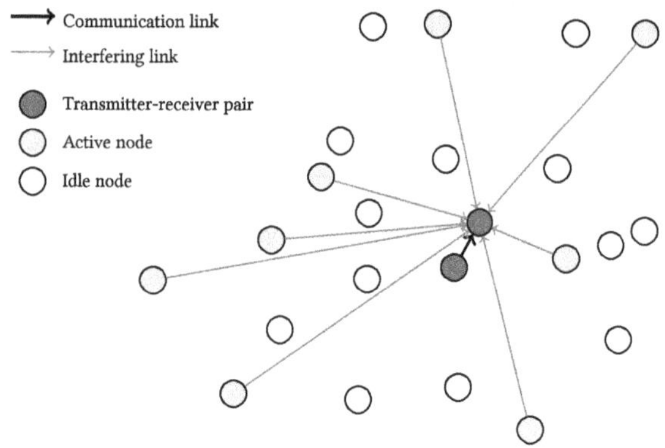

Figure 1: Network scenario.

expected fraction of nodes transmitting at a given slot is $p\,\mathbb{E}[L]$; values of p and η are chosen to ensure $p\,\mathbb{E}[L] \leq 1$.

A common wireless link model is used. The distance between s and r is called d_{sr}. The transmission power of each node is κ. The power attenuation over distance is modeled with a path gain

$$\ell(d_{sr}) = \min\left(1, \left(\frac{d_{sr}}{d_0}\right)^{-\alpha}\right).$$

The path loss exponent α is constant across all slots, and reference distance d_0 needed for normalization is assumed to be $d_0 = 1\,\text{m}$. The effects of multipath propagation are modeled by Nakagami-m fading [12]. A block fading channel is assumed, in which the small-scale fading is independent in each slot and remains constant for the duration of a slot (as in [13]). The reception power arising from a transmission from s to r is $p_r(t) = \kappa\,\ell(d_{sr})\,h_{sr}^2(t)$, where $h_{sr}(t)$ is Nakagami distributed. This transmission experiences co-channel interference from all other active nodes. The interference power at receiver r in slot t is

$$I_r(t) = \sum_{u \in \Phi \setminus \{s\}} \kappa\,\ell(d_{ur})\,h_{ur}^2(t)\,1_u(t)\,, \tag{1}$$

where the indicator function $1_u(t) \in \{0, 1\}$ states whether node u is active (contributes to interference) in slot t or not. The signal-to-interference ratio (SIR) is $\gamma_r(t) = \frac{p_r(t)}{I_r(t)}$. A link is in outage if and only if its SIR is below a certain threshold θ subject to the physical layer. The outage probability at r in slot t is $Q(t) = \mathbb{P}[\gamma_r(t) < \theta] = 1 - \mathbb{P}[\gamma_r(t) \geq \theta]$, whose solution is given by [14, Theorem 3].

The temporal dependance in (1) is caused by the fact that nodes are static (at unknown locations) and messages can be longer than one slot. This setup corresponds to Case (2, 1, 2) in [13]. By learning the traffic patterns in the network, a transmitter-receiver pair should be able to predict its future interference situation and schedule transmissions to reduce outage. The following two sections describe how we do such prediction and timing adjustments.

3 INTERFERENCE PREDICTION

Setup Phase. Upon a setup request from node r (or periodically), close-by nodes insert pilot symbols into their transmissions. Based on these pilots, r estimates the average reception powers from its k strongest interferers $u_1, u_2, \ldots, u_k$ and collects these values in a sorted way in a vector. The first vector element is the strongest interference value; the kth is the weakest. The k-tuple of the indicator functions for the k strongest interferers is the *transcode* $T(t) = (1_{u_1}(t), 1_{u_2}(t), \ldots, 1_{u_k}(t))$. For each distinct transcode, r adds up the estimated power values of the active nodes to yield its expected interference power. Overall, 2^k interference values are calculated and stored in a table, called *Rx-Table*, together with their transcodes. Note that k is a design parameter of the technique.

The setup phase is also used to estimate the Nakagami fading parameter m for the link between receiver r and its transmitter s. Methods proposed in [8, 18] can be applied to do so and get the estimate $\hat{m}$. We use maximum likelihood estimation in our work.

Learning Phase. Once the setup has been completed, all nodes transmit as usual. In order to learn, node r measures the experienced interference in each slot. These measured values are compared to the interference values in the *Rx-Table*. In each slot, we choose from the *Rx-Table* the transcode that corresponds to the largest interference value being smaller than the measured value. These estimated transcodes along with their measured interference values are stored for each slot t.

This data is used for two kinds of purpose at the end of the learning phase. First, r estimates the message lengths L_i and transmission probabilities p_i. This is done by analyzing the bit pattern in the estimations of the $1_{u_i}(t)$ for each of the k interferers u_i. Second, all interference values with the same transcode are averaged. These average values are stored in an *Int-Table* together with their transcodes. Ideally, the learning phase is long enough to allow the *Int-Table* to contain all 2^k lines. If lines are missing, they will be taken from the *Rx-Table*. Both tables consist of 2^k lines and hence do neither introduce high memory nor high search cost for k-values of interest ($k \leq 5$). The main difference between the two is that the *Int-Table* also accounts for the contribution of far away interferers.

Once the initial learning has been completed, the receiver enters the prediction phase. The *Int-Table* entries may be continuously refined while interference values keep being measured. This gives flexibility to the design by allowing to accommodate slow variations in the propagation scenario, arising e.g. from moving obstacles.

Prediction Phase. Node r predicts in each slot t for each of the k strongest interferers whether this interferer will be active in the next slot $t+1$ or not. To do so, it uses a record of the n most recently detected transcodes to predict the transcode $\hat{T}(t+1)$. It then gets the overall interference prediction $\hat{I}(t+1)$ for this transcode from the *Int-Table*. The value n should be larger than the longest message of these interferers. Algorithm 1 summarizes the prediction. For each of the strongest interferers, the predictor checks if interferer u_i is active in the current slot t. If not, the prediction will be that this interferer will remain inactive in slot $t+1$. If yes, the predictor counts as to how long the interferer has been transmitting. If this length is an integer multiple of the estimated message length $\hat{L}_i$ (acquired in the learning phase), the prediction is that the interferer will be inactive in slot $t+1$. Otherwise, the prediction is that it will remain active. Once this is done for all k interferers, the predicted transcode $\hat{T}(t+1)$ is constructed, and the corresponding predicted interference $\hat{I}(t+1)$ is read from the *Int-Table*.

Algorithm 1 Interference Prediction

for $i = 1, \dots, k$ **do**
  if $1_{u_i}(t) = 0$ **then**
    $\hat{1}_{u_i}(t+1) = 0$
  else
    Count = 1
    while ($1_{u_i}(t-\text{Count}) == 1$) **do**
      Count ++
    end while
    if (Count mod $\hat{L}_i$) == 0, **then**
      $\hat{1}_{u_i}(t+1) = 0$
    else
      $\hat{1}_{u_i}(t+1) = 1$
    end if
  end if
end for
search: *Int-Table* entry for $\hat{T}$
return: $\hat{I}(t+1)$

4 SLOT SELECTION

We utilize interference prediction to choose the best slot from $(\tau+1)$ following slots to start the transmission of a message. Our goal is to transmit as soon as possible constrained on an outage probability threshold ξ. This *slot selection based on interference prediction* $\mathcal{S}_{\text{IP}}$ works as follows (see Algorithm 2).

Node r predicts the interference for the next slot using Algorithm 1 and uses $\hat{I}(t+1)$ to calculate the predicted outage $\hat{Q}(t+1)$. For Nakagami-m fading with an estimated parameter $\hat{m}$, we have:

$$\hat{Q}(t+1) = \frac{1}{\Gamma(\hat{m})}\,\gamma\left(\hat{m}, \frac{\theta\,\hat{I}(t+1)}{\ell(d_{sr})}\,\hat{m}\right), \tag{2}$$

with gamma function $\Gamma(\cdot)$ and incomplete gamma function $\gamma(\cdot,\cdot)$. Depending on the predicted outage and ξ, a decision on whether to transmit in slot $t+1$ is made. If $\hat{Q}(t+1) \le \xi$, the predictor selects this slot. Otherwise, the decision is delayed by one slot. If no suitable slot is found within the transmission interval τ, the last slot $t+\tau+1$ is chosen.

Algorithm 2 Slot Selection Based on Interference Prediction $\mathcal{S}_{\text{IP}}$

Initiate a τ-slots transmission interval count
for $j = 1, \dots, \tau+1$ **do**
  Get $\hat{I}(t+j)$ from Algorithm 1
  Compute expected $\hat{Q}(t+j)$ from (2)
  if $\hat{Q}(t+j) \le \xi$, **then**
    Transmit
    exit **for**
  end if
  if $j = \tau+1$ **then**
    Transmit
  end if
end for

Low ξ leads on average to high delay W, as the predicted outage $\hat{Q}(t+1)$ is unlikely to reach its target ξ (and vice versa). It is important to note that lowering ξ does not necessarily result in lower outage. This is because, at low ξ, the end of the transmission interval is reached very frequently. The node is then forced to transmit in the last slot even if the threshold is not met; it thus missed an earlier slot with lower outage probability.

5 NUMERICAL EVALUATION

To investigate the performance achieved with $\mathcal{S}_{\text{IP}}$, we simulate a network with node density λ in a square area of size $A = 10{,}000\ \text{m}^2$. Due to the stationarity of the PPP and Slivnyak's theorem [5], we can assume that r is located in the middle of the area. Each other node transmits as described in Section 2 with parameters $p = 0.1$ and $\mathbb{E}[L] = 5$ using a fixed transmit power $\kappa = 1$ mW. The path loss exponent is $\alpha = 3$. We compare $\mathcal{S}_{\text{IP}}$ with *random slot selection* $\mathcal{S}_{\text{Rand}}$, which choses the first slot randomly from a uniform distribution between 0 and τ. Both selection schemes use the same τ. Simulations are performed over 20, 000 slots with a learning phase of 1, 000 slots and are averaged over 10, 000 independent realizations of Φ. All simulations are made using the R project for statistical computing.

The proper functioning of interference prediction is illustrated in Fig. 2, which compares the predicted and measured interference for 100 slots in a single realization of Φ. The predicted interference is close to the true interference for most slots with a mean square error of MSE = 0.068 $(\text{mW})^2$. Deviations are mainly caused by fading and interference from some close nodes starting new transmissions.

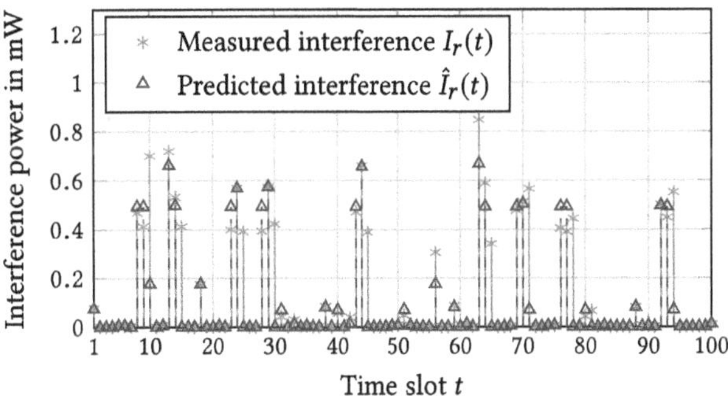

Figure 2: Measured and predicted interference power values

Impact of Node Density on Outage: Fig. 3 shows the impact of λ on outage. $\mathcal{S}_{\text{IP}}$ has a lower outage rate than $\mathcal{S}_{\text{Rand}}$ for all λ-values. The relative difference decreases with increasing λ because if nodes are far apart (sparse network, low λ), the few closest nodes can be easily distinguished, leading to good interference prediction; if nodes are close together (dense network, high λ), the distinction between closest neighbors degrades, resulting in poor interference prediction and consequently a smaller benefit in terms of outage.

Impact of Mean Delay on Outage: Fig. 4 shows the outage over the mean delay $\overline{W}$ for $\mathcal{S}_{\text{IP}}$. Since delay cannot be controlled directly, we vary ξ from 0 (high delay expected) to 1 (low delay expected). For random slot selection, the mean delay is always $\overline{W} = \tau/2$ — the line just indicates the outage rate for comparison. For reference, we show the results of $\mathcal{S}_{\text{IP}}$ fed with true interference values to make perfect slot selection. The main result is that $\mathcal{S}_{\text{IP}}$ always outperforms $\mathcal{S}_{\text{Rand}}$ in terms of outage (except for the extreme cases $\overline{W} = 0$ and τ, where all have the same outage because $\mathcal{S}_{\text{IP}}$ always

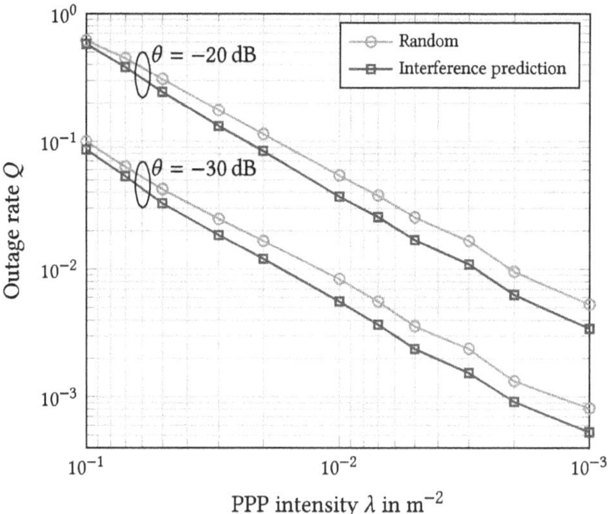

Figure 3: Outage over PPP intensity λ with $m = 3.5$, $p = 0.09$, $\tau = 6$, $k = 5$, and $\mathbb{E}[L] = 5.5$. We use here a larger area of $A = 1\,\text{km}^2$ to have enough active nodes for low λ.

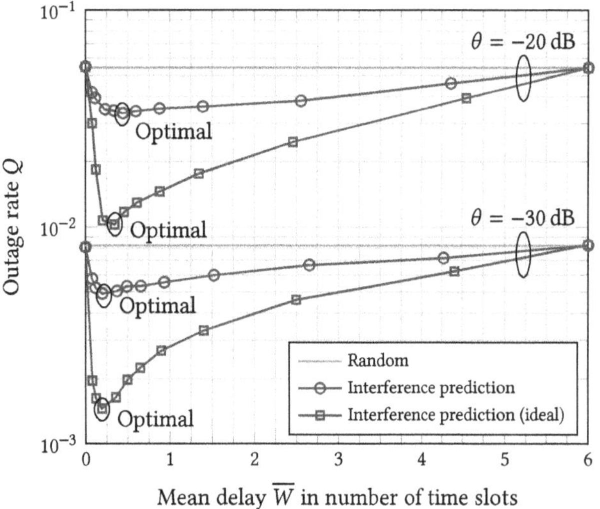

Figure 4: Outage over mean delay $\overline{W}$ with $m = 3.5$, $\tau = 6$, $\lambda = 10^{-2}$, $p = 0.1$, $k = 5$, and $\mathbb{E}[L] = 5$.

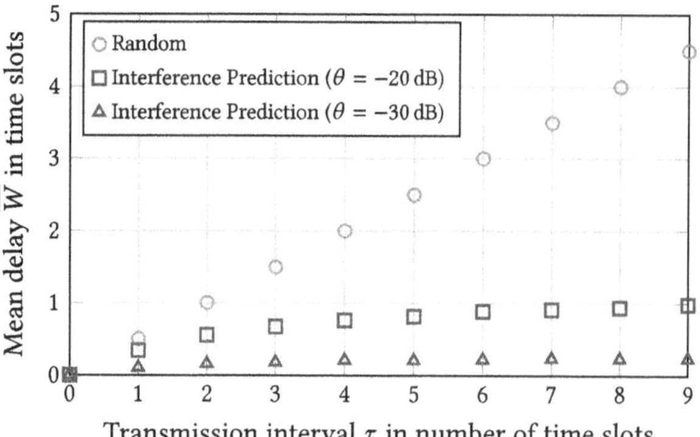

Figure 5: Mean delay over transmission interval τ with $m = 3.5$, $\lambda = 10^{-2}$, $p = 0.1$, $k = 5$, and $\mathbb{E}[L] = 5$.

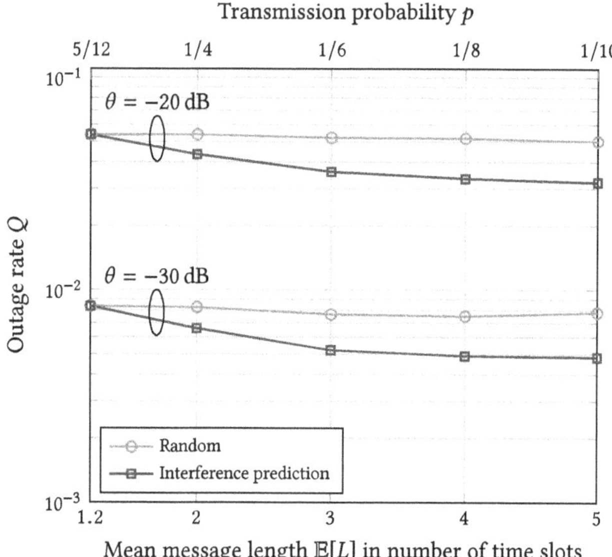

Figure 6: Outage over mean message length $\mathbb{E}[L]$ with $m = 3.5$, $\lambda = 10^{-2}$, $k = 5$, and $\tau = 9$

chooses the first or last slot, respectively). Note that an optimal operation point exists, which will be used in the following.

Impact of Transmission Interval on Delay: Fig. 5 shows that the mean delay of S_{IP} is lower than that using S_{Rand} for all values of τ (except for $\tau = 0$, where both have zero delay). The mean delay using interference prediction increases with increasing τ over the full range of the plot (which shows that S_{IP} sometimes uses the entire transmission interval to find a suitable slot). Nevertheless, this increase is much slower than the one using S_{Rand}.

Impact of Message Length on Outage: Fig. 6 studies the impact of $\mathbb{E}[L]$ on outage. We vary $\mathbb{E}[L]$ but keep $p\mathbb{E}[L]$ constant (at 0.5), thus having on average a constant fraction of active nodes and hence constant interference. The benefit of interference prediction is good for long messages but low for short ones. As short messages go along with high p, the technique is unable to predict nodes that become active in the next slot; the predictor underestimates the interference, resulting in outage close to random slot selection. Long messages, in turn, help the interference prediction.

Impact of Fading on Outage and Delay: To analyze the sensitivity of S_{IP} against fading, we evaluate the outage rate for different values of the Nakagami parameter m (Fig. 7). Recall that the severeness of fading increases with decreasing m. As expected even without interference, the outage rate decreases for increasing m.

Two types of S_{IP} are used: First, we optimize ξ individually for each m in terms of outage, where this optimal ξ is obtained by simulations (recall Fig. 4). Second, since the optimal ξ depends on

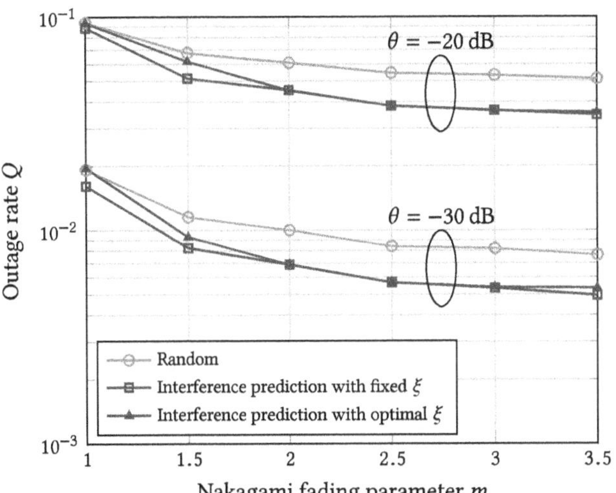

Figure 7: Outage over Nakagami fading parameter m with $\lambda = 10^{-2}$, $p = 0.1$, $k = 5$, $\tau = 6$, and $\mathbb{E}[L] = 5$.

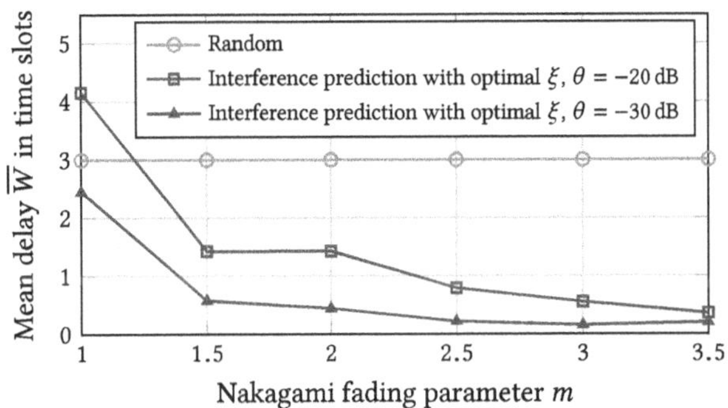

Figure 8: Mean delay over Nakagami fading parameter m with $\lambda = 10^{-2}$, $p = 0.1$, $k = 5$, $\tau = 6$, and $\mathbb{E}[L] = 5$.

many parameters and takes effort to be determined, we keep ξ constant over all m (we set ξ to its optimal value for $m = 2$). As expected, the first approach yields a lower outage rate than the second one. The difference is significant for strong fading (low m) but becomes negligible for weak fading (high m).

Both $\mathcal{S}_{\text{IP}}$ types outperform $\mathcal{S}_{\text{Rand}}$ independent of the severeness of the fading — the actual gain depends on m — meaning that the proposed slot selection scheme is somehow robust against fading. However, recall that the MSE in the actual interference prediction significantly depends on m. This is related to the predictor design, as it does not make use of fading channel estimation.

Finally, Fig. 8 shows the mean delay over m for optimally chosen ξ. $\mathcal{S}_{\text{IP}}$ has shorter mean delays than $\mathcal{S}_{\text{Rand}}$ for almost all m. Only when m is close to 1, the delay increases, as the interference prediction degrades significantly.

6 CONCLUSIONS AND OUTLOOK

Slot selection based on a simple interference prediction technique performs well in certain scenarios, especially in sparse networks with long messages. The gains in outage and delay show the potential of interference prediction as a building block in wireless systems. The performance strongly depends, however, on a proper choice of the outage threshold ξ. The proposed technique underestimates interference because transcode estimation does not consider newly started transmissions. It is expected that advanced learning techniques will improve interference prediction (probably at the cost of increased complexity). Further work is needed to design such advanced techniques, discuss their integration into the protocol stack, and assess their practicability in real systems. Comparisons with related interference management concepts, such as carrier sense medium access with backoff, must be made.

ACKNOWLEDGMENTS

This work was supported by grant P24480-N15 of the Austrian Science Fund (FWF) and grant 20214/26481/38805 of the KWF.

REFERENCES

[1] Yirui Cong, Xiangyun Zhou, and Rodney A. Kennedy. 2015. Interference prediction in mobile ad hoc networks with a general mobility model. *IEEE Trans. Wireless Commun.* 14, 8 (2015), 4277–4290.

[2] Elisabeth D. Carvalho and Dirk T. M. Slock. 1997. Cramer-Rao bounds for semi-blind, blind and training sequence based channel estimation. In *Proc. Workshop on Signal Process. Adv. in Wireless Commun.* IEEE, Paris, France, 129–132.

[3] Radha K. Ganti and Martin Haenggi. 2009. Spatial and temporal correlation of the interference in ALOHA ad hoc networks. *IEEE Commun. Lett.* 13, 9 (2009), 631–633.

[4] Martin Haenggi. 2009. Outage, local throughput, and capacity of random wireless networks. *IEEE Trans. Wireless Commun.* 8, 8 (2009), 4350–4359.

[5] Martin Haenggi. 2013. *Stochastic Geometry for Wireless Networks.* Cambridge University Press, Cambridge, United Kingdom.

[6] Martin Haenggi and Roxana Smarandache. 2013. Diversity polynomials for the analysis of temporal correlations in wireless networks. *IEEE Trans. Wireless Commun.* 12, 11 (2013), 5940–5951.

[7] Il M. Kim, Byung C. Shin, and Dong J. Lee. 2000. SIR-based call admission control by intercell interference prediction for DS-CDMA systems. *IEEE Commun. Lett.* 4, 1 (2000), 29–31.

[8] Young C. Ko and Mohamed S. Alouini. 2003. Estimation of Nakagami-m fading channel parameters with application to optimized transmitter diversity systems. *IEEE Trans. Wireless Commun.* 2, 2 (2003), 250–259.

[9] Kin K. Leung. 2002. Power control by interference prediction for broadband wireless packet networks. *IEEE Trans. Wireless Commun.* 1, 2 (2002), 256–265.

[10] Andreas Müller and Philipp Frank. 2010. Cooperative interference prediction for enhanced link adaptation in the 3GPP LTE uplink. In *Proc. Vehicular Technology Conf. (VTC).* IEEE, Taipei, Taiwan.

[11] Bertrand Muquet, Marc D. Courville, and Pierre Duhamel. 2002. Subspace-based blind and semi-blind channel estimation for OFDM systems. *IEEE Trans. Signal Process.* 50, 7 (2002), 1699–1712.

[12] Minoru Nakagami. 1958. The m-distribution — A general formula of intensity distribution of rapid fading. In *Proc. Symp. on Statistical Methods in Radio Wave Propag.* Pergamon Press, Los Angeles, USA, 3–36.

[13] Udo Schilcher, Christian Bettstetter, and Günther Brandner. 2012. Temporal correlation of interference in wireless networks with Rayleigh block fading. *IEEE Trans. Mobile Comput.* 11, 12 (2012), 2109–2120.

[14] Udo Schilcher, Stavros Toumpis, Martin Haenggi, Alessandro Crismani, Günther Brandner, and Christian Bettstetter. 2016. Interference functionals in Poisson networks. *IEEE Trans. Inf. Theory* 62, 1 (2016), 370–383.

[15] Arnold L. Swindlehurst and Geert Leus. 2002. Blind and semi-blind equalization for generalized space-time block codes. *IEEE Trans. Signal Process.* 50, 10 (2002), 2489–2498.

[16] Ralph Tanbourgi, Harpreet S. Dhillon, Jeffrey G. Andrews, and Friedrich K. Jondral. 2014. Effect of spatial interference correlation on the performance of maximum ratio combining. *IEEE Trans. Wireless Commun.* 13, 6 (2014), 3307–3316.

[17] Fredrik Tufvesson and Torleiv Maseng. 1997. Pilot assisted channel estimation for OFDM in mobile cellular systems. In *Proc. Vehicular Technology Conf. (VTC).* IEEE, Phoenix, AZ, USA, 1639–1643.

[18] Qi T. Zhang. 2002. A note on the estimation of Nakagami-m fading parameter. *IEEE Commun. Lett.* 6, 6 (2002), 237–238.

LABeL: Link-based Adaptive BLacklisting Technique for 6TiSCH Wireless Industrial Networks

Vasileios Kotsiou
ICube Lab, CNRS / University of Strasbourg
Illkirch, France
kotsiou@unistra.fr

Georgios Z. Papadopoulos
IMT Atlantique, IRISA, UBL
Rennes, France
georgios.papadopoulos@imt-atlantique.fr

Periklis Chatzimisios
CSSN Research Lab, Alexander TEI of Thessaloniki
Thessaloniki, Greece
peris@it.teithe.gr

Fabrice Théoleyre
ICube Lab, CNRS / University of Strasbourg
Illkirch, France
theoleyre@unistra.fr

ABSTRACT

Industrial applications require more and more low-power operations, low-delay, deterministic communications as well as end-to-end reliability close to 100%. However, traditional radio technologies are sensitive to external interference, which degrades the reliability and introduces unpredictable delays due to collision detection and retransmissions. Therefore, recent standardization efforts focus on slow channel hopping strategies to provide strict Quality of Service (QoS) for the Industrial Internet of Things (IIoT). By keeping nodes time-synchronized and by employing a channel hopping approach, IEEE 802.15.4-TSCH (Time-Slotted Channel Hoping) aims at providing high-level network reliability. However, some radio channels still suffer from high external interference and need to be *blacklisted*. Since the interference pattern is rather dynamic, unpredictable and highly localized, we here propose heuristics to decide which channels to blacklist. To avoid deafness, the transmitter and the receiver must also agree on a consistent blacklist. Furthermore, since the external interference may be time-dependent as well, we also propose mechanisms to decide when a channel has to be blacklisted or on the contrary recovered. Our thorough experimental evaluation based on OpenWSN and FIT IoT-LAB highlight the relevance of this approach: with a localized blacklisting strategy, we increase by 20% packet delivery rate for the worst links.

KEYWORDS

IoT; IEEE 802.15.4-2015; TSCH; Channel Hopping; Radio Characterization; Interference; Blacklisting; Experimental Evaluation;

1 INTRODUCTION

Wireless deployments are becoming broadly used and enable an Internet access for any user (and thing). Indeed, during the last years we have experienced the emergence of a new paradigm called Internet of Things (IoT) in which smart, uniquely identifiable and connected objects cooperatively construct a (wireless) network of things [2]. Those things can be deployed nearly everywhere, at homes, universities, cities, agricultural fields, even in human bodies.

Among the previously mentioned deployments, the Industry 4.0 is an emerging concept aiming at re-using the IoT automation to make the production chains more profitable by maximizing flexibility and adaptability in the factories. Industrial applications, such as vehicle automation, smart grid, automotive industry or airport logistics, share similar network performance requirements of including low-latency and high network reliability.

To provide Quality of Service (QoS) for industrial-like wireless networks, IEEE 802.15.4-2015 standard was published in 2016 [1]. Time-Slotted Channel Hoping (TSCH) is among the Medium Access Control (MAC) schemes defined in this standard. TSCH aims at low-power, deterministic and reliable wireless industrial networks. At its core, TSCH relies on scheduling by employing time synchronization to solve the contention in the wireless medium. To achieve low-power operations, a node turns its radio *ON* only when it transmits or receives a frame. Furthermore, TSCH supports a channel hopping approach to efficiently combat the noisy environments.

Number of research works related with radio characterization demonstrate that most of the IEEE 802.15.4 radio channels suffer from external interference in the 2.4 *GHz* band (e.g. [9, 14, 15, 25]). In particular, the IEEE 802.11 channels 1, 6 and 11 are extensively used and, thus, they interfere and heavily impact most of the IEEE 802.15.4 channels [11, 26]. As it is shown in Fig. 1, the 15, 20 and 25-26 IEEE 802.15.4 channels do not interfere with the popular IEEE 802.11 channels. In such harsh environments, channel hopping solutions are essential to combat external interference [26].

Since the overlapped channels may perform badly during long periods [11], the system should *blacklist* them in the channel hopping sequence. For instance, WirelessHART provides the possibility to *block* globally the bad channels [20] by removing them from the frequency hopping sequence for all the nodes. Blacklisting improves both reliability and energy efficiency, by reducing the amount of packet losses. However, we still have to propose localized strategies to detect and blacklist dynamically those bad channels.

In this paper, we focus on frequency hopping based approaches, and we aim at identifying the importance of implementing link-based blacklisting methods. We then propose LABeL, a Link-based Adaptive BLacklisting algorithm. To evaluate our mechanism, we

MSWiM '17, , November 21-25, 2017, Miami, FL, USA.

ACM ISBN ISBN 978-1-4503-5162-1/17/11...$15.00
https://doi.org/https://doi.org/10.1145/3127540.3127541

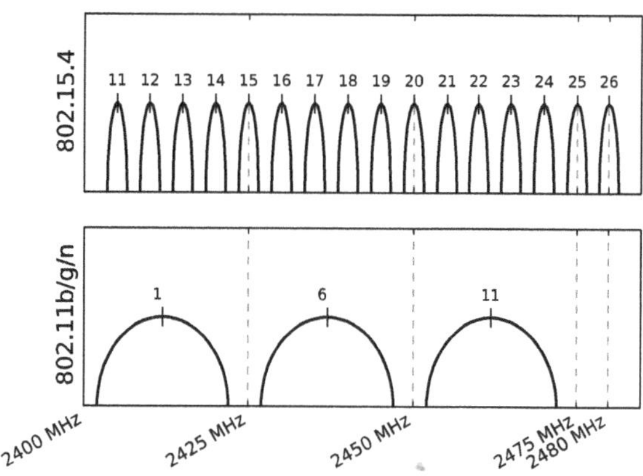

Figure 1: Overlapping IEEE 802.15.4 and IEEE 802.11 channels.

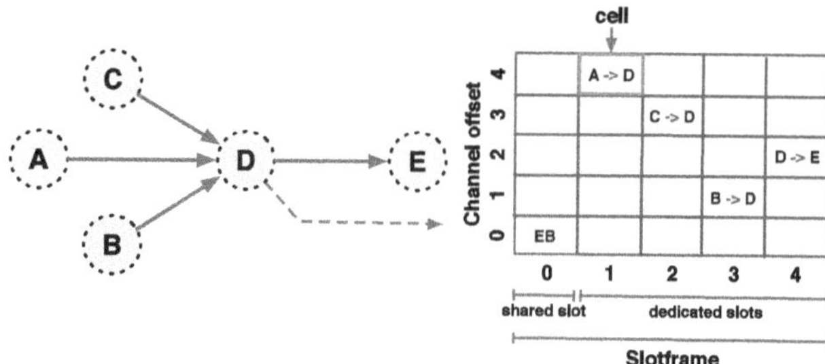

Figure 2: An example of TSCH scheduling for node D. A → D stands for *'A transmits to D'*, while Enhanced Beacon (EB) cells are used for broadcast and advertisement frames.

conduct a thorough experimental campaign, over the large Future Internet of the Things IoT-LAB platform based on M3 nodes and OpenWSN project that comes with a full 6TiSCH IoT stack, i.e., IEEE 802.15.4-TSCH, IPv6, 6TiSCH, Routing over Low Power and Lossy Networks (RPL), Constrained Application Protocol (CoAP). Our thorough experimental results highlight a significant increase of Packet Delivery Ratio (PDR), by 20% for the worst links.

The contributions of this paper are as follows:

(1) We provide an algorithm to determine dynamically which physical channels to blacklist. A set of *bad* channels is identified for each radio link. Since we do not exploit a *fixed* threshold value, we are able to identify bad channels even for weak links;
(2) We present a method to passively probe the bad channels, while limiting their impact on the energy consumption and the reliability;
(3) By exploiting 6P control packets, we detail techniques to maintain consistent blacklists for both the transmitter and the receiver and, thus, to avoid deafness [13];
(4) We propose a method to modify the frequency hopping sequence. This way, we make the collisions not repetitive, when two radio links use the same timeslot with a different channel offset and different blacklists;
(5) We experimentally validate our approach in the FIT IoT-LAB indoor testbed with the OpenWSN stack.

2 BACKGROUND & RELATED WORK

2.1 Channel Hopping-based Standards

Using a different physical channel for successive transmissions allows to reduce the impact of external interference and to improve the network reliability [26]. Indeed, the standardization bodies have proposed to use channel-hopping techniques, which allow subsequent packets to be transmitted over different frequencies, mainly to be utilized for industrial wireless networks. More specifically, the failed packet will be retransmitted through another physical channel, to increase the probability of successful reception, particularly in presence of narrow band external interference. Note that such protocols require strict guarantees in terms of time synchronization between the nodes within the wireless network [16].

IEEE 802.15.4-2015 has proposed the TSCH mode, largely inspired from the previous ISA100.11a [10] and WirelessHART [21] standards. In TSCH networks, time is divided into timeslots of equal length. At each timeslot, a node may transmit or receive a frame, or it may turn to sleep mode for saving energy. A set of timeslots constructs a slotframe. Each timeslot is labelled with an Absolute Sequence Number (ASN), a variable which counts the number of timeslots since the network was established. Based on the ASN and the schedule, the nodes in the TSCH network decide when to transmit or receive a frame.

IEEE 802.15.4-2015 TSCH implements a channel hopping approach to combat noise and interference and, thus, to achieve high network reliability [26]. To do so, TSCH presents a deterministic scheduling approach in which each cell consists of a pair of timeslot and channel offset for collision avoidance. The standard maintains a schedule, and assigns a set of cells to each radio link. At the beginning of each timeslot, the channel offset is translated into a physical channel using the ASN value:

$$frequency = F\left(\left(ASN + channelOffset\right) \% \ nFreq\right) \quad (1)$$

where ASN denotes the Absolute Sequence Number of the timeslot, $channelOffset$ the channel offset of the current cell, and $nFreq$ is the number of available channels (e.g., 16 when using IEEE 802.15.4-compliant radios at 2.4 GHz with all channels in use) [27]. Finally, note that each cell can be either dedicated (contention-free) or shared (contention-based approach).

In Fig. 2, a TSCH schedule is illustrated. The Enhanced Beacons (EBs) are broadcast packets and use the first (shared) cell (with contention). All the other cells are dedicated, one transmission opportunity being here allocated per slotframe to each active radio link.

2.2 Blacklisting Techniques

Blacklisting consists in identifying the channels which exhibit the lowest reliability to avoid using them for the transmissions. Without channel hopping, it consists for each radio link in negotiating the most efficient channel to use for *all* its transmissions [22].

Channel hopping allows to minimize the impact of these *bad* channels [26]. However, they still negatively impact the number of (re)-transmissions and the reliability. Thus, blacklisting for slow frequency hopping consists in excluding the *bad* channels from the frequency hopping sequence. This technique has been used by several standards such as IEEE 802.15.4-2015 [1] and WirelessHART [20].

2.2.1 Detecting bad channels. Blacklisting a channel may also reduce the network capacity, since the same traffic has to be forwarded through a smaller number of channels. Thus, we have to carefully select the channels to blacklist, i.e., their usage has to significantly degrade the reliability.

Hanninen *et al.* [8] propose to blacklist a channel if the associated packets exhibit an average Received Signal Strength Indicator (RSSI) value below a given threshold. However, RSSI has been shown to inaccurately estimate link quality for both indoor [23] and outdoor [17] environments. Sha *et al.* [19] blacklist the channels when the link reliability is below a certain threshold and they also exploit the fact that adjacent channels often exhibit a similar behavior.

To recover, Tang *et al.* [22] remove a channel from the blacklist after a fixed period: the channel has to be probed again to be (re)-blacklisted. Thus, the blacklist is periodically flushed, and the node has to re-estimate the link quality, it keeps on continuously oscillating, needing time to re-blacklist a bad channel. We rather propose to adopt a *continuous* approach, *updating* the link quality of bad channels with a limited impact on data packet losses.

Chiti *et al.* [4] use a spectrum sensing technique during a few dedicated timeslots to identify which channels to blacklist. However, such method needs specific cells, during which no other node is allowed to transmit, thus, wasting bandwidth and energy.

2.2.2 Global vs. localized blacklisting. Bluetooth was also exploiting frequency hopping to improve the reliability. Zacharias *et al.* investigated the co-existence of Wi-Fi and Bluetooth networks [28], and proposed to blacklist the concerned WLAN channels for Bluetooth. However, only 1-hop topologies are considered.

In WirelessHART, the blacklisting solution is applied globally, where certain channels are blocked for the whole wireless industrial network [20]. Such approach may be suboptimal since a physical channel exhibits very location-dependent characteristics [11]. Even more, a *weak* radio link will be more impacted by external interference: the Signal-to-Noise-plus-Interference Ratio (SINR) margin is smaller. Thus, a per-link blacklist should be preferred to avoid wasting bandwidth.

In ISA100.11a [18], a localized blacklist may also be implemented. The node has the right to transmit during a cell if the channel offset does not give a blacklisted physical channel. Else, the node has to *skip* the cell until the channel offset gives an authorized physical channel. However, such approach has a very negative impact on the delay and the throughput: the transmitter has to defer its transmission until the frequency hopping sequence provides a non-blacklisted channel (in the next slotframe).

Du *et al.* [5] proposed a localized blacklisting method in TSCH, in which a pair of nodes negotiate the most accurate channels to use based on link quality indicators. To this aim, specific timeslots are reserved to measure the noise level on each physical channel. A node then exchanges with its neighbors its blacklist to agree on the channels to use. In this study, we do not dedicate additional resource to probe each channel. We also modify the pseudo-random sequence to avoid repetitive collisions when two interfering radio links do not use the same blacklist.

2.3 6TiSCH Overview

The 6TiSCH IETF working group aims to define a set of protocols to operate IPv6 (i.e., 6LoWPAN) over a reservation based MAC layer (i.e., TSCH). 6TiSCH defines the way to modify the schedule, using the protocol 6P. In a distributed scheme, the Scheduling Function (e.g., SF0 [6]) will decide how many cells to reserve with a neighbor. A 6P transaction then engages, transmitted through the shared cells, or specific dedicated cells if some are already present in the schedule. A two-way handshake is provided in 6P:

(1) The transmitter sends a 6P request in unicast, with a list of available cells. This request is acknowledged by the receiver;
(2) The receiver verifies a sufficient part of these cells are available in its schedule. It then constructs a 6P reply transmitted in unicast, acknowledged by the transmitter.

When the transaction has completed, both the transmitter and the receiver have modified consistently their schedule. In particular, the loss of acknowledgements is neglected: the 6P unicast packet has already reserved the medium and the level of external interference may be considered stable during a timeslot.

Alternatively, 6TiSCH also supports a global schedule computed by the Path Computation Element (PCE) and pushed to each node.

In this study, we design and develop LocAd, a localized and adaptive blacklisting scheme for TSCH. To this aim, we employ the OpenWSN, an implementation of a full protocol stack based on IoT standards (i.e., IEEE 802.15.4-TSCH, IPv6, 6TiSCH, RPL, CoAP).

3 PROBLEM STATEMENT & APPROACH

External interference may severely affect some IEEE 802.15.4 channels [26], requiring to blacklist the *bad* channels. However, the performance of a given physical channel depends heavily on the geographical location, and even on the link's characteristics [11].

We propose here to implement a *link-based* blacklisting algorithm, i.e., LABeL: the transmitter and the receiver have to agree on the blacklisted channels to not use for their transmissions. Different pairs of nodes would blacklist different channels resulting in increased frequency re-use. More specifically, each pair monitors the link quality across all the 16 available channels at 2.4 *GHz*, and decides which channels to utilize. Consequently, in this study, we focus on addressing the following challenges:

Overhead: We here implement a passive method to detect *bad* channels. No probing packets are required, increasing both the level of interference and the energy consumption. Instead, we use the data packets to continuously re-evaluate the quality of channels in order to appropriately insert or remove from the blacklist;

Time-variant: Under dynamic environments, the list of bad channels may change so frequently that blacklisting it would have no effect on the performance [11]. Control packets have to be exchanged to update the blacklist, which would annihilate the benefit of reducing the number of (re)transmissions to deliver a data packet to the next hop. We experimentally verify that the PDR is actually improved with a localized adaptive blacklisting approach;

Inconsistency management: Two nodes agreeing on the list of bad channels, requires signaling (i.e., additional control packets). Since some control or acknowledgement packets may be lost, some inconsistencies may arise. As a result, they may operate with a different frequency hopping sequence, leading to potential deafness. We will propose robust mechanisms integrated to 6P in order to make the transactions reliable.

Minimization of collisions: When two interfering radio links use a different blacklist, they may collide even if they do not use the same channel offset, since Equation 1 depends on the blacklist's content (i.e., the number of available channels). We propose to modify the frequency hopping sequence to make the collisions less repetitive.

In this paper, we both propose the mechanisms to implement a link-based blacklist, and we evaluate thoroughly the blacklisting technique in a realistic testbed to demonstrate the advantages of such approach.

4 LOCALIZED AND PER-LINK ADAPTIVE BLACKLISTING UNDER IEEE 802.15.4-TSCH

A global blacklist exploits a list of *bad* channels that provide a low reliability due to the presence of interference. However, this list is location and time-dependent [11]: while a channel may perform badly for some radio links, it may provide a close to perfect reliability for some other radio links. Moreover, the same radio channel may perform well during the afternoon and night, however, its performance may drop during the day-time, due to the Wi-Fi activity.

The impact of external interference depends on the SINR margin of the radio link [7]. When the transmitter and the receiver are close to each other, the level of external interference has to be higher to impact the reliability. Thus, we here present an algorithm to incorporate a **localized** and **per-link** blacklist into IEEE 802.15.4-TSCH.

4.1 Deciding which channels to blacklist

In this study, we propose LABeL to identify the channels to blacklist, i.e., the set of channels that impact negatively the performance of the radio link and/or the network. According to our previous work, relying on RSSI or LQI metric is not representative of the channel quality [11]. Therefore, we focus on measuring the PDR performance, denoting accurately the ability of the link to deliver successfully the data packets.

To this aim, each node in a TSCH network computes the PDR of unicast data packets **independently** for each neighbor and channel. More precisely, a node counts the number of Acknowledgements (ACKs) and the number of packets transmitted to a particular neighbor N. Since we are interested in a per channel behavior, we compute this PDR value independently for each channel and neighbor:

$$PDR(N, c) = \frac{nb_{ack}(N, c)}{nb_{tx}(N, c)} \tag{2}$$

with $nb_{ack}[N, c]$ the number of ACKs received from N through the channel c, and $nb_{tx}[N, c]$ the number of packets transmitted to N.

We can note that a node that uses several tracks to the same neighbor may compute the average PDR for *all* the tracks. Indeed, external interference will impact equally each track, and we can aggregate the traffic of several tracks to more accurately identify the *bad* channels.

Most of the proposals use a fixed threshold value (e.g., [8], [19]): any radio channel that provides a PDR inferior to a pre-defined threshold value is blacklisted. However, the *average* PDR is very radio link-dependent: when the received signal strength is low, packets may be dropped even if no external interference is present. Low quality links are frequent in many deployments, while high quality links are often not sufficient to maintain a connected topology [12]. We have consequently focus on an **adaptive** approach in which this threshold depends on the link, and is not fixed a priori globally.

The Window Mean Exponential Weighted Moving Average estimator (WMEWMA) has been proved to accurately estimate the link quality [3]. Indeed, packet losses represent a stochastic variable and need to be *smoothen*. We consequently propose to use WMEWMA to independently measure the PDR for each channel. For this sake, a node counts the number of transmitted messages, and the number of acknowledgments received correctly. In this paper, each node computes the PDR for the last 16 transmitted packets for a given channel, and updates accordingly the smoothed PDR metric.

Algorithm 1 describes formally LABeL, our link-based and adaptive blacklisting approach. We first compute the average PDR of each channel independently, using the extended WMEWMA estimator (lines 3-4). Then, we identify the best channel, providing the highest PDR (lines 5-7), which allows us to define a dynamic PDR threshold value PDR_{th} to identify bad channels (lines 9-19). Note that we dynamically adapt PDR_{th} in order to maintain at minimum 3 whitelisted channels on each wireless link. Then, we update the blacklist. In particular, a given channel is considered as bad if it provides a PDR lower than PDR_{th} (lines 21-23). Inversely, a channel is removed from the blacklist if its PDR metric significantly exceeds the threshold value (lines 24-26).

Note that constructing a link-based blacklist requires only for the transmitter to collect the ratio of acknowledged packet. In particular, the blacklist considers both directions, for respectively the data frame and the acknowledgement transmissions. Thus, computing the blacklist does not need to send explicit control and probe packets, and does not generate any overhead. Note that the blacklist is updated continuously, i.e., at each data transmission, while 6P control packet is exchanged, only when the blacklist is modified.

4.2 Modifying the frequency hopping sequence

After identifying the blacklisted radio channels, we next have to exploit this blacklisting mechanism with TSCH. In particular, the employed physical channel is decided at the beginning of each cell, using Equation 1 (see Section 2.1).

Note that ISA100.11a [18] proposes to use a localized blacklist. A node follows the frequency hopping sequence. However, when the transmitter detects that the physical channel associated to a cell is blacklisted, it postpones its transmission (i.e., for the following

Algorithm 1: Blacklist construction

```
Data: blacklist (current blacklist),
  nb_tx[CH] and nb_ack[CH] (nb. of transmitted packets and received ACKs
  over each channel)
  α (WMEWMA's parameter)
  T (threshold to consider a channel bad)
Result: blacklist (new list of bad channels)
// PDR for each channel
best ← 0;
for c ∈ Channels do
    // WMEWMA of the PDR with the last 16 transmitted packets
    PDR_last16 ← nb_ack[c] / nb_tx[c];
    PDR_wmewma[c] = α PDR_wmewma[c] + (1 − α) PDR_last16;
    // Remembers the PDR of the best channel
    if best ≤ PDR_wmewma[c] then
        best ← PDR_wmewma[c];
    end
end
// Adaptive Threshold Calculation
repeat
    numch ← 0 ;
    weight ← weight − 0.01 ;
    T ← best * weight ;
    for c ∈ Channels do
        if PDR_wmewma[c] < T then
            numch ← numch + 1 ;
        end
    end
until numch ≥ 3;
// threshold PDR to define which channels perform
   significantly worse than the best one
PDR_th ← T * best
// For each channel, verifies it performs similarly to the
   best one (or not)
for c ∈ Channels do
    // To blacklist
    if PDR_wmewma[c] < PDR_th and c ∉ blacklist then
        blacklist ← blacklist + {c};
    end
    // To recover
    if PDR_wmewma[c] > PDR_th and c ∈ blacklist then
        blacklist ← blacklist − {c};
    end
end
return blacklist;
```

slotframe, 101 timeslots in TSCH). Since the number of channels and the slotframe length are mutually prime numbers, the physical channel associated with the same cell in the next slotframe will be different. However, such technique presents two major drawbacks:

Delay: Since the transmission is postponed for the next slotframe, blacklisting would consequently increase the end-to-end delay. The jitter is also increased due to the fact that the delay increases if the channel offset leads to a blacklisted channel;

Bandwidth: Blacklisting a channel prevents to use the cell in all the corresponding slotframes. Thus, if X% of the channels are blacklisted, the radio link can only use (100-X%) of the radio bandwidth.

Let us assume that we adapt directly Eq. 1, where *nFreq* would be the number of non blacklisted channels, and *F*() would map the values to the physical channels. Let us now consider two mutually interfering wireless links that use the same timeslot but a different channel offset. These links, would never collide, if they do not employ any blacklisting. However, if they use different blacklists, *different* channel offsets may map to the *same* physical channel.

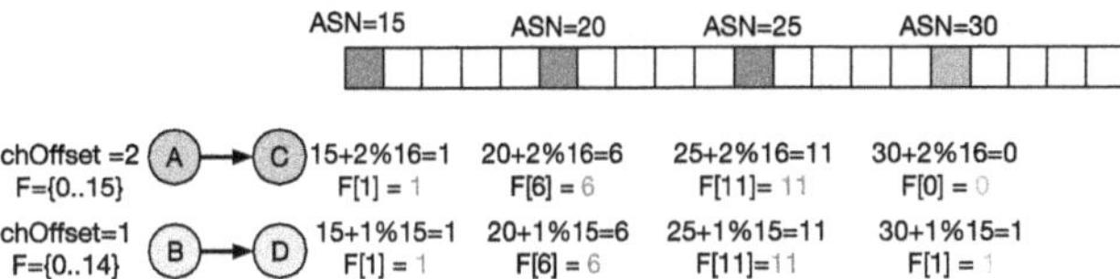

Figure 3: Colliding cells which use a different channel offset if we use the eq. 1 just changing the channel set — F[] denotes the set of *good* channels (the channel 15 is blacklisted for the link $B \rightarrow D$), the link $A \rightarrow C$ (resp. $B \rightarrow D$) is assigned the channel offset 2 (resp. 1).

Let's consider the scenario illustrated in Fig. 3. The pair A/C has no blacklisted channel, while B/D blacklisted the channel 15. Since the modulo changes, we may create several collisions in consecutive slotframes even when blacklisting only one channel.

Therefore, we propose to adapt the frequency hopping method, making the collisions non repetitive. We aim to minimize the number of collisions among interfering links that use a different channel offset if their blacklist differs slightly. To do so, we apply first the Equation 1 to compute the radio channel to use. Then, the algorithms makes the distinction between the following cases:

C1: **Good channel**: If the physical channel is not blacklisted, let's use it;

C2: **Blacklisted channel**: If the physical channel is blacklisted, let's select pseudo-randomly a good channel. The pseudo-random function must use a common knowledge between the receiver and the transmitter to avoid deafness. We propose to select the channel accordingly:

$$frequency = F\Big(\big(ASN + channelOffset + k\big) \ \% \ nFreq\Big) \quad (3)$$

with k the minimum integer value such that 'frequency' corresponds to a *good* channel. Since ASN, $channelOffset$, $nFreq$ and the blacklist are common to the receiver and the transmitter, they will lead to a consistent decision.

Since we keep the same modulo operator, two cells with different channel offsets will never collide if the channel hopping sequence leads to a good channel. A collision may occur probabilistically if at least one of the radio links leads to a blacklisted channel during the corresponding slotframe. The probability of collision is then uniformly distributed among all the channels. In other words, such repartition may be considered like external interference and over-provisioned cells should be already reserved for retransmissions to cope with this situation.

4.3 Modifying the Channel Hopping Sequence to Passively Monitor the Quality of Bad Channels

We continuously estimate the PDR performance for all channels, including the blacklisted ones. Indeed, since the radio conditions may change during the deployment [11], we should recover a radio channel from a blacklist to whitelist, when its PDR performance exceeds the threshold value (Algorithm 1, line 24). However, dedicating resource (control packets) to probe bad channels is not recommended since it would be costly in terms of energy consumption and additional unnecessary traffic. Note that is such case, the probe has to be done for each blacklisted channel for each radio link.

In this study, we rather propose to monitor the link quality using a passive method, exploiting directly the reliability statistics of data packets. However, a bad channel should be probed less frequently than a good channel since it has a negative impact on both the reliability and the energy consumption.

Therefore, we modify the previous second rule (C2) when computing the channel hopping sequence. More precisely, when Equation 1 returns a blacklisted channel:

C2.1: With the probability p, let's transmit the packet through this *bad* channel to keep on re-estimating the link quality for *all* channels;

C2.2: Otherwise, the transmitter and receiver select pseudo-randomly a good channel, applying the original C2 rule (cf. section 4.2).

A small p value means that the blacklisted channels will be probed infrequently. Re-estimating the quality consumes less resource, but requires a longer time to detect link quality change.

4.4 How to agree on a consistent blacklist in the transmitter and the receiver?

Recall, as previously detailed, each node calculates the number of ACKs received from a neighbor to compute the PDR. The transmitter then identifies the blacklisted channels according to their PDR by applying Algorithm 1. Hereafter, we should ensure that the transmitter and the receiver have the same blacklists, else they would use a different pseudo-random frequency hopping sequence, leading to a "deafness".

We focus here on providing a full blacklisting-enabled 6TiSCH stack. Thus, to this aim, the transmitter sends to the receiver its blacklist using a reliable method since the receiver is not aware of the actual statistics computed by the transmitter, and cannot construct the same blacklist. We here propose to exploit 6P to exchange the blacklists for each radio link (*e.g.*, *A*, *B*). More precisely, the transmitter *A* sends its blacklist in a 6P control packet. Note that 6P packets are transmitted through the shared cells and are prone to collisions: B needs to send an acknowledgement.

The IEEE 802.15.4 Information Elements (IEs) are a convenient option to include the backlist in the 6P packets. In our implementation, a node maintains for each of its active neighbors (i.e., to which it transmits packets) two blacklists:

(1) `tx-tmp`: the last backlist computed according to Algo. 1, not yet acknowledged by the receiver;
(2) `tx`: the last blacklist which was transmitted **and** acknowledged by the receiver.

Thus, we guarantee to use consistent blacklists for both sides. The list `tx-tmp` is used to construct a 6P IE. When the corresponding ACK is received, `tx-tmp` is copied in `tx` and then destroyed. Each node maintains different blacklists with each of its children. We thus achieve to define an adaptive, localized and per-link (per child) blacklisting algorithm.

Table 1: Experimental setup.

Topology	Parameter	Value
	Testbed site	Strasbourg site
	# of nodes	10
	# of Experiments	120
	Link Distance	[2.0 – 14.3] *meters*
Experiment	**Parameter**	**Value**
	Duration	120 *min*
	Payload size	48 bytes
Protocol	**Parameter**	**Value**
CoAP	CBR (*Unicast*)	1 *pkts*/3 *sec*
RPL	DAO period	50 *s*
	DIO period	8.5 *s*
TSCH	Slotframe length	101
	NShared cells	5
	Timeslot duration	15 *ms*
	Maximum retries	3
Queues	Timeout	8 *s*
	Queue size	10 packets
	incl. data packets	Maximum 6 packets
Hardware	**Parameter**	**Value**
	Antenna model	Omnidirectional
	Radio propagation	2.4 *GHz*
	802.15.4 Channels	11 *to* 26
	Modulation model	AT86RF231 O-QPSK
	Transmission power	0 *dBm*

We assume that the loss of acks when the packet is received can be neglected. If the ack is lost, the blacklists may become inconsistent, and the transmitter at some time will try to update its blacklist.

5 EXPERIMENTAL PERFORMANCE EVALUATION

In this Section, we present a thorough experimental campaign over the FIT IoT-LAB platform[1] that is part of the FIT[2], an open large-scale and multiuser testing infrastructure for IoT-related systems and applications. Note that FIT IoT-LAB is a shared platform with potential concurrent experiments.

5.1 FIT IoT-LAB Platform

We conducted our study over the FIT IoT-Lab testbed, which belongs to the half real-world testbed category since several Wi-Fi Access Points (APs) are co-located. Thus, under such a realistic indoor environment, the nodes are subjected to external interference originated from Wi-Fi-based devices.

5.2 Experimental Setup and Parameters

In our experimental campaign, we employed M3 nodes, based on a STMicroelectronics 32-bit ARM Cortex-M3 micro-controller (ST2M32F103REY) that embeds an AT86RF231 radio chip, providing an IEEE 802.15.4 compliant PHY layer.

[1] https://www.iot-lab.info/
[2] https://fit-equipex.fr/

We focused on a 1-hop scenario with 10 M3 nodes to focus on the performance of a given radio link. We performed 120 experiments, while each experiment lasted for 120 *min*. The transmitter (leaf) node implements a Constant Bit Rate (CBR) application model, by transmitting 1 data packet every 3 *seconds*, at 0 *dBm* transmission power, resulting in more than 2000 *pkts* transmissions in total per experiment. We chose a 48 *bytes* data size, which corresponds to the general information used by monitoring applications (e.g., node ID, packet sequence, sensed value). The details of the setup are exposed in Table 1. We systematically plotted the 95% confidence intervals (each radio link denoting a dataset).

To conduct our experiments, we employed OpenWSN[3], an open-source implementation of a full protocol stack based on IoT standards (IEEE 802.15.4-TSCH, IPv6, 6TiSCH, RPL, CoAP). In particular, we used the modified implementation of OpenWSN[4] for distributed scheduling with traffic isolation [24], to reserve a set of cells *per* flow.

5.3 Blacklisting Methods to Compare

We compared the following blacklisting methods:

- **Default:** TSCH network operates in standard mode and uses only channel hopping to defeat external interference;
- **Global Blacklisting**: We blacklist statically the three channels which are the most impacted by the interfering Wi-Fi networks – channel 12, 13 and 14;
- **Local-Fixed**: We blacklist all channels that exhibit a PDR lower than a fixed threshold value. This blacklist is then used in LocAd to modify the pseudo-random channel hopping sequence. Note that if all 16 radio channels present a performance lower that the pre-defined threshold, we select the channel with the best PDR value.
- **Local-Adaptive: LABeL**: The blacklist is computed based on Algo. 1. It is established as a per link basis, selecting the channels which perform significantly worse than the best ones. Thus, a channel is blacklisted not anymore only because it performs poorly, but more importantly if it exhibits a PDR significantly lower than the best channels for the *same* link. In other words, we avoid penalizing the links with a mediocre quality.

5.4 Studied Metrics

We measured the following metrics to evaluate the network performance:

- **Packet Delivery Ratio (PDR):** The ratio of the number of frames correctly acknowledged by the receiver and the number of frames transmitted by the transmitter. The PDR is measured at the MAC layer: one packet with one retransmission results a PDR of 50%;
- **Delay:** The average time between the generation of a packet and the reception of the corresponding acknowledgement. This average delay is computed only for the packets successfully delivered to the receiver;
- **Jitter:** The average difference for a given flow between its actual end to end delay and its average value;
- **Blacklist size:** The number of channels present in the blacklist;
- **ETX:** The average number of transmissions and retransmissions for each data frame. This metric is relative to the energy consumption: more cells and transmissions are required to deliver each data packet.

6 PERFORMANCE EVALUATION

6.1 Reliability

We first focus on the reliability performance and measure the PDR provided by a given link (Fig. 4a). To investigate the impact of the signal strength by grouping together the links with approximatively the same geographical length (in our testbed, the signal strength and the geographical length are quite strongly correlated variables).

For short (and strong) links, PDR is very high (≈100%) whatever the employed blacklisting technique (Fig. 4a). However, blacklisting technique improves slightly the PDR, even for strong links.

Weaker links tend to be more sensitive to external interference since their SINR margin is smaller. The *bad* channels, with a large level of external interference, impact negatively the reliability. All the blacklisting techniques improve in some extent the PDR. The global blacklisting provides the lowest improvement: some channels perform *badly* only for *some* radio links while they are blacklisted globally. Local blacklisting with a fixed threshold value is also suboptimal: a weak radio link tends to exhibit a low average PDR for all its channels. Thus, a medium PDR does not mean that a channel should be blacklisted. LABeL, computing dynamically the threshold value for the PDR, according to the best channels, is more effective to blacklist only the less efficient channels.

Next, we measured the Expected Transmission Count (ETX) in Fig. 4b. ETX is related to the energy efficiency since a node has less packets to transmit on average to deliver correctly a data packet. As can be observed, LABeL, the link-based adaptive scheme, provides an ETX below 1.1, making on average links more robust (14% less transmissions compared to without backlisting).

6.2 Blacklist size

We measured the average number of channels present in the blacklist (Fig. 5). The global blacklist is not represented since we fixed statistically its composition, including the three channels most impacted by Wi-Fi.

Our results demonstrate that the stronger the links, the fewer the blacklisted channels. Besides, we can verify that using a fixed threshold is suboptimal and aggressive: it tends to blacklist also channels which are close to the best ones, but below the fixed threshold. It is straightforward that using weaker links means also blacklisting more channels, whatever the blacklisting method is.

6.3 Delay

We finally consider the delay (in number of timeslots) between the packet's generation and the reception of the acknowledgement from the receiver (Fig. 6a). The global backlisting technique does not succeed to blacklist the worst channels: some keep on providing a low reliability and the packet has to be retransmitted. Indeed, it increases the average delay, while the standard deviation is much larger: some radio links are very negatively impacted by the non-blacklisted bad channels. On the contrary, local blacklisting allows

[3] http://www.openwsn.com

[4] branch *"track"* of https://github.com/ftheoleyre/openwsn-fw/ and https://github.com/ftheoleyre/openwsn-sw/

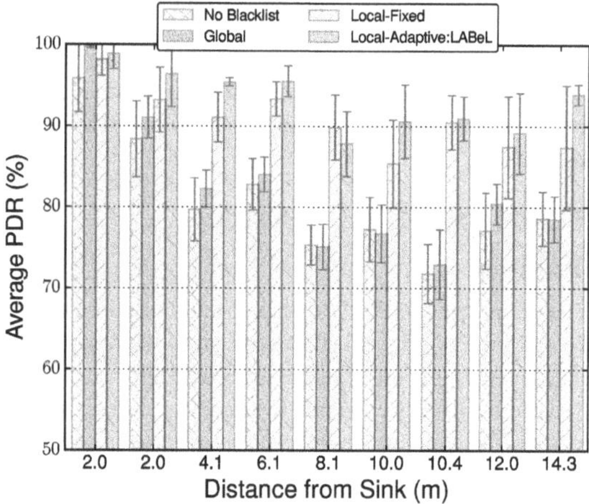

(a) Packet Delivery Ratio.

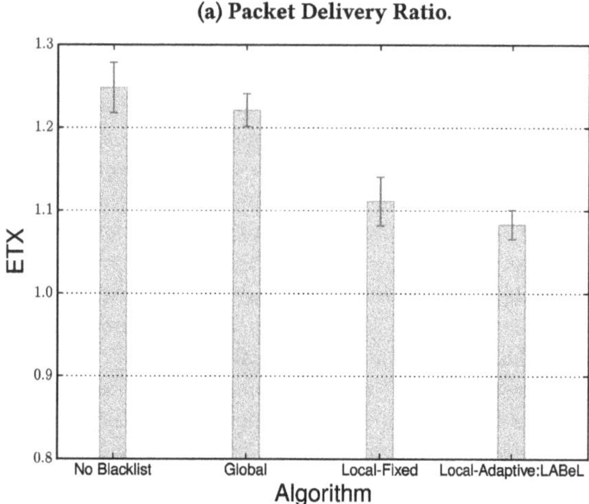

(b) Average number of transmissions before receiving an ack.

Figure 4: Per link reliability achieved with the different blacklisting methods.

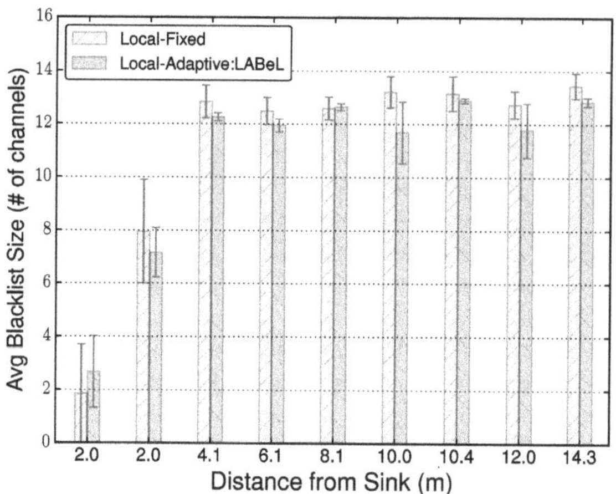

Figure 5: Average number of channels present in the blacklist.

to block the usage of the worst channels and to reduce the amount of retransmissions, thus, it reduces the delay.

In the Industrial Internet of Things (IIoT), a deterministic and predictable performance is required. Therefore, we focus specifically in Fig. 6b on jitter. While the non-blacklisting technique provides the highest jitter due to retransmissions, LABeL successfully identifies and exploits only the best channels and provides decreased jitter values.

7 CONCLUSIONS & FUTURE WORK

Recent standardization efforts such as WirelessHART, ISA100.11a and IEEE 802.15.4, focus on channel hopping strategies to improve the performance of industrial networks. Thus, we need algorithms able to *blacklist* a set of *bad* channels to use only the most reliable one. Since we face a very location and link-dependent performance, we here propose LABeL, a localized and link-based adaptive blacklisting technique. By employing the WMEWMA estimator paired with a dynamic PDR threshold, we identify the bad channels. We also modify the pseudo-random channel hopping sequence to keep on probing the *bad* channels to recover, while minimizing the amount of bandwidth and energy required for measurement. Furthermore, we propose to modify the translation of a channel offset in a physical frequency to minimize the amount of collisions among interfering radio links and making them less repetitive. Our thorough experimental evaluation based on OpenWSN (implementation of 6TiSCH stack) and FIT IoT-LAB platform, exhibits that LABeL, an adaptive and link-based blacklisting technique, improves the reliability performance (by 20%) as well as it reduces the unnecessary traffic in the network while improving the jitter performance.

In the future, we plan to extend our experimental evaluation by also considering outdoor testbeds as well as other channel hopping protocols. Identifying the bad channels represents a challenging task. For instance, blacklisting the channels providing a bad PDR may lead to a bias if only a few packets are forwarded through a given link. Thus, it would be interesting to study methods that do not rely directly on the PDR.

REFERENCES

[1] 2016. IEEE Standard for Low-Rate Wireless Personal Area Networks (LR-WPANs). *IEEE Std 802.15.4-2015 (Revision of IEEE Std 802.15.4-2011)* (April 2016). https://doi.org/10.1109/IEEESTD.2016.7460875

[2] Luigi Atzori, Antonio Iera, and Giacomo Morabito. 2010. The internet of things: A survey. *Computer networks* 54, 15 (2010), 2787–2805.

[3] Nouha Baccour, Anis Koubâa, Luca Mottola, Marco Antonio Zúñiga, Habib Youssef, Carlo Alberto Boano, and Mário Alves. 2012. Radio Link Quality Estimation in Wireless Sensor Networks: A Survey. *ACM Trans. Sen. Netw.* 8, 4, Article 34 (Sept. 2012), 33 pages. https://doi.org/10.1145/2240116.2240123

[4] F. Chiti, R. Fantacci, and A. Tani. 2017. Performance Evaluation of An Adaptive Channel Allocation Technique for Cognitive Wireless Sensor Networks. *IEEE Transactions on Vehicular Technology* 66, 6 (June 2017), 5351 – 5363. https://doi.org/10.1109/TVT.2016.2621140

[5] P. Du and G. Roussos. 2012. Adaptive time slotted channel hopping for wireless sensor networks. In *CEEC*. IEEE. https://doi.org/10.1109/CEEC.2012.6375374

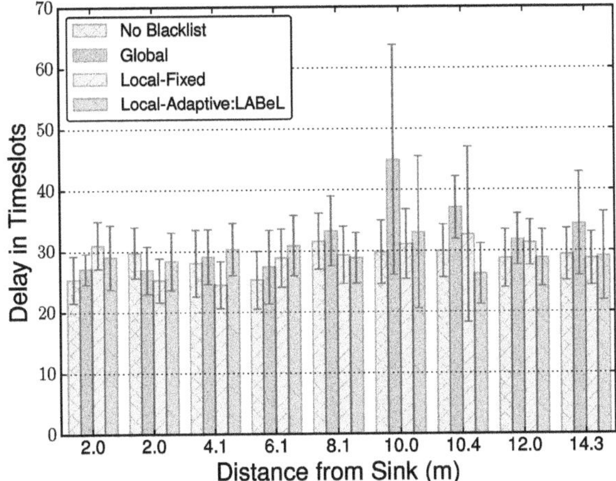

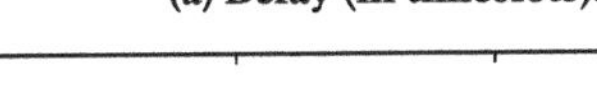

(a) Delay (in timeslots).

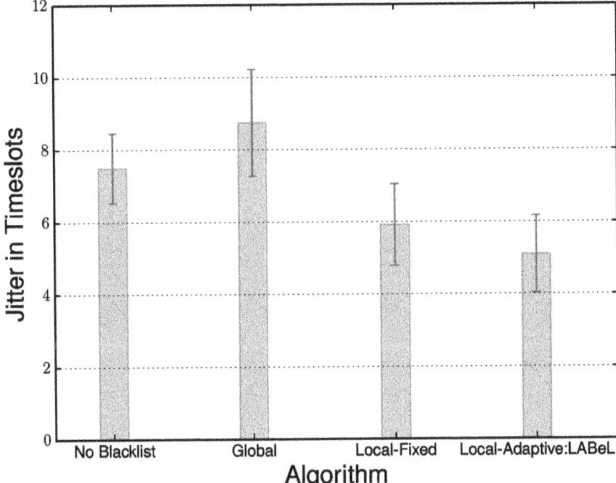

(b) Jitter (in timeslots).

Figure 6: Time required for a given link to receive an ack for a transmitted packet.

[6] D. Dujovne, LA. Grieco, MR. Palattella, and N. Accettura. 2016. *6TiSCH 6top Scheduling Function Zero (SF0)*. draft 2. IETF.

[7] Andrea Goldsmith. 2005. *Wireless Communications*. Cambridge University Press.

[8] Markku Hänninen, Jukka Suhonen, Timo D Hämäläinen, and Marko Hännikäinen. 2011. Link Quality-Based Channel Selection for Resource Constrained WSNs. In *GPC*. Springer.

[9] Anwar Hithnawi, Hossein Shafagh, and Simon Duquennoy. 2014. Understanding the Impact of Cross Technology Interference on IEEE 802.15.4. In *International Workshop on Wireless Network Testbeds, Experimental Evaluation and Characterization (WiNTECH)*. ACM, 49–56. https://doi.org/10.1145/2643230.2643235

[10] ISA-100.11a-2011:. May 2011. Wireless Systems for Industrial Automation:Process Control and Related Applications. *International Society of Automation (ISA) Std.* 1 (May 2011).

[11] V. Kotsiou, G. Z. Papadopoulos, P. Chatzimisios, and F. Theoleyre. 2017. Is Local Blacklisting Relevant in Slow Channel Hopping Low-Power Wireless Networks?. In *Proceedings of the IEEE International Conference on Communications (ICC)*.

[12] Y. Liu, Y. He, M. Li, J. Wang, K. Liu, and X. Li. 2013. Does Wireless Sensor Network Scale? A Measurement Study on GreenOrbs. *IEEE Transactions on Parallel and Distributed Systems* 24, 10 (Oct 2013), 1983–1993. https://doi.org/10.1109/TPDS.2012.216

[13] G. Z. Papadopoulos, J. Beaudaux, A. Gallais, P. Chatzimisios, and T. Noel. 2014. Toward a Packet Duplication Control for Opportunistic Routing in WSNs. In *Proc. of the IEEE Global Communications Conference (GLOBECOM)*. 94–99.

[14] G. Z. Papadopoulos, A. Gallais, G. Schreiner, E. Jou, and T. Noel. 2017. Thorough IoT testbed Characterization: from Proof-of-concept to Repeatable Experimentations. *Elsevier Computer Networks* 119 (2017), 86–101.

[15] G. Z. Papadopoulos, A. Gallais, G. Schreiner, and T. Noel. 2016. Importance of Repeatable Setups for Reproducible Experimental Results in IoT. In *PE-WASUN*. ACM.

[16] G. Z. Papadopoulos, A. Mavromatis, X. Fafoutis, N. Montavont, R. Piechocki, T. Tryfonas, and G. Oikonomou. 2016. Guard Time Optimisation and Adaptation for Energy Efficient Multi-hop TSCH Networks. In *WF-IoT*. IEEE.

[17] Bogdan Pavkovic, Fabrice Theoleyre, Dominique Barthel, and Andrzej Duda. 2010. Experimental Analysis and Characterization of a Wireless Sensor Network Environment. In *PE-WASUN*. ACM.

[18] S. Petersen and S. Carlsen. 2011. WirelessHART Versus ISA100.11a: The Format War Hits the Factory Floor. *IEEE Industrial Electronics Magazine* 5, 4 (Dec 2011), 23–34. https://doi.org/10.1109/MIE.2011.943023

[19] M. Sha, G. Hackmann, and C. Lu. 2011. ARCH: Practical Channel Hopping for Reliable Home-Area Sensor Networks. In *RTAS*. IEEE. https://doi.org/10.1109/RTAS.2011.36

[20] Jianping Song, Song Han, A.K. Mok, Deji Chen, M. Lucas, and M. Nixon. 2008. WirelessHART: Applying Wireless Technology in Real-Time Industrial Process Control. In *RTAS*. IEEE.

[21] WirelessHART Specification. 2008. 75: TDMA Data-Link Layer. *HART Communication Foundation Std., Rev* 1 (2008).

[22] Lei Tang, Yanjun Sun, Omer Gurewitz, and David B. Johnson. 2011. EM-MAC: A Dynamic Multichannel Energy-efficient MAC Protocol for Wireless Sensor Networks. In *Proceedings of the Twelfth ACM International Symposium on Mobile Ad Hoc Networking and Computing (MobiHoc '11)*. ACM, New York, NY, USA, Article 23, 11 pages. https://doi.org/10.1145/2107502.2107533

[23] L. Tang, K. C. Wang, Y. Huang, and F. Gu. 2007. Channel Characterization and Link Quality Assessment of IEEE 802.15.4-Compliant Radio for Factory Environments. *IEEE Transactions on Industrial Informatics* 3, 2 (May 2007), 99–110. https://doi.org/10.1109/TII.2007.898414

[24] F. Theoleyre and G. Papadopoulos. 2016. Experimental Validation of a Distributed Self-Configured 6TiSCH with Traffic Isolation in Low Power Lossy Networks . In *MSWiM*. ACM.

[25] L. Tytgat, O. Yaron, S. Pollin, I. Moerman, and P. Demeester. 2015. Analysis and Experimental Verification of Frequency-Based Interference Avoidance Mechanisms in IEEE 802.15.4. *IEEE/ACM Transactions on Networking* 23, 2 (April 2015), 369–382. https://doi.org/10.1109/TNET.2014.2300114

[26] Thomas Watteyne, Ankur Mehta, and Kris Pister. 2009. Reliability Through Frequency Diversity: Why Channel Hopping Makes Sense. In *PE-WASUN*. ACM.

[27] T. Watteyne, M. Palattella, and L. Grieco. 2015. Using IEEE 802.15.4e Time-Slotted Channel Hopping (TSCH) in the Internet of Things (IoT): Problem Statement. RFC 7554. (2015).

[28] S. Zacharias, T. Newe, S. O'Keeffe, and E. Lewis. 2012. Coexistence measurements and analysis of IEEE 802.15.4 with Wi-Fi and bluetooth for vehicle networks. In *International Conference on ITS Telecommunications*. IEEE, 785–790. https://doi.org/10.1109/ITST.2012.6425289

WiFO: A Hybrid WiFi Free-Space Optical Communication Networks of Femtocells

Qiwei Wang
Spencer Liverman
Yu-jung Chu
Anindita Borah
Songtao Wang
wangqi@oregonstate.edu
livermas@oregonstate.edu
chuy@oregonstate.edu
boraha@oregonstate.edu
wangso@oregonstate.edu
School of Electrical Engineering and Computer Science
Oregon State University
Corvallis, Oregon

Thinh Nguyen
Arun Natarajan
Alan X. Wang
thinq@eecs.oregonstate.edu
nataraja@eecs.oregonstate.edu
wang@eecs.oregonstate.edu
School of Electrical Engineering and Computer Science
Oregon State University
Corvallis, Oregon

ABSTRACT

The recent growth of markets for smart homes and the Internet of Things (IoT) create a significant demand in wireless access capacity. Consequently, much of current research has focused on efficient utilization of RF (Radio Frequency) spectrum. In this paper, an orthogonal approach using Free Space Optic (FSO) technology is proposed to increase capacities of indoor wireless networks. Specifically, we describe WiFO, a novel wireless indoor communication system based on the femtocell architecture that integrates both RF and FSO technologies. WiFO aims to increase the wireless capacities while retaining the mobility offered by the existing WiFi networks. Our preliminary prototype shows promising results to significantly boost up the capacity of the existing WiFi networks.

CCS CONCEPTS

• **Networks** → **Network performance modeling**; **Network experimentation**; **Wireless local area networks**;

KEYWORDS

WiFi; Free-Space Optics; Wireless Communication; Channel Characterization; System Prototype

1 INTRODUCTION

As the number of wireless devices continues to grow exponentially to over seven billions, providing adequate bandwidth for these devices from the limited shared radio frequency (RF) spectrum is becoming increasingly difficult. This leads to recent research on temporal and spatial spectrum allocation to utilize the RF resource more effectively [3, 12]. These approaches rely on many technological advances in RF circuitry and algorithms [8]. On the other hand, advances in free-space optical (FSO) technology promise a complementary approach to increase wireless capacity with minimal changes to the existing wireless technologies. Importantly, the FSO technology does not interfere with the RF transmissions. That said, such high data rates are currently achievable only with point-to-point and not well integrated with existing WiFi networks. This drawback severely limits the mobility of FSO wireless devices. This paper describes WiFO, a novel communication system that integrates both FSO and WiFi technologies to provide high capacity while retaining seamless mobility for its users.

Over the past several years, WiFi has become an indispensable wireless access technology. However, its limited capacity is becoming a critical issue with the growing number of Internet devices such as phones and tablets. Consider the popular WiFi standard 802.11g which has a theoretical maximum rate of 54 Mbps. However, it typically operates at only a fraction of the capacity, e.g., 15 20 Mbps due to MAC protocol overhead and distances between a device and the access point (AP). A quick calculation shows that WiFi fails to provide adequate bandwidth for many settings, e.g., a conference venue with 40 people in a room. With many people in a small area, the overall effective bandwidth for 802.11g is only a few megabits, e.g., 10 Mbps. Thus, each user will have an average of 250 Kbps which is unacceptable for video streaming applications.

WiFO Solution Approach. WiFO aims to overcome the WiFi capacity overload problem by enhancing wireless capacity using the complement FSO technology which does not interfere with WiFi transmissions. Our current WiFO prototype can provide up to 50 Mbps via FSO local transmissions alone. Furthermore, unlike stand-alone FSO technology, WiFO is tightly integrated with existing WiFi infrastructure to provide seamless mobility and allows wireless devices to receive data from both FSO and WiFi channels simultaneously based on their channel conditions.

2 RELATED WORK

Recent advances in FSO technologies have led to the development of RF/FSO hybrid communication systems. The majority of this research direction has focused on building a high-capacity, point-to-point links for outdoor settings. For example, Bouchet et al. [1] have studied an RF/FSO hybrid communication system and characterized the loss rates with respect to distances, weather conditions,

MSWiM '17, November 21–25, 2017, Miami, FL, USA

ACM ISBN 978-1-4503-5162-1/17/11...$15.00
https://doi.org/10.1145/3127540.3127557

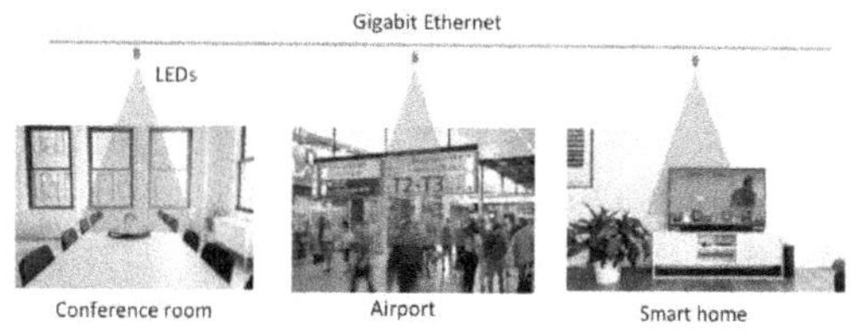

Figure 1: Use scenario

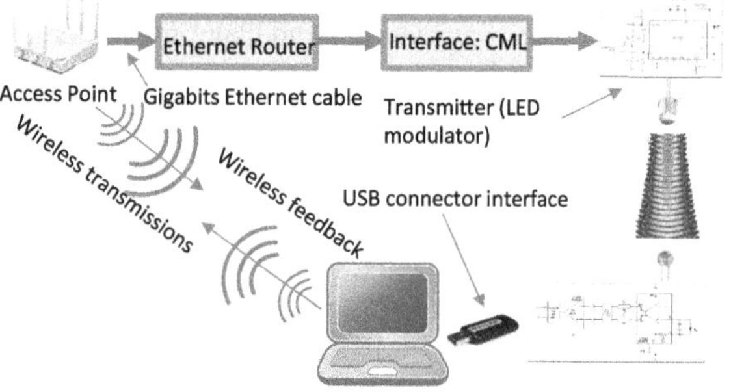

Figure 2: WiFO architecture

and scintillation. Wang et al. [10] analyzed throughput and delay for hybrid RF/FSO networks. In addition, there are many works on indoor free-space optical communication systems that can provide high speed data links for a small number of users [5, 7]. In [2], the authors proposed a point-to-point system architecture based on board-level and chip-level optical interconnects for supercomputers. However, the most imperative issues such as WiFi network congestion and dynamic allocation of bandwidth for a large number of users have not been considered. In addition, these high bandwidth FSO communication systems require expensive semiconductor laser diodes, Mach-Zehnder modulators (MZMs), and single-mode opticalfi bers. Such an approach adds a significant cost to upgrade the existing WiFi networks. On the other hand, there are approaches that use white light emitting diodes (WLEDs) for simultaneous illumination and indoor FSO communication [6]. Notably, Light-Fidelity (LiFi) [4] is a communication system that is based on visible light communication(VLC) technologies. Although these solutions are potentially energy efficient, it is not clear whether they can be of high bandwidth. Importantly, it is difficult to integrate the expensive LED illumination system with the power system. Another promising approach is the hybrid LiFi/WiFi system introduced in [11]. Unlike WiFO, in this hybrid system, LiFi and WiFi channels are not fully integrated but accessed by separate APs. Each user is connected to only one of them at a time. To the best of our knowledge,WiFO [9] is thefi rst system that integrates WiFi and FSO technologies to achieve high bandwidth and seamless mobility using inexpensive components.

3 SYSTEM ARCHITECTURE

In this section, we provide an overview of WiFO system architecture and its operations. Since the downlink traffic is often orders of magnitude larger than that of uplink traffic, WiFO is designed to increase the downlink capacity of an existing WiFi infrastructure. Specifically, the AP in WiFO is responsible for delivering data from the Internet to wireless devices in its network using both FSO and WiFi channels simultaneously. On the other hand, when a wireless device sends data to the Internet (uplink), it is handled using the existing WiFi mechanisms without the assisted FSO transmissions.

WiFO design is based on the femtocell architecture consisting of an array of triangular-lattice FSO transmitters (LEDs) deployed in the ceiling to provide coverage for thefl oor area directly below. The LEDs are connected through a high-speed Gigabit Ethernet network and controlled by a smart AP. To transmit data, each FSO transmitter creates an invisible light cone about one square meter directly below in which the data can be received. Digital bits "1" and "0" are transmitted by switching the LEDs on and off rapidly. Fig. 1 shows a few use cases for WiFO that include airport terminals, offices, or entertainment centers.

WiFO uses inexpensive FSO technologies, with the transmitters and receivers using LEDs and silicon photodiodes (PDs) that cost less than $20. In addition, they operate around 20 mW with good SNR and well within the eye safety (850 nm). Importantly, the current WiFO prototype can provide 50 Mbps for transmission range (3 to 5 meters), without interfering with the WiFi transmissions. This implies that a 10 Gigabit backbone Ethernet can theoretically modulate 200 LEDs at 50 Mbps each. Another version of WiFO prototype is being developed, and can provide up to 1 Gbps per user. We now describe some salient features of the current WiFO system.

Closed-Loop Architecture. Fig. 2 shows the WiFO architecture for the down-link scenarios. All the data packets from the Internet to the devices in a WiFi network arefi rst traversed through the AP. For each IP packet of a givenfl ow, the AP will decide whether to send it on the WiFi or FSO channels. If it decides to send the packet on the FSO channel to a particular receiver, the data will be encoded appropriately, and broadcast on the Gigabit Ethernet network with the appropriate information to allow the right FSO transmitter to receive the data. Upon receiving the data, the transmitter relays the data to the intended receiver below it. If the AP decides to send the data on the WiFi channel, then it directly broadcast the data through the usual WiFi protocol. Upon receiving the data from the FSO channel, the receiver decodes the data, and sends a feedback/ACK to the AP via the WiFi channel, completing a closed-loop transmission.

AP-centric Design. The AP handles all the sophisticated functions, e.g., which channels to send the data on, how to encode the data, as well as setting the FSO and WiFi transmission parameters. Fig. 3 shows an example of WiFO deployment in a library at Oregon State University. A centralized smart AP (our prototype currently implemented AP using a specialized server) manages both WiFi (red) and FSO (blue) hotspots through a Gigabit Ethernet links. Specifically, the smart AP handles all incoming data packets from the Internet. This architecture allows for better performance through the joint optimization of multiplefl ows while keeping the wireless devices simple. The AP-centric architecture is designed based on the cross-layer optimization approach with minimal modifications to the existing WiFi mechanisms. An important consequence of this design is that all existing applications are agnostic to the implementations of the lower OSI layers. Consequently, they operate seamlessly with WiFO.

Cross Layer Optimization. Given the current conditions of the FSO and WiFi channels, the WiFO performance depends on the joint optimization that produces optimal system parameters and

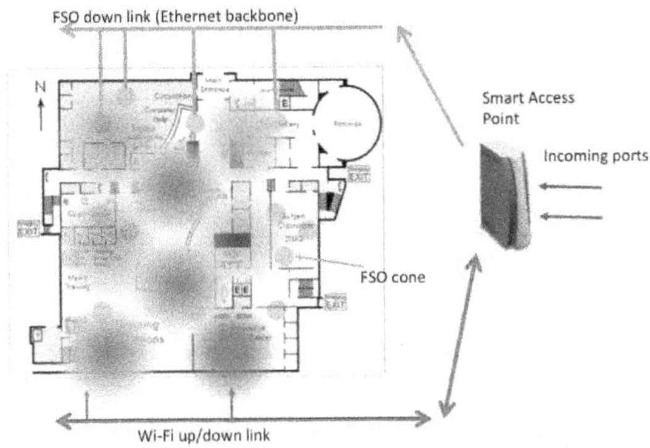

Figure 3: Deployment of WiFO in a building

policies. In WiFO, the transmission rates to FSO and WiFi channels are allocated dynamically at the packet levels. The rate allocation directly dictates the designs of various algorithmic components and parameters in the WiFO system. At the physical layer, we use OOK for modulation with channel coding. At the link layer, packet scheduling policy is used to allocate packets optimally to the FSO or WiFi queues, effectively performing rate allocation over the two channels.

Channel Feedback. Feedback channel is critical to the WiFO's bandwidth and mobility. Unfortunately, sending the feedback from a receiver via the FSO channel is problematic due to difficult deployment and interferences with the forward channel. Therefore, we employ a novel feedback scheme that uses WiFi transmissions to report the channel conditions on the FSO channel (see Fig. 2). Specifically, the WiFO system implements a control channel that is used for sending periodic SNR feedback, as well as the ACK messages for the FSO transmissions, from a mobile receiver to the AP using high-priority WiFi control channels.

Mobility. The FSO signal from each FSO transmitter can be modeled as a Gaussian beam withfi xed divergent angle as shown in Fig. 4(a) and the overall FSO coverage from an array of triangular-lattice FSO transmitters (LEDs) is shown in Fig. 4(b). To support mobility as a receiver moves from one light cone to another, WiFO employs an association protocol in which a receiver is associated with a FSO transmitter when it is in the transmitter's light cone. Multiple receivers can associate with a single FSO transmitter. The transmitter associated with a receiver is responsible for transmitting data for that receiver. To establish association, each FSO transmitter broadcasts a beacon signal that consists of its unique ID periodically. A receiver will automatically associate with a transmitter that provide highest SNRs. Upon receiving the beacon signal from a transmitter, the receiver sends back an *alive* heartbeat message that includes the essential information such as the transmitter ID and receivers' MAC address to the AP using the WiFi channel. The smart AP then updates a table whose entries consisting of the receiver's MAC addresses, the transmitter IDs and transmitter's MAC addresses. These information are used to forward the data of a receiver to the appropriate transmitters. If the AP does not receive a heartbeat from a receiver for some period of time, it will disassociate that receiver, i.e., remove its MAC address from the table. We note that the association protocol requires messages to be

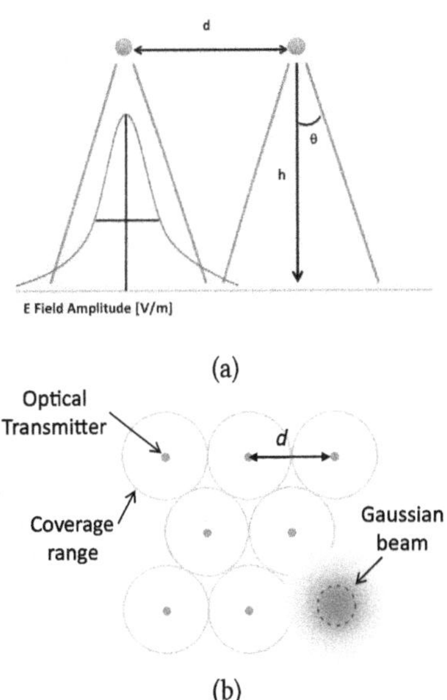

Figure 4: (a) Coverage of optical transmitters with a divergent angle of θ; and (b) Configuration of the optical transmitter array.

exchanged between the AP and the receiver. Since the FSO channel is a one-directional channel, the exchanged messages during the association protocol are sent on the WiFi channels. When a receiver moves out out a light cone, all its downlink data will be transmitted on WiFi channel until it moves into a new light cone and establishes a new association. Importantly, a salient feature of WiFO is the dynamic rate allocation for the simultaneous transmissions of data on both WiFi and FSO channels. As such, when the quality of one channel is low, most of data will be sent on the other good channel automatically. This mechanism will result in non-interrupted transmission when a receiver moves to another light cone as the rate allocation is performed continuously at the link layer.

Due to the limited space, we will not discuss many components above such as cross layer optimization and mobility in details. Instead, we will focus on describing a WiFO prototype, its basic functionalities, and overall performance from both hardware and software perspectives.

4 WIFO PROTOTYPE

The potential of hybrid WiFi/FSO systems is experimentally demonstrated with the WiFO prototype. FSO communication link of WiFO was assembled using only commercially available parts. In a practical indoor office environment, the distance between the ceiling and an end user's desk is approximately 2.8 meters. The FSO transmitter and receiver pair prototype were designed to maximize data throughput and SNR at such distances. Fig. 5 shows afl ow chart detailing the high level implementation of the WiFO prototype described below.

4.1 Transmitter

The transmitter in this prototype design consists of two main components: a BeagleBone Black board and a LED driver circuit. The BeagleBone Black has a 1 GHz Texas Instrument AM335x CPU, 512 MB memory, and two programmable real-time units (PRUs) that

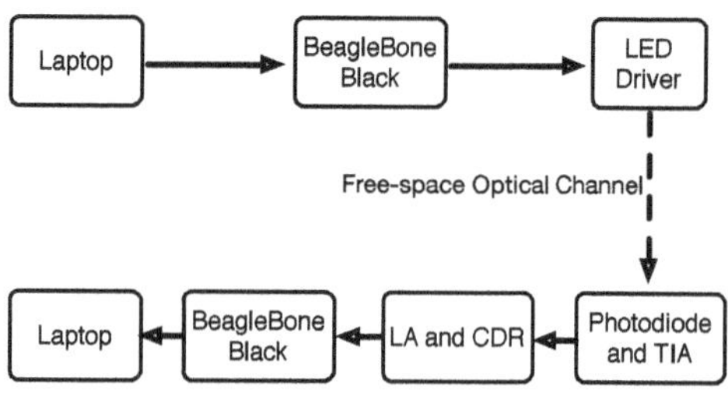

Figure 5: Systemfl owchart

can access onboard general-purpose input/output (GPIO) pins at a maximum speed of 200 MHz. The BeagleBone also supports WiFi, which allows for the sending and receiving of data over the WiFi channel. Importantly, the PRU of the BeagleBone Black is used to implement various functions at the physical and link layers. The digital output from the BeagleBone is then fed into the transmitter circuit that drives the LEDs. The LED driver circuit is shown in Fig. 7 and is designed to maximize the modulation depth of the LED luminary. A table showing the LED driver's component values is shown in Table 1. When the driver switches from a logic high state to a logic low state, transistors Q1 and Q2 short the terminals for the LED thereby reducing the LED's RC delay resulting in a faster optical fall time. The normalized frequency response of this LED driver is shown in Fig. 6.

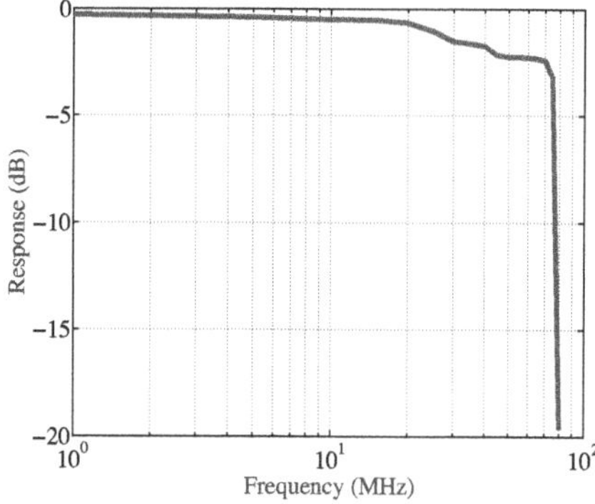

Figure 6: Normalized frequency response

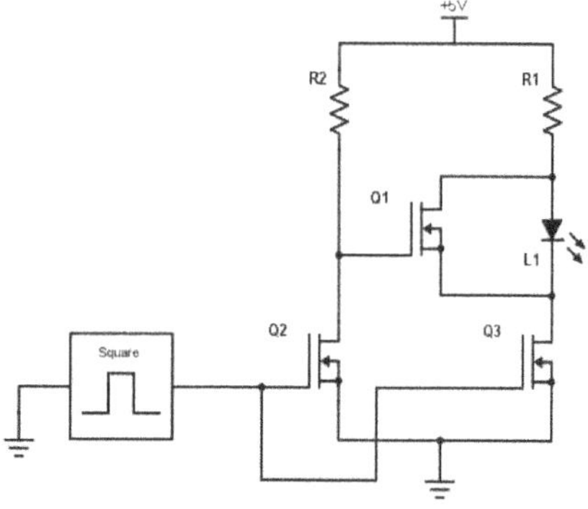

Figure 7: Transmitter circuit schematic

Symbol	Description	Part Number/Value
Q1	Shorts L1 when pulled high	A07404
Q2	Trigger for Q1	A07404
Q3	LED driver	RSU002N06
L1	LED source	VSMY2850
R1	Current limiting resistor	12Ω
R1	Pull up resistor	$20k\Omega$

Table 1: FSO transmitter components

4.2 Receiver

The receiver in this prototype design can be broken into three components. Thisfi rst component is a PIN photodiode, which is paired with a transimpedance amplifier (TIA). This component converts the optical signal into an electrical voltage and provides some initial gain. In this prototype design a photodiode that has been prepackaged with a domed lens was chosen to increase the receiver's viewing angle. The second component involves a series of amplifiers and a clock data recovery circuit (CDR). In this component, a limiting amplifier (LA) is used to saturate the data signal before it is processed by the CDR. The CDR then recovers the clock signal and outputs both a clock and data signal to the receiving BeagleBone. Thefi nal component is a second BeagleBone Black microcontroller, which is used to sample the data and provide a digital readout to the receiving laptop. The BeagleBone samples the data using the clock signal outputted from the CDR circuit. Table 2 details each of the components used in the receiver module. Fig. 8 shows the completed FSO prototype as tested and provides close up views of the transmitter and receiving modules. Fig. 9 shows the eye diagram at the receiver when a 30 MHz square wave is transmitted.

Symbol	Description	Part Number
PD	Photodiode	S6968-01
TIA	Transimpedance amplifier	OPA857
LA	Limiting amplifier	ADN2890
CDR	Clock-Data Recovery circuit	ADN2915

Table 2: FSO receiver components

4.3 System Software

Currently, we design our own network protocol stacks for FSO transmissions. Below is a short description of each layer.

Physical layer: The FSO channel uses On/Off Keying (OOK) modulation scheme. Low optical intensity stands for 0 and high intensity stands for 1. At the transmitter, optional Manchester code can be enabled for self-clocking. At the receiver, the BeagleBone samples the signal at the rising/dropping edge of the clock signal generated by the CDR. We note that unlike diffused light communication, the FSO channel of WiFO does not suffer from multi-path fading, and has a relatively higher SNR due to its line of sight transmission with focused LED beams. We observe that the majority of bit error is not due to thermal noise nor fading. Instead, the error

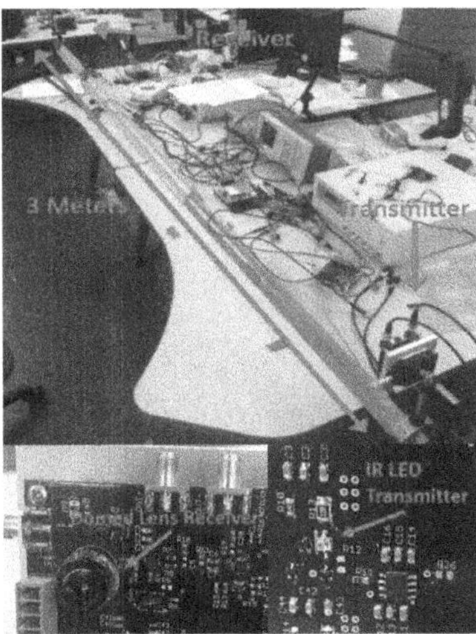

Figure 8: WiFO setup

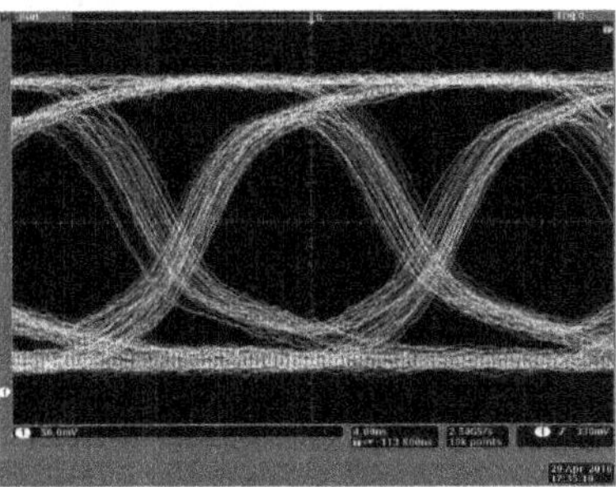

Figure 9: Eye diagram at 30 Mhz

is due to inter-symbol interference (ISI) caused not by the channel, but by the response of the LED transmitter, similar to that of wired communication. Our current LED can modulate a square signal cleanly up to 30 MHz (or 60 Mbps). When modulating at higher rates, the signals become distort and results in decoding errors.

Data link layer: An FSO link frame consists of two parts: 32 bits preamble, and 612 bytes of payload. The preamble is used to distinguish between frames.

Network layer: Unlike a regular network layer protocol, the WiFO network layer not only routes and delivers packets to its destination, it also handles the movement of the receiver between light cones. A network layer packet consists of a 12-byte packet header and 600 bytes of data from upper layers. The packet header includes 4 bytes of packet ID, 4 bytes of optic transmitter ID and 4 bytes of receiver ID. The packet ID is used to help the receiver identify lost packets and sends ACK messages to the transmitter accordingly. The FSO transmitter ID is for the receiver to identify the optic transmitter and send this information back to the server/AP. The receiver ID is important when multiple receivers are under same FSO transmitter. When a packet is received, the receiver discard the packet if the receiver ID in the header and its ID does not match.

Also in this layer, a specifically designed mobility protocol is implemented as described below:

- The AP always records all receivers' status, including IP address, delivered packet ID and associated optical transmitters
- All FSO transmitters send whatever packets assigned to it by the AP. When idle, each FSO transmitter sends a beacon signal periodically.
- When a new receiver enters the network, itfi rst connects to the AP via the existing WiFi channel. If the receiver receives a packet/beacon from a certain FSO transmitter, it will send an ACK via WiFi to the AP. After a simple handshake, the AP will now update the receiver profile by associating the FSO transmitter with the receiver. Until the association is deleted, the FSO transmitter is responsible for delivering the packets to the receivers in its coverage.
- When a receiver receives a packet/beacon from a transmitter, it compares its FSO transmitter ID with previous one. If different, an ACK will be sent to the AP, and the AP updates the receiver profile.
- When a receiver does not receive a beacon for a while, it sends a timeout ACK to the AP as a signal that it moves out of the FSO cone. The AP then updates the receiver profile.

Transport Layer: Since the FSO channel is a one-way channel, to implement the FSO link reliability, ACK messages are sent over the WiFi channel. Specifically, for every 10 packets received successfully via the FSO channel, an ACK is sent over the WiFi channel from the receiver to the transmitter.

Currently, for experimental reasons, network, transport layer protocols, and mobility protocol are implemented at the application layer via pre-encapsulation method, and are then sent down the lower levels/device drivers. Specific drivers for the FSO transmitter/receiver are being developed as a Linux kernel module. Once applied, any network application will be able to access WiFO system without significant modification.

5 SYSTEM EVALUATION

In this section, we show the system related performance metrics including FSO channel bit error rate (BER), throughput and delay. The FSO channel BER is evaluated by sending packets consisting of pseudo-random data using a BeagleBone Black transmitter at 25 Mbps. A receiver BeagleBone Black samples the data at the rising/dropping edge of the generated clock signal from a Clock and Data Recovery (CDR) board. Reed-Solomon codes of multiple rates are applied to evaluate the performance. As shown in Fig. 10, the FSO transmitter is located at the end of a 3-meter rail. The receiver is able to move along this rail and another perpendicular lateral rail. Also, the transmitter is mounted on a rotatable stage so that the rotation angle can be altered. In the following results, the rotation angle is 0° when not specified.

Fig. 11 shows the BER performance without any forward error correction (FEC) code. The result is evaluated at the distances from 1.5 meters to 2.8 meters. At each distance, BER is measured at the lateral offset of 4 centimeters (considered as the beam center due to the geometry of our setup), 10 centimeters, 20 centimeters, 30 centimeters, 40 centimeters and 50 centimeters. The minimum BER can be detected is 10^{-7} due to the sample size. Within the error range, following results are observed:

- At the beam center, the BER increases as distance increases.
- A larger lateral offset results in a higher BER.

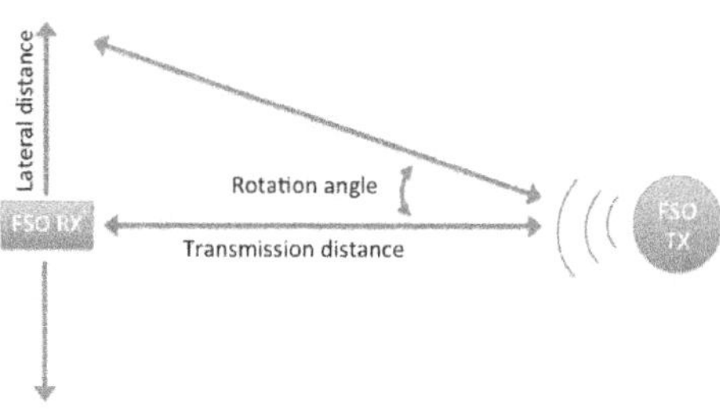

Figure 10: Experimental setup

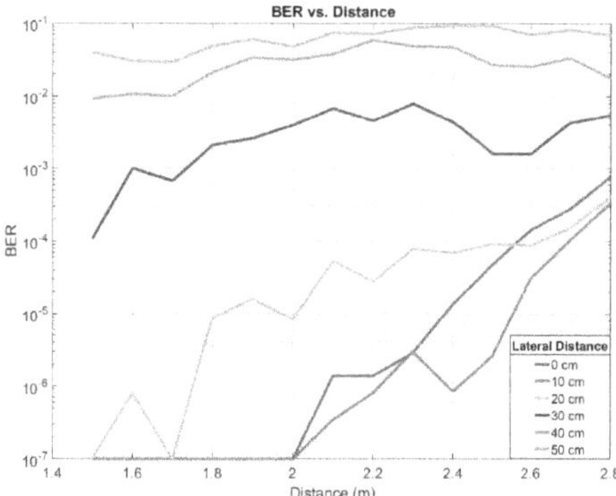

Figure 11: Overall bit error rate measurements

- When the distance is small (< 2 meters), the BER is considerably low (< 10^{-7} when close to the center).
- When the distance is large, the BER is still acceptable (< 10^{-3}) if the receiver is close enough to the beam center. Note that using sufficiently strong FEC, the BER can be significantly reduced.
- The BER performance is not strictly monotonic with the lateral offset. This can be explained by the shape of the Gaussian beam. When the distance increases, the beam width increases as well. As the receiver moves away from the transmitter, the received optical power may decrease due to the distance, or increase due to the widened beam-width. This is obvious at the distance of 2.4 meters with a lateral offset of 10 centimeters. A "dip" of BER can be observed as the receiver "moves into the light cone" at this point.
- When the receiver is at the center, the BER performance is not always the best. At some long distance, the best BER happens at 10 centimeters lateral offset. The reason is that the transmitter uses 4 LEDs placed at 4 corners of the PCB board. While each of them emits a Gaussian beam, the combined beam shape is not Gaussian anymore due to the location of the LEDs.

Fig. 12 and Fig. 13 show the BER results when multiple rates of Reed-Solomon codes are applied. In Fig. 12, it is clear that at a lateral offset of 10 centimeters, using a relatively weak FEC code (RS(255, 247)) already produces acceptable BER. We note that the BER is improved significantly even when distance is 2.8 meters. Furthermore, if a stronger FEC code (RS(255, 223)) is applied, the BER is essentially 0. Fig. 13 shows the results at the edge of the light cone with a lateral offset of 30 centimeters. While the BER is almost all above 10^{-4} with uncoded data, the performance becomes acceptable when a stronger code is applied.

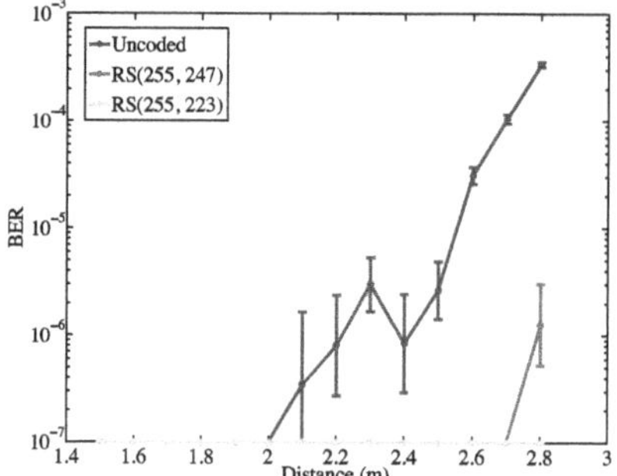

Figure 12: BER at 10 centimeter lateral offset with Reed-Solomon codes

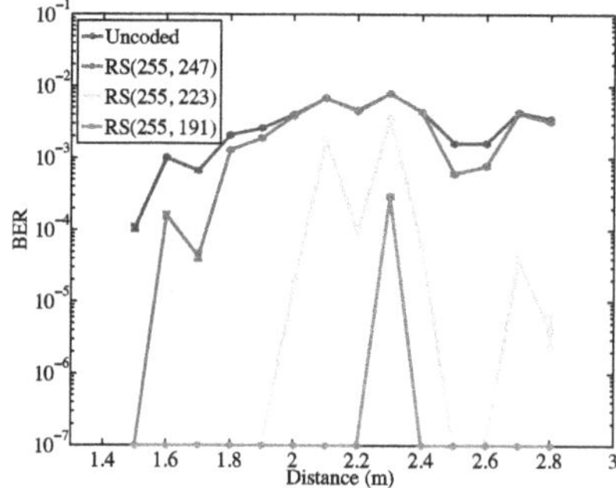

Figure 13: BER at 30 centimeter lateral offset with Reed-Solomon codes

Fig. 14 and Fig. 15 show the BER measurement at the distances of 2.1 meters and 2.8 meters, respectively, with multiple lateral offsets. For both cases, with a strong code RS(255, 191), the BER is below 10^{-7} for lateral offset less than 30 centimeters. At the distance of 2.8 meters, a relatively weaker code RS(255, 223) can still bring the BER down to 10^{-6} even at 30 centimeters offset.

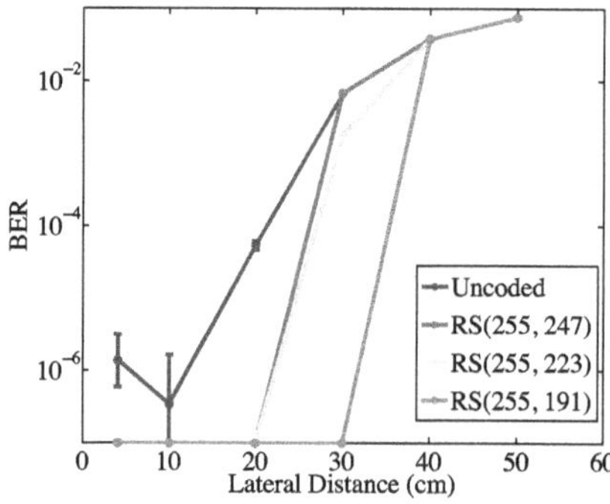

Figure 14: BER at 2.1 meters with Reed-Solomon codes

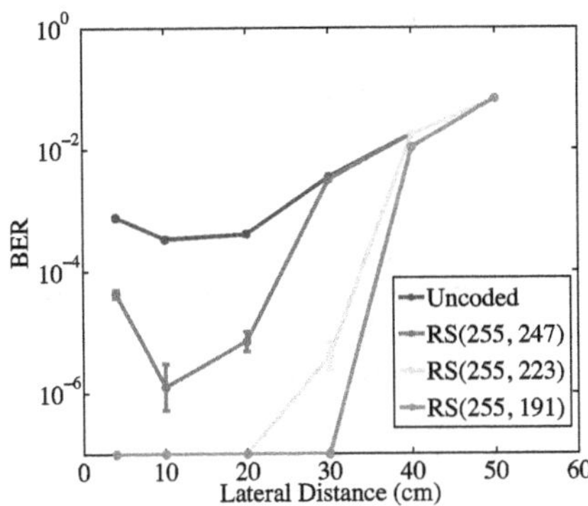

Figure 15: BER at 2.8 meters with Reed-Solomon codes

We now consider the performance of WiFO under ambient light. The FSO channel is designed to transmit/receive data using invisible light whose wavelength is centered at 850 nm. Most of the noise power from room ambient light will befi ltered out at the receiver. In Fig. 16, the BER is measured with and without room ambient light. It is clear that no significant impact on the WiFO performance is observed with the existence of ambient light.

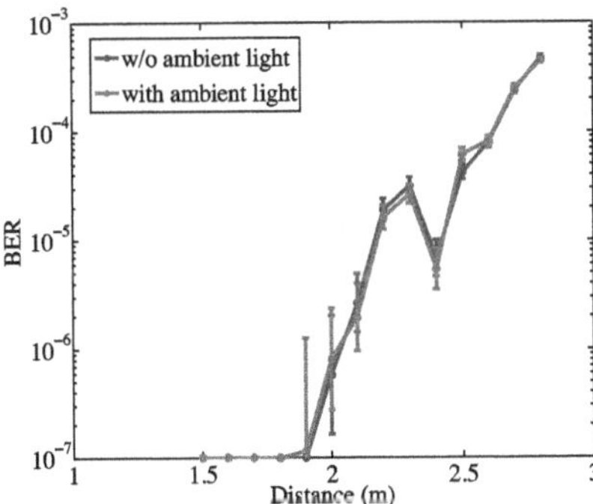

Figure 16: BER comparison with room ambient light

Fig. 17 shows the BER performance at different transmission speeds. 10^8 random generated bits were transmitted from the digital I/O board through the FSO channel, then received with the same board for comparison. The minimum detectable BER was 10^{-8}. The measurements were taken at 1.6 meters, 2 meters and 2.4 meters. As the graph shows, the BER increases with the transmission speeds. When the transmission rate is less or equal to 30 Mbps, the BER is acceptable at all 3 different distances. Fig. 18 shows the maximum achievable bit rate with some BER requirements. Previous graphs showed that a channel with BER less than 10^{-4} usually can be efficiently improved by FEC with a reasonable redundancy. In this case, WiFO is able to achieve 20 Mbps at the furthest transmission distance, while at shorter distances 30 Mbps or above is achievable. When the BER requirement is set higher at 10^{-8}, 20 Mbps bit rate is still achievable for all the considered distances. We note again the most the bit error at high speed is due to limitation of the modulation frequency of the LEDs. The new version of WiFO replaces LEDs with VCSELs that can provide up to 1 Gbps.

Fig. 19 shows the BER results when the rotation angle of the transmitter is set at 0°, 15°, 30° and 45° and the receiver is placed at the center of the beam. As seen, the BER is getting larger as the rotation angle increases. At the distance of 2 meters, the channel with a 15° rotation angle is still reliable with BER less than 10^{-7}, while with 30° or larger angle the bit rate is significantly larger since the receiver is outside the light cone.

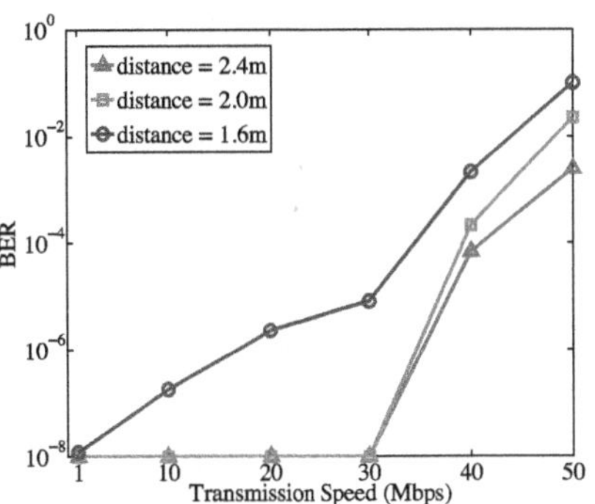

Figure 17: BER comparison with different transmission rates

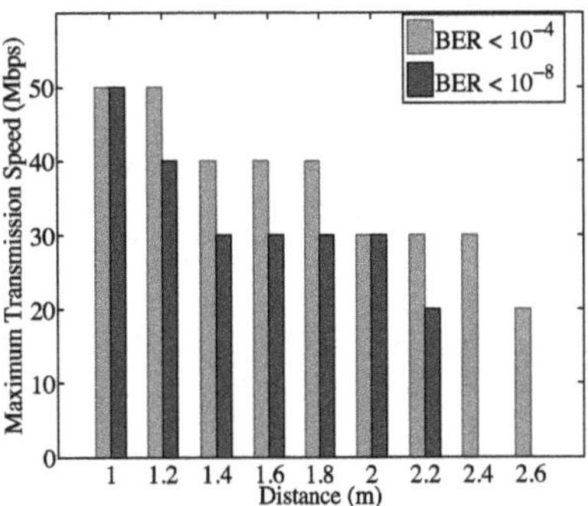

Figure 18: Maximum achievable rate with BER requirements

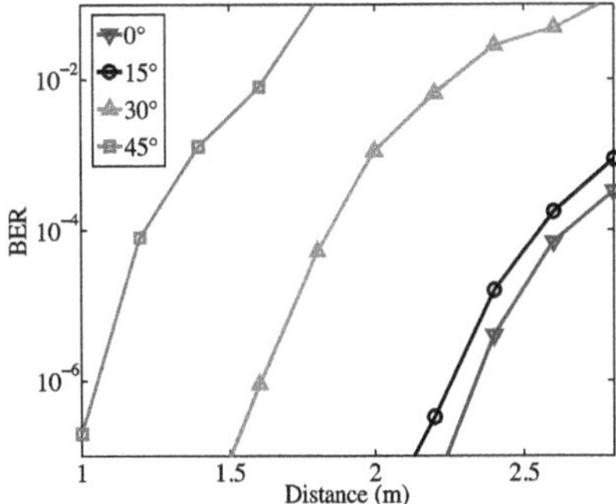

Figure 19: BER comparison with different transmitter rotation angle

All above results show that in a normal indoor scenario, with proper FEC coding, using FSO transmission alone, WiFO is able to transmit data at the distance of about 3 meters when the receiver is placed within the light cone of about 60 centimeters diameter.

Now we consider an experiment that involves simultaneous data transmissions on both WiFI and FSO channels. We designed the experiment to model a heavily congested scenario in a WiFi network. To accomplish this, heavy WiFi background traffic is generated artificially while two network applications are running. Application one uses WiFi channel while application two is allowed to use the FSO channel. The throughput for FSO channel is shown in Fig. 20. As seen, the WiFi throughput varies due to the artificial background traffic, which starts at around 110 seconds and ends at around 270 seconds. The throughput of application one is approximately 8 Mbps when the artificial background traffic is off, and about 3.5 Mbps when artificial background traffic is on. On the other hand, the throughput of application two is able to maintain its desired throughput of as an approximately constant rate of 12 Mbps through the use of the FSO channel. In fact, WiFO is designed to allow applications with higher priority to send their packets on the FSO channels to avoid WiFi congestion. We note thefluctuation in FSO channel throughput is mainly because of the delay of the ACK packets, which are sent through WiFi channels.

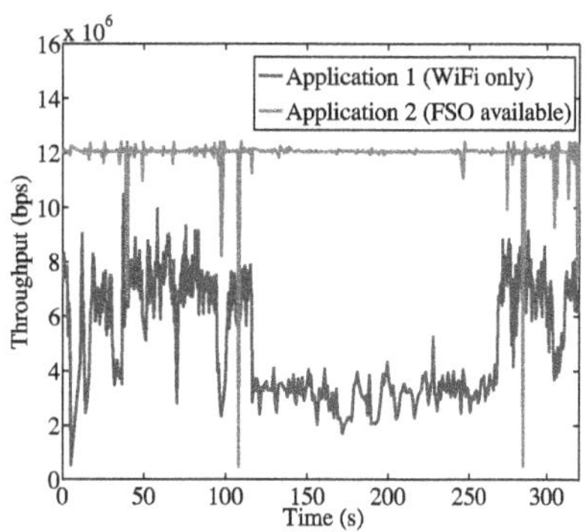

Figure 20: Throughput comparison between WiFi and FSO

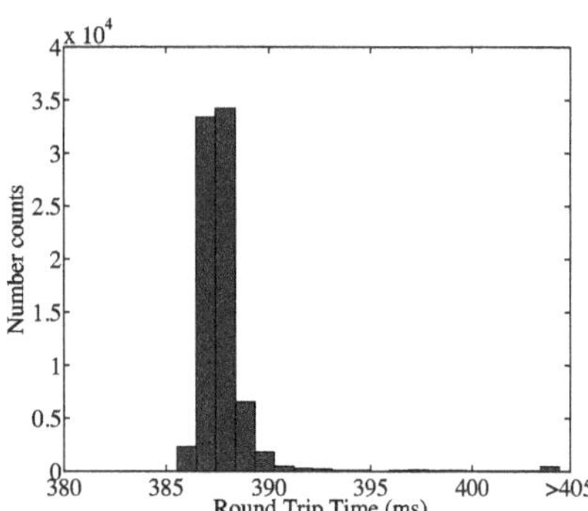

Figure 21: Histogram of round trip time for FSO channel

Fig. 21 shows the histogram of the round trip time for FSO channel. The round trip time is the elapsed time from the moment a 600 byte frame starts being transmitted on the FSO channel until the transmitter receives the WiFi acknowledgment packet. 80000 data frames were sent through FSO channel and an ACK packet was sent back through WiFi without any background traffic for each frame. As seen, the most of the measured round trip time is in the range of 385-390 ms, yielding a throughput no less than 12.3 Mbps, even with this simple Send-and-Wait protocol.

Table 3 shows the transition time for the current experiment hardware setup and mobility protocol implementation. When the receiver moves into a light cone, the time between thefi rst beacon signal and thefi rst FSO data packet is recorded as the transition time from WiFi to FSO. On the other hand, the transition time from FSO to WiFi is measured as the time difference between the receiver timeout and thefi rst WiFi packet. As before, the data is gathered with and without artificial heavy background traffic. In all cases, the transition time is fewer than 100 ms, which is small enough for even latency-sensitive applications. The transition time from WiFi to FSO is usually less than 2 ms, which provides a considerably smooth transition without noticeable latency.

	FSO to WiFi	WiFi to FSO
light traffic	49.10 ms	1.59 ms
heavy traffic	87.02 ms	1.64 ms

Table 3: Transition time (30 average)

6 CONCLUSION

In this paper, we presented architecture and implementation of WiFO, a novel communication system that integrates both RF and FSO technologies. WiFO aims to increase the wireless capacities while retaining the mobility offered by the existing WiFi systems. Our preliminary investigation demonstrates that a hybrid WiFi/FSO system is a promising approach to increase the capacity of existing WiFi networks.

7 ACKNOWLEDGMENT

The work is supported by National Science Foundation under Grant NSF:EARS 1547450.

REFERENCES

[1] O. Bouchet, M. El Tabach, M. Wolf, D. O'brien, G. Faulkner, J.W. Walewski, S. Randel, M. Franke, S. Nerreter, K.-D. Langer, J. Grubor, and T. Kamalakis. 2008. Hybrid wireless optics (HWO): Building the next-generation home network. In *CNSDSP 2008*. 283–287.

[2] F.E.Doany et.al. 2012. Terabit/s-Class Optical PCB Links Incorporating 360-Gb/s Bidirectional 850 nm Parallel Optical Transceivers. *J. Lightwave Technol.* 30 (2012), 560–571.

[3] FCC Spectrum Policy Task Force. 2002. Report of the spectrum efficieny working group. In *Online. Available at http://www.fcc.gov/sptf/reports.html.*

[4] H. Haas, L. Yin, Y. Wang, and C. Chen. 2016. What is LiFi? *Journal of Lightwave Technology* 34, 6 (March 2016), 1533–1544. https://doi.org/10.1109/JLT.2015.2510021

[5] H.Al Hajjar, B.Fracasso, and D.LerouxIndoor. 2013. optical wireless Gbps link dimensioning. In *National Fiber Optic Engineers Conference, Anaheim, CA, Mar. 17-21.*

[6] M. Kavehrad. 2010. Sustainable energy-efficient wireless applications using light. *IEEE Communication Magazine* (2010), 66–73.

[7] K.Wang, A.Nirmalathas, C.Lim, and E.Skafidas. 2012. Ultra-broadband indoor optical wireless communication system with multimodefi ber. *Optics Letters* 37 (2012), 1514–1516.

[8] J. Mitola III and G.Q. Maguire Jr. 1999. Cognitive radio: making software radios more personal. *Personal Communications, IEEE* 6, 4 (1999), 13–18.

[9] A. Wang Q. Wang, T. Nguyen. 2014. Channel Capacity Optimization for an integrated Wi-Fi and Free-space Optic Communication System (WiFiFO). In *17th ACM MSWiM 2014.* ACM.

[10] Di Wang and Alhussein A. Abouzeid. 2011. Throughput and Delay Analysis for Hybrid Radio-frequency and Free-space-optical (RF/FSO) Networks. *Wirel. Netw.* 17, 4 (May 2011), 877–892. https://doi.org/10.1007/s11276-011-0321-3

[11] Y. Wang, X. Wu, and H. Haas. 2015. Distributed load balancing for Internet of Things by using Li-Fi and RF hybrid network. In *2015 IEEE 26th Annual International Symposium on Personal, Indoor, and Mobile Radio Communications (PIMRC).* 1289–1294. https://doi.org/10.1109/PIMRC.2015.7343497

[12] Qing Zhao and B.M. Sadler. 2007. A Survey of Dynamic Spectrum Access. *Signal Processing Magazine, IEEE* 24, 3 (may 2007), 79 –89. https://doi.org/10.1109/MSP.2007.361604

The Importance of Adjacent Channel Interference: Experimental Validation of ns-3 for Dense Wi-Fi Networks

Andra M. Voicu, Laurent Lava, Ljiljana Simić
RWTH Aachen University
Institute for Networked Systems
{avo,lla,lsi}@inets.rwth-aachen.de

Marina Petrova
KTH Royal Institute of Technology
School of Information and Communication Technology
petrovam@kth.se

ABSTRACT

In its evolution to provide ever higher data rates, the Wi-Fi standard has incorporated sophisticated PHY-layer techniques, which has in turn increased the complexity of network-wide interference relationships. Proper modelling of the resulting inter-device interactions is crucial for accurately estimating Wi-Fi network performance, especially in the contemporary context of traffic and network densification. Event-driven simulators like the open-source ns-3 are in principle able to capture these interactions, however it is imperative to validate, against experimental results, whether their underlying models reflect the network behaviour in practice. In this paper we first perform experiments in a large-scale indoor testbed to validate the IEEE 802.11ac Wi-Fi model in ns-3, for various channel width and allocation configurations. Our results show that ns-3 captures Wi-Fi co-channel interactions with reasonable precision, but fails to model adjacent channel interference (ACI), which our experiments show to be critical in dense networks. We therefore propose and implement an ACI model in ns-3. Importantly, our model successfully captures the qualitative behaviour of the CSMA/CA mechanism when transmissions on adjacent channels occur. Further, our ACI implementation significantly improves the accuracy of both the network and per-device throughput estimates for the considered dense IEEE 802.11ac network compared to the basic ns-3 Wi-Fi model without ACI. For example, without ACI modelling, ns-3 overestimates the aggregate network throughput by up to 230%, whereas with our ACI implementation the aggregate throughput estimate is no more than 65% higher than the experimental results.

KEYWORDS

measurements; IEEE 802.11ac; ns-3; adjacent channel interference

1 INTRODUCTION

Projections of future wireless networks envision extreme densification for coping with the data traffic growth [12]. The already ubiquitous IEEE 802.11 Wi-Fi is a representative example of target technologies for densification, as it is easy to deploy, manage, and access. However, densification would also raise inter-device coexistence issues by increasing the level of interference that wireless technologies would have to manage. Coexistence in indoor environments can be particularly problematic for Wi-Fi, due to the various existing deployments (e.g. public hotspot, business, residential), corresponding to diverse interference conditions.

Wi-Fi has traditionally managed interference by distributed time-sharing of spectrum among devices. However, this MAC layer approach alone no longer suffices to mitigate interference and achieve the high throughput performance required in dense networks. Consequently, the latest Wi-Fi standards, i.e. IEEE 802.11n and 802.11ac [9], evolved by increasing the complexity of the PHY layer through, e.g. channel aggregation, MIMO techniques, and better modulation and coding schemes. It is thus increasingly challenging to characterize the interference conditions in such networks, especially for dense deployments. Moreover, some Wi-Fi features are vendor-specific and/or optional (e.g. rate adaptation mechanisms, frame aggregation, beamforming), introducing heterogeneous devices even within the same technology.

It is nevertheless crucial to reliably estimate the efficiency of these recently proposed techniques from a network-wide perspective, in order to determine if they can meet the demands of future deployments. The underlying network models should therefore be sufficiently accurate to provide relevant and realistic performance estimates. Existing network-level Wi-Fi analytical models are not able to faithfully capture in detail the complex interactions within real modern Wi-Fi networks, as they either consider only Wi-Fi nodes within carrier sense (CS) range of each other [6], or are based on stochastic geometry, which provides overly coarse network performance estimates [11]. Simulators in general provide more accurate results, at the cost of potentially long simulation time and computational complexity. Monte-Carlo-based simulations, e.g. [16], typically require a moderate simulation time and provide more detailed long-term average per-device performance than purely analytical models, but their time granularity is not fine enough to capture short-term metrics. Consequently, in this paper we focus on an event-driven network simulator, i.e. the open-source ns-3 [2], as such simulators currently offer the best opportunities to estimate the network-wide performance within a reasonable time compared to potentially infeasible real-life measurements, while being able to provide sufficient accuracy and time granularity.

With the rapid evolution of the IEEE 802.11 standard to include sophisticated features, network simulator models become easily outdated. We argue that the ultimate validation of such models is comparison against experimental results for commercial devices, as they directly show the network behaviour in practice. Existing experimental validation of the ns-3 Wi-Fi module [5, 7, 10, 13] is

MSWiM'17, November 21–25, 2017, Miami, FL, USA

ACM ISBN 978-1-4503-5162-1/17/11...$15.00.
DOI: http://dx.doi.org/10.1145/3127540.3127548

based on legacy standards prior to IEEE 802.11n, which do not implement any advanced features key for emerging dense deployments, e.g. channel aggregation, MIMO effects, frame aggregation, or rate adaptation. Importantly, to the best of our knowledge none of the existing experimental validations of the ns-3 Wi-Fi model evaluates adjacent channel interference (ACI). By contrast, in this paper we focus on IEEE 802.11ac as the most recent and complex Wi-Fi standard, which is also indicative of the evolution direction of future dense networks.[1] Furthermore, we argue that including ACI in Wi-Fi models especially for dense networks is critical.

Our contributions are threefold:

(i) we validate the accuracy of ns-3 simulations against extensive experiments in a dense IEEE 802.11ac Wi-Fi network;
(ii) we evaluate the effect of Wi-Fi ACI on the aggregate and per-device throughput for different channel configurations;
(iii) we implement a Wi-Fi ACI model, which we have made publicly available [1], to accurately capture the interactions among adjacent channel transmissions through the CSMA/CA mechanism in ns-3.

Our experimental results show that ns-3 estimates with reasonable precision the Wi-Fi network aggregate throughput for co-channel transmissions, but fails to model ACI, which we show has a major impact in dense networks. Also, our ACI model implementation in ns-3 significantly improves the accuracy of the estimated throughput compared to the basic ns-3 Wi-Fi model without ACI.

This paper is organized as follows. Section 2 presents our Wi-Fi ACI model and implementation. Section 3 presents the validation methodology. Section 4 presents and discusses the results. Section 5 summarizes related work and Section 6 concludes the paper.

2 WI-FI ACI MODEL & IMPLEMENTATION

In this section we present a general model[2] for ACI in IEEE 802.11ac networks and the implementation of this model in ns-3.26.

2.1 ACI Model

We assume the ACI experienced by a Wi-Fi receiver is due to imperfections in both Wi-Fi transmitter and receiver operating on adjacent channels. The ACI is estimated based on the transmit spectrum masks specified for IEEE 802.11ac [9], for each supported channel bandwidth, i.e. 20, 40, 80, and 160 MHz. These spectrum masks, which define the worst standard-compliant transmitter, are assumed to characterize the filters at both Wi-Fi transmitter and receiver, such that we obtain an upper bound value of the ACI.[3]

We calculate the fraction of the transmit power causing ACI to a receiver on an adjacent channel as

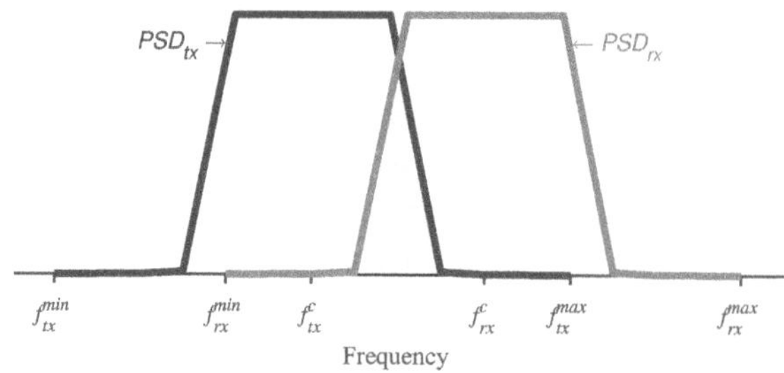

Figure 1: Illustrative example of normalized power spectral density functions for the transmitter (blue) and receiver (red), corresponding to two Wi-Fi devices operating on adjacent channels of equal bandwidth. The fraction of the transmit power causing ACI is determined by the overlapping area (yellow) of the two power spectral density functions, calculated as in (1). Terms f_{tx}^c and f_{rx}^c are the channel centre frequencies for the transmitter and receiver, respectively.

$$OF = \frac{\int_{max\{f_{tx}^{min},f_{rx}^{min}\}}^{min\{f_{tx}^{max},f_{rx}^{max}\}} PSD_{tx}(f) \times PSD_{rx}(f)\, df}{\int_{f_{tx}^{min}}^{f_{tx}^{max}} PSD_{tx}\, df}, \tag{1}$$

where $PSD_{tx}(f)$ is the normalized power spectral density of the transmitter, $PSD_{rx}(f)$ is the equivalent normalized power spectral density of the receiver on an adjacent channel, f_{tx}^{max} is the frequency above which $PSD_{tx}(f)$ can be considered negligible, f_{rx}^{max} is the frequency above which $PSD_{rx}(f)$ can be considered negligible, f_{tx}^{min} is the frequency below which $PSD_{tx}(f)$ can be considered negligible, and f_{rx}^{min} is the frequency below which $PSD_{rx}(f)$ can be considered negligible. The function $PSD_{tx}(f)$ is defined for IEEE 802.11ac by the spectrum mask in [9] for the considered channel width and channel centre frequency. We note that we select f_{tx}^{max} and f_{tx}^{min}, such that the spectrum mask spans two adjacent channels either side of the considered channel. The function $PSD_{rx}(f)$ can be determined analogously for the receiver. Equation (1) is thus the fraction of the transmit power corresponding to the overlapping area between spectrum masks centred on adjacent channels, as shown in Fig. 1.

The ACI at the receiver is then calculated as

$$P_{ACI} = OF \times P_{tx} \times L^{-1}, \tag{2}$$

where P_{tx} is the transmit power of a transmitter on an adjacent channel and L is the path loss.

2.2 Implementation of ACI in the Wi-Fi Module of ns-3

In order to implement the IEEE 802.11ac ACI model in Section 2.1 in ns-3.26, we first introduce the function *overlapFactorToBeDecoded*, which calculates the fraction of transmit power OF causing ACI. This function is defined in the file *yans-wifi-channel.cc* of the Wi-Fi module. We further modify the Wi-Fi module in ns-3.26, in order to take into account ACI and also co-channel interference between

[1]We note, however, that our general findings, especially with respect to ACI modelling, can also be extended to previous widespread standard amendments (e.g. IEEE 802.11n), which are simpler variants with lower data rates and less robustness to interference due to lack of beamforming.

[2]Our Wi-Fi ACI model is also applicable to other IEEE 802.11 standards, if the respective specified transmit spectrum mask in [9] is assumed. Also, the spectrum masks for IEEE 802.11a, 802.11n, and 802.11ac in the 5 GHz band are identical for the same bandwidth.

[3]We note that in practice the Wi-Fi transmit and receive filters may be more efficient, resulting in lower ACI values than the ones estimated by this model. As we do not know the exact spectrum masks of these filters, we estimate these as consistent with our empirical observation that strong ACI is due to transmissions occurring up to two channels apart. Importantly, if the actual specifications of the filters are known, our model can provide an estimate that matches even better the experimental results.

Algorithm 1 Logic added to *YansWiFiChannel::Send*

```
for all RXs do                                          ▷ already in ns-3
    if TX ≠ RX then                                     ▷ already in ns-3
        if TX's channel included in RX's channel then
            OF ← 0 dB                          ▷ co-channel interference
        else
            calculate OF in dB based on (1)                       ▷ ACI
        end if
        calculate P_rx in dBm                           ▷ already in ns-3
        P_rx = P_rx + OF
        schedule packet from TX to RX                   ▷ already in ns-3
    end if
end for
```

channels that are only partly overlapping (e.g. a 20 MHz channel overlapping with the primary or the secondary 20 MHz channel of a 40 MHz channel), as follows.

We modify the function *YansWiFiChannel::Send* in the *yans-wifi-channel.cc* file to send packets to Wi-Fi receivers operating on different channels (i.e. adjacent or partly overlapping), by adding the logic shown in Algorithm 1 in pseudocode, where P_{rx} is the received power. Specifically, we distinguish two cases: (i) the transmitter's band is included in the receiver's band, such that the receiver detects the transmission as co-channel (irrespective of being able to decode the received packet or not); and (ii) the transmitter and receiver are operating on different channels, so OF must be calculated. In the function *YansWiFiChannel::Receive* in file *yans-wifi-channel.cc* we also add the channel centre frequency and width as associated parameters for the received packet.

Up to this point we modified the code such that a packet is scheduled to be detected at the receiver for any of the co- or adjacent channel transmission cases. Next, we modify function *YansWiFiPhy::StartReceivePreambleAndHeader* in file *yans-wifi-phy.cc* to decode an incoming packet only if: the received power level is above the minimum sensitivity[4] of -82 dBm [9]; the receiver's channel bandwidth is at least as large as the transmitter's channel bandwidth (i.e. the receiver can capture the entire transmitted packet); and the transmitter's channel coincides with the receiver's primary channel (i.e. we assume that if the transmitter's channel coincides with the receiver's secondary channel, packet decoding is not possible). Otherwise the scheduled packet is not decoded, but may either trigger the clear channel assessment (CCA) busy mode if its power level exceeds the energy detect (ED) threshold of -62 dBm, or may simply cause SINR-decreasing interference if its power level is below -62 dBm [9]. The logic added in ns-3 is shown in Algorithm 2 in pseudocode.

3 MODEL VALIDATION METHODOLOGY & SCENARIOS

In order to validate the ns-3 Wi-Fi simulation model in general, and our ACI model specifically, we perform extensive measurements

Algorithm 2 Logic added to *YansWiFiPhy::StartReceivePreambleAndHeader*

```
...                                                     ▷ already in ns-3
case RX state = YansWiFiPhy::IDLE
if (P_rx > CS threshold) && (RX bandwidth ≥ TX bandwidth)
   && (TX & RX have same primary channel) then
    try to decode PLCP header                           ▷ already in ns-3
else
    drop packet                                         ▷ already in ns-3
    ...
end if
break
```

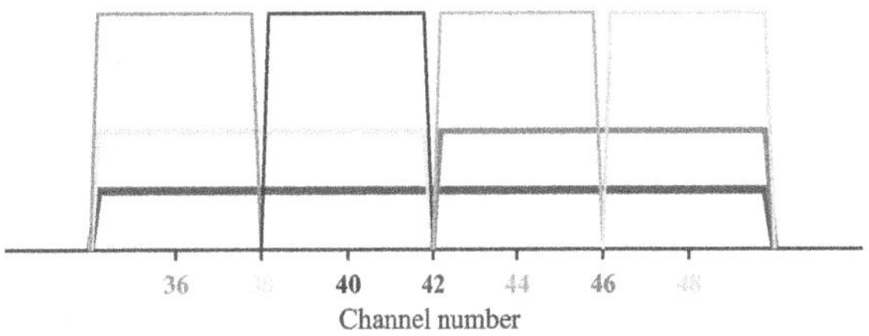

Figure 2: IEEE 802.11ac non-DFS channels for our scenarios, where the channel number determines the channel centre frequency $f^{c}_{Ch.No.} = 5\ GHz + 5\ MHz \times ChannelNumber$ [9]. There are 4×20 MHz channels (i.e. 36–magenta, 40–blue, 44–orange, 48–green), 2×40 MHz channels (i.e. 38–cyan, 46–red), and 1×80 MHz channel (i.e. 42–brown).

and simulations where we consider up to twelve IEEE 802.11ac access points (APs), each with one associated client, in three different indoor office scenarios, for different channel configurations. We match the measurement and simulation parameters as closely as possible, in order to obtain comparable results. In this section we describe the considered scenarios, the experimental testbed, and our simulation parameters.

3.1 Validation Scenarios

3.1.1 Two-Link Variable Distance Scenario. We assume two IEEE 802.11ac AP-client pairs operating on adjacent 20 MHz channels, i.e. the first pair on channel 36 and the second pair on channel 40. Fig. 2 shows the considered channels.[5] The distance between each AP and its associated client is always 1 m, whereas the distance d between the two pairs is varied from 1 m to 20 m along a hallway with line-of-sight conditions. Fig. 3 shows the placement of the AP-client pairs. We thus seek to test if the implemented ACI model matches the measurements when the ACI is strong enough to cause the two pairs to share the spectrum in time based on the CSMA/CA mechanism (i.e. exceeds -62 dBm) and when the ACI is lower and only causes SINR-decreasing interference (i.e. below -62 dBm). The

[4]We note that the minimum sensitivity is misleadingly named *EnergyDetectionThreshold* in ns-3. In the IEEE terminology the minimum sensitivity is the CS threshold and the ED threshold is the CCA mode 1 threshold [9]. We adopt the IEEE terminology.

[5]The IEEE 802.11ac channels are non-overlapping channels in the 5 GHz band. However, the IEEE 802.11ac spectrum masks [9] span a wider frequency range than that corresponding to the channel widths.

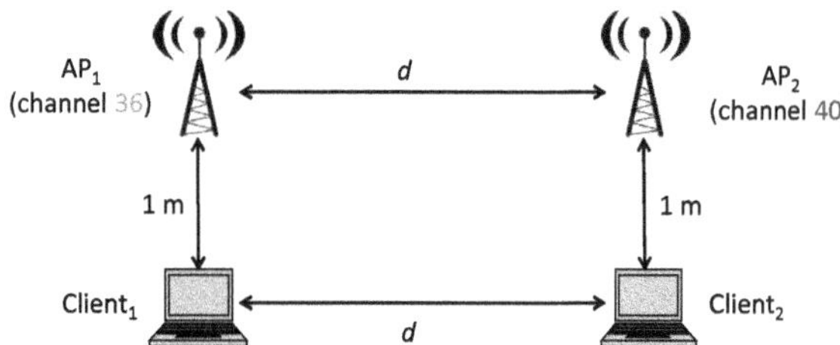

Figure 3: Node placement and channel allocation for the *two-link variable distance scenario*, where distance d is varied from 1 m to 20 m. $Client_1$ is associated to AP_1 and $Client_2$ is associated to AP_2. The channel color code matches Fig. 2, i.e. 36–magenta, 40–blue.

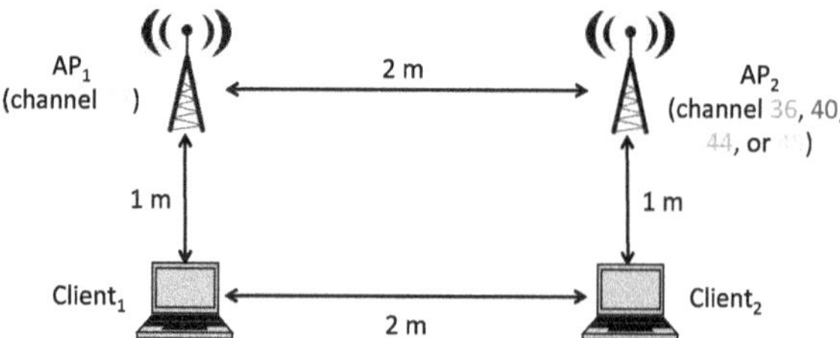

Figure 4: Node placement and channel allocation for the *two-link sliding channel scenario*. $Client_1$ is associated to AP_1 and $Client_2$ is associated to AP_2. The channel color code matches Fig. 2, i.e. 38–cyan, 36–magenta, 40–blue, 44–orange, 48–green.

free space path loss model is assumed for our simulations[6] and 6 measurement/simulation repetitions were performed for each d.

3.1.2 Two-Link Sliding Channel Scenario. We assume two IEEE 802.11ac AP-client pairs with fixed locations, as shown in Fig. 4. The first AP-client pair is always operating on the 40 MHz channel 38, whereas the second AP-client pair is operating on a 20 MHz channel with a varying center frequency, i.e. channel number 36, 40, 44, or 48. As shown in Fig. 2, we thus slide a 20 MHz channel with respect to the 40 MHz channel 38, such that the 20 MHz channel: (i) overlaps with the primary channel of the 40 MHz channel; (ii) overlaps with the secondary channel of the 40 MHz channel; (iii) is adjacent to the 40 MHz channel; or (iv) is separated by 20 MHz from the 40 MHz channel. Importantly, this scenario aims at validating our ns-3 implementation of both ACI and interactions between nodes operating on partly overlapping channels, according to our model in Section 2.2. For the simulations, the free space path loss model is assumed between each pair of nodes, due to the short distance between the nodes. We performed 10 measurement/simulation repetitions for each channel configuration.

3.1.3 Dense Network Scenario. This scenario has twelve IEEE 802.11ac AP-client pairs located in a single room, corresponding to the testbed and results in [14]. The number of active AP-client pairs (i.e. between which data traffic is transmitted) varies from one to twelve, where twelve captures extreme network densification, as may be expected in the future. For simplicity, we place the APs in a single room, such that they are within CS range of each other. The AP-client pairs are each allocated a channel as shown in Fig. 2, with three different overall network channel configurations: 4×20 MHz channels, 2×40 MHz channels, and 1×80 MHz channel. Fig. 5 shows the approximate placement and channel allocation for each AP-client pair within the room, for each of the three channel configurations. We note that the channel allocation strategy was chosen such that the separation between co-channel APs is maximized [14]. The turn-on order of the APs is marked by numbers in Fig. 5 and the distance between each AP and its associated client is always 1 m. In order to determine simulation path losses that match better the real path losses for this particular testbed deployment, we first measure the received power at the client side, for the beacon frames from each AP (the *iwlist* tool was used to extract this information). We then assume the same measured received signal power for the simulations, by applying the resulting path loss for the considered transmit power. Also, for an AP we assume that the path loss from each of the other APs is the same respective path loss as from each of the other APs to its associated client. Furthermore, for a client we assume that the path loss from each of the other clients is the same respective path loss as from each of the other APs. We note these approximations are reasonable, as the clients are located only 1 m away from the AP that they are associated with and all the nodes are within a single room and on each other's line-of-sight, so only negligible average path loss variations are expected. We performed 6 measurement/simulation repetitions for each number of active AP-client pairs, for each channel configuration.

[6]We note this approximation is necessary, since it is not straightforward to measure the received signal strength at an AP from the interfering non-co-channel AP. As the two APs operate on adjacent channels, they are not able to decode each other's frames, so readily-available tools like *iwlist*, which report the signal strength based on the decoded beacons, cannot be used. Although we could use a spectrum analyser, we would not be able to identify which transmitter the energy detected at the receiver comes from.

3.2 Measurement Testbed and Simulation Parameters

The testbed consists of up to twelve IEEE 802.11ac AP-client pairs. The clients are Asus PCE-AC68 wireless adapters connected to a PC with Linux driver version 6.30.223.248 and the APs are Asus RT-AC87U routers connected to blade servers [14]. The specifications of the IEEE 802.11ac devices are given in Table 1. The complete testbed includes four blade servers, each supporting three APs, which are connected to a main control PC via an Ethernet switch. The clients are also connected to the control PC via Ethernet connections, for automated traffic generation and experiment control [14].

For both measurements and simulations we assume UDP downlink saturated traffic. For the experiments, constant bit rate (CBR) traffic was generated with *iperf*, with a rate of 800 Mbps, which was empirically found to saturate the links [14]. For *iperf* the default application-layer payload of a packet is 1470 bytes long. These values were also adopted for the ns-3 simulations. Each measurement/simulation repetition for each scenario lasted 10 s.

For each measurement repetition, the downlink throughput per AP is calculated at the client with the *capinfos* tool in Wireshark, such that the application payload bytes, but also the headers bytes included in the frame are taken into account (the frame size is 1514 [14]). For the simulation results we measure the throughput

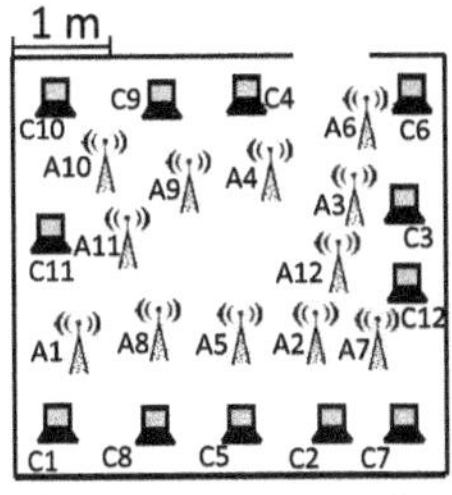

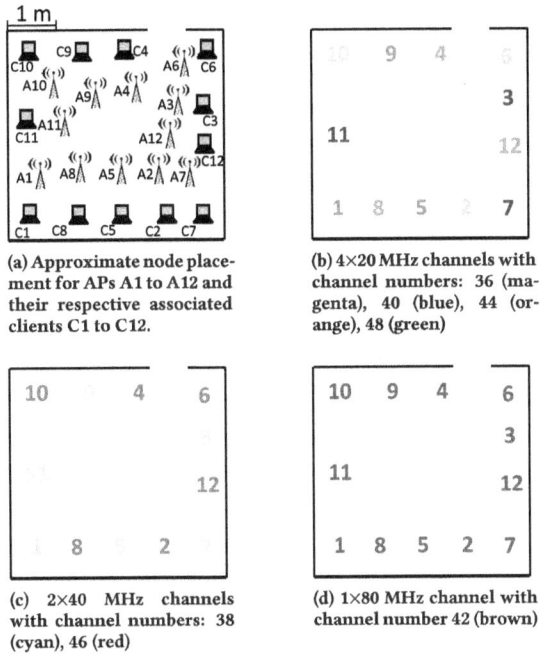

(a) Approximate node placement for APs A1 to A12 and their respective associated clients C1 to C12.

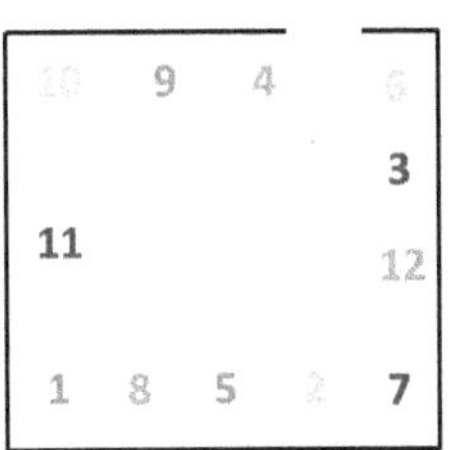

(b) 4×20 MHz channels with channel numbers: 36 (magenta), 40 (blue), 44 (orange), 48 (green)

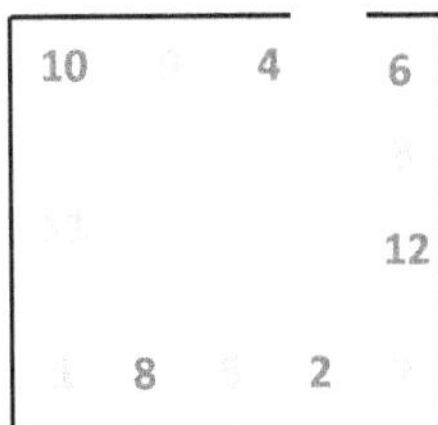

(c) 2×40 MHz channels with channel numbers: 38 (cyan), 46 (red)

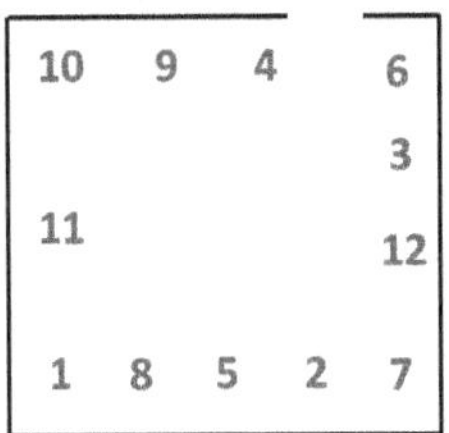

(d) 1×80 MHz channel with channel number 42 (brown)

Figure 5: Placement (approximate) and channel allocation for the twelve IEEE 802.11ac AP-client pairs, for the *dense network scenario*, for different channel configurations. The numbers indicate the turn-on order of the AP-client pairs. The channel color code matches the one in Fig. 2.

per client by counting the received data frames that are forwarded by the MAC layer to upper layers in ns-3 and we take into account the total number of bytes in a frame including the header, i.e. 1532 bytes out of which 1470 bytes are application-layer payload bytes.

Furthermore, for the simulations we assume the *ideal* PHY rate adaptation in ns-3, unless specified otherwise, which assumes the transmitter has perfect knowledge of the channel interference conditions and selects the optimal modulation and coding scheme that results in the maximum possible data rate. We note that we also present a short selection of simulation results for the *minstrel* rate adaptation, which is implemented in practice in the Linux kernel [15] and thus in many Linux-based Wi-Fi devices. However, we show in Section 4.3 that the *minstrel* rate adaptation does not approximate well the measurement results for the considered testbed. Other simulation parameters are summarized in Table 2.

4 RESULTS AND ANALYSIS

4.1 Two-Link Variable Distance Scenario

Fig. 6 shows the aggregate throughput for the *two-link variable distance scenario* in Section 3.1.1, for measurements and ns-3 simulations with and without ACI, when the two APs operate on adjacent channels 36 and 40, respectively. The measurement results show that the aggregate throughput increases overall with the distance d between the two APs. Furthermore, up to d=12 m, the median aggregate throughput is at most 220 Mbps (i.e. the throughput

Table 1: IEEE 802.11ac testbed equipment specifications

	Client: PCE-AC68	AP: RT-AC87U
Peak data rate	1.3 Gbps	1.734 Gbps
Spatial streams	3×3 MIMO	4×4 MIMO
Beamforming	no	yes
Channel width	20/40/80 MHz	20/40/80 MHz
DFS support	no	yes
Transmit power	18-22 dBm	19 dBm
Chipset	BCM4360	QT3840BC+QT2518B
MPDU aggregation	32 frames with implicit block ACK requests (empirically determined [14])	

Table 2: ns-3 simulation parameters for APs and clients

Parameter	Value
MPDU aggregation	32 frames (implicit block ACK requests)
Transmit power	Client: 22 dBm; AP: 19 dBm
Beamforming	no
Number of antennas	Client: 3; AP: 4
IEEE 802.11 MAC	CS threshold of -82 dBm ED threshold of -62 dBm
Noise figure (NF)	7 dB

of a single IEEE 802.11ac link with three spatial streams), which suggests that the ACI between the two AP-client links is strong enough to trigger CSMA/CA's ED threshold and thus cause the APs to share the spectrum in time. At d=13 m a jump in the aggregate throughput occurs (from 220 to 330 Mbps), suggesting that the received signal strength from the other AP is below the ED threshold, so the APs can transmit at the same time and the ACI only causes a decrease in SINR. This shows that for practical deployments, ACI has a strong impact on the contention between Wi-Fi devices.

The ns-3 simulation results without ACI severely overestimate the aggregate throughput as a constant 530 Mbps, irrespective of the distance between the APs, i.e. up to 365 Mbps higher median aggregate throughput compared to the measurement results. By contrast, the aggregate throughput for ns-3 with ACI follows a similar trend as the measurement results, i.e. exhibits a jump where the APs no longer share the spectrum in time. We emphasize that this is a key result, as it shows that our ACI model captures the qualitative behaviour of CSMA/CA for adjacent channel transmissions. However, the throughput jump for ns-3 with ACI occurs at a shorter distance than for the measurements, i.e. d=8 m, as our propagation model does not incorporate the antenna gains in the measured direction, since they are not known. Consequently, the received signal strength level is lower for the simulations compared to the measurements, so the range of distances over which the two APs defer to each other is also smaller. Nevertheless, the distance at which the jump occurs can be easily adjusted in ns-3, if the correct antenna gains are known. We note that this parameter mismatch does not significantly affect the results for our subsequent scenarios, where the nodes are placed within very close proximity.

Also, the throughput for ns-3 with ACI is only up to 105 Mbps and up to 190 Mbps higher than the measured throughput for $d \leq 7$ m

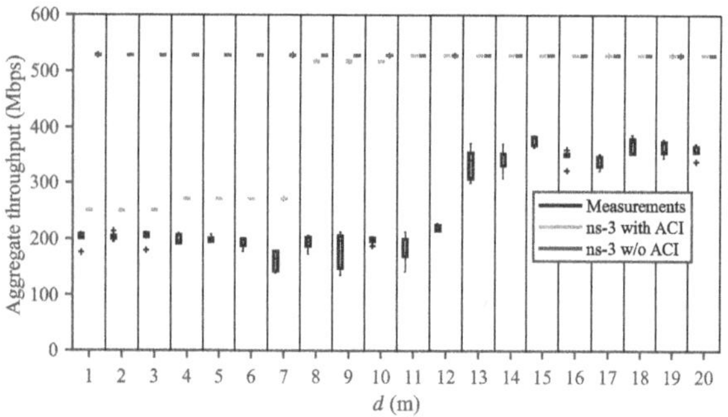

Figure 6: Aggregate throughput for the *two-link variable distance scenario*, for measurements and ns-3 simulations with and without ACI (*ideal* rate adaptation).

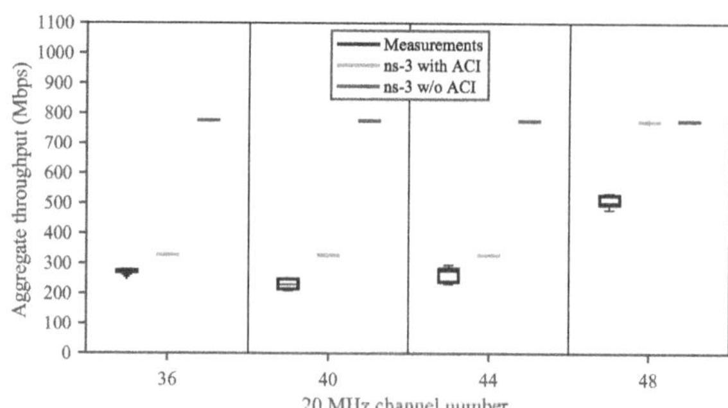

Figure 7: Aggregate throughput for the *two-link sliding channel scenario*, for measurements and ns-3 simulations with and without ACI (*ideal* rate adaptation).

and $d \geq 13$ m, respectively. This difference in throughput compared to the measurements for these distances can be explained by the MIMO channel conditions, which are assumed to be ideal in ns-3 (i.e. the throughput is obtained by multiplying the throughput of one stream with the number of streams), but vary in practice. The simulations in ns-3 with and without ACI provide the same throughput, if the APs interfere with each other by decreasing each other's SINR (i.e. $d \geq 11$ m). We note that for $8 \leq d \leq 10$ m, the throughput for ns-3 with ACI is slightly lower than that without ACI, as an AP may defer to the acknowledgements sent by the client associated with the other AP, but not to the data frames of the other AP, as the clients transmit with a higher power.

The overall results for this simple *two-link variable distance scenario* demonstrate two important aspects: (i) ACI has a major impact in real Wi-Fi deployments and should therefore be modelled for simulation-based Wi-Fi performance estimation, and (ii) our ACI implementation in ns-3 accurately captures the qualitative behaviour of CSMA/CA for adjacent channel transmissions and provides significantly more realistic results than the basic ns-3 Wi-Fi module.

4.2 Two-Link Sliding Channel Scenario

Fig. 7 shows the aggregate throughput for the *two-link sliding channel scenario* in Section 3.1.2, for measurements and ns-3 simulations with and without ACI. The measurement results show that for the considered short distance between APs (i.e. 2 m), the aggregate throughput has only a small variation with a median value of 230-270 Mbps (i.e. only slightly higher than the throughput of a 20 MHz single link), when the second AP operates on channels 36, 40, or 44. This suggests that the APs defer to each other via CSMA/CA for the cases where the channel of the second AP (i) is overlapping with the primary channel, (ii) is overlapping with the secondary channel, or (iii) is adjacent to the channel of the first AP. If the second AP operates on channel 48, the measured throughput is significantly higher (i.e. median of 505 Mbps), indicating that the 40 MHz and the 20 MHz channels are decoupled.

The ns-3 aggregate throughput without ACI is constant at 780 Mbps, regardless of the frequency separation between the 40 MHz and the 20 MHz channels, consistent with the assumption that the channels are fully decoupled. The ns-3 results with ACI reproduce the behaviour of the experimental deployment much more accurately, with a difference of only up to 100 Mbps (instead of 550 Mbps without ACI) for the cases where the two channels are coupled. If the channels are not coupled, the ns-3 results with and without ACI are the same, showing that our ACI implementation has the expected behaviour. The difference between the ns-3 results with ACI and the measurement results can be attributed to the different MIMO channel conditions experienced in practice.

The results for this scenario thus show that our modifications for Wi-Fi in ns-3 not only estimate the effects of ACI more accurately, but also capture the effects of the CSMA/CA mechanism between APs operating on partly overlapping channels of 20 and 40 MHz.

4.3 Dense Network Scenario

Fig. 8 shows the aggregate throughput for the *dense network scenario* in Section 3.1.3 with different channel configurations, for measurements and ns-3 with and without ACI. We emphasize that in this scenario we comprehensively validate the ns-3 simulation results against the large-scale dense Wi-Fi network testbed. Let us first consider the 1×80 MHz channel configuration in Fig. 8(a). The measured aggregate throughput reaches its maximum for a single active AP-client pair and gradually decreases when the number of active pairs increases, due to increased contention among APs, which increases the Wi-Fi MAC protocol overhead. The ns-3 aggregate throughput with and without ACI is 110 Mbps higher than the measured throughput for one active AP-client pair and decreases to a difference of only 10 Mbps for twelve active pairs. This marginal difference can be explained by the MIMO channel conditions, as for the *two-link scenarios*. Thus, this baseline channel configuration validates ns-3 for co-channel Wi-Fi transmissions and shows that our ACI implementation behaves correctly for this reference case.

Let us now consider the 2×40 MHz channel configuration in Fig. 8(b), focusing on ACI between two adjacent 40 MHz channels. The measured aggregate throughput is almost constant at about 400 Mbps (i.e. the throughput of a single 40 MHz link), irrespective of the number of active AP-client pairs, showing that both co- and adjacent channel interference trigger the spectrum time-sharing CSMA/CA mechanism. Although the aggregate throughput typically decreases slightly with increased contention (due to higher

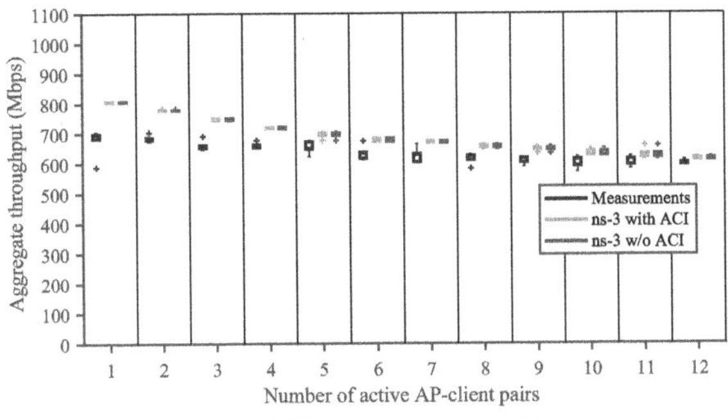

(a) 1×80 MHz channel configuration

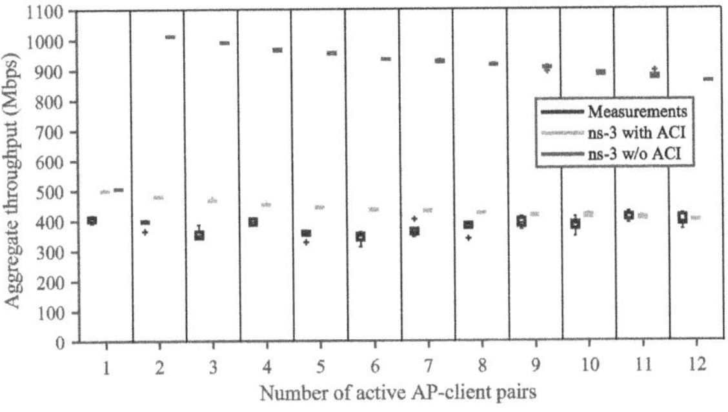

(b) 2×40 MHz channel configuration

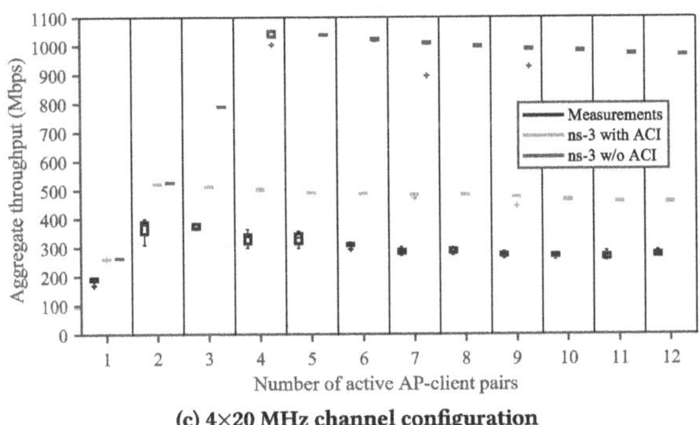

(c) 4×20 MHz channel configuration

Figure 8: Aggregate throughput for the *dense network scenario*, for measurements and ns-3 simulations with and without ACI (*ideal* rate adaptation).

MAC overhead), this effect was not observed, likely due to beamforming, which may reduce contention by minimising the spatial regions where interference is experienced. The ns-3 model without ACI can capture interactions only between co-channel APs and therefore provides a median aggregate throughput up to 615 Mbps higher than the measured one. By contrast, our ns-3 ACI model shows a median aggregate throughput only up to 115 Mbps higher than the measured one. The remaining difference can be explained by different MIMO channel conditions.

Fig. 8(c) shows the aggregate throughput for the 4×20 MHz channel configuration, which captures the most complex ACI interactions in this scenario. The measured aggregate throughput reaches 400 Mbps for two active AP-client pairs and gradually decreases to 280 Mbps with the increase in active pairs. This shows that the aggregate throughput does not reach that of four uncoupled saturated links, corresponding to the four different 20 MHz channels. Instead, the maximum is reached for only two active AP-client pairs on channels separated by a large frequency (i.e. channels 36 and 48), such that ACI is negligible. For more than two active pairs, ACI becomes dominant by exceeding the ED threshold and creating contention between APs on adjacent channels. Especially channels 40 and 44 are expected to suffer from increased contention (as shown in Fig. 10(b) and discussed subsequently), due to having two adjacent channels each. This also results in a higher MAC overhead, reflected by the decrease in the throughput curve. The aggregate throughput for ns-3 without ACI is about 1000 Mbps for more than four active pairs (i.e. approximately four times the single-link throughput and up to 700 Mbps, i.e. 230%, higher than the measured throughput), consistent with its assumption that the four channels are decoupled. The aggregate throughput for ns-3 with ACI estimates the measured results more accurately (at most 200 Mbps, i.e. 65%, higher) and the remaining difference in the results can stem from varying MIMO channel conditions in practice.

In order to understand in more detail the complex interactions in such dense networks, Fig. 9 shows the per-client throughput, for the 2×40 MHz channel configuration, for measurements and ns-3 with and without ACI. The measured client throughput in Fig. 9(a) decreases in general for all clients as the number of active links increases. For two active AP-client pairs on adjacent channels, the client throughput is about half the client throughput of one active pair, clearly showing that ACI causes contention between APs. However, there is a difference of 60 Mbps between the two simultaneously active pairs, which could be explained by different MIMO channel conditions and beamforming effects in the downlink, which may create contention in only some spatial regions. A similar trend is also observed for a higher number of active pairs. The client throughput for ns-3 with ACI (Fig. 9(b)) decreases more uniformly with the increase in active pairs, as no beamforming is implemented and MIMO conditions are considered ideal. For ns-3 without ACI (Fig. 9(c)), the client throughput values are typically twice the measured values. This shows that our ACI implementation in general significantly improves ns-3 accuracy, but that further extensions should take into account more realistic models for beamforming and MIMO.

Fig. 10 shows the client throughput for the 4×20 MHz channel configuration, for measurements and ns-3 with and without ACI. The measured throughput (Fig. 10(a)) decreases in general with the increase in active AP-client pairs operating on a co- or adjacent channel. However, some clients experience starvation even for a low number of active pairs, e.g. the third client for three active pairs. This shows that some APs defer to ACI from both one and two channels apart, such that they suffer from near-starvation, if operating on the middle channels [14]. The ns-3 results with ACI (Fig. 10(b)) show a similar behaviour when the number of active AP-client pairs increases on co- and adjacent channels. For example, for twelve active pairs, the throughput for clients 3, 4, 7, 8, 11, 12, which operate on the middle channels 40 and 44, is much lower than for the other clients, which operate on the edge channels 36 and 48.

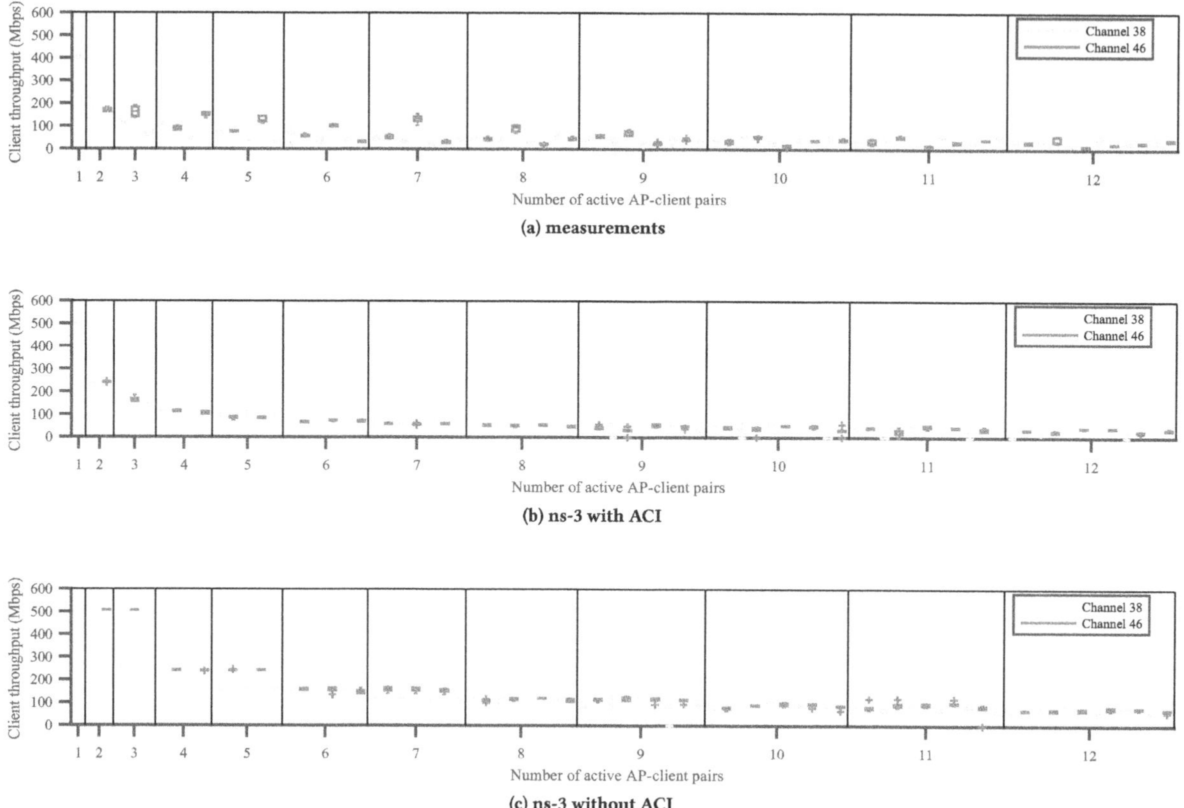

(a) measurements

(b) ns-3 with ACI

(c) ns-3 without ACI

Figure 9: Individual client throughputs for the *dense network scenario* vs. number of active AP-client pairs, for the 2×40 MHz channel configuration, for measurements and ns-3 simulations with and without ACI (*ideal* rate adaptation). The channel color code matches Fig. 2.

The ns-3 results without ACI (Fig. 10(c)) consistently overestimate the throughput compared to the measurements.

Importantly, these results show that our ACI implementation captures with better accuracy not only the overall aggregate network performance, but also the per-device behaviour of the CSMA/CA mechanism when adjacent channel transmissions occur.

4.4 Discussion and Future Enhancements

The validation results show overall that our ACI implementation in ns-3 is reasonably accurate when estimating the Wi-Fi throughput for the considered channel configurations and networks. However, the ACI model on its own cannot capture the entire set of interference conditions, which are influenced by a multitude of factors, e.g. beamforming, MIMO, some of which are left at the choice of the vendors. Therefore, more measurement results are needed in the future for developing models that incorporate the behaviour of commercial devices produced by different vendors.

Furthermore, we note that a widely-implemented vendor-specific feature of Wi-Fi is the rate adaptation mechanism. This mechanism may thus also cause the throughput difference between our measurements and ns-3 with ACI, alongside MIMO channel conditions. The rate adaptation mechanism used by our testbed devices is a vendor-specific proprietary implementation, such that its details are not known. Therefore, in our ns-3 simulations we assumed so far *ideal* rate adaptation which selects the optimal PHY rate. Let us now instead examine *minstrel* as a popular example of a more realistic rate adaptation mechanism, currently implemented in the Linux kernel and also available in ns-3 [15]. In order to evaluate whether assuming *minstrel* in ns-3 estimates the experimental results more accurately, in Fig. 11 we present the aggregate throughput for measurements and ns-3 with and without ACI, with *minstrel* rate adaptation, for the 1×80 MHz and 4×20 MHz channel configurations. Fig. 11(a) shows that for the reference 1×80 MHz configuration with only co-channel transmissions, the *minstrel* mechanism underestimates the median aggregate throughput by up to 550 Mbps (i.e. much worse than for *ideal*), which shows that *minstrel* does not provide accurate estimates for our IEEE 802.11ac testbed, for the baseline channel configuration. For the 4×20 MHz configuration, the aggregate throughput in Fig. 11(b) shows that ns-3 with ACI and *minstrel* appears to estimate more accurately the measurement results (only up to 110 Mbps difference) than with *ideal* in Fig. 8(c) (up to 200 Mbps difference). However, this is an example where a single, isolated experimental validation result can be misleading. We have already shown that for the basic co-channel configuration

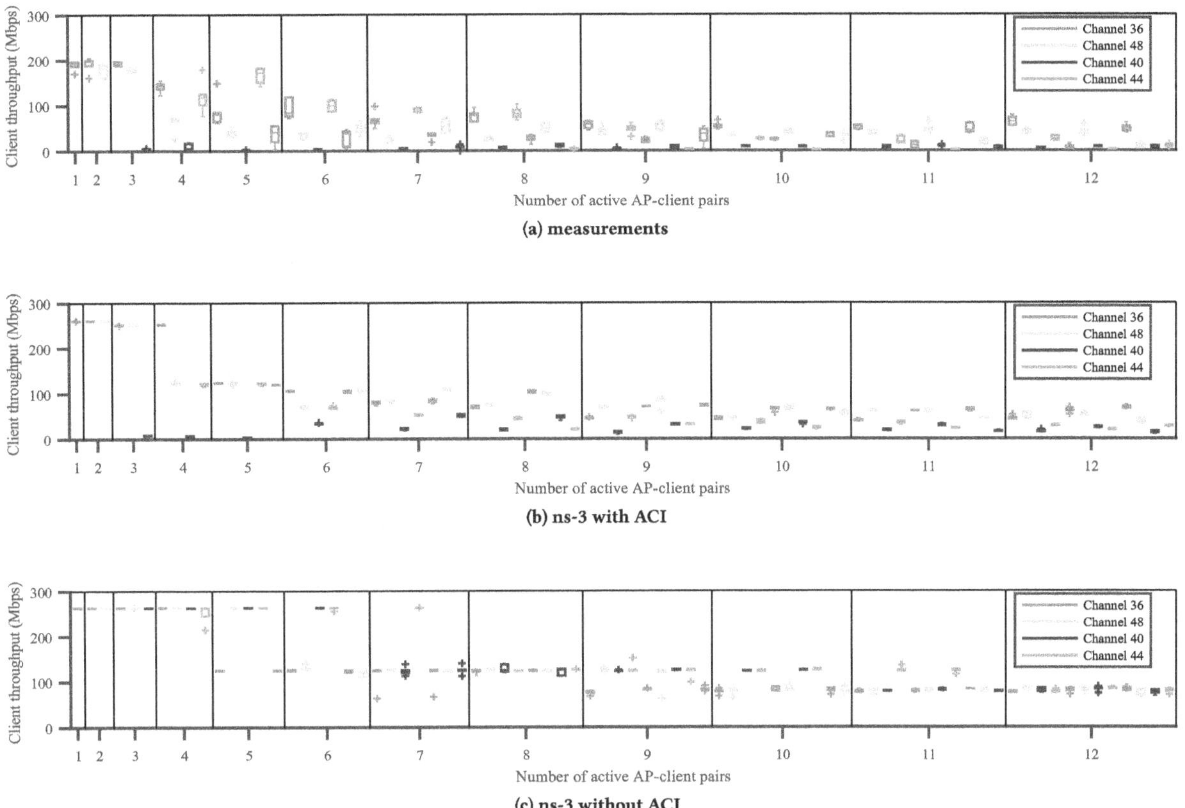

Figure 10: Individual client throughputs for the *dense network scenario* vs. number of active AP-client pairs, for the 4×20 MHz channel configuration, for measurements and ns-3 simulations with and without ACI (*ideal* rate adaptation). The channel color code matches Fig. 2.

minstrel does not provide a good estimate. It is thus most likely that for the 4×20 MHz configuration the compound errors of the various aspects of the simulation model (e.g. MIMO channel conditions and rate adaptation) result in compensating each other, such that the simulations coincidentally match the measurements.

Consequently, we argue that, especially for evolved standards like IEEE 802.11ac and dense deployments with complex inter-device interactions, it is critical to choose adequate measurement devices and scenarios. Importantly, they should enable differentiation of the effects in the network, such that they can be mapped individually to simulation models, in order to produce reliable results. Furthermore, it is crucial to test commercial devices from different vendors, especially since many of the features in today's and future wireless networks are optional and/or proprietary, so these devices may behave significantly different. Finally, the level of detail to which a simulator should model realistic networks and the acceptable error margin currently remain open questions.

5 RELATED WORK

Bianchi's analytical model for CSMA/CA [6] provides a fairly accurate estimate of the overall network performance, but this model assumes only fixed data rates and co-channel Wi-Fi devices within each other's CS range, so that co-channel interference from outside the CS range or from adjacent channels is not considered. Wi-Fi network models based on stochastic geometry, e.g. [11], estimate the overall system-level interference bounds by taking into account co-channel interference, but provide only a coarse average estimate, where some important per-device effects of the CSMA/CA protocol cannot be analysed, e.g. overhead due to backoff time. Moreover, this model assumes simple idealised network topologies and neglects link-specific propagation conditions. The Monte-Carlo-based Matlab simulation model in [16] unified and extended the Wi-Fi models in [6] and [11], by considering Wi-Fi devices within and outside each other's CS range, incorporating individual path losses for each link, considering ideal rate adaptation, and the CSMA/CA protocol overhead obtained analytically. Although this model estimates a sufficiently accurate long-term average throughput, the performance of individual devices cannot be readily analysed with fine time granularity or quantified by time metrics. In this paper we thus focused on the open-source, event-driven ns-3 network simulator, as it affords a more fine-grained simulation of Wi-Fi.

Existing experimental validations of the ns-3 Wi-Fi module have evaluated the PHY layer [13], the MAC layer [5], cross-layer interactions [10], and the interference model [7], but assumed standards

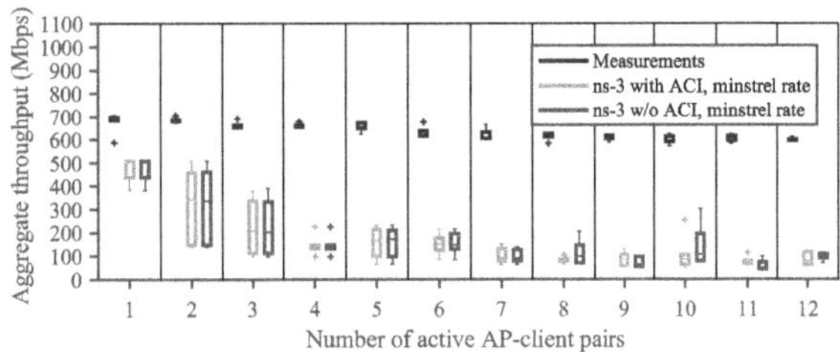

(a) 1×80 MHz channel configuration

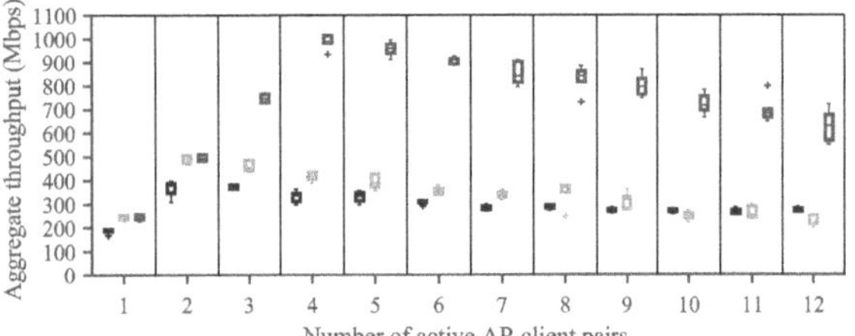

(b) 4×20 MHz channel configuration

Figure 11: Aggregate throughput for the *dense network scenario* vs. number of active AP-client pairs, for measurements and ns-3 simulations with and w/o ACI, with *minstrel*.

prior to IEEE 802.11n, which do not implement any advanced features, e.g. channel aggregation, MIMO effects, frame aggregation, or rate adaptation. Also, these models do not consider ACI effects or dense deployments. By contrast, we considered a large-scale indoor IEEE 802.11ac Wi-Fi deployment under ACI conditions.

The authors in [8] propose an analytical ACI model for OFDM signals in general, which captures time and frequency shifts per symbol. By contrast, we assumed an ACI model suitable for ns-3. An ACI model similar to ours is presented in [4] for IEEE 802.11a, but the model in [4] assumes an ideal receiver and is validated through a simple testbed and an emulated wireless medium. By contrast, we considered imperfections in both transmitter and receiver and we used up to 24 IEEE 802.11ac commercial devices transmitting over the air. 3GPP also presents a Wi-Fi ACI model [3]. This model considers the combined imperfections in the transmitter and receiver by means of adjacent channel interference ratio (ACIR), i.e. an attenuation of the transmit power in the adjacent channel, where ACIR is 20.64 dB to 24.47 dB. The equivalent of ACIR in our model is $-OF$, where OF is defined in (1) and is typically -17 dB, for the first adjacent channel. Namely, we assumed less efficient Wi-Fi receivers than [3], in order to obtain an upper bound of ACI, as discussed in Section 2.1.

6 CONCLUSIONS

In this paper we presented an extensive experimental validation of the IEEE 802.11ac Wi-Fi model in the ns-3 network simulator, for three different channel configurations, i.e. 1×80 MHz, 2×40 MHz, and 4×20 MHz. We focused on ACI for three different scenarios: *two-link variable distance*, *two-link sliding channel*, and *dense network* with up to twelve Wi-Fi AP-client pairs. We also implemented and validated a new publicly-available ACI model for IEEE 802.11ac in ns-3. Our measurement results showed that ns-3 approximates with sufficient accuracy the Wi-Fi network performance for co-channel transmissions. However, the empirical results also showed that ACI has a major impact especially in dense networks where it increases contention between Wi-Fi devices. Furthermore, our ACI model implementation in ns-3 was shown to accurately capture the interactions among adjacent channel transmissions through the CSMA/CA mechanism and to provide a significant improvement in aggregate and per-device throughput accuracy over the basic ns-3 model without ACI. For example, our implementation reduced the error for the aggregate throughput with respect to the measurements from at most 230% to at most 65% in the considered dense deployments. Our ongoing work is focusing on validating Wi-Fi performance in ns-3 also for heterogeneous width and partially overlapping channel configurations. The experimental validation results also indicate that better modelling of MIMO effects would further enhance the accuracy of the ns-3 model for emerging Wi-Fi deployments.

ACKNOWLEDGMENTS

The authors would like to thank Dr. Janne Riihijärvi for providing help with configuring the testbed and conducting measurements.

REFERENCES

[1] *iNETS Wi-Fi adjacent channel interference model for ns-3.* https://github.com/avoinets/Wi-Fi-ACI-in-ns-3
[2] ns-3. https://www.nsnam.org/
[3] 3GPP. 2015. Study on Licensed-Assisted Access to unlicensed spectrum (Release 13), TR 36.889, V13.0.0 . (June 2015).
[4] V. Angelakis, S. Papadakis, V. Siris, and A. Traganitis. 2008. Adjacent channel interference in 802.11a: Modeling and testbed validation. In *IEEE RWS.*
[5] N. Baldo, M. Requena-Esteso, J. Núñez Martínez, M. Portolès-Comeras, J. Nin-Guerrero, P. Dini, and J. Mangues-Bafalluy. 2010. Validation of the IEEE 802.11 MAC model in the ns3 simulator using the EXTREME testbed. In *ACM SIMUTools Proceedings.*
[6] G. Bianchi. 2000. Performance analysis of the IEEE 802.11 distributed coordination function. *IEEE J. Sel. Areas Commun.* 18, 3 (Mar. 2000), 535–547.
[7] P. Fuxjaeger and S. Ruehrup. 2015. Validation of the NS-3 interference model for IEEE802.11 networks. In *IEEE WMNC Proceedings.*
[8] M. Gudmundson and P.-O. Anderson. 1996. Adjacent channel interference in an OFDM system. In *IEEE VTC Proceedings.*
[9] IEEE. 2016. IEEE Standard for Information technology—Telecommunications and information exchange between systems; Local and metropolitan area networks—Specific requirements; Part 11: Wireless LAN Medium Access Control (MAC) and Physical Layer (PHY) Specifications. (Dec. 2016).
[10] G. Kremer, D. Kremer, P. Berthou, and P. Owezarski. 2013. Configuration schemes and assessment of NS3 models using a wireless testbed. (April 2013). https://hal.archives-ouvertes.fr/hal-00817453/
[11] H. Q. Nguyen, F. Baccelli, and D. Kofnam. 2007. A stochastic geometry analysis of dense IEEE 802.11 networks. In *IEEE INFOCOM Proceedings.*
[12] Nokia. 2016. Ultra dense network (UDN) white paper. (2016). http://resources.alcatel-lucent.com/asset/200295
[13] G. Pei and T. Henderson. 2009. Validation of ns-3 802.11b PHY model. (May 2009). https://www.nsnam.org/~pei/80211b.pdf
[14] L. Simić, J. Riihijärvi, and P. Mähönen. 2017. Measurement study of IEEE 802.11ac Wi-Fi performance in high density indoor deployments: Are wider channels always better?. In *IEEE WoWMoM Proceedings.*
[15] ns-3 Network Simulator. 2016. ns-3 Model Library, Release ns-3.26. (Oct. 2016). https://www.nsnam.org/docs/release/3.26/models/ns-3-model-library.pdf
[16] A. M. Voicu, L. Simić, and M. Petrova. 2016. Inter-technology coexistence in a spectrum commons: A case study of Wi-Fi and LTE in the 5-GHz unlicensed band. *IEEE J. Sel. Areas Commun.* 34, 11 (Nov. 2016), 3062–3077.

Carrier-Sense Multiple Access with Collision Avoidance and Detection

J.J. Garcia-Luna-Aceves
Computer Engineering Department, University of California, Santa Cruz, CA 95064
PARC, Palo Alto, CA 94304
jj@soe.ucsc.edu

ABSTRACT

Carrier-Sense Multiple Access with Collision Avoidance and Detection (CSMA/CAD) is introduced and analyzed. The new protocol operates in a single channel and consists of taking advantage of self-interference cancellation to enable collision detection (CD) in the context of collision-avoidance (CA) handshakes in multi-hop wireless networks. It is shown that CSMA/CAD eliminates the collisions of data packets in the presence of hidden terminals. The throughput of CSMA/CAD is analyzed and compared with the throughput of CSMA, CSMA/CA, and dual busy-tone multiple access (DBTMA). The analysis results show that CSMA/CAD provides better performance than the other channel-access schemes aimed at combating hidden terminals, and that the throughput degradation due to hidden terminals in CSMA/CAD is limited compared to CSMA.

CCS CONCEPTS

• **Networks** → **Network protocols**; *Link-layer protocols*; *Network performance analysis*;

KEYWORDS

channel access; collision avoidance; carrier-sense multiple access

ACM Reference Format:
J.J. Garcia-Luna-Aceves . 2017. Carrier-Sense Multiple Access with Collision Avoidance and Detection. In *Proceedings of MSWiM '17, Miami, FL, USA, November 21–25, 2017*, 9 pages.
https://doi.org/10.1145/3127540.3127551

1 INTRODUCTION

Carrier-sense multiple access (CSMA) [17] is arguably the most widely used method for the sharing of radio channels in wireless local-area networks or ad-hoc networks in which wireless nodes establish a network without the need for centralized control or preexisting infrastructure. CSMA provides far better throughput than ALOHA [1] when all nodes sharing a common channel can hear one another. However, the performance of CSMA quickly degrades in the presence of hidden terminals [19] and as a result many approaches have been proposed and implemented to address the performance problems of CSMA in ad-hoc networks.

Section 2 provides a review of prior work aimed at reducing or eliminating the negative effects of hidden terminals on contention-based channel access. This work has assumed that nodes are endowed with half-duplex radios, and has focused on the use of busy tones (e.g., [14, 19]) and collision-avoidance (CA) handshakes between transmitters and receivers over a single channel (e.g., [3, 11, 13, 16]). Recently, however, the feasibility of self-interference cancellation (SIC) techniques at the physical layer [7] has opened up the possibility of using collision detection in ad-hoc networks. However, as our review of prior work reveals [6], few proposals exist on how to take advantage of SIC at the medium-access control (MAC) layer.

The main contribution of this paper is the introduction, verification, and analysis of **CSMA/CAD** (*Carrier-Sense Multiple Access with Collisions Avoidance and Detection*).

Section 3 describes CSMA/CAD, which combines collision-avoidance (CA) handshakes aimed at eliminating hidden-terminal problems with collision detection (CD) enabled by SIC and aimed at reducing the negative effects of signaling packets colliding at receivers due to inevitable propagation delays.

In contrast to prior proposals focusing on enabling full-duplex exchange of data packets between neighboring nodes, CSMA/CAD simply focuses on making the collision-avoidance handshake much more effective. However, it constitutes a building block for more sophisticated channel-access disciplines enabling full-duplex data exchange between neighboring nodes.

Section 4 shows that CSMA/CAD eliminates the collision of data packets with other transmissions even in the presence of hidden terminals.

Sections 5 to 7 analyze the throughput of CSMA/CAD and compare it against the throughput of previous proposals based on collision avoidance and busy tones. The results show that CSMA/CAD is more efficient than prior solutions, because it reduces the signaling overhead and latencies incurred by nodes in avoiding data-packet collisions compared to collision-avoidance approaches or busy-tone methods.

Section 8 presents our conclusions and proposes future research areas.

MSWiM '17, November 21–25, 2017, Miami, FL, USA

ACM ISBN 978-1-4503-5162-1/17/11... $15.00
https://doi.org/10.1145/3127540.3127551

2 RELATED WORK

Tobagi and Kleinrock introduced CSMA [17] and were the first to address the hidden-terminal problem present in CSMA [19]. In the presence of hidden terminals, the performance of CSMA degrades to the same performance attained with ALOHA because a transmitter is unable to sense the transmissions from hidden sources.

The Busy-Tone Multiple Access (BTMA) approach proposed by Tobagi and Kleinrock [19] eliminates multiple-access interference around a central receiver. The available channel is partitioned into a data channel and the busy-tone channel. The central receiver, which has radio connectivity with all other nodes in the system, transmits a busy tone over the busy-tone channel as soon as it detects carrier in the data channel resulting from transmissions from any subset of transmitters. This reduces the vulnerability period of a data packet to a time interval proportional to the channel propagation delay and the time needed by the transmitters to detect the busy tone from the central receiver.

Several busy-tone protocols have been proposed, such as RI-BTMA (Receiver-Initiated Busy Tone Multiple Access) [22] and DTBMA (Dual Busy Tone Multiple Access) [14]. In RI-BTMA, the channel is divided into a data channel and a control channel. When the receiver detects the preamble of the transmission by the sender, it transmits its busy tone in the control channel. DBTMA adopts a similar approach but uses two busy tones. The available bandwidth is partitioned into a data channel and two control channels for the transmission of busy tones from transmitters and receivers. A transmitter aborts its transmission if it detects a receiver busy tone or a transmitter busy tone, and the receiver busy tone helps eliminate hidden-terminal interference.

A number of approaches have been proposed based on handshakes between transmitter and receiver using small signaling packets. The basic approach is called *collision avoidance* and has been proposed for wired and wireless networks [3, 16]. Karn proposed Multiple Access with Collision Avoidance (MACA) [16], which consists of a transmitter sending a request-to-send (RTS) packet to an intended receiver and the receiver sending a clear-to-send (CTS) packet if the RTS is successful. MACA does not use carrier sensing and does not perform well in the presence of hidden terminals, even tough the protocol was designed in part to solve that problem. Many variants have been proposed and analyzed since the introduction of these early works on collision avoidance. In some schemes the transmitter initiates the handshake [10–12] and in others the receiver does [13]. The IEEE 802.11 distributed coordination function (DCF) combines carrier sensing with the RTS-CTS handshake followed by a data packet and an ACK in successful cases.

CSMA with collision detection (CSMA/CD) was introduced as part of the original Ethernet design [18]. With CSMA/CD, a transmitter listens for carrier before transmitting; if no carrier is found and the transmitter starts a new transmission, and listens during its own transmission and aborts it upon detecting a collision with other signals in the channel. The development of self-interference cancellation (SIC) techniques at the physical layer (e.g., see [4, 7]) opens up the possibility of using communicating radios that can detect interference by comparing their output with the signal they receive, or even operating in full-duplex (FD) mode while accessing a common channel.

A few approaches have already been proposed that take advantage of SIC at the MAC layer, and focus on attaining FD operation for data exchange. Some proposals aim at exploiting FD operation to allow nodes to transmit concurrently as primary or secondary transmitters and receivers and allow relaying nodes to receive transmissions while forwarding their own [6, 8, 15]. Other proposals [5, 9] focus on the interplay between the up-link and down-link with an access point of a wireless LAN or base stations in 5G wireless networks. The fact that SIC enables a node to implement collision detection has not been fully exploited, and the interplay between collision-avoidance and collision-detection techniques in ad-hoc networks has not been addressed in the past.

3 CSMA/CAD

A silent receiver does not benefit from full-duplex communication when it receives multiple concurrent transmissions. However, self-interference cancelation (SIC) can be used to make collision avoidance more efficient. Using SIC while sending an RTS and CTS enables a node to detect the presence of interference within one maximum propagation delay from the start of the interfering signals, and this is the fastest-possible feedback that can be given to the sender of an RTS or a CTS. Furthermore, this feedback is provided without incurring any transmit-to-receive turnaround latency or the need for secondary channels. Hence, collision detection can improve the performance of collision avoidance substantially.

Rather than attempting to enable FD operation for the bidirectional dissemination of data packets, CSMA/CAD eliminates the collision of data packets at their intended receivers while minimizing the latencies incurred in securing collision-free handshakes between transmitters and receivers.

We describe the operation of CSMA/CAD for the case in which transmitters do not persist attempting to access the channel after detecting carrier or collisions. In a nutshell, a node uses carrier sensing before sending an RTS, and uses collision detection while transmitting an RTS or a CTS. If either carrier is detected before an RTS is sent or a collision is detected while an RTS or CTS is being sent, the node backs off, and aborts its ongoing transmission. The successful reception of a CTS from the receiver prompts the transmitter to send a data packet and to wait for the ACK from the receiver. A successful RTS-CTS handshake ensures that a data packet and its associated acknowledgment (ACK) are received without multiple-access interference (MAI).

Figure 1 illustrates the state machine of non-persistent CSMA/CAD assuming that at most one packet is passed to the MAC layer for transmission at any given time.

A node that is just initialized waits for a period of time equivalent to a DIFS (DCF inter frame space) as defined in IEEE 802.11. After that time, the node transitions to the PASSIVE state and waits for a local packet or carrier. This waiting period ensures that a node entering an ad-hoc network learns about ongoing packet transmissions if they exist. If a node is in PASSIVE state, there is no carrier in the channel, and the node receives a packet to send, then it starts transmitting an RTS to the intended receiver and transitions to the RTS state. Alternatively, if the node detects carrier, it transitions to the REMOTE state.

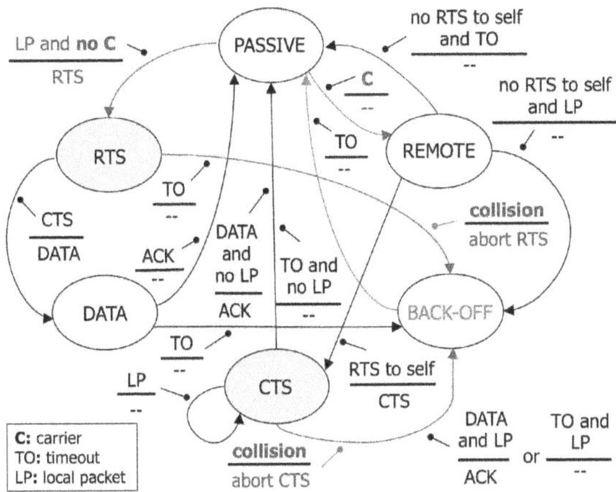

Figure 1: Non-persistent CSMA/CAD

If a node detects a collision while sending an RTS, it aborts the RTS and injects a short jamming bit sequence before transitioning to the BACK-OFF state. Once a node sends an RTS without collisions, it waits for a CTS from the receiver for an RTS-timeout time. If no CTS is received, the node assumes that a collision occurred and transitions to the BACK-OFF state to transmit its RTS at a future time. If a CTS is received correctly, the node transmits a data packet and transitions to the DATA state to wait for an ACK from the receiver. The node transitions to the BACK-OFF state if no ACK is received within an ACK timeout that is long enough to allow the node to receive and decode an ACK.

If a node is in the REMOTE state and decodes an RTS from a transmitter intended for itself (shown as "RTS to self" in Fig. 1), it starts sending its CTS to the transmitter and transitions to the CTS state.

If a node detects a collision while transmitting its CTS, it aborts the transmission, injects a short jamming bit sequence, and transitions to the BACK-OFF state. If the node is able to transmit its entire CTS, then it waits for a data packet and remembers whether or not it has a local packet to send. If a data packet is received from the transmitter, the node sends an ACK accordingly. The node transitions to the PASSIVE state if there is no local packet to send, or to the BACK-OFF state if it has a local packet to send. Similarly, the node transitions to PASSIVE or BACK-OFF state depending on whether it has a packet to send if a CTS timeout elapses with no data packet being received from the transmitter. The length of a CTS timeout is long enough for the node to be able to start decoding a valid data packet.

If the node is in REMOTE state and does not receive an RTS intended for itself (denoted by "no RTS to self" in Fig. 1) after a timeout interval, the node transitions to the PASSIVE state if it has no local packet to send, or to the BACK-OFF state if it has a local packet to send. The timeout interval in the REMOTE state is long enough to allow a complete handshake between another receiver and a transmitter to take place without interference from the node itself.

Once a node transitions to the BACK-OFF state, it computes a random back-off time, and transitions to the PASSIVE state after that time has elapsed. An exponential back-off discipline can be used to account for unsuccessful re-transmission attempts for the same data packet and limit congestion. However, it is not shown for simplicity.

4 CORRECTNESS OF CSMA/CAD

Theorem 4.1 below shows that, under a number of assumptions, CSMA/CAD ensures that all data packets and ACKs are delivered to their intended receivers without colliding with other transmissions around those receivers. The assumptions used are the following: (a) There are at least two nodes in the network, and a node knows the addresses of its neighboring nodes through some means external to the protocol; (b) all nodes execute the CSMA/CAD protocol correctly; (c) the propagation delay t_p between any two neighboring nodes is $0 < t_p \leq \tau$; (d) a node requires a transmit-to-receive and receive-to-transmit turn-around time of at most ω seconds; (e) the transmission time of an RTS and a CTS packet is γ, the transmission time of a data packet is δ, and the transmission time for an ACK is α; and (f) the time needed for a node with an ongoing transmission to detect a collision and transmit a jamming bit pattern is $\eta < \gamma$.

THEOREM 4.1. *CSMA/CAD ensures that no data packets or their ACKs collide with any other transmissions.*

PROOF. For a data packet from transmitter T to be sent to receiver R, a successful RTS-CTS handshake must first take place between T and R, i.e., R must receive the RTS from T free of collisions and T must receive the CTS from R free of collisions. Accordingly, the rest of the proof must show that, if an RTS-CTS handshake succeeds, any neighbor of T or R must back off long enough to allow the data and ACK sent between T and R to be received free of MAI.

For a successful RTS-CTS handshake to occur between T and R, T must be in PASSIVE state when it has a packet to send, and it must transmit its RTS without detecting a collision. Let t_0 be the time when node T sends its RTS to node R. Any neighbor n_T of T receives the entire RTS from T at time $t_T = t_0 + \gamma + t_p$, where $0 < t_p \leq \tau$.

Because T sends its entire RTS without detecting collisions, n_T must either transition to the REMOTE or the BACK-OFF state. If $n_T \neq R$ then it must defer for a back-off time T_{BT} of at least $\gamma + \delta + \alpha + 3\omega + 4\tau$ seconds if it is in the REMOTE state, or defer for a much longer time if in the BACK-OFF state. Accordingly, n_T cannot attempt to transmit any packet until time $t_{NT} \geq t_T + \gamma + \delta + \alpha + 3\omega + 4\tau$.

Therefore, given that $t_0 + \gamma < t_T$, it must be true that

$$t_{NT} > t_0 + 2\gamma + \delta + \alpha + 3\omega + 4\tau \quad (1)$$

A neighbor n_R of R other than T receives the entire CTS from R at time t_R, where $t_0 + 2\gamma < t_R \leq t_0 + 2(\gamma + \tau) + \omega$, because a propagation delay is $0 < t_p \leq \tau$ and R incurs at most ω seconds of turnaround time processing an RTS.

Because R sends its CTS without detecting collisions, neighbor n_R must transition to the REMOTE or the BACK-OFF state. Accordingly, n_R must defer for at least a back-off time T_{BR} in the REMOTE state after receiving the CTS from R, where $T_{BR} \geq \delta + \alpha + 3\omega + 4\tau$, or defer for a much longer time in the BACK-OFF state. Hence, n_R cannot attempt to transmit any packet until time $t_{NR} \geq t_R + T_{BR}$. Therefore, given that $t_0 + 2\gamma < t_R$, it follows that

$$t_{NR} > t_0 + 2\gamma + \delta + \alpha + 3\omega + 4\tau \quad (2)$$

Node R receives the entire data packet from T at time

$$t_{RD} \leq t_0 + 2\gamma + \delta + 2\omega + 3\tau \quad (3)$$

From Eqs. (2) and (3), it must be the case that $t_{RD} < t_{NR}$ and node n_R cannot interfere with the reception of the data packet from T. On the other hand, node T must receive the entire ACK from R at time

$$t_{TA} \leq t_0 + 2\gamma + \delta + \alpha + 3\omega + 4\tau \quad (4)$$

From Eqs. (1) and (4), it must be true that $t_{TA} < t_{NT}$ and node n_T cannot interfere with the reception of the ACK from R. It follows from this argument that no MAI exists for the reception of a data packet and its ACK; therefore, the theorem is true. □

5 THROUGHPUT IN FULLY-CONNECTED NETWORKS

We assume the same traffic model first introduced by Kleinrock and Tobagi [17] to analyze CSMA/CAD, CSMA/CA, DBTMA, and CSMA with ACKs. According to the model, there is a large (essentially infinite) number of nodes that constitute a Poisson source sending RTS's or data packets to the the channel with an aggregate rate of λ packets per unit time. We assume the use of priority acknowledgments (ACK) in all protocols, because they are needed in practice to account for transmission errors not due to multiple-access interference. For brevity, we only address the non-persistent versions of the protocols.

The throughput attained by a channel-access protocol is a function of the physical and medium-access control (MAC) layers. However, for the channel-access protocols we consider, the physical-layer overhead is roughly the same for each packet transmission in all the protocols. For simplicity, we assume that the transmission time of any control or data packet includes the overhead induced by the physical layer. A fixed receive-to-transmit and transmit-to-receive turnaround time of ω seconds is assumed, and the same assumptions stated in Section 4 for packet sizes apply.

Nodes have at most one data packet to sent at any time, which results from the MAC layer having to submit one packet for transmission before accepting the next packet. For the case of CSMA/CAD, it is assumed that the time needed for a node to detect a collision with its own transmission and send a jamming bit sequence lasts η seconds. In our model $\eta \ll \gamma$, because η is simply the time needed to identify the presence of a non-zero signal after SIC is applied to the received signal, plus the transmission of a short bit sequence that has to be larger than the error-checking field of a packet (e.g., 48 bits).

When a node has to retransmit a packet it does so after a random retransmission delay that, on the average, is much larger than the time needed for a successful transaction between a transmitter and a receiver and such that all transmissions of RTS's or data packets can be assumed to be independent of one another.

The channel is assumed to introduce no errors, and nodes are assumed to detect carrier and, depending on the protocol, collisions or busy tones perfectly. To further simplify the problem, we assume that two or more transmissions that overlap in time in the channel must all be retransmitted (i.e., there is no power capture by any transmission), and that any packet propagates to all nodes in exactly τ seconds.

The protocols are assumed to operate in steady state, with no possibility of collapse, and hence the average utilization of the channel is given by [17]

$$S = \frac{\overline{U}}{\overline{B} + \overline{I}}. \quad (5)$$

where $\overline{B}$ is the expected duration of a busy period, defined to be a period of time during which the channel is being utilized; $\overline{I}$ is the expected duration of an idle period, defined as the time interval between two consecutive busy periods; and $\overline{U}$ is the time during a busy period that the channel is used for transmitting user data successfully. This model is only an approximation of the real case, in which a small number of nodes may access the same channel, and transmissions and retransmissions are correlated because of the relationships between them. However, our analysis provides a good baseline for the comparison of the various channel-access protocols and the relative benefits of the joint use of collision avoidance and detection compared to other techniques.

5.1 CSMA/CAD

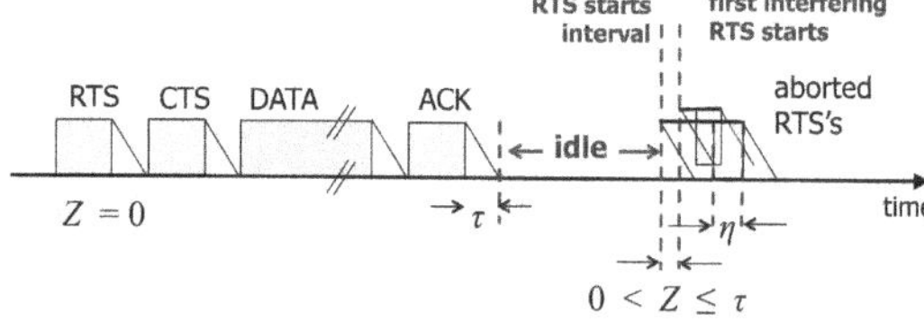

Figure 2: Transmission periods in CSMA/CAD

Figure 2 shows the transmission periods that may occur in a fully-connected ad-hoc network for the non-persistent CSMA/CAD protocol. As the figure illustrates, the utilization of the channel consists of idle periods, successful busy periods during which data packets are sent as part of successful collision-avoidance handshakes, and collision intervals resulting from the collision of two or more RTS's sent within one propagation delay of one another. No turnaround delays are incurred because a node listens while it transmits.

THEOREM 5.1. *The throughput of CSMA/CAD with a non-persistent transmission strategy is*

$$S_{CAD} = \frac{\delta}{\delta + 2\gamma + \alpha + 2\tau - \eta - \frac{1}{\lambda} + e^{\lambda\tau}(\frac{2}{\lambda} + \eta + 2\tau)} \quad (6)$$

PROOF. A transmitter in CSMA/CAD uses carrier sensing before transmitting an RTS and collision detection while transmitting the RTS. Accordingly, the probability that an RTS is sent without multiple access interference (MAI) and a successful transmission period occurs equals the probability that no arrivals of other RTS's take place within τ seconds from the start of the RTS. This probability is $P_S = e^{-\lambda\tau}$, and the probability that a collision interval occurs is simply $1 - P_S = 1 - e^{-\lambda\tau}$.

If an RTS does not collide with any other transmission, a CTS, a data packet, and an ACK follow. This occurs with probability P_S and takes $2\gamma + \delta + \alpha + 4\tau$ seconds.

If an RTS collides with other RTS's, then all the nodes that sent RTS's detect the collision, abort their RTS transmissions, and send jamming bit sequences. By assumption, the time needed to detect a collision and the transmission of the jamming bit sequence takes η seconds.

Any node sending an RTS that interferes with the first RTS of a collision interval starts receiving the carrier from the first RTS in τ seconds after the first RTS starts, takes η seconds to detect the collision and transmit a jamming pattern, and its own transmission propagates in τ seconds to all nodes. Therefore, the time incurred by any interfering RTS is $\eta + 2\tau$ from the start of the collision interval.

On the other hand, the node that starts a collision interval with its RTS detects a collision τ seconds after the first interfering RTS starts. Accordingly, the length of a collision interval is given by $Z+\tau+\eta+\tau$, where Z is a random variable that varies from 0 to τ and represents the time between the arrival of the RTS that starts the collision interval and the arrival of the *first* RTS that creates a collision.

Given that arrivals of RTS's are Poisson distributed, it is not possible to have two or more arrivals of RTS's into the channel exactly at the same time; therefore, $Z = 0$ occurs when an RTS is successful. Accordingly, the length of an average busy period equals

$$\begin{aligned} \overline{B} &= \overline{Z} + (1 - e^{-\lambda\tau})(\eta + 2\tau) + e^{-\lambda\tau}(2\gamma + \delta + \alpha + 4\tau) \\ &= \overline{Z} + \eta + 2\tau + e^{-\lambda\tau}(\delta + 2\gamma + \alpha + 2\tau - \eta) \end{aligned} \quad (7)$$

For Z to last more than z seconds, it must be the case that no arrival occurs in the first z seconds of a collision interval, that is, $P(Z > z) = P\{\text{no arrivals in } [0, z]\} = e^{-\lambda z}$. Therefore, the cumulative distribution function of Z is

$$F_Z(z) = P(Z \leq z) = 1 - P(Z > z) = 1 - e^{-\lambda z} \quad (8)$$

Z assumes non-negative values, and hence its mean can be computed using $F_Z(z)$ in Eq. (8) as follows:

$$\overline{Z} = \int_0^\infty (1 - F_Z(t))dt = \int_0^\tau e^{-\lambda t}dt = \frac{1}{\lambda}\left(1 - e^{-\lambda\tau}\right) \quad (9)$$

Substituting $\overline{Z}$ in Eq. (7) we have

$$\overline{B} = e^{-\lambda\tau}\left(\delta + 2\gamma + \alpha + 2\tau - \eta - \frac{1}{\lambda}\right) + \eta + 2\tau + \frac{1}{\lambda} \quad (10)$$

The average length of an idle period $\overline{I}$ in CSMA/CAD is just the average inter-arrival time of RTS's, which equals $1/\lambda$, because inter-arrival times are exponentially distributed with parameter λ. The average time period used to transmit useful data $\overline{U}$ is simply the useful portion of a successful busy period, i.e., $\delta P_S = \delta e^{-\lambda\tau}$. Substituting the values of $\overline{U}$, $\overline{B}$, and $\overline{I}$ into Eq. (5) we obtain Eq. (6). □

5.2 CSMA/CA

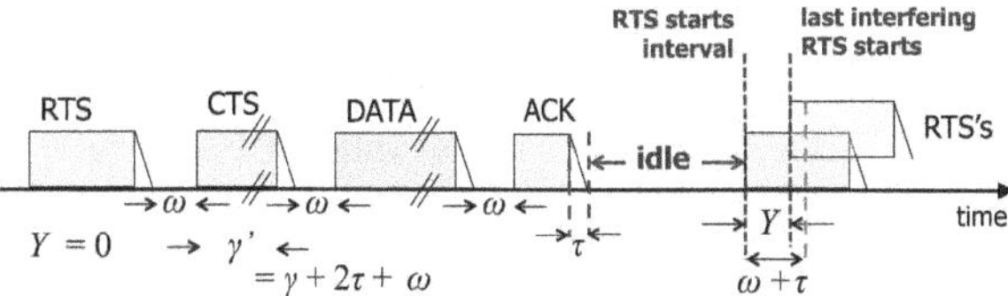

Figure 3: Transmission periods in CSMA/CA

We obtain the throughput of non-persistent CSMA/CA to evaluate the benefit of embedding collision detection in the collision-avoidance handshake. Figure 3 illustrates the transmission periods for non-persistent CSMA/CA assuming priority ACKs. Complete RTS's are transmitted during a collision interval, and the length of a CTS must last at least the duration of an RTS plus a round-trip time and transmit-to-receive turn-around time required for the radios to avoid the possibility of collisions of data packets with other transmissions [11]. As a result, collision intervals are longer in CSMA/CA than in CSMA/CAD.

The following theorem provides the throughput of non-persistent CSMA/CA. We assume that the minimum length of a CTS is equal to $\gamma' = \gamma + 2\tau + \omega$, where ω is the turn-around time. Our result differs slightly from prior results [10, 11] because of the use of ACKs and a simplification of the protocol we use as CSMA/CA compared to FAMA protocols.

THEOREM 5.2. *The throughput of non-persistent CSMA/CA is*

$$S_{CA} = \frac{\delta}{\delta + \gamma + \alpha + 4\omega + 5\tau + \frac{1}{\lambda} + e^{\lambda(\omega+\tau)}(\gamma + 2\tau + \omega)} \quad (11)$$

PROOF. A node using CSMA/CA must sense the channel before sending an RTS, and then it incurs a turnaround time ω during which the node is unable to listen to the channel. Therefore, the vulnerability period of an RTS is $\omega + \tau$, and the probability that an RTS succeeds and a successful transmission period occurs equals $P_S = e^{-\lambda(\omega+\tau)}$. It also follows that a collision interval occurs with probability $1 - P_S = 1 - e^{-\lambda(\omega+\tau)}$.

If an RTS is sent without MAI, then a CTS, a data packet and an ACK follow. This takes $\gamma + \gamma' + \delta + \alpha + 3\omega + 4\tau = 2\gamma + \delta + \alpha + 4\omega + 6\tau$ seconds and occurs with probability P_S.

If an RTS collides with other RTS's, then no receiver is able to decode any RTS. As Fig. 3 illustrates, the length of a collision interval is given by $Y + \gamma + \tau$, where Y is a random variable that varies from 0 to $\omega + \tau$ and represents the time between the arrival of the first RTS and the last RTS in a collision interval.

$Y = 0$ occurs when an RTS is successful, which follows from the assumption that packet arrivals are Poisson distributed. Therefore, the length of an average busy period equals

$$\overline{B} = \overline{Y} + (1 - e^{-\lambda(\omega+\tau)})(\gamma + \tau) + e^{-\lambda(\omega+\tau)}(2\gamma + \delta + \alpha + 4\omega + 6\tau) \quad (12)$$

If the time period between the start of the the first and the last RTS in a collision interval equals y seconds, then there are no more arrivals of RTS's in the remaining time of the vulnerability period of the first RTS of the collision interval, i.e., $\omega + \tau - y$ seconds. Accordingly, $P(Y \leq y) = F_Y(y) = e^{-\lambda(\omega+\tau-y)}$. Therefore, the average value of Y equals

$$\overline{Y} = \int_0^{\infty} (1 - F_Y(t))dt = \int_0^{\omega+\tau} \left(1 - e^{-\lambda(\omega+\tau-t)}\right) dt = \omega + \tau - \frac{1 - e^{-\lambda(\omega+\tau)}}{\lambda} \quad (13)$$

Substituting Eq. (13) in Eq. (12) we have

$$\overline{B} = e^{-\lambda(\omega+\tau)} \left(\delta + \gamma + \alpha + 4\omega + 5\tau + \frac{1}{\lambda}\right) + \gamma + \omega + 2\tau - \frac{1}{\lambda}$$

The average time period used to transmit useful data $\overline{U}$ is just $\delta P_S = \delta e^{-\lambda(\omega+\tau)}$. As in CSMA/CAD, the average length of an idle period $\overline{I}$ is $1/\lambda$. Substituting the values of $\overline{U}$, $\overline{B}$, and $\overline{I}$ into Eq. (5) we obtain Eq. (11). □

5.3 DBTMA

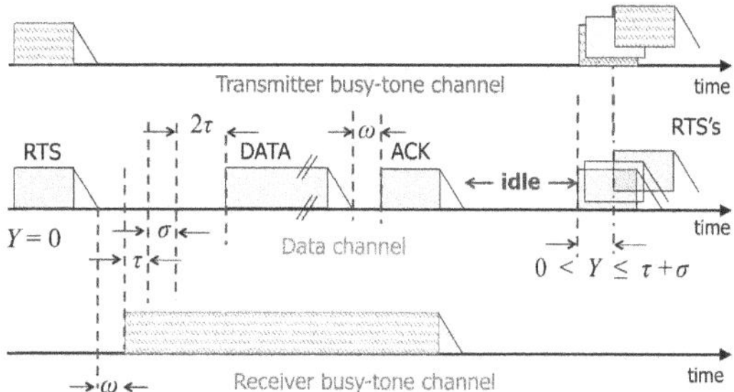

Figure 4: Transmission periods in DBTMA

We compute the throughput of DBTMA to account for non-trivial turnaround times and the use of ACKs, and to correct modeling inconsistencies in the results by Haas and Deng [14]. Fig. 4 illustrates the transmission periods in DBTMA.

We assume that the data channel is assigned a percentage of the total bandwidth equal to $0 < \beta < 1$, with each busy-tone channel having an equal portion of the remaining bandwidth. The time needed for a node to detect the presence of a busy tone from a transmitter or a receiver is σ seconds. We assume that busy tones are detected perfectly, and that the probability of false busy-tone detection is 0. For simplicity we assume that receive-to-transmit latencies are the same for the data and control channels. As with the other MAC protocols we consider, a receiver sends an ACK after the successful reception of a data packet. Following the design of DBTMA in [14], a transmitter waits a round-trip time after detecting the busy tone from its receiver before sending a data packet (see Fig. 4).

The analytical result for the throughput of DBTMA reported in [14] assumes that colliding RTS's arrive to the channel uniformly distributed in the duration of a collision interval. However, this cannot be true with the arrival of RTS's being Poisson distributed in order to compute success probabilities and the average length of idle periods. Furthermore, receive-to-transmit turnaround times in the receiver busy-tome channel must be taken into account. The following theorem provides the throughput of DBTMA assuming that the total available bandwidth is the same as in the other channel-access protocols.

THEOREM 5.3. *The throughput of non-persistent DBTMA over a data channel using only β (with $0 < \beta < 1$) of the total available bandwidth is*

$$S_{DBT} = \frac{\delta}{\delta + \alpha + \beta^{-1}\left(2\omega + \sigma + 5\tau + \frac{1}{\lambda}\right) + He^{\lambda(\tau+\sigma)}} \quad (14)$$

where $H = \gamma + \beta^{-1}[\sigma + 2\tau]$

PROOF. A node decides that the channel is busy in DBTMA if it detects a busy tone in one of the control channels. Because a busy tone is a narrow-band signal, a non-negligible tone-detection delay σ is incurred *after* the signal propagates in τ seconds to the node receiving the signal. Hence, the vulnerability period of an RTS is $\tau + \sigma$ seconds, because a transmitter sends a transmit busy tone at the same time that it transmits an RTS in the data channel. Given that RTS arrivals are Poisson distributed with parameter λ, the probability with which an RTS is sent without MAI and a successful transmission period occurs is $P_S = e^{-(\tau+\sigma)}$. Correspondingly, the probability that acollision interval occurs is $1 - P_S = 1 - e^{-\lambda(\tau+\sigma)}$.

If an RTS does not collide with other transmissions, the receiver starts transmitting its receive busy tone after a turnaround time, and its busy tone takes τ seconds to propagate and σ seconds to be detected by the transmitter. After that, the transmitter waits 2τ seconds and starts sending its data packet and the receiver transmits its ACK accordingly. Therefore, the time incurred in a successful handshake using busy tones is $\delta + \gamma + \alpha + 2\omega + \sigma + 6\tau$ seconds.

If an RTS collides with other RTS's, then all the transmit busy tones and RTS's involved in the collision are transmitted in their entirety, but no receiver is able to decode any of them given that we assume no capture effect for busy tones.

As Fig. 4 illustrates, the length of a collision interval in DBTMA is $Y + \gamma + \tau$, where Y is a random variable that varies from 0 to τ and represents the time between the arrival of the first and the last RTS in the collision interval, similar to the case of CSMA/CA.

$Y = 0$ necessarily implies that an RTS is successful, because arrivals of RTS's are Poisson distributed. Hence, the length of an average busy period equals

$$\begin{aligned}\overline{B} &= \overline{Y} + (1 - e^{-\lambda(\tau+\sigma)})(\gamma + \tau) \\ &\quad + e^{-\lambda(\tau+\sigma)}(\delta + \gamma + \alpha + 2\omega + \sigma + 6\tau) \\ &= \overline{Y} + \gamma + \tau + e^{-\lambda(\tau+\sigma)}(\delta + \alpha + 2\omega + \sigma + 5\tau)\end{aligned} \tag{15}$$

Given that the vulnerability period of the first RTS in a collision interval is $\tau + \sigma$, $F_Y(y) = P(Y \leq y)$ equals the probability that no RTS arrivals occur in the remaining $\tau + \sigma - y$ seconds of the vulnerability period of the first RTS of the collision interval. Therefore,

$$F_Y(y) = P\{\text{no arrivals in } \tau + \sigma - y\} = e^{-\lambda(\tau+\sigma-y)} \tag{16}$$

Because Y assumes non-negative values, we have that

$$\overline{Y} = \int_0^{\tau+\sigma} \left(1 - e^{-\lambda(\tau+\sigma-t)}\right) dt = \tau + \sigma - \frac{1 - e^{-\lambda(\tau+\sigma)}}{\lambda} \tag{17}$$

Substituting Eq. (17) in Eq. (15) we obtain

$$\begin{aligned}\overline{B} &= \tau + \sigma - \frac{1 - e^{-\lambda(\tau+\sigma)}}{\lambda} \\ &\quad + \gamma + \tau + e^{-\lambda(\tau+\sigma)}(\delta + \alpha + 2\omega + \sigma + 5\tau) \\ &= e^{-\lambda(\tau+\sigma)}\left(\delta + \alpha + 2\omega + \sigma + 5\tau + \frac{1}{\lambda}\right) + \gamma + \sigma + 2\tau - \frac{1}{\lambda}\end{aligned}$$

The average length of an idle period $\overline{I}$ is $1/\lambda$, because RTS arrivals are Poisson distributed with parameter λ. On the other hand, the average time period used to transmit useful data $\overline{U}$ is $\delta P_S = \delta e^{-\lambda(\tau+\sigma)}$.

The data-channel capacity in DBTMA is reduced by the amount of bandwidth needed for the two busy-tone channels. To account for this, the transmission time for data packets and signaling packets must be normalized to the length of a data packet enjoying the entire channel bandwidth. Accordingly, substituting the values of $\overline{U}$, $\overline{B}$, and $\overline{I}$ into Eq. (5) and multiplying each packet length by β we obtain Eq. (14). □

5.4 CSMA with Priority ACKs

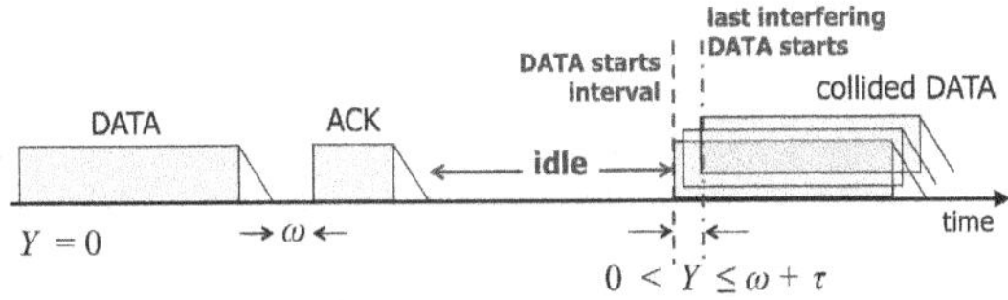

Figure 5: Transmission periods in CSMA

The original throughput results for non-persistent CSMA by Kleinrock and Tobagi [17] assume an ideal secondary channel over which ACKs are sent in 0 time. We consider the throughput of non-persistent CSMA with priority ACKs to provide a level-playing field for the comparison of all the MAC protocols. Figure 5 illustrates the transmission periods in non-persistent CSMA with priority ACKs, and the following theorem specifies its throughput.

THEOREM 5.4. *The throughput of non-persistent CSMA with priority ACKs is*

$$S_{CS} = \frac{\delta}{\alpha + \omega + \tau + \frac{1}{\lambda} + e^{\lambda(\omega+\tau)}(\delta + \omega + 2\tau)} \tag{18}$$

PROOF. The proof is presented in [20] using different terminology and assuming zero turnaround times. In our model, the vulnerability period of a data packet is $\omega + \tau$ rather than just τ, and the proof for this case is similar to the proof of Theorem 5.2. □

6 IMPACT OF HIDDEN TERMINALS

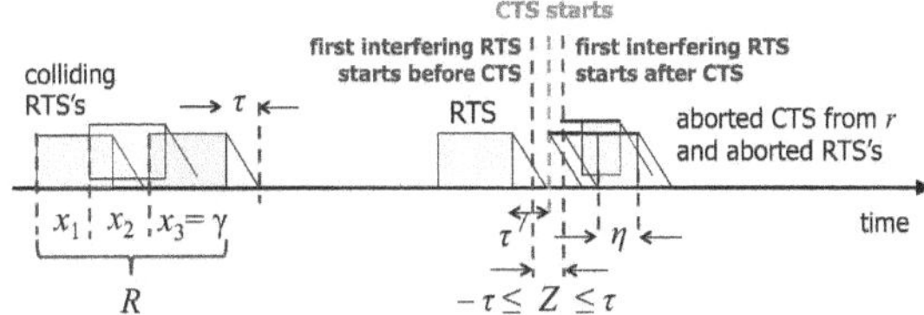

Figure 6: Effect of hidden terminals in CSMA/CAD

We analyze the impact of hidden terminals on the performance of CSMA/CAD. To simplify our modeling problem, we assume a star network in which all traffic is sent to a central receiver r and all nodes other than r are hidden from one another, which constitutes a worst-case performance scenario for CSMA/CAD, because it renders carrier sensing and collision detection useless for the transmission of RTS's. However, together with the results of the previous section, it provides sufficient insight on the efficacy of CSMA/CAD. Other than the fact that all sources are hidden from one another, the assumptions made in Section 5 apply to this case. Figure 6 illustrates the collision intervals that may occur in non-persistent CSMA/CAD with the assumptions we make.

THEOREM 6.1. *The throughput of CSMA/CAD with a non-persistent transmission strategy at a central receiver r with a large population of sources hidden from each other is*

$$S_{CAD} \approx \frac{\delta}{H + e^{\lambda\tau}[\, e^{\lambda\gamma}\left(\tau + \frac{1}{\lambda}(e^{\lambda\gamma} - 1)\right) + J\,]} \tag{19}$$

with $J = \frac{1}{\lambda} + \gamma + \eta + 2\tau$ *and* $H = \delta + \gamma + \alpha + \tau - \eta$

PROOF. A node aborts its RTS or CTS if it detects a collision. By assumption, transmitters are hidden from one another, and hence an RTS is vulnerable for its entire length and arrives successfully at receiver r with probability $P_{SR} = e^{-\lambda\gamma}$. On the other hand, receiver r sends its CTS successfully with probability $P_{SC} = e^{-\lambda\tau}$, because it can detect any RTS that collides with its CTS in one propagation delay.

With Poisson arrivals, having no arrivals in a given time interval is independent of having no arrivals in another non-overlapping time interval. Hence, given that RTS arrivals are Poisson distributed and a data packet is sent only if an RTS and the corresponding CTS are sent successfully, we have $\overline{U} = \delta P_{SR} P_{SC} = \delta e^{-\lambda(\gamma+\tau)}$.

On the other hand, the value of $\overline{I}$ is the same as in Theorem 5.1, i.e., $\overline{I} = 1/\lambda$.

A busy period is an RTS collision interval (RCI) if the first RTS suffers MAI with probability $1 - P_{SR}$. An RCI lasts $\tau + R$ seconds, where R is a random variable whose value depends on the number of RTS's involved in the collision interval and the inter-arrival times of those RTS's.

For an RCI to have k RTS's, some RTS's must arrive during the transmission time of each of the first $k-1$ RTS's and no RTS arrives during the transmission time of the last RTS in the RCI. With the simplifying assumption that there is an infinite number of transmitters around receiver r, this corresponds to the geometric random variable in which the probability of successfully ending the RCI is the probability that no RTS arrives during the γ seconds, or $e^{-\lambda\gamma}$. Therefore, the average number of RTS's in an RCI is $e^{\lambda\gamma}$.

The inter-arrival times between consecutive RTS's in an RCI are exponentially distributed and each can be at most γ seconds. Therefore, the average $\overline{X}$ of such times is

$$\overline{X} = \int_0^\infty (1 - F_X(t))dt = \int_0^\gamma e^{-\lambda t}dt = \frac{1}{\lambda}\left(1 - e^{-\lambda\gamma}\right) \quad (20)$$

It thus follows that the average value of R is given by

$$\overline{R} = e^{\lambda\gamma}\overline{X} = \frac{e^{\lambda\gamma}}{\lambda}\left(1 - e^{-\lambda\gamma}\right) = \frac{e^{\lambda\gamma} - 1}{\lambda} \quad (21)$$

If an RTS arrives at its receiver r with no MAI (with probability P_{SR}) and the CTS succeeds (with probability P_{SC}), the length of the busy period is $\overline{T} = \delta + 2\gamma + \alpha + 4\tau$.

If a CTS from r fails (with probability $1 - P_{SC}$), it must collide with RTS's sent within the period of time starting with the reception of the RTS at r and ending τ seconds from the start of the CTS, after which all neighbors of r detect the carrier of the CTS from r.

Any neighbor of r creating MAI for the CTS must abort its transmission after detecting collision with the CTS, and node r must abort its transmission after detecting a collision with the *first* interfering RTS. The average length of a CTS collision interval is then $\overline{C} = \gamma + \tau + \overline{Z} + \eta + \tau$, where Z is a random variable that varies from $-\tau$ to τ and represents the time between the arrival of the CTS from receiver r and the arrival of the first RTS causing MAI to the CTS.

The longest CTS collision interval occurs when $Z = \tau$ and for simplicity we approximate $\overline{C} \approx C_{max} = \gamma + \eta + 3\tau$. This is safe to use because it results in a lower bound for the throughput. We can then express $\overline{B}$ as follows:

$$\overline{B} \approx e^{-\lambda\gamma}\left(\overline{T}e^{-\lambda\tau} + C_{max}(1 - e^{-\lambda\tau})\right) + (1 - e^{-\lambda\gamma})(\overline{R} + \tau) \quad (22)$$

Substituting the values of $\overline{T}$, C_{max}, and $\overline{R}$ into Eq. (22), and then substituting the values of $\overline{U}$, $\overline{B}$, and $\overline{I}$ into Eq. (5) we obtain Eq. (19). □

7 PERFORMANCE COMPARISON

For simplicity, we assume a channel data rate of 1 Mbps even though higher data rates are common today. MAC-level lengths of signaling packets are similar to those used in IEEE 802.11 DCF, and we assume that an RTS and an ACK is 40 bytes. The time needed to detect collisions and send a jamming signal (η) in CSMA/CAD is roughly twice the duration of a jamming signal in CSMA/CD, or 84-bit time. A CTS in CSMA/CAD has the same length of an RTS. On the other hand, to ensure floor acquisition using CTS's in the version of CSMA/CA we use for comparison, the length of a CTS equals the length of an RTS plus a round-trip time and a transmit-to-receive turnaround time ω, which equals $20\mu s$. The busy-tone detection time σ in DBTMA is 100 μs, which corresponds to a probability of correct busy-tone detection close to 1 according to the model presented in [19]. We use $\beta = .9$ to take into account the fact that DBTMA dedicates most of the available bandwidth to the data channel.

We normalize the results to the length of a data packet by making $G = \lambda \times \delta$ and $a = \tau/\delta$; and by using the normalized value of each other variable, which equals its ratio with δ (e.g., the normalized RTS length is γ/δ).

7.1 Results for Fully-Connected Scenario

We compare the throughput (S) versus the offered load (G) attained by CSMA/CAD, CSMA/CA, DBTMA, and CSMA based on Eqs. (6), (11), (14), and (18).

Figure 7 shows the results for a local-area scenario that highlights the performance of the protocols when latencies are very short and signaling overhead is small relative to the time needed to transmit data packets. Physical distances are around 500 meters, and the duration of a data packet is 1500 bytes, which is an average-length IP packet and takes 0.012s to transmit at 1 Mbps. We use a normalized propagation delay of $a = 1 \times 10^{-4}$.

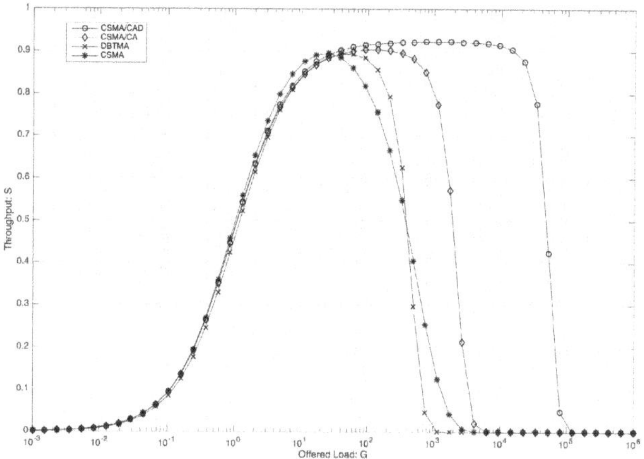

Figure 7: S vs. G in fully-connected scenario

As the results indicate, the throughput attained with DBTMA, CSMA/CA, and CSMA/CAD surpasses the throughput of CSMA with priority ACKs at high loads. This results from the fact that the three protocols reduce the length of collision intervals compared to CSMA. DBTMA suffers from the latencies incurred in detecting busy tones and the reduced bandwidth available for the transmission of data packets compared to CSMA/CA and CSMA/CAD.

CSMA/CAD is more stable at higher loads because of the reduced overhead associated with using SIC to detect collisions compared to using a long CTS as an in-band busy tone, or requiring a separate control channel to transmit busy tones. Overall, CSMA/CAD provides the highest throughput of the channel-access schemes capable of eliminating MAI due to hidden terminals. This is because CSMA/CAD provides the fastest feedback to transmitters when MAI occurs, which results in the shortest collision intervals.

7.2 Results with Hidden Terminals

Fig. 8 shows the throughput of CSMA/CAD with and without hidden terminals using Eq. (19) and Eq. (6), respectively. The same parameter values of the fully-connected scenario are used. We do not consider CSMA/CA, DBTMA, and CSMA because modifications would be required in these protocols to eliminate MAI on ACKs, which must be used in practice.

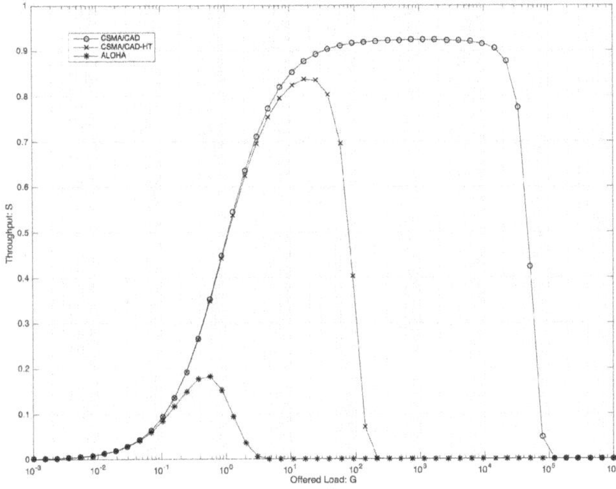

Figure 8: S vs. G with hidden terminals

The results in Fig. 8 clearly show that CSMA/CAD provides a marked improvement over CSMA even if ACKs in CSMA are assumed to be delivered without MAI and in 0 time, which results in the same throughput as ALOHA [19]. The degradation in the throughput of CSMA/CAD resulting from hidden terminals is due primarily to RTS's being vulnerable for their entire transmission time, rather than just a propagation delay. As should be expected, this is more apparent at higher loads.

8 CONCLUSIONS

We introduced CSMA/CAD (Carrier-Sense Multiple Access with Collision Avoidance and Detection) and showed that no data packets or ACKs sent into the channel can collide with other transmissions. We compared the throughput attained with CSMA/CAD with the throughput of CSMA/CA, DBTMA, and CSMA with priority ACKs for the case in which nodes use a non-persistent transmission strategy. Our results show that using collision detection as an integral part of the collision-avoidance handshake among nodes of ad-hoc networks has clear advantages over the other techniques.

Our future work focuses on: (a) the impact of persistence in the transmission of signaling packets, (b) the use of back-off strategies to address congestion, (c) full-duplex data exchanges between neighbors that successfully complete a collision-avoidance handshake, and (d) the analysis of CSMA/CAD in multi-hop networks using approximate models [2, 21].

ACKNOWLEDGMENTS

This work was supported in part by the Jack Baskin Chair of Computer Engineering at UC Santa Cruz.

REFERENCES

[1] N. Abramson. The aloha system–another alternative for computer communications. *Proc. Fall Joint Computer Conference 1970.*
[2] M. Carvalho and J. J. Garcia-Luna-Aceves. A scalable model for channel access protocols in multihop ad hoc networks. *Proc. ACM MobiCom 2004.*
[3] A. Colvin. Csma with collision avoidance. *Computer Communications*, 6(5):227–35, 1983.
[4] D. Bharadia, E. McMilin, and S. Katti. Full duplex radios. *Proc. ACM SIGCOMM 2013.*
[5] H. Ahn et al. Hidden chain: A full-duplex mac protocol using hidden terminal relationships in wlans. *Proc. IEEE WONS 2016.*
[6] K.M. Thilina et al. Medium access control design for full duplex wireless systems: Challenges and approaches. *IEEE Communications Magazine*, 2015.
[7] M. Jainy et al. Practical, real-time, full duplex wireless. *Proc. ACM MobiCom 2011.*
[8] S. Goyal et al. A distributed mac protocol for full duplex radio. *IEEE 2013 Asilomar Conf.*
[9] X. Zhang et al. Full-duplex transmission in phy and mac layers for 5g mobile wireless networks. *IEEE Communications Magazine*, 2015.
[10] C. Fullmer and J. J. Garcia-Luna-Aceves. Floor acquisition multiple access (fama) for packet-radio networks. *Proc. ACM SIGCOMM 1995.*
[11] C. Fullmer and J. J. Garcia-Luna-Aceves. Solutions to hidden terminal problems in wireless networks. *Proc. ACM SIGCOMM 1997.*
[12] R. Garces and J. J. Garcia-Luna-Aceves. Floor acquisition multiple access with collision resolution. *Proc. ACM MobiCom 1996.*
[13] J. J. Garcia-Luna-Aceves and A. Tzamaloukas. Receiver-initiated collision avoidance in wireless networks. *Wireless Networks*, 2002.
[14] Z. Haas and J. Deng. Dual busy tone multiple access (dbtma)–a multiple access control scheme for ad hoc networks. *IEEE Trans. Commun.*, 2002.
[15] A. R. K. Tamaki and Y. Sugiyama. Full duplex media access control for wireless multi-hop networks. *Proc. VTC Spring 2013.*
[16] P. Karn. Maca–a new channel access method for packet radio. *Proc. ARRL/CRRL Amateur Radio 9th Computer Networking Conference*, 1990.
[17] L. Kleinrock and F. Tobagi. Packet switching in radio channels: Part i - carrier sense multiple-access modes and their throughput-delay characteristics. *IEEE Trans. Commun.*, 1975.
[18] R. Metcalfe and D. Boggs. Ethernet: Distributed packet switching for local computer networks. *CACM*, 1976.
[19] F. Tobagi and L. Kleinrock. Packet switching in radio channels: Part ii - the hidden terminal problem in carrier sense multiple-access modes and the busy-tone solution. *IEEE Trans. Commun.*, 1975.
[20] F. Tobagi and L. Kleinrock. The effect of acknowledgment traffic on the capacity of packet-switched radio channels. *IEEE Trans. Commun.*, 1978.
[21] Y. Wang and J. J. Garcia-Luna-Aceves. Collision avoidance in multi-hop ad hoc networks. *Proc. IEEE MASCOTS 2002.*
[22] C. Wu and V. Li. Receiver-initiated busy tone multiple access in packet radio networks. *Proc. ACM SIGCOMM 1987.*

Multi-Channel Continuous Rendezvous in Cognitive Networks

Cledson Oliveira de Sousa
MidiaCom Labs, UFF
Niterói, Brazil
cledson@midiacom.uff.br

Diego Passos
MidiaCom Labs, UFF
Niterói, Brazil
dpassos@ic.uff.br

Ricardo Campanha Carrano
MidiaCom Labs, UFF
Niterói, Brazil
carrano@midiacom.uff.br

Célio Albuquerque
MidiaCom Labs, UFF
Niterói, Brazil
celio@ic.uff.br

ABSTRACT

The rapid growth of wireless networking technologies, the emergence of several new devices that offer or need Internet interconnection, and a pent-up demand for wide band access, especially away from the big cities, are hampered by the problem of the frequency spectrum exhaustion for telecommunications services. A more efficient use of the spectrum passes through solutions, such as the improvement and deployment of radios with cognitive ability. In this context, the problem of neighbor discovery extends not only for the initial *blind rendezvous*, but also for the maintenance of periodical encounters of neighbors after such initial encounter. At this stage, it will be necessary for a node that has already found a peer to interrupt its data communication, so that nodes can become aware of changes in their surroundings and the network can support the addition of new nodes. The contribution of this paper is the creation of asynchronous, distributed and robust schedules to guarantee multiple continuous rendezvous and communication opportunities between two or more cognitive radios using control channels, employing frequency hopping with new sequences and mappings based on combinatorial design theory.

KEYWORDS

Frequency reuse, cognitive radios, multi-channel rendezvous.

ACM Reference format:
Cledson Oliveira de Sousa, Diego Passos, Ricardo Campanha Carrano, and Célio Albuquerque. 2017. Multi-Channel Continuous Rendezvous in Cognitive Networks. In *Proceedings of MSWiM '17, Miami, FL, USA, November 21–25, 2017,* 8 pages.
https://doi.org/10.1145/3127540.3127552

1 INTRODUCTION

Although we have observed a rapid spread of wireless communications, we have also witnessed the exhaustion of radio-frequency spectrum caused, in part, by the lack of flexibility of the licensing model used by government regulation agencies and the pollution of the wavebands that do not require license for operation, the Industrial Scientific and Medical (ISMs) being the most patent example. At such frequency bands, forced by circumstances, a multiplicity of devices are required to operate. Moreover, there are large portions of the spectrum already granted remaining idle, such as in sparsely-populated regions, or simply not operated due to market issues [16].

Thanks to significant hardware and software advances in digital signal processing, there are promising computational solutions that attempt to solve the spectrum scarcity issue. Among those, we can cite the Dynamic Spectrum Access (DSA) and the usage of radios with cognitive ability, ie., radios that able to dynamically find and operate opportunistically at idle channels.

This efficiency improvement comes from the frequency reuse, since Cognitive Radios (CR) are able to scan the spectrum, searching for those bands that, despite being licensed, remain idle. These are what are commonly refereed to as white spaces or spectrum holes [1]. The reuse of such spaces depends on the presence or not of the licensed Primary Users (PUs), that, due to the dynamics of wireless environments, changes over time. These changes result in problems of temporal and spectral diversity. In others words, two unlicensed secondary users (SUs) that want to communicate, must, without previous knowledge of spectral occupation or any central aid, scan a subset of vacant frequencies and find one or more common channels at a same instant, which constitutes a communication opportunity. Such problem is commonly called *blind rendezvous* [20].

Cognitive Radios need to sense the spectrum and vacate the channel in case of PU detection to protect PUs from harmful interference. To achieve this fundamental feature, CR users usually share information with each other by using a common medium for control message exchange. This common medium is known as a common control channel (CCC) [1].

The single CCC approach, in which only one channel is used to exchange control messages, is a simple way to guarantee the control rendezvous and set up future data transmission. Figure 1 illustrates the operating scenario of a single dedicated CCC.

The main disadvantage of the single CCC approach is its susceptibility to the dynamics of the wireless communication environment. The presence of the PU in the control channel can not only degrade the overall flow of the SUs' communication, but if the transmission period of the PU is long, it may even block access to the channel for the SUs. Interference or jamming attacks can also disrupt the SUs' communication and this behavior can hinder or block the

MSWiM '17, November 21–25, 2017, Miami, FL, USA

ACM ISBN 978-1-4503-5162-1/17/11...$15.00
https://doi.org/10.1145/3127540.3127552

establishment of new rendezvous. A solution for this situation is to provide communication in multiple control channels. However despite facilitating the maintenance of network connectivity, increasing the number of control channels can result in unacceptable levels of control overhead.

In this work we consider the problem of multi-channel rendezvous by assuming each CR follows a cyclic frequency hop sequence, called a schedule, in which it alternates between the data channel and each of the control channels. Such a schedule must be constructed in a way that guarantees that any two nodes will have some overlapping time in each control channel in every cycle.

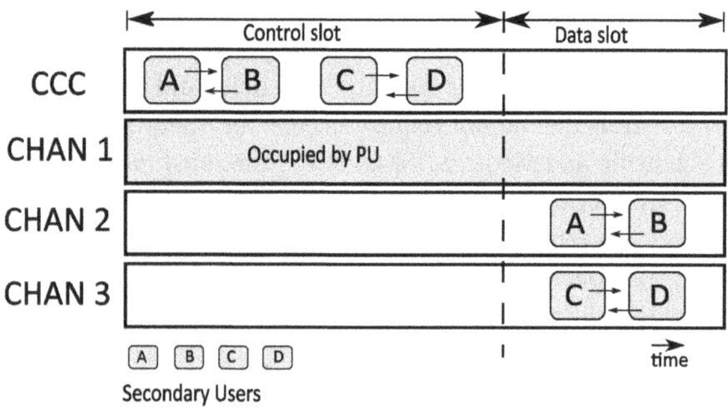

Figure 1: This example shows a single CCC as a dedicated control channel visited by secondary users during control slots. CHAN 1 is occupied by the PU, CHAN 2 and CHAN 3 are dedicated to communication between SUs. The SUs hop from the CCC to one of those channels during data slots.

Synchronism between nodes would make the overlap of frequency hop sequences trivial, but, typically, cognitive devices are embedded with inexpensive and inaccurate clocks, which makes synchronization in cognitive networks a difficult and costly task [13]. Thereby, we opt to employ an asynchronous approach.

In summary, blind rendezvous is a well studied problem, as seen in [10, 12, 18], but the continuous multi-channel rendezvous is scarcely visited in literature. For example, it is mentioned in [3] and only recently addressed in [6]. In this context, the contribution of this paper is the proposal of heuristics that can operate on known schedules for the control channel scenario, and output more robust multi-channel schedules for continuous time rendezvous with low control overhead.

This text is organized as follows. In Section 2, we describe the scenario considered in this paper in more detail. Next, in Section 3, we introduce theoretical concepts and definitions. Related work is presented in Section 4. Later, in Section 5, we discuss the concept of Block Designs, the mathematical basis of our proposed schedules for continuous rendezvous. The next section details our proposal, followed by a section presenting an evaluation. Finally, in Section 8, we present our conclusions and ideas for future work.

2 THE SCENARIO

After the first rendezvous, cognitive radios operating as secondary users must return periodically to the control channel for collaborating, admitting new nodes, exchanging information regarding the PU activity, and contacting known nodes for establishing new control or data channels in case a PU becomes present. A subset of the channels already chosen at the first rendezvous could be used to set up a robust multi-channel schedule and accomplish these functions through continuous rendezvous.

In our scenario, two or more radios coexist and share the same licensed band. The licensed spectrum is divided in a set G of orthogonal channels, with N of those being control channels, while one is chosen as a dedicated data channel.

Our schedule will traverse the channels of set G, in fixed size time slots. All radios operate under the same schedule S, which is a sequence of v slots, of which k are control slots. Notice that, although all nodes operate under the same schedule, due the lack of synchronism, at a given moment of time, the nodes may be in different slots and therefore, in different channels. Thus, two nodes operating under the same schedule will likely not rendezvous at all control slots of a cycle. We define the number of control slots in which two nodes rendezvous in each cycle λ.

Given two radios R_1 and R_2 equipped with a single half-duplex radio interface, and programmed with the same schedule S, we would like to guarantee multi-channel rendezvous in each cycle.

In Figure 2, we present a fragment of a schedule starting at slot 11. These radios rendezvous at two different control slots in each cycle. All control slot in a schedule S belong to a specific control set K_i and should be allocated to the respective control channel, C_{C0} or C_{C1} by predefined control sets K_0 and K_1 to guarantee the rendezvous.

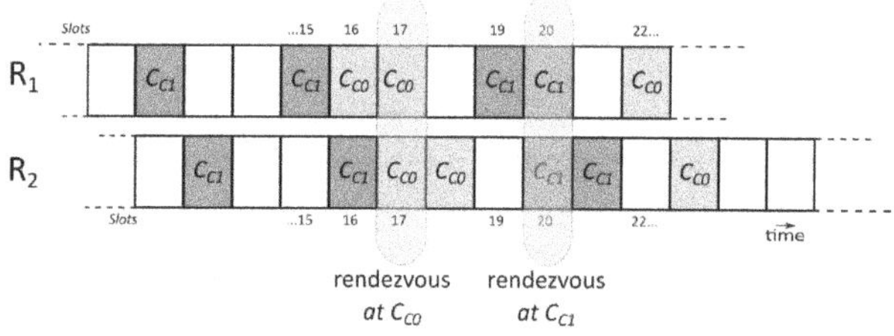

Figure 2: Two radios R_1 and R_2 operating under a same schedule with 59 slots and 29 control slots (Grey). In this example, there are rendezvous in C_{C0} at slot 17, and in C_{C1} at slot 20. There is an offset $\theta = 1$ between the two nodes. The white slots represent the data slots.

3 DEFINITIONS, TERMINOLOGY AND METRICS

Typically, in sequence-based CCC approaches, nodes divide time into cycles, consisting of a sequence of fixed-size control and data slots, dictated by a schedule, which defines a frequency hopping sequence [15]. In order to be used in asynchronous CCC, such schedule should guarantee that any two nodes will rendezvous in both dimensions, time and frequency, irrespective of their radios' time offset. In this section, we will present some definitions, terminology and metrics related to these schedules, namely: control overhead, upper bound rendezvous, Expected Time To Rendezvous (ETTR), Maximum Time To Rendezvous (MTTR) and Rotation Closure Property (RCP).

In all definitions and figures, we assume that the slots of the radios are border-aligned, ie., starting and ending together, which in fact, would require synchronization. However, as demonstrated theoretically in [14], with simulations in [3], and experimentally in [4], if a schedule satisfies a property called Rotation Closure Property, the alignment between slots is not a requirement for the rendezvous to occur. Also note that two cognitive nodes programmed to operate under the same schedule, due to asynchrony, might actually operate under rotations of the same schedule. Such rotations are dictated by their internal clock offsets. Schedule rotation is a key factor to understand the RCP, and only by satisfying RCP, a schedule can deterministically guarantee the rendezvous. See an RCP definition bellow.

Definition 1. ***Rotation Closure Property*** *— A schedule S presents the Rotation Closure Property, if, and only if, the intersection between itself and any of its rotations has at least one common control slot.*

In this paper, we are interested in N multi-channel rendezvous, which means that a schedule S can also be understood as a set of v slots and a collection of disjoint sub control sets $K = \{K_i, K_j, ..., K_N\}$. Thereby, if each sub control set of K satisfies RCP individually, the schedule satisfies RCP for all N control channels. It is important to draw attention to the fact that a design is defined as a set together with a family of subsets whose members are chosen to satisfy some set of properties [8], and can have several different schedules, with disjoint control sets or not. We are interested in the disjoint case here.

In the example shown in Figure 2, radio R_1 operates under a schedule S with two distinct sub control sets $K_0 = \{..., 16, 17, 22, ...\}$ mapped to control channel C_{C0} and $K_1 = \{..., 12, 15, 19, 20, ...\}$ mapped to control channel C_{C1}. R_2 operates under the same schedule S, but rotated by one slot, ie., $\theta = 1$. Note that $K_0 \cap K_1 = \emptyset$. Thereby, we want to construct a collection $K = \{K_0, K_1, ..., K_N\}$ $\forall K_i, K_j, K_i \cap K_j = \emptyset$, and all sub control sets of K satisfy RCP individually.

From these definitions, we determine metrics to measure schedule efficiency. The **control overhead** is defined as the fraction of time that each node spends on control channels. The Time To Rendezvous (**TTR**) for a given pair of nodes is simply the number of slots elapsed until rendezvous, which is a function of both the used schedule and the offset between the internal clocks of the nodes. Since two nodes may present arbitrary clock offsets, more useful metrics would be to consider the average and worst cases. Thus, we define the **ETTR** to be the average TTR, considering all possible time offsets. Similarly, **MTTR** is the worst-case TTR for all possible time offsets.

4 RELATED WORK

Rendezvous approaches can be classified in two main branches, aided and unaided, and the latter can be divided in synchronous or asynchronous, and with or without control channels. This section seeks to situate and compare our proposal and scenario using this general classification already established in literature, as in [15] and [20].

Some rendezvous proposals make use of Quorum Systems (QS) to create control channel-based schedules and to promote rendezvous in Cognitive Radio Networks (CRN). A Quorum is a set system where the intersection of any two sets is never null. The rotations of a schedule based on Quorum Systems are sets of the Quorum. Thus, RCP is guaranteed. However, the proposals in [3], [5] and [17], are able to guarantee rendezvous for only one channel, not being applicable for multi-channel rendezvous. Further, such approaches present high control overhead when compared to Block Designs of the same length [4].

In SeqR [9], the authors create channel hop sequences by first selecting a random permutation P of N channels, and repeating it $P(N + 1)$ times in the sequence, interspersed by each element of P. For example, for $N = 3$, and choosing $\{1, 2, 3\}$ as a permutation of the channels, we obtain the sequence $\{1, 1, 2, 3, 2, 1, 2, 3, 3, 1, 2, 3\}$. While this mechanism guarantees rendezvous, it does not guarantee rendezvous in all available channels, which reduces its robustness against interference and channel occupancy. It is important to notice that SeqR is concerned with the blind rendezvous problem, instead of the continuous rendezvous considered in this paper. Notice that the channel hopping sequences created by SeqR do not include the data channel. Indeed, SeqR assumes that the rendezvous is only a concern at an initial setup stage of the network. After that, nodes are assumed to remain fixed at the data channel. As an illustration, Figure 3 shows an example of a SeqR schedule, highlighting the rendezvous in channel 2, but failing to provide rendezvous on channels 1 and 3 in a same cycle.

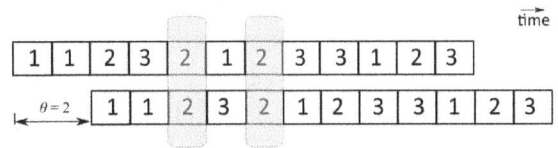

Figure 3: Example of two nodes A and B operating under a schedule created with SeqR with offset $\theta = 2$, showing the case with 2 rendezvous on channel 2.

DRDS in [12] and CRSEQ [18] are also rendezvous mechanisms that achieve multi-channel rendezvous. They present bounded time to rendezvous, but are not interested in continuous rendezvous as our scenario defined in Section 2.

The authors in [6] address the problem of continuous multi-channel rendezvous and propose a channel-hopping schedule called Shift-based Channel Hopping for Continuous Rendezvous (SCHCR), which is based in SeqR, without distinguishing control and data channels: ie., they assume any channel can be used to send both data and control information. So far, all the mechanisms mentioned in this section deal with several ways of creating hop sequences to achieve rendezvous in bounded time. Some are quorum-based, others use permutation and others use combinatorial designs, as in [12], but none uses specifically Balanced Incomplete Block Designs (BIBD) [21]. In [2], we find for the first time the application of BIBD for the construction of a rendezvous mechanism in CRANs. The authors' proposal concerns data and control transmission, but it does not use CCC concept, treating all channels as possible opportunities for both, data and control transmissions. It can be noticed that none of those solutions can be readily employed for the continuous rendezvous scenario presented in Section 2.

5 BLOCK DESIGNS

Combinatorial design theory deals with the existence, construction and properties of systems of finite sets, whose arrangements satisfy general concepts of balance and/or symmetry [8]. The application of such mathematical framework in our work hinges on the ability to partition the time into a set of slots divided in two subsets, control and data slots, such that, two non-synchronized radios operating under a frequency hopping sequence, defined by these designs, are guaranteed to have overlapping times at the control slots (ie., they are guaranteed to rendezvous).

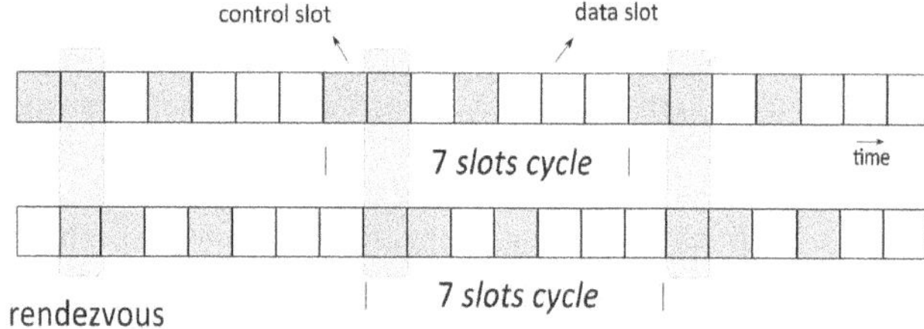

Figure 4: Example of Block Design with a periodic cycle of 7 slots, where there are 3 control slots and 4 slots used for data transmission. This specific design guarantees one rendezvous per cycle.

We now, briefly introduce the formal definition of a BIBD or simply Block Designs, adapted for our context, composed of slots and cycles.

Definition 2. ***Block Designs*** — *Let* $v, k, \lambda \in \mathbb{Z}^{+} | \ v > k \geq 2$. *A Block Design* $BD - \{v, k, \lambda\}$ *is a pair* $(Y, \mathcal{A})$ *which satisfies the following properties* [11]:

(1) *Y is a set of slots of cardinality v that forms a cycle,*
(2) $\mathcal{A}$ *is a collection of two subsets of Y, called blocks,*
(3) *one block contains k control slots , while the other contains* $v - k$ *data slots,*
(4) *any pair of different blocks must contain* λ *rendezvous.*

So, the relationship between Y, a schedule S and a $BD - \{v, k, \lambda\}$, can be exemplified in the following particular case, which is illustrated in Figure 4. Henceforth, for brevity, we will express the BDs just as $\{v, k, \lambda\}$.

- Example: given $Y = \{0, 1, 2, 3, 4, 5, 6\}$, there is a BD $\{7, 3, 1\}$, which has a particular schedule $S = [7, \{0, 1, 3\}]$, whose cycle has a total of 7 slots in which 3 control slots are allocated at positions $\{0, 1, 3\}$ in the same single frequency, and data slots are allocated at positions $\{2, 4, 5, 6\}$. For any schedule rotation $\vec{S}^{\theta}$ of S, there is exactly one overlap per cycle as depicted in Figure 4, for $\theta = 1$.

Note that there are many other possible designs. Some more elaborate with $\lambda = 3$, 4 and 17 are shown in Table 1.

Table 1: Some known more elaborated designs.

BDs	Schedules
$\{15, 7, 3\}$	$S = [15, \{0, 1, 2, 4, 5, 8, 10\}]$
$\{19, 9, 4\}$	$S = [19, \{1, 4, 5, 6, 7, 9, 11, 16, 17\}]$
$\{4369, 273, 17\}$	$S = [4369, \{1, 2, 46, 55, 112, 123, ..., 4344, 4356, 4362\}]$

Although we use BIBDs as the basis for this work, notice that they are not trivially applicable to the multi-channel schedules since their blocks specify two kinds of slots (eg., control and data). In order to adapt block designs to our specific scenario, we propose heuristics that can start with a block design and output an efficient multi-channel schedule.

6 OUR PROPOSAL

This paper proposes a set of heuristics that can take one or more existing designs and generate new designs suitable for providing multi-channel continuous rendezvous. By systematically employing those heuristics, we obtain three new kinds of designs, called C-designs, M-designs and H-designs. The first design arises from the application of what we refer to as Reverse Engineering (RE), while the second exploits the concept of Constructive Sum (CS), our extension of the constructive sum theorem in [11], and the third combines the first two. We also create the concept of mapping functions $\mathcal{M}$, which designate which channels will be allocated to the control slots.

On a scenario where we want to promote multi-channel rendezvous, we can allocate the channels to control slots in many possible ways, but in the absence of analytic means to prove that a given a tuple (*Design*, $\mathcal{M}$, *S*) provides rendezvous at all channels within every cycle, for all offsets, we would have to explore all possible mapping functions. However, in order to reduce the scope of discovering successful $\mathcal{M}$ functions, since the number of possible schedules grows exponentially with cycle length (N^k), we divided our mapping functions into two groups:

(1) **regular**, mapping function that groups $2 < g < k/2$ consecutive control slots at a same frequency. Notice that there are schedules where k is not multiple of the group size. In these cases the remaining slots are allocated on the last channel; and
(2) **irregular**, all other combinations that group g control slots using different frequencies.

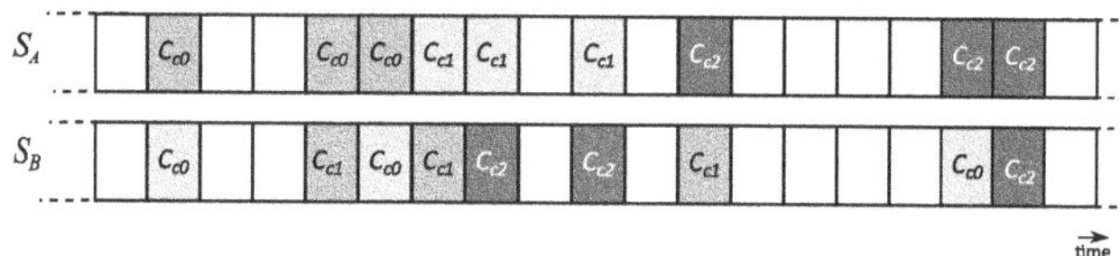

Figure 5: Schedule S_A with a regular mapping function that allocates each three consecutive control slots, to the same control channel, alternating between three control channels for each group. The mapping used on schedule S_B, on the other hand, is irregular.

As an example of those two distinct mappings, Figure 5 illustrates two schedules S_A and S_B, originated from the same BD with $\lambda = 9$, operating respectively, in a regular mapping function that allocates the same channel C_{ci} for each three consecutive control slots, and an irregular mapping that does not obey a regular allocation. Notice that the number of possible irregular mappings grows exponentially with the number of control slots k. For this reason, in this paper we will focus on regular mappings, although we intend to pursue a deeper investigation on irregular mappings in the future.

Once defined the use of regular mappings to allocate control slots, the next step is the discovery of a suitable tuple (*BD*, $\mathcal{M}$, *S*), that:

(a) ensures rendezvous on all channels within every cycle regardless the offset in bounded time,
(b) is efficient in terms of as overhead, ETTR and MTTR.

To verify the feasibility of our designs and schedules, we have implemented a simulator that generates and tests schedules and rotations. For each design, the simulator computes the parameters presented in Table 2. It also implements our heuristics for constructing new designs, and checks the existence of disjoint control sets. Those functionalities, that will be explained in more details in the next sections, are illustrated in Algorithms 1 and 2. Both algorithms use the text_RCP function, which is responsible for testing the RCP property for each offset and reporting the results.

Table 2: Simulator input parameters and output metrics.

Parameter	Description
Design type	BD CD, MD and HD
v	Cycle length.
k	# control slots.
λ	# rendezvous per cycle.
overhead	% of slots used to control (k/v).
Functions $\mathcal{M}_{k,N,g}$	used $\mathcal{M}$ functions and parameters k, N, g.
$\mathcal{R}_{C_{cn}}$	Rendezvous per channel.
ETTR C_{cn}	ETTR per control channel.
MTTR C_{cn}	MTTR per control channel.
Flawed offsets per C_{cn}	Total of failed offset per control channel

6.1 Traditional Block Designs with $\lambda > 1$ and Regular Mappings

BD-based schedules, as in [4] and [7], fit well for neighbor discovery techniques which employ nodes operating at a single frequency and require rendezvous only in time dimension. Regular mapping introduces the idea of grouping a number of consecutive slots allocating them to a same frequency, creating schedules that provides multi-channel rendezvous.

The first and most didactic example of the application of a regular mapping function over a Block Design is the schedule obtained from the BD $\{59, 29, 14\}$. A fragment of this schedule is illustrated in Figure 2. Using a regular mapping function that allocates two different channels, alternating each two consecutive control slots to the same frequency, there are rendezvous on both control channels C_{C0} and C_{C1} for all possible offsets. Therefore, this BD-based schedule obeys the RCP, using this regular mapping $\mathcal{M}$ and two control channels. Nevertheless, this design is not efficient, resulting in almost 50% of control overhead. In Section 7, we present results for more efficient designs.

In order to use a more specific and compact notation, from this point on, we will refer to a regular mapping function that maps k control slots to N control channels, grouped in g consecutive slots as $\mathcal{M}_{k,N,g}$. Thus, the function employed in the example of Figure 2, can be represented by $\mathcal{M}_{29,2,2}$. Notice that the regular mapping function $\mathcal{M}$ does not influence the control overhead, since it does not change the number of control slots.

A result of the use of regular mappings to Block Designs is the emergence of some schedules with redundant control slots. If we observe the intersection of such a schedule with rotations of itself, we often notice the occurrence of multiple rendezvous opportunities per channel and per cycle, while a single opportunity suffices. The opposite also happens: some mappings do not achieve rendezvous in all channels in all offsets. So, we create heuristics to overcome these obstacles, that combine two or more designs, increase or reduce the number of control slots, in a such a manner that we obtain more efficient designs in terms of rendezvous and control overhead.

6.2 Constructive Sum

Based on the concept of disjoint control sets (difference families) [19] and on the theorem of constructive sum [11], we extend this theorem for our purposes, proposing a deterministic heuristic we call Constructive Sum (CS).

If we obtain two designs with the same length v and with two disjoint control sets K_1 and K_2, we can create a new design $\{v, k_1 + k_2, (\lambda_1, \lambda_2)\} \therefore |K_1| = k_1, |K_2| = k_2$, which will allow us to ensure multiple channel rendezvous. Here (λ_1, λ_2) indicates the number of rendezvous in each of the two different control channels. We can then apply a new constructive mapping function $\mathcal{M}_c$, that associates uniquely each slot $s_i \in K_1$ to C_{C1} and each slot $s_j \in K_2$ to C_{C2}. Constructive sum is simply a merge of two disjoint control sets. This property is also valid for n designs.

6.3 Reverse Engineering

Reverse Engineering is a technique that can fix both the cases, where we have more control slots than required for multi-channel rendezvous and where we have less control slots than needed. We present this technique in the form of two distinct heuristics: Subtractive Reverse Engineering ($\text{RE}^{(-)}$) and Additive Reverse Engineering ($\text{RE}^{(+)}$).

Subtractive RE – The goal is to reduce the overhead. Choose BD pairs with low overhead e.g. 20% of control overhead. If they have different cycle lengths, reduce the longest design keeping the RCP satisfied, so that they match in size. Then we carefully remove redundant control slots, obtaining, at the end, two disjoint control sets, without loosing RCP property. Before the first step, we choose among all rotations of both BDs, that pair which offers less coincident slots. At the end of these steps, we obtain two more efficient designs in terms of control overhead with two mutually exclusive schedules. Algorithm 1 shows the steps for $\text{RE}^{(-)}$.

Additive RE – First, select a BD with low overhead and few flawed offsets (say $k/10$) for a N-channel rendezvous through regular mapping, and then replace data slots with new control slots to these BD, on failed positions. Run mapping function until there are no more flawed offsets, so that we have, at the end, a new design, incurring in only a small increase in the control overhead, but now satisfying RCP for N-channel rendezvous. Algorithm 2 shows the steps for $\text{RE}^{(+)}$. We call these evolutions of BDs, C-Designs (CD).

Algorithm 1 : Subtractive Reverse Engineering

Input:
length of BD_1 and BD_2 ▷ used designs
S_1, S_2 ▷ schedules
K_1, K_2 ▷ control sets
Output:
C-Design ▷ new $\{v, K', \lambda\}$

adjust BD_1 and BD_2 cycle lengths, testing RCP
counter ← 0
while $K_1 \cap K_2 \neq \varnothing$ **do**
  s ← lowest slot in $K_1 \cap K_2$
  if counter is even **then**
    $s \in K_1$ becomes data slot
    counter++
  else
    $s \in K_2$ becomes data slot
    counter++
  if test_RCP(S_1, S_2) is False **then**
    return fail
return (C-design)

Algorithm 2 : Additive Reverse Engineering

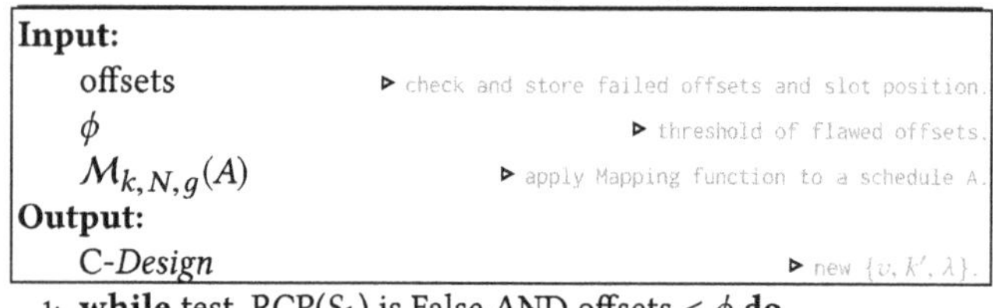
Input:
offsets ▷ check and store failed offsets and slot position.
ϕ ▷ threshold of flawed offsets.
$\mathcal{M}_{k,N,g}(A)$ ▷ apply Mapping function to a schedule A.
Output:
C-Design ▷ new $\{v, K', \lambda\}$.

while test_RCP(S_1) is False AND offsets $< \phi$ **do**
  add control slot in S_1 failed position
  $\mathcal{M}_{k,N,g}(S_1)$
return (C-design)

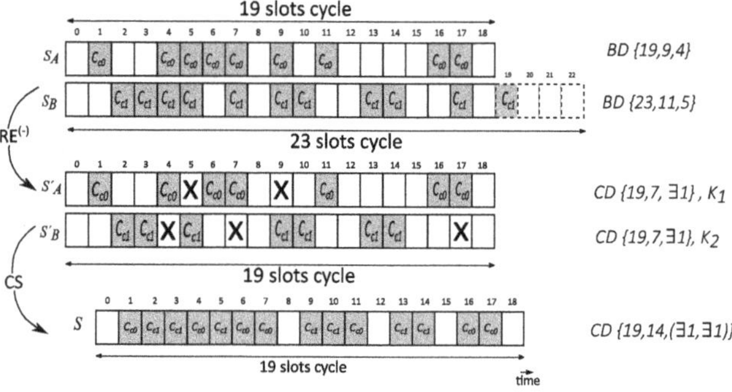

Figure 6: The process of creating C-Designs, through the application of $RE^{(-)}$ in two BDs, showing the removal of surplus slots, eliminating intersection of control slots (marked with an X), for subsequent use of Constructive Sum, creating a new C-Design with two meetings each cycle. Note that a single design like CD $\{19, 7, \exists 1\}$ can have more than one control set, represented here by K_1 and K_2.

The example in Figure 6 [1] explains $RE^{(-)}$ and CS. Take schedules S_A and S_B. As, for example BDs $\{19, 9, 4\}$ and $\{23, 11, 5\}$. We proceed by reducing the length of S_B to match the length of S_A (by eliminating dashed slots), applying the $RE^{(-)}$ heuristic on both schedules, and alternately removing the coincident and redundant slots (slots marked with **X**), until there are no more intersections (which means disjoint control sets), and simultaneously checking, at each iteration, if there are still rendezvous for all offsets in each schedule. At the end of these steps, we have a C-Design with two different control sets. Notice that the resulting control sets after $RE^{(-)}$ are disjoint, and this feature will allow us to use them with another heuristic: Constructive Sum. The simplest RE case is illustrated as a diagram in Figure 7(a).

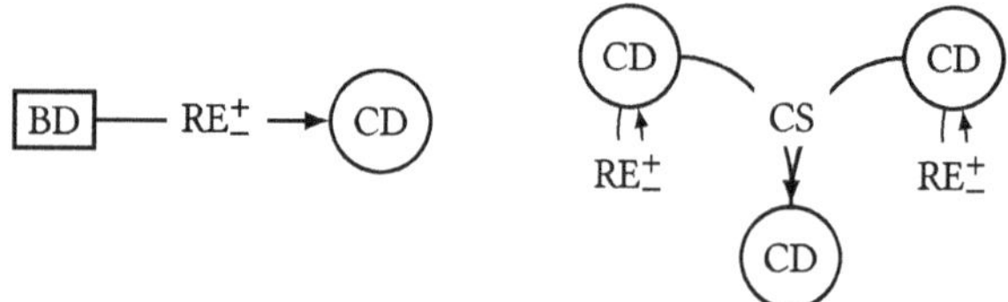

(a) A CD may be obtained from a BD through additive and subtractive Reverse Egineering heuristic.

(b) A CD can be obtained from the constructive sum of two CDs.

Figure 7: Figures (a) and (b) show how C-designs, that allow multi-channel rendezvous, may be constructed.

The idea behind case $RE^{(+)}$ is the opposite of $RE^{(-)}$. In the first phase, we search for any failed BD for N-channel rendezvous in few offsets (threshold ϕ), checking failed slots for each offset. Then, instead of removing a control slot, we replace some data slot by control slots in the largest gap between two control slots until achieving a successful new Design for N-channel rendezvous. Take, for example, BD $\{1562, 312, 62\}$. This specific BD does not have any regular mapped schedule that reaches 3-channel rendezvous. The best case achieved through regular mapping is a schedule with 2 flawed offsets (offsets where there are no rendezvous for one or more control slots) for C_{C2} and C_{C1}. However, replacing 9 data slots by new control slots, we achieve a CD $\{1562, 321, 62\}$ that is successful for 3-channel rendezvous for all offsets. Notice that we can also combine case $RE^{(-)}$ and $RE^{(+)}$ to form new designs, as exemplified in the diagram in Figure7(b).

6.4 Heuristics Summary

For a matter of nomenclature and better understanding we summarize here the resultant designs of our heuristics:

Merged Designs are obtained by applying Constructive Sum to two or more Block Designs that present two or more disjoint control sets. That is the case of BDs $\{553, 24, 1\}$ and $\{871, 30, 1\}$, since both BDs, individually, present two schedules with no control set intersection. So, we can apply $\mathcal{M}_c$ to such schedules forming, respectively MD $\{553, 48, (1, 1)\}$ and $\{871, 60, (1, 1)\}$.

Hybrid Designs are also formed through Constructive Sum, but combining two different designs, which is the case of HD $\{871, 147, (1, 1, \exists 1)\}$, that is formed by MD $\{871, 60, (1, 1)\}$, and a CD $\{871, 87, \exists 1\}$.

C-Designs can also be obtained by CS. Schedules formed with same dimensions, CD {19, 7, ∃1}, but with distinct control sets.

[1] We introduce here a new notation (∃1) to the parameter equivalent to λ for BDs. This means that, after merging, at least one rendezvous per channel per cycle will be guaranteed, instead of exactly one, as with BDs.

Applying the Constructive Sum, and $\mathcal{M}_C$ map function forms the schedule S from CD $\{19, 14, (\exists 1, \exists 1)\}$ with 2-channel rendezvous, ie., at least one slot rendezvous in each channel, for every cycle, regardless of the offset between nodes. Such schedules that present different number of rendezvous per cycle are known as unbalanced.

To enlighten the reader about the number of possibilities and combinations explored in this paper, we summarize our contributions regarding the new designs and their constructions through forming diagrams: Figures 7(a), 7(b), 8(a) and 8(b) show through those diagrams, the construction of mentioned designs. The label of the oriented edges indicates the acronym of heuristic employed, the forms linked to non-oriented edges indicate the forming designs. Figures of different blocks linked to oriented end of the edge represent the resultant designs.

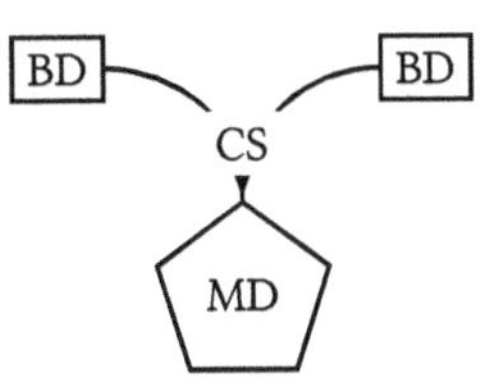

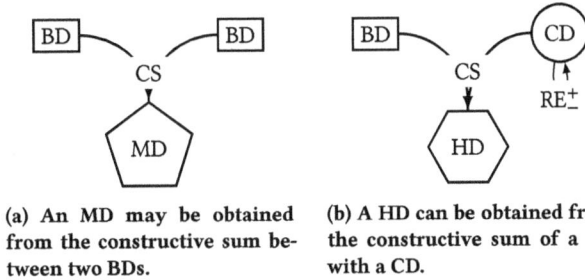

(a) An MD may be obtained from the constructive sum between two BDs.

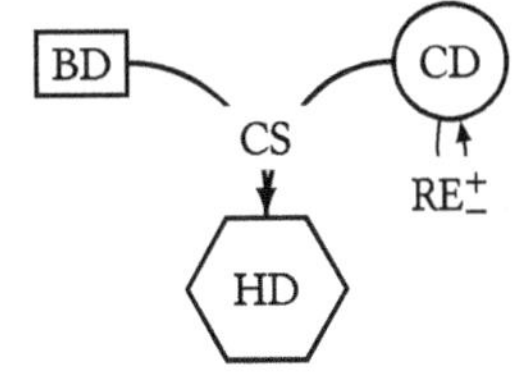

(b) A HD can be obtained from the constructive sum of a BD with a CD.

Figure 8: Figures (a) and (b) show respectively how are obtained MD and HD designs, that allow multiple rendezvous.

To complete the understanding of the differences between new heuristics, designs and their relation to the mapping functions, we present Table 3, showing which mapping functions are used to generate other designs. The restriction of combinations of these elements occurs due to the nature of the designs. For example, once a design has been created by constructively summing two original designs with preassigned channels, there is no sense in using regular mappings. To define in one statement, the regular mapping functions are designed to allow multiple rendezvous in designs not built for this purpose, while constructive mappings have been created already with the purpose of multi-channel rendezvous in mind.

Table 3: Forming designs, applicable mapping functions and their creating heuristics.

		Mapping Functions		Heuristics	
		Regulars	Constructive	Rev. Engineering	Constructive Sum
Designs	CD	✓	✓	✓	✓
	MD		✓		✓
	HD		✓		✓
	BD	✓			

7 RESULTS

Our numerical analysis tests RCP for all possible schedule offsets using any $\mathcal{M}$ function, grouping channels from 2 up to $\lfloor k/2 \rfloor$, starting at the smallest BD $\{19, 9, 4\}$ up to the longest $\{4369, 273, 17\}$. We have tested possible schedules and their rotations, using these four types of designs: BD, CD, MD and HD. In this process we have found almost 150 schedules to compare and use. To be didactic, we will present our results arranging them by design, starting with the direct application of regular mappings to high λ Block Designs, dividing in two groups, first, results for 2-channel rendezvous and control overhead $\leq$ 25%, then all results for 3-channel rendezvous. Later in this section we show the results of our new heuristics.

Table 4: Table with BD-based schedules that effectively guarantee the rendezvous of two radios in two different channels (overhead ≤ 25%).

v	k	λ	overhead	$\mathcal{M}$ function	$\overline{\mathcal{R}_{C_{c0}}}$	ETTR C0	MTTR C0	$\overline{\mathcal{R}_{C_{c1}}}$	ETTR C1	MTTR C1
341	85	21	0.25	$\mathcal{M}_{85,2,2}$	5.17	41.35	330	5.42	31.41	335
677	169	42	0.25	$\mathcal{M}_{169,2,2}$	10.42	60.07	668	10.67	55.73	673
781	156	31	0.20	$\mathcal{M}_{156,2,2}$	7.79	61.32	765	7.79	53.00	633
1562	312	62	0.20	$\mathcal{M}_{312,2,2}$	15.58	61.32	1556	15.58	53.00	1536

7.1 Results for Block Designs

Table 4 shows four different BDs that are able to guarantee rendezvous in two control channels, while incurring in $\leq$ 25% overhead. The table shows the values for v, k, λ, control overhead and the mapping function $\mathcal{M}$. $\overline{\mathcal{R}_{C_{ci}}}$ indicates the average number of rendezvous in a given channel and the ETTR and MTTR in both control channels 0 and 1.

Table 5 lists all BD-based schedules that support 3-channel rendezvous (at least 1 each channel per offset). We wish to pursue the reduction of the control overhead for multi-channel rendezvous in the following sections.

Table 5: BD-based schedules that guarantee multi-channel (3) rendezvous, with their respective overhead and $\mathcal{M}$ functions.

v	k	λ	overhead	$\mathcal{M}$ functions	v	k	λ	overhead	$\mathcal{M}$ functions
199	99	49	0.5	$\mathcal{M}_{99,3,4}$	419	209	104	0.5	$\mathcal{M}_{209,3,11}$
251	125	62	0.5	$\mathcal{M}_{125,3,4}$	431	215	107	0.5	$\mathcal{M}_{215,3,5}$
255	127	63	0.5	$\mathcal{M}_{127,3,3}$	439	219	109	0.5	$\mathcal{M}_{219,3,10}$
263	131	65	0.5	$\mathcal{M}_{131,3,6}$	443	221	110	0.5	$\mathcal{M}_{219,3,17}$
271	135	67	0.5	$\mathcal{M}_{135,3,3}$	463	231	115	0.5	$\mathcal{M}_{231,3,12}$
283	141	70	0.5	$\mathcal{M}_{141,3,3}$	467	233	116	0.5	$\mathcal{M}_{233,3,12}$
307	153	76	0.5	$\mathcal{M}_{153,3,3}$	479	239	119	0.5	$\mathcal{M}_{239,3,3}$
331	165	82	0.5	$\mathcal{M}_{165,3,3}$	487	243	121	0.5	$\mathcal{M}_{243,3,13}$
347	173	86	0.5	$\mathcal{M}_{173,3,3}$	491	245	122	0.5	$\mathcal{M}_{245,3,11}$
359	179	89	0.5	$\mathcal{M}_{179,3,3}$	511	255	127	0.5	$\mathcal{M}_{255,3,10}$
367	183	91	0.5	$\mathcal{M}_{183,3,3}$	523	261	130	0.5	$\mathcal{M}_{261,3,3}$
379	189	94	0.5	$\mathcal{M}_{189,3,4}$	587	293	146	0.5	$\mathcal{M}_{293,3,13}$
383	191	95	0.5	$\mathcal{M}_{191,3,10}$	1023	511	255	0.5	$\mathcal{M}_{511,3,11}$

7.2 Results for Reverse Engineering Heuristic

As already mentioned, Block Designs do not fit well for multi-channel rendezvous, but we can overcome this difficulty using new heuristics to add some particularly positioned control slots with a small increase in control overhead. An example of this new heuristic is the reuse of BD $\{1562, 312, 62\}$. This specific BD reaches 2-channel rendezvous as seen in the first row of Table 6, which shows, among others parameters, some flawed per offset (2) when applying the $\mathcal{M}_{312,3,3}$ mapping. In this particular case adding 9 more control slots modifies the original BD. Using this new control

Table 6: Table showing result of employing the Reverse Engineering heuristic on Block Designs.

Type	v	k	λ	*overhead*	$\mathcal{M}$ function	$\overline{\mathcal{R}_{C_{c0}}}$	ETTR C_{c0}	MTTR C_{c0}	Flawed offsets C_{c0}	$\overline{\mathcal{R}_{C_{c1}}}$	ETTR C_{c1}	MTTR C_{c1}	Flawed offsets C_{c1}	$\overline{\mathcal{R}_{C_{c2}}}$	ETTR C_{c2}	MTTR C_{c2}	Flawed offsets C_{c2}
BD	1562	312	62	0.20	$\mathcal{M}_{312,3,3}$	7.05	188.97	1431	0	6.66	190.42	1363	2	7.05	167.93	1482	2
CD	1562	321	$(\exists 1, \exists 1, \exists 1)$	0.21	$\mathcal{M}_{321,3,3}$	7.05	175.01	1412	0	7.46	167.20	1360	0	7.46	156.81	1211	0

Table 7: Table showing results of new designs created by the Constructive Sum heuristic.

Type	v	k	λ	*overhead*	$\mathcal{M}$ function	$\overline{\mathcal{R}_{C_{c0}}}$	ETTR C_{c0}	MTTR C_{c0}	Flawed offsets C_{c0}	$\overline{\mathcal{R}_{C_{c1}}}$	ETTR C_{c1}	MTTR C_{c1}	Flawed offsets C_{c2}	$\overline{\mathcal{R}_{C_{c2}}}$	ETTR C_{c2}	MTTR C_{c2}	Flawed offsets C_{c2}
HD	871	147	$(1, 1, \exists 1)$	0.16	$\mathcal{M}_C$	1	434.53	870	0	1	434.53	870	0	8.68	46.11	805	0
MD	553	48	$(1, 1)$	0.08	$\mathcal{M}_C$	1	275.54	552	0	1	275.54	552	0	–	–	–	–
MD	871	60	$(1, 1)$	0.06	$\mathcal{M}_C$	1	434.53	870	0	1	434.53	870	0	–	–	–	–

set, the design is not a BD, but a CD $\{1562, 321, (\exists 1, \exists 1, \exists 1)\}$, that satisfies RCP for all 3 control channels.

Through $RE^{(+)}$ heuristic, the number of rendezvous has increased and ETTR was reduced in both control channels 1 and 2, incurring only a small increase of 1% in the overhead, comparing to the original BD. These result are in Table 6.

7.3 Results for Constructive Sum Heuristic

A new hybrid design HD is formed by a constructive sum of two different schedules obtained from the same BD $\{871, 30, 1\}$, since it has two disjoint control sets, that forms a new design $\{871, 60, (1, 1)\}$. This new design is then added constructively to the CD $\{871, 87, \exists 1\}$ forming an HD $\{871, 147, (1, 1, \exists 1)\}$. In Table 7, the overhead column shows for HD, that we reach 16% for 3-channel rendezvous, which is less than 1/3 of the best results for regular mappings with BDs. Table 7 also shows metrics of these designs. Still in Table 7, a design named MD was assembled from the constructive sum of two BDs $\{553, 24, 1\}$ with disjoint sets of K, and presents 8% overhead. MD $\{871, 60, (1, 1)\}$ that shares the same property of previous BD achieves 6% overhead. The three schedules shown in Table 7 were created using $\mathcal{M}_C$.

8 CONCLUSION

In this work, we have evaluated two mapping functions, two heuristics, four types of designs and about hundreds of schedules. For all BDs tested, only the indicated in Table 5, with 50% overhead, offer guaranteed rendezvous on three different channels for all offsets. New heuristics for new designs, new mapping functions and different combinations of those abstractions were proposed, and novel schedules were found to guarantee multi-channel rendezvous with 16% overhead for 3-channel rendezvous, as shown in Table 7. Our schedules achieved control overhead of 6% and 8% for 2-channel rendezvous. Those promising results encouraged us to continue in this line of research, and part of our future plans is to reduce to lower levels the control overhead for multiple rendezvous. Additionally, since the ETTR is an important metric for rendezvous efficiency, our study will also focus on finding designs that reduce it. We also plan to implement these mechanisms in SDR (Software Defined Radios), in order to compare our simulated results to real experiments.

REFERENCES

[1] Ian F. Akyildiz, Won-Yeol Lee, Mehmet C. Vuran, and Shantidev Mohanty. 2006. NeXt generation/dynamic spectrum access/cognitive radio wireless networks: A survey. *Computer Networks* 50, 13 (sep 2006), 2127–2159. https://doi.org/10.1016/j.comnet.2006.05.001

[2] Majid Altamimi, Kshirasagar Naik, and Xuemin Shen. 2010. Parallel link rendezvous in ad hoc cognitive radio networks. *GLOBECOM - IEEE Global Telecommunications Conference* (2010). https://doi.org/10.1109/GLOCOM.2010.5683741

[3] Kaigui Bian, Jung-Min Park, and Ruiliang Chen. 2009. A quorum-based framework for establishing control channels in dynamic spectrum access networks. In *Proceedings of the 15th annual international conference on Mobile computing and networking*. ACM, 25–36.

[4] Ricardo C. Carrano, Diego Passos, Luiz C. S. Magalhães, and Célio VN Albuquerque. 2013. Nested block designs: Flexible and efficient schedule-based asynchronous duty cycling. *Computer Networks* 57, 17 (2013), 3316–3326.

[5] Chih-Min Chao and Hsiang-Yuan Fu. Providing complete rendezvous guarantee for cognitive radio networks by quorum systems and latin squares. In *Wireless Communications and Networking Conference (WCNC), 2013 IEEE*. IEEE, 95–100.

[6] Yen-Wen Chen, Po-Yin Liao, and Ying-Cheng Wang. 2016. A channel-hopping scheme for continuous rendezvous and data delivery in cognitive radio network. *Peer-to-Peer Networking and Applications* 9, 1 (2016), 16–27.

[7] Sangil Choi, Wooksik Lee, Teukseob Song, and Jong-Hoon Youn. 2015. Block Design-Based Asynchronous Neighbor Discovery Protocol for Wireless Sensor Networks. *Journal of Sensors* (2015), 1–12. https://doi.org/10.1155/2015/951652

[8] Charles J. Colbourn and Jeffrey H. Dinitz. 2006. *Handbook of combinatorial designs*. CRC press.

[9] Luiz A. DaSilva and Igor Guerreiro. 2008. Sequence-based rendezvous for dynamic spectrum access. In *3rd IEEE DySPAN*. 1–7.

[10] Luiz A. DaSilva and Thomas Ryan. 2009. Rendezvous in Cognitive Radio Network. In *Cognitive Radio Technology* (2 ed.), Bruce Fette (Ed.). Elsevier, 635–644.

[11] Jeffrey H. Dinitz and Douglas R. Stinson. 1992. *Contemporary design theory: A collection of Surveys*. Vol. 26. John Wiley & Sons.

[12] Zhaoquan Gu, Qiang-Sheng Hua, Yuexuan Wang, and Francis C. M. Lau. 2013. Nearly optimal asynchronous blind rendezvous algorithm for cognitive radio networks. In *(SECON), IEEE Communications Society Conference*. 371–379.

[13] Zaw Htike, Choong Seon Hong, and Sungwon Lee. 2013. The life cycle of the rendezvous problem of cognitive radio ad hoc networks: a survey. *Journal of computing science and engineering* 7, 2 (2013), 81–88.

[14] Jehn-Ruey Jiang, Yu-Chee Tseng, Chih-Shun Hsu, and Ten-Hwang Lai. 2005. Quorum-based asynchronous power-saving protocols for IEEE 802.11 ad hoc networks. *Mobile Networks and Applications* 10, 1-2 (2005), 169–181.

[15] Brandon F. Lo. 2011. A survey of common control channel design in cognitive radio networks. *Physical Communication* 4, 1 (2011), 26–39.

[16] Michael J. Marcus, Paul Kolodzy, and Andrew Lippman. 2006. Why Unlicensed Use of Vacant TV Spectrum Will Not Interfere with Television Reception. *New America Foundation Issue Brief, July* (2006), 22–31.

[17] Sylwia Romaszko and Petri Mahonen. 2011. Quorum-based channel allocation with asymmetric channel view in cognitive radio networks. In *Proceedings of the 6th ACM workshop on Performance monitoring and measurement of heterogeneous wireless and wired networks*. ACM, 67–74.

[18] Jongmin Shin, Dongmin Yang, and Cheeha Kim. 2010. A channel rendezvous scheme for cognitive radio networks. *IEEE Communications Letters* (2010), 954.

[19] Douglas R. Stinson. 2007. *Combinatorial designs: constructions and analysis*. Springer Science & Business Media.

[20] Nick C. Theis, Ryan W. Thomas, Luiz DaSilva, et al. 2011. Rendezvous for cognitive radios. *IEEE Transactions on Mobile Computing* 10, 2 (2011), 216–227.

[21] Frank Yates. 1936. Incomplete randomized blocks. *Annals of Eugenics* 7, 2 (1936), 121–140.

Rendezvous with Utilities in Cognitive Radio Networks

Lin Xiao
Tsinghua University
Beijing, China
jackielinxiao@gmail.com

Gu Zhaoquan
Tsinghua University and the University of HongKong
HongKong, China
demin456@gmail.com

ABSTRACT

In constructing the cognitive radio networks, a fundamental process is to establish a communication link on a same channel for every two users, which is referred to as *rendezvous*. Most studies focus on minimizing the time to rendezvous after they start the process synchronously or asynchronously. However, to the best of our knowledge, no work has considered the possibility that the users may achieve different utilities when they rendezvous on different channels for communication. The utility originates from the quality of the specific channel that two users rendezvous on, and it is influenced by the channel's bandwidth, transmission rate, stability, etc. In this paper, we formally formulate the problem of maximizing rendezvous utilities and propose a novel method by extending the channels to promote the users to achieve higher rendezvous utilities. We propose channel extension algorithms for both symmetric and asymmetric rendezvous scenarios, where the users may have the same or different sets of rendezvous channels respectively. These algorithms are built on the construction of Disjoint Relaxed Difference Set (DRDS) in [5], and we show the efficiency of achieving rendezvous on the channel with high utility theoretically. Moreover, we conduct thorough simulations to evaluate our algorithms and the results also corroborate our theoretical analyses.

CCS CONCEPTS

•**Networks** → **Cognitive radios;** *Network protocol design;*

KEYWORDS

Rendezvous, Utility, Cognitive Radio Network

1 INTRODUCTION

With the proliferation of wireless network applications, spectrum resources are becoming more and more scarce. However, this scarcity has an imbalance between the licensed and unlicensed portions of the spectrum. The unlicensed spectrum is overcrowded by the rapidly growing number of wireless devices while the licensed spectrum (like TV spectrum) is relatively under-utilized[1]. To allow dynamic access of the licensed spectrum has been seen as an efficient way to share the resources and reduce the imbalance. The Cognitive Radio Networks (CRNs) hence emerge as new paradigm. There are normally two types of users in Cognitive Radio Networks: the users who own the licensed spectrum are referred to as primary users (PUs) and those who can only access licensed spectrum opportunistically are called secondary users (SUs). In the CRN, the SUs are equipped with cognitive radios to sense and access the vacant licensed spectrum that is not occupied by the PUs. This approach is promising in alleviate the spectrum scarcity problem. Unless otherwise specified, "user" in this paper refers to SU.

In the CRNs, two users need to find a common channel from the unoccupied licensed spectrum to establish a link for communication. This process is usually referred to as "rendezvous". Generally speaking, the licensed spectrum is assumed to be divided into N non-overlapping channels. The user can sense the spectrum and utilize the *available* channels that are not occupied by nearby PUs. We call it *symmetric rendezvous*[5] if the users have the same set of available channels, while it is called *asymmetric rendezvous* when the users have different sets of available channels[7, 8]. Both scenarios are considered in this paper.

Time is assumed to be divided into slots of equal length and the users can choose any available channel for a rendezvous attempt in a time slot. If two neighboring users happen to choose the same available channel in the same time slot, they rendezvous on the channel. Since the users can start the rendezvous process simultaneously or at different time slots, which are referred to as *synchronous* or *asynchronous* scenarios respectively, the proposed algorithms in the paper work for both scenarios.

Rendezvous problem has been widely studied and most of the previous studies are to minimize the time to rendezvous [4–9]. However, to the best of our knowledge, no work has ever considered the objective of achieving different levels of **utilities** when the users rendezvous on different channels. Actually, the quality of a channel can be affected by the bandwidth, transmission rate, and stability, thus rendezvous on different channels for communication may result in different utilities of communication quality. In this paper, we initiate the study of maximizing rendezvous utility for achieving better communication quality. In handling the maximizing rendezvous utility problem, we face the following challenges:

MSWiM'17, November 21-25, 2017, Miami, FL, USA
© 2017 ACM. ISBN 978-1-4503-5162-1/17/11...$15.00
DOI: http://dx.doi.org/10.1145/3127540.3127546

1) To begin with, the channel with high utility may not be available for a specific user and the channel utility information has to be utilized in a smart way;
2) Second, the users may have asymmetric sets of available channels, they have to choose from all these available channels during the attempts such that two users can always rendezvous if they share some common ones;
3) Finally, the users may start the algorithms at different time slots, how to tackle the asynchronous start-up is also a vital problem.

In this paper, our proposed algorithm addresses all these issues. Concretely, we adopt the Disjoint Relaxed Different Set (DRDS) method[5] as a cornerstone to achieve higher rendezvous utilities. A DRDS consists of multiple Relaxed Difference Sets (RDS), where each RDS corresponds to a specific channel and the elements in the RDS are the time slots when the user accesses the channel (cf. section 4.1 for details). The intuitive idea of our algorithm is to extend the channels into multiple virtual channels according to their utility values, and then adopt the DRDS method for rendezvous. The channels with higher utilities can be shown to have more opportunities to engage in rendezvous.

The contributions of this paper are threefold:

1) First, we initiate the study of rendezvous utility, and formulate the maximizing rendezvous utilities problem. We believe that this problem depicts the real network scenarios more precisely where the users can achieve different qualities when they rendezvous on different channels;
2) Second, we design efficient channel extension algorithms that build upon the DRDS construction. We present the detailed theoretical analyses for the symmetric rendezvous scenarios, no matter the users are synchronous or asynchronous; For the asymmetric scenario, we present a modified channel extension algorithm. The performance in asymmetric scenario is difficult to analyze since one users channel of high utility may not be available for the other user. Therefore empirical analyses are provided for the algorithm in the asymmetric scenario.
3) Third, we conduct extensive simulations on different kinds of rendezvous scenarios and the results also corroborate our analyses.

The rest of the paper is organized as follows. The next section presents some important related studies on the rendezvous problem. We introduce the system model and problem formulation in Section 3. We propose a channel extension rendezvous algorithm and detailed analyses for the symmetric scenario in Section 4. In Section 5, the algorithm is adapted to solve the problem in asymmetric rendezvous scenarios. We provide the simulation results in Section 6 and conclude the paper in Section 7.

2 RELATED WORK

Most distributed rendezvous algorithms can be categorized into two types: global sequence (GS) based algorithm [2, 5, 7, 8] and local sequence (LS) based algorithm [4, 6, 11, 12]. GS based algorithms construct a hopping sequence on the basis of all N (global) channels, and users accessing channels by the sequence can rendezvous on every (commonly available) channel no matter when they start the process. For example, Jump Stay (JS) algorithm is proposed in [8] where a sequence of length $O(N^3)$ is constructed from two types of patterns: *jump pattern* and *stay pattern*. An Enhanced JS method is proposed in [7] which reduces the sequence length to $O(N^2)$. LS based algorithms construct hopping sequences on the basis of local available channels, and rendezvous is also guaranteed. In [4], a sequence of length $O(|C_A|^2)$ is constructed where C_A represents user A's available channel set. However, this method utilizes user's identifier to construct the sequence. A special construction of length $O(|C_A|^2 \log\log N)$ time slots is proposed in [6], where edge coloring and moving pointer methods are adopted. Generally speaking, the GS based algorithms have a better performance when the number of available channels is large. The LS based algorithms have shorter time to rendezvous when the number of available channels is small.

In this paper, we build the algorithm on the Disjoint Relaxed Different Set (DRDS) method, a type of GS based algorithm, which divides time slots into disjoint sets and each set is a relaxed difference set (RDS). It has been proven that a DRDS corresponds to a global sequence (GS) that guarantees the users can rendezvous on every channel asynchronously[5]. However, there is not a unified approach to generate the DRDS for arbitrary number of time slots and the optimal construction of such GS remains open. In [5], a DRDS is generated for $3P^2$ slots where P is the smallest prime number larger than N. Another approach constructing a DRDS for $(2P + \lfloor \frac{P}{2} \rfloor)P$ time slots is introduced in [13].

3 SYSTEM MODEL AND PROBLEM FORMULATION

We consider a CRN where the secondary users coexist with the primary users (PUs). Assume the licensed spectrum is divided into N non-overlapping channels as $C = \{1, 2, ..., N\}$. The users are equipped with cognitive radios to sense the channels and we call a channel *available* to a particular user if it is not occupied by any nearby PUs. Denote the channels that are available for user i as $C_i \subseteq C$. Time is assumed to be divided into slots of equal length $2t$ where $t = 10ms$ is sufficient to establish a communication link [10]. The user can choose any available channel for a rendezvous attempt in a time slot. Considering two neighboring users A, B with available channel sets $C_A \bigcap C_B \neq \emptyset$, they achieve **rendezvous** only if they both access a same channel in the same time slot. Since different channels have different utilities if they are utilized for communication, we denote the utility of channel $i \in [1, N]$ as R_i. In traditional rendezvous problems, all channels are assumed to have the same utility and we are to design efficient algorithms for more general situations to achieve high utilities for rendezvous. In this paper, we mainly focus on the rendezvous between two users.

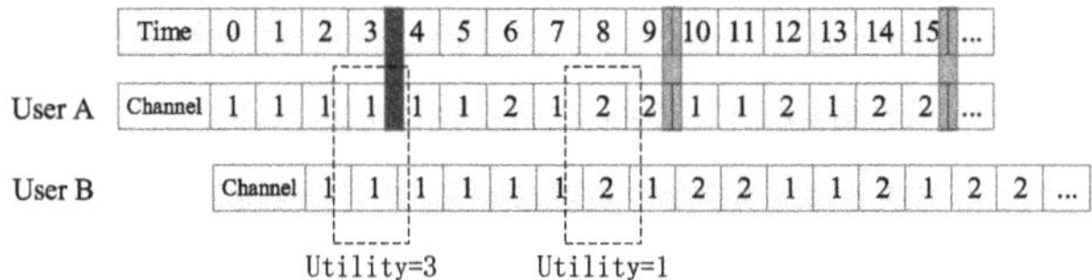

Figure 1: An Example of Rendezvous with Utilities on Different Channels

Considering the example in Fig. 1, suppose the utilities of channel 1 and 2 are $R_1 = 3$ and $R_2 = 1$ respectively, and two users choose the channels by the designed sequence. At time slot $t = 3$, two users can rendezvous on channel 1 to get an utility of 3, but the utility is only 1 at time $t = 8$ when they both access channel 2. In this paper, we are to design rendezvous algorithms such that the users can achieve a high utility when they rendezvous. Denote the rendezvous algorithm as f, and we introduce a new metric to evaluate the algorithm.

Definition 3.1. **Rendezvous Utility at time t** is the utility achieved by two users at time slot t during the rendezvous process. Denote the channels user A, B access at t are CH_A^t, CH_B^t respectively, the rendezvous utility on channel i of algorithm f at time t is defined as:

$$R_f(i,t) = I_{i,t} \cdot R_i = \begin{cases} R_i & ,if\ CH_A^t = CH_B^t = i \\ 0 & ,otherwise \end{cases} \quad (1)$$

where $I_{i,t}$ is an indicator variable that depicts whether users A and B achieve rendezvous on channel i at time t.

For a given period T of the chosen channel sequence by algorithm f, the users can rendezvous on a channel in multiple time slots. We define:

Definition 3.2. **Rendezvous Utility (RU) on channel i in the period of length T** is the average of achieved utilities over length T when they rendezvous on channel i in the period:

$$R_f(i,T) = \frac{1}{T}\sum_{t=1}^{t=T} R_f(i,t) = \frac{TR_i(T) \times R_i}{T} \quad (2)$$

where $TR_i(T)$ denotes how many times of rendezvous happen on channel i during period T.

For any algorithm f, denote $MTTR_f$ as the maximum time to rendezvous for any two neighboring users (this implies they are guaranteed to rendezvous within $MTTR_f$ time slots). Therefore, we choose $T = MTTR_f$ to evaluate the rendezvous utility $R_f(i,T)$. For the remainder of the paper, we denote $Rf(i, MTTR_f)$ as $R_f(i)$ for short. We define the rendezvous utility of algorithm f as:

Definition 3.3. **Rendezvous Utility of algorithm f** is the sum of rendezvous utilities on all channels:

$$R_f = \sum_{i \in C} R_f(i). \quad (3)$$

In this paper, we aim to design efficient algorithms such that the users are guaranteed to rendezvous and they could achieve high rendezvous utility. We formally formulate the problem as follows:

Problem: Given a channel set $C_i \subseteq C$, design a channel hopping strategy f such that for any two users A and B running the same algorithm f with available channels $C_A, C_B \subseteq C$, $C_A \bigcap C_B \neq \emptyset$, the rendezvous is guaranteed and overall rendezvous utility R_f is maximized.

4 RENDEZVOUS UTILITY FOR SYMMETRIC SCENARIO

In this section, we formally introduce our algorithm for Rendezvous with Utilities.

4.1 Rendezvous with DRDS Construction

To begin with, we introduce the Disjoint Relaxed Difference Set (DRDS) construction for rendezvous. It has been shown that a DRDS corresponds to a good channel chosen sequence that guarantees rendezvous for any asynchronous users[5]. Our algorithm uses DRDS as the cornerstone, and we introduce the process of the DRDS construction.

The intuition of DRDS algorithm is to generate a collection of disjoint sets where each set is a Relaxed Difference Set (RDS) that corresponds to a channel. In addition, the elements in the RDS represent the time slots to access the channel for the user.

Definition 4.1. A set $D = \{a_1, a_2, \cdots, a_k\} \subseteq Z_n$ (the set of all nonnegative integers less than n) is called a Relaxed Difference Set (**RDS**) if for every $d \neq 0 \pmod n$, there exists at least one ordered pair (a_i, a_j) such that $a_i - a_j \equiv d \pmod n$, where $a_i, a_j \in D$.

In a RDS, the differences of any two elements inside the set could cover any value in $(0, n)$, where n is the length of the constructed sequence, and the difference values correspond to different asynchronous situations. For example, $\{1, 2, 4\}$ is a RDS under Z_7: the differences of 1 and 2 correspond to 1 (i.e. $2 - 1$) and 6 (i.e. $1 - 2 \mod 7$); the differences of 1 and 4 correspond to 3 ($i.e. 4 - 1$) and 4 (i.e. $1 - 4 \mod 7$); the differences of 2 and 4 correspond to 2 (i.e. $4 - 2$) and 5 (i.e. $2 - 4 \mod 7$). Therefore, the difference values of the set cover all integers from 1 to 6 (0 is omitted since it refers to the synchronous situation). We rewrite the DRDS construction of [5] as follows:

When $n = 3P^2$, divide Z_n into P disjoint subsets $Z_n = U_0 \bigcup U_1 \bigcup \cdots \bigcup U_{P-1}$, where $U_j = Z_{3P(j+1)} \setminus Z_{3P \cdot j}$. Let $D_i = T_{i0} \bigcup T_{i1} \bigcup \cdots \bigcup T_{i,P-1}$ where $T_{ij} \subseteq U_j$. For each U_j, let $q_j = j^2$ and $p_{ij} = \frac{(i-q_j)(P+1)}{2} \mod P$. Choose the $(P + p_{ij})$-th and $(2P + p_{ij})$-th number of U_j to compose T_{ij}. They are $t_{j0} = 3Pj + P + p_{ij}, t_{j1} = 3Pj + 2P + p_{ij}$. Then T_{ij} is constructed:

After the DRDS is generated, each user chooses the channel for rendezvous attempt on the basis of each RDS in the set: in each time slot, the user finds out the RDS it belongs to and chooses the channel correspondingly. For example, if

$RDS_1 = \{0, 1, 2, 3, 6, 13, 16, 22, 25\}$, at time slots $t = 3$ and $t = 6$, the user chooses channel 1. Judging from the construction, the sequence consists of P frames and each frame has a length of $3P$ slots. In each frame, the user stays on a fixed channel for the first P slots and hops on the channels for the remaining $2P$ slots. Notice that, the subsequences in the second and third P slots are the same. For each frame, the first P time slots are referred to as the **static segment** and the remaining two copies of P time slots are referred to as the **dynamic segments**.

4.2 Channel Extension based Rendezvous Algorithm

When we consider the symmetric scenario where both users have the same set of available channels, an important fact is that they may start the rendezvous process at any time (i.e. they are synchronous or asynchronous). We propose the Channel Extension based Rendezvous Algorithm (CERA) to enlarge the rendezvous utility. The intuitive idea is: a channel with higher utility is extended to more virtual channels so that two users may rendezvous on the high-utility channel with more chances.

Algorithm 1 Channel Extension based Rendezvous Algorithm

Input: The set of available channels C_A, and the utility for all available channels: $R_A = \{R_i, \forall i \in C_A\}$.
Output: The channel chosen sequence S.

```
Denote the virtual channel set as VC. Initially, VC = ∅
for each channel i ∈ C_A do
    Extend channel i into E_i virtual channels :VC_i^j ∈ VC_i, j ∈ {1, 2, ..., E_i};
    VC = VC ∪ VC_i;
end for
Design RDS for each VC_i^j ∈ VC_i (denoted as RDS_i^j) with the introduced DRDS construction;
for each channel i ∈ C_A do
    RDS_i = ∅;
    for each virtual channel VC_i^j ∈ VC_i, j > 0 do
        RDS_i = RDS_i^j ∪ RDS_i, ∀VC_i^j ∈ VC_i;
    end for
end for
Construct the channel chosen sequence S based on DRDS = {RDS_i, ∀i ∈ C_A};
```

As described in Alg. 1, we first extend each channel i to E_i virtual channels (E_i is a function of R_i that can be chosen from different powers of R_i). Then we design a RDS for each virtual channel and merge these RDSes of the virtual channels to the original ones correspondingly. Finally, the users can choose the channels based on the generated RDS.

We use an example to illustrate the construction of our algorithm. Consider two users A and B running Alg. 1, suppose there are two channels $C = \{1, 2\}$ with different utilities $R_1 = 2$ and $R_2 = 1$. We define $E_i = R_i$, channel 1 is extended to $R_1 = 2$ virtual channels, while there is only $R_2 = 1$ virtual channel for the other channel. Then, we construct the DRDS with 3 virtual channels and merge the RDS of virtual channel 1 together. Then, the sequence is generated. Three RDS for the virtual channels are generated as:

$$RDS(VC_1^1) = \{0, 1, 2, 3, 6, 13, 16, 22, 25\};$$
$$RDS(VC_1^2) = \{5, 8, 9, 10, 11, 12, 15, 21, 24\};$$
$$RDS(VC_2) = \{4, 7, 14, 17, 18, 19, 20, 23, 26\}.$$

where $RDS(VC_i^j)$ represents the constructed RDS for the j-th virtual channel of channel i. The merged sets are:

$$RDS_1 = \{0, 1, 2, 3, 6, 13, 16, 22, 25, 5, 8, 9, 10, 11, 12, 15, 21, 24\};$$
$$RDS_2 = \{4, 7, 14, 17, 18, 19, 20, 23, 26\}.$$

Then the users can choose the channel according to the generated DRDS$=\{RDS_1, RDS_2\}$ as shown in Fig. 2, where channel 1 is extended into 2 virtual channels $\{1, 2\}$ and channel 2 is considered as virtual channel 3 in constructing the sequence for the extended scheme. Then, the time slots corresponding to channels 1 and 2 are merged into a single RDS for choosing the channel. Those slots in the black shadow form the static segment while the slots in the blue shadow form the dynamic segment. When $t = 0$, user A chooses channel 1; when $t = 4$, user A chooses channel 2. Notice that, the virtual channel 2 is actually a copy of channel 1, and both users can actually access channel 1 in more time slots during a period.

4.3 Performance Analysis

Suppose one user is δ slots later than the other, since the users access the channel according to the sequence of length T periodically, where T is the length of the constructed sequence, we assume $\delta \in [0, T)$. Denote $\hat{N} = \sum_{i \in [1,N]} E_i$ as the number of extended virtual channels, and P as the smallest prime number no less than $\hat{N}$. The sequence length is thus $T = 3P^2$ according to the construction. We derive the correctness of guaranteeing rendezvous during T time slots and derive the rendezvous utility on the basis of the number of rendezvous on each channel i.

Rewrite $\delta = \theta \times P + \varepsilon, 0 \le \theta < 3P, 0 \le \varepsilon \le 3P$, we compute the times of rendezvous on each channel i in the period of T time slots for different situations.

From the algorithm, channel i has been extended E_i times.

LEMMA 4.2. *When $0 \le \delta < P$, the times of rendezvous on channel i (denoted as $TR_i^1(T)$) follows: $P - \delta \le TR_i^1(T) \le P - \delta + \min\{E_i, \delta\}$.*

PROOF. When $0 \le \delta < P$, we know that $\theta = 0, 1 \le \varepsilon = \delta < P$. There are two kinds of situations that two users might rendezvous:

a) Two users rendezvous in static-static phase, i.e. both users access the channels in the static segment, since they choose the same channel i. The times of rendezvous in this phase are $P - \delta$;

b) Two users might rendezvous on the dynamic-static phase or on the static-dynamic phase, i.e. one user accesses

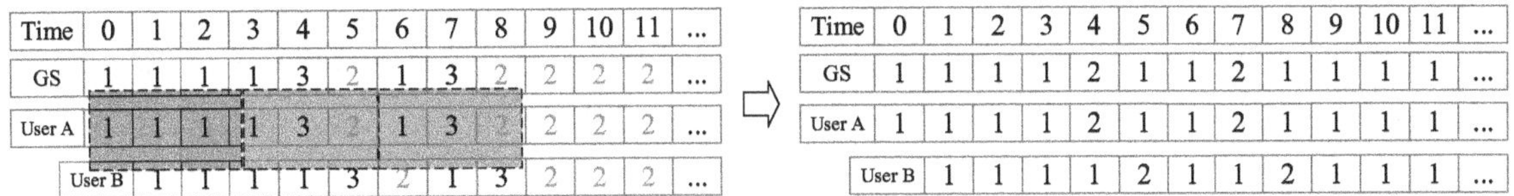

Figure 2: Example of Alg. 1

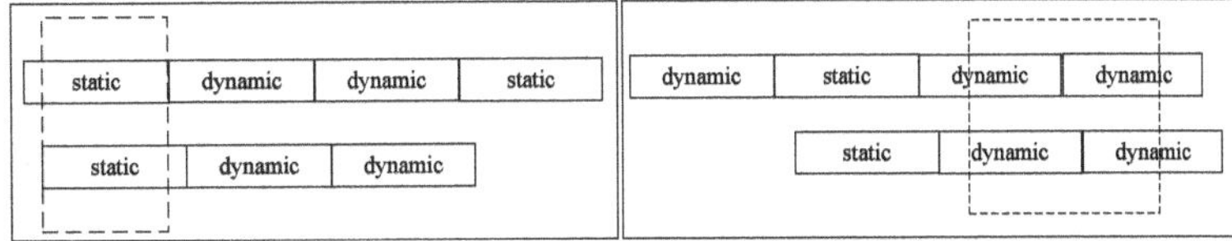

Figure 3: Illustrations for Analysis, Scenario One (Left) and Scenario Two (Right)

channels in the static segment, while the other accesses channels in the dynamic segment. However, rendezvous cannot be guaranteed for sure. If they can achieve rendezvous luckily, the times for rendezvous should be at most $\min\{E_i, \delta\}$ (since there are at most E_i copies of channel i in the intersection part of the dynamic segment, and the overlapping part contains at most δ time slots).

Combining these, we can derive the lower and upper bounds for the times of rendezvous when $0 \le \delta < P$ (denoted as $TR_i^1(T)$):

$$P - \delta \le TR_i^1(T) \le P - \delta + \min\{E_i, \delta\}. \tag{4}$$

Therefore, the lemma holds. □

LEMMA 4.3. *When $P \le \delta$ and $0 \le \delta(\bmod 3P) \le P$, the times of rendezvous on channel i (denoted as $TR_i^2(T)$) follows: $E_i \le TR_i^2(T) \le E_i + \min\{E_i, \delta \bmod P\}$.*

PROOF. When $P \le \delta$ and $0 \le \delta(\bmod 3P) \le P$, there are two kinds of situations that two users might rendezvous:

a) Two users rendezvous in the dynamic-dynamic phase, i.e. both users access channels in the dynamic segment. Suppose two users access channel i_a and i_b at time $t + \delta = 3P\theta_a + \varepsilon_a$ and $t = 3P\theta_b + \varepsilon_b$, where $P \le \varepsilon_b < 2P$. We can derive:

$$3P\theta_a + \varepsilon_a \equiv 3P(\theta + \theta_b) + \varepsilon + \varepsilon_b \bmod 3P^2$$

and $P \le \varepsilon_a < 3P$. Then,

$$\begin{cases} \theta_a \equiv (\theta + \theta_b) \bmod P \\ \dfrac{(i_a - \theta_a^2)(P+1)}{2} \equiv \dfrac{(i_b - \theta_b^2)(P+1)}{2} + \varepsilon \bmod P \end{cases}$$

For any given δ, θ and ε are fixed constants, thus:

$$(i_a - i_b) - 2\varepsilon - \theta^2 \equiv 2\theta \cdot \theta_b \bmod P.$$

When two users rendezvous, $i_a, i_b \in VC_i$, i.e. they are the extension of a specific channel. The equation has a unique solution based on [3]. Therefore, this leads to E_i times of rendezvous.

b) Two users might rendezvous in two dynamic-static phases, but it is not guaranteed for sure. Similar as the second situation of Lemma 1, the maximum times of rendezvous is $\min\{E_i, \delta \bmod P\}$.

Combining these, we can derive the lower and upper bounds for the times of rendezvous on channel i when $P \le \delta$ and $0 \le \delta(\bmod 3P) \le P$ (denoted as $TR_i^2(T)$):

$$E_i \le TR_i^2(T) \le E_i + \min\{E_i, \delta \bmod P\}. \tag{5}$$

Therefore, the lemma holds. □

LEMMA 4.4. *When $P \le \delta$ and $P \le \delta(\bmod 3P) \le 2P$, the times of rendezvous on channel i (denoted as TR_i^3) follows: $2E_i \le TR_i^3(T) \le 2E_i + \min\{E_i, \delta \bmod P\}$.*

LEMMA 4.5. *When $P \le \delta$ and $2P \le \delta(\bmod 3P) \le 3P$, the times of rendezvous on channel i (denoted as TR_i^4) follows: $E_i \le TR_i^4(T) \le E_i + \min\{E_i, \delta \bmod P\}\}$.*

Due to page limits, we leave the proofs of lemma 4.4 and lemma 4.5 in the appendix.

THEOREM 4.6. *The times of rendezvous of users A and B on a specific channel $i \in C_A \cap C_B$ in T are $TR_i(T) = \Theta(E_i^2)$.*

PROOF. Consider that the δ value follows an uniform distribution on interval $[0, T)$. Combining the four lemmas above, for any given δ, the lower bound for rendezvous times on channel i is E_i. Since the channels are extended with E_i times, the overall times of rendezvous are $E_i \times E_i = E_i^2$. □

On the basis of Theorem 1, we compare the achieved utility in a period of T time slots with the method that we simply adopt the DRDS construction for rendezvous, i.e. no channel extension is conducted. The length of the constructed sequence is $t = 3P'^2$ where P' is the smallest prime number no less than N. The rendezvous utility in $T = 3P'^2$ for channel extension is:

$$R_E = \Theta\left(\frac{\sum_{i\in[1,N]} E_i^2 R_i}{3(\sum_{i\in[1,N]} E_i)^2}\right) \tag{6}$$

By plugging in $E_i = 1, \forall i \in [1, N]$, the rendezvous utility of the no channel extension algorithm is:

$$R_O = \Theta\left(\frac{\sum_{i\in[1,N]} R_i}{3N^2}\right) \tag{7}$$

When E_i is a polynomial function of R_i, such as a simple situation: $E_i = cR_i$ (utility-proportional scheme where c is a constant). We have:

$$R_E = \frac{\sum_{i\in[1,N]} c^2 R_i^3}{3(\sum_{i\in[1,N]} cR_i)^2} = \frac{\sum_{i\in[1,N]} R_i^3}{3(\sum_{i\in[1,N]} R_i)^2}. \tag{8}$$

5 RENDEZVOUS UTILITY FOR ASYMMETRIC SCENARIO

Considering the asymmetric situation where the users have different sets of available channels, one user's channel of high utility may not be available for the other user. Therefore, we need elaborate efforts to modify the channel extension based rendezvous algorithm for symmetric scenario. In this section, we present the modifications and the basic idea is to split the constructed RDS of the unavailable channels into the RDS of the other available channels.

Algorithm 2 Modified Channel Extension based Rendezvous Algorithm

Input: The set of all channels C, The set of available channels C_A, and the utility of all available channels: $R_A = \{R_i, \forall i \in C_A\}$.

Output: The channel chosen Sequence: S.

Run the Channel Extension based Rendezvous Algorithm (Alg. 1) for all channels in C and get the RDS of all virtual channels $VC_i, \forall i \in C$: RDS_i^j and $\forall j \in \{1, 2, ..., R_i\}$;
Denote the virtual channels to assign as $\widetilde{VC} = \{\}$;
for $i \in C \setminus C_A$: **do**
  Merge the virtual channels to $\widetilde{VC} = \widetilde{VC} \cup VC_i$
end for
for $VC_i \in \widetilde{VC}$: **do**
  Assign virtual channel VC_i to $j \in C_A$ randomly: $RDS_j = RDS_j \cup RDS(VC_i)$;
end for
Construct the channel sequence S according to the RDSes of $i \in C_A$;

Since two users do not have prior knowledge about each other's available channels, we still extend all channels according to the rendezvous utility of each channel. Then, the time slots of unaccessible channels will be split to the available channels randomly. The Modified Channel Extension based Rendezvous Algorithm (MCERA) is described in Alg. 2. It first extends channels into virtual channels and uses DRDS construction to get the RDSes of all virtual channels. Then it merges virtual channels of unavailable channels to a set and randomly assigns them to the available channels, including the virtual extensions of them.

One simple idea is to assign the RDS of unavailable virtual channels to available ones as symmetric rendezvous. However, since the available channels of two users can be different, the available channels of two users may have different RDSes, which may not necessarily increase the times of rendezvous on high-utility channels. In this paper, we conduct thorough simulations to show the efficiency of our algorithm and the results will be presented in Section 6.

Table 1: Rendezvous Utilities for Symmetric Scenarios (Integer Utilities)

#common channels	DRDS	CERA($R^{0.5}$)	CERA(R^1)	CERA(R^2)
0.2N	0.6679	0.8407	1.0000	1.4086
0.4N	0.3413	0.4314	0.5000	0.7388
0.6N	0.1963	0.2305	0.2288	0.2685
0.8N	0.1997	0.2514	0.2691	0.3589

Table 2: Rendezvous Utilities in Symmetric Local Settings (Fractional Utilities)

#common channels	DRDS	CERA($R^{0.5}$)	CERA(R^1)	CERA(R^2)
0.2N	0.6286	0.6278	0.7442	1.1641
0.4N	0.3196	0.3075	0.3399	0.4011
0.6N	0.2194	0.2213	0.2487	0.3137
0.8N	0.1850	0.1832	0.1981	0.2277

6 SIMULATION RESULTS

We conduct extensive simulations for both symmetric and asymmetric rendezvous scenarios and use DRDS algorithm [5] (the state-of-art rendezvous algorithm) without channel extension as a baseline for comparison. We assume that the utility of each channel is chosen from $[1, 5]$ randomly. In the simulations, two users start the rendezvous process at randomly generated time slots in the simulation and we provide average performances here.

6.1 Utility for Symmetric Scenario

We conduct simulations on different portions of common channels in both symmetric and asymmetric settings. For each setting, we choose three different ways to extend the channels, including $R_i^{0.5}$, R_i and R_i^2 (DRDS can be seen as a special case of CERA where each channel is extended equally). We consider the cases when users have different fractions of common channels ranging from $0.2N$ to $0.8N$ with step of $0.2N$. We list the results of rendezvous utilities when two users have different numbers of common channels in different scenarios in Table 1. The increase of common channels may lead to higher chances that unavailable channels are mapped to the available channels. Meanwhile, more common channels also make it more difficult to rendezvous on the same specific channel. Therefore, the utilities gaining from the algorithm can be fluctuating when the number of common channels is increasing. For the asymmetric scenario, both MCERA and DRDS algorithms map the unavailable channels to available ones, the chances of rendezvous on common channels may decrease when the number of common channels is increasing. The results indicate that MCERA still leads to superior rendezvous utilities in asymmetric scenarios.

Moreover, we present times of rendezvous when common channels are $0.6N$ in Fig 4. The number of all channels (N) is set to 15 and 20 for symmetric and asymmetric settings. The channels with zero times of rendezvous are not common channels for the two users and clearly users tend to rendezvous more frequently on high-utility channels.

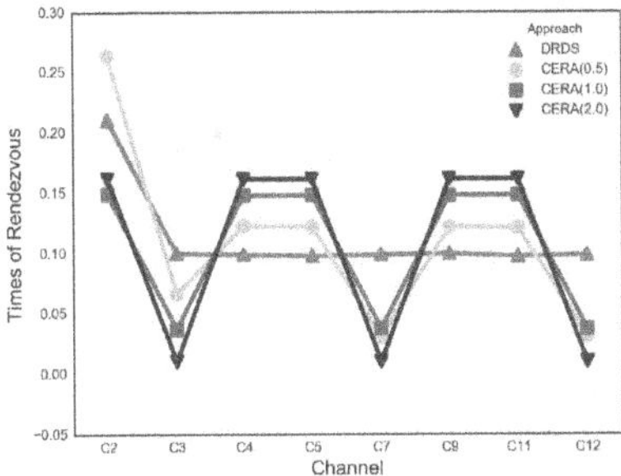

Figure 4: Times of Rendezvous for the Symmetric scenario: $C_A = C_B \subset C$; The common channels of A and B and the utilities of these channels are $\{C_2 : 3, C_3 : 1, C_4 : 3, C_5 : 3, C_7 : 1, C_9 : 3, C_{11} : 3, C_{12} : 1\}$

As shown in the experiment, the results indicate that fewer common channels increases the chances of rendezvous and the utility of rendezvous is therefore increased. This is due to the setting that two users have same set of channels to access and more common channels may cause mismatching of the hopping channels at same time slots.

6.1.1 Impact of extension methods. We further conduct experiments on the symmetric channels with different ways of channel extension. Since our algorithm first extends the global channels and assigns the unavailable channels to those available channels later, the available channels are still assigned with time slots proportionally with the channels' utilities. The results of utilities and times of rendezvous both support the fact that higher utility-power channel extension leads to more chances of rendezvous on the high-utility channels, thus leading to higher utilities of rendezvous.

6.2 Utility for Asymmetric Scenario

In the asymmetric scenario, users have different sets of available channels. This causes more difficulties: first, users are not aware of the common channels they have and can not run the algorithm based on the common channels; second, users do not have access to global channels and have to find ways to adapt the algorithm to the locally available channels. In this scenario, we conduct experiments with different portions of common channels and extend the channels with different ways. We present the results of the experiment and display the impacts of common channels and channel extension methods here. The number of global channels N is set to 20.

6.2.1 Impact of common channels. We alter the common channels from 0.2 of global channels to 0.8 of global channels with a stepsize of portion 0.2. The results of utility are presented in Table 3 and the results of times of rendezvous are presented in Fig 5. It can be seen that the algorithm achieves relative low utility when the number of common channels is only 0.2N. The utilities are relatively higher when the common channels are greater. However, the increase is not monotone. The increase of common channels may lead to higher chances that unavailable channels are mapped to the available channels. Meanwhile, more common channels also make it more difficult to rendezvous on the same specific channel. Therefore, the utilities gaining from the algorithm are not increasing continually but fluctuating when the number of common channels is increasing.

Table 3: Rendezvous Utilities in Asymmetric Local Settings (Integer Utilities)

#common channels	DRDS	MCERA($R^{0.5}$)	MCERA(R^1)	MCERA(R^2)
0.2N	0.1576	0.1927	0.2187	0.2978
0.4N	0.1210	0.1637	0.1929	0.2437
0.6N	0.1154	0.1370	0.1684	0.2168
0.8N	0.1025	0.1233	0.1384	0.1910

Table 4: Rendezvous Utilities in Asymmetric Local Settings (Fractional Utilities)

#common channels	DRDS	MCERA($R^{0.5}$)	MCERA(R^1)	MCERA(R^2)
0.2N	0.1300	0.1275	0.1444	0.2031
0.4N	0.0975	0.1033	0.1120	0.1675
0.6N	0.1157	0.1144	0.1298	0.1674
0.8N	0.1261	0.1191	0.1456	0.1702

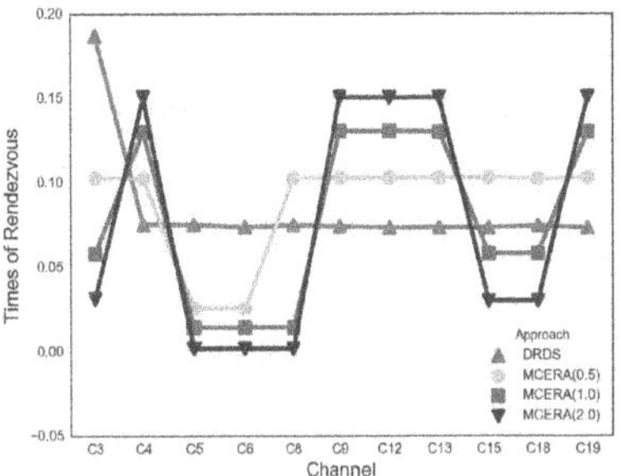

Figure 5: Times of Rendezvous for the Asymmetric scenario: $C_A \neq C_B \subset C$; The common channels of A and B and the utilities of these channels are $\{C_3 : 3, C_4 : 5, C_5 : 1, C_6 : 1, C_8 : 1, C_9 : 5, C_{12} : 5, C_{13} : 5, C_{15} : 3, C_{18} : 3, C_{19} : 5\}$

6.2.2 Impact of extension methods. As the extension of channels can impact the performances of our algorithm, we try to evaluate the impact in the both settings here. It is not difficult to see from the results that the algorithm can achieve better utilities when the channel extension methods choose to extend higher-utility channels to more virtual channels.

The results illustrate that our algorithm is effective since the channel extension method increases the utilities in an significant extent. Moreover, the algorithm provides a good intuition for increasing the utility of rendezvous: extend the

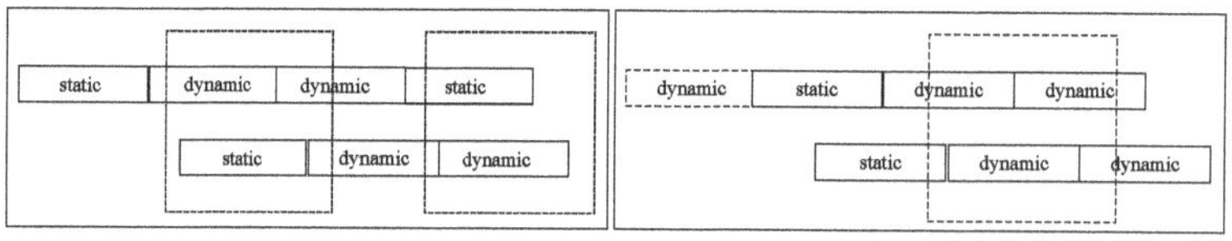

Figure 6: Illustrations for Analysis, Scenario Three (Left) and Scenario Four (Right)

channels with higher utilities locally, even when the accessible channels are not symmetric, the method can still improve the utilities compared to existing methods.

7 CONCLUSION

In this paper, we initiate the study of maximizing rendezvous utility. For each channel in the commonly available channels of two users, both of them can achieve a corresponding utility of rendezvous. The utility is channel-related and the properties of channels like bandwidth, transmission rate, the stability may affect the utility that both users can achieve when they rendezvous on them. We design a channel extension algorithm for the problem and use the DRDS (Disjoint Relaxed Difference Sets) as a cornerstone to build our algorithm. In our algorithm, the channels with higher utilities are extended into more virtual channels and more Disjoint Relaxed Difference Sets are constructed. Therefore, the algorithm guarantees that users can rendezvous on high-utility channels more frequently in a period and thus achieve higher utilities. We conduct extensive simulations in different scenarios, the results support our analysis well and we believe the method can be extended into other scenarios.

REFERENCES

[1] Ian F Akyildiz, Won-Yeol Lee, Mehmet C Vuran, and Shantidev Mohanty. 2006. NeXt generation/dynamic spectrum access/cognitive radio wireless networks: A survey. *Computer networks* (2006).
[2] Guey-Yun Chang and Jen-Feng Huang. 2013. A fast rendezvous channel-hopping algorithm for cognitive radio networks. *IEEE Communications Letters* (2013).
[3] Charles J Colbourn and Jeffrey H Dinitz. 2006. *Handbook of combinatorial designs*. CRC press.
[4] Zhaoquan Gu, Qiang-Sheng Hua, and Weiguo Dai. 2014. Fully distributed algorithms for blind rendezvous in cognitive radio networks. In *MobiHoc*.
[5] Zhaoquan Gu, Qiang-Sheng Hua, Yuexuan Wang, and Francis CM Lau. 2013. Nearly optimal asynchronous blind rendezvous algorithm for cognitive radio networks. In *SECON*.
[6] Zhaoquan Gu, Haosen Pu, Qiang-Sheng Hua, and Francis C M Lau. 2015. Improved rendezvous algorithms for heterogeneous cognitive radio networks. In *INFOCOM*.
[7] Zhiyong Lin, Hai Liu, Xiaowen Chu, and Yiu-Wing Leung. 2013. Enhanced jump-stay rendezvous algorithm for cognitive radio networks. *IEEE Communications Letters* (2013).
[8] Hai Liu, Zhiyong Lin, Xiaowen Chu, and Yiu-Wing Leung. 2012. Jump-stay rendezvous algorithm for cognitive radio networks. *IEEE Transactions on Parallel and Distributed Systems* (2012).
[9] Barbeau Michel, Cervera Gimer, Garcia-Alfaro Joaquin, and Kranakis Evangelos. 2014. A new analysis of the cognitive radio jump-stay algorithm under the asymmetric model. In *ICC*.
[10] Vitalio Alfonso Reguera, Erik Ortiz Guerra, Richard Demo Souza, Evelio MG Fernandez, and Glauber Brante. 2014. Short channel hopping sequence approach to rendezvous for cognitive networks. *IEEE Communications Letters* (2014).
[11] Ching-Chan Wu and Shan-Hung Wu. 2013. On bridging the gap between homogeneous and heterogeneous rendezvous schemes for cognitive radios. In *MobiHoc*.
[12] Shan-Hung Wu, Ching-Chan Wu, Wing-Kai Hon, and Kang G Shin. 2014. Rendezvous for heterogeneous spectrum-agile devices. In *INFOCOM*.
[13] Bo Yang, Meng Zheng, and Wei Liang. 2016. A time-efficient rendezvous algorithm with a full rendezvous degree for heterogeneous cognitive radio networks. In *INFOCOM*.

A PROOFS FOR LEMMA 4.4 AND LEMMA 4.5

Lemma 4.4: When $P \leq \delta$ and $P \leq \delta(\bmod 3P) \leq 2P$, the times of rendezvous on channel i (denoted as TR_i^3) follows: $2E_i \leq TR_i^3(T) \leq 2E_i + \min\{E_i, \delta \bmod P\}$

PROOF. The details can be reflected in Fig. 6. When $P \leq \delta$ and $P \leq \delta(\bmod 3P) \leq 2P$: There are two kinds of situations that two users might rendezvous:

3a) Two users might rendezvous in dynamic-dynamic phase, however it is not guaranteed. The maximum of times of rendezvous are $\min\{E_i, \delta \bmod P\}$;

3b) Two users can rendezvous in two dynamic-static phases, where one user stays on channel i for the static segment, and the other user is hopping along a full permutation of all the channels. There must exist one pair of channels (i, i) that appears between two sequences. Therefore, the maximum of times of rendezvous on channel i are $2E_i$.

Therefore we can derive the lower and upper bounds for the times of rendezvous for Scenario Three (denoted as $TR_i^3(T)$):

$$2E_i \leq TR_i^3(T) \leq 2E_i + \min\{E_i, \delta \bmod P\} \tag{9}$$

. □

Lemma 4.5: When $P \leq \delta$ and $2P \leq \delta(\bmod 3P) \leq 3P$, the times of rendezvous on channel i follows: $E_i \leq TR_i^4(T) \leq E_i + \min\{E_i, \delta \bmod P\}\}$

PROOF. The details can be reflected in Fig. 6. When $P \leq \delta$ and $2P \leq \delta(\bmod 3P) \leq 3P$, this case is quite similar to the second case where $P \leq \delta$ and $0 \leq \delta(\bmod 3P) \leq P$. There is only one situation that two users are guaranteed to rendezvous.

Two users can rendezvous in dynamic-dynamic phase. Similar to the second scenario, we can derive the lower and upper bounds for the times of rendezvous for Scenario Four (denoted as $TR_i^4(T)$):

$$E_i \leq TR_i^4(T) \leq E_i + \min\{E_i, \delta \bmod P\}\} \tag{10}$$

. □

Improving BLE Distance Estimation and Classification Using TX Power and Machine Learning: A Comparative Analysis

Mimonah Al Qathrady, Ahmed Helmy
Computer and Information Science and Engineering Department
Gainesville, Florida, USA
{mimonah,helmy}@ufl.edu

ABSTRACT

Distance estimation and proximity classification techniques are essential for numerous IoT applications and in providing efficient services in smart cities. Bluetooth Low Energy (BLE) is designed for IoT devices, and its received signal strength indicator (RSSI) has been used in distance and proximity estimation, though they are noisy and unreliable. In this study, we leverage the BLE TX power level in BLE models. We adopt a comparative analysis framework that utilizes our extensive data library of measurements. It considers commonly used state-of-the-art model, in addition to our data-driven proposed approach. The RSSI and TX power are integrated into several parametric models such as *log shadowing* and *Android Beacon library models*, and machine learning models such as *linear regression, decision trees, random forests* and *neural networks.* Specific mobile apps are developed for the study experiment. We have collected more than 1.8 millions of BLE records between encounters with various distances that range from 0.5 to 22 meters in an indoor environment. Interestingly, considering TX power when estimating the distance reduced the mean errors by up to 46% in parametric models and by up to 35% in machine learning models. Also, the proximity classification accuracy increased by up to 103% and 70% in parametric and machine learning models, respectively. This work is one of the first studies (if not the first) that analyze in depth the TX power variations in improving the distance estimation and classification.

CCS CONCEPTS

• **Networks → Location based services;** • **Human-centered computing →** *Ubiquitous and mobile computing; Mobile phones;*

1 INTRODUCTION

Internet of Things (IoT) is the expected architecture of our interaction with the physical world in the smart cities, and billions of dollars are allocated for its solutions [7]. Distance estimation and proximity classification are major building blocks in numerous IoT applications such as crowd monitoring, infection tracing [14], localization, and mapping. BLE is built specifically for IoT [5]. It is an energy efficient version of Bluetooth and overcomes its limitations. BLE advertisements can be sent without establishing a connection, and they are used for proximity and range estimation. As a result, BLE has the potential to become an alternative for indoor localization [3, 8]. Much of the previous BLE models have used RSSI as the primary parameter in their positioning or distance estimation [4, 10, 19]. However, experimental studies show that RSSI is unreliable in determining the distance accurately [1]. On the other hand, BLE's transmission (TX) power level can be included in the advertisement. Consequently, we extensively investigate the gain of integrating TX power level with RSSI into the BLE models. We target two main goals in this paper; first to improve encounter distance estimate using BLE, and second to improve encounter proximity classification using BLE.

First, in terms of distance estimation, this study covers several parametric and machine learning models. Parametric models are *log shadowing*[1], as the more general model that describes the relationship between distance and the RSSI [9], and *Android Beacon library models*[2] that got over 150 million installations [12]. Machine learning models include *linear regression* [6], *decision trees* [17], *random forests* [11] and *neural networks* [15]. *Linear regression* is used to model the relationship between variables. *Decision trees* and *random forests* are not affected by the nonlinear relationship between parameters. *Random forests* are more complicated than *decision tree*, but they are more powerful. *Neural networks* are capable of understanding the patterns and generalizing the result.

The second main goal of this paper is proximity classification. Identifying nearby objects provides valuable contextual knowledge to the smart applications. The distances where the encounters are classified to be proximate depends on the application needs, and it varies from one study to another. For example, it is defined as the distance within three meters for social interaction [16], while 3 feet is known to be the unsafe distance from an infected patient [18], and has to be identified during infection tracing. There are some BLE proximity studies, such as how its parameters affect the detection system [16]. However, the level of comparative analysis in this paper has not been previously presented in any of the BLE proximity studies. In our work, we have leveraged BLE TX power levels in the models and evaluated them under different definitions of proximity classifications that range from encounter within half a meter to encounters within three meters. Overall, our work contributions are summarized as follows:

- We have integrated BLE TX power levels with RSSI in several BLE distance estimation and proximity classification models: parametric and machine learning models.
- We have built a framework that systemically studies and analyzes in-depth incorporating Tx power into the models,

MSWiM '17, November 21–25, 2017, Miami, FL, USA

ACM ISBN 978-1-4503-5162-1/17/11...$15.00
https://doi.org/10.1145/3127540.3127577

[1]It is also called path-loss model
[2]It is also called Alt Beacon Library

and evaluated them under various TX power levels with two states: as regular models that use only RSSI, and when they incorporate the TX power. They are assessed for their distance estimation and proximity classification accuracy.
- We have collected over 1.8 million BLE records with known distances from an indoor environment. We developed two specific Android applications for this study: a scanner and an advertiser. The advertiser sends BLE advertisements with various TX power levels: high, medium, low and ultra low. The scanner scans TX power along with RSSI. The distances ranges are up to 22 meters, which are longer than many of the previous studies. The tools and data will be shared with the community to establish reproducibility.
- Significant results have been reached. For instance, the mean distance estimation error is reduced by up to 46% in parametric models and by up to 35% in machine learning models when considering TX power. Also, the proximity classification accuracy has been increased by up to 103% and 70% in parametric and machine learning models respectively.

The analysis results in hybrid models which consist of several other models that produced the best result under each TX power level. The rest of the paper is organized as follows: In section 2, we discuss the comparative analysis framework. The results are presented in section 3. The conclusion and future work are provided in section 4.

2 COMPARATIVE ANALYSIS FRAMEWORK

As in figure 1, our proposed framework consists of four main components: the models, the training and testing data, the evaluation and the adaptive hybrid models. These components are discussed in more details in the rest of this section.

2.1 Models

The investigated models include parametric models and machine learning models.

2.1.1 Parametric Models. They use equations to estimate the distance. We analyze two parametric models: *log shadowing*, and *Android Beacon library models* (old and new versions). For the purpose of this study, we define two kinds of the referenced *RSSI*: $RSSI_1$ and $RSSI_{TX}$. $RSSI_1$ is used with regular models, and it is the average *RSSI* when the distance is one meter between the BLE devices regardless of the advertised TX power. $RSSI_{TX}$ is used with TX power integrated models, and it is the average RSSI when the distance is one meter between the devices, but it depends on the TX power. As a result, we have a vector of $RSSI_{TX}$, a particular value for each TX power.

A. Regular Parametric Models: They use *RSSI* and $RSSI_1$ as the main parameters in their equation. The *log shadowing model (LogR)* uses the following equation:

$$distance = 10^{\frac{RSSI-RSSI_1}{-10n}}, \qquad (1)$$

where n is the path-loss exponent, n = 2 in free space [3].
Android Beacon Models use the following formula:

$$distance = A \times (\frac{r}{t})^B + C, \qquad (2)$$

where r is the RSSI measured by the device, and t is the referenced RSSI. A, B, and C are constants. We have found two library versions based on the coefficients. The old version *(oldBconR)*, as its coefficients were presented in the previous research [2, 4], and assigns the following values to the coefficient: A=0.89976, B= 7.7095, and C= 0.111. The new version *(newBconR)* is the most recent version of the default coefficients as in the library code [12], where A=0.42093, B=6.9476 and C= 0.54992.

B. TX Power Integrated Parametric Models: We have adjusted the models to consider TX power level. Therefore, the scanner reads TX power in the received BLE advertisement along with RSSI. The TX power *log-shadowing* model *(LogTx)* estimates the distance using the following equation:

$$distance = 10^{\frac{RSSI-RSSI_{TX}}{-10n}}, \qquad (3)$$

where $RSSI_{TX}$ depends on the scanned TX power. For example, when TX power=high, the model then uses the value in $RSSI_{TX}$ vector that corresponds to the high TX power. The *Android libraries* are also adjusted in this work to consider the TX power in their equations. The libraries check the received BLE TX power and RSSI to estimate the distance. Then, they use the $RSSI_{TX}$ value that corresponds to the TX power level. The old version *(oldBconTX)* estimate the distance using the following equation:

$$distance = 0.89976 \times (\frac{RSSI}{RSSI_{TX}})^{7.7095} + 0.111. \qquad (4)$$

While the new version *(newBconTX)* use the equation:

$$distance = 0.42093 \times (\frac{RSSI}{RSSI_{TX}})^{6.9476} + 0.54992. \qquad (5)$$

Note that the *Android Beacon Library* currently does not scan for TX power [12]. However, in this study, we have implemented the TX power integrated model and compared it to the regular version of the library under each TX power level.

2.1.2 Machine Learning Models. We study four machine learning models for distance estimation between BLE devices. The models are the *linear regression (LR), decision trees (DT), random forests (RF) and neural networks (NN).* There are two modes of the machine models: regular and TX power integrated.

A. Regular Machine Learning Model: The models are trained on RSSI regardless of the TX power. As a result, they only use BLE advertisement RSSI to estimate the distance. For example, in *linear regression*, the distance is computed as:

$$distance = A \times RSSI + C, \qquad (6)$$

where A and C are defined from the training phase. *Decision trees and random forests* split based on RSSI values, and the *neural networks* will have RSSI as an input layer.

B. TX Power Integrated Machine Learning Models: TX power level is combined in the machine learning distance estimation models using two different ways:

1) RSSI and TX power as input training features: the models are

[3] n=2 provides better estimation with our data than n=1.6 to n=1.8

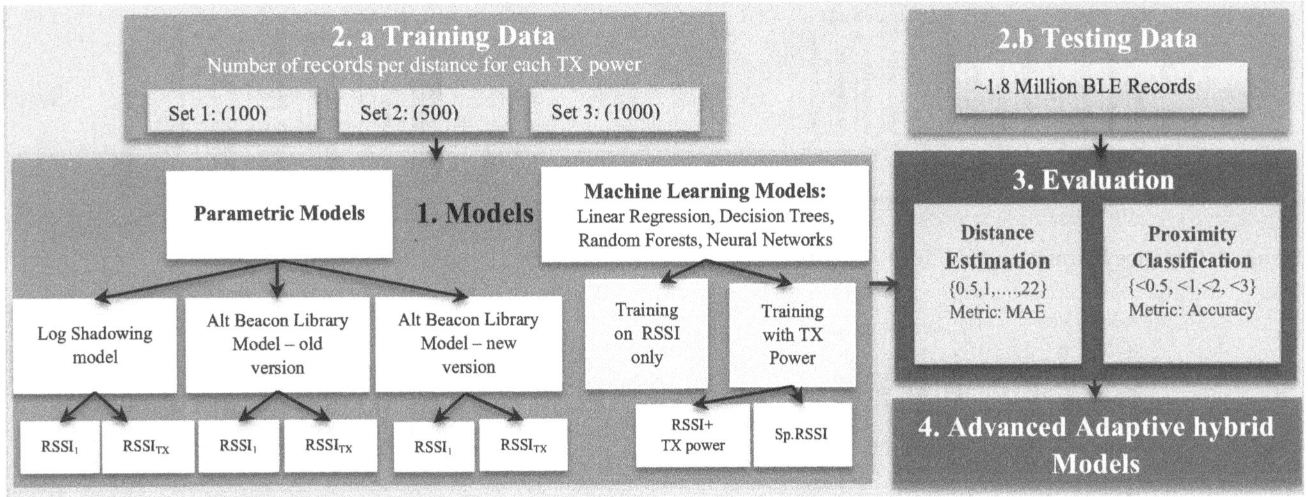

Figure 1: The Comparative analysis framework. It consists of four main components.1. Models: parametric or machine learning, each model is evaluated as a regular model and when TX power is combined with it. 2. Datasets including a. training dataset, and b. the testing dataset. 3. Evaluation: models are evaluated by using a) *MAE* for distance estimation, and b) accuracy of classifying, and 4. Hybrid Models: consist of the best models performed in each TX power.

trained on RSSI and TX power. For instance, the *linear regression* equation will contain TX power and RSSI variables.

$$distance = A \times TXpower + B \times RSSI + C \tag{7}$$

Also, the *decision trees and random forests* have TX power and RSSI in their decision nodes, while the *neural networks* will include TX power in their input layers. To estimate the distance, both RSSI and TX power are plugged into the trained model.

2) *Training specific model for each TX power data (sp.RSSI):* the RSSI training data are separated based on their TX power. Then, a particular model is trained for each group using the RSSI only. Therefore, we will have four models from each machine learning model. For example, we will have four *linear regression* models: one model for each TX power level. To estimate the distance, the TX power is checked, and then its corresponding model is used to calculate the distance based on RSSI. Also, there will be four *decision trees and four random forests*: a tree and a forest for each TX power level. Also, we will have *four different neural networks.* For instance, the neural networks that are used when TX power is high will be different than the *neural networks* that will be used when the BLE TX power = medium.

The upper limit for the predicted distances is set to 30 meters.

2.2 Collected Data

2.2.1 Data Collection and Experiments. Two specific Android applications are developed to collect BLE records with known distances: an advertiser and a scanner. The advertiser sends the advertisements using different TX power levels. The scanner records the BLE RSSI along with TX power. The experiment is run in an indoor environment, specifically in the CSE department hallway, with no obstacle between the devices, which have been placed at predefined distances from a half to 22 meters {0.5,1,2,....,22}. More than 1.8 million records that are sent from our advertisers are collected.

2.2.2 Training Data. They consist of three sets of data with different sizes. The purpose is to investigate if the training size affects the modeling result. The number of records for each TX power (total 4) at each distance (total 23) is shown in figure 1. There are 9,200, 46,000, and 92,000 records in the 1st, 2nd and 3rd set, respectively. These training sets are used to train the machine learning models. Also, the parametric models parameters are extracted from the training sets such as $RSSI_1$ and $RSSI_{TX}$.

2.2.3 Testing Data. The testing data are around 1.8 million BLE records. They do not include the data used for training.

2.3 Evaluation

2.3.1 Distance estimation. The mean absolute error (*MAE*) is used to measure how close the estimated distance is to the real one.

2.3.2 Proximity classification. We consider the following distance classification in meters: half or less, one or less, two or less and three or less. The result of distance estimation is used for classification. If the distances set is *Pd={0.5,1,2,3,....,N}*, and the proximate distance of interest is Pd_i, then the estimated distance '*d*' between objects is classified as proximate if:

$$d <= \frac{Pd_i + Pd_{i+1}}{2} \tag{8}$$

The models' accuracy is their ability to classify the proximate distance accurately, which is given by:

$$Accuracy = \frac{TP + TN}{S}, \tag{9}$$

where *TP* is the true positive cases with the distances less than or equal the proximate distance, and they are classified as *proximate.* *TN* is the true negative cases with distances more than the proximate distance, and they are classified as *not proximate.* *S* is the testing data size.

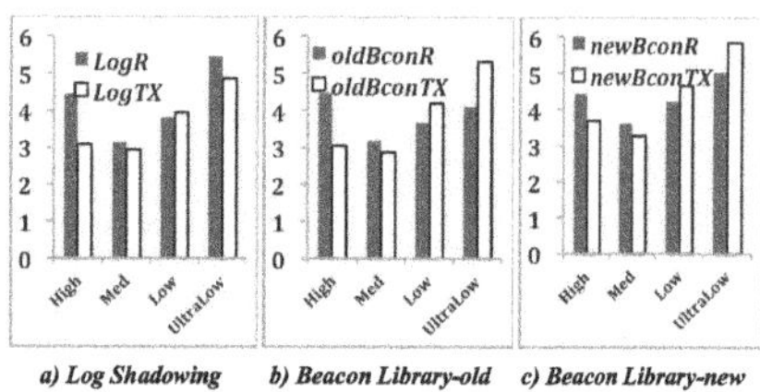

Figure 2: Distance Estimation *MAE* for Parametric Models.

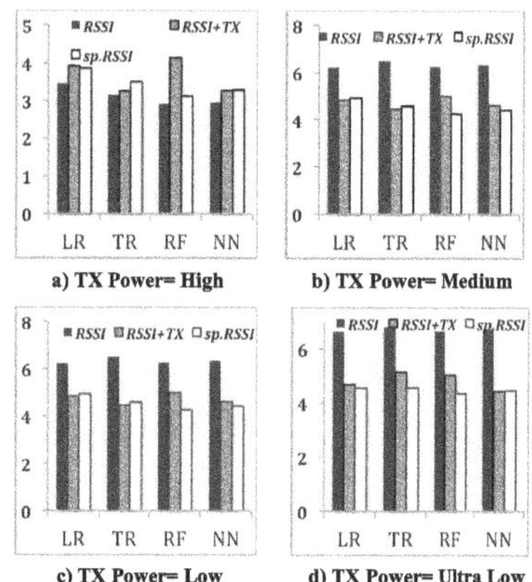

Figure 3: Distance Estimation *MAE* for Machine Learning Models. LR *Linear Regression*, DT: *Decision Trees*, RF: *Random Forests*, NN: *Neural Networks*.

2.4 Advanced Adaptive Hybrid Models

Our comparative analysis resulted in hybrid models that are sensitive to the TX power. One is used when the goal is to reduce the distance estimation error. The other is used when the proximity classification is the primary goal. Details of the hybrid models are omitted for brevity. For details please see [13].

3 COMPARATIVE ANALYSIS RESULT

This section discusses the models' distance estimation *MAE* and classification accuracy.

3.1 Distance Estimation

3.1.1 Parametric Models. As shown in figure 2, the models have similar patterns in most cases. TX power integrated model with medium TX power reduced *MAE* by 46%, 35% and 30% in *log shadowing, Android Beacon library (new), Android Beacon library (old)* models, respectively, than using the models' regular versions with ultra low power. Consequently, if an IoT application needs distance estimation, our result suggests using medium TX power with TX power integrated model.

3.1.2 Machine Learning Models. They have similar *MAE* pattern in most cases as in figure 3. Considering TX power improved the models with all TX power levels, with the exception of the high level. For example, with ultra low power, TX power integrated model *MAE* is reduced by up to 35%.
Random Forest that trained on RSSI only produces the least mean

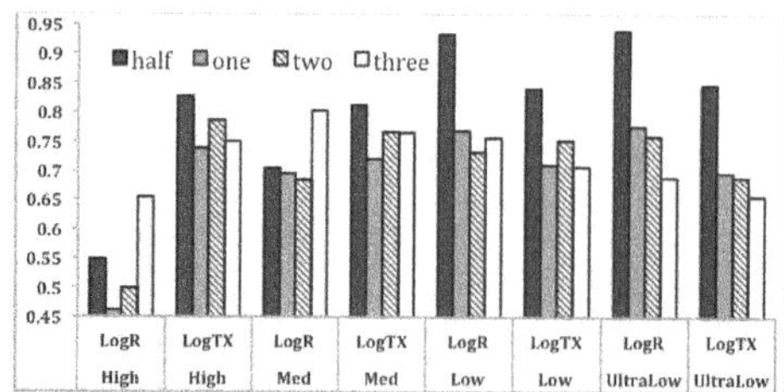

a) *Log Shadowing Model*

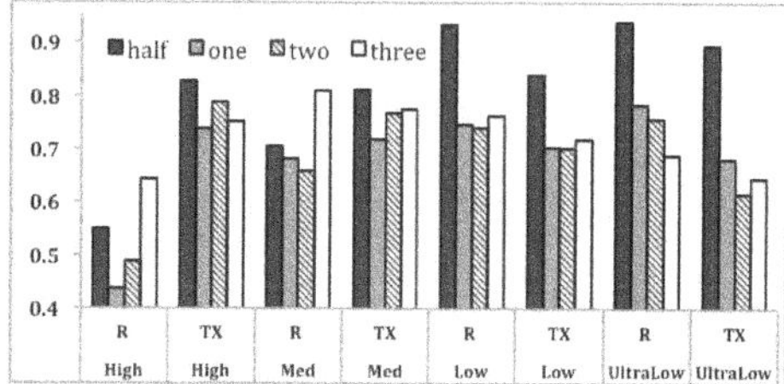

b) *Alt Beacon Library Model (old version)*

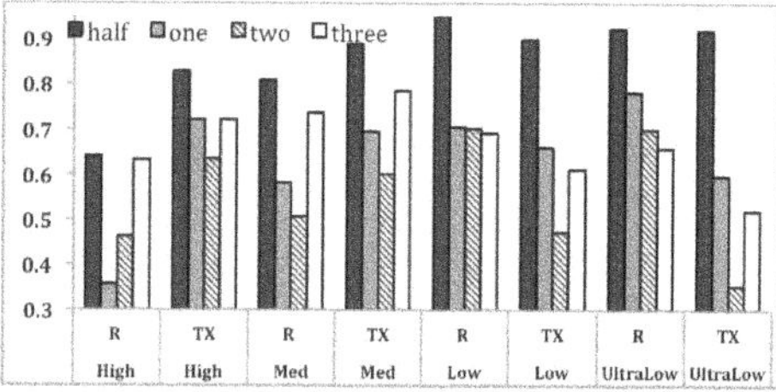

c) *Alt Beacon Library Model (new version)*

Figure 4: Proximity Classification *Accuracy* for Parametric Models. R: Regular Models, TX: TX Power Integrated Models.

error with high TX power. However, parametric models outperform machine learning with other TX power levels. *TX power integrated Android Beacon library*-old is the best with *medium* TX power, while its regular version is the best when TX power is *low or ultra low*.

3.2 Proximity Classification

3.2.1 Parametric Models. Low and ultra low TX power levels yield the best result, up to 95% accuracy, when classifying encounters using regular *Android Beacon library* (new) within half a meter as in figure 4. Therefore, if an IoT application requires classifying close encounters, then our result suggests using low or ultra low TX power. Another finding is regular models with high TX power produced unreliable classification. However, integrating TX power in the model improved their accuracy. For example, *Android Beacon library* (new) classifying encounters within one meter improved by 103% accuracy when combining TX power into the same model. The models can classify encounters that are within half a meter accurately, but their accuracy is decreased with other distances classification.

3.2.2 Machine Learning Model. Figure 5 shows their classification accuracy. As the case with parametric models, the encounters within half a meter can be classified with up to 95% accuracy when using low or ultra low power with TX power integrated *linear*

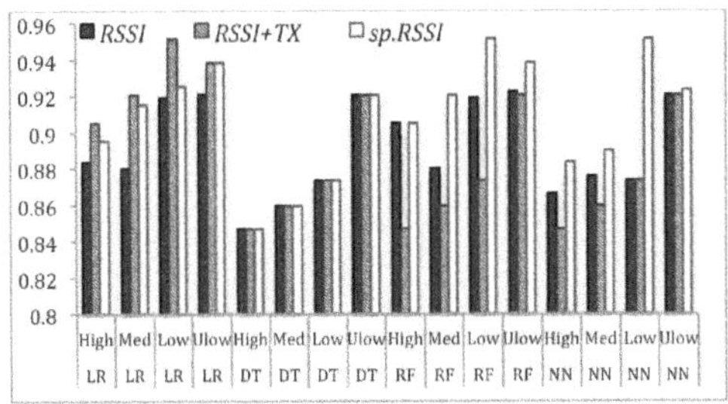

a) Within Half a Meter

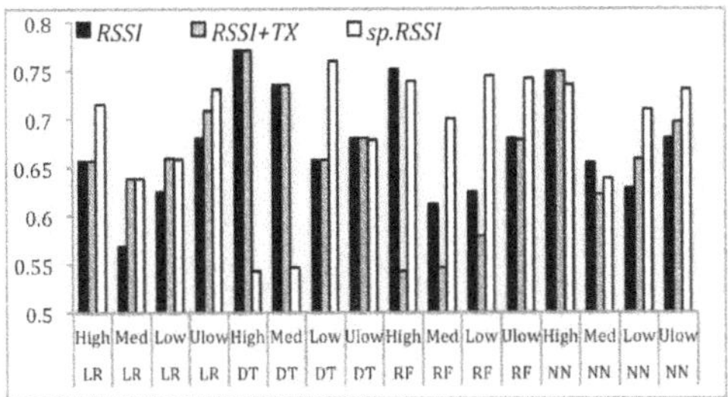

b) Within One Meter

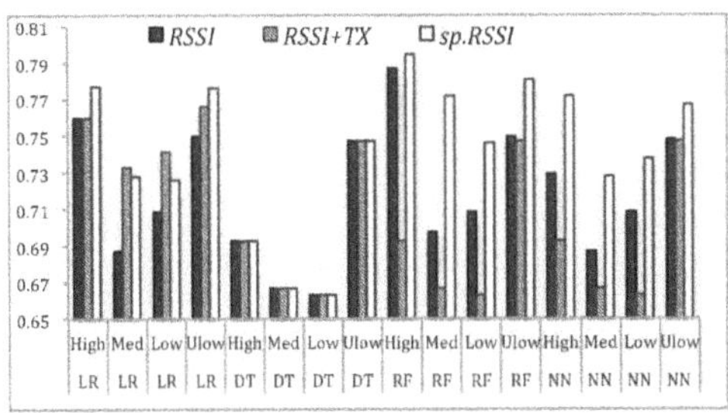

c) Within Two Meters

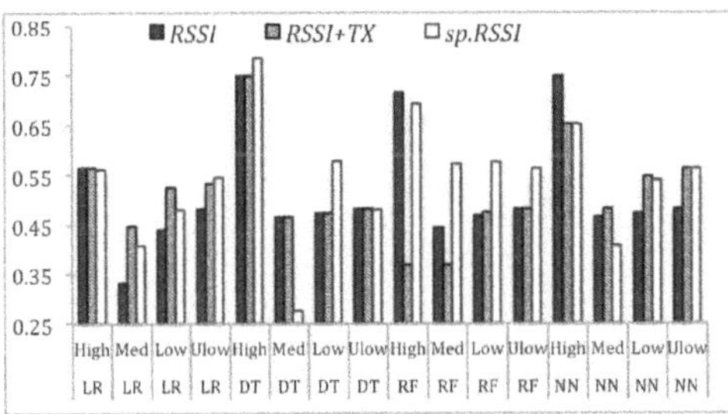

d) Within Three Meters

Figure 5: Proximity Classification *Accuracy* for Machine Learning Models. LR: *Linear Regression,* DT: *Decision Trees,* RF: *Random Forests,* NN: *Neural Networks.*

regression, random forests or *neural networks* models. Also, the accuracy decreased when classifying other distances. Integrating TX power improved the accuracy in some cases, and the maximum improvement has been observed when classifying encounters that are within three meters. For example, in *linear regression,* the accuracy is improved by 70% when considering TX power and using high level than using a regular model with medium TX power.

3.3 Training Data Size

The different training sets results have similar pattern in most cases. Though, a slight improvement was noticed with the largest set.

4 CONCLUSION AND FUTURE WORK

This work combines TX power into BLE distance estimation models. Then, an extensive comparative analysis between regular and TX power integrated models is conducted. The distance estimations *MAE* is reduced by up to 46%. Also, considering TX power improved the classification accuracy in some cases by up to 103% accuracy. Our study reached significant conclusions; for example, the medium TX power is the best with parametric models when the distance estimation is of interest. However, low and ultra low TX power provide the best accuracy classification of encounters within half a meter. Also, the result of this investigation prompts hybrid models that are adaptive to the TX power and consist of other models. While our experiment is performed indoor with no obstacle between objects, we expected leveraging TX power would also improve the distance estimation and classification in other indoor environments. We plan to study this in the future.

ACKNOWLEDGMENTS

This work was partially funded by Najran University, Saudi Arabia, and NSF 1320694.

REFERENCES

[1] A.Kwiecien, M.Mackowski, M.Kojder, and M.Manczyk. 2015. Reliability of bluetooth smart technology for indoor localization system. In *International Conference on Computer Networks.* Springer, 444–454.
[2] M. S. Aman, H. Jiang, C. Quint, K. Yelamarthi, and A. Abdelgawad. 2016. Reliability evaluation of iBeacon for micro-localization. In *(UEMCON).* IEEE, 1–5.
[3] S Bertuletti, A Cereatti, U Della, M Caldara, and M Galizzi. 2016. Indoor distance estimated from Bluetooth Low Energy signal strength: Comparison of regression models.. In *Sensors Applications Symposium (SAS).* IEEE, 1–5.
[4] H. Cho, J. Ji, Z. Chen, H. Park, and W. Lee. 2015. Accurate Distance Estimation between Things: A Self-correcting Approach. *Open Journal of Internet Of Things (OJIOT)* 1, 2 (2015), 19–27.
[5] Bluetooth Low Energy. *https://www.bluetooth.com/what-is-bluetooth-technology/how-it-works/low-energy.*
[6] Julian J Faraway. 2002. Practical regression and ANOVA using R. (2002).
[7] Here's how the Internet of Things will explode by 2020. *www.businessinsider.com/iot-ecosystem-internet-of-things-forecasts-and-business-opportunities-2016-2.*
[8] Z. Jianyong, L. Haiyong, C. Zili, and L. Zhaohui. 2014. RSSI based Bluetooth low energy indoor positioning. In *(IPIN).* IEEE, 526–533.
[9] J.Xu, W.Liu, F.Lang, Y.Zhang, C.Wang, et al. 2010. Distance measurement model based on RSSI in WSN. *Wireless Sensor Network* 2, 8 (2010), 606–616.
[10] K.Urano, K. Hiroi, K. Kaji, and N. Kawaguchi. 2016. A Location Estimation Method using BLE Tags Distributed Among Participants of a Large-Scale Exhibition. In *MOBIQUITOUS.* ACM, 124–129.
[11] Andy Liaw and Matthew Wiener. 2002. Classification and regression by randomForest. *R news* 2, 3 (2002), 18–22.
[12] Android Beacon Library. *https://altbeacon.github.io/android-beacon-library/.*
[13] M. Al Qathrady and A.Helmy. *https://www.cise.ufl.edu/˜qathrady/reports/BLE.pdf.*
[14] M. Al Qathrady, A. Helmy, and K. Almuzaini. 2016. Infection tracing in smart hospitals. In *(WiMob).* IEEE, 1–8.
[15] Brian Ripley, William Venables, and Maintainer Brian Ripley. 2016. Package 'nnet'. *R package version* (2016), 3–7.
[16] R.Tabata, A.Hayashi Arisa, S.Tokunaga, S.Saiki, M.Nakamura, and S.Matsumoto. 2016. Implementation and evaluation of BLE proximity detection mechanism for Pass-by Framework.. In *Computer and Information Science.* IEEE/ACIS, 1–6.
[17] Terry M Therneau, Beth Atkinson, Brian Ripley, et al. 2010. rpart: Recursive partitioning. R package version. *R package version* 3 (2010), 1–46.
[18] www.cdc.gov/hicpac/2007IP/2007ip part1.html. *CDC.*
[19] Y. Zhuang, J. Yang, Y. Li, L. Qi, and N. El-Sheimy. 2016. Smartphone-based indoor localization with bluetooth low energy beacons. *Sensors* 16, 5 (2016), 596.

GRM: Group Regularity Mobility Model

Ivan O. Nunes[1,2], Clayson Celes[1], Michael D. Silva[1], Pedro O.S. Vaz de Melo[1], Antonio A.F. Loureiro[1]
[1]Department of Computer Science - Federal University of Minas Gerais - Brazil
[2]School of Information and Computer Sciences - University of California Irvine - USA
{ivanolive,claysonceles,micdoug,olmo,loureiro}@dcc.ufmg.br

ABSTRACT

In this work we propose, implement, and evaluate Group Regularity Model (GRM), a novel mobility model that accounts for the role of group meetings regularity in human mobility. We show that existing mobility models for humans do not capture the regularity of human group meetings present in real mobility traces. We characterize the statistical properties of such group meetings in real mobility traces and design GRM accordingly. We show that GRM maintains the typical pairwise contact properties of real traces, such as contact duration and inter-contact time distributions. In addition, GRM accounts for the role of group mobility, presenting group meetings regularity and social communities' structure. Finally, we evaluate state-of-art social-aware protocols for opportunistic routing and show that their performance in synthetic traces generated by GRM is similar to their performance in real-world traces.

1 INTRODUCTION

Mobility models have fundamental importance for mobile networking prototyping. They enable the generation of synthetic trajectories for mobile nodes in simulated environments, which can then be used to evaluate the performance of newly designed networking protocols. The validation of such protocols in real-world large scale experiments is often unfeasible due to the financial and operational limitations. In recent years, several mobility models were proposed with the goal of reproducing statistical properties of human mobility [21]. Examples of such properties include human walks and displacements, the spatial regularity of human mobility, human trajectories and transportation, pairwise encounter patterns, and also group mobility.

Although earlier studies [7, 14, 15] on mobility modeling have focused on reproducing the regularity of human contacts, those models only focus on reproducing the regularity of pairwise interactions. Such models do not account for the role and regularity of group meeting, which is also a fundamental building block for mobility modeling [21]. Unfortunately, existent group mobility models focus on modeling groups that remain together throughout the whole simulation time. Therefore, such models are not representative of the statistical regularity of human interactions, i.e., groups of people that meet regularly. This limitation is specially harmful to the validation of opportunistic forwarding protocols, because the social-aware strategies [12, 16, 17] have remarked themselves as the most effective for this types of protocols. Recent studies [5, 18, 19] have shown that the regularity of group meetings, which is present in real-world traces, play an important role for content forwarding in mobile opportunistic networks.

Aiming at addressing the aforementioned issues, in this work we propose the Group Regularity Mobility (GRM) Model[1]. GRM is the first mobility model to consider the role of group meetings and their regularity to simulate human mobility. We show that GRM retains important real-world mobility properties, such as social community structure in the mobile network, group meetings regularity, and statistical patterns of inter-contact time and contact duration.

2 BACKGROUND AND RELATED WORK

Existing ***group mobility models*** focus on modeling groups that remain together throughout the whole simulation time. Examples of models like that are Reference Point Group Mobility (RPGM) [11] and Reference Velocity Group Mobility (RVGM) [22]. On the other hand, mobility models that model the regularity of human contact patterns [7, 14, 15] only consider pairwise contacts, ignoring the fact that human social contacts often happen in groups, involving more than two entities. Therefore, none of these models exhibit the statistical contact properties nor the social structure that is exhibited in real-world mobility.

In recent years, some studies have focused on modeling human mobility using spatial and temporal statistical patterns that were observed in real-world mobility traces. Lee et al. [15] presented the Self-similar Least Action Walk (SLAW) mobility model that captures the following properties: truncated power-law distributions of flights, pause-times and inter-contact times, attractive force to more popular places, and heterogeneously defined areas of individual mobility. The model uses these features to represent the mobility of people who share "common gathering places", i.e., places that most people visit during their daily lives.

In Small World in Motion (SWIM) [14], Kosta el al. present a mobility model based on the intuition that people go more often to nearby or popular places. This intuition is supported by Gonzalez et al. [9] observation about the spatial and temporal regularity in

MSWiM '17, November 21–25, 2017, Miami, FL, USA

ACM ISBN 978-1-4503-5162-1/17/11...$15.00
https://doi.org/10.1145/3127540.3127570

[1]GRM synthetic mobility traces containing 100, 1000, and 2000 mobile nodes are available together with a demo video of GRM working on top of The ONE Simulator [13] at:
https://www.dropbox.com/sh/792mi849nf3dvam/AAAR4RofaLBfoFaxmeONe-H4a?dl=0

GRM source code is available at:
https://github.com/ivanolive/GRM

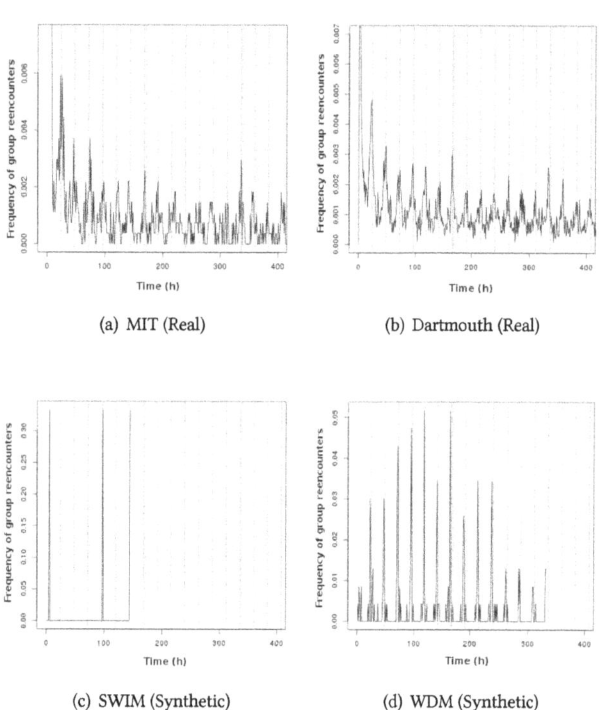

(a) MIT (Real) (b) Dartmouth (Real)

(c) SWIM (Synthetic) (d) WDM (Synthetic)

Figure 1: Comparison of group meetings regularity in real and synthetic mobility traces

human movement. SWIM assigns each node with a home location and computes a visitation probability to each possible destination in the simulation space. The visitation probability in computed according to (i) the popularity of each possible destination, and (ii) the distance of each location to the node's home location (closest destinations have higher probabilities).

SLAW and SWIM produce inter-contact time and contact duration distributions that follow the ones found in real mobility traces. However, both models consider only pairwise contacts, ignoring group mobility or synchronized relationships among more than two people. In this direction, Ekman et al. [7] introduced the Working Day Movement Model (WDM), which simulates daily routines of people considering their commutes between home and workplace and also group meetings. Unfortunately, group meetings in WDM occur always after work hours and are always among the same set of people.

In order to show these drawbacks, we compare SLAW, SWIM and WDM traces with real mobility traces, with the goal of verifying if group meetings' regularity properties are captured by such models. Specifically, we want to verify if such models capture group re-encounters and their evolution over time, i.e., groups' dynamics. To that purpose, we apply the methodology for detecting and tracking mobile groups, proposed in [19], to the real mobility traces, MIT and Dartmouth. MIT [6] and Dartmouth [10] traces are proximity contact registers containing 80 and 1200 users respectively. In the

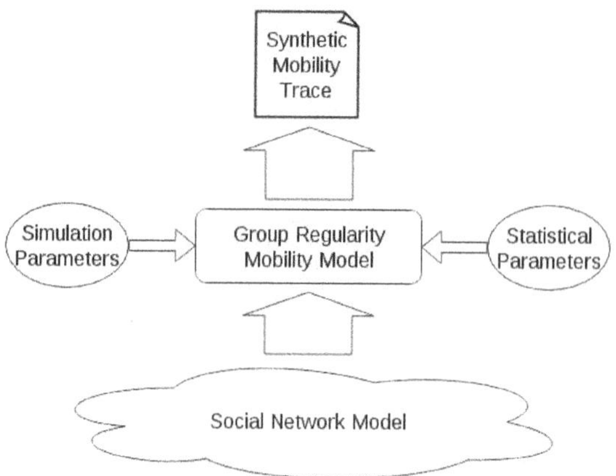

Figure 2: GRM Model Framework

MIT trace, users reside in two university buildings and were monitored for almost one year. Contacts were registered when two users were less than 10 meters apart. The Dartmouth trace registered contacts between students in a university campus for two months using Wi-Fi connectivity logs.

Figs. 1(a) and 1(b) show the Probability Density Function (PDF) of group re-meetings along the time for the real-world traces. In both traces we can verify the presence of periodicity in groups' re-encounters. Also, the mass of probability is concentrated in peaks around the red dotted lines, which represent periods of 24 hours. Finally, observe that in both cases higher peaks are present around the green dashed lines, which represent periods of seven days. This pattern in the group re-meetings' PDF. shows that group meetings present daily and weekly periodicity. It is noteworthy that such pattern happens in both real traces, even though they are from different places, have different number of nodes, and used different data collection methods.

As we did for the real traces, we apply the same group detection and tracking methodology to traces generated by the three synthetic models (SLAW, SWIM, and WDM). Figs. 1(c) and 1(d) present the results for the SWIM and WDM models, respectively. The contact trace generated by SWIM (Fig. 1(c)) do not present any group meeting regularity. Out of the detected groups, only three group re-meetings were registered in a period of 15 days. The result for the contact trace generated by the SLAW model presented an analogous behavior, i.e., no regularity in group meetings. In the WDM trace (Fig. 1(d)) we can observe that group re-meetings happen precisely in periods of 24 hours and with much higher frequencies than in real mobility traces. This behavior is observed because WDM firstly defines a set of places, called offices, and then distributes nodes to transition between pre-defined subsets of offices with daily periodicity. Therefore, nodes with intersections in their lists of offices will always form groups with exaggerated meeting regularity.

By analyzing the group meetings regularity of the synthetic models, we conclude that none of them represents well the group mobility patterns. GRM is an evolution of the aforementioned models, including all of their properties and also group meeting regularity and social context.

3 THE GRM MODEL

In this section, we describe GRM in details. Fig. 2 illustrates the GRM framework. In this section we go over each of the building blocks that are contained within the model. GRM receives as input a social graph, which can be a real social graph, given as input by the user, or generated by a synthetic social network model. GRM implementation has native support for several social network models including Barabasi-Albert [1], Gaussian Clustering [3], and Random Partition Graph [8] models. The social network is used to define which nodes will be present at each group meeting event, i.e., the groups' structures, as discussed later on. The idea of providing the social network as an input for the model is to give flexibility for the mobility modeling and the social network modeling to evolve separately. GRM will adapt to any social network given as input and produce a mobility trace as output.

In addition to the social network, GRM receives a set of simulation configurations, such as the size of the simulated area, the simulation duration, the number of nodes, and the number of groups. Finally, it also receives a set of statistical parameters, which are the parameters for the statistical distributions contained in the model. Such statistical parameters vary in different real mobility traces, depending on the scenario. Therefore, the values of these parameters can be given as input to the model directly, or via automated extraction from existing real-world mobility traces, allowing GRM to mimic and augment the scenario and mobility behavior of a given real-world trace. The synthetic traces generated by GRM are fully compatible and are ready to run on top of the ONE simulator [13]. The summary for the notation we will use to describe GRM is provided in Table 1.

Table 1: Notation summary

Notation	Description
T	The trace duration
$NodesSet$	The set of all network nodes
G_i	The ith group of nodes in the trace
$\|\|G_i\|\|$	The number of group members of G_i
T_{G_i}	The existence period of group G_i
μ_{G_i}	The average inter-meeting time for G_i
$Meeting_{G_i}(t)$	The time for the tth meeting of G_i
Dur_{G_i}	The duration of G_i group meetings
$u \sim U(a,b)$	$u \in \mathbb{R}$ is a value randomly selected with uniform probability in the interval $[a,b]$
$\eta \sim N(\mu,\sigma^2)$	$\eta \in \mathbb{R}$ is a value randomly selected with a Gaussian distribution of mean μ and variance σ^2
$\rho \sim PL(\alpha,\beta)$	$\rho \in \mathbb{R}$ is a value randomly selected with a truncated power law distribution with exponent α and the exponential cut-off value β
$P_{att}[U_j,G_i]$	The probability of user U_j attending to a meeting of group G_i
$P_{\text{place}}(C_j,G_i)$	The probability of a meeting of group G_i to happen at the C_j cell

3.1 Group Meeting Times

To properly design a group regularity mobility model, there must be a representative statistical model for group meeting times. Due to group meetings' periodicity, presented in Fig. 1, we model group meeting times as follows.Each group G_i in the model receives an average inter-meeting time, μ_{G_i}. The value of μ_{G_i} is randomly generated according to a power-law distribution with exponential cut-off. This way of generating μ_{G_i} is based on the fact that inter-contact times of real mobility traces follow this distribution (as discussed in Secs. 1 and 2). The power-law exponent (α_{gmt}) and the exponential cut-off value (β_{gmt}) are statistical parameters given as input to the model. Then, a series of meeting times for group G_i is recursively generated with Gaussian inter-meeting times, as in Eq. 1:

$$\mu_{G_i} \sim PL(\alpha_{\text{gmt}},\beta_{\text{gmt}})$$
$$Meeting_{G_i}(t) = \begin{cases} u \sim U(0,T) & \text{if } t = 0 \\ Meeting_{G_i}(t-1) + \eta \sim N(K \times \mu_{G_i},\sigma^2) & \text{if } t > 0 \end{cases} \tag{1}$$

In the simulation, each group G_i has its own μ_{G_i}. The variance σ^2 is a simulation parameter for all groups, allowing higher or lower variation on the group meetings punctuality, according to the Gaussian distribution variance properties.

Following the recursive equation for group meetings generation, each group will then have its set of meetings determined as:

$$\bigcup_{j=0}^{\lceil \frac{T_{G_i}}{K \times \mu_{G_i}} \rceil} Meeting_{G_i}(j), \tag{2}$$

where T_{G_i} denotes the period of time throughout which the group G_i will exist. GRM considers that each group G_i has its own regularity factor, which is represented by the scale factor K in Eq. 1. For instance, most of the groups with $K = 24h$ will usually meet every 24, 48, 72 hours, and so on, following the power-law probability function of μ_{G_i}. K is a multiplier that will generate the periodical behavior of real traces, depicted in Fig. 1 of Sec. 2, while the value of μ_{G_i}, generated by a truncated power law, will generate statistically representative inter-contact times.

Since each group has its own K value, the distribution for the values of K is given to the model as a simulation parameter. An example would be: "The simulation will have 500 groups. Seventy percent of these groups will have K =24h, 15% will have K =7 days, and 15% K = 6h". In Sec. 4 we show that this example of configuration for the K distribution generates group re-meetings that are very similar to the ones observed in the MIT and Dartmouth traces.

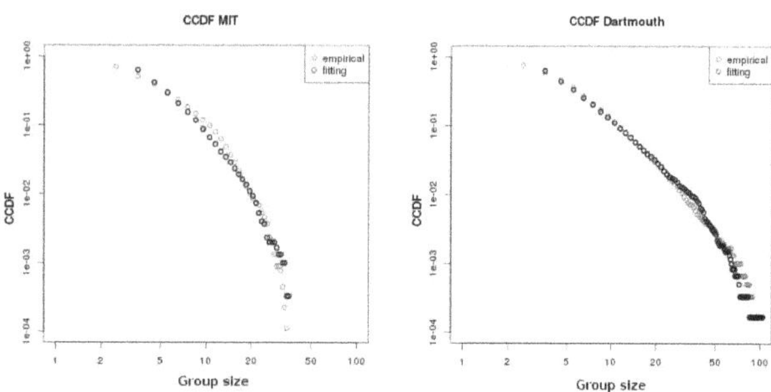

(a) $\alpha = 2.24; \beta = 30.4$. Average group size of 6.06

(b) $\alpha = 2.42; \beta = 54.6$. Average group size of 6.96

Figure 3: Group sizes: empirical data from MIT and Dartmouth traces and their fitting to data generated by power laws of exponents α and exponential cuts β.

3.2 Group Meetings Durations

After defining the group meeting times, we now must define the duration of a group meeting, i.e., the time that the involved nodes will spend together. To do so, we inherit the findings of previous studies (as discussed in Secs. 1 and 2), which show that contact durations follow truncated power laws. Therefore, as we did for μ_{G_i} in Eq. 1, we define the meeting durations as:

$$Dur_{G_i} \sim PL(\alpha_{\text{dur}}, \beta_{\text{dur}}), \tag{3}$$

where α_{dur} and β_{dur} are statistical parameters of GRM.

3.3 Groups' Structure and Social Context

Finally, here we discuss how we define which nodes will be at each meeting, i.e., the groups' compositions. The first step to define group structures is to verify the group sizes in real mobility traces. In Fig. 3, we show that group sizes in the MIT and Dartmouth traces follow power laws with exponential cuts. Therefore, the number of group members in G_i is defined as:

$$||G_i|| \sim PL(\alpha_{\text{size}}, \beta_{\text{size}}), \tag{4}$$

where α_{size} and β_{size} are the last couple of statistical parameters of GRM. GRM defines the network nodes that will compose a given group G_i using the size $||G_i||$, defined by Eq. 4, and a probabilistic snowball sampling algorithm [2]. To do so, a node n is randomly selected, with uniform probability, from the set of network nodes. The snowball algorithm randomly selects a set of neighbors of n. Next, it select a random set of the neighbors of the neighbors of n, and so on, until the set of selected nodes reach the predetermined size $||G_i||$. The selected set of nodes will compose the group G_i. The snowball sampling is performed in the inputted social network, thus preserving the social context of such network. In summary, the structural composition of a group is defined as:

$$\begin{aligned} Node_n &= U(NodesSet) \\ Members_{G_i} &= \text{Snowball}(Node_n, ||G_i||, SocialGraph) \end{aligned} \tag{5}$$

At this point, it is worth to emphasize that, as it happens in reality, one node may participate of several social groups. In addition, the number of possible group structures is combinatorial in relation to the number of nodes. In practice, the number of groups detected in a real mobility trace is bigger than the number of nodes. For instance, around 5000 different groups were detected in the Dartmouth trace that monitors only 1200 nodes.

Also, in reality, it is not reasonable to expect every node always attend to every meeting of a given group. In GRM, each user U_j, that is a member of the group G_i, receives a probability $P_{att}[U_j, G_i]$ of attending to a G_i meeting as:

$$P_{\text{att}}[U_j, G_i] = \frac{\text{Known}(User_j, G_i, SocialGraph)}{||G_i||} \tag{6}$$

The intuition behind the P_{att} probability is that people have higher probability to attend to meetings of social groups in which they know more nodes. The *Known* function returns the number of nodes in G_i that have social edges with U_j in the inputted social network *SocialGraph*. Using such modeling, each social group in the trace will have a different composition at each meeting, but, at the same time, maintaining most of its structure throughout all of its meetings. Such behavior is also presented in social relationships of real life [19].

3.4 Mobility and Meeting Places

The final step of GRM is to generate the network nodes' mobility based on the group meetings defined in the previous sections. GRM mobility is inspired by the SWIM mobility model [14]. However, instead of defining the nodes' trajectories based on individual decisions, the group defines its meeting places to provide common benefit to its members.

As in SWIM, GRM defines a home for each node with uniform probability. Then the simulation space is divided in equally sized square cells, and each group G_i assigns to each cell C_j a weight $W(C_j, G_i)$, which is proportional to the average distance of that cell to the homes of each of the members of G_i:

$$W(C_j, G_i) = \frac{1}{||G_i||} \sum^{U_k \in G_a} dist(Home(U_k), C_j) \tag{7}$$

Similarly to the SWIM model, in GRM the *dist* function has power-law decay with the euclidean distance, which enables the generation of truncated power-law flights in the users displacements [9]. Finally, each cell C_j receives a probability of hosting the group G_i meeting as:

$$P_{\text{place}}(C_j, G_i) = \frac{W(C_j, G_a)}{\sum_{i=0}^{N_{\text{cells}}} W(C_i, G_a)} \tag{8}$$

where N_{cells} denote the total number of cells in the simulation space.

In GRM, nodes transition between their homes and their group meetings. If the next group meeting is to happen before the necessary time for a node to arrive at home, nodes transition directly between the two meeting places.

4 EVALUATION

In this section, we show that mobility traces generated by GRM maintain the typical characteristics of real mobility that are fundamental for mobile opportunistic networking protocols. The first properties we evaluate in GRM are pairwise inter-contact time and contact duration. Inter-contact time measures the time between

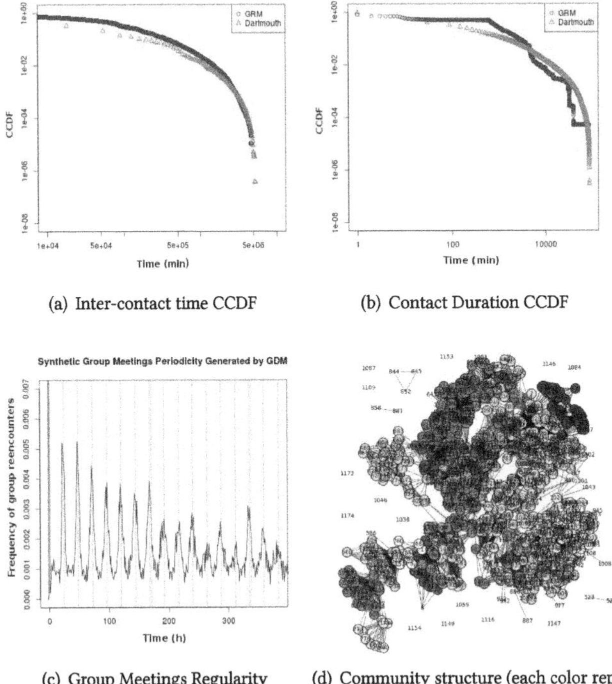

(a) Inter-contact time CCDF

(b) Contact Duration CCDF

(c) Group Meetings Regularity

(d) Community structure (each color represents a different community)

Figure 4: Important properties for opportunistic forwarding extracted from GRM.

the contacts of pairs of nodes. This is important because, in mobile networks, these contacts are the opportunities to forward messages to other nodes. Conversely, contact duration is important because it determines the amount of data that can be transferred during a given contact. Several studies, such as [4, 14], have used a wide number of real-world traces to show that the inter-contact time and contact duration in human mobility distributions follow truncated power laws.

Fig. 4(a) compares the distribution of inter-contact times for GRM and Dartmouth traces. We see that the inter-contact time distribution of GRM conforms with the one presented in the Dartmouth trace. Both of them follow power laws with exponential cut-offs, also conforming with the results for real-world mobility reported in previous studies. In Fig. 4(b), we see that the contact duration distribution also follows a power law, conforming with the distributions shown in real human mobility.

Fig. 4(c) shows that GRM indeed simulates well the regularity of group meetings. We see that the distribution of group re-meeting times is very similar to the ones of real mobility traces (recall Figs 1(a) and 1(b)). It presents peaks at periods of 24 hours and 7 days, remarking the presence of daily and weekly periodicity. This result confirms that GRM fulfill its purpose of properly modeling the role of group meetings regularity in human mobility.

Finally, Fig. 4(d) presents a very important result. It illustrates communities detected in the GRM trace using the Clique Percolation Method [20]. Such result confirms that, by generating regular group meetings, composed of members who share social bonds (defined in the social network input), the social community structure emerges naturally in the mobile network. Therefore, the traces generated by GRM also account for the influence of social context in human mobility.

In addition to the properties discussed in this section, we have also evaluated state-of-the-art social-aware opportunistic routing strategies, namely GROUPS-Net [17] and Bubble-Rap [12], in traces generated by GRM. We found that their performance in GRM is similar to that presented in real-world traces. Due to space limitation, these results are not presented here, but are available at GRM public repository (https://github.com/ivanolive/GRM).

5 CONCLUSION

In this work, we have designed and evaluated GRM, a novel mobility model to represent group meetings regularity and its impact on human mobility. We show that GRM preserves the properties of human mobility that are fundamental for opportunistic networking, namely, ICT and Contact Duration distributions, social community structures, and group meetings regularity.

REFERENCES

[1] Albert-László Barabási and Réka Albert. 1999. Emergence of scaling in random networks. *science* 286, 5439 (1999), 509–512.
[2] Sven Berg. 1988. Snowball sampling. *Encyclopedia of statistical sciences* (1988).
[3] U. Brandes et al. 2003. Experiments on graph clustering algorithms. In *European Symposium on Algorithms*. Springer, 568–579.
[4] A. Chaintreau et al. 2007. Impact of Human Mobility on Opportunistic Forwarding Algorithms. *IEEE TMC* 6, 6 (June 2007), 606–620. https://doi.org/10.1109/TMC.2007.1060
[5] N. Cruz and H. Miranda. 2015. Recurring contact opportunities within groups of devices. In *12th EAI Mobiquitous*. 160–169.
[6] Nathan Eagle and Alex Pentland. 2006. Reality mining: sensing complex social systems. *Personal and ubiquitous computing* 10, 4 (2006), 255–268.
[7] Frans Ekman et al. 2008. Working day movement model. In *Proceedings of the 1st ACM SIGMOBILE workshop on Mobility models*. ACM, 33–40.
[8] Santo Fortunato. 2010. Community detection in graphs. *Physics reports* 486, 3 (2010), 75–174.
[9] Marta Gonzalez et al. 2008. Understanding individual human mobility patterns. *Nature* 453, 7196 (2008), 779–782.
[10] Tristan Henderson et al. 2008. The changing usage of a mature campus-wide wireless network. *Computer Networks* 52, 14 (2008), 2690–2712.
[11] Xiaoyan Hong et al. 1999. A Group Mobility Model for Ad Hoc Wireless Networks. In *2nd ACM MSWIM*. 53–60.
[12] Pan Hui et al. 2011. Bubble rap: Social-based forwarding in delay-tolerant networks. *IEEE TMC* 10, 11 (2011), 1576–1589.
[13] Ari Keränen et al. 2009. The ONE simulator for DTN protocol evaluation. In *Proceedings of the 2nd international conference on simulation tools and techniques*. 55.
[14] Sokol Kosta et al. 2014. Large-scale synthetic social mobile networks with SWIM. *IEEE TMC* 13, 1 (2014), 116–129.
[15] Kyunghan Lee et al. 2009. Slaw: A new mobility model for human walks. In *INFOCOM 2009, IEEE*. 855–863.
[16] Yong Li et al. 2014. Social-aware D2D communications: qualitative insights and quantitative analysis. *Communications Magazine, IEEE* 52, 6 (2014), 150–158.
[17] Ivan O. Nunes, Clayson Celes, Pedro O.S. Vaz de Melo, and Antonio A.F. Loureiro. 2017. GROUPS-NET: Group meetings aware routing in multi-hop D2D networks. *Computer Networks* (2017), 94 – 108.
[18] I. O. Nunes, Clayson Celes, Pedro O.S. Vaz de Melo, and Antonio A.F. Loureiro. 2017. GROUPS-NET: Group meetings aware routing in multi-hop D2D networks. *Computer Networks* 127, Supplement C (2017), 94 – 108.
[19] I. O. Nunes et al. 2016. Group Mobility: Detection, Tracking and Characterization. In *IEEE ICC*.
[20] Gergely Palla et al. 2005. Uncovering the overlapping community structure of complex networks in nature and society. *Nature* 435, 7043 (2005), 814–818.
[21] Joanne Treurniet. 2014. A Taxonomy and Survey of Microscopic Mobility Models from the Mobile Networking Domain. *ACM Computing Surveys (CSUR)* 47, 1 (2014), 14.
[22] K. H. Wang and Baochun Li. 2002. Group mobility and partition prediction in wireless ad-hoc networks. In *IEEE ICC 2002*.

Quality of Experience-Aware Mobile Edge Caching through a Vehicular Cloud

Luigi Vigneri
EURECOM
450 Route des Chappes
Biot, France 06410
luigi.vigneri@eurecom.fr

Thrasyvoulos Spyropoulos
EURECOM
450 Route des Chappes
Biot, France 06410
spyropou@eurecom.fr

Chadi Barakat
INRIA Sophia Antipolis
2004 Route des Lucioles
Valbonne, France 06902
chadi.barakat@inria.fr

ABSTRACT

Densification through small cells and caching in base stations have been proposed to deal with the increasing demand for Internet content and the related overload on the cellular infrastructure. However, these solutions are expensive to install and maintain. Instead, using vehicles acting as mobile caches might represent an interesting alternative. In our work, we assume that users can query nearby vehicles for some time, and be redirected to the cellular infrastructure when the deadline expires. Beyond reducing costs, in such an architecture, through vehicle mobility, a user sees a much larger variety of locally accessible content within only few minutes. Unlike most of the related works on delay tolerant access, we consider the impact on the user experience by assigning different retrieval deadlines per content. In our paper, we provide the following contributions: (i) we model analytically such a scenario; (ii) we formulate an optimization problem to maximize the traffic offloaded while ensuring user experience guarantees; (iii) we propose a variable deadline policy; (iv) we perform realistic trace-based simulations, and we show that, even with low technology penetration rate, more than 60% of the total traffic can be offloaded which is around 20% larger compared to existing allocation policies.

1 INTRODUCTION

The large diffusion of handheld devices is leading to an exponential growth of the mobile traffic demand which is already overloading the core network [7]. To deal with such a problem, several works suggest to store content in small cells (SCs) or user equipments. Recently, it has been proposed the use of private or public transportation as storage points and mobile relays (*vehicular cloud*) [1, 2, 24] controlled by mobile network operators (MNOs) through a cellular interface. In urban environments, the number of vehicles is expected to be considerably higher than in any envisioned SC deployment. Hence, the sheer number of vehicles along with the lower cost involved make this an interesting alternative.

In this paper, we exploit such a vehicular cloud to store popular content to offload part of the mobile traffic demand. In our model, a user can query nearby vehicles to download a content with low delay (and at low cost for the MNO). However, since caches will be quite small compared to the daily catalogue, the user might not be inside the range of any cache storing the requested content at that time. To alleviate this, we propose that each request can be delayed for a small amount of time, if there is a local cache miss. Conversely, if the content is not found within a deadline, the user will be redirected to the cellular infrastructure. While the idea of delay tolerance has already been extensively discussed in literature, in this work we introduce three fundamental novelties:

Vehicle storage capacity "virtually" extended. Most of related works [4, 6, 19] *require the user to move* to encounter new base stations and see new caches. This is problematic as most users exhibit a nomadic behavior, staying in the same location for long periods. As a result, such delayed offloading architectures require deadlines in the order of half to a couple of hours to demonstrate performance benefits [4, 18, 19]. Instead, when caches are on vehicles, especially in a dense urban environment, a user will see a much larger number of caches within the same amount of time, thus *virtually extending the size of the accessible local storage.* This leads to better hit rates with considerably smaller deadlines.

Variable deadlines. The majority of edge caching related works aims at policies that exclusively minimize the load on the cellular infrastructure. In most delayed offloading settings, the worst-case delay guarantee offered to the user is usually *fixed* for all content requests and set to large values. Conversely, in this work we allow the operator to *set different deadlines for different content.* This variability in the deadlines brings two advantages: first, it allows to increase the percentage of the traffic offloaded as we will see in the rest of the paper; second, these deadlines can be adapted according to the specific characteristics of the content (e.g., size) to improve user Quality of Experience (QoE) as we explain below.

User QoE-Aware offloading. We evaluate the user QoE according to the experienced *slowdown* which has recently become popular [13]. This metric relates the waiting delay with the "net" download time. For example, a user requesting a web page of a few megabytes (normally taking some seconds) will be quite frustrated if she has to wait an extra 1-2 minutes to encounter a vehicle caching that web page. However, a user downloading a large video or software file might not even notice an extra 1-2 minutes delay. Specifically, in our framework an MNO can calibrate the user experience by setting a required slowdown which upper bounds the tail behavior of the response time. Tuning the waiting time per content ensures maximum offloading with little QoE degradation.

While there are a number of additional architectural and incentive-related questions to consider, the main focus of this paper is on the modelling of the above scenario and on the formulation of a related

MSWiM'17, November 21–25, 2017, Miami, FL, USA
 ISBN 978-1-4503-5162-1/17/11...$15.00.
DOI: 10:1145/3127540:3127555

(nontrivial) optimization problem. The main contributions of the paper can be summarized as follows:

- We model the problem of maximizing the percentage of traffic offloaded through the vehicular cloud considering the user QoE (captured by the slowdown metric) and a large range of realistic conditions (e.g., content of heterogeneous size), and we solve the corresponding optimization problem.
- We validate our findings using simulations with real traces for vehicle mobility and content popularity. We show that, in an urban scenario, our system can achieve considerable offloading gains with modest technology penetration (less than 1% of vehicles participating in the cloud) and low mean slowdown (that leads to average deadlines of a few minutes).
- We study the impact of different user QoE guarantees on operator- and user-related performance, and compare variable and fixed deadline policies.

The rest of the paper is organized as follows: in Section 2, we compare our work with the previous literature; in Section 3, we define the system model with the main assumptions; then, in Section 4, we present the mathematical formulation of the problem, and we solve a reasonable approximation (since the original problem is hard); we validate our results through real trace-based simulations in Section 5; finally, we conclude our paper with a summary and future work in Section 6.

2 RELATED WORK

Caching at the edge of the network has been deeply investigated by researchers lately [11, 21]. Golrezaei *et al.* [11] propose to replace backhaul capacity with storage capacity at the SC access points (APs), called *helpers*; the challenge faced by the authors was in the analysis of the optimum way of assigning content to the helpers in order to minimize the expected download time. Poularakis *et al.* [21] focus their attention on video requests trying to optimize the service cost and the delivery delay; in their framework, pre-stored video files can be encoded with two different schemes in various qualities. While such distributed caching schemes for SCs provide very interesting theoretical insights and algorithms, they face some key shortcomings. A large number of SCs is required for an extensive enough coverage by SCs, which comes at a high cost [3]. E.g., in a macro-cell of a radius of a few kilometers, it is envisioned to place 3-5 SCs, of range a few hundred meters. By contrast, in an urban environment, the same area will probably contain thousands of vehicles. Furthermore, the smaller size of edge caches and the smaller number of users per cell raise the question whether enough overlap in user demand would be generated locally to have a high enough hit ratio, when real traffic is considered.

To alleviate the aforementioned problem of requests overlap at a low cost, a number of works introduce delayed access. This can be seen as an enforced delay until a WiFi access point is encountered to offload the cellular connection to a less loaded radio access technology [4, 19], or until to reach peer nodes in a P2P infrastructure [6]. For example, Balasubramanian *et al.* [4] develop a system to augment mobile 3G capacity with WiFi, using two key ideas: delay tolerance and fast switching. This enforced delay virtually extends the coverage of WiFi APs, allowing a larger ratio of connections to be offloaded than the mere physical coverage of WiFi APs allows. In other works [6, 10] a different deadline is assigned to each content. However, these deadlines are problem input parameters and cannot be used to improve performance (e.g., the amount of data offloaded, QoE) as we do in our paper. Nevertheless, these approaches *require the user to move* in order to encounter new base stations and new caches. User mobility is often nomadic and slow, requiring the respective algorithms to enforce very large delays (often in the order of hours) before any performance improvement is perceived by the operator. Instead, in our paper we present two main novelties: (i) having the SC and cache move, the operator can offload up to 60% of its traffic with minimum QoE impact; (ii) while other works consider pre-assigned deadlines, we allow variable delay tolerance per content, and also allow the operator to optimize it (by setting an upper limit on the slowdown).

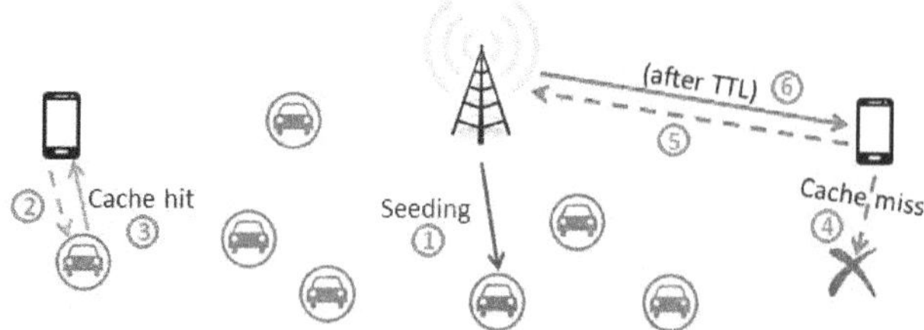

Figure 1: Communication protocol.

In a previous work, we have dealt with the idea of vehicular cloud used to offload part of the traffic and accessible by handheld devices [24]. However, the paper only mentions initial thoughts about the architecture without dealing with QoE or variable deadlines. The hype around vehicular networks as part of the cellular infrastructure has been confirmed by car manufacturers [1] or by the launch of new companies [2] that offer network connectivity to public and private transportation.

3 SYSTEM MODEL

3.1 Content access protocol

We consider a network with three types of nodes:

- *Infrastructure nodes* ($\mathcal{I}$): base stations or macro-cells; their role is to seed content into vehicles and to serve user requests when the deadline expires.
- *Helper nodes* ($\mathcal{H}$): vehicles such as cars, buses, taxis, trucks, etc., where $|\mathcal{H}| = h$; these are used to store popular content and to serve user requests at low cost through a direct vehicle to mobile node link.
- *End user nodes* ($\mathcal{U}$): mobile devices such as smartphones, tablets or netbooks; these nodes request content to $\mathcal{H}$ and $\mathcal{I}$ nodes (the last ones are only contacted when the deadline expires and the content is still not entirely downloaded).

The basic protocol is made up of three phases (Fig. 1):

- ($\mathcal{I} \rightarrow \mathcal{H}$): $\mathcal{I}$ nodes place content in $\mathcal{H}$ nodes according to the chosen allocation policy. This policy is the main outcome of this paper. We refer to this phase as *seeding* which is repeated at the beginning of operator selected time windows to adjust to varying content access patterns. If seeding is performed during off-peak times, the seeding cost can be considered equal to 0. In our work we will focus on this scenario[1].

- ($\mathcal{H} \rightarrow \mathcal{U}$): an end user node can request content i to the vehicles that are inside her communication range[2]. If content i is found, then the $\mathcal{U}$ node can download bytes from the vehicle during the contact. If the download is not terminated, then the requesting mobile user will query nearby vehicles for a time equal to y_i. This deadline is decided for that content i by the allocation policy during the seeding phase. The related local access cost is null.
- ($\mathcal{I} \rightarrow \mathcal{U}$): in case of a content not successfully downloaded within a time y_i, the $\mathcal{U}$ node's request will be served (partially or entirely) by the cellular infrastructure. The related cost is equal to the number of bytes downloaded from $\mathcal{I}$ nodes.

3.2 Main assumptions

A.1 - Catalogue. Let $\mathcal{K}$ be the set of all possible contents that users might request (also defined as "catalogue"), where $|\mathcal{K}| = k$. Let further c be the size of the cache in each vehicle. We make the natural assumption that $c \ll k$. A content $i \in \mathcal{K}$ is of size s_i (in MB) and is characterized by a popularity value ϕ_i measured as the expected number of requests within a seeding time window from all users and all cells.

A.2 - Inter-meeting times. We assume that the inter-meeting times $T_{ij}(t)$ between a user requesting content $i \in K$ and a vehicle $j \in H$ are IID random variables characterized by a known cumulative distribution function (CDF) $F_T(t) = \mathbf{P}[T_{ij} \leq t]$ with mean rate λ. This model does not make any assumption on the individual user and vehicle mobility patterns and can capture a number of inter-contact time models proposed in related literature such as exponential, Pareto, or mixed models [15].

A.3 - Cache model. Let x_i denote the number of vehicles storing content i. The vector $\mathbf{x}$ will be the control variable for our optimal cache allocation problem. We also assume $\mathcal{H}$ nodes to *store the whole content*, i.e., fractional storage is not allowed.

A.4 - Chunk download. Let b_{ij} be the number of bytes downloaded from content i by a $\mathcal{U}$ node during the jth meeting. b_{ij} are positive IID continuous random variables having equal mean μ and variance σ^2. Let further M_i be a random variable counting the number of contacts within y_i. Then, we define $B_i \triangleq \sum_{j=1}^{M_i} b_{ij}$ as the number of bytes downloaded within y_i for content i.

A.5 - QoE metric. First, we define $t_i \triangleq s_i/r$ as the *net* download time of content i by a user, i.e., the amount of time it takes to download the content (excluding any potential waiting time to encounter vehicles holding the content), where r is the download rate from the cellular infrastructure. As for videos, t_i can be thought of as the video duration (and r as the playout rate). Then, we introduce the *maximum slowdown per content* imposed by our system when the content is fetched from the infrastructure that ties content download time to its size as $\omega_i \triangleq \frac{y_i+t_i}{t_i} = 1 + \frac{y_i}{s_i/r}$. The larger ω_i is, the worse the impact of the allocation policy on user experience. This is in fact a *worst case* metric, because if the content is downloaded before the deadline expires, say at some time $d_i < y_i$ (i.e., there is a cache hit), the real slowdown is lower and equal to $1 + \frac{d_i}{t_i}$. Nevertheless, we choose to use the maximum slowdown in our theoretical framework as a more conservative approach for the user, and keep analysis simpler. Furthermore, since the operator's goal is to consider the global QoE (and not only per request), we consider a weighted average of the maximum slowdown according to the content popularity defined as

$$\Omega(\mathbf{y}) = \frac{1}{\sum_{i=1}^{k} \phi_i} \cdot \sum_{i=1}^{k} \phi_i \cdot \omega_i.$$

For simplicity, we will refer to $\Omega(\mathbf{y})$ as *mean slowdown*. An MNO can use this metric to calibrate the global user QoE of the system by setting a parameter $\omega_{max} > 1$ that upper bounds the mean slowdown. This value can be seen as a sort of "budget" available to the MNO that can be reallocated between contents. Moreover, it can set a maximum tolerable deadline y_{max} to avoid excessively large deadlines for specific content.

We summarize the notation used in the paper in Table 1.

[1]The generic case (i.e., non-null seeding cost) is a straightforward extension when seeding time windows are large enough to amortize content seeding.

[2]The communication range size depends on the physical layer technology used between $\mathcal{U}$ and $\mathcal{H}$ nodes.

Table 1: Notation used in the paper.

CONTROL VARIABLES	
x_i	Number of replicas stored for content i
y_i	Deadline for content i
CONTENT	
k	Number of content in the catalogue
ϕ_i	Number of requests for content i
s_i	Size of content i
c	Buffer size per vehicle
MOBILITY	
T_{ij}	Inter-meeting time between $\mathcal{U}$ and $\mathcal{H}$ nodes
λ	Mean inter-meeting rate with vehicles
M_i	Number of contacts within y_i
h	Number of vehicles
CHUNK DOWNLOAD	
b_{ij}	Bytes downloaded per contact
μ	Mean of b_{ij}
σ^2	Variance of b_{ij}
B_i	Total bytes downloaded for content i
f_{B_i}	Probability density function of B_i
F_{B_i}	Cumulative density function of B_i
QOE PARAMETERS	
r	Download rate from cellular infrastructure (or playout rate for videos)
Ω	Mean slowdown
y_{max}	Maximum deadline
ω_{max}	Upper bound on the mean slowdown

4 OPTIMAL CONTENT ALLOCATION

4.1 Offloading optimization problem

The operator's goal is to define a policy to maximize the bytes offloaded through the vehicular cloud while satisfying storage capacity and user QoE requirements. This policy should infer the optimal content allocation $\mathbf{x}$ and the optimal deadlines $\mathbf{y}$ to assign to the content catalogue. The number of bytes offloaded through the vehicular cloud *per request* is either equal to s_i, if the content is entirely downloaded from vehicles, or to B_i, otherwise. For popular content, we can consider the expected value of this quantity since the envisioned number of requests during a seeding time window is large. The following lemma captures these considerations in the objective function $\Phi(\mathbf{x}, \mathbf{y})$ to be optimized:

LEMMA 4.1. *Given the previous assumptions, the amount of bytes offloaded through the vehicular cloud during a seeding time window is given by*

$$\Phi(\mathbf{x}, \mathbf{y}) \triangleq \sum_{i=1}^{k} \phi_i \cdot \mathrm{E}\left[\min\{B_i, s_i\}\right], \tag{1}$$

COROLLARY 4.2. *The objective function $\Phi(\mathbf{x}, \mathbf{y})$ is equivalent to*

$$\Phi(\mathbf{x}, \mathbf{y}) \equiv \sum_{i=1}^{k} \phi_i \cdot \int_0^{s_i} \left(1 - F_{B_i}(t)\right) dt, \tag{2}$$

where F_{B_i} is the CDF of B_i.

PROOF. The objective function can be written as follows:

$$\begin{aligned}\Phi(\mathbf{x}, \mathbf{y}) &= \sum_{i=1}^{k} \phi_i \cdot \mathrm{E}\left[\min\{B_i, s_i\}\right] \\ &= \sum_{i=1}^{k} \phi_i \cdot \left(\int_0^{s_i} t \cdot f_{B_i}(t)\, dt + \int_{s_i}^{+\infty} s_i \cdot f_{B_i}(t)\, dt\right),\end{aligned}$$

where f_{B_i} is the PDF of B_i. The first integral becomes equal to

$$s_i \cdot F_{B_i}(s_i) - \int_0^{s_i} F_{B_i}(t)\, dt$$

by integration by parts, while the second integral is trivially equal to

$$s_i \cdot (1 - F_{B_i}(s_i)).$$

After simplifying the null terms, we obtain Eq. (2). □

We formulate an optimization problem based on the following ideas: an ideal content allocation should replicate content with higher popularity in many different vehicles in order to increase the probability to find it from a requesting user. Trivially, more replicas lead to smaller waiting times. However, if the *marginal* gain from extra replicas is nonlinear, it might be better to also have some less popular content at the edge. As the storage capacity of each vehicle is limited, our objective is thus to find the optimal replication factor per content to minimize the total load on the cellular infrastructure while accounting for end users QoE:

PROBLEM 1. *The solution to the following optimization problem maximizes the bytes offloaded through the vehicular cloud:*

$$\begin{aligned}&\underset{\mathbf{x}\in X^k, \mathbf{y}\in Y^k}{\mathit{maximize}} \quad \sum_{i=1}^{k} \phi_i \cdot \int_0^{s_i} \left(1 - F_{B_i}(t)\right) dt \qquad (3)\\ &\mathit{subject\ to} \quad \mathbf{s}^t \cdot \mathbf{x} \le c \cdot h, \\ &\qquad\qquad\quad \Omega(\mathbf{y}) \le \omega_{max},\end{aligned}$$

where $X \triangleq \{a \in \mathbb{R} \mid 0 \le a \le h\}$ and $Y \triangleq \{b \in \mathbb{R} \mid 0 \le b \le y_{max}\}$.

Each vehicle has a storage constraint and cannot store more than c contents. However, instead of considering h individual storage constraints, we only consider the global cache capacity of the vehicular cloud that corresponds to improve the tractability of the problem. Although the global capacity constraint introduces an error in the problem formulation, such an error is expected to be low when caches are large compared to the mean content size as we will explain at the end of this section (see randomized rounding).

Solving Problem (1) requires the knowledge of F_{B_i} and, therefore, of B_i. We prove that the following theorem holds:

LEMMA 4.3. *B_i can be approximated by a compound Poisson process as the number of vehicles participating in the vehicular cloud increases, if the mean inter-meeting rate with such vehicles is small.*

PROOF. Assume that user m requests content i. Let $\{T_{ij}(t), t > 0, j \in \mathcal{H}$ s.t. $x_{ij} = 1\}$ be x_i identical and independent renewal processes corresponding to the inter-contact times with vehicles storing content i. The CDF of T_{ij} is $F_T(t)$ with mean λ (see Assumption A.2). Let further $\{T_i(t), t > 0\}$ be the superposition of these processes. According to the Palm-Kintchine theorem [16], $\{T_i(t)\}$ approaches a Poisson process with rate $\lambda \cdot x_i$ if x_i large[3] and λ small. A Poisson process can be defined as a counting process that represents the total number of occurrences up to time t. Thus, the total number of contacts within the deadline $M_i = \{T_i(y_i)\}$ is again a Poisson process.

Remember that $B_i \triangleq \sum_{j=1}^{M_i} b_{ij}$. Observe that the reward (bytes downloaded) in each contact is independent of the inter-contact times, i.e., M_i and b_{ij} are independent, and b_{ij} are IID random variables with same distribution. Since M_i is a Poisson process, then B_i is a compound Poisson process. □

LEMMA 4.4. *The first two moments of B_i are given by:*

$$\begin{aligned}\mathrm{E}[B_i] &= \mu \cdot \lambda \cdot x_i \cdot y_i, \\ Var[B_i] &= (\mu^2 + \sigma^2) \cdot \lambda \cdot x_i \cdot y_i.\end{aligned}$$

PROOF. The expected value of a compound Poisson process can be computed using conditional expectation, where the expectation is calculated using the Wald's equation. Similarly, it is possible to compute the moment of second order of B_i, and then its variance using the total law of variance. □

LEMMA 4.5. *The CDF of B_i is given by*

$$F_{B_i}(s_i) = 1 - \mathcal{L}^{-1}\left\{e^{(b^*_{ij}(s)-1)\cdot\lambda\cdot x_i\cdot y_i}/s\right\}(s_i), \tag{4}$$

where $b^*_{ij}(s)$ is the Laplace transform of b_{ij}.

PROOF. A *random* sum of identically distributed random variables has a Laplace transform that is related to the transform of the summed random variables and of the number of terms in the sum

$$B^*_i(s) = M^*_i(b^*_{ij}(s)),$$

where B^*_i (resp. b^*_{ij}) is the Laplace transform of B_i (resp. b_{ij}) and M^*_i is the $\mathcal{Z}$-transform of M_i. Since the number of meetings within y_i is Poisson distributed (see proof of Lemma 4.3), we can write $B^*_i(s)$ as follows:

$$B^*_i(s) = e^{(b^*_{ij}(s)-1)\cdot\lambda\cdot x_i\cdot y_i}.$$

Moreover, it is well known that the CDF of a continuous random variable X is given by $F_X(x) = \mathcal{L}^{-1}\left\{\frac{\mathcal{L}\{f_X\}}{s}\right\}(s_i)$ where

[3] While this assumption (i.e., x_i large) might not always be true, exponential inter-meeting times have been largely used in literature and considered as a good approximation, especially in the tail of the distribution [9].

$\mathcal{L}^{-1}\{F(s)\}(t)$ is the inverse Laplace transform of $F(s)$. Thus, $F_{B_i}(s_i)$ corresponds to Eq. (4). □

All the quantities needed to solve the optimization problem are known, and can be plugged in Eq. (3). However, due to the large number of contents to consider, the related maximization problem cannot be solved efficiently. For this reason, further insights, approximations and specific scenarios will be discussed in the rest of the paper.

4.2 QoE-Aware Caching (QAC)

Problem (1) is a mixed-integer nonlinear programming (MINLP) problem. MINLP refers to optimization problems with continuous and discrete variables and nonlinear functions in the objective function and/or the constraints.

Theorem 4.6. *Problem (1) is an NP-hard combinatorial problem.*

Proof. The problem is NP-hard since it includes mixed-integer linear programming as a subproblem [14]. □

What is more, this problem is in general non-convex. This means that the solution can be computed by global optimization methods, but this is generally not an efficient solution as it does not scale to a large number of contents. Similarly to a number of works we consider the *continuous relaxation* of a MINLP which is identical to the mixed-integer problem without the restriction that some variables must be integer. The continuous relaxation brings two fundamental advantages: first, it is possible to evaluate the quality of a feasible set of solutions; second, it is much faster to optimize than the mixed-integer problem. According to this relaxation, we also introduce a new objective function $\Phi_{qac}(\cdot)$ that approximates Eq. (1) in order to convert the problem in a convex optimization problem, hence improving tractability.

Lemma 4.7. *Eq. (1) can be approximated by*

$$\Phi_{qac}(\mathbf{x},\mathbf{y}) = \sum_{i=1}^{k} \phi_i \cdot \min\{\mathrm{E}[B_i], s_i\}.$$

Corollary 4.8. *Let $e \triangleq \Phi_{qac} - \Phi$ be the error introduced by Lemma 4.7. The following statements hold:*

(1) *For a given $\mathrm{E}[B_i]$, as the content size s_i tends to 0 or becomes large, the approximation becomes exact, i.e., e tends to 0.*
(2) *The error e is equal to*

$$e = \sum_{i=1}^{k} \phi_i \cdot \left[\alpha(s_i) \cdot |s_i - \mathrm{E}[B_i]| + \sigma_{B_i} \cdot f_{B_i}(s_i)\right],$$

where $\alpha(s_i) = \min\{F_{B_i}(s_i), 1 - F_{B_i}(s_i)\}$.

Proof. (1) The following equivalences are true:

$$\lim_{s_i \to 0} \Phi_{qac} = \lim_{s_i \to 0} \Phi = \sum_{i=1}^{k} \phi_i \cdot s_i$$

$$\lim_{s_i \to +\infty} \Phi_{qac} = \lim_{s_i \to +\infty} \Phi = \sum_{i=1}^{k} \phi_i \cdot \mathrm{E}[B_i].$$

(2) It is easy to see that

$$\mathrm{E}[\min\{B_i, s_i\}] = F_{B_i}(s_i) \cdot \mathrm{E}[B_i|B_i \le s_i] + s_i \cdot (1 - F_{B_i}(s_i)). \quad (5)$$

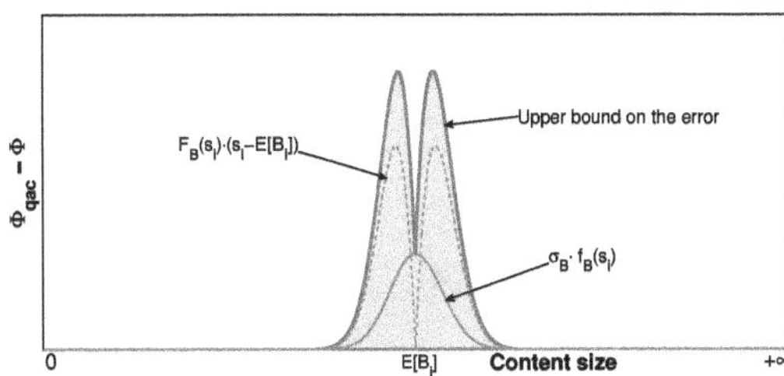

Figure 2: Error introduced by $\Phi_{qac}(\mathbf{x},\mathbf{y})$ in Lemma 4.7 for a fixed value of $\mathrm{E}[B_i]$.

$\mathrm{E}[B_i|B_i \le s_i]$ corresponds to the truncated mean of B_i upper bounded by s_i. If the number of meetings within y_i is large, B_i can be considered as a normal distribution [23]. Thus, we can write its truncated mean as:

$$\mathrm{E}[B_i|B_i \le s_i] = \mathrm{E}[B_i] - \sigma_{B_i} \cdot \frac{f_{B_i}(s_i)}{F_{B_i}(s_i)},$$

where σ_{B_i} is the standard deviation of B_i, and can be inferred from Corollary 4.4[4]. If $\mathrm{E}[B_i] > s_i$, the error e introduced by Φ_{qac} can be evaluated as follows:

$$e = \sum_{i=1}^{k} \phi_i \cdot |\min\{\mathrm{E}[B_i], s_i\} - \mathrm{E}[\min\{B_i, s_i\}]|$$
$$= \sum_{i=1}^{k} \phi_i \cdot (s_i - \mathrm{E}[\min\{B_i, s_i\}]). \quad (6)$$

Then, we compute the second term of Eq. (6) from Eq. (5), and, after some calculations, we obtain:

$$e = \sum_{i=1}^{k} \phi_i \cdot [(1 - F_{B_i}(s_i)) \cdot (\mathrm{E}[B_i] - s_i) + \sigma_{B_i} \cdot f_{B_i}(s_i)].$$

Similarly, we compute e when $\mathrm{E}[B_i] \le s_i$. □

A qualitative analysis of e can be found in Fig. 2, where we can see that the error is concentrated in the region where $s_i \approx \mathrm{E}[B_i]$, and it tends to 0 otherwise. Using the above approximation, Problem (1) can be converted in a *convex* optimization problem that can be solved extremely efficiently and reliably:

Problem 2. *Consider the approximation introduced by Lemma 4.7. Then, the solution to the following convex optimization problem maximizes the bytes offloaded through the vehicular cloud:*

$$\underset{\tilde{\mathbf{x}} \in \tilde{X}^k, \tilde{\mathbf{y}} \in \tilde{Y}^k}{\text{maximize}} \quad \log\left(\sum_{i=1}^{k} \phi_i \cdot e^{\tilde{x}_i + \tilde{y}_i}\right),$$
$$\text{subject to } \tilde{x}_i + \tilde{y}_i \le \log\left(\frac{s_i}{\mu \cdot \lambda}\right), \quad \forall i \in K,$$
$$\sum_i s_i \cdot e^{\tilde{x}_i} \le c \cdot h,$$
$$\Omega(\tilde{\mathbf{y}}) \le \omega_{max},$$

where $\tilde{x}_i \triangleq \log x_i$, $\tilde{y}_i \triangleq \log y_i$, $\tilde{X} \triangleq \{a \in \mathbb{R} \mid -\infty \le a \le \log h\}$, $\tilde{Y} \triangleq \{b \in \mathbb{R} \mid -\infty \le b \le \log y_{max}\}$.

[4] Note that $\sigma_{B_i} \neq \sigma$ that is the standard deviation for a single contact.

Proof. We rewrite the objective function $\Phi_{qac}(\cdot)$ in an equivalent form that removes the min function:

$$\Phi_{qac}(\mathbf{x},\mathbf{y}) = \sum_{i=1}^{k} \phi_i \cdot \min\{\mathrm{E}[B_i], s_i\} = \sum_{i=1}^{k} \phi_i \cdot \mathrm{E}[B_i], \quad \text{s. t. } \mathrm{E}[B_i] \leq s_i, \ \forall i \in K, \qquad (7)$$

where the equivalence is true since the related maximization problem will choose the control variables $\mathbf{x}$ and $\mathbf{y}$ such that $0 \leq \mathrm{E}[B_i] \leq s_i$ as any scenario where $\mathrm{E}[B_i] > s_i$ is suboptimal. Remember that $\mathrm{E}[B_i] = \mu \cdot \lambda \cdot x_i \cdot y_i$ from Lemma 4.4. According to Eq. (7), Problem (1) becomes

$$\begin{aligned} \underset{\mathbf{x}\in X^k, \mathbf{y}\in Y^k}{\text{maximize}} \quad & \sum_{i=1}^{k} \phi_i \cdot x_i \cdot y_i, \\ \text{subject to} \quad & x_i \cdot y_i \leq \frac{s_i}{\mu \cdot \lambda}, \quad \forall i \in K, \\ & \mathbf{s}^t \cdot \mathbf{x} \leq c \cdot h, \\ & \Omega(\mathbf{y}) \leq \omega_{max}. \end{aligned}$$

The above optimization problem is a *geometric program* (GP). A GP is an optimization problem where the objective is a posynomial function[5] and the constraints are posynomial or monomial functions. The main trick to solve a GP efficiently is to convert it to a nonlinear but *convex* optimization problem, since efficient solution methods for general convex optimization problem are well developed [5]. The conversion of a GP to a convex problem is based on a logarithmic change of variables and on a logarithmic transformation of the objective and constraint functions. We apply the following transformations to the above optimization problem:

$$\tilde{x_i} \triangleq \log x_i \ \Leftrightarrow\ e^{\tilde{x}_i} \triangleq x_i; \qquad \tilde{y_i} \triangleq \log y_i \ \Leftrightarrow\ e^{\tilde{y}_i} \triangleq y_i.$$

We obtain a problem expressed in terms of the new variables $\tilde{\mathbf{x}}$ and $\tilde{\mathbf{y}}$. By taking the logarithm of the objective function and of the constraints, it can be proved that the related problem is convex [5]. □

While this problem seems more complicated in its formulation, NLP is far trickier and always involves some compromise such as accepting a local instead of a global solution. Conversely, a GP can actually be solved efficiently with any nonlinear solver (e.g., MATLAB, SNOPT) or with common optimizers for GP (e.g., MOSEK, GPPOSY). Finally, we use *randomized rounding* [22] on the content allocation which is a widely used approach for designing and analyzing such approximation algorithms. We expect the rounding error to be low since the number of copies per content is usually large (then the decision whether rounding up or down has only a marginal effect in the objective function). To validate this, in Table 2 we compare the objective value from our allocation to the one corresponding to the continuous solution of Problem (2) (we report the percentage of traffic offloaded). As the latter is an upper bound on the optimal solution of the mixed-integer problem, the actual performance gap is bounded by the values shown in Table 2. We refer to this policy as QoE-Aware Caching (*QAC*).

[5]A posynomial function $f(x)$ is a sum of monomials: $f(x) = \sum_{k=1}^{K} c_k x_1^{a_{1k}} x_2^{a_{2k}} \cdots x_n^{a_{nk}}$, where $c_k > 0$.

Table 2: Estimated offloading gains of rounded allocation vs. continuous relaxation for different cache sizes (in percentage of the catalogue size).

Cache size	0,1%	0,2%	0,5%	1%
Rounded (QAC)	34,25%	44,10%	52,88%	60,75%
Continuous	34,29%	44,12%	52,89%	60,75%

5 PERFORMANCE EVALUATION

5.1 Simulation setup

We build a trace-driven MATLAB simulator to validate our theoretical findings. Our tool simulates YouTube requests in the centre of San Francisco over five days. We use the following traces:

- *Vehicle mobility.* We use the Cabspotting trace [20] to simulate the vehicle behaviour; this trace records the GPS coordinates for 531 taxis in San Francisco with granularity of 1 minute. To improve the accuracy of our simulations, we increase the granularity to 10 seconds by linear interpolation.
- *User mobility.* We use synthetic traces based on SLAW mobility model [17]. According to this model, users move in a limited and defined area around popular places. The mobility is nomadic where users alternate between pauses (heavy-tailed distributed) and travelling periods at constant (but random) speed.
- *Content.* We infer the number of requests per day from a database with statistics for 100.000 YouTube videos [25]. To increase the number of simulations and to provide sensitivity analysis for content size, buffer capacity and cache density, we randomly select 10.000 contents from the catalogue.

Inline with proposed protocols for vehicle communications (e.g., 802.11p, LTE ProSe), we consider short (100 m) or long (200 m) communication ranges between $\mathcal{U}$ and $\mathcal{H}$ nodes. As most wireless protocols implement some *rate adaptation* mechanism, our simulator also varies the communication rate according to the distance between the user and the vehicle she is downloading from, with a *mean* of 5 Mbps. We also set r = 1 Mbps which approximates the streaming of a 720p video (remember that r corresponds to the playout rate in the case of videos - see Assumption A.5). We set the cache size per vehicle in the range 0,1-1% of the total catalogue which is an assumption that has also been used in other works [12, 21] (we use 0,2% as a default value). We generate content size from either a truncated normal or a bounded Pareto distribution[6] (instead of using the content size from the YouTube trace) in order to experiment different characteristics of the catalogue. Finally, we consider ω_{max} = 3 which corresponds to an average deadline of *only* a few minutes (compared to video durations that can go up to 1,5 hours).

Our simulator works as follows: first, it generates a set of content requests concentrated at day-time; inter-arrival times between successive requests are exponentially distributed according to the IRM model [8] which is the de facto standard in the analysis of storage systems. Next, the simulator associates to each request the coordinates (and the mobility according to the SLAW model) of the user requesting the content. Then, it allocates content in

[6]Since content size and popularity are not correlated (from the analysis of the trace), we randomly assign content size to the catalogue.

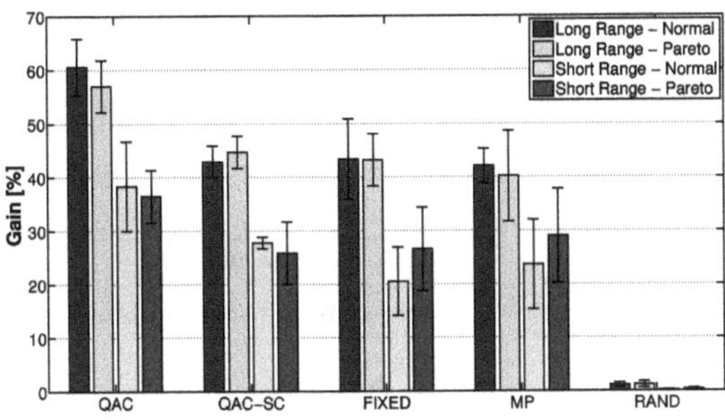

Figure 3: Offloading gains.

caches according to different allocation policies. For each request, a user downloads chunks of video when she is in the communication range of a vehicle storing the requested content. When the deadline expires, the potential remaining bytes are downloaded from the cellular infrastructure.

We consider and compare the following allocation policies:

- *QAC.* This policy solves the optimization problem with a reasonable approximation for content of generic size. This policy is described in Section 4.2.
- *FIXED.* This policy solves the optimization problem when a content can be downloaded with large probability in on contact, and deadlines are fixed. This policy is suitable for content of small size and is described in Vigneri *et al.* [24].
- *QAC-SC.* This policy solves the optimization problem of *FIXED* when deadlines are variable. The problem is biconvex and is solved numerically.
- *MP.* This policy stores the most popular content in vehicle buffers until caches are full while any other content gets 0 copies. Deadlines are fixed. This policy is optimal for sparse scenarios where caches do not overlap.
- *RAND.* Content is allocated randomly with fixed deadlines.

5.2 Caching policies evaluation

In Fig. 3 we plot the amount of data offloaded for different allocation policies. This plot also includes the 95% confidence interval. The fraction of traffic offloaded by *QAC* is much larger (additional gains of around 20%) than any other policy in any situation. For instance, when long range communications are considered, offloading gains are in the order of 60% for *QAC*, and no more than 40% for *QAC-SC*, *FIXED* and *MP*. *RAND* policy performs poorly in any scenario. It is also interesting to note that, while *QAC-SC* is expected to benefit from the deadline variability, it performs similar to fixed deadline policies since the assumption that a content can be downloaded in one contact is unrealistic for content of 200 MB. Not substantial differences have been observed for different content size distributions: however, from additional experiments we have noticed that, as the coefficient of variation of the content size distribution decreases (i.e., contents have similar size), the percentage of traffic offloaded by variable and fixed deadline policies becomes similar.

Fig. 4 depicts the fraction of data offloaded by the vehicular cloud as a function of number of vehicles, buffer size and mean content size for long range communications when content size distribution is truncated normal. Specifically, in Fig. 4a we perform sensitivity analysis according to the number of vehicles h in the cloud which varies from 100 to 500. When h is larger than 200, more than 40% of the traffic can be offloaded by *QAC*. While the number of envisioned connected vehicles in the centre of San Francisco is expected to be much larger, the low technology penetration rate analyzed still provides considerable amount of data offloaded. This result is important to promote the start up phase of the vehicular cloud. However, it is interesting to note that in a sparse scenario ($h = 100$), *QAC* performs poorly. This happens because the value of $\mathrm{E}[B_i] = \lambda \cdot \mu \cdot x_i \cdot y_i$ that has been used in *QAC* holds only if the number of vehicles participating in the vehicular cloud is large (see Lemma 4.3). What is more, from Corollary 4.8, the error of the approximation used by *QAC* is proportional to the standard deviation of B_i which increases in a sparse environment.

Fig. 4b compares different buffer capacities per vehicle. Buffer size goes from the 0,1% to the 1% of the catalogue (where $h = 531$). Interestingly, considerable performance gains can be achieved with very reasonable storage capacities. Here the simulations are performed on a set of 10.000 contents, but in a scenario with a larger realistic catalogue (e.g., 1000 times larger), it seems doable to store 0,1-0,5% of the contents needed to achieve good savings. E.g., if one considers an entire Torrent catalogue (~3 PB) or the entire Netflix catalogue (~3 PB), a mobile helper capacity of about 3 TB (0,1%) already suffices to offload more than 40% of the total traffic for long range communications (while around 30% for fixed deadline policies). Furthermore, as the buffer capacity increases, *QAC-SC* offloads much more traffic than *FIXED*, while this is less evident when the cache size per vehicle is lower. Basically, as the cache size increases, offloading gains are mainly provided by the deadline variability rather than the cache policy chosen.

In Fig. 4c we analyze the effect of content size by varying the mean content size from 30 MB to 200 MB. As expected, for small content, *QAC-SC* offloads more traffic than any other policy. After this threshold, since the assumption of entire download of a content during a contact becomes inaccurate, this policy offloads less traffic. A similar behavior can be seen for *FIXED* that uses the same assumption. What is important to notice, however, is that the traffic offloaded by *QAC* is stable for any content size.

Finally, we perform an analysis of the user QoE by allowing different values of ω_{max}. In Fig. 5, we show the upper bound on the mean slowdown ω_{max} that an MNO should set in order to reach some specific offloading gains, from 30% to 60%. We consider long range communications, and content size drawn from a truncated normal distribution with mean 200 MB, but similar results can be obtained for short range communications or other content size distributions. The required mean slowdown to offload more traffic increases slowly for variable deadline policies while we notice an exponential growth for fixed deadlines. Basically, Fig. 5 can be seen as a description of the effect produced by additional gains on the QoE: for instance, an MNO should double the value of ω_{max} (100% increase) with *FIXED* policy to offload 10% more traffic, while the mean slowdown only increases in the range of 15-40% for *QAC* and *QAC-SC* to have the same improvement in the offloading gains. This low impact on the slowdown highlights the advantages introduced by variable deadlines. Knowing the function that ties user

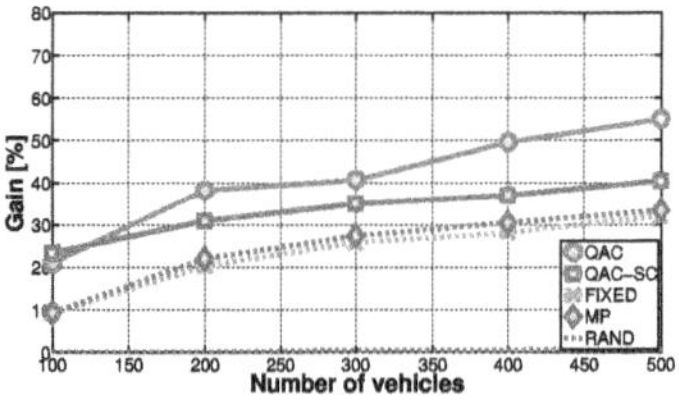

(a) Offloading gain vs. h ($c = 0, 2\% \cdot k$).

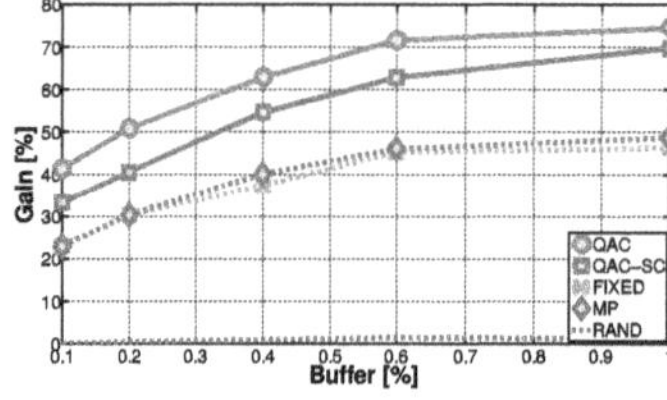

(b) Offloading gain vs. c ($h = 531$).

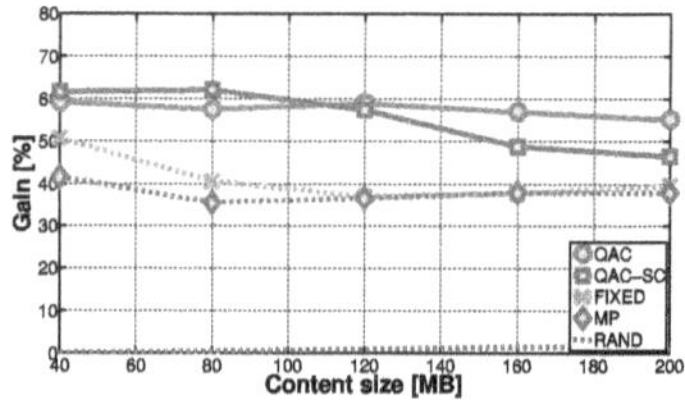

(c) Offloading gain vs. mean content size.

Figure 4: Fraction of traffic offloaded as a function of vehicle density (Fig. 4a), buffer capacity (Fig. 4b) and mean content size (Fig. 4c) for long range communications.

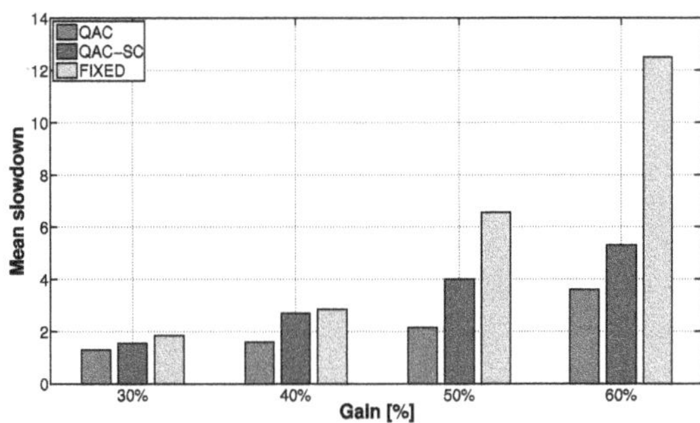

Figure 5: Mean slowdown needed to reach specific offloading gains for long range communications.

experience and slowdown (e.g., linear, logarithmic) can lead to a better interpretation of the plot. However, this behavioural analysis goes beyond the scope of the paper.

6 CONCLUSION AND FUTURE WORK

Compared to similar works in mobile edge computing, this work introduces several contributions: (i) it considers mobile relays (vehicles) that virtually increase the cache size seen by pedestrian users; (ii) while the majority of the works consider fixed deadlines, our paper deals with variable deadlines by introducing a QoE metric; (iii) the generic model includes per chunk-level downloads from vehicles. In the paper, we propose a caching policy that can be adopted by MNOs. This policy has been largely validated analytically and through real trace simulations. The comparison with traditional approaches shows a large increment in the percentage of traffic offloaded. We have also given insights to an operator on how to set the QoE parameters. As future work, it would be interesting to tune the user QoE taking into account the content *type* along with the content size. While we have shown that *QAC* performs well in the majority of the situations, it would be interesting to study closer approximations for the generic formulation of the problem.

ACKNOWLEDGMENT

This work was funded by the French Government (National Research Agency, ANR) through the "Investments for the Future" Program reference #ANR-11-LABX-0031-01.

REFERENCES

[1] BMW Vehicular CrowdCell. https://goo.gl/FBzemq, 2016.
[2] Veniam. https://veniam.com/, 2017.
[3] N. Alliance. NGMN 5G White Paper. https://www.ngmn.org/uploads/media/NGMN_5G_White_Paper_V1_0.pdf, 2015.
[4] A. Balasubramanian, R. Mahajan, and A. Venkataramani. Augmenting Mobile 3G Using WiFi. In *Proceedings of the 8th International Conference on Mobile Systems, Applications, and Services (MobiSys)*, pages 209–222. ACM, 2010.
[5] S. Boyd and L. Vandenberghe. *Convex Optimization.* Cambridge University Press, New York, NY, USA, 2004.
[6] H. Cai, I. Koprulu, and N. B. Shroff. Exploiting double opportunities for deadline based content propagation in wireless networks. In *Proceedings IEEE INFOCOM*, pages 764–772, April 2013.
[7] Cisco. Cisco visual networking index: Global mobile data traffic forecast update. 2016-2021.
[8] E. G. Coffman and P. J. Denning. *Operating systems theory*, volume 973. Prentice-Hall Englewood Cliffs, NJ, 1973.
[9] V. Conan, J. Leguay, and T. Friedman. Characterizing Pairwise Inter-contact Patterns in Delay Tolerant Networks. In *Proceedings of the 1st International Conference on Autonomic Computing and Communication Systems (Autonomics)*, pages 19:1–19:9. ICST, 2007.
[10] G. Gao, M. Xiao, J. Wu, K. Han, and L. Huang. Deadline-Sensitive Mobile Data Offloading via Opportunistic Communications. In *13th Annual IEEE International Conference on Sensing, Communication, and Networking (SECON)*, June 2016.
[11] N. Golrezaei, A. G. Dimakis, and A. F. Molisch. Wireless Device-to-Device Communications with Distributed Caching. *CoRR*, abs/1205.7044, 2012.
[12] N. Golrezaei, A. F. Molisch, A. G. Dimakis, and G. Caire. Femtocaching and device-to-device collaboration: A new architecture for wireless video distribution. *IEEE Communications Magazine*, 51(4):142–149, 2013.
[13] M. Harchol-Balter. *Performance Modeling and Design of Computer Systems: Queueing Theory in Action.* 2013.
[14] R. Kannan and C. L. Monma. On the computational complexity of integer programming problems. In *Optimization and Operations Research.* Springer, 1978.
[15] T. Karagiannis, J. Y. L. Boudec, and M. Vojnovic. Power Law and Exponential Decay of Intercontact Times between Mobile Devices. *IEEE Transactions on Mobile Computing*, (10):1377–1390, Oct 2010.
[16] S. Karlin and H. Taylor. *A First Course in Stochastic Processes.* Elsevier Science, 2012.
[17] K. Lee, S. Hong, S. J. Kim, I. Rhee, and S. Chong. SLAW: A New Mobility Model for Human Walks. In *IEEE INFOCOM*, pages 855–863, April 2009.
[18] K. Lee, J. Lee, Y. Yi, I. Rhee, and S. Chong. Mobile Data Offloading: How Much Can WiFi Deliver? *IEEE/ACM Transactions on Networking*, April 2013.
[19] F. Mehmeti and T. Spyropoulos. Is it worth to be patient? Analysis and optimization of delayed mobile data offloading. In *IEEE INFOCOM Conference on Computer Communications*, pages 2364–2372, April 2014.
[20] M. Piorkowski, N. Sarafijanovic-Djukic, and M. Grossglauser. DAD data set epfl/mobility (v. 2009-02-24). http://crawdad.org/epfl/mobility/, Feb 2009.
[21] K. Poularakis, G. Iosifidis, A. Argyriou, and L. Tassiulas. Video delivery over heterogeneous cellular networks: Optimizing cost and performance. In *IEEE INFOCOM Conference on Computer Communications*, April 2014.
[22] P. Raghavan and C. D. Tompson. Randomized rounding: A technique for provably good algorithms and algorithmic proofs. *Combinatorica*, 7(4):365–374, 1987.
[23] H. Schmidli. Lecture Notes on Risk Theory.
[24] L. Vigneri, T. Spyropoulos, and C. Barakat. Storage on wheels: Offloading popular contents through a vehicular cloud. In *IEEE 17th International Symposium on A World of Wireless, Mobile and Multimedia Networks (WoWMoM)*, 2016.
[25] M. Zeni, D. Miorandi, and F. De Pellegrini. YOUStatAnalyzer: a tool for analysing the dynamics of YouTube content popularity. In *Proc. 7th International Conference on Performance Evaluation Methodologies and Tools*, Torino, Italy, 2013.

Cost-Effective Processing in Fog-Integrated Internet of Things Ecosystems

Wei Bao
School of Information Technologies, University of Sydney
wei.bao@sydney.edu.au

Wei Li
School of Information Technologies, University of Sydney
liwei@it.usyd.edu.au

Flavia C. Delicato
Department of Computer Science, Federal University of Rio de Janeiro
fdelicato@gmail.com

Paulo F. Pires
Department of Computer Science, Federal University of Rio de Janeiro
paulo.f.pires@gmail.com

Dong Yuan
School of Electrical and Information Engineering, University of Sydney
dong.yuan@sydney.edu.au

Bing Bing Zhou
School of Information Technologies, University of Sydney
bing.zhou@sydney.edu.au

Albert Y. Zomaya
School of Information Technologies, University of Sydney
albert.zomaya@sydney.edu.au

ABSTRACT

The emerging Internet of Things (IoT) paradigm creates a growing need to analyze a significant amount of data produced by the interconnected IoT devices. Since IoT devices have limited computation capabilities, Fog Computing is a natural complement, to provide distributed, location-aware, and easy-to-access computation resources. In this work, we address the problem of application processing and data offloading in a Fog-integrated IoT ecosystem. By leveraging the Lyapunov optimization technique, we design an online and distributed system control policy called the Distributed Weighted Backpressure (DWB) policy that asymptotically minimizes the cost of IoT devices. A three-way tradeoff among queue backlogs, communication cost, and computation cost is then investigated. Finally, simulation study has been conducted to validate the correctness and usefulness of the proposed DWB policy.

KEYWORDS

Internet of Things; fog computing; data processing; stochastic optimization.

1 INTRODUCTION

The emergence of the Internet of Things (IoT) will soon make a substantial impact on our daily lives by enabling several novel applications in a variety of domains [1]. IoT is characterized by an enormous number of physical objects, instrumented with sensor/actuator devices, all connecting to and requesting services from the Internet. Such an IoT paradigm creates a growing need to store and analyze significant quantities of data produced by the interconnected objects (things). Nevertheless, IoT devices have limited computing and energy resources, and hence are not able to perform sophisticated processing and storage of large amounts of data. Therefore, IoT is perfectly aligned with Fog Computing – with easy-to-access computation nodes – to create a new generation of highly smart services in application domains such as Smart Healthcare, Smart Home, and Intelligent Transportation. In the same way as cloud data centers, Fog nodes are strongly based on virtualization, but differently from the former, they are less powerful devices and placed closer to the end user, thus providing better delay performance, which is a key requirement for time critical applications. Moreover, the distributed nature of the Fog nodes, in opposite to the centralized nature of the more expensive cloud data centers, promotes better scalability and resilience to the whole system. However, despite the benefits provided by the integration of Fog Computing and IoT, we have encountered new challenges to coordinate such a large-scale integrated system [24], [12]. A most direct question is: in which part of the systems (IoT or Fog) shall we process the applications? It is easy to think of processing all applications in the Fog since IoT devices are limited by their computation capacities. However, over-utilization of the Fog may result in unnecessary data transmission and response delay since in some cases, data could be immediately and locally processed and discarded right away. As a consequence, the full offload approach is non-optimal and the above question cannot be answered in a straightforward way. Many factors, such as communication overhead, computation workload, channel states, and cost in communication and computation, must also be taken into account. Of course, answering the above question is only a first step. Our ultimate goal is to devise a holistic solution that controls and manages the Fog-integrated IoT ecosystem, to achieve a long-term efficient utilization of the system as a whole, minimizing possible performance bottlenecks, while guaranteeing the satisfaction of application requirements.

Our motivation in this work is to investigate the service provision and offloading problem in an Fog-integrated IoT ecosystem.

MSWiM '17, November 21–25, 2017, Miami, FL, USA

ACM ISBN 978-1-4503-5162-1/17/11...$15.00
https://doi.org/10.1145/3127540.3127547

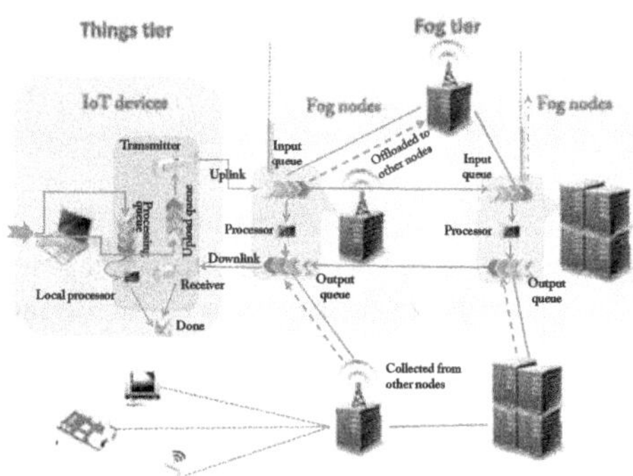

Figure 1: The Fog-integrated IoT ecosystem.

As shown in Fig. 1, the system comprises arbitrarily large numbers of IoT devices in the Things tier and Fog nodes in the Fog tier. Each device generates a specific type of application, in terms of different communication overhead and computation workload. Such applications can be processed either locally or offloaded to the Fog nodes. The outcomes of the offloaded applications will finally return to the source IoT devices. Our study is broadened to consider the content-aware processing [18], where each type of applications can only be processed at a certain set of Fog nodes. Each IoT device should decide if its applications should be processed locally or offloaded to the Fog tier, and each Fog node should further decide which applications it should process and which should be further offloaded to another Fog node.

In this work, by taking advantages of Lyapunov optimization techniques, we propose an online, distributed, and cost-effective solution, referred to as the Distributed Weighted Backpressure (DWB) policy, to operate the Fog-integrated IoT ecosystem. The benefit of our proposed DWB policy is three-fold. First, DWB is an online solution, and is thus suitable for systems which are unaware of their future status (e.g, unpredictable workload, channel states, etc.). Second, our solution is fully distributed, which means each node/device can make its own decision based on its local information only, without recourse to a global view of the system. Thus, DWB is scalable in large-scale networks. Third, DWB asymptotically minimizes the long-term average cost of IoT devices, where cost denotes a "general cost" encompassing for instance the usage of transmission/computing modules at the things. Another contribution of this work is that we are able to characterize a three-way tradeoff among queue backlogs (representing the number of applications "in-flight"), communication cost, and computation cost. This feature makes our approach more advanced compared with most existing Lyapunov optimization analyses where only a two-way tradeoff between queue backlogs and one cost term can be characterized.

The rest of the paper is organized as follows. Section 2 introduces the system model and problem definition. Section 3 provides a detailed description of our proposed DWB policy, and Section 4 presents the optimal cost analysis and tradeoff between communication and computation. In Section 5, simulation results are presented to further demonstrate the performance of our proposed policy. Section 6 reviews related work. A brief conclusion is drawn in Section 7.

2 SYSTEM MODEL

Table 1: Selected definitions of variables.

$A_j(t)$	Number of arrival apps at thing j.
$a_j(t)$	Number of apps to be processed locally at thing j.
$b_j(t)$	Number of apps to be offloaded at thing j.
$h_j(t)$	Uplink channel state at thing j.
$g_j(t)$	Downlink channel state at thing j.
$R_{i\to k}(t)$	Link capacity of link $i \to k$.
$C_i(t)$	Computation capacity of node i.
$x_j(t)$	Number of jobs can be processed at thing j.
$c_{i,j}(t)$	Number of type-j apps can be processed at node i.
$u_{j\Rightarrow i}(t)$	Number of apps can be uploaded from thing j to node i.
$\mu_{i\to k,j}(t)$	Number of unprocessed type-j apps can be transmitted from node i to k.
$\nu_{i\to k,j}(t)$	Number of processed type-j apps can be transmitted from node i to k.
$d_{i\Rightarrow j}(t)$	Number of processed type-j apps can be transmitted from node i to thing j.
$V_j(t)$	Number of unprocessed jobs queued at thing j upon arrival.
$U_{i,j}(t)$	Number of processed type-j apps stored at node i.
$W_j(t)$	Number of unprocessed jobs queued at thing j to be uploaded.
$Q_{i,j}(t)$	Number of unprocessed type-j apps stored at node i.

2.1 Fog Nodes and Things Modeling

As shown in Fig. 1, we study a Fog-integrated IoT ecosystem with Fog nodes and things. Let $\mathcal{I} = \{1, 2, \ldots, I\}$ denote the set of Fog nodes. Let $\mathcal{J} = \{1, 2, \ldots, J\}$ denote the set of things. For simplicity, Fog nodes are referred to as nodes, and the set of things and Fog nodes are referred to as the Things tier and Fog tier respectively. Nodes are interconnected via wired links, and each thing connects to one node via wireless link. Let $\mathcal{F}(j)$ denote the node to which thing j is connected. Let $\mathcal{U}(i)$ denote the set of things connected to node i. $\mathcal{F}(j) = i$ if and only if $j \in \mathcal{U}(i)$. We allow nodes with no things connected (i.e. $\mathcal{U}(i) = \emptyset$). We assume that each thing generates one type of applications, where each type implies a different communication and computation workload, as well as a different execution cost for the system. Note that this assumption can be easily extended to accommodate the scenario where each thing generates multiple types of applications, simply through adding another subscript to indicate the type of applications. However, for presentation convenience, we consider one type of applications at one thing. The applications generated at thing j are referred to as type-j applications. A partial list of nomenclature is given in Table Table

2.2 Application Arrivals at Things

The system operates in slotted time $t \in \{0, 1, 2. \ldots\}$. At time t, $A_j(t)$ applications arrive at thing j. We assume that $A_j(t)$ are independent and identically distributed (i.i.d.) over different t. Let $\mathbb{E}[A_j(t)] = \lambda_j$ denote the average arrival rate. Applications are either processed at the thing's local processor or uploaded to the node to which the thing is connected (which may be further offloaded to another node). The thing should split $A_j(t)$ applications into two streams: $a_j(t)$ of the $A_j(t)$ applications are delivered to its local processor and $b_j(t)$ applications are uploaded. $a_j(t)$ and $b_j(t)$ are decision variables. We have

$$A_j(t) = a_j(t) + b_j(t). \tag{1}$$

2.3 Applications Processed at Local Processors

At time t, $a_j(t)$ applications arrive at the local processor of thing j. However, due to the limited capacity of the local processor, the applications may not be processed immediately. Unprocessed applications are stored at a queue $V_j(t)$ first, and then processed at the local processor. Let $x_j(t)$ denote the amount of applications that can be processed at the local processor (i.e. computation capability offered by the local processor). $x_j(t)$ is a decision variable at each timeslot. Then $V_j(t)$ evolves as follows.

$$V_j(t+1) = \left[V_j(t) - x_j(t)\right]^+ + a_j(t), \tag{2}$$

where $[\cdot]^+$ represents $\max[\cdot, 0]$ throughout this paper. Processing applications introduces a cost. Let $\phi_j(t) = \phi_j(x_j(t))$ denote the cost if $x_j(t)$ applications are processed. Here the cost denotes a "general cost" encompassing for instance the usage of computing modules at the thing (e.g., energy, hardware degradation, etc.).

Let β_j denote the computation load of one type-j application. $c_{j,\max}$ is the computation capacity at the local processor. The overall computation load cannot exceed the computation capacity, and thus we have

$$\beta_j x_j(t) \leq c_{j,\max}. \tag{3}$$

2.4 Applications Uploaded to Fog Tier

At time t, $b_j(t)$ applications are identified to be uploaded to the Fog tier. Due to the limited capacity of the upload link, the applications are firstly stored at a queue $W_j(t)$, and then uploaded. Thing j can only upload applications to its connected node $\mathcal{F}(j)$. Let $u_{j \Rightarrow \mathcal{F}(j)}(t)$ denote the number of applications that can be uploaded (i.e. communication capability offered by the wireless link from thing j to node $\mathcal{F}(j)$). $u_{j \Rightarrow \mathcal{F}(j)}(t)$ is a decision variable. Then, $W_j(t)$ evolves as follows.

$$W_j(t+1) = \left[W_j(t) - u_{j \Rightarrow \mathcal{F}(j)}(t)\right]^+ + b_j(t). \tag{4}$$

Let $h_j(t)$ denote the uplink channel state of thing j at t, which represents the communication capacity of the wireless link from thing j to node $\mathcal{F}(j)$. $h_j(t)$ is i.i.d. Let α_j denote the communication load of one (unprocessed) type-j application. The overall uploading amount cannot exceed the capacity.

$$\alpha_j u_{j \Rightarrow \mathcal{F}(j)}(t) \leq h_j(t). \tag{5}$$

Note that by considering the different states of the channel, the inherent unpredictability (e.g., noise and channel gain) of wireless communication is already being considered in our model. Uploading applications also introduces a cost. Let $\varphi_j(t) = \varphi_j(u_{j \Rightarrow \mathcal{F}(j)}(t), h_j(t))$ denote the cost if $u_{j \Rightarrow \mathcal{F}(j)}(t)$ applications are uploaded.[1]

2.5 Processing Applications in Fog Tier

Fog nodes are interconnected via wired communication links, which are modeled as a directed graph. Let $\mathcal{L}$ denote the link set. We use $i \to k \in \mathcal{L}$ to denote the directed link from node i to k. Unprocessed applications and processed applications can be transmitted via these links. In this way, applications can be offloaded from one node to another one, and thus the processing capabilities at different nodes can be better utilized.

In this work, we are able to accommodate the content-aware processing [18]. Let $\mathcal{P}(i)$ denote the set of application types that can be processed at node i. In other words, type-j applications can be processed at node i if and only if $j \in \mathcal{P}(i)$.

At time t, let $\mu_{i \to k,j}(t)$ denote the number of unprocessed type-j applications that can be offloaded from node i to k. $\mu_{i \to k,j}(t) = 0$ if $i \to k \notin \mathcal{L}$. Let $c_{i,j}(t)$ be the number of type-j applications that can be processed at node i (computation capability offered by node i to process type-j applications). Note that $c_{i,j}(t) = 0$ if $j \notin \mathcal{P}(i)$. $\forall i \in \mathcal{I}, \forall j \in \mathcal{J}$, we define $Q_{i,j}(t)$ as the number of unprocessed type-j applications stored at node i. $Q_{i,j}(t)$ evolves as follows

$$Q_{i,j}(t+1) \leq \left[Q_{i,j}(t) - \sum_{k:i \to k \in \mathcal{L}} \mu_{i \to k,j}(t) - c_{i,j}(t)\right]^+ + \sum_{k:k \to i \in \mathcal{L}} \mu_{k \to i,j}(t) + u_{j \Rightarrow i}(t), \tag{6}$$

where $u_{j \Rightarrow i}(t)$ is the number of applications that can be uploaded from thing j to node i. If $j \notin \mathcal{U}(i)$, $u_{j \Rightarrow i}(t) = 0$. If $j \in \mathcal{U}(i)$, $u_{j \Rightarrow i}(t) = u_{j \Rightarrow \mathcal{F}(j)}(t)$.

$C_i(t)$ is the computation capacity at node i. $C_i(t)$ is i.i.d. over different timeslots. The overall computation load cannot exceed the computation capacity, and thus we have

$$\sum_{j \in \mathcal{P}(i)} \beta_j c_{i,j}(t) \leq C_i(t). \tag{7}$$

Note that if $j \notin \mathcal{P}(i)$, type-j applications cannot be processed at the node i. However, they are allowed to enter node i to be further forwarded to another node. At each timeslot t, $\mu_{i \to k,j}(t)$ and $c_{i,j}(t)$ are decision variables.

2.6 Processed Applications in Fog Tier

Processed applications will return to the original thing, i.e. type-j processed applications are transmitted back to thing j. We define $U_{i,j}(t)$ as the number of processed type-j applications stored at node i. Let $\nu_{i \to k,j}(t)$ denote the number of processed type-j applications that can be transmitted from node i to k (communication capability offered by link $i \to k$). $U_{i,j}(t+1)$ evolves as follows

$$U_{i,j}(t+1) \leq \left[U_{i,j}(t) - \sum_{k:i \to k \in \mathcal{L}} \nu_{i \to k,j}(t) - d_{i \Rightarrow j}(t)\right]^+ + \sum_{k:k \to i \in \mathcal{L}} \nu_{k \to i,j}(t) + c_{i,j}(t), \tag{8}$$

where $d_{i \Rightarrow j}(t)$ is the number of processed type-j applications that can be transmitted from node i to thing j (i.e. download capability offered by the wireless link from node i to thing j). If $j \in \mathcal{U}(i)$, $d_{i \Rightarrow j}(t) = d_{\mathcal{F}(j) \Rightarrow j}(t)$; if $j \notin \mathcal{U}(i)$, $d_{i \Rightarrow j}(t) = 0$.

As discussed in Section 2.4, each unprocessed type-j application has a communication load α_j. In addition we assume that each processed type-j application has a communication load γ_j. Let $R_{i \to k}(t)$ denote the link capacity of link $i \to k \in \mathcal{L}$. $R_{i \to k}(t)$ is i.i.d. The transmission load of unprocessed and processed applications over

[1] The assumptions on channel state and cost can accommodate the following scenario: The channel capacity is modeled as $B \log(1 + \frac{P(t)g(t)}{N(t)})$, where B is the bandwidth of the wireless channel, $g(t)$ and $N(t)$ are channel gain and noise level (i.i.d. random variables), and $P(t)$ is the decision variable representing the transmission power. The uploading cost can be an arbitrary function of $P(t)$.

link $i \rightarrow k$ cannot exceed the link capacity.

$$\sum_{j \in \mathcal{J}} \alpha_j \mu_{i \rightarrow k,j}(t) + \sum_{j \in \mathcal{J}} \gamma_j \nu_{i \rightarrow k,j}(t) \leq R_{i \rightarrow k}(t). \tag{9}$$

At each time t, $\nu_{i \rightarrow k,j}(t)$ is a decision variable.

2.7 Applications Downloaded to Things

The downlink from node $\mathcal{F}(j)$ to thing j is operated by a wireless link. Let $g_j(t)$ denote the downlink channel state of thing j at t, which represents the communication capacity of the wireless link from node $\mathcal{F}(j)$ to thing j. $g_j(t)$ is i.i.d. The overall downloading amount cannot exceed the capacity, thus we have

$$\gamma_j d_{\mathcal{F}(j) \Rightarrow j}(t) \leq g_j(t). \tag{10}$$

Downloading applications also introduces a cost. Let $\psi_j(t) = \psi_j(d_{\mathcal{F}(j) \Rightarrow j}(t), g_j(t))$ denote the cost if $d_{\mathcal{F}(j) \Rightarrow j}(t)$ applications are downloaded. Note that we assume that uplinks and downlinks of different things are operated in orthogonal channels (e.g., different frequency bands or different timeslot through using LTE category 0 or 1), such that $h_j(t)$ and $g_j(t)$ are independent.

2.8 Overall Cost

Let $P(t)$ denote the overall cost at t, then we have

$$P(t) = \sum_{j \in \mathcal{J}} \left[\phi_j(t) + \varphi_j(t) + \psi_j(t) \right]. \tag{11}$$

Note that in this work, we focus on the cost generated at things. This is because the things are equipped with less resource (e.g., battery capacity and computation capacity), so that reducing the cost at the Things tier is prioritized.

Our goal is to minimize the long term average cost, and guarantee the stability of all queues. Therefore, we reach the following problem **P**:

$$\min \lim_{T \to \infty} \frac{1}{T} \sum_{t=0}^{T-1} \mathbb{E}(P(t)), \tag{12}$$

$$\text{s.t. All queues are mean rate stable.} \tag{13}$$

$$(1)(3)(5)(7)(9)(10).$$

In this work, we assume that problem **P** is feasible, i.e. there exists at least one control policy that all queues are mean rate stable.

2.9 System Control Policy and System State

The aim of this work is to design a system control policy to determine the control variables $a_j(t)$, $b_j(t)$, $u_{j \Rightarrow \mathcal{F}(j)}(t)$, $d_{\mathcal{F}(j) \Rightarrow j}(t)$, $x_j(t)$, $\forall j \in \mathcal{J}$; $\mu_{i \rightarrow k,j}(t)$, $\nu_{i \rightarrow k,j}(t)$, $\forall i \rightarrow k \in \mathcal{L}$, $\forall j \in \mathcal{J}$; and $c_{i,j}(t)$ $\forall i \in \mathcal{I}, \forall j \in \mathcal{J}, j \in \mathcal{P}(i)$, at each timeslot.

The (joint) queue state of the system at t is defined as $\mathbf{Z}(t) \triangleq \{V_j(t), W_j(t), Q_{i,j}(t), U_{i,j}(t), \forall j \in \mathcal{J}, \forall i \in \mathcal{I}\}$. The system state is $\mathbf{s}(t) \triangleq \{A_j(t), h_j(t), g_j(t), R_{k \rightarrow l}(t), C_i(t), \forall j \in \mathcal{J}, \forall i \in \mathcal{I}, \forall k \rightarrow l \in \mathcal{L}\}$. Note that the system states at different timeslots are independent.

An S-only policy is defined as a system control policy at each time t, which depends only on the system state at t and is irrelevant to the queue state. On the other hand, a queue-aware policy depends on both the system state and queue state at t.

3 LYAPUNOV OPTIMIZATION AND DWB

In this section, we discuss the solution to problem **P** and propose the Distributed Weighted Backpressure (DWB) policy. First, we notice that the arrivals of applications may be bursty and unpredictable, and thus the system is unaware of the workload in future timeslots. The system may also need to react promptly to the workloads, and thus an online solution is desired for instant service provisions. Furthermore, since our aim is to optimize a long-term average objective, and satisfy the queue stability and several instantaneous constraints, Lyapunov optimization is an ideal technique to be leveraged for solving the problem.

3.1 Lyapunov Function Definition

We define the Lyapunov function at time t as

$$L(\mathbf{Z}(t)) \triangleq \sum_{\substack{i \in \mathcal{I}, \\ j \in \mathcal{J}}} Q_{i,j}^2(t) + \sum_{\substack{i \in \mathcal{I}, \\ j \in \mathcal{J}}} U_{i,j}^2(t) + \sum_{j \in \mathcal{J}} V_j^2(t) + \sum_{j \in \mathcal{J}} W_j^2(t).$$

Please note that we can assign different weights to different queues to accommodate different priorities on different nodes, things, and application types, which only slightly changes the subsequent analysis. However, for presentation convenience, we do not consider the weights in the rest of this work.

In the next step, we define the Lyapunov drift as

$$\Delta(\mathbf{Z}(t)) \triangleq \frac{1}{2} \mathbb{E}\left[L(\mathbf{Z}(t+1)) - L(\mathbf{Z}(t)) | \mathbf{Z}(t) \right]. \tag{14}$$

$\Delta(\mathbf{Z}(t))$ is further characterized and bounded in (15), in which B is defined as an upper bound of (16). Note that (16) is bounded since $a_j(t)$, $b_j(t)$, $x_j(t)$, $u_{j \Rightarrow \mathcal{F}(j)}(t)$, $d_{\mathcal{F}(j) \Rightarrow j}(t)$, $\mu_{i \rightarrow k,j}(t)$, and $\nu_{i \rightarrow k,j}(t)$ are all bounded in a practical system.

$$\begin{aligned} \Delta(\mathbf{Z}(t)) \leq B - \mathbb{E}\Bigg\{ & \sum_{i \in \mathcal{I}, j \in \mathcal{J}} Q_{i,j}(t) \Bigg[\sum_{k: i \rightarrow k \in \mathcal{L}} \mu_{i \rightarrow k,j}(t) + c_{i,j}(t) \\ & - \sum_{l: l \rightarrow i \in \mathcal{L}} \mu_{l \rightarrow i,j}(t) - u_{j \Rightarrow i}(t) \Bigg] + \sum_{i \in \mathcal{I}, j \in \mathcal{J}} U_{i,j}(t) \\ & \Bigg[\sum_{k: i \rightarrow k \in \mathcal{L}} \nu_{i \rightarrow k,j}(t) + d_{i \Rightarrow j}(t) - \sum_{l: l \rightarrow i \in \mathcal{L}} \nu_{l \rightarrow i,j}(t) - c_{i,j}(t) \Bigg] \\ & + \sum_{j \in \mathcal{J}} V_j(t)[x_j(t) - a_j(t)] + \sum_{j \in \mathcal{J}} W_j(t) \left[u_{j \Rightarrow \mathcal{F}(j)}(t) - b_j(t) \right] \Bigg| \mathbf{Z}(t) \Bigg\}. \end{aligned} \tag{15}$$

$$\begin{aligned} B \leq \frac{1}{2} \mathbb{E}\Bigg\{ & \sum_{i \in \mathcal{I}, j \in \mathcal{J}} \Bigg[\Bigg(\sum_{k: i \rightarrow k \in \mathcal{L}} \mu_{i \rightarrow k,j}(t) + c_{i,j}(t) \Bigg)^2 + \\ & \Bigg(\sum_{l: l \rightarrow i \in \mathcal{L}} \mu_{l \rightarrow i,j}(t) + u_{j \Rightarrow i}(t) \Bigg)^2 + \Bigg(\sum_{k: i \rightarrow k \in \mathcal{L}} \nu_{i \rightarrow k,j}(t) + d_{i \Rightarrow j}(t) \Bigg)^2 \\ & + \Bigg(\sum_{l: l \rightarrow i \in \mathcal{L}} \nu_{l \rightarrow i,j}(t) + c_{i,j}(t) \Bigg)^2 \Bigg] + \\ & \sum_{j \in \mathcal{J}} \left[(x_j(t))^2 + (a_j(t))^2 + \left(u_{j \Rightarrow \mathcal{F}(j)}(t) \right)^2 + (b_j(t))^2 \right] \Bigg| \mathbf{Z}(t) \Bigg\}. \end{aligned} \tag{16}$$

3.2 Lyapunov Drift Plus Cost

In order to satisfy the queue stability and to minimize the overall cost, we study the Lyapunov drift plus cost, shown in (17). θ is a tunable weight, representing the relative importance of "cost minimization" compared with "queue stability". Larger θ implies higher priority in cost minimization but lower priority in queue stability. A tradeoff between queue backlog and cost minimization can be characterized by adjusting θ, which will be studied in Section 3.4. We have

$$\Delta(\mathbf{Z}(t)) + \theta \mathbb{E}\left[P(t)|\mathbf{Z}(t)\right] \tag{17}$$

$$\leq (15) + \theta \cdot \mathbb{E}\left\{ \sum_{j\in\mathcal{J}} \left[\phi_j(t) + \varphi_j(t) + \psi_j(t)\right] \middle| \mathbf{Z}(t) \right\} \tag{18}$$

$$= B - \mathbb{E}\left[\mathrm{Obj}(t)|\mathbf{Z}(t)\right], \tag{19}$$

in which Obj(t) is defined in (20).

$$\begin{aligned}\mathrm{Obj}(t) = &\sum_{i\in\mathcal{I}, j\in\mathcal{J}} Q_{i,j}(t)\Bigg[\sum_{k:i\to k\in\mathcal{L}} \mu_{i\to k,j}(t) + c_{i,j}(t) \\ &- \sum_{l:l\to i\in\mathcal{L}} \mu_{l\to i,j}(t) - u_{j\Rightarrow i}(t)\Bigg] + \sum_{i\in\mathcal{I}, j\in\mathcal{J}} U_{i,j}(t)\cdot \\ &\Bigg[\sum_{k:i\to k\in\mathcal{L}} \nu_{i\to k,j}(t) + d_{i\Rightarrow j}(t) - \sum_{l:l\to i\in\mathcal{L}} \nu_{l\to i,j}(t) - c_{i,j}(t)\Bigg] \\ &+ \sum_{j\in\mathcal{J}} V_j(t)\left[x_j(t) - a_j(t)\right] + \sum_{j\in\mathcal{J}} W_j(t)\left[u_{j\Rightarrow\mathcal{F}(j)}(t) - b_j(t)\right] \\ &- \theta \sum_{j\in\mathcal{J}} \left[\phi_j(t) + \varphi_j(t) + \psi_j(t)\right].\end{aligned} \tag{20}$$

3.3 One-Timeslot Optimization and DWB

In this subsection, we maximize the term $\mathbb{E}\left[\mathrm{Obj}(t)|\mathbf{Z}(t)\right]$. This can be achieved with an opportunistic optimization approach, i.e., to maximize Obj(t) at each timeslot[15]. As a consequence, we reach the optimization problem **P0**, the solution to which leads to our proposed Distributed Weighted Backpressure (DWB) policy. **P0** is formally stated as follows[2]

$$\max \ \mathrm{Obj}(t), \tag{21}$$
$$\text{s.t. } (1)(3)(5)(7)(9)(10).$$

In order to solve the above problem **P0**, we first rearrange the objective function as follows

$$\begin{aligned}&\sum_{\substack{l\to k\in\mathcal{L}\\ j\in\mathcal{J}}} \left\{\mu_{l\to k,j}(t)\left[Q_{l,j}(t) - Q_{k,j}(t)\right] + \nu_{l\to k,j}(t)\left[U_{l,j}(t) - U_{k,j}(t)\right]\right\} \\ &+ \sum_{i\in\mathcal{I}, j\in\mathcal{P}(i)} c_{i,j}(t)\left[Q_{i,j}(t) - U_{i,j}(t)\right] \\ &+ \sum_{j\in\mathcal{J}} \left[u_{j\Rightarrow\mathcal{F}(j)}(t)\left[W_j(t) - Q_{\mathcal{F}(j),j}(t)\right] - \theta\varphi_j(u_{j\Rightarrow\mathcal{F}(j)}(t), h_j(t))\right] \\ &+ \sum_{j\in\mathcal{J}} \left[d_{\mathcal{F}(j)\Rightarrow j}(t)U_{\mathcal{F}(j),j}(t) - \theta\psi_j(d_{\mathcal{F}(j)\Rightarrow j}(t), g_j(t))\right] \\ &+ \sum_{j\in\mathcal{J}} \left[V_j(t)x_j(t) - \theta\phi_j(x_j(t))\right] \\ &- \sum_{j\in\mathcal{J}} \left[V_j(t)a_j(t) + W_j(t)b_j(t)\right].\end{aligned} \tag{22}$$

We observe that the sum-form objective function (22) and the constraints (1), (3), (5), (7), (9), and (10) are separable [2]. Therefore, the optimization problem **P0** can be decomposed into independent subproblems **SP1**, **SP2**, ..., **SP6** (to be discussed next). The original problem is optimized if and only if subproblems **SP1**, **SP2**, ..., **SP6** are optimized individually. This is a key step in this paper leading to a distributed solution to the original complicated problem.

3.3.1 *Problem* SP1 *and Solution, Transmission Control at Link $l \to k$.*

By combining the first line of (22) and constraint (9), we reach the following subproblem at each link $l \to k \in \mathcal{L}$:

$$\begin{aligned}\max_{\substack{\mu_{l\to k,j}(t), \nu_{l\to k,j}(t),\\ \forall j\in\mathcal{J}}} \ &\sum_{j\in\mathcal{J}} \Big\{\mu_{l\to k,j}(t)\left[Q_{l,j}(t) - Q_{k,j}(t)\right] \\ &+ \nu_{l\to k,j}(t)\left[U_{l,j}(t) - U_{k,j}(t)\right]\Big\},\end{aligned} \tag{23}$$

$$\text{s.t.} \ \sum_{j\in\mathcal{J}} \alpha_j \mu_{l\to k,j}(t) + \sum_{j\in\mathcal{J}} \gamma_j \nu_{l\to k,j}(t) \leq R_{l\to k}(t), \tag{24}$$

which is a linear programming problem, leading to the optimal solution as follows:

Case 1. If $\max_j \left(\frac{Q_{l,j}(t)-Q_{k,j}(t)}{\alpha_j}\right) \leq 0$ and $\max_j \left(\frac{U_{l,j}(t)-U_{k,j}(t)}{\gamma_j}\right) \leq 0$, the optimal solution is $\mu_{l\to k,j}(t) = 0, \nu_{l\to k,j}(t) = 0, \forall j$. The link will be idle in this case.

Case 2. Otherwise, if $\max_j \left(\frac{Q_{l,j}(t)-Q_{k,j}(t)}{\alpha_j}\right) \geq \max_j \left(\frac{U_{l,j}(t)-U_{k,j}(t)}{\gamma_j}\right)$, let $j^* = \arg\max_j \left(\frac{Q_{l,j}(t)-Q_{k,j}(t)}{\alpha_j}\right)$, and the optimal solution is $\mu_{l\to k,j^*}(t) = \frac{R_{l\to k}(t)}{\alpha_{j^*}}, \mu_{l\to k,j}(t) = 0, \forall j \neq j^*, \nu_{l\to k,j}(t) = 0, \forall j$. In this case, the full link capacity of $l \to k$ will be allocated to type-j^* unprocessed applications.

Case 3. Otherwise, if $\max_j \left(\frac{U_{l,j}(t)-U_{k,j}(t)}{\gamma_j}\right) > \max_j \left(\frac{Q_{l,j}(t)-Q_{k,j}(t)}{\alpha_j}\right)$, let $j^{**} = \arg\max_j \left(\frac{U_{l,j}(t)-U_{k,j}(t)}{\gamma_j}\right)$, and the optimal solution is $\nu_{l\to k,j^{**}}(t) = \frac{R_{l\to k}(t)}{\gamma_{j^{**}}}, \nu_{l\to k,j}(t) = 0, \forall j \neq j^{**}, \mu_{l\to k,j}(t) = 0, \forall j$. In this case, the full link capacity of $l \to k$ will be allocated to the type-j^{**} processed applications.

The above solution to **SP1** is referred to as *DWB at link $l \to k$*. It means that each link $l \to k$ greedily transmits the type of unprocessed or processed applications which maximizes the term $\left(\frac{Q_{l,j}(t)-Q_{k,j}(t)}{\alpha_j}\right)$ or $\left(\frac{U_{l,j}(t)-U_{k,j}(t)}{\gamma_j}\right)$. All other unprocessed or processed applications will not be transmitted. Note that Problem **SP1** is solved in a distributed fashion. For each link $l \to k$, we only need to know the local information: the differences between the queue backlogs (i.e. backpressures), $Q_{l,j}(t) - Q_{k,j}(t)$ and $U_{l,j}(t) - U_{k,j}(t)$, $\forall j$. The solution is interpreted as a *weighted backpressure* scheme where each link transmits the type of application with the greatest backpressure multiplied by its weight ($1/\alpha_j$ or $1/\gamma_j$).

3.3.2 *Problem* SP2 *and Solution, Computation Control at Node i.*

By combining the second line of (22) and constraint (7), we reach

[2]The decision variables are shown in Section 2.9. All decision variables are non-negative.

the following subproblem at each node i

$$\max_{c_{i,j}(t),\forall j\in\mathcal{P}(i)} \sum_{j\in\mathcal{J}} c_{i,j}(t)\left[Q_{i,j}(t)-U_{i,j}(t)\right], \tag{25}$$

$$\text{s.t.} \sum_{j\in\mathcal{P}(i)} \beta_j c_{i,j}(t) \le C_i(t). \tag{26}$$

The optimal solution to **SP2** is as follows: If $\max_{j\in\mathcal{P}(i)} \left(\frac{Q_{i,j}(t)-U_{i,j}(t)}{\beta_j}\right) > 0$, let $j^* = \arg\max_{j\in\mathcal{P}(i)} \left(\frac{Q_{i,j}(t)-U_{i,j}(t)}{\beta_j}\right)$, and the optimal solution is $c_{i,j^*}(t) = \frac{C_i(t)}{\beta_{j^*}}$, $c_{i,j}(t) = 0, \forall j \neq j^*$. Otherwise, the optimal solution is $c_{i,j}(t) = 0, \forall j \in \mathcal{P}(i)$.

The above solution to **SP2** is referred to as *DWB at node i*. It means that each node i should greedily process the type of applications that maximize the term $\frac{Q_{i,j}(t)-U_{i,j}(t)}{\beta_j}$. Problem **SP2** can be solved at each node in a distributed fashion. At each node, we only need to know the local backpressures, $Q_{i,j}(t)-U_{i,j}(t), \forall j$. The above solution can also be interpreted as a *weighted backpressure* scheme where each node processes the type of application with the greatest backpressure multiplied by its weight $(1/\beta_j)$.

3.3.3 Problem SP3 and Solution: Uploading Control at Thing j.

By combining the third line of (22) and constraint (5), we reach the following subproblem at each thing j

$$\max_{u_{j\Rightarrow\mathcal{F}(j)}(t)} u_{j\Rightarrow\mathcal{F}(j)}(t)\left[W_j(t)-Q_{\mathcal{F}(j),j}(t)\right] - \theta\varphi_j(u_{j\Rightarrow\mathcal{F}(j)}(t), h_j(t)), \tag{27}$$

$$\text{s.t. } \alpha_j u_{j\Rightarrow\mathcal{F}(j)}(t) \le h_j(t). \tag{28}$$

Problem **SP3** is a single-variable optimization problem that can be solved by standard numerical-search methods.

In this paper, we are interested in studying the on/off scenario: $u_{j\Rightarrow\mathcal{F}(j)}(t)$ can be either 0 or $\frac{h_j(t)}{\alpha_j}$, leading to a cost of 0 or φ_j respectively. In this scenario, the optimal solution is

$$u_{j\Rightarrow\mathcal{F}(j)}(t) = \begin{cases} \frac{h_j(t)}{\alpha_j}, & \text{if } \frac{h_j(t)}{\alpha_j}\left[W_j(t)-Q_{\mathcal{F}(j),j}(t)\right] - \theta\varphi_j \ge 0, \\ 0, & \text{otherwise.} \end{cases} \tag{29}$$

The above solution to **SP3** is referred to as *DWB at uplink of thing j*. It is operated at each thing in a distributed fashion. We only need to know the local information $h_j(t)$ and $W_j(t)-Q_{\mathcal{F}(j),j}(t)$.

3.3.4 Problem SP4 and Solution: Downloading Control at Thing j.

By combining the fourth line of (22) and constraint (10), we reach the following subproblem at each thing j

$$\max_{d_{\mathcal{F}(j)\Rightarrow j}(t)} d_{\mathcal{F}(j)\Rightarrow j}(t) U_{\mathcal{F}(j),j}(t) - \theta\psi_j(d_{\mathcal{F}(j)\Rightarrow j}(t), g_j(t)), \tag{30}$$

$$\text{s.t. } \gamma_j d_{\mathcal{F}(j)\Rightarrow j}(t) \le g_j(t). \tag{31}$$

Similar to **SP3**, **SP4** is a single-variable optimization problem that can be solved by standard numerical-search methods.

Still, we are interested to study the on/off scenario: $d_{\mathcal{F}(j)\Rightarrow j}(t)$ can be either 0 or $\frac{g_j(t)}{\gamma_j}$, leading to a cost of 0 or ψ_j respectively. In this scenario, the optimal solution is

$$d_{\mathcal{F}(j)\Rightarrow j}(t) = \begin{cases} \frac{g_j(t)}{\gamma_j}, & \text{if } \frac{g_j(t)}{\gamma_j} U_{\mathcal{F}(j),j}(t) - \theta\psi_j \ge 0, \\ 0, & \text{otherwise.} \end{cases} \tag{32}$$

The above solution to **SP4** is referred to as *DWB at downlink of thing j*. It is operated at each thing in a distributed fashion.

3.3.5 Problem SP5 and Solution: Computation Control at Thing j.

By considering the fifth line of (22) and constraint (3), we reach the following subproblem at each thing j

$$\max_{x_j(t)} V_j(t)x_j(t) - \theta\phi_j(x_j(t)), \tag{33}$$

$$\text{s.t. } \beta_j x_j(t) \le c_{j,\max}. \tag{34}$$

SP5 is a single-variable optimization problem, which can be solved by standard numerical-search methods.

We are interested to study the on/off scenario: $x_j(t)$ can be either 0 or $\frac{c_{j,\max}}{\beta_j}$, leading to a cost of 0 or ϕ_j, respectively. In this scenario, the optimal solution is

$$x_j(t) = \begin{cases} \frac{c_{j,\max}}{\beta_j}, & \text{if } V_j(t)\frac{c_{j,\max}}{\beta_j} - \theta\phi_j \ge 0, \\ 0, & \text{otherwise.} \end{cases} \tag{35}$$

The above solution to **SP5** is referred to as *DWB at processor of thing j*. It is operated at each thing in a distributed fashion.

3.3.6 Problem SP6 and Solution: Arrival Partition of Thing j.

By combining the sixth line of (22) and constraint (1), we reach the following subproblem at each thing j

$$\min_{a_j(t), b_j(t)} V_j(t)a_j(t) + W_j(t)b_j(t), \tag{36}$$

$$\text{s.t. } a_j(t) + b_j(t) = A_j(t). \tag{37}$$

The optimal solution is as follows: If $V_j(t) \le W_j(t)$, $a_j(t) = A_j(t)$, $b_j(t) = 0$; otherwise, $a_j(t) = 0$, $b_j(t) = A_j(t)$. The above solution to **SP6** is referred to as *DWB in arrival partition of thing j*. It is operated at each thing in a distributed fashion.

3.3.7 Summary of Solutions to SP1–SP6.

Through the above discussion, we derive a distributed online queue-aware policy, the DWB policy, which minimizes the drift plus cost at each timeslot. In the next subsection, we aim to investigate the optimality of the DWB policy.

3.4 Optimality Analysis

In this subsection, we study the performance of our proposed DWB policy. As discussed in Section 2.8, we have assumed that the original optimization problem is feasible. Therefore, there exists an S-only policy that achieves the following conditions[8] (ϵ is some non-negative value)

$$\mathbb{E}\left[\sum_{k:i\to k\in\mathcal{L}} \mu_{i\to k,j}(t) + c_{i,j}(t) - \sum_{l:l\to i\in\mathcal{L}} \mu_{l\to i,j}(t) - u_{j\Rightarrow i}(t) \middle| \mathbf{Z}(t)\right] \ge \epsilon, \forall i\in\mathcal{I}, \forall j\in\mathcal{J}, \tag{38}$$

$$\mathbb{E}\left[\sum_{k:i\to k\in\mathcal{L}} \nu_{i\to k,j}(t) + d_{i\Rightarrow j}(t) - \sum_{l:l\to i\in\mathcal{L}} \nu_{l\to i,j}(t) - c_{i,j}(t) \middle| \mathbf{Z}(t)\right] \ge \epsilon,, \forall i\in\mathcal{I}, \forall j\in\mathcal{J}, \tag{39}$$

$$\mathbb{E}\left[x_j(t) - a_j(t) | \mathbf{Z}(t)\right] \ge \epsilon, \forall j\in\mathcal{J}, \tag{40}$$

$$\mathbb{E}\left[u_{j\Rightarrow\mathcal{F}(j)}(t) - b_j(t) | \mathbf{Z}(t)\right] \ge \epsilon, \forall j\in\mathcal{J}. \tag{41}$$

Note that for an S-only policy, $\mathbb{E}[\cdot|\mathbf{Z}(t)] = \mathbb{E}[\cdot]$. Among the S-only policies satisfying (38)–(41), there is an optimal one that minimizes the long-term average cost $\lim_{T\to\infty} \frac{1}{T}\sum_{t=0}^{T-1} \mathbb{E}(P(t))$, denoted by $\Psi(\epsilon)$. Under such optimal S-only policy, substituting (38)–(41) into (15) leads to

$$\Delta(\mathbf{Z}(t)) + \theta\mathbb{E}[P(t)|\mathbf{Z}(t)] \le B + \theta\Psi(\epsilon) - \epsilon\overline{Q}(t), \tag{42}$$

where we define $\overline{Q}(t) \triangleq \sum_{i\in\mathcal{I},j\in\mathcal{J}} Q_{i,j}(t) + \sum_{i\in\mathcal{I},j\in\mathcal{J}} U_{i,j}(t) + \sum_{j\in\mathcal{J}} V_j(t) + \sum_{j\in\mathcal{J}} W_j(t)$, representing the overall queue backlog in the system, i.e. the number of applications "in-flight".

The DWB policy opportunistically minimizes drift plus penalty at each timeslot, thus (42) is satisfied if the DWB policy is employed.

Summing (42) over all $t \in \{0, 1, \ldots, T-1\}$, taking expectation, and letting $T \to \infty$ yields

$$\lim_{T\to\infty} \frac{1}{T}\sum_{t=0}^{T-1} \mathbb{E}(P(t)) \le \Psi(\epsilon) + \frac{B}{\theta}, \tag{43}$$

$$\lim_{T\to\infty} \frac{1}{T}\sum_{t=0}^{T-1} \mathbb{E}(\overline{Q}(t)) \le \frac{B + \theta(\Psi(\epsilon) - \Psi^*)}{\epsilon}, \tag{44}$$

where Ψ^* is the optimal cost achieved by any policies (including queue-aware policies).

Note that (43) and (44) hold for arbitrary possible ϵ. Therefore, (43) stands when $\epsilon = 0$. In addition, the optimal cost Ψ^* can be achieved by an S-only policy with $\epsilon = 0$, and hence $\Psi^* = \Psi(0)$ [8, 15]. As a consequence, we have

$$\lim_{T\to\infty} \frac{1}{T}\sum_{t=0}^{T-1} \mathbb{E}(P(t)) \le \Psi(0) + \frac{B}{\theta}, \tag{45}$$

$$\lim_{T\to\infty} \frac{1}{T}\sum_{t=0}^{T-1} \mathbb{E}(\overline{Q}(t)) \le \frac{B + \theta(\Psi(\epsilon) - \Psi(0))}{\epsilon}. \tag{46}$$

(45)–(46) demonstrate an $[O(1/\theta), O(\theta)]$ tradeoff between the cost and queue backlogs. If a large θ is chosen, the average cost under the DWB policy can be pushed arbitrarily close to the optimal cost (i.e., asymptotically optimal). However, if θ is too large, the number of outstanding applications is also large. By tuning the parameter θ, we are able to balance the cost and queue backlogs.

4 TRADEOFF BETWEEN COMMUNICATION AND COMPUTATION

In Section 3, we proposed the DWB policy and characterized the tradeoff between queue backlog and cost. We further note that the cost is composed of communication cost, i.e., the cost of uploading and downloading applications to the Fog tier, and computation cost, i.e., the cost of processing applications at local processors. This motivates us to further characterize the tradeoff between communication cost and computation cost. In this section, we investigate the optimal cost $\Psi(0)$ under different values of φ_j, ψ_j, and ϕ_j. Since $\Psi(0)$ can be achieved by an optimal S-only policy [8, 15], we focus on S-only policies in this section. (Please note that the proposed DWB is not an S-only policy: the S-only policy is considered in this section for the purpose of analyzing $\Psi(0)$.) Let $\Psi(0) = \sum_{j\in\mathcal{J}} \Psi_j(0)$, where $\Psi_j(0)$ is the optimal cost of thing j.

4.1 Optimal Cost Analysis

It can be shown that in order to achieve $\Psi(0)$, an equivalent S-only optimization problem should be studied, which can then be decomposed into sub-problems in which each thing minimizes its average per-timeslot cost by making decisions on the average numbers of offloaded and locally processed applications per timeslot, denoted by $\lambda_{1,j}$ and $\lambda_{2,j}$ respectively. $\lambda_{1,j} + \lambda_{2,j}$ is equal to λ_j. For those offloaded applications, in order to achieve the minimum cost, they are uploaded when the uplink channel ($j \Rightarrow \mathcal{F}(j)$) is "as good as" possible. In other words, these applications are uploaded when the channel condition is greater than a threshold value $h_{0,j}$. For the same reason, processed applications are downloaded when the downlink channel is greater than a threshold value $g_{0,j}$. $\lambda_{1,j}$ must be equal to the average number of uploaded/downloaded applications per timeslot, i.e. $\lambda_{1,j} = \frac{\int_{h_{0,j}}^{\infty} \text{pdf}_{h_j}(x)x\text{d}x}{\alpha_j} = \frac{\int_{g_{0,j}}^{\infty} \text{pdf}_{g_j}(x)x\text{d}x}{\gamma_j}$, where $\text{pdf}_{h_j}(\cdot)$ and $\text{pdf}_{g_j}(\cdot)$ denote the probability density functions (pdfs) of channel states $h_j(t)$ and $g_j(t)$. On the other hand, each locally processed application will result in a cost of $\frac{\phi_j\beta_j}{c_{j,\max}}$, leading to an average per-timeslot computation cost of $\frac{\lambda_{2,j}\phi_j\beta_j}{c_{j,\max}}$.[3] In summary, the optimal cost $\Psi_j(0)$ is derived if each thing j optimizes the following problem $\mathbf{SP}'$

$$\min_{\substack{h_{0,j}, g_{0,j},\\ \lambda_{1,j}, \lambda_{2,j}}} \left(\varphi_j \int_{h_{0,j}}^{\infty} \text{pdf}_{h_j}(x)\text{d}x + \right. \tag{47a}$$

$$\left. \psi_j \int_{g_{0,j}}^{\infty} \text{pdf}_{g_j}(x)\text{d}x + \frac{\lambda_{2,j}\beta_j\phi_j}{c_{j,\max}}\right),$$

$$\text{s.t. } \lambda_{1,j} = \frac{\int_{h_{0,j}}^{\infty} \text{pdf}_{h_j}(x)x\text{d}x}{\alpha_j}, \tag{47b}$$

$$\lambda_{1,j} = \frac{\int_{g_{0,j}}^{\infty} \text{pdf}_{g_j}(x)x\text{d}x}{\gamma_j}, \tag{47c}$$

$$\lambda_{1,j} + \lambda_{2,j} = \lambda_j, \tag{47d}$$

$$0 \le \lambda_{1,j} \le \lambda_{1,j,\max}, 0 \le \lambda_{2,j} \le \lambda_{2,j,\max}, \tag{47e}$$

where (47e) specifies the limited capacity of the wireless links and local processors.

By examining the KKT conditions of $\mathbf{SP}'$, we can derive the optimal solutions as follows. First, let $h^*_{0,j}$, $g^*_{0,j}$, and $\lambda^*_{1,j}$ denote the solutions to the following equations.

$$\frac{\alpha_j\varphi_j}{h_{0,j}} + \frac{\gamma_j\psi_j}{g_{0,j}} = \frac{\beta_j\phi_j}{c_{j,\max}}, \tag{48}$$

[3] At the Fog tier, the optimal S-only policy must also satisfy link capacity constraints (the average communication load is no greater than the average link capacity at each link $l \to k$), computation capacity constraints (the average computation load is no greater than the average computation capacity at each Fog node j), and flow conservation constraints (the average input is equal to average output at each queue $Q_{i,j}(\cdot)$ and $U_{i,j}(\cdot)$). In this analysis, we focus on the scenario that the Fog tier has enough computation and link capacity so that even if all applications are uploaded, the Fog tier is able to accommodate all of them. These constraints are guaranteed to be satisfied. Moreover, since processing applications at the Fog tier does not generate cost, the optimal cost is not relevant to how the applications are transmitted and processed at this tier, but only related to uploading cost, downloading cost, and local processing cost at things.

$$\lambda_{1,j} = \frac{\int_{h_{0,j}}^{\infty} \text{pdf}_{h_j}(x)x\text{d}x}{\alpha_j} = \frac{\int_{g_{0,j}}^{\infty} \text{pdf}_{g_j}(x)x\text{d}x}{\gamma_j}. \tag{49}$$

Note that (49) implies that a larger $h_{0,j}$ leads to a larger $g_{0,j}$, and thus smaller $\frac{\alpha_j\varphi_j}{h_{0,j}} + \frac{\gamma_j\psi_j}{g_{0,j}}$. Therefore, there is a unique solution to (48)–(49). If $\lambda_j - \lambda_{2,j,\max} \le \lambda_{1,j}^* \le \lambda_{1,j,\max}$, then $h_{0,j}^*$ and $g_{0,j}^*$ are the optimal solutions to **SP′**. Otherwise, if $\lambda_{1,j}^* < \lambda_j - \lambda_{2,j,\max}$ (resp. $\lambda_{1,j} > \lambda_{1,j,\max}$), the optimal $\lambda_{1,j}$ is $\lambda_j - \lambda_{2,j,\max}$ (resp. $\lambda_{1,j,\max}$), and the optimal $h_{0,j}$ and $g_{0,j}$ values are derived by substituting the optimal $\lambda_{1,j}$ into (49).

The solution to Problem **SP′** can be interpreted through the concept of *marginal cost.* Given $h_{0,j}$ and $g_{0,j}$, $\frac{\alpha_j\varphi_j}{h_{0,j}}$ is the marginal cost of uploading one more application, and $\frac{\gamma_j\psi_j}{g_{0,j}}$ is the marginal cost of downloading one more application, and thus $\frac{\alpha_j\varphi_j}{h_{0,j}} + \frac{\gamma_j\psi_j}{g_{0,j}}$ is the marginal cost of offloading one more application. The marginal cost increases as $\lambda_{1,j}$ increases. At the optimal point, the marginal cost of offloading one application is equal to the cost of processing the application locally (if the constraint (47e) is not violated).

Let $c_{u,j}(\lambda)$ denote the marginal cost of uploading one more application under $\lambda_{1,j} = \lambda$, and $c_{d,j}(\lambda)$ denote the marginal cost of downloading one more application,[4] and $c_{c,j} = \frac{\beta_j\phi_j}{c_{j,\max}}$ is the cost of processing one application locally.

The optimal cost $\Psi_j(0)$ can be concluded as follows:

Case 1: If $c_{u,j}(\lambda_j-\lambda_{2,j,\max})+c_{d,j}(\lambda_j-\lambda_{2,j,\max}) > c_{c,j}$, the optimal $\lambda_{1,j} = \lambda_j - \lambda_{2,j,\max}$, and

$$\Psi_j(0) = \int_0^{\lambda_j-\lambda_{2,j,\max}} (c_{u,j}(\lambda) + c_{d,j}(\lambda))\text{d}\lambda + \lambda_{2,j,\max}c_{c,j}. \tag{50}$$

Case 2: If $c_{u,j}(\lambda_{1,j,\max}) + c_{d,j}(\lambda_{1,j,\max}) < c_{c,j}$, the optimal $\lambda_{1,j} = \lambda_{1,j,\max}$, and

$$\Psi_j(0) = \int_0^{\lambda_{1,j,\max}} (c_{u,j}(\lambda) + c_{d,j}(\lambda))\text{d}\lambda + (\lambda_j - \lambda_{1,j,\max})c_{c,j}. \tag{51}$$

Case 3: Otherwise, the optimal $\lambda_{1,j}$ is the solution to $c_{u,j}(\lambda) + c_{d,j}(\lambda) = c_{c,j}$ (denoted by $\lambda_{1,j}^*$), and

$$\Psi_j(0) = \int_0^{\lambda_{1,j}^*} (c_{u,j}(\lambda) + c_{d,j}(\lambda))\text{d}\lambda + (\lambda_j - \lambda_{1,j}^*)c_{c,j}. \tag{52}$$

4.2 Further Discussions on the Optimal Cost

From (46), we are also motivated to further study the term $\Psi(\epsilon) - \Psi(0)$. According to (38)–(41), $\Psi(\epsilon)$ is achieved by an S-only policy if at each thing j, we have $\lambda_{1,j}+\lambda_{2,j} = \lambda_j+\epsilon$, $\lambda_{1,j} = \frac{\int_{h_{0,j}}^{\infty} \text{pdf}_{h_j}(x)x\text{d}x}{\alpha_j} + \epsilon$, and $\lambda_{1,j} = \frac{\int_{g_{0,j}}^{\infty} \text{pdf}_{g_j}(x)x\text{d}x}{\gamma_j} + \epsilon$. In addition, the average per-timeslot cost of local processing of an application becomes $\frac{(\lambda_{2,j}+\epsilon)\phi_j\beta_j}{c_{j,\max}}$.

As a consequence, if $c_{u,j}(\lambda_j-\lambda_{2,j,\max})+c_{d,j}(\lambda_j-\lambda_{2,j,\max}) > c_{c,j}$, the incremental applications will be offloaded, and the incremental cost is $3\epsilon\bar{c}_j$, where $\bar{c}_j = c_{u,j}(\lambda_j - \lambda_{2,j,\max}) + c_{d,j}(\lambda_j - \lambda_{2,j,\max})$. Otherwise, the incremental applications will be locally processed, and the incremental cost is $3\epsilon\bar{c}_j$, where $\bar{c}_j = c_{c,j}$. Therefore, we have

$$\Psi(\epsilon) - \Psi(0) = 3\epsilon \sum_{j\in\mathcal{J}} \bar{c}_j, \tag{53}$$

which can be used to further simplify (46):

$$\lim_{T\to\infty} \frac{1}{T} \sum_{t=0}^{T-1} \mathbb{E}(\overline{Q}(t)) \le \frac{B}{\epsilon} + 3\theta \sum_{j\in\mathcal{J}} \bar{c}_j. \tag{54}$$

By combining (45) and (54), we observe a three-way tradeoff among queue backlogs, communication cost, and computation cost. First, there is $[O(1/\theta), O(\theta)]$ tradeoff between the overall cost and queue backlogs. Then, the overall cost can be rewritten in the form of (50)–(52), where the tradeoff between computation cost and communication cost is quantified through the marginal cost.

Note that in this section, we further characterize $\Psi(\epsilon)$ and $\Psi(0)$ through focusing on S-only policies. In the analysis, we require additional information (e.g. the distributions of channel states) to characterize the optimal costs. However, such information is not required in the implementation of the designed DWB policy – each thing, communication link, and node only needs to know its local information and perform local operations.

5 SIMULATION STUDY

In this section, we present simulation studies to validate our proposed model and DWB policy.

5.1 Simulation Setup

We focus on a Fog-integrated IoT ecosystem as introduced in Section 2, which consists of 50 IoT devices and 30 Fog nodes. For illustration purpose, we only present the performance of three IoT devices and the three Fog nodes connected to them. The IoT devices are indexed by 1, 2, and 3, and they are responsible for processing applications APP-1, APP-2, and APP-3 respectively. The parameters of these devices and nodes are set as follows. Each timeslot lasts 10 seconds. The numbers of arriving APP-1, APP-2, and APP-3 are uniformly distributed in [20 – 30], [30 – 50], and [20 – 40] each timeslot respectively. $\{\alpha_1, \alpha_2, \alpha_3\} = \{2, 1, 4\}$ Mbits. $\{\beta_1, \beta_2, \beta_3\} = \{4, 4, 4\} \times 10^9$ CPU cycles. $\{\gamma_1, \gamma_2, \gamma_3\} = \{1, 1, 4\}$ Mbits. We set uplink cost $\{\varphi_1, \varphi_2, \varphi_3\} = \{1, 1, 1\}$, downlink cost $\{\psi_1, \psi_2, \psi_3\} = \{1, 1, 1\}$, and local processor cost ϕ_1, ϕ_2, and ϕ_3 are all equal to a tunable value η. Its impact on the system performance will be studied. The processing capacities of things are $\{c_{1,\max}, c_{2,\max}, c_{3,\max}\} = \{60, 60, 100\} \times 10^9$ CPU cycles per timeslot. The uplink and downlink channel states h_1, h_2, h_3, g_1, g_2, and g_3 are uniformly distributed in [3 – 8], [3 – 8], [8 – 10], [1.5 – 4], [2 – 4], and [6 – 10] Mbps respectively. The computation capacities of Fog nodes are all set to 500×10^9 CPU cycles per timeslot and the communication capacities of the wired links are set to 100Mbps. All data points are averaged over 500 simulation rounds, and each round includes 7×10^4 timeslots.

[4] We can define function $\widehat{\lambda}_j(h_{0,j}) = \frac{\int_{h_{0,j}}^{\infty} \text{pdf}_{h_j}(x)x\text{d}x}{\alpha_j}$ and $\widehat{\lambda}_j^{-1}(\cdot)$ is the inverse function of $\widehat{\lambda}_j(\cdot)$. Then, we have $c_{u,j}(\lambda) = \frac{\alpha_j\varphi_j}{\widehat{\lambda}_j^{-1}(\lambda)}$. Similarly, we can define function $\widetilde{\lambda}_j(g_{0,j}) = \frac{\int_{g_{0,j}}^{\infty} \text{pdf}_{g_j}(x)x\text{d}x}{\gamma_j}$ and $\widetilde{\lambda}_j^{-1}(\cdot)$ is the inverse function of $\widetilde{\lambda}_j(\cdot)$. Then, we have $c_{d,j}(\lambda) = \frac{\gamma_j\psi_j}{\widetilde{\lambda}_j^{-1}(\lambda)}$.

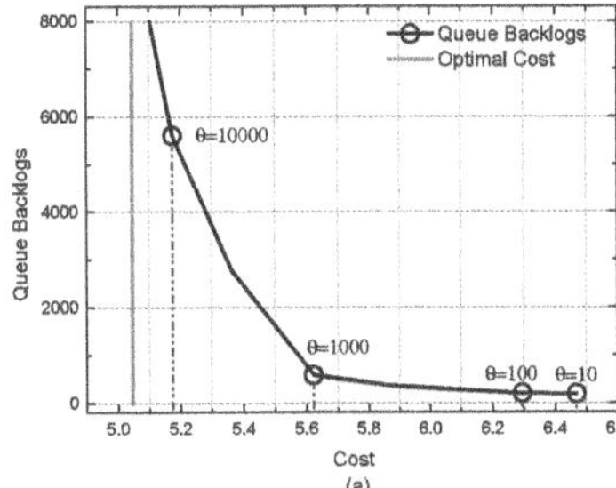

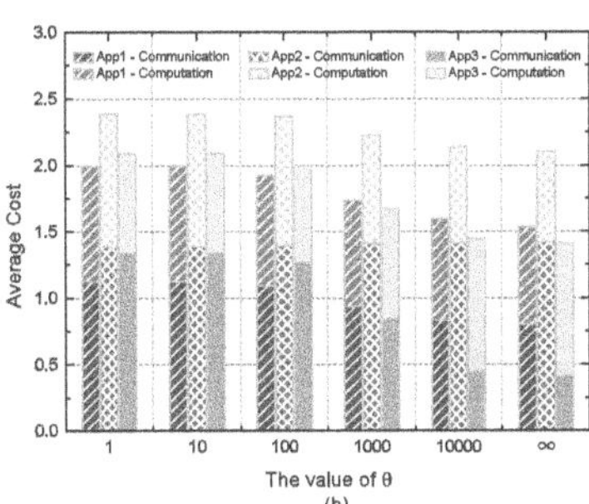

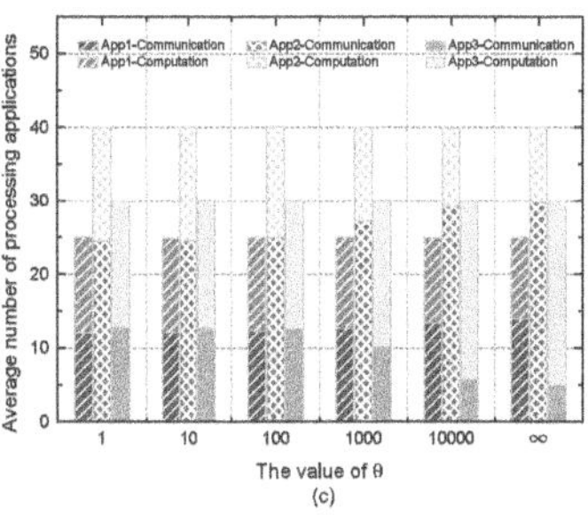

Figure 2: θ-related experiments with $\eta = 1$.

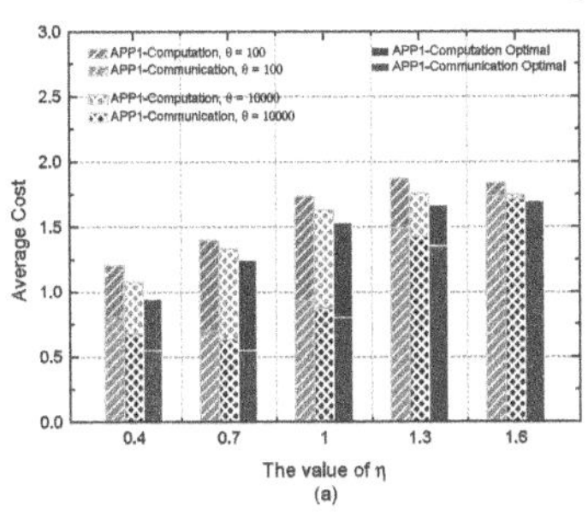

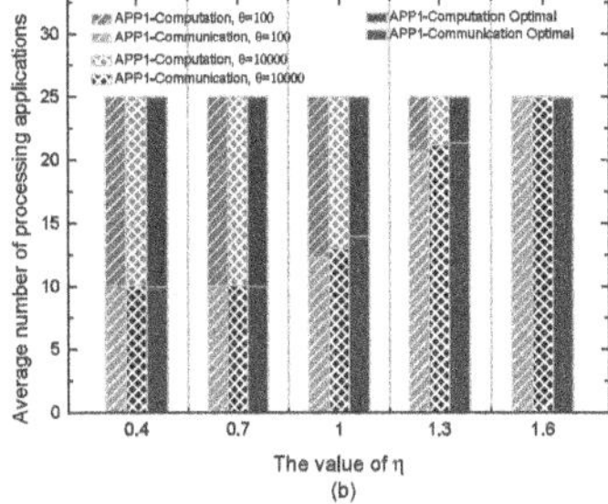

Figure 3: η-related experiments.

5.2 Simulation Results

The θ-related experiments. With the increment of θ, the tradeoff between overall cost and queue backlogs is shown in Fig. 2(a). The theoretically optimal cost ($\theta \longrightarrow \infty$) is shown as the vertical red line, which is gradually approached by the black curve when θ increases. In Fig. 2(b), the cost at the IoT devices is investigated, and in Fig. 2(c), the average numbers of applications locally computed and offloaded per timeslot under different θ are investigated. The overall cost decreases when θ increases, validating our analysis in Section 3. We observe that the local computation ratios of APP-1 and 2 are decreased, while the computation ratio of APP-3 is increased as θ increases. This is because when θ is smaller, the cost minimization part is less weighted compared with queue stability, so that applications are locally processed or offloaded impatiently, without waiting for a chance when the cost can be minimized. For APP-1 and 2, at the optimal point, offloading is less expensive compared with computation, and thus if θ decreases, some applications (should be offloaded) are impatiently to be locally processed, leading to higher local computation ratios. For APP-3, at the optimal point, computation is less expensive. If θ decreases, some applications (should be locally computed) are impatiently offloaded, leading to a higher offloading ratio.

The η-related experiments (changing computation costs). The effect of η is studied in Fig. 3. We set $\theta = 100$ and 10000 in the simulation for each selected η, and also present the theoretically optimal cost ($\theta \longrightarrow \infty$) for reference. As observed from Fig. 3(a), the total cost of performing the applications in the system is increased when η increases. Meanwhile, along with the increment of η, the number of local computation of the applications becomes smaller since computation cost is increased, as depicted in Fig. 3(b).

6 RELATED WORK

There has been a significant research interest in integrating cloud computing and IoT over the past decade, much of which focused on system implementations, such as cloud support for the IoT [7], device virtualization and service provisioning [19], and computation offloading in mobile clouds [3]. With the popularity of Fog Computing, Fog-integrated IoT systems start drawing attentions. The authors in [12] proposed a theoretical model for such systems. The joint optimization of service provisioning, data offloading, and task scheduling were studied, with the goal of minimizing the system resource usage while meeting the defined QoS requirements. In [20], the authors mathematically characterized a Fog computing network in terms of power consumption, service latency, CO_2 emission, and cost. The paper focused on the interactions between Fog layer and Cloud layer only. The authors in [22] studied the problem of service migration and workload scheduling in Fog Computing systems to minimize operational costs while providing required QoS. They modeled the system as a Markov decision process. In [23], the authors studied the joint task scheduling and resource management issue in Fog Computing supported systems and aimed to minimize the task completion time while improving the user experience. The above papers did not consider the possibility of processing applications locally and the offloading cost from the things' point of view. To the best of our knowledge, ours is the first work that proposes a distributed online control policy in a Fog-integrated IoT ecosystem.

Lyapunov optimization is a promising approach to solve resource allocation, traffic routing, and scheduling problems in wireless ad hoc networks and processing networks. There are several papers focusing on the traffic routing and scheduling in wireless ad hoc networks based on the Lyapunov optimization framework [14, 16], while they have not considered the task processing in the networks. [5] considered a mobile crowdsourcing scenario, where mobile devices upload data via different data collectors, while the data processing and computation is not considered in that work. The focus of the authors was on the data transmission and on exploiting idle capacities of mobile devices to upload data from other users, creating marketplace for mobile Internet access. However, for typical IoT applications, it is critical to consider also data processing, and the decision on where to process is a key issue that can affect the system performance. IoT devices, although constrained in resources, are nevertheless able to perform part of the application workload, and such capability needs to be considered to achieve a cost-effective solution.

For processing networks, [6, 9] considered offloading one application from a mobile device to a cloud data center. [11, 13, 17] studied processing networks with limited numbers of network nodes, while we allow arbitrarily large numbers of things and nodes in the system. Since IoT systems can scale to potentially hundreds to thousands of nodes, considering a large number of devices is a key requirement for any realistic, efficient and effective solution.

The paper [21] studied a network with many users and computation nodes, but those cloud nodes are not interconnected so that a task cannot be further offloaded from one computation node to another. [4, 10] focused on task processing and offloading scenarios in a wired network, while the influence of wireless communications and their impact on the users' cost cannot be characterized. Among the above papers, only [13] has considered that the outcomes of processed applications should finally return to the things.

7 CONCLUSION

We believe that Fog Computing and IoT are complementary technologies, and their synergistic combination enables the creation of innovative, value-added applications and services for the end user. In particular, the privileged location of Fog devices, close to the user, enabling location-aware processing and providing services with low latency and high availability, makes such technology very attractive for a wide range of applications. However, there are still a number of challenges to be overcome to get the most out of the IoT-Fog combination. In this paper, we addressed one of such challenges. We thoroughly investigate the problem of application processing and offloading in a Fog-integrated IoT ecosystem. We proposed an online, distributed, and cost-effective system control policy referred to as the Distributed Weighted Backpressure (DWB) policy to address this problem. A three-way tradeoff among queue backlogs, communication cost, and computation cost was then analyzed. Simulation study was conducted, validating the correctness and usefulness of the proposed DWB policy.

8 ACKNOWLEDGEMENT

This work was supported in part by the University of Sydney DVC Research/Bridging Support Grant DE170100906, CNPq 307378/2014-4, FAPERJ 213967, and Australian Linkage Grant LP160100406.

REFERENCES

[1] Luigi Atzori, Antonio Iera, and Giacomo Morabito. 2010. The Internet of Things: A survey. *Computer Networks* 54, 15 (Jun. 2010), 2787–2805.

[2] Stephen Boyd, Lin Xiao, Almir Mutapcic, , and Jacob Mattingley. [n. d.]. Notes on Decomposition Methods. ([n. d.]). https://see.stanford.edu/materials/lsocoee364b/08-decomposition_notes.pdf

[3] S. Deng, L. Huang, J. Taheri, and A. Y. Zomaya. 2015. Computation Offloading for Service Workflow in Mobile Cloud Computing. *IEEE Trans. on Parallel and Distributed Systems* 26, 12 (Dec. 2015), 3317–3329. https://doi.org/10.1109/TPDS.2014.2381640

[4] Apostolos Destounis, Georgios S. Paschos, and Iordanis Koutsopoulos. 2016. Streaming Big Data meets Backpressure in Distributed Network Computation. In *Proc. of IEEE INFOCOM*. San Francisco, CA.

[5] Ngoc Do, Cheng-Hsin Hsu, and Nalini Venkatasubramanian1. 2012. CrowdMAC: A Crowdsourcing System for Mobile Access. In *Proc. of International Middleware Conference*. Montreal, Canada.

[6] Weiwei Fang, Xiaoyan Yin, Yuan An, Naixue Xiong, Qiwang Guo, and Jing Li. 2015. Optimal scheduling for data transmission between mobile devices and cloud. *Elsevier Information Sciences: an International Journal* 301, C (Apr. 2015), 169–180.

[7] Claudio M. De Farias, Wei Li, Flávia C. Delicato, Luci Pirmez, Albert Y. Zomaya, Paulo F. Pires, and José N. De Souza. 2016. A Systematic Review of Shared Sensor Networks. *Comput. Surveys* 48, 4, Article 51 (Feb. 2016), 50 pages. https://doi.org/10.1145/2851510

[8] Leonidas Georgiadis, Michael J. Neely, and Leandros Tassiulas. 2006. Resource Allocation and Cross-Layer Control in Wireless Networks. *Foundations and Trends in Networking* 1, 1 (2006), 1–144.

[9] Dong Huang, Ping Wang, and Dusit Niyato. 2012. A Dynamic Offloading Algorithm for Mobile Computing. *IEEE Trans. on Wireless Communications* 11, 6 (Apr. 2012), 1991–1995.

[10] L. Huang and M. J. Neely. 2011. Utlity Optimal Scheduling in Processing Networks. In *Proc. of IFIP Performance*. Amsterdam, Netherlands.

[11] Song Li, Yangfan Zhou, Lei Jiao, Xinya Yan, Xin Wang, and Michael Rung-Tsong Lyu. 2015. Towards Operational Cost Minimization in Hybrid Clouds for Dynamic Resource Provisioning with Delay-Aware Optimization. *IEEE Trans. on Services Computing* 8, 3 (May–Jun. 2015), 398–409.

[12] Wei Li, Igor Santos, Flavia C. Delicato, Paulo F. Pires, Luci Pirmez, Wei Wei, Houbing Song, Albert Zomaya, and Samee Khan. 2016. System Modelling and Performance Evaluation of a three-tier Cloud of Things. *Future Generation Computer Systems, accepted* (2016). http://www.sciencedirect.com/science/article/pii/S0167739X16302047

[13] Yuyi Mao, Jun Zhang, and Khaled B. Letaief. 2016. Dynamic Computation Offloading for Mobile-Edge Computing with Energy Harvesting Devices. arXiv:1605.05488 [cs.IT] (2016).

[14] Michael J. Neely. 2006. Energy optimal control for time-varying wireless networks. *IEEE Trans. on Information Theory* 52, 7 (Jul. 2006), 2915–2934.

[15] Michael J. Neely. 2010. *Stochastic Network Optimization with Application to Communication and Queueing Systems*. Morgan & Claypool Publishers.

[16] Michael J. Neely, Eytan Modiano, and Chih-Ping Li. 2008. Fairness and Optimal Stochastic Control for Heterogeneous Network. *IEEE/ACM Trans. on Networking* 16, 2 (Apr. 2008), 396–409.

[17] Yipei Niu, Bin Luo, Fangming Liu, Jiangchuan Liu, and Bo Li. 2015. When Hybrid Cloud Meets Flash Crowd: Towards Cost-Effective Service Provisioning. In *Proc. of IEEE INFOCOM*. Hong Kong, China.

[18] Y. Qi, K. Wang, J. Fong, Y. Xue, J. Li, W. Jiang, and V. Prasanna. 2011. FEACAN: Front-end acceleration for content-aware network processing. In *Proc. of IEEE INFOCOM*. Shanghai, China. https://doi.org/10.1109/INFCOM.2011.5935021

[19] I. L. Santos, L. Pirmez, F. C. Delicato, S. U. Khan, and A. Y. Zomaya. 2015. Olympus: The Cloud of Sensors. *IEEE Cloud Computing* 2, 2 (Mar. 2015), 48–56. https://doi.org/10.1109/MCC.2015.43

[20] S. Sarkar, S. Chatterjee, and S. Misra. 2015. Assessment of the Suitability of Fog Computing in the Context of Internet of Things. *IEEE Trans. on Cloud Computing, accepted* (2015). https://doi.org/10.1109/TCC.2015.2485206

[21] Rahul Urgaonkar, Ulas C. Kozat, Ken Igarashi, and Michael J. Neely. 2010. Dynamic Resource Allocation and Power Management in Virtualized Data Centers. In *Proc. of IEEE Network Operations and Management Symposium*. Osaka, Japan.

[22] Rahul Urgaonkar, Shiqiang Wang, Ting He, Murtaza Zafer, Kevin Chan, and Kin K. Leung. 2015. Dynamic service migration and workload scheduling in edge-clouds. *Performance Evaluation* 91 (2015), 205–228. https://doi.org/10.1016/j.peva.2015.06.013 Special Issue: Performance 2015.

[23] D. Zeng, L. Gu, S. Guo, Z. Cheng, and S. Yu. 2016. Joint Optimization of Task Scheduling and Image Placement in Fog Computing Supported Software-Defined Embedded System. *IEEE Trans. on Computers, accepted* (2016). https://doi.org/10.1109/TC.2016.2536019

[24] Ben Zhang, Nitesh Mor, John Kolb, Douglas S. Chan, Ken Lutz, Eric Allman, John Wawrzynek, Edward Lee, and John Kubiatowicz. 2015. The Cloud is Not Enough: Saving IoT from the Cloud. In *7th USENIX Workshop on Hot Topics in Cloud Computing*. Santa Clara, CA.

QoS-Aware Task Offloading in Distributed Cloudlets with Virtual Network Function Services

Mike Jia
Research School of Computer Science
The Australian National University
Canberra, ACT, Australia 2601
u5515287@anu.edu.au

Weifa Liang
Research School of Computer Science
The Australian National University
Canberra, ACT, Australia 2601
wliang@cs.anu.edu.au

Zichuan Xu
School of Software
Dalian University of Technology
Dalian, China 116024
z.xu@dlut.edu.cn

ABSTRACT

Pushing the cloud frontier to the network edge has attracted tremendous interest not only from cloud operators of the IT service/software industry but also from network service operators that provide various network services for mobile users. In particular, by deploying *cloudlets* in metropolitan area networks, network service providers can provide various network services through implementing virtualized network functions to meet the demands of mobile users. In this paper we formulate a novel task offloading problem in a metropolitan area network, where each offloaded task requests a specific network function with a maximum tolerable delay and different offloading requests may require different network services. We aim to maximize the number of requests admitted while minimizing their admission cost within a finite time horizon. We first show that the problem is NP-hard, and then devise an efficient algorithm through reducing the problem to a series of minimum weight maximum matching in auxiliary bipartite graphs. We also consider dynamic changes of offloading request patterns over time, and develop an effective prediction mechanism to release and/or create instances of network functions in different cloudlets for cost savings. We finally evaluate the performance of the proposed algorithms through experimental simulations. Experimental results indicate that the proposed algorithms are promising.

KEYWORDS

cloudlets; task offloading; request QoS requirement; functionality service virtualization; request admission cost minimization; network function virtualization; offloading algorithms; wireless metropolitan area networks; resource allocation of cloudlets.

1 INTRODUCTION

Mobile devices such as smart phones and tablets have become the main communication tools of users for business, social networking, and personal banking. Due to their portable size, the computing/storage and energy powering these mobile devices are critical, making their processing and storage ability very limited. One promising technique is to offload their tasks to nearby cloudlets via WiFi or bluetooth for processing. For example, an inspector takes a photo of a stranger in his monitoring area, and uploads the photo to the cloudlets to verify the identity of the stranger, assuming that there is a database of personal identities on the cloudlets. Cloudlet technology also looks particularly promising for emerging augmented reality (AR) applications and products. In the recent 2017 F8 Developers Conference, Facebook CEO Mark Zuckerberg laid out a vision of the near future where artists could display virtual artwork in public spaces [1], and friends could share virtual notes and objects with each other, using their mobile devices. From these examples, it can be seen that different offloading tasks have different network functions and quality of service requirements. As different network functions in cloudlets are implemented by different virtual machines (referred to as Virtualized Network Functions (VNFs)), we may group all offloading tasks with the same network function services together and implement them in virtual machines. To share the computing resources among offloaded tasks with the same network service while meeting their individual QoSs, network service providers usually instantiate some instances of the VMs of each network function service in each cloudlet.

Provisioning network services in a mobile edge cloud, having instantiated instances of network function services in its cloudlets, poses several challenges. That is, how many instances are to be instantiated at which cloudlets, such that the computing resource of cloudlets can be maximally utilized while the cost and delay of instance instantiation can be minimized? How should offloaded tasks be assigned to different cloudlets while meeting their QoSs? and how can the admission cost of offloaded task requests be minimized by utilizing existing instances of their requested network function services? Finally, how can the number of required instances be predicted, and how should the creation and removal of instances be managed in the network? In this paper we will address these challenges, by comprehensively studying the problem of task offloading with network function service requirements in a mobile edge cloud. To the best of our knowledge, we are the first to explore the possibility of utilizing existing VNF instances of network function services in cloudlets for cost-effective task offloading while meeting different QoS requirements of offloaded tasks, by formulating a novel QoS-aware task offloading optimization problem, and providing an optimization framework. To respond to dynamic changes of offloading request patterns over time to further reduce request admission costs, we also develop an effective prediction mechanism to predict the instance demands in the future through the removal and creation of different numbers of VNF instances of each network function service at each cloudlet.

MSWiM '17, November 21–25, 2017, Miami, FL, USA

ACM ISBN 978-x-xxxx-xxxx-x/YY/MM...$15.00
https://doi.org/10.1145/nnnnnnn.nnnnnnn

The main contributions of this paper are as follows. We first formulate a novel QoS-aware task offloading problem in a wireless metropolitan area network consisting of Access Points (APs) and cloudlets (servers) that are co-located with the APs, where each offloading task request has a specific network function requirement with a given tolerable delay, and different offloading tasks request have different VNFs. We assume some instances of the VNFs have already been instantiated on the cloudlets, and others can be dynamically created if there are sufficient resources in cloudlets. We aim to maximize the number of offloading requests admitted within a finite time horizon while minimizing the admission cost of requests and meeting their individual end-to-end delay requirements. We achieve this by fully making use of the VNF instances in the cloudlets to reduce the admission cost and shorten the response time of the requests. We then devise an efficient online algorithm for offloading request admissions through a non-trivial reduction that reduces the problem to a series of minimum-weight maximum matching problems in auxiliary bipartite graphs. We also investigate offloading request patterns over time, and develop an effective prediction mechanism that can predict the numbers of instances of each network function at different cloudlets, through releasing the occupied resources by idle VNF instances back to the system, and creating new VNF instances of other highly demanded network functions in cloudlets to meet the need of future offloading task requests. We finally evaluate the performance of the proposed algorithms through experimental simulations. Experimental results demonstrate that the proposed algorithms are promising.

The remainder of the paper is arranged as follows. Section 2 will survey the state-of-the-arts on this topic, and detail the difference of this work from previous studies in task offloading. Section 3 will introduce the system model, notations and problem definition. Section 4 will devise algorithms for the problem. Section 5 will provide some experimental results on the performance of the proposed algorithm, and Section 6 concludes the paper.

2 RELATED WORK

Offloading tasks to cloudlets has been extensively studied in the past several years. Generally, the model for application offloading systems [2, 3] in mobile cloud computing consists of a client component on a mobile device, and a server component on the cloudlet to remotely execute offloaded tasks from the device. As the options for user applications are too numerous for server components to be stored in the cloudlet, most works [2, 4, 5] assume the use of virtual machines (VM) as a platform for task offloading. A VM image of a mobile device is transferred to the cloudlet, and tasks are remotely executed on the device's VM in the cloudlet, using task offloading operations. Once a task on the VM in the cloudlet has been executed, the result will be returned to its user.

Most previous studies assumed that each user connects to a dedicated VM in the cloudlet, without consideration of whether an existing VM for the same application could be used to serve multiple users. However, as many emerging applications and services are location-specific, it is more realistic to assume that multiple users in a local area will request the same computing service from cloudlets. In [6], the authors introduced a mobile task offloading architecture specifically for mobile augmented reality in a museum setting. In their model, a user turns on his mobile device's camera to capture a scene. The location and direction of the camera are calculated for each captured video frame and the data is sent to a nearby cloudlet where a rendering process generates the 2D image of a virtual exhibit, which is then overlayed on top of the original video frame. The resulting image is then sent back to the user's device for display, creating the impression of seeing the virtual exhibit in the real world through the camera viewport. Since the processing of each user video frame can be modeled as an individual task, it is possible for a VM instance on a cloudlet to serve multiple users. However, it then becomes a challenge to assign users to existing VM instances, or create additional instances to serve more users while ensuring the QoS requirement of each user is met, as they share computing resources on the cloudlet.

In recent years, several studies focused on network planning problems in deploying cloudlets for public use. For example, Jia et al [7] considered the assignment of user requests to different cloudlets in a WMAN, by developing a heuristic for it. Jia et al [8] also dealt with minimizing the maximum delay among offloaded tasks in a distributed cloudlet network through balancing the workload between cloudlets. Xu et al [9, 10] devised assignment algorithms for user offloading requests to different cloudlets, by proposing efficient approximation and online algorithms with performance guarantees. Xia et al [11] considered opportunistic task offloading under link bandwidth, mobile device energy, and cloudlet computing capacity constraints. Xia et al [12] studied the location-aware task offloading problem for mobile devices. All of these mentioned studies assumed that each offloaded task will be assigned the amounts of computing resources they demanded, there is no consideration for whether there are already VMs in cloudlets for serving them, not to mention whether such services meet their QoS requirements. However, the emergence of AR applications and IoT computing strongly suggest that many offloaded tasks may request for the same type of services in the near future. If the VM for that service has been established, the offloading cost will be less expensive and the service can be carried out immediately.

3 PRELIMINARIES

In this section, we first introduce the system model and notations, and then define the problems precisely.

3.1 System model

Given a WMAN $G = (V \cup C, E)$ where V is the set of AP nodes and E is the set of links between AP nodes. There is a subset of nodes $C \subseteq V$ of cloudlets co-located with the AP nodes. Each cloudlet $c_j \in C$ has computing capacity cap_j with $1 \leq j \leq m$ and $m = |C|$. Assuming that time is divided into equal time slots. The amounts of available resources at the beginning of different time slots varies, due to request admissions and departures. Let $cap_j(t)$ be the available computing capacity of cloudlet c_j at time slot t with $1 \leq j \leq m$.

Computing resource in the cloudlets is used to instantiate a certain number of VNFs to implement offloading requests from mobile users. We thus assume that there is a set of network functions $f_i \in \mathcal{F}$ with $1 \leq i \leq N$ and $N = |\mathcal{F}|$, which are virtualized and implemented in VMs in cloudlets. If the implementation of an offloading request with a network function $f_i \in \mathcal{F}$ demands *the basic resource unit* of f_i, we term this implementation as *an instance* of network function f_i for the request, or *an VNF instance* of f_i; otherwise (if the implementation of the request needs x (≥ 1) times the basic resource unit of f_i), we term that the request implementation takes x instances of f_i for each $f_i \in \mathcal{F}$. We further assume that each cloudlet has instantiated some instances of virtualized network functions. Denote by $n_{ij}(t)$ the number of instantiated instances of f_i in cloudlet c_j at time slot t.

Each mobile device can offload its tasks to cloudlets in G, via APs. Consider a set of requests for offloading their tasks to the cloudlets in G for processing, each request with a specified network service will be implemented in a VM of that function, which is termed as an instance of the specified virtualized network function (VNF). Let $S(t)$ be the set of user requests at time slot t. Each user request $r_k \in S(t)$ is represented by a tuple $(id_k, loc_k, VNF_k, \lambda_k, d_k)$, where id_k is the request identity, loc_k is the location of the request user, VNF_k is the computing service that r_k requests, which in fact is a virtualized network function, $\lambda_k \geq 0$ is the packet rate of r_k, and d_k is the end-to-end delay requirement of r_k.

3.2 End-to-end delay requirements of offloading requests

The end-to-end delay experienced by each admitted request r_k include the queuing delay that it spent in waiting for an available instance of its VNF, processing delay by its assigned VNF instance, instantiation delay of creating a new VNF when necessary, and network latency from its location loc_k to its assigned cloudlet c_j.

Queuing delay and processing delay: each offloaded packet with packet rate λ_k of r_k will be queued in the VM of VNF_k in a cloudlet prior to its processing by the VM, which will incur both queuing and processing delays when each packet passes through the VM of the VNF. To differentiate user requests with different delay requirements, the requests in each cloudlet c_k are partitioned into N groups with each group consisting of requests for the same service. We thus assume that there is an $M/M/n$ queue at each cloudlet for each type of service $f_i \in \mathcal{F}$. Each group of requests will eventually be processed by instances of network service $f_i \in \mathcal{F}$, with $1 \leq i \leq N$. The average queuing delay of the $M/M/n$ queue for function f_i at cloudlet c_j thus is

$$\tau_{kj}(\lambda) = \frac{1}{n_{ij}(t)\mu_i - \lambda}, \tag{3.1}$$

where λ is the sum of packet rates of all requests that require VNF f_i and are assigned to cloudlet c_j, and μ_i is the data processing rate of VNF f_i. Considering that the data processing rate of VNF f_i is μ_i, the processing delay of f_i thus is $\frac{1}{\mu_i}$.

Instantiation delay: without loss of generality, we assume that the instantiation delay of an VNF instance is a given constant d_i^{ins} for VNF f_i.

Network latency: assuming that data traffic in network G is transferred via a shortest path between each pair of source and destination, the network latency of request r_k thus is the accumulative delay incurred in the edges of a shortest path p_{loc_k, c_j} from its source location loc_k to its assigned cloudlet c_j. Let $d(e)$ be the delay of link e of network G, the network latency d_k^{net} thus is

$$d_k^{net} = \sum_{e \in p_{loc_k, c_j}} d(e). \tag{3.2}$$

The end-to-end delay D_k experienced by a request r_k for VNF f_i at cloudlet c_j thus can be calculated by

$$D_k = \begin{cases} \tau_{kj} + \frac{1}{\mu_i} + d_k^{net}, & \text{if } n_{ij}(t) > 0 \\ d_i^{ins} + \frac{1}{\mu_i} + d_k^{net}, & \text{otherwise.} \end{cases} \tag{3.3}$$

The end-to-end delay requirement of each offloading request r_k thus is

$$D_k \leq d_k. \tag{3.4}$$

3.3 The admission cost

For each request $r_k \in S(t)$ with network function f_i ($= VNF_k^i$), its implementation can either make use of some of existing VNF instances of f_i in a cloudlet c_j if it joins in other admitted requests with the same network function f_i, and the delay requirements of all requests can be met. Specifically, let R_{ij} be the set of offloaded requests with network function f_i in cloudlet c_j when r_k is being considered, and assume that the admission of r_k to R_{ij} will not violate the delay constraint of any of them. The operational cost of admitting r_k in c_j then is the cost sum of its data packet transmission cost (between its location via its nearby AP) and cloudlet c_j and its processing cost $c(VNF_k^i)$ at c_j. Otherwise (the addition of r_k resulting in the violation of computing or delay constraints of requests in R_{ij}), if there are available computing resources in cloudlet c_j, we then allocate the demanded resources for r_k by increasing the number of instances for VNF_k^i in c_j, the admission cost $w(r_k)$ of r_k per packet thus is the cost sum of its packet transmission cost, the creation of new instances for r_k, and its processing cost in c_j.

3.4 Problem definition

Given a WMAN $G(V \cup C, E)$, a set of user requests $S(t)$ at time slot t with each request having an end-to-end delay requirement, and a finite time horizon T, assume that the set of network functions by the requests in $S(t)$ is $\mathcal{F}$, and some instances of each network function $f \in \mathcal{F}$ have already been installed in cloudlets C, *the operational cost minimization problem* in G is to find a schedule of request admissions such that as many requests as possible are admitted during a monitoring period of T while the cumulative operational cost of admitted requests is minimized, subject to the computing resource capacity constraint, and end-to-end delay requirement of each user request.

Theorem 3.1. *The operational cost minimization problem in $G(V \cup C, E)$ is NP-hard.*

Proof We consider an extreme case where there are only two cloudlets in the network with identical computational capacities. We assume that each request in $S(t)$ has a different service (i.e., a different network function), we can ignore the delay requirement of each request. Our task is to assign the requests to the two cloudlets to see whether all of the requests can be admitted. Clearly, for each request $r_k \in S(t)$, we need to create a VM for implementing its network function that is associated with computing resource demand c_k, subject to the computing capacity constraints on the two cloudlets.

We reduce the well-known summation problem to the mentioned assignment problem in polynomial time as follows. Given n positive integers $a_1, a_2, \ldots, a_n$, the summation problem is to partition the n integers into two subsets such that the sum of integers in each subset is equal, which is NP-hard. As the special case of the minimum operational cost problem is equivalent to the summation problem, the operational cost minimization problem thus is NP-hard too.

4 ONLINE ALGORITHM

In this section we first consider admissions of requests in $S(t)$ in the beginning of each time slot t. We then deal with dynamic request admissions within a finite time horizon T, by proposing an efficient online algorithm for the operational cost minimization problem in WMAN $G(V \cup C, E)$.

4.1 Algorithm for offloading requests at each time slot

Given a set of arrived requests $S(t)$ in the beginning of each time slot t, we aim to admit as many requests in $S(t)$ as possible while minimizing the admission cost of the admitted requests and meeting their delay requirements. The basic idea behind our algorithm is to reduce the operational cost minimization problem in G to a series of minimum weight maximum matching problems in a set of auxiliary bipartite graphs. Each matched edge in the maximum matching of an auxiliary bipartite graph corresponds to an assignment of offloading requests to cloudlets in the network G, where the end-to-end delay requirement of each admitted request can be met. The detailed description of this reduction is as follows.

For each cloudlet c_j, we construct a bipartite graph $G_j(t) = (X_j \cup \{x_{0,j}\}, Y_j, E_j; w)$, where X_j is the set of VNF instances in cloudlet c_j, and $x_{0,j}$ represents available resources for creating new instances for any of network functions in c_j, and Y_j is the set of requests $r_k \in S(t)$. There is an edge in E_j between a node $v_{ij} \in X_j$ and $r_k \in Y_j$ if sharing the resources for r_k does not violate the resource and delay requirements of other running requests for the network function. Specifically, there is an edge between $r_k \in X_j$ and the instance node of f_i in cloudlet c_j if (i) the VNF of r_k is f_i; (ii) the demanded instance of f_i by r_k is no greater than $n_{ij}(t)$; (iii) the addition of r_k into the set of admitted requests sharing the instance does not violate the delay constraints of other admitted requests in R_{ij}; and (iv) the total delay incurred by the assignment of r_k is no greater than d_k. The weight assigned to this edge is the cost of implementing request r_k in cloudlet c_j, which consists of the routing cost between the mobile device location and the cloudlet and the cost of processing the packet at the VNF instance of f_i. There is an edge between r_k and $x_{0,j}$ if its demanded computing resource is no greater than $cap_j(t)$ and its delay is no greater than d_k (including the instance creation delay). The weight of the edge thus is the sum of the routing cost, the processing cost and the instance creation cost for the request.

Assume that there are m cloudlets in G. An auxiliary bipartite graph $G(t) = \bigcup_{j=1}^{m} G_j(t) = (X(t), Y(t), E(t); w)$ is then derived from G, where $X(t) = \cup_{j=1}^{m}(X_j \cup \{x_{0,j}\})$, $Y(t) = \sum_{j=1}^{m} Y_j = \{r_1, r_2, \ldots, r_n\}$, and $E(t) = \cup_{j=1}^{m} E_j$.

To admit requests in $S(t)$ in the beginning of each time slot t, the admission algorithm proceeds iteratively. Let $G_1(t) = G(t)$. Within iteration l with $1 \leq l \leq m$, a minimum weight maximum matching M_l in $G_l(t)$ is found. Then, allocate the demanded resources for the requests in M_l, remove all matched requests in M_l from $S(t)$, update the available instances and cloudlet resources at each cloudlet in the network, and construct the next auxiliary bipartite graph $G_{l+1}(t)$. This procedure continues until there are no matchings in $G_{l+1}(t)$.

The union of all found minimum weight maximum matchings $\cup_{l=1}^{m} M_l$ forms a solution to the problem, i.e., each matched edge corresponds to an admission of a request in $S(t)$. The weighted sum $\sum_{l=1}^{L} c(M_l)$ of the edges in $\cup_{l=1}^{L} M_l$ is the implementation cost of admitted requests in $S(t)$, where L is the number of iterations which depends on requests in $S(t)$. Alternatively, $L \leq \max_{1 \leq l \leq L}\{deg(G_l(t))\}$ which $deg(G_l(t))$ is the maximum degree of nodes in auxiliary graph $G_l(t)$. The details are given in `Algorithm 1`.

Algorithm 1 Admission_Algorithm_Each_Time_Slot $(G(t), S(t))$

Require: m cloudlets with each having its available resource capacity $cap_j(t)$, the number of instances of VNFs of each $f_i \in \mathcal{F}$, and a set of requests $S(t)$ at each time slot t.

Ensure: maximize the number of requests admitted (i.e., a subset $S'(t) \subseteq S(t)$) for each time slot t while minimizing the total admission cost. For each request r_k, if it is admitted, then to which cloudlet it will be sent and to which instance of VNF it should join/or create will be given in the solution.

```
/* perform request admissions for requests in S(t) */
M_t ← ∅; cost_t ← 0; /* the assignment of requests in S(t) while minimizing their implementation cost cost_t */
Construct the weighted bipartite graph G(t);
G_1(t) ← G(t); l ← 1; cost_t ← 0;
while there is a minimum weight maximum matching M_l in G_l(t) do
    Find the minimum weight maximum matching M_l in G_l(t), by invoking an efficient algorithm for the weighted maximum matching;
    if M_l ≠ ∅ then
        M_t ← M_t ∪ M_l;
        c(M_l) ← Σ_{e∈M_l} w(e);
        cost_t ← cost_t + c(M_l);
        Allocate resources to the requests in M_l;
        Update the amounts of available resources and instances of each network function at each cloudlet;
        S(t) ← S(t) \ r(M_l); /* Remove requests in M_l from S(t), where r(M_l) is the set of requests in M_l */
        l ← l + 1;
        Construct G_l(t) according to the updated resources, instances of VNFs, and the request set S(t);
return M_t corresponds to the assignment of requests in S(t), while cost_t is their implementation cost.
```

4.2 Online algorithm for the minimum operational cost problem

In the previous subsection, we considered the admissions of offloading requests within one time slot. In reality, requests arrive into or depart from the system dynamically, request admissions at the current time slot should take into account their impact on the admissions of requests in future.

Notice that on one hand, new VNF instances of some network functions have been created to admit newly arrived requests. On the other hand, idle VNF instances will be released back to the system if they will not be used in the near future. Two types of simple solutions can be adopted to handle such resource releases: (1) never release VNF instances in case of being used by future requests; (2) immediately release VNF instances that become idle. The first solution is based on the rationale that some VNF instances will be shared with subsequent admitted requests. Thus, in spite of the departures of some admitted requests, their occupied resources (or VNF instances) will still be kept by their VMs without releasing back to the system. Consequently, more and more VNF instances of each network function in the system will become idle, while the available resources at each cloudlet become more scarce. This will incur unnecessary operational costs, while at the same time preventing new requests from being admitted due to the lack of VNF instances or computing resources. The second solution is to avoid maintaining idle instances of VNFs. However, if a VNF instance is demanded by a request right after its release, the delay requirement of an admitted request might be violated, considering that creating a new instance for it will incur a delay. To avoid such situations, we make VNF creation and release decisions based on a smart prediction method that predicts the idle VNF instance releases and new VNF instance creations, such that the operational cost is minimized while the delay requirements of admitted requests are still met.

In the following we propose a prediction mechanism to predict idle VNF instance releases and new VNF instance creations to respond to changing request patterns over time. Thus, the system will perform resource collection, by releasing the occupied resources by idle VNF instances back to the system if the cost overhead on maintenance of these idle VNFs is beyond a given threshold after a certain time slots. Specifically, let $n_{ij}(t)$ be the number of VNF instances of f_i in cloudlet c_j at time slot t, its actual usage number is $n'_{ij}(t)$ ($\leq n_{ij}(t)$), the number of idle VNF instances of f_i in cloudlet c_j in time slot t thus is

$$\delta_{ij}(t) = n_{ij}(t) - n'_{ij}(t). \tag{4.1}$$

Let each idle instance of f_i in cloudlet c_j incur a fixed cost γ_{ij} at each time slot, and there is a given cost overhead threshold θ ($\geq n_0 \cdot \max_{f_i \in \mathcal{F}}\{c(f_i)\}$). The system will release the occupied resources by idle VNF instances at a specific time slot if the accumulative cost of these idle VNF instances at that time slot is greater than the given threshold θ. Clearly, at least n'_{ij} VNF instances of f_i should be kept in order to meet the end-to-end delay requirements of the running requests in $R_{ij}(t)$. However, consider the worst scenario where an VNF instance of f_i is just released back to the system at the current time slot, only to have the same instance be created again at the next time slot to accommodate a new request. To avoid this, we develop an efficient prediction method to determine the expected number of instances of each network function to be kept in the system. To determine which idle VNF instances should be released to the system, we make use of historic offloading request traces (patterns) at each cloudlet to predict the number of VNF instances needed of each network function in that cloudlet in future. Specifically, we adopt an auto-regression method to predict the number of VNF instances $\hat{n}_{ij}(t)$ of f_i in cloudlet c_j at the next time slot,

$$\hat{n}_{ij}(t) = \alpha_1 n_{ij}(t-1) + \alpha_2 n_{ij}(t-2) + \ldots + \alpha_k n_{ij}(t-k), \tag{4.2}$$

where $\alpha_{k'}$ (> 0) is a constant with $0 \leq \alpha_{k'} \leq 1$, $\sum_{l=1}^{t} \alpha_l = 1$, and $\alpha_{k_1} \geq \alpha_{k_2}$ if $k_1 < k_2$. Thus, the number of VNF instances of f_i in cloudlet c_j should be kept after time slot t is $\max\{\hat{n}_{ij}(t), n'_{ij}(t)\}$.

Similarly, if the number of VNF instances of a network function f_i keeps growing at each time slot, by adding extra computing resources to its VM, more VNF instances of that network function will be created. This incurs an extra cost at each instance creation. Instead, we may create the expected number of VNF instances at once to meet its future need, instead of adding computing resources for each new request to its VM incrementally. This can be achieved by using the similar auto regression method. That is, let $a_{ij}(t)$ be the number of new VNF instances of f_i in cloudlet c_j added at time slot t. If the number of instances added since the last time slot t_0 exceeds a given threshold Ξ, i.e., $\sum_{l=t_0}^{t} a_{ij}(l) \geq \Xi$, then the predicted number of new instances $\hat{a}_{ij}$ of f_i added at time slot t is

$$\hat{a}_{ij}(t) = \beta_1 a_{ij}(t-1) + \beta_2 a_{ij}(t-2) + \ldots + \beta_k a_{ij}(t-k), \tag{4.3}$$

where Ξ is the given threshold, $\beta_{k'}$ (> 0) is a constant with $0 \leq \beta_{k'} \leq 1$, $\sum_{l=1}^{k} \beta_l = 1$, and $\beta_{k_1} \geq \beta_{k_2}$ if $k_1 < k_2$. Thus, the number of VNF instances of f_i after time slot t installed in cloudlet c_j should be $\hat{a}_{ij}(t) + n_{ij}(t)$.

So far we assumed that there are sufficient resources at each cloudlet to meet the need of creating different VNF instances. However, if there are not enough residual resources at each cloudlet to meet different instance creations, then which VNF instances should we create? To fairly allocate the computing resource for instance creations, we proportionally scale down the number of instances of each different network functions at each cloudlet. In other words, let RC_j be the residual computing resource and DI_j the total computing resource demanded by different instance creations in cloudlet c_j. If $DI_j \leq RC_j$, this implies that all needed numbers of VNF instances can be created; otherwise, let $\mu_j = \frac{RC_j}{DI_j}$ be the ratio, for each requested number of VNF instances, e.g., the total computing resource for creating $a_{ij}(t)$ VNF instances for f_i is $a_{ij}(t)C(f_i)$, then we actually create $a'_{ij}(t) = \lfloor \frac{a_{ij}(t)C(f_i)\cdot\mu_j}{C(f_i)} \rfloor$ VNF instances for f_i at c_j. The details are given in Algorithm 2.

5 PERFORMANCE EVALUATION

In this section we evaluate the performance of the proposed algorithms by experimental simulations. We also study the impact of different parameters on algorithmic performance.

5.1 Experimental settings

We assume that a WMAN $G(V, E)$ follows a network topology [7] consisting of 100 APs, where the network is generated using the Barabasi-Albert Model [13], and there are 20 cloudlets randomly deployed in G. Each cloudlet c_j has a computing capacity cap_j within the range from 2,000 to 4,000 MHz [14]. We allow 20 network functions to be available on the cloudlets, where each instance of a network function requires between 40 and 400MHz. We assume that the delay of a link between two APs in the network is between 2 milliseconds (ms) and 5ms [15]. The running time obtained is based on a machine with a 3.4GHz Intel i7-4770 CPU and 16GiB RAM.

Algorithm 2 Admission_Algorithm_Finite_Horizon $(G(t), S(t))$

Require: m cloudlets with each having its available resource capacity $cap_j(t)$, a number of instances of VNFs of each $f_i \in \mathcal{F}$, and a set of requests $S(t)$ at each time slot t for a finite time horizon $1 \leq t \leq T$, each idle instance of VNF f_i has a cost γ_{ij} and the given cost threshold Ξ.

Ensure: maximize the number requests admitted (i.e., a subset $S'(t) \subseteq S(t)$) for all t during the finite time horizon T with $1 \leq t \leq T$ while minimizing the total operational cost. For each request r_k, if it is admitted, then to which cloudlet it will be sent and to which instance of VNF it should join/or create will be given in the solution.

$cost \leftarrow 0$; $M \leftarrow \emptyset$; /* the total cost of admitted task offloading requests to the system during a period of T, and request assignment M */;

for all t with $1 \leq t \leq T$ **do**

/* STAGE one: (a) perform release some occupied resources by idle instances if needed */

$l_{ij} \leftarrow t_0$ /* The resource release procedure was performed in the last time slot t_0 with $t_0 < t$ */;

for each cloudlet c_j **do**

for each $f_i \in \mathcal{F}$ **do**

if $\sum_{l=t-l_{ij}}^{t} \delta_{ij}(l) \cdot \gamma_{ij} \geq \theta$ **then**

Predict the number $\hat{n}_{ij}(t)$ of instances of f_i to be kept in c_j by Eq. (4.2);

Keep $\max\{n'_{ij}(t), \hat{n}_{ij}(t)\}$ instances of f_i in cloudlet c_j;

Release the occupied resources by the rest $n_{ij}(t) - \max\{n'_{ij}(t), \hat{n}_{ij}(t)\}$ instances of f_i in cloudlet c_j;

Update the amounts of available resources at cloudlet c_j;

$l_{ij} \leftarrow t$; /* reset the start time slot of the next idle VNF instances of f_i release in c_j */

/* STAGE two: (b) increase the number of instances of a network function f_i */;

$I_{ij} \leftarrow t_0$ /* the number of instances of f_i was increased in the last time slot t_0 with $t_0 < t$ */;

for each cloudlet c_j **do**

for each $f_i \in \mathcal{F}$ **do**

if $\sum_{l=t-I_{ij}}^{t} a_{ij}(l) \cdot \gamma_{ij} \geq \Xi$ **then**

Predict the number of instances of f_i to be increased $\hat{a}_{ij}$ by Eq. (4.3);

Let RC_j be the residual computing resource of cloudlet c_j, and DI_j be the total computing resource needed by creating new instances;

if $RC_j < DI_j$ **then**

There will be $\lfloor \frac{RC_j}{DI_j} \cdot (n_{ij}(t) + \hat{a}_{ij}(t)) \rfloor$ instances of f_i in cloudlet c_j at time slot t;

else

There will be $n_{ij}(t) + \hat{a}_{ij}(t)$ instances of f_i in cloudlet c_j at time slot t;

Update the available resources at cloudlet c_j;

$I_{ij} \leftarrow t$; /* reset the start time slot of the next VNF instance increase of f_i in cloudlet c_j*/

/* STAGE two: perform request admissions for the requests in $S(t)$ */

M_t and $cost_t$ will be returned by applying `Algorithm` 1 to $G(t)$;

$M \leftarrow M \cup M_t$; $cost \leftarrow cost + cost_t$.

return M corresponds to the assignment of requests, while $cost$ is the total admission cost to the system during a period of T;

Unless otherwise stated, the default settings for network parameters will be as follows. The default number of requests per time slot is 1,000, each request has a packet rate between 10 and 80 packets per seconds (similar to the range of application frame rates in typical interactive applications [16]), and a delay bound d_k between 0.2 and 1.2 seconds. The network function requested by each request is randomly selected from the 20 different network functions.

Using the hourly price of a general purpose m3.xlarge Amazon EC2 instance as reference, we assume the operating cost is 0.25 per MHz in each time slot, while the cost of instantiating a new function instance varies between 20 to 50. We assume the cost of transferring a packet between two APs to be proportional to the latency, and so the cost of transferring a packet along a network link varies between 0.002 and 0.005.

We evaluate the proposed algorithms against a greedy baseline which is described as follows. The greedy algorithm assigns each request r_k to the cloudlet with the highest rank in terms of the product of its available number of service chain instances and the inverse of the implementation cost of admitting r_k in the cloudlet. The rationale of this method is to find a cloudlet with high number of available service chain instances and low implementation cost, such that as many as requests are admitted while the implementation cost is minimized. We refer to this highest-rank-first baseline heuristic and the proposed algorithm as HRF and ALG respectively. Each experiment plot is the average of 100 simulation runs.

5.2 Algorithm performance within a single time slot

We first investigate the performance of the proposed algorithm ALG and algorithm HRF within a single time slot, by varying the number of requests within the time slot from 600 to 2,400 and creating some instances of each NFV in each cloudlet randomly.

Fig. 5.1 shows the results. From Fig. 5.1 (a), we can see that algorithm ALG admits much more requests than algorithm HRF, while also delivering a lower operation cost, as seen from Fig. 5.1 (b). The reason is as follows.

As both algorithms target requests with the cheapest resource requirements, an increasing number of low cost requests are admitted as we scale the number of initial requests. However, because algorithm ALG matches (assigns) several requests to cloudlets simultaneously, multiple instances of network functions are placed among the cloudlets, spreading the workload when subsequent requests for the network function are admitted. In contrast, as algorithm HRF admits requests one by one, new queues for network functions are instantiating less frequently. As a result, many requests with tight delay tolerances fail to be admitted by a cloudlet that has already instantiated their requested network functions, and thus fewer requests are admitted compared to algorithm ALG.

Initially, when the number of requests is low, algorithm HRF delivers a slightly lower operation cost compared to algorithm ALG, as HRF has instantiated fewer new queues and instances. However, as the number of admitted requests increases, the operation cost delivered by algorithm HRF increases sharply as the algorithm is forced to allocate resources for more expensive requests. The operation cost delivered by algorithm HRF plateaus, as HRF reaches the limit in the number of requests it can admit. In contrast, the growth in operation cost delivered by algorithm ALG is much slower, as the initially higher operation cost from instantiating more queues

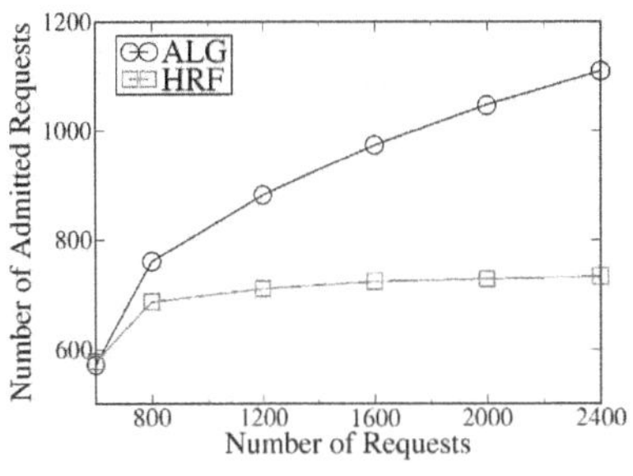

(a) The number of requests admitted by different algorithms

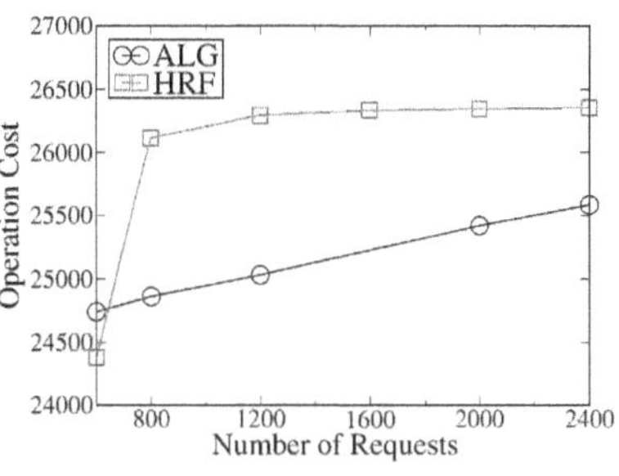

(b) Operation cost delivered by different algorithms

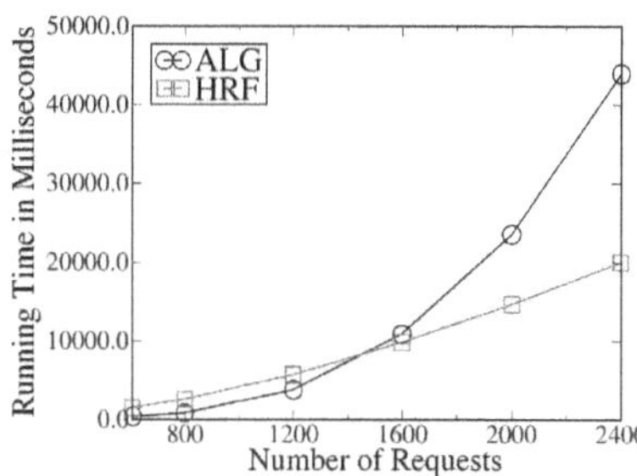

(c) Running time of different algorithms in milliseconds

Figure 5.1: Performance of Algorithm ALG and HRF when the number of requests varies from 600 to 2400, while the number of cloudlets in the network is 20.

and network instances allows subsequent requests be more cheaply admitted to the network.

Fig. 5.1 (c) illustrates the running time of algorithms ALG and HRF with the growth of the number of user requests. As can be seen, the running time increases dramatically for both algorithms with the number of requests, while the running time of algorithm ALG increases at a faster rate than that of algorithm HRF.

We next evaluate the performance of algorithms ALG and HRF within a single time slot, by varying the number of cloudlets between 4 and 24, while creating some instances of each NFV in each cloudlet randomly. Fig. 5.2 shows the result.

From Fig. 5.2. (a) we can see that algorithm ALG admits more requests than algorithm HRF. Since low cost requests are admitted into the network first, the remaining requests are increasingly expensive and require more cloudlet resources to meet their demands. Due to algorithm ALG instantiating multiple network function instances on different cloudlets, requests that have short delay tolerances are more easily admitted, resulting in a higher number of admitted requests compared to algorithm HRF.

Fig. 5.2. (b) displays the operation cost of the cloudlets when the number of requests is 1,500, and the number of cloudlets in the network ranges from 4 to 24. Both algorithms have similar plots, and deliver operation costs that have an approximately linear correlation with the number of cloudlets. While algorithm ALG delivers a slightly higher operation cost compared to algorithm HRF as the number of cloudlets increases, it should be noted that algorithm ALG admits significantly higher numbers of requests compared to algorithm HRF.

Fig 5.2. (c) illustrates the running time of algorithm ALG and algorithm HRF as the number of cloudlets in the network increases. The running time of algorithm HRF increases linearly with the number of cloudlets. Interestingly the running time of algorithm ALG decreases slightly as the number of cloudlets increases. This is because the number of requests admitted in each round of matching is limited to the number of cloudlets. As the number of cloudlets increases, more requests are admitted per round of matching, resulting in fewer rounds of matching and a shorter running time. However it is clear that the change in running time when increasing the number of cloudlets is negligible compared to changes in the number user requests, as the number of requests is orders of magnitude larger than the number of cloudlets.

5.3 Online algorithm performance

We now consider a time horizon consisting of 100 time slots. The number of requests in each time slot samples the Poisson distribution with a mean of 500, and each admitted request spans 1 to 5 time slots randomly.

Fig. 5.3(a) shows the accumulative number of requests admitted by algorithms ALG and HRF across the time horizon. We can see that algorithm ALG outperforms algorithm HRF by an average of 31%, due to more efficient allocation of resources. Fig. 5.3(b) shows the accumulative operation cost delivered by algorithms ALG and HRF across the time horizon. We can see that algorithm ALG has a lower operation cost compared to algorithm HRF by an average of 90%.

Fig. 5.4 illustrates how the idle cost threshold affects the total number of admitted requests and the total operation cost across a time horizon consisting of 100 slots. Both plots show an increase in total admitted requests and total operation cost with the threshold. A low threshold results in the prediction model being more frequently invoked, and since the cloudlet must maintain at least enough network function instances to handle existing requests, overusing the prediction mechanism can lead to over-provisioning resources to network function instances. As resources are constrained, this restricts the number of requests that can be admitted. As the threshold increases, resources are more efficiently allocated within each time slot, leading to a slight increase in admitted requests. However operation cost also increases with the threshold, as when the prediction model is less frequently used, fluctuation in the number of required instances across time slots are more common and incur additional instantiation costs.

6 CONCLUSIONS

In this paper, we studied a novel task offloading problem in a wireless metropolitan area network, where each offloading task has a maximum tolerable delay and different requests need different types of services from the cloudlets in the network. We focused on maximizing the number of offloading request admissions while minimizing their admission cost within a given time horizon. To this

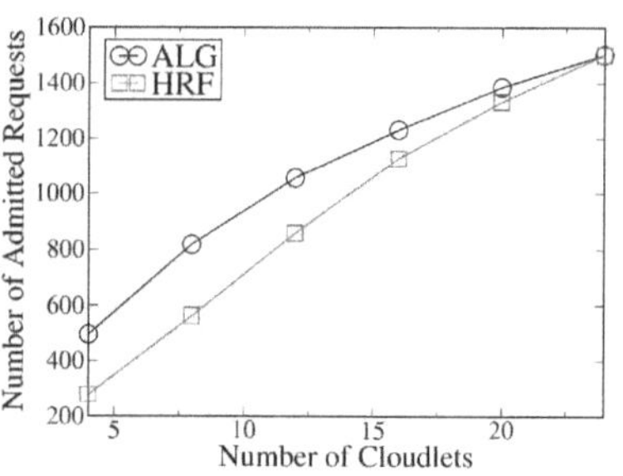

(a) The number of requests admitted by different algorithms

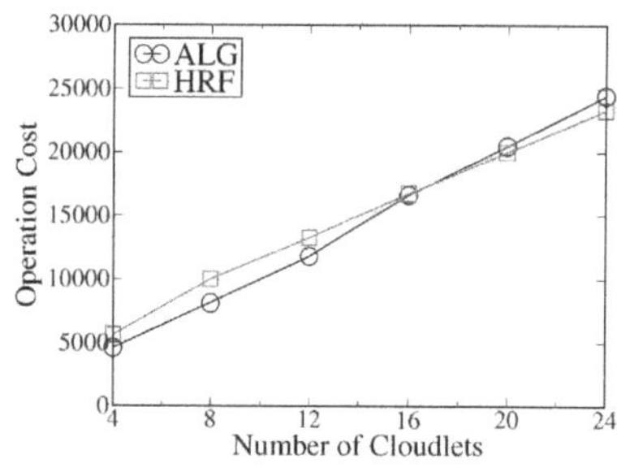

(b) Operation cost delivered by different algorithms

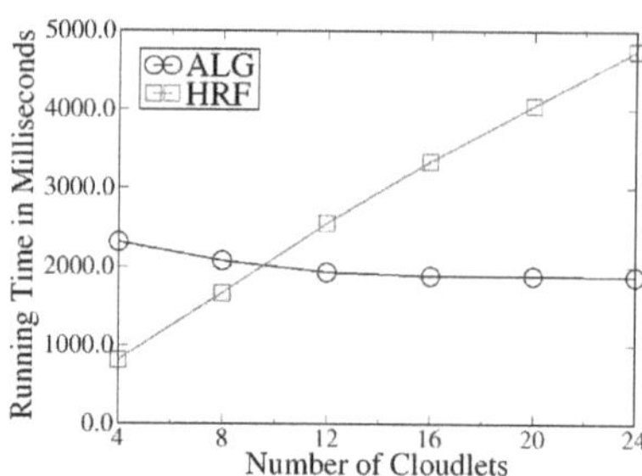

(c) Running time of different algorithms in milliseconds

Figure 5.2: Performance of algorithms ALG and HRF when the number of cloudlets in the network varies from 4 to 24 while the number of requests is fixed at 1,500.

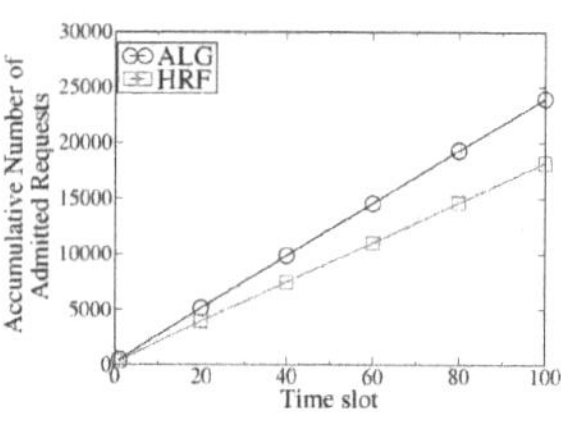

(a) The accumulative number of requests admitted by different algorithms

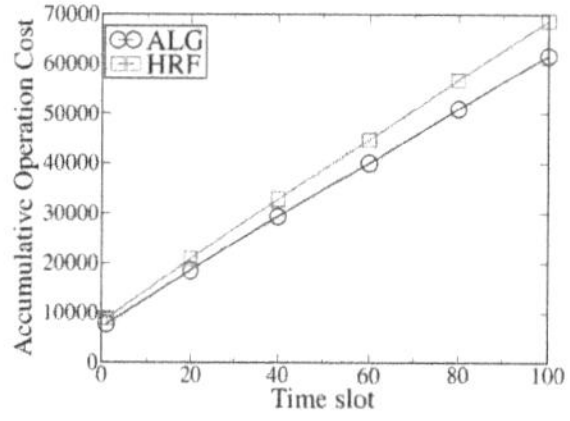

(b) The accumulative operation cost delivered by different algorithms

Figure 5.3: Performance of algorithms ALG and HRF for a time horizon with 100 time slots, where the number of requests in each time slot follows a Poisson distribution with a mean of 500.

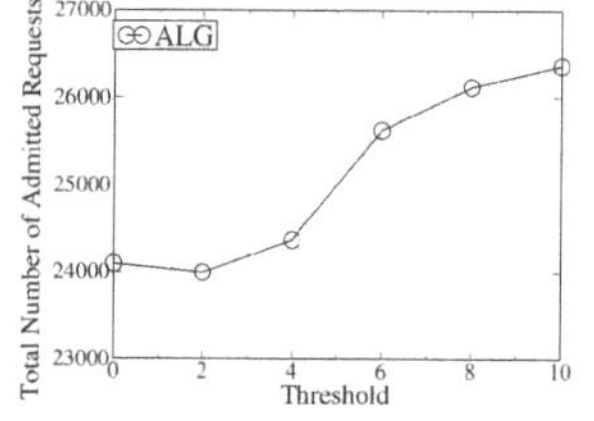

(a) The total number of requests admitted by algorithm ALG

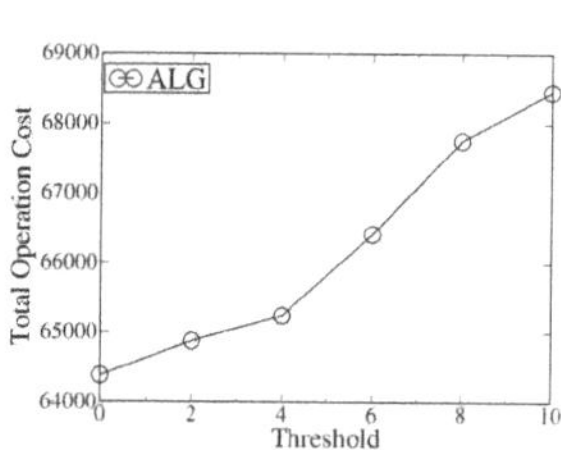

(b) The total operation cost delivered by algorithm ALG

Figure 5.4: Threshold impact on the performance of algorithm ALG for a time horizon with 100 time slots.

end, we developed an efficient algorithm for the problem through a novel reduction that reduces the problem to a series of minimum weight maximum matching problems in auxiliary bipartite graphs, and an effective prediction mechanism to predict instance releases and creations in different cloudlets within the network for further cost savings. We finally evaluated the performance of the proposed algorithm through experimental simulations. Experimental results indicate that the proposed algorithm is promising.

REFERENCES

[1] "Facebook f8 developers conference 2017," https://www.fbf8.com/, 2017, accessed: 2017-04-25.

[2] B.-G. Chun, S. Ihm, P. Maniatis, M. Naik, and A. Patti, "Clonecloud: elastic execution between mobile device and cloud," *Proceedings of the sixth conference on Computer systems.* ACM, 2011.

[3] E. Cuervo, A. Balasubramanian, D.-k. Cho, A. Wolman, S. Saroiu, R. Chandra, and P. Bahl, "Maui: making smartphones last longer with code offload," *Proceedings of the 8th international conference on Mobile systems, applications, and services,* ACM, 2010.

[4] S. Kosta, A. Aucinas, P. Hui, R. Mortier, and X. Zhang, "Thinkair: Dynamic resource allocation and parallel execution in the cloud for mobile code offloading," *INFOCOM, 2012 Proceedings IEEE*, IEEE, 2012.

[5] E. Y. Chen and M. Itoh, "Virtual smartphone over ip," *Proc of World of Wireless Mobile and Multimedia Networks (WoWMoM)*, IEEE, 2010.

[6] B. G. Rodrıguez-Santana, A. M. Viveros, B. E. Carvajal-Gámez, and D. C. Trejo-Osorio, "Mobile computation offloading architecture for mobile augmented reality, case study: Visualization of cetacean skeleton," *International Journal of Advanced Computer Science & Applications*, vol. 1, no. 7, pp. 665–671.

[7] M. Jia, J. Cao, and W. Liang, "Optimal cloudlet placement and user to cloudlet allocation in wireless metropolitan area networks,' To appear in *IEEE Transactions on Cloud Computing*, IEEE, 2015.

[8] M. Jia, W. Liang, Z. Xu, and M. Huang, "Cloudlet load balancing in wireless metropolitan area networks," in *Proc of INFOCOM*, IEEE, 2016.

[9] Z. Xu, W. Liang, W. Xu, M. Jia, and S. Guo, "Capacitated cloudlet placements in wireless metropolitan area networks," *Proc. of 2015 IEEE 40th Conference on Local Computer Networks (LCN)*, IEEE, 2015.

[10] Z. Xu, W. Liang, W. Xu, M. Jia, and S. Guo, "Efficient algorithms for capacitated cloudlet placements," *IEEE Transactions on Parallel and Distributed Systems*, vol. 27, no. 10, pp. 2866–2880, IEEE, 2016.

[11] Q. Xia, W. Liang, and W. Xu, "Throughput maximization for online request admissions in mobile cloudlets," *Proc of 2013 IEEE 38th Conference on Local Computer Networks (LCN)*, IEEE, 2013.

[12] Q. Xia, W. Liang, Z. Xu, and B. Zhou, "Online algorithms for location-aware task offloading in two-tiered mobile cloud environments," *Proc of 2014 IEEE/ACM 7th International Conference on Utility and Cloud Computing (UCC)*, IEEE, 2014.

[13] R. Albert, H. Jeong, and A.-L. Barabási, "Internet: Diameter of the world-wide web," *Nature*, vol. 401, no. 6749, pp. 130–131, 1999.

[14] "Hewlett-packard company - enterprise computer server systems and network solutions," https://www.hpe.com/au/en/servers.html/, 2017, accessed: 2017-04-25.

[15] S. Knight, H. X. Nguyen, N. Falkner, R. Bowden, and M. Roughan, "The internet topology zoo," *IEEE Journal on Selected Areas in Communications*, vol. 29, no. 9, pp. 1765–1775, IEEE, 2011.

[16] M. Satyanarayanan, P. Bahl, R. Caceres, and N. Davies, "The case for vm-based cloudlets in mobile computing," *Pervasive Computing, IEEE*, vol. 8, no. 4, pp. 14–23, 2009.

Providing Computing Services through Mobile Devices in a Collaborative Way - A Fog Computing Case Study

Danilo Costa Marim Segura
University of Sao Paulo (USP)/ICMC
Sao Carlos, Sao Paulo, Brazil
dcmsdancosta@usp.br

Rafael de Souza Stabile
University of Sao Paulo (USP)/ICMC
Sao Carlos, Sao Paulo, Brazil
stabilerafael@usp.br

Sarita Mazzini Bruschi
University of Sao Paulo (USP)/ICMC
Sao Carlos, Sao Paulo, Brazil
sarita@icmc.usp.br

Paulo Sergio Lopes de Souza
University of Sao Paulo (USP)/ICMC
Sao Carlos, Sao Paulo, Brazil
pssouza@icmc.usp.br

ABSTRACT

The increasing number of mobile devices, such as smartphones, tablets and laptops, and also advances in their computing power enabled them to be considered as computing resources, having their proximity explored. The use of nearby resources for computing is growing year by year and it is called Fog Computing. The elements on the edge of the Internet are exploited once the computer service providers could be unavailable or overloaded. This work focuses on using mobile devices to provide computing services by using an heuristic called Adapted Maximum Regret, which tries to minimize energy and avoid unreliable devices. There is also a top-level meta-heuristic which has global information and interconnects different clusters of devices on the edge of the Internet to guarantee QoS. We conducted a set of experiments that demonstrated we should avoid devices with a high degree of failures to save more energy when allocating tasks as well as to decrease the applications response time and communication through adjustments in the selection algorithm of external agglomerates.

CCS CONCEPTS

• **Information systems** → *Mobile information processing systems*; • **Human-centered computing** → **Mobile computing**;

KEYWORDS

Mobile Grid, Fog Computing

1 INTRODUCTION

Mobile devices, such as smartphones, tablets, and laptops are increasingly becoming part of people's life and also changing their lifestyle. The mobile applications explore the proximity with the user and offer tools for personal organization, entertainment, among others. According to Gartner, in the first quarter of 2017, about 379.977.300 units were sold over the world, that is, an increasing of 9% when comparing to the same period of 2016 [1].

Advances in wireless networks as well as in the Internet technologies allowed to mitigate some of the local restrictions on mobile devices, which expanded not only their computational potential but also their possibility to save energy by using remote computational services [5, 6, 9].

However, with Internet of Things (IoT), the integration of mobile devices on the Internet becomes more popular. The data generated by these devices can result in a lot of traffic on the network, downgrading the application performance. It may also be difficult to reach the required QoS, mainly in applications that are sensitive to network variations, such as real-time monitoring (healthcare, smart cities, etc). Besides that, centralized cloud providers may become unavailable for many reasons. This can cause the complete or partial failure of mobile applications that explore offloading computational processing offered by these virtual infrastructure [4].

In this paper, we propose a two-level architecture. The lower level (level 1) is composed of clusters of mobile devices interconnected by a wireless access point (AP), like a network of a university campus. Each cluster is coordinated by an elected leader while the mobile leaders are responsible for locally allocate the tasks over the devices by using an adapted heuristic. This heuristic tries to minimize energy consumption considering some restrictions on the device mobility. On the other hand, the higher level (level 0) is responsible for aggregating all the clusters in level 1. When an application if offloaded by one cluster, the broker chooses the cluster in which the application must be executed. The cluster selection algorithm considers QoS requirements adapted to mobile environments.

The main contributions of this paper are:

(1) The proposal of an architecture that allows mobile devices to be used as computational resources by considering their battery and mobility limitations;
(2) The possibility of collaboration among mobile devices that are close to each other by offering computational services and take advantage of their low latency;
(3) The establishment of a connection between energy saving and mobility: when an unreliable device is avoided, more energy is saved, since reschedulings are reduced.

[1] http://www.gartner.com/newsroom/id/3725117

MSWiM '17, November 21–25, 2017, Miami, FL, USA

ACM ISBN 978-1-4503-5162-1/17/11...$15.00
https://doi.org/10.1145/3127540.3127578

(4) The proposal of two metrics with global information that may be combined and applied in service oriented architectures in order to connect mobile devices that don't know each other, however may collaborate.

The rest of this paper is organized as follows. Section 2 presents some related work that focus on the use of devices that are near in order to process applications. Section 3 presents the and the algorithms proposed. Section 4 shows how the system is evaluated and how the experiments are designed. In Section 5, the results are presented. Finally, Section 6 brings the conclusion of this paper and discusses limitations and future work.

2 RELATED WORK

The advances in mobile devices allowed them to be considered as computational resources. In this kind of environment, energy consumption and high level of mobility and disconnections are key concepts and must be addressed. The related works aim to explore the proximity of lightweight devices, such as smartphones and tablets, in order to avoid the use of large processing centers, like dedicated servers in cloud computing.

Huerta-Canepa and Lee, in [8], identify the need to use nearby mobile resources, as the most powerful remote resource may become inaccessible. They develop a framework that decides if a certain part of a mobile application shall be offloaded. By using Hadoop to develop a prototype, the authors conclude this pervasive environment brings advantages, even though it is a preliminary work. However, they do not address energy consumption minimization and mobility characteristics of this kind of environment.

In [11], Morsy and El-Rewini proposed a dynamic distributed which uses different kinds of computing resources, taking energy consumption and the reliability of the grid elements into consideration. The authors define specialized nodes named WiGOs (Wireless Grid Operators) to make scheduling decisions on the architecture, and they use graphs with weighted edges (energy and reliability) to represent the connections between a local network and other resources. With experiments in GridSim v4.1, the authors conclude that this approach is efficient when compared to optimal baseline solutions. The authors do not evaluate the interaction between energy minimization and reliability and the heuristics do not aim at minimizing energy and meeting deadlines, but at maximizing the user's throughput [11].

The authors of the work proposed in [13] were motivated by the advance of smart devices in the last decade. They mention that the mobile cloud computing can be negatively influenced by network issues. They propose a genetic algorithm to schedule tasks among thin and thick clients, improving user's QoS. The authors proposed a DAG to model the tasks and their processing, in which the edges represent both computing and networking costs, and a genetic algorithm based on natural evolution is applied to solve the model. As results, the authors compare the algorithm proposed with a classic greedy algorithm, and show that their approach can obtain good results in relation to environment costs, and their solution performs very well. Nevertheless, the authors do not consider how to manage energy saving and mobility at the same time, and how this can affect the applications QoS.

The authors of the work presented in [3] proposed an algorithm to provide increase of QoS of data stream processing applications. They presented an architecture named Storm, which solves scheduling over intermittent mobile grids, and contains the following elements: WorkerMonitor, QoSMonitor, BootstrapScheduler and AdaptiveScheduler. The AdaptiveScheduling, holding QoS information, is responsible for taking decisions of local offloading, and the BootstrapScheduler monitors the applications and restarts them when necessary. To evaluate this approach, the authors compared the proposed scheduler dQoS to a centralized and baseline algorithm named cRR, and verified that dQoS improved the applications performance, even pointing some instability in scenarios with complex topologies. However, the approach did not take into account how to handle with the mobility of resources when considering energy spending.

3 METHODOLOGY

As illustrated in Figure 1, the proposed architecture has two levels. In Level 1, we can see the agglomerates of mobile devices. The mobile devices in each agglomerate are interconnected through an Access Point (AP), and has a leader elected by a Bully Election Algorithm adapted to wireless networks, as proposed by some authors [12, 15]. Level 1 communicates with Level 0 through the Internet layer, and each agglomerate in Level 1 may or may not be on the same sub-net.

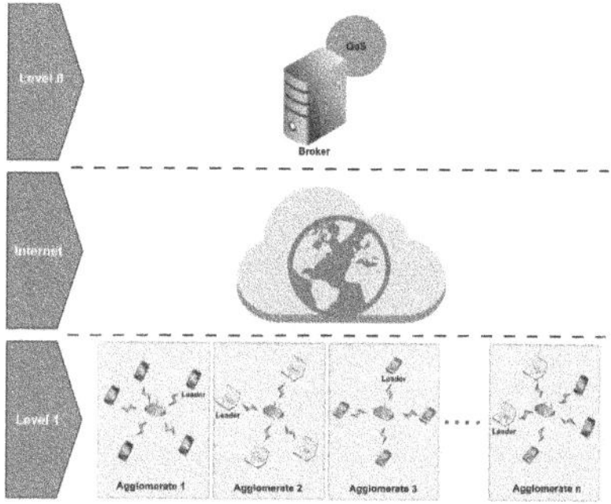

Figure 1: Propposed Architecture

Level 0 is a specialized node, which has global information of all the agglomerates in Level 1, including their processing capacities, energy efficiency, network quality, reliability, etc. The decision of defining a two-level approach is to allow different devices cluster to collaborate each other, once every aglomeratte is placed in a particular network, and a Broker can serve as a resource discoverer as well.

The applications requests are generated by the nodes in Level 1 and each request is composed of a bunch of tasks. When a node requests a service, the agglomerate leader is responsible for checking if the service may be offered internally by its agglomerate and if the processing deadline, which is a QoS statement, is guaranteed. In case the service may be attended internally, the leader must schedule the tasks over the nearby nodes. At this point, energy is the main concern to be addressed.

We propose a linear programming model to solve the scheduling. Equation 1 is the objective function and it aims to minimize the resources energy (mobile devices). Equation 2 checks the deadline and the resources capacity to process all the i tasks. Equation 3 associates a task to only one resource (there is no task replication), Equation 4 defines the domain of the binary variable x_{ij}, and Equation 5 is a restriction to avoid resources that present reliability factors that are lower than a threshold *epsilon*, which is directly associated with the reliability of a node i. The notations are summarized in Table 1.

$$Min \quad E = \sum_{i=1}^{m} \sum_{j=1}^{n} e_{ij} x_{ij} \tag{1}$$

$$s.t. \quad \sum_{j=1}^{n} t_{ij} x_{ij} \leq min\{d, c_i/p_i\}, \forall i \tag{2}$$

$$\sum_{i=1}^{m} x_{ij} = 1, \forall j \tag{3}$$

$$x_{ij} \in \{0, 1\} \forall i, j \tag{4}$$

$$m_i >= \epsilon \tag{5}$$

Table 1: Model notation

Parameter	Description
q_i	Processing power of node i (in MIPS)
p_i	Estimated energy consumption of a node i (W)
c_i	Battery capacity of a node i (J)
w_j	Workload of the task j (MI, Millions of Instructions)
d	Deadline of the application
t_{ij}	Execution time of the task j in the node i
e_{ij}	Energy consumption of the task j in the node i (J)
m_i	Reliability factor of the node i

The linear programming model gives us the optimal solution, however, preliminary experiments show that its executing time is impracticable, once this problem belongs to the NP-hard subclass. This way, a less complex heuristic has been proposed, named Adapted Maximum Regret (AMR), which is an adaption of the Maximum Regret heuristic proposed by [1]. The main idea of this algorithm is to verify the amount of extra energy to be spent for each task if it was not assigned to the most energetically favorable resource, which minimizes the global energy to be spent.

In case the subset of resources for a task j is empty, this task receives a very low value of "regret" (r_j). It numerically represents the necessity of allocating a task to the best resources in order to spend less energy. However, in case there is just one element of the subset F_j, the regret r_j receives a great positive value. If none of the previous conditions is satisfied, the r_j is the difference between the two highest values of f_{ij}, and task j^* is assigned to the resource with the highest value of r_j i^*.

The reliability factor of resources is used to avoid nodes that present a constant failure rate, and it is set according to a threshold ϵ that could be adjusted. If $\epsilon = 0$, there are no limitations on the available resources. When $\epsilon = m$, where m is the maximum number of resources that may be eliminated from the scheduling without affecting the feasibility of the problem, the AMR only considers the resources with the best reliability factor.

In the first moment, we set all the reliability factors by using a normalized distribution with average 0.5 and standard deviation 0.1. It is a first estimation for this metric. If the selected node fails when receiving the task, its reliability factor is penalized, and if the allocation is successful, there is an increase on m_i. As the system continues its operation, the mobility factor value suits reality. The probability values are defined according to reference values found on [10]. Each node receives a failure probability when a task is assigned, and the defined values may be 0.02 (low), 0.15 (medium) and 0.25 (high).

However, it is not always possible to execute the application internally in Level 1, which makes the exportation of requests necessary from Level 1 to Level 0. Once the request is externally offloaded, the broker must select an agglomerate to process it. In order to make this decision, it is necessary to address some metrics to choose an agglomerate that presents good and sufficient computational power, energy efficiency and reliability.

In the global selection algorithm there are two different metrics: metric A and metric B. Metric A focuses on the application QoS (response time), taking into account (i) the normalized value of average processing capacity in MIPS, (ii) the normalized capacity of external communication and (iii) the normalized capacity of internal communication. The agglomerates that consider Metric A are ordered descendingly, ie, the first is the best one.

Metric B takes the expected energy consumption of each agglomerate into consideration. The complement of the normalized energy consumption and the average of the reliability factor are used to calculate Metric B. The reliability factor is included in this metric due to the impact of the failures on the energy consumption.

This metric is computed by using the K parameter, which decides how many resources will be considered in the agglomerate list. If $K = 1$, only the first element of the agglomerate list is considered, prioritizing Metric A. As K increases, Metric B is gradually prioritized, once only the best elements according to Metric B will be selected. The maximum value of K is n.

Both ϵ (reliability factor restriction in Level 1) and K (selection algorithm adjustment in Level 0) are important. They must be changed and evaluated in order to measure the impact on the energy consumption and on the applications responsiveness. A model that represents the proposed has been created by using a queueing network model, implemented on the SimPack/Sim++ Simulation Toolkit [7].

4 DESIGN OF EXPERIMENTS

The proposed architecture was evaluated based on a 30-agglomerate scenario, divided into three groups: the first one presents 10 nodes per agglomerate, the second one, 20 nodes and, the third one, 30 nodes. Some characteristics of each agglomerate, such as average of MIPS and residual energy per node, vary arbitrarily.

This variation allows not only the Adapted Maximum Regret Heuristic inside the agglomerates but also the Global Selecting Algorithm in the Broker to influence the response variables, once it is a heterogeneous scenario. Besides that, five different types of application have been designed, and each of them is decomposed into independent tasks. Each application has a predominant characteristic.

The design and the execution of experiments and the analysis of results followed the methodology proposed by Jain [2]. A full factorial experiment model was conducted, with two factors and three levels in each factor, leading to a combination of $3^2 = 9$ experiments. Besides that, the experiments have been replicated 30 times, in order to establish a confidence level of 95%. The factors are (1) ϵ, with levels 0, $m/2$ and m, where m is the maximum number of elements that can be eliminated without avoiding the feasibility of the allocation, and (2) K, with levels 0, $n/2$ and n, where n is the total amount of possible agglomerates to be external selected.

The ϵ factor is the adjustment of the reliability factor restriction in the Adapted Maximum Regret Heuristic. This variation aims to verify how the heuristic saves energy when unreliable devices are avoided during the scheduling process. When $\epsilon = 0$, there is no restriction related to the reliability factor of the devices. As ϵ gets higher (max. m), the restriction forces the heuristic to consider only the subset with the best devices, according to their mobility factor.

Apart from the ϵ factor, the K factor is the calibration of the global algorithm in order to select the agglomerates. If $K = 1$, only Metric A is considered and it tries to select the best agglomerates considering their processing power and their network quality. As K gets higher (max. n), Metric B is proportionally prioritized and it tries to save energy and select the most reliable agglomerate.

The response variables were chosen in order to allow a precise analysis of how much the ϵ and K variations affect them. They are described below:

- **Total Energy Spent (TES):** is the arithmetic mean of the energy spent in Joules of all the mobile devices in all the agglomerates;
- **Average Response Time (ART):** is the arithmetic mean of the applications response time in seconds, from the time of request to the response. This variable was grouped by application classes, and each application (1-5) has its own mean;
- **Average Communication Time (ACT):** is the arithmetic mean of the time spent on communication in seconds. Similarly to ART, each application class has its own mean.

5 RESULTS

The responsible variables will be analyzed in the next subsections considering the execution of the applications in the proposed. The applications and settings were defined in Section 4.

5.1 Total Energy Spent

Figure 2 presents the TES values according to the variation of ϵ and K. In the situations where $\epsilon = m/2$ and $K = n/2$, and $\epsilon = m$ and $K = n/2$, the TES reaches the best result, which means that the intermediate value of both factors, as well as the intermediate value of K with the maximum value of ϵ, results in the greatest global energy saving.

This behavior shows an interesting trade-off: as K increases, the global algorithm starts prioritizing the lowest energy consumption and most reliable resources. However, agglomerates with good computing capacity and with good network quality are not options anymore, which results in an energy increase, once the applications take more time to be processed and communication becomes more expensive.

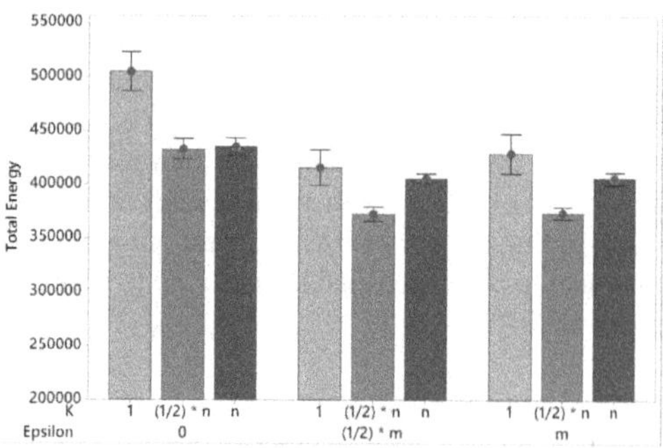

Figure 2: Total Energy Spent - Factors ϵ and K

5.2 Response and Communication Times

In a previous analysis, we verified that only factor K influences both the ART and the ACT response variables. Thus, we focused on this factor while evaluating how time varies in function of K.

Analyzing the ART for application 1 (Figure 3), we can observe that when $K = n/2$, the ART is lower when compared to other levels of K. So, we see a trade-off when K restricts half of the preselected elements in the global heuristic. However, when $K = n$, the lowest energy consumption and highest reliability factor resources are overloaded by the global heuristic. Besides that, the ACT also contributes to the ART degradation in this application, as we can see in the Figure 4.

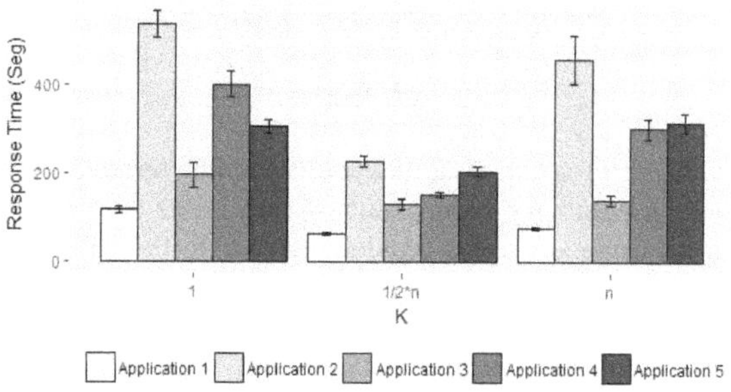

Figure 3: Average Response Time for all applications

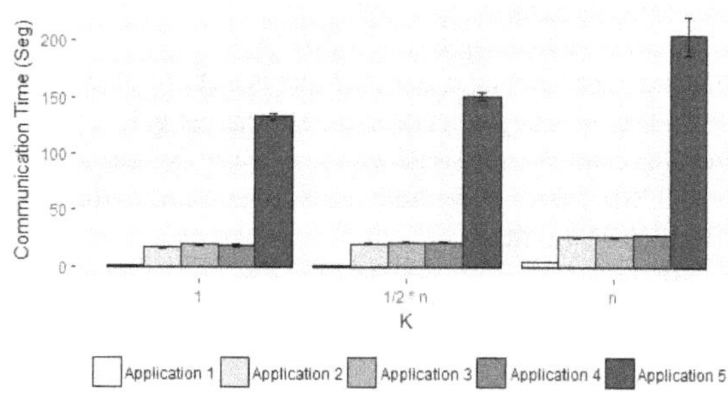

Figure 4: Average Communication Time for all applications

Considering the ACT for application 1, in Figure 4 we can see a huge increase (about 4 times) when K varies from $n/2$ to n, even though this application has few communication requirements. This can be explained by the prioritization of metric B of the global algorithm, which ignores the network quality of the agglomerates.

As illustrated in Figure 3, the ART of application 2 reaches the best result when $K = n/2$ and it is approximately half of the two other levels. This happens since both metric A and metric B are considered at the same time, which is a trade-off of metrics. When we analyze the ACT for application 2, there is an increase once metric A is gradually less prioritized, as presented in Figure 4.

The ART of Application 3, which is composed of a lot of tasks, reaches the highest value (Figure 3) when $K = 1$, due to fact that only the best agglomerate, with the best computing power and network quality, is candidate. Thus, this decision statistically leads to agglomerates with high rates of failure. In case K varies from $n/2$ to n, the ACT increases. As shown in Figure 4, there are no statistical differences in the ART. That is, when the clusters that have the most reliable devices are prioritized by Metric B, there is no difference in the total time for a lot of tasks.

Regarding the ART of Application 4, we can see from Figure 3 that the execution time of the applications is higher, once the relation between the processing deadline and the application size in MIPS makes the externally selected clusters overloaded. When $K = n/2$, the ART is reduced dramatically in relation to other levels. This may be considered another trade-off, since it prioritizes the clusters that present lower energy consumption, better processing, network quality, and higher reliability. The three last items are considered complementary metrics. Figure 4 represents the ACT, and again the communication cost gets higher as K increases.

Lastly, for Application 5, we can see in Figure 3 that when $K = n/2$, the ART reaches its best result, once both of the QoS metrics of the global algorithm are considered. Thus, as this application is communication predominant, when $K = n$, the ACT (Figure 4) increases sharply in relation to $K = 1$ and to $K = n/2$ and it contributes to the increase of the ART when $K = n$, once ART contains ACT.

6 CONCLUSIONS

Using mobile devices is a challenge. Aspects such as energy limitations, mobility and communication must be addressed despite the development of mobile devices over time. Taking advantages of both nearby and "lightweight" devices is the main reason of this Fog Computing study case and it avoids computing services to be executed on overloaded cloud servers.

This work presented a two-level approach for computational services composed of mobile devices that are on the edge of the Internet and it considers their energy restrictions and their high failure rate due to mobility. Results showed that the adjustments in ϵ restriction and in K saved the devices energy, and a trade-off in both variables was observed, which lead to better results not only in response time but also in communication.

Our contribution is in Fog Computing and, as it considered energy restricted devices as computational resources, this approach may be applied to many scenarios such as urban networks, university campus or home networks. Our proposal minimized the impact over the devices energy and it presented better results when unreliable nodes were avoided. We also proposed two global metrics that can be mixed to interconnect different groups of devices. However, our work has limitations on the workload generated, once there are too many requests. These requests imply an overload, which can be observed on the ART response variable.

As future work, we can list the following possibilities: (i) aiming to get better results and to save energy, evaluate other heuristics, such as the Greedy heuristic, also proposed by [1]; (ii) create a multi-objective model, in which reliability is not a restriction anymore, but a second objective; (iii) create a prototype with real applications to be deployed in real devices; (iv) unify the QoS metrics at Level 0 and add more important information to this context. A more detailed information about the parameters, the simulation and the experiments can be found in [14].

ACKNOWLEDGMENTS

The authors would like to acknowledge the financial support provided by FAPESP, CNPq and CAPES.

REFERENCES

[1] Luiz César Borro. 2013. *Escalonamento em grades móveis: uma abordagem ciente do consumo de energia.* Master's thesis. Universidade de São Paulo.

[2] Per Nikolaj D Bukh and Raj Jain. 1992. The art of computer systems performance analysis, techniques for experimental design, measurement, simulation and modeling. (1992).

[3] Valeria Cardellini, Vincenzo Grassi, Francesco Lo Presti, and Matteo Nardelli. 2015. On QoS-aware scheduling of data stream applications over fog computing infrastructures. In *Computers and Communication (ISCC), 2015 IEEE Symposium on.* IEEE, 271–276.

[4] Amir Vahid Dastjerdi, Harshit Gupta, Rodrigo N Calheiros, Soumya K Ghosh, and Rajkumar Buyya. 2016. Fog Computing: Principals, Architectures, and Applications. *arXiv preprint arXiv:1601.02752* (2016).

[5] M.D. Dikaiakos, D. Katsaros, P. Mehra, G. Pallis, and A Vakali. 2009. Cloud Computing: Distributed Internet Computing for IT and Scientific Research. *Internet Computing, IEEE* 13, 5 (Sept 2009), 10–13. https://doi.org/10.1109/MIC.2009.103

[6] Hoang T Dinh, Chonho Lee, Dusit Niyato, and Ping Wang. 2013. A survey of mobile cloud computing: architecture, applications, and approaches. *Wireless communications and mobile computing* 13, 18 (2013), 1587–1611.

[7] Paul A Fishwick. 1992. SimPack: getting started with simulation programming in C and C++. In *Proceedings of the 24th conference on Winter simulation.* ACM, 154–162.

[8] Gonzalo Huerta-Canepa and Dongman Lee. 2010. A virtual cloud computing provider for mobile devices. In *Proceedings of the 1st ACM Workshop on Mobile Cloud Computing & Services: Social Networks and Beyond.* ACM, 6.

[9] Priya A Kotwal and Adwitiy R Singh. 2012. Evolution and effects of mobile cloud computing, middleware services on cloud, future prospects: A peek into the mobile cloud operating systems. In *Computational Intelligence & Computing Research (ICCIC), 2012 IEEE International Conference on.* IEEE, 1–5.

[10] Antonios Litke, Dimitrios Skoutas, Konstantinos Tserpes, and Theodora Varvarigou. 2007. Efficient task replication and management for adaptive fault tolerance in mobile grid environments. *Future Generation Computer Systems* 23, 2 (2007), 163–178.

[11] Hazem Morsy and Hesham El-Rewini. 2013. Adaptive scheduling in a mobile ad-hoc grid for time-sensitive computing. In *Computer Systems and Applications (AICCSA), 2013 ACS International Conference on.* IEEE, 1–8.

[12] Sung-Hoon Park, Tae-Gyu Lee, Hyung-Seok Seo, Seok-Jin Kwon, and Jong-Ho Han. 2009. An Election Protocol in Mobile Ad Hoc Distributed Systems. In *Information Technology: New Generations, 2009. ITNG '09. Sixth International Conference on.* 628–633. https://doi.org/10.1109/ITNG.2009.61

[13] Pham Phuoc Hung and Eui-Nam Huh. 2015. An adaptive procedure for task scheduling optimization in mobile cloud computing. *Mathematical Problems in Engineering* 2015 (2015).

[14] Danilo Costa Marim Segura. 2016. *Integrando grades móveis em uma arquitetura orientada a serviços.* Master's thesis. Universidade de São Paulo.

[15] S. Vasudevan, J. Kurose, and D. Towsley. 2004. Design and analysis of a leader election algorithm for mobile ad hoc networks. In *Network Protocols, 2004. ICNP 2004. Proceedings of the 12th IEEE International Conference on.* 350–360. https://doi.org/10.1109/ICNP.2004.1348124

Hardening Opportunistic HIP

Adel Fuchs
Dept. of Computer Science and Engineering
Jerusalem College of Technology
Jerusalem, Israel 93721
adelfuchs@gmail.com

Ariel Stulman
Dept. of Computer Science and Engineering
Jerusalem College of Technology
Jerusalem, Israel 93721
stulman@jct.ac.il

Andrei Gurtov
Dept. of Computer and Information Science
Linköping University
Linköping, Sweden 58183
andrei.gurtov@liu.se

ABSTRACT

As mobile and multi-homed devices are becoming ubiquitous, the need for a dynamic, yet secure communication protocol is unavoidable. The Host Identity Protocol (HIP) was constructed to meet this requirement; to provide significantly more secure mobility and multi-homing capabilities. HIP opportunistic mode, which is to be used when other, more trusted mechanisms are lacking, is based on a leap of faith (LoF) paradigm. In this paper, we analyze different Man in the middle (MiTM) attacks which might occur under this LoF, and propose a set of tweaks for hardening opportunistic HIP (HOH) that strengthen opportunistic mode's security.

CCS CONCEPTS

• **Security and privacy → Mobile and wireless security**; *Security protocols*;

KEYWORDS

HIP, security, leap-of-faith, mobility, multihoming

1 INTRODUCTION

The Host Identity Protocol (HIP) [4, 7] is a multi-homing and mobility solution for IPv4 [20] and IPv6 [3] based communications [15, 17]. HIP achieves its abilities by separating a host's identity from its location, which are both regularly represented by a single IP address. Under HIP, the dynamic and multiple IP addresses remain pure locators while the steady and single identity is represented by a separate Host Identifier (HI), a pair of self-generated public and private keys[6, 26]. This identifier is commonly represented by the Host Identity Tag (HIT), a hash of the public key. Due to this identity/locator split, nodes can change their IP addresses during a communication session without losing their connections; allowing for both mobility and multi-homing. The mapping between actual network addresses and host identifiers is controlled by a new protocol layer, which is sandwiched between the network and transport layers.

Security primitives are natively integrated into HIP. HIP packets are authenticated and protected using IPsec ESP [8, 11]. Prior to a session initiation, identity information of both parties is attained via external means such as DNSSEC [14, 16, 19]. This allows for subsequent authentication of the session.

In some existing situations and environments, where no third party exists to provide authentication, the identity of the hosts cannot be verified. For such situations, HIP provides an opportunistic mode. This mode offers a leap of faith (LoF) [18, 22] based security, in which the protocol assumes that an attacker is not present during the initial handshake. Consequently, the use of this mode is recommended only for otherwise secure environments.

With no prior knowledge of each other's identity, the opportunistic mode is especially vulnerable to MiTM attacks. A LoF can be easily defeated during the handshake between the two communicating parties. With handshake messages passing through an attacker, manipulations, allowing the rest of the conversation to be decrypted and tainted, are easily executed.

In this paper, we analyze various attack scenarios on the opportunistic mode (Section 3), with a focus on MiTM attacks. We then propose a method for hardening opportunistic HIP (HOH) (Section 4), partially based on Spraying Diffie-Hellman [23] (see Section 2.2), which significantly alleviates MiTM attacks on opportunistic mode. Discussion of HOH and concluding remarks are presented in sections 5 and 6, respectively.

2 BACKGROUND

2.1 Host Identity Protocol

2.1.1 HIP Base Exchange. Every communication between two HIP-aware hosts begins with a four way handshake, known as a Base Exchange (BEX) [2]. The BEX implements the standard authenticated Diffie-Hellman (DH) exchange [21, 27], so that two parties can generate an ephemeral symmetric session key and create a security association (SA). The four messages, I1, R1, I2 and R2, denote the sender of the packet, Initiator ($\mathbb{I}$) or Responder ($\mathbb{R}$), and their ordinal number. In a standard session, all messages contain the HITs of $\mathbb{I}$ and $\mathbb{R}$, but only the parameters of the last three messages are authenticated by the HITs. Commonly, I1 may be sent through a rendezvous server (RVS) [13] which maps between HITs and IP addresses. After receiving I1, $\mathbb{R}$ replies with R1 which contains its DH public key. Similarly, I2 contains the DH public key of $\mathbb{I}$. Finally, R2 is sent as a final acknowledgment, which completes the BEX. R1 and I2 may optionally include a LOCATOR_SET parameter [1], which contains multiple IP addresses which the sender wants to advertise. Receiving a BEX message with this parameter, forces the receiver to send the next BEX message to the preferred LOCATOR specified in the LOCATOR_SET. Figure 1 illustrates a truncated

MSWiM '17, November 21–25, 2017, Miami, FL, USA

ACM ISBN 978-1-4503-5162-1/17/11...$15.00
https://doi.org/10.1145/3127540.3127571

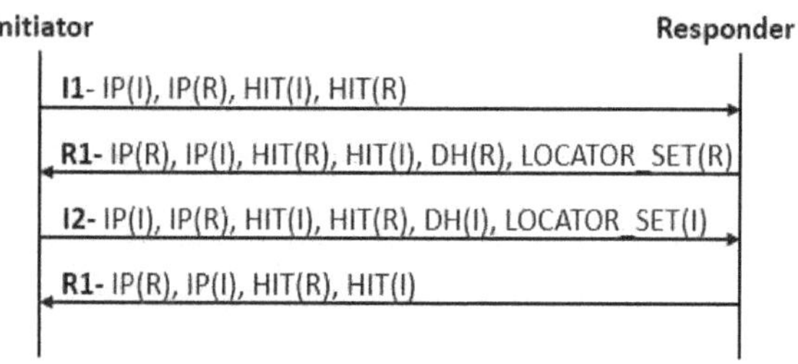

Figure 1: HIP Base exchange

BEX, including only parameters necessary for understanding this paper.

2.1.2 Opportunistic Mode. In addition to the standard BEX, parties can establish HIP associations opportunistically: without $\mathbb{I}$ knowing HIT($\mathbb{R}$). This opportunistic mode is based on a leap of faith (LoF) [22], in which $\mathbb{I}$ assumes no attacker ($\mathbb{A}$) is present during the initial communication, and the IP it knows functions as identity as well. For all subsequent communications, authentication is based on the keys which were exchanged during in the initial handshake. Initialization of this mode is performed by $\mathbb{I}$, sending an I1 packet with HIT($\mathbb{R}$) set to 0. As an outcome of this mode's limitations, RVS services cannot be supported.

Opportunistic mode does not use any predetermined Public-Key Infrastructure (PKI) or other predetermined trusted relationships between hosts [10]. This has explicitly been left out of the HIP architecture, as it is expected that each system using HIP may want to implement such functionality differently.

As specified in [5], LoF drawbacks can be partially mitigated when certificates [25] are supported at $\mathbb{R}$'s side, or by prompting the user using a graphical interface [10] to explicitly accept the connection.

2.2 Spraying Diffie Hellman (SDH)

SDH, proposed by Stulman, et al. [23], is a variant of the Diffie-Hellman key exchange, which minimizes MiTM attacks caused by lack of prior knowledge among communicating parties. SDH was originally constructed for mobile ad hoc networks (MANETs), where attackers can inject and alter the key exchange (KE) data. It attempts to turn active adversaries into passive ones by spreading (or *spraying*) pieces of each DH messages in different, ever-changing paths.

Even spread and *random spread* are the two main spreading approaches of SDH [24]. The former spreads each message uniformly among the host's neighbors, while the latter selects the different paths randomly. In terms of MiTM attacks, *even spread* is shown to perform better, while *random spread* is preferred if denial of service (DoS) is of utter importance. Both methods, however, have similar achievements as network size increases.

3 MITM

3.1 Setting the stage

The current work focuses on topologies with stationary infrastructure and multi-homed HIP hosts. Each host has a multitude of network interface cards (NIC), each referred by a different IP address (the basis for multi-homing). By extension, though, the entire technique can be applied to mobile hosts with a single NIC as well. Due to movement, they appear to the network as a single host with multiple NICs.

Our threat model assumes an attacker can (and has) take over specific nodes in the different networks a host is connected to. Moreover, we assume that the attacker has active capabilities such as deleting, inserting, or otherwise changing any packet traveling through it. One cannot assume passive attackers alone, for which alternative techniques exist for setting up confidential sessions.

3.2 Attacks

3.2.1 Direct. There are various ways an attacker can take over opportunistic communications, performing a MiTM attack. It is important to note, that since I1 contains HIT($\mathbb{I}$) and R1 contains $\mathbb{R}$'s DH public key, fake I2 and R2 will lead to a MITM attack only if $\mathbb{A}$ already took over the BEX in the first two messages.

Manifestation of the MiTM attacks on the opportunistic mode, can be grouped into 2 sets of possibly contradicting scenarios, referred to henceforth as 1a, 1b, 2a and 2b. Under all combinations, thereof, in contrast to hosts' HITs which are not known, we do assume that $\mathbb{I}$ knows $\mathbb{R}$'s IP address, otherwise the handshake cannot begin:

(1) Does $\mathbb{R}$ know (at the network level) $\mathbb{I}$'s IP address? That is, does $\mathbb{R}$ recognize a legitimate initiator IP?
   (a) The first scenario assumes that both $\mathbb{I}$ and $\mathbb{R}$ know each other's IP addresses. Furthermore, it may be the case that $\mathbb{R}$ not only recognizes a legitimate IP address, but has an incentive to verify $\mathbb{I}$'s identity.
   An example for this, described by Komu and Lindqvist in [12], are IRC servers [9] that force the IRC connection to timeout if they are not able to find out the client's identity. Another appropriate situation, is when the network contains publicly-reachable services with a stable IP address. As a matter of fact, any two mobile hosts wanting to communicate directly with each other when IP's are known, can be included in this scenario.
   (b) The opposing scenario assumes that $\mathbb{R}$ is not familiar with $\mathbb{I}$'s IP address. Alternatively, it has no incentive to identify $\mathbb{I}$ based on its IP address, and is willing to service anyone.
   It must be noted, that although $\mathbb{I}$'s identity is not critical in the network layer, it is certainly necessary on some higher layer. Otherwise, of course, security would be of no concern. Thus, some means of identification (e.g. user name and password) must be provided by $\mathbb{I}$ on higher layers before $\mathbb{R}$ agrees to transfer secret information to its communication partner.

(2) Does 𝔸 intercept I1?
  (a) 𝔸 intercepts I1 from 𝕀 to ℝ. Here the attack is simple: she sends a different I1 to ℝ, and sends her own R1 to 𝕀.
  (b) 𝔸 intercepts R1 but not I1. For this attack, she must send a different R1 to 𝕀 and simultaneously start a new BEX with ℝ, posing as 𝕀.

Under all attack scenarios, 𝔸 sets the preferred address in the LOCATOR_SET of R1 and I2 to her own IP address. Consequently, 𝔸's interference in the first two messages forces the rest of the messages to be directed through her.

Putting together 2a with 1a and 1b, allowing 𝔸 to intercepts I1, the attack schema can be seen in Figure 2, where X of IP(X) must be replaced with I and A, respectively. Figure 3 depicts the attack scenarios 1a and 1b when I1 is not caught by 𝔸 (scenario 2b). Here too, X of IP(X) must be replaced by I and A, respectively.

We point out that scenario 1b+2a generates the most powerful attack. 𝔸 can transfer I1 to ℝ after not only changing 𝕀's HIT, but setting the source IP address to her own. Subsequently, there is no risk that R1 will ever attempt at reaching 𝕀 before being infected by 𝔸, as ℝ had never received any information about 𝕀.

4 MITIGATION

In this section we propose multi-factor hardening techniques, collectively named Hardening Opportunistic HIP (HOH), to minimize MiTM attacks on HIP's opportunistic mode. HOH proposes various heuristics and transformations of HIP, which can individually or together achieve better security for the opportunistic mode.

HOH is partially based on SDH, with some differences. SDH spreads a single packet among different routes, capitalizing on topology changes of the network. HOH, on the other hand, spreads complete packets among different networks, taking advantage of the multi-homing feature of HIP. Hence, assuming the attacker has not compromised all networks, HOH would work on stationary networks. Of the two spraying techniques put forth in [24], HOH uses *even spread* since it was suggested it performs better against MiTM, in situations where few alternative routes exist.

Throughout the description, by *spreading* or *spraying* we mean the operation of sending a message from a source IP address that differs from both the source addresses of previously sent messages and the destination addresses of previously received messages.

With respect to attack scenarios of Section 3.2.1, the hardening steps can be divided on which of the four groups (1a+2a, 1a+2b, 1b+2a, 1b+2b) it comes to deal with. All steps are collectively illustrated in Figure 4, in which $Enc(\alpha,\beta)$ represents encryption of α using the key β.

4.1 Ignore requests of a peer to change its preferred LOCATOR

For all scenarios of Section 3.2, HOH suggest that a host ignores location information received from the other peer, fearing that data may be forged. Thus, when the sender has a legal IP address of the receiver, it should be used for all BEX messages. Only after the BEX is completed successfully, a host may consider the peer's other LOCATORS assuming that the association is already secure. This ameliorates the original opportunistic mode deficiency, where malicious LOCATORS in R1 or I2 cause the rest of the BEX to be routed directly to 𝔸. Spraying I2 and R2 (see Section 4.2) cannot help without this limitation, as topology manipulation will cause a de-spraying and routing directly to 𝔸.

4.2 Spread BEX messages

Another technique that can be employed to alleviate the attacks when all assumptions exist, is by spreading I2 and R2 between different networks available to hosts. This would decrease the probability that all messages will pass through 𝔸. Correlation of messages must be based on the sender's HIT which is embedded in all messages.

As further clarification, we note that there is no contradiction between our requirement to ignore LOCATOR information (Section 4.1) and spraying I2 and R2 on multiple interfaces, as they pertain to different sides of the handshake. Ignoring LOCATORS deters a host from accepting new address information regarding the other host. It does not inhibit oneself from using its own multiple interfaces for spreading messages.

Contrary to I2 and R2, spreading R1, although permitted by HIP, is of undetermined consequence. In the current setup it will destroy the only information that 𝕀 can use to correlate R1 with the corresponding I1 (R1's source IP address), disconnecting the BEX before it even had a chance to begin. Adding a random correlation number in both messages I1 and R1, solves this problem.

Spreading R1, however, might do more harm than good. If I1 is caught (scenario 2a), sending R1 through a different network decreases the probability that it will likewise be caught by 𝔸. On the other hand, if I1 has not been caught (scenario 2b), spreading R1 increases the probability that it will be caught by 𝔸. Since ℝ has no way of knowing whether I1 was caught or not, the effectiveness of spraying R1 is not predictable; hence, step 4.3.

4.3 Create a dependency between I1 and R1.

For cases where I1 managed to escape attack (scenario 2b), it would be beneficial if we were able to use that in order to detect an attack on R1. Thus, HOH suggests a *dependency* between I1 and R1 to be created.

For a *dependency,* I1 should include a public key in addition to the sequence number already there. For each opportunistic BEX it triggers, 𝕀 saves a triplet containing a sequence number, a public key and its corresponding private key. In R1, ℝ should encrypt the DH public key parameter with the public key it received in I1. As a result, 𝔸 who only caught R1, cannot encrypt properly her own DH parameter.

This *dependency* does not break HIP's architectural requirement that ℝ should not maintain state until after receiving I2 (to diminish DoS attacks), as the state created by the *dependency* is kept by 𝕀, not ℝ. This extension will also eliminate the negative consequence occasionally caused by spraying R1 (see Section 4.2).

4.4 Abort BEX if mismatched R2 arrives

When 𝕀's IP is known by ℝ (scenario 1a), it is useful to add that a renegade R2 message that arrives while establishing a BEX, should cause the BEX to terminate. As 𝔸 cannot change 𝕀's IP, R2 might

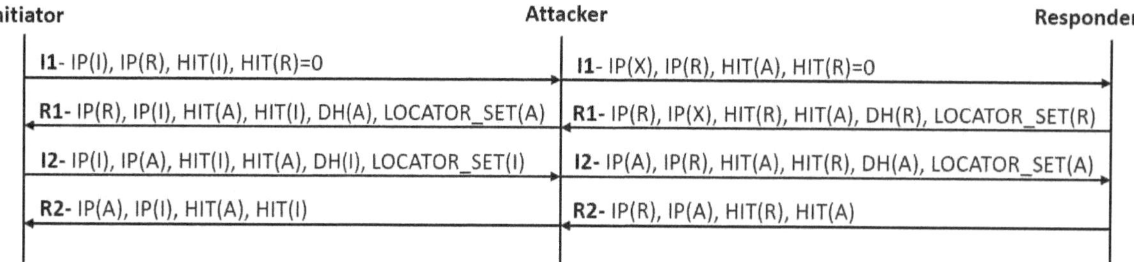

Figure 2: Attack scenarios where $\mathbb{A}$ intercepts I1 (2a)

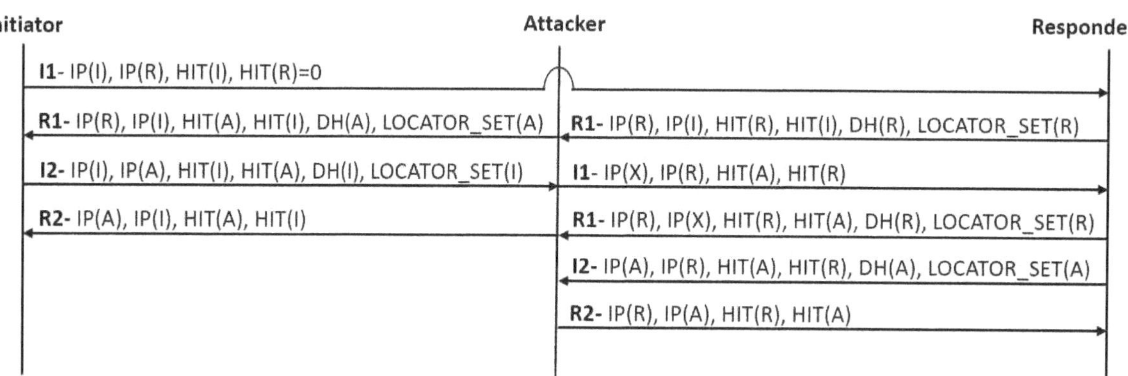

Figure 3: Attack scenarios where I1 eludes $\mathbb{A}$ (2b)

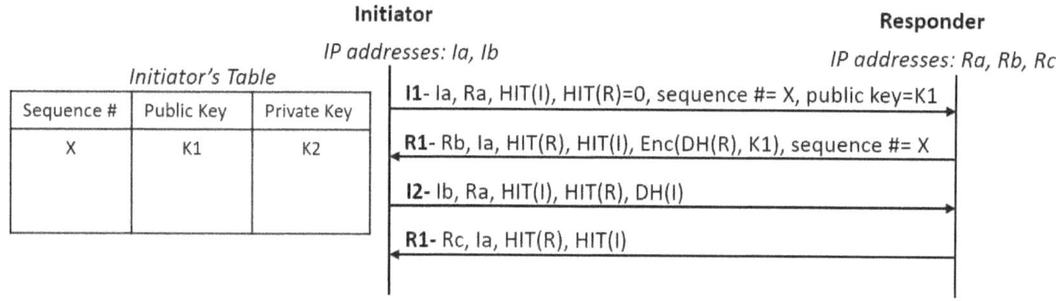

Figure 4: BEX, according to HOH

(due to multiple routes or spraying of Section 4.2) circumvent $\mathbb{A}$ and reach $\mathbb{I}$ untainted. This can be categorized as a warning to $\mathbb{I}$ that it may be communicating via a MiTM.

It is worthwhile to note two points:

(1) We consider only unfamiliar R2 messages, because for all other unfamiliar BEX messages escaping $\mathbb{A}$, communications will be aborted by $\mathbb{A}$ herself as not enough keying information has been received.
(2) The spreading of R2 in step 4.2 is not necessary unless this mitigation step has been performed. As R2 has no new keying information, it does not matter whether $\mathbb{A}$ receives this message or not. Therefore, the spraying of R2 is necessary only for protecting $\mathbb{I}$.

5 DISCUSSION

5.1 Pros, cons and cost

As most security supplements, HOH as well, has its disadvantages. HOH's spreading approach seemingly increases the DoS attack surface. Spreading messages in different networks and over multiple paths, increases the probability that at least one of the four BEX messages will encounter the attacker. This, however, is not a big problem if any other message beside I1 is dropped. HIP provides timeouts and re-transmission of messages for such situations. Using HOH will cause the subsequent message to travel on an alternate path, which might not be under $\mathbb{A}$'s control.

Another issue not addressed by HOH is an I1 flooding attack on $\mathbb{R}$. HIP was designed to withstand this attack by allowing R1 messages to be pre-computed. With HOH dependency scheme (Section 4.3), this feature is abandoned. The dependency requires the DH parameter of R1 to be encrypted with the public key sent in I1; precluding pre-computation, and adding a costly computation to $\mathbb{R}$.

Additionally, an outcome of ignoring request of location change (Section 4.1) is limited mobility during the BEX. This limitation, however, is negligible as BEX is a quick handshake, such that most hosts would not have a chance to change their topological location anyway.

Another issue, albeit small, is the cost factor associated with HOH. Network traffic slightly increases due to the additional parameters in I1 and R1 which slightly increase message size. In addition, an expensive encryption computation is added to each R1 created, precluding a *compute once* scheme currently employed by HIP.

All of these drawbacks are not security failures; rather, weaknesses in quality of service (QoS) and usability. [10] already stated that usability and security are often seen as contradicting goals. As the opportunistic mode, by definition, provides a *better than nothing* security, increasing the security of this mode should be done with awareness that usability might be degraded.

A last deficiency with HOH, which is true for all LoF schemes (such as SDH), was already alluded to by Stulman, et al. [23]. LoF protocols do not solve the lack of authentication, but they merely make the attacker's job harder. This implies that one does not know who he is really talking to. They are probabilistic schemes, giving security with a weighted tag attached. They should only be treated as such.

6 CONCLUSION AND FUTURE RESEARCH

The opportunistic mode of HIP is beneficial and necessary. It opens up HIP to multiple domains, including, for example, ad-hoc environments where pre-configuration of HITs is problematic. The immediate consequence of the opportunistic mode, however, facilitates vulnerabilities such as MiTM and DoS. The *better than nothing* security model, guaranteeing security at least as good as existing unprotected IP-based communications, does not mean that one should not make an attacker's job harder.

In this paper, we analyzed a variety of MiTM implementation, and proposed HOH for hardening the *better than nothing* paradigm. By no means, however, did we lock-down security of opportunistic mode. This is a feat for future research, and might not be attainable at all. We also leave the assessment of HOH for a further publication, to evaluate how much harder the attacks have become.

ACKNOWLEDGEMENT

The authors would also like to acknowledge the contribution of the COST Action IC1303 - AAPELE, Architectures, Algorithms and Platforms for Enhanced Living Environments.

REFERENCES

[1] Jari Arkko, Thomas Henderson, and Christian Vogt. Host mobility with the host identity protocol. 2017.

[2] Tuomas Aura, Aarthi Nagarajan, and Andrei Gurtov. Analysis of the hip base exchange protocol. In *Australasian Conference on Information Security and Privacy*, volume 21, pages 481–493. Springer, 2005.

[3] Steve Deering and Robert Hinden. Rfc 2460: Internet protocol, 1998.

[4] Andrei Gurtov. *Host identity protocol (HIP): towards the secure mobile internet*, volume 21. John Wiley & Sons, 2008.

[5] Andrei Gurtov and Tom Henderson. The host identity protocol (hip) experiment report. 2012.

[6] Andrei Gurtov, Miika Komu, and Robert Moskowitz. Host identity protocol: identifier/locator split for host mobility and multihoming. *Internet Protocol J*, 12(1):27–32, 2009.

[7] Thomas Henderson, Tobias Heer, Petri Jokela, and Robert Moskowitz. Host identity protocol version 2 (hipv2). 2015.

[8] Petri Jokela. Using the encapsulating security payload (esp) transport format with the host identity protocol (hip). 2008.

[9] Christophe Kalt. Rfc 2813: Internet relay chat: Server protocol. *Network Working Group, IETF. En ligne.< http://tools. ietf. org/html/rfc2813*, 2000.

[10] Kristiina Karvonen, Miika Komu, and Andrei Gurtov. Usable security management with host identity protocol. In *AICCSA*, pages 279–286, 2009.

[11] S Kent. Rfc 4303. *IP Encapsulating Security Payload (ESP)*, 2005.

[12] Miika Komu and Janne Lindqvist. Leap-of-faith security is enough for ip mobility. In *2009 6th IEEE Consumer Communications and Networking Conference*, pages 1–5. IEEE, 2009.

[13] J Laganier and L Eggert. Rfc 5204: Host identity protocol (hip) rendezvous extension. *Request for Comments*, 5204, 2011.

[14] Paul Mockapetris. Rfc 1034: Domain names: concepts and facilities (november 1987). *Status: Standard*, 6, 2003.

[15] P Nikander, T Henderson, C Vogt, and J Arkko. Rfc 5206: End-host mobility and multihoming with the host identity protocol. *Request for Comments*, 5206, 2008.

[16] P Nikander and J Laganier. Rfc 5205: Host identity protocol (hip) domain name system (dns) extension. *Request for Comments*, 5205, 2008.

[17] Pekka Nikander, Jukka Ylitalo, and Jorma Wall. Integrating security, mobility and multi-homing in a hip way. In *NDSS*, volume 3, pages 6–7, 2003.

[18] Viet Pham and Tuomas Aura. Security analysis of leap-of-faith protocols. In *International Conference on Security and Privacy in Communication Systems*, pages 337–355. Springer, 2011.

[19] Oleg Ponomarev and Andrei Gurtov. Using dns as an access protocol for mapping host identifiers to locators. In *Routing in Next Generation Workshop, Madrid, Spain*, 2007.

[20] Jon Postel et al. Rfc 791: Internet protocol. 1981.

[21] E Rescorla. Rfc 2631: Diffie-hellman key agreeement method. *RTFM Inc., juin*, 1999.

[22] Ph D Peter Sjödin. Efficient leap of faith security with host identity protocol.

[23] Ariel Stulman, Jonathan Lahav, and Avraham Shmueli. Spraying diffie-hellman for secure key exchange in manets. In *Cambridge International Workshop on Security Protocols*, pages 202–212. Springer, 2013.

[24] Ariel Stulman and Alan Stulman. Spraying techniques for securing key exchange in large ad-hoc networks. In *Proceedings of the 11th ACM Symposium on QoS and Security for Wireless and Mobile Networks*, pages 29–34. ACM, 2015.

[25] Samu Varjonen and Tobias Heer. Host identity protocol certificates. 2011.

[26] Samu Varjonen, Miika Komu, and Andrei Gurtov. Secure and efficient ipv4/ipv6 handovers using host-based identifier-locator split. In *Software, Telecommunications & Computer Networks, 2009. SoftCOM 2009. 17th International Conference on*, pages 111–115. IEEE, 2009.

[27] Zachary Zeltsan, Sarvar Patel, Igor Faynberg, and Alec Brusilovsky. Password-authenticated key (pak) diffie-hellman exchange. 2010.

DADCA: An Efficient Distributed Algorithm for Aerial Data Collection from Wireless Sensors Networks by UAVs

Bruno Olivieri
Pontifical Catholic University
Rua Marques de São Vicente 225, Gávea
Rio de Janeiro, RJ, Brazil 22.543-060
bolivieri@inf.puc-rio.br

Markus Endler
Pontifical Catholic University
Rua Marques de São Vicente 225, Gávea
Rio de Janeiro, RJ, Brazil 22.543-060
endler@inf.puc-rio.br

ABSTRACT

Unmanned Aerial Vehicles (UAVs) are increasingly used as data collectors for Wireless Sensors Networks (WSN) on the ground. Most current research proposes optimizations for the itinerary creation of a single UAV. Our work, however, proposes a distributed algorithm for collecting WSN data using a dynamic set of UAVs. The algorithm takes into account the fact that UAVs could leave or join the group due to either recharging requirements or malfunctions. In our work we also consider the fact that UAVs only have medium-range communication capabilities (a few meters) in order to deliver collected data. Compared to the computationally costly and non-real-time Traveling Salesman Problem (TSP) approach, our algorithm delivers approximately 13% more efficient sensory visiting at certain scenarios without using the optimized tour.

CCS CONCEPTS

• **Networks → Sensor networks**; **Mobile ad hoc networks**; Network mobility; • **Theory of computation → Distributed algorithms**; • **Computer systems organization → Sensor networks**; **Sensors and actuators**; *Robotic control*;

KEYWORDS

UAV, WSN, Data Collection, Data Mule, Swam, Optimization

ACM Reference format:
Bruno Olivieri and Markus Endler. 2017. DADCA: An Efficient Distributed Algorithm for Aerial Data Collection from Wireless Sensors Networks by UAVs. In *Proceedings of MSWiM'17, November 21–25, 2017, Miami, FL, USA*, , 8 pages.
DOI: http://dx.doi.org/10.1145/3127540.3127553

1 INTRODUCTION

Visitation of Points of Interest (POI) is a fundamental problem in mobile robot systems [14], including Unmanned Aerial Vehicles (UAVs). UAVs can be used to collect sensor' data in hazardous areas or in regions that may be difficult for humans to reach. More recently there has recently been growing interest in data collection by groups of collaborative UAVs [4].

MSWiM'17, November 21–25, 2017, Miami, FL, USA
 ACM ISBN 978-1-4503-5162-1/17/11...$15.00
DOI: http://dx.doi.org/10.1145/3127540.3127553

Wireless sensor networks (WSNs) are often deployed to collect environmental data for different kinds of applications (e.g. seismic monitoring, wildlife tracking, soil and air condition control, etc.). However, in many cases it is very difficult, or even impossible, to connect WSNs straight to its data destination. For such cases this connection can be achieved by some UAVs that visit some WSNs periodically and relay the data to the proper destination. Retrieval of sensor data from WSNs to a proper destination is a topic of high relevance to the future of sensing systems. Therefore, several research projects have focused at the use of UAVs for collecting WSN data, and majority of these works have proposed optimized UAV itineraries amongst WSN nodes for single UAVs [5] and takes into account a single tour to collect data.

The use of (UAVs) as mobile relay nodes for WSNs significantly reduces the sensor nodes' energy consumption, as the UAVs spare the WSN nodes from the multi-hop communication among them[2]. In fact this approach turns out to be a very cost-effective approach to monitoring an area and gathering the data from all sensor nodes of a wide-scale WSN [20]. Jeng *et. al.* [11] discuss the impacts and benefits of WSN data collection using UAVs along this line. Their work has shown a method to find a more efficient in WSN data collection through the use of UAVs than collection of the same data by ground vehicles. The authors in [23] have demonstrated that the use of mobile agents (robots) for collecting data probed by sensor nodes significantly increases the system's lifetime by reducing the consumption of energy that the sensing nodes would otherwise use for communication.

In order to collect data from WSNs with UAVs, several studies have suggested diverse approaches for optimizing a cost function modeling to certain aspects of this task, such as the total cost of distance traveled [3]; the amount of energy used by the sensors' radios [10]; or the cost of trajectory updates [12]. In most cases the strategies are based on variations of the Traveling Salesman Problem (TSP) or the Vehicle Routing Problem (VRP) [18][24], which are acknowledged as being NP-Complete problems. In general, all these works aim to optimize the best tour for visiting a desired set of Points of Interests (POI) or sink nodes in WSN scenarios. Such optimization means a relevant computational effort for planning the entire visitation order.

In related works the cost function (for data collection) to be optimized takes into consideration a single visit at each WSN sink sensor. For repeated data collection, therefore, these works suggest repeating the calculated tour or does not considerate multiple visits. We, on the other hand, propose a cyclic visitation of a set of sink nodes during a period of time T, taking into consideration the possibility that the group of UAVs may increase or decrease due to UAV malfunctions or extra deployment of UAVs.

In this paper we propose a WSN data collection algorithm using groups of UAVs visiting sink nodes and collecting data available at these nodes. Our approach does not aim to find the short or best tour for UAV visitation of the sensor nodes. Instead, each of the UAVs flies with a dynamic tour which is updated whenever it detects new variables upon a *rendez-vous* with other UAVs. We mean as *rendez-vous* a desired and controlled meet-up of UAVs. A valid *rendez-vous* occurs when two and only two UAVs meet-up in opposite directions. The exchanged variables are related to number of UAV in working and collected data.

The communication paradigm used relies only on *ad-hoc* communication between UAVs, sensors and the Ground Station (*GS*). This work takes into consideration the possibility that during the cyclic visitation period *T*, some UAV malfunctions and reinforcements may occur. This work presents as its main contributions:

- A distributed algorithm for maintaining a data collection from sink nodes by UAVs through a period of time;
- Comparisons of results with classical strategies which have given of up to 13% improvement when compared with a straight TSP approach regarding the amount of collected data;
- Scalability evaluations regarding the number of sink nodes to collect data.;
- Data collection delay analysis regarding our algorithm and TSP based strategies.

This work is organized as follows: Section 2 presents motivation and state of the art; Section 3 presents the problem; Section 4 presents strategies for collect data from sink nodes with UAVs, which are evaluated and discussed in Section 5. Section 6 presents final remarks and for future work.

2 BACKGROUND

2.1 Motivation

When deploying a WSN at large-scale and in remote regions, the use of mobile data collectors (mobile sink nodes) represent an interesting option. It allows to overcome possible WSN partitions, avoids, or reduces, WSN routing and provides higher adaptivity of the itinerary to the availability of data and the residual energy at each WSN node as investigated in several researches as [1][6][22]. Additionally, mobile sink usage — especially with UAVs — is the most convenient method for accessing each sensor node in a large-scale WSN [20].

Some authors [7][21] [25] have proposed the use of one UAV as a data collector. However, a single UAV acting as a mobile sink node has some drawbacks. For example, it represents a single point of failure at which possible malfunctions may compromise the entire WSN operation.

Another drawback is the latency that is related to the time that a single UAV would spend to pass through all nodes. The use of multiple UAVs can enhance malfunctions tolerance because the dynamic group of UAVs could compensate some UAVs malfunction in the group.

A group of UAVs can reduce the overall latency because it can enable a divide and conquer approach. A divide and conquer approach can reduce the tour a UAV, causing a faster delivery of collected data.

2.2 State of Art

Qadori *et. al.* discuss on [19] a series of Multi-mobile agent itinerary planning algorithms for data gathering in wireless sensor networks. Multi-mobile agents are software agents for connected WSNs.

Multi-agents (MA) have benefits compared with the summarization protocols of single agent approaches. Different MA data collecting algorithms were compared regarding the approach used to prioritize divide and conquer, determine the number of MA and make itinerary plans. Their work indicates a lack of researchers regarding investigations of collaboration between MA to perform the data collection together. Instead of collaboration, cited researches use several MA working in parallel independently[19]. We do a parallel with MA navigating through a WSN and UAV navigating between sink nodes.

Sensor data collection using UAVs forked a large array of research proposing itinerary planning techniques of various sorts: (i) some propose techniques based on the TSP or the VRP [18][24]; (ii) others focus at Genetic algorithm optimization (GA) as in [15][26]; (iii) yet anothers employ Particle Swarm Optimization (PSO) as in [28][9]; and some also are (iv) TSP-like approaches, that take into consideration the radio range as neighborhood heuristics [2][28]. However, all these works consider only a single UAV.

With respect to data collection through multiple-UAVs, is usual to group WSN sensor nodes in clusters.

UAVs can collect data from clustered sensors in the same way that MA can navigate from sensor to sensor in a WSN. Both cases consist of an itinerary plan to collect data. Further, to apply one of the itinerary planning strategies previously mentioned, as in [27] [26], a single UAV is sent for each cluster of nodes. This may decrease the delay of data collection by the UAVs, but it does not address the central point of failure problem, since a single UAV is dispatched to each cluster. As discussed in [19], which is specifically about MA, multi-UAV approaches still have some lack of investigation regarding cooperation between UAVs.

All related works in this paper take into account the data collection in a single moment. It means, at some point a UAV pass through all sink nodes to collect data after the desired period. It is reasonable that there are applications that would need data during a period *T*. For example, we present the following scenario: After a nuclear accident at a nuclear plant, some emergency tasks need to be placed as soon as possible. For some period after the accident - 72 hours per say - is crucial to maintaining continuum radiation reads from a huge and dangerous area. For instance, several radiation sensors are disposed around the plant. Thus UAV are used to collect data straight from sensors or sink nodes.

For the best of our knowledge, still a lack of investigation take into consideration the data collection on a cyclic data collection during the entire period *T* rather than a single pass after the end of the period *T*.

In our work we aim to explore collaboration between UAVs performing data collection and to compare our approach and algorithm with aforementioned related works when applying multiple

UAVs. The collaboration between UAVs is responsible to dynamically resize each individual UAV tours upon a UAV malfunction or reinforcement. Such resize process prevent uncovered sink nodes after a UAV leaving the data collection. It also prevents irregular delivery delays. The collaboration is also responsible for forwarding messages between UAVs to reach the GS without the necessity of a UAV displacement to GS to deliver its collected data.

3 PROBLEM DEFINITION

This section defines the problem and its variables. UAV's mobility characteristics are the same as *Dubin' Car* and are represented as a quadcopter, which is a vehicle capable of moving in tridimensional space in any direction. Our scenarios take into consideration that each UAV is capable of avoiding collisions. Each UAV, sink node and the *GroudStation GS* has a radio with r range for communication between them. Any communications only occurs through a *rendez-vous*. We asume that the Sink Nodes are positioned on a $\mathbb{R}^3$ surface, and their number is always larger than the set of UAVs. The ordered path taken by each UAV while visiting sink nodes is called a *tour*. These sink nodes are disconnected from the *GS* and from each other sensors. They are either isolated sensor nodes or else, cluster heads for a portion of the entire WSN. UAVs have just one radio interface, as do the WSN sensor nodes. This means that the data collected is not sent immediately to *GS*, but must be relayed between UAVs until it reaches the *GS* or is delivered when one UAV moves close enough to *GS*.

Cyclic visitation is the recurrent execution of a same tour, when required, during a T period. The T period is measured only while all UAVs perform the cyclic visitation; thus the pre-processing time is neglected. This is because of the fact that our strategy does not require any pre-processing time, whereas the benchmark strategies do. We are therefore not comparing optimization techniques utilized in other strategies. The entire process presupposes that information about the sink nodes' positions are available to *GS*, and it proceeds as follows:

i *GS* initializes v UAVs and sends them to perform their data collections;
ii The v UAVs perform the data collections during the T established period;
iii A UAV moves with constant speed and collects data only if sink nodes are at a distance of less than r;
iv When a UAV fails or needs to be recharged, it immediately ceases its activities. It may or may not resume activity.

During period T the set of p sink nodes generate an amount of data presented in (1) and each single sink node i has its own data tax generation C_i. C_i^T represents the amount of data generated after a T period by an i sink node.

$$C_i^T = \sum_0^T C_i \qquad (1)$$

For each instant t of T that a sink node exchanges data with a UAV, an T value $\overline{C}_i^T$ is added on the C_i tax as in (2). $\overline{C}_i^T$ is the total amount of transmitted data by a sink node i after a T period is multiplied by a transmission tax ρ.

$$\overline{C}_i^T = \sum_0^t C_i * \rho \qquad (2)$$

When T finishes, the average collected data C_{avg}^T is calculated by adding all the remaining data and dividing the sum by the number of sink nodes. The tax of collected dataTD^T (4) is obtained by dividing C_{avg}^T by the total of generated data C_i^T of all sink nodes p.

$$C_{avg}^T = \frac{\sum_{i=0}^{i=p} C_i^T - \overline{C}_i^T}{p} \qquad (3)$$

$$TD^T = \frac{C_{avg}^T}{\sum_{i=0}^{i=p} C_i^T} \qquad (4)$$

4 VISITATION STRATEGIES

This paper compares two strategies that perform data collections with UAVs during a period T. Figure 1 illustrates a possible arrangement of sink nodes during a period T. Let sink node A represents Ground Station (*GS*). It shows the costs that shift between one sink node and another. These costs can be interpreted as distances or as even more complex costs (*e.g.* composite costs using more than one value such as distance and barriers).

The first strategy uses the non-optimized tour routine. It is our proposal for a distributed approach. Relying on a non-optimized tour, the UAVs autonomously divide the entire original tour into sub-tours upon *rendez-vous*. The second strategy relies on obtaining the best tour by applying a TSP approach. This second strategy provides a benchmark as a representation of all other optimization strategies from related works on this paper.

4.1 Distributed Strategy (DADCA)

This paper proposes an online strategy that runs as a distributed strategy. Online is used in a meaning that the strategy is not pre-processed and can vary it own behavior. It is called *DADCA* which stands for Distributed Aerial Data Collection Algorithm. It extends and adapts the algorithm originally proposed by Kingston *et. al.* [13]. Their algorithm controls a set of UAVs surveilling a linear path in $\mathbb{R}^2$ that represents a boundary such as a frontier or a pipe-line. All UAVs travel over the path in a zigzag pattern between the first and

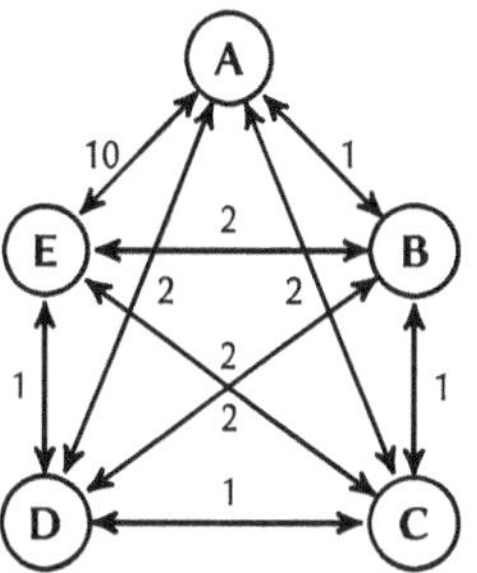

Figure 1: A possible arrangement of sink nodes and the costs to a UAV fly between them.

the last limits, from left to right, without taking into consideration points of interest such as sink nodes.

In our approach we create a non-optimized tour and the data collection is performed without running a full Hamiltonian Cycle. It performs the collection by using the tour as modeled by Kingston. All sink nodes are positioned in an order, the tour order. Let *Original Tour* be the first generated tour on each UAV. All UAVs generate the same *Original Tour*, which acts as a main global *Original Tour* that all further sub-tours are related to.

A UAV goes from the *GS* then from the each sink node in the *Original Tour* to the last one. Once the UAV reaches this last one, it inverts the tour order and follows through all sink nodes. The UAV remains, following such a pattern until the end of the period T, or until a *rendez-vous* with other UAVs, or a malfunction. Figure 2 presents a possible solution for this strategy for the arrangement shown in Figure 1 with a single UAV.

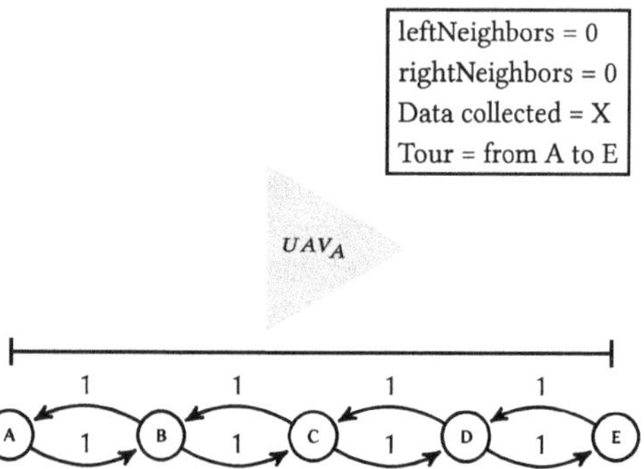

Figure 2: A possible solution of presented graph by *DADCA* with a single UAV collection data from all sink nodes. The logical segment above sink nodes represents the UAV tour from A to E.

If more than one UAV is active when two UAVs are moving in opposite directions related to the *Original Tour*, they will eventually be within radio range at some point, as shown in Figure 3. This is what we call a *rendez-vous*, and at this moment the UAVs exchange current information about known UAVs, collected data, and then adjust the sub-tours accordingly.

To explain the *rendez-vous*, let UAV_A be the first UAV sent and let UAV_B be the second one. When UAV_A begins to collect data, its tour is from A to E, and when it reaches E it begins its return. At some point UAV_B began with the same *Original Tour*, as shown in Figure 4. Thus they exchange their own data. They are capable of understanding which UAV comes from the nearest side regarding *GS*. This UAV is called left UAV. It receives the other UAV data in order to deliver on *GS*. Both UAVs compute new sub-tours to take into consideration the ideal division of the *Original Tour* with known available UAVs working at that moment.

From this moment, both UAVs move to the nearest intersection from both sub-tours. Both UAVs then move in opposite directions until find the end of all sink nodes in the same direction, or another UAV performing another *rendez-vous*, until the end of period T, or a malfunction, as shown in Figure 5. The UAVs move to the nearest intersection in order to accelerate the division of the *Original Tour*

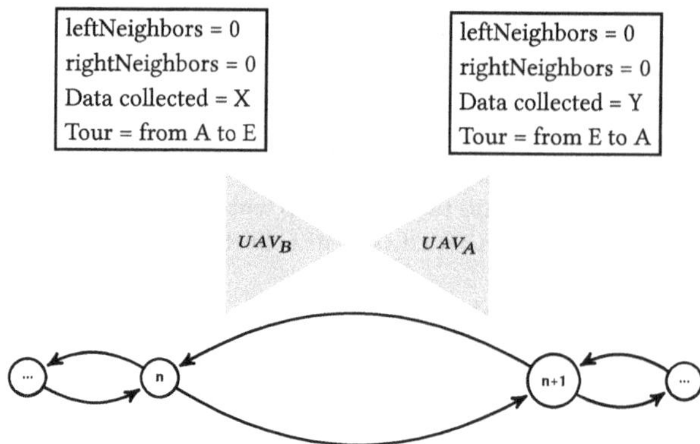

Figure 3: Two UAVs running *DADCA* a moment before a *rendez-vous*. Each one with an independent tour and no references about other UAVs.

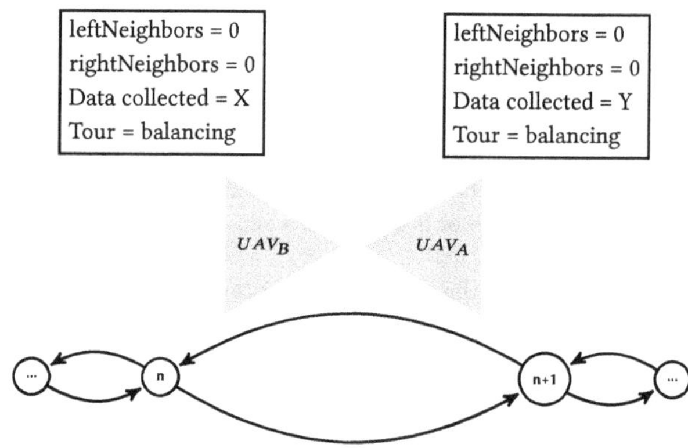

Figure 4: Two UAVs running *DADCA* a moment after a *rendez-vous*. Each one updating its data with data from the other.

between all UAVs, as proven in [13]. The hole idea is maintain the UAVs doing a zigzag pattern in a same tour. When two UAVs meets they update each other.

The visitation model has therefore been adapted from Kingston *et. al.*. Similarly, the tour was not known by the UAVs before commencing their flight. However, we were not accustomed to following a linear path, but to visiting sink nodes. In *DADCA* each UAV receives an unordered list of sink nodes by *GS* and creates their own tours without any *GS* processing. The *Original Tour* is obtained by a greedy algorithm which runs at $\theta(p^2)$ by searching the nearest sink node not added in the tour and add it (considering the number os sink nodes as p). Our extension is capable of (re)calculating their tours in $\mathbb{R}^3$ with tour intersections. In addition to resilience and to malfunctions, we are able to receive new UAVs at any point in the tour, not only at the first and the last sink nodes, as in [13].

4.2 Optimization Strategy (TSP-based)

Similar to Burman *et. al.* [3] and Ho *et. al.* [10], this strategy executes visitations to all sink nodes through the shortest possible tour.

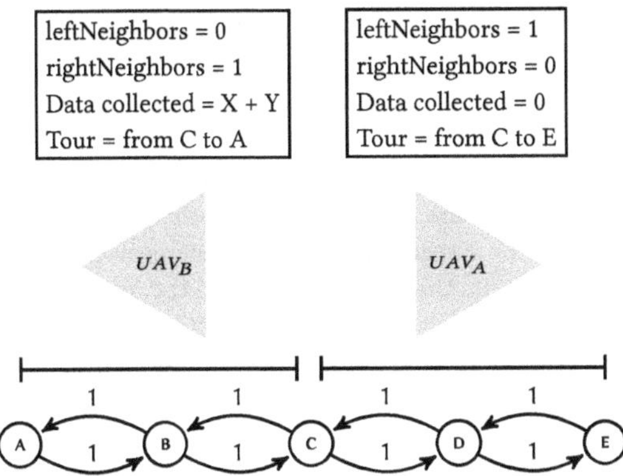

Figure 5: Two UAV running *DADCA* after defined the shared border for the last *rendez-vous*. Is this case, sink node *C*. Both go to *C* and then go to opposite sides. Logical Left UAV carries data from Right UAV.

It represents several modern optimization approaches for collecting data with UAVs [2][3][10][17][16]. This directly addresses the TSP problem. All UAVs, which are equidistant between each other, perform their data collections by following the best tour through a Hamiltonian Cycle. Figure 6 presents a possible solution of this strategy for the arrangement shown in Figure 1.

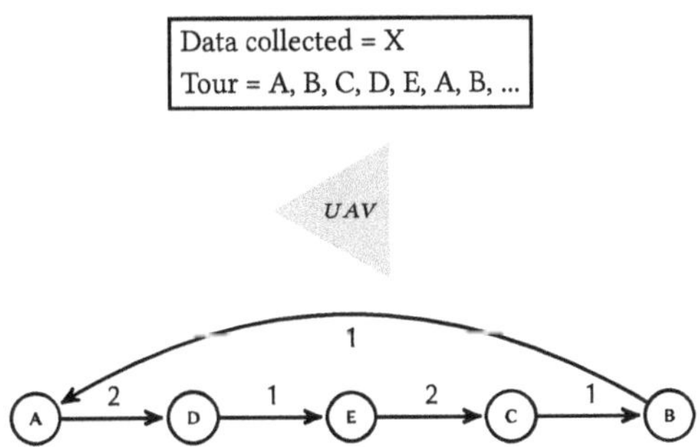

Figure 6: A possible solution of the graph presented by the strategy TSP–*based*. A UAV does a Hamiltonian Cycle through all sink nodes with the best tour regarding the costs.

On the complete graph $G(V, E)$: the vertices V are sink nodes, and the edges E represent the cost of a UAV flight between two vertices V. Obstacles and prohibited flight zones can be represented by the costs attached to the edges of this graph. As a complete graph, it is reasonable to assume that it is difficult to compute the best tour for addressing the TSP problem with a high number of sink nodes.

5 EVALUATION AND DISCUSSIONS

In order to compare the aforementioned strategies, we implemented all of them in the distributed algorithms simulator Sinalgo. Each algorithm was executed against the same set of 100 maps created with random entries of sink node locations. We calculated TD^T for each simulation result after a period T. This process was repeated for different numbers of UAVs, as well as for sets of 2, 4, 8 and 16. The confidence interval was above 98% and presented as follows.

The simulated area was equivalent to $100km^2$ and the UAV speed equivalent to $10m/s$. The communication radius r was equivalent to $100m$. The best tour computation of TSP–*based* was executed with the linear programming solver[8]. As previously mentioned, the time spent with the TSP solution was ignored in order to compare just the data collection results.

The radio communication was not taken as perfect. Some real radio issues were introduced. An interference model was set and it was assumed that the intensity of an electric signal decays exponentially with the distance from the sender. Further, there was a 10% chance of a package being lost. Radio range was not perfect; it varied randomly from 90% of r to 100% of r in each direction of each sink node or UAV.

Table 1 shows the TD^T means for each set of simulations regarding the amount of collected data. A comparison, taking as the benchmark the TSP tour, is presented in Table 2 with TSP–*based* taken as 100%. Thereafter in Table 3 we present all TD^T results with a statistical analysis for simulations with 2 UAVs. Mean data were used in Tables 1 and 2. Standard deviations of all results were calculated. Min and Max represents the best and the worst results of each strategy. The median value divides the results into two equal intervals with the same amount of results. The Lower Quartile (Q1) divides the 25% worst results as an upper boundary and divides the 75% better results as a lower boundary. Conversely, the Upper Quartile (Q3) divides the 25% better results as a lower boundary and divides the 75% worst results as an upper boundary.

To compare the results of our approach with related works we compared the tax TD^T (4). One of our goals is to be relatively close to optimization strategies without the computational effort. Figure 7 presents the results of the simulations performed with 20 Sink Nodes and sets of 2, 4, 8 and 16 UAVs. The graph presents two results: (1) *DADCA* obtained by the distributed strategy proposed in this work and (2) TSP–*based* obtained by executing the TSP-based strategy representing several related works. Figure 7 shows that asymptotic behavior was the same for both results. This occurs because the same cost function was applied for all cases versus the same period T. Higher results on the axis Y means that the medium data accumulation of the point was lower, so the visit rate TD^T was higher. This was, in other words, a better result.

After several runs performing a zigzag pattern without following the Hamiltonian Cycle, our proposal, the strategy *DADCA*, gives better results than TSP–*based*. The results of *DADCA* with results up to 13% better than the TSP–*based* as shown in Table 2. Although the method adopted in *DADCA* has one less edge - because it does not utilize a Hamiltonian Cycle - there is no guarantee that it will be better than the optimized tour computed in TSP–*based*. Originally, we did not aim to reach better results than TSP. We certainly aim to be reasonably close to it. After several runs, however, the average case showed better results for *DADCA*.

Moreover, any optimization-based strategies (e.g. TSP–*based*) need time for processing the best tour before the operation and this requires a δ period. If we take into consideration δ, our proposed

Table 1: TD^T mean results.

	2 UAVs	4 UAVs	8 UAVs	16 UAVs
TSP−*based*	3.30	6.61	13.17	26.18
DADCA	3.71	7.29	14.43	28.50

Table 2: TD^T mean results comparison.

	2 UAVs	4 UAVs	8 UAVs	16 UAVs
TSP−*based*	100%	100%	100%	100%
DADCA	113%	110%	110%	109%
Diff	**13%**	**10%**	**10%**	**9%**

Table 3: TD^T statistics results comparison concerning 2 UAVs

	DADCA	TSP−*based*
Simulation Maps	100	100
Mean	3.71	3.30
Std Deviation	0.51	0.29
Min	2.61	2.38
Q1 (25%)	3.30	3.11
Median (50%)	3.72	3.30
Q3 (75%)	4.03	3.44
Max	4.80	4.07

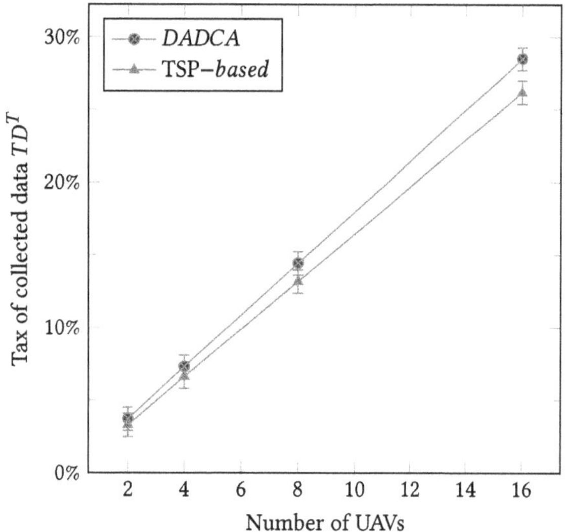

Figure 7: Simulation with 20 sink nodes and 2, 4, 8 e 16 UAVs. Higher values at y axis are better.

strategy *DADCA* would have the same period δ for its results to be enhanced against TSP−*based*. This fact would improve the performance of *DADCA* substantially. The *DADCA* strategy performs a relaxed computation for its tour, being executed in $\theta(p^2)$. It is plausible to say that it can be computed aboard the UAVs just after the launch, allowing immediate launching.

Furthermore, the strategy *DADCA* is able to go into operation immediately, without the need for pre-processing. This could be a key factor regarding collecting data from environments if there are a larger number of sink nodes. In this case that would cause a long pre-processing time regarding NP-Complete problems.

Figure 7 presents the mean results, and the averages from 100 simulated maps. However, the use of average values could result in inaccurate interpretations. For this reason Table 3 presents statistical values regarding the simulation results. Figure 8 presents plots of the Table 3 data in a Box Plot graph.

In Figure 8 the Lower Quartile (Q1) of *DADCA* has practically the same level of the TSP−*based* median. This means that half the number of the worst results of TSP−*based* are equal to only 25% of the worst results of TSP−*based*. *DADCA* Median is higher than the TSP−*based* Upper Quartile (Q3); this means that the half or 50% of the best results of *DADCA* are better than 75% of the TSP−*based* results. Furthermore, the *DADCA* Upper Quartile (Q3) has practically the same level of TSP−*based* max results; this means that 25% of the *DADCA* results are better than all of the TSP−*based* results.

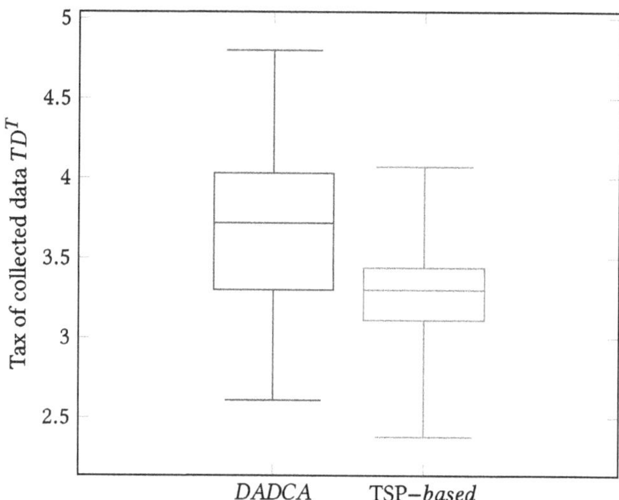

Figure 8: This figure presents the Table 3 data in a Box Plot Graph. It shows the statistics interpretation of simulation results with 2 UAVs and 20 sink nodes. Higher values at y axis are better.

Figure 9 presents six other evaluations scenarios. Each one with 20, 40, 60, 80, 100 and 200 sink nodes. For each scenario, there was used 4 distinct number of UAVs regarding the total amount of sink nodes: 50% of sink nodes; 25%; 10% and 5%. Each simulation ran with 30 distinct maps each with a confidence level of 95%. Axis y presents TD^T. It is possible to note that the results of data retrieval follow linearly the scenarios. It is important to notice that the better values in bigger sets of UAVs it also due the fact the area still the same, it means $100km^2$. Thus it are more dense scenarios.

Furthermore, Figure 10 presents the processing time that each UAV takes at t_0 for an amount of sink nodes. Axis x represents

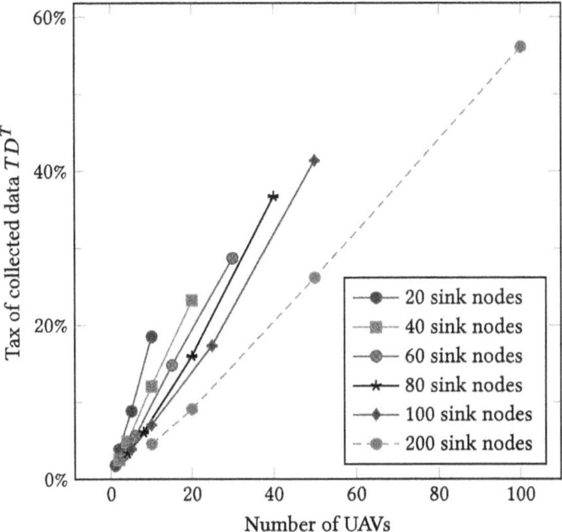

Figure 9: Simulation concerning several sink nodes and several UAVs. Is possible to note that the asymptotic behavior still the same for several distinct number of sink nodes.

the number of UAVs and axis y the time um milliseconds. It means the preparation time that a UAV would need to begin the data collection. As previously mentioned the asymptotic behavior grows responsibly with the number of sink nodes to visit and collect data. Moreover, it is scalable in contrast of TSP–*based*. As TSP–*based* is NP-Complete, we were not able to process the evaluation in Figure 9 with plausible time. All evaluations in this paper were processed in a computer powered by a processor XEON-E3-1220-V3.

Furthermore, we bring some qualitative advantage regarding malfunctions and reinforcements. At any moment during T a UAV could either return or enter the data collection activity utilizing the *Original Tour* from the other UAVs. This happens without any centralized or *off-line* processing occurring dynamically.

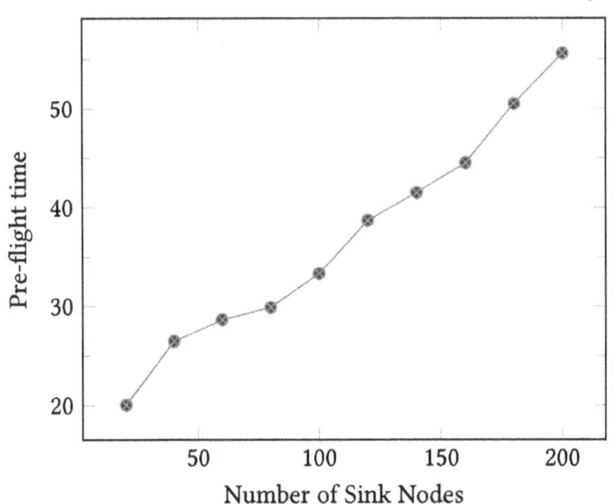

Figure 10: Processing time for 20, 40, 60, 80, 100 and 200 sink nodes. Axis y presents results in milliseconds

The *DADCA* presents better results regarding the amount of messages collected. However, to investigate the arriving flow of messages on *GS* perspective we present the following details. UAVs movements affects message delivery time on each strategy. It means, the message delay from a sink node to the *GS* is affected by the UAV trajectory which carries the message.

The Figure 11 presents the mean delay of the simulations presented on Table 2 and Table 1 as well in Figure 7. In Figure 11 each point of the Series presents the mean delay of 100 simulations with the presented number of UAVs.

On the TSP–*based* results in Figure 11 is possible to note the stability of results. Indeed, the results are almost on the same level. The small variations in low UAVs numbers are related to the time to launch of UAVs. The linear behavior happens due the fact of tour of UAVs are the same all time. All UAVs do the same Hamiltonian Cycle through all sink nodes. On each instant t_n of T that a UAV is carrying a message collected until t_{n-1}, this message is near to *GS* than a instant $t_{\{n<=(n-1)\}}$. In other words, on the TSP–*based* a collected data is always going to *GS*.

DADCA results in Figure 11 presents a different behavior in relation of TSP–*based* results. With a few UAVs *DADCA* a worst result than TSP–*based*. As the number of UAVs is increased the results show a tendency to equip. This occurs because the *DADCA* have two kind of movements. As the tour is a linear path, a UAV could be going from *GS* to the end or the inverse (from the end to *GS*). It affects the delay in two ways. A UAV going on *GS* direction deliver its collected messages to *GS* of pass it away to another UAV which will deliver. A UAV going on *GS* opposite direction is increasing its messages delays. We call it a *waste of message dislocation*. Each meter pushed in the opposite direction must be traversed again during the return. Increasing the number of UAVs, there is a greater number of *rendez-vous*. With a greater number of *rendez-vous* more often the UAVs deliver its collect data to another UAV that will eventually deliver to the *GS*.

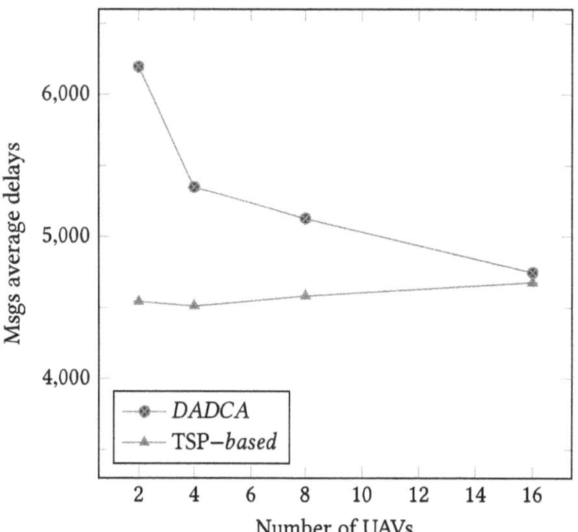

Figure 11: Average delays to messages from sink nodes reaches *GS*. Smaller values at y axis are better.

To use *DADCA* instead of TSP–*based* strategies with a few number of UAVs need to be analyzed. There is a trade-off between the amount of collected data versus the time to receive them. For cases with a higher number of UAVs *DADCA* will perform similar to TSP–*based* strategies.

6 CONCLUSION AND FUTURE WORK

In order to investigate and support the future of sensing systems we have extended the algorithm proposed by [13] to be used in data collection from WSNs. We have improved the dynamics of *rendez-vous* in order to employ three-dimensional environments, tour intersections and carrier data. We have also evaluated its performance against classic strategies with best tour approaches. The results of simulations showed a reduction of up to 13% of the total cost evaluated in relation to a TSP–*based* tour.

This research is still ongoing and new factors will be analyzed. Visitation costs from the perspective of the UAVs will also be analyzed, particularly when their flight dynamics during the zigzag pattern remains more costly than a continuous flight. We are currently investigating flying dynamics costs with regard to the zigzag pattern. Three other aspects are still under analysis: (1) the dynamism of the number of sink nodes with regard to their respective positions; (2) data throughput from the perspective of the *GS* and (3) characteristics of the V2V communication employed, such as throughput versus communication range.

REFERENCES

[1] Kemal Akkaya, Mohamed Younis, and Meenakshi Bangad. 2005. Sink repositioning for enhanced performance in wireless sensor networks. *Computer Networks* 49, 4 (2005), 512–534.

[2] Temesgen Seyoum Alemayehu and Jai-Hoon Kim. 2017. Efficient Nearest Neighbor Heuristic TSP Algorithms for Reducing Data Acquisition Latency of UAV Relay WSN. *Wireless Personal Communications* 1, 1 (feb 2017), 1–15. DOI: https://doi.org/10.1007/s11277-017-3994-9

[3] Jerry Burman, Joao Hespanha, Upamanyu Madhow, Jason Isaacs, Sriram Venkateswaran, and Tien Pham. 2012. Autonomous UAV persistent surveillance using bio-inspired strategies. In *SPIE Defense, Security, and Sensing*. International Society for Optics and Photonics, Baltimore, Maryland, USA, 13. DOI: https://doi.org/10.1117/12.920018

[4] Ting Chen, Duncan Campbell, Luis Felipe Gonzalez, and Gilles Coppin. 2015. Increasing Autonomy Transparency through capability communication in multiple heterogeneous UAV management. In *2015 IEEE/RSJ International Conference on Intelligent Robots and Systems (IROS)*. IEEE, Brisbane, Autralia, 2434–2439. DOI: https://doi.org/10.1109/IROS.2015.7353707

[5] Rone Ilídio da Silva and Mario A. Nascimento. 2016. On best drone tour plans for data collection in wireless sensor network. In *Proceedings of the 31st Annual ACM Symposium on Applied Computing - SAC '16*. ACM Press, New York, New York, USA, 703–708. DOI: https://doi.org/10.1145/2851613.2851854

[6] Abhimanyu Das and Debojyoti Dutta. 2005. Data acquisition in multiple-sink sensor networks. *ACM SIGMOBILE Mobile Computing and Communications Review* 9, 3 (2005), 82–85.

[7] Aysegul Tuysuz Erman, Lodewijk van Hoesel, Paul Havinga, and Jian Wu. 2008. Enabling mobility in heterogeneous wireless sensor networks cooperating with UAVs for mission-critical management. *IEEE Wireless Communications* 15, 6 (2008), 38–46.

[8] Redouane Ezzahir, Christian Bessiere, Mustapha Belaissaoui, and El Houssine Bouyakhf. 2007. DisChoco: A platform for distributed constraint programming. In *Proceedings of the IJCAI*, Vol. 7. Citeseer, 16–21.

[9] Yangguang Fu, Mingyue Ding, Chengping Zhou, and Hanping Hu. 2013. Route Planning for Unmanned Aerial Vehicle (UAV) on the Sea Using Hybrid Differential Evolution and Quantum-Behaved Particle Swarm Optimization. *IEEE Transactions on Systems, Man, and Cybernetics: Systems* 43, 6 (nov 2013), 1451–1465. DOI: https://doi.org/10.1109/TSMC.2013.2248146

[10] Esten Ingar Grotli, P. B. Sujit, Tor Arne Johansen, Joao Borges de Sousa, Dac-Tu Ho, Esten Ingar Grotli, P. B. Sujit, Tor Arne Johansen, and Joao Borges De Sousa. 2013. Performance evaluation of cooperative relay and Particle Swarm Optimization path planning for UAV and wireless sensor network. In *2013 IEEE Globecom Workshops (GC Wkshps)*. IEEE, Atlanta, USA, 1403–1408. DOI: https://doi.org/10.1109/GLOCOMW.2013.6825191

[11] Hoon Jeong, Changwon Lee, Jaehong Ryu, Byeong-Cheol Choi, and JeongGil Ko. 2015. Communicating "in the Air"- Studying the Impact of UAVs on Sensor Network Data Collection. In *Proceedings of the 13th ACM Conference on Embedded Networked Sensor Systems - SenSys '15*. ACM Press, New York, New York, USA, 435–436. DOI: https://doi.org/10.1145/2809695.2817901

[12] S.V. Kashuba, V.I. Novikov, O.I. Lysenko, and I.V. Alekseeva. 2015. Optimization of UAV path for wireless sensor network data gathering. In *2015 IEEE International Conference Actual Problems of Unmanned Aerial Vehicles Developments (APUAVD)*. IEEE, Kyiv, Ukraine., 280–283. DOI: https://doi.org/10.1109/APUAVD.2015.7346621

[13] Ryan S Kingston, Derek and Beard, Randal W and Holt. 2008. Decentralized Perimeter Surveillance Using a Team of UAVs. *IEEE Transactions on Robotics* 24, 6 (dec 2008), 1394–1404. DOI: https://doi.org/10.1109/TRO.2008.2007935

[14] Vijay (University of Pennsylvania) Kumar, Subhrajit Bhattacharya, and Robert Ghrist. 2014. Multi-robot Coverage and Exploration on Riemannian Manifolds with Boundary. *International Journal of Robotics Research* 33, 1 (2014), 113–137.

[15] Pawel Ladosz, Hyondong Oh, and Wen-Hua Chen. 2017. Trajectory Planning for Communication Relay Unmanned Aerial Vehicles in Urban Dynamic Environments. *Journal of Intelligent & Robotic Systems* 1, 1 (jan 2017), 1–19. DOI: https://doi.org/10.1007/s10846-017-0484-y

[16] Andriy Mazayev, Noélia Correia, and Gabriela Schütz. 2016. Data Gathering in Wireless Sensor Networks Using Unmanned Aerial Vehicles. *International Journal of Wireless Information Networks* 23, 4 (dec 2016), 297–309. DOI: https://doi.org/10.1007/s10776-016-0319-y

[17] Shintaro Mori. 2016. Cooperative sensing data collecting framework by using unmanned aircraft vehicle in wireless sensor network. In *2016 IEEE International Conference on Communications (ICC)*. IEEE, Kuala Lumpur, Malaysia, 1–6. DOI: https://doi.org/10.1109/ICC.2016.7511187

[18] Domenico Pascarella, Salvatore Venticinque, and Rocco Aversa. 2013. Agent-based design for UAV mission planning. In *Proceedings - 2013 8th International Conference on P2P, Parallel, Grid, Cloud and Internet Computing, 3PGCIC 2013*. IEEE, Compiegne, France, 76–83. DOI: https://doi.org/10.1109/3PGCIC.2013.18

[19] Huthiafa Q Qadori, Zuriati A Zulkarnain, Zurina Mohd Hanapi, and Shamala Subramaniam. 2017. Multi-mobile agent itinerary planning algorithms for data gathering in wireless sensor networks: A review paper. *International Journal of Distributed Sensor Networks* 13, 1 (jan 2017), 155014771668484. DOI: https://doi.org/10.1177/1550147716684841

[20] Sarmad Rashed and Mujdat Soyturk. 2017. Analyzing the Effects of UAV Mobility Patterns on Data Collection in Wireless Sensor Networks. *Sensors* 17, 2 (feb 2017), 413. DOI: https://doi.org/10.3390/s17020413

[21] Francesco Restuccia and Sajal K Das. 2015. Lifetime optimization with QoS of sensor networks with uncontrollable mobile sinks. In *World of Wireless, Mobile and Multimedia Networks (WoWMoM), 2015 IEEE 16th International Symposium on a*. IEEE, IEEE, Boston, MA, USA, 1–9.

[22] Arun A Somasundara, Aditya Ramamoorthy, and Mani B Srivastava. 2004. Mobile element scheduling for efficient data collection in wireless sensor networks with dynamic deadlines. In *Real-Time Systems Symposium, 2004. Proceedings. 25th IEEE International*. IEEE, IEEE, Lisbon, Portugal, 296–305.

[23] Onur Tekdas, Volkan Isler, Jong Hyun Lim, and Andreas Terzis. 2009. Using mobile robots to harvest data from sensor fields. *IEEE Wireless Communications* 16, 1 (2009), 22–28.

[24] Dinesh Thakur, Maxim Likhachev, James Keller, Vijay Kumar, Vladimir Dobrokhodov, Kevin Jones, Jeff Wurz, and Isaac Kaminer. 2013. Planning for opportunistic surveillance with multiple robots. In *2013 IEEE/RSJ International Conference on Intelligent Robots and Systems*. IEEE, Vancouver, Canada, 5750–5757. DOI: https://doi.org/10.1109/IROS.2013.6697189

[25] Damla Turgut and Ladislau Bölöni. 2009. Heuristic approaches for transmission scheduling in sensor networks with multiple mobile sinks. *Comput. J.* 1, 1 (2009), bxp110.

[26] Chengliang Wang, Fei Ma, Junhui Yan, Debraj De, and Sajal K. Das. 2015. Efficient Aerial Data Collection with UAV in Large-Scale Wireless Sensor Networks. *International Journal of Distributed Sensor Networks* 2015, 11 (nov 2015), 1–19. DOI: https://doi.org/10.1155/2015/286080

[27] Jin Wang, Jiayi Cao, Sai Ji, and Jong Hyuk Park. 2017. Energy-efficient cluster-based dynamic routes adjustment approach for wireless sensor networks with mobile sinks. *The Journal of Supercomputing* 1, 1 (jan 2017), 1–14. DOI: https://doi.org/10.1007/s11227-016-1947-9

[28] Wei Wang, Haoshan Shi, Pengyu Huang, Fuping Wu, Dingyi Fang, Xiaojiang Chen, and Xiaoyan Yin. 2015. An Efficient Variable Dimension PSO Algorithm for Mobile Node Tour Planning in WSN. In *Proceedings of the 1st Workshop on Context Sensing and Activity Recognition - CSAR '15*. ACM Press, New York, New York, USA, 47–52. DOI: https://doi.org/10.1145/2820716.2820723

Experimental Study of Packet Loss in a UWB Sensor Network for Aircraft

Daniel Neuhold
University of Klagenfurt, Austria

Jorge F. Schmidt
University of Klagenfurt, Austria
and Lakeside Labs GmbH, Austria

Jirka Klaue
Airbus, Hamburg, Germany

Dominic Schupke
Airbus, Munich, Germany

Christian Bettstetter
University of Klagenfurt, Austria
and Lakeside Labs GmbH, Austria

ABSTRACT

There is a strong demand in the aviation industry to replace cables in airplanes by wireless connectivity to gain flexibility and reduce weight. Such in-plane wireless communications must be reliable and robust against interference. As part of our activities in this domain, we present a proof-of-concept for an ultra-wideband (UWB) sensor network deployed in a mockup of a small passenger cabin of a commercial aircraft with a few passengers and report experimental results on the packet loss rate with off-the-shelf IEEE 802.15.4-2011 compliant UWB transceivers. It is shown that a combination of spatial and temporal diversity can significantly lower the packet loss rate of different link types without degrading throughput.

KEYWORDS

Ultra-wideband communications, Wireless sensor networks, Aircraft measurements, Reliability, Packet loss, Diversity.

ACM Reference format:
Daniel Neuhold, Jorge F. Schmidt, Jirka Klaue, Dominic Schupke, and Christian Bettstetter. 2017. Experimental Study of Packet Loss in a UWB Sensor Network for Aircraft. In *Proceedings of MSWiM '17, Miami, FL, USA, November 21–25, 2017,* 6 pages.
https://doi.org/10.1145/3127540.3127549

1 INTRODUCTION

Wireless technologies are rarely used for on-board machine-type communications in today's commercial airplanes. A common fear is that wireless systems cannot compete with traditional wiring in terms of reliability in such critical infrastructure — and indeed, an aircraft cabin is a challenging scenario for wireless communications. To give two examples, the sheer number of people located in a small space results in severe signal shadowing, and the carried wireless devices they carry may cause interference. Despite these concerns and challenges, the industry's need for more cost efficient and greener airplanes is triggering research toward the deployment of in-aircraft wireless networks [9, 11–16]. Use cases include wireless connectivity of hundreds of sensors in passenger cabins and cargo areas.

From an economical perspective, the removal of cables makes planes lighter and has the potential to speed up the production process and lower operating costs [1, 14]. The deployment flexibility of wireless systems is expected to reduce maintenance costs by avoiding time-consuming repairs in the wiring subject to significant mechanical stress. Beyond this, wireless connections may enable completely new services that are impossible with wires. From the perspective of carbon dioxide emissions, a key factor determining the fuel-saving capabilities of airplanes is their weight. As the fuselage weight is being decreased by the use of lighter high-tech materials, the weight of wires in today's airplanes remains fixed, thus becoming a non-negligible fraction (2–5 %) of the overall weight [1]. To give an example, over 500 km of wires are deployed in an Airbus A380 [17]. Removing a significant portion of wires is expected to eventually lower emission values.

A key question in this context is: Which technology to use for an in-aircraft wireless sensor network (WSN)? Commonly used WSN solutions (e.g., Zolertia Z1) rely on nodes with low computational power and deliver inadequate data rates. The unlicensed frequency bands used by such technologies are crowded, as most passengers in a typical flight use 802.11 or Bluetooth. Interference in such bands is a major concern in the aviation industry; it may prevent guaranteeing a certain quality of service (QoS).

A promising candidate to tackle these problems is *ultra-wideband* (UWB) technology. Its high data rates over short distances, high-precision localization, and very low power consumption (a key feature for sustainable operation with harvested energy [6]), together with the fact that current UWB [2] targets frequency bands that do not overlap with mass communication systems, are some features that favor UWB deployment [19]. Moreover, the IEEE 802.15.4-2011 UWB standard contemplates a transmission channel that is likely to comply with in-aircraft wireless regulations. Although the spectrum mask for Wireless Avionics Intra-Communication (WAIC) [1] is not yet defined, a compliance with regard to a characteristic −5 dBm transmission, with a typical out-of-band attenuation profile, and a bandwidth restriction to 200 MHz, seems to be attainable with the IEEE 802.15.4-2011 UWB standard. It must be noted that regulation in some countries (e.g., Australia) forbids UWB operation on board an aircraft, but studies in this domain may contribute to revising these regulations if UWB proves to be a good solution.

We follow this path and deploy an off-the-shelf IEEE 802.15.4-2011 compliant UWB testbed [5] with up to 17 nodes in a mockup

MSWiM '17, November 21–25, 2017, Miami, FL, USA

ACM ISBN 978-1-4503-5162-1/17/11.
https://doi.org/10.1145/3127540.3127549

of a passenger cabin with a few passengers. Our deployment serves as a proof-of-concept of a WSN in a cabin environment close to reality. It provides first results in network performance accounting for the constraints imposed by commercially available UWB hardware. Different to other experimental contributions in this domain, which mainly focus on channel sounding [13, 15], our objective is to assess the reliability in terms of packet loss achieved by diversity. We first perform a characterization of the propagation effects: we measure the path loss for line-of-sight links (hallway and head panel deployment) and characterize the shadowing for the obstructed links (armrest and floor heights). We also take into account the non-ideal radiation pattern of our antennas. Based on this characterization, we take the perspective of the entire network and analyze simple diversity schemes. We show that the use of code division multiplexing within a time division multiple access (TDMA) scheme, combined with spatial diversity, reduces packet loss without degrading the throughput. The node positioning allows some insight into the system dimensioning.

Our contributions can be summarized as follows: First, we present a proof-of-concept of a UWB-WSN in a passenger cabin mockup of a commercial aircraft. Second, we characterize the path loss and shadowing experienced by commercial UWB nodes in this environment and quantify the loss induced by a single passenger and seat row to be 3 and 6 dB, respectively. Third, we provide packet loss rates for empty and occupied cabins at different flight stages. Fourth, we give insight into the node deployment and system dimensioning.

The paper is organized as follows: Section 2 describes the system, including hardware, network architecture, and multiple access and diversity. Section 3 presents and discusses experimental results on attenuation and packet loss. Section 4 covers related work. Section 5 contains conclusions and outlook to future work. The paper is based on our preliminary results on UWB aircraft sensor networks, presented as extended abstracts and posters [11, 12].

2 SYSTEM

This study is part of our ongoing efforts to develop a WSN that will replace a number of wired systems in commercial airplanes. We focus on the passenger cabin being the most challenging scenario from the networking perspective. A major challenge is the heterogeneity of system and environment: Applications include seat occupation sensors, security-critical fire and smoke detectors, advanced lighting features, localization of items, and many others. These applications have different priorities and QoS requirements. Some transmissions are periodic, others are event driven. Different parts of the cabin exhibit differences in terms of node density, number of reflexive objects, and degree of mobility.

2.1 Hardware Platform

Our network builds on IEEE 802.15.4-2011 UWB compliant transceivers commercialized by DecaWave [5]: the EVK1000 boards (see Fig. 1). The main application and purpose of these boards is indoor localization; they are not calibrated for reliable and efficient data communication. Hence, significant development efforts were needed to adapt these boards to our use case. The newly developed software enables us to meet the aircraft-related QoS requirements and makes off-the-self nodes meet certain system demands. Even though different nodes may have different functions, as we employ research kits, all of our nodes consist of the same hardware and differ solely in the software. This enables us to dynamically switch nodes to take over different tasks in different setups.

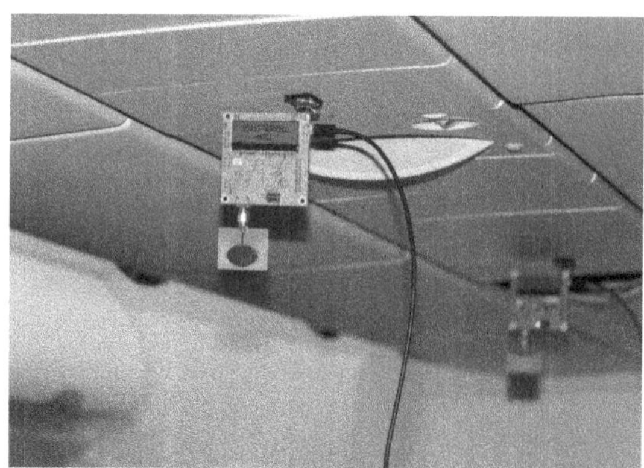

Figure 1: Deployment of DecaWave transceivers in a cabin mockup for test purposes at Airbus in Ottobrunn/Munich.

A characterization of the antennas is needed to ensure that unintended signal attenuation, due to the relative orientation of the antennas, is avoided. Such characterization determines the maximally permitted tilt axes so as not to compromise the quality of the measurements. Our antennas (Fig. 1) exhibit a deep notch on their vertical axis and have maximum gain on their perpendicular direction. Nodes are deployed in a way that the relative antenna orientation is aligned optimally with the main lobe.

2.2 Network Architecture

Fig. 2 shows the architecture of the network. An aircraft may have hundreds of sensor nodes, which monitor the environment and report their data to one of several wireless data concentrators (WDCs). The WDCs are connected to the application server, which collects, merges, and ultimately controls the system. There are two types of WDC: access points (APs) and listeners. APs are mounted along the hallway ceiling to establish a cellular network with full coverage of the cabin. They are responsible for controlling, monitoring, and keeping time alignments among nodes and listeners. Listeners are deployed at strategic locations to improve the coverage; they are connected to the APs and provide spatial diversity between nodes and APs. Whenever appropriate, data is sent to the human machine interface for visualization and/or action by the aircraft crew.

2.3 Multiple Access and Diversity

2.3.1 Multiple Access. Sensor nodes are expected to rely on energy harvesting to reduce maintenance costs. It is thus of importance to employ protocols that enable duty-cycling and deep-sleep functionality. Furthermore, the aviation industry needs QoS support in terms of reserved channels with requirements on delay and packet loss. Taking this into account, channel resources are arranged into time slots with scheduling performed by the APs. One slot in this time division multiple access (TDMA) scheme is reserved as a common slot to broadcast control information to all nodes. It can be used to notify or reconfigure nodes, e.g., when a

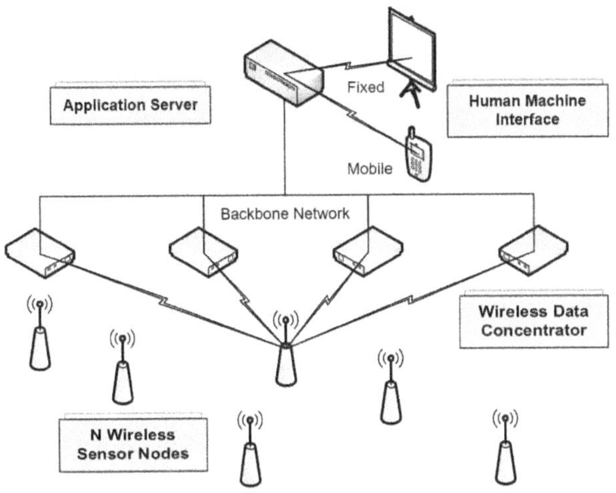

Figure 2: Network architecture.

new node joins the network or when priorities or data rates change. At initialization, each AP executes a node discovery to detect and accommodate nodes in its coverage area. Each node synchronizes its time to its AP. The slot duration is fixed, the TDMA frame scales with the number of nodes, and nodes periodically transmit in their allocated slot. It is assumed that the maximum frame length is short enough to meet the response time targets.

Various factors influence the packet loss, e.g., shadowing and small-scale fading. We investigate as to which types of diversity can be used to efficiently improve the system reliability. We study the benefits of (1) spatial diversity implemented with listeners that overhear transmissions, and (2) temporal diversity in combination with code division multiplexing to enable simultaneous transmissions.

2.3.2 Spatial Diversity. An approach to increase reliability is to add listeners as additional WDCs to provide alternative signal paths. We spatially separate all WDCs as far apart as possible to have independent shadowing conditions. In our experiments, we place one AP in the center of the cabin and four listeners in the corners. We found that this deployment strategy provides both sufficient spatial diversity to overcome fading events and enough alternative receivers to handle the shadowing (see Section 3). With this spatial distribution of receivers, nodes transmit redundant information to all WDCs located at different positions. The cost for this reliability enhancement is an increasing number of WDCs. It is therefore of interest to deploy not more listeners than really needed.

2.3.3 Temporal Diversity. Reliability can be further improved — alternatively, the number of listeners can be reduced — if multiple quasi-orthogonal pseudo noise (PN) codes are used to allow several nodes to transmit in the same slot without message corruption. This is similar to code division multiple access (CDMA), but CDMA cannot be implemented due to limitations of our hardware. Our nodes can be configured to decode a single PN but not all PNs used simultaneously. Because of this limitation, we cannot use the PN to obtain multi-user diversity. Nevertheless, the utilization of different PNs still enables nodes to send redundant messages without reducing the throughput. In our implementation, each listener decodes a different PN, so messages are sent to different WDCs sequentially on each redundant transmission.

As shown in Fig. 3, each node transmits the same message in several consecutive slots altering the PN from slot to slot. This increases the reliability if the channel changes significantly from one slot to the next. Nodes are clustered into groups of size equal to the number N of PNs used. Within groups, nodes alter their PNs in a sequential manner. Redundancy in a factor of N is obtained with each node transmitting periodically in N consecutive slots. In our implementation, we associate each listener to one of these $N = 4$ nodes. As nodes change their PN at each transmission attempt, all nodes transmit their messages to all listeners.

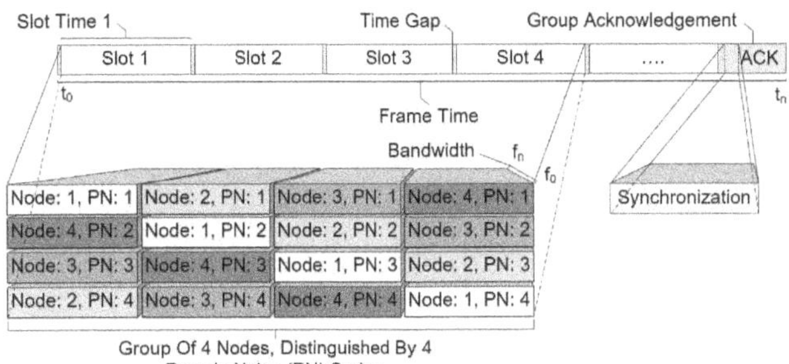

Figure 3: TDMA with code division redundancy for $N = 4$.

This scheme can be exploited in fast fading channels. If the channel variation was slow, it is likely that a bad channel condition persists during many slots. We know, however, from our measurements that severe channel fade periods are short compared to the slot duration. The longest fade events are observed during the flight stage when there is very little movement of passengers. In this stage, the combination of spatial and temporal diversity is important.

Note that code division can also be used to increase the data rate instead of reliability. This tradeoff adds flexibility to the design.

3 EXPERIMENTAL RESULTS

Two different node deployments in a business class compartment (6.3 m long, 5.1 m wide) with extended foot room are used to conduct our tests. The first setup is used to characterize the propagation scenario in terms of path loss and shadowing, and gives insight into feasible communication ranges. The second setup is used to evaluate packet loss between nodes and WDCs for realistic deployment positions; it is used to assess the reliability gains of diversity. Small-scale fading is induced by moving passengers.

3.1 Propagation Features

We use the testbed setup in Fig. 4 to investigate the attenuation due to path loss and shadowing to estimate the maximum cell size. Shadowing describes the attenuation caused by absorption from objects obstructing the line of sight (LOS) path.

3.1.1 Hallway Test. A fixed AP is deployed in a cabin hallway without passengers (see upper part of Fig. 4) with a transmitting node moving away from the AP as shown. Fig. 5 shows the received power over distance. A path loss exponent of about 2 is found by least square fitting the mean reception power over distance to

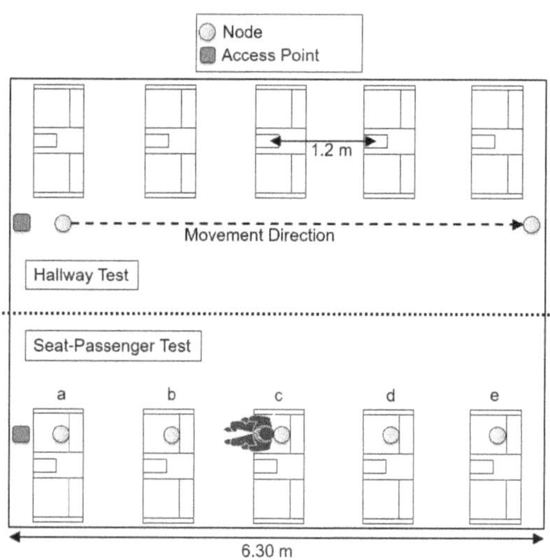

Figure 4: Point-to-point testbed in the hallway and on seats with and without a passenger.

the singular path loss model. There are significant power drops whenever the node passes a seat row in its movement. Since this effect is observed consistently at each seat row, we conjecture that these fluctuations result from the narrow hallway and the small space between the transceiver and the seat when passing by.

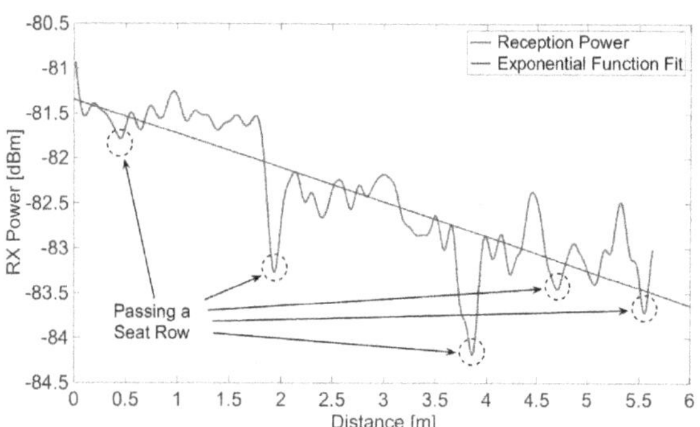

Figure 5: Path loss in a cabin mockup under LOS condition.

3.1.2 Seat-Passenger Test. Let us now quantify the shadowing caused by stationary objects. The majority of objects in a cabin are seats and passengers. The setup is illustrated in the bottom part of Fig. 4. A passenger sits on the right seat in row *c* for about 220 seconds, then stands up and moves out of the cabin. He or she reenters the cabin after 130 additional seconds and repeats the procedure for each other row. Measurements are made on the point-to-point link from the sensor node on the seat to the AP without any other node turned on. Fig. 6 shows that a significant power drop occurs if the signal travels through an occupied seat. When the passenger stands up and leaves the cabin, the signal level increases by 3 dB. This is consistent with the findings in [8] for human body attenuation and complies to our own measurements. The attenuation of a seat

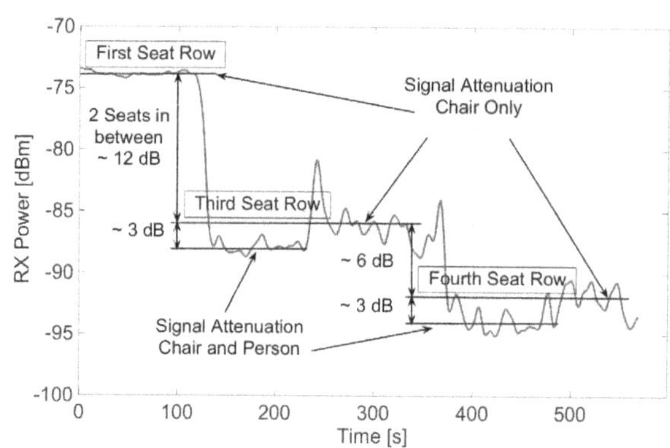

Figure 6: Shadowing in a cabin: Attenuation caused by seats and passengers.

is measured to be 6 dB. As the number of obstructing seat rows increases, the received signal power decreases.

3.2 Packet Loss

The packet loss is assessed in a scenario with 12 sensor nodes and 5 WDCs as shown in Fig. 7. There are three nodes on each seat: one at the floor, one at the armrest/seat, and one at the head panel/ceiling. The AP and the four listeners (L1-L4) are deployed at the ceiling. All these positions correspond to practically feasible deployment locations. People in the mockup mimic passengers in different flight phases. A packet loss is accounted for whenever the received signal power falls below the −105 dBm sensitivity of our nodes.

3.2.1 Impact of Moving Passengers. Passengers obstruct links between senders and receivers, leading to a degraded reception power, which in some cases leads to packet loss. The received power levels are very different to those observed in an empty cabin [12], as shown in Fig. 8 for an armrest node.

3.2.2 Comparison of Deployment Positions. It is of interest for the network design to investigate the impact of the node positioning heights, taking into account that passengers might stand up during boarding, flight, and preparation for de-boarding. Our cabin mockup has almost no packet loss when being empty (see Fig. 9(a)). Packet losses become more frequent if passengers are in the cabin. Fig. 9(b) shows the results in all three flight phases with eight passengers. As passengers take their seats, the packet loss rate increases considerably for nodes at the armrest. This is consistent with our earlier results and is due to the fact that human bodies imply a significant attenuation. As most passengers remain seated during the flight, no major changes are observed for floor and ceiling nodes until the de-boarding phase. Nodes on the floor have a more stable performance. The lowest loss rate occurs for nodes on the ceiling, as most passengers do not obstruct the ceiling links even when walking. The loss rate for the ceiling nodes increases when passengers grab their baggage at the end of the flight. All results are somehow expected in this way; they illustrate the importance of a system that is capable of coping with severe shadowing independently of deployment position or flight stage.

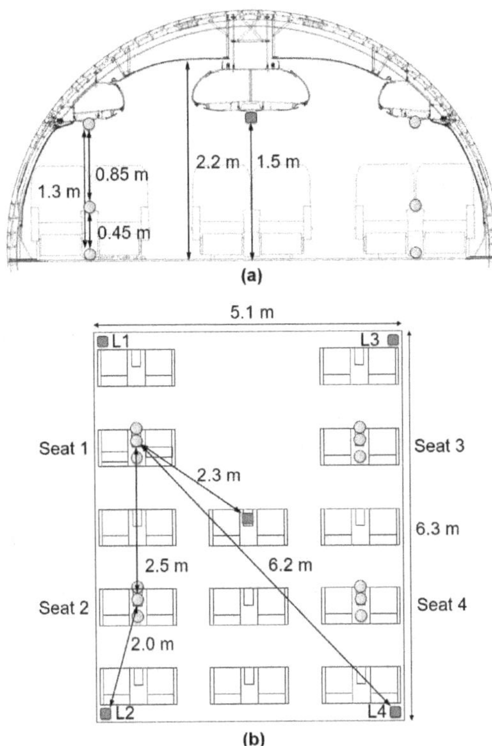

Figure 7: One-cell testbed with 12 nodes, 1 AP, 4 listeners.

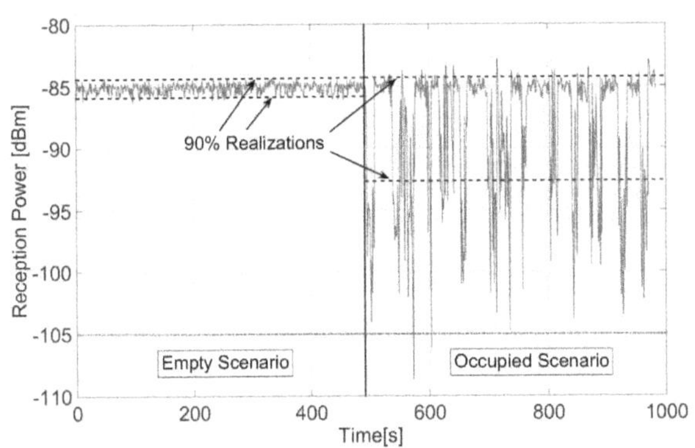

Figure 8: Received signal strength with or without mobility.

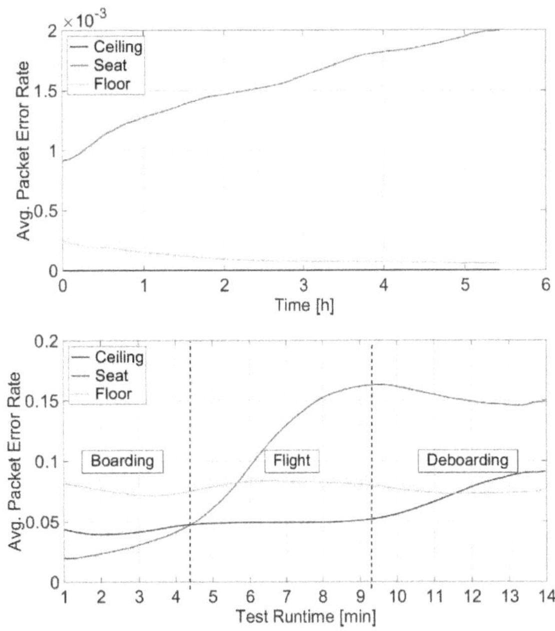

Figure 9: Average packet error rates for different deployment heights in an (a) empty and (b) occupied cabin.

3.2.3 Reliability by Diversity. We study as to how spatial and temporal diversity makes the system more reliable. The measurement runs for 30 minutes with eight people moving in the cabin. Their behavior mimics a realistic flight phase and causes link outages. Measurement results are averaged over the deployed nodes independent of their height. Results are shown in Fig. 10. The x-axis shows the reception power averaged over all available links.

The top plot shows the packet loss percentage in the TDMA baseline scenario. The loss increases and reaches 100 % well before the average receiver signal strength falls below the receiver sensitivity. In the middle and bottom plots, the stacked bars show the minimum number of listeners needed to successfully recover the lost packets from the top plot. Using spatial diversity (middle plot), the bars show the share of losses that are avoided if using one (dark blue), two (light blue), three (green), or four (yellow) extra listeners, respectively. The same colors are used in the bottom plot, which shows results for the combination of spatial and temporal diversity.

Let us give some examples. Below an average reception power of −99 dBm almost all packets are lost in the baseline case. Spatial diversity recovers all packet errors up to an average reception power of −94 dBm by adding one listener. At −100 dBm almost no packets are recoverable using only one listener, but quite some packets are recoverable with a second listener, and even more with a third one. Finally, as the reception power falls below −104 dBm (close to sensitivity), packets are only recoverable using four listeners.

Reliability is further improved with the use of temporal diversity implemented as multiple PN codes in addition to spatial diversity (bottom plot). Bars are lower in this case because the use of temporal diversity leads to fewer packet losses to be recovered by adding additional listeners. For example, for an average reception power of −95 dBm the 40 % packet loss of the baseline scenario is reduced to 20 % due to temporal diversity. This smaller percentage of lost packets determines the need of only one additional listener (bottom) compared to two listeners (middle) to recover all errors at this power level. The movement of passengers is somehow exploited to increase reliability, as an obstructed link is likely to be unobstructed after a short period. Results show that full packet error recovery is reached at minimum reception power of −86 dBm with no listener (top), −94 dBm with spatial diversity using only one listener (middle), and −96 dBm with spatio-temporal diversity and one listener (bottom).

From the design perspective, the limit to the number of redundant codes is given by the cross-correlation properties of the codes

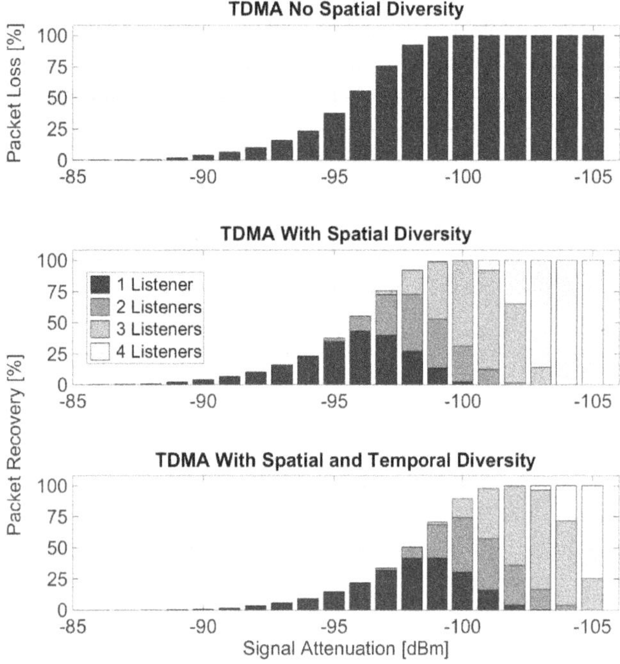

Figure 10: Packet errors for TDMA (top) and improvements by spatial diversity (middle) and spatio-temporal diversity (bottom). An overall number of 600 packets are sent per bar.

and the hardware capabilities. In our case, this yields four different codes. The limit in the degree of spatial diversity is driven by the economical cost of the installation. We can identify that the cell size fixes the average reception power (i.e., the bar to use in Fig. 10). This implies a tradeoff between the number of cells and the number of listeners needed per cell for a given reliability target. The study of this tradeoff is non-trivial and beyond the scope of this paper.

4 RELATED WORK

Most related work on UWB focuses on localization [4], tracking [10], and military applications [16]. WSNs for airplanes have been investigated for condition monitoring (e.g., to monitor mechanical parts with special interest on engines [3, 18]). There are some papers on channel sounding in airplanes. The work in [13] focuses on channel characterizations of UWB in a cabin. These measurements cover a wide range of frequency bands, including the WAIC band. Similar work was done in [15] with a further comparison of cabin and office environments. A main difference to our work is that both mentioned papers are performed with expensive channel sounding equipment, which only allows consecutive measurements to cover different locations in the cabin, and does not account for the effects of practical hardware shortcomings. In this context, the present paper is a continuation of our preliminary work [12] assessing channel features using off-the-shelf transceivers. The influence of passengers was analyzed in [9], where a UWB network was deployed to measure and compare empty and occupied cabins.

5 CONCLUSIONS AND OUTLOOK

This paper presented a proof-of-concept for a UWB sensor network in a mockup of an aircraft passenger cabin. Our experimental assessment of reliability demonstrates that spatial and temporal diversity can significantly lower the packet loss rate in this scenario. Full packet error recovery is reached at minimum signal attenuation of −85 dBm with no listener, −94 dBm using one listener, and −100 dBm using three listeners. Temporal diversity reduces the number of required listeners for a given reception power.

Future work will provide results in real and fully-occupied airplanes. The real-time protocol EchoRing [7] is an interesting alternative to our approach and should be investigated in the context of airplanes. From a more general perspective, there is a need for domain-specific interference management and security solutions with low complexity on nodes powered by energy harvesting.

ACKNOWLEDGMENTS

This work was supported by Airbus, Alpen-Adria-Universität Klagenfurt, and Lakeside Labs GmbH; it was funded by the Carinthian Economic Promotion Fund (KWF) under grant 20214/26481/38805.

REFERENCES

[1] Technical characteristics and operational objectives for wireless avionics intra-communications (WAIC). Report ITU-R M.2197, Nov. 2010.
[2] Standard for local and metropolitan area networks-Part 15.4: Low-Rate Wireless Personal Area Networks. IEEE Std 802.15.4, Sep. 2011.
[3] H. Bai, M. Atiquzzaman, and D. Lilja. Wireless sensor network for aircraft health monitoring. In *Proc. Int. Conf. Broadband Networks*, 2004.
[4] K. Balac, M. Akhmedov, M. Prevostini, and M. Malek. Topology optimization of wireless localization networks. In *Proc. European Wireless*, 2016.
[5] DecaWave UWB-WSN platform. http://www.decawave.com/.
[6] J. M. Dilhac and M. Bafleur. Energy harvesting in aeronautics for battery-free wireless sensor networks. *IEEE Aerosp. Electron. Syst. Mag.*, 29(8):18–22, 2014.
[7] C. Dombrowski and J. Gross. Echoring-meeting hard real-time constraints by decentralized wireless networks. In *Proc. NetSys*, Cottbus, Germany, Mar. 2015.
[8] I. Dove. Analysis of Radio Propagation Inside the Human Body for in-Body Localization Purposes. Master's thesis, University of Twente, 2014.
[9] M. Jacob, K. L. Chee, I. Schmidt, J. Schuur, W. Fischer, M. Schirrmacher, and T. Kurner. Influence of passengers on the UWB propagation channel within a large wide-bodied aircraft. In *Proc. European Conf. on Antennas and Propagation*, pages 882–886. IEEE, 2009.
[10] J. Ko et al. Target tracking algorithms for UWB radar network. In *Proc. Int. Conf. Radioelektronika*, pages 319–324. IEEE, 2016.
[11] D. Neuhold, J. Schmidt, U. Schilcher, G. Brandner, C. Bettstetter, J. Klaue, and D. Schupke. Poster: Towards an ultra-wide band sensor network for aircraft applications. In *Prof. ACM Int. Conf. on Embedded Wireless Syst. and Networks (EWSN)*, pages 217–218, 2016.
[12] D. Neuhold, J. F. Schmidt, C. Bettstetter, J. Klaue, and D. Schupke. Experiments with UWB aircraft sensor networks. In *Proc. IEEE INFOCOM Workshops*, pages 948–949, April 2016.
[13] H. Saghir, C. Nerguizian, J. Laurin, and F. Moupfouma. In-cabin wideband channel characterization for WAIC systems. *IEEE Trans. on Aerospace and Electronic Syst.*, 50(1):516–529, 2014.
[14] C. Sanchez. Wireless sensor networks on-board aircrafts: Design and implementation of the medium access control protocol. Master's thesis, Universitat Politecnica de Catalunya, 2013.
[15] I. Schmidt, J. Jemai, R. Piesiewicz, R. Geise, M. Schwark, T. Kurner, M. Schirrmacher, and P. Thielker. UWB propagation channels within an aircraft and an office building environment. In *Proc. IEEE Int. Symp. Antennas Propagation.* IEEE, 2008.
[16] C. Spiliotopoulos and A. Kanatas. Path-loss and time-dispersion parameters of UWB signals in a military airplane. *IEEE Antennas Wireless Propag. Lett.*, 8:790–793, 2009.
[17] D. Vujic. Wireless sensor networks applications in aircraft structural health monitoring. *Istraz. i Proj. za privredu*, 13(2):79–86, 2015.
[18] R. K. Yedavalli and R. K. Belapurkar. Application of wireless sensor networks to aircraft control and health management systems. *J. Control Theory Appl.*, 9(1):28–33, 2011.
[19] J. Zhang, P. Orlik, Z. Sahinoglu, A. Molisch, and P. Kinney. UWB systems for wireless sensor networks. *Proceedings of the IEEE*, 97(2):313–331, Feb 2009.

Lifetime-Aware Data Collection Using A Mobile Sink in WSNs with Unreachable Regions

Chuanyao Nie
The University of New South Wales
Sydney, Australia
cnie@cse.unsw.edu.au

Hui Wu
The University of New South Wales
Sydney, Australia
huiw@cse.unsw.edu.au

Wenguang Zheng
Tianjin University of Technology
Tianjin, China
wenguangz@tjut.edu.cn

ABSTRACT

Using mobile sinks to collect sensed data in WSNs (Wireless Sensor Network) is an effective technique for significantly improving the network lifetime. We investigate the problem of collecting sensed data using a mobile sink in a WSN with unreachable regions such that the network lifetime is maximized and the total tour length is minimized, and propose a polynomial-time heuristic, an ILP-based (Integer Linear Programming) heuristic and an MINLP-based (Mixed-Integer Non-Linear Programming) algorithm for constructing a shortest path routing forest for the sensor nodes in unreachable regions, two energy-efficient heuristics for partitioning the sensor nodes in reachable regions into disjoint clusters, and an efficient approach to convert the tour construction problem into a TSP (Travelling Salesman Problem). We have performed extensive simulations on 100 instances with 100, 150, 200, 250 and 300 sensor nodes in an urban area and a forest area. The simulation results show that the average lifetime of all the network instances achieved by the polynomial-time heuristic is 74% of that achieved by the ILP-based heuristic and 65% of that obtained by the MINLP-based algorithm, and our tour construction heuristic significantly outperforms the state-of-the-art tour construction heuristic EMPS.

KEYWORDS

Wireless sensor networks; network lifetime; mobile sinks; unreachable regions; clustering; routing forest

1 INTRODUCTION

A WSN may consist of several hundreds to thousands of low cost, low-power sensor nodes which are deployed in an area to perform specific tasks. Each sensor node collects the local information, processes it, and sends it to a sink (base station). Sensor nodes are typically battery powered and not practical to get recharged or replaced after deployment, especially in hostile environments [2]. Therefore, maximizing the network lifetime is an important goal when designing a WSN. Sensor nodes communicate with each other by using radio signals. Experiments show that most energy of a sensor node is consumed in communication [16]. Consequently, it is important to minimize the energy consumption of sensor nodes in communication.

In traditional WSNs, multi-hop routing is used to transfer the data sensed by each sensor node to its designated static sink. In such WSNs, the sensor nodes near a sink need to relay much more data than other sensor nodes, resulting in much shorter lifetimes [25]. In order to reduce the extra energy consumption of relaying data for sensor nodes, researchers have proposed using mobile sinks to collect sensed data from sensor nodes. In WSNs with mobile sinks, a mobile sink can travel to sensor nodes to collect data directly, significantly reducing the energy consumption of relaying data and prolonging the network lifetime.

In WSNs with a mobile sink, the problem of constructing a tour for the mobile sink to collect data is critical for prolonging the network lifetime and reducing the cost of data collection. However, the problem of minimizing the tour length of the mobile sink is NP-hard [28]. Many tour construction approaches (algorithms, heuristics and approximation algorithms) have been proposed [4, 17, 29]. One major problem with all the existing approaches that use a mobile sink to collect sensed data from sensor nodes is that they assume the mobile sink can go to anywhere in the sensed area. This assumption is not realistic as there may have some obstacles in the sensed regions, such as rivers, canyons and mountains, preventing the mobile sink from directly collecting data sensed by the sensor nodes in those regions.

In WSNs with unreachable regions, the sensor nodes in the regions with obstacles need to send their data to the sensor nodes the mobile sink can reach via a routing topology. In the areas without obstacles, the sensor nodes may have different loads (amount of data to be sent) as some of them need to relay the data of the sensor nodes in the regions with obstacles. For those sensor nodes with lower loads, they can form clusters so that the mobile sink can collect the data of all the sensor nodes of each cluster by travelling to each cluster head only without reducing the network lifetime, resulting in a shorter tour length for the mobile sink. There are three major challenges in such WSNs. The first challenge is to find a good routing topology for all the sensor nodes in the regions with obstacles such that their sensed data can be routed to sensor nodes reachable by the mobile sink and the maximum load of all the sensor nodes is minimized. The second challenge is to create clusters for the sensor nodes in the regions without any obstacles and select a cluster head for each cluster such that the network lifetime will not decrease due to clustering. The third challenge is to construct a tour for the mobile sink to collect data from all the cluster heads such that the total tour cost is minimized.

In this paper, we investigate the network lifetime-aware data collection problem for WSNs with unreachable regions using a

MSWiM'17, November 21-25, 2017, Miami, FL, USA
 ISBN 978-1-4503-5162-1/17/11...$15.00
DOI: http://dx.doi.org/10.1145/3127540.3127544

mobile sink. To the best of our knowledge, our work is the first one considering unreachable regions. We make the following major contributions:

(1) We propose a polynomial-time heuristic, an ILP-based heuristic and an MINLP-based algorithm for constructing a shortest path routing forest via which the sensed data of each sensor node in an unreachable region can be sent to a sensor node in reachable regions.
(2) We propose two energy efficient clustering heuristics to form clusters for the sensor nodes in reachable regions.
(3) We propose an efficient approach to convert the tour construction problem into a TSP.
(4) We have performed extensive simulations on 100 instances with 100, 150, 200, 250 and 300 sensor nodes in an urban area and a forest area. The simulation results show that the average lifetime of all the network instances achieved by the polynomial-time heuristic is 74% of that achieved by the ILP-based heuristic and 65% of that obtained by the MINLP-based algorithm. We also compare our tour construction heuristic with the state-of-the-art tour construction heuristic EMPS [26]. The simulation results show that our tour construction heuristic significantly outperforms EMPS.

The remainder of this paper is organized as follows. Section 2 summarizes the related work. Section 3 describes the network model. Section 4 proposes a polynomial-time heuristic, an ILP-based heuristic and an MINLP-based algorithm for constructing a shortest path routing forest. Section 5 presents two energy efficient clustering heuristics for constructing clusters for the sensor nodes in reachable regions. Section 6 proposes an efficient approach to convert the tour construction problem into a TSP. Section 7 shows the simulation results and analysis. Lastly, Section 8 proposes future research problems and concludes this paper.

2 RELATED WORK

Data collection in WSNs depends on sink mobility. Sink mobility can be classified into three categories, namely, uncontrollable mobility, restricted mobility, and unrestricted mobility [5]. In the first category [8, 21], mobile sinks are often mounted on some animals moving randomly to collect data from the sensor nodes. The major challenge is to dynamically maintain a routing topology such that the network lifetime is maximized. In the second category, mobile sinks are often attached to vehicles that are constrained to move along certain roads for data collection [7, 22]. Since the tour of mobile sinks is known in advance, the major challenge is to construct an efficient static routing topology for the sensor nodes far from the tour to send their data to the sensor nodes near the tour. In the last category, a mobile sink is attached to a vehicle and the tour of the vehicle is constructed at the design stage. All the previous approaches in this category assume that the mobile sink can go to anywhere in the sensed area. Therefore, the major challenge is to design an optimal tour for the mobile sink to improve the network performance. The problem investigated in this paper belongs to the last category with additional unreachable regions. The subsequent survey will focus on the last category.

Many tour construction approaches for WSNs with mobile sinks under unrestricted mobility have been proposed. All the previous approaches can be classified into two categories, namely, single optimization objective approaches and multiple optimization objective approaches.

2.1 Single Optimization Objective Approaches

One of the optimization objective of the tour design approaches is to prolong the network lifetime. Lou et al. [11] assume that the sensor nodes are densely deployed within a circle and there is only one sink for data collection, and give a theoretical analysis on why using a mobile sink will have a longer network lifetime than using a static sink. They conclude that the tour of the mobile sink should follow the periphery of the network. Furthermore, they propose a multi-hop routing heuristic that significantly improves the network lifetime. Ma et al. [13] propose an energy-efficient heuristic for designing a tour for the mobile sink. The tour is constructed iteratively based on geometric distribution of the sensor nodes. In each iteration, the mobile sink chooses a location to stop for balancing the workload of the sensor nodes. They use the Dijkstra shortest path algorithm to construct a multi-hop routing forest for each sensor node to send its data to the mobile sink. Basagni et al. [1] formulate the tour design problem into an MILP (Mixed Integer Linear Programming) problem. The solution of the MILP problem determines the tour of the mobile sink, assuming that each sensor node sends its data to the mobile sink via multi-hop routing. Furthermore, they propose a distributed, localized heuristics named GMRE (Greedy Maximum Residual Energy) for moving the sink from its current location to the next one, and a simple distributed mobility scheme for the sink to move randomly throughout the network. Tashtarian et al. [24] jointly determine the optimal tour of the mobile sink and the routing topology from sensor nodes to the mobile sink. They propose an algorithm that considers the tour of the mobile sink as a connected line segments and formulate the tour design problem into an MINLP problem.

Another optimization objective of tour construction is to minimize the tour length of the mobile sink. Ma et al. [28] prove that the problem of minimizing the tour length of the mobile sink is NP-hard, and propose a greedy heuristic for constructing the tour of the mobile sink considering the location of each sensor node together with the distance between neighbour sensor nodes, where each sensor node sends its data to the mobile sink directly. Tang et al. [23] propose a tour design algorithm that formulates the tour design problem into an ILP problem, and propose a heuristic. The heuristic chooses some anchor points by considering the locations of all the sensor nodes and their transmission ranges. The mobile sink traverses all the anchor points to collect data from each sensor node directly.

2.2 Multiple Optimization Objective Approaches

Nakayama et al. [17] propose a heuristic to achieve better network lifetime and provide fault-resilience in case of malfunctions of some sensor nodes due to attacks. Sensor nodes are partitioned into clusters and the mobile sink traverses through the cluster centers to collect data. The clusters are constructed by dividing the sensed area into geometric rectangles. The tour of the mobile sink is designed by using an approximate solution of TSP.

Xing et al. [27] propose a heuristic to achieve a balance between the network lifetime and data collection delay. The heuristic selects a subset of sensor nodes as the rendezvous nodes, and uses multi-hop routing for other nodes sending their data to the rendezvous nodes. The mobile sink traverses all the rendezvous nodes to collect data.

Jerew et al. [9] propose a clustering-based heuristic for finding a tour of the mobile sink such that the energy consumption of the sensor nodes within any cluster is balanced and the tour length of the mobile sink is bounded by a given value. The heuristic equally divides the sensed area into sub-areas by radial lines from the center of the sensed area. Each sensor node sends its data to the cluster head, and the mobile sink traverses all the cluster heads to collect data.

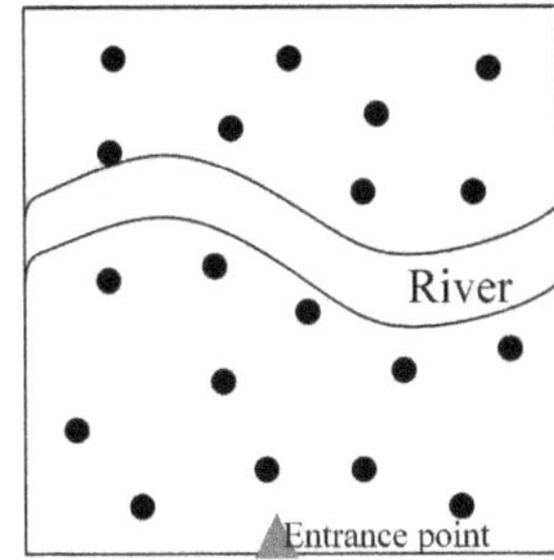

Figure 1: An example of the distribution of sensor nodes in a sensed area

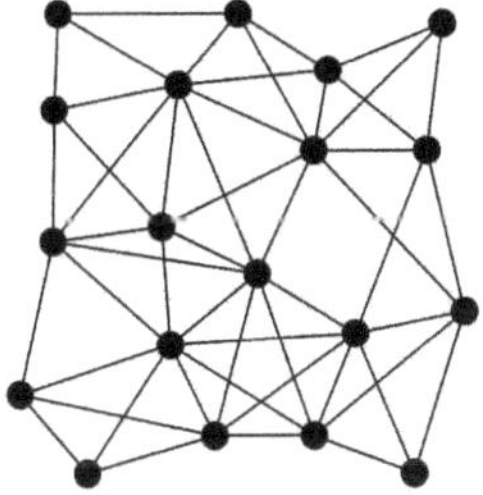

Figure 2: The connectivity graph of the sensor nodes in Figure 1

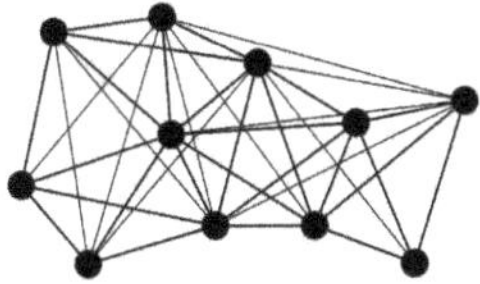

Figure 3: The reachability graph of the sensor nodes in Figure 1

Liang et al. [10] propose a time-sensitive data gathering approach for WSNs with a mobile sink such that the network lifetime is maximized, subject to a set of constraints on the mobile sink: the maximum travel distance, the maximum distance of each movement, and the minimum sojourn time at each sojourn location. This approach chooses a subset of sensor nodes as sojourn nodes by constructing a load-balanced spanning forest. Other sensor nodes send their data to the sojourn nodes via the routing forest. This approach uses LP (Linear Programming) to determine the tour of the mobile sink and the sojourn time at each sojourn location.

Yang et al. [30] propose a tour construction approach considering the network lifetime, the maximum hops from sensor nodes to the mobile sink, and the maximum tour length of the mobile sink. A subset of sensor nodes are selected as polling points that buffer locally the aggregated data and upload the data to the mobile sink when it arrives. A multi-hop routing heuristic is proposed for other sensor nodes sending their data to the polling points such that the packet relay is bounded within a given number of hops.

Zhao et al. [31] propose a distributed clustering-based approach to achieve better network lifetime and lower data collection delay. This approach constructs clusters such that each cluster has two cluster heads. They construct clusters by considering the location and the residual energy of each sensor node. Two sensor nodes with the highest residual energy are selected as cluster heads within a cluster. A mobile sink equipped with two antennas collects data from the two cluster heads simultaneously using MU-MIMO (Multi-User Multiple-Input and Multiple-Output) technique.

Yue et al. [29] propose an approach for data collection in WSNs with a mobile sink to maximize the network lifetime and minimize the tour length of the mobile sink. This approach partitions the sensor nodes into clusters considering the sensor nodes distribution. Then, it formulates the tour design problem into a TSP and uses the artificial bee colony algorithm to solve the TSP. Wang et al. [26] propose another clustering-based tour design heuristic to prolong the network lifetime and reduce the data transmission delay. Sensor nodes are partitioned into clusters considering the residual energy and the location of each sensor node. The tour of the mobile sink is designed based on the residual energy of each cluster head.

3 NETWORK MODEL

The target WSN consists of a set $V = \{v_1, v_2, \cdots, v_n\}$ of n sensor nodes, deployed on a sensed area to continuously monitor the environment. The locations of all the sensor nodes are fixed and known. All the sensor nodes are identical with the same transmission range and the same initial energy level. Each sensor node generates one packet of data per time unit. Each sensor unreachable from the mobile sink sends its data to a sensor node reachable from the mobile sink via a routing topology.

We use an undirected graph, named connectivity graph, to represent the wireless connectivity between sensor nodes in the WSN. The connectivity graph G_c is defined as follows: $G_c = (V, E_c)$, where $E_c = \{(v_i, v_j)$: v_i and v_j can communication with each other via wireless communication directly$\}$. We assumed that the connectivity graph is connected. Figure 1 shows an example of the distribution of sensor nodes in a sensed area. Figure 2 shows the connectivity graph of the sensors in Figure 1.

We use a mobile sink to collect data from all the sensor nodes. However, there are obstacles in the sensed area such that the mobile sink cannot travel to some sensor nodes to collect their data directly. We use another undirected graph, named reachability graph, to represent the reachability between sensor nodes when the mobile sink collects data. The reachability graph G_r is defined as follows: $G_r = (V', E_r)$, where V' is a set of sensor nodes that the mobile sink can travel to and $E_r = \{(v_i, v_j)$: the mobile sink can travel between v_i and v_j $\}$. We assume that the reachability graph is connected. Figure 3 shows an example of the reachability graph for the sensor nodes reachable from the mobile sink in Figure 1.

Based on the reachability graph, all the sensor nodes are partitioned into two categories, namely, reachable sensor nodes and unreachable sensor nodes. The reachable sensor nodes are the sensor nodes in the reachability graph and the unreachable sensor nodes are the sensor nodes not in the reachability graph. The unreachable sensor nodes need to send their data to the reachable sensor nodes via a routing topology. We construct a shortest path forest for the unreachable sensor nodes to send their data to the reachable sensor nodes. In the shortest path forest, each root is a reachable sensor node and all the other nodes are unreachable sensor nodes. We partition the reachable sensor nodes into disjoint clusters. Each cluster has a cluster head. Other nodes in each cluster send their data and the data received from unreachable sensor nodes to their cluster head. The mobile sink travels to all the cluster heads to collect data via a tour.

We consider the energy consumption of each sensor node in transmitting and receiving data only. For each sensor node, α is the energy consumed to receive one packet, and β is the energy consumed to transmit one packet. The lifetime of a WSN is the elapsed time when the first sensor node uses up it energy.

4 SHORTEST PATH ROUTING FOREST CONSTRUCTION

In this section, we propose a polynomial-time heuristic, an ILP-based heuristic and an MINLP-based algorithm for constructing a shortest path routing forest for the unreachable sensor nodes to send their data to reachable sensor nodes.

4.1 Candidate Graph Construction

Our polynomial-time heuristic, ILP-based heuristic and MINLP-based algorithm for constructing a shortest path routing forest are based on a candidate graph $G_p = (V_p, E_p)$ that satisfies the following constraints:

(1) G_p is a directed acyclic graph.
(2) Each source node in G_p, a node with zero in-degree, denotes a sensor node reachable from the mobile sink and each non-source node represents a sensor node unreachable from the mobile sink.
(3) Each path from a source node to a non-source node is a shortest path.

The candidate graph is constructed as follows:

(1) Partition the sensor nodes in the connectivity graph into disjoint layers $L_i (i = 1, 2, \cdots, k)$ as follows:
   (a) The first layer L_1 consists of all the reachable sensor nodes each of which has at least one edge to an unreachable sensor node in the connectivity graph.
   (b) The nodes in layer $L_i (i = 2, 3, \cdots, k)$ consists of all the unreachable sensor nodes each of which has at least one edge to a node in layer L_{i-1} in the connectivity graph.
(2) The set V_p of vertices of the candidate graph consists of all the sensor nodes in all the layers.
(3) The set E_p of edges of the candidate graph is constructed as follows:
   - For each layer $L_i (i = 1, 2, \cdots, k-1)$, do the following:
     - For each sensor node v_s in layer L_i, if there is a node v_t in L_{i+1} such that the edge (v_s, v_t) is in the connectivity graph, add the directed edge (v_s, v_t) to E_p.

Figure 4 shows an example of converting the connectivity graph to a candidate graph.

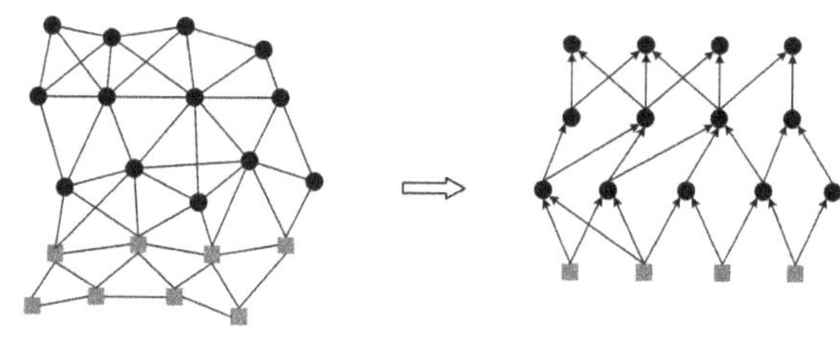

Figure 4: An example of the candidate graph construction

We introduce the following notations:

- PS_i: a set of all the immediate predecessors of v_i in the candidate graph. Each sensor node in PS_i is a candidate parent of v_i in the shortest path forest.
- CS_i: a set of all the immediate successors of v_i in the candidate graph. Each sensor node in CS_i is a candidate child of v_i in the shortest path forest.

It can be easily seen that the candidate graph can be constructed in $O(e)$ time, where e is the number of edges in the connectivity graph.

4.2 Polynomial-Time Heuristic

Our polynomial-time heuristic constructs a shortest path forest incrementally. It starts with the bottom layer L_k and works towards the second layer L_2, where k is the longest path length of the candidate graph. When working with a specific layer L_m, it assigns a parent node from the nodes in layer L_{m-1} to each sensor node in layer L_m, aiming at minimizing the maximum energy consumption of all the sensor nodes in layer L_{m-1}.

We introduce the following additional notations:

- $size(v_i)$: the number of sensor nodes in the subtree rooted at the sensor node v_i in the partial shortest path forest constructed so far.
- e_i: the energy consumed by the sensor node v_i per unit time under the current partial shortest path forest. Initially, e_i is equal to β. Each time when v_i is selected as the

parent of a sensor node v_j, e_i is updated as follows: $e_i = e_i + size(v_j) * \alpha + size(v_j) * \beta$.

We define two types of priorities: a priority for each sensor node in layer L_m and a priority for each sensor node in layer L_{m-1}. The priority $P_1(v_i)$ of each sensor node v_i in layer L_m is a 2-tuple defined as follows:

$$P_1(v_i) = (|PS_i|, e_i), \tag{1}$$

where $|PS_i|$ is the number of sensor nodes in the set PS_i of candidate parents of v_i. The priority $P_2(v_j)$ of each sensor node v_j in layer L_{m-1} is a 2-tuple defined as follows:

$$P_2(v_j) = (e_j, |CS_i|), \tag{2}$$

where $|CS_i|$ is the number of sensor nodes in the set CS_i of candidate children of v_i.

For both types of priorities, the lexicographical order is used to compare two priorities, and a smaller tuple implies a higher priority. Note that the priority of each sensor node may be changed dynamically during the parent selection process.

Our heuristic works for each layer $L_m(m = k, k-1, \cdots, 2)$ as follows:

(1) For each sensor node v_i in layer L_m, compute its priority $P_1(v_i)$.
(2) Select a sensor node v_s which has the highest priority $P_1(v_s)$ among all the sensor nodes in layer L_m without a parent in the partial shortest path forest.
(3) For each sensor node v_j in v_s's candidate parent set PS_s, compute the priority $P_2(v_j)$.
(4) Select a sensor node v_t which has the highest priority $P_2(v_t)$ among all the sensor nodes in PS_s as the parent of v_s.
(5) Update e_t of v_t as follows:
   - $e_t = e_t + size(v_s) * \alpha + size(v_s) * \beta$.

Next, we analyse the time complexity of our polynomial-time heuristic as follows:

(1) It takes $O(e)$ to compute the priorities of all the sensor nodes, where e is the number of edges in the candidate graph.
(2) We can use two priority queues for all the sensor nodes in each layer, one for $P_1(v_j)$'s and one for $P_2(v_j)$'s. Therefore, it takes $O(\log(|L_m|)$ time to select a sensor node v_s which has the highest priority $P_1(v_s)$ and $O(\log(|L_{m-1}|)$ time to select a sensor node v_t which has the highest priority $P_2(v_t)$, where $|L_m|$ and $|L_{m-1}|$ are the numbers of sensor nodes in L_m and L_{m-1}, respectively. Therefore, the total time complexity for selecting all the parents is $O(n \log n)$, where n is the number of sensor nodes in the candidate graph.

As a result, the time complexity of our polynomial-time heuristic is $O(e+n \log n)$.

4.3 ILP-Based Heuristic

Similar to our polynomial-time heuristic, our ILP-based heuristic constructs a shortest path forest in a bottom up way. The difference is that our ILP-based heuristic formulates the problem of assigning a parent to each sensor node in layer $L_m(m=k, k-1, \cdots, 2)$ as an ILP problem.

Next, we show how to use ILP to find a locally optimal assignment of a parent in layer L_{m-1} for each sensor node in layer $L_m(m=k, k-1, \cdots, 2)$.

For each edge (v_j, v_i) in the candidate graph, where v_j is in layer L_{m-1} and v_i is in layer L_m, we introduce a binary decision variable $X_{j,i}$ as follows:

$$X_{j,i} = \begin{cases} 1 & v_j \text{ is selected as the parent of } v_i \\ 0 & \text{otherwise} \end{cases} \tag{3}$$

Therefore, for each sensor node v_i in layer L_m, we have the following parent selection constraint:

$$\sum_{v_j \in PS_i} X_{j,i} = 1 \tag{4}$$

The above constraint implies that among all the candidate parents of v_i, only one sensor node can be selected as the parent of v_i.

For each sensor node $v_j \in L_{m-1}$, we have the following constraint on e_j:

$$e_j = \beta + \sum_{v_i \in CS_j} X_{j,i} * size(v_i) * (\alpha + \beta) \tag{5}$$

The optimization objective function is to minimize the maximum total energy consumption of all the sensor nodes in layer L_{m-1} as follows:

$$\min \max_{v_j \in L_{m-1}} \{e_j\} \tag{6}$$

4.4 MINLP-Based Algorithm

Our MINLP-based algorithm formulates the problem of constructing a shortest path forest as an MINLP problem. For each layer $L_m(m=k, k-1, \cdots, 2)$, we assign a parent in L_{m-1} to each sensor node in L_m such that the maximum energy consumption per time unit of all the sensor nodes is minimized. Next, we show how to use MINLP to find an optimal assignment of a parent for each sensor node in layer $L_m(m=k, k-1, \cdots, 2)$.

Similar to the ILP-based heuristic, for each sensor node v_i, we have the following parent selection constraint:

$$\sum_{v_j \in PS_i} X_{j,i} = 1 \tag{7}$$

The binary decision variable $X_{j,i}$ is defined in the same way as in the ILP-based heuristic.

For each sensor node v_j, if it is in layer L_k, it is a leaf node in the routing forest. Therefore, we have the following constraint on $size(v_j)$:

$$size(v_j) = \begin{cases} 1 & v_j \text{ is in layer } L_k \\ \sum_{v_i \in CS_j} X_{j,i} * size(v_i) + 1 & \text{otherwise} \end{cases} \tag{8}$$

For each sensor node v_j, we have the following constraint on e_j:

$$e_j = \beta + \sum_{v_i \in CS_j} X_{j,i} * size(v_i) * (\alpha + \beta) \tag{9}$$

Our optimization objective function is as follows:

$$\min \max_{v_j \in L_1} \{e_j\} \tag{10}$$

where L_1 is a set of all the sensor nodes in the first layer. The reason is that the sensor node with the maximum energy consumption per time unit must be in the first layer.

5 CLUSTER CONSTRUCTION

Via a shortest path forest, all the unreachable sensor nodes send their data to reachable sensor nodes. As a result, reachable sensor nodes may have different loads. In order to minimize the total tour cost, we need to construct clusters such that adjacent reachable sensor nodes with low loads form a cluster without reducing the network lifetime.

Next, we propose two energy efficient clustering heuristics, namely Cluster-Expansion heuristic and Cluster-Merge heuristic.

We introduce the following additional notations:

- w_i: the weight of a reachable sensor node v_i, which is the number of packets v_i needs to send per time unit. If a reachable sensor node v_i is a root node of a tree in the shortest path routing forest, its weight w_i equals to the total number of sensor nodes of the tree. Otherwise, $w_i = 1$.
- cw_i: the weight of a cluster c_i, which is the sum of the weights of all the sensor nodes in cluster c_i.
- w_{max}: the maximum weight of all the reachable sensor nodes.

The objective of our clustering heuristics is to construct clusters such that the number of clusters is minimized while the maximum weight of all the clusters is not greater than w_{max}.

5.1 Cluster-Expansion Heuristic

Given a cluster c_i of sensor nodes and a sensor node v_j that is not in c_i, v_j is a neighbour node of c_i if v_j is adjacent to a sensor node in c_i in the connectivity graph.

Our Cluster-Expansion heuristic incrementally expands a cluster by adding a neighbour sensor node to the cluster providing that the cluster weight is not greater than w_{max}. It works as follows:

1. Repeat the following steps until each reachable sensor node is in a cluster:
   (a) Find a reachable sensor node v_p which has the lowest weight and is not in any cluster.
   (b) Create a new cluster c_s containing v_p only.
   (c) $cw_s = w_p$.
   (d) Repeat the following steps until c_s is finalized:
      (i) Find a neighbour node v_q of cluster c_s which has the lowest weight.
      (ii) If $cw_s + w_q \leq w_{max}$, add v_q to cluster c_s and update the cluster weight: $cw_s = cw_s + w_q$. Otherwise, c_s is finalized.

Next, we analyse the time complexity of our Cluster-Merge heuristic. Creating a cluster c_i takes $O(|c_i|e_i)$ time, where $|c_i|$ is the number of sensor nodes in c_i, and e_i the total degree of all the reachable sensor nodes in c_i. Therefore, creating all the clusters takes $O(ne)$ time, where n is the number of reachable sensor nodes and e is the number of edges in the connectivity graph of all the reachable sensor nodes.

5.2 Cluster-Merge Heuristic

Our Cluster-Merge heuristic converts all the reachable sensor nodes into a Voronoi Diagram [20]. Let P be a set of n distinct points called sites. The Voronoi Diagram [20] of P is the subdivision of the plane into n cells, one for each site. A point q lies in the cell of a site $p_i \in P$ if and only if the Euclidean distance between q and p_i is less than the Euclidean distance between q and p_j ($p_j \in P$ and $i \neq j$). The edges of the Voronoi Diagram are all the points in the plane that are equidistant to the two nearest sites. Figure 5 shows an example of converting reachable sensor nodes into a Voronoi Diagram.

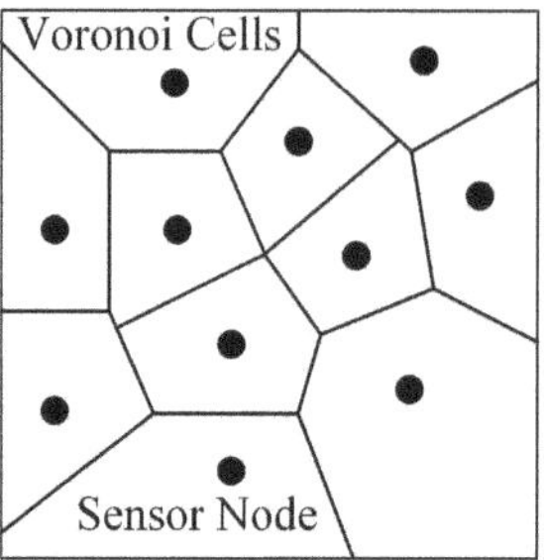

Figure 5: An example of the Voronoi Diagram

A sensor node v_i is a neighbour of a sensor node v_j if the Voronoi cells of v_i and v_j share a Voronoi edge. A cluster c_i is a neighbour of a cluster c_j if there are two sensor nodes $v_s \in c_i$ and $v_t \in c_j$ such that v_s is a neighbour of v_t.

Our Cluster-Merge heuristic works as follows:

1. Create the Voronoi Diagram for all the reachable sensor nodes.
2. For each reachable sensor node v_i, create a cluster c_s containing v_i and set the weight cw_s of c_s to w_i.
3. Repeat the following steps until no two clusters can be merged into a single cluster.
   (a) Find a cluster c_p with the lowest weight.
   (b) Find a neighbour cluster c_q of c_p such that c_q has the lowest weight among all the neighbour clusters of c_p.
   (c) If $cw_p + cw_q \leq w_{max}$, merge c_q and c_p into a new cluster c_t: $c_t = c_p \cup c_q$, and set the weight cw_t of c_t to $cw_p + cw_q$.

Next, we analyse the time complexity of our Cluster-Merge heuristic as follows:

1. It takes $O(n \log n)$ time to construct the Voronoi Diagram for all the reachable sensor nodes [3], where n is the number of reachable sensor nodes.
2. We can use an adaptable priority queue for all the clusters. Therefore, it takes $O(\log m)$ time to find a cluster with the lowest weight, where m is the number of clusters.
3. We need to maintain a connectivity graph for all the clusters, which takes $O(e)$ time, where e is the number of edges in the Voronoi Diagram for all the reachable sensor nodes.
4. Finding a neighbour cluster c_q with the lowest weight of a cluster c_p takes $O(deg(c_p))$ time, where $deg(c_p)$ is the degree of c_p in the connectivity graph of clusters. Since the total degree of all the clusters is no more than $2e$, the

total time complexity of finding all the neighbour clusters is $O(e)$.

(5) The time complexity of merging all the clusters is $m \log m$.

As a result, the time complexity of our Cluster-Merge heuristic is $O(e+n \log n)$.

6 TOUR CONSTRUCTION

After creating clusters for all the reachable sensor nodes, we need to find a tour for the mobile sink to collect the data from all the cluster heads such that the total tour cost, namely, the total tour length, is minimized. The problem of finding a tour such that the total tour length is minimized is NP-hard [28]. Assume that the mobile sink is at an entrance point at the beginning. The tour starts at the entrance point, traverses all the cluster heads and returns to the entrance point.

Next, we propose a heuristic for selecting the cluster head of each cluster and constructing a tour for the mobile sink to collect data from all the cluster heads.

Given two clusters c_s and c_t, c_s is a neighbour cluster of c_t if there are two sensor nodes $v_p \in c_s$ and $v_q \in c_t$ such that there is an edge between v_p and v_q in the connectivity graph. Notice that this definition is different from that in Section 5.2.

We introduce the following additional notations:

- H_i: the set of neighbour clusters of a cluster c_i.
- $d_{min}(v_i, v_j)$: the minimum travel distance between a sensor node v_i and a sensor node v_j.

For each sensor node v_i in a cluster c_s, we introduce a variable $sum(v_i)$ that is calculated as follows:

$$sum(v_i) = \sum_{c_t \in H_s} \sum_{v_j \in c_t} d_{min}(v_i, v_j) \tag{11}$$

For each cluster c_s, we calculate $sum(v_i)$ for each sensor node v_i in c_s. The sensor node v_{ch_s} in c_s with the smallest value of $sum(v_{ch_s})$ is selected as the cluster head of c_s.

Assume that there are l clusters. Let $V_{CH} = \{v_{ch_1}, v_{ch_2}, \cdots, v_{ch_l}\}$ be a set of all the cluster heads. In order to construct the tour of the mobile sink, we construct another undirected graph, namely cluster head reachability graph. In the cluster head reachability graph $G_{CH} = (V_{CH} \cup \{EP\}, E_{CH})$, the set of vertices consists of all the cluster heads and the entrance point EP. The set E_{CH} of edges consists of all the edges between each pair of cluster heads and the edges between the entrance point and each cluster head. We formulate the tour construction problem as a TSP as follows:

- Given the cluster head reachability graph, construct a tour for the mobile sink to visit each cluster head exactly once and return to the entrance point such that the total tour length is minimized.

We apply the algorithm proposed in [6] to solve this TSP problem.

7 SIMULATION RESULTS

To the best of our knowledge, our work is the first one that investigates the lifetime-aware data collection problem in WSNs with unreachable regions using a mobile sink. Our clustering heuristics do not change the maximum load of all the reachable sensor nodes. Therefore, they do not affect the network lifetime. We use two performance metrics to evaluate the performance of our proposed heuristics and algorithm, network lifetime and tour length. As defined in Section 3, the network lifetime is the elapsed time when the first sensor node depletes its energy. The tour length is the total distance of the tour for the mobile sink to collect data from all the cluster heads. We use the network lifetime metric to evaluate our polynomial-time heuristic, ILP-based heuristic, and MINLP-based algorithm for constructing a shortest path forest, and the tour length metric to evaluate our clustering heuristics. We use the state-of-the-art heuristic EMPS [26] to compare the performance of our tour construction heuristics based on the Cluster-Expansion Heuristic and the Cluster-Merge Heuristic.

7.1 Setup

We select two real sensed areas, Clear Island Lake, Gold Coast, Queensland, Australia, and Royol National Park, New South Wales, Australia, from Google Maps. Subsequently, we call these two sensed areas the urban area and the forest area, respectively. We generate 100 network instances in the two areas, and vary the number of sensor nodes from 100 to 300 with an increment of 50. For each scenario with a fixed number of sensor nodes, we generate 10 instances. For each instance, sensor nodes are randomly deployed in a $1000m * 1000m$ square area, and the entrance point of the mobile sink is located at the bottom center of the area. Each sensor node generates one packet of data per time unit. The initial energy of each sensor node is $1KJ$. The transmission range is fixed to $200m$. The energy consumed to receive one packet of data is $\alpha = 0.001\ KJ$ while the energy consumed to transmit one packet of data is $\beta = 0.002\ KJ$. Figure 6 and Figure 7 show examples of the distribution, the connectivity graph, and the reachability graph of 200 sensor nodes in the urban area and the forest area.

The hardware platform is Intel Core i5-3470 with a clock speed of 3.20 Ghz, a memory size of 8 GB and a cache size of 8192 MB. The solver for the ILP problems is *Intlinprog* Solver of MATLAB and the solver for the MINLP problems is *MIDACO* Solver [12].

7.2 Simulation Results

Figure 8 and Figure 9 show the network lifetimes achieved by the polynomial-time heuristic, the ILP-based heuristic and the MINLP-based algorithm for constructing a shortest path routing forest in the urban area and the forest area. The simulation results show that the heuristic obtains comparable network lifetimes compared with the ILP-based heuristic and the MINLP-based algorithm.

Comparing the polynomial-time heuristic with the ILP-based heuristic, the minimum ratio between the network lifetime obtained by the polynomial-time heuristic and the network lifetime obtained by the ILP-based heuristic is 57% while the maximum ratio is 89%. The average ratios for the urban area and the forest area are 80% and 68%, respectively. The average ratio for all the instances is 74%.

In comparison between the polynomial-time heuristic and the MINLP-based algorithm, the minimum ratio between the network lifetime obtained by the polynomial-time heuristic and the network lifetime obtained by the MINLP-based algorithm is 53% while the maximum ratio is 84%. The average ratios for the urban area and the forest area are 71% and 59%, respectively. The average ratio for all the instances is 65%.

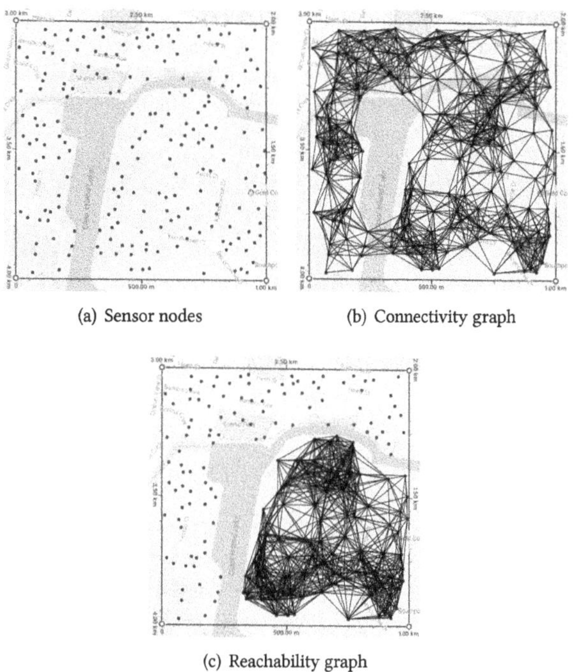
(a) Sensor nodes (b) Connectivity graph

(c) Reachability graph

Figure 6: An example of 200 sensor nodes in the urban area

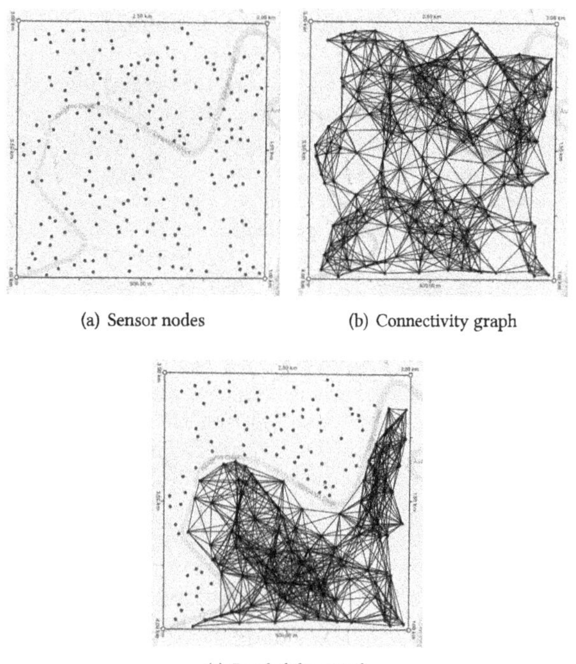
(a) Sensor nodes (b) Connectivity graph

(c) Reachability graph

Figure 7: An example of 200 sensor nodes in the forest area

In comparison between the ILP-based heuristic and the MINLP-based algorithm, the minimum ratio between the network lifetime

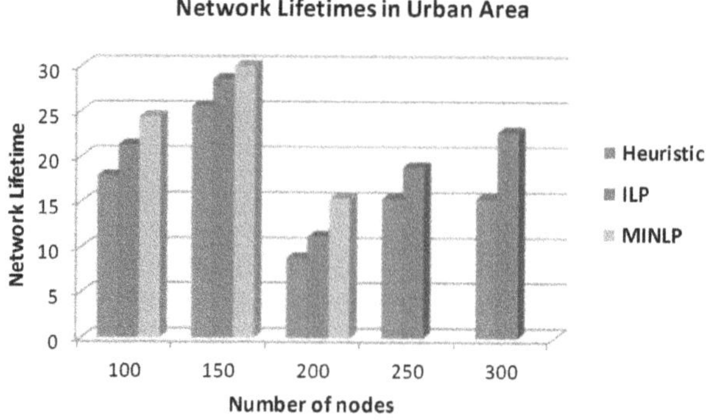

Figure 8: Network lifetimes in the urban area

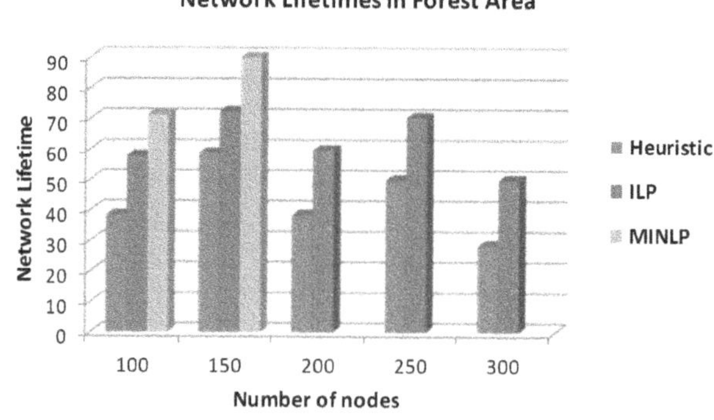

Figure 9: Network lifetimes in the forest area

obtained by the ILP-based heuristic and the network lifetime obtained by the MINLP-based algorithm is 73% while the maximum ratio is 94%. The average ratios for the urban area and the forest area are 85% and 80%, respectively. The average ratio for all the instances is 82%.

Figure 10 and Figure 11 show the running times of the polynomial-time heuristic, the ILP-based heuristic and the MINLP-based algorithm for constructing a shortest path routing forest in the urban area and the forest area. The simulation results show that the polynomial-time heuristic and the ILP-based heuristic always construct a shortest path routing forest in a reasonable amount of time for all the instances while the MINLP-based algorithm does not scale. For example, in the urban area, the MINLP-based algorithm fails to construct the shortest path routing forest for the instances with more than 250 nodes in 3 days. The reason that the ILP-based heuristic takes a reasonable amount of time is that each layer has a limited number of sensor nodes, resulting in a small number of decision variables and constraints. On the other hand, the MINLP problem is a well-known NP-complete problem, and our MINLP problem has much more decision variables and constraints than the corresponding ILP problem. Consequently, our MINLP-based algorithm does not scale.

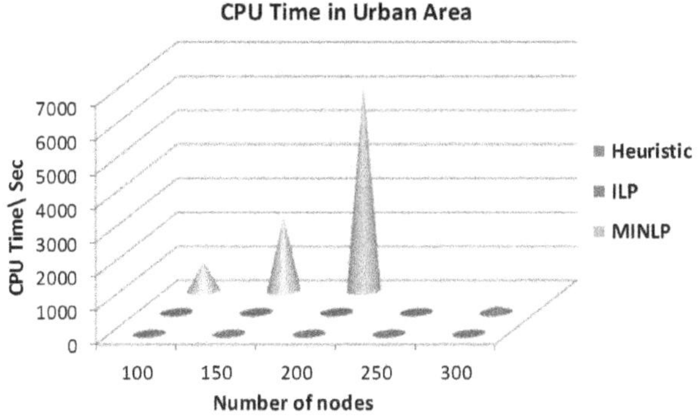

Figure 10: Running times for the urban area

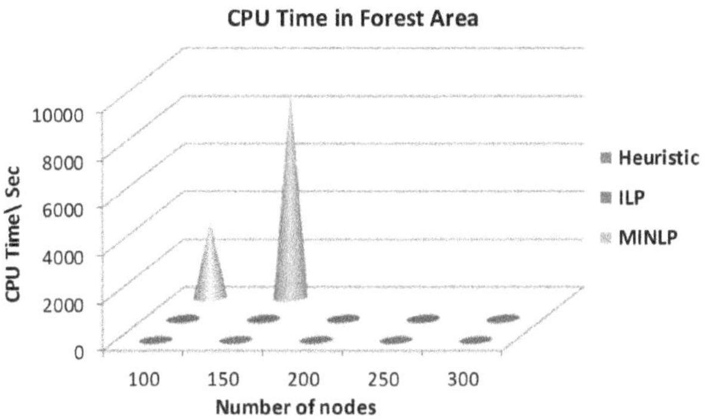

Figure 11: Running times for the forest area

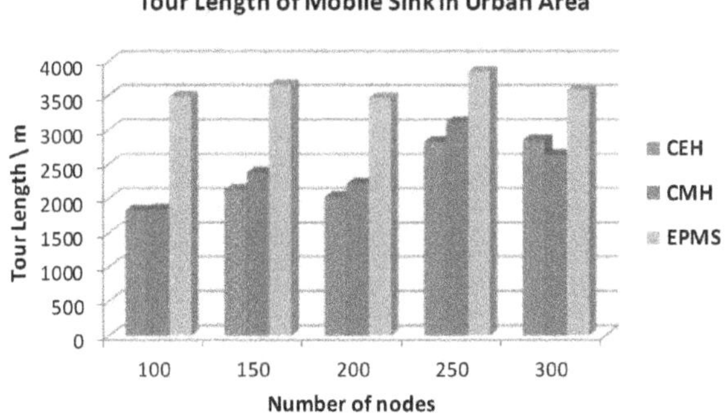

Figure 12: Tour length of the mobile sink in the urban area

Figure 12 and Figure 13 show the tour lengths of the mobile sink with our tour construction heuristic based on the Cluster-Expansion Heuristic (CEH), our tour construction heuristic based on the Cluster-Merge Heuristic (CMH), and the state-of-the-art heuristic EMPS [26], in the urban area and the forest area, respectively.

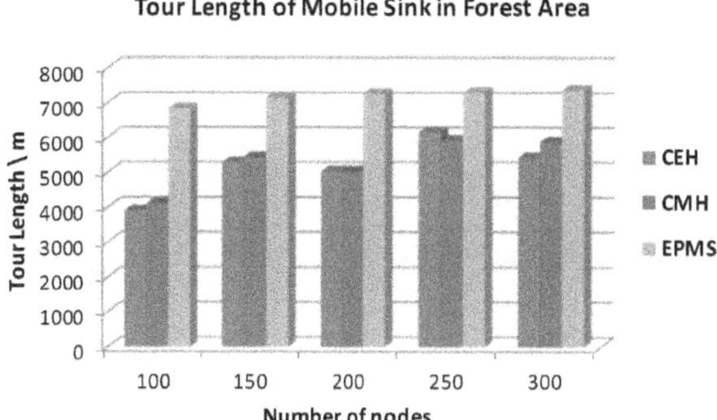

Figure 13: Tour length of the mobile sink in the forest area

The simulation results show that both our tour construction heuristics based on the Cluster-Expansion Heuristic and the Cluster-Merge Heuristic achieve better performance than the EMPS heuristic. Comparing our tour construction heuristic based on the Cluster-Expansion Heuristic with the EMPS heuristic, the maximum improvement, the minimum improvement, and the average improvement are 48%, 17%, and 32%, respectively. Comparing our tour construction heuristic based on the Cluster-Merge Heuristic with the EMPS heuristic, the maximum improvement, the minimum improvement, and the average improvement are 47%, 19%, and 30%, respectively.

There are two key reasons that our tour construction heuristics outperform the EMPS heuristic. Firstly, when selecting the cluster head of each cluster, our heuristics use an efficient model considering the distance between clusters. Secondly, our tour construction heuristics formulate the tour design problem into a TSP, further reducing the tour length of the mobile sink.

8 CONCLUSION

We investigate the network lifetime-aware data collection problem for WSNs with unreachable regions using a mobile sink and propose a set of efficient heuristics and algorithm for constructing a shortest path routing forest, clusters and a tour for the mobile sink to collect data. We have evaluated our heuristics and algorithm using 100 network instances with 100, 150, 200, 250 and 300 sensor nodes randomly distributed in the urban area and the forest area. The simulation results show that our heuristics for constructing a shortest path forest performs well and our tour construction heuristics significantly outperform the state-of-the-art approach EMPS.

In this paper, we assume that data from each sensor nodes must be delivered to the mobile sink. In some applications such as computing the average temperature sensed by all the sensor nodes, data aggregation may reduce the resulting packet size significantly. For those applications, a different energy consumption model must be derived. We will investigate the tour construction problem for those applications in the future research. Furthermore, we assume there is no packet loss during the wireless transmission. This assumption is not realistic. The transmission between two sensor nodes may not be always reliable. Another future research problem is to construct a routing forest and a tour for the mobile sink by considering link quality.

REFERENCES

[1] Stefano Basagni, Alessio Carosi, Emanuel Melachrinoudis, Chiara Petrioli, and Z Maria Wang. 2008. Controlled sink mobility for prolonging wireless sensor networks lifetime. *Wireless Networks* 14, 6 (2008), 831–858.

[2] Deborah Estrin, Lewis Girod, Greg Pottie, and Mani Srivastava. 2001. Instrumenting the world with wireless sensor networks. In *International Conference on Acoustics, Speech, and Signal Processing (ICASSP)*, Vol. 4. IEEE, 2033–2036.

[3] S Fortune. 1986. A sweepline algorithm for voronoi diagrams. In *Annual Symposium on Computational Geometry*. ACM, 313–322.

[4] Shashidhar Rao Gandham, Milind Dawande, Ravi Prakash, and Subbarayan Venkatesan. 2003. Energy efficient schemes for wireless sensor networks with multiple mobile base stations. In *Global Telecommunications Conference (GLOBECOM)*, Vol. 1. IEEE, 377–381.

[5] Yu Gu, Fuji Ren, Yusheng Ji, and Jie Li. 2016. The evolution of sink mobility management in wireless sensor networks: A survey. *IEEE Communications Surveys and Tutorials* 18, 1 (2016), 507–524.

[6] Keld Helsgaun. 2000. An effective implementation of the Lin–Kernighan traveling salesman heuristic. *European Journal of Operational Research* 126, 1 (2000), 106–130.

[7] Bret Hull, Vladimir Bychkovsky, Yang Zhang, Kevin Chen, Michel Goraczko, Allen Miu, Eugene Shih, Hari Balakrishnan, and Samuel Madden. 2006. CarTel: a distributed mobile sensor computing system. In *International Conference on Embedded Networked Sensor Systems*. ACM, 125–138.

[8] Sushant Jain, Rahul C Shah, Waylon Brunette, Gaetano Borriello, and Sumit Roy. 2006. Exploiting mobility for energy efficient data collection in wireless sensor networks. *Mobile Networks and Applications* 11, 3 (2006), 327–339.

[9] Oday Jerew, Kim Blackmore, and Weifa Liang. 2012. Mobile base station and clustering to maximize network lifetime in wireless sensor networks. *Journal of Electrical and Computer Engineering* 12, 1 (2012), 121–134.

[10] Weifa Liang, Jun Luo, and Xu Xu. 2013. Network lifetime maximization for time-sensitive data gathering in wireless sensor networks with a mobile sink. *Wireless Communications and Mobile Computing* 13, 14 (2013), 1263–1280.

[11] Jun Luo and J Hubaux. 2005. Joint mobility and routing for lifetime elongation in wireless sensor networks. In *IEEE International Conference on Computer Communications (INFOCOM)*, Vol. 3. IEEE, 1735–1746.

[12] Schlueter M, Gerdts M, and Rckmann J. 2012. A Numerical Study of MIDACO on 100 MINLP Benchmarks. *Optimization* 61, 7 (2012), 873–900.

[13] Ming Ma and Yuanyuan Yang. 2007. SenCar: an energy-efficient data gathering mechanism for large-scale multihop sensor networks. *IEEE Transactions on Parallel and Distributed Systems* 18, 10 (2007), 1476–1488.

[14] Sabbir Mahmud and Hui Wu. 2012. Lifetime Aware Deployment of K Base Stations in WSNs. In *ACM International Conference on Modeling, Analysis and Simulation of Wireless and Mobile Systems (MSWiM)*. 89–98.

[15] Sabbir Mahmud, Hui Wu, and Jingling Xue. 2011. Efficient Energy Balancing Aware Multiple Base Station Deployment for WSNs. In *European Conference on Wireless Sensor Networks (EWSN)*, Pedro José Marrón and Kamin Whitehouse (Eds.). Springer Berlin Heidelberg, Berlin, Heidelberg, 179–194.

[16] Vivek Mhatre and Catherine Rosenberg. 2004. Design guidelines for wireless sensor networks: communication, clustering and aggregation. *Ad-hoc Networks* 2, 1 (2004), 45–63.

[17] Hidehisa Nakayama, Nirwan Ansari, Abbas Jamalipour, and Nei Kato. 2007. Fault-resilient sensing in wireless sensor networks. *Computer Communications* 30, 11 (2007), 2375–2384.

[18] Chuanyao Nie and Hui Wu. 2016. Lifetime-aware clustering and dag-based routing in WSNs. In *ACM Symposium on QoS and Security for Wireless and Mobile Networks*. ACM, 77–86.

[19] Chuanyao Nie, Hui Wu, and Wenguang Zheng. 2016. Latency and lifetime-aware clustering and routing in wireless sensor networks. In *Local Computer Networks (LCN)*. IEEE, 164–167.

[20] J Sack and Jorge Urrutia. 1999. *Handbook of computational geometry*. Elsevier.

[21] Rahul C Shah, Sumit Roy, Sushant Jain, and Waylon Brunette. 2003. Data mules: modeling and analysis of a three-tier architecture for sparse sensor networks. *Ad Hoc Networks* 1, 2 (2003), 215–233.

[22] Hugues Smeets, Chia-Yen Shih, Marco Zuniga, Tobias Hagemeier, and Pedro José Marrón. 2013. TrainSense: a novel infrastructure to support mobility in wireless sensor networks. In *European Conference on Wireless Sensor Networks*. Springer, 18–33.

[23] Jiqiang Tang, Hongyu Huang, Songtao Guo, and Yuanyuan Yang. 2015. Dellat: delivery latency minimization in wireless sensor networks with mobile sink. *J. Parallel and Distrib. Comput.* 83, 2 (2015), 133–142.

[24] Farzad Tashtarian, Khosrow Sohraby, and Amir Varasteh. 2017. Multihop data gathering in wireless sensor networks with a mobile sink. *International Journal of Communication Systems* 30, 12 (2017), 1099–1131.

[25] Can Tunca, Sinan Isik, M Yunus Donmez, and Cem Ersoy. 2014. Distributed mobile sink routing for wireless sensor networks: A survey. *IEEE Communications Surveys and Tutorials* 16, 2 (2014), 877–897.

[26] Jin Wang, Yiquan Cao, Bin Li, Hyejin Kim, and Sungyoung Lee. 2016. Particle swarm optimization based clustering algorithm with mobile sink for WSNs. *Future Generation Computer Systems* 76, 3 (2016), 452–457.

[27] Guoliang Xing, Tian Wang, Weijia Jia, and Minming Li. 2008. Rendezvous design algorithms for wireless sensor networks with a mobile base station. In *ACM International Symposium on Mobile Ad Hoc Networking and Computing*. ACM, 231–240.

[28] Yuanyuan Yang and Ming Ma. 2008. Data gathering in wireless sensor networks with mobile collectors. In *IEEE International Symposium on Parallel and Distributed Processing*. IEEE, 1–9.

[29] Yinggao Yue, Jianqing Li, Hehong Fan, and Qin Qin. 2016. Optimization-based artificial bee colony algorithm for data collection in large-scale mobile wireless sensor networks. *Journal of Sensors* 16, 6 (2016), 132–144.

[30] Miao Zhao and Yuanyuan Yang. 2012. Bounded relay hop mobile data gathering in wireless sensor networks. *IEEE Trans. Comput.* 61, 2 (2012), 265–277.

[31] Miao Zhao, Yuanyuan Yang, and Cong Wang. 2015. Mobile data gathering with load balanced clustering and dual data uploading in wireless sensor networks. *IEEE Transactions on Mobile Computing* 14, 4 (2015), 770–785.

Serial In-network Processing for Large Stationary Wireless Sensor Networks

Mohammed Amine Merzoug
Department of Computer Science
Faculty of Exact Sciences
University of Bejaia
06000 Bejaia, Algeria
amine.merzoug@univ-batna2.dz

Azzedine Boukerche
PARADISE Research Lab.
University of Ottawa
Ottawa, Canada
boukerch@site.uottawa.ca

Ahmed Mostefaoui*
FEMTO-ST Institute, DISC Dept.,
Univ. of Burgundy-Franche-Comte
Belfort 90000, France
ahmed.mostefaoui@univ-fcomte.fr

ABSTRACT

In wireless sensor networks, a serial processing algorithm browses nodes one by one and can perform different tasks such as: creating a schedule among nodes, querying or gathering data from nodes, supplying nodes with data, etc. Apart from the fact that serial algorithms totally avoid collisions, numerous recent works have confirmed that these algorithms reduce communications and considerably save energy and time in large-dense networks. Yet, due to the path construction complexity, the proposed algorithms are not optimal and their performances can be further enhanced. To do so, in the present paper, we propose a new serial processing algorithm that, in most of the cases, approximates the optimal number of hops (i.e., it requires $n-1$ communications to traverse a network of n nodes). The extensive OMNeT++ simulations confirm the outperformance and efficiency of the proposal in terms of scalability and energy/time consumption.

CCS CONCEPTS

• **Mathematics of computing → Paths and connectivity problems**; • **Networks → In-network processing**; **Sensor networks**;

KEYWORDS

In-network data aggregation; sensor query processing; serial data fusion; wireless sensor networks

1 INTRODUCTION

Usually in wireless sensor networks, the mission of the randomly deployed sensor nodes is to respond as quickly and efficiently as possible to the queries of the sink node (e.g., maximum sensed value, alive nodes count, etc.). To meet this goal and ensure communication efficiency, numerous recent research works have proposed a more effective alternative to the in-network structure-based approaches [5, 8, 15], namely the serial localized algorithms [3, 9, 11, 13, 14].

*Dr. A. Mostefaoui is a visiting Professor at PARADISE Research Lab.

MSWiM '17, November 21–25, 2017, Miami, FL, USA

ACM ISBN 978-1-4503-5162-1/17/11...$15.00
https://doi.org/10.1145/3127540.3127568

The three main features that differentiate serial algorithms from their structure-based counterparts are:

- Compact operation: in fact, one of the main reasons behind the bad performance of structure-based approaches is their mode of operation. Actually, these approaches operate in three separate phases: structure construction, query dissemination, and data processing. For example, at first, a spanning tree must be created. Once the whole network is covered, a query can be spread throughout the tree ordering nodes to perform a certain processing on data. After query dissemination, data processing starts from leaf nodes and goes up towards the root/sink. Performing these three phases separately not only increases energy consumption but also delays the response time. With regard to serial algorithms, energy and time are considerably saved through the combination of the three previous phases into one step. While the path is being gradually laid out throughout the network, at the same time, the query is disseminated and data is processed.
- Collision-free: in serial algorithms, the desired task is executed sequentially by each node while the network is gradually traversed. Hence, serial algorithms are inherently collision-free and no elaborated MAC layer is needed in these algorithms. As regards tree-based approaches, the network in this case is traversed in a parallel fashion. So, from a theoretical point of view, we can say that this feature would give an advantage to tree-based approaches and enhances their response time. In reality however, as many recent works have shown [3, 11], the parallel traversal creates a lot of collisions, which considerably wastes time and dissipates energy especially in large-dense networks. In fact, even the tree construction process is deeply affected by collisions.
- Structure-free: unlike structure-based approaches, serial algorithms do not rely on any pre-established structure (no path is built in advance). Instead, each time a query is issued, a new path will be gradually built by each traversed node. This characteristic makes serial algorithms more resistible to topology changes and links/nodes failures. On the contrary, the main concern in structure-based approaches is topology changes because rebuilding or fixing a structure that covers a large dense network, is a very time and energy-consuming task.

1.1 Motivation

The major challenge faced when designing a serial algorithm is ensuring the traversal of the entire network while reducing time and energy consumption. Recently, several localized serial algorithms have been proposed in the literature [3, 11, 13]. Despite their interesting features and outperformance compared to structure-based approaches, these serial algorithms require an extra overhead to construct the path. So, our primary objective is to develop a scalable serial algorithm that shortens the traversal path and reduces communications to the maximum extent possible. We aim the optimal number of communications (i.e., $n-1$ packets to traverse a network of n nodes). No extra overhead or control packets must be required. Second, the proposed algorithm has to be able to traverse any connected network and ensure the visit of all nodes regardless of the topology (hole topology, regular or irregular topology, sparse or large-scale topology, etc.).

1.2 Contribution

We present in this paper a new serial processing algorithm, called GSS (for Geometric Serial Search). In this algorithm, no control packets are required, in fact, just one data packet that can be issued by any node, moves from node to node and traverses the entire network. As confirmed by the obtained OMNeT++ simulation results, in most of the cases, GSS approximates the optimal traversal path, which means that GSS scales well in large networks and significantly saves energy and time. For example, for a network of 500 nodes, GSS requires approximately 510 packets to visit each and every node. As the present paper shows, we have also compared GSS with other existing approaches. The obtained results confirm the efficiency and superiority of our proposal.

The remainder of this paper is organized as follows. In the next section, we specify the problem. Section 3 details the proposed solution. Section 4 presents and discusses the simulation results. Finally, the paper is concluded by Section 5.

2 PROBLEM SPECIFICATION

We consider a finite set of n stationary wireless sensor nodes, and we make the following assumptions. We suppose that the network is connected. Further, we assume that all nodes are aware of their locations through GPS or any other localization technique [4]. Finally, each node is aware of its one-hop neighbors and their corresponding locations.

Our objective is to start from any node and be able to traverse the entire network using one single packet. This latter must jump sequentially from node to node and browse the network while reducing communications to the extent possible. That is, minimizing or avoiding the visit of any node more than once. Also, in order to reduce communications, the next hop of the packet must be determined locally by each traversed node using only its local pre-collected one-hop neighbors table (no extra communications or collaboration between nodes should be required). In simple words, the problem that we are trying to solve can be boiled down to a distributed graph traversal. We recall that perfectly, a network with n connected nodes, should be traversed using exactly $n-1$ communications. Thus, theoretically, the path must cross every node precisely once. But, realistically, not every graph or network contains such optimal Hamiltonian path [14], and even if it does, determining that path constitutes an NP-complete problem [6].

3 PROPOSED SOLUTION

This section describes the proposed algorithm and details its behavior through illustrative examples.

3.1 Traversal tool

The whole operation of our proposal is based on a geometric form called *rolling-ball* (or *rolling-disc*) [10]. To summarize, a rolling-ball is a virtual circle that is hinged at a node and must be empty of any other node. Figure 1 shows a rolling-ball hinged at node N_1 with $c_1 \in \mathbb{R}^2$ as its center and $r/2$ as its radius (where r is the communication range of nodes [2]).

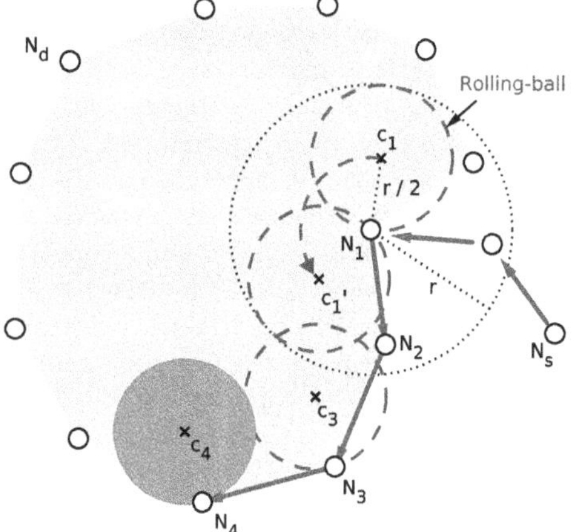

Figure 1: Rolling-ball.

Originally the rolling-ball has been used as a solution for the void problem encountered in geographic routing [10]. For instance, as demonstrated in Figure 1, in order to reach the destination N_d, node N_1 which is a local minimum creates a rolling-ball and spins it counterclockwise. The first touched neighbor, i.e., node N_2, in its turn, spins the received rolling-ball and determines the next hop. The process is repeated at each visited node until the greedy routing is resumed or until the whole boundary is traversed.

In this paper we make use of the rolling-ball as a network traversal tool. The reason behind this option resides in the fact that the rolling-ball is localized and other than the one-hop neighbors table of its owner, it does not require any other information to move to the next node. The second reason behind this choice is to guarantee the visit of all nodes in the network.

3.2 Initialization of the algorithm

In our algorithm, the node that launches the serial processing, which we refer to as the *trigger node*, can be any node in the network. Saying that the trigger node can be anywhere and knowing that the rolling-ball must be all the time empty of nodes, signifies that two cases are possible: the trigger node can be external or internal. The definition of external and internal nodes is given as follows:

Definition 3.1. External and internal Node
Given a set of wireless nodes with a communication range r, a node N_i is said to be external (resp. internal), iff at least one rolling-ball (resp. no rolling-ball) with radius $r/2$ can be hinged at this node.

Definition 3.1 simply means that an internal node cannot hold a rolling-ball while an external one can. Therefore, as Algorithm 1 shows, an external trigger node is considered as the starting point of the traversal, whereas an internal one is not. Actually, in the case of an internal trigger node, a starting point must be determined. In order to efficiently find a starting point (i.e., a random external node in the network), several techniques can be utilized. The goal is to find an external node as quickly as possible, because minimizing communications reduces the overall required time and energy.

Algorithm 1 Initialization

```
if (current_node.isExternal()) then
    call Algorithm 2;
else
    // current_node is internal
    Calculate boundary_point coordinates;
    Find nearest neighbor to boundary_point;
    Send init_packet to this neighbor;
    Upon receiving init_packet: current_node calls
    Algorithm 1;
end if
```

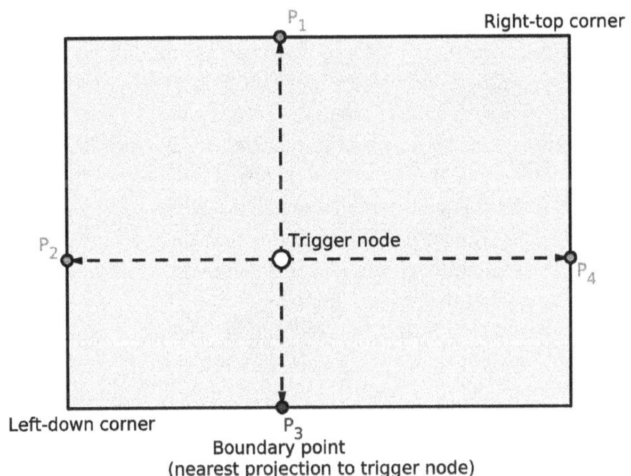

Figure 2: Boundary point determination by internal trigger node.

The technique used to find an external node may differ according to the considered scenario. To illustrate this, let us assume that the field in which nodes are deployed is a rectangle. And let us assume that this rectangle is defined by two points: *left-down* and *right-top* corners. In this situation, the best way to find an external node is to aim the external boundary of the network. To do so, as Figure 2 shows, the internal trigger node calculates its perpendicular projection on each side of the rectangle. Once calculated, the internal trigger node picks the closest perpendicular projection and determines the nearest neighbor to this point. Finally, as shown in Algorithm 1, an initialization packet has to be sent to this neighbor. Upon receiving the initialization packet, the destination node resumes the execution of Algorithm 1 (i.e., it checks if it is external or internal, and acts accordingly).

Note that the initialization packet does not have always to go all the way to the external boundary of the network. For example, if a hole is encountered halfway (i.e., an external node has been found), this condition is sufficient to stop the execution of Algorithm 1.

3.3 Algorithm's key idea

The idea of our traversal algorithm is to launch a rolling-ball (processing packet) and let it visit the network node by node (Figure 3). In order for this technique to work, initially, all nodes must be *unmarked* and each time a node is traversed, it has to be *marked*. In addition to that, in order to correctly determine the next hop, each node must keep track of its unmarked neighbors. In fact, thanks to the broadcast communication model used in wireless networks, this process does not require any additional communications or overhead other than the processing packet. Because, when a node forwards the processing packet to the next hop, all its neighbors can receive it and hence can update their neighbors table (locally mark the source of the received packet).

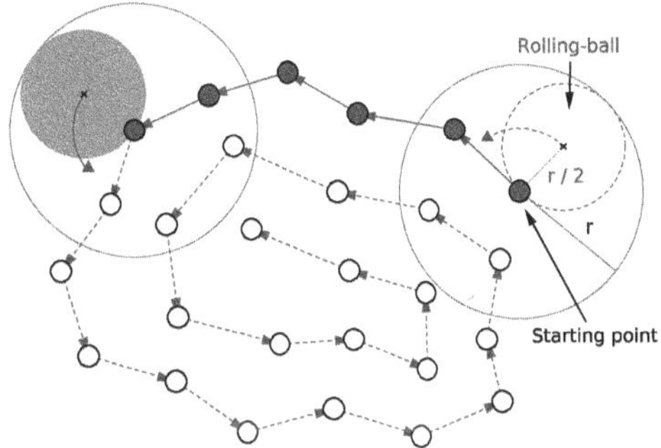

Figure 3: Traversal process using the rolling-ball.

3.4 Connectivity issue

The main issue faced by our distributed algorithm is ensuring the connectivity of the unmarked nodes while saving energy and time. In general, the problem arises in the case where a node that is essential for the unmarked nodes connectivity, marks itself. For example, as Figure 4 shows, if node N_6 and the subsequent nodes in the path mark themselves, data processing will end at node N_{15}, while nodes N_{16}, N_{17} and N_{18} have not been visited yet. We underline that processing termination is detected at a node when the neighbors of this latter have all been marked.

To solve the connectivity problem, we have introduced two new states for nodes. Thus, each node will have four possible states: unmarked, potential-cut, actual-cut, and marked. The unmarked, potential-cut, and actual-cut nodes are considered as **alive**, while the marked ones are seen as dead (they do not participate in the traversal process).

To keep things clear, we are going to start by introducing the concept of actual-cut nodes. As we go along, we will explain why the concept of potential-cut nodes has been introduced.

Definition 3.2. Actual-cut node
An actual-cut node in a connected network is a node whose removal (marking) disconnects the set of alive nodes into two or more sub-sets.

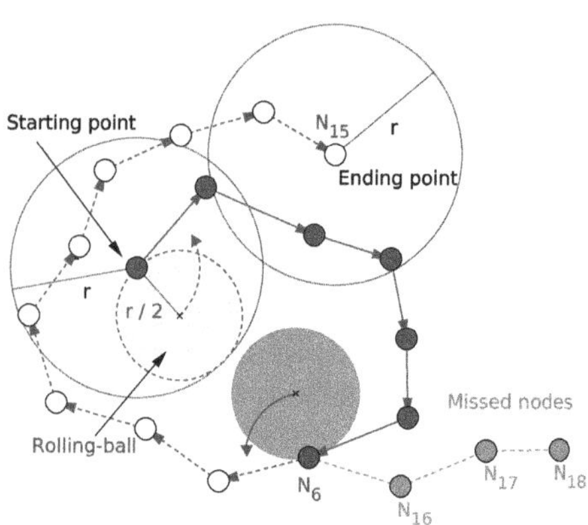

Figure 4: Connectivity issue

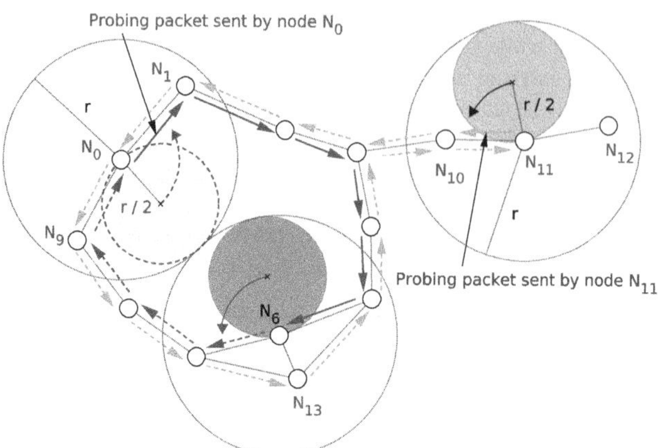

Figure 5: Concept of actual and potential-cuts

The goal behind determining the actual-cuts is to avoid network partitioning and hence ensuring the traversal of all nodes. For example, in Figure 4, node N_6 and the subsequent nodes in the path (except node N_{15}) are all actual-cuts and must remain involved in the traversal process. Once an actual-cut is no longer needed (to ensure the connectivity), it passes to the *marked* state.

In fact, having a network topology overview, it is easy to correctly determine the actual-cuts. For example, as Figure 5 shows, having an overview, it is easy to say that node N_{11} is an actual-cut while N_0 is not. As a matter of fact, being able to correctly determine the actual-cuts, the steps described above are sufficient to traverse any connected network while considerably saving both time and energy. Nevertheless, the assumption of having a network topology overview, holds only in two cases: (1) the algorithm is executed by nodes that have each a global knowledge about the network topology or (2) the algorithm is executed in a centralized fashion by one entity possessing a global knowledge. Despite their advantages or disadvantages, these two cases are out of scope of this paper. In the remainder, we treat only the distributed version of the algorithm in which each node must rely only on its immediate one-hop neighbors. For instance, as shown in Figure 5, all that node N_0 and node N_{11} are aware of, is that they have two neighbors that cannot communicate with each other without their help. That is to say, both nodes see the same thing.

With that being said, we conclude that a node cannot locally determine if it is an actual-cut. In other words, Definition 3.2 cannot be fulfilled locally and necessitates communications and collaboration between nodes. A first intuitive solution for determining the actual-cuts consists of using probing (or control) packets. Before explaining this solution, let us first define what is a potential-cut.

Definition 3.3. Potential-cut node
A potential-cut node in a connected network is a node whose removal (marking) disconnects the set of its one-hop alive neighbors into two or more sub-sets.

For example, in Figure 5, nodes N_0 and N_{11} are potential-cuts while node N_6 is not (i.e., it can be marked). We underline that unlike the actual-cuts case, a node can locally (i.e., using its one-hop neighbors table) determine if it is a potential-cut. Note also that an actual-cut is necessarily a potential-cut but the opposite is not true.

For a potential-cut to determine if it is an actual-cut, this node can issue a rolling-ball probing packet that due to its nature will make a tour and come back to it. When the probing packet gets back to its sender, this latter based on which side the packet has come back from, can properly decide if it is an actual-cut. As a simple illustrative example, let us consider Figure 5. In order for node N_0 and node N_{11} to decide if they are actual-cuts, these two nodes send a probing packet and wait to receive it back. Once this is done, N_{11} concludes that it is an actual-cut because the probing packet got back from the same side (there is no other path connecting its neighbors). Whereas, N_0 concludes that there is another path connecting its neighbors and hence it can mark itself and pass the processing packet to the next hop.

Without entering into details, we can say that from one side, the solution of probing packets solves the connectivity problem but from the other side, it violates the localized design of our distributed algorithm and forces it to spend an extra overhead (i.e., extra time and energy). We recall that our objective is to propose a distributed algorithm that excludes any use of control packets and relies only on the processing packet and the local one-hop neighbors table of each node.

The solution that we propose to determine the actual-cuts makes use of the processing packet itself. This latter besides its ordinary role, plays the role of a probing packet, which considerably reduces communications and saves both energy and time. The solution can be explained briefly as follows. If a node detects (locally) that it is a potential-cut then instead of issuing a probing packet, this node changes its status to *potential-cut* and forwards the processing packet. Given its nature, the processing packet will certainly get back to its sender. Once revisted, the node decides whether (1) it becomes actual-cut, (2) remains as a potential-cut, or (3) marks itself (no longer needed for the traversal). Our serial processing technique is summarized in Algorithm 2, which can be divided into three big steps:

(1) **Processing packet received for the first time:** (*statements 3 to 9*). When a node receives the processing packet for the

Algorithm 2 Serial data processing

```
1: The starting point (which must be an external node):
     change its state to potential-cut or marked;
     forwardProcessingPacket();
2: Upon receiving the processing packet, the destination node
   executes the following steps:
3: if (current_node.state == unmarked) then
4:    // Processing packet received for the first time.
5:    process_data();
6:    change_state(); // to potential-cut, actual-cut or marked.
7:    forwardProcessingPacket();
8:    return;
9: end if
10:
11: // Processing packet has already been received.
12: if (not current_node.isPotentialCut()) then
13:    // current_node is no longer a potential-cut
14:    current_node.state = marked;
15:    forwardProcessingPacket();
16: else
17:    if (current_node.state == actual_cut) then
18:       call Algorithm 4;
19:    else
20:       // current_node.state == potential_cut
21:       call Algorithm 3;
22:    end if
23: end if
```

Algorithm 3 Code executed by potential-cuts

```
1: if (current_node.canBecomeActualCut()) then
2:    current_node.state = actual_cut;
3:    forwardProcessingPacket();
4:    return;
5: end if
6: switch (previous_hop.state){
7:    case marked: {
8:       if (processing_pkt came back from the same set
9:       and this set still contain alive nodes){
10:         current_node.state = actual_cut;
11:      }
12:      break;
13:   }
14:   case potential_cut: {
15:      if (processing_pkt came back from the same set){
16:         current_node.state = actual_cut;
17:      }
18:      else {
19:         Cut link with previous_hop;
20:         Change state to marked or potential-cut;
21:         sendCycleBreakPacket(previous_hop);
22:         return;
23:      }
24:   }
25: }
26: forwardProcessingPacket();
```

first time, it executes the required task (query), changes its state to *potential-cut, actual-cut* or *marked*, and finally forwards the processing packet to the next hop. We mention that a node can become actual-cut if it is potential-cut just to ensure the connectivity of other actual-cuts. In other terms, a potential-cut can become actual-cut, if without considering its actual-cut neighbors, it is not a potential-cut.

(2) **Processing packet has already been received and node is no longer a potential-cut:** (*statements 12 to 15*). Being no longer a potential-cut means also that the node cannot be either an actual-cut. In such a case, the current node marks itself and forwards the processing packet to the next hop. We underline that `isPotentialCut()` method applies Definition 3.3.

(3) **Processing packet has already been received and node is still potential-cut:** (*statements 16 to 23*). Being a potential-cut according to `isPotentialCut()` method, means that the current node can be also an actual-cut. In this situation, the node refers to its local stored state and executes the corresponding code. The steps executed by potential-cuts and the ones executed by actual-cuts are described respectively in Algorithm 3 and Algorithm 4.

As mentioned earlier, when a potential-cut receives the processing packet back, it can decide to whether become actual-cut, remain potential-cut or mark itself. In fact, a potential-cut determines its next state according to two factors: the state of its immediate neighbors, and the side (set) from which the processing packet has come back. The code executed by a potential-cut (Algorithm 3) can be divided into three main steps:

(1) **Current node can become actual-cut:** (*statements 1 to 5*). As mentioned earlier, a node can become actual-cut if it is potential-cut only to ensure the connectivity of other actual-cuts. In other words, a potential-cut can become actual-cut, if without considering its actual-cut neighbors, it is not a potential-cut.
If the potential-cut can become actual-cut, it changes its state accordingly, forwards the processing packet, and stops the execution of Algorithm 3. In the opposite case (i.e., node is not an actual-cut), the execution of Algorithm 3 continues according to the previous-hop state (i.e., marked or potential-cut).

(2) **Current node cannot become actual-cut and previous-hop is a marked node:** (*statements 7 to 13*). To determine its state, besides the state of the previous-hop, in this case, the current node relies also on which set the processing packet has come back from. If the processing packet came back from the same set it was sent to, and this set still contain alive neighbors, then the current node is ensuring the connectivity of this set. So, it changes its state to actual-cut (statement 10) and forwards the processing packet (statement 26). The opposite case means that, (1) the processing

packet came back from the same set, but this set does not contain any alive neighbors, or (2) processing packet came back from a different set. In both cases, the current node remains as a potential-cut and forwards the processing packet to the next hop (statement 26).

(3) **Current node cannot become actual-cut and previous-hop is a potential-cut:** (*statements 14 to 24*). Here also, to determine its state, besides the state of the previous-hop, the current node relies also on which set the processing packet has come back from. Actually, if the processing packet came back from the same set (to which it was sent), then there is no need to check if this set still contain alive neighbors because the previous-hop is alive. In such a case, the current node changes its state to actual-cut (statement 16) and forwards the processing packet (statement 26). The opposite case (i.e., the processing packet came back from a different set) means that there is a cycle that must be broken.
To well illustrate the cycle break process, let us consider the example depicted in Figure 6(a). In this example, node N_0 which is the trigger node changes its state to potential-cut and forwards the processing packet. This latter makes a tour and comes back to N_0 from N_7 which is also a potential-cut. In this case, to break the cycle, as Figure 6(b) shows, node N_0 executes the following steps:
- It cuts its link with node N_7
- After cutting the link with the previous-hop, N_0 cannot be marked, so it remains as a potential-cut.
- The last step consists of sending a cycle break packet to the previous-hop. This packet, as Figure 6(b) shows, orders the previous-hop and other nodes to cut the proper links.

Once the cycle has been broken, the previous-hop, i.e., node N_7 continues the traversal by forwarding the processing packet.

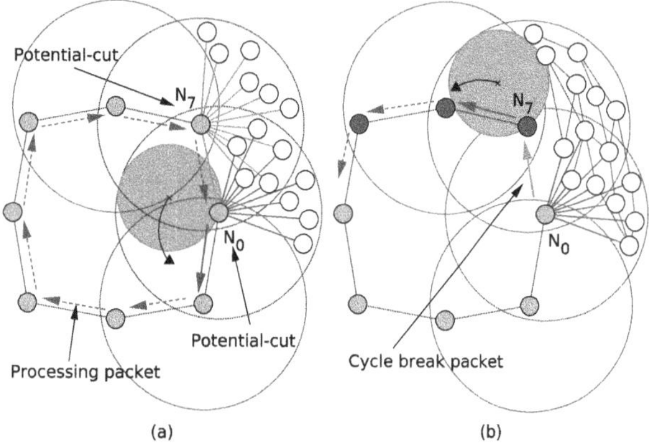

Figure 6: Example of cycle break.

In the previous paragraphs, we have treated the cases where the previous-hop can be marked or potential-cut, but we did not talk about the case of a previous actual-cut. We mention that even if the previous-hop is an actual-cut then this does not mean that the current node can become actual-cut. In fact, if the previous-hop is an actual-cut and the current node cannot become actual-cut, the execution of Algorithm 3 will jump to statement 26 (i.e., current node remains potential-cut and forwards the processing packet).

The fact that a node is an actual-cut does not mean that it will remain in this state. Similarly as a potential-cut, when an actual-cut receives the processing packet back, it decides to whether remain actual-cut, become again a potential-cut or mark itself. The next state of an actual-cut is determined by the state of its immediate neighbors and the set from which the processing packet has come back. The steps followed by an actual-cut when it receives back the processing packet, are summarized in Algorithm 4.

Algorithm 4 Code executed by actual-cuts

```
switch (previous_hop.state){
  case marked: {
    if (set for which current_node is actual-cut
    contains no alive nodes){
        current_node.state = potential_cut;
    }
    break;
  }

  case potential_cut: {
    if (processing_packet came back from a different
    set than the one it was sent to){
        Cut link with previous_hop;
        Change state to marked or potential-cut;
        sendCycleBreakPacket(previous_hop);
        return;
    }
  }

  case actual_cut: {
    if (processing_packet came back from a different
    set than the one it was sent to){
        current_node.state = potential_cut;
    }
    break;
  }
}

forwardProcessingPacket();
```

4 SOLUTION EVALUATION

Given the fact that numerous research works have already shown the superiority of serial algorithms over structure-based ones [3, 11], in this paper, we consider only serial algorithms. More exactly, we chose to compare our solution with three other serial algorithms, namely: the Peeling Algorithm (PA) [11], the Greedy and Boundary Traversal algorithm (GBT) [3], and the well-known depth-first search algorithm (DFS).

In summary, the Peeling Algorithm uses a *curved-stick* [12] as a network traversal tool and must start from the external boundary of the network. The term peeling came from the fact that each time, the visited node is removed from the external boundary. As

Table 1: Simulation parameters

Parameter	Value(s)
Number of nodes	100, 150, 200, ..., 500
Deployment field	1000 x 1000 m^2
Nodes deployment	Uniform
Location of the trigger node	Random
Transmission range of nodes	150 m
Processing packet size	50 Bytes

regards GBT, this algorithm operates in two alternative distinct modes: greedy forwarding and boundary traversal. At first, the path is extented towards the unvisited nodes as long as possible, and when there is no more left unvisited neighbors, the boundary traversal will be launched. During boundary traversal, if a non-visited node is encountered, the greedy mode will be resumed. This way, GBT switches between the two modes until visiting all nodes. DFS extends the path as far as possible towards the unmarked nodes, and when it gets stuck at some node (all neighbors have been marked), it goes back to the parent of that node and so forth.

4.1 Evaluation metrics and simulation settings

To evaluate the performance of all four algorithms, we have opted for OMNeT++ along with Castalia [1]. The first considered evaluation metric is the total number of packets required to process data. In fact, given the serial nature of the evaluated algorithms, this metric is the most important because it affects the two other metrics, which are the time and energy necessary for data processing.

By processing time, we mean the time elapsed between the instant when the trigger node launches data processing and the moment when it receives the processed data. In the chosen simulation scenario, while being traversed one by one, nodes have been queried to compute the *average sensed value* in the network.

As regards processing energy, this metric represents the total energy dissipated by all nodes to process data. The energy consumed by the radio of each node has been estimated using the model proposed by Heinzelman [7]. In this well-known energy consumption model, in order to send a k-bit packet a distance d, the radio consumes $E_{TX}(k,d) = E_{elec} * k + \epsilon_{amp} * k * d^2$, and it consumes $E_{RX}(k) = E_{elec} * k$ to receive this packet. Where:

- E_{elec} = 50 nJ/bit: energy for running the transmitter/receiver circuitry.
- ϵ_{amp} = 100 pJ/bit/m^2: energy for running the transmitter amplifier.

The parameters used in the simulations are summarized in Table 1.

4.2 Evaluation results

The number of packets spent by GSS (proposed algorithm), PA (Peeling Algorithm) [11], GBT (Greedy and Boundary Traversal) [3] and DFS (Depth-First Search) to process data are shown in Figure 7. This figure shows also the number of packets that an optimal algorithm (if it existed) would have spent. As a matter of fact, the number of packets used by both, the optimal theoretical algorithm and DFS, have been depicted to serve as a reference to measure the effectiveness of the evaluated serial algorithms in terms of communications. We recall that an optimal algorithm traverses a network of n connected nodes using $n-1$ packets, whereas DFS, due to its backtracking behavior, requires $2*(n-1)$ packets.

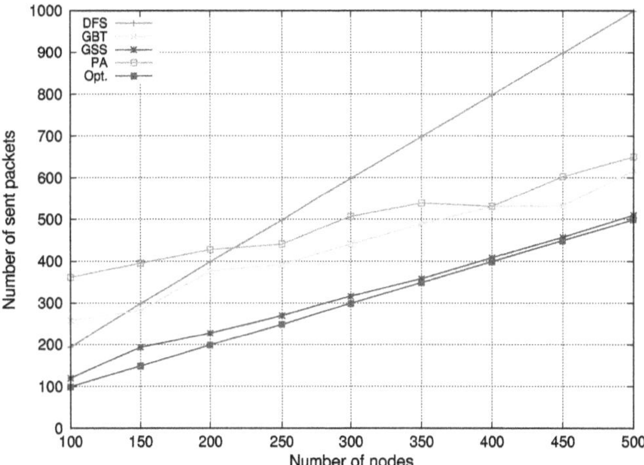

Figure 7: Required communications (sent data and control packets).

As Figure 7 demonstrates, our proposal is clearly superior. Actually, GSS outperforms all the other algorithms and spends a number of packets that is very close to the optimal algorithm's number. We can say that the denser the network, the better the performance of GSS will be. In low density networks, GSS is slightly different than the optimal algorithm because in such networks, cycles have a high occurrence probability. In such scenarios, due to the limited knowledge of nodes, the processing packet has to make a tour in order to be able to detect the existence of a cycle. In spite of that, the performance of GSS is not drastically affected as it is the case for PA and GBT. In fact, as demonstrated in Figure 7, in sparse networks, even DFS outperforms PA and GBT.

The good performance of GSS comes from the idea used to solve the connectivity issue and overcome the limited knowledge of nodes. This solution attributes a twofold role to the processing packet: at the same time it serves as a network traversal tool and as a probing packet.

The time and energy consumed by the four algorithms to process data are depicted respectively in Figure 8 and Figure 9. Given its sequential behavior, the more a serial algorithm requires packets, the longer it will take to finish and the more energy it will consume. As Figure 8 and Figure 9 show, since GSS requires less communications, it outperforms the other algorithms it in terms of processing time and energy.

5 CONCLUSION AND FUTURE WORK

Lately, serial in-network processing has proven its efficiency in large-dense networks. However, due to the complexity of path building process, the proposed solutions are not optimal and require an extra overhead. To overcome this drawback, we have proposed in this paper a new scalable serial processing algorithm that reduces

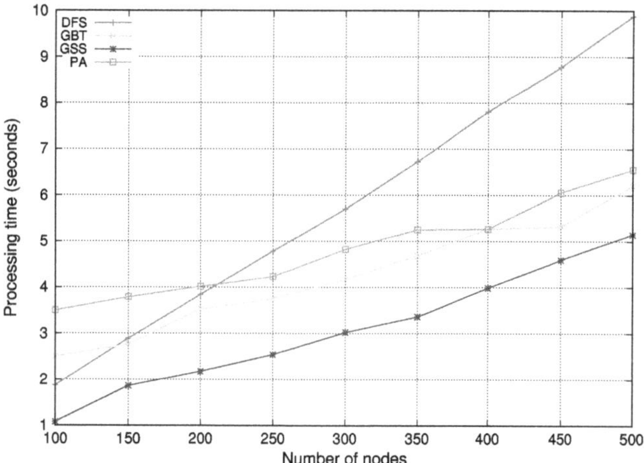

Figure 8: Processing time.

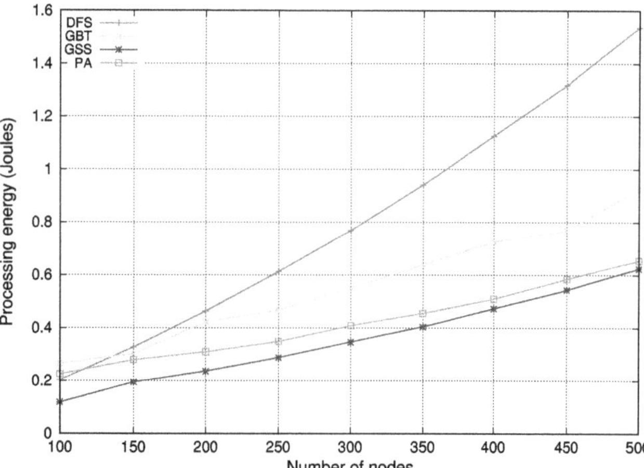

Figure 9: Processing energy.

further the processing time and energy. The extensive simulations have demonstrated that the proposed solution approximates the optimal number of hops. The obtained results have confirmed also that the proposed algorithm traverses all nodes in the network and does not loop.

As a future work, we plan to formally prove the correction of the proposed algorithm. More specifically, prove that (1) it is free of looping, and (2) it visits all connected nodes. First, in order to prove that GSS terminates and does not loop indefinitely, we base on the fact that all cycles (which can be generated due to the use of potential and actual-cuts) are detected and properly removed. Second, in order to prove that GSS visits all nodes, we base on the fact that the network is initially connected and its connectivity is maintained throughout the traversal.

REFERENCES

[1] OMNeT++ : Simulation Environment. http://www.omnetpp.org/. (????).

[2] Azzedine Boukerche, Xin Fei, and Regina B Araujo. 2007. An optimal coverage-preserving scheme for wireless sensor networks based on local information exchange. *Computer Communications* 30, 14 (2007), 2708–2720.

[3] A Boukerche, A Mostefaoui, and M Melkemi. 2016. Efficient and robust serial query processing approach for large-scale wireless sensor networks. *Ad Hoc Networks* 47 (2016), 82–98.

[4] Azzedine Boukerche, Horacio Oliveira, Eduardo F. Nakamura, and Antonio A. F. Loureiro. 2007. Localization systems for wireless sensor networks. *IEEE Wireless Communications* 14, 6 (2007), 6–12.

[5] Elena Fasolo, Michele Rossi, Jorg Widmer, and Michele Zorzi. 2007. In-network aggregation techniques for wireless sensor networks: a survey. *IEEE Wireless Communications* 14, 2 (2007).

[6] Michael R. Garey and David S. Johnson. 1983. *Computers and Intractability: A Guide to the Theory of NP-completeness.* W. H. Freeman, New York.

[7] Wendi B. Heinzelman, Anantha P. Chandrakasan, and Hari Balakrishnan. 2002. An application-specific protocol architecture for wireless microsensor networks. *IEEE Transactions on Wireless Communications* 1, 4 (2002), 660–670.

[8] Mo Li, Yajun Wang, and Yu Wang. 2011. Complexity of data collection, aggregation, and selection for wireless sensor networks. *IEEE Trans. Comput.* 60, 3 (2011), 386–399.

[9] Stephanie Lindsey and Cauligi S Raghavendra. 2002. PEGASIS: Power-efficient gathering in sensor information systems. In *Aerospace conference proceedings, 2002. IEEE*, Vol. 3. IEEE, 3–3.

[10] Wen-Jiunn Liu and Kai-Ten Feng. 2009. Greedy routing with anti-void traversal for wireless sensor networks. *IEEE Transactions on Mobile Computing* 8, 7 (2009), 910–922.

[11] Ahmed Mostefaoui, Azzedine Boukerche, Mohammed Amine Merzoug, and Mahmoud Melkemi. 2015. A scalable approach for serial data fusion in Wireless Sensor Networks. *Computer Networks* 79 (2015), 103–119.

[12] Ahmed Mostefaoui, Mahmoud Melkemi, and Azzedine Boukerche. 2012. Routing through holes in wireless sensor networks. In *Proceedings of the 15th ACM international conference on Modeling, analysis and simulation of wireless and mobile systems.* ACM, 395–402.

[13] Swapnil Patil, Samir R Das, and Asis Nasipuri. 2004. Serial data fusion using space-filling curves in wireless sensor networks. In *Sensor and Ad Hoc Communications and Networks, 2004. IEEE SECON 2004. 2004 First Annual IEEE Communications Society Conference on.* IEEE, 182–190.

[14] Michael G. Rabbat and Robert D. Nowak. 2005. Quantized incremental algorithms for distributed optimization. *IEEE Journal on Selected Areas in Communications* 23, 4 (2005), 798–808.

[15] Ramesh Rajagopalan and Pramod K. Varshney. 2006. Data Aggregation Techniques in Sensor Networks: A Survey. *IEEE Comm. Surveys & Tutorials* 8 (2006), 48–63.

Live Synthesis of Vehicle-Sourced Data Over 4G LTE

Wenlu Hu
Carnegie Mellon University
wenlu@cmu.edu

Ziqiang Feng
Carnegie Mellon University
zf@cs.cmu.edu

Zhuo Chen
Carnegie Mellon University
zhuoc@cs.cmu.edu

Jan Harkes
Carnegie Mellon University
jaharkes@cs.cmu.edu

Padmanabhan Pillai
Intel Labs
padmanabhan.s.pillai@intel.com

Mahadev Satyanarayanan
Carnegie Mellon University
satya@cs.cmu.edu

ABSTRACT

Accurate, up-to-date maps of transient traffic and hazards are invaluable to drivers, city managers, and the emerging class of self-driving vehicles. We present LiveMap, a scalable, automated system for acquiring, curating, and disseminating detailed, continually-updated road conditions in a region. LiveMap leverages in-vehicle cameras, sensors, and processors to crowd-source hazard detection without human intervention. We build a real-time simulation framework that allows a mix of real and simulated components to be tested together at scale. We demonstrate that LiveMap can work well at city scales within the limits of today's cellular network bandwidth. We also show the feasibility of accurate, in-vehicle, computer-vision-based hazard detection.

CCS CONCEPTS

•Networks → Application layer protocols; Mobile networks; *Network performance modeling; Network experimentation;* **•Software and its engineering → Distributed systems organizing principles;** *Middleware; Operating systems; Client-server architectures;* **•Information systems → Sensor networks; Mobile information processing systems;** *Geographic information systems;*

KEYWORDS

Vehicular Systems; Automotive Systems; Maps; Cloudlet; Edge Computing; Cloud Computing; Situational Awareness; Driverless Cars

1 Introduction

Every day, millions of drivers benefit from real-time synthesis of GPS location data that is periodically transmitted by participating vehicles (Figure 1). In this paper, we examine future extensions of this concept to provide fine-grain, deep-zoom details about road conditions and hazards such as *"Dead deer in left lane at GPS location (x,y), here is an image;"* or, *"Fog detected at GPS location (x,y), visibility down to 30 feet, here is a short video clip."* Receiving map overlays with such details in near real-time could greatly improve the situational awareness of many stakeholders such as driverless vehicles, drivers, road-maintenance crews, emergency personnel, and law enforcement officers [23]. We look to a future when such reports can be algorithmically-generated, without human assistance, from video cameras and other sensors on a vehicle.

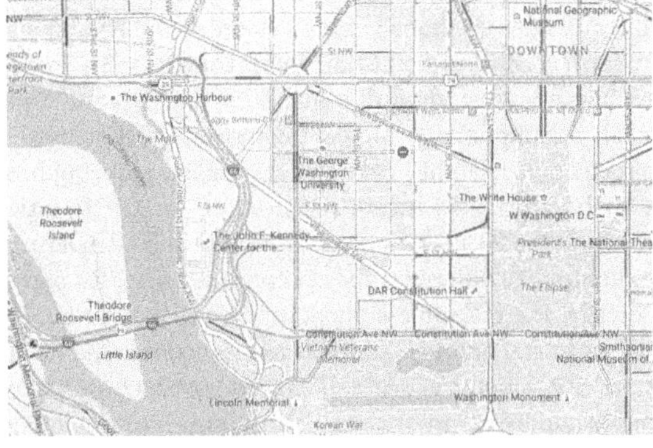

Green: normal Orange: slow Red: very slow

Figure 1: Traffic Overlay on Google Maps

This paper focuses on *LiveMap,* a scalable mobile information system that synthesizes vehicular update streams in real-time. Our informal scalability goal is tens of thousands of vehicles over a county-sized coverage area. For the foreseeable future, 4G LTE offers the most plausible wide-area Internet connectivity from a moving vehicle. The demand for this resource is intense, and its spectrum-limited supply is scarce [9]. Hence, the crucial requirement for our system is to be frugal in terms of wireless transmission. Peak bandwidth demand as well as total volume of data transmitted should be minimized, while offering timely synthesis.

A simple implementation strategy would be to ship the video from moving vehicles over 4G LTE to the cloud or a regional data collection point for real-time video analytics and generation of map overlays. Unfortunately, this is not scalable in terms of wireless network usage. For example, consider rush hour in Manhattan over the two-block by two-block coverage area of a small cell. Using an average vehicle size of 5 m and a separation of 5 m, such an area can accommodate roughly 400 vehicles. If each vehicle streams SD video at 3.0 Mbps (Netflix's estimate [17]), the total aggregate uplink demand in the cell would be 1.2 Gbps. This clearly exceeds the stated capacity of 500 Mbps for LTE Advanced technology [16]. Streaming HD or 4K video rather than SD video would improve the quality of the video analytics and expose finer-grain features, but would worsen the bandwidth problem. Non-urban areas have much lower density of vehicles, but their cells are larger.

Scalability can be greatly improved by performing video analytics on board each vehicle at an edge computing device called a

MSWiM '17, November 21–25, 2017, Miami, FL, USA

IBSN 978-1-4503-5162-1/17/11.
DOI: https://doi.org/10.1145/3127540.3127543

cloudlet [24]. Only the extracted information, encoded in a standardized format such as XML or JSON, needs to be shipped over 4G LTE to the data collection center. For example, analysis of a single video frame that is multiple megabytes in size may result in output that is just a few hundred bytes in size. This reduction in bandwidth demand by 4 to 5 orders of magnitude is crucial for scalability. In practice, the system would require an image or short video clip to be uploaded for each detected event, for further analysis and confirmation purposes. Even with this, the bandwidth savings from processing in the vehicle over streaming all video to the regional data collection point will be tremendous. Of course, a critical requirement is that a vehicle's cloudlet be powerful enough to transform continuous real-time input from its video and other sensors into a low-bandwidth semantic update stream. This is a reasonable assumption with today's computing technology.

We focus on scalability issues in this paper, ignoring broader issues such as privacy, incentive structure for participation in LiveMap, and the HCI issues involved in optimally delivering synthesized output to different types of consumers. In this paper, we first describe the real-time simulation framework we have built to allow us to run and test a mix of real and simulated instances of system components at scale. We then describe how we model LiveMap components in our simulation framework, followed by an evaluation of bandwidth consumption for different upload policies. Finally, we demonstrate the feasibility of in-vehicle hazard detection by building detectors to find deer and potholes.

2 Background and Related Work

Research on vehicular communication and computing spans nearly two decades. A major theme has been *vehicle to vehicle (V2V)* use cases. These focus on transient information (lifetimes of milliseconds to seconds), whereas LiveMap involves persistence of sensor information and map information over timescales of minutes to hours to days. Second, the response times involved differ by two or more orders of magnitude: a few milliseconds or less for V2V use cases, versus LiveMap's best-effort response times of hundreds of milliseconds to a few seconds to detect and report an observation. Thus, LiveMap is "near real-time" rather than "hard real-time."

Closely related to V2V use cases is the entire body of wireless networking research on *vehicular ad hoc networking (VANET)*. LiveMap does not rely on VANET technologies, but instead relies on the widely-used 4G LTE technology. The unique challenges of using LTE for vehicular use cases have been discussed by Araniti et al [6], and their insights apply to our work.

Driverless vehicles are another hot topic in vehicular research. Many of the V2V safety use cases mentioned above are relevant to driverless vehicles. Rapid sensing and actuation for collision avoidance are essential for any driverless vehicle. At the same time, proactive actions based on detailed map information are (whenever possible) better than reactive just-in-time actions. As Autor points out [7], "A Google car navigates through the road network primarily by comparing its real-time audio-visual sensor data against painstakingly hand-curated maps that specify the exact locations of all roads, signals, signage, and obstacles." The creation of these detailed maps, which change rapidly over time, is a large hidden cost of driverless vehicular technology. LiveMap could cheaply and continuously crowd-source the creation of these detailed maps.

Closest in spirit to LiveMap are commercial map services such as Waze [28]. LiveMap can be viewed as a Waze-like system that automates the sensing, reporting, and synthesis of events. Instead of relying on human input, LiveMap is based on sensor data that is locally processed to generate map update reports. It would be simple to extend LiveMap to also allow human input.

Independent of vehicular contexts, there is a huge body of work on data aggregation in sensor networks [12, 15, 26].That work has tended to focus on small low-cost sensors where the dominant constraint is the energy cost of sensing, processing and transmission. In contrast, energy usage for processing and transmission is only a minor consideration in LiveMap. Relative to the energy consumed in accelerating and maintaining a vehicle and its occupants at highway speeds, the energy used by LiveMap is modest. Bandwidth demand on 4G LTE is the dominant theme for LiveMap.

3 Simulation Framework

3.1 Goals and Requirements

Our intention is to build a prototype implementation of the LiveMap system and test it at scale. As it is impractical to actually implement, deploy, and connect even a small set of vehicles with cameras and computation, and drive them around a city, we instead rely on realistic simulations to provide scale. However, we would like to be able to plug in a few instances of real, implemented components, and have them interact with the large number of simulated components. This will allow us to both run the system at large scale and to test the actual implemented application code. Our primary focus is on system scalability, so accuracy of sensing models or low-level details of the network are less critical. Based on these considerations, we derive the following requirements:

- simulate vehicles and applications that communicate with fixed infrastructure
- support real maps and realistic traffic patterns
- allow interfacing with real implementations of system components by executing in real time
- support county- or city-scale simulations

The rest of this section details the simulation system that we have designed and implemented to meet these requirements.

3.2 Vehicle Simulation

We began our investigations with the Veins [25] system, which is intended for the study of connected vehicular systems. It provides accurate modeling of vehicular communication networks, and includes models for V2V communication and for LTE. Furthermore, it also provides a straightforward way to run custom application logic on each simulated vehicle, a key need for our work.

Veins itself is built on top of SUMO [8] and Omnet++ [27]. SUMO is an open-source vehicle simulation framework that is widely used to study traffic patterns and smart vehicle coordination, and has been shown to realistically simulate traffic patterns on maps of real cities. Omnet++ provides full network stack simulation and is used to provide accurate models of connectivity and communication among vehicles and to fixed infrastructure.

Although Veins is functionally well-suited to our goals, it suffers from performance issues. Its architecture separates the SUMO and

Omnet++ components into different processes, thus incurring inter-process communication overhead at each simulation step. Further, the network is modeled much more precisely than we need. Hence, we also investigate using SUMO alone, extending it with just the features we need.

3.3 Maps and Traffic Patterns

SUMO and, by extension, Veins have excellent support for using real maps in simulations. SUMO provides a tool, NETCONVERT, to convert the map data from OpenStreetMap [18] to the SUMO format. OpenStreetMap is a crowd-sourced map of the world, open and free to the public. Although this converting process is not perfect, e.g., the locations and changing cycles of traffic lights are guessed, it does allow simulations on almost any real road network.

In addition to the maps, we also need realistic traffic patterns as input models to the simulator. The largest publicly available input model is the TAPAS Cologne dataset [5]. It describes traffic in the city of Cologne, Germany for a whole day, derived from observed traveling habits and information about the infrastructure of the area. Rush hours in this dataset have up to 14,000 vehicles on the road at the same time, providing us with a clear scalability target.

3.4 Real-time Simulation

A key goal of our work is to mix real and simulated components together. As a consequence, we need a simulation system that can run in real time. In other words, the simulated time step equals the real-world elapsed time for that step. Both SUMO and Veins are designed for offline simulations. To interface the simulated world to the real components, we ensure that the simulation time of SUMO is synchronized with real, wall-clock time by adding a high-precision sleep to SUMO simulation steps. This modification adds just enough sleep to the end of each simulation step to allow wall-clock time to catch up to simulation time.

Of course, this works only when the simulation step takes no more time to execute than the corresponding real world time period. How well does this hold true? When running Veins with a few hundred cars and a time step of 100 ms, we note that most steps take just a few milliseconds to execute. However, some take significantly longer, more than 100 ms, and violate the requirement that elapsed time be less than simulated time. The largest spikes are due to writing of logs, $O(n^2)$ heartbeat messaging, and synchronized introduction of new vehicles into the simulation. We reconfigure Veins to eliminate these issues, and also pin the simulation process to a dedicated processor core to reduce context switching. However, more subtle, periodic spikes persist, as shown in Figure 2(a). After investigation, we determined these are due to the way the simulator loads input data — every 200 simulation steps, it loads inputs for the next set of steps. By preloading all inputs, we finally eliminate these spikes, as shown in Figure 2(b). Note that these plots reflect our modification that introduces a high-precision sleep after every step that executes too quickly, bringing the step time up to the desired value. The ideal curve would be a straight line at 100 ms.

As the execution time of a step depends on the size of the simulation, this limits the scale of real-time simulation. Figure 3 compares the execution time of a single simulation step to the real-world time it represents for Veins as the number of vehicles is increased. The

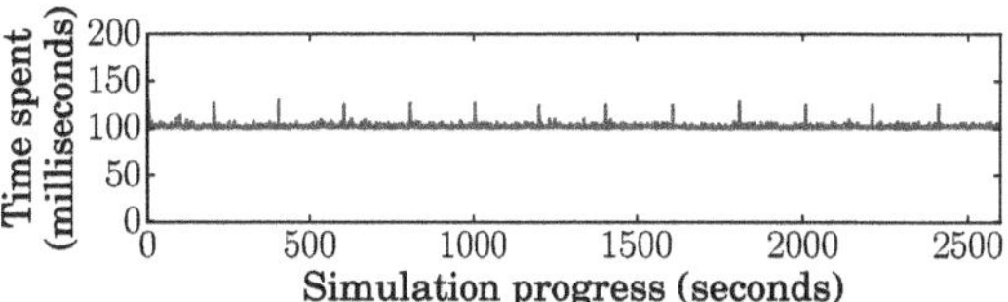

(a) Periodic spikes in Veins execution time

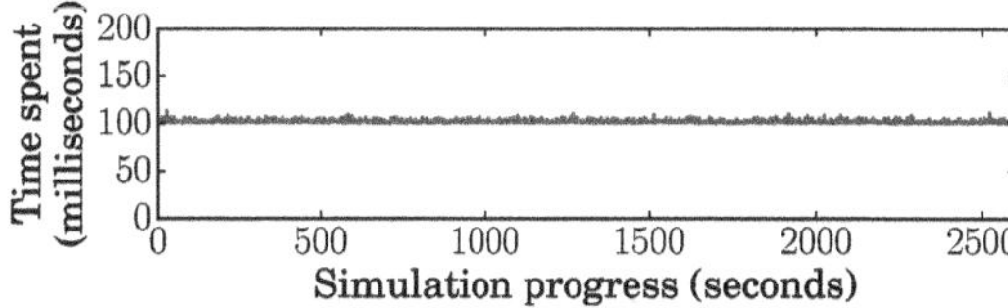

(b) Consistent execution times with fully pre-loaded input data

Figure 2: Execution Time Variability in Veins

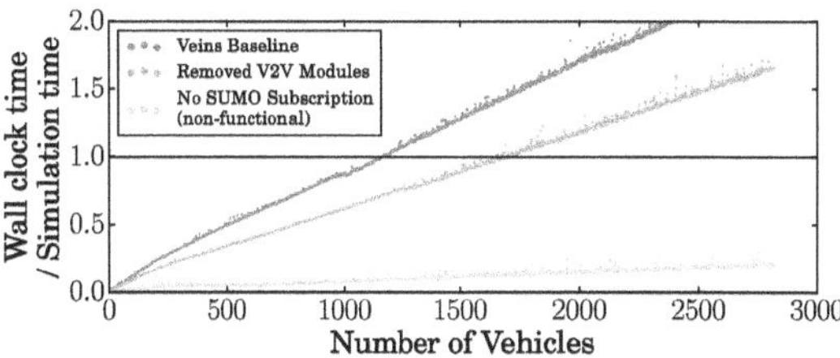

Figure 3: Scalability of Veins

Y axis presents execution time of each simulation step, normalized by the step size (100ms). Real-time simulation can only be achieved when this ratio is below 1, as shown by the horizontal line. As we can see, Veins can run in real-time for up to 1200 vehicles on a 3.6 GHz CPU (turbo clock rate). As Veins is largely sequential, increasing the number of CPU cores does not improve scalability.

As LiveMap does not involve V2V communications, we modified Veins to eliminate V2V-related functionality, in the hope of increasing scalability. This configuration supports real-time simulation of up to 1700 vehicles. This disappointing result shows that Veins will likely not suffice for our goal of county-scale simulations.

Further investigations showed the bottleneck to be due to transferring data between the SUMO simulation and the rest of Veins, which run in separate processes. To evaluate this bottleneck, we disabled the inter-process data transfer, using dummy data instead. The third curve in Figure 3 is for this non-functional system and indicates that real-time simulation at significantly higher scales is possible without the multi-process architecture imposed by Veins.

3.5 Scaling to County-size Inputs

To allow real-time simulation with more than 1700 vehicles, we must forego Veins and Omnet++, and instead use SUMO alone. We retest scalability with SUMO alone, plotting the execution time of a simulation step relative to the length of time that the step represents as the number of vehicles is increased. Figure 4 shows that SUMO can simulate up to 20,000 vehicles while maintaining real-time performance on the same 3.6 GHz CPU (turbo clock rate) as in the Veins experiments. We note that this does not include any LiveMap code or network communication. With careful implementation of application logic for the vehicles, and use of real networking between the simulated vehicles and external components, we are able to scale SUMO-based, real-time simulations of LiveMap to 14,000 simultaneous vehicles needed for the Cologne dataset, for most LiveMap configurations. For some variants that require more processing time, we slightly increase the step size to keep the simulation real-time.

Further scaling of SUMO is limited by its architecture. The SUMO core simulation is single-threaded, and prior attempts to parallelize it have not been very successful [14]. A faster simulation model provided by SUMO, the mesoscopic model, only outputs aggregated information at the road level and is not useful for LiveMap, where the locations of individual vehicles along roads are important. Despite these limitations, we are able to use SUMO to demonstrate LiveMap at the scale of a city.

3.6 Simulating In-vehicle Application Logic

We extend SUMO to add support for custom application logic that is run on each vehicle. The application logic for LiveMap implements a model for sensing of road hazards, an application-level data cache, protocols to maintain the cache, and logic to decide when and what updates based on sensed hazards should be sent. Our SUMO extension permits a single application callback method, which is invoked once per vehicle, per simulation step. This requires the application logic to use a polled, event-driven style, and to explicitly keep track of state of activities across simulation steps. To avoid slowing the simulation, the application method is required to return quickly, and avoid long running computations or blocking calls. To support slow operations and blocking calls (e.g., network communication operations), our system provides a means of deferred execution – the operations are queued and executed in the background by a worker thread pool. It is up to the application method to check if the deferred operation has completed in a future invocation. Finally, we use multiple threads to run the application callbacks concurrently. These implementation choices add some complexity and introduce some nondeterminism into the simulation, but ensure that real-time performance is minimally impacted.

For network communications in our simulation, we use an actual wired connection instead of network models to avoid their impact on the real-time performance. This setup can be seen as an upper bound of the cellular network and may have an impact on simulation accuracy. As shown in Section 5, this impact is very small in terms of the metrics important to LiveMap.

4 Modeling LiveMap

4.1 LiveMap Components

LiveMap is a distributed sensing and aggregation system intending to provide situational awareness across a region. It primarily consists of a large number of vehicles with multiple sensors, typically cameras, and significant compute capability in the form of in-vehicle cloudlets. These vehicles observe, detect, and report anomalies and hazards. For this paper, all of the vehicles and corresponding in-vehicle cloudlets are simulated, but the LiveMap software is real.

We refer to the coverage area of a single instance of LiveMap as its *zone*. A centralized entity called the *zone cloudlet* is responsible for the zone. We use the term *in-vehicle cloudlet* in the rest of the paper to distinguish in-vehicle cloudlets from zone cloudlets. A zone cloudlet fuses inputs from all in-vehicle cloudlets in its zone, curates the data to ensure quality control, enforces security and privacy policies, and selectively disseminates the synthesized knowledge to participants. A zone cloudlet may be physically replicated for survivability, and standard failover protocols can be used to create a high-availability LiveMap service for each zone. A working prototype zone cloudlet has been implemented. It interacts with the simulated in-vehicle cloudlets over network connections.

How large a zone should LiveMap target? It is within a single zone that LiveMap offers the best situational awareness — i.e., the most up to date and timely sharing of information across participating entities. While it is tempting to consider the entire planet as one giant zone, there are many reasons why smaller zones are advisable. In particular, the granularity and resolution of detail of synthesized information has to be fine enough to base the second-to-second actions of driverless vehicles. For a vehicle traveling at 70 mph (roughly 100 feet per second), hazards as small as a one-foot pothole or an even smaller rock are worthy of attention over the many hundred feet of the road that will be covered in the next few seconds. At such a fine spatial and temporal granularity, with the end-to-end latency of today's networking technologies as a guide and the speed of light as a lower bound, it is hard to see how to create a single zone that spans the entire planet. What appears feasible is a federation of many smaller zones. Across that federation, the spatial and temporal granularity of knowledge propagation may be significantly lower than within a single zone. Even if observers outside a zone can "zoom in" to details within that zone, there will be significant lag in seeing updates. Our intuition which is validated through the results presented later is that a city-sized or county-sized coverage area is feasible today, and the focus of our simulation work. As the end-to-end latency of networking technologies improves, and as our experience with LiveMap implementation matures, it is conceivable that a typical zone may expand to a medium-sized US state.

4.2 Vehicle-Zone Interactions

Figure 5 shows the interactions between an in-vehicle cloudlet and its currently-associated zone cloudlet. All of the data streams shown are implemented over TCP connections. In a real deployment, these will be secured using standard SSL/TLS mechanisms. The in-vehicle cloudlet performs edge analytics on external sensor inputs (e.g., video cameras, possibly multiple per vehicle) and internal sensor readings (such as speed, engine performance parameters, occupant alertness, etc.). These edge analytics transform the high data rate of raw sensor data into a semantic update stream of much lower bandwidth. Several decentralized transmission control mechanisms, described in Section 5.3, can be used to determine whether a specific update is likely to be redundant because of reports from other vehicles. The updates deemed redundant are suppressed, while the rest are transmitted to the zone cloudlet (arrow ① in Figure 5).

The transmission control mechanism in a vehicle may sometimes be too aggressive. Some data deemed redundant by an in-vehicle cloudlet may, in fact, be valuable to the zone cloudlet. From time to time, a zone cloudlet may explicitly request more information or ask for confirmation of an observation from another vehicle

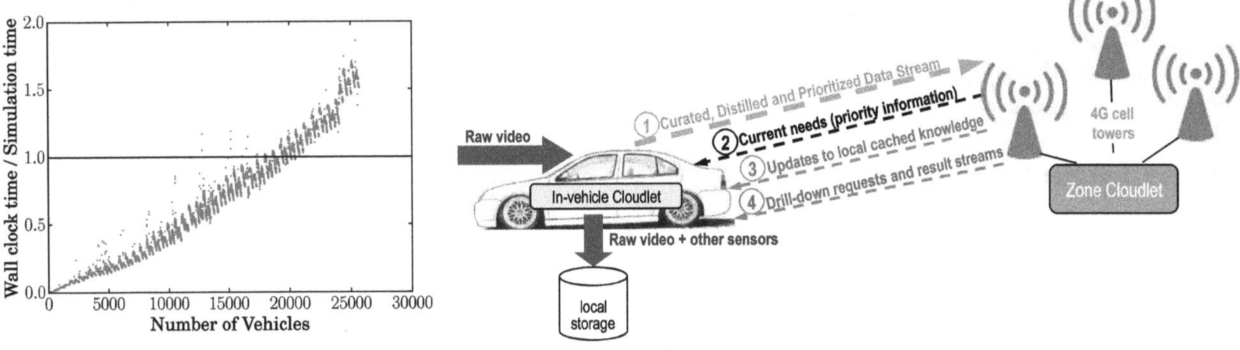

Figure 4: SUMO Scalability

Figure 5: Vehicle-Zone Interactions

(arrow ② in Figure 5). This request is an implicit hint to reduce the throttling of updates by a in-vehicle cloudlet. Each in-vehicle cloudlet caches data from the zone cloudlet. The communication to maintain cache consistency is shown as arrow ③ in Figure 5.

Raw sensor data is buffered in local storage at the in-vehicle cloudlet for a finite period of time. Retention is valuable if a need arises later to re-process the data with fresh analytics, or to drill down for more details. For example, if a public service alert is issued for a lost child, it may be valuable to search for the child's face and clothing in the retained video data from vehicles that recently passed through relevant neighborhoods. At an average of 3 GB per hour for HD video [17], almost two weeks of video can be stored in a modest 1 TB disk, that costs only $50 today. In Figure 5, arrow ④ corresponds to these ad hoc interactions between the zone cloudlet and in-vehicle cloudlet. An authorization mechanism and policy to determine who can present such requests will be needed in a real-world implementation. More details on how vehicle-zone interaction is implemented in our prototype can be found in Section 5.1.

4.3 Synthetic Hazard Generation

To the best of our knowledge, there are no existing large datasets of road hazards from which we can mine sophisticated statistical patterns. Therefore we create our own synthetic road hazard event generator. We model events with the following assumptions and constraints. First, we assume different types of road hazards (e.g., "dead deer" vs. "car accident") are independent and happen according to type-specific probabilities. Thus, for example, we can configure hazard profiles with a large number of disabled cars, but just a few deer sightings. We also assume that events happening on different road segments are independent. Furthermore, in each unit of time, the number of events of a particular type that happen on a road segment follows a Poisson distribution. Thus, the probability that k events happen is $P(k) = e^{-\lambda}\frac{\lambda^k}{k!}$, where λ is the expected number of events in one unit of time. We modify this slightly so that the expected number of events on a road segment depends on its "area," which is determined by its length and the number of lanes. Therefore, a three-lane highway will in average have 3 times the number of events as a similar length single-lane road. Finally, we constrain particular hazard types to only happen on specific types of roads, e.g., a "car accident" cannot happen on a cycleway.

Our hazard generator takes two files as input: a *hazard profile*, containing statistical parameters and constraints, and an OpenStreetMap file of a region. It also takes in the starting and ending times of a simulation and a time unit. By default, we use a time unit of one second. It then produces a trace log of road hazards, each with a timestamp, coordinates, and duration.

We would like the same hazard profile to be applicable to any map without modification, so that we can generate hazard traces for two different cities with similar statistical characteristics. Hence the parameters and constraints specified in the hazard profile are independent of the map (e.g., New York or Cologne). For a certain hazard type e, we specify a parameter β_e, and a list of road types it is allowed to occur on. On each road segment, its Poisson parameter is $\lambda_e = \beta_e \cdot area$. For each time unit, we generate events for each road segment and each hazard type independently. The final outputs are merged and sorted by time for playback.

4.4 Sensing Model

The simulated vehicles in our system execute the complete LiveMap application logic and protocol explained in Section 4.2. They do not, however, execute real video analytics code to detect hazards. To use real analytics code, the simulation framework would need to generate realistic camera views, including realistic portrayals of synthetic hazards and other vehicles in the system, for each vehicle at each timestep, and then execute the relatively expensive analytics algorithms to detect the hazards. This would be impractical, and greatly limit the scalability of the simulation.

Since we are primarily interested in testing scalability of the the LiveMap system, and not accuracy of analytics, we instead use a simple, fast sensing model to decide when simulated vehicles detect hazards. We assume each vehicle is equipped with multiple cameras that can view in all directions. The in-vehicle cloudlet is assumed to perform computer vision algorithms to detect events of interest (e.g., stopped cars, obstacles, etc.). The feasibility of such analytics is demonstrated in Section 6. Our model approximates sensing with omnidirectional cameras: within a configurable radius (50 m default), any hazard is assumed to be seen and detected. At each simulation step for each vehicle, the list of currently active hazards from the generated trace is consulted, and a sublist of active hazards within the detection radius of the vehicle's current position are returned by the simulated analytics. Other application logic decides if these need to be reported to the zone cloudlet, according to a variety of policies explored in Section 5.3.

5 Zone Cloudlet Prototype and Evaluation

To study our ideas on improving scalability and bandwidth use of automobile-based sensing, we have implemented a prototype of a zone cloudlet that serves a large collection of in-vehicle cloudlets at city or county scales. Although we test this server prototype with simulated in-vehicle cloudlets, the design and implementation of the server is fully independent of the simulation framework. The same server prototype can serve a large collection of real vehicles without modification. This feature is valuable when we extend the simulation to include real vehicles in the future.

As cellular bandwidth is the scarce resource in the system, we use this prototype to explore ways to lower the bandwidth needed. We seek quantitative answers to the following questions:

- How much bandwidth do LiveMap updates consume?
- How effective are different bandwidth throttling policies?
- What is the bandwidth-accuracy tradeoff?
- How well do caching and cache-based policies perform?
- How close can we get to the theoretical lower bound?

5.1 Zone Cloudlet Implementation

The zone cloudlet service is a typical TCP server written in Python. The service listens for incoming communications from vehicles, and sends messages to concurrent handlers for processing. Although there may be tens of thousands of active vehicles, only a small fraction of them will be in communication with the zone cloudlet at the same time, limiting the level of concurrency needed. These handlers update an in-memory Redis database [3] of the current state of the world. Each current road hazard is stored as an entry in the database, and an index of its location is created to facilitate fast search. We use the Gevent library [1] to provide a coroutine-based concurrency implementation underneath a thread-like API. Since the service is I/O bound, the coroutine approach works well. When the workload fully utilizes one CPU core, we spawn multiple processes of the same server and use a HAProxy load balancer [2] to coordinate them. We separate the information flow into two phases, data acquisition and data dissemination, and study them separately. Data transferred for acquisition is mostly on the uplink and data for data dissemination is mostly on the downlink.

The most naïve approach for data acquisition is to let vehicles report every road hazard they observe to the zone cloudlet. This approach provides the most accurate map (high coverage and low staleness), but transfers the most bytes and consumes the most bandwidth. We call this approach `upload-all` and use it as a baseline. The other extreme is the unattainable but ideal `oracle-driven` approach, where each hazard is reported exactly once, and on the earliest observation. This gives a lower bound on the bandwidth demand of any approach that provides full coverage.

We design and implement three other data acquisition approaches. The first is a probabilistic approach called `upload-X%`. With this approach, whenever a vehicle observes a hazard, it throws a die to decide whether or not to report this hazard. The upload happens X% of the time, statically configured across all vehicles. The second approach, `throttle-by-traffic`, uses a dynamic upload probability that is inversely proportional to the vehicle density in a 50m x 50m grid cell. The zone cloudlet tracks the traffic density of each cell, based on reports from the vehicles as they enter a new grid cell, and sends this aggregated information back to the vehicles.

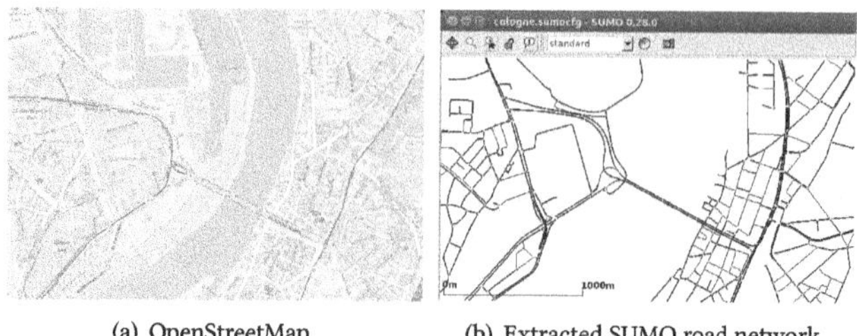

(a) OpenStreetMap (b) Extracted SUMO road network

Figure 6: Parts of the Map in the Cologne Dataset

The third approach is deterministic. The `throttle-by-cache` approach requires vehicles to maintain a cache of the live map of the surrounding area. The cache contains a subset of the map grid cells where each cell is 50m x 50m. When vehicles observe a hazard, they consult their cache and only upload new observations. To keep the cache up to date, vehicles refresh their cache when leaving the cached area, or when they receive an invalidation callback from the zone cloudlet indicating the cache may be stale. The callback mechanism is implemented on top of a modified Paho MQTT library [13], a low-bandwidth publish-and-subscribe system for IoT applications. We modify its asynchronous I/O multiplexing mechanism from `select` to `poll` to work for the scale of our experiments. The Pub/Sub channels correspond to grid cells. The vehicles subscribe to channels related to the cells in their cache, and the zone cloudlet publishes "cache invalid" messages to the corresponding channels when appropriate.

In addition to maintaining a live map, the zone cloudlet disseminates the acquired information to vehicles. If the network supports broadcast messages, the most efficient way to disseminate data is to broadcast a message to all vehicles when the zone cloudlet first learns about a road hazard. If broadcast is not available, a substitute can be emulated broadcast: the zone cloudlet sends one message to each vehicle for every road hazard. Dissemination can also be done with callback caching. With callback caching, the vehicles do not know about all hazards on the map, but they know the ones in their surroundings. With the `throttle-by-cache` acquisition option, callback caching is automatically assumed.

5.2 Experimental Setup

We run our zone cloudlet services and vehicle simulation framework in two virtual machines (VMs) on the same physical host, emulating near-perfect networking between vehicles and the zone cloudlet. The tradeoff between fidelity and scalability/practicality is discussed in more detail in Section 3. The host machine is a server with two Intel®Xeon®E5-2699 v3 processors (2.30 GHz, turbo 3.6 GHz, total of 36 cores, 72 hyper threads) and 128 GB memory. The zone cloudlet VM is configured with 4 GB memory and 8 VCPUs, and

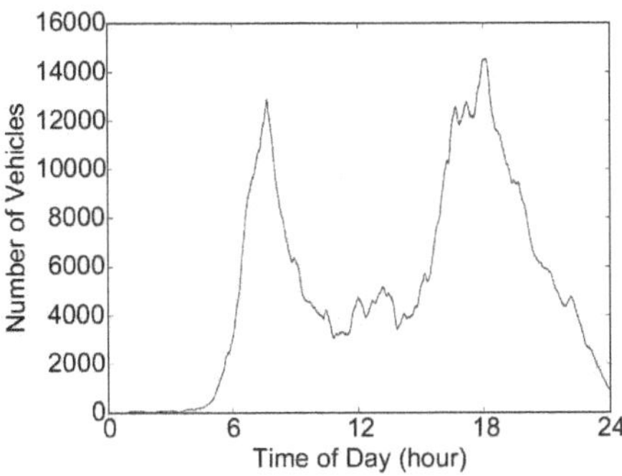

Figure 7: Traffic Statistics of TAPAS Cologne Dataset

Map area	1110 sq km
Vehicle total	462,000 vehicles
Peak traffic	14,000 vehicles
Median trip length	11 minutes

Figure 8: Summary of the Cologne Dataset Statistics

the simulation VM is configured with 8 GB memory and 32 VCPUs. These are ample resources for our experiments.

We use the TAPAS Cologne dataset (introduced in Section 3.3) for our experiments unless otherwise specified. Figure 6 shows the OpenStreetMap excerpt as well as the extracted road network for SUMO corresponding to this dataset. As suggested by the dataset provider, we reduce traffic demands to 30% of the realistic value to avoid city-wide traffic jams. This is a limit of the dataset itself and the current traffic simulation technology. Even with this reduction, it is still the largest available dataset to the best of our knowledge. Figure 7 shows the number of vehicles in the simulation as the simulation progresses. The rush hours are 6 am to 8 am and 4:30 pm to 8pm. The number of vehicles peaks at 7 am with around 13,000 vehicles and again at 6 pm with around 14,000 vehicles. Figure 8 shows a summary of statistics about this dataset.

We measure the bandwidth consumed, bandwidth efficiency, and the accuracy of the live map constructed. Bandwidth efficiency is measured by *duplication*, the percentage of messages that repeat previously-reported information. A few (two to three) messages for a particular hazard are useful in helping the zone cloudlet verify crowd-sourced information and resolve conflicts. Thus, a good duplication value may be between 50% and 67%, while a much higher one means a waste of resources. LiveMap accuracy is described by hazard *coverage*, the percentage of road hazards that are reported to the zone cloudlet, and information *staleness*, the average latency between when a road hazard appears and when the zone cloudlet receives the first report about it.

A 2.0 MB video file is submitted with each hazard report, equivalent to approximately 10 seconds of SD video or 2.4 seconds of HD video. [17]. Experiments are run three times with different random seeds, and median results presented. The simulation step is set to 200 ms to account for the computing time of LiveMap. Fidelity is slightly sacrificed for scalability and practicality of the simulation.

5.3 Bandwidth Saving - Acquisition

Figure 9 shows how the different approaches perform. The baseline approach, `upload-all`, has the best map accuracy and largest resource consumption by definition. The 1.9-minute staleness is mostly due to the time between when a hazard appears and when the first vehicle passes the area and notices it. The `upload-50%` approach lowers the peak bandwidth and bytes transferred approximately by half, at the cost of 3% on coverage, and 0.7 minute of staleness. `upload-10%` further reduces the peak bandwidth and bytes transferred to 10% of that of the baseline. 73% of the road hazards still get reported with 4.1-minute staleness. By controlling the upload probability in `upload-X%` approaches, we can tune this simple approach to fit different network bandwidth budgets with modest sacrifice of map accuracy.

Approach	Peak BW (Mbps)	Bytes Sent (GB)	Duplication	Coverage	Staleness (minutes)
upload-all	1362	77	98%	100%	1.9
upload-50%	657	38	97%	95%	2.6
upload-10%	295	7	90%	73%	4.1
throttle-by-traffic[a]	809	63	98%	98%	2.1
throttle-by-cache[b]	1037	17	89%	100%	2.0
oracle-driven	153	2	0%	100%	1.9

[a]The number of traffic update messages is very large. 16% of the messages are not sent because of the limited number of threads in the simulation.
[b]The simulation step is relaxed to 500ms to account for more computing time.

Figure 9: Bandwidth Saving Techniques for Data Acquisition (Cologne Scenario)

The `throttle-by-traffic` approach has near-perfect hazard coverage and staleness. This approach significantly reduces peak bandwidth, but not the total bytes transferred. Typically peak bandwidth is required when many vehicles are in the area when a hazard appears, and multiple vehicles simultaneously report it. With `throttle-by-traffic` because of high vehicle density, these vehicles upload with only a small probability, thus significantly reducing peak bandwidth. As peaks do not occur very often, the total bytes transferred mostly depends on the other situations where the vehicle density is smaller. Whenever the vehicle density is below 50 vehicles per cell per hour, vehicles report all detected hazards. So this approach does not significantly save bytes transferred.

The `throttle-by-cache` also has near-perfect coverage and staleness. It reduces the total bytes transferred to 22% of that of the baseline, including the extra bytes needed to fetch and maintain cache. A hazard that has already been reported by another vehicle is not likely to be reported again. However, this does not reduce peak bandwidth significantly. When a hazard appears in a high-traffic area, multiple vehicles may report it before there is time for the information to appear in their caches, contributing to peak bandwidth and duplication. Although `throttle-by-cache` has the least duplication other than oracle, it is still significant at 89%.

The `throttle-by-traffic` and `throttle-by-cache` approaches are both very useful because of their high accuracy, as shown by coverage and staleness. They are also efficient in reducing peak bandwidth and total bytes transferred separately. A combination of them might be able to reduce both peak bandwidth and bytes transferred at the same time, while providing high accuracy. We are exploring this possibility in continuing studies.

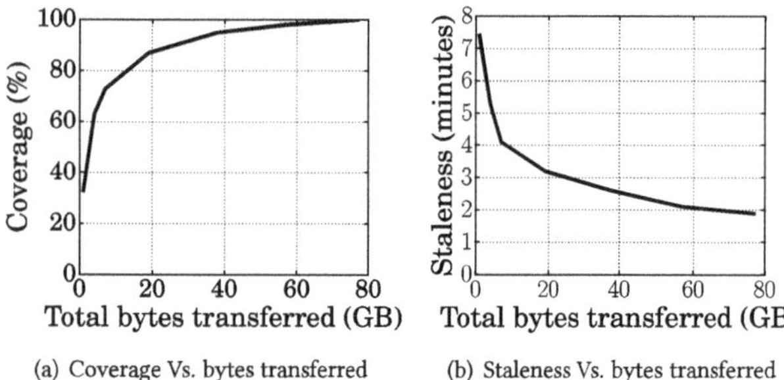

(a) Coverage Vs. bytes transferred (b) Staleness Vs. bytes transferred

Figure 10: Upload-X% Tradeoff (Cologne Scenario)

Technique	Bytes Transferred
Broadcast	61 KB
Emulated broadcast	567 MB
Callback caching	524 MB

Figure 11: Bandwidth Saving Techniques for Data Dissemination (Cologne Scenario)

5.4 Sensitivity to Acquisition Parameters

Some of the above approaches have tunable parameters that may affect the performance of the approach, such as the upload probability in `upload-X%` and the inverse proportion coefficient in `throttle-by-traffic`. These parameters serve as tuning knobs of the tradeoff between resources consumed (characterized by peak bandwidth and bytes transferred) and map accuracy (characterized by coverage and staleness). When these parameters change, it is straightforward to expect peak bandwidth and bytes transferred to change approximately proportionally. But it is difficult to predict how other metrics change, as the relationship is not linear.

We take `upload-X%` as an example to study this tradeoff. We experiment with varying values of upload probability and present the tradeoff curve in Figure 10. As we lower the upload probability, fewer bytes are transferred and fewer hazards are covered, and it takes longer for the zone cloudlet to learn about hazards. The first half of the bytes can be saved at a low cost of coverage and staleness. To further reduce the bytes transferred to a quarter of its original value, the staleness has to increase from 1.9 minutes to 3.3 minutes and coverage decreases from 100% to 87%. Further reduction in the number of bytes transferred comes at an even larger cost. The "knees" of the curves suggest a good operating range between 10 GB and 40 GB transferred, which corresponds to an upload probability between 10% to 50%. In this range, coverage is between 74% to 96% and staleness ranges from 2.6 to 4.1 minutes.

5.5 Bandwidth Saving - Dissemination

Figure 11 shows the performance of the data dissemination approaches. Surprisingly, similar numbers of bytes are transferred for callback caching and emulated broadcast. This is due to coarse-grain cache invalidation; if any cells change, vehicles will refresh the whole cache. These design choices reduce the number of messages sent, but transfer extra bytes for refreshing up-to-date portions of the cache. If we make caching granularity smaller and have vehicles only refresh the invalid cells, we will able to reduce this overhead significantly. If caching granularity is too small, the system will suffer from frequent inefficient small fetches of data. We will investigate the optimal cache granularity in continuing studies.

Approach	Peak BW (Mbps)	Bytes Sent (GB)	Duplication	Coverage	Staleness (minutes)
upload-all	2077	61	99%	100%	1.3
upload-10%	235	6	95%	84%	3.6
throttle-by-traffic[a]	792	61	99%	100%	1.3
throttle-by-cache	1186	3	74%	100%	1.3

[a] 2% of the messages are not sent due to limited number of threads in the simulation.

Figure 12: Bandwidth Saving Techniques for Data Acquisition (Luxembourg Scenario)

5.6 Sensitivity to Input Traffic Model

To verify the generalizability of our previous results, we run the same experiments on another input model, the Luxembourg SUMO Traffic Scenario [10]. It features a map of the Luxembourg City and traffic in this area for a whole day. The traffic patterns are synthesized with the SUMO ACTIVITYGEN tool, which takes detailed demographics data as an input. The dataset provides four variants of the traffic model with different mobility models and traffic light models. We choose the variant with the most traffic and run the experiments from 6 am to 9 am. The peak traffic is around 5200 vehicles at 8 am.

Figure 12 shows that the results are similar to those from the Cologne experiments. `upload-10%` reduces peak bandwidth and bytes transferred to 10% of their baseline values as expected. 84% of the hazards still get reported to the zone cloudlet, which is higher than that in the Cologne scenario, and it takes 2.3 minutes longer than the baseline for the zone cloudlet to learn about hazards. The `throttle-by-traffic` approach has perfect coverage and staleness, and significantly reduces peak bandwidth to 32% of the baseline. This reduction is much bigger than in the Cologne scenario. On the other hand, bytes transferred are not saved, unlike in the Cologne case. These differences may be due to the different traffic patterns of the two scenarios. Despite the differences, this approach is effective in significantly reducing peak bandwidth in both scenarios. `throttle-by-cache` still has the perfect coverage and staleness as expected. Comparing to the baseline, only 5% of the bytes are transferred. Peak bandwidth is also reduced by half.

Experiments on more input models can give us more insights. Unfortunately, to the best of our knowledge, there are no other large-scale per-vehicle traffic datasets publicly available. However in general, we believe `throttle-by-traffic` will consistently be more effective at reducing peak bandwidth, and `throttle-by-cache` will be more effective at reducing total bytes transferred. We plan to study hybrid approaches that combine these ideas.

6 Feasibility of In-vehicle Hazard Detection

Computer-vision based video analytics to detect road hazards is a critical component of LiveMap. Such analytics need to be fast enough to run on the in-vehicle cloudlets, yet provide reasonably good accuracy. False positives will result in unnecessary updates

Dataset	# of Images	Labeled by
Google Deer Dataset	340	us
ImageNet Deer Dataset	691	ImageNet
Google Pothole Dataset	34	us
ImageNet Pothole Dataset	267	us

Figure 13: Summary of Training Datasets

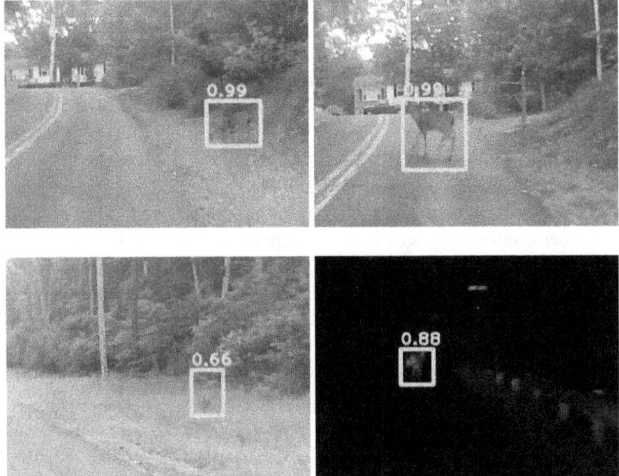

Figure 14: Examples of Deer Detection Results

and video transmitted to the zone cloudlet, wasting precious bandwidth. On the other hand, with too many false negatives, hazards are not detected and the system becomes useless. In this section, we demonstrate the feasibility of in-vehicle hazard detection by implementing a fast, reasonably accurate system for detecting deer and potholes.

Our implementation uses the state-of-the-art, neural-network-based Faster R-CNN [22] algorithm. To generate training data, we manually labeled deer and potholes in the videos and images found from the web. We employ the transfer learning approach [19] to reduce the total number of hand-labeled training images and total amount of training time needed for our detector. Figure 13 summarizes the datasets we used for training.

Running on a machine with a modern NVIDA Tesla K40 GPU, our detectors are able to operate at 7 frames per second (FPS). This confirms that today's computing technology is able to process video streams fast enough for LiveMap. The two proof-of-concept hazard detectors described below are representative of what is achievable today. Any computer vision work that improves road hazard detection will complement our work. When better detectors are available (for example, those created by entities such as RoadBotics [4] and Lost And Found [20]), they can be easily plugged into LiveMap to improve the accuracy and speed of hazard detection.

6.1 Example: Deer Detection

Obtaining appropriate data for training the object detector is a non-trivial task. A simple online search often returns images that do

Figure 15: Examples of Pothole Detection Results

not have the right camera view for a vehicle mounted camera. This could lead to low detection accuracy. Therefore, we had to manually filter images to find ones with the right views (e.g., dashcam views) before including them in the training dataset. Our training data for deer detection comes from two sources. We first searched for "deer on road" in Google Image Search, and manually selected and annotated 340 valid images (Figure 13). We then included 691 annotated deer images from ImageNet [11]. Videos from YouTube did not provide good training data, as many of them are compilation videos deer-car collisions, without normal poses and views of deer.

In the precision-recall curve of a 10-fold cross-validation, the area under the curve of our detector is 87.8%. This is comparable to the reported accuracy of state-of-the-art object detection work today [22]. Figure 14 shows the detection results on example frames from a 2-minute YouTube dashcam video [21]. The full video with annotations of detection results can be found at https://youtu.be/_GrP42359z8.

6.2 Example: Pothole Detection

Using a similar procedure as we followed for deer detection, we obtain several thousand images of potholes from ImageNet and Google. However, potholes are much harder to detect than deer, due to their greater variation in shape, and change in appearance with distance and viewing angles. The potholes at a distance can also be really small, only a few pixels in each dimension. This required us to perform a more careful screening of our raw dataset based on viewing angle, finally resulting in 267 images from ImageNet and 34 images from Google (Figure 13). To help reduce false positive rate with this fairly small set of images, we included the deer images as negative samples in our training set for the pothole detector.

Our trained pothole detector is sensitive to the viewing angle and distance to the pothole. So on still images, it typically only detects a subset of potholes. However, it performs well on YouTube dashcam videos like in Figure 15. A full video with annotated potholes can be found at https://youtu.be/U7_QAVbiF8U. Although some potholes may not be detected at a distance, they will likely be caught when the vehicle moves closer, leading to a hazard report in subsequent frames. In the video mentioned above, 913 unique potholes appear and 74% of them are detected in at least one frame. In addition, of the reported potholes, 75% are true positives.

7 Conclusion

A live, continuously-updated map overlayed with road conditions and hazards can provide the situational awareness needed to enable self-driving vehicles, empower human drivers and optimize city services. We have proposed LiveMap, an automated approach to this goal that employs in-vehicle processing of video and sensor data to detect road conditions, and uses a central zone cloudlet to manage, aggregate, and disseminate a unified view onto regional conditions. We have shown that LiveMap can scale to city or county scales within the limits of today's 4G LTE network bandwidth. We have also demonstrated the feasibility of in-vehicle computer-vision-based hazard detection.

Our evaluations of LiveMap are based on a novel mixed simulation framework that allows real implemented components and simulated ones to operate together. This effectively provides us the best of both worlds, allowing us to test real components and code, at system scales only practical in simulation. A key necessary requirement is that our simulation framework executes in real time. We are able to meet the real-time requirements at city scale simulation. Looking ahead, further scaling is limited by the single-threaded architecture of the core SUMO traffic simulator. To scale real-time simulation to hundreds of thousands of vehicles, significantly faster processor cores or an efficient multi-threaded implementation of SUMO will be needed. Finally, to better understand how LiveMap performs in the real world, we hope to deploy real vehicles instrumented with cameras, and in-vehicle cloudlets, and to construct a fully-operational instance of LiveMap.

Acknowledgements

This research was supported by the National Science Foundation (NSF) under grant number CNS-1518865. Additional support was provided by Intel, Google, Vodafone, Deutsche Telekom, Verizon, Crown Castle, NTT, and the Conklin Kistler family fund. Any opinions, findings, conclusions or recommendations expressed in this material are those of the authors and do not necessarily reflect the view(s) of their employers or the above-mentioned funding sources.

REFERENCES

[1] Gevent. http://www.gevent.org/.

[2] HAProxy. http://www.haproxy.org/.

[3] Redis. https://redis.io/.

[4] RoadBotics. https://www.roadbotics.com/.

[5] TAPAS Cologne Scenario. http://sumo.dlr.de/wiki/Data/Scenarios/TAPASCologne, Accessed May 11, 2017.

[6] G. Araniti, C. Campolo, M. Condoluci, A. Iera, and A. Molinaro. LTE for vehicular networking: a survey. *IEEE Communications Magazine*, 51(5):148–157, May 2013.

[7] D. H. Autor. Why Are There Still So Many Jobs? The History and Future of Workplace Automation. *Journal of Economic Perspectives*, 29(3):3–30, Summer 2015.

[8] M. Behrisch, L. Bieker, J. Erdmann, and D. Krajzewicz. Sumo–simulation of urban mobility: an overview. In *Proceedings of SIMUL 2011, The Third International Conference on Advances in System Simulation*. ThinkMind, 2011.

[9] R. N. Clarke. Expanding mobile wireless capacity: The challenges presented by technology and economics. *Telecommunications Policy*, 38:693–708, 2014.

[10] L. Codeca, R. Frank, and T. Engel. Luxembourg sumo traffic (lust) scenario: 24 hours of mobility for vehicular networking research. In *Vehicular Networking Conference (VNC), 2015 IEEE*, pages 1–8. IEEE, 2015.

[11] J. Deng, W. Dong, R. Socher, L.-J. Li, K. Li, and L. Fei-Fei. Imagenet: A large-scale hierarchical image database. In *Computer Vision and Pattern Recognition, 2009. CVPR 2009. IEEE Conference on*, pages 248–255. IEEE, 2009.

[12] H. R. Dhasian and P. Balasubramanian. Survey of data aggregation techniques using soft computing in wireless sensor networks. *International Journal of Information and Computation Technology*, 3(3):167–174, 2013.

[13] Eclipse. Paho. https://www.eclipse.org/paho/, Accessed May 18, 2017.

[14] K.-H. Kastner, R. Keber, P. Pau, and M. Samal. Real-time traffic conditions with sumo for its austria west. In *Simulation of Urban MObility User Conference*, pages 146–159. Springer, 2013.

[15] V. Kumar and S. Madria. Secure Data Aggregation in Wireless Sensor Networks. In T. Hara, V. I. Zadorozhny, and E. Buchmann, editors, *Wireless Sensor Network Technologies for the Information Explosion Era*, pages 77–107. Springer, Berlin, Heidelberg, 2010.

[16] LteWorld. LTE Advanced: Evolution of LTE. http://lteworld.org/blog/lte-advanced-evolution-lte, August 2009. Retrieved: 2016-1-11.

[17] Netflix Help Center. How can I control how much data Netflix uses? https://help.netflix.com/en/node/87. Accessed November 26, 2016.

[18] OpenStreetMap Foundation. OpenStreetMap. https://www.openstreetmap.org, Accessed May 19, 2017.

[19] S. J. Pan and Q. Yang. A Survey on Transfer Learning. *IEEE Transactions on Knowledge and Data Engineering*, 22(10):1345–1359, October 2010.

[20] P. Pinggera, S. Ramos, S. Gehrig, U. Franke, C. Rother, and R. Mester. Lost and found: detecting small road hazards for self-driving vehicles. In *Intelligent Robots and Systems (IROS), 2016 IEEE/RSJ International Conference on*, pages 1099–1106. IEEE, 2016.

[21] W. Quinn. Deer on the road dec 2015. https://www.youtube.com/watch?v=JPSQUkT8rZY.

[22] S. Ren, K. He, R. Girshick, and J. Sun. Faster r-cnn: Towards real-time object detection with region proposal networks. In *Advances in neural information processing systems*, pages 91–99, 2015.

[23] M. Satyanarayanan. Edge Computing for Situational Awareness. In *Proceedings of the 23rd IEEE International Symposium on Local and Metropolitan Area Networks (LANMAN 2017)*, Osaka, Japan, June 2017.

[24] M. Satyanarayanan, P. Bahl, R. Cáceres, and N. Davies. The Case for VM-Based Cloudlets in Mobile Computing. *IEEE Pervasive Computing*, 8(4), 2009.

[25] C. Sommer, R. German, and F. Dressler. Bidirectionally Coupled Network and Road Traffic Simulation for Improved IVC Analysis. *IEEE Transactions on Mobile Computing*, 10(1):3–15, January 2011.

[26] A. Tripathi, S. Gupta, and B. Chourasiya. Survey on Data Aggregation Techniques for Wireless Sensor Networks. *International Journal of Advanced Research in Computer and Communication Engineering*, 3, July 2014.

[27] A. Varga and R. Hornig. An overview of the omnet++ simulation environment. In *Proceedings of the 1st international conference on Simulation tools and techniques for communications, networks and systems & workshops*, page 60. ICST (Institute for Computer Sciences, Social-Informatics and Telecommunications Engineering), 2008.

[28] Waze. http://waze.com, Accessed Nov 22, 2016.

Performance Model for 4G/5G Heterogeneous Networks with Different Classes of Users

Narcisse Nya
Sorbonne Universités, UPMC Univ Paris 06, CNRS, LIP6
UMR 7606, 4 place Jussieu 75005 Paris
narcisse.nya@lip6.fr

Bruno Baynat
Sorbonne Universités, UPMC Univ Paris 06, CNRS, LIP6
UMR 7606, 4 place Jussieu 75005 Paris
bruno.baynat@lip6.fr

ABSTRACT

In this paper, we analyze flow level performance of mobile users in 4G/pre-5G cellular networks such as LTE and LTE-A. To this end, we develop a two-levels model that provides users' performance in a cell and end-to-end performance in the network. At a cell-level, the model is a multi-class PS queue that captures mobility of users between zones of a cell, through a simple mobility model, that is decoupled from the cell model itself, enabling to directly apply the approach to more realistic mobility patterns. At a network-level, the model is a simple Discrete Time Markov Chain that reproduces the routing of mobile users between the different cells of the system. We first show that this model is consistent with known analytical bounds corresponding to a system with either static users or users having an infinite speed. The outcomes of our model confirm that mobility may improve both users and cells performance, and enable to quantify the gain. The model also shows that, while inter-cell mobility balances the load between cells, it does not lead to such improvement of throughput as intra-cell mobility.

KEYWORDS

LTE/LTE-A networks, Performance evaluation, Mobility, Processor Sharing queues, Markov processes, Data traffic.

1 INTRODUCTION

LTE/LTE-A are the latest standards in the mobile network technology tree that previously realized the GSM/EDGE and UMTS/HSxPA technologies. The main advantage with LTE is the improvement of end-user experience. One of the key of this improvement is the use of Adaptive Modulation and Coding (AMC) [17]. Its basic idea is to select an optimal combination of modulation and coding scheme (MCS) according to channel quality so as to achieve the highest spectral efficiency at all times [14]. More precisely, the UE periodically sends CQI feedbacks as an indication of the data rate which can be supported by the downlink channel. This helps the eNodeB to select appropriate modulation scheme and code rate for downlink transmission. As such, modulation and/or coding can change with time for a given user depending on its location and its channel quality. This is especially true when users are mobile, highlighting the influence of mobility on user and network performance. This capability of dynamically controlling the rate, combined with the relative delay tolerance of data applications, opens up the possibility of scheduling transmissions so as to obtain efficiency gains of throughput. A particularly attractive approach is to use channel-aware scheduling strategies [6] [8], which schedule the transmissions to various users when their instantaneous channel conditions are relatively favorable. While channel variations are considered to have a predominantly adverse impact for constant-rate voice connections, they provide the opportunity to improve the throughput for elastic data transfers [3], [13] and even schedulers with fair resource sharing strategy can take advantage of channel variation or users' mobility.

Only few authors study the performance of users taking into account their mobility. In [9], authors identify two limit regimes of infinitely fast and infinitely low channel variations. They show that these limit regimes provide simple bounds of performance at flow-level. [7] also develops lower and upper bounds for flow-level performance measures, and show that mobility tends to increase the overall capacity of the network. In [12], authors analyze networks with several interacting base stations, and show that mobility increases the stability region of the system. Authors of [16] model an OFDMA system jointly using Proportional Fairness (PF) and Hierarchical Modulation (HM), by a multi-dimensional Markov chain, and show that in the presence of HM, a simple cyclic service, such as Round Robin, yields better performance than PF. [11] proposes a Whittle model to evaluate the impact of mobility of users on performance of cellular networks. Unfortunately, in this model the mobility is influenced by a congestion in the network. In particular, when the network approaches instability, user mobility is being frozen. Authors of [2] assess the impact of users mobility on cell performance, under a fair and an opportunistic scheduling scheme. They show in particular that under both scheduling policies, mobility improves throughput performance at cell edge. But as the Markovian process associated with their model is no longer reversible in the case where mobile users fairly share resources, they can only develop closed-form expressions in two limiting cases, namely when users are static and when users have a theoretical infinite speed. The most related works is [5] where authors evaluates users performance for realistic speeds. Considering the particular case of a network of statistically identical cells with users moving at the same speed, they propose an analysis based on a multiclass Processor-Sharing (PS) model.

In this paper we develop a model for performance evaluation of users in LTE/LTE-A heterogeneous networks visited by different class of users. We extend the analitycal results of [5] to more general cellular networks and Several users classes. At a cell-level, the

MSWiM '17, November 21–25, 2017, Miami, FL, USA

ACM ISBN 978-1-4503-5162-1/17/11...$15.00
https://doi.org/10.1145/3127540.3127554

model is based on multi-class Processor Sharing (PS) queue, that captures mobility of users through the distribution of the time a given user physically stays in different coding zones of the cell. At a network-level, the model is a simple Discrete Time Morkov Chain (DTMC), that reproduces the routing of mobile users between the different cells of the system. Contrarily to previous studies, our model does not rely on the numerical analysis of complex Markov chains, or on limiting assumptions such as infinite speed of users, and as such is one of the first tractable and accurate approximations for LTE/LTE-A heterogeneous networks. Thanks to our model, we quantify the gain of speed on both the performance of the cell and the end-to-end performance of users in network, and investigate the influence of times and data traffic distributions.

The remainder of the paper is organized as follows. Section 2 presents system and traffic assumptions. Section 3 develops the PS queue model and the DTMC and all performance parameters of interest. Section 4 present performance results of the model. The model is validated through simulation in Section 5 and section 6 investigates the impact of times and data distributions on performance. Finally, Section 7 concludes the paper.

2 SYSTEM AND TRAFFIC DESCRIPTION

2.1 The system: a network of LTE macrocells

We consider a heterogeneous LTE network composed of N macrocells. Without loss of generality and to simplify notations, we assume that each cell has one antenna. Each antenna provides service to the users located in the corresponding cell through a shared downlink. For a given number of active users in cell n, resources (Resource Blocks in LTE) of the antenna are equally divided among these users. The achievable throughput, i.e., a throughput that can be achieved by a user that is alone in a given cell depends on its radio conditions to the serving eNodeB and fading variation, but also to others neighboring eNodeB. In fact, according to Adaptive Modulation and Coding (AMC) in use in LTE system, the eNodeB dynamically change the Modulation and Coding Scheme (MCS) to the channel conditions. Thus, the cell n of the network can be divided into J_n transmission zones of equal radio conditions, each characterized by an achievable throughput [10]. Each zones corresponds to a MCS used for transmission, users in the same region have the same average radio condition and thus, use the same MCS. We recall that the network is heterogeneous, therefore the number of zones is not identical between cells. A user of zone (j, n), i.e., currently present in region j, $j = 1, ..., J_n$, of cell n, $n = 1, ..., N$, will obtain a throughput $C_{j,n}$, if he is alone in this cell. Even if it is not necessary for the developments in this work, we can assume as, e.g., in [18] and [15], that the J_n transmission zones of cell n form concentric circles of radius $R_{j,n}$, where zone 1 is the central zone and zone J_n is the peripheral zone. This assumption is use just to illustrate how the input parameters of the model can be related to users speed in this special case, any other structural model of the cell, e.g., hexagonal cells with sectorization, can alternately be used without affecting the developments of the model.

2.2 Mobility model and traffic assumption

Users are mobile, therefore, users connected to a eNodeB, i.e., present in one cell, have the ability to change zone (modulation oder efficiency) by migration to another one in the same cell or change cell during their transfer. Specifically, we consider an arbitrary number of K types of users, each type corresponding to a given statistical flow size Σ^k to transfer and mobility speed V^k, $k = 1, ..., K$. The mobility model we consider is the following. It is important to emphasize that it is a physical mobility model of users that is decoupled from the utilization of the resources of cells by users. We denote by $\Theta^k_{j,n}$ the physical sojourn time of a type-k user in region j of cell n at each visit of this region, that is the time duration he physically stays in zone (j, n) starting form the moment he appears in that zone (either because he begins its download in that zone, or because he enters the zone from neighboring zones or cells), and ending when he leaves the zone (still being active or not) for a neighboring zone or cell, or leave definitively the network. We consider that new connection demands arrive in cell n of the network according to a Poisson process of rate Λ_n. A user that carries a new connection demand has a probability $p_{j,n}$ to be initially in zone (j, n) and thus to start its download in region j of cell n and probability q^k to be a type-k user. As a result, new connection demands of type-k users arrive in zone (j, n) according to a Poisson process of rate $\Lambda^k_{j,n} = p_{j,n}q^k\Lambda_n$. We define $P_{j\to i,n}$, the probability that a user (whatever its type) that physically (i.e., active or not) exits zone (j, n) move to a neighboring zone (i, n) of the same cell. We note by $P_{j\to 0,n}$ the probability that a user exits cell n from zone (j, n), and by $P_{0\to j,n}$, the probability that a user enters in cell n by zone (j, n). Note that when zones form concentric circles, users can only leave and enter in a cell from zone J_n. We also define $\Psi_{m\to n}$ the probability that a user (whatever his type) that physically (i.e., active or not) exits cell m move to cell n.

We focus our attention on the so-called data traffic in downlink, corresponding mainly to file transfer, web pages downloads and emails. As soon as a new request arrives, it triggers the start of a new data transmission (in the zone where the request appears). This transmission ends when the user has completed its transfer whatever the number of zones or cells he has visited meanwhile.

We first consider that random variables Σ^k and $\Theta^k_{j,n}$ are exponentially distributed. The first assumption is necessary for the derivations presented below. As a matter of fact, and because of the memoryless property of the exponential distribution, assuming an exponential volume enables us to forget the amount of data already transferred by a user in previous zones or cells as long as he is still active and moves to another zone or cell. This drastically simplify the analysis. On the other hand, assuming exponential sojourn time in each zone is only made for simplification purposes. The impact of these assumptions will be investigated in Section 6.

2.3 Estimation of parameters when zones are concentric circles

Considering the special case where zones of cells form concentric circles, we show in this section how we can estimate the traffic and mobility parameters. Let us consider cell n with J_n transmission zones, zone (j, n) being of radius $R_{j,n}$. First, the surface of zone (j,n) is $S_{j,n} = \pi(R_{j,n}^2 - R_{j-1,n}^2)$, for $j > 1$, and $S_{1,n} = \pi R_{1,n}^2$. If arrivals of new connection demands are uniformly distributed over the whole surface of the cell, the probability $p_{j,n}$ that a new connection demand whatever its type appears in zone (j,n), is proportional to the surface of zone (j,n):

$$p_{j,n} = \frac{S_{j,n}}{\pi R_{J_n,n}^2}. \quad (1)$$

Concerning the mean sojourn time $\mathbb{E}(\Theta_{j,n}^k)$ of type k users in zone (j,n), we can reasonably assume that it is proportional to the square root of the surface of the zone and inversely proportional to the speed V^k of users:

$$\mathbb{E}(\Theta_{j,n}^k) = K\frac{\sqrt{S_{j,n}}}{V^k}, \quad (2)$$

When zones form concentric circles, a user that physically exists zone (j,n), $j = 2, \ldots, J_n - 1$ and $n = 1, \ldots, N$, has a probability $P_{j\to j-1,n}$ to move to zone $(j-1,n)$, and a probability $P_{j\to j+1,n}$ to move to zone $(j+1,n)$ (with, of course, $P_{j\to j-1,n} + P_{j\to j+1,n} = 1$). For zone 1, obviously, $P_{1\to 2,n} = 1$. And from zone J_n, a user can either move back to zone $J_n - 1$ with a probability $P_{J_n\to J_n-1,n}$, or exit the cell with a probability $P_{J_n\to 0,n}$. All these probabilities clearly depend both on the radius $R_{j,n}$ of zones and on the real mobility of users. However, without additional assumptions on physical mobility of users, we can use the following approximation:

$$P_{j\to j-1,n} = \frac{R_{j-1,n}}{2R_{j,n}}, j > 1. \quad (3)$$

This is a linear approximation that respects obvious limits: when $R_{j-1,n} \to 0$, $P_{j\to j-1,n} \to 0$, and when $R_{j-1,n} \to R_{j,n}$, $P_{j\to j-1,n} \to \frac{1}{2}$.

Note that probabilities $p_{j,n}$, $P_{j\to i,n}$ and $\Psi_{m\to n}$, as well as mean sojourn times $\mathbb{E}(\Theta_{j,n}^k)$, are input parameters for the PS queue model. Any alternative expressions resulting from a realistic physical mobility model of users, can be alternately used without changing the development presented below.

3 MODEL

3.1 Model of an isolated macrocell

For the sake of simplicity, we first consider in this section only the intra-cell mobility. Users in the same cell have the ability to change their transmission zones (modulation order efficiency) by migration to another zone. However, users can not leave the cell before completing their download, i.e., in the considered cell denoted by n, $P_{J_n\to 0,n} = 0$ and $P_{J_n\to J_n-1,n} = 1$. Conversely, active users can not enter the cell coming from neighboring cells.

The model represents this cell n occupancy by a multi-class Processor Sharing queue with $J_n * K$ classes. Each class of the queue corresponds to one zone of the cell and one type of users. Customers of class $(j,n)^k$ arrive to the queue according to a Poisson process of rate $\lambda_{j,n}^k$, $j = 1, \ldots, J_n$ and $k = 1, \ldots, K$. It is important to note that, $\lambda_{j,n}^k$ is different from the rate $\Lambda_{j,n}^k$ of new connection requests of type k users that appear in zone (j,n), as it must include arrival of users that move from other zones of cell n while still being active. If we denote by $\Lambda_{j\to i,n}^k$ the average number of type-k active users moving from zone (j,n) to zone (i,n) by unit of time, we have:

$$\begin{cases} \lambda_{1,n}^k = \Lambda_{1,n}^k + \Lambda_{2\to 1,n}^k \\ \lambda_{j,n}^k = \Lambda_{j,n}^k + \Lambda_{j-1\to j,n}^k + \Lambda_{j+1\to j,n}^k, j = 2, \ldots, J_n - 1 \\ \lambda_{J_n,n}^k = \Lambda_{J_n,n}^k + \Lambda_{J_n-1\to J_n,n}^k \end{cases} \quad (4)$$

Class-$(j,n)^k$ rate can in turn be expressed as:

$$\mu_{j,n}^k = \frac{C_{j,n}}{\bar{x}_{j,n}^k}, \quad (5)$$

where $\bar{x}_{j,n}^k$ is defined as the average volume actually transferred by type-k user at each visit of zone (j,n). As a result, we are left to estimate input parameters of the PS queue, namely $\lambda_{j,n}^k$ and $\mu_{j,n}^k$ or more precisely all $\Lambda_{j\to i,n}^k$ and $\bar{x}_{j,n}^k$.

If parameters $\lambda_{j,n}^k$ and $\mu_{j,n}^k$ are known, standard results for the stationary multi-class Processor Sharing queue can be readily applied to calculate the average throughput $\bar{\gamma}_{j,n}$ obtained by users (whatever their types) in zone (j,n) of the cell during their transfer, that is,

$$\bar{\gamma}_{j,n} = C_{j,n}(1 - \rho_n), \quad (6)$$

where ρ_n is the load of the cell and it is given by:

$$\rho_n = \sum_{j=1}^{J_n}\sum_{k=1}^{K} \rho_{j,n}^k \text{ with } \rho_{j,n}^k = \frac{\lambda_{j,n}^k}{\mu_{j,n}^k}. \quad (7)$$

In order to estimate the first missing parameters $\bar{x}_{j,n}^k$, required in the expression of $\mu_{j,n}^k$, we use the methodology developed in [4] for a cell with a single zone, and apply it to each zone individually. As shown in [4] in the special case where Σ^k and $\Theta_{j,n}^k$ are exponentially distributed, $\bar{x}_{j,n}^k$ is related to the average throughput $\bar{\gamma}_{j,n}$ obtained by users in zone (j,n) and to the average time $\mathbb{E}(\Theta_{j,n}^k)$ a type-k user physically spends in zone (j,n), as:

$$\bar{x}_{j,n}^k = \frac{\mathbb{E}(\Sigma^k)\mathbb{E}(\Theta_{j,n}^k)\bar{\gamma}_{j,n}}{\mathbb{E}(\Sigma^k) + \mathbb{E}(\Theta_{j,n}^k)\bar{\gamma}_{j,n}}. \quad (8)$$

We now need to estimate the missing parameters $\Lambda_{j\to i,n}^k$ appearing in the expressions of $\lambda_{j,n}^k$. If we denote by $h_{j,n}^k$ the handover probability of type-k users from zone (j,n), i.e., the probability that a type-k active user leaves zone (j,n) without having completed its transfer, we can express $\Lambda_{j\to j+1,n}^k$ and $\Lambda_{j\to j-1,n}^k$ as:

$$\begin{cases} \Lambda_{j\to j+1,n}^k = \lambda_{j,n}^k h_{j,n}^k P_{j\to j+1,n}, j = 1, \ldots, J_n - 1 \\ \Lambda_{j\to j-1,n}^k = \lambda_{j,n}^k h_{j,n}^k P_{j\to j-1,n}, j = 2, \ldots, J_n \end{cases} \quad (9)$$

The handover probabilities $h_{j,n}^k$ can in turn be expressed as:

$$h_{j,n}^k = \int_0^{+\infty} \mathbb{P}\left[\Theta_{j,n}^k \le \frac{y}{\bar{\gamma}_{j,n}}\right] f_{\Sigma^k}(y)\, dy. \quad (10)$$

Assuming that Σ^k and $\Theta_{j,n}^k$ are exponentially distributed, the previous integral readily gives [4]:

$$h_{j,n}^k = \frac{\mathbb{E}(\Sigma^k)}{\mathbb{E}(\Sigma^k) + \mathbb{E}(\Theta_{j,n}^k)\bar{\gamma}_{j,n}}. \quad (11)$$

We finally end up with a system of 7 dependent equations (4-7 , 8, 9, 11) that will be solved using a fixed-point iterative technique.

3.2 Performance bounds and stability

The performance of the system we consider where mobile users physically moving in the cell with some speed V^k, is bounded by that of two systems in which all users have the same speed. In the first one, users are all static ($V^{st} = 0$), and in the second one, users have an infinite speed ($V^{\infty} = \infty$).

Let us denote by $\mathbb{E}(\Sigma) = \sum_{k=1}^{K} q^k \mathbb{E}(\Sigma^k)$ the average size of data to be downloaded by a user (whatever its type) in the system. The model corresponding to the first system where users are stationary, is the classical multi-class PS queue with parameters $\lambda_{j,n} = \Lambda_{j,n}$ and $\mu_{(j,n)} = \frac{C_{j,n}}{\mathbb{E}(\Sigma)}$. It corresponds to a cell with a single zone having an equivalent capacity C^{st} equal to the harmonic mean of $C_{j,n}$:

$$\frac{1}{C^{st}} = \sum_{j=1}^{J_n} \frac{p_{j,n}}{C_{j,n}}, \tag{12}$$

$p_{j,n}$ being the probability that a new connection demand appears in zone (j,n). We define the load of this system as:

$$\rho_n^{st} = \frac{\mathbb{E}(\Sigma) \sum_{j=1}^{J_n} \lambda_{j,n}}{C^{st}}. \tag{13}$$

The necessary and sufficient condition for the stability of this system is therefore:

$$\rho_n^{st} < 1, \text{ i.e., } \Lambda_n = \sum_{j=1}^{J_n} \lambda_{j,n} < \frac{C^{st}}{\mathbb{E}(\Sigma)}. \tag{14}$$

As shown in [9], the second system where users have an infinite speed, is equivalent to a single-class PS queue with an arrival rate $\Lambda_n = \sum_{j=1}^{J_n} \Lambda_{j,n}$, and a service rate $\mu^{\infty} = \frac{C^{\infty}}{\mathbb{E}(\Sigma)}$ where C^{∞} equal to the arithmetic mean of the capacity of each zone: $C^{\infty} = \sum_{j=1}^{J_n} p_{j,n} C_{j,n}$. The necessary and sufficient condition for the stability of this second system is thus:

$$\rho_n^{\infty} < 1, \text{ i.e., } \Lambda_n = \sum_{j=1}^{J_n} \Lambda_{j,n} < \frac{C^{\infty}}{\mathbb{E}(\Sigma)}. \tag{15}$$

Theorem 2 of [9] proves that, if the cumulative distribution function (c.d.f) associated with the random variable of data size is concave (which is the case of exponential distribution), the load ρ of our system described in Section 3.1 is bounded as follow:

$$\rho_n^{\infty} \leq \rho_n \leq \rho_n^{st}. \tag{16}$$

It follows from equation 16 and theorem 1 of [9] that $\Lambda_n < \frac{C^{\infty}}{\mathbb{E}(\Sigma)}$ is a necessary and sufficient condition for the stability of the system described in Section 3.1.

3.3 Model of a network of several macrocells

We now present the model for a network composed of N heterogeneous macrocells. A user present in one cell of the network has the ability to change zone, he can also leave the cell without completing his transfer. Similarly, some active users can enter any cell of the network from others cells, with some data volume remaining to be transferred.

Users present in cell n may leave it either because they have completed their transfer and leave definitely the network or because they have made a handover to neighboring cells due to their mobility and still being active. Note that handovers can occur only on cell edge, i.e., in zone J_n of cell n. Conversely users that arrive in cell n from neighboring cells start their transmissions in this cell at cell edge, i.e., in zone J_n. Because the size Σ^k of data to be transferred by type-k users is exponentially distributed, when active user makes a handover the data remaining to be transferred has the same distribution as the original one (memoryless property of the exponential distribution). As result to account for a cell involved in a network of several macrocells, we can simply rewrite system 4 and add to arrival rates $\lambda_{J_n,n}^k$ (with $k = 1, ..., K$) of classes corresponding to the external zone of the cell, the rate of type-k active users leaving neighboring cells to cell n:

$$\begin{cases} \lambda_{1,n}^k = \Lambda_{1,n}^k + \Lambda_{2\to1,n}^k \\ \lambda_{j,n}^k = \Lambda_{j,n}^k + \Lambda_{j-1\to j,n}^k + \Lambda_{j+1\to j,n}^k, j = 2, ..., J_n - 1 \\ \lambda_{J_n,n}^k = \Lambda_{J_n,n}^k + \Lambda_{J_n-1\to J_n,n}^k + \sum_{m=1,m\neq n}^{N} v_{m\to n}^k, \end{cases} \tag{17}$$

where $v_{m\to n}^k$ is the average number of type-k active users that leave cell m to cell n by unit of time. Therefore, the total arrival rate of type-k users at cell n becomes,

$$\lambda_n^k = \Lambda_n^k + \sum_{m=1,m\neq n}^{N} v_{m\to n}^k. \tag{18}$$

where $\Lambda_n^k = q_k \Lambda_n$ is the rate of new connection demands of type-k in cell n.

The question now becomes: how to estimate $v_{m\to n}^k$? Let H_m^k be the handover rate of type-k users in cell m, i.e., the probability that a type-k active user present in cell m needs to migrate to other cells before completing its service. We can express $v_{m\to n}^k$ as:

$$v_{m\to n}^k = \lambda_m^k H_m^k \Psi_{m\to n}, \tag{19}$$

The handover probability H_m^k is calculated as the ratio between the average number of type-k active users leaving the cell m by unit of time (from zone J_m) without having completed their transfer and the total number of type-k users that leave the cell by unit of time:

$$H_m^k = \frac{\bar{Q}_{J_m,n}^k \frac{P_{J_m\to0,m}}{\mathbb{E}(\Theta_{J_m,m}^k)}}{\lambda_m^k}, \tag{20}$$

with

$$\bar{Q}_{J_m,m}^k = \frac{\rho_{J_m,m}^k}{1-\rho_m}, \tag{21}$$

where ρ_m and $\rho_{J_m,m}^k$ are computed as in equation 7.

We finally end up with a system of 7 dependent equations (5, 7, 17-21) that will be solved using a fixed-point iterative technique.

4 PERFORMANCE RESULTS

4.1 Performance of type-k users in isolated macrocell

We now derive from the model of Section 3.1, the performance of type-k active users in the considered cell. From classical results of PS queues, we can calculate the average number of customers of each class, corresponding to the average number of active users of each type in each zone of the cell, that is:

$$\bar{Q}^k_{j,n} = \frac{\rho^k_{j,n}}{1-\rho_n}, \quad (22)$$

thus the average number of type-k users in the cell is:

$$\bar{Q}^k = \sum_{j=1}^{J_n} \bar{Q}^k_{j,n}. \quad (23)$$

From Little law, we derive the average time $\bar{R}^k$ spent by a type-k active user in the cell, starting from the moment where he appears in the cell (because of a new connection demand), and ending when he finishes its transfer:

$$\bar{R}^k = \frac{Q^k}{\sum_{j=1}^{J_n} \Lambda^k_{j,n}}. \quad (24)$$

We then calculate the average throughput $\bar{\gamma}_k$ obtained by a type-k active user during his transfer in the cell:

$$\bar{\gamma}^k = \sum_{j=1}^{J_n} \bar{\gamma}_{j,n} \alpha^k_{j,n}, \quad (25)$$

where $\alpha^k_{j,n} = \frac{\bar{Q}^k_{j,n}}{\bar{Q}^k}$ is the proportion of type-k active users present in zone (j,n).

4.2 Performance of type-k users in the network

We now turn our attention to the end to end performance of users in a network of heterogeneous macrocells. Let us define as $\omega^k(m,n)$ the probability that a type-k user leaves cell m to cell n while downloading an incomplete file. For instance, in Figure 1 (omitting the blue arrows and state s), $\omega^k(1,2)$ corresponds to the probability of a type-k users leaving cell 1 (i.e., C_1 in the figure) to cell 2 (resp. C_2).

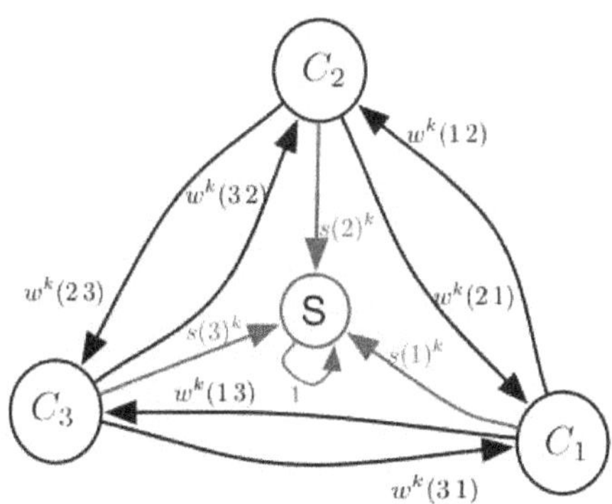

Figure 1: Studied topology.

$\omega^k(m,n)$ is simply the handover probability H^k_m of type-k users in cell m multiplied by the probability $\Psi_{m\to n}$ for a user to move to cell n when he leaves cell m.

$$\omega^k(m,n) = H^k_m \Psi_{m\to n}. \quad (26)$$

In order to derive the end to end performance of a user in the network, we first have to calculate the number of times a user visits each cell before completing his download. Our approach consists in representing the network topology as a Discrete-Time Markov Chain (DTMC), where each cell represents a state of the DTMC and the probabilities $\omega^k(m,n)$ represent its transition probabilities. However, we must also consider the fact that a user eventually finishes its download. this means that, a user in the network will reach a state from where it does not download anymore and therefore, does not perform any other handover. We represent such behavior by an absorbing state denoted by s in the figure. Once reached there, the user has finished his download and will no longer use the network service for that particular file. Note that, if the user has another file to download, we consider that as a new arrival at the system. The resulting absorbing DTMC is represented in Figure 1 with state s representing the absorbing state. $s^k(n)$ corresponds to the probability that a type-k user finishes his download while in cell n. In other words, $s^k(n)$ is the probability of reaching the absorbing state s, with $s^k(n) = 1 - H^k_n$. This is a absorbing Markov chain, which is not irreducible. The corresponding transition matrix can be written as a bloc matrix form [19]: $M^k = \begin{pmatrix} I & 0 \\ A^k & B^k \end{pmatrix}$ where I is identity square matrix, 0, a matrix of zeros, the square matrix B^k describes the probabilities of motion among the transient states of the chaine, i.e., the probabilities of motion among cells of the network ($B^k_{m\,n} = \omega^k(m,n)$), while the matrix A^k gives the probabilities of absorption in one step i.e., A^k_m the probabilities to end the download. The expected number of times the chain spends in transient state n starting in transient state m, i.e., the expected number of times a type-k user visits cell n conditioned by the fact that he began his transfer in cell m, is given by the element $F^k_{m\,n}$ of the fundamental matrix F^k. The fundamental matrix F^k can be expressed as (see [19] for more details):

$$F^k = (I - B^k)^{-1}. \quad (27)$$

Let denote by $\bar{T}^k$ the average sojourn time of a type-k user in the network during his transfer. Because the size Σ^k of data to be transferred by a user is exponentially distributed, $\bar{T}^k$ can be expressed as:

$$\bar{T}^k = \sum_{n=1}^{N} \bar{R}^k_n \sum_{m=1}^{N} F^k_{m\,n} \frac{\Lambda^k_m}{\sum_{i=1}^{N} \Lambda^k_i}, \quad (28)$$

where $\bar{R}^k_n$ is the mean time a type-k user spend in cell n at each visit of the cell, $\bar{R}^k_n$ is expressed in equation 24. $\frac{\Lambda^k_m}{\sum_{i=1}^{N} \Lambda^k_i}$ is the probability for a type-k user to start his service in the network in cell m and $\sum_{m=1}^{N} F^k_{m\,n} \frac{\Lambda^k_m}{\sum_{i=1}^{N} \Lambda^k_i}$ is the number of times a type-k user visits cell n during his transfer. Therefore, the end to end throughput obtain by a type-k user during its download in network is given by:

$$\bar{\Gamma}^k = \frac{\mathbb{E}(\Sigma^k)}{\bar{T}^k}. \quad (29)$$

The type-k handover probability in the network, i.e, the probability for a type-k user to change cell during his transfer, is given by:

$$\bar{H}^k = \sum_{n=1}^{N} H^k_n \beta_n \text{ with } \beta_n = \frac{\sum_{m=1}^{N} F_{m\,n} \frac{\Lambda_m}{\sum_{i=1}^{N} \Lambda_i}}{\sum_{n=1}^{N} \sum_{m=1}^{N} F_{m\,n} \frac{\Lambda_m}{\sum_{i=1}^{N} \Lambda_i}} \quad (30)$$

where β_n is the probability for a type-k user to visits cell n during his transfer.

The average number $\bar{n}_c^k$ of cells visited by a type-k user and the average number $\bar{n}_h^k$ of handovers performed by a type-k user before completed his download can be expressed as:

$$\bar{n}_c^k = \sum_{n=1}^{N} \sum_{m=1}^{N} F_{m\,n}^k \frac{\Lambda_m^k}{\sum_{i=1}^{N} \Lambda_i^k} \quad \text{and} \quad \bar{n}_h^k = \bar{n}_c^k - 1. \tag{31}$$

5 EXPERIMENTS RESULTS

We validate the model by comparing the results provided by the model to those delivered by a home-made discrete-event simulator developed in Matlab. We consider a network of $N = 3$ cells. For simplicity as explained in section 2.1, zones of cells form concentric regions based on path-loss only as function of distance of user from his eNodeB. We reproduced in simulation the traffic assumptions and the mobility model described in Sections 2.3. Each cell uses a number of 100 Ressource Blocks for the downlink channel and cell 1 (resp. 2 and 3) offer to users four MCS (28, 23, 16, 6) (resp. three MCS (28, 23, 16) and two MCS (28, 23)). This results in transmission zones with corresponding capacity presented in the Table 1 [1]. For the surface of zones, we use the radius presented in Table 1 corresponding to concentric circles model of cells. We assume that the network is visited by two types of users, which move at speed $V^1 = 5$ km/h and $V^2 = 50$ km/h, the average size of data for each type of users is set to $\mathbb{E}(\Sigma^1) = 20$ MB and $\mathbb{E}(\Sigma^2) = 10$ MB. The probability for a user to be of each type is $q^1 = 0.6$, $q^2 = 0.4$. The remaining parameters, i.e, the probability for a user to start his download in zone j of a given cell, the transition probability between zones of a cell and between cells, and the sojourn time in zone j of a given cell at each visit, are calculated according to the estimations given in Section 2.3.

Table 1: Cells parameters

Cells	Zone 1	Zone 2	Zone 3	Zone 4
Cell 1: Radius (m)	$R_1 = 100$	$R_2 = 150$	$R_3 = 200$	$R_4 = 250$
Capacity (Mbits/s)	$C_1 = 75$	$C_2 = 51$	$C_3 = 31$	$C_4 = 10$
Cell 2: Radius	$R_1 = 100$	$R_2 = 150$	$R_3 = 200$	
Capacity (Mbits/s)	$C_1 = 75$	$C_2 = 51$	$C_3 = 31$	
Cell 3: Radius (m)	$R_1 = 100$	$R_2 = 150$		
Capacity (Mbits/s)	$C_1 = 75$	$C_2 = 51$		

5.1 Performance results of users in isolated cell

Considering the first cell (cell with four transmission zones), we first illustrate the performance results in the simple case of an isolated cell, corresponding to the model of Section 3.1.

Figures 2 and 3 show comparison of throughput and sojourn time in the cell for each type of users as a function of load ρ^∞. We observe that the predicted model is very close to simulation results with a relative error about 6% in average and less that 10% in the worst case. As explained in section 3.2, mobile users' throughput is bounded by the throughput obtained when all users are static (lower bound) and the throughput obtained with infinite speed (upper bound). As expected, users mobility improve capacity, i.e., the throughput obtained by a user if he is alone in the cell, which is about 21 Mbits/s for type-1 users and about 23 Mbits/s for type-2 users. Mobility also improve users' throughput (type-2 users have

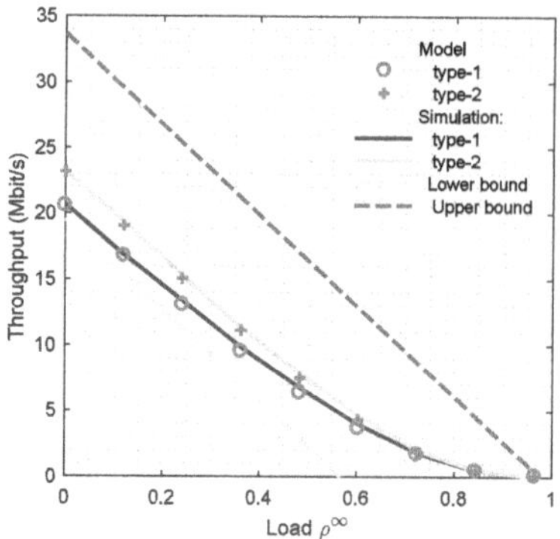

Figure 2: Throughput obtained by an active user of each type in the isolated cell as a function of the cell load.

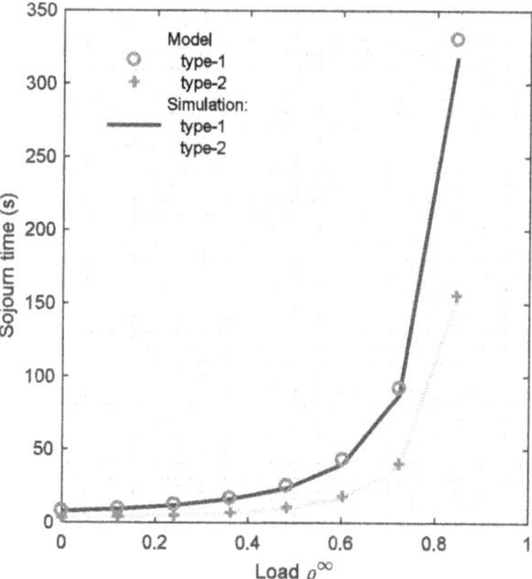

Figure 3: Sojourn time of an active user of each type in the isolated cell as a function of the cell load.

better throughput than type-1 users) and stability condition which is $\Lambda < 0.15$ for the system with only static users and $\Lambda < 0.27$ when users are mobile. In this latter case, observe that the stability condition does not depend on users speed. The reason of this improvement is that, even if a user that physically exits a zone is more likely to move to zone with poor channel conditions, when a user moves to a zone with favorable conditions, he have a better chance to complete his transfer before leaving the zone. Thereby, the average number of active users moving from zone with good channel conditions to zones with poor channel conditions by unit of time is lower than the average number of active users moving in the opposite direction. And this phenomenon is increasing with users' speed since the frequency of zone change increases with speed.

5.2 Performance results of users in the network

We now present some numerical results for end to end user performance in the network with the 3 heterogeneous macrocells presented in Section 5.. Without additional assumptions on physical

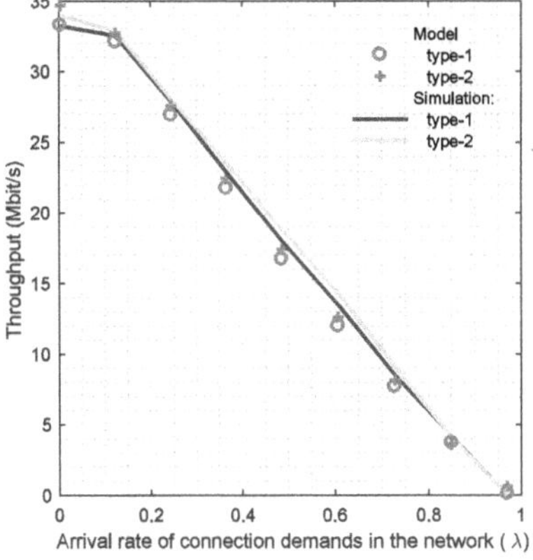

Figure 4: Throughput obtain by each type of user in the network as a function of the total arrival rate of new connection demands in the network.

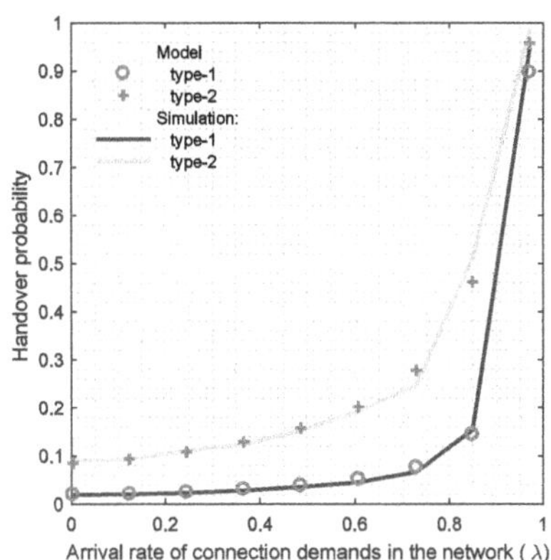

Figure 5: Handover probability of each type of user in the network as a function of the total arrival rate of new connection demands in the network.

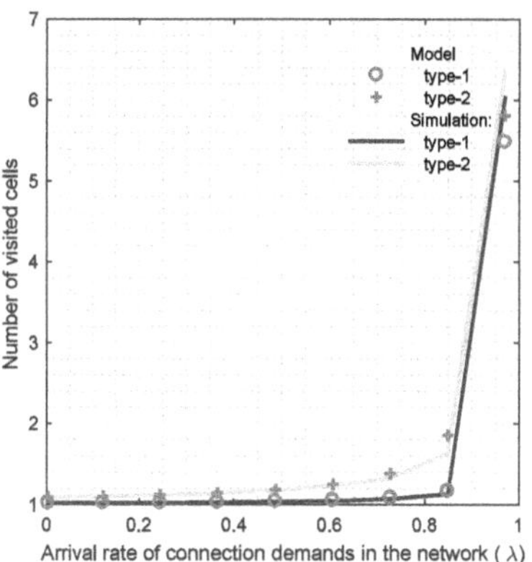

Figure 6: Number of cells visited by each type of user as a function of the total arrival rate of new connection demands in the network.

mobility of users, when a active user exit one cell without have completed the download, he have the same probability to migrate to each of the $N-1$ others cells. Therefore, $\Psi_{m\to n} = \frac{1}{N-1}$, i.e, $\Psi_{m\to n} = \frac{1}{2}$, $m,n \in \{1,2,3\}$.

Figures 4 show the throughput obtained by users of each type during the transfer in the network as a function of the total arrival rate $\lambda = \sum_{n=1}^{N} \Lambda_n$ of new connection demands in the network. Observe that the predicted model remain close to simulation with an average relative error of 8.5%.

Note that the throughput obtained by the two type of users is greater than throughput obtain in Section 5.1 with only intra cell mobility. This show the impact of the heterogeneity of cells (cells 2 and 3 have better channel conditions than cell 1). In fact, when the network is not in the high load $\lambda < 0.8$, users in zones of cells 2 and 3, obtain better throughput due to capacity of zones. They also have better chance to complete their transfers before changes zone or cell as can be seen in Figure 5 where the handover probability remain less than 0.5 and in Figure 6 where the number of cells visited by a active user is less than 2. Therefore in this two cells (cells 2 and 3), the gain due to intra-cell mobility is not longer significant. Also note that the difference of throughput between the two type of users is less than the difference of throughput with only intra cell mobility. This is because after a handover, users always start transmission in the new cell in cell edge which is the zone with the smallest capacity whereas in the case of the isolated cell users at the edge always move to a zone of better capacity. As show in figure 5 (where the probability to change cell during the transfer is more important for type-2 than type-1 users) and in figure 6 (where type-2 users visit more cells than type-1 users), type-2 users are more impacted by the inter-cells mobility. Therefore, the gain due to intra-cell mobility is attenuated by inter-cells mobility.

6 IMPACT OF DISTRIBUTION

All the results presented so far, assume exponential distributions of users sojourn time $\theta^k_{(j,n)}$ in each zone and volume of data Σ^k a user want to transfer. We now investigate the impact of these assumptions on users' performance in the network. We consider the same parameters as in Subsection 5.2 and we present curves for type-2 users only, curves for type-1 users show the same behavior.

6.1 Impact of users sojourn time distributon

Figures 7, and 8 compare user throughput and handover probability of type-2 users in the network why considering an exponential distributions of the volume of data Σ^k to be transferred by a type-k user and different distributions of users sojourn time $\theta^k_{(j,n)}$. These curves show the sensibility of performance parameters to the distribution of users sojourn time $\theta^k_{(j,n)}$. Thereby, it would be interesting to propose a development of the model with other distributions of users sojourn time in each zones.

6.2 Impact of distribution of data to be transfert

Figures 9 and 10 compare user throughput and handover probability of type-2 users in the network why considering an exponential distributions of users sojourn time $\theta^k_{(j,n)}$ and different distributions of data volume Σ^k to be transferred by a type-k user. On these curves, one can note the insensitivity of the performance parameters to the distribution of the volume of data, which is reminiscent of the insensitivity of PS queues to the distributions of data. It might be interesting to look if our model which is based on the PS queues without being a classical PS queue, retains the insensitivity property.

7 CONCLUSION

In this paper we have presented a model based on PS queue and DTMC for performance evaluation of heterogeneous LTE/LTE-A network with intra-and inter-cell mobility of users. We have shown that this model is consistent with known analytical bounds corresponding to static users or users with an infinite speed, and provides a very good accuracy for more general speeds. Our model confirms that mobility may improve performance of users in a given cell, and enables to quantify the gain. It also provides end-to-end performance of users among a network of heterogeneous

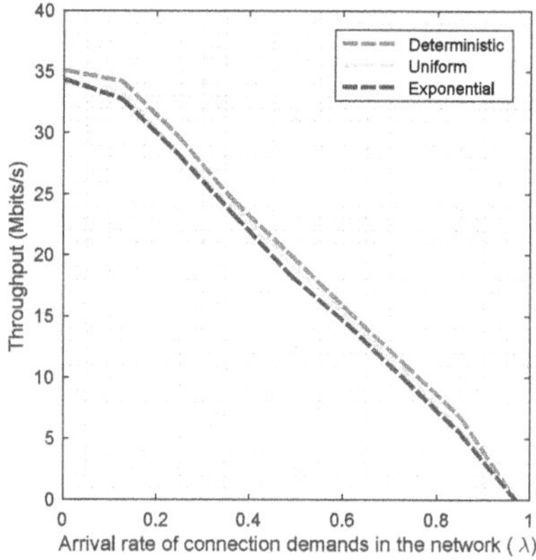

Figure 7: Throughput obtained by a type-2 user as a function of the total arrival rate of connection demands in the network and distribution of sojourn time.

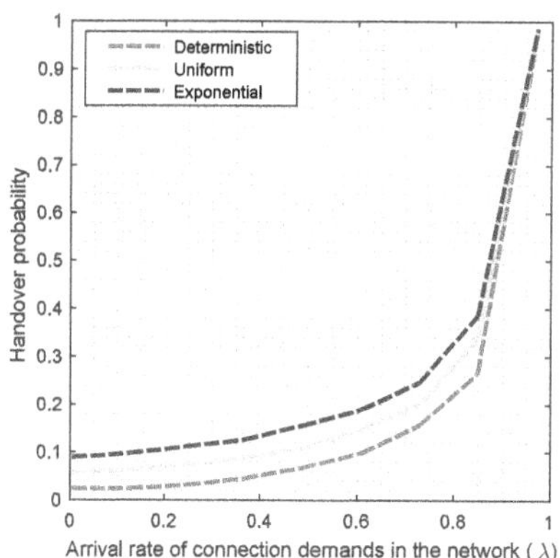

Figure 8: Handover probability of type-2 user as a function of the total arrival rate of new connection demands in the network and distribution of sojourn time.

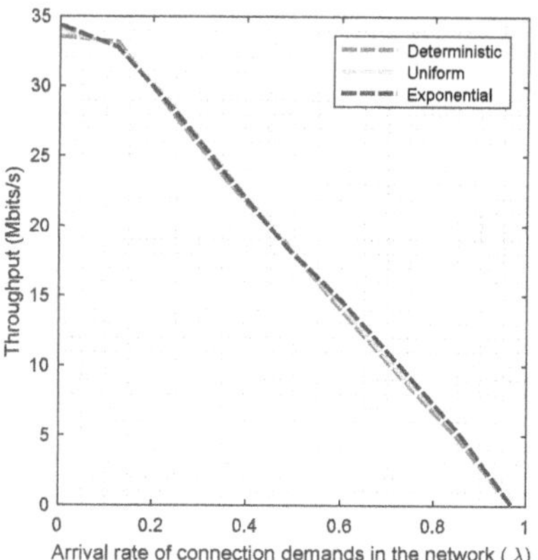

Figure 9: Throughput obtained by a type-2 user as a function of the total arrival rate of connection demands in the network and distribution of data volume.

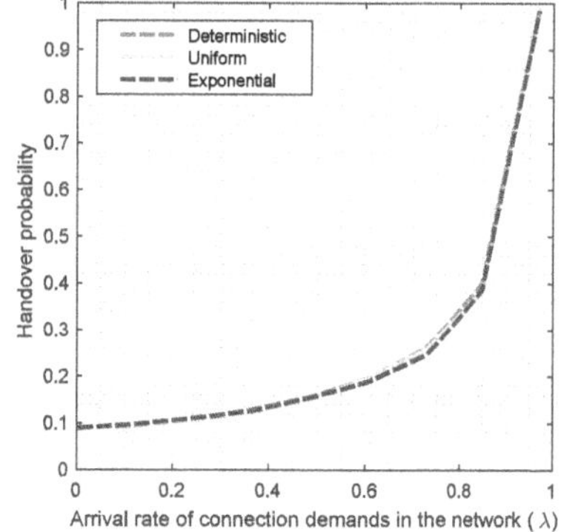

Figure 10: Handover probability of type-2 user as a function of the total arrival rate of new connection demands in the network and distribution of data volume.

cells, and shows that, while inter-cell mobility balances the load between the cells, it does not lead to such improvement of throughput as intra-cell mobility. we consider only data traffic in this paper. It would be interesting to extend the approach consisting in decoupling the mobility model from the cell and network model to a system with data and real time traffic.

ACKNOWLEDGMENTS

The authors would like to thank Dr. Thiago Abreu for valuable comments and helpful suggestions.

REFERENCES

[1] 3GPP. [n. d.]. 3GPP TS 36.213 V9.2.0 (2010-06): Physical layer procedures. ([n. d.]).

[2] Nivine Abbas, Thomas Bonald, and Berna Sayrac. 2015. Opportunistic gains of mobility in cellular data networks. In *13th International Symposium on Modeling and Optimization in Mobile, Ad Hoc, and Wireless Networks (WiOpt), 2015*. IEEE, 315–322.

[3] Urtzi Ayesta, Martin Erausquin, and Peter Jacko. 2010. A modeling framework for optimizing the flow-level scheduling with time-varying channels. *Performance Evaluation* 67, 11 (2010), 1014–1029.

[4] Bruno Baynat, R-M Indre, Narcisse Nya, Philippe Olivier, and Alain Simonian. 2015. Impact of mobility in dense LTE-A networks with small cells. In *IEEE Vehicular Technology Conference (VTC Spring)*. IEEE, 1–5.

[5] Bruno Baynat and Narcisse Nya. 2016. Performance Model for 4G/5G Networks Taking into Account Intra-and Inter-Cell Mobility of Users. In *Local Computer Networks (LCN), 2016 IEEE 41st Conference on*. IEEE, 212–215.

[6] Paul Bender, Peter Black, Matthew Grob, Roberto Padovani, Nagabhushana Sindhushyana, and S Viterbi. 2000. CDMA/HDR: a bandwidth efficient high speed wireless data service for nomadic users. *IEEE Communications magazine* 38, 7 (2000), 70–77.

[7] Thomas Bonald, Sem Borst, Nidhi Hegde, Matthieu Jonckheere, and Alexandre Proutiere. 2009. Flow-level performance and capacity of wireless networks with user mobility. *Queueing Systems* (2009).

[8] Thomas Bonald, Sem Borst, and Alexandre Proutiere. 2005. Inter-cell scheduling in wireless data networks. In *Wireless Conference 2005-Next Generation Wireless and Mobile Communications and Services (European Wireless), 11th European*. VDE, 1–7.

[9] Thomas Bonald, Sem C Borst, and Alexandre Proutière. 2004. How mobility impacts the flow-level performance of wireless data systems. In *INFOCOM 2004. Twenty-third AnnualJoint Conference of the IEEE Computer and Communications Societies*. IEEE.

[10] Thomas Bonald and Alexandre Proutière. 2003. Wireless downlink data channels: user performance and cell dimensioning. In *Proceedings of the 9th annual international conference on Mobile computing and networking*. ACM, 339–352.

[11] Thomas Bonald and Alexandre Proutiere. 2011. A queueing analysis of data networks. In *Queueing Networks*. Springer, 729–765.

[12] Sem C Borst, Nidhi Hegde, and Alexandre Proutiere. 2009. Mobility-driven scheduling in wireless networks. In *INFOCOM 2009*. IEEE, 1260–1268.

[13] Sem C Borst, Alexandre Proutiere, and Nidhi Hegde. 2006. Capacity of Wireless Data Networks with Intra-and Inter-Cell Mobility.. In *INFOCOM*.

[14] Andrea J Goldsmith and Soon-Ghee Chua. 1998. Adaptive coded modulation for fading channels. *IEEE Transactions on Communications* (1998).

[15] Khalil Ibrahimi, Rachid El-Azouzi, Sujit K Samanta, and El-Houssine Bouyakhf. 2009. Adaptive modulation and coding scheme with intra-and inter-cell mobility for hsdpa system. In *2009 Sixth International Conference on Broadband Communications, Networks, and Systems*. IEEE, 1–8.

[16] Anis Jdidi and Tijani Chahed. 2011. Flow-level performance of proportional fairness with hierarchical modulation in OFDMA-based networks. *Computer Networks* (2011).

[17] Stefania Sesia, Matthew Baker, and Issam Toufik. 2011. *LTE-the UMTS long term evolution: from theory to practice*. John Wiley & Sons.

[18] Chadi Tarhini and Tijani Chahed. 2012. QoS-oriented resource allocation for streaming flows in IEEE802. 16e Mobile WiMAX. *Telecommunication Systems* 51, 1 (2012), 65–71.

[19] IWard Whitt. 2007. IEOR 4701: Professor Whitt Lecture Notes, Monday, July 16, 2007 Introduction to Markov Chains. (2007).

Joint User Association and Backhaul Routing for Green 5G Mesh Millimeter Wave Backhaul Networks

Agapi Mesodiakaki
Karlstad University
Universitetsgatan
65188 Karlstad, Sweden
agapi.mesodiakaki@kau.se

Enrica Zola
UPC-BarcelonaTECH
Jordi Girona 1-3
08034 Barcelona, Spain
enrica@entel.upc.edu

Andreas Kassler
Karlstad University
Universitetsgatan
65188 Karlstad, Sweden
andreas.kassler@kau.se

ABSTRACT

With the advance offi fth generation (5G) networks, network density needs to grow significantly in order to meet the required capacity demands. A massive deployment of small cells may lead to a high cost for providingfi ber connectivity to each node. Consequently, many small cells are expected to be connected through wireless links to the umbrella eNodeB, leading to a mesh backhaul topology. This backhaul solution will most probably be composed of high capacity point-to-point links, typically operating in the millimeter wave (mmWave) frequency band due to its massive bandwidth availability. In this paper, we propose a mathematical model that jointly solves the user association and backhaul routing problem in the aforementioned context, aiming at the energy efficiency maximization of the network. Our study considers the energy consumption of both the access and backhaul links, while taking into account the capacity constraints of all the nodes as well as the fulfillment of the service-level agreements (SLAs). Due to the high complexity of the optimal solution, we also propose an energy efficient heuristic algorithm (Joint), which solves the discussed joint problem, while inducing low complexity in the system. We numerically evaluate the algorithm performance by comparing it not only with the optimal solution but also with reference approaches under different traffic load scenarios and backhaul parameters. Our results demonstrate that Joint outperforms the state-of-the-art, while being able tofi nd good solutions, close to optimal, in short time.

CCS CONCEPTS

• **Networks → Network resources allocation; Network performance modeling; Mobile networks;**

KEYWORDS

5G; Backhaul; Green Heterogeneous Networks; LTE-Advanced; Millimeter Wave (mmWave); Traffic Routing; User Association;

MSWiM '17, November 21–25, 2017, Miami, FL, USA

ACM ISBN 978-1-4503-5162-1/17/11...$15.00
https://doi.org/10.1145/3127540.3127560

1 INTRODUCTION

The next generation of mobile networks, i.e.,fi fth generation (5G), requires a significant increase in capacity to meet the bandwidth demands of high quality augmented and virtual reality (4K/8K) services. In 5G, we will most likely see the use of massive multiple-input multiple-output (MIMO), combined with new modulation and coding techniques and the exploitation of new spectrum blocks to satisfy capacity needs. In addition, much smaller cell sizes are expected, leading to the massive deployment of small cells (SCs) to provide localized capacity on demand. In order to provide coverage, umbrella eNodeBs (eNBs) are about to be used, which will offload traffic to SCs, when needed [1]. Smaller cell sizes result in higher signal-to-interference-plus-noise ratio (SINR), which enhances the network capacity. Moreover, frequencies can be reused by SCs that are far from each other, thus improving the area spectrum efficiency.

However, providing optical connections to each SC may lead to prohibitive costs for network operators. Therefore, researchers are working on wireless backhaul (BH) solutions that could provide the required capacity, while relaying the user equipment (UE) traffic towards the core network of the operator. Consequently, millimeter wave (mmWave) technology is an interesting candidate to backhaul the SC user traffic because of the massive amount of spectrum available in the 60, 70 or 80 GHz band. The dense deployment of SCs will also lead to short point-to-point BH links among neighboring SCs operating in the line-of-sight (LOS) range. The small mmWave wavelengths enable high antenna gains, required to compensate the much higher path loss at these frequency bands [2].

As most eNBs have already afi ber connection to the core network, the multi-hop mesh BH may re-use this connection. As a result, such a heterogeneous network (HetNet) will be comprised of umbrella eNBs and overlaid SCs that will relay UE data through the multi-hop mesh BH network over diverse paths towards the core network reachable through the eNB sites. The mesh structure increases reliability and link redundancy, which enables a fast repair in case of link outages using e.g. software defined networking based fast failover techniques [3].

While such a HetNet provides afl exible framework, there are several challenges to be solved in order to optimize the network deployment and operation. Firstly, the users may connect to multiple SCs or eNBs. While typically such association is based on simple metrics such as signal quality [4, 5], different SCs may have different BH capacity available, since they may serve different traffic volumes and UE population. In parallel, connecting to different SCs may require the UE to request different amount of physical resource blocks (PRBs), to guarantee its rate demand, due to different SINR conditions. Consequently, user association strategies need to be developed that take into account both the required access network resources as well as the BH capacity [6, 7]. Secondly, each SC may have multiple available paths in the multi-hop wireless BH, which may have different characteristics in terms of capacity. In addition, each SC BH link may require a different amount of energy to serve the traffic demand. To that end, key operator goals are to reduce the total energy consumption of both access network and BH to save costs and reduce the total CO_2 consumption of the network.

In this paper, we tackle the joint problem of energy-efficient user association and BH routing for 5G HetNets with point-to-point mmWave mesh BH links. Wefi rst develop a mathematical optimization model based on mixed integer linear programming (MILP) that minimizes the total power consumption of the access network and BH links subject to constraints on both the achievable user rate as well as the maximum cell and BH link capacity. The outcome of the model provides the optimal user association and BH routing strategy. As the model is complex to solve for large instances, we develop a novel fast energy-efficient solution, called Joint. The heuristic favors the most energy-efficient associations, taking into account both the access network and BH routing. In parallel, it considers the number of PRBs needed to guarantee the UE rate demands. In particular, the proposed algorithm calculates the total power consumption (both in the access and BH links) for every possible association of a UE and promotes the association with the lowest power. In the case of SCs with more than one alternative BH paths, it takes into account the BH traffic of the already associated UEs and favors the path that involves the minimum power. Thereby, load balancing is achieved. Furthermore, Joint limits the number of potential cells to associate with so as to reduce the computational complexity. Our numerical evaluations demonstrate that the proposed algorithm canfi nd very good solutions in short time and outperforms several other heuristics in terms of energy efficiency over a large number of traffic scenarios and BH parameters.

The remainder of this paper is structured as follows. In Section 2, we review the related work. In Section 3.1, wefi rst describe the system model under study. Then, the proposed analytical model as well as the heuristic for the joint user association and BH traffic routing problem are given in Sections 3.2 and 3.3, respectively. Section 4 presents the simulation scenarios as well as our numerical evaluation results. Finally, Section 5 concludes the paper.

2 RELATED WORK

A key aspect in dense wireless networks is to solve the user association problem, which decides which UE will be associated with which base station. When a massive amount of SCs is connected through wireless BH, the problem becomes even more complex, as the UE association also impacts the BH traffic, and consequently, the BH utilization and power consumption. Hence, new joint UE association and BH routing approaches are required to optimize the network operation. These solutions should target at high network energy efficiency, while achieving low computational complexity.

However, most approaches proposed so far try to either optimize the user association without taking into account the BH parameters and constraints or to solve the routing problem without considering the different association options. For instance, LTE-Advanced (LTE-A) employs the reference signal received power (RSRP) and the reference signal received quality (RSRQ) metrics to decide the UE associations [4]. Nevertheless, those metrics, which maximize the instantaneous SINR, do not maximize the network throughput, since only a small portion of UEs connect to SCs. As an extreme solution to this problem, a UE may connect to the base station from which it experiences the minimum path loss (MPL), as proposed in [5]. Although this approach achieves maximum traffic offloading to SCs, it presents very low spectrum efficiency. Common to the aforementioned approaches is that they assume that the BH is not the bottleneck (neither in terms of capacity nor in terms of energy), which, however, may not be the case for 5G multi-hop mesh BH.

To that end, researchers have recently studied BH-aware association strategies. For instance, [6] proposes an analytical framework that encompasses both access and BH, considering network parameters such as base station load, spectral efficiency, BH link capacity and topology. In [7], the joint problem of user association and resource allocation is studied, while taking into account the BH capacity and the energy budget of base stations. Still, those BH-aware approaches do not focus on the total energy efficiency maximization of the network, which, however, is expected to be a key objective of next generation networks.

Being the closest to our work, in [8], an energy-efficient association algorithm is proposed, which considers the power consumption of both the access and BH links. Nevertheless, this work does not jointly optimize the user association and BH routing, as it only considers tree BH topologies, where only a single path is available for the connection of each SC to the umbrella eNB site. Hence, in 5G scenarios, where SC BH routing is expected to play a key role due to the massive amount of hotspot traffic to be handled, it can result in poor performance (as it will be shown later in Section 4).

3 JOINT USER ASSOCIATION AND BACKHAUL TRAFFIC ROUTING

In this section, wefi rst describe the system model under study. Thereafter, we formulate the joint user association and BH traffic routing problem as a MILP targeting at minimizing the total power consumption of both the BH and access links (ALs), while satisfying the BH and AL capacity constraints as well as the rate demands of UEs. Finally, we develop a heuristic solution, called Joint, that is able to provide good solutions, close to the optimal obtained through the model, in short time.

3.1 System Model

The topology under study consists of a set $\mathcal{E}$ of umbrella eNBs. In the same area, a set $\mathcal{S}$ of SCs is also deployed (see Fig. 1). The SCs are connected to each other and to the eNB through a set $\mathcal{L_{BL}}$ of mmWave BH links, thereby forming a mesh BH network. A set $\mathcal{U}$ of UEs tries to access the network, each one requiring a specific rate d_u based on its strict guaranteed bit rate (GBR) service [9]. For the access network, we assume a set of microwave ALs, between the UEs and their serving cells (i.e., eNBs and/or SCs), denoted by $\mathcal{L_{AL}}$. Flat channels are also considered and we, therefore, employ constant power allocation, i.e., the maximum transmitted power of each cell is divided equally in its PRBs. Furthermore, the user may associate only with one cell at a time. We focus on downlink transmissions, with the source nodes co-located with the eNBs and

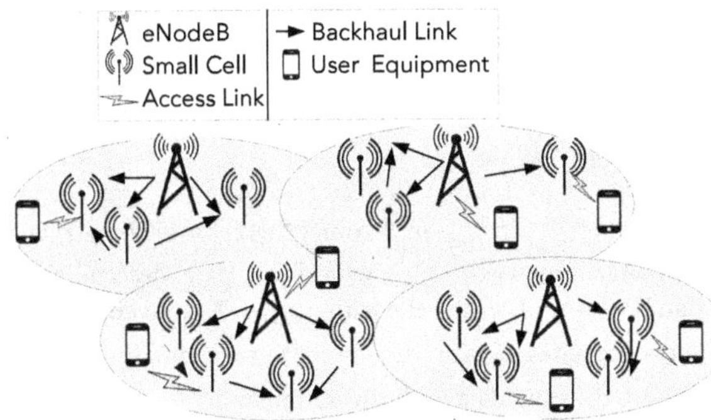

Figure 1: System model.

the sinks with the UEs. Hence, each UE may download data from an eNB directly or from a SC s; in the latter case, the traffic is thus routed from the eNB through the mesh BH and then to UE u.

3.2 Proposed Analytical Model

As already discussed, the goal of the problem is to minimize the total power (both in the AL and BH) that the eNB and the SCs consume, while guaranteeing the download rate d_u of each UE u. Under the constraint satisfaction of the UE rate demands, the power consumption minimization is equivalent to the maximization of the network energy efficiency. This metric (measured in bits/Joule) is defined as the total throughput of the network divided by the total power consumption [10]. To that end, the MILP can be written as

$$argmin \sum_{i \in \mathcal{E} \cup \mathcal{S}} p_i, \tag{1}$$

where p_i is the total power consumption at cell i (i.e., eNB or SC).

The solution to our MILP jointly selects the optimal: 1) user association map and 2) routing on the BH links, so that the total power consumed in the network is minimized. The set of constraints related to thefl ows that pass through the network links are provided in Section 3.2.1, while Section 3.2.2 provides the power constraints for the eNBs and SCs, together with the applied power model.

3.2.1 Flow Conservation Constraints. In this work, we assume non-splittablefl ows. Hence, the *single-path routing constraint* is assumed for thefl ow of each UE u which can be written as

$$\sum_j x^u_{(i,j)} - \sum_j x^u_{(j,i)} = \begin{cases} 1, & \text{if } i = \text{source} \\ -1, & \text{if } i = u \text{ (sink)} \\ 0 & \text{otherwise} \end{cases} \tag{2}$$
$$\forall\, u \in \mathcal{U},\ \ \forall\, i \text{ and } j \in \mathcal{E} \cup \mathcal{S} \cup \mathcal{U},$$

where $x^u_{(i,j)}$ is a binary link vector that is 1 when UE u uses link (i, j) and 0 otherwise. For this decision variable we have

$$x^u_{(i,u)} \in \{0,1\},\ \forall\, u \in \mathcal{U},\ \ \forall\, j \in \mathcal{E} \cup \mathcal{S},$$
$$x^u_{(i,j)} \in \{0,1\},\ \forall\, u \in \mathcal{U},\ \ \forall\, i \text{ and } j \in \mathcal{E} \cup \mathcal{S}, \tag{3}$$

with the former constraint referring to any AL $(i, u) \in \mathcal{L}_{\mathcal{AL}}$, and the latter to any BH link $(i, j) \in \mathcal{L}_{\mathcal{BL}}$.

We have to ensure that each UE u connects to only one cell in the network; this is expressed by the *single association rule* as follows

$$\sum_{(i,u) \in \mathcal{L}_{\mathcal{AL}}} x^u_{(i,u)} = 1, \quad \forall\, u \in \mathcal{U}. \tag{4}$$

Table 1: Analytical model notation table.

Symbol	Description
$\mathcal{E}$	Set of eNodeBs
$\mathcal{S}$	Set of small cells
$\mathcal{U}$	Set of user equipments
$\mathcal{L}_{\mathcal{AL}}$	Set of access links (ALs)
$\mathcal{L}_{\mathcal{BL}}$	Set of backhaul (BH) links
p_i	Total power of cell i, sum of the power in the ALs of cell i (p_i^{AL}) and in the BH links exiting i (p_i^{BH})
$x^u_{(i,j)}$	Binary indicator of the use of link (i,j) by UE u
$BW_{(i,j)}$	Bandwidth of the BH link (i,j)
BW_{PRB}	Bandwidth of a physical resource block (PRB)
$c_{(i,u)}$	Number of PRBs used for the access link (AL) (i,u)
$c_{i_{max}}$	Max. number of PRBs at cell i
d_u	Download rate demand of user u
$SE_{(i,u)}$	Maximum achievable spectrum efficiency for $SINR_{(i,u)}$
$\Delta^{AL}_{p_i}$	Slope of the load-dependent AL power of cell i
Δ^{BH}_{p}	Slope of the load-dependent BH power
$N^{AL}_{TRX_i}$	Number of AL transceiver chains at cell i
$N^{BH}_{TRX_{(i,j)}}$	Number of BH transceiver chains for link (i,j)
$p^{AL}_{max_i}$	Max. transmit power of the AL transceiver of cell i
$p^{BH}_{max_{(i,j)}}$	Max. transmit power of the BH transceiver of link (i,j)
$p^{AL}_{out_i}$	RF output power for the AL at cell i
$p^{BH}_{out_{(i,j)}}$	RF output power for the BH link (i,j)
$p^{AL}_{0_i}$	Min. non-zero power consumption of cell i
$p^{BH}_{0_{(i,j)}}$	Min. non-zero power consumption of BH link (i,j)
$\beta_{(i,j)}$	Path loss and gain dependent parameter of BH link (i,j)
$L_{TX_{(i,j)}}, L_{RX_{(i,j)}}$	Losses of the transmitter and receiver of BH link (i,j)
$G_{TX_{(i,j)}}, G_{RX_{(i,j)}}$	Gain of the transmitter and receiver of BH link (i,j)
$PL_{(i,j)}$	Path loss of BH link (i,j)
LM	BH link margin
N_{TH}	Thermal noise
NF	Receiver noisefi gure

UEs that connect to the same cell share its available resources. Each UE will be assigned a given number of PRBs, $c_{(i,u)}$, according to its demand and cell availability, which is calculated as

$$c_{(i,u)} = \left\lceil \frac{d_u}{BW_{PRB} SE_{(i,u)}} \right\rceil, \tag{5}$$

where BW_{PRB} denotes the bandwidth of a PRB and $\lceil \cdot \rceil$ is the ceiling operator. Then, $SE_{(i,u)}$ is the maximum achievable spectrum efficiency with effective $SINR_{(i,u)}$, given by [[11], Eq. 5.12]. Finally, $x^u_{(i,u)}$, as already mentioned, is the link vector (in this AL case, it is equal to 1, when UE u is associated with cell i, and 0 otherwise).

We can thus write the *capacity constraint for an AL* as follows

$$\sum_{u \in \mathcal{U}} x^u_{(i,u)} c_{(i,u)} \leq c_{i_{max}},\ \forall\, i \in \mathcal{E} \cup \mathcal{S}, \tag{6}$$

where $c_{i_{max}}$ is the maximum number of PRBs of cell i.

3.2.2 Power Model. The total power of each cell i (eNB or SC) consists of two terms: the power consumed in its ALs (p_i^{AL}); and the power consumed by all the BH links exiting cell i (p_i^{BH}). That is

$$p_i = p_i^{AL} + p_i^{BH} \qquad \forall i \in \mathcal{E} \cup \mathcal{S}. \tag{7}$$

In the following, the power model used for the AL and the one used for the BH link are detailed.

For the **power model in the access link**, the linear approximation in [12] is considered, for which the relationship between the variable RF output power $p^{AL}_{out_i}$ and the power consumption at cell i are nearly linear as follows

$$p^{AL}_i = N^{AL}_{TRX_i}(p^{AL}_{0_i} + \Delta^{AL}_{p_i} p^{AL}_{out_i}), \qquad \forall i \in \mathcal{E} \cup \mathcal{S}, \tag{8}$$

where $N^{AN}_{TRX_i}$ is the number of transceiver chains of cell i, and $p^{AL}_{0_i}$ represents the minimum non-zero output power of the AL transceiver at cell i; $\Delta^{AL}_{p_i}$ is the slope of the load-dependent power consumption, which takes different values based on the used type of the antenna [12]; $p^{AL}_{out_i}$ is the power consumption of the transceiver for the ALs between cell i and all the associated UEs, given by

$$p^{AL}_{out_i} = \frac{p^{AL}_{max_i}}{c_{i_{max}}} \sum_{u \in \mathcal{U}} \left(x_{(i,u)} c_{(i,u)}\right), \tag{9}$$

where $p^{AL}_{max_i}$ is the maximum transmit power of the ALs of cell i.

A similar approach is adopted for the **BH power model**. Again, the power of each BH transceiver has two parts: a static ($p^{BH}_{0_{(i,j)}}$), and a variable that scales with the aggregate ratefl owing over the BH link. The power of all the BH links exiting cell i is thus given by

$$p^{BH}_i = \sum_{(i,j) \in \mathcal{L_{BL}}} N^{BH}_{TRX_{(i,j)}} \left(p^{BH}_{0_{(i,j)}} + p^{BH}_{out_{(i,j)}} \Delta^{BH}_p\right). \tag{10}$$

where, similar to the AL power model, $N^{BH}_{TRX_{(i,j)}}$ is the number of transceiver chains of BH link (i, j); Δ^{BH}_p is the slope of the load-dependent BH power consumption; $p^{BH}_{0_{(i,j)}}$ is the minimum non-zero BH power and $p^{BH}_{out_{(i,j)}}$ is the RF transceiver output power of BH link (i, j) at cell i [2]. Then, $p^{BH}_{max_{(i,j)}}$ stands for the maximum transmission power of BH link (i, j) at cell i, for which we have

$$0 \leq p^{BH}_{out_{(i,j)}} \leq p^{BH}_{max_{(i,j)}}. \tag{11}$$

Finally, $p^{BH}_{out_{(i,j)}}$ is given by

$$p^{BH}_{out_{(i,j)}} = \left(2^{\frac{\sum_{u \in \mathcal{U}} x^u_{(i,j)} d_u}{BW_{(i,j)}}} - 1\right) \beta_{(i,j)}, \tag{12}$$

where $BW_{(i,j)}$ is the bandwidth of the BH link (i, j) and $\sum_{u \in \mathcal{U}} d_u x^u_{(i,j)}$ is the aggregated traffic that passes through it. Moreover, parameter $\beta_{(i,j)}$ results by subtracting from the total losses the gains of the transmitter and the receiver of the BH link (i, j) and is measured in Watt. Specifically, in the case of a mmWave link, $\beta_{(i,j)}$ is given by

$$\begin{aligned} \beta_{(i,j)(dBm)} = {} & (L_{TX_{(i,j)}} + L_{RX_{(i,j)}} + PL_{(i,j)} + LM + NF)_{(dB)} \\ & + N_{TH(dBm)} - G_{TX_{(i,j)}(dBi)} - G_{RX_{(i,j)}(dBi)}, \end{aligned} \tag{13}$$

where $L_{TX_{(i,j)}}$, $L_{RX_{(i,j)}}$ and $G_{TX_{(i,j)}}$, $G_{RX_{(i,j)}}$ are the losses and the antenna gains, respectively, of the BH link (i, j). The parameter $PL_{(i,j)}$ stands for the path loss of the link (sum of free space path loss, rain and gas attenuation [2]), LM is the link margin, N_{TH} is the thermal noise, and NF is the noisefi gure of the receiver.

As Eq. 12 is non-linear, we approximate it using a piecewise linear interpolation function. Depending on the scenario, we have used 6 or 7 line segments to linearize and approximate the power consumed by the transceiver of a BH link.

Algorithm 1 Joint: Proposed Heuristic Algorithm

Input: $\mathcal{E}, \mathcal{S}, \mathcal{U}, \mathcal{L_{AL}}, \mathcal{L_{BL}}, SINR_{(i,u)}, BW_{PRB}, BW_{(i,j)}, c_{i_{max}}, d_u, \Delta^{AL}_{p_i}, \Delta^{BH}_p, N^{AL}_{TRX_i}, N^{BH}_{TRX_{(i,j)}}, p^{AL}_{max_i}, p^{BH}_{max_{(i,j)}}, p^{AL}_{0_i}, p^{BH}_{0_{(i,j)}}, \beta_{(i,j)}, \theta_{PRB}, \mathcal{U}_{assoc}$

```
1: Calculate c_(i,u) from (5) ∀u ∈ U, i ∈ E ∪ S
2: Calculate p^tot_t(i,u) = p^AL_(i,u) + p^BH_tu from (8)-(12) ∀u ∈ U, i ∈ E ∪ S
3: Sort all UEs by w_P D_p(k+1,k) + w_PRB D_PRB(k+1,k) descendingly
4: Candidates ∀ UE u: all cells with c_(i,u) ≤ c*_(i,u) given by (15)
5: Sort candidates of each UE u by p^tot_t(i,u) ascendingly
6: Choose the candidate with the minimum p^tot_t(i,u)
7: while UE u is not associated do
8:   if chosen BS i has sufficient spectrum resources then
9:     if no link of BH route t exceeds its capacity then
10:      Associate UE u to BS i and use BH path t
11:      Update available PRBs of BS i and current BH traffic
12:    else if there is an alternative BH link route then
13:      Choose the next BH route in the sorted list
14:    else
15:      Move to the next candidate i
16:    end if
17:  else
18:    Move to the next candidate i
19:  end if
20: end while
```

3.3 Joint: Proposed Heuristic Algorithm

3.3.1 Algorithm Design. The solution of the MILP of Section 3.2 induces high complexity in the system, which increases significantly with an increasing number of UEs and cells. Notice that an exhaustive search would require the examination of $(|\mathcal{E}|+|\mathcal{S}|)^{|\mathcal{U}|}$ different combinations, which results in prohibitive complexity ($O(n^n)$). Therefore, in the following, we propose an energy-efficient heuristic algorithm called Joint, which aims to optimize jointly the user association and BH traffic routing problem.

In order to decide the user association and BH traffic routing decision of a UE at a specific instant, Joint (summarized in Algorithm 1), calculates i) the number of PRBs needed to satisfy the UE QoS and ii) the total power consumption for every possible association (lines 1-2). The proposed algorithm favors the association with the lowest power (lines 5-6) as long as this is feasible in terms of spectrum and BH capacity (lines 8-9). The total power calculation refers to both the AL and BH. In the case of BH, for SCs with more than one alternative paths, Joint takes into account the BH traffic of the already associated UEs and favors the path that involves the minimum power consumption. Thereby, load balancing is achieved.

A key parameter for the algorithm performance is the order in which different UE associations will be examined. Therefore, the algorithm calculates for every UE the differences between theirfirst best choice from the second in terms of power consumption, their second from their third and so on, denoted by $D_{p_{(k+1,k)}} = p_{(k+1,u)} - p_{(k,u)}$. The UEs with the highest differences are examinedfi rst. The rationale for that is that these associations are more important compared to others, as in case they are not possible (e.g., if the maximum capacity of the cell is reached), they will provoke a higher

Table 2: Operation example. PRBs needed to satisfy QoS.

Cell index	PRBs	Cell index	PRBs	Cell index	PRBs
eNB	4	SC 3	7	SC 6	8
SC 1	18	SC 4	5	SC 7	4
SC 2	12	SC 5	6	SC 8	7

loss in energy efficiency. The same procedure is followed also for the number of PRBs, i.e., $D_{PRB_{(k+1,k)}}=c_{(k+1,u)}-c_{(k,u)}$.

Both criteria are very important: thefi rst (i.e., power) in order to achieve higher energy efficiency and the second (i.e., number of PRBs) to ensure that there will be no unsatisfied UE. Therefore, Joint decides the UE order by sorting them by $(w_P D_{P_{(k+1,k)}} + w_{PRB} D_{PRB_{(k+1,k)}})$ in descending order (line 3). The parameters w_P and w_{PRB} refer to the applied normalized weights for power and PRBs, respectively, and are calculated as [13]

$$w_i = \theta_i \left(D^U_{i_{(k+1,k)}} - D^N_{i_{(k+1,k)}} \right)^{-1}, \tag{14}$$

where θ_i is the factor that express the preference on criterion i and the fraction refers to the normalization coefficient. The exponents U and N refer to the Utopia and Nadir points of $D_{i_{(k+1,k)}}$, respectively.

To reduce the algorithm overhead, for each UE, Joint considers only the cells that involve fewer PRBs than $c^*_{(i,u)}$ (line 4), given by

$$c^*_{(i,u)} = min\left(\frac{c_{(i,u)_{min}}}{\theta_{PRB}}, c_{i_{max}} \right), \tag{15}$$

with $c_{(i,u)_{min}}$ referring to the association with the cell that requires the fewest PRBs to guarantee the GBR service of UE u. For best performance, parameter θ_i should be adapted to UE traffic conditions so as to guarantee that no UE is blocked.

3.3.2 Operation example. Let us decide the association of UE u according to Joint, given that its GBR demand is d_u= 100 Mbps. Based on $SINR_{(i,u)}$, we calculate from (5) the PRBs needed in each case, denoted as $c_{(i,u)}$. Let us assume the PRB demands of Table 2. Notice that we do not include the rest of the cells in the table, since the received SINR from them is so low that the demand in PRBs to satisfy the UE rate demand exceeds their maximum capacity.

Then, let us assume that the system is highly overloaded and thus θ_{PRB}=0.8 (θ_P=0.2). Hence, the set of candidates will involve PRBs fewer or equal to $c^*_{(i,u)}=c_{(i,u)_{min}}/\theta_{PRB}$=4/0.9=4.44. As a result, the set of candidates of UE u is $\{eNB, SC\ 7\}$. For them, the total variable power consumption $p^{tot}_{t_{(i,u)}}=p^{AL}_{(i,u)}+p^{BH}_{t_u}$ is calculated as follows.

i) For i=eNB
- For the calculation of $p^{AL}_{(i,u)}$, from (8) and (9), we have

$$p^{AL}_{(i,u)} = N^{AL}_{TRX_i} \Delta^{AL}_{p_i} \frac{p^{AL}_{max_i}}{c_{i_{max}}} c_{(i,u)}, \tag{16}$$

  with $N^{AL}_{TRX_i}$ =8, $\Delta^{AL}_{p_i}$ =4.7, $p^{AL}_{max_i}/c_{i_{max}}$ =0.3981 W and $c_{(i,u)}$=4, we have $p^{AL}_{(i,u)}$=59.8753 W.
- As already explained, $p^{BH}_{t_u}$=0 in the case of the eNB, and thus, $p^{tot}_{t_{(i,u)}}=p^{AL}_{(i,u)}$=59.8753 W.

ii) For i=SC 7
- For the calculation of $P_{AN_{(i,u)}}$, similar to the case of the eNB, we have from (16), with $N^{AL}_{TRX_i}$ =8, $\Delta^{AL}_{p_i}$ =4, $p^{AL}_{max_i}/c_{i_{max}}$ =0.01 W and $c_{(i,u)}$=4, that $p^{AL}_{(i,u)}$=1.28 W.
- For the calculation of $p^{BH}_{t_u}$, let us assume a simple case, where SC 7 has two alternative paths, i.e., t=1,2, with the following characteristics.
  - BH route t=1 consisting of two BH links, L1 and L2, i.e., $\mathcal{L}^u_{t=1} = \{L1, L2\}$, with
    BW_{L1} = 750 MHz and β_{L1} =-57.25 dBm,
    BW_{L2} = 100 MHz and β_{L2} =-62.45 dBm.
    Moreover, assuming that there is a set of already associated UEs ($\mathcal{U}_{assoc}$), the current BH traffic that passes through each link is assumed to be equal to $\sum_{u\in\mathcal{U}_{assoc}} d_u x^u_{L1} = \sum_{u\in\mathcal{U}_{assoc}} d_u x^u_{L2}$ = 100 Mbps.
  - BH route t=2 consisting of two BH links, L3 and L4, i.e., $\mathcal{L}^u_{t=2} = \{L3, L4\}$, with
    BW_{L3} = 500 MHz and β_{L3} =-55.29 dBm,
    BW_{L4} = 200 MHz and β_{L4} =-66.34 dBm.
    The current traffic of these BH links is assumed to be equal to $\sum_{u\in\mathcal{U}_{assoc}} d_u x^u_{L3}$ =300 Mbps and $\sum_{u\in\mathcal{U}_{assoc}} d_u x^u_{L4}$ =100 Mbps.

  Subsequently, we calculate $p^{BH}_{t_u}$ for every route.

▷ We calculate the target SINR for each link l of route t as

$$SINR_l = 2^{\frac{(\sum_{i\in\mathcal{U}_{assoc}} d_i x^t_l)+d_u}{BW_l}} - 1. \tag{17}$$

Then, we calculate $p^{BH}_{t_u}$ from (10) and (12) as

$$p^{BH}_{t_u} = \sum_{l\in\mathcal{L}^u_t} N^{BH}_{TRX_l} \Delta^{BH}_p SINR_l \beta_l, \tag{18}$$

where $N^{BH}_{TRX_l}$=1, Δ^{BH}_p =4 for all BH links and β_l is converted in W. As a result,
- BH route t=1, $P_{BH^{t=1}_u}$ =2.09 ×10$^{(-9)}$ W
- BH route t=2, $P_{BH^{t=2}_u}$ =2.89 ×10$^{(-9)}$ W

Hence, the minimum $p^{tot}_{t_{(i,u)}}$ corresponds to SC 7 and BH link route t=1. This would be the association and BH routing decision for UE u in each case, as long as SC 7 has at least 4 PRBs available and the maximum capacity of the involved BH links is not reached (please note that in the considered example, the latter constraint is not exceeded, since the transmitted power of the involved BH links, when considering the aggregate traffic that passes through them, is much lower than the maximum P^{BH}_{max} = 33 dBm).

4 EVALUATION

In this section, wefi rst describe the simulation scenario and parameters used in our study. Then, we evaluate the performance of the proposed solutions by comparing it with state-of-the-art algorithms, while gaining insights into the algorithm performance.

4.1 Simulation Scenario

For the performance evaluation, for the sake of simplicity and without loss of generality, we focus on a single eNB sector, as depicted in Fig. 2. SCs are also deployed in hotspot areas of the sector, thus forming two SC clusters [14]. Each cluster consists of 8 SCs [14]. In particular, the SC cluster centers are uniformly distributed in the sector area and the SCs are uniformly distributed in a 100 m radius from each cluster center. The allowable distances among cells as well as among cells and UEs are assumed as described in [14]. The

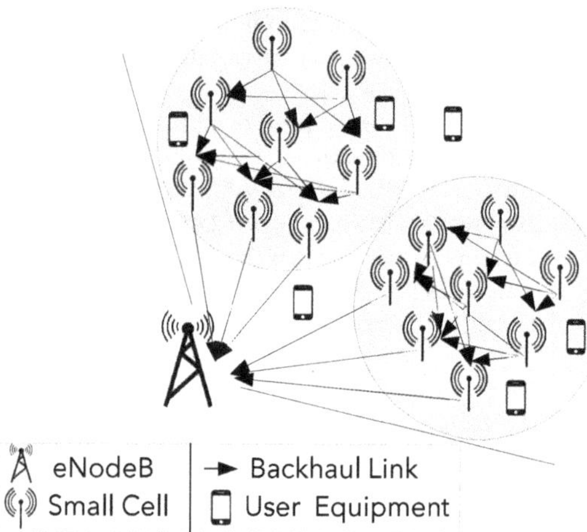

Figure 2: Simulation scenario.

SCs of each cluster are divided according to their distances from the eNB site to the following categories: cluster traffic aggregators (one hop from eNB), intermediate nodes (two hops from eNB) and distant nodes (three hops from eNB). Specifically, 3 aggregators, 3 intermediate and 2 distant nodes are considered in each cluster. Moreover, the mesh BH link connections of Fig. 2 are assumed.

Furthermore, we consider UE hotspot distribution, with 2/3 uniformly located in 100 m from the cluster centers and 1/3 uniformly distributed in the eNB sector area. In terms of their service demands, 70% of UEs require 0.2 Gbps of GBR, 20% 0.4 Gbps and 10% 0.8 Gbps.

As for the frequency allocation: in the access network the eNB uses orthogonal channels compared to the SCs. However, SCs belonging to different clusters reuse the same frequencies and, as a result, interfere to each other; in the BH, by virtue of its static nature, we assume that the frequency allocation takes place during the initial phase so that the generated interference is mitigated.

The rest of the simulation parameters are summarized in Table 3, where h is the antenna height and C_H its correction factor. Moreover, $L_{TX_{(i,j)}}$=$L_{RX_{(i,j)}}$=5 dB, LM=15 dB and N_{TH}=-174 dBm/Hz. A log-normal random variable is used to model shadowing with mean equal to 0 dB and variance 8 dB for the eNB and 10 dB for the SCs.

The algorithms that will be compared in the next section are:

- **Optimal**: It refers to the proposed analytical solution of Section 3.2, which jointly optimizes the UE association and BH routing problem. Implemented in CPLEX, it uses exhaustive Branch-and-Cut search algorithm,fi nding the optimal solution at the expense of potential long search time.
- **Joint**: The proposed energy-efficient heuristic algorithm Joint (Section 3.3), which aims at jointly optimizing the aforementioned problem, while considering both the BH and ALs. For the performance evaluation, we initially select θ_P=1 to maximize energy efficiency and we decrease it by a step equal to 0.02 in case the algorithm returns unsatisfied UEs. This procedure continues until there is no unsatisfied UE or if the other extreme case has been reached, i.e., θ_{PRB}=1.
- **MPL**: It associates the UEs with the cells from which they have the lowest path loss [5]. Given that this algorithm only considers the ALs, for a fair comparison we combine it with the following BH traffic routing algorithms:

Table 3: Parameters used in the performance evaluation.

Parameter	AL: eNB	AL: SC	BH link
Frequency f (GHz)	2		73
Available BW (MHz)	20 (100 PRBs)		500
N_{TRX}	8 (MIMO 8x8)[4]		variable
p_0 (W)	130 [12]	6.8 [12]	3.9 [12]
p_{max} (W)	39.8107 [14]	1 [14]	1.9953 [15]
Δ_p	4.7 [12]	4.0 [12]	variable
Path Loss	69.55+26.16 $\log f$-13.82 $\log h$-C_H+ (44.9-6.55 $\log h$) $\log(d_{iu_{(km)}})$ [16]		Eq. 6-11 in [2]
C_H	0.8+ (1.1 $\log f$- 0.7) h_{UE} -1.56 $\log f$ [16]	0	-
h (m)	25 [14]	2.5 [1]	-
	h_{UE}=1.5 [14]		
NF (dB)	9 [14]		6 [15]
G_{TX}, G_{RX} (dBi)	17[14]	5 [14]	43 [2]

  - **random**: In case of a SC with multiple alternative BH paths, a random selection is made.
  - **min power with LB**: The BH path with the lowest power consumption is selected, given the traffic of the already associated UEs. Thereby, load balancing is achieved.
  - **shortest path**: The shortest BH path is selected.
- **EE-random**: The energy-efficient algorithm that was proposed in [8], which considers both the BH and ALs. As EE-random considers no BH traffic routing, we randomly select a path from the available ones.
- **SINR**: The UEs connect to the cells with the highest received signal power [4]. Again, given that SINR only focuses on the ALs, for a fair comparison, we combine SINR with the three different BH traffic routing algorithms as in the case of MPL.

Finally, two different cases will be studied. In thefirst Δ_p^{BH}=4 and N_{TRX}^{BH}=1, while in the second Δ_p^{BH}=4000 and N_{TRX}^{BH}=8000. In thefi rst case, we examine a simple scenario where the BH consists of point-to-point LOS mmWave BH links of one transceiver chain. This solution will most probably be thefi rst step towards 5G. On the other hand, the second case examines a scenario with massive MIMO BH deployments consisting of thousands of antennas in order to cope with the increasing traffic demands.

4.2 Simulation Results

In Fig. 3, the average total energy efficiency of all algorithms for different numbers of UEs is shown for (Δ_p^{BH}=4, N_{TRX}^{BH}=1) and for (Δ_p^{BH}=4000, N_{TRX}^{BH}=8000). As it can be noticed, in both cases, Joint outperforms the state-of-the-art (up to 95% energy efficiency gain), while achieving performance close to Optimal. It is worth noting that for the second case, i.e., with high traffic-dependent BH energy parameters, the deviation from the Optimal increases up to 14%. This stems from the fact that the system gets very loaded, resulting in most cells reaching their maximum capacity. Hence, the order that the UEs will be examined by Joint becomes very important, as not all the UEs can be associated to their best choice. Therefore, Joint

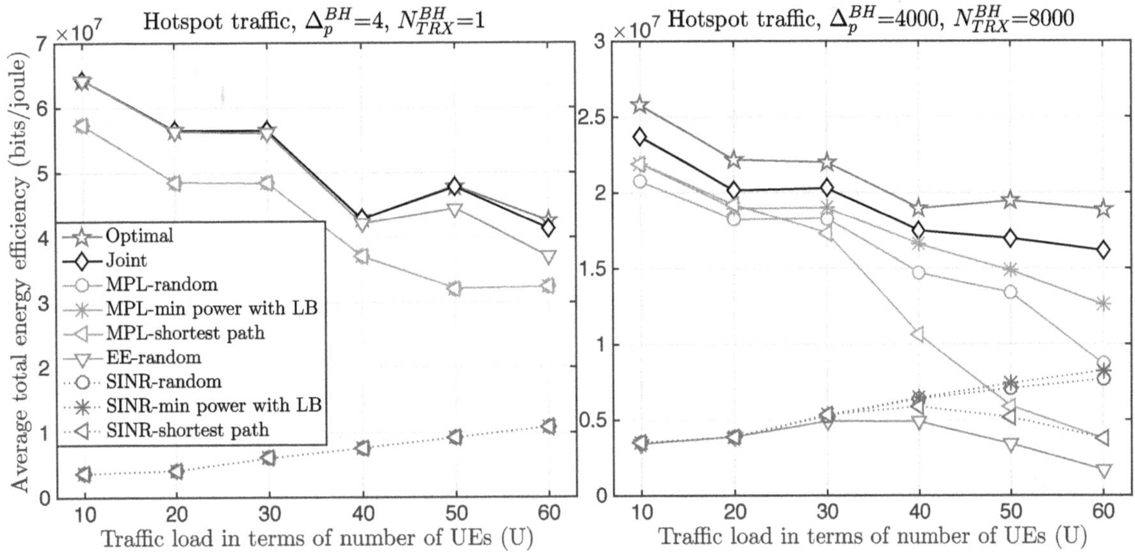

Figure 3: Average total energy efficiency versus traffic load for different Δ_p^{BH} and N_{TRX}^{BH} values.

selects θ_{PRB}=1 in order to favor the connections that require less PRBs, so as to minimize the probability of having unsatisfied UEs. In the case of Optimal, however, all different feasible combinations are examined, thus leading to optimal energy efficiency.

As for the rest of the algorithms, although EE-random achieves very good performance in thefi rst case (up to 13% decrease compared to Optimal), in the second its energy efficiency deteriorates significantly. This is due to the fact that, in the second case, due to the very high traffic-dependent BH energy parameters, EE-random favors the connection with the eNB. This results in very high AL power consumption, with the eNB reaching its maximum capacity. In addition, unlike Joint, the order that the UEs will be examined is not optimized so as to further improve the energy efficiency performance of the algorithm. Once the eNB capacity is reached, EE-random associates the UEs to the SC with the lowest AL and BH power, while having already assigned a random BH path among the alternatives ones to each SC. Nevertheless, the fact that EE-random does not jointly optimize user association and BH routing results in very high BH power consumption, and consequently very low energy efficiency. Especially under high load, it leads to non-zero blocking probability unlike the rest of the algorithms. Specifically, in the second case, for U=40 EE-random presents 0.25% blocking probability, 1% for U=50 and 4.75% for U=60.

MPL achieves worse performance in thefi rst case than the aforementioned algorithms (up to 33% decrease compared to Optimal) mainly for two reasons. Firstly, as the UE association is independent of the SINR, the UEs get associated to cells that require more PRBs to guarantee the GBR, thereby resulting in higher AL power consumption. Secondly, due to hotspots, the UEs are actively pushed to SCs, given that they provide the lowest path loss. This results to the increase of the generated BH traffic, and consequently, to high BH energy consumption. Finally, SINR presents low performance (up to 95% lower energy efficiency than Optimal), since the UEs are connected only based on their SINR. Hence, the UEs may connect to SCs that are located far away from the eNB site, thus involving higher BH energy consumption. Moreover, even in low traffic conditions, there are more UEs connected to the eNB than the rest of the algorithms, resulting in much higher AL power consumption (the power per PRB is much higher for the eNB than the SCs). The differences among different routing algorithms for both MPL and SINR become evident only in the second case, since the BH energy impact becomes much more important than in thefi rst case. As it can be noticed, shortest path and minimum power with load balancing achieve the worst and the best performance, respectively. This is due to the fact that when the latter is applied, the traffic is more evenly distributed in the BH links. On the other hand, with shortest path, the shortest links will become heavy loaded and consequently much more energy hungry due to the exponential increase of the BH power consumption with the increase of traffic.

To gain further insights into the algorithm performance, we depict in Table 4 the utilization percentage (%) of the AL and BH links grouped by their distance from the eNB site when U=30 and (Δ_p^{BH}=4000, N_{TRX}^{BH}=8000). For each group, the mean value and the standard deviation are shown. As it can be seen, Joint and Optimal distribute the traffic in a very similar way for both the AL and BH links. However, especially in the BH case, due to its load balancing feature, Joint presents lower standard deviation in the percentage utilization among the links of each group. This is of high importance, as load balancing provides better utilization of BH resources and lower possibility of BH link bottlenecks.

Regarding the rest of the algorithms, as already commented, EE-random presents high eNB utilization, due to the high traffic-dependent BH energy parameters, that disfavor the connection to SCs. Still, in this example, many SC PRBs are also utilized. This is mainly due to the fact that, as the eNB reaches its capacity limit, the UEs connect to SCs, from which they may require more PRBs to satisfy their GBR. This implies a high increase in the AL utilization, but not in the BH link one, which is smaller than the other algorithms. SINR and MPL present high eNB and SC utilization, respectively, as already explained. As for the different BH traffic routing algorithms,

Table 4: Access and backhaul link utilization percetange (%) for U=30 and (Δ_p^{BH}=4000, N_{TRX}^{BH}=8000).

Algorithm	AL links							BH links					
	eNB	1-hop SCs		2-hop SCs		3-hop SCs		1-hop links		2-hop links		3-hop links	
		Mean	Std	Mean	Std	Mean	Std	Mean	Std	Mean	Std	Mean	Std
Optimal	6.65	29.3	5.87	24.48	8.62	28.11	8.53	10.62	11.3	2.29	1.05	1.33	0.8
Joint		29.7	2.73	25.77	7.96	29.23	7.57	10.69	3.07	2.21	0.5	1.31	0.66
EE-random	98.1	37.21	6.84	40.22	10.9	28.88	8.92	7.53	7.81	1.13	0.48	0.44	0.2
MPL-random								10.66	2.5	2.05	0.56	1.33	0.55
MPL-min power with LB	9.2	24.67	1.87	25.55	9.2	31.49	3.09	10.62	2.4	2.04	0.55	1.31	0.53
MPL-shortest path								10.61	3.3	1.99	1.49	1.3	1.13
SINR-random								7.75	1.59	1.52	0.5	1.01	0.59
SINR-min power with LB	96.1	15.13	5.11	10.47	3.68	13.18	0.6	7.72	1.55		0.39	1	0.5
SINR-shortest path									2.08	1.48	1.18	0.99	0.9

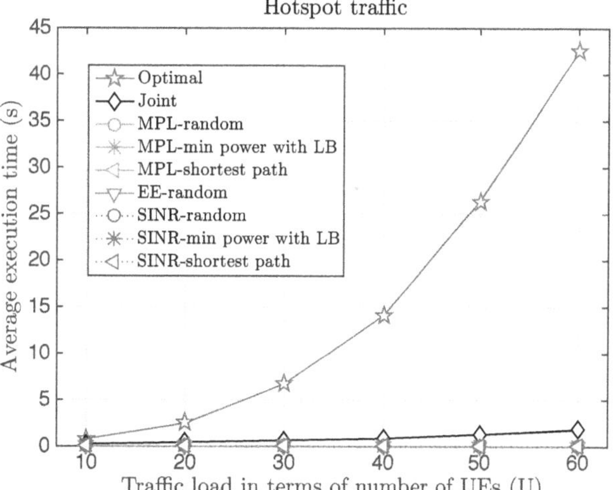

Figure 4: Average execution time for all algorithms and traffic-dependent backhaul energy parameters.

note that minimum power with LB presents lower deviation from the mean value of each group, due to its load balancing feature. On the contrary, shortest path presents the highest standard deviation, as it tends to create uneven BH links in terms of traffic load.

Finally, in order to demonstrate the algorithm performance in terms of complexity, we depict in Fig. 4 the average execution time in seconds for all the algorithms. As it can be noticed, Joint presents slightly higher execution time than the rest of the algorithms, but still much lower than the Optimal. Therefore, Joint allows to calculate solutions of very good quality in short time.

5 CONCLUSION

In this paper, we focused on the joint user association and backhaul traffic routing problem, in a heterogeneous 5G network with mesh millimeter wave backhaul links. The aforementioned problem was formulated with the aim of minimizing the total power consumption of both the access and backhaul links, while satisfying the rate demands of users. To this end, a mixed integer linear problem has been formulated. Given the high complexity of the optimal solution, we also proposed a low-complexity algorithm that targets at optimizing the joint problem so as to achieve high energy efficiency. The proposed joint solution was compared both with the optimal as well as with references approaches, and it was shown that it can achieve considerable performance gains, very close to optimal. As future work, we plan to study the aforementioned problem in a scenario where switching-off both the base stations and backhaul links is enabled to achieve further energy saving gains.

ACKNOWLEDGMENTS

Part of this work has been funded by the Knowledge foundation of Sweden (KKStiftelsen) through the project SOCRA and the Spanish Government and ERDF through CICYT project TEC2013- 48099-C2-1-P.

REFERENCES

[1] "NGMN 5G white paper," NGMN Alliance, v. 1.0, Feb. 2015.

[2] A. Mesodiakaki *et al.*, "Energy Efficient Line-of-Sight Millimeter Wave Small Cell Backhaul: 60, 70, 80 or 140 GHz?", in *Proc. 17th IEEE WoWMoM*, Jun. 2016.

[3] J. Vestin *et al.*, "Low Frequency Assist for mmWave Backhaul - The case for SDN resiliency mechanisms", in *Proc. IEEE ICC*, May 2017.

[4] *E-UTRA and E-UTRAN; Overall description; Stage 2*, 3GPP TS 36.300, v. 11.5.0, Rel. 11, Mar. 2013.

[5] D. Fooladivanda and C. Rosenberg, "Joint resource allocation and user association for heterogeneous wireless cellular networks," *IEEE Trans. Wireless Commun.*, vol. 12, no. 1, pp. 248-257, Oct. 2012.

[6] N. Sapountzis, T. Spyropoulos, N. Nikaein, and U. Salim, "User association in over- and under- provisioned backhaul HetNets," *Eurocom Research Report*, 16-318, Apr. 2016.

[7] Q. Han, B. Yang, C. Chen, and X. Guan, "Backhaul-aware joint user association and resource allocation for energy-constrained HetNets," *IEEE Trans. Veh. Technol.*, vol. 66, no. 1, pp. 580-593, Jan. 2017.

[8] A. Mesodiakaki *et al.*, "Energy and spectrum efficient user association in millimeter wave backhaul small cell networks," *IEEE Trans. Veh. Technol*, vol. 66, no. 2, pp. 1810-1821, Feb. 2017.

[9] *Study on Small Cell enhancements for E-UTRA and E-UTRAN; Higher layer aspects*, 3GPP TR 36.842, v. 12.0.0, Rel. 12, Dec. 2013.

[10] K. Samdanis, A. Maeder, M. Meo and C. Verikoukis, *Green Communications: Principles, Concepts and Practice*, John Wiley & Sons, 2015.

[11] E. Dahlman, S. Parkvall and J. Sköld, *4G: LTE/LTE- Advanced for Mobile Broadband*, Academic Press, ISBN: 012385489X, 2011.

[12] G. Auer *et al.*, "How much energy is needed to run a wireless network?," *IEEE Wireless Commun.*, vol. 18, no. 5, pp. 40-49, Oct. 2011.

[13] O. J. Grodzevich and O. Romanko, "Normalization and other topics in multi-objective optimization," in *Proc. FM-IPSW*, Aug. 2006.

[14] *Small cell enhancements for E-UTRA & E-UTRAN-Physical layer aspects*, 3GPP TR 36.872, v. 1.0.0, Rel. 12, Aug. 2013.

[15] www.gotmic.se, Documents: gTSC0020, gAPZ0039, gRSC0016, gRSC0015, gTSC0023, gAPZ0042.

[16] T. S. Rappaport, *Wireless Communications: Principles and Practice*, (2nd ed.), Prentice Hall, pp. 153-154, 2002.

Acrux: Indoor Localization Without Strings

Jean-Gabriel Krieg
IRIT-INPT/ENSEEIHT
University of Toulouse
Toulouse, France
jeangabriel.krieg@enseeiht.fr

Gentian Jakllari
IRIT-INPT/ENSEEIHT
University of Toulouse
Toulouse, France
jakllari@enseeiht.fr

Hadrien Toma
ENSICAEN
Caen, France
hadrien.toma@ecole.ensicaen.fr

Andre-Luc Beylot
IRIT-INPT/ENSEEIHT
University of Toulouse
Toulouse, France
beylot@enseeiht.fr

ABSTRACT

We present Acrux, the first indoor localization system to achieve meter level accuracy while relying exclusively on a single fix and the sensors commonly found in off-the-shelf smartphones. Acrux uses dead-reckoning, the approach that gives probably the best chance at a completely autonomous indoor localization system. Unfortunately, it has not been mastered on smartphones beyond a few dozen meters due to its inherent integration drift. As a result, all dead-reckoning based solutions in literature require periodic recalibration using input from outside – attaching strings preventing indoor localization from becoming mainstream. While it is virtually impossible to completely eliminate integration drift, Acrux is the first solution to succeed in dead-reckoning with meter level accuracy for several hundred meters, enough to relax the requirement for periodic recalibration in most indoor scenarios. To accomplish this, Acrux replaces step-counting, the standard approach for measuring distance using sensors, with an approach that measures the speed of locomotion. Although a straightforward accurate estimation of motion speed using the erroneous sensors found on smartphones is infeasible, Acrux combines a novel approach with measurement based analysis to achieve that. Leveraging its excellent dead-reckoning capability, Acrux is shown to provide indoor localization with median error between 0.7 m and 1.2 m and 98% percentile error of 3 m in a dozen of scenarios in 4 different buildings – without any recalibration.

KEYWORDS

Indoor localization; Dead reckoning; Inertial navigation system

1 INTRODUCTION

Someone named Alice, smartphone in her hand, enters an area with weak or no satellite coverage – inside a building, subway station, urban canyon – and losses the GPS fix. An app on the phone picks up where the GPS left off and continues to provide accurate fixes to help Alice get to her destination. The app is standalone and autonomous – it relies on the smartphone's sensors only. While this scenario might sound well within our technological capabilities, it is currently impossible.

Extending the localization experience enabled by GPS in most outdoors areas to areas with weak or no satellite reception – the last-mile localization problem – has been the subject of intense research and development in recent years. A majority of the proposed solutions rely on the smartphone's Wi-Fi transceiver and available Wi-Fi infrastructure [5, 14, 19, 26]. However, a training phase, known as fingerprinting, is required for every environment – an onerous task that has to be repeated every time the Wi-Fi infrastructure is updated. Crowdsourcing has been proposed [5, 8, 23] to remove the pain from fingerprinting. However, crowd-based approaches suffer from a chicken-egg problem: early adaptation hinges on the quality of the solution while the quality of the solution hinges on a high number of adapters. Other RF-based solutions relax the requirement for fingerprinting but require specialized hardware [28] and/or the deployment of dedicated servers [16, 17], creating a high barrier to entry. With the increase in sophistication of the smartphone hardware many responded by designing indoor localization systems that leverage the motion and/or audio/video sensors. In principle, equipped with inertial sensors, Alice should be able to track her trajectory once outside the GPS' reach and using the last GPS fix continue generating accurate fixes until reaching her destination. This approach, commonly known as dead-reckoning, has been in use since the days of Christopher Columbus for determining longitude [7] but it suffers from integration drift [10]. No solution currently exists that can make it work for more than a few dozen meters on a commodity smartphone [5, 6, 18]. As a result, the common approach is to perform periodic recalibration every few dozen meters: using the Wi-Fi infrastructure [5], an accurate geometry of the location [6, 18] and/or crowdsourcing [23].

We present Acrux[1] the first system that relies exclusively on the smartphone's sensors and a single fix to address the last-mile localization problem. Acrux achieves this by improving the accuracy of dead-reckoning by several times when compared to state of the art solutions thanks to two innovations. First, we make an

MSWiM'17, November 21–25, 2017, Miami, FL, USA

ACM ISBN 978-1-4503-5162-1/17/11...$15.00.
DOI: http://dx.doi.org/10.1145/10.1145/3127540.3127545

[1]Acrux is the brightest star in the Southern Cross, used for navigation purposes in the Southern Hemisphere much like Polaris is used in the Northern Hemisphere.

observation that becomes the foundation of this work's novel contribution. The natural language contains several nonsynonymous terms for describing human motion indoors: strolling, rushing, walking, running. Obviously, this is because we, as humans, have noticed differences in the body mechanics and speed of locomotion. Yet, the dead-reckoning schemes proposed so far consider all human motion indoors as simply "walking" and try to estimate the distance a user has "walked" since the last fix. A system that would first identify if a user is strolling, walking, rushing or running – which we collectively refer to as *elementary locomotions* – and then estimate the distance she could travel given the elementary locomotion would benefit from higher granularity and thus have the potential to be significantly more accurate. Second, instead of following the common approach of estimating the distance traveled by counting steps and multiplying by an estimate of step size, something notoriously difficult to measure accurately[18, 27], Acrux estimates the speed of movement. Speed is less variable – people walking together may have very different step sizes but they progress at similar speeds.

Translating these observations into an accurate and efficient localization system running entirely on a commodity smartphone entails several challenges: (i) While humans can easily distinguish the different elementary locomotions, how can Acrux do so relying purely on the inertial sensors that are erroneous and are further affected by how/where users carry their phones; (2) Even if Acrux is capable of recognizing with accuracy the different elementary locomotions when given enough sensor readings, how will it be able to determine each elementary locomotion in real-time and on a smartphone with limited processing power running on battery; (3) How does Acrux use this information to compute speed and direction so as to fully map a user's trajectory; (4) What happens when a user moves between floors.

In short, we address these challenges by first identifying unique patterns in the inertial sensor readings, vertical acceleration in particular, that unequivocally identify each elementary locomotion, regardless of the particular user's height and weight. Using the identified patterns, we design and implement an algorithm that can recognize an elementary locomotion on a commodity smartphone using only 1 s of sensor readings. This information is combined with the user's cadence for accurately estimating the speed of locomotion. To estimate the direction of locomotion, Acrux combines the knowledge of the current elementary locomotion with an approach for correcting bias into a light-weight and accurate algorithm. Finally, combining vertical acceleration, barometer readings and knowledge of regulations regarding the angle of inclination of stairs and escalators, Acrux is able to accurately track a user as she moves between floors.

Our main contributions may be summarized as follows:

- Inspired by how humans perceive pedestrian locomotion indoors, we introduce the concept of elementary locomotion for improving the accuracy of dead-reckoning based localization (§ 3). We leverage this concept to design and implement an algorithm that runs entirely on a commodity smartphone and can accurately estimate the speed of locomotion.
- We design a light-weight approach that relies on elementary locomotion based filtering and bias correction for accurately tracking a user's direction of locomotion (§ 4).

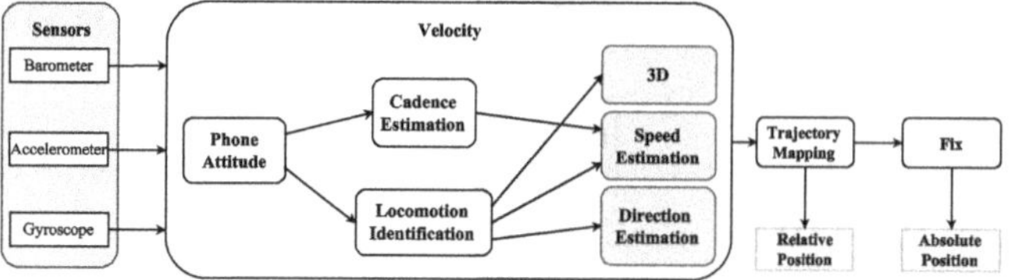

Figure 1: The Architecture of Acrux.

- We extend Acrux in "3D" (§ 5), enabling it to provide localization fixes when a user moves between floors.
- We develop Acrux on the Android OS and carry out extensive experiments on 4 commodity smartphones and 4 different indoor locations, including two subway stations (§ 6). Measurements on a 5 km path show that the best step-counting strategy deviates from the truth by 1 m after 99 m and by 55.29 m at the end of the path; Acrux deviates by 1 m after 557 m and by 8.33 m at the end of the 5 km path – an improvement of over 5.6×. Dozens of scenarios in 4 different buildings showed median errors between 0.7 and 1.2 m and 98% percentile error of 3 m.

2 OVERVIEW OF ACRUX

Fig. 1 shows a high-level depiction of Acrux's architecture. The heart of Acrux is utilizing the readings from the accelerometer, gyroscope and barometer for computing the smartphone user's motion velocity. When Acrux determines the phone has lost the GPS lock[2], it does two things. First, it stores a *fix* consisting of the coordinates and global direction. Second, it establishes its own frame of reference. Once inside the building, all localization computations are done in its own frame of reference and converted into global coordinates using the initial fix. As the raw gyroscope and accelerometer readings are in the phone's frame of reference, the *Phone Attitude* component[3] converts the readings into the user's frame of reference before passing them onto the rest of Acrux.

There are three key components that utilize the sensors readings for accurately computing velocity: the *Speed Estimation* component (§ 3), the *Direction Estimation* component (§ 4) and what we refer to as *3D* (§ 5), the component for tracking a user as she transitions between floors. This includes a user taking the stairs, escalator (standing or walking) as well as the elevator. In the following, we describe each component in detail.

3 ESTIMATING SPEED

In this section, we describe how Acrux estimates the speed of locomotion, one of the two components required for computing the velocity. Acrux uses a two step algorithm that first limits the range of possible speed values and then guesses the actual speed. To limit the range of possible speed values, Acrux deconstructs human motion into *elementary locomotions* and then solves the challenge of identifying these locomotions in real time while relying exclusively on inertial sensors. Acrux's solution requires a single signature per

[2]This information can be extracted from the phone's operating system. Android, for example, exposes a very detailed state of the GPS.

[3]There are more sophisticated systems for accurately computing the phone's attitude [30]. However, as Acrux relies on patterns in the sensor readings rather than their absolute values, a heavier, albeit more accurate, system is not necessary.

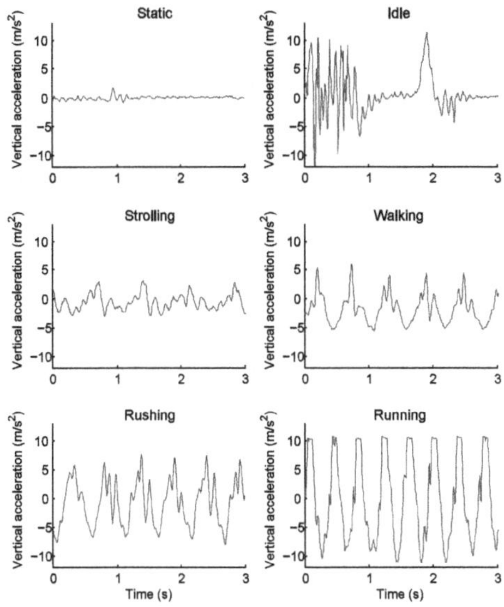

Figure 2: Vertical acceleration readings for every elementary locomotion.

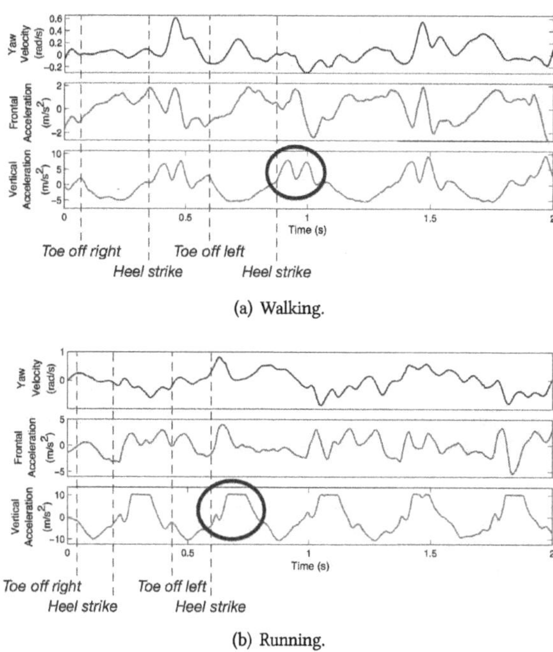

(a) Walking.

(b) Running.

Figure 3: Acceleration and gyroscope readings (most relevant dimensions shown) with phone in the right hand. Clear and distinct patterns emerge in the vertical acceleration readings for walking and running, respectively.

elementary locomotion and only 1 s of sensor readings; no per user training is required. Once the elementary locomotion is identified, Acrux measures the user's current cadence and uses it to estimate the speed of locomotion. In the following, we describe both steps in detail.

3.1 Identifying the Elementary Locomotions

Inspired by how humans perceive pedestrian motion indoors, reflected in the nonsynonymous terms of the natural language, Acrux deconstructs human motion into 6 *elementary locomotions*: (1) ***Static*** – no movement; (2) ***Idle***: random movement with no localization change, e.g. while sitting in a food court at the mall; (3) ***Strolling***; (4) ***Walking***; (5) ***Rushing*** and (6) ***Running***.

We leverage the sensor readings in response to the distinct body mechanics inherent in every elementary locomotion to build a *signature* for every elementary locomotion. Acrux stores the signature and when requested it can identify the user's current elementary locomotion by comparing the phone's sensor readings to the stored signatures. The challenge, however, is building a single signature per elementary locomotion, regardless of a user's height, weight or gender.

3.1.1 Building a Signature per Elementary Locomotion. Fig. 2 shows the vertical accelerations collected on a Nexus 5 phone when a user is performing one of the 6 elementary locomotions. When the foot strikes the ground, an unmistakable vertical acceleration is generated throughout the entire body and can be sensed by the phone no matter where it is placed and/or how it is being held, making vertical acceleration the most reliable indicator of locomotion. It is immediately clear that beyond the obvious differences in the actual values, the readings exhibit distinct *patterns* for every locomotion and with some analysis one should be able to identify unique signatures. In the interest of brevity, we describe in detail the process for identifying signatures for walking and running; the process is the same for strolling and rushing. Fig. 3 shows the time series of the sensor readings generated when a user is walking and running. Zooming in on the vertical acceleration, right after the heel strikes the ground, reveals a significant difference in the shapes of the respective time series – both present two peaks but while for walking the peaks are similar in size that is not the case for running. The reason for this difference lies in how most people run and walk with shoes. When running, most people [13], including the user in this experiment, land hard on their heels, which end up absorbing most of the energy. When walking, people still land on their heels but the landing is more soft and flat so the energy is transferred more uniformly on the foot, explaining the similar peaks. These basic locomotion mechanics do not depend on a person's height, weight or gender. For example, approximately 75% of shod runners heel strike [13]. Therefore, the patterns observed in Fig. 3 are used by Acrux as signatures for walking and running, respectively, for all users. Experimental results in § 6.3 show that these signatures cut across user gender, height and weight.

Finally, as Fig. 2 shows, there is no signature for static and idle so when Acrux does not identify a particular signature it knows the user is either idle or static. To distinguish these two locomotions, Acrux uses the fact that an idle user generates far stronger readings than a completely static one.

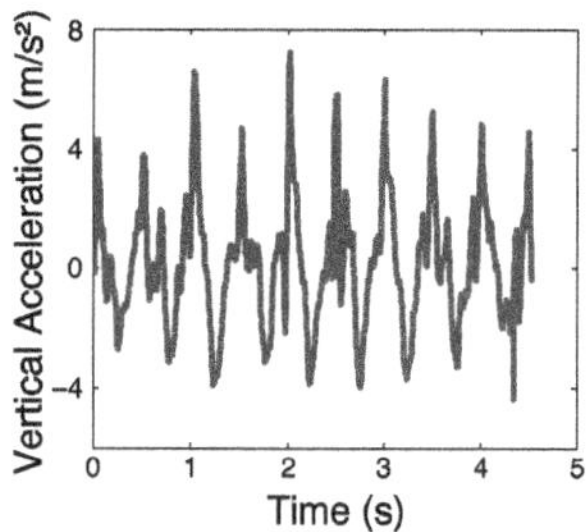

(a) Vertical Acceleration of a rushing user

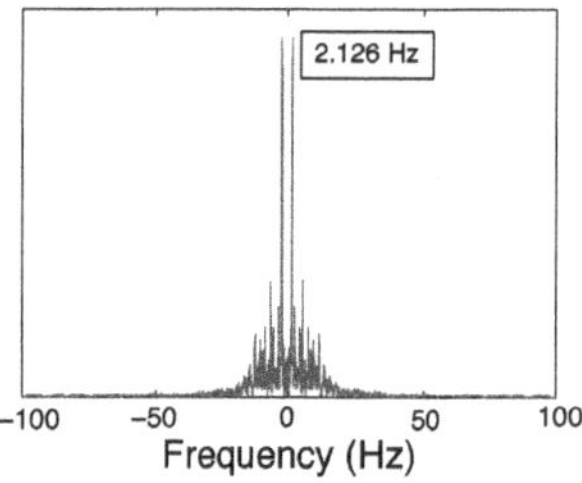

(b) Fast Fourier Transform of the vertical acceleration

Figure 4: Retrieving the cadence (steps/sec) using FFT. The FFT predicts around 2 steps/sec which, as can be seen by the vertical acceleration readings, is the correct value.

Algorithm 1: Real Time Speed Estimation.

```
input    : 1 s sensor readings (A(k))_{k ∈ [[1;p]]}
output   : The current speed.
begin
    p = 6; //Accelerometer & gyroscope
    m = 4; //Number of stored signatures
    W[6] = {0.4, 0.2, 0.05, 0.2, 0.1, 0.05};
    locomotion = IDLE; //Default locomotion
    score = 0.4; //Minimum recognition score
    for || k = 1 → p do
        z(k) = frequency_analysis(A(k));
    //STEP 1: Identify the elementary locomotion.
    for i = 1 → m do
        for || k = 1 → p do
            r(i)(k) = r_Pearson(X(i, k), z(k));
        score_loc = r(i)^T × W;
        if score_loc > score then
            score = score_loc;
            locomotion = i;
    //STEP 2: Compute the cadence.
    cadence = compute_cadence(z(0));
    return speed[locomotion][cadence];
```

3.1.2 Storing the Signatures. Let $A_{i,k}(t)$ be the 5 s[4] temporal realization of elementary locomotion i from sensor reading k, where $i \in [\![1;m]\!]$ and $k \in [\![1;p]\!]$. For the current version, $m = 4$, for strolling, walking, rushing, running and $p = 6$: 3 readings from the accelerometer and 3 from the gyroscope.

- The signal is truncated, centered and zero-padded.
- Each signal is converted into the frequency domain, $\mathcal{A}_{i,k} = FFT\left(A_{i,k}\right)$, and normalized: $\mathcal{A}_{i,k}\big|_{norm}$
- All signals are entered on a matrix: $\mathcal{X} = \left(\mathcal{A}_{i,k}\right)_{i\in[\![1;m]\!],k\in[\![1;p]\!]}$.

3.1.3 Real Time Elementary Locomotion Identification. When running on a phone, Acrux periodically collects sensor readings and looks for signatures so as to identify the current elementary locomotion. For this it needs to, one, decide how much data it needs for identifying a particular signature and, two, a quick and efficient way of searching the data for signatures. Fig. 3 gives an easy answer to the first question – 1 to 2 seconds of sensor readings contain more than enough patterns. The challenge is identifying them in real time.

Matching current sensor readings to a signature: Instead of searching the sensor readings for a particular signature, Acrux simply compares a sample of the current readings with the stored signatures (§ 3.1.2) and returns the closest match. The input readings are first processed and then converted into the frequency domain using FFT. The processing consists of truncating the signal for removing the edge effects and mean value and then zero-padding so the signal's length is a power of two[5]. The readings are compared to the stored signatures using the Pearson coefficient. For two signals x and y, each of length n, the Pearson coefficient, r, is defined as follows:

$$\begin{cases} r_{Pearson}(x,y) = \frac{xy^T - n\bar{x}\bar{y}}{v_x v_y} \\ \text{where: } v_x = \sqrt{\left[\sum_{i=1}^{n} x_i^2\right] - n\bar{x}^2} \end{cases}$$

Once the Pearson coefficient is computed for all 6 readings, we get a scalar correlation score by multiplying with a weighting vector reflecting the relative importance of each reading in identifying locomotions. As mentioned in § 3.1.1, the vertical acceleration is the most reliable indicator of locomotion. Based on this and hours of trial and errors, Acrux implementation uses 0.4, 0.2, 0.05 for the accelerometer's vertical, frontal and side readings and 0.2, 0.1, 0.05 for the gyroscope's yaw, pitch and roll. If the scalar correlation score for a particular candidate locomotion is at least 0.4, it is considered a good potential fit. If no candidate locomotion scores at least 0.4, indicating no locomotion pattern in the sensor readings, it returns idle by default[6]

3.1.4 Accuracy in Practice. To test the accuracy of our approach for identifying elementary locomotions, we carry the following experiment. A single user travels a 200 m distance while holding a Nexus 5 phone running Acrux and is asked to switch between the 6 elementary locomotions, as the user perceives them, every 10 s. Acrux tries to identify the elementary locomotions using readings from a fixed time window. This time window is varied from 0.25 to 2.5 s and a separate experiment is carried out for every value. We collect the data and compare offline what Acrux identified as elementary locomotion with what the user was actually doing. The data showed (graph not shown for lack of space) that a 1 s sample was enough for Acux to identify the elementary locomotion with over 90% accuracy. When the sampling window is stretched out to 2.5 s the accuracy approaches 100%. For the performance evaluation (§ 6) we used a 1 s[7] window as it presents a good tradeoff between accuracy and speed.

[4] As is evident from Figures 2 and 3, a few seconds contain more than enough patterns. We tested and got good results with as little as 2 s but as it costs next to nothing we chose to be conservative and sampled for 5 s.

[5] It enables computing the FFT using two different processes: one for the even part and one for the odd part of the signal.

[6] When the readings are close to 0 Acrux decides the current locomotion is static and does not trigger Algorithm 1.

[7] The fact that the signatures are 5 s (§ 3.1.2) is not an issue as the matching is done in the frequency domain (§ 3.1.3).

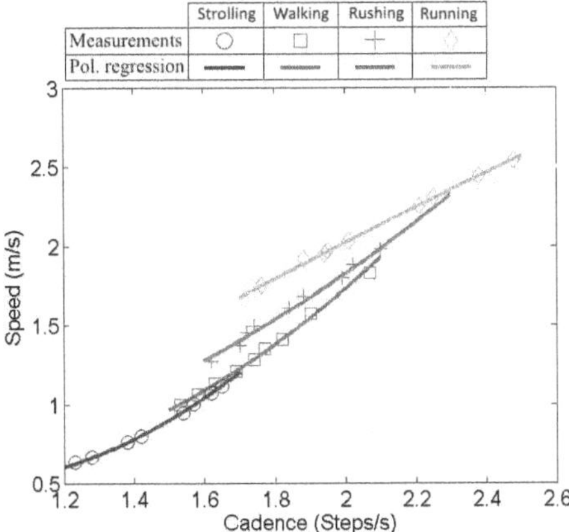

Figure 5: Speed as function of the elementary locomotion and cadence. Polynomial regression is used to create a continuous mapping.

3.2 Combining Elementary Locomotion and Cadence for Estimating Speed

Even after deconstructing human motion indoors into 6 elementary locomotions, there is still some variability in the speed within each locomotion. When strolling, the locomotion speed cannot be as high as when running but it can still vary. Further analysis, however, revealed that changing speed while staying within a given locomotion was accomplished by changing cadence, the number of steps per second. Fortunately, as Fig. 4 shows, the cadence can be estimated by simply converting the vertical acceleration readings into the frequency domain and looking at the highest peak.

We use a measurement based analysis to compute the relationship between cadence and speed for every elementary locomotion. Several volunteers are given a Nexus 5 phone that is measuring cadence and asked to perform each of the elementary locomotions for 20 m while we use a chronometer to measure their speed of motion. Fig. 5 shows the measured speed values as function of cadence and elementary locomotion. Acrux uses polynomial regression to create a continuous mapping.

The complete algorithm Acrux uses for estimating speed is shown in Algorithm 1. Obviously the most challenging part is the elementary locomotion identification, lines 9 – 15. The elementary locomotion is combined with the cadence using the mapping shown in Fig. 5 to return the current speed, line 17.

4 ESTIMATING DIRECTION

In principle, the MEMS (microelectro-mechanical-system) gyroscope and compass with which the commodity mobile devices are equipped should make it straightforward to calculate the global direction in which a user is moving. Unfortunately, the gyroscope readings are influenced by what we refer to as *parasitic movements*: body movements, such as swing of arms, side-to-side sway, etc. that do not necessarily take place because a user has changed direction. To make matters worse, the compass available on mobile devices is itself erroneous. Several solutions have been proposed for addressing this two-fold challenge [24, 27]. Fortunately, Acrux does not need the instantaneous global direction of locomotion but rather the direction in its own frame of reference (§ 2). It uses the initial fix to convert all local calculations into global values, entirely circumventing the compass. As a result, Acrux employs a light-weight solution needing only the gyroscope. It relies on two ideas for resolving the issues arising from using a MEMS gyroscope: leveraging the current elementary locomotion for filtering out parasitic movements, and bias correction.

4.1 Locomotion Based Filtering

The gyroscope measurements are impacted not only by changes in direction but also by how a user moves. To filter out the impact of these movements, Acrux makes use of its locomotion signatures. When it needs to estimate direction, it first identifies the current elementary locomotion and then subtracts the yaw velocity of the particular locomotion from the current gyroscope values. Specifically, it first converts the current yaw velocity into the frequency domain and then subtracts from its highest peak the highest peak of the stored signature (already in the frequency domain § 3.1.2). This gives Acrux a filtered version of the yaw velocity that is a better indication of the actual direction changes.

4.2 Bias Correction

Let $\dot{\theta}_m(t_n)$ denote the measured and filtered (§ 4.1) yaw velocity at time t_n. Because of the bias and noise introduced by the MEMS gyroscope, we get:

$$\dot{\theta}_m(t_n) = \dot{\theta}(t_n) + b(t_n) + \eta(t_n) \tag{1}$$

where $\dot{\theta}(t_n)$ represents the correct yaw velocity, $b(t_n)$ represents the bias introduced by the gyroscope and $\eta(t_n)$ represents the white Gaussian noise.

Thus, estimating the correct yaw velocity using Eq. (1) reduces to the problem of estimating the bias. We can re-write Eq. (1) in recursive form for $i = 1, 2, 3 \ldots n$ as follows:

$$\dot{\theta}_m(t_i) - \dot{\theta}(t_{i-1}) = \dot{\theta}(t_i) - \dot{\theta}(t_{i-1}) + b(t_i) + \eta(t_i)$$

Taking expectations, we get:

$$\mathbb{E}\left[\dot{\theta}_m(t_i) - \dot{\theta}(t_{i-1})\right] = \mathbb{E}\left[\dot{\theta}(t_i) - \dot{\theta}(t_{i-1})\right] + \mathbb{E}\left[b(t_i)\right]$$

Assuming no abrupt changes in the direction of locomotion, that is, $\mathbb{E}\left[\dot{\theta}(t_i) - \dot{\theta}(t_{i-1})\right] = 0$, leads to:

$$\mathbb{E}\left[b(t_i)\right] = \mathbb{E}\left[\dot{\theta}_m(t_i) - \dot{\theta}(t_{i-1})\right] \tag{2}$$

Finally, using the fact that at time t_n, $\mathbb{E}\left[b(t_i)\right] = \frac{1}{n} \times \sum_{i=1}^{n} b(t_i)$, Acrux can estimate the bias of the MEMS gyroscope as follows:

$$\begin{aligned} b(t_n) &= n \times \mathbb{E}\left[b(t_i)\right] - \sum_{i=1}^{n-1} b(t_i) \\ &= n \times \mathbb{E}\left[\dot{\theta}_m(t_i) - \dot{\theta}(t_{i-1})\right] - \sum_{i=1}^{n-1} b(t_i) \end{aligned} \tag{3}$$

As base case for Eq. (3), we assume $\dot{\theta}(t_0) = 0$.

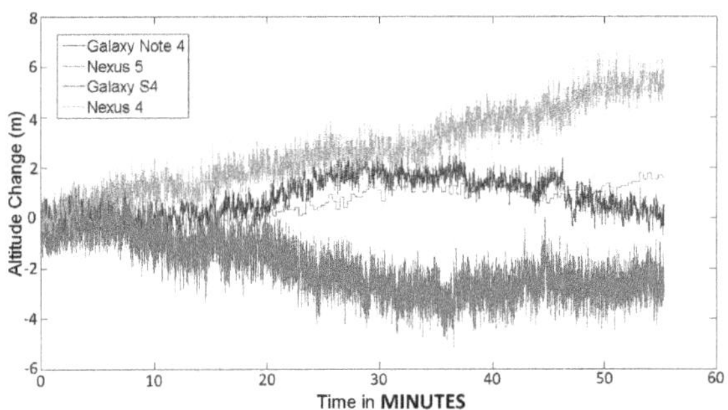

Figure 6: Altitude change estimates over tens of MINUTES using the barometer sensor readings from 4 different smartphones left stationary.

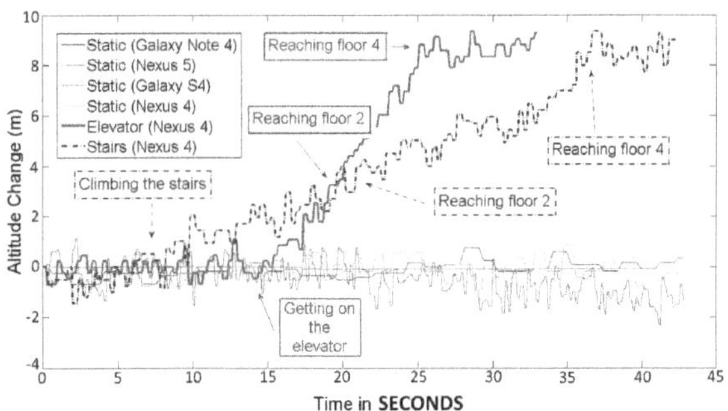

Figure 7: Altitude change estimates over tens of SECONDS, the time it normally takes to change floors using one of the vertical transportation modes. Data is from 6 smartphones – one with a user taking the elevator, one with a user taking the stairs and 4 left stationary. At this time scale, the drift in barometer readings (4 static devices) is too low compared to the changes due to a user's changing floors (2 devices changing floors).

5 LOCALIZATION IN 3D: STAIRS, ESCALATORS, ELEVATORS

To continue tracking a user's trajectory as she moves between floors in a multilevel building, Acrux needs to address the following three challenges. One, estimating the altitude change. Two, detecting the vertical transportation mode – stairs, escalator, elevator. Three, estimating the displacement given the user's vertical transportation mode. In the following, we explain how Acrux addresses each of these challenges.

5.1 Estimating Altitude Changes Using the Barometer Sensor Readings

Acrux calculates the changes in altitude by leveraging the barometer sensor and adapting the barometric formula as follows:

$$\Delta z = -\frac{\Delta p}{\rho g} \tag{4}$$

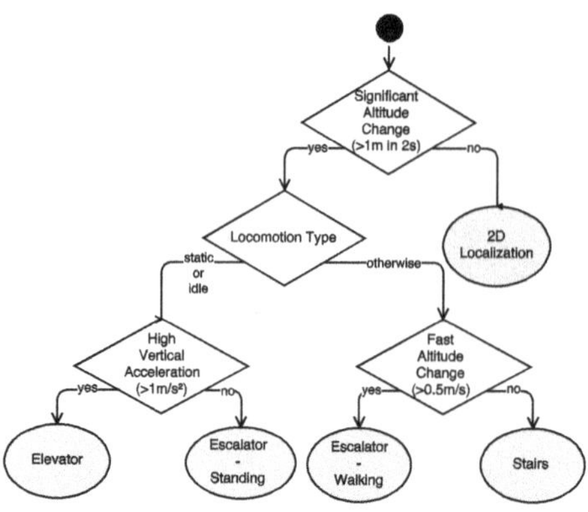

Figure 8: Detecting Vertical Transportation Mode.

where Δz is the differential altitude, Δp is the pressure differential, ρ is the air density and g is the earth's gravity.

Unfortunately, the air density, ρ, can be highly variable due to, among other things, changes in room temperature. Fig. 6 shows altitude estimations when using Equation 4 with the barometer readings from 4 different mobile devices left stationary for approximately an hour on a table in our building. The data shows that over time the barometer readings for the same exact location drifts by amounts corresponding to several meters, the equivalent of one or more floors. Clearly, one cannot rely on the absolute barometer readings for identifying the exact floor a user is on. A similar conclusion is also reached in [22, 29] which, as a result, introduce training and output from outside in the form of fingerprinting or crowdsourcing to achieve accurate floor placement.

Fortunately, Acrux's goal is not exact floor placement but dead-reckoning. It only needs to know if a user has changed floors not the exact floor she is on, which would require the exact number of floors she has changed since entering the building. A floor change using any of the vertical transportation modes takes place in a matter of seconds, time during which, as Fig. 7 shows, the change in barometer readings due to changing floors is much higher than the drift. Therefore, by analyzing altitude changes taking place over a few seconds, Acrux can tell if a user is changing floors, the vertical transportation mode § 5.2 used and the displacement between two floors § 5.3 so as to compute the next fix.

5.2 Detecting Vertical Transportation Mode

To detect the vertical transportation mode, Acrux uses the decision tree shown in Fig. 8. When it detects a high altitude change over few seconds (>1m in 2 seconds), it knows the users has taken a vertical transportation mode. It then identifies the elementary locomotion and if it is static or idle it decides the user is either on an elevator or standing on an escalator. To distinguish these two, it looks at the vertical acceleration; if it is high ($> 1m/sec^2$) the user is in an elevator otherwise she is standing on an escalator. If the elementary locomotion is not static or idle the user is either climbing the stairs or is walking on an escalator. To distinguish these two, Acrux uses the fact that a user who is walking on an escalator will normally change altitude significantly faster than someone taking the stairs.

5.3 Estimating Displacement for Every Vertical Transportation Mode

To generate fixes while on an elevator, Acrux only needs to update the vertical axis value. For this it simply computes the attitude change since the last fix using Equation 4. In the case of escalators, generating fixes using the altitude change only is not possible as the movement is both across the vertical as well as the horizontal axis. However, with a little research we found that the angle of inclination of an escalator is regulated and is typically 30° [3]. Using this information and simple trigonometry we can compute the displacement in the horizontal axis and continue generating accurate fixes in 3D. Finally, generating fixes while a user is taking the stairs is a bit more complex – a user taking a spiral staircase, for example, is continually changing direction while climbing. To address this, Acrux makes use of its direction estimation module in addition to the altitude change and the fact that the angle of inclination of stairs is also regulated and is typically 30°.

6 SYSTEM EVALUATION

6.1 Implementation

We implemented Acrux following a *write once, run anywhere* approach. Towards this, we used PhoneGap [4], a mobile development framework that enables application development for mobile devices using JavaScript. It allowed us to implement a responsive user interface in HTML5 and CSS3 and a unified back-end in JavaScript. What is more, with PhoneGap we were able to implement part of Acrux as a native process which allowed for a robust interface with the sensors. Finally, we used Couchbase [2] for building a fast and efficient database on a mobile device following the NoSQL approach.

6.2 Methodology

We evaluate Acrux in real-life experiments using 10 users, 4 different mobile devices and 4 different buildings. The mobile devices include an HTC Google Nexus 5 with Android 5.0 Lollipop, an HTC Google Nexus 9 tablet with Android 5.0 Lollipop, a Samsung Galaxy S5 with Android 4.4.2 Jelly Bean and a Sony Xperia E3 with Android 4.4 Jelly Bean. The 4 different buildings include a two-story office building, a five-story university building and two subway stations. Collecting the ground truth proved challenging as we do not have access to detailed architecture drawings of the buildings in which we carried out the experiments, the subway stations in particular. Instead we do the following. For every experiment we use two volunteers per mobile device: one carrier and one "shadower". During an experiment, the phone carrier selects arbitrarily an end point and "walks"[8] there at normal pace; along the way the "shadower" marks the floor once a second. Acrux also outputs fixes once a second. After the carrier reaches the end point, we use a meter and a protractor to measure the coordinates of every mark on the floor – the set of all these coordinates constitutes the ground truth. The elementary locomotion signatures Acrux uses throughout the experiments are from a single user, as described in § 6.3.

[8]When not clear from the context, we use the quotation marks to distinguish walking as in someone getting from point A to point B on foot from walking, the elementary locomotion.

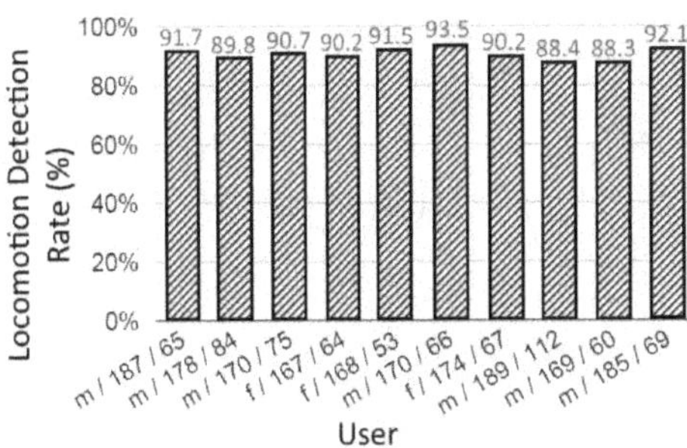

Figure 9: Correct locomotion detection rates for the 10 volunteers participating in the experimental evaluation. Acrux uses a single signature per elementary locomotion throughout the experiment. The x-axis describes each volunteer using the format sex/height(cm)/weight(kg).

6.3 Accuracy Across Different Users

A basic premise of this work is that the elementary locomotions generate unique signatures in the inertial sensor readings that do not depend on someone's height, weight or gender. Hence we start the performance evaluation by testing this premise.

Method: Using the approach described in § 3.1.1 and § 3.1.2, we build elementary signatures for each of the 10 volunteers participating in the experiments. We select at random the signatures from one volunteer, make them Acrux's only signatures for the rest of this experimental study and throw away the rest. Each volunteer is then asked to travel a 200 m distance while holding a Nexus 5 phone freely at hand and switching between the 6 elementary locomotions, as they perceive them, every 10 s. Acrux tries to identify the elementary locomotions using readings from a 1 s fixed time window. We collect the data and compare offline what Acrux identified as elementary locomotion with what the user was actually doing.

Results: Fig. 9 shows the correct elementary locomotion detection rates for the 10 volunteers along with information as to their gender, height and weight. We observe that, using a single signature per elementary locomotion, Acrux is capable of correctly detecting the elementary locomotions of a diverse set of users with an accuracy between 88.3% and 93.5%.

For a look under the covers, Fig. 10 shows a sampling of the vertical acceleration readings collected for 3 of the volunteers during the above experiment (including more readings from all the volunteers would make the plot illegible but similar behavior was observed). We observe remarkably similar signatures, despite the differences in gender, height and sex, which is the underlying reason for the results of Fig. 9.

6.4 Acrux vs. Traditional Dead-Reckoning

In this experiment, we evaluate Acrux's capability to accurately measure distance, the most challenging part in dead-reckoning, and compare it against step-counting, the approach traditionally adopted for pedestrian dead-reckoning.

Comparison: Ideally, we would compare Acrux to full-fledged implementations of state-of-the-art, step-based systems [18, 27].

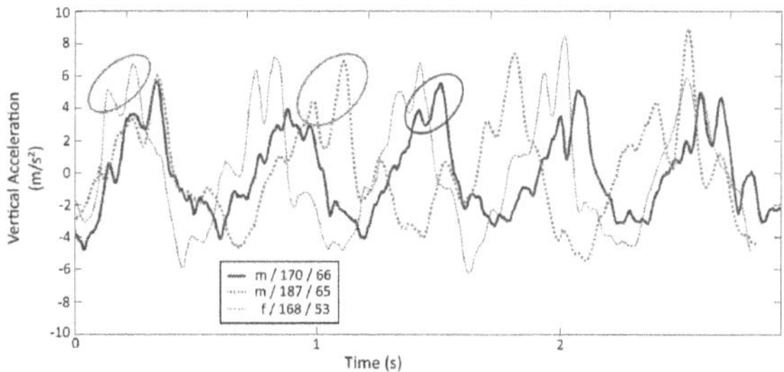

Figure 10: A sample of vertical readings from 3 of the 10 volunteers, taken while Acrux had identified walking as elementary locomotion.

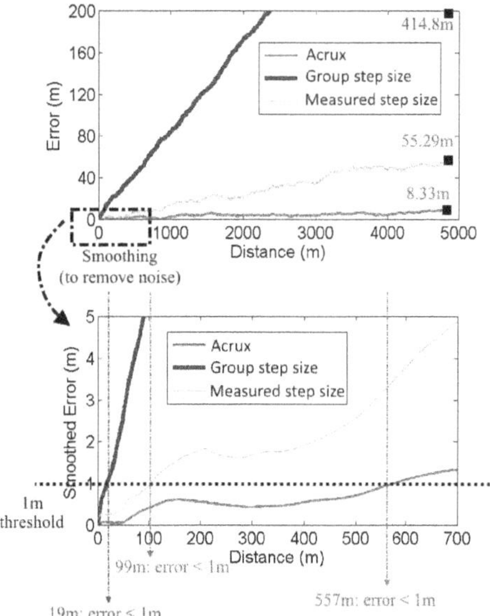

Figure 11: Acrux vs Step Count. The error is relative to the true path. The x-axis shows the distance from the starting point, measured on the true path, when the error is computed.

Unfortunately, none of these systems are available as open-source and we find it infeasible to faithfully implement them based simply on the paper descriptions. However, we can bound their accuracy using an approach we refer to as the Measured step size and compare against this bound.

[18, 27] start with a generic model assuming a linear relationship between step size and step frequency for any user. Then, the slope and constant term of the linear function are estimated on a per user basis. [18] uses a particular filtering based approach requiring the user to physically turn several time in order to converge as well as input from the user. [27] selects and improves the parameters of the linear equation using a feedback loop involving map (e.g. floor plan) matching. The sophistication of these approaches and the help from outside they need highlight the difficulty facing any step-based approach. Most important, a system assuming a linear relation between step size and step frequency and needing to learn

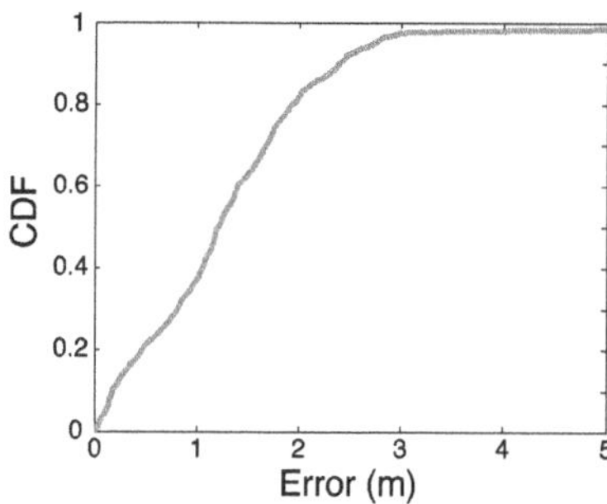

Figure 12: CDF of absolute localization error at the end of the trajectory computed over 460 trajectories (46 distinct start-end points and 10 different users) of lengths between 80 and 120 m.

crucial parameters as the user walks cannot be more accurate than the Measured step size approach.

Method: Ten volunteers are asked to "walk" as they normally would for 25 m and every step they take is measured. The average over all sizes measured for a particular user is selected as her step size. Then a volunteer is selected arbitrarily among the 10 and is asked to "walk" the same way down a boulevard for 5 km while trying to avoid turns and changes in direction – to avoid other components designed for estimating direction from affecting the outcome – using the same shoes and outfit as during the 25 m walk. Using Android's special purpose App, we track the step count at regular intervals and store it along with a timestamp for offline processing. The error for step-counting is computed by comparing the ground truth distance to the product of the step count with either the step size of the volunteer taking the 5 km walk – the **Measured step size** approach – or the average step size over the 10 volunteers – the **Group step size** approach.

Results: Fig. 11 (top graph) shows that after 5 km, Acrux's deviation from the truth is 8.33 m while step counting using the Measured step size approach deviates by 52.29 m – over 6.5 times as much as Acrux. This is due to the fact that no two steps are the same even if everything else – user, outfit, environment – is kept the same. Thus, the Measured step size approach will suffer from errors, which considering the large number of steps one takes, will accumulate fast over distance. Step counting using as step size the average over 10 people gives the unacceptable result of 414.8 m deviation from the true distance.

For a better understanding, we zoom in on the data for which all approaches exhibit an error of just over 1 m. As the bottom graph in Figure 11 shows, Acrux can dead-reckon for 557 m before the deviation from the truth reaches 1 m, while the Measured and Group step size approaches hit the same error after 19 and 99 m, respectively.

6.5 Large Scale Measurements in the Wild

In this experiment, we evaluate Acrux's localization accuracy across a large and diverse set of paths, users and indoor locations.

Method: We select arbitrarily 46 different start-end pairs in 4 locations – 32 at an office building, 12 at a university building

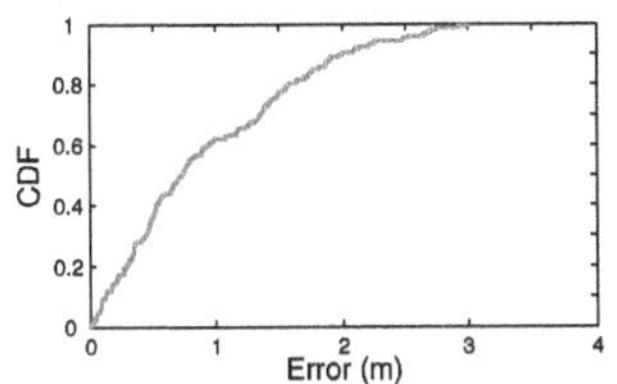

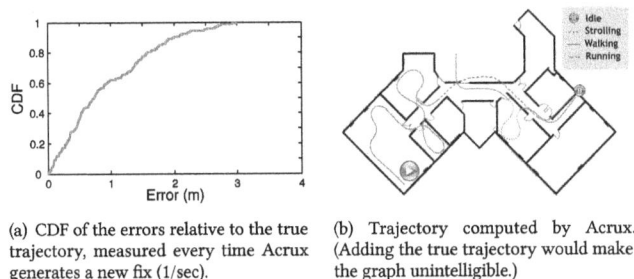

(a) CDF of the errors relative to the true trajectory, measured every time Acrux generates a new fix (1/sec).

(b) Trajectory computed by Acrux. (Adding the true trajectory would make the graph unintelligible.)

Figure 13: Acrux "trying to keep pace" with a user following a complex trajectory inside an office building. The whole trajectory is around 400 m.

and one at each subway station (carrying out experiments at a busy subway station proved challenging). The 10 phone carriers participating in the experiment are each given the same phone[9], a Nexus 5, and are asked to go from the start to the end point "walking" as they would in a normal situation. Similarly, they are told to hold the phones as they normally would – in hand or pocket. Once the experiment concluded we had data from 460 trajectories of lengths between 80 – 120 m.

Results: Fig. 12 shows the cumulative distribution function (CDF) of the error for Acrux across all 460 trajectories. The data shows that Acrux attains a median and 98% percentile error of 1.2 and 3 m, respectively.

6.6 Catch Me If You Can

In this experiment, we evaluate Acrux's ability to map a complex user trajectory inside an office building.

Method: A single user is invited to follow a purposefully complex trajectory (Fig. 13(b)) inside an office building while carrying a smartphone in her pocket. In particular, the user is invited to take many turns, a major source of localization errors, and to switch pace between strolling, walking and even running. At some point she pauses to talk to a colleague. The whole trajectory is about 400 m.

Results: Fig. 13(a) shows that despite the challenging scenario, Acrux is able to successfully map the true trajectory. The median error is only 0.7 m and never exceeds 3 m.

6.7 Going Upstairs

In this experiment, we evaluate Acrux's ability to localize a user as she moves across different floors inside a building.

Method: A user selects one of the 4 devices available and takes the stairs, shown in Fig. 14, to the second floor of the office building. In this particular experiment we did not compute a ground truth and instead relied on visual verification.

Results: Fig. 14 shows the trajectory mapped by Acrux superimposed on the picture of the staircase. Considering the small size of the stair riser, 15 cm, one can visually verify the high accuracy with which Acrux follows a user's every step as she is climbing up the stairs.

[9]This is a deliberate choice so as to aggregate the data without introducing device specific noise.

Figure 14: Acrux follows a user's every step as she is climbing the stairs.

Application	Power (mW)	Battery Life (Nexus 5)	Battery Life (Tablet)
Acrux	452	5.09 h	14.8 h
BaselineRF	480	4.80 h	14.0 h

Table 1: The energy performance of Acrux is compared to that of BaselineRF, an application that does only a passive WiFi scan every time Acrux is called to generate a localization fix.

6.8 Impact on Battery Life

Finally, we evaluate Acrux's performance in terms of energy consumption, a crucial metric for an application running on battery powered devices.

Method: Starting with fully charged batteries, Acrux is left running and generating fixes 1/sec on a tablet and smartphone until the batteries die. Meanwhile, we measure its power consumption using the Android App Power Tutor [1]. To contextualize Acrux's energy performance, we compare it to BaselineRF, a simple application we developed to establish a baseline for the energy consumption of RF-based localization schemes. Every time Acrux generates a localization fix, BaselineRF simply performs a passive (listen only) WiFi scan. An actual RF-based localization scheme needing to generate a localization fix would most probably have to perform more tasks than simply looking for access points, thereby consuming more energy than BaselineRF.

Results: Table 1 shows that Acrux draws less power than BaselineRF. This excellent energy performance is due to the fact that Acrux does not make use of the WiFi card, relying instead on sensors, such as the accelerometer, shown to be energy efficient [15].

7 RELATED WORK

While the literature on indoor localization is rich most works fall into four overlapping categories.

RF-based solutions: A majority of indoor localization solutions rely on the WiFi transceivers on mobile devices and ubiquitous availability of WiFi hot spots [5, 14] to generate accurate fixes indoors. Based on how the distance to the access points is estimated, the proposed solutions can be categorized in two large groups. In one group there are solutions that leverage the IEEE 802.11 MAC protocol, especially the fact that certain transmissions take place after exactly SIFS time, to estimate the propagation delay between the mobile device and an access point [12, 20, 21, 25]. However, these solutions require nanosecond accuracy, and extensive measurements on popular WiFi chipsets [11] have shown very large dispersions in the values of the PHY SIFS, reaching 1 µs for the 802.11b Broadcom Samsung. The second group of solutions uses the propagation characteristics of the WiFi signal to estimate the distance between a mobile device and access points in range. However, a majority of these solutions need require fingerprinting [14], a tedious and time-consuming process. Recently, Ubicarse [17] and SpotFi [16] have relaxed the requirement for fingerprinting and demonstrated decimeter level accuracy. Nevertheless, they still require accurate coordinates from multiple access points, CSI (Channel State Information) from the mobile device to the AP and dedicated servers to perform complex computations required for generating every localization fix for every device in the range of a particular WiFi network.

RF-based solutions with dedicated infrastructure and/or hardware: Using dedicated hardware and/or infrastructure can lead to indoor localization systems with cm-level accuracy [28], however, as with the fingerprinting solutions it creates a high barrier to entry that so far no solution has been able to overcome.

Non RF-based solutions: Given the increasing sophistication of the smartphone hardware, several solutions have proposed taking advantage of the inertial sensors to build dead-reckoning based localization schemes [6, 18]. However, all the dead-reckoning based schemes require periodic recalibration [18, 27].

Crowdsourcing based solutions: Most solutions belonging in the three previous categories could be improved by using crowdsourcing [8, 9, 23]. While these solutions are very promising they are hindered by a chicken-egg problem – early adaptation relies on the system's performance while the system's performance relies on large scale adaptations.

8 CONCLUSION AND FUTURE WORK

We presented Acrux, an indoor localization system that can dead-reckon with meter level accuracy for several hundred meters, a several times improvement over the state-of-the-art, and more important, long enough to cover most distances traveled by pedestrians outside of GPS coverage. This is accomplished thanks to an innovative algorithm for estimating the speed of locomotion inspired by how humans perceive pedestrian locomotion indoors combined with careful measurement based analysis. We have developed Acrux on the Android OS and through experiments in 4 different buildings shown that it can offer meter level indoor localization with the minimum outside input – a single fix.

This work is not the last chapter on Acrux. While this version focused on the 6 basic elementary locomotions, future work will focus on breaking down the elementary locomotions into sub-locomotions based on things such as walking surface, crowd density, time of the day, geography, etc. Coupled with more sophisticated classification algorithms, this has the potential to significantly improve the robustness and reliability of Acrux.

REFERENCES

[1] 2015. Android App Power Tutor. (2015). http://powertutor.org/
[2] 2015. Couchbase Documentation. (2015). http://docs.couchbase.com/
[3] 2015. Escalator. (2015). http://en.wikipedia.org/wiki/Escalator#Operation_and_layout
[4] 2015. PhoneGap 4 Documentation. (2015). http://docs.phonegap.com/
[5] Krishna Chintalapudi, Anand Padmanabha Iyer, and Venkata N. Padmanabhan. 2010. Indoor Localization Without the Pain. In *ACM MobiCom*.
[6] I. Constandache, R.R. Choudhury, and I. Rhee. 2010. Towards Mobile Phone Localization without War-Driving. In *IEEE INFOCOM*.
[7] Mark Denny. 2012. *The Science of Navigation: From Dead Reckoning to GPS*. Johns Hopkins University Press, Baltimore, MD.
[8] Jiang Dong, Yu Xiao, Marius Noreikis, Zhonghong Ou, and Antti Ylä-Jääski. 2015. iMoon: Using Smartphones for Image-based Indoor Navigation. In *ACM SenSys*.
[9] Ruipeng Gao, Mingmin Zhao, Tao Ye, Fan Ye, Yizhou Wang, Kaigui Bian, Tao Wang, and Xiaoming Li. 2014. Jigsaw: Indoor Floor Plan Reconstruction via Mobile Crowdsensing. In *ACM MobiCom*.
[10] Jacques Georgy, Aboelmagd Noureldin, Michael J. Korenberg, and Mohamed M. Bayoumi. 2010. Modeling the Stochastic Drift of a MEMS-based Gyroscope in Gyro/Odometer/GPS Integrated Navigation. *Trans. Intell. Transport. Sys.* 11, 4 (Dec. 2010), 856–872.
[11] Domenico Giustiniano, Theodoros Bourchas, Maciej Bednarek, and Vincent Lenders. 2015. Deep Inspection of the Noise in WiFi Time-of-Flight Echo Techniques. In *ACM MSWiM*.
[12] S.A. Golden and S.S. Bateman. 2007. Sensor Measurements for Wi-Fi Location with Emphasis on Time-of-Arrival Ranging. *Mobile Computing, IEEE Transactions on* 6, 10 (Oct 2007).
[13] Hiroshi Hasegawa, Takeshi Yamauchi, and William J. Kraemer. 2007. Foot strike patterns of runners at the 15-km point during an elite-level half marathon. *Journal of Strength and Conditioning Research* 21, 3 (August 2007).
[14] Suining He, Tianyang Hu, and S.-H. Gary Chan. 2015. Contour-based Trilateration for Indoor Fingerprinting Localization. In *ACM SenSys*.
[15] Samuli Hemminki, Petteri Nurmi, and Sasu Tarkoma. 2013. Accelerometer-based Transportation Mode Detection on Smartphones. In *ACM SenSys*.
[16] Manikanta Kotaru, Kiran Joshi, Dinesh Bharadia, and Sachin Katti. 2015. SpotFi: Decimeter Level Localization Using WiFi. In *ACM SIGCOMM*.
[17] Swarun Kumar, Stephanie Gil, Dina Katabi, and Daniela Rus. 2014. Accurate Indoor Localization with Zero Start-up Cost. In *ACM MobiCom*.
[18] Fan Li, Chunshui Zhao, Guanzhong Ding, Jian Gong, Chenxing Liu, and Feng Zhao. 2012. A Reliable and Accurate Indoor Localization Method Using Phone Inertial Sensors. In *ACM UbiComp*.
[19] Hongbo Liu, Yu Gan, Jie Yang, Simon Sidhom, Yan Wang, Yingying Chen, and Fan Ye. 2012. Push the Limit of WiFi Based Localization for Smartphones. In *ACM MobiCom*.
[20] Alex T. Mariakakis, Souvik Sen, Jeongkeun Lee, and Kyu-Han Kim. 2014. SAIL: Single Access Point-based Indoor Localization. In *ACM MobiSys*.
[21] D.D. McCrady, L. Doyle, H. Forstrom, T. Dempsey, and M. Martorana. 2000. Mobile ranging using low-accuracy clocks. *Microwave Theory and Techniques, IEEE Transactions on* 48, 6 (Jun 2000), 951–958. https://doi.org/10.1109/22.846721
[22] Kartik Muralidharan, Azeem Javed Khan, Archan Misra, Rajesh Krishna Balan, and Sharad Agarwal. 2014. Barometric Phone Sensors: More Hype Than Hope!. In *ACM HotMobile*.
[23] Anshul Rai, Krishna Kant Chintalapudi, Venkata N. Padmanabhan, and Rijurekha Sen. 2012. Zee: Zero-effort Crowdsourcing for Indoor Localization. In *ACM MobiCom*.
[24] Nirupam Roy, He Wang, and Romit Roy Choudhury. 2014. I Am a Smartphone and I Can Tell My User's Walking Direction. In *ACM MobiSys*.
[25] Souvik Sen, Dongho Kim, Stephane Laroche, Kyu-Han Kim, and Jeongkeun Lee. 2015. Bringing CUPID Indoor Positioning System to Practice. In *WWW*.
[26] Souvik Sen, Božidar Radunovic, Romit Roy Choudhury, and Tom Minka. 2012. You Are Facing the Mona Lisa: Spot Localization Using PHY Layer Information. In *ACM MobiSys*.
[27] Z. Xiao, H. Wen, A. Markham, and N. Trigoni. 2015. Robust Indoor Positioning With Lifelong Learning. *IEEE Journal on Selected Areas in Communications* 33, 11 (Nov 2015), 2287–2301.
[28] Jie Xiong and Kyle Jamieson. 2013. ArrayTrack: A Fine-grained Indoor Location System. In *NSDI*.
[29] Haibo Ye, Tao Gu, Xianping Tao, and Jian Lu. 2014. B-Loc: Scalable Floor Localization Using Barometer on Smartphone. In *IEEE MASS*.
[30] Pengfei Zhou, Mo Li, and Guobin Shen. 2014. Use It Free: Instantly Knowing Your Phone Attitude. In *ACM MobiCom*.

Pre-Crowdsourcing: Predicting Wireless Propagation with Phone-Based Channel Quality Measurements

Rita Enami, Yan Shi, Dinesh Rajan, and Joseph Camp
Southern Methodist University
{renami,shiy,rajand,camp}@smu.edu

ABSTRACT

Conducting in-field performance analysis for wireless carrier coverage and capacity evaluation is extremely costly, in terms of equipment, manpower, and time. Hence, there is a growing number of opportunities that exist for crowdsourcing via smart applications, firmware, and cellular standards. These facilities offer carriers feedback about user-perceived wireless channel quality. Crowdsourcing provides the ability to rapidly collect feedback with dense levels of penetration using client smartphones. However, mobile phones often fail to capture the fidelity and high sampling rate of more advanced equipment (e.g., a channel scanner) used when drive testing for analysis of propagation characteristics. In this work, we study the impact of various effects induced by user equipment (UE), when sampling signal quality. These shortcomings include averaging over multiple samples, imprecise quantization, and non-uniform and/or less frequent channel sampling. We specifically, investigate the accuracy of characterizing large-scale fading using crowdsourced data in presence of the aforementioned phone measurement shortcomings. To do so, we conduct extensive in-field experiments across heterogeneous devices and environments to empirically quantify the perceived channel characteristics by phone measurements. Analyzing the quality of the smartphone measurements in LTE indicates that the inferred radio propagation models, is comparable with models obtained by advanced equipment.

KEYWORDS

crowdsourced mobile network measurement; LTE; path loss evaluation; radio propagation model

1 INTRODUCTION

Cellular network providers need to collect and analyze radio signal measurements continuously to improve network performance and optimize network configuration. Available methods to obtain the signal measurements consist of drive testing, network-side-only tools, dedicated testbeds, and crowdsourcing [12]. The former three methods are extremely resource intensive. For example, one common approach for capturing radio signal measurements is to outfit a backpack with six mobile phones running various applications and network protocols alongside an expensive mobile channel scanner (see Fig. 1) for network engineers to gather data on foot. Vehicles are often used for an even greater numbers of and potentially higher-powered and more costly devices and allowing higher levels of mobility in a targeted region. In congested areas with various technologies (*e.g.*, LTE, GSM, UMTS, and TETRA) the problem becomes worse: to get an acceptable quality of service, data collection should be repeated multiple times per roll out of each technology to appropriately configure the network [31]. Further complicating matters, physical changes to the environment such as construction of new buildings or highways can render the obtained data useless.

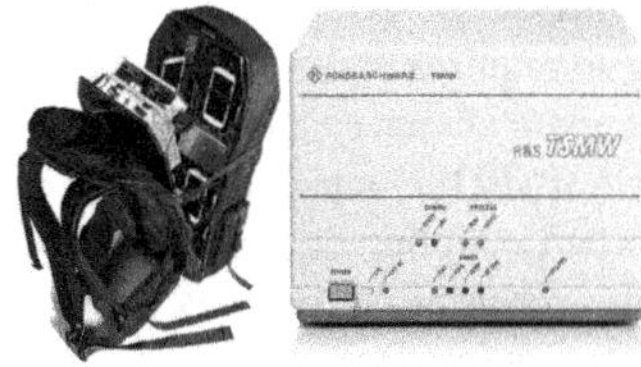

Figure 1: Typical Rohde & Schwarz backpack for walk/drive testing (left) and TSMW channel scanner (right) [8].

Crowdsourcing is an economical alternative to these resource-intensive methods that has the additional benefit of considering the in-situ performance at the end user device. Consequently, many carriers are rolling out smart applications, firmware, and standardization efforts to crowdsource perceived channel state by user equipment (UE). Furthermore, LTE release 10 in 3GPP TS 37.320 has developed a Minimization of Drive Test (MDT) specification to monitor the network Key Performance Indicators (KPIs) via crowdsourcing. While there is less control of the factors leading to a recorded channel quality, there are many advantages to crowdsourcing this information in terms of lessening the need for costly equipment, reduced in-field man hours, rapid scalability of data sets, and penetration into restricted physical locations. These advantages have sparked a number of works where crowdsourcing has been utilized to identify network topology [7], perform real-time network adaptation [28], characterize Internet traffic [27], detect network events [4], fingerprint and georeference physical locations [23], assess the quality of user experience [15], and study network neutrality [10]. To evaluate the wide area wireless network performance [11] and in-context performance [32], the bandwidth, latency, and throughput are previously-crowdsourced KPIs [25, 29].

However, mobile phones possess a number of shortcomings when compared to a channel scanner in reporting channel quality, such as: *(i)* averaging over multiple samples which can flatten channel fluctuations [29] with manufacturer-specific methodologies to estimate the received signal power [5], *(ii)* coarse quantization which can impose a unit step for minuscule changes, *(iii)* sampling

MSWiM '17, November 21–25, 2017, Miami, FL, USA

ACM ISBN 978-1-4503-5162-1/17/11...$15.00
https://doi.org/10.1145/3127540.3127563

at non-uniform intervals when crowdsourcing information as opposed to long, consecutive testing periods recorded when drive testing, and *(iv)* clipping that results from less sensitive receivers with fringe network connectivity.

The accuracy of the received signal reporting by mobile phones as compared to a channel scanner was evaluated in [17], but the effect of averaging was not considered. Hence, while a crowdsourcing framework for characterizing wireless environments would have tremendous impact on drive testing costs, we believe that a first step in doing so requires understanding the viability of mobile phones to replace more advanced measurement equipment.

In this work, we study the impact of various effects induced by user equipment, when sampling signal quality. These shortcomings include averaging over multiple samples, imprecise quantization, and non-uniform and/or less frequent channel sampling. We specifically, investigate the accuracy of characterizing large-scale fading using crowdsourced data in presence of the aforementioned phone measurement shortcomings. To do so, we perform extensive in-field experimentation to quantify the impact of each of these four effects when evaluating the viability of mobile phones to characterize large-scale fading effects. This metric is commonly used by carriers for deployment planning, frequency allocation, and network adaptation. Our results indicate that the inferred propagation parameters by smartphone measurements in GSM and LTE networks is comparable to those obtained by the advanced equipment that are frequently used by drive testers (*e.g.*, channel scanners). In particular, our work consists of the following three contributions.

First, we set forth a framework to evaluate the impact of strictly using mobile phones (as opposed to a channel scanner) in propagation prediction. As depicted in Fig. 2, we consider how the averaging, uniform and non-uniform downsampling over time and space, and quantization of mobile phone channel quality samples at both the firmware and API level affect the path loss characterization. At the API level, we have designed an Android application, called WiEye, which can be used by users globally as an economical spectrum analyzer. Additionally, WiEye functions as a crowdsourcing tool, which has captured over 250 million signal quality measurements from over 60 thousand users (protected by an IRB) and has a global footprint. At the firmware level, we are able to capture signal quality directly from the hardware via a Rohde & Schwarz tool called Qualipoc.

Second, we compare the perceived channel quality across the channel scanner, multiple mobile phone models, and various levels of the software stack. To do so, we perform extensive local experiments across downtown, single-family residential, and multi-family residential regions and directly compare the received channel quality as reported by the channel scanner to mobile phone firmware-level and API-level data, where each mobile phone measurement considered has a corresponding channel scanner measurement for comparison. We are also interested the range over which each user-side device and software is able to receive cellular base station transmissions (*i.e.*, their sensitivities) to understand where clipping of crowdsourced data might occur.

Third, we quantify the impact on inferring propagation characteristics from the various calculations and imperfections that mobile phones can perform on received channel quality before reporting it to the user. To do so, we consider numerous data sets

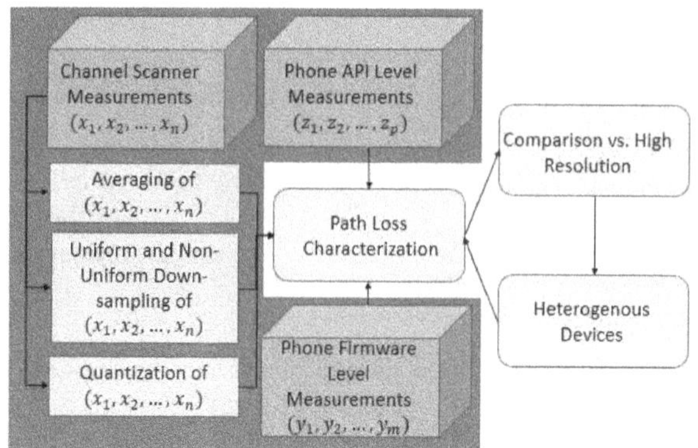

Figure 2: Pre-processing and post-processing of collected data by channel scanner and mobile phones.

from the channel scanner in the aforementioned environmental contexts and impose these imperfections to understand their role by evaluating against the root mean-squared error of path loss prediction from the original channel scanner data set in that region. Our results show that the fading parameters obtained by mobile phone samples are sufficiently comparable to the advanced drive testing equipment, paving the way for crowdsourcing as a viable solution for in-field performance analysis.

The remainder of the paper is organized as follows. In Section 2, we experimentally quantify the channel quality reporting differences of mobile phones versus a channel scanner. In Section 3, we analyze the role of mobile phone imperfections in terms of path loss prediction. We discuss related work in Section 4 and conclude in Section 5.

2 IN-FIELD CALIBRATION OF RECEIVED SIGNAL POWER FROM MOBILE PHONES

The purpose of this study is to compare the ability of mobile phone measurements, captured either at the API level or the firmware level, to an advanced measurement tool, the channel scanner, in characterizing wireless channels in terms of path loss. Before doing so, in this section, we compare and calibrate the raw measurements provided by diverse mobile phones at different levels of the software stack with data provided by a channel scanner.

API-Level Phone Data. At the API level, we modify our Android application WiEye, which we designed to crowdsource measurements, to log signal quality measurements at the highest sampling rate that the operating system will allow (1 Hz). Since WiEye can be installed on any Android-based phone, we can compare API-level measurements across a wide array of devices. In our study, we use four different mobile phones: (*i.*) Samsung S5, (*ii.*) Nexus 5, (*iii.*) Google Pixel, and (*iv.*) Samsung S8. While the former two phones are not the latest models, they provide a comparison across multiple generations, and the Samsung S5 is the phone that allows a firmware-based tool that we will now discuss.

Firmware-Level Phone Data. At the firmware level, we have purchased a software tool called Qualipoc from Rohde & Schwarz, which allows signal strength measurements to be reported directly from the chipset. Qualipoc can receive the channel quality information from many diverse technologies, such as LTE, GSM, and

WCDMA. The sampling rate of the Qualipoc is approximately 3 Hz. Unlike the channel scanner, the mobile phones continuously search for the best visible base station on which to camp by measuring the signal power received from base stations, affecting both the API-level and firmware-level measurements.

Channel Scanner Data. For a piece of equipment that is commonly used by drive testers to gather signal quality measurements in the field, we have acquired a Rohde & Schwarz TSMW Channel Scanner. The TSMW can passively and continuously monitor numerous technologies in 30 MHz - 6 GHz frequency range, with a sampling rate of 500 Hz. The scanner is controlled by Romes software (version 4.89), which is installed on a laptop connected via wire to the TSMW.

In-Field Measurement Setup and Calibration. Since the difference between the aforementioned devices might vary across regions, we conducted the measurement campaign in three diverse regions of Dallas, Texas with regards to their terrain type: single-family residential, multi-family residential, and downtown. All five device types are connected to the same network operator for direct comparison and perform measurements in parallel on a co-located roof of a car. In each region, we observed 11 base stations.

We first would like to understand the range of signal quality sensitivities of each device for measurements taken at the same time and location. To do so, we applied a post-processing procedure on the entire collected data set. Since the sampling rate of the channel scanner is higher than that of Qualipoc (firmware) or WiEye (API), we extract the samples from channel scanner data set, which are the closest in time to that of WiEye and Qualipoc. The matching process consists of two steps: (*i.*) grouping measurements based on the transmitting base station, and (*ii.*) downsampling channel scanner data to have the same number of samples as the Qualipoc and WiEye's data set, where each mobile phone sample has a corresponding channel scanner measurement in time. If the channel scanner did not report a measurement within one second of the mobile phone measurement, we do not consider that data point in our comparison.

Table 1 shows the minimum, maximum, and range of the received signal power for all of these measurements across all cell towers in each region. As it is seen from the results, the widest range (77) and greatest sensitivity (-134 dBm) is captured by the channel scanner with the least range (71) and sensitivity (-128 dBm) captured by WiEye. The reduced range experienced by the mobile phone will cause some clipping on the extreme ends of the connectivity ranges, especially with poor signal quality.

Table 1: Field-tested range of reported signal quality (dBm) from channel scanner (TSMW), Qualipoc, and WiEye.

Device	Min	Max	Range
Channel Scanner	-134	-56	77
Qualipoc Phone	-129	-55	74
WiEye Phone	-128	-57	71

Next, we again consider this downsampled data set which matches the time stamps across devices to consider the difference in reported signal quality per signal quality sample across devices. Table 2 shows the difference of WiEye compared to the matched channel scanner measurement and Qualipoc compared to the matched channel scanner measurement across the three region types. This measurement shows the bias that a mobile phone induces on a crowdsourced data set as compared to more advanced equipment. We also report the mean reported signal strength per region for completeness.

Table 2: Average signal quality bias reported from Qualipoc and WiEye with matched channel scanner measurement.

Device	Qualipoc	WiEye
Location	dBm Diff. (Mean)	dBm Diff. (Mean)
Downtown	-1.5 (-75.6)	-4.4 (-78.5)
Single-Family	-1.3 (-82.5)	-3.8 (-85.0)
Multi-Family	-1.9 (-78.4)	-4.1 (-80.3)

We observe that the difference in reported received signal level is on average 1.57 dBm higher on the channel scanner versus Qualipoc across the three regions with a range of 1.3 to 1.9. In contrast, the difference in reported received signal level is on average 4.43 dBm higher on the channel scanner versus WiEye across the three regions with a range of 4.1 to 4.8. These biases directly affect the path loss characterization as a higher reported channel quality will lower the path loss exponent versus a lower reported channel quality will raise the path loss exponent. In the following section, we will consider the role of this bias as well as multiple other mobile phone imperfections.

3 EVALUATING MOBILE PHONE IMPERFECTIONS ON PATH LOSS PREDICTION

One of the most common metrics which drive testers use to evaluate a given region is path loss. Since we ultimately want to use mobile phone measurements in a crowdsourcing manner to obtain the same metric, we need to understand the role of mobile phone imperfections on evaluating the path loss of a given environment. In particular, reported signal quality from mobile phones will have the following effects: averaging, uniform and non-uniform downsampling, and different resolutions caused by quantization. In this section, we first provide some background with path loss modeling and then will experimentally evaluate the role of these mobile phone imperfections on path loss modeling.

3.1 Modeling Large-Scale Fading: Path Loss

Large-scale fading refers to the average attenuation in a given environment to transmission through and around obstacles in an environment for a given distance [24]. Path loss prediction models are defined in three different categories: empirical, deterministic, and semi-deterministic. Empirical models such as [14] and [22] are based on measurements and use statistical properties. However, the accuracy of these models is not as satisfying as deterministic models to estimate the channel characteristics. These models are widely-used because of their low computational complexity and simplicity. Deterministic models or geometrical models using the Geometrical Theory of Diffraction to predict the path loss. To consider the losses due to diffraction, detailed knowledge of the terrain is needed to calculate the signal strength such as [16] and [30]. These models are accurate, however their computational complexity is high and need detailed information about the region of interest. Semi-deterministic models applied in [6] and [9] are based on empirical models and deterministic aspects. In our study, we use the empirical method since it is the type of modeling that would be most appropriate to leverage crowdsourcing. The large-scale fading is a function of distance (d) between the transmitter and the receiver and the γ as the path loss exponent, where the path loss exponent varies due to the environmental type from 2 in free space to 6 in indoor environments. Some typical values are 2.7-3.5 in typical urban scenarios and 3-5 in heavily shadowed urban environments [24]. In this work, we focus on the inferred path loss exponent from mobile phone measurements, where a linear regression model is used to calculate the path loss exponent.

3.2 In-Field Per Sector Analysis of Inferred Path Loss Exponent Across Devices

As discussed in Section 2, our experimental analysis spans three region types (single-family residential, multi-family residential, and downtown) with multiple mobile phone types at the API-level (WiEye), with mobile phones at the firmware level (Qualipoc), and with a channel scanner (TSMW). All of these devices report which base station sector is transmitting the received signal. Since prior work has shown per sector performance can differ [11], we first consider the path loss exponent from each sector in a single-family residential region from the channel scanner to show an example of the diversity a single base station can have across sectors.

Fig. 3a depicts the spatial distribution of signal strength measurements from a channel scanner for a base station in the single-family residential region. The measurement locations across the three sectors are represented by red dots. We perform linear regression on each sector's signal strength measurements independently to find the path loss exponent for that sector. In Fig 3b, we see that the path loss exponent of sector (a) to sector (c) ranges from 3.1 to 3.4, even from the same base station.

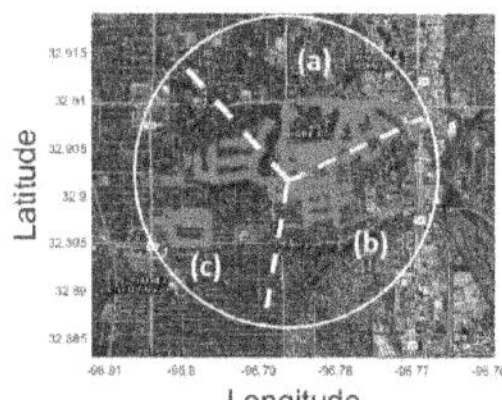

(a) Collected measurement from a base station in the single family region.

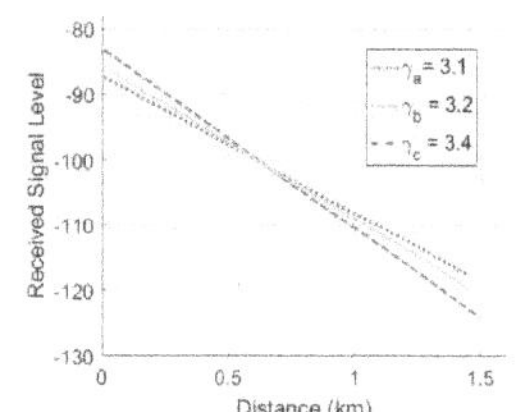

(b) The regression line fit to the measurements of each sector.

Figure 3: Collected measurements from three sectors around a base station (left) related path loss exponents of each (right).

We now focus on a single mobile phone (Samsung Galaxy S5) to directly compare the path loss exponent inferred from the received signal quality reported at the API and firmware levels to that reported by the channel scanner in the same environment. We consider the most densely measured sector from each region type in our comparison and calculate three different path loss exponents. First, we consider the path loss exponent γ_X as calculated from all measurements in the chosen sector for device X, where X is T for TSMW, Q for Qualipoc, or W for WiEye. Second, we downsample the TSMW measurements according to the matching process mentioned in Section 2, where the TSMW measurement with the closest time stamp to the mobile phone measurement is chosen for Qualipoc and then for WiEye. This second calculated path loss exponent is represented by $\gamma_{Q'}$ and $\gamma_{W'}$, respectively and allows the path loss exponent to be considered for the same number of measurements as Qualipoc and WiEye but with the signal strength readings from the TSMW. Third, we consider a similar path loss exponent as $\gamma_{X'}$ but considers the average bias that each tool would induce on each of the TSMW's signal strength measurements from Table 1 and denoted as $\gamma_{Q''}$ and $\gamma_{W''}$, respectively. The third calculated path loss exponent would subtract this average bias to each of the channel scanner's measurements before calculating the path loss exponent.

These three γ values are shown in Table 3. There are a few interesting effects that we observe in the comparison across these path loss exponents. First, by comparing γ_T with $\gamma_{Q'}$ and $\gamma_{W'}$, even when the same device is used (TSMW) to capture the signal strength measurements, downsampling the number to match the mobile phones raises the estimate of the path loss exponent in every environment. This effect could be explained by the inclusion of lower quality measurements (*i.e.*, considering the measurements that were clipped from the mobile phone measurements), which in turn lowers the path loss exponent. Second, by comparing each mobile phone measurement type (Q and W) across $\gamma_{X'}$ and $\gamma_{X''}$, we observe that the consideration of the bias brings the estimate even closer to that of the TSMW (γ_T). For the firmware level measurements, the average difference between γ_Q and γ_T in actual, matched, and compensated calculations are 0.1, 0.08, and 0.03, respectively. For the API level measurements, the average difference between the γ_W and γ_T in actual, matched and compensated calculations are 0.15, 0.05, and 0.03, respectively. Hence, the API level measurements have the largest error in path loss calculation from its raw measurements and require the most compensation.

To depict the difference in received signal power between the channel scanner, firmware, and API level, we depict the distribution of the Received Signal Received Power (RSRP) values obtained by each tool for a specific base station sector in Fig. 4a. To evaluate the distance between each curve, we can use the KolmogorovâĂŞSmirnov test (KS test). The ks distance between channel scanner curve and Qualipoc and WiEye curves are 0.11 and 0.13, respectively. Also, the difference between the CDF's median of the channel scanner (-77 dBm), Qualipoc (-78.8 dBm), and WiEye (-79.5 dBm) are about 1.8 dB and 2.5 dB, respectively. This is along the line of bias discussed in Table 1, especially for the firmware measurements but shows that the API level samples are subject to other effects such as averaging of samples, which will be explored in greater depth in the following section.

Table 3 also brings up an important issue with crowdsourcing regarding how many measurement samples are required to form an accurate estimate of the path loss exponent. Assume that X_i is the channel scanner signal measurements corresponded to a

Table 3: Path loss characteristics obtained by three devices in three modes: actual, matched, compensated mode.

Region	TSMW		Qualipoc					WiEye				
	Samples	γ_T	ΔQ&T (dB)	Samples	γ_Q	γ_Q'	γ_Q"	ΔW&T (dB)	Samples	γ_W	γ_W'	γ_W"
Single-Family	2063	3.1	1.4	620	3.23	3.17	3.15	3.8	293	3.31	3.19	3.15
Multi-Family	1961	3.41	0.9	970	3.48	3.42	3.44	3.1	350	3.51	3.38	3.42
Downtown	11634	3.85	1.2	512	3.97	3.87	3.85	3.5	225	4.00	3.89	3.88

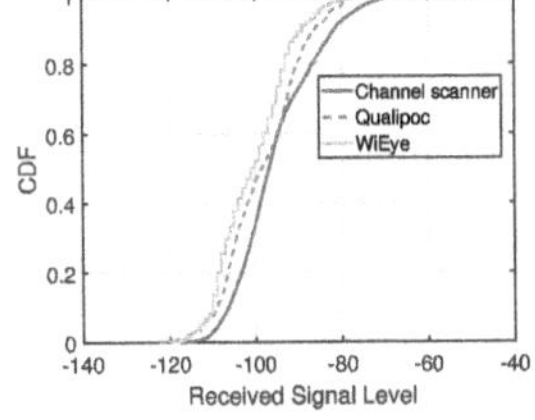

(a) CDF of RSRP of channel scanner versus Qualipoc and WiEye.

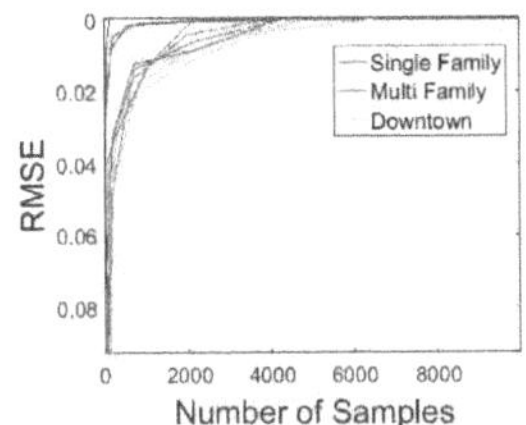

(b) The impact of decreasing the number of samples on the ks-distance

Figure 4: Verifying the number of measurements in each region to estimate the γ accurately.

sector, where i shows the number of samples. Then, if we select different number of samples from our reference data set, then we can calculate the ks-distance between the new dataset, Y_m, and the reference distribution, where m represents the number of samples of the new data set.

The difference between the path loss exponent obtained by the reference data set and downsampled data set in terms of ks-distance is depicted in Fig. 4b. The starting point for m is 50 and increases by 50 to 3000 total number of samples for six densely-measured sectors across the three regions. Here, the error is depicted as the Root Mean-Squared Error (RMSE). We observe that the distance between the downsampled data set and the reference data set increases when the number of measurements drops below approximately 800 to 1000 samples. Also, the maximum RMSE between the path loss exponent is about 0.03 when the number of samples is less than 1000. Furthermore, the figure shows that decreasing the number of measurements in a single-family area has a lower impact on the ks-distance as compared to multi-family or downtown area. This effect can be credited to the relative homogeneity of the geographical features in the single-family area as opposed to the more heterogeneous multi-family or downtown regions. In the following section, we will explore the issue of downsampling uniformly and non-uniformly over time and space to understand another imperfection that is introduced with crowdsourcing signal strengths from mobile phones.

3.3 Impact of Mobile Phone and Crowdsourcing Limitations on Path Loss Estimation

In this section the impact of different shortcomings with mobile phone measurements (averaging, temporal downsampling, and quantization) and imperfections that arise with crowdsourcing wireless signal strengths (non-uniform downsampling in both time and space) as opposed to drive testing in a known physical pattern with a known periodic sampling frequency in a particular region under test. In this subsection (3.3) and Section 3.4, we use signal strength samples from the channel scanner exclusively in our analysis and emulate each mobile phone imperfection in isolation to evaluate the impact of that effect.

3.3.1 Averaging of the Received Signal Power. Network interfaces often use some form of hysteresis to suppress sudden fluctuations in channel state that might lead to overcompensation in adaptive protocols. Many times this hysteresis is performed by averaging multiple received signal qualities before reporting it to the higher layers (*e.g.*, within the firmware) and/or the user (*e.g.*, within the operating system in support of API calls). Each device uses its own policy (often proprietary) to take a specific number of samples over a certain period of time.

Even if two devices are in the same environment in close proximity and experience virtually the same channel quality fluctuations, differences in averaging window sizes could be interpreted as diverse fading behaviors. More importantly, when crowdsourcing signal strengths, we are forced to accept the averaging behavior of a broad range of devices. Hence, we seek to characterize the impact of differing averaging windows on the interpretation of large-scale fading. For the purposes of our work, we will be comparing multiple devices (the aforementioned heterogeneous mobile phones against a channel scanner).

A mobile phone in an LTE network is required to measure the Reference Signal Received Power (RSRP) and Reference Signal Received Quality (RSRQ) level of a serving cell at least every Discontinuous Reception (DRX) cycle to see if the cell selection criteria is satisfied [3]. To do so, a filter is applied on the RSRP and RSRQ of the serving cell to continuously keep tracking of the quality of the received signal. Within the set of measurements used for the filtering, two measurements shall be spaced by no longer than DRX cycle/2 [2]. On the other hand, a mobile phone receives multiple resource elements and measures the average power of resource elements. However, the number of resource elements in the considered measurement frequency and period over which measurements are taken to determine RSRP by the mobile phone depends on the manufacturer.

Hence, we seek to empirically quantify the degree to which a range of averaging windows (*i.e.*, the number of samples used in the average reported) affects the calculation of the path loss exponent parameter. We depict the variation of the γ parameter in Fig. 5 when we vary the averaging window from 0.25 to 6s on the collected measurements by the channel scanner, which corresponds to a window size of 0 to 200 samples. We averaged the RMSE corresponded to each window size over multiple base stations in each region. As we see, by increasing the filter size, the maximum error in three regions is about 0.1.

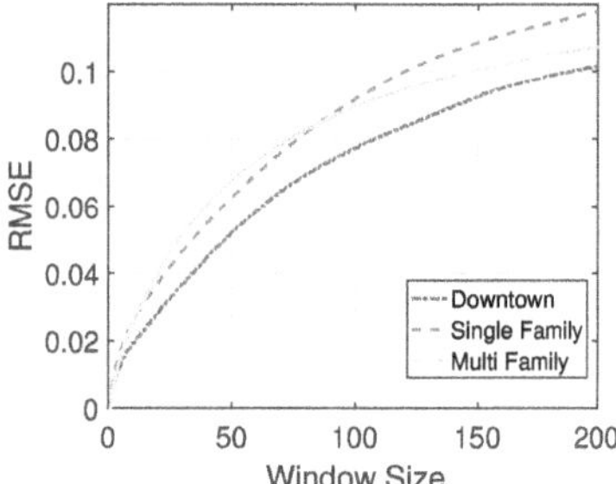

Figure 5: The impact of averaging on the path loss exponent (γ).

3.3.2 Non-Continuous Measurement Periods. When crowdsourcing information, users may be willing to participate in offering their data. However, there are data usage and battery consumption issues that preclude prolonged, continuous measurements of detailed signal strength values. One option may be to uniformly reduce the number of samples per unit time for a given user over an extended period. Another option could be to aggregate small numbers of samples at different time periods and space from one or more users to compose an aggregate channel effect. We now study both the former (uniform downsampling) and latter (non-uniform downsampling).

Uniform Downsampling Impact on The Channel Characteristic. The channel scanner samples the channel quality at approximately 500 times per second as opposed to about 3 and 1 Hz with the Qualipoc and WiEye, respectively. In this scenario, as the mobile phone preserves energy and/or data usage the question becomes: how would the γ parameters further diverge from the results shown in Table 3? In other words, the previous result showed the extreme of matching the same number of samples or having a very different number of samples, but not the trend in between.

To study this issue, we first examine the calculated γ parameter from a particular sector of a base station in each region, when using uniform and non-uniform down-sampling. We gradually reduce the number of samples obtained by channel scanner to eventually reach the same number of samples recorded by WiEye. At each step, we calculate the error in path loss exponent calculation with respect to our reference value, which is obtained by considering the highest resolution in channel scanner data set. To do so, we reduce the number of samples by i, where $i \in 1,..,n$ and $n = \frac{\#Channel\,scanner's\,records}{\#Phone\,records'}$. As we reduce the data set by i samples, we are able to leverage i data sets for a given i to increase the confidence in the result and show the variation of error in the figure.

Fig. 6a shows the error in terms of path loss calculation by reducing the signal samples received from a cell sector of a base station in the downtown area. By increasing the time interval between samples, the γ and resulting variation thereof are affected. We observe that the error caused by uniformly downsampling can reach up to 0.03 in this specific cell. We see that it is not getting very far from the reference γ. Although the RMSE over each 10 steps has some variation, it does not increase the error dramatically. Furthermore, by decreasing the number of samples, the variation of channel characteristic estimation is not as stable as when we have more data points.

Fig. 6b shows the impact of uniformly downsampling on the channel characteristics on each of the three different regions (single-family residential, multi-family residential, and downtown). The maximum variation over all three regions is depicted as the variation of the RMSE at each point. Of particular note in this result is that downtown shows more sensitivity to downsampling and the single-family residential region shows the least sensitivity.

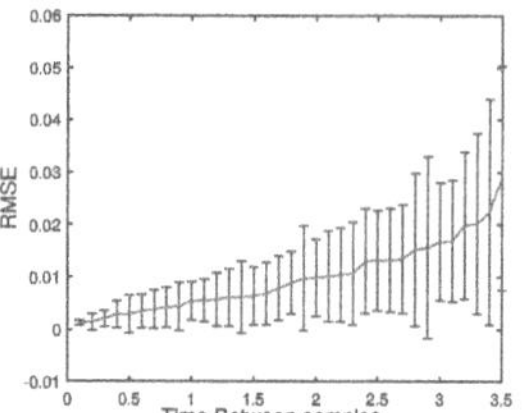

(a) Uniformly Downsampling (Downtown).

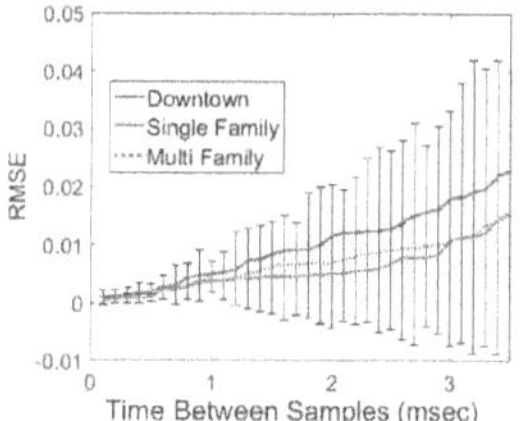

(b) Uniform Downsampling from a Sector in Three Regions.

Figure 6: Uniformly downsampling the measurements of a sector in downtown (left) and across all three regions (right).

Non-Uniformly Downsampled Data Sets. In a second scenario, perhaps the crowdsourced measurements are not coming from a single user which has uniformly throttled the number of measurements recorded or reported but from multiple users in the same area. Controlling for device differences for now (we will study this issue in Section 3.5), the newly composed data set for mobile phone measurements Y has a non-uniform sampling period in time and space compared to drive testing the region with a channel scanner. As before, how far would the estimate of γ_Y be to that of the estimated γ when mobile phone signal strength readings are dispersed through time and space? Assume that a sufficiently large number of users in a similar area have crowdsourced measurements. Assuming the number of measurements from the non-uniformly sampled data set matches that of the uniformly sampled data set, what would be the effect of the difference downsampling types?

The non-uniform distributed measurements are studied with two types of distributions: *(a)* temporal and *(b)* spatial. For non-uniform temporal downsampling, we reduce the number of samples randomly based on the time stamp of the received signal measurements from the channel scanner dataset. Fig. 7a depicts the impact of the non-uniform downsampling data respect to time on the path loss exponent from a cell sector in downtown. It shows that by increasing the number of samples, the error respect to the reference value decreases. However, in general it has caused a higher value in terms of RMSE for the same number of measurements as compared to uniform downsampling.

For non-uniform spatial downsampling, we select the most populated sector in each region. Then, we chose the measurements based on three clusters which are randomly distributed over the region. Then, we increased the number of the selected measurements in each cluster. Finally, we compared the path loss exponent of the aggregated samples from non-uniformly distributed clusters with the γ computed from all measurements from the channel scanner in the same region. A comparison between the uniform downsampling and non-uniform distributed measurements in space for three regions is depicted in Fig. 7b. The clustered scenario shows a higher error than the uniformly-distributed one. In addition, we observe that the corresponded error to the downtown is higher than two other regions. We have found that the location of the selected

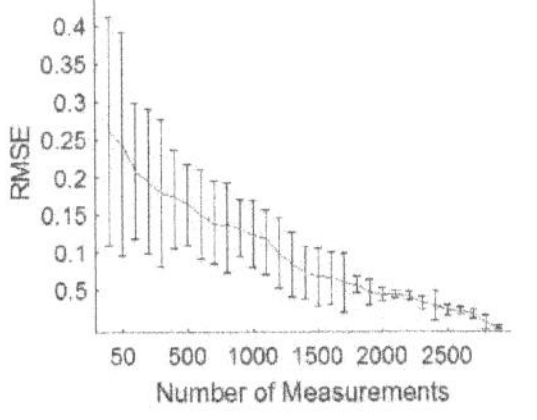

(a) Non-Uniformly downsampling selection in time.

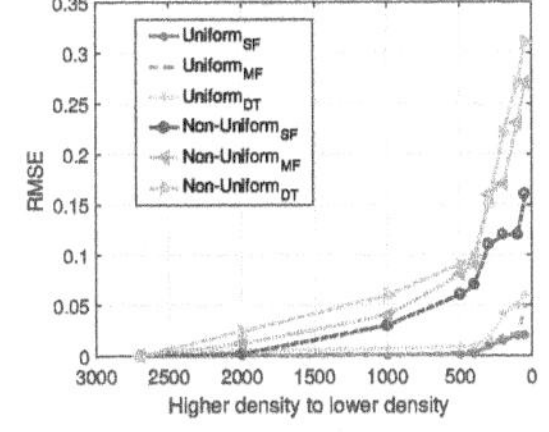

(b) Non-Uniform (space) vs. Uniform (space).

Figure 7: Non-uniform downsampling of a sector in downtown (left) and non-uniformly downsampling in space compared to uniformly (right).

clusters in the non-uniform scenario is significant and attempts to depict the results here. To do so, we again select the most populated sector in a region. Then, we determine the location of three clusters of measurements based on Fig. 8. We start by choosing 50 measurements in each cluster and we increase it by 50 until we have 3000 measurements. The left figure shows a model which is more dispersed through a sector. The middle scenario covers the left and top left area of the sector. In the right scenario, all measurements have a grouping on the left of the sector. We measured the average of the RMSE for each scenario. The results show the 0.083, 0.15, and 0.3 as the average of the RMSE for each aforementioned scenario. In other words, a spatially well-distributed group of user measurements would contribute to a better result to predict the path loss exponent. Also, the type of cluster distribution has impact on the number of measurements that are needed to estimate the channel condition. With this result and the current developments in the LTE standard (10) about the Minimization of Drive Test function [1], a carrier could more strategically poll users in a given area and/or at a certain time to reduce the resources necessary for their users to crowdsource and increase the likelihood of success of such an effort.

3.3.3 Quantization of the Received Signal Power. Android reports the quality of the common pilot channel received signal quality for LTE in terms of Arbitrary Strength Units (ASU) with 98 quantized levels. The received signal level has a range of -44 dBm to -140 dBm and is mapped to "0 to 97" with the resolution of 1 dBm. Since the obtained signal strength by a channel scanner has much greater granularity, the question becomes: what role does quantization have on the path loss exponent? We have considered the quantization impact on path loss estimation as defined as the difference between the estimated γ compared to the highest resolution setting as measured by the channel scanner and found it to be negligible (*e.g.*, less than 1 percent of the RMSE). We will show this effect in Fig. 9a of the following subsection, which considers the joint effect of all of these imperfections.

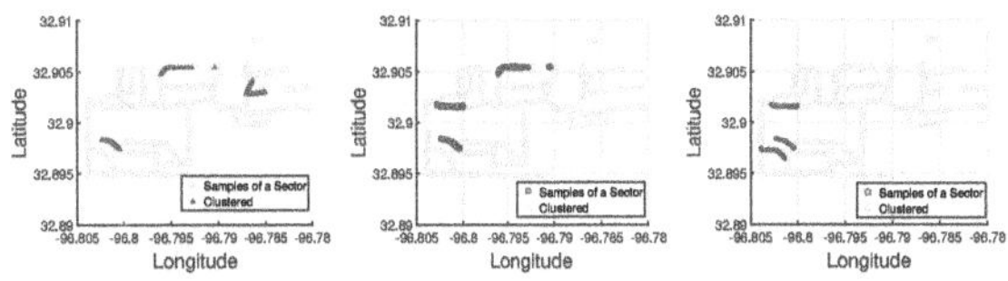

(a) RMSE = 0.083 (b) RMSE = 0.15 (c) RMSE = 0.39

Figure 8: Impact of the non-uniformly downsampling in space.

3.4 Joint Analysis of Mobile Phone Factors on Path Loss

Up to this point, we applied each of the challenges with phone measurements individually. We now jointly consider the mobile phone imperfections impact (averaging, uniform and non-uniform downsampling in space and time, and quantization) on the γ estimation. To do so, we extract the collected data by the channel scanner obtained from a specific cell sector from three regions. Then, we apply the averaging on signal samples which are quantized already. Then, we downsampled (uniformly and non-uniformly in time and space) from the averaged and quantized values. At each step, we obtain the RSME from the path loss exponent calculated from the channel scanner's samples with the highest resolution. Fig. 9a depicts the relative error, caused by each shortcoming in compare with the other issues. Fig. 9b shows the percentage of RMSE caused by each individual issue respect to the reference γ. There are two inter-

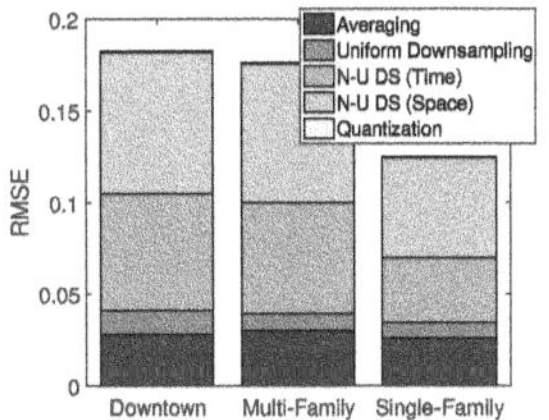

(a) Relative impact of mobile phone factors on RMSE of γ.

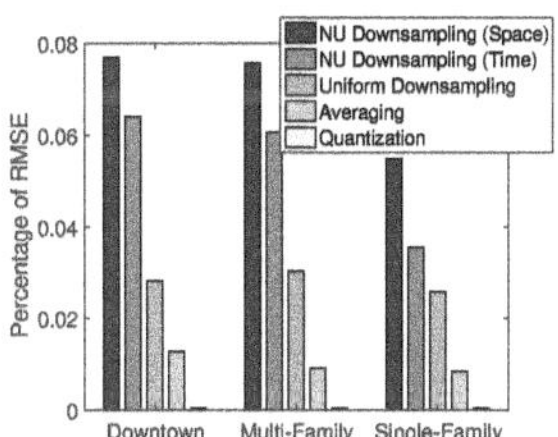

(b) Impact of each factor on percentage of RMSE of γ.

Figure 9: Joint impact of mobile phone imperfections relatively (left) and per effect (right).

esting findings from these result: *(i)* either form of non-uniformly downsampling is clearly the most dominant effect in predicting the path loss exponent, and *(ii)* the two non-uniform downsampling techniques (time and space) have approximately equivalent performance (despite the noisiness of non-uniform downsampling noted earlier). The latter finding offers great hope for crowdsourced data sets to be influential in characterizing the path loss characteristics of an environment.

3.5 Impact of Heterogeneous Mobile Phones and Users on Path Loss Characterization

When crowdsourcing signal quality from mobile phone users, there is a diversity in hardware and software of the devices. Even two co-located mobile phones at the same time may report very different signal qualities due to different RF front ends. In this section, we study the impact of heterogeneous devices on the estimated path loss exponent. Up to this point, we have considered a single type of mobile phone, Samsung Galaxy 5S, due to its ability to support both Qualipoc and WiEye. Here, we use WiEye across three other mobile phones (4 total) with a two-phase approach. First, we consider the signal strength samples from all the devices to calculate the path loss exponent and evaluate the accuracy compared to the path loss exponent from the channel scanner signal quality samples. Second, we account for the per-region-type bias introduced by each mobile phone in terms of dBm as compared to the raw measurements of the channel scanner. Lastly, we calculate the path loss exponent based on strictly crowdsourced data from WiEye users in different regions around the world and examine the geographical features of these areas.

3.5.1 Calibrating Diverse Phone Models and Setup. In this experiment, four Android phones described in Table 4 are used to collect signal strength data from the three aforementioned areas in Dallas (single-family residential, multi-family residential, and downtown). We installed our development version of WiEye, which logs signal strength samples at 1 Hz, on the following four phones: Samsung GS5, Nexus 5X, Samsung S8, and Google Pixel. Each phone was co-located alongside the channel scanner on the roof of a car. The duration of the experiment was 360 minutes.

Table 4: Measurement tools configuration and field-tested range of reported signal quality (dBm) from channel scanner (TSMW) and WiEye of four phones.

Tool	Model/OS	Chipset	Min	Max	Range
Channel Scanner	TSMW/-	-	-130	-52	78
W_1	Samsung GS5/A5	MSM8974AC	-118	-54	64
W_2	Nexus 5X/A5	MSM8974	-119	-58	61
W_3	Google Pixel/A7	MSM8996	-120	-57	63
W_4	Samsung GS8/A7	MSM8996	-121	-54	67

We first analyze the RSRP differences of the four phones in terms of the minimum, maximum, and resulting range of dBm reported across all measurements to understand the relative sensitivities. While a few hours of driving does not guarantee the full range of signal strengths, during this time, we observe that the greatest range of values is achieved by the Samsung S8 (67 dBm) as reported by WiEye and the least range of values belonged to the Nexus 5X (61 dBm). As a point of comparison, the TSMW Channel Scanner achieved a range of 78 dBm for the temporally-matched samples.

3.5.2 Inferring Path Loss Across Devices. We now will use each phone to predict γ for four observed base stations in aforementioned regions. The dBm offset bias between the average received signal level by each phone and the channel scanner is shown in Table.5 per region.

We observe that on average the difference in reported received signal level by the scanner is 3 dBm higher versus the phones across the three regions with a range of 1.46 to 4.1 dBm. As we depicted before, the biasses directly affect the path loss characterization. The lower reported channel quality corresponds to a higher value in obtained path loss exponent, while a higher reported channel quality corresponds to a lower path loss exponent. We now consider the calculated path loss exponent from the signal strength samples of each of the four phones, the calculated path loss exponent from the aggregated data set of the reported signal strength samples from all phones, and then the calculated path loss exponent from the compensated signal strength samples of all phones, considering the bias.

Table 6 shows the obtained path loss characteristics of one specific sector in three different regions, when we consider only a single phones' RSRP and all phones' RSRP. As a point of reference, we also include the γ from the channel scanner RSRP data. We observe that the obtained γ using the data set of each phone are relatively close to one another. We see that the Samsung S8 phone has the closest γ value between all four phones to the channel scanner. In other words, the device that receives the larger range is more accurate in terms of the γ estimation. The comparison shows that considering all RSRP data across device types actually increases the accuracy as compared to any given phone against the path loss exponent calculated from the channel scanner RSRP. Hence, we find that γ is predicted by using the RSRP from a *diverse* set of mobile phones. In addition, we compensated the signal strength of the aggregated dataset by using the 3 dBm obtained in the previous section. We find that the compensated results in terms of γ are extremely close (with 2.7 %, 0.3 %, and 0.6 % error for single-family residential, multi-family residential, and downtown, respectively) to the obtained results by the channel scanner.

3.5.3 Inferring the Path Loss from Crowdsourcing. We now use crowdsourced measurements taken from our widely-distributed WiEye application on the Google Play store. We estimate the path loss exponent of regions around the world without physically drive testing those areas. Based on some of our highest user density, we have selected four environments with diverse geographical features: (i) tall buildings and trees in Dresden, Germany, (ii) low buildings and no trees in Artesia, New Mexico, (iii) mostly trees with a few homes in Macon, Georgia, and (iv) mostly free space in Thiersheim, Germany. The aerial view of each of these environments can be seen in the top figures of Fig 10. In Fig. 10, the bottom figures show the number of crowdsourced signal strength samples and their spatial location as captured by our Android application overlayed on a more basic map of the same area displayed in the aerial view on the top. Using these signal quality measurements from each region, we have computed the path loss exponent γ, which can be seen in the caption of each subfigure. We have ordered the figures from left to right where we see the path loss exponent is decreasing from left to right. In particular, γ_a equals 3.3 with the most diverse and complex environment with tall buildings and trees, γ_b equals 2.7 with an environment that has similar, small building types but no trees, γ_c equals 2.5 with mostly trees and a few homes, and γ_d equals 2.1 with mostly free space. Therefore, the geographical features and complexity in the environment match the γ behavior we would expect, and the channel factors were derived strictly using crowdsourced measurements. Of particular note that in these measurements alone we saw a fairly dramatic change in the γ. In fact, we observed a range of 2.1 to 4.0 of the path loss exponent throughout this paper, which would constitute extremely different network designs across this range of propagation scenarios.

Table 5: Average signal quality bias reported from heterogeneous phones as reported by WiEye with matched channel scanner measurement.

Device	W_1 (GS5)	W_2 (N5X)	W_3 (Pixel)	W_4 (GS8)
Location	dBm Diff. (Mean)	dBm Diff. (Mean)	dBm Diff. (Mean)	dBm Diff. (Mean)
Downtown	4.4 (-78.5)	2.1(-76.2)	3.2 (-77.3)	1.6 (-75.7)
Single Family	3.8 (-85.0)	2.4 (-83.6)	2.5(-83.7)	1.7 (-82.9)
Multi Family	4.1 (-80.3)	2.7 (-79.1)	3.5 (-80)	1.1 (-77.6)

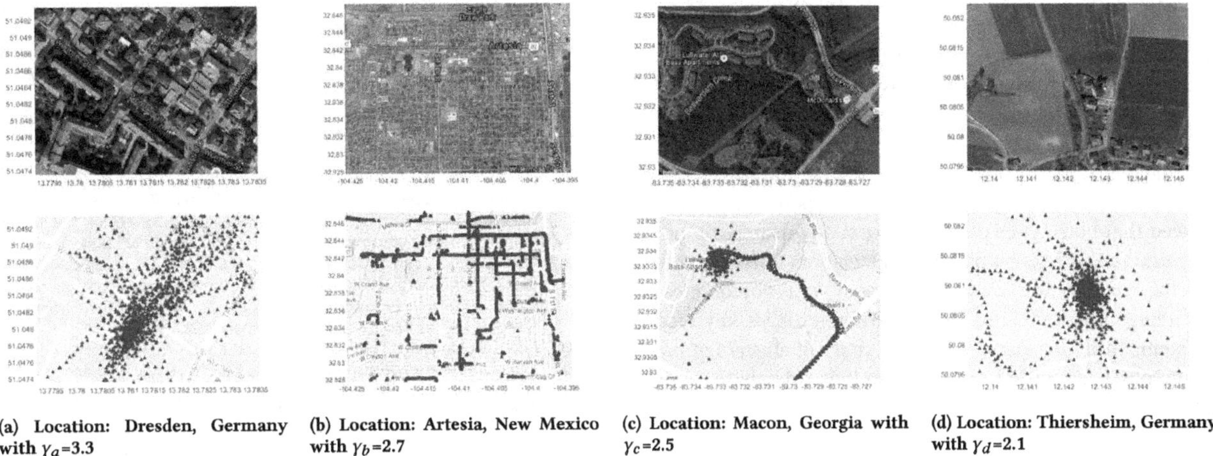

(a) Location: Dresden, Germany with γ_a=3.3 (b) Location: Artesia, New Mexico with γ_b=2.7 (c) Location: Macon, Georgia with γ_c=2.5 (d) Location: Thiersheim, Germany with γ_d=2.1

Figure 10: Path Loss Analysis for Crowdsourced Data Sets in Four Different Regions.

Table 6: Path loss characteristics obtained by four devices in three modes: matched, aggregated, compensated mode.

Device	Single Family	Multi-Family	Down-town
Channel Scanner	3.01	3.33	3.61
W_1 (GS5)	3.21	3.50	3.80
W_2 (N5X)	3.18	3.54	3.78
W_3 (Pixel)	3.38	3.58	3.90
W_4 (GS8)	3.19	3.47	3.75
Aggregated	3.27	3.53	3.83
Compensated	3.09	3.34	3.63

4 RELATED WORK

The Minimization of Drive Tests (MDT) initiative in the 3GPP standard has been created to exploit the ability of smartphones to collect radio measurements in a wide range of geographical areas to enhance the coverage, mobility, capacity optimization, and path loss prediction [1]. Also, a few measurements studies have been conducted to use API-level measurements to estimate different Key Performance Indicators (KPIs) of the cellular networks [13, 21, 25, 29]. They each measured KPIs in terms of throughput, received signal power, and delay and involved regular users to provide the measurements (*i.e.* crowdsourcing) across a large geographical region in some cases. In contrast, we focus on characterizing the wireless channel using diverse end user devices at different levels of the software stack. Predicting the cellular network coverage by using the crowdsourced data has been studied in a few studies. For example, network coverage maps using crowdsourced data is studied in [18]. However, the authors provided the observed received signal level without a discussion of the differences across end user devices. In addition, anther work used a similar idea of using crowdsourced data along with interpolation techniques to predict the coverage area [19]. Although, the impact of location inaccuracy and data distribution of the interpolation techniques was investigated, the impact of the imperfections of end user devices was not explored. Furthermore, others proposed the Bayesian Prediction method to improve the coverage estimation obtained by drive test and MDT measurements, but the results were strictly based on advanced devices as opposed to mobile phone measurements [26]. The provided X-map's accuracy, from simulated data in [20] has been evaluated in terms of the position inaccuracy, UE inaccuracy, and number of measurements. However, to analyze crowdsourced data, using in-field experimentation is important to distinguish between the performance of more advanced equipment versus a mobile phone in channels similar to those experienced by user devices.

To estimate the channel quality, we are using RSRP as our metric from the LTE standard. It was previously observed by [5] that the reported value by a mobile phone in terms of RSRP is influenced by averaging but did not consider the compounding effects. Similarly, [17] depicts that the received signal power by commercial phones is comparable to an advanced tool. While this is close in nature, we also consider many of the spatial and temporal downsampling effects that would cause imprecise estimation of the path loss estimation for a given environment.

5 CONCLUSION

In this work, we take a first step towards crowdsourcing wireless channel characteristics in LTE cellular networks (and beyond) by considering the relationship between received signal strength measurements of diverse mobile phones at the firmware and API level versus advanced drive testing equipment. In particular, we performed extensive experimentation across four mobile phone types, two pieces of software, and a channel scanner in three representative geographical regions: single-family residential, multi-family residential, and downtown. With these devices and in-field measurements, we evaluated the effects of averaging over multiple samples, uniform and non-uniform downsampling (in time and space), quantization, and crowdsourcing on the path loss exponent estimation. We showed that both types of non-uniform downsampling have the most dramatic effects on path loss calculation. Conversely, we showed the quantization impact can largely be ignored since it showed a negligible influence on our estimation. One key result of note stems from the spatial non-uniformity of clusters of measurements observed within our crowdsourcing database, which required far more measurements than more uniformly spaced measurements. Using the MDT specification of LTE release 10 carriers could request specific measurement locations and times from users to be far more efficient in polling signal quality. Finally, we showed four regions around the globe and predicted the channel characteristics of these regions from our crowdsourced data. In summary, we lay a strong foundation for understanding a large majority of the issues involved with crowdsourcing channel characteristics.

ACKNOWLEDGMENTS

This work was in part supported by NSF grants: CNS- 1150215, CNS-1320442, and CNS-1526269. Also, we would like to thank Rhode & Schwarz for their extensive support in this measurement campaign.

REFERENCES

[1] 3GPP. 2011. *ETSI TS 137 320 "Radio measurement collection for Minimization of Drive Tests (MDT)".*

[2] 3GPP. January 2011. *ETSI TS 136 133 "Evolved Universal Terrestrial Radio Access (E-UTRA); Requirements for support of radio resource management ".*

[3] 3GPP. November 2011. *ETSI TS 136 304 "Evolved Universal Terrestrial Radio Access (E-UTRA); User Equipment (UE) procedures in idle mode".*

[4] Zachary S Bischof, John S Otto, Mario A Sánchez, John P Rula, David R Choffnes, and Fabián E Bustamante. 2011. Crowdsourcing ISP characterization to the network edge. In *Proc. of ACM SIGCOMM Measurements Up the Stack.*

[5] Joe Cainey, Brendan Gill, Samuel Johnston, James Robinson, and Sam Westwood. 2014. Modelling download throughput of LTE networks. In *Local Computer Networks Workshops (LCN Workshops), 2014 IEEE 39th Conference on.* IEEE, 623–628.

[6] Gerald K Chan. 1991. Propagation and coverage prediction for cellular radio systems. *IEEE transactions on vehicular technology* 40, 4 (1991), 665–670.

[7] Alessandro Checco, Carlo Lancia, and Douglas J Leith. 2014. Using Crowdsourcing for Local Topology Discovery in Wireless Networks. *arXiv preprint arXiv:1401.1551* (2014).

[8] Rohde & Schwarz GmbH & Co.KG. [n. d.]. *Radio Network Analyzer Operating Manual.*

[9] U Dersch and WR Braun. 1991. *A physical radio channel model.* Technical Report. IEEE CH2944-7/91/0000/0289.

[10] Marcel Dischinger, Massimiliano Marcon, Saikat Guha, P Krishna Gummadi, Ratul Mahajan, and Stefan Saroiu. 2010. Glasnost: Enabling End Users to Detect Traffic Differentiation.. In *Proc. of USENIX NSDI.*

[11] Aaron Gember, Aditya Akella, Jeffrey Pang, Alexander Varshavsky, and Ramon Caceres. 2012. Obtaining incontext measurements of cellular network performance. In *Proceedings of the 2012 ACM conference on Internet measurement conference.* ACM, 287–300.

[12] Utkarsh Goel, Mike P Wittie, Kimberly C Claffy, and Andrew Le. 2016. Survey of end-to-end mobile network measurement testbeds, tools, and services. *IEEE Communications Surveys & Tutorials* 18, 1 (2016), 105–123.

[13] Nicolas Haderer, Fawaz Paraiso, Christophe Ribeiro, Philippe Merle, Romain Rouvoy, and Lionel Seinturier. 2015. A Cloud-Based Infrastructure for Crowdsourcing Data from Mobile Devices. In *Crowdsourcing.* Springer, 243–265.

[14] Masaharu Hata. 1980. Empirical formula for propagation loss in land mobile radio services. *IEEE transactions on Vehicular Technology* 29, 3 (1980), 317–325.

[15] Tobias Hoßfeld, Michael Seufert, Matthias Hirth, Thomas Zinner, Phuoc Tran-Gia, and Raimund Schatz. 2011. Quantification of YouTube QoE via crowdsourcing. In *Proc. of IEEE Multimedia (ISM).*

[16] Fumio Ikegami and Susumu Yoshida. 1980. Analysis of multipath propagation structure in urban mobile radio environments. *IEEE transactions on Antennas and Propagation* 28, 4 (1980), 531–537.

[17] Mads Lauridsen, Ignacio Rodriguez, Lucas Chavarria Gimenez, Preben Mogensen, et al. 2016. Verification of 3G and 4G received power measurements in a crowdsourcing Android app. In *Wireless Communications and Networking Conference (WCNC), 2016 IEEE.* IEEE, 1–6.

[18] Jaymin D Mankowitz and Andrew J Paverd. 2011. Mobile device-based cellular network coverage analysis using crowd sourcing. In *EUROCON-International Conference on Computer as a Tool (EUROCON), 2011 IEEE.* IEEE, 1–6.

[19] Massimiliano Molinari, Mah-Rukh Fida, Mahesh K Marina, and Antonio Pescape. 2015. Spatial interpolation based cellular coverage prediction with crowdsourced measurements. In *Proceedings of the 2015 ACM SIGCOMM Workshop on Crowdsourcing and Crowdsharing of Big (Internet) Data.* ACM, 33–38.

[20] Michaela Neuland, Thomas Kurner, and Mehdi Amirijoo. 2011. Influence of different factors on X-map estimation in LTE. In *Vehicular Technology Conference (VTC Spring), 2011 IEEE 73rd.* IEEE, 1–5.

[21] Ashkan Nikravesh, Hongyi Yao, Shichang Xu, David Choffnes, and Z Morley Mao. 2015. Mobilyzer: An open platform for controllable mobile network measurements. In *Proceedings of the 13th Annual International Conference on Mobile Systems, Applications, and Services.* ACM, 389–404.

[22] Yoshihisa Okumura, Eiji Ohmori, Tomihiko Kawano, and Kaneharu Fukuda. 1968. Field strength and its variability in VHF and UHF land-mobile radio service. *Rev. Elec. Commun. Lab* 16, 9 (1968), 825–73.

[23] Anshul Rai, Krishna Kant Chintalapudi, Venkata N Padmanabhan, and Rijurekha Sen. 2012. Zee: zero-effort crowdsourcing for indoor localization. In *Proc. of ACM MobiCom.*

[24] Theodore S Rappaport et al. 1996. *Wireless communications: principles and practice.* Vol. 2. Prentice Hall.

[25] Sanae Rosen, Sung-ju Lee, Jeongkeun Lee, Paul Congdon, Z Morley Mao, and Ken Burden. 2014. MCNet: Crowdsourcing wireless performance measurements through the eyes of mobile devices. *IEEE Communications Magazine* 52, 10 (2014), 86–91.

[26] Berna Sayrac, Janne Riihijärvi, Petri Mähönen, Sana Ben Jemaa, Eric Moulines, and Sébastien Grimoud. 2012. Improving coverage estimation for cellular networks with spatial bayesian prediction based on measurements. In *Proceedings of the 2012 ACM SIGCOMM workshop on Cellular networks: operations, challenges, and future design.* ACM, 43–48.

[27] Yuval Shavitt and Eran Shir. 2005. DIMES: Let the Internet measure itself. *ACM SIGCOMM CCR* 35, 5 (2005), 71–74.

[28] Jinghao Shi, Zhangyu Guan, Chunming Qiao, Tommaso Melodia, Dimitrios Koutsonikolas, and Geoffrey Challen. 2014. Crowdsourcing access network spectrum allocation using smartphones. In *Proc. of ACM Hot Topics in Networks.*

[29] Sebastian Sonntag, Jukka Manner, and Lennart Schulte. 2013. Netradar-Measuring the wireless world. In *Modeling & Optimization in Mobile, Ad Hoc & Wireless Networks (WiOpt), 2013 11th International Symposium on.* IEEE, 29–34.

[30] Joram Walfisch and Henry L Bertoni. 1988. A theoretical model of UHF propagation in urban environments. *IEEE Transactions on antennas and propagation* 36, 12 (1988), 1788–1796.

[31] SeungJune Yi, SungDuck Chun, YoungDae Lee, SungJun Park, and SungHoon Jung. 2012. *Radio Protocols for LTE and LTE-advanced.* John Wiley & Sons.

[32] Jongwon Yoon, Sayandeep Sen, Joshua Hare, and Suman Banerjee. 2015. WiScape: A Framework for Measuring the Performance of Wide-Area Wireless Networks. *IEEE Transactions on Mobile Computing* 14, 8 (2015), 1751–1764.

Rate-Compatible Transmission Schemes Based on Parallel Concatenated Punctured Polar Codes

Bowen Feng, Jian Jiao, Sha Wang, Shaohua Wu, Shushi Gu, Qinyu Zhang
Harbin Institute of Technology (Shenzhen)
Shenzhen, Guangdong, China 518055
hitfbw@hotmail.com,wangsha0701@foxmail.com,{jiaojian,hitwush,gushushi,zqy}@hit.edu.cn

ABSTRACT

In this paper, an improved random puncturing pattern of polar codes is proposed, where only the frozen bits can be selected to puncture. Compared to the existing random puncturing schemes, our improved random puncturing scheme can achieve 0.2-1dB decoding performance improvement. Then, an optimized rate-compatible hybrid automatic repeat request (HARQ) transmission scheme is proposed based on parallel concatenated punctured (PCP) polar codes. By analyzing the overhead of the previous successful decoded coding block in our rate-compatible HARQ scheme, two methods of determining the optimal initial code-rate of each new PCP polar coding block are proposed over a time-varying channel. Simulation results show that the average number of retransmissions is about 1.5 times in our proposed rate-compatible HARQ schemes with a 2-level PCP polar encoding construct, which reduces half of the average number of retransmissions than the existing rate-compatible polar coding scheme.

CCS CONCEPTS

•**Theory of computation** →*Error-correcting codes;*

KEYWORDS

Polar codes; puncturing algorithm; rate-compatible transmission; Hybrid ARQ

1 INTRODUCTION

Polar codes is a breakthrough of coding theory, which is proposed by Arikan [1]. The emerging polar codes can achieve the capacity of any memoryless symmetric channel [2, 3]; the encoding and decoding complexity are $O(N\log_2 N)$, where N is block length [4]. Polar codes will be applied in fifth-generation (5G) communication systems due to these attractive features [5].

Due to the time-varying nature of wireless channels in the future 5G communications, the quality of the channel is unknown to the transmitter in many communication scenarios [6] and the conventional fixed-rate coding schemes can not perform well [7]. In particular, polar codes need to be constructed according to the channel capacity to has good approaching performance [8, 9], and the original polar coding scheme can not perform well over an unknown channel. Moreover, the block length of original polar codes is restricted to the power of 2. Polar codes with any arbitrary lengths and rates can be constructed by puncturing [10–12]. However, the performance of these punctured codes is worse than the conventional polar codes.

Recently, a capacity-achieving rateless polar coding scheme has been proposed in [13] to realise the polar codes over an unknown channel by transmitting coded bits incrementally, until all the information bits can be decoded reliably by a backward decoding strategy according to the *nested* encoding property [13]. However, the code-rate in each transmission is $R_m = R_1/m$, where R_1 is the rate of the first transmission and m is the number of retransmissions, so the scheme is not truly rateless. [14] proposed a capacity-achieving rate-compatible polar (RCP) coding scheme, by using a sequential encoders and decoders to construct different block length polar codes.

In this paper, we propose a rate-compatible HARQ transmission scheme with two parallel concatenated punctured (PCP) polar coding schemes for continuously transmitting of multiple PCP polar coding blocks. In Section 2 we present preliminaries of polar codes, and propose our system model. We design an improve random puncturing (IRP) polar coding algorithm that limited the puncturing patterns in the frozen bit set in Section 3, which can provide better performance than the existing random puncturing schemes. Furthermore, by analyzing the performance of our HARQ transmission scheme over a time-varying channel in Section 4, we present two methods of determining the optimal initial code-rate of each new PCP polar coding block by the overhead of the previous successful decoded coding block. Section V presents the simulation results of our IRP methods and rate-compatible HARQ schemes. Finally, we conclude the paper in Section 6.

MSWiM'17, November 21–25, 2017, Miami, FL, USA
© 2017 ACM. ISBN 978-1-4503-5162-1/17/11...$15.00
DOI: https://doi.org/10.1145/3127540.3127562

2 PRELIMINARIES AND SYSTEM MODEL

2.1 Polar codes

Let $C(N, R, \boldsymbol{A})$ denote a polar code of block length $N = 2^n$ $(n \geq 0)$ and rate R with information set $\boldsymbol{A}$, where $R =$

K/N and K is the number of information bits. N polarized sub-channels $\{W_N^{(i)}\}$ $(i = 1, 2, ..., N)$ can be obtained by channel combining and splitting operation on N independent discrete memoryless channels (DMCs). For a source message vector $u_1^N = (u_1, u_2, ..., u_N)$, K information bits are transmitted in "good" sub-channels with indices $\boldsymbol{A}$, while frozen bits are transmitted in "bad" sub-channels with indices in complementary set $\boldsymbol{A}^c$. A polar codeword $x_1^N = (x_1, x_2, ..., x_N)$ is generated as

$$x_1^N = u_1^N \boldsymbol{G}_N = u_1^N \boldsymbol{B}_N \boldsymbol{F}^{\otimes n}, \tag{1}$$

where $\boldsymbol{B}_N$ is the permutation matrix, $\boldsymbol{F} = \begin{bmatrix} 0 & -1 \\ 1 & 0 \end{bmatrix}$ is known as standard kernel and $\boldsymbol{F}^{\otimes n}$ is the nth Kronecker power of $\boldsymbol{F}$.

Successive cancellation (SC) decoding algorithm is proposed in the original decoding for polar codes [1], the SC decoder generates the estimate $\hat{u}_1^N$ of u_1^N by calculating the likelihood ratio (LR) of the channels outputs $y_1^N = (y_1, y_2, ..., y_N)$. The LR of the i-th bits is calculated by

$$L_N^{(i)}(y_1^N, \hat{u_{i-1}}) = \frac{W_N^{(i)}(y_1^N, \hat{u}_{i-1}|0)}{W_N^{(i)}(y_1^N, \hat{u}_{i-1}|1)}, \tag{2}$$

and

$$\hat{u}_i = \begin{cases} 0 & L_N^{(i)}(y_1^N, \hat{u_{i-1}}) \geq 1 \\ 1 & \text{otherwise} \end{cases}, \tag{3}$$

where $\hat{u_{i-1}}$ denotes an $(i-1)$ dimensional vector.

2.2 System Model

We denote $\boldsymbol{C} = C(N, R_i, \boldsymbol{A}_i)|_{i \in 1,2,...,J}$ as a family of nested polar codes, which can be constructed in a sequence of degraded channels $W_1, W_2, ..., W_J$, where all coded block have the same block length that are restricted to 2^n and their information bit set arte nested such that $\boldsymbol{A}_1 \supseteq \boldsymbol{A}_2 \supseteq \ldots \supseteq \boldsymbol{A}_J$.

In order to construct arbitrary block length and code-rate polar codes, our propose an improved random puncturing (IRP) algorithm for the nested polar codes and construct the PCP polar codes. Let $\boldsymbol{C} = \{C(N_i, R_i, \boldsymbol{A}_i^{(i)})\}|_{i \in \{1,2,...,J\}}$ denotes a sequence of PCP polar codes, and the code-rate and block length satisfy

$$R_i = \frac{k}{\sum_{j=1}^{i} N_j}. \tag{4}$$

Moreover, for each block length $N_i, i \in \{1, 2, ..., J\}$, we can construct a sequence of *punctured nested* polar codes $\boldsymbol{C} = \{C(N_i, R_j, \boldsymbol{A}_j^{(i)})\}|_{j=i}^{J}$ with code-rate $R_i, ..., R_J$.

An example of the encoder and decoder structure of a 3-level PCP polar codes is shown in Fig. 1. The encoder in Fig. 1(a) transmit polar codes with code-rates from high to low until the receiver can decode reliably. The corresponding decoder in Fig. 1(b) starts backward decoding if the last PCP coding block is decoded, then the decoded bits are used as frozen bits in the previous polar coding blocks according to the nested property until all information bits are decoded successfully. Let $N_1 = 16$, $R_1 = 3/4$, $R_2 = 1/2$, $R_3 = 1/4$. The 1st polar coding block $C(N_1, R_1, \boldsymbol{A}_1^{(1)})$ is transmitted in

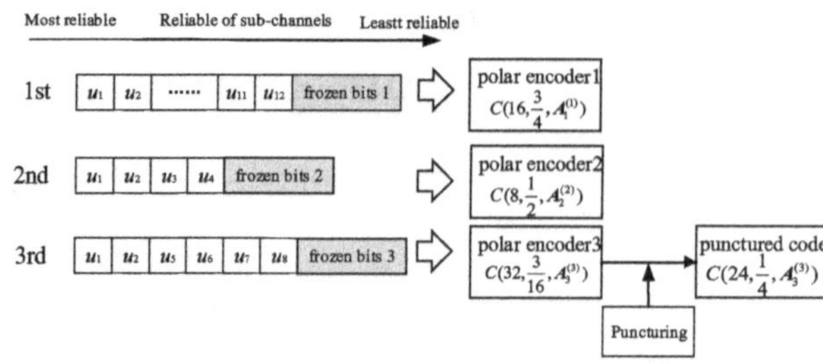

(a) Encoder structure

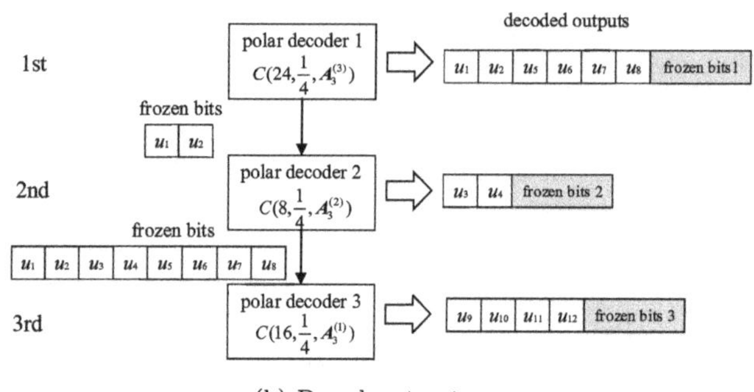

(b) Decoder structure

Figure 1: Encoder and decoder structure of a 3-level PCP polar coding scheme, where $N_1 = 16, N_2 = 8, N_3 = 24$.

1st transmission round as shown in Fig. 1(a), where $u_1^{12} = \{u_1, ..., u_{12}\}$ are information bits. If the 1st transmission fails to decode, the 2nd polar coding block $C(N_2, R_2, \boldsymbol{A}_2^{(2)})$ is transmitted, where $N_2 = 8$ can be calculated according to (2), and the information bits are $u_1^4 = \{u_1, u_2, u_3, u_4\}$. If the 2nd transmission also fails to decode, then the 3rd transmission is performed. According to (2), we can get $N_3 = 24$ which is not satisfy the power of 2 and can not be obtained by the conventional polar encoder, which the polar coding block is need to punctured. We choose a mother polar code with block length $N_M = 32$, then the number of information bits in the 3rd transmission is $N_3 R_3 = 6$, and the code-rate is $R_M = 3/16$. Now we can get the 3rd polar code $C(N_3, R_3, \boldsymbol{A}_3^{(3)})$ by puncturing 8 code bits, where the information bits is $\{u_1, u_2, u_5, u_6, u_7, u_8\}$.

The backward decode starts by recovering $C(N_3, R_3, \boldsymbol{A}_3^{(3)})$ and the corresponding information bits $\{u_1, u_2, u_5, u_6, u_7, u_8\}$. The the decoded bits $\{u_1, u_2\}$ are used as frozen bits in $C(N_2, R_2, \boldsymbol{A}_2^{(2)})$ and turned to $C(N_2, R_3, \boldsymbol{A}_3^{(2)})$, where the remanning information bits $\{u_3, u_4\}$ can be decoded with the code-rate R_3. Finally, the decoded bits in the 3rd and 2nd coding blocks are used as frozen bits in $C(N_1, R_1, \boldsymbol{A}_1^{(1)})$ to decode the remanning information bits $\{u_9, u_{10}, u_{11}, u_{12}\}$. Therefore, we have decoded all bits and complete the transmission of this block.

Note that it needs m encoders and m decoders to construct a m-level PCP polar code, the system structure will be complex when m is large. In addition, if the PCP polar codes for other blocks still be constructed with a same initial rate R_1, then the other blocks are still need m retransmissions. To address this problem, a rate-compatible HARQ transmission scheme to transmit multiple blocks continuously with simple structure of PCP polar codes will be described later.

3 IMPROVED RANDOM PUNCTURING PATTERN OF POLAR CODES

Puncturing is used to obtain polar codes with arbitrary code rates and block lengths by deleting some code bits, and the deleted bits will not be transmitted over the channel. Decoding of punctured polar codes can be accomplished in the same way as non-punctured codes by setting the LLRs to zero at the puncturing positions.

A punctured polar codes of length $[N_M]_p$ can be obtained by puncturing $N_M - [N_M]_p$ codewords from a mother code with length $[N_M]_p$, which is equivalent to move $N_M - [N_M]_p$ columns and $N_M - [N_M]_p$ rows from generation matrix $\boldsymbol{G_N}$. The indices of moving columns i are the same as the puncturing positions, and the indices of the puncturing rows are $j = \prod(i)$ [11], where $\prod(\cdot)$ is a bit-reversal function.

Let $u_{\boldsymbol{A}}$ and $u_{\boldsymbol{A}^c}$ denote the information bit set and frozen bit set of source block u_1^N. Then (1) can be rewritten as

$$\begin{aligned} x_1^N &= u_{\boldsymbol{A}} \boldsymbol{G}_N(\boldsymbol{A}) + u_{\boldsymbol{A}^c} \boldsymbol{G}_N(\boldsymbol{A}^c) \\ &= \sum_{i \in \boldsymbol{A}} u_i \times \boldsymbol{R}_i + \sum_{i \in \boldsymbol{A}^c} 0 \times \boldsymbol{R}_i, \end{aligned} \tag{5}$$

where $\boldsymbol{G}_N(\boldsymbol{A})$ is the sub-matrix of $\boldsymbol{G}_N$ formed by the row with indices in $\boldsymbol{A}$, and $\boldsymbol{G}_N(\boldsymbol{A}^c)$ is defined in the same fashion.

It is worth noting that the rows in previous item of (3) contains the information bits that need to be transmitted, and the latter item is 0, which will not affect the decoding performance if corresponding rows are moved. So we can limit the puncturing positions in the set $\prod(\boldsymbol{A}^c)$.

Let a mother polar code with length N_M and rate R_M, and the punctured code with block length $[N_M]_p$. Define $\boldsymbol{p}$ is the puncturing pattern and $|\boldsymbol{p}| = N_M$. A new improved random puncturing (IRP) pattern is described as follows:

Stage1: Initialize the vector $\boldsymbol{p}$ as all ones;

Stage2: $N_M - [N_M]_p$ bits are randomly selected in set $\prod(\boldsymbol{A}^c)$, and then set those positions of vector $\boldsymbol{p}$ as zeros. The positions corresponding to 0 in $\boldsymbol{p}$ will be punctured.

4 RATE-COMPATIBLE HARQ TRANSMISSION SCHEME BASED ON PCP POLAR CODES

In this section, we aim to design a rate-compatible HARQ transmission scheme via PCP polar coding blocks, where two methods are proposed to optimized the initial code-rate of each block by using IRP algorithm.

Table 1: The relationship between the initial rate and the number of retransmissions over time-varying channel

Initial code-rate	Channel condition	Result
R_1	ameliorate	$(m-1)$ retransmissions at most
	deteriorate	$(m+1)$ retransmissions at least
R_m	ameliorate	only 1 transmission
	deteriorate	2 retransmissions at least

4.1 Analysis of Initial Rate and Number of Retransmissions

We first introduce how to simplify the system structure of PCP polar codes and realise the transmission of multiple blocks over a time-varying channel. Assuming the 1st PCP polar coding block was transmitted with the initial code rate R_1, and successfully decoding with decreasing code rate R_m, the number of retransmissions corresponding to different initial rates is shown in Table 1.

Therefore, the key to simplify the system structure of PCP polar codes is to choose an optimal initial rate that close to the unknown channel capacity $I(W)$ from 1. Considering R_m is closer to the channel capacity than R_1, if the next transmission PCP polar coding block with initial rate R_m, then the expected number of retransmissions can be reduced. Although the exact $I(W)$ is unknown for transmitter, it still can have better performance with R_m which has better estimation to the channel state information.

A capacity interval is defined as $I(W) \in [R_m, R_{m-1})$ after the first block is transmitted, where R_m is final rate and R_{m-1} is last rate that cannot be supported by channel. Then the initial rate for the second block can be chosen according to $[R_m, R_{m-1})$. Similarly, we can get such interval after the transmission of each block and choose an optimal rate according to the interval for next block. The rate is close to the channel capacity which will reduce the number of transmissions and simplify the system structure of PCP polar codes for each block.

4.2 Rate-Compatible HARQ Transmission Scheme

Based on the above analysis, in the following, two different rate-compatible HARQ transmission schemes for multiple blocks with simplified structure of PCP polar codes are proposed. In our schemes, each block will be transmitted by encoding PCP polar codes that described in Section 2.2.

First, we define some parameters: ΔR denotes an estimate difference of two adjacent code-rates in a PCP polar coding block; $C(N_k^{(n)}, R_k^{(n)}, \boldsymbol{A}_k^{(n)})$ is the polar codes as k-th retransmission in n-th block; $I^{(n)}(W) \in [R_L^{(n)}, R_U^{(n)})$ is the interval of channel capacity after the n-th block is transmitted successfully, where $I^{(n)}(W)$ is current capacity, $R_L^{(n)}$ and $R_U^{(n)}$ represent the lower and upper limits of the channel capacity with the initial value $R_L^{(0)} = 0$, $R_U^{(0)} = 1$, respectively.

Scheme 1

The first capacity interval $I^{(1)}(W) \in [R_L^{(1)}, R_U^{(1)})$ will be returned to the sender after this data block is transmitted successfully. Then $R_L^{(1)}$ is used as initial rate to construct of the polar code $C(N_1^{(2)}, R_L^{(1)}, \boldsymbol{A}_1^{(2)})$, if the receiver cannot decode, it proves that the channel condition deteriorates. So $R_L^{(1)}$ is used as the initial rate directly. Then construct a OPCPP code block with lower rate $R_2^{(2)} = R_L^{(1)} - \Delta R$ in the second transmission, and a 2-level OPCPP codes for the second block can be constructed. If $R_2^{(2)} = R_L^{(1)} - \Delta R$ is supportable by channel, then the current capacity interval is $I^{(2)}(W) \in [R_L^{(1)} - \Delta R, R_L^{(1)})$ to transmitted the third block.

If the code $C(N_1^{(2)}, R_L^{(1)}, \boldsymbol{A}_1^{(2)})$ can be decoded, then this block is transmitted successfully only by 1 transmission, and we set the current channel capacity interval is $I^{(2)}(W) \in [R_L^{(2)}, R_U^{(2)})$, where $R_L^{(2)} = R_L^{(1)}$ and $R_U^{(2)} = R_U^{(1)}$.

The transmission of the third block is according to the result of the second block and we will discuss in two cases. If the second block was transmitted by 2 retransmissions and return $I^{(2)}(W) \in [R_L^{(1)} - \Delta R, R_L^{(1)})$, then $R_L^{(2)} = R_L^{(1)} - \Delta R$ will be used to as the initial rate $R_1^{(3)}$ in the transmission of the third block. If the second block was transmitted only by 1 transmission and return $I^{(2)}(W) \in [R_L^{(1)}, R_U^{(1)})$, we will use $R_U^{(1)} = R_L^{(1)} + \Delta R$ as $R_1^{(3)}$ in the transmission of the third block.

In the transmission of the fourth block, the initial rate $R_1^{(4)}$ will be determined in the similar method as the third one. Such that when the third one is transmitted by 2 retransmissions, then $R_1^{(3)} = R_L^{(2)}$ which is the low limit of the second capacity interval; when the third one is transmitted by 1 transmission, then $R_1^{(3)} = R_U^{(2)}$ that is the upper limit of the second capacity interval, which is also equal to $R_1^{(2)} + \Delta R$.

In summary, if the $(n-1)$-th block is transmitted only 1 transmission, the initial rate of the n-th one is $R_1^{(n)} = R_1^{(n-1)} + \Delta R$ which is shown in lines 6−8 of the pseudo codes listed in **Algorithm 1**; if the $(n-1)$-th block is transmitted more than 1 transmission, the initial rate of the n-th one is $R_1^{(n)} = R_L^{(n-1)}$ which is shown in lines 2 − 4 of the pseudo codes listed in **Algorithm 1**.

Scheme 2

In scheme 1, we use $R_1^{(n-1)} + \Delta R$ as the initial rate of the n-th block where $R_1^{(n-1)}$ is the initial rate of the $(n-1)$-th one when it was transmitted by 1 transmission. There are two problems need consider: if the channel condition deteriorates such that $I^{(n)}(W) < I^{(n-1)}(W)$, it will be need to constructed 3-level PCP polar code for the block; If channel conditions ameliorates with small scale or unchanging such that $I^{(n)}(W) \approx I^{(n-1)}(W)$, $R_1^{(n)} + \Delta R$ is too large than current channel capacity $I^{(n+1)}(W)$ especially with a large ΔR. So we will proposed a new scheme base on scheme 1 where we consider to improved rate by puncturing.

We defined $C([N_k^{(n)}]_p^j, [R_k^{(n)}]_p^j, [\boldsymbol{A}_k^{(n)}]_p^j, P_j)$ as the j-th punctured polar code from them mother code $C(N_k^{(n)}, R_k^{(n)}, \boldsymbol{A}_k^{(n)})$,

Algorithm 1: Scheme 1, Calculation of Optimal Initial Code-Rate

```
   Input: The final code-rate of first block R_L^(1)
   Output: The optimal initial code-rate for n-th block R_1^(n)
1  for i = 2 : 1 : n do
2      Construct polar code C(N_1^(i), R_L^(i-1), A_1^(i));
3      if code C(N_1^(i), R_L^(i-1), A_1^(i)) cannot be decoded then
4          R_1^(i) = R_L^(i-1);
5      end
6      else
7          R_1^(i) = R_L^(i-1) + ΔR;
8      end
9  end
10 return R_1^(n);
```

where $P_j = j\delta$ is the number of punctured bits in step j and δ is a pre-selected number of puncturing bits.

Algorithm 2: Scheme 2, Calculation of Optimal Initial Code-Rate

```
Input: The final code-rate of first block R_L^(1)
Output: The optimal initial code-rate for n-th block
Num ← 0;
for i = 2 : 1 : n do
    if Num ← 0 then
        R_1^(i) = R_L^(i-1);
    end
    else
        if R_1^(i-1) is not punctured rate then
            R_1^(i) = R_L^(i-1);
        end
        else
            when R_1^(i)=[R_M]_p^j, where j is the times of
             puncturng;
            j ← j + 1;
            R_1^(i) = [R_M]_p^j;
        end
    end
    if R_1^(i) is supportable by channel then
        Num ← 1;
    end
    else
        Num ← 0;
    end
end
return R_1^(n);
```

The way to transmit the first and second block in scheme 2 is same as scheme 1, and we will not repeat them. When the transmitter obtain the interval $I^{(2)}(W) \in [R_L^{(2)}, R_U^{(2)})$ after the transmission of first two blocks. If the second block was transmitted more than 1 transmission, then the rate $R_L^{(2)}$ used to as the third initial rate $R_1^{(3)}$.

Otherwise, if the second block was transmitted only by 1 transmission, we will construct and transmit a punctured polar code $C([N_1^{(3)}]_p^1, [R_L^{(1)}]_p^1, [\boldsymbol{A}_1^{(2)}]_p^1, P_1)$ from mother code $C(N_1^{(3)}, R_L^{(1)}, \boldsymbol{A}_1^{(2)})$, and $R_1^{(3)} = [R_L^{(1)}]_p^1$, where $P_1 = \delta$ is the number of punctured bits. Noting that, both punctured code and mother code use the same pair of encoder and decoder, which means puncturing will not increase the complexity of system. If $R_1^{(3)} = [R_L^{(1)}]_p^1$ is un-supportable by channel, then construct a PCP polar code block with lower rates in the later transmission.

If $R_1^{(3)} = [R_L^{(1)}]_p^1$ is supportable by channel, we will construct punctured code $C([N_1^{(3)}]_p^2, [R_L^{(1)}]_p^2, [\boldsymbol{A}_1^{(2)}]_p^2, P_2)$ by continue puncturing from mother code $C(N_1^{(3)}, R_L^{(1)}, \boldsymbol{A}_1^{(2)})$, where $[N_1^{(3)}]_p^2$,$[R_L^{(1)}]_p^2$ denotes the length and rate of 2nd punctured code. In the transmission of the fourth block, the initial rate $R_1^{(4)} = [R_L^{(1)}]_p^2$.

When $(n-1)$-th block is transmitted successfully, the corresponding channel capacity interval $[R_L^{(n-1)}, R_U^{(n-1)})$ is feedback, the n-th block will be transmitted according to the above method. The detail pseudo codes of scheme 2 is listed in **Algorithm 2**.

From the above analysis we can see the difference between both two scheme is the way to obtain higher rate as initial rate of current after previous was transmitted by 1 transmission. Due to the performance loss is inevitable by puncturing, scheme 2 is worse than scheme 1 in terms of polar code performance at the same rate. However, it is possible to compensate for the increase in the number of retransmissions brought about by scheme 1 when the channel change with small scale.

In summary, the main idea of our rate-compatible HARQ schemes are according to the final code-rate of the previous transmitted block to determine an optimal initial code-rate close to current channel capacity for remaining blocks. As the transmission of blocks increases, the estimate of unknown channel will be more accurate. Furthermore, each block can be transmitted by less retransmission than that use the same initial rate $R_1^{(1)}$ except the first one which will simplify the system structure.

4.3 Parameter Optimization

We defined two parameters in our rate-compatible schemes: a pre-selected number of puncturing bits δ, and an estimated difference of two adjacent code-rates in a PCP polar coding block ΔR. Both of them have crucial effects on the efficiency and reliability of scheme. For example, when δ is small, the target rate can be found by puncturing many times and increase the number of retransmissions. Conversely, if δ is too large, the performance of punctured polar codes will be poor. In this Section, we will discuss the optimal parameters selection.

Table 2: The relationship between the block length of punctured polar codes $[N_M]_p$ and the number of puncturing bits P.

Parameter	Value				
$[R_M]_p$	0.5	0.6	0.7	0.8	0.9
$[N_M]_p$	1024	853	731	640	568
P	0	171	293	384	456
$[N_M]_p$	2048	1706	1462	1280	1137
P	0	342	586	768	911

a. Puncturing step δ

Table 2 shows the relationship between the block lengths of punctured codes $[N_M]_p$ and the number of puncturing bits P, where the mother polar codes with code-rate $R_M = 0.5$, and block lengths are N_M=1024 and N_M=2048, respectively. It can be seen that the larger punctured rates are, the more bits need to be punctured, but there is no specific function relationship between them.

In this paper, we choose a half of punctured bits when punctured rate is $[R_M]_p = R_M + 0.1$ as δ. Such as, if $N_M = 1024$, then $\delta = \lfloor \frac{171}{2} \rfloor$; if $N_M = 2048$, then $\delta = \lfloor \frac{342}{2} \rfloor$. We can obtain the conclusion in *Corollary 1*.

COROLLARY 1. *The times of puncturing j and corresponding punctured rate $[R_M]_p^j$ are independent on the block length of mother code N_M.*

PROOF. we choose the half of the number of puncturing codewords when puncturing rate is $[R_M]_p = R_M + 0.1$ as δ. We can get (6) and (7) because the number of information bits does not change after puncturing.

$$R_M N_M = (R_M + 0.1)(N_M - 2\delta) \tag{6}$$

$$\delta = \frac{1}{2}(N_M - \frac{R_M N_M}{R_M + 0.1}) \tag{7}$$

Puncturing rates $R_M < [R_M]_p < 1$ and the number of puncturing codewords $1 \leq P < N_M - N_M R_M$. The number of puncturing times is $P = j\delta$ after j times puncturing. j and $[R_M]_p^j$ are such that

$$j < \frac{N_M - R_M N_M}{\delta} = 20(R_M + 0.1)(1 - R_M), j \in Z \tag{8}$$

$$[R_M]_p^j = \frac{R_M N_M}{N_M - j\delta} = \frac{2(R_M + 0.1)R_M}{2(R_M + 0.1) - 0.1j} \tag{9}$$

□

b. Rate difference ΔR

The relationship between the mother rate R_M and the first punctured rate $[R_M]_p^1$ is shown in Fig. 2 when the puncturing step δ is chosen by (7), the difference is about 0.05. In order to facilitate the analysis we record as

$$[R_M]_p^1 = R_M + 0.05 \tag{10}$$

it is easy to prove $[R_M]_p^1 = \frac{1}{2}(R_M + (R_M + \Delta R))$. Due to the first punctured rate $[R_M]_p^1$ is slightly larger than mother rate R_M and the number of punctured bits required to be less which not causes larger performance loss. Moreover,

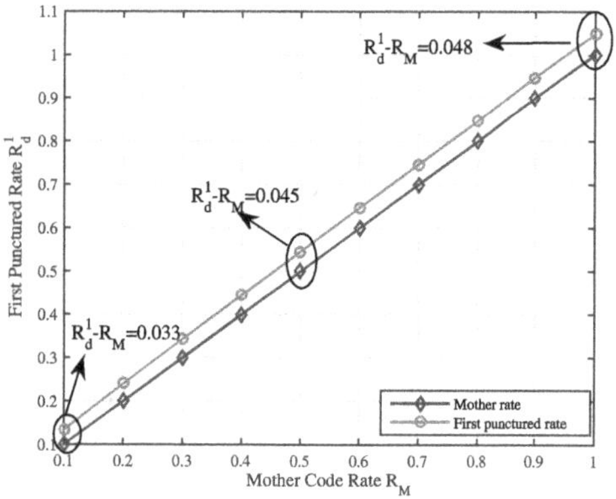

Figure 2: The relationship between mother code rate R_M and the first punctured rate $R_p^{(1)}$.

Table 3: Parameters for BER and FER simulations

Parameters	Value
Block length of mother polar codes N_M	1024
Code-rate of mother polar codes R_M	0.5
Code-rate of punctures polar codes $[R_M]_p$	0.6, 0.7, 0.8
Polar decoding algorithm	SC
Modulation	BPSK

when channel condition change with small scale, the first punctured rate $[R_M]_p^1$ will close to current channel capacity.

Combined with the above analysis, δ and ΔR can be chose as the relationship in (11).

$$\delta = \frac{1}{2}(N_M - \frac{R_M N_M}{R_M + \Delta R}) \tag{11}$$

(11) describes the relationship of δ and ΔR, however, finding an optimal solution of δ and ΔR is still an open problem.

5 SIMULATIONS AND NUMERICAL RESULTS

5.1 Comparison of Decoding Performance of Improved Puncturing Algorithm

In this section, we first simulated the performance of the bit error rate (BER) and frame error rate (FER) of our improved random puncturing algorithm and compared with existing punctured polar coding schemes over binary-input additive white Gaussian noise (BI-AWGN) channel, the simulation parameters are given in Table 3.

As Fig.3 and Fig.4 shows, the improved random puncturing algorithm (IRP) outperforms than other two algorithms, where the performance loss is catastrophic under stop-tree puncturing (STP) algorithm [10], because STP algorithm which is more suitable under BP decoding. And when the punctured rate is $[R_M]_p = 0.6$, the performance of punctured

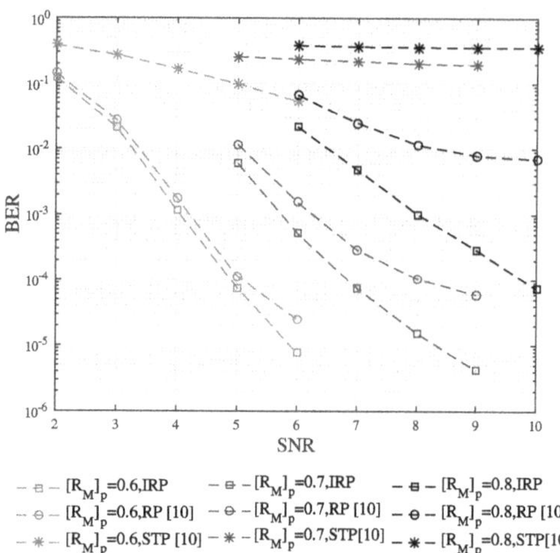

Figure 3: The BER performance over BI-AWGN channel with punctured code rate 0.6, 0.7, 0.8 under different puncturing algorithms where mother code is with length $N_M = 1024$ and rate $R_M = 0.5$.

codes under IRP obtains a gain 0.2dB at BER 10^{-4} and 0.2dB at FER 10^{-2} than random puncturing (RP)[10]. With the increase of puncturing rate, the advantages of our proposed IRP algorithm are more obvious. When punctured rate is $[R_M]_p = 0.7$, the IRP algorithm outperforms RP algorithm and obtains a gain of about 1dB at BER 10^{-4} and 0.3dB at FER 10^{-2}, respectively. Moreover, RP algorithm suffers from an error-floor when punctured rate is $[R_M]_p = 0.8$, which no longer happens in our IRP algorithm.

5.2 Comparison of Rate-Compatible HARQ Schemes via Polar Codes

We simulate the number of retransmissions of multiple blocks with the Rate-Compatible Polar (RCP) scheme [14] and our proposed two PCP polar coding HARQ schemes over slow fading channel, the simulation parameters are shown in Table 4, and δ is determined as (7). In the RCP scheme, all initial rates of subsequent blocks are equal to $R_1^{(1)}$, while they are determined as the method in [14]. The result is shown in Fig. 5, where the vertical axis is the average of the number of retransmissions, and the horizontal axis is the index of block, and lines with marker "$*$" denotes the results of RCP scheme while marker "$\circ$" and "$\star$ " denotes the results of our proposed OPCPP scheme1 and scheme2.

Fig. 5 shows that the average number of retransmissions for the first block is equal under both of the three schemes. In the RCP scheme, due to all blocks have the same initial rate, the average retransmissions for subsequent blocks is substantially equal to that of the first block. The red line with marker "$*$" in Fig. 5(a) shows the average retransmissions is about 5.5 times for the RCP scheme when $I^{(1)}(W) =$

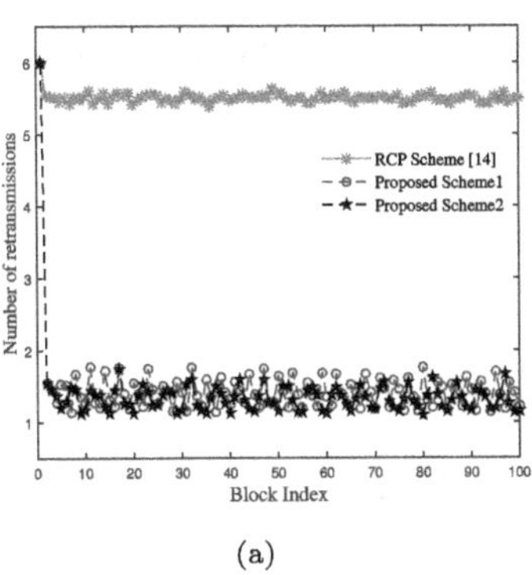

(a)

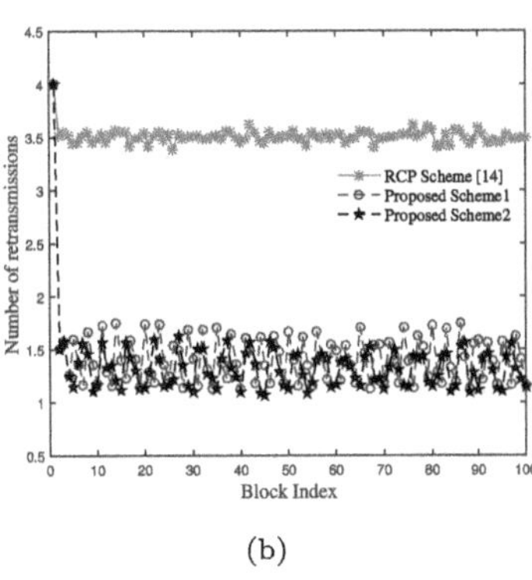

(b)

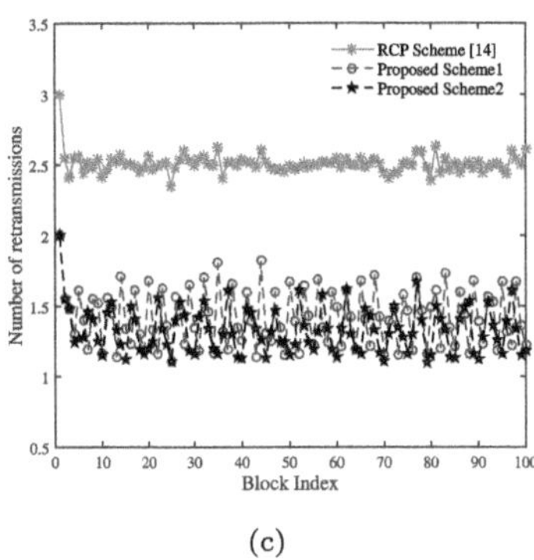

(c)

Figure 5: Comparison of average number of retransmissions of 100 packets in RCP scheme, and of our proposed rate-compatible HARQ schemes with different initial channel capacity $I^{(1)}(W)$: (a) $I^{(1)}(W) = 0.3$; (b) $I^{(1)}(W) = 0.5$; (c) $I^{(1)}(W) = 0.7$.

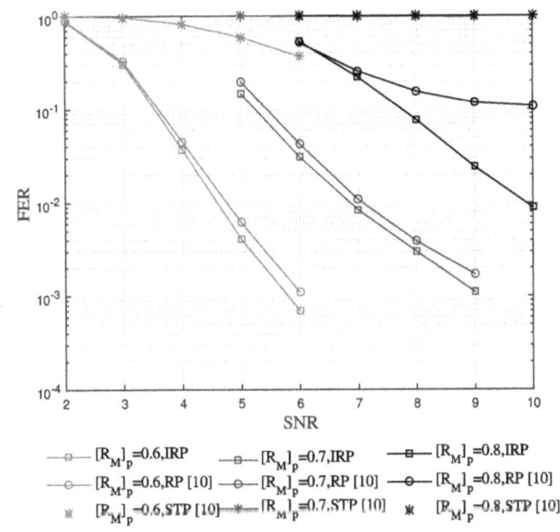

Figure 4: The FER performance over BI-AWGN channel with punctured code rate $0.6, 0.7, 0.8$ under different puncturing algorithms where mother code is with length $N_M = 1024$ and rate $R_M = 0.5$.

Table 4: Parameters for retransmissions simulations.

Parameters	Value
Initial channel capacity $I^{(1)}(W)$	0.3, 0.5, 0.7
The first initial code-rates $R_1^{(1)}$	0.8
Code-rate difference ΔR	0.1
The number of blocks	100
Monte Carlo simulation times	100

0.3. In addition, the average retransmissions for subsequence blocks are strongly depend on the difference between $R_1^{(1)}$ and the $I^{(1)}(W)$. As the blue line and black line with marker "$*$" shows the average retransmissions reduce to 3.5 times and 2.5 times when $I^{(1)}(W) = 0.5$ and $I^{(1)}(W) = 0.7$, respectively, which are shown in Fig. 5(b)(c). In addition, the number of encoder and decoder required is the same number of retransmissions in the RCP scheme.

In both our proposed PCP polar coding HARQ schemes, the average retransmissions of subsequent blocks are all about 1.5 times under different as all lines with marker "$\circ$" and "$\star$ show, our proposed PCP polar coding HARQ schemes need less retransmission times than the RCP scheme, especially $I^{(1)}(W) = 0.3$. In addition, the number of retransmissions can ignore the influence of $I^{(1)}(W)$ in this scheme which is more flexible than RCP scheme over time-varying channel. Moreover, in PCP polar coding HARQ scheme, each one of subsequence blocks can be transmitted with 2-level PCP polar codes at most and puncturing pattern dose not increase number of encoders and decoders, so the number of encoders and decoders for subsequence blocks is only 2 at most, which the structure of PCP polar coding scheme is simpler than the RCP scheme.

5.3 Comparison of decoding performance of two PCP polar coding schemes with same initial code-rates

In this subsection, we compare the decoding performance of our proposed two PCP polar coding HARQ schemes with the same initial code-rates in one block transmission in Section 4.2, which means the initial encoding code-rate is $R_1^{(n)} = R_L^{(n-1)} + \Delta R$ in scheme 1, and the same initial code-rate in scheme 2 is by using IRP algorithm. We will show that the performance is different when the same initial code-rate are obtain in different ways in the two schemes, the simulation parameters ΔR is selected as $\Delta R = 0.1$, then $\delta = 57$ which is according to (7).

Assuming the final code-rate of the previous block is $R_L^{(1)} = 0.4$ and the block length of polar code is 512, let $C_1 =$

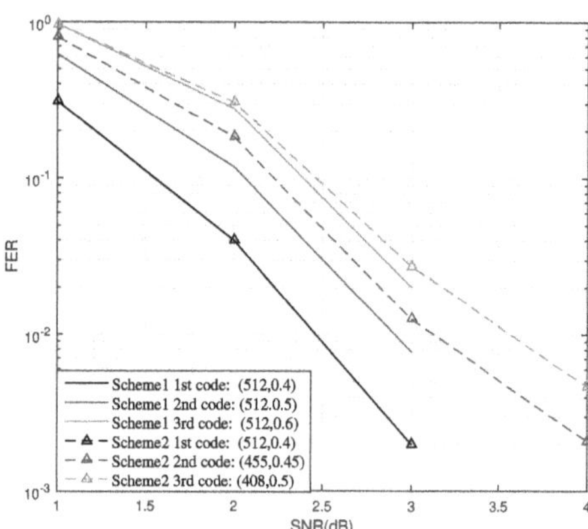

Figure 6: Comparison of FER performance with the same initial code-rate of PCP polar codes in Scheme 1 and Scheme 2.

$(512, 0.4)$ denotes this polar code. In scheme 1, the next block will be transmitted with initial rate $R_1^{(2)} = 0.4 + \Delta R = 0.5$ and $R_1^{(3)} = R_1^{(2)} + \Delta R = 0.6$ is the initial rate of the third transmission, then polar codes $(512, 0.5)$ and $(512, 0.5)$ are the second and third transmissions' initial code-rate, respectively. In scheme 2, $(455, [R_L^{(1)}]_p^1)$ and $(408, [R_L^{(1)}]_p^2)$ are the second and third transmissions' initial code-rate in scheme 2, where $[R_L^{(1)}]_p^1 = 0.45$ and $[R_L^{(1)}]_p^2 = 0.5$

As Fig. 6 shows, the first initial polar codes in both two scheme have the same FER performance, and performance of the second polar codes in scheme 1 obtains about 0.1 dB gain than scheme 2, while the two performance of the third codes are basically the same.

6 CONCLUSION

In this paper, we proposed a rate-compatible HARQ transmission scheme via PCP polar coding. First, we designed an improve random puncturing algorithm that limited the puncturing patterns in the frozen bits of polar codes, which can obtain about 0.2-1 dB better decoding performance than the existing random puncturing schemes. Then, by analyzing the overhead of the previous successful decoded coding block in our rate-compatible HARQ scheme, two methods to obtain the optimal initial code-rates of each new PCP polar coding block are proposed over slow fading channels. Simulation results show that the mean number of retransmissions is about 1.5 times in both of our proposed rate-compatible HARQ schemes, with a 2-level PCP polar encoding construct, which reduces half of the mean number of retransmissions than the existing rate-compatible polar coding scheme. The future works of our rate-compatible HARQ schemes are described as follows. The PCP polar codes in this paper can combine with a channel estimation algorithm, which we can selected a more aggressive initial code-rate to further enhance the transmission efficiency.

ACKNOWLEDGMENT

This work was supported in part by the National Natural Sciences Foundation of China (NSFC) under Grant 61771158, 61701136, 61525103 and 61371102, the Natural Scientific Research Innovation Foundation in Harbin Institute of Technology under Grant HIT. NSRIF. 2017051, and the Shenzhen Fundamental Research Project under Grant JCYJ201603281 63327348 and JCYJ20150930150304185.

REFERENCES

[1] E. Arikan. Channel polarization: A method for constructing capacity-achieving codes for symmetric binary-input memoryless channels. *IEEE Transactions on Information Theory*, 55(7): 3051–3073, 2009.

[2] R. Mori, T. Tanaka. Performance and construction of polar codes on symmetric binary-input memoryless channels. In *2009 IEEE International Symposium on Information Theory*, pages 1496–1500, 2009.

[3] E. Abbe, A. Barron.Polar coding schemes for the AWGN channel. In *IEEE International Symposium on Information Theory Proceedings*, pages 194–198, 2011.

[4] M. Mondelli, R. Urbanke, and S. H. Hassani. Unified scaling of polar codes: Error exponent, scaling exponent, moderate deviations, and error floors. In *2015 IEEE International Symposium on Information Theory*, pages 1422–1426, 2015.

[5] M. Mondelli, S. H. Hassani, I. Maric. Capacity-achieving rate-compatible polar codes for general channels. In *2017 IEEE Wireless Communications and Networking Conference Workshops (WCNCW)*, San Francisco, USA, May 2017.

[6] H. Kim. Coding and modulation techniques for high spectral efficiency transmission in 5g and satcom. In *2015 Signal Processing Conference*, pages 2746–2750, 2015.

[7] S. Chen, K. Peng, Y. Zhang, J. Song. Near capacity LDPC coded MU-BICM-ID for 5G. In *International Wireless Communications and Mobile Computing Conference (IWCMC)*, pages 1418–1423, 2015.

[8] B. Feng, J. Jiao, S. Wang, S. Wu, and Q. Zhang. Construction of polar codes concatenated to space-time block coding in mimo system. In *2016 IEEE 84th Vehicular Technology Conference (VTC-Fall)*, pages 1–5, 2016.

[9] B. Feng, J. Jiao, S. Gu. Efficient Design of Polar Coded STTD Systems over Rician MIMO Channels. In *Proceeding of the 6th International Conference on Communications, Signal Processing, and Systems (CSPS)*, Harbin, China, July 2017.

[10] A. Eslami, H. Pishro-Nik. A practical approach to polar codes. In *IEEE International Symposium on Information Theory Proceedings*, pages 16–20, 2011.

[11] L. Zhang, Z. Zhang, X. Wang, and Q. Yu. On the puncturing patterns for punctured polar codes. In *IEEE International Symposium on Information Theory*, pages 121–125, 2014.

[12] S. Wang, J. Jiao, B. Feng. Design of Rateless Transmission Scheme based on Punctured Polar Codes. In *Proceeding of the 6th International Conference on Communications, Signal Processing, and Systems (CSPS)*, Harbin, China, July 2017.

[13] B. Li, D. Tse, K. Chen, H. Shen. Capacity-achieving rateless polar Codes. In *IEEE International Symposium on Information Theory (ISIT)*, pages 46–50, 2016.

[14] S. N. Hong, D. Hui, and I. Mari. Capacity-achieving rate-compatible polar Codes. In *International Symposium on Information Theory (ISIT)*, pages 41–45, 2016.

An Uncertain Continuous Collaborative Users Finding Algorithm for Location Privacy Protection *

Extended Abstract†

Zhang Lei
College of Computer Science and Technology, Harbin Engineering University, 150001
College of Information and Electronic Technology, Jiamusi University, 154007
P. R. China
8213662@163.com

Ma Chunguang*
College of Computer Science and Technology, Harbin Engineering University, 150001
P. R. China
machunguang@hrbeu.edu.cn

Yang Songtao
College of Information and Electronic Technology, Jiamusi University, 154007
P. R. China
songtao_y@163.com

Li Zengpeng
College of Computer Science and Technology, Harbin Engineering University, 150001
P. R. China
zpleefly@126.com

ABSTRACT

[1] The centralized and distributed models are the main system architecture of privacy protection in location-based services (LBS). In the model of centralized, the trusted third party (TTP) is used to provide location privacy, but it is usually thought as the point of attack and the bottleneck of service, which makes the distributed model attract more attention. However, although a large number of algorithms were proposed under this model, they were mainly focussed on the protection of the snapshot query and difficult to provide privacy in the continuous query. Especially that, with the difference of anonymous users, the adversary can get rid of the anonymous users and identify the issuer, and then the privacy of the issuer will be revealed. In order to deal with this problem, we propose an uncertain continuous collaborative users finding algorithm (UCCUFA), which utilizes the uncertainty cells of region grid and the collaborative users to provide query results to make the issuer hiding behind the collaborative users. In this algorithm, all query results are provided by collaborative users, and no information interacted between the issuer and the LBS server during the procedure of continuous query. At last, we utilize the security analysis and experimental results further verify the effectiveness of location privacy protection and the performance efficiency of our proposed algorithm.

MSWiM '17, November 21–25, 2017, Miami, FL, USA

ACM ISBN 978-1-4503-5162-1/17/11..$15.00
https://doi.org/10.1145/3127540.3127572

CCS CONCEPTS

• *Security and privacy~Privacy-preserving protocols*

KEYWORDS

Location-based service, privacy protection, collaborative users, uncertainty cells

1 INTRODUCTION

In order to protect location privacy, Gruteser et al. [1] proposed the k-anonymity in 2003, which utilized the TTP to provide location privacy protection. Then several similar algorithms were proposed such as p-sentivity[2] and l-diversity [3]. For consideration of flaws of TTP, Ghinita et al. [4] utilized the device of mobile users, and based on the computational private information retrieval (PIR) achieved a zero information leakage scheme. Chow et al. [5] utilized collaborative users to achieve k-anonymity in mobile devices. With the development of LBS, the user prefers to utilize the continuous query instead of the snapshot one. Therefore, based on the TTP, Zhang et al. [6] utilized the similarity attributes to cut off the correlation of real locations into a trajectory. For the un-trusted of TTP, Schelegel et al. [7] utilized the encrypted message transferred between the TTP and collaborative users and achieve the secure interaction. Gao et al. [8] assumed the collaborative users have the same direction of moving with the issuer and achieve the trajectory anonymity. However, existing algorithms usually performance better in snapshot service. In the continuous query, the issuer may provide a series of real locations, and the adversary can utilize the differential of users in each query to correlate the real location and generate a location trajectory. Then with the trajectory the adversary may obtain even more private information about the issuer. In order to cope with this problem, we propose an algorithm called continuous collaborative users finding short for UCCUFA to protect the privacy in continuous query.

2 PRELIMINARIES

2.1 Adversary Model

The location privacy protection scheme will produce several anonymous regions as depicted in figure 1. In this figure, we can see that the issuer A requires four times queries with 4-anonymous in continuous location, and she selects B, C and D in the first anonymous region. Then she selects C, D and E in the second query and so on. Thus, we can see that anonymous users in per-query are different from each other except the issuer, and the adversary can correlate the real trajectory by getting rid off the anonymous user. As in continuous query, the anonymous user may have different directions and velocity, which makes the anonymous user who can be used in the vicinity is metabolic and leads the differentiation. So the adversary can easily correlate discrete locations into trajectory and identify the real location. This condition further threatens the privacy of the issuer.

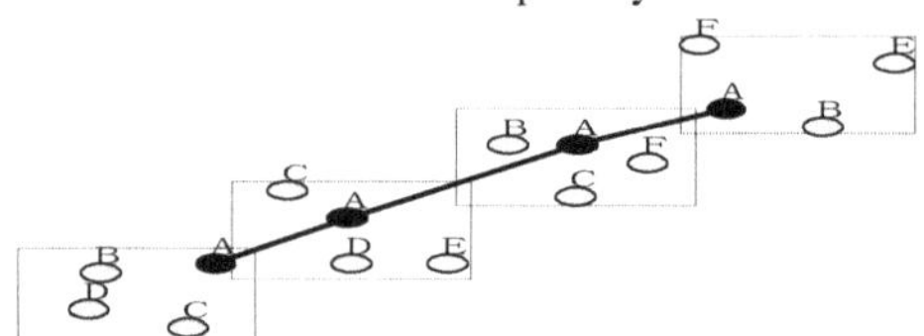

Figure 1: The figure of continuous anonyous.

In this paper, we assume the un-trusted LBS server as the adversary, as it may sell the information for commercial advantages or be breached by the adversary. Because of the LBS server can get all information of the user while requiring for the LBS, it has all the background knowledge used for correlating the personal privacy. Thus, we consider all attack especially the above attack is launched by the LBS server.

2.2 The Basic Idea

In order to cope with real locations can be correlated in continuous queries, the simplest conception is to select all the same anonymous users in per-query. However, it is difficult to achieve, as the anonymous user also has his own direction and velocity. Therefore, we utilize the cached result of collaborative user, and select useful collaborative users along the routing, and then hiding the issuer behind collaborative users all the times. Furthermore, we also divide the region into a grid to simplify the procedure of collaborative users finding as well as an uncertain expanding algorithm to further generalization the real trajectory.

3 THE UCCUFA

3.1 The Expanding of Uncertainty Cells

The purpose of uncertainty cells expanding is to solve the problem of cells correlation. With expanded cells, the adversary cannot get the real cell trajectory. Furthermore, the uncertainty expanding can also be used to find the collaborative user in muti-hop regions. The procedure of uncertainty cells expanding can be summarized as making each cell achieve the k-anonymity. For example, the issuer divides the region into a grid as depicted in figure 2a, her routing is denoted as the arrow line. Once the issuer wants 4-anonymity continuous queries in the routing, she has to expand the cell based on the cell of (x_u,y_u) firstly. The expanding cell is the cell next to (x_u,y_u) in a random direction. Then the second expanding cell is based on the cell which has been chosen in the last expanding as depicted in figure 2b. Repeat above operation until all the potential cells in the grid along the routing is expanded. Then we will see the final expanding cells in figure 2c, and the issuer has to find the collaborative users in these cells.

3.2 Procedure of Collaborative Users Finding

From the expanding we can see the issuer has to select the collaborative user in muti-hop regions. So the procedure of collaborative users finding can be seen as the procedure of the collaborative user deals with the received message and the details can be seen in figure 3. In the routing, the issuer first finds a collaborative user in the cell of her locates. The collaborative user who receives the message has to decide whether to be partied in the group, if so she transmits this message to the expanding cell in her vicinity and finding another collaborative user, else she drops this message. Then this user submits the received message to the LBS server, and preserves the received query result. If the issuer wants the query result in the current cell, the user who has preserved the result can provide it, and the issuer does not need to submit the query to the LBS server. Once the cell in the routing does not have any collaborative user, the UCCUFA is failure. If the cell is not in the routing, the issuer can execute the uncertainty expanding another time until finding enough collaborative users.

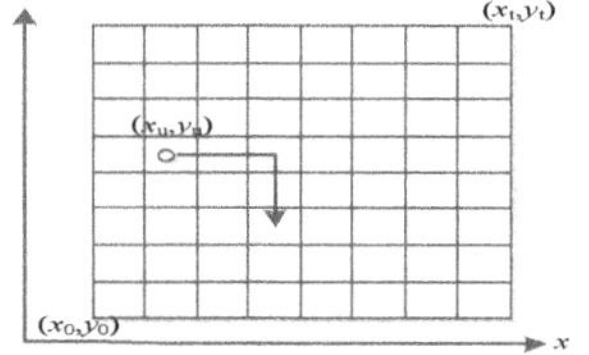

(a)The cells of continuous moving.

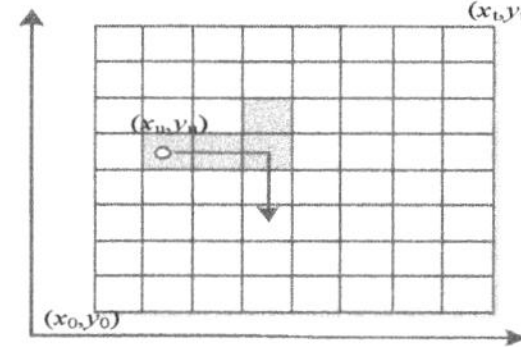

(b)The uncertainty of initial cell.

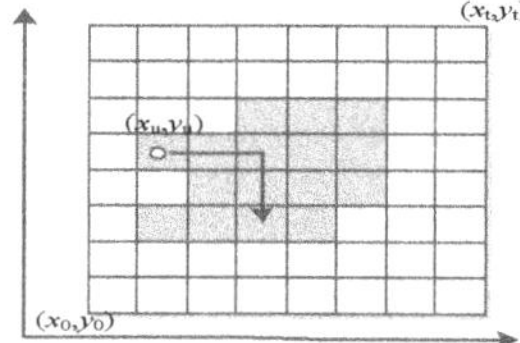

(c)The uncertainty of continuous cells.

Figure 2: The procedure of cells uncertainty expanding.

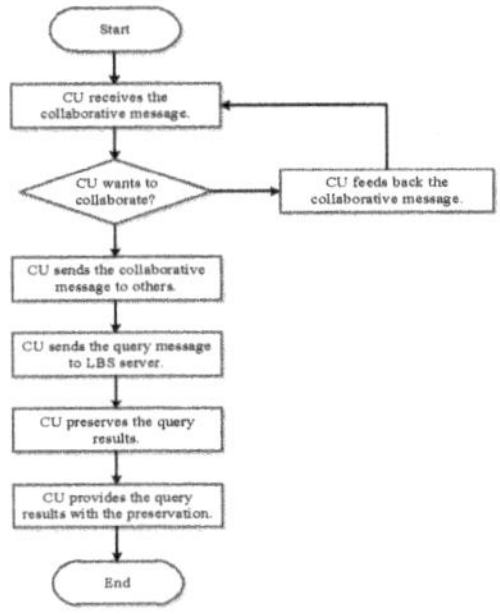

Figure 3: The procedure of the collaborative user.

3.3 Security Analysis

The security of UCCUFA can be reflected by the probability of the adversary guess the real trajectory. As we have depicted in the adversary model, the adversary can guess the real trajectory by getting rid off collaborative users. However, in UCCUFA the issuer does not submit any query to the LBS server and gets the query result from other collaborative users, which makes the adversary cannot correlate any location. For snapshot query, our algorithm requests the collaborative user who received the message also finds at least other k-1 users, these users can generalize the real cell, let alone the real location. Consider that the issuer wants n times query with k-anonymity, under the policy of UCCUFA, the issuer can generate at least $n*k$ cells in the best condition and at least n cells in the worst condition. However, the worst condition cannot exist, as the issuer can drop this result and initiate another expanding. Thus, collaborative users can be dispersed in at least $n*k/2$ cells, and the trajectories will increase into at least $n*k!/2$. This is difficult for the adversary identifies the real trajectory from the set of trajectories.

For the security of guessing the real location in per-query, as collaborative users also submit the query, which makes the adversary cannot distinguish who is the issuer. For other queries, each potential collaborative user has to find other users according to the principle of UCCUFA, and these users further generalize the real location of the issuer. Furthermore, as all results feed back from collaborative users during the routing, there is no interaction with the LBS server and further obscure the real location. At last, as the collaborative user submits the query with its own location, which makes the LBS server obtain a set of locations, and as we have depicted in the above example, the set contains at least $n*k/2$ locations, the success probability of guessing the real one may be $2/(n*k)$. Obviously, it is difficult for the adversary to identify the real location in per-query.

4 EXPERIMENTAL VERIFICATION

In order to demonstrate the superiority of UCCUFA, we check its performance in both of privacy protection effectiveness and the algorithm execution efficiency. We utilize the location data in BerlinMOD Data Set and implemented all algorithms by matlab 7 on a laptop with Intel Core i5 1.70 GHz CPU, 4 GB RAM memory, and Windows 7×64 ultimate operating system. Algorithms used in comparison contain R-cloak [9], QFPIR [10] and random-QBE [11] in snapshot query protection. In the continuous query, we utilize MobiCrowd [12], LTPPM and IRDA. At last, we can see the better algorithm will show a better performance in both of location privacy and algorithm execution. The superiority of our proposed algorithm can be seen from the level of location privacy protection and the performance of algorithm execution. The privacy level is measured by entropy in snapshot query and the variance of average pair entropy in continuous query. The performance of the algorithm can be seen in the average running time and the success anonymity ratio.

4.1 Experimental Results

From Figure 4, we can see that the UCCUFA can acquire the maximum value of entropy as algorithms of R-cloak, QFPIR and random-QBE. Thus, we can regard the UCCUFA as good as other algorithms.

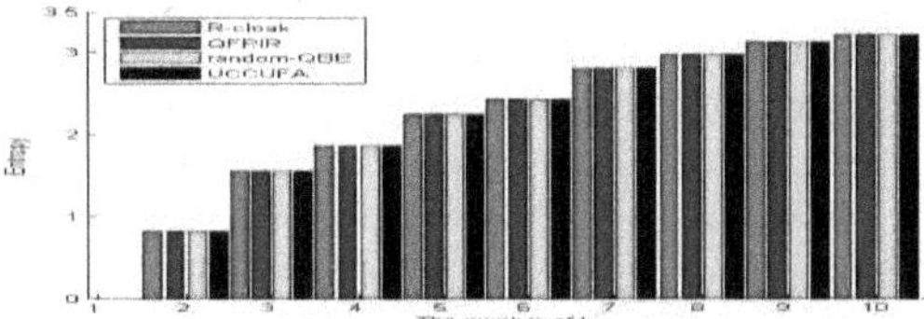

Figure 4: The entropy of snapshot query.

In Figure 5a, we can see the value of the variance of average pair entropy. As two locations in the routing of continuous query may be correlated by the adversary, and these correlations may affect the value of pair entropy then affect the value of the variance of average pair entropy, all algorithms may generate the value. In Figure 5b, we can also see algorithms of MobiCrowd and LTPPM have generated the value.

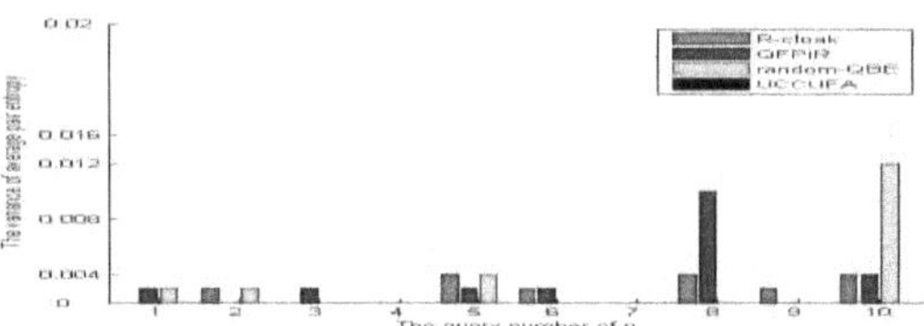

(a) The variance of average pair entropy in snapshot query.

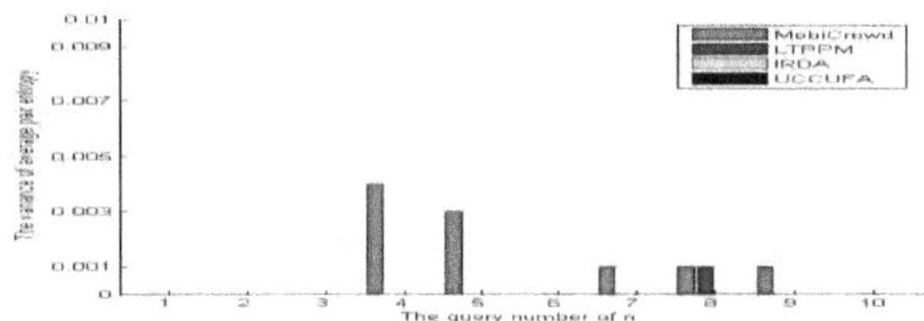

(b) The variance of average pair entropy in continuous query.

Figure5: The variance of average pair entropy in different algorithms.

This is because the user has to submit the query to the LBS server directly if there is no collaborative user. At last, we can see values of UCCUFA and IRDA are all equal to zero, as the user gets the query result from the collaborative user and has no interaction with the LBS server during the routing.

In Figure 6, we can see the average running time of different algorithms. In this figure,the average running time of UCCUFA is lower than others. Because of that this algorithm does not have to find collaborative users in per-query, and does not have to consider the anonymity of profile attributes as the query result is achieved from the collaborative users and there is no interaction with the LBS server.

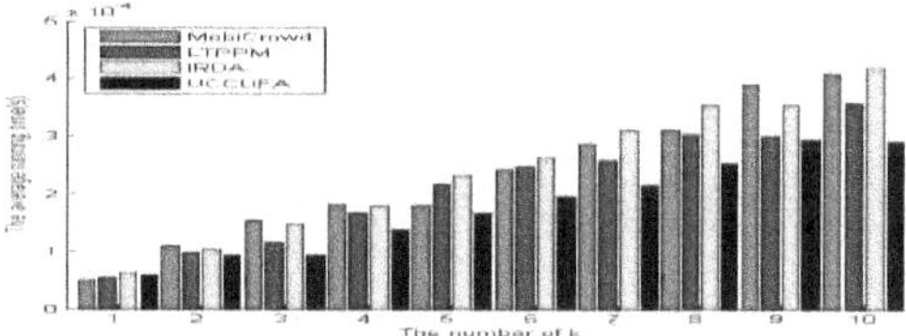

Figure 6: The average running time of different algorithms.

In Figure 7, the success anonymity ratio of different algorithms is shown. In this figure, as the collaborative user in UCCUFA can transfer the query to other collaborative user one by one, and the collaborative user can also initiate the procedure of another collaborative user finding, which makes this algorithm can find enough collaborative user and leads the higher of success anonymity ratio.

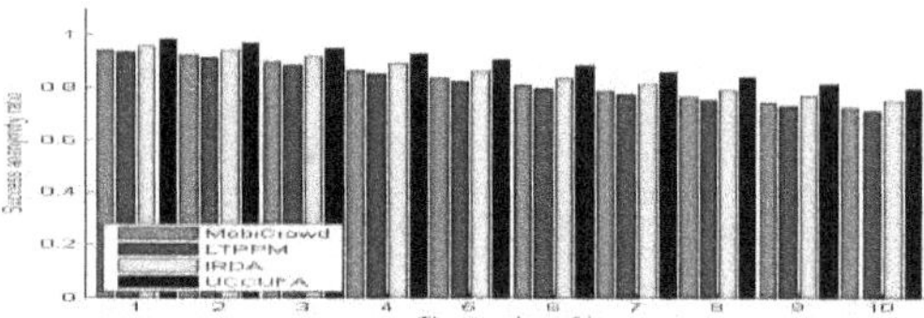

Figure 7: The success anonymity ratio of different algorithms.

5 CONCLUSION

In this paper, we propose the UCCUFA to cope with the problem of distributed architecture scheme insufficient in privacy protection of the continuous query. This algorithm utilizes the uncertainty expanding of cells in grid and muti-hop collaborative users finding to achieve the continuous location privacy protection. At last, we use security analysis as well as experimental results further verify the effectiveness of location privacy protection and the performance efficiency of our proposed algorithm, and this algorithm also has a better performance in the balance of privacy and the quality of service.

ACKNOWLEDGMENTS

This work was supported by the National Natural Science Foundation of China (Grant No. 61472097), the Specialized Research Fund for the Doctoral Program of Higher Education (Grant No. 20132304110017), the Natural Science Foundation of Heilongjiang Province of China (Grant No. F2015022)

REFERENCES

[1] CHOW, C.-Y., MOKBEL, M.F., and LIU, X., 2006. A peer-to-peer spatial cloaking algorithm for anonymous location-based service. In *Proceedings of the Proceedings of the 14th annual ACM international symposium on Advances in geographic information systems* (Arlington, Virginia, USA2006), ACM, 1183500, 171-178. DOI= http://dx.doi.org/10.1145/1183471.1183500.

[2] FUYU, L., HUA, K.A., and YING, C., 2009. Query l-diversity in location-based services. In *Mobile Data Management: Systems, Services and Middleware, 2009. MDM '09. Tenth International Conference on*, 436-442. DOI= http://dx.doi.org/10.1109/MDM.2009.72.

[3] GAO, S., MA, J.F., SHI, W.S., and ZHAN, G.X., 2015. LTPPM: a location and trajectory privacy protection mechanism in participatory sensing. *Wireless Communications & Mobile Computing 15*, 1 (Jan), 155-169. DOI= http://dx.doi.org/Doi 10.1002/Wcm.2324.

[4] GHINITA, G., KALNIS, P., KHOSHGOZARAN, A., SHAHABI, C., and TAN, K.-L., 2008. Private queries in location based services: anonymizers are not necessary. In *Proceedings of the Proceedings of the 2008 ACM SIGMOD international conference on Management of data* (Vancouver, Canada2008), ACM, 121-132. DOI= http://dx.doi.org/10.1145/1376616.1376631.

[5] GRUTESER, M. and GRUNWALD, D., 2003. Anonymous usage of location-based services through spatial and temporal cloaking. In *Proceedings of the 1st international conference on Mobile systems, applications and services* ACM, San Francisco, California, 31-42. DOI= http://dx.doi.org/10.1145/1066116.1189037.

[6] LEI, Z., CHUNGUANG, M., SONGTAO, Y., and XIAODONG, Z., 2016. Location privacy protection model and algorithm based on profiles generalization. *Systems engineering and electronics 38*, 12, 2894-2900.

[7] MA, C., ZHANG, L., YANG, S., ZHENG, X., and KE, P., 2016. Achieve personalized anonymity through query blocks exchanging. *China Communications 13*, 11, 106-118.

[8] NIU, B., ZHU, X.Y., LI, Q.H., CHEN, J., and LI, H., 2015. A novel attack to spatial cloaking schemes in location-based services. *Future Generation Computer Systems-the International Journal of Grid Computing and Escience 49*, 2015 (Aug), 125-132. DOI= http://dx.doi.org/10.1016/j.future.2014.10.026.

[9] REBOLLO-MONEDERO, D., FORNE, J., SOLANAS, A., and MARTINEZ-BALLESTE, A., 2010. Private location-based information retrieval through user collaboration. *Computer Communications 33*, 6 (Apr 15), 762-774. DOI= http://dx.doi.org/10.1016/j.comcom.2009.11.024.

[10] SCHLEGEL, R., CHOW, C.Y., HUANG, Q., and WONG, D.S., 2015. User-Defined privacy grid system for continuous location-based services. *Ieee Transactions on Mobile Computing 14*, 10 (Oct), 2158-2172. DOI= http://dx.doi.org/10.1109/tmc.2015.2388488.

[11] SHOKRI, R., THEODORAKOPOULOS, G., PAPADIMITRATOS, P., KAZEMI, E., and HUBAUX, J.P., 2014. Hiding in the mobile crowd: location privacy through collaboration. *Ieee Transactions on Dependable and Secure Computing 11*, 3 (May-Jun), 266-279. DOI= http://dx.doi.org/10.1109/tdsc.2013.57.

[12] SU, H., ZHENG, K., WANG, H., HUANG, J., and ZHOU, X., 2013. Calibrating trajectory data for similarity-based analysis. In *Proceedings of the 2013 ACM SIGMOD International Conference on Management of Data* ACM, 833-844.

Reverse Engineering Human Mobility in Large-scale Natural Disasters

Milan Stute, Max Maass, Tom Schons, and Matthias Hollick
Secure Mobile Networking Lab
Technische Universität Darmstadt
Darmstadt, Germany
firstname.lastname@seemoo.tu-darmstadt.de

ABSTRACT

Delay/Disruption-Tolerant Networks (DTNs) have been around for more than a decade and have especially been proposed to be used in scenarios where communication infrastructure is unavailable. In such scenarios, DTNs can offer a best-effort communication service by exploiting user mobility. Natural disasters are an important application scenario for DTNs when the cellular network is destroyed by natural forces. To assess the performance of such networks before deployment, we require appropriate knowledge of human mobility.

In this paper, we address this problem by designing, implementing, and evaluating a novel mobility model for large-scale natural disasters. Due to the lack of GPS traces, we reverse-engineer human mobility of past natural disasters (focusing on 2010 Haiti earthquake and 2013 Typhoon Haiyan) by leveraging knowledge of 126 experts from 71 Disaster Response Organizations (DROs). By means of simulation-based experiments, we compare and contrast our mobility model to other well-known models, and evaluate their impact on DTN performance. Finally, we make our source code available to the public.

KEYWORDS

Mobility model, disaster response, DTN

1 INTRODUCTION

Around the globe, we observe a continuous increase in natural disaster occurrences [11]. When a disaster strikes, the communication infrastructure is often destroyed or unavailable in the immediate aftermath which hinders effective disaster relief work [5, 7].

In the humanitarian sector, messaging applications have proved extremely helpful for both organizations as well as individuals as they facilitate coordination and broadcasting information to the public [6]. Smartphone-based DTNs present themselves as an attractive technology for message-based communication in disaster scenarios where the communication infrastructure is disrupted or destroyed as these devices are readily available [17]. DTNs are facilitated by user mobility as user devices act as data mules to carry messages from a to b. Clearly, the underlying human mobility greatly affects DTNs performance as disconnected network partitions are unable to communicate.

Current works on DTNs usually conduct simulation-based performance evaluations but are lacking realistic mobility models for large-scale natural disasters. This lack can be attributed to the unavailability of public mobility traces due to security and privacy concerns of cellular network operators as well as DROs. In this paper, we approach the problem by creating a disaster scenario mobility model based on expert knowledge. In particular, we make the following contributions which are relevant for both the opportunistic and ad hoc network as well as the disaster response communities:

- We model the mobility of disaster response teams as well as the local population in real large-scale natural disasters. Our model is based on expert knowledge, such as operational reports and conducted interviews, gathered from 126 individuals from 71 DROs.
- We characterize our mobility model and compare it with two other widely used models via simulation. In addition, we demonstrate the impact of mobility on DTN performance.
- We provide an open source implementation [23] of our *Natural Disaster* mobility model as well as two exemplary scenarios: the *2010 Haiti earthquake* [5] and the *2013 Typhoon Haiyan* [7].

The rest of the paper is structured as follows: we first revisit the state-of-the-art of mobility models and DTN simulation in Section 2. We explain our approach in Section 3. Then, we present our mobility model and scenario design in Section 4 and their implementation in Section 5. We analyze and evaluate the impact of our mobility model in Section 6 and, finally, conclude in Section 7.

2 RELATED WORK

Generic mobility models such as Random Waypoint (RWP) have been used to study the performance of mobile wireless networks such as DTNs. However, these models do not capture the non-randomness of human mobility and, therefore, produce questionable results when trying to understand network performance in realistic scenarios. To alleviate this problem, multiple works (see Table 1) have sought to create domain-specific models: [2] proposes *Disaster Area* which models disaster scenarios based on traces collected at a fire fighter manoeuvre. This model has been used multiple times to evaluate performance of mobile networks, e. g., [12, 20]. [10] proposes a micro-movement pattern generation framework for

MSWiM '17, November 21–25, 2017, Miami, FL, USA

ACM ISBN 978-1-4503-5162-1/17/11...$15.00
https://doi.org/10.1145/3127540.3127542

Table 1: Related publications on disaster and emergency response mobility models. (*) indicates a work that proposes a new model. Our work is printed in bold.

Work	Nodes	Area (m^2)	Duration	Mobility Model
[16]	100	1000	25 min	*Event–Role* *
[2]	150	350 × 200	27.7 h	*Disaster Area* *
[12]	≤ 80	700 × 600	10 min	*Disaster Area* [2]
[1]	≤ 200	≤ 550 × 500	30 min	*Disaster Area* [2]
[20]	200	550 × 500	5 min	*Disaster Area* [2]
[9]	150	350 × 200	1.1 h	*Disaster Area* [2]
[10]	100	6000 × 5000	35 h	*Search & Rescue* *
[25]	234	N/A	4 days	*Natural Disaster* *
–	**500**	**5000 × 7000**	**7 days**	***Natural Disaster*** *

search-and-rescue missions. [9] states the need for expert knowledge to create realistic scenarios. [25] is closest related to our work as they attempt to model a large-scale post-disaster scenario. However, they claim that "no documents/reports happen to describe the disaster operation in as detail as required to reproduce the scene by a simulator." In our work, we tackle precisely this problem and reverse-engineer human mobility at a granularity-level suitable for a simulator by using information from public and non-public documents and by conducting interviews with various International Disaster Response (IDR) experts.

3 METHODOLOGY

GPS mobility traces are the "holy grail" for creating accurate mobility models. Unfortunately, such ground truth data during and post disaster especially from Disaster Response Teams (DRTs) are not (publicly) available. This is due to the plain lack of records, strict data privacy laws, mobile network operators protecting their valuable business assets, as well as security concerns of DROs who do not wish to disclose sensitive location information of their staff, especially when operating in armed-conflict areas.

As a consequence, we follow an alternative approach: we base our mobility model on "soft" data, in particular, expert knowledge of various DROs. In order for this method to yield acceptable results, we need to ensure that (1) the model input is sufficiently fine-grained for extracting mobility patterns, (2) the model is verified by a group of experts.

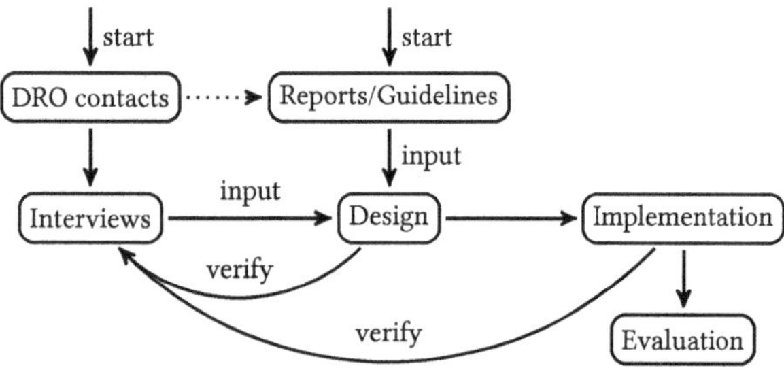

Figure 1: Our process for information gathering, model design and implementation, verification, and evaluation.

Unfortunately, documentation of the events during a disaster is often incomplete: media coverage of high-profile disaster is vast but articles typically lack technical details. Also, first responders and disaster relief workers are supposed to create daily reports but can often invest only minimal time as they prioritize actual life-saving work. This often leads incomplete or imprecise documentation unusable for our purposes. To understand IDR and eventually derive our mobility model, we gathered information from

(1) DRO policies, guidelines, strategies and fieldbooks partly gathered from online disaster response platforms, and
(2) individual (on-site) interviews with disaster relief experts.

Our approach is visualized in Fig. 1. During the process, we contacted 298 and received feedback from 126 IDR experts (42 % response rate). From the responders, we received additional information about their humanitarian activities, past mission reports, and pointers to other experts and contacts better suited for replying to our inquiry. In addition, we received access to exclusive online platforms and forums such as the Virtual On-Site Operations Coordination Centre (VOSOCC) of the UN Office for the Coordination of Humanitarian Affairs (OCHA), reliefweb.int, and humanitarianresponse.info. They contain field handbooks and guidelines for in-field operations which are not publicly accessible. Furthermore, we were able to conduct 15 on-site interviews with IDR experts and former disaster relief workers. Those experts were also involved in the verification loop from design to implementation.

4 DESIGN

In this section, we review past candidate events which qualify for our methodology. We then provide a detailed time-line of events for one recent high-profile disaster: 2013 Typhoon Haiyan. The same information for the 2010 Haiti earthquake is available in [22] but was omitted here for brevity. From the description and a number of policy documents and guidelines provided by DROs, we extract structured elements such as the different actors and their activities which we finally pour into a novel generic mobility model.

4.1 Scenario Selection Criteria

Table 2 lists recent natural disasters and their scale. We found that the following six factors are key for the creation of scenarios and models for DTN research in the area of natural disasters: (1) the number of *affected people* and (2) the size of the affected *area* both define the scope of the disaster; (3) *geographic conditions* are important as impassable natural obstacles such as rivers or lakes would partition the network and render a DTN deployment unusable; (4) the availability of *infrastructure* (bridges, airports, power plants, cellular network, etc.) after the disaster; and (5) strong international *response* by DROs as they are the sources for (6) sufficient, fine-grained *information* on the event. The latter is the most important factor for us as we base our model and scenario design solely on written and oral reports. Note that we did not include all presented factors in Table 2 due to space reasons, but provide an extended version in [22].

Table 2: Large-scale natural disasters in the last ten years. Ratings range from low (*) to high (***). Our scenarios are printed in bold. We selected Typhoon Haiyan as the running example for this paper.

Disaster	Year	Country	Killed	Injured	Displaced	Area (km^2)	Response	Information
Nepal earthquake	2015	Nepal	9 000	22 000	2 600 000	3 610	***	***
Cyclone Pam	2015	Vanuatu	24	30	3 300	12 190	**	**
Ludian earthquake	2014	China	617	2 400	229 700	1 487	*	*
Typhoon Haiyan	**2013**	**Philippines**	**6 300**	**28 689**	**6 000 000**	**71 503**	***	***
Christchurch earthquake	2011	New Zealand	185	2 000	–	1 426	**	***
East Africa drought	2011	East Africa	260 000	–	5 720 000	2 346 466	***	***
Tropical storm Washi	2011	Philippines	1 292	2 002	430 900	104 530	**	*
Tohoku earthquake	2011	Japan	15 894	6 152	340 000	83 955	**	***
Haiti earthquake	**2010**	**Haiti**	**316 000**	**300 000**	**895 000**	**27 750**	***	***
Afghanistan blizzard	2008	Afghanistan	926	100	–	652 864	*	*
Sichuan earthquake	2008	China	69 195	374 643	5 000 000	485 000	**	***
Cyclone Nargis	2008	Myanmar	138 000	–	800 000	676 578	**	**

4.2 2013 Typhoon Haiyan

We chose to re-create human mobility of the 2013 Typhoon Haiyan as media coverage and response was high, and communication infrastructure was dysfunctional during the first days. In this section, we will give an overview of the disaster and describe the situation in detail during the first week (days zero to six). The following information was gathered through interviews[1] with multiple first responder eyewitnesses from different relief organizations, as well as press articles about the relief efforts.

Summary. Typhoon Haiyan lasted from November 3rd to 11th, 2013 and was one of the strongest tropical cyclones ever recorded [18]. Even though typhoon Haiyan had devastating effects on large portions of Southeast Asia, for the purpose of this work we will focus on the aftermath of November 8th when Typhoon Haiyan hit the Philippines at 04:40 local time. Haiyan was the deadliest and most damaging Philippine typhoon on record and left more than one million houses partially or totally damaged, killing at least 6 300 people and leaving numerous injured and homeless [15]. Typhoon Haiyan was ranked as a category 5 typhoon, the highest category by the definition of the Saffir–Simpson Hurricane Wind Scale (SSHWS), implying that "catastrophic damage will occur" and "most of the area will be uninhabitable for weeks or months." After the storm had passed, widespread damage became visible with power lines cut off, roads blocked by fallen debris, and trees and buildings collapsed under the strong winds [19]. A 2013 preliminary estimate [14] calculated the total damage related to typhoon Haiyan to be around 2.86 billion US$. Figure 2 depicts the city of Tacloban and its surroundings, which were severely hit by Typhoon Haiyan, and is intended to provide visual guidance to the reader for a better understanding of the upcoming sections.

Right after the disaster had hit the Philippines, many officials concluded that even though early warnings had been issued to the population of potentially affected areas, only few people actually evacuated. This was likely related to the high number of smaller typhoons the Philippines experience every year, which led to the population underestimating the severity of the coming typhoon. Warnings were broadcast on TV and radio, but went largely unheeded. The typhoon was accompanied by the biggest storm surge ever experienced within the Philippines, reportedly reaching between four to six meters in height [24]. This resulted in fast-rising tides and surge water brought by the typhoon, which led to many additional fatalities [4].

Day 0. In the aftermath of the typhoon, the immediate arrival of DRTs was hindered by the severe damage the airport had sustained. Therefore, many DRTs were rerouted to the airport of the nearby island of Cebu, which was still operational. From there, they had to travel to Tacloban using other means, which took around 8 hours. This slowed down the initial arrival of DRTs considerably. Despite the damage, a number of airplanes and helicopters managed to land in Tacloban, delivering aid and personnel. The newly arrived DRTs registered at the Reception/Departure Centre (RDC) before proceeding into the city to reach the On-Site Operations Coordination Centre (OSOCC). There were also a number of storm chasers and typhoon experts already on the ground when Haiyan made landfall. In search of scientific evidence, they moved through the city before, during and after the typhoon. (For our mobility model, we will assume that they are distributed randomly throughout the city.) The local population spent the storm in their homes or shelters. After the storm had passed, eyewitnesses report that most of the population seemed to wander around the perimeter of their home or shelter area, overwhelmed by the destruction caused by the storm, or trying to help their neighbors. (For our mobility model, we will assume their locations to be randomly spread throughout the city.) At the end of the day, DRTs and experts alike returned to their respective sleeping spots.

Day 1 to 3. On the first day after the disaster, the US Navy deployed radar equipment to the Tacloban airport, allowing it to be re-opened in short order. This allowed a greater number of DRTs and relief goods to arrive close to the city, leading to more travel between the airport and the city. Arriving DRTs reported at the RDC and then proceeded to the OSOCC, which was located in the city center. Afterwards, they traveled to the base camp of

[1] Interview notes are available upon request.

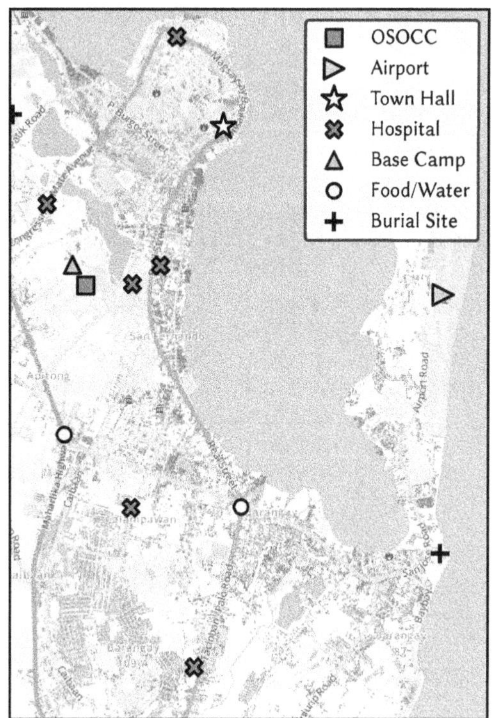

Figure 2: City of Tacloban with locations of IDR-relevant sites in the early aftermath of 2013 Typhoon Haiyan.

their organization and began their relief efforts. The initial focus of most DRTs lies with Search and Rescue Operations (SROs), as the likelihood of finding survivors drops with every hour. Urban Search and Rescue Teams (USRTs) have a large number of different search strategies. (For the purpose of the movement model, we implement a basic strategy: a start area is chosen, and the team searches every house along that street before spreading out to the next street in the direct neighborhood.) Eyewitnesses indicate that during the first three days, the civilian population was mostly concerned with search for food and the rebuilding of their homes or temporary shelters. Healthy survivors assisted with local search and rescue efforts and cleared the street from debris, staying in the general area of their homes or shelters. Injured survivors were transported to one of the partially operational city hospitals, which were quickly filled to capacity. As the government still remained in office, the relief organizations had to coordinate with country officials. This led to some traffic between the city hall and OSOCC. The United Nations (UN) rented a hotel as a temporary office location for the duration of the rebuilding efforts.[2] All DRTs continued to return to their respective base camps for the night.

Day 4 to 6. SROs were reduced and came to a stop at the end of the first week, as the chance of finding survivors drops significantly after several days. After about one week, most of the USRTs are replaced by teams specialized in other forms of disaster relief. The distribution of food and clean water remained a challenge, as the infrastructure was severely damaged by the typhoon. Much of the local population had to collect food and water from distribution points around the city on a daily basis. The local population assisted DRTs in clearing the roads of debris to allow trucks to pass through them. The government also ordered the removal of dead bodies to prevent the spread of diseases. The US Marines started flying out injured locals and exhausted relief workers alike. At the same time, new DRTs were still arriving via the airport, following the same procedure as previously described.

After Week 1. We stop our description of the events after the first week. At this time, locals had slowly begun to resume a semblance of their normal lives, and the scenario gradually transforms into a scenario of daily routine, where a dedicated mobility model no longer applies. For the same reason, we did not consider that most DROs have a rotation mechanism for their employees, which prevents them from becoming mentally and physically exhausted from the demanding work in disaster relief.

4.3 Natural Disaster Mobility Model

Based on the information gathered for specific disasters, we extract recurring behavioral patterns of the various entities involved in disaster relief work. To this end, we define *roles* and role-specific *activities*, and also consider movement *speed*.

Roles. We identified the main stakeholders in natural disaster-struck areas (scenario-independent) and defined the following seven roles with distinct behavioral patterns: (1) healthy local population, (2) injured local population, (3) Disaster Response Teams (DRTs) from DROs, (4) dedicated Urban Search and Rescue Teams (USRTs), (5) scientists (storm chasers, typhoon experts, etc.), (6) UN officials, and (7) government officials.

Activities. To create a model, we further need to define activities that regularly occur in disaster areas that can be attributed to specific roles. Figure 3 summarizes the various activities by showing the coarse locations of each role during the course of the first week. What follows is a detailed but non-exhaustive description of important activities that have been identified during the interviews with IDR experts.

Activities applying to everyone. In the evening, everyone goes to their respective base camp, home, or shelter to sleep. Those arriving via the airport (e. g., DROs), at the day of arrival, first go to the RDC for registration, then visit the OSOCC, and finally set up the base camp or sleeping place.

Activities applying to DROs and DRTs. After arriving and registering at the airport, they go to the OSOCC or the town hall for a situation briefing and then start to help the affected population with one of the following activities: (*i*) collect dead bodies and organize burials; (*ii*) walk the main streets of the city and clean streets from debris, such that supplies can be delivered; or (*iii*) go to food and water distribution centers to serve the locals until the end of the day. Besides that, they regularly visit the UN hotel, the OSOCC site, the base camp, or town hall to meet with officials and other DROs.

Activities applying to UN and government officials. Officials regularly (at least daily) visit the OSOCC, the town hall or base camp, for a situation briefing and meet other officials and DROs. During the day, they perform reconnaissance missions to get an situation overview such as infrastructural damage. This information is used

[2] We were asked not to publish the location of the hotel, so we randomly chose a hotel in the city for the purposes of the simulation.

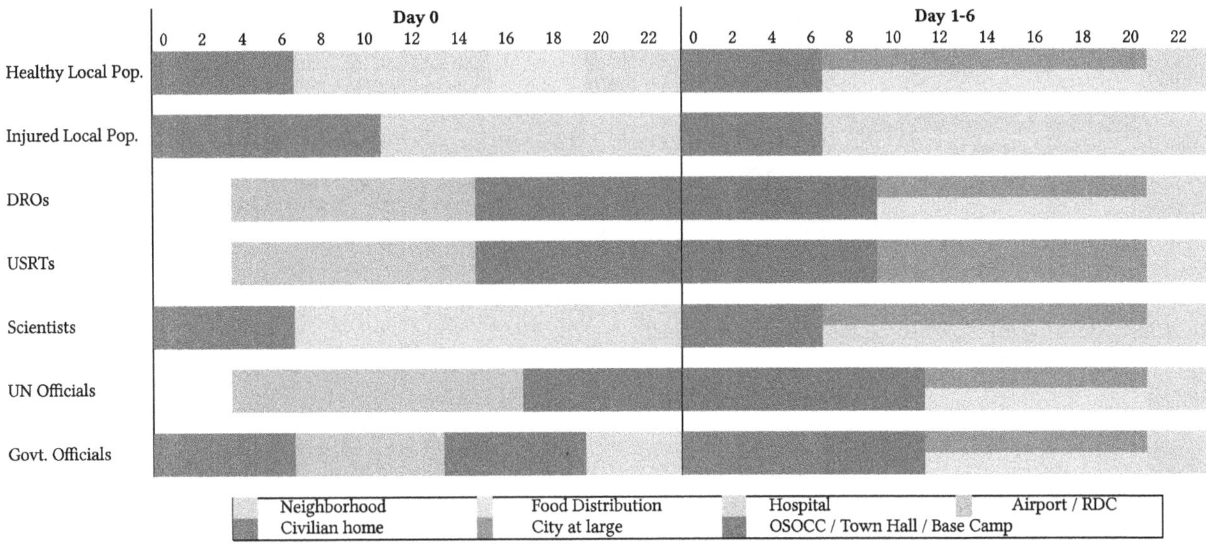

Figure 3: Activity-based location of different groups over time. Time values are indicative, i. e., activities do not start exactly at the same time but with a random jitter of one or two hours.

to provision help. Also, they organize the disaster relief efforts with other officials and DROs such as setting up food and water distribution spots, organizing burials, etc.

Activities applying to scientists. Within the first two to three days, they collect scientific evidence from the disaster site before the cleaning of the rubble and debris starts. When their job is done, they either leave the area via the airport, or decide to volunteer and help the DROs.

Activities applying to USRT. After arriving and registering at the airport, they go to the OSOCC for a situation briefing and SRO planning. When starting an SRO, USRTs go to the chosen location in the morning and then search every house in that street. When done, they repeat with next street in the direct neighborhood. Usually, SROs are stopped after one week as the chances to find survivors diminish, and USRTs fly back home.

Activities applying to healthy local population. According to eye witnesses, most locals stay at home or try to find friends and family members within the immediate surroundings after the disaster has struck. Later on the first day, they stay in the proximity of their homes to assess the damage and to help their neighbors. Then, they start to look for food and water, for example, at distribution centers where they will return on a daily basis. The rest of the day, they either volunteer for cleaning operations (we model this by slowly roaming around the city), or as replacement of security personnel to patrol the area.

Activities applying to injured local population. Depending on the severeness, the injured stay at home if they are unable to move, or try to go to the closest hospital as soon as possible. Upon arrival, they stay at the hospital if its capacity is not exhausted or leave to find another one otherwise.

Typhoon Haiyan Arrival Times. Most scientists, particularly storm chasers and typhoon experts were already present prior to the occurrence of the disaster. Furthermore, government officials were already present prior to the disaster, while UN officials arrived after the disaster had struck. DROs and USRTs mainly arrived via the airport during the first days after the disaster as they were delayed due to the damaged airport. However, some had been prepositioned to locations close to the affected area and arrived on day zero.

Movement Speed. For the purpose of this work, we consider walking the only viable form of movement. This is due to the fact that within disaster-struck areas, debris, flood/surge water, or earthquakes often render streets completely unusable for cars and trucks until they can be repaired. This means that all entities move approximately at walking speed. Nevertheless, there are slight differences depending on the entity's role. For example, injured individuals and heavily equipped USRTs will be slower than normal. Note that our model could be extended to support faster-traveling vehicles, but would require additional scenario-specific information currently unavailable to us, such as who has access to vehicles and which streets are passable.

5 IMPLEMENTATION

In this section, we briefly describe the implementation of our generic Natural Disaster *mobility model* and the workflow for generating specific *scenarios.* This is a trade-off between code re-usability (reoccurring behavioral patterns of certain groups such as DROs and the local population) and acknowledging the uniqueness of every disaster (terrain, streets, point of interests (POIs), arrival times, population density, etc.)

Mobility Model. We implement our mobility model directly as a module for the Opportunistic Network Simulator (ONE) [8] as we are concerned with DTN simulation. Our model implements the different roles and activities as defined in Section 4. These roles and activities have been observed in different disasters (Table 2) and as such are generally independent of the scenario instance. Nevertheless, our model can only operate on a specific *scenario.*

Scenario. A *scenario* describes the prevailing conditions of a specific post-disaster situation. In particular, the scenario comprises

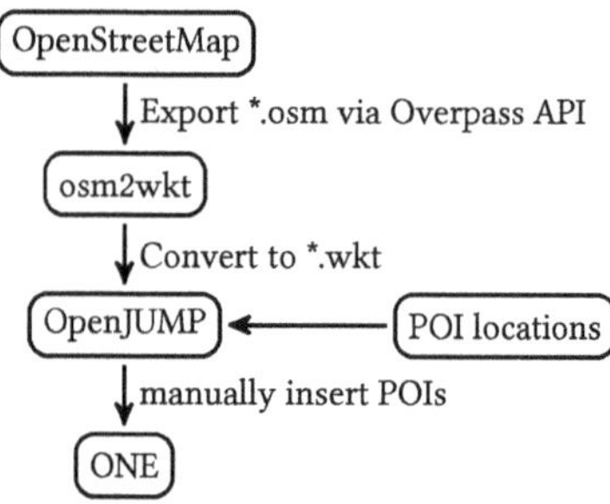

Figure 4: Technical workflow for generating a *scenario*'s map data for our Natural Disaster mobility model.

the number of actors as well as a street map including different POIs of the affected area. We generate the map data using a number of tools shown in Fig. 4: we start with exporting OpenStreetMap data and converting it to the Well-Known Text (.wkt) file format using *osm2wkt* [13]. Finally, we use *OpenJUMP* to add POI locations, such as the OSOCC, airports, and hospitals as shown in Fig. 2. The .wkt files can then be processed by our mobility model implemented in the ONE. In this paper, we only focus on the area around the city of Tacloban which was severely hit by Typhoon Haiyan. However, we have also implemented a scenario for the 2010 Haiti earthquake (Port-au-Prince and surroundings) which is discussed in [22] and included in our source code [23]. Using our model, workflow, and explanations in [22], third parties are able to create additional scenarios. In addition, our implementation is open to extensions such as more detailed activities, vehicle support, etc.

6 EVALUATION

In this section, we want to (*i*) visually validate our mobility model (*ND*), (*ii*) identify qualitative differences between *ND* and other contemporary models, (*iii*) assess the impact that different mobility models have DTN performance, and finally (*iv*) give actionable advice to DTN protocol designers. To this end, we compare *ND* with two other widely used models: the Random Waypoint Mobility model (*RWP*) and a map-based RWP model (*Map*) where waypoint selection is still random, but node movement is confined to a street grid. We selected the *epidemic* DTN routing protocol for the network performance analysis as its simple design facilitates reasoning about the results. For all experiments, we rely on the ONE simulator v1.6.0 [8]. Each experiment is averaged over 10 independently seeded runs. We summarize the most important simulation settings in Table 3 and refer to our source code [23] for all details. For reproducibility, we also publish our experiment data set [21].

We note the limitation of our simulation setup with only 500 nodes. Even though our mobility model supports an arbitrary number of nodes, current network simulators (ONE, ns-2/3, etc.) do not scale to a large number of nodes, e. g., the population size in an urban area (order of 10^6). However, as we will show, we can demonstrate qualitative differences between the different mobility models already with a rather low number of nodes. We also note that in our traffic model, sources and destinations as well as messages sizes are arbitrarily chosen. A realistic communication model would be incredibly useful but is orthogonal to our work.

Table 3: The ONE Simulation Settings

Scenario	Dimensions	$5000 \times 7000\,\mathrm{m}^2$ (Tacloban)
	Simulation time	7 days
	Nodes	500
Mobility	Model	*RWP, Map, ND*
	Speed (m/s)	0.5–1.5 ≈ walking speed
Routing	Algorithm	*Epidemic*
	Buffer size	20 MB
Taffic	Msg. interval	8–12 s
	Msg. TTL	6 h
	Msg. size	50–100 KB
Comm.	PHY rate	2 Mbit/s ≈ Bluetooth
	Radio range	10 m

6.1 Characterizing Mobility

We are interested in the spatial node distribution and encounters that occur during a disaster since they both affect the applicability of a DTN: node hot spots can function as communication hubs where messages are quickly exchanged, while nodes that have a lot of encounters can act as "data mules" and transport messages over larger distances.

Spatial Node Distribution. We visualize the spatial node distribution of the three mobility models using a scatter-plot heatmap in Fig. 5. In Fig. 5a, we identify the typical non-uniform center-weighted distribution [3] of the *RWP* model. From a practical perspective, this means that nodes are moving across inaccessible areas, for example, a bay. In contrast, *Map* and *ND* (Figs. 5b and 5c) essentially "redraw" the underlying street grid. Here, the nodes' movements are confined to streets and paths and are thus no longer moving across water. However, node distribution in *Map* across streets appears generally uniform. There are only minor hot spots at street intersections which are expected since movement trajectories cross there. In general, nodes are located with similar probabilities at any point in the map. Figure 5c shows that *ND* exhibits characteristic hot spots that can be mapped to certain POIs in the street map (Fig. 5d) where many nodes stay for a longer period of time. Most prevalent are the locations of the OSOCC and the base camp as they are frequented by DRTs and officials. In addition, we can also make out other hot spots at the city hall and the food and water distribution points. In the simulation, the airport is the location for inactive nodes, that is, those nodes that have not yet arrived and those that have already left. The hot spots around the airport can therefore be considered an artifact as the simulator does not support removing nodes from a running simulation.

Encounters. An *encounter* is a transmission opportunity which occurs if two nodes move in each other's transmission range. DTNs performance highly depends on the number of encounters a node makes while moving around. For example: if a node encounters the destination of any currently carried message, it can directly deliver it. The advantage of direct delivery is that it prevents the replication overhead to intermediate nodes in form of radio transmissions and storage consumption. So, in a scenario where communicating parties are generally physically close to one another, or at least meet regularly, a DTN deployment could exclusively rely on direct

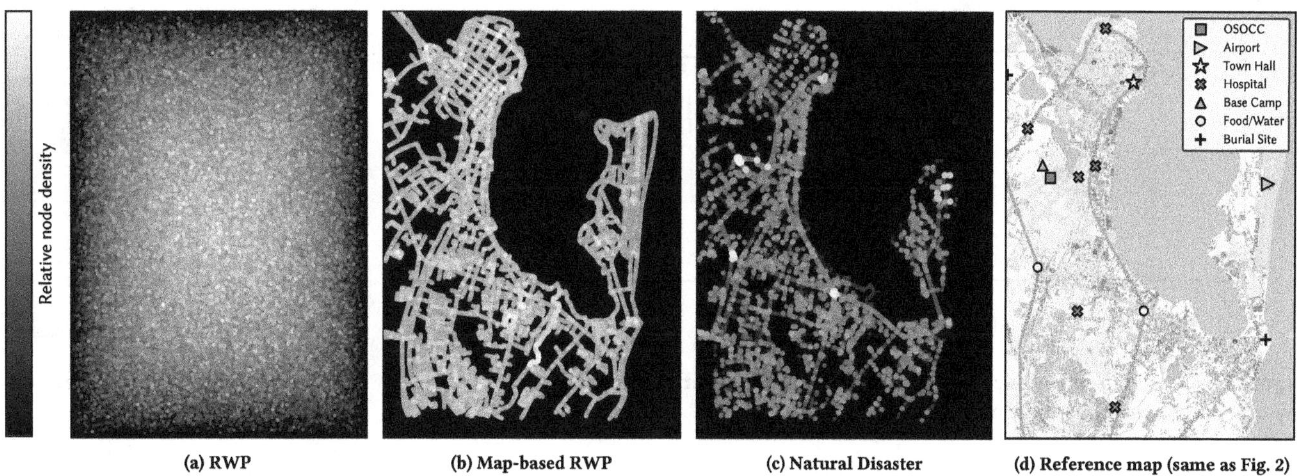

(a) RWP (b) Map-based RWP (c) Natural Disaster (d) Reference map (same as Fig. 2)

Figure 5: Spatial node distribution in different mobility models averaged over 7 days. Node counts are sampled from a grid of 10 × 10 m squares. Circle sizes and colors scale logarithmically with node count to highlight hot spots.

deliveries. Therefore, assessing the encounter characteristics of the underlying mobility model in a scenario is of utmost importance to understand which protocols are suitable for a natural disaster scenario. In Fig. 6, we observe that in *ND*, the local population groups (healthy and injured) make significantly fewer contacts than the other groups. Especially the injured encounter very few other nodes. On the other hand, DRO teams as well as government and UN officials make significantly more contacts due to regular meetings at the OSOCC, in the town hall, and in the base camps. In the *RWP* and *Map* models, the number of encounters solely depends on the average velocity of the user role. For example, injured as well as heavily equipped USRTs move slower than the other groups. The generally low number of encounters of *RWP* can be explained by the low node density in combination with the low transmission range: as the nodes freely move around the large area, nodes only infrequently move into each others transmission range.

6.2 Characterizing Network Performance

We evaluate the impact of our mobility model on network performance. For this, we measure the delivery rate and delay, the buffer occupancy, as well as the delivery rate for the different roles.

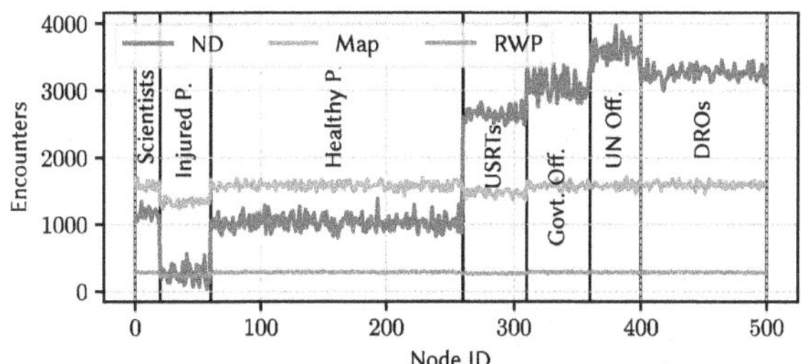

Figure 6: Number of encounters per node (1 week).

In Fig. 7, we observe that the delivery delay short in *ND*, meaning that about 80 % of all delivered messages are delivered within three hours, which appears to be due to the regular meetings at certain POIs. However, we can see in Fig. 9 that delivery success is highly heterogeneous with respect to the user role in *ND*. We observe that the most successful communication partners are the ones that make the most encounters, in particular, DROs, USRTs, and government/UN officials. These are the groups that can rely on message deliveries the most and are, thus, the main beneficiaries of the communication network. On the other hand, less mobile nodes, especially the injured population, are poorly connected to the rest. Without special treatment (e. g., via prioritization), these users will be insufficiently served by the network. In *RWP* and *Map*, performance is almost uniform across the different group (not shown here). The overall delivery success of *ND* is lower than for *Map* which is likely due to the fact that at night, when mobility is low, only few messages are delivered. This is supported by Fig. 8 which shows that buffer occupancy is depending on the time of day. During the night, undelivered messages expire and nodes remove them from their buffers. Starting around noon, buffers refill with new messages as nodes travel across the map and collect messages from others, leading to more message deliveries during the day. Note that the delivery success over time is not shown here for space reasons, but follows the same cyclic behavior as the buffer occupancy.

7 CONCLUSION

DTNs could greatly facilitate disaster response communications as they allow message-based communication even in the absence of supporting infrastructure. However, so far, the communication community has yet to prove the practicality of DTNs for such scenarios. In this paper, we have shown the feasibility of reverse engineering human mobility solely by written or oral reports and have extract general as well as scenario-specific features and patterns. Based on two exemplary scenario, we were able to assess the performance of DTNs in large-scale natural disasters as a backup for

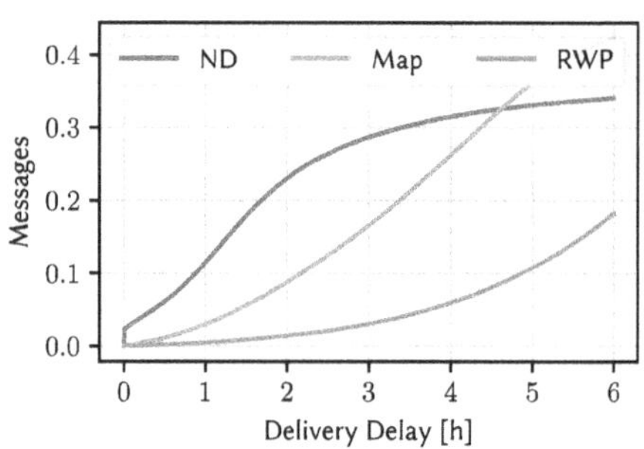

Figure 7: Message delivery success and delay as a cumulative distribution function.

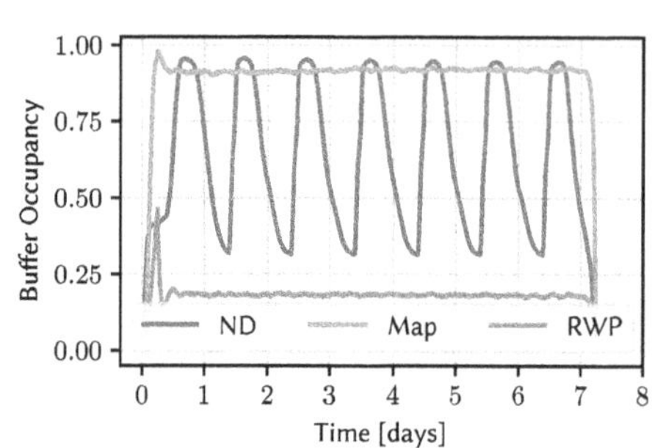

Figure 8: Buffer occupancy over time.

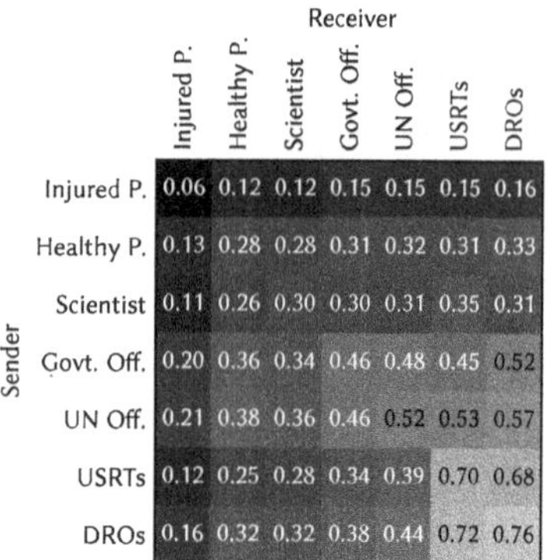

Figure 9: Delivery rates between roles (*ND*).

infrastructure-based communication, and develop a tool for future works in this area. In particular, we observed that a DTN deployment could be most useful for disaster relief workers due to regular meetings, while the population benefits to a lesser degree. Based on these observations, we give advice to DTN designers such as preferring frequently traveling nodes as relays and exploiting hot spots by deploying fixed DTN nodes to serve as information exchange hubs. In the future, we could increase the level of detail in our mobility model, for example, by including vehicles. Our network performance evaluation could be extended, which would require to increase the scalability of current simulators to support simulations with significantly more nodes. Finally, a realistic communication model of all users in a disaster scenario would complement our mobility model since communication patterns and user mobility are the two main factors influencing DTN performance.

ACKNOWLEDGMENTS

The authors would like to express their sincere gratitude towards all cooperating individuals from the following national and international organizations: Caritas (AT), Berufsfeuerwehr Bochum (DE), Johanniter (DE), Red Cross (DE), Technisches Hilfswerk (DE), emergency.lu (LU), Humanitarian Intervention Team (LU), Ministry of Foreign Affairs (LU), Concern Worldwide, Plan International, ZOA International, Emergency Telecommunication Cluster (ETC), Global Disaster Alert and Coordination System (GDACS), Office for the Coordination of Humanitarian Affairs (OCHA), United Nations Organizations (UNO), United Nations Office for Disaster Risk Reduction (UNISDR), World Food Program (WFP), and many others who wished to remain anonymous.

This work has been co-funded by the LOEWE initiative within the NICER project, and by the DFG as part of project C.1 within the RTG 2050 "Privacy and Trust for Mobile Users."

REFERENCES

[1] N. Aschenbruck, M. Frank, P. Martini, and J. Tolle. 2004. Human Mobility in MANET Disaster Area Simulation – A Realistic Approach. In *IEEE LCN*.

[2] N. Aschenbruck, E. Gerhards-Padilla, and P. Martini. 2009. Modeling mobility in disaster area scenarios. *Elsevier Performance Evaluation* 66, 12 (2009).

[3] C. Bettstetter, G. Resta, and P. Santi. 2003. The node distribution of the random waypoint mobility model for wireless ad hoc networks. *IEEE Transactions on Mobile Computing* 2, 3 (July 2003), 257–269.

[4] Dailymotion. 2013. Megastorm: Worlds Biggest Typhoon. (2013). http://www.dailymotion.com/video/x186qfd_megastorm-worlds-biggest-typhoon_shortfilms

[5] H. Goldstein. 2010. Engineers Race to Restore Communications after Haiti Quake. *IEEE Spectrum* (19 Jan. 2010).

[6] ICRC, The Engien Room, and Block Party. 2017. *Humanitarian Futures for Messaging Apps*. Technical Report.

[7] IRIN News. 2013. Life-saving radio begins broadcasting in typhoon-hit Tacloban. (2013). http://www.irinnews.org/report/99132/life-saving-radio-begins-broadcasting-typhoon-hit-tacloban

[8] A. Keränen, J. Ott, and T. Kärkkäinen. 2009. The ONE simulator for DTN protocol evaluation. In *ICST Conference on Simulation Tools and Techniques (SIMUTools'09)*.

[9] S. Krug, S. Schellenberg, and J. Seitz. 2015. Impact of Traffic and Mobility Patterns on Network Performance in Disaster Scenarios. In *ACM CHANTS*.

[10] S. Krug, M. F. Siracusa, S. Schellenberg, P. Begerow, J. Seitz, T. Finke, and J. Schroeder. 2014. Movement patterns for mobile networks in disaster scenarios. In *IEEE WoWMoM*.

[11] J. Leaning. 2013. Natural Disasters, Armed Conflict, and Public Health. *The New England Journal of Medicine* (2013).

[12] A. Martín-Campillo, J. Crowcroft, E. Yoneki, and R. Martí. 2013. Evaluating opportunistic networks in disaster scenarios. *Journal of Network and Computer Applications* 36, 2 (March 2013).

[13] C. P. Mayer. 2010. osm2wkt – OpenStreetMap to WKT Conversion. http://www.chrismc.de/osm2wkt. (2010).

[14] NDRRMC. 2013. Final Report – Effects on Typhoon "Yolanda" (Haiyan). (Nov. 2013). http://www.ndrrmc.gov.ph/attachments/article/1329/FINAL_REPORT_re_Effects_of_Typhoon_YOLANDA_(HAIYAN)_06-09NOV2013.pdf

[15] NDRRMC. 2013. Situation Update - Effects of Yolanda. (2013). https://web.archive.org/web/20161208214400/http://www.ndrrmc.gov.ph/attachments/article/1177/Update/%20Effects/%20TY/%20YOLANDA/%2017/%20April/%202014.pdf

[16] S. C. Nelson, A. F. Harris III, and R. Kravets. 2007. Event-driven, role-based mobility in disaster recovery networks. In *ACM CHANTS*.

[17] H. Nishiyama, N. Ito, and N. Kato. 2014. Relay-by-smartphone: realizing multihop device-to-device communications. *IEEE Communications Magazine* 52, 4 (2014).

[18] NPR. 2013. Why Typhoon Haiyan Caused So Much Damage. (2013). http://www.npr.org/2013/11/11/244572227/why-typhoon-haiyan-caused-so-much-damage

[19] International Charter on Space and Major Disasters. 2013. Activation – Typhoon Haiyan in the Philippines. (2013). https://www.disasterscharter.org/web/guest/-/typhoon-haiyan-in-the-philippin-5

[20] D. G. Reina. 2012. Modeling and assessing ad hoc networks in disaster scenarios. *Journal of Ambient Intelligence and Humanized Computing* (2012).

[21] M. Schmittner. 2017. Experimental Data for Natural Disaster Mobility Model and Typhoon Haiyan Scenario. (2017). https://doi.org/10.5281/zenodo.836815

[22] T. Schons. 2017. Design, Implementation and Evaluation of Realistic Scenarios and Movement Models for Natural Disasters Using Simulation for Delay Tolerant Networks. (Jan. 2017).

[23] T. Schons. 2017. Natural Disaster Mobility Model and Scenarios Source Code. (2017). https://github.com/seemoo-lab/natural-disaster-mobility

[24] The Telegraph. 2013. Super Typhoon Haiyan smashes into Philippines. (2013). http://www.telegraph.co.uk/news/worldnews/asia/philippines/10434846/Super-Typhoon-Haiyan-smashes-into-Philippines.html

[25] M. Y. S. Uddin, D. M. Nicol, T. F. Abdelzaher, and R. H. Kravets. 2009. A post-disaster mobility model for Delay Tolerant Networking. In *Winter Simulation Conference (WSC)*.

SMAFramework

Urban Data Integration Framework for Mobility Analysis in Smart Cities

Diego O. Rodrigues
University of Campinas
Campinas, Brazil
diego@lrc.ic.unicamp.br
University of Ottawa
Ottawa, Canada
doliv040@uottawa.ca

Azzedine Boukerche
School of Electrical Engineering and Computer Science, University of Ottawa
Ottawa, Canada
boukerch@site.uottawa.ca

Thiago H. Silva
Dept. of Informatics, Federal University of Technology of Paraná
Curitiba, Brazil
thiagoh@utfpr.edu.br

Antonio A. F. Loureiro
Dept of Computer Science, Federal University of Minas Gerais
Belo Horizonte, Brazil
loureiro@dcc.ufmg.br

Leandro A. Villas
Institute of Computing, University of Campinas
Campinas, Brazil
leandro@ic.unicamp.br

ABSTRACT

Smart cities emerge as a topic to cover how the technology of information and communication can be used in the urban centers to monitor its dynamics and allow the improvement of services for the citizens. In these urban centers, different methodologies are used in order to collect data and provide them to applications. These data come from several heterogeneous sources, thus there is an effort to integrate and standardize them before their use. Also, a significant amount of this data has spatio-temporal annotations, which may be used to analyze the city dynamics, such as the mobility flow. Due to these characteristics of the data generated in urban centers, and also the possibilities brought by their use and analyses, this work presents a novel approach to collect, integrate and perform some analysis tasks in mobility data from smart cities. Thus, the SMAFramework can analyze mobility patterns based on a Multi-Aspect Graph (MAG) data structure. To show the potential of the framework, it is proposed a method to analyze the saptio-temporal correlation between data from two different data sources in the same city. Real data collected from social media and a taxi system of the city of New York are used to evaluate this method. The obtained results allowed to understand some of the applicabilities of the framework and also provided some insights on how to use the framework to resolve specific problems when analyzing mobility in urban environments.

CCS CONCEPTS

•**Computing methodologies** → *Modeling methodologies;*

KEYWORDS

Smart Cities, Mobility Analysis, Big Data, Urban Data

MSWiM'17, November 21–25, 2017, Miami, FL, USA
© 2017 ACM. ACM ISBN 978-1-4503-5162-1/17/11...$15.00.
DOI: http://dx.doi.org/10.1145/3127540.3127569

1 INTRODUCTION

Recently, the complexity of cities has increased considerably due to several factors such as the bigger number of inhabitants living in urban environments [15]. With that, urban computing has emerged as a topic in computer science envisioning the application of information and communication technology to improve services provided to city dwellers [15, 19, 31]. Through the improvement of city services, the new cities, also called smart cities, have the opportunity to offer a better quality of life to their inhabitants in different aspects, ranging from more efficient city mobility and less bureaucratic and transparent governmental processes.

In order to achieve that, it is fundamental to obtain data to better understand the city functioning. Data generated by cities can be originated from different sources. For example, one typical approach is to use the traditional sensor networks that can be seen as a sensing layer of a particular phenomenon. There are several types of sensors available nowadays, and the combination of different sensor networks may allow the understanding of complex phenomena. However, building sensor networks may not be scalable in certain circumstances, for instance, to cover a metropolitan area [24]. Thus, a useful alternative is to consider user participation in the sensing process, where users with their mobile devices act as sensors in the city. This approach has become practical due to the decrease of the prices of mobile devices (e.g., smartphones) and the popularization of location-based social networks, such as Twitter, Instagram, and Foursquare [7, 24].

Several approaches have been used to analyze data collected from single urban data sources and led to remarkable results. However, methodologies to explore data from multiple sources still need to be further investigated [17, 25]. Particularly, to combine urban data to obtain more precise insights about the city impose several issues, among them data integration [17, 25, 32]. This issue is especially critical for spatio-temporal data, data of a phenomenon containing geographic coordinates and annotations about the time when it happened.

Knowing that representing and integrating different sources of spatio-temporal data is a challenge [8, 30], the goal of this study is to propose a novel framework, called SMAFramework, to help city planners and others on these issues. The framework eases the process of dealing with multiple heterogeneous sources providing an approach to standardize these data in order to facilitate information extraction regarding urban mobility. This framework envisions to provide different tools to help professionals as city planners, researchers, and engineers to extract insights about urban mobility dynamics to better plan the city to its citizens. In this paper, we propose one of these tools and, to show the potential of the framework, we design an algorithm based on fuzzy-logic scores to evaluate spatio-temporal correlations between entries from different sensing layers of an area. The approach, entitled Fuzzy Matcher, aims to provide a tool for evaluating urban areas in space and time – rather than performing an aggregated analysis not aware of the time variance – where data collected from different sources are highly correlated; or evaluate areas where this correlation does not exist but could be stimulated. We use real data from New York City using two distinct data sources: (i) spatio-temporal annotated tweets (i.e., short messages shared in the Twitter platform); and (ii) trips performed in the New York City using yellow taxis. We demonstrate how to explore the proposed framework using our datasets to establish a better positioning of the taxis, which could, potentially, improve taxi services to users and increase revenue for taxi drivers.

This work is organized as follows. Section 2 presents the related work. Section 3 describes how data is collected and represented. Section 4 presents and explains the framework architecture. Sections 5 and 6 present the algorithm developed to demonstrate the applicability of the proposed framework. Section 7 presents the results of mobility analysis exploring our framework in our studied real-world urban datasets, showing the potential for new services and applications. Finally, Section 8 summarizes the contributions obtained with the proposed methods and presents some future directions.

2 RELATED WORK

The use of graphs to represent mobility data is recurring in the literature. This recurrence allied to the need of representing the time variance of this data has resulted in different graph-based models with time representation support. The most common examples of these models are: (i) Snapshot based [6, 26], where the graph is formulated as N disconnected graphs where each graph represents a moment in time, with all its connections and nodes; (ii) Continuous Time Intervals [3], where the links between the nodes are described as functions in a certain fashion that allows to identify whether the edge exists or not given a specific moment in time; (iii) Spatio-Temporal Edges [11, 16], which use two kinds of links to represent the interactions between the nodes (spatial edges and temporal edges); (iv) Time Mixed Edges [9], similar to the Spatio-Temporal Edges, however, in this model the existence of mixed edges (i.e., edges that connect nodes in different moments of time and locations in space) are allowed; and finally (v) the Multi Aspect Graphs [10, 28]. One of the advantages of selecting the MAG to represent the smart city data is its capability of representing all kinds of connections present in the other graphs. Table 1, extended from the paper of Wehmuth, et al. [28], shows a representation map indicating for each model the other models that can be represented with its definition. Also, the last column was added to emphasize that only the MAG has native support for multilayer.

Table 1: Representation map for the different models used to extend the graphs with time variance data

	Snapshots	CTI	STE	TME	MAG	Multilayer Support
Snapshots	X	X				
CTI	X	X	X			
STE	X	X	X			
TME		X		X		
MAG	X	X	X	X	X	X

Furthermore, other frameworks for mobility analysis, based on different models, have emerged in the literature. These frameworks were developed focusing not only on mobility in the cities, but also other scenarios as discussed below. Thakur & Helmy [27] investigate how current mobility models are adequate to represent the human mobility. Also, the authors propose a framework, namely COBRA, which extends the mobility model metrics to match with real traces. The framework aims to create a model for mobility to allow simulation of network protocols dependent on that mobility. To evaluate their framework, the authors use some network protocols, combined with other mobility models and also traces from real world in specific environments within the city (e.g., university campus, parks). This framework uses archived data collected from the scenarios when using real world data, this data also can be combined from different sources or scenarios in order to create more complex models. Their framework was not built with the purpose of analyzing mobility, but, instead, model it, thus it lacks some of the needed features to perform analysis tasks, such as the layer-based structure (i.e., all data collected are mixed together), and the possibility to use real time data.

Patroumpas [18] propose a methodology to model traces of generic positional information. That model introduces a sliding window operator that allows an incremental examination of streamed motion traces. On top of this model, there is a query language able to express spatio-temporal queries to retrieve data stored in the sliding window format. That work presents the approach as a tool to analyze online streamed data, but does not show how it can be used to stored data, which is an important source of mobility data. For example, some of the mobility data cannot be published in real time due to privacy constraints and/or other issues (e.g., the New York Yellow Taxis Trip dataset used in this paper), thus the unique way to work with this data is by collecting it from archived sources. These two ways of accessing data, streamed and archived approaches, may be used to ensure the exploration of the data available, and, thus, frameworks that can handle both formats have extra advantages, such as the ones following.

Silva et al. [25] discuss the concept of sensing layer division for different types of data available in geographical regions. The authors focus on analyzing data about urban regions provided by users using their portable devices through location-based social networks platforms (e.g., Twitter). They provide a generic way of structuring data for analyses, however, the abstract model is not specialized, i.e., does not contain functions to help for instance in mobility analysis.

Besides, the time dimension in that model presents some limitations. In our work, the focus is on creating a tool to analyze mobility patterns, thus the structure of the data is well defined and all the sensing layers can be standardized in a common data structure (i.e., the MAG structure).

In order to perform maritime traffic analysis, Salmon & Ray [22] introduce a spatio-temporal framework capable of analyzing archived and streamed data sources. The proposed architecture is oriented to receive data in real time as data streams. The authors explore also a query specification standard, which allows the creation of persistent and one-time queries, reflecting respectively queries that will stay listening to new incoming data, or queries that will run over the data already stored. That study is focused on maritime traffic, where the data comes from sensors, but it is not shown how data from different sources can be used in that model.

The SMAFramework, proposed in this paper, is focused on analyzing data generated in cities observing their characteristics, such as the high heterogeneity of the data sources, which may be archived or streamed in several different standards. The architecture is extensible, allowing to collect data from data sources not currently present in the framework in a plug-and-play fashion. Its focus is on mobility, allowing defining more specifically details for this purpose. Table 2 summarizes the contents of this section and indicates the differences from the models and frameworks discussed and our proposed model. Also in Table 2, it is possible to identify the number of different sensing layers supported by the model.

Table 2: Summary of related work emphasizing the differences from other studies and the SMAFramework

	Archived Data	Streamed Data	Unified Data Structure	Combination of Data Sources	Number of Independent Layers
Thakur & Helmy (2013)	X			X	1
Patroumpas et. al. (2013)		X	X	X	1
Silva et. al. (2014)	X	X		X	N
Salmon & Ray (2016)	X	X	X		1
SMAFramework (2017)	X	X	X	X	N

3 URBAN SENSING LAYERS AND ITS REPRESENTATION

One way to classify data generated in a city is to use sensing layers. Silva et al. [25] define sensing layers as datasets describing specific aspects of a given geographical location. The raw data in these layers must be collected and processed in order to be used for analysis purposes. An example of sensing layer is data collected from the Twitter platform, which provides *tweets* that may be spatio-temporal annotated. These annotations can be used to identify the position of the person by the time of sharing a message. This is done using the latitude, longitude and time fields of the tweet. Also, more sophisticated analysis can extract other information from the content field of the message.

Each sample of data in the sensing layer includes a time interval when the data was generated, a location where it was produced, a specialty data and one or more IDs (or UIDs – user ids) to represent the entity who created the data. The specialty data could be the message in the tweet, or the photo itself shared in a photo sharing service. In this work, we consider the data location itself as the specialty data. This division of sensing layers brings a series of advantages in different applications of urban computing because it helps to extract useful information [25]. Currently, many approaches explore data from single sensing layers and get useful results. However, data combination of different sources, as complementary data, to improve results is an emerging research topic when studying data in urban areas. The unification of these datasets is not a trivial task, thus resulting in different efforts proposing models and frameworks capable of representing and aiding the use of these datasets.

Zheng [32] identifies some features that may facilitate the success of a framework to represent and analyze urban data. That model must be able to (i) integrate data from heterogeneous sources: organizing the data in an efficient way for retrieval and mining, while keeping the consistency of the data for each independent source; (ii) allow cross-domain data combination to allow knowledge extraction that cannot be extracted from single data sources; and (iii) be able to manipulate sequences of time-stamped locations coordinates. Also, according to Plale and Kouper [20] as data is becoming more and more ubiquitous, being generated in different devices and objects, one important aspect of dealing with these data is to keep track of the lifecycle of it. Thus, it is interesting to a framework to retain information about how the data is created and how it is transformed through it's use. To allow the full control of this lifecycle the framework and its data model must answer questions as how the collection of data is made (e.g., real-time, in batches) and how these data is stored and used for analysis [13, 20].

Inspired by the concept of sensing layers and by features needed to facilitate the success of a model to represent data from urban centers, we propose the use of a Multi Aspect Graph (MAG) [10, 28] to represent the data inside the framework. To establish a structure to the data increases the number of methodologies that can be applied to extract knowledge from mobility data [32]. The MAG is an extension of the Graph model that allows the representation of different data features by using the so-called aspects. The selection of a graph-based structure to represent the data is made due to the convenience of these models to represent the city road infrastructure [21] easing the combination of the collected data with representations of the city infrastructure in the form of maps or city roads networks [2]. Also, some extensions in the graph-base models, such as the MAG, has evolved its capabilities of representing spatio-temporal variations, as mobility flows [11, 12, 16]. In the literature, there are different descriptions of the model, but the models proposed by Kivela et.al. [10] and Wehmuth et.al. [28] are the most well accepted by the academic community. Both models are equivalent with a few peculiarities distinguishing them. In the proposed framework, the model presented by Kivela et.al. [10] was used because of its simpler and clearer mathematical definition, what reflects in being better referenced in the literature. Figure 1 shows a representation of a MAG indicating how some of the real-world characteristics are mapped to the structure in the framework. Specifically, as for example, Twitter and Taxi Trips are shown as data sources mapped as layers in the MAG.

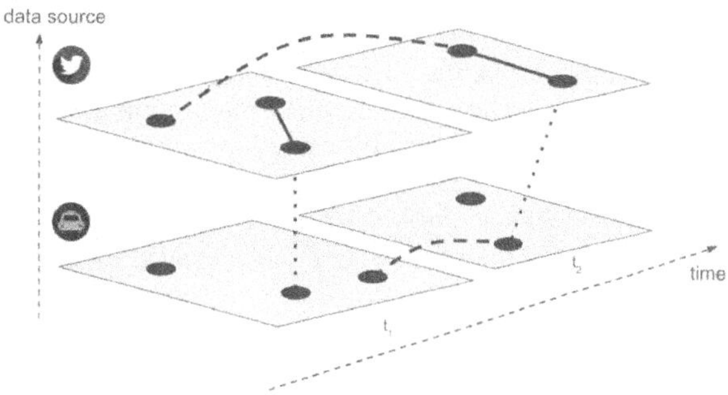

Figure 1: Sample representation of a MAG structure

In Figure 1, it is shown a MAG with two aspects. An aspect is one axis where layers can be created, each of these layers is represented as a square in Figure 1. The first aspect, represented vertically, is the data source aspect, thus every surface (i.e., elementary layer, or row of layers) contains data from a different source. It is important to mention that even the same source can produce information for different layers when the source produces entries that represent different specialties (e.g., an entry from a taxi trip can represent either the presence of a person or the presence of a vehicle in a given location). The second aspect, represented horizontally, is the time. In the model, the time is discretized, so every elementary layer in the temporal axis represents a moment in time when the data was generated. Every node in the graph is a piece of collected data and the links connecting them represent their relationships. The model allows the representation of any kind of relationship, which is able to adapt to different analysis cases, what is accomplished by using labels to identify the links.

In the example, three kinds of relationships are shown. The thick dashed line represents a movement of the data producer, thus two nodes connected by a thick dashed line have the same UID. The thin dashed lines represent nodes in different layers, which were created by the same entity. Finally, the solid lines represent contacts that happen instantly (i.e., quick enough to not use more than one time step), one example could be a tweet sent to another user, it will leave the first user and arrive to the second probably not taking more than one second. Since the data was collected in different sources, their UID may not be the same, thus this kind of connection must be created through analysis tasks. These links can be created when the UIDs in different layers are the same, or when the map of UIDs in different layers is known, however, it is not clear yet how these connections can be created when this information is not present (i.e., it is an open question, especially when studying user-based sensors [25]). Yet, our work shows initial insights on possibilities of creating these connections. We call this mapping of sensors/users in different layers as the Cross-layer sensor/user mapping problem. As shown in the Figure 1 the MAG structure keeps the information about the data source used to collect the data and also allows the storage of time sequenced data, which are important characteristics to a model used by city mobility analytics tools [13, 20]. Also, the division into data layers is important when managing data sources with different access privileges, for sample the MAG can accommodate private and public data, allowing the definition of specific data sharing policies.

According to Kivela et al. [10], the MAG is a model that uses a composition of aspects and layers to add information to graphs. The aspects are the dimensions (i.e., axis) in which the layers are in. Every aspect a has a family of elementary layers L_a, which represent a unique value of one aspect of the data (e.g., one moment in time in the temporal axis permeating all the data sources). This way, if we have d aspects, we can define all the elementary layers as $L = \{L_a\}^d_{(a=1)}$. Thus, the set of all layers in the graph is the Cartesian product of all elementary layers $L_1 \times L_2 \times \cdots \times L_d$. Since any of the nodes in V can be in any layer, the set of nodes that are present in the graph is $V_m \subseteq V \times L_1 \times L_2 \times \cdots \times L_d$. Any of the edges in the graph can connect two different nodes in any layer or aspect. Thus, the set of edges is $E_m \subseteq V_m \times V_m$. Using this information, we can define a MAG as $M = (V_m, E_m, V, L)$.

One advantage of using the MAG model is because it keeps some of the characteristics of the traditional static graphs. The traditional graphs were used to represent static information, and also sometimes to do analytical tasks over aggregated area over time (i.e., not time-aware analysis), but some peculiarities of the mobility data, for example, cannot be expressed in a timeless fashion. Since these graphs have been used to represent mobility data before the advance of time-varying graphs, some of the techniques and methodologies already available may be reused. This model is also adequate to represent the division of the sensing layers to facilitate the development of the proposed framework and enables the execution of analysis tasks over the data.

4 SMAFRAMEWORK: SMART CITIES MOBILITY ANALYSIS FRAMEWORK

In this section, we introduce the framework to aid developers, researchers and city planners to analyze mobility data generated in the city environment. In order to accomplish that, the framework helps gathering data from the different sources available in the city and standardize them to facilitate data management and analysis. Furthermore, the framework also provides a base structure to perform trivial and common tasks to deal with any data, including mobility (e.g., clean invalid data, remove duplicates and filter data). Nowadays, every data scientist working with mobility data tends to build his/her own solution, which raises a challenge on data standardization among others, preventing its reuse in an easy way. Providing a tool that allows users to avoid rebuilding these procedures and also perform them in an optimized way can, potentially, help to save time to work on more specific details of their analysis. Finally, the framework also envisions to provide ways to deal with some challenges regarding mobility data analysis tasks. More specifically, matching traces in different sensing layers and analyzing the correlation of layers from different perspectives.

Figure 2 shows the framework architecture. At the top, it is shown the city generating data through different sources. Every icon inside the cloud represents a different source of raw data that is being collected to be analyzed, using Data Extractors. These Data Extractors are pieces of software that collect the raw data from its source and adequate it in a basic initial format called Entries. For example, a Data Extractor can use an API to collect data from a social media platform and put it in the Entry format. This data may also be provided in different ways rather than through APIs. The objective of the

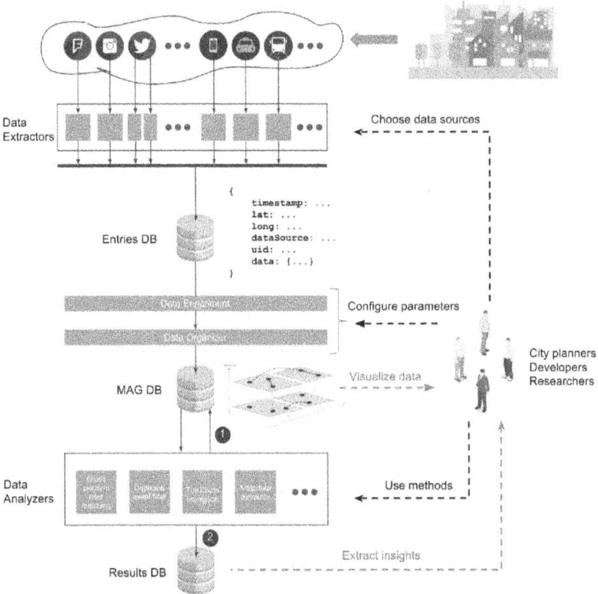

Figure 2: The SMAFramework architecture

Data Extractors consists in looking at these peculiarities of each data source and performing the initial data extraction step. In the example shown in Figure 2, the Twitter source is been explored by two Data Extractors that can, for instance, be a stream extractor, collecting real-time data, and another archived extractor, collecting stored data in other formats.

Every entry represents sample data, space and time annotated that will be stored in the framework. These samples consist of geolocation (i.e., latitude and longitude), time, data source and user ids, i.e., represent the entity, which generated the sample. In the absence of information indicating the UID, the framework will generate values assuming that every entry was created by different entities. Also, these samples may contain additional data that might help eventual analysis cases. These entries are initially stored in the database, as shown in Figure 2. Once in database, there are common tasks that read the entries and organize them into the MAG structure and perform data enrichment both according to the users' configurations. These tasks can add more data samples that were not initially in the entries, but can be inferred. For example, Mahrsi et al. [14] present two ways of enriching data from bus system traces. In those scenarios, it is known when the users take a bus, but it is not known when they leave it. Thus, in order to infer this information, the authors raise two assumptions: (i) closest-stop – for a given transaction, the passenger arrives in the closest station of the one where the next transaction starts; and (ii) daily-symmetry – for the last transaction of the day, the passengers arrive in the closest station of the one they used to do the first departure of the day.

After the Data Organizer and Data Enrichment steps, the data can be structured on the MAG model. This structure will be stored by the framework in a so-called MAG database. At this point, the data can be checked by the users of the framework, for example, using a visualization tool. On top of the MAG structure, the Data Analyzers run tasks that help the extraction of knowledge from the mobility collected data. Similar to the Data Extractors, the data analyzers can be conveniently added to extend the framework and adequate it to the user needs. The results of the analysis tasks executed are finally stored in the Results Database, where the users of the framework can extract information as totalizators, summaries, rates, meta-data and so on.

The framework is organized in a 3-step pipeline of the data, i.e., first entries, then the MAG and finally the results, to reduce the amount of work needed to add a new module. Thus, if users need to use the Data Analyzers that already exist in a new data source, they can only deploy the Data Extractor to be able to do it. A similar situation occurs in the case where the user is going to use the already supported data sources, but with a new Data Analyzer. This design eases the extension of the framework, that can be performed by the addition of new modules; this capacity of been easily extended to add new features to the SMAFramework and keep the model updated, which is a important characteristic to deal with data analysis [2, 13] a recent field where new methodologies and kinds of analysis are developed in a reasonable frequency. The division of the framework architecture in layers also organizes it in a way that makes easier to add new layers between the existing ones to improve metrics as performance and/or scalability, for sample adding a caching layer may enhance the data access performance.

The MAG structure and the Data Analyzers are the core of the framework. These modules allow the framework users to explore the data and extract knowledge. The Data Analyzers can perform two types of tasks: they can change the MAG structure to allow the visualization of certain patterns, or also can output summarized results to a result database. Since these analyzers are a key part of the framework, the present paper shows a use case with a proposed Data Analyzer called Fuzzy Matcher. This analyzer aims to create spatio-temporal matches between two different sensing layers, and its full description appears in the next section.

5 FUZZY MATCHER

The analysis provided by the SMAFramework can provide important insights for different city stakeholders. For instance, citizens helping other people to better use the resources available in the city; or city managers, aiding themselves to build the policies to manage the city. To show a use case exploring the framework, we propose a Data Analyzer, called Fuzzy Matcher, to investigate spatio-temporal correlation of data from different sensing layers.

Fuzzy Matcher is an algorithm that identifies spatio-temporal matches between nodes of the MAG from different sensing layers of the smart city. After the identification of the match, the algorithm also evaluates a temporal and spatial score of the matches. This score is evaluated based on the spatio-temporal distance between the matching nodes and a dispersion function. While using this procedure from the framework, the users are able to specify parameters such as distance, time precision, and also distance and time depreciation function. The change of this function can be used to adapt the analysis for specific cases. For example, the way crowds move in a city may vary according to a particular scenario. A crowd as a parade, for instance, tends to walk longer distances to make its cause more visible, whereas a crowd attending a concert does not move a lot. The way that crowds, and other mobility flows, behave in the city can be better described by different dispersion functions.

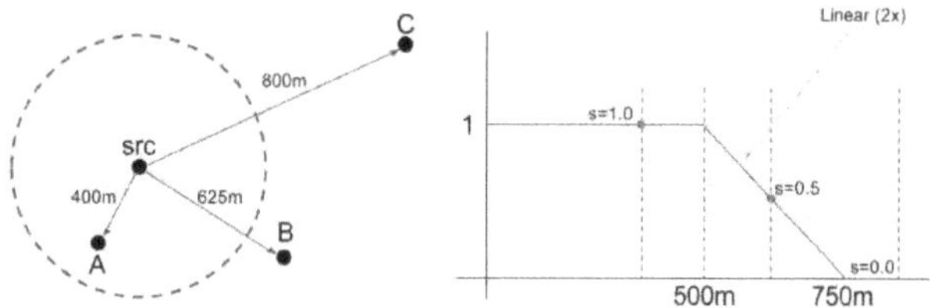

Figure 3: Fuzzy matching process

Figure 3 shows how the Fuzzy Matcher algorithm works and also how its parameters are used. The distance precision D, time precision T, and the temporal and spatial depreciation functions $td(t)$ and $sd(d)$, respectively, where d and t are the spatial and temporal distances, are used to create a curve to evaluate the score of the match. The spatial score is given by $SS(d) = f(d)/D$ where $f(d) = \{D$, if $d < D$; $sd(d - D)$, otherwise$\}$, and similarly for the temporal score: $TS(t) = f(t)/T$ where $f(t) = \{T$, if $t < T$; $st(t - T)$, otherwise$\}$. For example, given the scenario in Figure 3, the match (SRC, B) has spatial score $SS(625) = 0.5$, for $D = 500$, and the spatial depreciation is a linear function (i.e., $sd(d) = D - d$). In the same scenario, since the pair (SRC, C) has $SS(800) = 0$, this pair does not become a match. The same is valid in case of $TS(t) = 0$.

Considering the proposition of this method, this work aims to add a few possibilities to aid researchers and developers in analyzing mobility data when compared to other methodologies. For instance, geographical databases offer a variety of tools to match spatial data, such as geo-located queries, that allow searching a specific area; or even observer functions that make possible to watch for changes in the database within a region. However, many of these approaches lack temporal awareness, not performing any analysis over time. Also, despite only matching samples, the Fuzzy Matcher provides scores to represent how strong/weak is a given match. By using these scores, thresholds can be identified to allow classification of the matches, for instance. Finally, Fuzzy Matcher introduces a way of using different depreciation functions to analyze datasets that might have different dispersion behaviors.

One of the issues related to finding matches in datasets is the algorithmic complexity. If the algorithm is built in a naive manner, its complexity can become $O(n^2)$. This result is obtained because of the naive necessity of comparing each one of the n interest nodes (i.e., nodes in a given target layer) with all the other $n-1$. This complexity might be a barrier to use the Fuzzy Matcher algorithm when it comes to huge datasets with dozens of millions of samples. To reduce the algorithmic complexity, we propose a method of walk through the dataset comparing samples to their neighbors. This method was built inspired in the Bucket Sort [4] algorithm, leading to the so-called Bucket Walk. The method is described as a three-dimensional walk in section 6, but it can be extended to any number of dimensions.

6 BUCKET WALK

In this paper, to reduce the $O(n^2)$ complexity of the Fuzzy Matcher algorithm, it is introduced the Bucket Walk approach to visit samples in the datasets and compare them with their neighborhood. In this section, the Bucket Walk is described as a three-dimensional method to walk through a dataset, however, the method can be extended to work with any number of dimensions. Also, this method is not bound to work only in the Fuzzy Matcher algorithm, rather it can be used with any algorithm that aims to compare dataset samples against their neighbors. The use of this walking method reduces significantly the time and memory usage to run the Fuzzy Matcher. This section shows some results collected from experiments using the Bucket Walk and the naive approach. The same experiments could not be obtained from the complete datasets since the naive experiments were taking much time to run and exhausting the memory even if some of the best servers are available to be used (i.e., 24 cores, 40Gb RAM). By using the Bucket Walk to execute Fuzzy Matcher, the server was able to perform the task saving significant resources (i.e., using 16 cores and 8Gb RAM) and time.

As mentioned, the Bucket Walk was built using as inspiration the Bucket Sort algorithm [4]. The Bucket Sort consists in splitting the samples to be sorted into smaller groups called buckets (or bins), sort the samples within the bins and then sort the bins themselves. In order to split the original dataset, the Bucket Sort creates hashes of the samples. For example, a hash function, when sorting strings, could be to get the very first character; each character would be mapped to one bin, so every string starting with the same character would be placed in the same bin. We argue that this approach can be extended to organize multi-dimensional data by creating buckets and hashes at each data dimension in the samples. For instance, the data analyzed in the Fuzzy Matcher is spatio-temporal aware, thus resulting in a 3D data model, with the latitude, longitude and time dimension – two spatial dimensions and one temporal.

The Bucket Walk consists in creating hashes to split the original dataset in a 3D space (i.e., latitude, longitude and time). Given this division, while walking through the dataset, it is possible to compare samples in neighbor buckets, rather than the whole dataset. We need to choose a hash function to use this approach, and its choice will affect the performance of the walk, and consequently, the algorithm that uses it (e.g., Fuzzy Matcher). One possibility of choosing the hash function is to define a base sample, which may or may not be in the dataset, and compute the distance of every sample to this base sample, and then get the integer part of the division of this distance by a factor K. This has to be done for the three dimensions of the data separately. If the base sample has the lowest (or highest) values for every dimension the result of the hash and split tasks will be a cube of data buckets. Every bucket will contain the samples that obtained the same result from the hash function. Once identified the base sample, the hash procedure has to be performed for every data sample, which means it is $O(n) \subset O(n^2)$ operation, then we do not have the complexity problems to run the hash over all data. Furthermore, if the base sample is not known initially, all data samples will have to be visited before performing the walk to identify it, resulting in a $O(n) \subset O(n^2)$ procedure, which also does not imply in any complexity increase compared to the naive approach.

The factor K, mentioned in the hash function, has also to be defined. To do so, it is necessary to look at how the neighborhood of a data sample is defined. In the Fuzzy Matcher algorithm, the neighborhood is defined by a custom function $f(x) = \{SS(x), TS(x)\}$, where the factor can be defined as $K = x$ when $f(x) = 0$. Conveniently, for the sample presented in Section 5, with the linear depreciation function and a precision $P = \{D, T\}$, $K = 2P$. Defining K this way allows the algorithm, for a given sample, to only compare data in adjacent buckets in the cube. It is important to note that two K values were obtained, one for spatial hash and another one for the temporal hash. This approach allows to have one different K value for each dimension.

Once obtained the hash function, the K factor splits the dataset samples into the cube of data buckets. The worst-case scenario would still result in a $O(n^2)$ complexity. This is the scenario where all data samples would be allocated to the same bucket. However, it is known that the usual distribution of the studied data has no such trend. To show this distribution, the proposed hash function was used to split the data samples in the experiments. These data samples were collected from the Twitter platform and the Yellow Taxis from the New York City, as previously mentioned, and contain respectively 399, 024 and 10, 580, 378 samples. More details about the datasets are provided in Section 7.

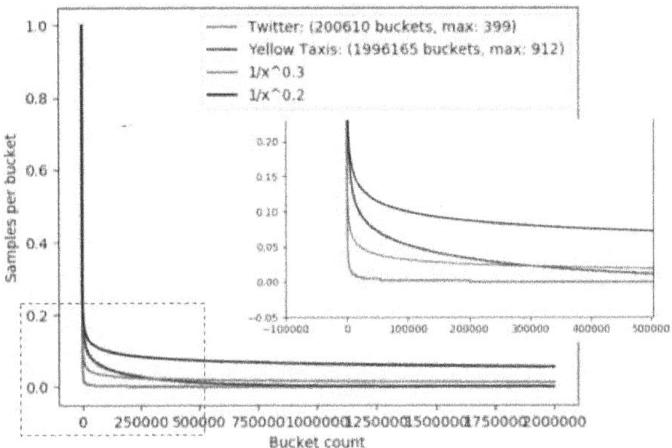

Figure 4: Distribution of the buckets usage

Figure 4 shows the distribution curve of data samples in buckets. In that figure, the horizontal axis represents the buckets while the vertical one represents the number of samples in the buckets. The buckets were sorted according to the number of samples in it. Also, to facilitate the visualization, a number of samples per bucket were normalized to the [0, 1] interval. The legends of Figure 4 show a number of buckets with at least one sample and the number of samples in the most popular bucket. It is visible that the datasets have a quite sparse distribution where most of the samples are centralized in a few buckets, but not all in the same bucket as described in the worst-case scenario. Indeed, the Twitter and Yellow Taxi curves can be approximated by an equation of the form: $D(x) = \frac{\alpha}{x^\beta+1}$, as shown in Figure 4, where the factors α and β will define the shape of the curve, also the +1 was ripped without loss of generality. By using this approximation we can estimate $n \simeq \sum_x \frac{\alpha}{x^\beta}$, resulting in:

$$n^2 \simeq \left(\sum_x \frac{\alpha}{x^\beta}\right)^2 = \sum_x \left(\frac{\alpha^2}{x^{2\beta}}\right) + 2\sum_{i>x} \left(\frac{\alpha^2}{(xi)^\beta}\right). \quad (1)$$

This way, the equivalent complexity will be:

$$O(n^2) = O\left[\sum_x \left(\frac{\alpha^2}{x^{2\beta}}\right) + 2\sum_{i>x} \left(\frac{\alpha^2}{(xi)^\beta}\right)\right] = O\left[\sum_x \left(\frac{\alpha^2}{x^{2\beta}}\right)\right]. \quad (2)$$

The last step in Equation 2 is only possible because of the Big-O notation, where only the higher order factors in a sum affect the algorithmic complexity. In Equation 2, there is still a quadratic term, as predicted in the worst-case scenario, however, this quadratic term is attenuated according to the samples distribution. For the specific datasets studied in this work, some upper bounds of the values of β were identified as $\beta \leq 0.3$ for Twitter, and $\beta \leq 0.2$ for the Yellow Taxis. These bounds were simply defined by observing the behaviors of the $\frac{1}{x^{0.3}}$ and $\frac{1}{x^{0.2}}$ curves. The obtained equation represents the expected result, where the full complexity of the algorithm is evaluated according to the sum of the complexity contained at each bucket. In this case, the value of α is the maximum number of samples in a single bucket. In the case that $\alpha = n$, i.e., the worst scenario, only one bucket exists, thus $x \in \{1\}$ and the complexity becomes again, as predicted, quadratic, as follows:

$$O\left[\sum_{x\in\{1\}} \left(\frac{n^2}{x^{2\beta}}\right)\right] = O\left(\frac{n^2}{1^{2\beta}}\right) = O(n^2). \quad (3)$$

Another advantage of using the Bucket Walk is the fact that it does not require all the data to be loaded into the memory of a server. Only chunks of data containing the buckets of a region to be analyzed need to be loaded, making it more convenient to run in low memory environments. Also, when running the algorithm over the whole dataset, the nodes within the same bucket can be analyzed in sequence, which facilitates the usage of a caching hierarchy. This works in a similar way of the Iteration Space Tiling optimization [29].

There are in the literature some other access methods that can be used to retrieve spatial and temporal data. For example, the R*-tree model [1] is based on tree structures commonly used to query spatial data samples. That method builds a tree with two types of nodes: leaves and pages. Starting from the top page, which covers all the samples, the search algorithm starts looking for a child page that covers the desired query. Once the algorithm identifies this page, the process will repeat recursively until the algorithm reaches a page with the leaf children. At this point, the algorithm will look at the leaf nodes to find the queried sample. In this model, the hierarchy is used to organize the nodes, however, even for sibling pages, there are no indications if they are from neighbor regions. The absence of a notion of neighborhood in the R-tree may result in repeated visits to the higher levels of the tree while performing the nearest neighbor queries [23]. In the Bucket Walk, this information of neighborhood is used to reduce the number of comparisons needed to execute the Fuzzy Matcher. There are still different extensions of the R-tree algorithm in the literature, which may improve its performance in the nearest neighbor queries, however, they are not using all the information of the search domain of the Fuzzy Matcher. For instance, a depreciation function to estimate the maximum search area is not used.

StreamCube [5] is another algorithm to search data samples that is aware of the spatial and temporal variations. It consists in organizing the data in a 3D cube, making it easier to access data querying over latitude, longitude and time. The difference of this approach to ours is that it queries items as continuous values. To quickly navigate over the data, StreamCube creates some hierarchical divisions based on temporal and spatial regions. In this hierarchy data items can be queried, for sample, over week periods, these periods can be accessed on a daily basis. In our solution, we use a hash strategy, leading to indexes that may result in a more efficient data access when compared with a continuous representation. In fact, indexes allow Fuzzy Matcher to have a better data access, retrieving less unneeded data.

7 EVALUATION

We use Fuzzy Matcher to analyze data collected from the two different data sources in New York City. In order to analyze the correlation of both datasets, we defined an area of interest that covers the Manhattan region and also some near neighborhoods. The first dataset consists of tweets collected during the month of January/2016. During that month, we extracted 399,024 tweets geo-annotated (i.e., tweets that contain information about the geo-location where it was shared). The second dataset is available on the NYC Open Data portal. It has information about the New York Yellow Taxi trips. In January/2016, there were 10,580,378 valid trips within the boundaries of our analysis.

The first experiment consists in using the Fuzzy Matcher scores to check the spatio-temporal correlation of zones of the city. In this experiment, we analyze if we can use Twitter data to better position taxis within the city so these taxis will be more accessible for the citizens, and also more trips will be requested. The Yellow Taxis in New York only provide their services through street-hails, thus they must be well positioned to have a better coverage of the city area, which consequently results in a more intelligent transportation system. Our hypothesis is that a region with a relevant number of tweets may indicate a significant amount of possible taxi users. In this way, Twitter data, collected in real time, may be used to indicate regions where taxis could be positioned to serve citizens, or to quickly identify changes in the city environment caused by events, such as demonstrations and traffic jams.

We used the Fuzzy Matcher algorithm to analyze the correlation of samples collected from Twitter and the Yellow Taxis sensing layers. The algorithm identifies spatio-temporal matches with a distance precision of 100 meters and a temporal precision of 2 hours. We use linear functions as depreciation functions in the Fuzzy Matcher[1]. The scores of the identified matches were evaluated and used to build a heatmap of the matches, shown in the left part of Figure 5. We used the Twitter data to build the heatmap shown in the right part of Figure 5. It is important to notice that the matches in the Fuzzy Matcher heatmap reflect the amount and scores of the identified matches, rather than only a given amount in the Twitter heatmap. This correlation does not exclude the possibility of having the same Twitter sample matching different Yellow Taxis samples. These two factors may lead to greater values in the Fuzzy Matcher heatmap than in the Twitter one, which is expected. Furthermore, the Fuzzy Matcher heatmap considers the time variation, i.e., the scores of a region only increase if this region has matches closer in time and space, rather than an aggregated analysis where the time is not considered.

Looking at the heatmaps in Figure 5, it is possible to identify that regions with higher volumes of tweets resulted in regions with higher volumes of matches. This information by itself is not enough to prove the initial hypothesis, however, it acts as an indicator of its validity. After looking over all the heatmap, there are some specific regions that may be highlighted, identified with circles in Figure 5. In these regions, there is a significant amount of tweets, however, the scores of the matches are not relevant. The first region to observe is the one indicated by the red circle A (top of left image). This represents the Central Park area and it is clear that taxis will not be available there since they cannot access the park area. In the other two red circles B and C of the left image, it is possible to notice a smaller amount of tweets that are not reflected in matches, and, apparently, there is no reason for this lack of matches. In this case, we require a more elaborated analysis of the datasets, complemented by other sources, to ensure that assigning more taxis to those regions may increase the number of requested trips.

The second experiment aims to provide initial insights on the study of the Cross-layer User Mapping problem, i.e., to map data generated from the same entities in different sensing layers. The experiment consists in finding trips of taxis that have fuzzy matches, with the Twitter layer, in the beginning and at the end of the trip. We argue that the algorithm may capture trips that were performed by the owner of a given Twitter account. To check this hypothesis, we initially generated data to simulate a scenario where users actually tweeted, took a taxi and then tweet again. In this scenario, 500 Twitter users sent 20,000 tweets in one day. Also, 5,000 taxi trips were generated. We, then, executed a procedure on top of the results obtained by the Fuzzy Matcher in the simulation scenario. We analyzed the user ids contained in the matches in both layers. Thus, if we have a persistent match generated by two fuzzy matches $P = \{(A, B), (C, D)\}$, where A, B, C and D are nodes in the MAG structure, and also, without loss of generality, A and C belong to the Twitter layer, and B and D to the Yellow Taxis layer. Then, for P, it is valid that $A.uid = C.uid$ and $B.uid = D.uid$. Figure 6 shows the results obtained in the simulation.

The Fuzzy Matcher algorithm allows the same Twitter layer node to match many Yellow Taxis nodes, and, thus, we can establish a lower bound of the distance, as depicted in Figure 6. To consider a persistent match and not only noise produced by the Fuzzy Matcher algorithm, the persistent match distance needs to be at least 500 meters. Also, to ensure that the data has no noise, we defined a max speed limit used in the persistent matches to be 27.8 meters/second, or 100 Km/h, which may still be high. We discarded trips leading to a taxi or a Twitter user moving faster than this speed. These distance and speed limits are based on usual speeds and distances practiced by taxis in big cities, however, these values were only meant to waive the noise in the data and may not have implications on the analysis. As it can be observed, the algorithm identifies the persistent matches, showing that it can be used to investigate this sort of correlation between the sensing layers. There were identified 229 persistent matches in the simulated scenario, where the top 10 most relevant matches (i.e., greater distance and match score) are shown. After the simulation, the same method was applied to real data from New York City, and the result is shown in Figure 7.

In the Yellow Taxi layer, the unique available information about the entity who generates the data is when a taxi starts a trip the same taxi will finish it. After finishing a trip, there is no information if the same taxi was, or not, used in another trip. Due to this limitation of the UID control in the Yellow Taxis dataset, every link represents a trip assumed to be performed by a different taxi. Also, colors

[1]Note that other functions could be used, however, the investigations of better configurations are out of the scope of the current study.

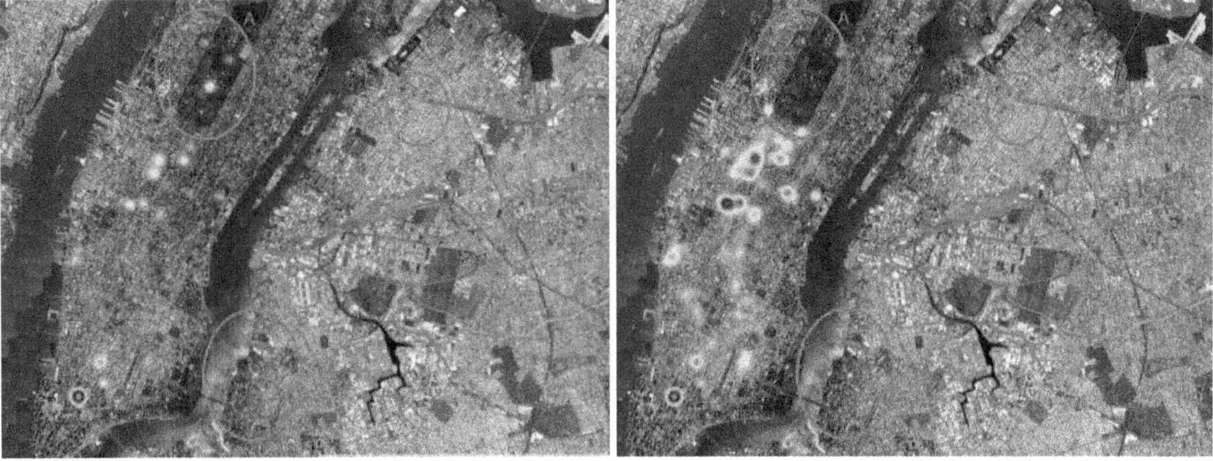

Figure 5: Heatmap of the twitter data distribution (left) and matches distribution (right)

Figure 6: Simulated scenario to evaluate hypothesis

Figure 7: Persistent matches indicated by Fuzzy Matcher

of the lines represent the day when the trip happened. Finally, the icons associated with the persistent matches represent the Twitter user who created the data entry that resulted in that match. At the end of the procedure, 20,368 persistent matches were identified after filtering the noise. Since the whole picture of the persistent matches is not visually insightful, in the Figure 7 we chose a slice of the data that allows to better understand the purpose of this analyses. The slice was taken focusing in a few users in the end of the month (i.e., January 25th to 31st). As it can be observed in the figure, it is possible to track the position of certain users in the city (e.g., the user represented by the red square). These positions were know only with the Twitter data, however, now it is possible to identify which transportation was been used by the users at a established time. This way, if another interaction of the same user is generated in the time window when the persistent match was taking place, we can infer that the user was still inside of the taxi in that location. This information helps to improve the understanding of the usage of the transportation system.

Figure 7 shows evidence that the Twitter data may be used to map trips in the Yellow Taxis sensing layer. Silva et al. [25] suggest the use of the Twitter UIDs to work as a global identifier for data generated by human entities in different sensing layers. We could show that the Fuzzy Matcher algorithm can be one of the tools used to help creating this map of entities in different sensing layers. The information present in the experiment may not be enough to ensure all the persistent matches that reflect a real person using a taxi. However, due to the high amount of persistent matches and the alignment of trips' start and end locations with the user's locations, we claim that some initial analysis toward the solution of the cross-layer user mapping problem can be obtained with the SMAFramework and the use of the Fuzzy Matcher algorithm. As mentioned before, the problem of mapping the same entities in different layers is still an open issue in the literature [25].

8 CONCLUSIONS

Solutions for urban computing are enabling cities to provide better services for their citizens and optimize the usage of city resources. This work contributes in this direction, by introducing the SMAFramework to analyze mobility data in smart cities. This framework focuses on collecting spatio-temporal annotated data from different data sources, merge and standardize them to facilitate their analysis. To show the applicability of the SMAFramework, we analyzed data collected from two distinct sources in New York City. For that, we proposed an algorithm for mobility analysis, called Fuzzy Matcher. This algorithm allows its users to analyze spatio-temporal correlation (i.e., alignment/closeness of data entries in space and time) between data collected from different data sources. We argue that this algorithm may have different use cases, such as helping to deal with the cross-layer user/sensor mapping problem. There is still open opportunities to extend the framework, including more Data Extractor, Data Analyzers and Data Enrichment tasks. Indeed, the architecture of the SMAFramework was proposed to ease the addition of new modules in a plug-and-play fashion to maintain its evolution.

ACKNOWLEDGMENTS

The authors would like to thank the grant 2015/07538-1, São Paulo Research Foundation (FAPESP) for the financial support.

REFERENCES

[1] Norbert Beckmann, Hans-Peter Kriegel, Ralf Schneider, and Bernhard Seeger. 1990. The R*-tree: an efficient and robust access method for points and rectangles. *ACM SIGMOD Record* 19, 2 (1990), 322–331. DOI: http://dx.doi.org/10.1145/93605.98741

[2] Alain Biem, Eric Bouillet, Hanhua Feng, Anand Ranganathan, Anton Riabov, Olivier Verscheure, Haris Koutsopoulos, and Carlos Moran. 2010. IBM Infosphere Streams for Scalable, Real-time, Intelligent Transportation Services. In *Proceedings of the 2010 ACM SIGMOD International Conference on Management of Data (SIGMOD '10)*. ACM, New York, NY, USA, 1093–1104. DOI: http://dx.doi.org/10.1145/1807167.1807291

[3] Arnaud Casteigts, Paola Flocchini, Walter Quattrociocchi, and Nicola Santoro. 2012. Time-Varying Graphs and Dynamic Networks. *CoRR* abs/1012.0 (2012), 20. DOI: http://dx.doi.org/10.1007/978-3-642-22450-8_27

[4] Thomas H Cormen, Clifford Stein, Ronald L Rivest, and Charles E Leiserson. 2001. *Introduction to Algorithms* (2nd ed.). McGraw-Hill Higher Education.

[5] Wei Feng, Chao Zhang, Wei Zhang, Jiawei Han, Jianyong Wang, Charu Aggarwal, and Jianbin Huang. 2015. STREAMCUBE: Hierarchical spatio-temporal hashtag clustering for event exploration over the Twitter stream. *Proceedings - International Conference on Data Engineering* 2015-May (2015), 1561–1572. DOI: http://dx.doi.org/10.1109/ICDE.2015.7113425

[6] Daniel Figueiredo, Philippe Nain, Bruno Ribeiro, Edmundo de Souza e Silva, Don Towsley, and Edmundo De Souza E Silva. 2011. Characterizing Continuous Time Random Walks on Time Varying Graphs. *Sigmetrics* cs.SI (2011), 1–30.

[7] Vanessa Frias-Martinez, Victor Soto, Heath Hohwald, and Enrique Frias-Martinez. 2012. Characterizing urban landscapes using geolocated tweets. *Proceedings - 2012 ASE/IEEE International Conference on Privacy, Security, Risk and Trust and 2012 ASE/IEEE International Conference on Social Computing, SocialCom/PASSAT 2012* (2012), 239–248. DOI: http://dx.doi.org/10.1109/SocialCom-PASSAT.2012.19

[8] Huiji Gao, Jiliang Tang, Xia Hu, and Huan Liu. 2013. Exploring temporal effects for location recommendation on location-based social networks. *Proceedings of the 7th ACM conference on Recommender systems - RecSys '13* (2013), 93–100. DOI: http://dx.doi.org/10.1145/2507157.2507182

[9] Hyoungshick Kim and Ross Anderson. 2012. Temporal node centrality in complex networks. *Physical Review E - Statistical, Nonlinear, and Soft Matter Physics* 85, 2 (2012), 1–8. DOI: http://dx.doi.org/10.1103/PhysRevE.85.026107

[10] Mikko Kivelä, Alex Arenas, Marc Barthelemy, James P. Gleeson, Yamir Moreno, and Mason A. Porter. 2014. Multilayer networks. *Journal of Complex Networks* 2, 3 (2014), 203–271. DOI: http://dx.doi.org/10.1093/comnet/cnu016

[11] Vassilis Kostakos. 2009. Temporal graphs. *Physica A: Statistical Mechanics and its Applications* 388, 6 (2009), 1007–1023. DOI: http://dx.doi.org/10.1016/j.physa.2008.11.021

[12] Tatiana Von Landesberger, Felix Brodkorb, Philipp Roskosch, Natalia Andrienko, Gennady Andrienko, Andreas Kerren, and Senior Member. 2016. Mobility Graphs: Visual Analysis of Mass Mobility Dynamics via Spatio-Temporal Graphs and Clustering. *IEEE Trans. Vis. Comput. Graph.* 22, 1 (2016), 11—20.

[13] Andre Luckow and Ken Kennedy. 2017. Chapter 5 âĂŞ Data Infrastructure for Intelligent Transportation Systems. In *Data Analytics for Intelligent Transportation Systems*. 113–129. DOI: http://dx.doi.org/10.1016/B978-0-12-809715-1.00005-5

[14] Mohamed K El Mahrsi, Etienne Côme, Latifa Oukhellou, and Michel Verleysen. 2016. Clustering Smart Card Data for Urban Mobility Analysis. (2016), 1–17.

[15] Taewoo Nam and Theresa A Pardo. 2011. Conceptualizing smart city with dimensions of technology, people, and institutions. In *Proceedings of the 12th Annual International Digital Government Research Conference on Digital Government Innovation in Challenging Times - dg.o '11*. ACM Press, New York, New York, USA, 282. DOI: http://dx.doi.org/10.1145/2037556.2037602

[16] Vincenzo Nicosia, John Tang, Cecilia Mascolo, Mirco Musolesi, Giovanni Russo, and Vito Latora. 2013. *Graph Metrics for Temporal Networks*. Springer Berlin Heidelberg, Berlin, Heidelberg, 15–40. DOI: http://dx.doi.org/10.1007/978-3-642-36461-7_2

[17] Zhaolong Ning, Feng Xia, Noor Ullah, Xiangjie Kong, and Xiping Hu. 2017. Vehicular Social Networks : Enabling Smart Mobility. *IEEE Communications Magazine* 5 (jan 2017), 49–55.

[18] Kostas Patroumpas. 2013. Multi-scale window specification over streaming trajectories. *Journal of Spatial Information Science* 7, 7 (2013), 45–75. DOI: http://dx.doi.org/10.5311/JOSIS.2013.7.132

[19] Soledad Pellicer, Guadalupe Santa, Andres L. Bleda, Rafael Maestre, Antonio J. Jara, and Antonio Gomez Skarmeta. 2013. A global perspective of smart cities: A survey. *Proceedings - 7th International Conference on Innovative Mobile and Internet Services in Ubiquitous Computing, IMIS 2013* (2013), 439–444. DOI: http://dx.doi.org/10.1109/IMIS.2013.79

[20] Beth Plale and Inna Kouper. 2017. Chapter 4 âĂŞ The Centrality of Data: Data Lifecycle and Data Pipelines. In *Data Analytics for Intelligent Transportation Systems*. 91–111. DOI: http://dx.doi.org/10.1016/B978-0-12-809715-1.00004-3

[21] M. Mazhar Rathore, Awais Ahmad, Anand Paul, and Uthra Kunathur Thikshaja. 2016. Exploiting real-time big data to empower smart transportation using big graphs. In *Proceedings of 2016 IEEE Region 10 Symposium (TENSYMP)*. 135–139. DOI: http://dx.doi.org/10.1109/TENCONSpring.2016.7519392

[22] Loic Salmon and Cyril Ray. 2016. Design principles of a stream-based framework for mobility analysis. *GeoInformatica* (2016), 1–25. DOI: http://dx.doi.org/10.1007/s10707-016-0256-z

[23] Mehdi Sharifzadeh and Cyrus Shahabi. 2010. VoR-Tree : R-trees with Voronoi Diagrams for Efficient Processing of Spatial Nearest Neighbor Queries âĹŮ. *Proceedings of the 36th International Conference on Very Large Data Bases* 3 (2010), 1231–1242. DOI: http://dx.doi.org/10.14778/1920841.1920994

[24] T.H. Silva, P.O.S. Vaz De Melo, J.M. Almeida, and A.A.F. Loureiro. 2014. Large-scale study of city dynamics and urban social behavior using participatory sensing. *Wireless Communications, IEEE* 21, 1 (Feb 2014), 42–51.

[25] T. H. Silva, P. O. S. V. de Melo, J. M. Almeida, A. C. Viana, Salles J., and A. A. F. Loureiro. 2014. Participatory Sensor Networks as Sensing Layers. 386–393. DOI: http://dx.doi.org/10.1109/BDCloud.2014.27

[26] J. Tang, S. Scellato, M. Musolesi, C. Mascolo, and V. Latora. 2010. Small-world behavior in time-varying graphs. *Physical Review E* 81, 5 (2010), 055101. DOI: http://dx.doi.org/10.1103/PhysRevE.81.055101

[27] Gautam S. Thakur and Ahmed Helmy. 2013. COBRA: A framework for the analysis of realistic mobility models. In *Proceedings - IEEE INFOCOM*. 3351–3356. DOI: http://dx.doi.org/10.1109/INFCOM.2013.6567163

[28] Klaus Wehmuth, Artur Ziviani, and Eric Fleury. 2014. A Unifying Model for Representing Time-Varying Graphs. *Computing Research Repository arXiv.org* I, January (2014), 1–28.

[29] M Wolfe. 1989. More Iteration Space Tiling. In *Proceedings of the 1989 ACM/IEEE Conference on Supercomputing (Supercomputing '89)*. ACM, New York, NY, USA, 655–664. DOI: http://dx.doi.org/10.1145/76263.76337

[30] Quan Yuan, Gao Cong, Zongyang Ma, Aixin Sun, and Nadia Magnenat Thalmann. 2013. Time-aware point-of-interest recommendation. *Proceedings of the 36th international ACM SIGIR conference on Research and development in information retrieval - SIGIR '13* (2013), 363. DOI: http://dx.doi.org/10.1145/2484028.2484030

[31] Yu Zheng, Licia Capra, Ouri Wolfson, and Hai Yang. 2014. Urban computing: concepts, methodologies, and applications. *ACM Transactions on Intelligent Systems and Technology (TIST)* 5, 3 (2014), 38.

[32] Y U Zheng. 2015. Trajectory Data Mining : An Overview. *ACM Trans. Intell. Syst. Technol.* 6, 3 (2015), 1–41. DOI: http://dx.doi.org/10.1145/2743025

Inferring Private Demographics of New Users in Recommender Systems

Mingxuan Sun
Louisiana State University
msun@csc.lsu.edu

Changbin Li
Louisiana State University
cli45@lsu.edu

Hongyuan Zha
Georgia Institute of Technology
zha@cc.gatech.edu

ABSTRACT

With the growing number of wireless and mobile devices ingrained into our daily lives, more and more people are interacting with online services that adopt recommender systems to suggest movies, news and points of interest. The private demographics of users such as age and gender in online recommender systems are very useful for many applications such as personalized ads, social study and marketing. However, users do not always provide details in their online profiles due to privacy concern. Most existing approaches can infer user private attributes based on sufficient interaction history but could fail for new users with few ratings. In this paper, we present a novel preference elicitation method, with which a recommender system asks cold-start users to rate selected items adaptively and infer the demographics rapidly via a few interactions. Specifically, latent user profiles are learned across the tasks of demographic inference and rating prediction simultaneously, which enables knowledge transfer through the two related tasks and improves the prediction accuracy for both tasks. The proposed method can also facilitate the understanding of the tradeoff between user privacy and the utility of personalization. Experimental results on real-world datasets demonstrate the performance of the proposed method in terms of the accuracy of both demographics inference and rating prediction.

CCS CONCEPTS

• **Information systems** → **Personalization;** • **Security and privacy** → *Web application security;*

KEYWORDS

Demographic inference; user modeling; recommender systems

1 INTRODUCTION

A user browses news at an airport, watches a movie in a cafe, and looks for a restaurant or a tourist attraction in a city. Mobile devices coupled with recommender systems have emerged as key tools for personalized information access and have enabled significant business applications such as mobile tourism [2, 4, 27, 30]. User demographics such as their age, gender and ethnicity information can improve recommendations and enable other richer services such as targeted advertisement and marketing. A recommender system may explicitly solicit user demographics through user registration. However, online users do not always provide such information due to privacy concern [3]. On the other hand, user interactions such as ratings in recommender systems may provide an alternative way to infer demographic information. For example, a Netflix user who likes romance comedy and child-friendly movies may indicate that she is a mom. Existing attempts include the famous de-anonymization of Netflix Prize dataset [19] that link private Netflix rating data with public databases such as IMDB to partially infer some user identities. Other attempts [29] suggest that it is possible to infer user gender with as high as 80% accuracy given sufficient user ratings in recommender systems.

Effectively inferring private attributes for users with few interactions is fundamentally important yet challenging. A large portion of users and items in relatively mature recommender systems are "cold". For example, Netflix movie dataset contains 100 million movie ratings from 480189 users over 17770 movies and most users typically rate only a small number of movies. Since most existing inference approaches largely depend on sufficient interaction history, they could fail for new users with few interactions [10, 23, 26].

A natural approach to circumvent cold-start scenario is to elicit new users' responses to a few selected questions and refine the estimation of user private attributes progressively. A lengthy exploration is intimidating, which may cause users to abandon the system at the very beginning. An adaptive process that queries users based on the previous responses is found to be more effective and variations of decision tree models [8] work well for this purpose. For example, a system queries new users "Do you like Sense and Sensibility?". Based on the answers, the users are then directed to one of the subtrees each of which is associated with another question. The system gradually refines the estimation of user profiles with higher confidence. Note that the primary goal of most web services is to attract and retain users, and thus the items selected to ask should be sufficient for both estimating user private attributes and improving recommendation accuracy at the same time.

In this paper, we propose a novel preference elicitation method for new users, which learns the tasks of both demographic inference and rating prediction in a single framework. Specifically, a decision tree with each node corresponding to a query item is constructed. Latent user profiles are learned across the tasks of demographic inference and rating prediction simultaneously at each node, which enables knowledge transfer through the two related tasks and improves the prediction accuracy gradually for both

MSWiM '17, November 21–25, 2017, Miami, FL, USA

ACM ISBN 978-1-4503-5162-1/17/11...$15.00
https://doi.org/10.1145/3127540.3127566

tasks. An iterative optimization algorithm is proposed to alternate between decision tree learning and latent profile construction. In addition, the similarity between different items is better captured in a lower dimensional-space based on lower-rank matrix factorization. As a result, the items selected to query users are more effective in improving both recommendation and demographic inference accuracy. Experimental results on three benchmark datasets including the Flixster dataset, the MovieLens dataset and the Bookcrossing dataset demonstrate that the proposed method outperforms existing ones in cold-start recommendations.

The potential success of demographic inference for new users have positive impacts on not only recommender systems but also end users. In particular, if new users are aware of the type of privacy threats, they can learn to control the amount of information to release to better balance between preserving privacy and gaining personalized information. We also discuss the tradeoff between user privacy and the utility of personalization. The former is captured by the prediction accuracy of demographics and the latter is captured by the recommendation accuracy.

Our contributions are two folds: (1) we propose a novel and effective method to simultaneously infer private information and enhance user preference prediction for cold-start users, which is critical for recommender systems. (2) The proposed method can help new users to preserve their privacy by not giving answers to certain questions while enjoying some benefits from personalization.

2 RELATED WORK

There has been extensive studies on demographic inference from various online human activities. Studies including [18] demonstrate that it is possible to infer private user attributes from online social networks given a small fraction of users who are willing to provide their private attributes such as location and interests. A variety of online activities are examined for demographic inference such as friendship on Facebook [15, 31], search queries [6], linguistic features of tweets [20, 22], and location check-ins [32].

Accurate demographic inference in recommender systems is challenging since most of the user information such as ratings is not as informative as activity information in Facebook, Twitter and LinkedIn. Until recently, studies such as [5, 29] make the first attempt and suggest that it is possible to infer user gender with as high as 80% accuracy given sufficient user ratings in recommender systems. Studies including [5, 9, 21, 29] also explore different ways to perturb user generated contents such as ratings and locations to prevent from private information leakage from the online security point of view.

The major difficulty in recommender systems is that the demographic prediction accuracy is affected by data sparsity since most users only provide a few ratings. Several studies [23, 24] focus on preference elicitation to improve rating prediction accuracy through an interview process using a static set of questions. Approaches such as [10, 24, 28, 33] explore variations of decision tree models to adaptively select items to query. Active learning methods [5, 7, 11–13] select questions to query users adaptively. However, these methods usually involve computationally expensive optimization procedures, which are not feasible for online user interactions. Our work focuses on an effective and efficient cold-start

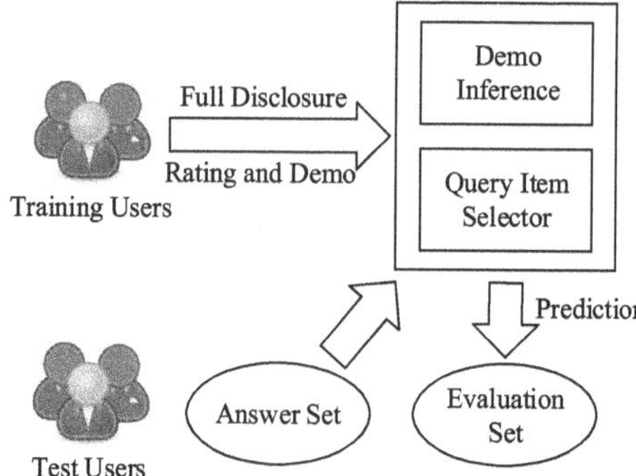

Figure 1: Evaluation framework for cold-start users.

recommendation method for both demographic inference and item recommendation.

Matrix factorization methods [14, 16, 17, 25] popularized by the Netflix competition winner [14] have been used to predict user ratings. Those methods seek to map users and items in a low-dimensional space to capture the intrinsic similarities. Content-based models such as [1, 26] utilize item features such as movie genre, directors and actors for cold-start recommendations. Our model is solely based on ratings and we adopt the latent factor based method for rating and demographic prediction.

3 MODEL

We describe the demographic inference model in the context of cold-start recommendation. We propose to construct an efficient rating elicitation process by exploring both demographics and ratings of warm-users in the training dataset. Our goal is to learn latent user profiles to best estimate both demographics and ratings. As described in Figure 1, the recommender system constructs a model to query users for better inferring private attributes based on training user data. At the visits of new users, the recommender system infers their demographic type and makes recommendations based on their answers to queries.

3.1 Simultaneous Rating Prediction and Demographic Inference

In cold-start scenario, the system queries the user's rating on several selected items and constructs a rough user profile, which is then used to predict ratings for other items and at the same time to infer demographics. We propose to model the user profile as a function of user responses to the questions formed in the decision tree. Assume that there are n possible items to ask and each response takes a value in the set $\{1, -1, 0\}$ corresponding to *like*, *dislike* and *unknown*, respectively. Let x_i be the response of user i, which is an n-dimensional vector. Let T denote the function mapping the user response x_i to the user profile that is $u_i = T(x_i)$. We also assume that there exists latent item features and denote each item feature by v_j for item j.

For rating prediction, we assume that the rating r given user and item profiles follows a Gaussian distribution, that is:

$$p(r_{ij}|u_i, v_j, \sigma^2) = \mathcal{N}(v_j^\top u_i, \sigma^2). \tag{1}$$

Similarly, we can assume priors on user and item profiles. For example, $p(v_j|\sigma_v^2) = \mathcal{N}(v_j|0, \sigma_v^2)$.

For demographic prediction, we assume that the demographic label y such as age or gender follows some distribution

$$y_i \in p(y_i|\theta^\top u_i), \tag{2}$$

where θ is the regressor for continuous label prediction or the classifier for discrete label prediction.

Given observed ratings $O = \{(i,j) \mid r_{ij} \text{ is observed}\}$ and demographic information $S = \{i \mid y_i \text{ is observed}\}$, where $i = 1, 2, \ldots, m$ and $j = 1, 2, \ldots, n$, our goal is to learn the function T, item profile v_j for each item j, and the regressor θ to minimize the negative log posterior of the model, which is equivalent to the following objective:

$$\min_{T,V,\theta} \lambda_r \sum_{(i,j)\in O} \ell_r(r_{ij}, T(x_i)^\top v_j) + \lambda_s \sum_{i\in S} \ell_s(y_i, T(x_i)^\top \theta) + \lambda_v ||V||^2 + \lambda_\theta ||\theta||^2, \tag{3}$$

where $\ell_r(\cdot,\cdot)$ and $\ell_s(\cdot,\cdot)$ denote the loss functions for ratings and demographic information respectively, and λ_r and λ_s are weights. The last two parameters λ_v and λ_θ are regularization terms for $V = [v_1, v_2, \ldots, v_n]$, a matrix containing all item profiles v_j, and θ is the regressor. For simplicity, we name θ the regressor, which actually means the classifier in the case of discrete variable prediction. Specifically, the probability model of rating r_{ij} and demographic information y_i is encoded through the choice of loss functions. Similarly, the prior over parameters v and θ can also be translated into the regularization penalties.

We assume that the rating is continuous, i.e., $r_{ij} \in \mathbb{R}$, while the demographics can be continuous, i.e., $s_i \in \mathbb{R}$ such as the age, or binary, i.e., $s_i \in \{0, 1\}$ such as the gender. For a continuous variable, the loss function represents least mean square error, that is

$$\ell(y, \hat{y}) = (y - \hat{y})^2. \tag{4}$$

For binary variable, the choice of loss function can be the logistic regression error or least mean square error, that is

$$\ell(y, \hat{y}) = (1 - y\hat{y})^2. \tag{5}$$

3.2 Alternative Optimization

The parameters in the objective function defined in equation (3) are learned through an alternative optimization following the two steps:

(1) Given item profile V and regressor θ, a decision tree T is learned such that:

$$\min_{T} \lambda_r \sum_{(i,j)\in O} \ell_r(r_{ij}, T(x_i)^\top v_j) + \lambda_s \sum_{i\in S} \ell_s(y_i, T(x_i)^\top \theta). \tag{6}$$

(2) Given $T(x)$, variables v_j and θ are learned such that

$$\min_{V} \sum_{(i,j)\in O} \ell_r(r_{ij}, T(x_i)^\top v_j) + \lambda_v ||V||^2, \tag{7}$$

$$\min_{\theta} \sum_{i\in S} \ell_s(y_i, T(x_i)^\top \theta) + \lambda_\theta ||\theta||^2. \tag{8}$$

The item profile v_j and the regressor θ can be initialized randomly. Another option for item profile initialization is through matrix factorization method such as [17] using training data. Given the decision tree T, a closed-form solution for the item profiles v_j ($j = 1, 2, \ldots, n$) exists:

$$v_j = \left(\sum_{(i,j)\in O} T(x_i)T(x_i)^\top + \lambda_v I \right)^{-1} \left(\sum_{(i,j)\in O} r_{ij} T(x_i) \right). \tag{9}$$

The regressor θ can be generally solved through gradient decent and updated as $\theta = \theta - \delta\Delta\theta$ where δ is the learning rate and $\Delta\theta$ is:

$$\Delta\theta = \sum_{i\in S} \ell_s'(y_i, \hat{y}_i) T(x_i) + \lambda_\theta w, \tag{10}$$

where $\hat{y}_i = T(x_i)^\top \theta$ consists of previous estimations.

The major challenge is that the number of possible items to query is very large, e.g., $n \sim 10^5$ in a movie recommender system. It is therefore computational prohibitive to search over all possible trees in order to get a global optimal solution to equation (6). We propose an efficient greedy algorithm to find an approximation.

3.3 Decision Tree Construction

Compared with classification and regression loss in traditional decision tree algorithms such as C4.5 and CART [8], our objective is to minimize the loss of both rating prediction and demographic inference as defined in equation (6). The decision tree is constructed in a top-down approach using training user data to minimize the loss recursively. A ternary decision tree to represent the mapping function T is suggested in previous work [10] to account for a large portion of users with no explicit responses.

Specifically, for each node in the decision tree, the best set of questions are learned by optimizing the objective defined in equation (6). Users are then split into three subsets L, D, and U according to the responses to those questions. The procedure is recursive until the decision tree grows to a certain depth. Starting from the root, given an item j to query, users are divided to three groups L, D, and U if the response value is $x_{ij} = 1, -1, 0$ corresponding to "like", "dislike" and "unknown". Generally, more than one item can be selected at each node to minimize user cognitive burden as suggested in [28]. In such cases, we assign each item with a weight and denote the n-dimensional weight vector by w, which defines a hyperplane to partition user responses into different groups. Users at the current node are split into group L if the answer $x_i^\top w$ is positive, group D if $x_i^\top w$ is negative, or group U when none of the questions are answered. To find the weight vector w that leads to the best split, we minimize the following function:

$$\begin{aligned} \min_{w} \lambda_r & \sum_{i\in L(w)} \sum_{(i,j)\in O} \ell_r(r_{ij}, u_L^\top v_j) + \lambda_s \sum_{i\in L(w)\cap S} \ell_s(y_i, u_L^\top \theta) \\ &+ \lambda_r \sum_{i\in D(w)} \sum_{(i,j)\in O} \ell_r(r_{ij}, u_D^\top v_j) + \lambda_s \sum_{i\in D(w)\cap S} \ell_s(y_i, u_D^\top \theta) \\ &+ \lambda_r \sum_{i\in U(w)} \sum_{(i,j)\in O} \ell_r(r_{ij}, u_U^\top v_j) + \lambda_s \sum_{i\in U(w)\cap S} \ell_s(y_i, u_U^\top \theta) \\ \text{s.t. } & ||w||_0 \le l, \end{aligned} \tag{11}$$

where u_L, u_D and u_U are the optimal user profiles at child nodes L, D and U. In addition, $\|w\|_0$ is the number of non-zeros and the constraint $\|w\|_0 \leq l$ determines that the number should be no greater than l. For simplicity, we assume one item to ask at each node, that is $l = 1$. We set all except the jth entry in weight vector w to 0. The problem boils down to finding the best single item to split users so as to minimize prediction loss. However, our framework can be easily generalized to multi-item split by adopting existing techniques as described in [28].

The optimal profiles u_L, u_D and u_U are the ones to minimize prediction loss in each child. Specifically, the profile u_L in group L is solved by:

$$u_L = \arg\min_u \lambda_r \sum_{i \in L(w)} \sum_{(i,j) \in O} \ell_r(r_{ij}, u_L^\top v_j) + \lambda_s \sum_{i \in L(w) \cap S} \ell_s(y_i, u_L^\top \theta) + \lambda_u \|u - u_p\|^2, \tag{12}$$

where λ_u is a regularization parameter for user profile u at the current node so that the profile is regularized towards u_p to avoid overfitting. The user profile u can be generally solved through gradient decent and updated as $u = u - \delta \Delta u$ where δ is the learning rate and Δu is:

$$\Delta u = \lambda_r \sum_{i \in L(w)} \sum_{(i,j) \in O} \ell_r'(r_{ij}, \hat{r_{ij}}) v_j + \lambda_s \sum_{i \in L(w) \cap S} \ell_s'(y_i, \hat{y_i}) \theta + \lambda_u (u - u_p), \tag{13}$$

where $\hat{r_{ij}} = u^\top v_j$ and $\hat{y_i} = u^\top \theta$ are previous estimations.

Specifically, for predicting both ratings and demographics such as age, we adopt least mean square error (L_2) as the loss function. In such cases, the user profile has a closed-form solution:

$$u_L = \left(\lambda_r \sum_{i \in L(w)} \sum_{(i,j) \in O} v_j v_j^\top + \lambda_s \sum_{i \in L(w) \cap S} \theta \theta^\top + \lambda_u I \right)^{-1} \left(\lambda_r \sum_{i \in L(w)} \sum_{(i,j) \in O} r_{ij} v_j + \lambda_s \sum_{i \in L(w) \cap S} y_i \theta + \lambda_u u_p \right). \tag{14}$$

The profiles u_D and u_U for the other two children can be computed in a similar way. In summary, we iterate over possible items and select the best one according to (11) for single-item split at each node. While for multi-item split, we alternatively optimize (11) using techniques as suggested in [28] and (12) until convergence. After the current node is constructed, we recursively construct its child nodes in a similar way.

3.4 Computational Complexity

We summarize the algorithm in Algorithms 1 and 2. For the tree construction, at each node, the complexity to compute latent profiles u_L, u_D and u_U for each possible split is $O(nk^2 + k^3)$ including inversing a square matrix of size k. There are totally n possible splits since we consider one item to query at each node. Using a similar analysis in [33], the time complexity of preparing matrix coefficients for all possible splits is $\sum_{i=1}^m |O_i|^2$ at each tree level, where $|O_i|$ is the number of ratings of user i and m is the number of users. The complexity for building the whole tree is thus $O(d \sum_{i=1}^m |O_i|^2 + \beta nk^3 + \beta n^2 k^2)$, where d is the depth of the tree and β is the total number of nodes in the decision tree. Usually, smaller parameter values for k and d are sufficient for good model performance. For example, the tree depth d is around 8 and k usually ranges from 10 to 20. The computational complexity for equation (9) is $O(nk^3 + n|O^j|k^2)$ where $|O^j|$ is the number of users who rate item j. Similarly, the complexity for updating the regressor θ is $O(k^3 + mk^2)$ with choices of loss functions in equation (4) and (5). The alternative optimization usually converges in a few iterations.

Algorithm 1 Alternative Optimization

Require: The training data $R = r_{ij}|(i,j) \in O$, $Y = y_i \in S$.
Ensure: Estimate decision tree T, item profile v_j ($j = 1, 2, \ldots, n$), and regressor θ.

Initialize v_j ($j = 1, 2, \ldots, n$) using [17].
Initialize θ randomly.
while not converge **do**
  Learn a decision tree T as in Algorithm 2.
  Update v_j by Equation (9).
  Update θ by Equation (10).
end while
return T, v_j ($j = 1, 2, \ldots, n$) and θ.

Algorithm 2 Greedy Tree Construction

function FitTree(AtNode)
Compute u_L, u_D and u_U using Equation (12).
Find the best split item or item set in Equation (11) using [28].
Split users into three groups $L(w)$, $D(w)$ and $U(w)$.
if square error reduces after split **and** depth < maxDepth **then**
  call FitTree($L(w)$), FitTree($D(w)$) and FitTree($U(w)$) to construct subtrees.
end if
return T with $T(x)$
end function

4 EXPERIMENTS

In the experiments, we would like to demonstrate that our multi-task model is effective in improving the prediction accuracy of both demographic inference and item recommendation with only a few sets of selected questions for cold-start users. We further discuss the tradeoff between user privacy and the utility of personalization, where the former is captured by the prediction accuracy of demographics and the latter is captured by the recommendation accuracy. The estimation framework is examined on three movie recommendation datasets: MovieLens, Flixster and Bookcrossing.

4.1 Experiment Setting

We evaluate the performance of our multi-task model in a cold-start setting. For each dataset, users are randomly split into a training set and a test set with 80%/20% ratio, respectively. The users in the training set are assumed to be warm-start users and their ratings and demographic information are visible to the system. Our model is learned and the set of items are constructed as the probing questions

Table 1: Dataset description.

Dataset	Users	Items	Ratings	Gender	Age
MovieLens	6, 040	3, 952	1, 000, 209	71%/29%	NA
Flixster	23, 488	5, 795	5, 625, 681	43%/57%	24
Book	5, 411	34, 963	384, 888	NA	35

based on training data. In contrast, the users in the test set are assumed to be cold-start users. Their ratings are further split into two disjoint sets: answer and evaluation sets that contain 80% and 20% ratings. We use the answer set to simulate cold-start user responses in the rating elicitation process. We use the evaluation set to evaluate the rating prediction accuracy for withheld items. Meanwhile, the demographic information of each user in the test set can be used to evaluate the demographic prediction accuracy. The evaluation process is summarized in Figure 1. In the rating elicitation process, we select items to query user responses. For simplicity, we ask for user binary responses and the question is in the form "Do you like movie *50 first date*?" Following the classic settings [10, 24, 33], we simulate test user responses as the following: the response is "like" if a user's rating is larger than 3 and "dislike" otherwise. The response is "unknown" if no rating is observed.

We seek to answer the following questions:

(1) Does the proposed algorithm outperform baselines in terms of the demographic prediction accuracy with respect to the number of query items?
(2) Does the multi-task model also enhance the recommendation accuracy?
(3) How many items to query are sufficient for demographic inference? What is the tradeoff between user privacy and the utility of personalization?

4.2 Dataset and Evaluation Metrics

The MovieLens dataset contains about 3, 900 movies, 6, 040 users and about 1 million ratings. In this dataset, about 4% of the user-movie interactions are observed and each user rates at least 20 movies. The ratings are integers ranging from 1 (dislike) to 5 (like). For the Flixster dataset, we select users with at least 20 ratings and movies with at least 60 ratings, which results in a subset of ratings for 5, 795 movies by 23, 488 users. The ratings are from 1 to 5. The Bookcrossing data is the most sparse dataset, with about 0.2% rating density. We select users with at least 20 ratings and movies with at least 4 ratings and obtain a subset of ratings for 34, 963 movies by 5, 411 users. The ratings are from 1 to 10 and we normalize the ratings to 1 to 5 in the same scale as the other two datasets for comparison. In terms of demographic information, the MovieLens dataset has gender and discrete age labels. The Flixster dataset has gender and continuous age labels. Both datasets have imbalanced gender distribution. There are about 71% males in MovieLens users and about 43% males in Flixster users. The Bookcrossing dataset has only continuous age labels. The mean age for Flixster and Bookcrossing are 24 and 35, respectively. In our experiments, we choose age regression tasks using Flixster and Bookcrossing data. We also choose Flixster and MovieLens for gender classification. For all three datasets, we compare the rating prediction accuracy. The details of each dataset are shown in Table 1.

The rating prediction performance is evaluated with the root mean square error (RMSE). For age regression, we use standard mean absolute error (MAE), rooted mean squared error (RMSE) and mean absolute percentage error (MAPE). The MAE measures the average of the absolute errors in test sets and the individual differences of each test data are weighted equally in the average. The RMSE measures the rooted squared error between truth and predicted values and then averaged over the samples. This means that the RMSE is most powerful to measure particularly undesirable large errors. The MAPE is more readable across different datasets. For gender classification, we use precision, recall and fscore to measure the performance for imbalanced binary classes.

4.3 Prediction Accuracy of User Demographics

In this section, we evaluate the performance of our multi-task model in terms of demographic prediction accuracy in cold-start settings to answer the first question in Section 4.1. We compare our model "TreeMulti" with 4 baseline methods named as "Mean", "Variance", "Weight". and "TreeSingle". The baseline "Mean" selects the top l items to query based on the mean ratings in the training dataset. The items with higher mean values indicate the "goodness". On the other hand, the baseline "Variance" picks the top ones with highest rating variance across users [24]. The third one "Weight" [29] first trains a regressor toward age using ratings in the training dataset and picks the item whose corresponding regression coefficient has highest absolute values. The last one "TreeSingle" [8] is single-task decision tree model to predict demographics from ratings.

Figure 2 compares the prediction accuracy of our model with baselines for age regression on two datasets. The first row of Figure 2 compares the performance on dataset Flixster. For all models, the age prediction error measured in MAE and RMSE decreases when the number of questions increases. Our model "TreeMulti" performs better than "TreeSingle" since the latent user profiles are learned through related tasks. Both tree models have big advantages over others especially within the first several questions. Specifically, our model achieves almost the same prediction accuracy within 5 questions as compared to 20 for others. Within 5 questions, we can predict age accuracy with MAE of 5 years, which is great considering a large range of users and sparse user responses. The model "Weight" also performs better than others in this sense and the model "Variance" performs only a little better than "Mean", which is reasonable since items with high means cannot help differentiating user types.

In the second row in Figure 2, we compare performance on dataset Bookcrossing and we see similar trends. Overall, the dataset Bookcrossing is more challenging for prediction than Flixster since the training set is extremely sparse with a rating density of around 0.2%. Our model "TreeMulti" still performs better than others with no major differences among the others.

Figure 3 compares the prediction accuracy of our model with several standard baselines for gender classification on datasets Flixster and MovieLens. The first row of Figure 3 compares the performance on dataset Flixster. For all methods, the gender prediction accuracy measured in precision, recall and fscore increase as more questions have been asked in general. The only exception is that method "Mean" decreases with more questions in precision metric. Our

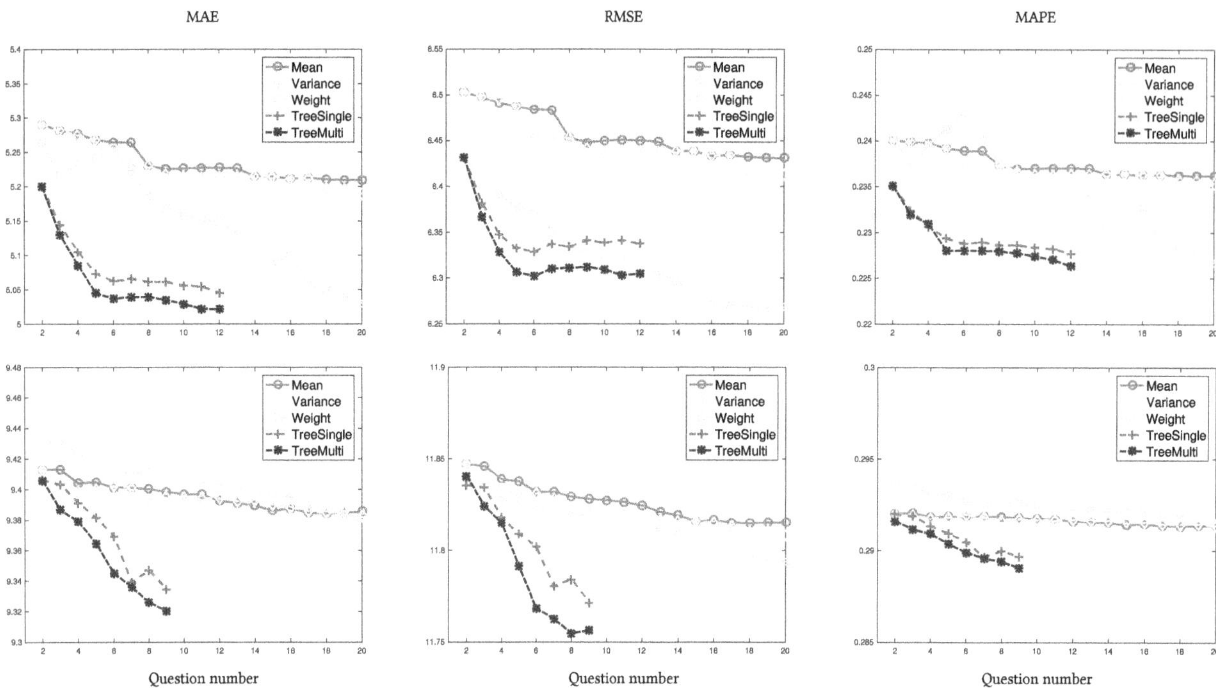

Figure 2: The age prediction metrics MAE and RMSE with respect to number of questions on two datasets Flixster (top row) and Bookcrossing (bottom row). For all models, the prediction error decreases as the number of questions increases. It shows that our methods "TreeMulti" performs better than baselines for both datasets.

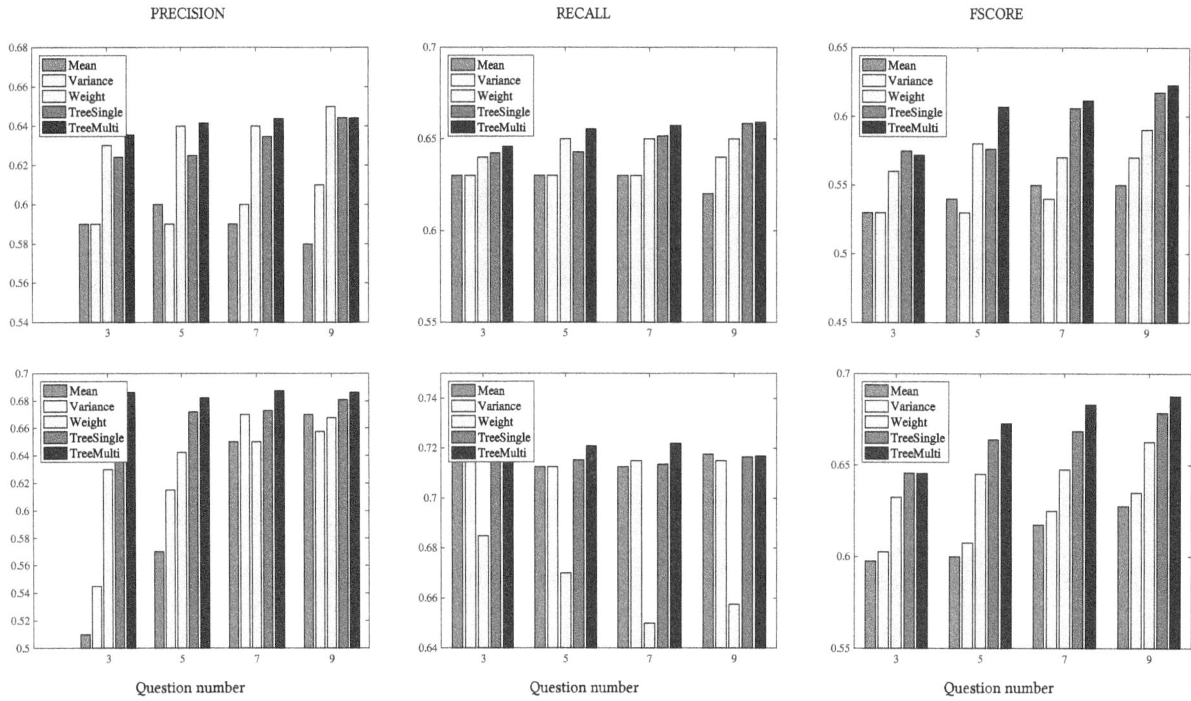

Figure 3: The gender prediction metrics precision, recall and fscore with respect to number of questions on datasets Flixster (top row) and MovieLens (bottom row). For all methods, the prediction accuracy increases as the number of questions increases. It shows that our method "TreeMulti" performs better than baselines for both datasets.

Table 2: Rating prediction error (RMSE) for cold-start users with respect to the number of query items on Datasets MovieLens, Flixster and Bookcrossing.

Data \Method		$n = 2$	$n = 3$	$n = 4$	$n = 5$	$n = 6$
Movie	TreeMulti	0.9247	0.9236	0.9226	0.9209	0.9212
	fMF	0.9310	0.9302	0.9282	0.9264	0.9241
	TreeMean	0.9447	0.9364	0.9320	0.9305	0.9302
Flixster	TreeMulti	0.8954	0.8946	0.8940	0.8939	0.8934
	fMF	0.9067	0.9050	0.9049	0.9048	0.9048
	TreeMean	0.9091	0.9089	0.9087	0.9085	0.9084
Book	TreeMulti	1.3462	1.3414	1.3383	1.3364	1.3356
	fMF	1.4094	1.4097	1.4040	1.4007	1.3938
	TreeMean	1.4865	1.4658	1.4605	1.4594	1.4590

model "TreeMulti" has a big advantage over others. Specifically, the prediction accuracy (fscore) of our model increases fastly from 3 to 5 questions and changes smoothly from 5 to 7 questions. The model "Weight" also performs better than others, followed by the model "Variance". Model "Mean" is the worst. The second row in Figure 3 compares gender classification performance on dataset MovieLens. Overall, the performance on MovieLens is better than Flixster. Our model "TreeMulti" performs better than others.

4.4 Recommendation Accuracy

We now evaluate our multi-task model in terms of rating prediction to answer the second question in Section 4.1. We compare our model with two state-of-the-art baselines. One is the bootstrapping tree model [10], denoted as "TreeMean", which predicts user-item ratings using the mean ratings at each node. The other is the strongest decision tree with matrix factorization, denoted as "fMF" [33]. The model estimates user/item profiles as latent factors and learn the profiles through matrix factorization. Our proposed algorithm differs from others in that it integrates both rating and user demographics through shared user profile learning, and thus enhances prediction accuracy.

For all three types of trees, we set the same maximum depth and regularization parameter $\lambda = 0.01$ for user and item profiles. We apply 5-fold cross validation to determine other parameters such as latent dimensions. The results on MovieLens, Flixster and Bookcrossing datasets are reported in Table 2. First of all, for all three models, the performance improves as the number of questions increases. The three algorithms generally are capable of refining user preference via adaptive rating elicitation for tackling cold-start problems. For all models, we can see that our "TreeMulti" model consistently outperforms others in all the three datasets.

In Tables 3 and 4, we present the query questions in user sessions using MovieLens dataset as well as the top-5 recommendations for them after the sessions. We can see that the recommended movies are quite related to the movies that the users liked based on their genres. In addition, the users who like romance or family movies more than drama or action movies are likely to be female. Those results illustrate that the elicitation process is reasonable.

Table 3: Examples of rating querying using MovieLens. The predicted gender for the case is Female.

No. Query Items	Query	Response
1	Terminator 2	Unknown
2	Sense and Sensibility	Like
3	Groundhog Day	Like

Rank	Movie Title
1	Casablanca
2	The Wrong Trousers
3	Life Is Beautiful
4	Much Ado About Nothing
5	Shakespeare in Love

Table 4: Examples of rating querying using MovieLens. The predicted gender for the case is Male.

No. Query Items	Query	Response
1	Terminator 2	Like
2	Dangerous Liaisons	Unknown
3	Independence Day	Like
4	Peter Pan	Dislike

Rank	Movie Title
1	The Matrix
2	Star Wars: Episode IV
3	Raiders of the Lost Ark
4	The Shawshank Redemption
5	Die Hard

4.5 Tradeoff between Privacy and Personalization

Experiments on three datasets MovieLens, Flixster and Bookcrossing show that our proposed method is sufficient to predict new user demographics using labeled training data from users who share private information. In particular, a recommender system can infer a new user's gender with 69% accuracy using as few as 10 selected queries. The result is promising given the fact that the reported gender accuracy for users with full rating history is 80% [29]. In addition, the prediction error of a new user's age in Flixster is smaller than 5 years in best-case scenario with no more than 12 queries. In general, the prediction accuracy depends on the rating density of training data. In comparison with MovieLens and Flixster, the prediction error of Bookcrossing user demographics is lower since the rating density of the training data is only round 0.2%.

In general, the more a user interacts with a recommender system, the more privacy threats the user is exposed to. However, the user will also gain more from personalized service. The experiment results from our proposed method show that favorable tradeoff for new users can be established. For example, as illustrated in Figure 3 and Table 2, a MovieLens user may choose to answer the first 3 questions and withhold the answers to the rest questions. As a result, the gender prediction accuracy will decrease from 69% to 64% with 7% reduction. Meanwhile, the recommendation error will change from 0.9209 to 0.9236 with only 0.3% increment. The experiments confirm that it is possible for new users to preserve their privacy by not giving answers to certain questions while still benefiting from personalization.

5 CONCLUSIONS

We proposed a novel and effective method to simultaneously infer private information and enhance user preference prediction for cold-start users, which is critical for recommender systems. Experimental results on three benchmark datasets including the Flixster dataset, the MovieLens dataset and the Bookcrossing dataset demonstrate that the proposed method outperforms existing ones. The proposed method can help new users to preserve their privacy by not giving answers to certain questions while enjoying some benefits from personalization. We further discuss the tradeoff between user privacy and the utility of personalization, which lays a solid foundation for future work of privacy-preserving recommender systems with full user control.

6 ACKNOWLEDGEMENT

We would like to thank the reviewers for their constructive and insightful comments. This work was supported in part by the Louisiana Board of Regents under Grant LEQSF(2017-20)-RD-A-29.

REFERENCES

[1] D. Agarwal and B.C. Chen. 2009. Regression-based latent factor models. In *Proc. of the 15th ACM SIGKDD International Conference on Knowledge Discovery and Data Mining*. 19–28.

[2] O. Averjanova, F. Ricci, and Q. N. Nguyen. 2008. Map-based interaction with a conversational mobile recommender system. In *Proc. of the Second International Conference on Mobile Ubiquitous Computing, Systems, Services and Technologies*. 212–218.

[3] N. F. Awad and M.S. Krishnan. 2006. The personalization privacy paradox: an empirical evaluation of information transparency and the willingness to be profiled online for personalization. *MIS quarterly* 30, 1 (2006), 13–28.

[4] L. Baltrunas, B. Ludwig, S. Peer, and F. Ricci. 2012. Context relevance assessment and exploitation in mobile recommender systems. *Personal and Ubiquitous Computing* 16, 5 (2012), 507–526.

[5] S. Bhagat, U. Weinsberg, S. Ioannidis, and N. Taft. 2014. Recommending with an agenda: active learning of private attributes using matrix factorization. In *Proc. of the 8th ACM Conference on Recommender systems*. 65–72.

[6] B. Bi, M. Shokouhi, M. Kosinski, and T. Graepel. 2013. Inferring the demographics of search users: social data meets search queries. In *Proc. of the International Conference on World Wide Web*. 131–140.

[7] C. Boutilier, R.S. Zemel, and B. Marlin. 2003. Active collaborative filtering. In *Proc. of the 19th Conference on Uncertainty in Artificial Intelligence*. 98–106.

[8] L. Breiman, J. Friedman, R. Olshen, and C. Stone. 1984. *Classification and Regression Trees*. Wadsworth and Brooks, Monterey, CA.

[9] J.A. Calandrino, A. Kilzer, A. Narayanan, E.W. Felten, and V. Shmatikov. 2011. "You Might Also Like:" Privacy Risks of Collaborative Filtering. In *Proc. of the IEEE Symposium on Security and Privacy*. 231–246.

[10] N. Golbandi, Y. Koren, and R. Lempel. 2011. Adaptive bootstrapping of recommender systems using decision trees. In *Proc. of the 4th ACM International Conference on Web Search and Data Mining*. 595–604.

[11] A.S. Harpale and Y. Yang. 2008. Personalized active learning for collaborative filtering. In *Proc. of the ACM SIGIR Conference*. 91–98.

[12] L. He, N.N. Liu, and Q. Yang. 2011. Active dual collaborative filtering with both item and attribute feedback. In *Proc. of the 25th AAAI Conference on Artificial Intelligence*.

[13] R. Jin and L. Si. 2004. A Bayesian approach toward active learning for collaborative filtering. In *Proc. of the 20th Conference on Uncertainty in Artificial Intelligence*. 278–285.

[14] Y. Koren. 2010. Factor in the neighbors: scalable and accurate collaborative filtering. *ACM Transactions on Knowledge Discovery from Data* 4, 1 (2010), 1–24.

[15] M. Kosinski, D. Stillwell, and T. Graepel. 2013. Private traits and attributes are predictable from digital records of human behavior. *Proceedings of the National Academy of Sciences* 110, 15 (2013), 5802–5805.

[16] B. Lakshminarayanan, G. Bouchard, and C. Archambeau. 2011. Robust Bayesian Matrix Factorisation. In *Proc. of the International Conference on Artificial Intelligence and Statistics*.

[17] N. D. Lawrence and R. Urtasun. 2009. Non-linear matrix factorization with gaussian processes. In *Proc. of the International Conference on Machine Learning*.

[18] A. Mislove, B. Viswanath, K.P. Gummadi, and P. Druschel. 2010. You are who you know: inferring user profiles in online social networks. In *Proc. of the ACM International Conference on Web Search and Data Mining*. 251–260.

[19] A. Narayanan and V. Shmatikov. 2008. Robust de-anonymization of large sparse datasets. In *Proc. of the IEEE Symposium on Security and Privacy*. 111–125.

[20] M. Pennacchiotti and A.M. Popescu. 2011. Democrats, republicans and starbucks afficionados: user classification in twitter. In *Proc. of the ACM SIGKDD International Conference on Knowledge Discovery and Data Mining*. 430–438.

[21] K. P. Puttaswamy and B. Y. Zhao. 2010. Preserving privacy in location-based mobile social applications. In *Proc. of the 11th Workshop on Mobile Computing Systems & Applications*. 1–6.

[22] D. Rao, D. Yarowsky, A. Shreevats, and M. Gupta. 2010. Classifying latent user attributes in twitter. In *Proc. of the 2nd international workshop on Search and mining user-generated contents*. 37–44.

[23] A.M. Rashid, I. Albert, D. Cosley, S.K. Lam, S.M. McNee, J.A. Konstan, and J. Riedl. 2002. Getting to know you: learning new user preferences in recommender systems. In *Proc. of the 7th International Conference on Intelligent User Interfaces*. 127–134.

[24] A.M. Rashid, G. Karypis, and J. Riedl. 2008. Learning preferences of new users in recommender systems: an information theoretic approach. In *SIGKDD Workshop on Web Mining and Web Usage Analysis*.

[25] R. Salakhutdinov and A. Mnih. 2008. Bayesian probabilistic matrix factorization using Markov chain Monte Carlo. In *Proc. of the International Conference on Machine Learning*.

[26] A. I. Schein, A. Popescul, L. H. Ungar, and D. M. Pennock. 2002. Methods and metrics for cold-start recommendations. In *Proc. of the ACM SIGIR Conference*. 253–260.

[27] M. Strobbe, O. Van Laere, S. Dauwe, B. Dhoedt, F. De Turck, P. Demeester, C. van Nimwegen, and J. Vanattenhoven. 2010. Interest based selection of user generated content for rich communication services. *Journal of Network and Computer Applications* 33, 2 (2010), 84–97.

[28] M. Sun, F. Li, J. Lee, K. Zhou, G. Lebanon, and H. Zha. 2013. Learning multiple-question decision trees for cold-start recommendation. In *Proc. of Conference on Web Search and Data Mining*.

[29] U. Weinsberg, S. Bhagat, S. Ioannidis, and N. Taft. 2012. Blurme: inferring and obfuscating user gender based on ratings. In *Proc. of the 6th ACM conference on Recommender systems*. 195–202.

[30] B. Zenker and B. Ludwig. 2009. ROSE: assisting pedestrians to find preferred events and comfortable public transport connections. In *Proc. of the 6th International Conference on Mobile Technology, Application & Systems*. 16.

[31] E. Zheleva and L. Getoor. 2009. To join or not to join: the illusion of privacy in social networks with mixed public and private user profiles. In *Proc. of the International Conference on World Wide Web*. 531–540.

[32] Y. Zhong, N.J. Yuan, W. Zhong, F. Zhang, and X. Xie. 2015. You are where you go: inferring demographic attributes from location check-ins. In *Proc. of the ACM International Conference on Web Search and Data Mining*. 295–304.

[33] K. Zhou, S. Yang, and H. Zha. 2011. Functional matrix factorizations for cold-start recommendation. In *Proc. of the ACM SIGIR Conference*. 315–324.

Scheduling Nodes in Underwater Networks using Voronoi Diagram

Eduardo P. M. Câmara Júnior
Universidade Federal de Minas Gerais
Belo Horizonte, Minas Gerais, Brazil
epmcj@dcc.ufmg.br

Luiz F. M. Vieira
Universidade Federal de Minas Gerais
Belo Horizonte, Minas Gerais, Brazil
lfvieira@dcc.ufmg.br

Marcos A. M. Vieira
Universidade de Federal Minas Gerais
Belo Horizonte, Minas Gerais, Brazil
mmvieira@dcc.ufmg.br

ABSTRACT

Underwater networks are used for monitoring water resources and underwater environments. Thus, it is important that the underwater sensor nodes cover the largest region possible, during the largest amount of time. This paper presents a method to perform node scheduling in underwater stratified networks. It aims to maintain the network active for longer, maintaining its connectivity. Voronoi Diagrams are used to decompose the space into regions around each node in order to determine which one should be scheduled to sleep. Simulation results show that the proposed method achieves the desired objectives, more than doubling the network lifetime while guaranteeing connectivity.

CCS CONCEPTS

• **Networks → Network algorithms**; *Network services*; *Wireless access networks*;

KEYWORDS

Node Scheduling; Voronoi Diagram; Underwater Network; Stratified Network

1 INTRODUCTION

The studies and monitoring activities in underwater environments are very relevant for human activities. As such environments have a major impact on our lives, whether through the water we drink or the climate changes they are responsible for, it is necessary to have a good knowledge about them. In this way, the collection of data from these environments is essential and can be performed using underwater networks.

This kind of network must provide communication between the underwater nodes, allowing them to adequately cover the environment. Unlike terrestrial networks, the equipment used in underwater networks are very expensive and their energy management are even more critical. Thus, it is necessary for the network nodes to cover the desired region for the longest possible time [21].

MSWiM '17, November 21–25, 2017, Miami, FL, USA

ACM ISBN 978-1-4503-5162-1/17/11...$15.00
https://doi.org/10.1145/3127540.3127565

This paper presents a method [1] to perform node scheduling in underwater stratified networks, where the sensor nodes and underwater devices are spread through layers at different depths. It aims to increase the network lifetime while guaranteeing its connectivity and also a data collection path from sensors to sink nodes. Voronoi diagrams are used in order to find the relevance of each node in the network and then select which ones can be temporarily deactivated. This maintains the delivery of sensed data collection and reduces the network energy consumption, prolonging the network lifetime. In addition, Voronoi diagrams can be computed in polynomial time without requiring computational costly techniques for scheduling nodes.

We evaluated the proposed model for node scheduling using Voronoi Diagram via simulations. The results show that the proposed solution achieves the desired objectives and lead to an increase of the network lifetime when it is used.

The main contributions of this paper are: the description of a method for node scheduling based on Voronoi diagrams that increases the network lifetime while guaranteeing connectivity and sensed data deliver, experimental multiple-parameters evaluation validating the proposed solution and demonstrating the benefits of it, and results that show that the network lifetime is increased.

This paper is organized as follows. Section 2 discusses the related work. Section 3 details the preliminary concepts. Section 4 describes the proposed method. Section 5 shows the evaluation and results. Finally, section 6 presents the conclusions and future work.

2 RELATED WORK

Due to the increasing attention given to underwater networks, many work have been developed to solve problems encountered in them.

Some data link layer protocols, such as Aloha [23], were developed for this kind of network. Other protocols were developed for the network layer, such as Pressure Routing [17], GEDAR [10], using opportunistic routing [11, 22], geographic routing [6], using depth control [9] or based in network centrality [8]. None of them investigates the scheduling of underwater nodes.

Routing techniques that consider nodes to be able to sleep for some time interval are presented in [5]. Protocols and algorithms to save network energy are presented in [7]. However, no one proposes the use of Voronoi diagrams to schedule nodes, saving their energy and increasing the network lifetime.

A schema to node scheduling in terrestrial sensor networks that uses Voronoi diagrams is developed in [24]. Through simulations,

[1]Code available at https://github.com/epmcj/uwnodescheduling .

the authors verify that it is able to save network energy without loosing sensing area. No study is presented for underwater networks or 3D networks with multiple node layers (stratified networks) nor uses the message exchange model presented here.

Voronoi diagrams are employed in solutions to other problems of underwater networks. The network coverage optimization problem is an example [25]. In [26] the authors propose a mechanism that uses Voronoi diagrams to adjust the depth of the nodes of a network and thus maximize its coverage. It is worth noting that neither can be used for node scheduling.

3 PRELIMINARY CONCEPTS

In this section, we present the preliminary concepts for this work. The network model considered is described first. Next, a brief description about Voronoi diagrams is given. Lastly, we describe the model used to estimate the packet delivery probability in an underwater network.

3.1 Network Model

When monitoring an environment, the nodes deployment should follow some organization. One possibility is to set some depths of interest and then spread the nodes along each one of them. A network that follows this model is called a stratified network. Without loss of generality, in this work we investigate the proposed method based on Voronoi diagrams in a stratified network. One can observe that every network can be stratified by considering all depths that have a node. Figure 1 shows an example of a stratified network with 3 layers, where points represent nodes and lines connect nodes that can exchange messages.

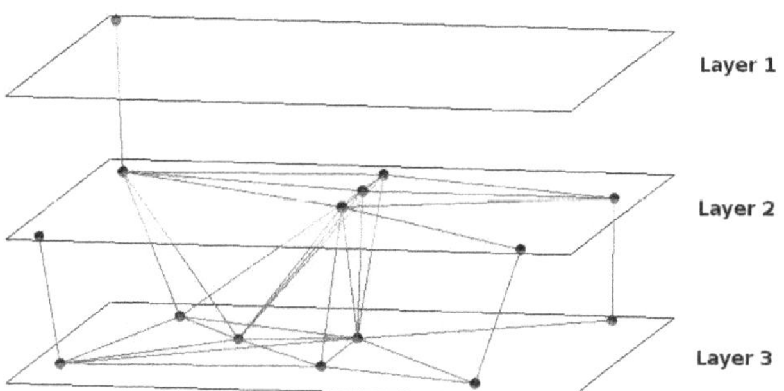

Figure 1: Stratified network example.

The data in the network are expected to flow from the bottom up. In other words, the nodes from the lower layers should send messages to the ones closest to the surface where sink nodes or gateways (also referred here as surface buoys) can be present and collect the data and transmit them to remote monitoring centers or even to the Internet. The Hydrocast routing algorithm [18] and DBR(Depth Based Routing) [27], for example, exploits the measured pressure levels (which is proportional to the nodes depth) in each node to route data to surface buoys.

Each network layer is considered as a 2D plan, since all nodes within it have the same depth. A layer must have at least one node and nodes in that layer should be able to communicate with one or more layers, otherwise the network would contain a disconnected component.

The position of the nodes can be evaluated in different moments of time. They might be global or relative to one point. Even though Global Positioning Systems (GPS) do not work properly in underwater environments [1], it is possible to use approaches based on localization techniques [13–15].

The network topology is considered as being dynamic. Thus, the nodes can be temporarily deactivated or permanently turned off.

3.2 Voronoi Diagram

A Voronoi diagram is a partitioning of a plane or space into regions based on distance to a set of points. It was defined by the mathematician Georgy Voronoi and have practical and theoretical applications.

Let $S = \{p_1, p_2, ..., p_n\}$ be a set of n distinct points (also called seeds or sites) in a Euclidean plane P. In a Voronoi diagram generated by S, each point p_i in S generates a region (called cell) such that any point inside it is closer to p_i than p_j, for all $j \neq i$ and $i, j \in \{1, ..., n\}$. Formally, a cell $V_i(S)$ can be defined as:

$$V_i(S) = \{q \in P \mid dist(p_i, q) \leq dist(p_j, q), \forall\, j \neq i\} \quad (1)$$

In some variations of the Voronoi diagram, the distance function may not be a simple euclidean distance. It can be limited by a value, resulting in a range-limited Voronoi partition, or be based in points weights, resulting in a weighted Voronoi partition [3].

The size of each Voronoi cell depends on the position of its site and the neighboring sites. If a site lies on the convex hull of S, then its corresponding cell is unbounded [12]. As sensor applications typically have interest in bounded fields F, the intersection between any cell $V_i(S)$ and F always leads to a bounded cell if the sensor nodes are represented by the points and then $S \subseteq F$.

Voronoi diagrams can be computed in polynomial time. Given n sites, the Voronoi diagram can be computed in $O(n \log n)$ time using $O(n)$ space [16].

Figure 2 shows Voronoi diagrams of an example of a stratified network with 3 layers. Each layer is considered as a plane that covers part of the monitoring region. The middle layer is highlighted in order to exemplify a Voronoi diagram. Each cell has one site. All points inside a cell are closer to the cell site than any other site.

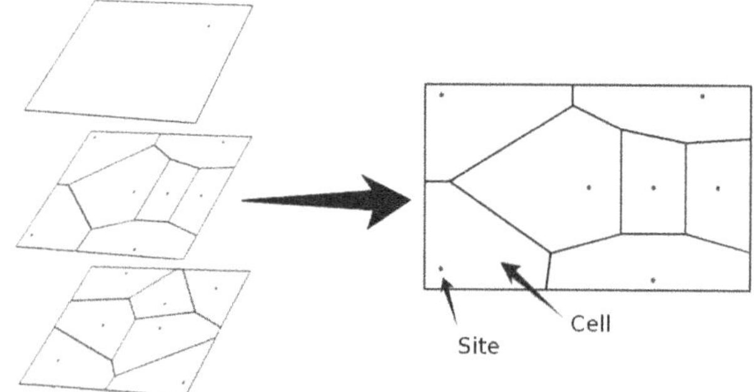

Figure 2: Example of a Voronoi Diagram of a bounded layer.

3.3 Packet Delivery Probability Estimation

In this subsection, we describe the underwater signal propagation model used to estimate the packet error rate [20]. It is mainly characterized by a signal attenuation and the aquatic ambient noise. A signal is attenuated when it travels through a distance d in an underwater acoustic channel. This attenuation, or path loss, is given by

$$A(d, f) = 10k \cdot \log d + 1000d \cdot \alpha(f) + 10 \quad (2)$$

where f is the signal frequency, d is the distance traveled by it, k is the spreading factor and $\alpha(f)$ is the absorption coefficient. In this formula, the path loss is expressed in dB. According to Stojanovic [20], the first and second terms represent, respectively, the spreading and the absorption loss. The geometry of propagation is described by the spreading factor (k). Its common values are $k = 2$ for spherical spreading, $k = 1$ for cylindrical spreading and $k = 1.5$ for practical spreading. The absorption coefficient can be calculated empirically using the Thorp's formula. When the frequency of the signal is above a few hundred Hz, the following formula is valid [2]:

$$10 \log \alpha(f) = 0.11 \frac{f^2}{1 + f^2} + 44 \frac{f^2}{4100 + f^2} + 2.75 \cdot 10^{-4} f^2 + 0.003, \quad (3)$$

where $\alpha(f)$ is expressed in dB/km for f in kHz.

In the ocean, the noise can be modeled as the sum of four sources: turbulence (N_t), shipping (N_s), waves (N_w) and thermal noises (N_{th}). Each one of these noise components can be expressed, in dB re μ Pa per Hz, as a function of frequency, in kHz, by the following empirical formulas [4]:

$$\begin{aligned} 10 \log N_t(f) &= 17 - 30 \log f \\ 10 \log N_s(f) &= 40 + 20(s - 0.5) + 26 \log f - 60 \log(f + 0.03) \\ 10 \log N_w(f) &= 50 + 7.5w^{\frac{1}{2}} + 20 \log f - 40 \log(f + 0.4) \\ 10 \log N_{th}(f) &= -15 + 20 \log f \end{aligned} \quad (4)$$

Different from turbulence and thermal noises, the shipping noise is modeled through the shipping activity factor s, with a value between 0 (low activity) and 1 (high activity). The waves noise represents the surface motion caused by the wind, where w is the wind speed in m/s.

Attenuation and noise values are used to evaluate the signal-to-noise ratio (SNR) that is observed when a signal of frequency f and power P is transmitted over a distance d. Considering Δf as the receiver noise bandwidth and counting only the path loss gains and losses, the narrow-band SNR is given by [20]

$$SNR(d, t) = \frac{P/A(d, f)}{N(f)\Delta f} \quad (5)$$

Once the SNR value is obtained, it is used in order to calculate the probability of bit errors over a distance. Using the BPSK (Binary Phase Shift Keying) modulation, where each symbol carries a bit, the Bit Error Rate (BER) is given by the formula [19]:

$$BER = \frac{1}{2}\left(1 - \sqrt{\frac{SNR(d, f)}{1 + SNR(d, f)}}\right) \quad (6)$$

The BER value is then used to estimate the Packet Error Rate (PER). For a packet with size of n bits, the probability of an error occurrence is given by

$$PER = 1 - (1 - BER)^n \quad (7)$$

Thus, the packet delivery probability is simply the complement of the PER and is represented by the second term in the formula above.

4 VORONOI SCHEDULING METHOD

This section describes the proposed method and illustrates one part of it using a small example.

4.1 Method description

The proposed method can be divided into steps. The first step consists of splitting the monitoring region between the nodes of the network. The Voronoi diagrams of each layer are used for this purpose. In these diagrams, the sites and their cells represent, respectively, the nodes and their monitoring areas. It is worth noting that every cell is bounded, since we consider that each layer is bounded by the monitoring region.

After determining the area for which each node is responsible, the next step consists of checking for nodes that can be disabled, or put in sleep mode for some time. By doing this, the energy of these nodes is spared for later use. In case of extending the network lifetime, they will potentially be used to replace some neighbor node that has run out of energy.

The verification of the second step is done layer by layer, starting with the one closest to the surface. The reason for starting this way is to always try to ensure that there are paths between the nodes and the sink. If a node has a monitoring area smaller than a given threshold and its absence does not disconnect any part of the network, then it can be deactivated. When this occurs, the region for which it was responsible for is divided between its neighbors. As a result, the Voronoi diagram of the layer containing the node is updated. After this update, a new verification in the layer is necessary. When there are no more nodes that can be deactivated in one layer, the verification moves to the next layer. The end of this step is reached when the deepest layer is checked. With this, the node scheduling is done. Algorithm 1 shows the pseudo-code of the node scheduling.

Algorithm 1 Node scheduling algorithm

```
for each layer do
    repeat
        voronoi ← CalculateVoronoi(layer)
        areas ← CalculateAreas(voronoi)
        smallest ← SmallestArea(areas)
        node ← NodeOfSmallestArea(voronoi, areas)
        if smallest < threshold & isNotEssencial(node) then
            PutToSleep(node)
            more_nodes ← true
        else
            more_nodes ← false
    until more_nodes ≠ true
```

Once the node scheduling is done, the network then becomes active and the nodes start sending data to the surface. At some point, some network nodes begin to become inaccessible by depleting their energy supplies. As soon as a network node dies, its monitoring area must be split between its active neighbors. To represent this change, the Voronoi diagram of the layer to which it belongs must be updated. This is similar to what is done in the second step of the node scheduling.

It is also necessary to check whether exists nodes that have lost contact with the sink. If this happens, it may be necessary to reactivate any of the previously nodes placed in sleep mode. This need can be verified by redoing the Voronoi diagram of the layer, considering all the nodes that still have energy. This includes both active and deactivated nodes. It is worth noting that there may be no alternatives in some cases. For example, a node has its energy depleted more quickly than the others if is the only one available to relay data from the nodes of the layers below its own. When it dies, and if there is not any node that can replace it, all the nodes that depend on it are no longer able to send data to the surface because there is no alternative route. This helps in the process of "death" of the network. The network is considered dead when only a small percentage of its nodes are still active and able to send messages to the surface nodes.

4.2 Example

To illustrates the verification step of the method, the topologies shown in Figures 3(a) e 3(b) are considered. Both are very similar, differing only in two connections: one between nodes 1 and 2 and another between nodes 4 and 5. These connections exist in the first but not in the second.

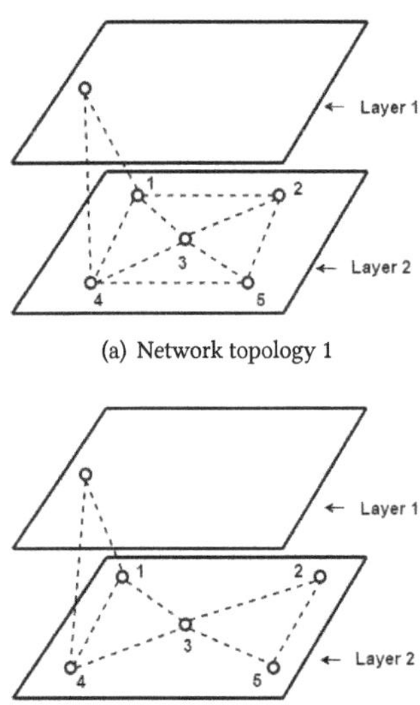

Figure 3: Example of two networks with similar topologies. Circles mean nodes and dashed lines represent connections between them.

The verification in both cases begins with layer 2, since the first has only the sink node. The Voronoi diagrams of this layer in both topologies are quite similar, being roughly represented by Figure 4(a). Assuming that the monitoring area of node 3 is smaller than a previously defined threshold, it is necessary to check whether it can be deactivated or not. In the first topology this is possible because all nodes that communicate with it are able to send data to the first layer node through others. But in the second it is not. Turning node 3 off would cause nodes 2 and 4 to lose communication with the rest of the network.

In the first case, after the deactivation of node 3, the Voronoi diagram of the second layer is updated and looks like the one shown in Figure 4(b). After that, in both cases, there are no more candidate nodes to be deactivated and the scheduling is complete.

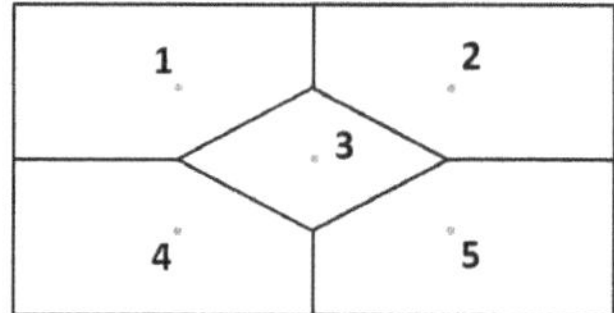

(a) Initial Voronoi diagram

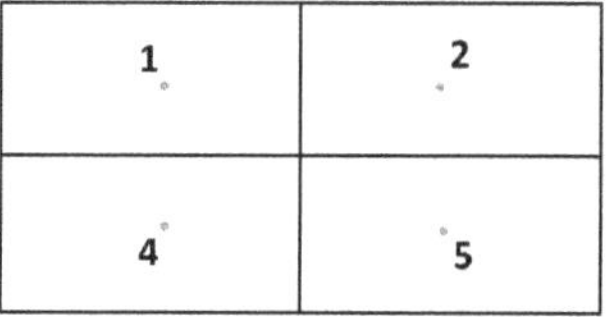

(b) Updated Voronoi diagram

Figure 4: Updating a Voronoi diagram when a node is deactivated.

5 EVALUATIONS

This section describes the settings and results of the experiments. The evaluation of the proposed method was done through simulations using MATLAB software.

5.1 Simulation Settings

Unless otherwise specified, all the experiments use a network whose nodes are distributed along five layers of $1500m \times 1500m$ each. The first layer is aways on the surface and has only the sink node, while the others have n nodes each. When required, n is varied in order to obtain different node density configurations.

The depth of each layer, except the one that contains the sink node, is randomly determined with the restriction that none gets isolated. This restriction means that the distance between any two subsequent layers can not be greater than the nodes transmission range. Therefore, one way to build a network that obeys this constraint is to incrementally add layers with increasing depths within a interval. It was used in the simulations with the interval $[t_{range}/2, t_{range}]$, where t_{range} is the nodes transmission range. The choice of this interval aims a better distribution of the layers so that they neither are so close nor too distant from each other.

Inside each layer, the nodes are uniformly distributed. The monitoring area threshold is defined as been a percentage of the nodes transmission area, as in [24]. It is considered that the network is dead when at least 50% of its nodes are not able to transmit data to the sink node.

The exchange of messages was simulated through a model where only one node transmits data at each unit of time. This model works as follow:

(1) A node is randomly chosen to send data to the sink node.
(2) The route between the two nodes that has the lowest number of hops is then determined.
(3) Next, the data transmission starts. The first node in the route tries to transmit to the second and so on. If a transmission succeeds, the receiver node sends back an acknowledgment. Otherwise the node may retransmit the message two more times.
(4) If the sink node receives the data or the transmission attempts are exhausted in some node, then the cycle starts again in step 1.

Figure 5 exemplifies a round of the message exchange model. First, the node 5 is chosen to send its data to the node 1, or the sink node (Figure 5(b)). Then the route between them is determined and has the node 3 in it (Figure 5(c)). If no failure occurs, then node 5 sends the data message to node 3 (Figure 5(d)), which then forwards it to the sink node (Figure 5(e)). After this, a new node is chosen (Figure 5(f)).

The packet delivery probability described in section 3.3 was used to verify whether a transmission was successful or not. The spreading factor k was set to value 1.5 (practical spreading). The wind speed and the shipping activity factor s were both consider as being null.

It was considered that only one node would be transmitting a message every minute. The size of the message packets was 500 bytes.

It was assumed that the nodes had transmitters with power equals to 1 W e frequency of 100 kHz. In some experiments their range was considered as being 250 meters. In others this value varied between 100 and 400 meters. The receivers noise bandwidth was 3 dB.

A summary of the parameter values used is shown in Table 1.

Table 1: Default parameter values used in the simulation.

Parameter	Value
Transmission rate	1 node/minute
Transmission frequency	100 kHz
Packet size	500 bytes
Transmission range	250 m
Transmission power	1 W
Receiver noise bandwidth	3 dB
Spreading factor (k)	1.5 (practical spread)
Wind speed (w)	0 m/s
Shipping activity factor (s)	0

The network energy consumption was modeled as follows:

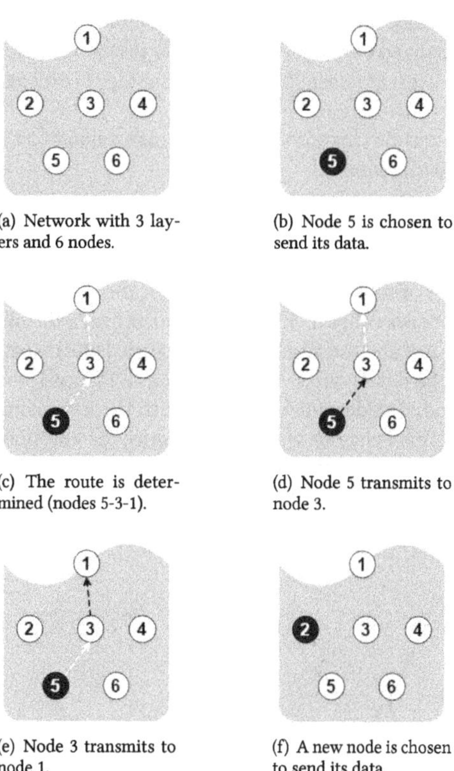

(a) Network with 3 layers and 6 nodes.
(b) Node 5 is chosen to send its data.
(c) The route is determined (nodes 5-3-1).
(d) Node 5 transmits to node 3.
(e) Node 3 transmits to node 1.
(f) A new node is chosen to send its data.

Figure 5: Example of running a round using the model for message exchange.

- At each unit of time, nodes consume some part of their energy. This consumption depends on their state. An active node spends more energy than a deactivated one.
- Data transmission only consumes power from the transmitting node. The reason is that nodes need to listen to the environment all the time when searching for new messages.

The values associated to the energy consumptions were used as percentages in the simulations. This allows greater generality, since the consumption varies from device to device. Thus, at the beginning of the simulation, each node of the network has 100% of its power capacity. It was also considered that the sink node had a higher power capacity than the other nodes. This is due to the fact that it is much easier to recharge a node that is on the surface than one that is submerged. For example, solar energy could be used to constantly recharge the sink node. The values of energy consumption are shown in Table 2.

Table 2: Energy consumption parameters used in the experiments.

State	Consumption (in %)
Transmitting	0.2
Activated	0.01
Deactivated	0.001

The network lifetime is measured based on the number of messages exchanged between the nodes. The reason for that is that, as said before, it is assumed that only one message is exchanged every minute.

All the results correspond to an average value of 30 runs with 95% confidence interval.

5.2 Results

First, we tried to verify the influence of the number of layers on the number of nodes deactivated. For this, the number of nodes in the network was kept at 200, the monitoring area threshold value was set at 20% and the number of layers varied until no more nodes could not be deactivated. As can be seen in Figure 6, the number of deactivated nodes quickly decays with the increasing number of layers. This behavior was expected since the addition of a new layer increases the network coverage area and thus it is necessary that more nodes become active.

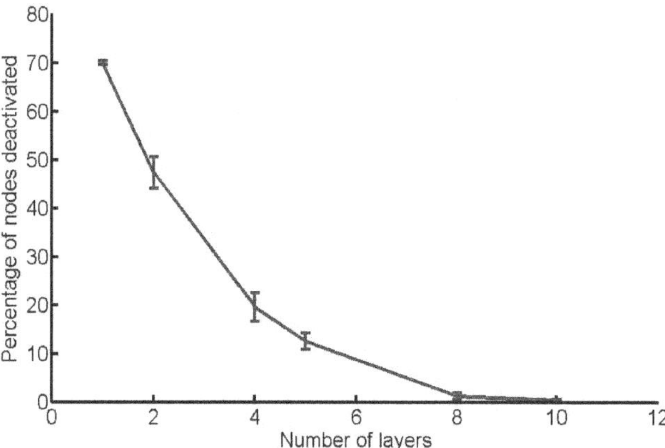

Figure 6: Percentage of nodes deactivated according to the number of network layers.

Figure 7 shows the relationship between the density of nodes per layer and the number of deactivated nodes, for the monitoring area thresholds of 5%, 10% and 20%. The transmission range varies in each one of the figures, assuming the values of 100, 250 and 400 m in Figures 7(a), 7(b) e 7(c), respectively. It is possible to see that, as expected, the percentage of deactivated nodes grows as node density increases in all the three cases. This growth can also be observed when the monitoring area threshold value is increased. The results also show that the transmission range directly impacts in the number of deactivated nodes. It may cause no node to be deactivated, as shown in Figure 7(a), or with more than 80% of the network been deactivated as shown in Figure 7(c).

In order to check the impact of the method in the network lifetime, the value of the monitoring area threshold was again considered as 20%. Figure 8 shows the relationship between the density of nodes per layer and the network lifetime, with and without the use of the proposed method. It is possible to see that the use of the proposed method leads to an increase in the network lifetime, especially when it has a high node density. In some cases, the time has doubled.

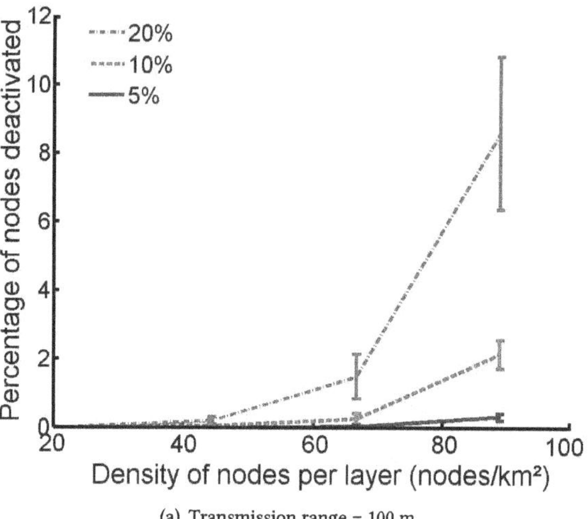

(a) Transmission range = 100 m.

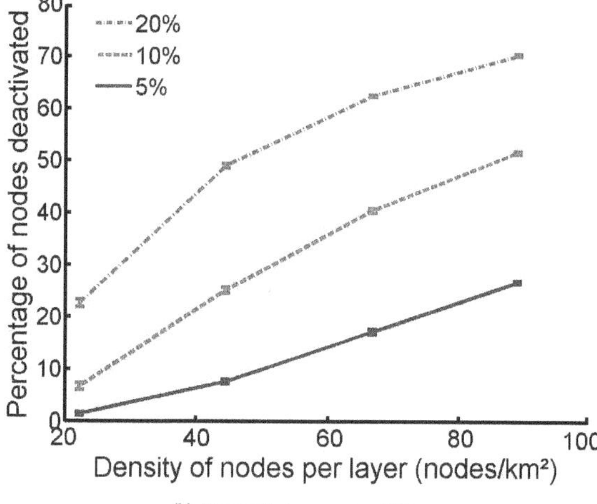

(b) Transmission range = 250 m.

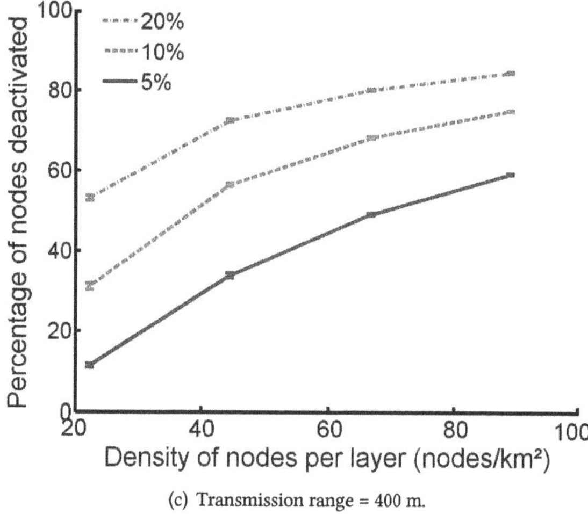

(c) Transmission range = 400 m.

Figure 7: Percentage of nodes deactivated per node density per layer, for three monitoring area thresholds and different transmission range values.

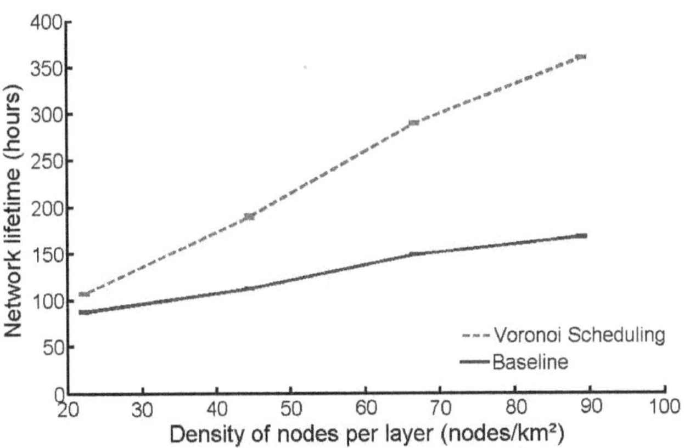

Figure 8: Network lifetime per node density per layer, with and without the proposed method.

Figure 9 shows the relationship between the number of data sent to the sink node and the density of nodes per layer, with and without using the proposed method. A data sent occurs every time a node is chosen to send its data to the surface. It can be observed that, as a consequence of the increase in the network lifetime, the use of the proposed method leads to an increase in the number of transmissions. It can also be noted that this increase is similar to that achieved in the network lifetime. The reason for this is that the both are measured based on the messages exchanged between the nodes.

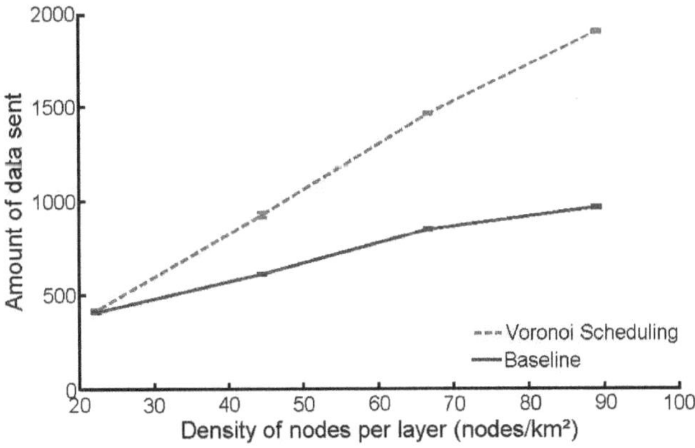

Figure 9: Amount of data sent per node density per layer, with and without the proposed method.

The relationship between the average number of messages per data sent, varying the density of nodes per layer, is shown in Figure 10. It is noticed that using the proposed method, the average number of messages per data sent is greater than without its use. This is mainly due to the fact that deactivating some nodes causes the distance between some neighboring nodes to be larger. With this increase, the probability of packet errors also increases and more retransmissions may be required to deliver the data correctly. This results in a small decrease in the network lifetime that, as can be seen in Figure 8, can never overcome the gains.

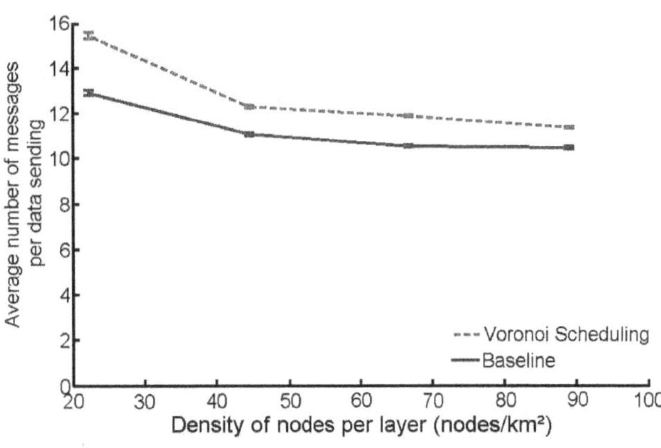

Figure 10: Average number of messages exchanged in a data sent to the sink node when node density per layer is varied, with and without the proposed method.

Figure 11 shows the percentage of the network nodes that are alive over time, with baseline and using the Voronoi scheduling. The number of nodes per layer was kept at 100 for this experiment. It is possible to notice the advantage of using our proposed method as the network nodes are kept alive for longer. The dotted line represents the threshold value for considering the network dead. Therefore, in the baseline case the network dies before 150 hours and with the Voronoi method it is extended till over 270 hours.

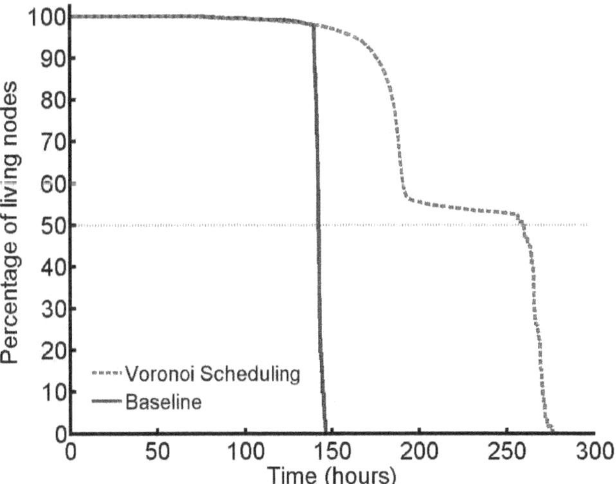

Figure 11: Percentage of living nodes over time. The dotted line represents the threshold value for the network to be considered dead.

6 CONCLUSIONS AND FUTURE WORK

This paper presents a method to perform the node scheduling in underwater stratified networks. It calculates the Voronoi diagrams of each one of the network layers in order to define the nodes that might be deactivated temporarily for further use. A node may be deactivated only if it does not disconnect other nodes from the network. We showed that using this method the network lifetime could be increased and connectivity between nodes maintained.

Simulations showed that the number of deactivated nodes grows with the number of nodes in the network, with their transmission range and with the monitoring area threshold. It was also possible to see that, even with an increase in the average number of messages per data sending, the proposed method is able to fulfill its goal of increasing network lifetime. In some cases, this increase has doubled the lifetime. Thus, this method is attractive for use in underwater sensor networks.

As future work, we intend to evaluate the use of this method when the network has a greater amount of data traffic. Besides, we plan to use weighted Voronoi Diagrams, where the cells are defined by a weighted distance, to model priority areas within the region to be monitored and thus allow a higher concentration of active nodes in them. We also intend to evaluate its use in three-dimensional underwater networks, where the nodes can be spread in a general way.

ACKNOWLEDGEMENT

The authors would like to thank the research agencies CNPq, CAPES and FAPEMIG for their financial support.

REFERENCES

[1] Ian F. Akyildiz, Dario Pompili, and Tommaso Melodia. 2005. Underwater acoustic sensor networks: research challenges. *Ad Hoc Networks* 3, 3 (2005), 257 – 279. https://doi.org/10.1016/j.adhoc.2005.01.004

[2] Leonid Brekhovskikh and Yury Lysanov. 1982. *Fundamentals of Ocean Acoustics.* Springer.

[3] Francesco Bullo, Jorge Cortés, and Sonia Martinez. 2009. *Distributed control of robotic networks: a mathematical approach to motion coordination algorithms.* Princeton University Press.

[4] Rodney FW Coates. 1989. *Underwater acoustic systems.* Halsted Press.

[5] Rodolfo WL Coutinho, Azzedine Boukerche, Luiz FM Vieira, and Antonio AF Loureiro. 2015. Modeling and Analysis of Opportunistic Routing in Low Duty-Cycle Underwater Sensor Networks. In *Proceedings of the 18th ACM International Conference on Modeling, Analysis and Simulation of Wireless and Mobile Systems.* ACM, 125–132.

[6] Rodolfo WL Coutinho, Azzedine Boukerche, Luiz FM Vieira, and Antonio AF Loureiro. 2016. Geographic and Opportunistic Routing for Underwater Sensor Networks. *IEEE Trans. Comput.* 65, 2 (2016), 548–561.

[7] Rodolfo WL Coutinho, Azzedine Boukerche, Luiz FM Vieira, and Antonio AF Loureiro. 2016. On the design of green protocols for underwater sensor networks. *IEEE Communications Magazine* 54, 10 (2016), 67–73.

[8] Rodolfo WL Coutinho, Azzedine FM Boukerche, Luiz Vieira, and Antonio Loureiro. 2016. A Novel Centrality Metric for Topology Control in Underwater Sensor Networks. In *Proceedings of the 19th ACM International Conference on Modeling, Analysis and Simulation of Wireless and Mobile Systems.* ACM, 205–212.

[9] Rodolfo WL Coutinho, Luiz F. M. Vieira, and Antonio A. F. Loureiro. 2013. DCR: Depth-Controlled routing protocol for underwater sensor networks. In *2013 IEEE Symposium on Computers and Communications (ISCC).* IEEE, 453–458.

[10] Rodolfo W. L. Coutinho, Azzedine Boukerche, Luiz F. M. Vieira, and Antonio A. F. Loureiro. 2014. GEDAR: geographic and opportunistic routing protocol with depth adjustment for mobile underwater sensor networks. In *2014 IEEE International Conference on Communications (ICC).* IEEE, 251–256.

[11] Rodolfo W. L. Coutinho, Azzedine Boukerche, Luiz F. M. Vieira, and Antonio A. F. Loureiro. 2016. Design guidelines for opportunistic routing in underwater networks. *IEEE Communications Magazine* 54, 2 (2016), 40–48.

[12] M. de Berg, O. Cheond, M. van Kreveld, and M. Overmars. 2008. *Computational Geometry: Algorithms and Applications* (3rd ed.). Springer-Verlag.

[13] Melike Erol, Luiz FM Vieira, Antonio Caruso, Francesco Paparella, Mario Gerla, and Sema Oktug. 2008. Multi stage underwater sensor localization using mobile beacons. In *Sensor Technologies and Applications, 2008. SENSORCOMM'08. Second International Conference on.* IEEE, 710–714.

[14] Melike Erol, Luiz FM Vieira, and Mario Gerla. 2007. Localization with Dive'N'Rise (DNR) beacons for underwater acoustic sensor networks. In *Proceedings of the second workshop on Underwater networks.* ACM, 97–100.

[15] Melike Erol, Luiz Filipe M Vieira, and Mario Gerla. 2007. AUV-aided localization for underwater sensor networks. In *Wireless Algorithms, Systems and Applications, 2007. WASA 2007. International Conference on.* IEEE, 44–54.

[16] S Fortune. 1986. A Sweepline Algorithm for Voronoi Diagrams. In *Proceedings of the Second Annual Symposium on Computational Geometry (SCG '86).* ACM, New York, NY, USA, 313–322. https://doi.org/10.1145/10515.10549

[17] Uichin Lee, Paul Wang, Youngtae Noh, Luiz Filipe M. Vieira, Mario Gerla, and Jun-Hong Cui. 2010. Pressure Routing for Underwater Sensor Networks.. In *INFOCOM 2010. The 29th Conference on Computer Communications. IEEE.* 1676–1684.

[18] Youngtae Noh, Uichin Lee, Saewoom Lee, Paul Wang, Luiz FM Vieira, Jun-Hong Cui, Mario Gerla, and Kiseon Kim. 2016. Hydrocast: pressure routing for underwater sensor networks. *IEEE Transactions on Vehicular Technology* 65, 1 (2016), 333–347.

[19] Theodore S Rappaport and others. 1996. *Wireless communications: principles and practice.* Vol. 2. Prentice Hall PTR New Jersey.

[20] Milica Stojanovic. 2007. On the relationship between capacity and distance in an underwater acoustic communication channel. *ACM SIGMOBILE Mobile Computing and Communications Review* 11, 4 (2007), 34–43.

[21] L Vieira, A Loureiro, A Fernandes, and Mario Campos. 2010. Redes de Sensores Aquáticas. *XXVIII Simpósio Brasileiro de Redes de Computadores e Sistemas Distribuídos, Gramado, RS, Brasil* 24 (2010).

[22] Luiz Filipe M Vieira. 2012. Performance and trade-offs of opportunistic routing in underwater networks. In *2012 IEEE Wireless Communications and Networking Conference (WCNC).* IEEE, 2911–2915.

[23] Luiz Filipe M Vieira, Jiejun Kong, Uichin Lee, and Mario Gerla. 2006. Analysis of aloha protocols for underwater acoustic sensor networks. *Extended abstract from WUWNet* (2006).

[24] MAM Vieira, LFM Vieira, Linnyer Beatrys Ruiz, Antonio Alfredo Ferreira Loureiro, Antônio Otávio Fernandes, and José Marcos S Nogueira. 2003. Scheduling nodes in wireless sensor networks: A Voronoi approach. In *Local Computer Networks, 2003. LCN'03. Proceedings. 28th Annual IEEE International Conference on.* IEEE, 423–429.

[25] Zhongsi Wang and Bang Wang. 2016. A novel node sinking algorithm for 3D coverage and connectivity in underwater sensor networks. *Ad Hoc Networks* (2016).

[26] Jiagao Wu, Yinan Wang, and Linfeng Liu. 2013. A Voronoi-Based Depth-Adjustment Scheme for Underwater Wireless Sensor Networks. *Int. J. Smart Sens. Intell. Syst* 6 (2013), 244–258.

[27] Hai Yan, Zhijie Jerry Shi, and Jun-Hong Cui. 2008. DBR: depth-based routing for underwater sensor networks. In *International conference on research in networking.* Springer, 72–86.

Energy-efficient HTTP Adaptive Streaming with Anticipated Channel Throughput Prediction in Wireless Networks

Liqiang Tao
Southern University of Science and Technology, China
Southeast University, China

Yi Gong*
Department of Electrical and Electronic Engineering,
Southern University of Science and Technology, China

Shi Jin
Southeast University, China

Junhui Zhao
Beijing Jiaotong University, China

ABSTRACT

Exploiting predicted channel information and designing energy-efficient content delivery protocols has started to draw attention, which is referred to as predictive, anticipatory, or context-aware resource allocation. In this paper, we investigate how predicted user rates can be exploited for streaming on-demand mobile video with dynamic adaptive streaming over HTTP(DASH). Specifically, we propose an edge-cloud assisted framework for prediction based DASH streaming; For optimal prediction scenario, we propose a lightweight algorithm to solve it; For imperfect prediction scenario, we model uncertainty in predicted user rates and propose a chance constraint programming method to dynamically allocate the risks, optimize QoE and system efficiency; For the multi-user scenario, we propose a quality-level-aware throughput gain maximization method to improve the network efficiency, fairness and QoE for all users under different prediction error variances; Simulation studies show that our method has a better performance than traditional methods in terms of average QoE, fairness and energy efficiency.

KEYWORDS

mobility assisted channel throughput prediction; radio access network; energy efficiency; video streaming; DASH

1 INTRODUCTION

In the HTTP-based adaptive streaming (or DASH) model that is commonly in use today, video is encoded at multiple discrete bit-rate levels, and each bit-rate stream is broken into multiple 2-10s short segments (or "chunks."). In DASH, the design of bit-rate adaptation logic for future segments is the most important factor to obtain the highest possible quality of experience (QoE). Recent measurement studies [7, 8] show that the performance of state-of-art DASH players has been found to be undesirable. For example, in [7], the authors reported the instability of video bit-rate selection, unfairness, and bandwidth under-utilization among three Microsoft Smooth Streaming clients sharing a 3-Mbps link. The root cause of these problems is the discrete nature of the video bit-rate level and the alternate ON-OFF traffic pattern in DASH-based systems [8]. The client may over-estimate its fair share of bandwidth if its ON state temporarily overlaps with the OFF state of other clients. At the same time, a client cannot estimate the available bandwidth during OFF periods, and this becomes a source of ambiguity to incorrectly determine its fair share of available bandwidth.

*Corresponding author: Yi Gong(gongy@sustc.edu.cn)

MSWiM '17, November 21–25, 2017, Miami, FL, USA

ACM ISBN 978-1-4503-5162-1/17/11...$15.00
https://doi.org/10.1145/3127540.3127574

Thus, a key metric that impacts the video bit-rate adaptation logic is the stability and predictability of the bandwidth. Current studies show that it is possible to accurately predict future available resources at short- and medium-term scales [3, 11]. In [5], the authors analyze two methods for throughput prediction, i.e., formula-based and history-based, and they find that history-based method is superior because of the difficulty associated with accurately measuring parameters in dynamic network environments, moreover, the use of simple heuristics to detect outliers and level shifts can significantly reduce the number of prediction errors. In [3], the authors propose a formula for short-term throughput prediction, and prediction errors increase with the predicted slot distance k. Some researchers use the hidden Markov model (HMM) to learn a throughput predictor for improving the TCP throughput stability, and they find that high throughput sessions tend to be more stable and predictable, and it is more similar in neighboring/recent time slots [11].

2 RELATED WORK

Current work has proposed buffer based [6] and rate based approaches [12]. In [14, 15], the authors use Markov model to predict and optimize future bit-rate adaptation logic. In [9], resource allocation for stored video delivery based on a knowledge of future wireless capacity is proposed; Based on [9], the authors in [13] propose an anticipatory future resource allocation scheme where the video quality and network resource allocation are jointly optimized; In [4], the author proposes the Fill algorithm, which can always find a feasible schedule whenever it exists. In [1], the author proposes predictive resource allocation method PGS (Predictive Green

Streaming) for HTTP adaptive streaming. In [2], the author proposes a chance-constrained predictive resource allocation method which optimizes QoE and energy efficiency in the probabilistic sense.

Based on the findings of existing literature, in this work, We try to solve prediction based DASH streaming problem, Specifically, the main contributions of our work are:

- We propose an edge-cloud assisted framework for prediction based DASH streaming. In the architecture, resource planning and allocation for all the users is executed in the BS side. The bit-rate adaptation logic is in the user's side. The operation of video streaming process is comply with the DASH standard.
- For imperfect prediction scenario, we model uncertainty in predicted user rates and propose a chance constraint programming method to dynamically allocate the risks, optimize QoE and system efficiency.
- For the multi-user scenario, we propose a quality-level-aware throughput gain maximization method to improve the network efficiency, fairness and QoE for all users under different prediction error variances.

3 SYSTEM MODEL

We consider a mobile edge-cloud assisted HTTP adaptive streaming architecture. A MEC (Mobile Edge Computing) server, which is directly integrated into access network, can monitor the network level context information(channel quality, traffic load). Each client is equipped with navigation hardware (or software) which facilitates user level context information (CQI, location and target destination) reporting to BS. Moreover, an external geographical radio-map database can be accessed by the predictive resource planning module. Based on these information, it predicts future channel capacity variation of each client within a finite look-ahead window. We assume that time is discrete, and is represented as a sequence of slots t_i with constant length τ, where τ is selected to be of the order of a few seconds. Further, we focus on slow variations in wireless capacity, e.g., the order of magnitude of a few seconds (large scale variation) before the capacity changes too much.

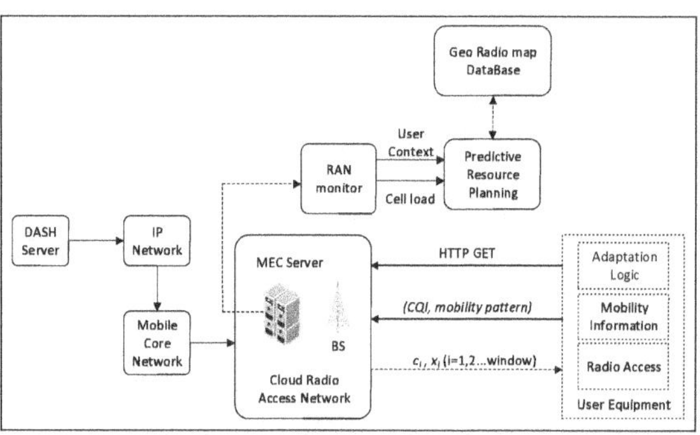

Figure 1: Proposed System Architecture.

Fig.1 shows the proposed architecture, the predictive resource planning module is a centralized resource arbitrator for all the users in the cell. It generates allocated time ratio x_i^t, capacity variation c_i^t for user i in slot t within the look-ahead window based on the network level and user level context information. The bit-rate adaptation logic is in the client, after getting the planned time ratio and capacity variation of each slot from the BS, the video streaming process can proceed with the standard DASH operation.

Let $c(t)$ be the average of the peak capacity at time t, and $r(t,k,j)$ be the actual transmission schedule for segment k with quality level j, such that $0 \leq r(t,k,j) \leq c(t)$. Let $\eta(t,k,j)$ characterize the channel utilization efficiency,

$$\eta(t,k,j) = \frac{r(t,k,j)}{c(t)} \tag{1}$$

A higher $\eta(t,k,j)$ results in a better channel efficiency. If $\eta(t,k,j) = 1$, segment k will be sent at times when the channel capacity is highest, and we can obtain the best transmission schedule. For segment k with level j, its channel utilization cost can be represented as

$$cost_u(k,j) = \int_0^T \frac{r(t,k,j)}{c(t)} dt \tag{2}$$

Where T is the video stream duration, our aim is to maximize average download segment quality level under given channel utilization cost and end user buffer constraint.

4 PROBLEM FORMULATION

Consider one or more HTTP servers that stream stored video to a mobile client via one (or more) base station(s), as shown in Fig. 1. The stream is divided into N small consecutive short video segments, and each segment is encoded at multiple bit-rate levels, $R = \{r_1 \cdots r_K\}$ as the set of K available bit-rate levels for each segment, and L is the time length of each segment. Let $q(\cdot) : R \to R^+$ be a non-decreasing function, which maps the selected bit-rate R_k to the video quality perceived by the user. The user can choose to download segment k at bit-rate $r \in R$. Let $d_k(r_j)$ denote the size of segment k encoded at bit-rate r_j; it typically increases with its effective compression rate f_k,

$$f_k(q_j) = d_k(r_j) \div L \tag{3}$$

The playback curve specifies the cumulative data needed for the video to be played back without interruptions. Let $l(t_i)$ and $u(t_i)$ respectively denote the minimum and maximum data that should be sent to client before t_i to prevent the buffer from being empty or overflow state. In HTTP Adaptive Streaming, the video playback can be paused only after an entire segment is displayed, so buffer underflows can occur at the jump points $t = \{0, L \cdots nL\}$. We denote the waiting times as $\tau_0, \tau_1 \cdots \tau_n$, and our rebuffing cost is defined as

$$cost_r = \sum_{i=0}^{n} \tau_i \tag{4}$$

The buffer occupancy $B(t)$ evolves as the segments are being downloaded and the video is being played. Let $B_k =$

$B(t_k)$ denote the buffer occupancy when the player starts to download chunk k; its dynamics can then be formulated as

$$B(t_{k+1}) = B(t_k) - \frac{d_k(R)}{Th_k} + L - \Delta t_k \quad (5)$$

$$where\ Th_k = \frac{1}{t_{k+1} - t_k - \Delta t_k} \int_{t_k}^{t_{k+1}-\Delta t_k} r(t)\, dt$$

When minimizing the channel utilization cost, we are constrained to ensure that the playback buffer does not decrease below 0. This can be captured by the following constraints,

$$\int_0^{t_i} \frac{r(t,k,j)}{f_k(q_j)} dt + b_0 \geq l(t_i) \quad (6)$$
$$k \in \{1 \dots N\}, j \in \{1 \dots K\}$$

, where b_0 is the initial buffer content that is not considered in the transmission schedule. We have the terminal condition

$$\int_0^{N\times L+\sum_{k=0}^{N}\tau_k} \frac{r(t)}{f_k(q_j)} dt + b_0 = l(t_N) = N \times L \quad (7)$$

Buffer overflows can occur at the time when the client is downloading one segment, $t_i \in [t_k, t_{k+1} - \Delta t_k]$, and it can be formulated as

$$\int_0^{t_i} \frac{r(t,k,j)}{f_k(q_j)} dt + b_0 \leq u(t_i) \quad (8)$$

$$u(t_i) = B_{max} - (B(t_k) - (t_i - t_k))$$

We summarize our overall goal in terms of the following maximization problem.
Given Channel Utilization Cost:

$$\sum_{k=1}^{N} \int_{i=0}^{T} \frac{r(t,k,j)}{c(t)} dt \quad (9)$$

Maximize:

$$\phi_N(q) = \sum_{k=1}^{N} q(R_k) - \beta \sum_{k=1}^{N} |q_k - m(q)| - \alpha \sum_{i=0}^{N} \tau_i \quad (10)$$

under constraints (5) – (10)

4.1 Optimization with Perfect Prediction

We observe that each slot can only be allocated to the segment whose deadline is before it. Assume the deadline of seg_{k+1} is $slot_k$, then $slot_k$ can only be allocated to $seg_{[k+1,k+2\dots N]}$. Thus,

$$c(k) = \sum_{i=k+2}^{N} c(k) \times \delta_i + c(k) \times \delta_{k+1} \quad s.t. \sum_{i=k+1}^{N} \delta_i \leq 1$$

We start from the last segment in the look-ahead window, such as seg_W and its deadline $slot_{deadline(W)}$. The slots are sorted based on their channel-utilization costs, from low cost to high cost. In step k, assume that the current segment is seg_{W-k} and its deadline is $slot_{W-k-1}$. We first check segments $[seg_{W-k+1}, seg_W]$, which will be given priority in the current slot ($slot_{W-k-1}$) if they were not allocated previously. Next, we allocate the current segment (seg_{W-k}) for the best video quality in $slot_{W-k-1}$. After that, we perform the following: (1) find seg_c with the maximum channel-utilization costs from $[seg_{W-k+1}, seg_W]$, and it will be re-allocated in a slot with minimum energy cost; (2) update $[slot_{W-k}, slot_W]$ if they can accommodate segments with better quality based on the order of the energy costs. At any time when the cost of the current slot is greater than or equal to the maximum cost found in residual slots, the process will return to the previous segment and its corresponding deadline slot. The process then continues until bandwidth has been allocated for the first segment in the predicted window.

There exists an energy quality tradeoff, and we re-allocate segment with better slots only if its quality downgrade, which resulted from the reallocation, will not be lower than a threshold.

4.2 Optimization with Imperfect Prediction

Owing to the time-varying characteristics of the wireless channel and interference, prediction errors are inevitable. Previous literature [2, 3, 11, 14] find that the prediction result in each slot of the look-ahead window can be modeled as a normal random variable,

$$th(i) \sim N(u_i, \sigma_i), i = 1 \dots W$$

where u_i is the average throughput in a $slot_i$ and σ_i is standard deviation.

At the beginning of each look-ahead window, each client knows its buffer length B_s. If $B_s \leq B_{min}$, it implies buffer length is very low and the problem reduces to select potential high efficient slot to transmit segments as fast as possible, in this case, we use the similar method similar to BBA2 [6]. Next, we discuss the scenario when $B_s > B_{min}$.

4.2.1 Joint Chance Constraint Decomposition.

We would like the buffer length to be stable around B_e with probability β at the end of the window, that is to say,

$$Pr\{B_s + \sum_{i=1}^{M} L - W \times \tau = B_e\} \geq \beta \quad (11)$$

M represent the number of segments which should be downloaded in the window,

$$M = \frac{B_e - (B_s - W \times \tau)}{L} \quad (12)$$

The joint download time constraints for all the segments in the look-ahead window can be expressed as follows,

$$Pr\{\bigcap_{\forall i \in \mathcal{M}} (d_i \leq \frac{\alpha_i \times W \times \tau}{M})\} \geq \beta \quad (13)$$

where $\alpha_i = 1, 2 \dots, M, \sum_{i=1}^{M} \alpha_i = M$

We denote the event of each segment download delay constraint as S_i and the complement set of S_i is S_i^c. The joint probability dissatisfaction constraint can be expressed as,

$$\sum_{\forall i \in \mathcal{M}} Pr\{S_i^c\} \leq 1 - \beta \quad (14)$$

The above equation implies that the joint probability is satisfied if the summation of individual probabilities of the compliment event is kept below the probability of constraint dissatisfaction. Accordingly, the joint chance constraint in (13) can be replaced by constraints (15) and (16),

$$Pr\{\frac{\alpha_i \times W \times \tau}{M} - d_i < 0\} \leq \xi_i, \forall i \in \mathcal{M} \tag{15}$$

$$\sum_{\forall i \in \mathcal{M}} \xi_i \leq 1 - \beta, \forall i \in \mathcal{M} \tag{16}$$

4.2.2 **Dynamic Risk Allocation**. There are two ways risk can be increased(decreased). First, downloading a segment with higher(lower) quality level. Second, choosing a slot with higher(lower) throughput variance σ_i.

a) segment risk allocation. Intuitively, higher quality level means higher risk level it should bear. When the quality level of each segment has been planned with $q_i, i = 1...M$. We fine-tune the risk level of each segment with,

$$\xi = (1 - \beta) \times \lambda_i \tag{17}$$
$$\lambda_i = \frac{q_i}{\sum_{i=1}^{M} q_i}$$

b) slot risk allocation. We sort slot from high to low according to E-V rule ("expected returns - variance of returns"),

$$u_i - \alpha \times \sigma_i \tag{18}$$

where $\alpha \in (0, 1)$, α is inversely proportional to current buffer length, a very small α implies that its current buffer length is very long and we can select slot with potential high expected throughput without consideration variance much, and vice versa.

After download of current segment, we re-evaluate the buffer status and calculate the total risks which should be allocated for subsequent segments in the window.

4.2.3 **QoE Optimization**. Based on the above analysis and the probabilistic download delay range of each segment, if segment k is downloaded in slot i, then,

$$Pr\Big\{th(i) < \frac{d_k(r_s) \times (M - M_{offset})}{(W - offset) \times \tau}\Big\} \leq \xi_k \tag{19}$$

where $offset$ is the time range which has been consumed in current window(initially, $offset = 0$). M_{offset} is the number of segments which have been actually downloaded within the time range of $offset$. The maximum bit-rate level r_s which would not violate the probabilistic constraint can be determined with the above formula. Algorithm 1 describes our complete idea for solving QoE optimization problem with imperfect channel throughput prediction, in 21 lines of algorithm 1, when the actual download delay is measured, risks will be recomputed and allocated for subsequent segments.

5 EXTENSION TO MULTI-USER SCENARIO

For multi-user scenarios with V mobile clients in the system, we consider QoE optimization and fairness. The average

Algorithm 1: Probabilistic scheduler()

```
Input: (u_i, σ_i), i = 1...W, segment, threshold
Output: scheduletable[Segnum]
1  initialize slot_map, schedule_table, β;
2  window ← WINIDOW; slotp ← 0;
3  repeat
4      {B_s, B_e} ← {Compute_buffer(slotp), f(B_s, predict_th)};
5      M ← ⌈(Be−(Bs−WINDOW*SLOT_TIME)) / SEG_TIME⌉;
6      next_to_schedule_table=Compute(SEG_INFO);
7      tlen ← next_to_schedule_table.len;
8      {α, risk[].epsn} ← {1 − B_s/B, (1 − β)/tlen};
9      for ;slotp ≤ window − 1; do
10         flag ← true;
11         for i = 0; i < tlen; i + + do
12             s = next_to_schedule_table[];
13             if !schedule[s].allocated then
14                 Schedule_Segment(slotp, s, risk[s].epsn);
15         for i = 0; i < tlen; i + + do
16             s = next_to_schedule_table[];
17             if schedule[s].slot = slotp and
               !schedule[s].allocated then
18                 flag = false;
19                 if Bs < B_min then
20                     schedule[s].level = 1;
21                 slotp=Actual_Download_Delay(slotp,s);
22                 ReComputeRisk(slotp);
23         if flag then
24             slotp+ = 1;
25     window+ = WINDOW;
26 until window ≤ SLOT_NUM − 1;
```

predicted throughput R_i for user i can be formulated as,

$$R_i = \frac{1}{W} \times \sum_{j=1}^{W} u_i(j) - \sigma_i(j) \tag{20}$$

The throughput gain gives an indication of the efficiency of the slot. For user i at slot j, it is represented as

$$e_i(j) = \frac{u_i(j) - \sigma_i(j)}{R_i} \tag{21}$$

Let $f_i(j)$ and B_{si} respectively represent the time ratio of user i at slot j and its buffer length at the beginning of a look-ahead window, in order to avoid buffer-constraint violations, we must consider the buffer status for each client at the beginning of a look-ahead window,

$$e_i'(j) = \begin{cases} \frac{e_i(j)}{log(1 + B_{si})} & B_{si} \in (0, B_{min}) \\ e_i(j) & B_{si} \in [B_{min}, B_{max}) \\ 0 & B_{si} \in [B_{max}, B) \end{cases} \tag{22}$$

The ratio of $slot_j$ allocated to $user_i$ can be formulated as,

$$f_i(j) = \frac{e_i'(j)}{\sum_{i=1}^{V} e_i'(j)} \tag{23}$$

Due to the discrete nature of throughput requirements for segments with different bit-rates, wastage of resource allocation will occur if the ratio of $f_i(j)$ can't amount to jump from one quality level to another. we further improve formula (23) by,

$$w_i(j) = \begin{cases} 0 \\ f_i(j) \\ f_i(j) + \beta_1 \\ f_i(j) - \beta_2 \end{cases} \tag{24}$$

In our single-user optimization method, only the best slot will be selected for transmission of the segment. If the slot was not selected at all, then $w_i(j) = 0$. The addition (subtraction) of $\beta_1(\beta_2)$ ensures that at least one quality level can be guaranteed, and reduces the unnecessary resource allocation as much as possible. The value of β can be determined by comparing the allocated bit-rates with what was actually consumed for downloading segments in each slot.

The total allocated bit-rates for user i is

$$\sum_{j=1}^{W} w_i(j) \times \tau \times BS_i(j) \tag{25}$$

With each slot ratio allocation in the look-ahead window being determined, the multi-user case is converted to single user problem and can be solved accordingly.

6 ALGORITHM COMPLEXITY

The proposed algorithm is divided into two parts: (1) predictive resource planning and allocation part which is located in the BS side, it generates predicted throughput and time ratio of each slot for each user; (2) bit-rate adaptation logic which is located in the user side; For the first part, the total time complexity is proportional to the window length and user number, plus the computation of formula (23) and (24), which lead to the time complexity with $O(V^2 \times W^2)$; For the second part, the most time consuming step is sorting slot from high to low and find the most efficient slot, its time complexity is proportional to $O(M \times W^2)$. So, the overall time complexity of the proposed algorithm is $O((V^2 + M) \times W^2)$.

Table 1: Simulation Parameters.

Parameter	Value
Video codec	H.264/AVC, ffmpeg, mp4box
Segment duration	2 second
Buffer Length	90 s
Slot Length	2 s
Window Length	10 slot
LTE TxPower	20 w
DlBandwidth	25 MHz
PathlossModel	FriisSpectrumPropagationLossModel
BS-to-UE distance	(0,10000 m)
number of user	5
Simulation time	600 s

7 NUMERICAL SIMULATION

7.1 Simulation Setup

We performed the simulation using an LTE module in the Network Simulator (ns-3) [10]. The simulation parameters are listed in Table I. We used a Big-Bucky-bunny video, which is 10 min with a resolution of $1920 \times 1080p$. We used FFmpeg and MP4Box to split the video into short segments with bit-rates(Mbps) {0.02,0.05, 0.08,0.12,0.2,0.36,0.56,0.75,1.02,1.33}. As the benchmark, we have implemented buffer-based methods, BBA (BBA1, BBA2 and BBAO) [6], prediction-based methods, Fill [4], and predictive green streaming (PGS) [1] in the ns-3 environment.

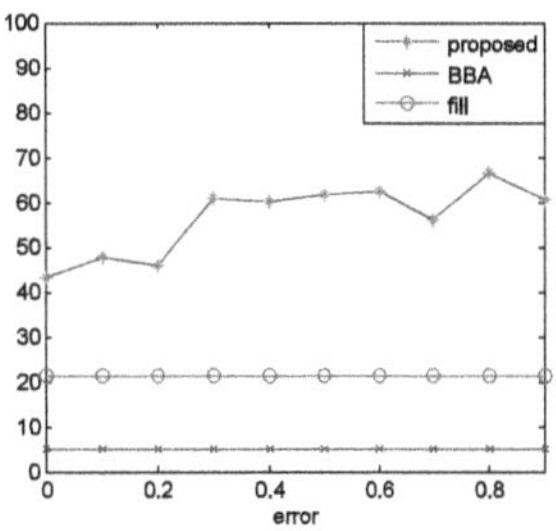

Fig. 6 channel efficiency

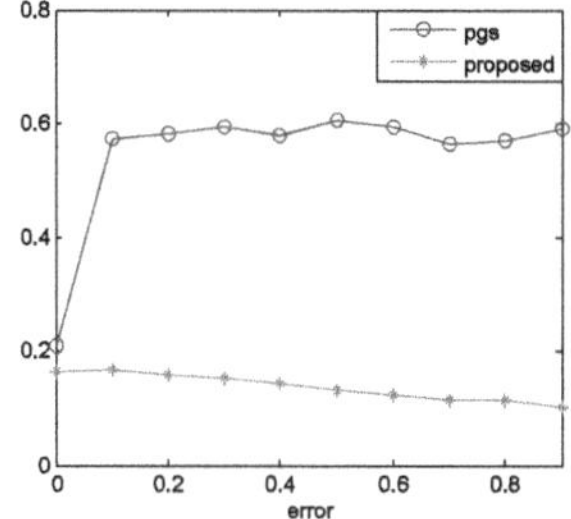

Fig. 7 channel cost

7.2 The Results of Perfect Prediction

As indicated in Fig. 2, the buffer-based algorithm (BBA) achieved the lowest video quality level. The average video quality level of Fill algorithm is clearly lower than the proposed method. This is because Fill only focuses on minimizing the playback interruption ratio, and does not consider whether the resource allocation is the most efficient. On the other hand, the proposed method only assigns wireless resources at its highest link capacity. Fig. 3 show that the proposed method has a minimum channel-utilization cost and highest average video quality level.

7.3 The Results of Imperfect Prediction

As indicated in Fig.5, with the increase of prediction error variance, the average video quality level decrease correspondingly. However, even with $\sigma = 0.9$, the proposed algorithm has average quality level 5.96656, and it is better than BBA algorithm which is not influenced by prediction error. when prediction error is zero, $\sigma = 0$, the average quality level of proposed algorithm is better then Fill algorithm.

In Fig.6, we use $ratio = q/t$ to evaluate channel utilization efficiency, where q is average quality level and t represents the downloading time length, we can see that, the proposed algorithm surpass the outcomes of BBA and Fill obviously under prediction error increases, this will save channel time and improve the average download video quality level.

The proposed algorithm can dynamically adjust risks according to the actual downloading time of previous segment, we use $u - \alpha \times \sigma$ to predict the throughput, when prediction error variance is small, the buffer variance will be stable as

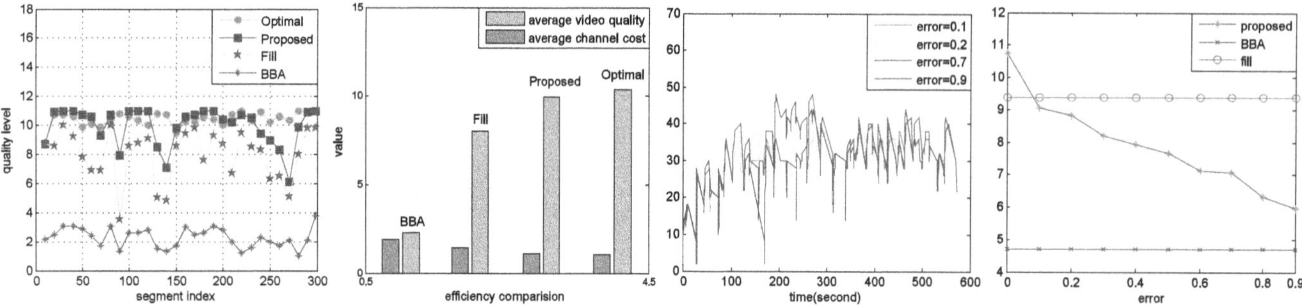

Fig. 2 Segment quality level Fig. 3 Average channel efficiency Fig. 4 buffer variation Fig. 5 quality compare

indicated in Fig.4, however, with the increase of prediction error variance, the variance of buffer becomes fiercely, the proposed algorithm try to follow the actual buffer variance and counteract the downside effects of prediction risks.

In PGS[1] , "target quality" is introduced as an assumption. It is an input parameter for the algorithm and used for computing needed resource for smooth playback. In Fig. 7, we can see that PGS has high channel cost compared to the proposed method. There are three reasons for this phenomenon, (1) PGS uses "target quality" as the basis to assign resource for each user, however, if the system can't satisfy "target quality" for some users, then its download time will become unpredictable, possibly very large, which may result in high channel utilization cost; (2) in each round of resource allocation, PGS first assigns resources to the user with the lowest buffer length, which may decrease the system performance in some scenarios; (3) if the capacity of the current slot exceeds 65%-95% of the total capacity of future slots, PGS allocates all of the remaining capacity of this slot to the user. However, 65%-95% is only an empirical value.

8 CONCLUSION

In this paper, we addressed the problem of predictive HTTP adaptive streaming in wireless networks. We propose an edge-cloud assisted framework for prediction based DASH streaming, and develop algorithms to optimize QoE and channel utilization cost. Preliminary results shows that the proposed architectures and algorithms can improve system performance significantly compared with traditional methods. As future work, we plan to implement the proposed model in our realistic test-bed, study and improve the performance in true mobile environment.

ACKNOWLEDGMENTS

This work was supported by Guangdong Science and Technology Program under Grant No. 2016A010101003 and Shenzhen Peacock Program under Grant No. KQJSCX20160226193545.

REFERENCES

[1] H. Abou-zeid, H. S. Hassanein, and S. Valentin. 2014. Energy-Efficient Adaptive Video Transmission: Exploiting Rate Predictions in Wireless Networks. *IEEE Transactions on Vehicular Technology* 63, 5 (2014), 2013–2026.

[2] R. Atawia, H. Abou-zeid, H. S. Hassanein, and A. Noureldin. 2016. Joint Chance-Constrained Predictive Resource Allocation for Energy-Efficient Video Streaming. *IEEE Journal on Selected Areas in Communications* 34, 5 (2016), 1389–1404.

[3] N. Bui and J. Widmer. 2014. Modelling throughput prediction errors as Gaussian random walks. In *Proc. KuVS (KuVs '14)*.

[4] M. Drxler, J. Blobel, P. Dreimann, S. Valentin, and H. Karl. SmarterPhones: Anticipatory download scheduling for wireless video streaming. In *2015 International Conference and Workshops on Networked Systems (NetSys)*.

[5] Qi He, Constantine Dovrolis, and Mostafa Ammar. On the Predictability of Large Transfer TCP Throughput. In *Proceedings of the 2005 Conference on Applications, Technologies, Architectures, and Protocols for Computer Communications (SIGCOMM '05)*.

[6] Te-Yuan Huang *et al.* A Buffer-based Approach to Rate Adaptation: Evidence from a Large Video Streaming Service. In *Proceedings of the 2014 ACM Conference on SIGCOMM (SIGCOMM '14)*.

[7] J. Jiang, V. Sekar, and H. Zhang. 2014. Improving Fairness, Efficiency, and Stability in HTTP-Based Adaptive Video Streaming With Festive. *IEEE/ACM Transactions on Networking* 22, 1 (2014), 326–340.

[8] Z. Li, X. Zhu, J. Gahm, R. Pan, H. Hu, A. C. Begen, and D. Oran. 2014. Probe and Adapt: Rate Adaptation for HTTP Video Streaming At Scale. *IEEE Journal on Selected Areas in Communications* 32, 4 (2014), 719–733.

[9] Z. Lu and G. de Veciana. Optimizing stored video delivery for mobile networks: The value of knowing the future. In *2013 Proceedings IEEE INFOCOM*.

[10] Giuseppe Piro, Nicola Baldo, and Marco Miozzo. 2011. An LTE Module for the Ns-3 Network Simulator. In *Proceedings of the 4th International ICST Conference on Simulation Tools and Techniques (SIMUTools '11)*.

[11] Yi Sun, Xiaoqi Yin, Junchen Jiang, Vyas Sekar, Fuyuan Lin, Nanshu Wang, Tao Liu, and Bruno Sinopoli. CS2P: Improving Video Bitrate Selection and Adaptation with Data-Driven Throughput Prediction. In *Proceedings of the 2016 ACM SIGCOMM Conference (SIGCOMM '16)*.

[12] G. Tian and Y. Liu. 2016. Towards Agile and Smooth Video Adaptation in HTTP Adaptive Streaming. *IEEE/ACM Transactions on Networking* 24, 4 (2016), 2386–2399.

[13] I. Triki, R. El-Azouzi, and M. Haddad. NEWCAST: Anticipating resource management and QoE provisioning for mobile video streaming. In *2016 IEEE 17th International Symposium on A World of Wireless, Mobile and Multimedia Networks (WoWMoM)*.

[14] Xiaoqi Yin, Abhishek Jindal, Vyas Sekar, and Bruno Sinopoli. A Control-Theoretic Approach for Dynamic Adaptive Video Streaming over HTTP. In *Proceedings of the 2015 ACM Conference on Special Interest Group on Data Communication (SIGCOMM '15)*.

[15] C. Zhou, C. W. Lin, and Z. Guo. 2016. mDASH: A Markov Decision-Based Rate Adaptation Approach for Dynamic HTTP Streaming. *IEEE Transactions on Multimedia* 18, 4 (2016).

GeoRIPE: Efficiently Harvesting Field Measurements for Map-Based Path Loss Modeling

Matthew Tonnemacher
Southern Methodist University
Dallas, Texas
mtonnemach@smu.edu

Dinesh Rajan
Southern Methodist University
Dallas, Texas
rajand@smu.edu

Joseph Camp
Southern Methodist University
Dallas, Texas
camp@smu.edu

ABSTRACT

Ensuring cellular coverage is an important and costly concern for carriers due to the expense of in-field experimentation (i.e., drive testing). With the ubiquity of smartphones, apps, and social media, there has been an explosion of crowdsourcing to understand a vast array of trends and topics at a minimal cost to the organization. While cellular carriers might seek to replace the expensive act of drive testing with the nearly cost-free crowdsourcing, questions remain as to: *(i)* the accuracy of crowdsourcing, considering the lack of user control, *(ii)* the detection of when drive testing might still be required, and *(iii)* the quantification of how many additional in-field measurements to perform for a certain accuracy level. In this work, we use geographical features of a region to reduce in-field propagation experimentation by predicting the number of measurements required to accurately characterize its path loss. In particular, we study the path loss prediction accuracy of drive testing and crowdsourcing by taking millions of measurements in a suburban and downtown region. We then use statistical learning to build a relationship between these geographical features and the measurements required. In doing so, we find that the number of measurements collected to achieve a certain path loss accuracy over the entire region can be reduced by up to 58% in a high density drive testing scenario.

1 INTRODUCTION

To address multi-fold increases in cellular demand, carrier cell sizes are shifting downwards to maximize network capacity. In doing so, the accurate and fine-grained coverage estimation of coverage becomes a critical issue for spatial reuse, intercell interference, and smooth handoffs between cells. Historically, in-field experimentation (i.e., drive testing) has been used to estimate the cellular propagation of a given region, which is costly for network operators due to the manpower and equipment required. The emergence of smartphones and their apps have offered a far cheaper alternative, recording in-field network observations directly from the cellular users (i.e., crowdsourcing). Crowdsourcing can allow network observations to be recorded in areas to which in-field testers may not have access.

MSWiM '17, November 21–25, 2017, Miami, FL, USA

ACM ISBN 978-1-4503-5162-1/17/11...$15.00
https://doi.org/10.1145/3127540.3127558

Despite the availability of crowdsourced measurements, network providers continue to use extensive drive-testing to validate network coverage and quality of service metrics. One of the main goals in supplementing crowdsourced measurements with drive testing measurements is to fill in the gaps of crowdsourcing. However, the drive testing process can be costly and time consuming, creating a market for network drive testing reports. Thus, collecting these measurements in an efficient manner is a high priority. The most direct approach would be to minimize the number of measurements that needs to be collected to achieve the accuracy requirements set. In this paper, we attempt to reduce the number of measurements required for accurate path loss characterization throughout a given region by understanding and exploiting the variation in geographical features. In order for this to happen, several questions need to be answered:

(1) What are the relationships between geographical features and signal strength measurement requirements?
(2) Can the number of measurements required to achieve a particular accuracy level be determined for a specific area?
(3) How can these spatial differences be exploited to reduce the total number of measurements required to meet a particular regional path loss characterization accuracy?

In this work, we use geographical features of a region to more efficiently collect signal strength measurements, thereby reducing the amount of time spent on in-field propagation experimentation. To do this, we first introduce GeoRIPE, a statistical learning framework to situationally predict the number of measurements required to meet a specified path loss characterization precision. With this framework, geographical feature distribution input is used to suggest measurement collection requirements in a grid-like fashion over the target region. Then, we developed and deployed an Android application to gather signal strength measurements from real users throughout the world. We use a specially modified version of this application to collect high-density drive testing measurements from two distinct region types in a major metropolitan area. By using commercially available smartphones, measurements gathered are comparable to those gathered using purely crowdsourcing. Next, we explore the effect of land use on path loss characterization, showing how geographical feature diversity plays a large role in determining regional measurement requirements. We show especially strong correlation between the number of measurements required to accurately characterize the path loss in a region and the geographical feature ratio of small, medium, and large buildings, foliage and free space in an area. Finally, we validate the framework by

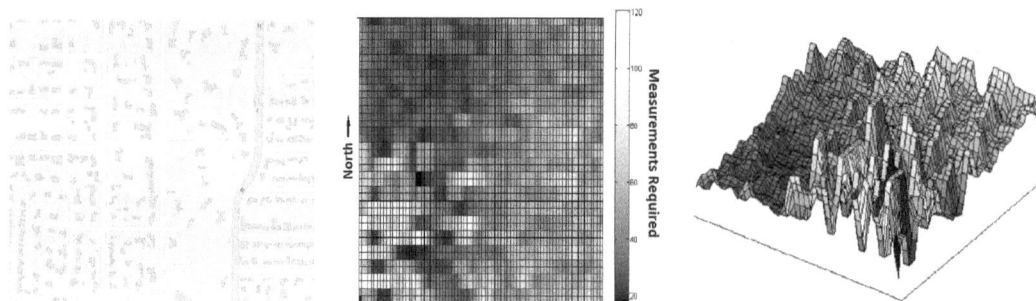

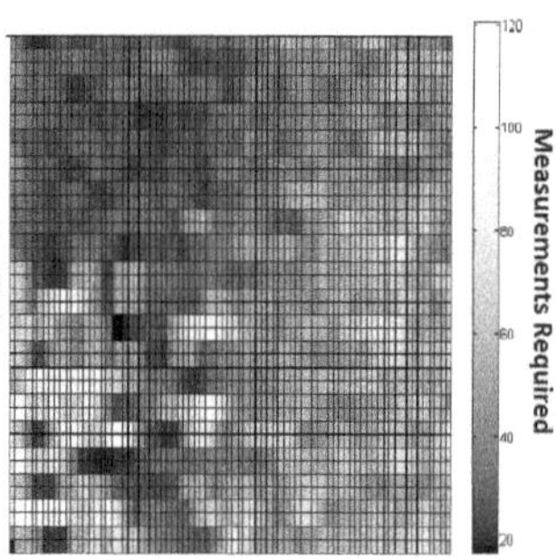

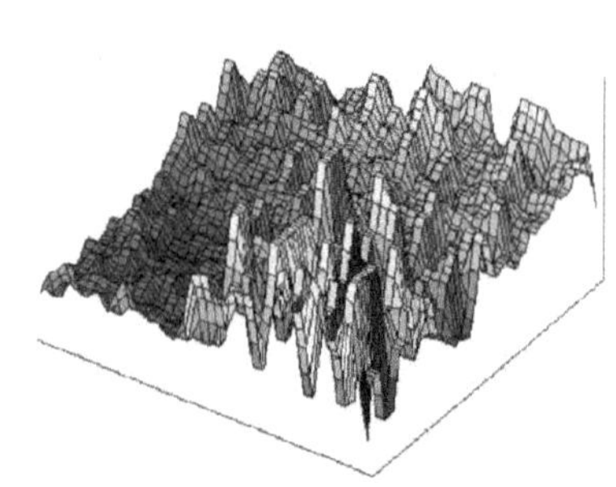

Figure 1: GeoRIPE Framework: using geographical features of a region (left) to infer the number of measurements required to predict path loss with a given accuracy level. The middle figure shows minimum measurements required (light is high, dark is low) of the same spatial distribution as the left-most figure. The right figure is a 3-D version of the middle figure.

comparing GeoRIPE to uniform measurement collection approach. We show that when fixing the accuracy requirement in path loss evaluation over the entire region, using the GeoRIPE framework can significantly reduce the required number of measurements that need to be taken to meet it.

2 GEORIPE FRAMEWORK

To illustrate the GeoRIPE[1] framework of using geographical features to reduce in-field propagation experimentation, we have depicted an aerial view of a region's terrain in the left-most image in Figure 1 with north on the top of the image. The terrain is classified into the following geographical features: buildings, dense foliage, and free space. Since in-field testing is expensive, our goal is to predict the least number of propagation measurements required to characterize the path loss in the region according to a specified level of accuracy. For example, the path loss of a region which has entirely free space (e.g., a desert) could be characterized with very few measurements. However, a diverse metropolitan region would require far more measurements to characterize.

The middle and right images of Figure 1 depict the end result of the GeoRIPE framework. The middle image depicts a two-dimensional overlay of the measurement density required to characterize the region shown in the left-most image. The southwest portion of the region is the lightest color, which means that it requires the greatest number of measurements to characterize due to the high concentration of buildings. In contrast, the northwest portion of the region is the darkest, which means that it requires the least number of measurements to characterize due to sparse building placement and less foliage. A three-dimensional version of the same figure can be seen in the right-most image to show the quantity of measurements required in each portion of the region.

A similar analysis could be done for a given region by an excessive amount of in-field testing and finding when each portion of the terrain converged to a particular level of path loss prediction accuracy. However, such an approach, by definition precludes any in-field testing reduction. While we take a very large number of measurements in certain regions in our work, we do so to train a statistical learning decision structure to infer the number of in-field measurements required. As a result, for any mix of such terrain features, we can avoid the two in-field testing extremes of: *(i)* too few measurements, resulting in an inaccurate path loss estimate, or *(ii)* too many measurements, resulting in excessive experimentation costs. We can then evaluate the viability of using crowdsourcing to lower the drive testing cost.

The GeoRIPE framework's measurement distribution prediction is made with path loss accuracy in mind. So, before we evaluate the framework itself, we first need to give some background on path loss models in general as well as what model we use for our analysis. Path loss models attempt to predict the electromagnetic propagation as a function of distance. Many of these models rely on *a priori* information, using environmental details, a theoretical foundation, empirical findings, or some combination of the three for their prediction [6, 11, 21]. Other techniques operate under the assumption that *a priori* information is insufficient. These models supplement an existing model with a correction factor or factors based on measurements collected throughout a region to be modeled and tend to be more accurate than their *a priori* counterparts [17]. These active measurement models consist of two fundamental components: *(i)* how the measurements are gathered, and *(ii)* how they are incorporated into the model.

2.1 Path Loss Measurement and Supplemented Models

W. C. Lee studied the initial theoretical methodology of gathering active measurements for modeling path loss [13]. Lee proposed arced measurements at incremental distances from the transmitter while averaging measurements that fall within 20 to 40 wavelengths of each other, a claim corroborated by Shin using IEEE 802.11b measurements some years later [20]. In practice, it is often difficult to collect measurements strictly following the theoretically ideal guidelines due to environmental inaccessibility. This can be due to permission limitations, such as access restricted buildings or construction sites, or infrastructure limitations, where equipment setups are subject to the same mobility freedoms as the vehicles in which they operate. With a crowdsourced approach, a greater access diversity can be achieved with the limitations of a lack of control over data validity and input distribution. Due to these practical considerations, our work considers geographical complexity and its role in characterizing a region, both with vehicle-based drive testing and app-enabled crowdsourcing.

[1]As a mnemonic for this work, consider that fruit should be in the field the appropriate amount of time before harvested (i.e., to be *ripe*). Similarly, we seek to find the minimum amount of time necessary for in-field experimentation to accurately predict the path loss of a region.

One of the more recent path loss models utilizing collected measurements is one proposed by Robinson et al. [18]. Using the Technology For All (TFA) network in Houston, TX, they utilized a modified Flexible Path Loss Exponent model with a terrain correction factor derived iteratively from collected measurements. The model is an extension of Friis' fundamental study [6] and can be written as:

$$P_{rx} = P_{tx} + 10\alpha \log(d) - 20 \log(f) - 20 \log\left(\frac{4\pi}{c}\right) \quad (1)$$

Here, P_{tx} and P_{rx} are the transmitted and received signal powers, respectively, α is the path loss exponent, f is the transmit frequency, d is the distance from the transmitter, and c is the speed of light. In their work, the authors use existing wireless mesh nodes and detailed terrain information to determine sections that are likely to share a similar path loss exponent. They then incrementally gather measurements around the borders of these sections in a push-pull algorithm to refine the coverage estimate of the mesh node.

2.2 Obtaining a Path Loss Exponent

In our statistical learning approach, it is necessary to train a classifier with path loss exponent observations derived from existing measurements to motivate predictions in areas that lack those same measurements. We borrow the idea of a spatially-dependent path loss exponent from Robinson et al. without the push-pull measurement adjustment algorithm, a reference node, and detailed terrain information (including material loss estimations). Instead, we use (1) in a square-shaped moving window over the region, using linear regression to obtain a path loss exponent for each window. Since the measurements are obtained from many different towers distributed over the area, each using potentially different transmit powers at different heights, we rely on a larger quantity of data to average out these inconsistencies. However, the accuracy (which we define as inversely proportional the standard deviation of obtained path loss exponents over several calculations using orthogonal measurements) is increased, which we rely on more heavily for our statistical learning framework. To calculate the metric of standard deviation on the path loss exponent, we divide the data considered into several independent sets, calculate path loss exponent for each independent set, and compute the standard deviation of the exponents derived. Again, this gives us a solid metric for path loss precision, even if the exponents themselves are biased by the data collection limitations.

3 IN-FIELD WIRELESS AND GEOGRAPHICAL DATA

In this section, we present our Android-based measurement gathering platform, which will be leveraged locally by us to gather a dense measurement set of wireless signal strengths in both a downtown region and suburban region. We also introduce the geographical feature data set that we use from the drive tested regions to establish a relationship between geodata and the attenuation of wireless signals. By using a smartphone based collection platform, we can gather Received Signal Strength Indicator (RSSI) measurements that relate more directly to user experience than measurements collected with traditional network analyzing hardware.

3.1 Local Measurement Collection

Over the span of two weeks (over 30 in-car hours), we collected 6.7 million drive testing measurements by placing LG Nexus 4 smartphones in a vehicle and thoroughly driving throughout two regions in a snake like pattern, covering all available roads in each region. Since we are using the measurements for studying region-based path loss characteristics, the specific cellular technology used is less important. Therefore, the measurements were collected on GSM networks as they are still the most prevalent. The measurements were obtained at a relatively constant speed of 30 mph in two different areas of the Dallas metropolitan area. The first area is a suburban region several miles north of the city center with lush greenery prevalent throughout and is predominantly residential. The second area is in downtown, where there is far less vegetation, and the buildings are far taller than the suburban structures with non-uniform heights. Our goal is to use these two distinct regions to examine how differences in feature distribution affect the number of required measurements to characterize path loss to a certain degree of accuracy in each region.

3.2 Received Signal Strength in Android API

Each cellular measurement contains an RSSI field for each visible cellular tower, a GPS location, an accuracy reading, and physical speed of the device. While we now obtain RSSI readings in terms of dBm, most of our measurements were taken when the API reported RSSI in terms of Arbitrary Strength Units (ASU), an android specific quantized signal strength metric, which quantizes obtained RSSI values for GSM to 32 different levels shown in the equation below from the Android API [9].

$$P_{rx}(dBm) = 2 * P_{rx}(ASU) - 113 \quad (2)$$

$$P_{rx}(ASU) = [0, 31] \quad (3)$$

We consider $P_{rx}(ASU) = 0$ and 31 unusable since they correspond to SNR in an unlimited range; an ASU value of 31 includes any RSSI value above −51 dBm. Not including these measurements, however, clips the natural distribution of RSSI readings at locations with measurements near the quantization limits. The lower and upper bounds set by omitting measurements where $P_{rx}(ASU) = 31$ and $P_{rx}(ASU) = 0$, respectively, move the average RSSI at certain distances from the tower. Distances closer to the tower that generally have higher RSSI measurements near the upper bound may have a lowered average RSSI. Conversely, distances farther from that tower that generally have lower RSSI measurements near the lower bound may have a heightened average RSSI. The bias in the movement of average RSSI near the boundaries could end up changing (likely reducing) the value of the obtained path loss exponent. While the exact values of RSSI and path loss exponents are likely affected by the quantization error, we are not evaluating absolute path loss accuracy, only relative accuracy in our experiments, so the bias does not affect our results.

3.3 Geographical Feature Data

In order to obtain geographical feature information, we utilized an open-access online resource, Open Street Maps (OSM) [1], to identify, outline, and label specific regional features and output them to an easily accessible data structure for parsing. To this end, we mapped hundreds of offices, parks, houses, and other features in both the suburban and downtown regions and grouped them into the feature category classes for our statistical learning system. With statistical learning, the number of training observations necessary for accurate divisions scales up proportionally with the number of features used in the training. Due to this so-called curse of dimensionality, as well as the limited number of possible features to label in each region considered, it is necessary to divide all possible geographical features into relatively few feature categories for processing. With this in mind, we selected five feature categories under which all features were labeled: small buildings, medium buildings, large buildings, high foliage, and open space. In this system, we define small buildings consist of buildings that are under 5 stories tall (ground footprint is not considered for the category, but is implicitly considered when calculating feature distributions in a region). Similarly, we define the range of medium buildings as being between 5 and 15 stories tall and large buildings as being over 15 stories tall. These building height tiers were chosen to give each feature type non-trivial representation in the learning algorithm. Finally, we consider high foliage areas in the regions are areas with a large number of trees, and open space is the area defined by the complement to the set of all other features combined and includes structures such as roads, parking lots, etc. It is important to note that the feature set we consider is far from ideal; with more detailed geo-spatial feature data that is currently unavailable to us (such as exact building and foliage canopy heights), the GeoRIPE framework's accuracy will only improve.

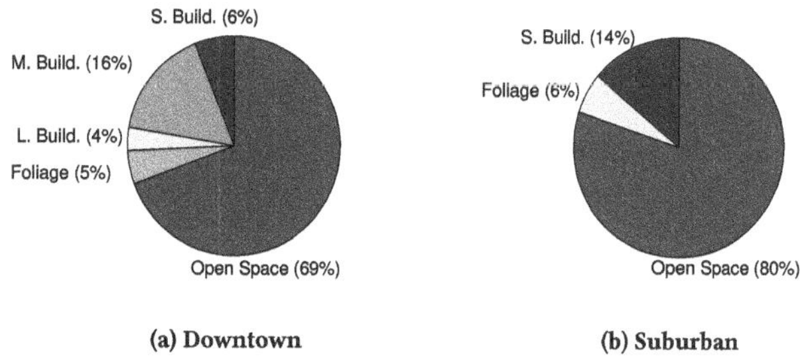

(a) Downtown (b) Suburban

Figure 2: Regional Feature Distributions

The overall ratio of features in the downtown and suburban regions we examine are shown in Figures 2a and 2b, respectively. These ratios represent the relative space occupied by each feature according the following equations:

$$s = [f_1, f_2, ..., f_5] \tag{4}$$

$$\sum_i s_i = 1 \tag{5}$$

where s is a weighted vector for the normalized occupancy of each of the 5 features in the full region in terms of total feature area. From this figure, we can see that the suburban area lacks medium and large buildings and has a higher percentage of open space than the downtown region, as anticipated. Ideally, we will be able to further differentiate and parse members of the open space set to derive additional feature categories in the future.

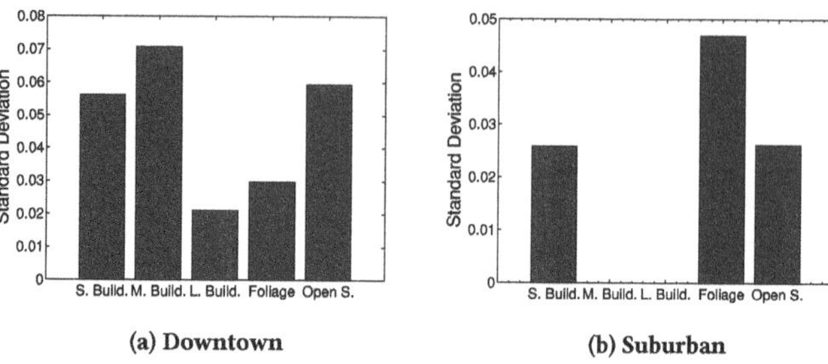

(a) Downtown (b) Suburban

Figure 3: Regional Feature Distribution Deviation

Primarily, we want to examine how the features change over each region. To do this, we calculated the ratio of features in a moving window over each region. Treating the percentage of each feature in the windows as a random variable, we then compute the standard deviation, giving us a picture of the feature variability as we move across each region. The standard deviation of features can be seen for the downtown and suburban regions in Figures 3a and 3b, respectively. From these figures, we can see that the variance of features in the suburban region is, overall, significantly smaller than in the downtown region. This is because, in the suburban region, the grouping of features are polarized (ex: houses in half the region, foliage in the other half), while the in the downtown region, neighboring areas have a higher diversity in their feature composition.

4 DENSITY-DEPENDENT TILING OF IN-SITU DATA

While we have examined the differences in geographical feature distribution of the two areas, we have yet to explore the impact of changing the size of the subregion, or tile, used to group measurements spatially. In this section, we explore the differences in path loss exponent changes between these regions, their relative subregions, and the trade off between tile size, measurement density, and measurement error in evaluating path loss.

4.1 Extreme 1: Highly-Sparse Crowdsourced Data

The first scenario is one in which the data set has very few measurements. In such a situation, we need all the measurements we have to assign a single path loss exponent to characterize an entire region, similar to the traditional approach. In other words, dividing the region into smaller areas to have more path loss precision cannot occur because there is a lack of a sufficient number of measurements to compose a path loss exponent estimate. The result here can be considered a rough average of path loss over the entire region; however, accuracy at any given area depends on the variability of the region itself. While a single exponent over an entire region may create a simpler coverage calculation, it may not be accurate, especially in more diverse region types such as large cities. When enough measurements are available, we can divide the region into independent tiles for characterization based on measurement density and region type instead. Figure 4 shows the suburban region is divided into 6 and 24 tiles for path loss evaluation, demonstrating the disparity in derived path loss exponents for the same area using different tile sizes. While some smaller tiles match the their large tile counterparts, others are different, alluding to diverse environmental characteristics.

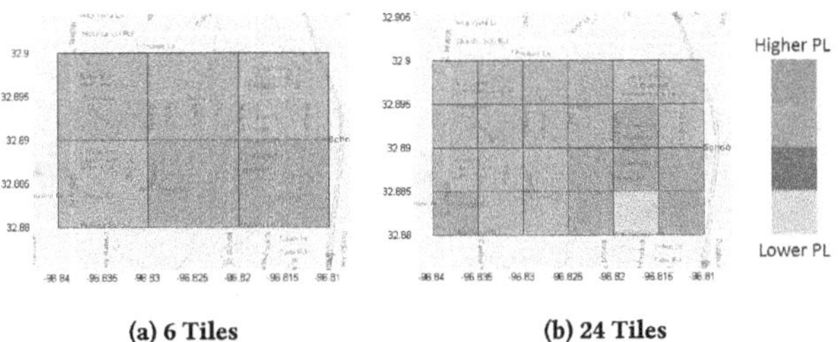

(a) 6 Tiles (b) 24 Tiles

Figure 4: Suburban region path loss divided into a) 6 and b) 24 tiles.

4.2 Extreme 2: Highly-Dense Crowdsourced Data

We now examine the other extreme, when a very large number of measurements are available. In this case, the tile size is not limited by measurement density or acceptable error. With highly-dense measurements (*e.g.*, as the number of measurements approach infinity), tile size is virtually unbounded, and the standard deviation of path loss approaches zero (orthogonal subsets measurements would regress to the same exponent when evaluating as the subset size approaches infinity). Instead, the variability of the terrain determines the effective lower bound on the terrain characterization resolution, preventing the tile size from going to zero. In other words, decreasing the title size resolution after a certain point does not provide any additional information about path loss in the region.

Region	Tiles	Diff. Mean	Diff. Variance
Downtown	6	0.0668	0.0040
	24	0.0944	0.0059
Suburban	6	0.0742	0.0029
	24	0.0464	0.0014

Table 1: Mean and variance of differences between neighboring tiles' path loss.

Depending on the nature of the region being analyzed, the mean and variance of the difference between neighboring tiles changes with the tile size. Table 1 shows the mean and the variance in path loss exponent calculation differences between neighboring tiles for both the downtown and suburban regions of different tile sizes. As the tile size decreases, we observe different behavior from the two region types. In the downtown region, the differential mean and variance increase with a smaller tile size, while in the suburban region, the opposite is true. For more diverse regions like downtown, using smaller tile sizes has a larger benefit in characterizing the spatial diversity of path loss. In less diverse regions like homogeneous neighborhoods, the differential path loss throughout the region does not require as high of a resolution; the path loss variability seen from smaller tile sizes is below the noise floor in generating the path loss exponents. Thus, the measurement density available along with the region type's path loss variability must be jointly considered in determining a minimum tile size for characterization.

4.3 General Case: In-Situ Tile Size Adaptation

In most cellular networks, it is likely that the set of available measurements is neither highly sparse nor infinitely dense. Instead, the system is generally in a state between these two extremes. Hence, choosing the tile size of the region becomes a critical issue since it is not initially clear if the measurement density or the terrain heterogeneity will drive the tile size.

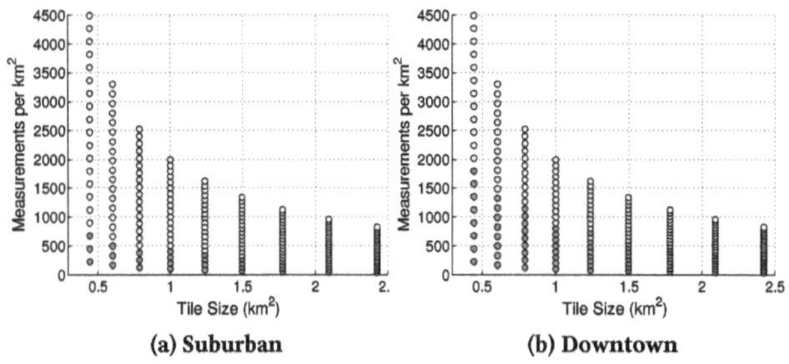

(a) Suburban (b) Downtown

Figure 5: Examining tile size versus measurement density over different land uses for a given acceptable error.

Given a set of measurements with a specific measurement density, a minimum tile size exists that remains below the reliability threshold. In Figures 5a and 5b we set a standard deviation threshold of 0.0125 for our path loss evaluation and examined the minimum tile size for different measurement densities available. In these figures the lighter points are below the threshold and darker, red dots are above the threshold. For both land use types, we see that as the measurement density increases, the minimum tile size achievable under the threshold decreases, enabling a finer grain resolution while maintaining the reliability we desired. However, the suburban region consistently requires a lower measurement density to be below the error threshold than the downtown region because the suburban region has a lower terrain variability. From these figures, we can see that to achieve a tile size of 1 km^2 under the error threshold, the suburban region requires a measurement density of 500 measurements per km^2 while the downtown region requires 800. This relationship between the different land uses holds for each other tile size as well. The measurement density required for a certain resolution of path loss increases with the heterogeneity of the region.

5 EXPERIMENTALLY EVALUATING MAP-BASED MODELING

Despite that fact that there have been several works that suggest measurement distribution and geographical features play an enormous role in the resulting path loss characterization of a region, there has not been a study showing how these metrics can be used to quantify the number of measurements required to characterize an area. In this section, we take a critical look at the impact of measurement distribution and geographical feature components on path loss precision. More specifically, we compare measurement distributions obtained from crowdsourcing versus drive testing measurements, examine geographical feature components of our two metropolitan region types, and correlate these feature distributions with both path loss exponents as well as the number of measurements required to obtain a certain precision in characterization. Our goal is to use regional geographical features to learn how to properly collect measurements, ensuring a predetermined precision in path loss characterization.

5.1 Path Loss Metric and Geographical Feature Correlation

Using geographical features as a region specific identifier, we want to understand how specific geographical features can be used to characterize path loss throughout a region. We now explore four different path loss related metrics to determine which had the closest relationship, and therefore the highest suitability, to be used as the target for our geographical feature based statistical learning approach. The four metrics we examine are path loss exponent (PLE), differential path loss exponent (DPLE), number of measurements required (MR) for path loss convergence, and the differential number of measurements required (DMR) for convergence. The MR and PLE metrics are calculated for a given region using Algorithm 1, which is initialized with parameters listed in Table 2. Algorithm 1 can be visualized as a sliding window filter moving across the region as illustrated in Figure 6. In this algorithm, the first two loops control the moving window as it shifts vertically and horizontally, respectively. For a given window at position v, h, we compute the path loss exponent directly with all available data, giving the PLE metric. Following that, we divide the data into G separate groups, calculate the path loss exponent in each group, and take the standard deviation over all exponents. We increase the number of measurements in each of these groups by S until the standard deviation is under a certain threshold (chosen to be whatever accuracy is acceptable, we chose 0.03 because that was about the point that an a linear increase in the number of measurements started to have diminishing returns). Additionally, When the standard deviation falls under this threshold, we record the measurements in each group as the MR metric.

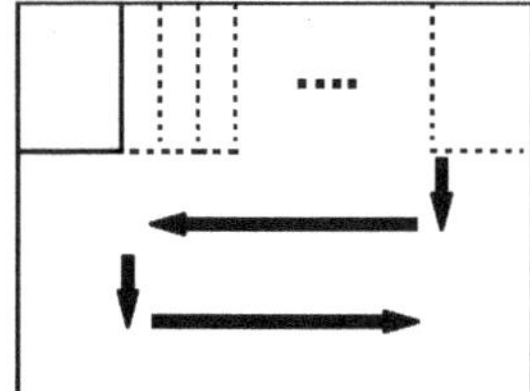

Figure 6: Visualization of Algorithm 1.

We use this algorithm to determine a map of the measurements required and path loss exponent metrics over a region. With our feature data for the region, we can derive a similar map of feature distributions using the same windowing method. The differential

Parameter	Setting	Description
W	$1km^2$	Moving window area
V	20	Number of vertical shifts
H	40	Number of horizontal shifts
σ	0.03	Desired std. dev.
S	20	Measurement step size
G	30	Number of orthogonal groups

Table 2: Spatial feature and path loss metric algorithm parameters.

```
Data: measurements (M)
Result: V by H PLE and MR matrices
Initialize Parameters;
for v ← 1 to V do
    for h ← 1 to H do
        PLE(v, h) ← ComputeExponent(∀M ∈ W);
        group(1..G) ← ∀M ∈ W split into G sets;
        P_size ← 0;
        while σ_temp ≥ σ do
            σ_temp ← ∞;
            P_size ← P_size + S;
            for g ← 1 to G do
                P ← P_size elements ∈ group(g);
                exponent(g) ← ComputeExponent(P);
            end
            σ_temp ← ComputeStdDev(exponent(1..G));
        end
        MR(v, h) ← P_size;
        W ← W horizontally shifted by 1;
    end
    W ← W vertically shifted by 1;
end
```

Algorithm 1: Algorithm for computing PLE and MR metrics.

metrics, differential path loss exponent and differential measurements required, can be easily derived from column and row differentiation of the PLE and MR matrices, respectively. A corresponding differential feature distribution map can be derived in the same manner. With matching metric and feature maps, we can correlate each metric with the corresponding feature map to obtain a sample Pearson correlation coefficient (the standard equation for correlating discreet groups) using Equation 6.

$$r_{ij} = \frac{\sum_{k=1}^{n}(x_{ik} - \bar{x_i})(y_{jk} - \bar{y_j})}{\sqrt{\sum_{k=1}^{n}(x_{ik} - \bar{x_i})^2 \sum_{k=1}^{n}(y_{jk} - \bar{y_j})^2}} \quad (6)$$

In this equation, n is the number of samples, x_{ik} is sample k of feature i, y_{jk} is the sample k of path loss metric j, and $\bar{x_i}$ and $\bar{y_j}$ are the average distribution of feature i and the average of path loss metric j, respectively.

We want to select a path loss metric to use as a training class for the statistical learning framework that has the highest correlation coefficients with the feature set to provide clear decision boundaries. The correlation coefficients for each of the path loss metrics in the downtown and suburban regions are shown Tables 3 and 4, respectively.

Metric	S. Building	M. Building	L. Building	Foliage	Open Space
PLE	-0.23	0.02	-0.05	0.17	0.18
DPLE	-0.05	-0.03	0.02	-0.04	0.07
MR	**-0.32**	**0.34**	**0.49**	-0.10	-0.23
DMR	-0.06	0.05	0.03	0.01	-0.02

Table 3: Downtown metric-feature correlation coefficients.

Metric	S. Building	M. Building	L. Building	Foliage	Open Space
PLE	**0.36**	NA	NA	**0.31**	**-0.38**
DPLE	-0.15	NA	NA	0.05	0.05
MR	**-0.53**	NA	NA	**0.44**	-0.27
DMR	-0.06	NA	NA	0.01	0.04

Table 4: Suburban metric-feature correlation coefficients.

We can see that the MR metric has the highest overall correlation coefficient magnitude and is likely the best contender for a simple decision tree based learning algorithm. Interestingly, we see that for the suburban region in particular, the correlation coefficient for the MR metric are negative with small buildings and positive with foliage, while positive with both for the PLE metric. This suggests that while increased buildings and foliage contribute to a larger path loss exponent (as expected), the number of measurements required to drop below the 0.03 path loss exponent standard deviation increases only with the percentage of foliage.

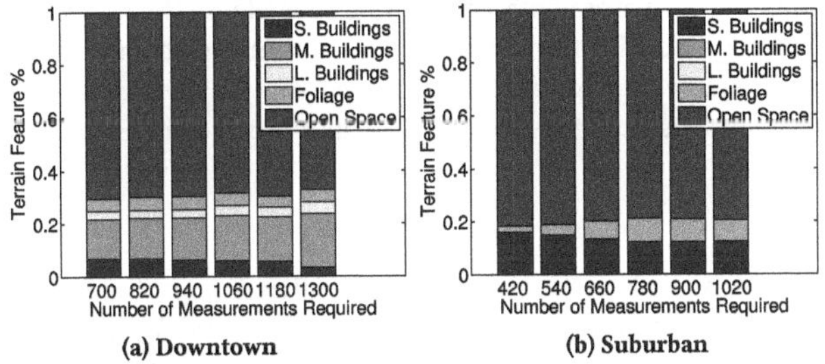

(a) Downtown (b) Suburban

Figure 7: Average feature distributions for different MR tiers.

From this result, we can see that while the small buildings feature increases the path loss exponent, it decreases received power variability, while the foliage feature increases received power variability. This trend is visualized for the downtown and suburban areas in Figures 7a and 7b.

To understand how each terrain feature affects the measurement requirements individually, we examined the trends of each feature distribution as the number of required measurements increases in Figure 8. From this figure, we can see that in the suburban region, the individual feature impact is quite clear; increases in the percentage of foliage and decreases in the percentage of small buildings increases the number of measurements required, while the open space component doesn't fluctuate much at all. Conversely, we

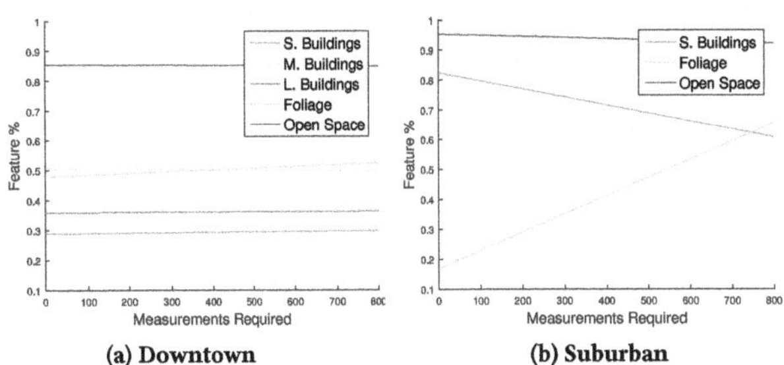

(a) Downtown (b) Suburban

Figure 8: Feature trends for increasing measurement requirements.

cannot induce distinct trends from the downtown region. We see in the suburban region, there are only two features driving the increase in measurement requirements, thus trends can be easily seen. In the downtown region, however, each feature apart from open space has an effect on the measurements, thus trends from individual factors cannot be so easily derived.

5.2 Classifier Training for MR Prediction

To validate the GeoRIPE framework, we divide the MR results for the downtown and suburban regions into 6 same-sized class bins. As seen in Figure 9, the class groupings are not homogeneous for either of the regions. Unsurprisingly, the downtown region class distribution has a higher mean number of required measurements than the suburban region due to its higher geographical complexity.

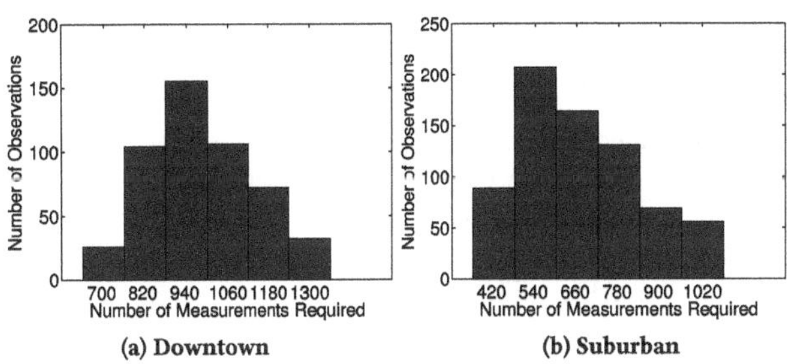

(a) Downtown (b) Suburban

Figure 9: Regional MR Class Distributions

Under these class groupings, the input terrain feature distributions used each measurement class grouping are shown in Figure 7. In reference to Figure 9, we see that the majority of the regional features fall into groups centered around 940 and 540 measurements for the downtown and suburban regions, respectively. Thus, these bins will have a higher weight under the learning framework.

To train each the decision tree classifier, it is important to allow equal training weights per class as much as possible to balance the tree and not over-fit the data. For this, we randomly selected an equal number of observations for resulting in each class to balance the observations per bin. We further divided this set of observations into two separate training and validation observation sets, again being sure to have equal class representation in each set. We then trained the decision tree classifier with the training set and predicted MR classes with the validation set.

Due to the linear relationship between the MR metric and class, it is important to look at not only the prediction accuracy in choosing the correct class, but also the distribution of predicted class offsets (how many classes away from the correct class) when the correct class is not chosen. This is because a lower average offset between the predicted and correct MR class is nearly as important as the accuracy in choosing the correct class. For example, predicting the adjacent class is not as detrimental to the measurement number estimation as predicting multiple classes away.

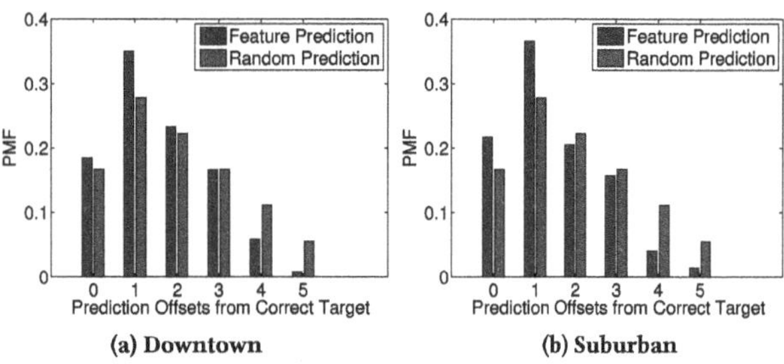

Figure 10: Regional Feature Versus Random Prediction Offsets

Figure 10 shows the class prediction offset magnitudes for using feature prediction to choose a class and choosing a random class (according to the frequency of occurrence). This result shows that for both the downtown and suburban region, the average predicted class offset is significantly lower using the feature prediction than choosing a class at random, even if there may not be a very high accuracy in actually predicting the correct class.

5.3 Uniform Drive Testing Comparison

Using our trained and validated decision tree classifier, we wanted to compare GeoRIPE to uniform drive testing in two scenarios. First is a dense uniform drive testing scenario, in which measurements are gathered according to the requirements of the subregion (window from Algorithm 1) with the highest geographical variability. More specifically, we experimentally found the number of measurements required in the worst case subregion to meet the accuracy threshold and uniformly take that number of measurements over every subregion. The other is a sparse uniform drive testing scenario, in which measurements are gathered according to the measurement requirements of the subregion with the lowest geographical variability. In this experiment, the goal is to stay under a predetermined path loss exponent standard deviation (corresponding to an accuracy that a network provider would require) while using the lowest amount of measurements. To do this, we divided the regions into several uniformly sized tiles and gathered several orthogonal sets of measurements from each tile according to the sparse, dense, and GeoRipe predicted number of measurements. For each orthogonal set in each scheme, we calculated the path loss exponent and took the standard deviation over all exponents for each of the three techniques. By doing this, we can compare the path loss exponent accuracy and the number of measurements required for each technique. For this experiment, we trained the GeoRIPE classifier to predict the measurements required for the standard deviation of 0.03 using half of the region, and predicted the number of measurements required for the for the other half. We repeated this experiment for both the downtown and suburban regions, and the results can be seen in Table 5.

Technique	Region	Average σ	Avg. Meas. per km^2
GeoRIPE	Downtown	0.0286	194
GeoRIPE	Suburban	0.0284	186
Sparse	Downtown	0.0631	40
Sparse	Suburban	0.0440	80
Dense	Downtown	0.0205	400
Dense	Suburban	0.0188	440

Table 5: GeoRIPE Standard Deviation and Measurements Compared to Sparse and Dense Uniform Drive Testing Scenarios

From this table, we can see that the sparse drive testing does not meet the required standard deviation of below 0.03 that we set at the start of the experiment. The dense drive testing does stay under the standard deviation requirement, using the minimum number of measurements to do so over all areas. Using GeoRIPE, the standard deviation requirement is also met, but it requires 58% fewer measurements than uniform dense drive testing to get all subregions below the threshold. From the GeoRIPE results, the effect of geographical complexity can be clearly seen; a lower standard deviation of path loss exponents is obtained using fewer measurements in the suburban region than the geographically more complex downtown region.

In addition to meeting the accuracy requirements using the least number of measurements, we wanted to evaluate the benefits of using the GeoRIPE framework over a uniform distribution that uses the same number of total measurements. To do this, we used measurements from the GeoRIPE distribution given by Equation 7.

$$p_x = \frac{M_x}{\sum_{\hat{x}}^{X} M_{\hat{x}}} \tag{7}$$

Here, x is a single section in the set of all tiles X, p_x is the fraction of measurements to be collected in section x, and M_x is the set of predicted MR values of tile x. We collected several orthogonal subsets of measurements in each tile for an increasing number of total measurements in each region and compared the accuracy of the two techniques. For each orthogonal subset in each tile, we calculated a path loss exponent and computed the standard deviation of the path loss exponents in each tile. The standard deviation for all tiles was averaged at each number of total measurements and the results were organized by standard deviation. For selected standard deviation, each of the techniques required a different number of measurements per km^2, resulting in Table 6.

From this table, we see that as the threshold for standard deviation is lowered, measurements required increases approximately 10% 'faster' using uniform drive testing. So, while the true value in using the GeoRIPE framework is predicting the number of measurements required over a region to meet a certain path loss exponent accuracy, the normalized GeoRIPE distribution also achieves the desired path loss accuracy with proportionally fewer measurements

σ	GeoRIPE # Meas.	Uniform # Meas.
0.050	64	64
0.045	80	84
0.040	96	108
0.035	128	138
0.030	178	196
0.025	252	276
0.020	400	436

Table 6: GeoRIPE versus Uniform Drive Testing Measurements to Achieve a Fixed σ

than the uniform counterpart. This result, however, only analyzes the average path loss over the entire region. Using a similar windowing method previously described, we wanted to see how many measurements it took to bring the standard deviation of the path loss exponent in all the windows to fall below these thresholds. We found that while the number of measurements for the GeoRIPE framework to accomplish this is similar to the numbers in Table 6, uniform drive testing required an average of 20% more measurements than the listed numbers. The biggest difference in this experiment is alluded to in Table 5, wherein GeoRIPE requires 58% fewer measurements to go below the standard deviation threshold than uniform drive testing.

6 RELATED WORK

Measurement Collection Approaches. Due to the low cost of crowdsourcing from smartphones, the technique has been used by many other groups to collect data about wireless networks. In a study by Huang et al. [12], LTE performance data was collected by creating an Android application named 4GTest. This application gained 3,000 users during 2 months of data collection and collected data that focused on media streaming by mobile clients. With this data, [12] was able to show that with the download speed increase seen with LTE networks, the traffic bottleneck shifted from the network to the processing power of the mobile devices. In [5], an Android application was again used to capture network speed data. This study focused on comparing the speeds of 802.11 networks to the speeds of LTE networks in major cities around the globe. Neidhardt et al. used a crowdsourced infrastructure to provide an open source and more accurate base station location and coverage estimation system [15]. While they had promising results on the base station localization aspect, they concede that cellular coverage estimation was lacking with their purely crowdsourced measurements, especially in urban environments with diverse terrain features. Our work focuses on the minimum measurement requirements according to different geographical features of a given region.

Measurement-Driven Path Loss Evaluation. There have been several measurement studies that strive to more accurately characterize path loss in specific region types. Hata et al. [11] and Okumura et al. [16] specifically focus on accurate characterization in urban regions. Using measurements gathered by [16] in Tokyo, Japan, Hata et al. empirically derived a path loss prediction formula with correction factors for various region types such as large-city urban, small-city urban, suburban, and open areas. Additionally, the Hata model considers base station transmitter height. Similar to the path loss prediction curves found by [16] in Japan, Allsebrook et al. [3] evaluated path loss prediction curves for three British cities: Birmingham, Bath, and Bradford. Akimoto et al. [2] derived a model based on gathered measurements in a rural area using the 2 and 5 GHz bands. Similarly, [8] studied measurements collected in a suburban neighborhood at 5.7 GHz as did [10] with measurements taken in Istanbul in the GSM-900 band. More recently, Robinson et al. sought to minimize the number of measurements necessary to accurately characterize mesh node coverage in the TFA network in Houston [18]. Their work uses an online push-pull measurement gathering approach, taking very few active measurements on an existing deployment based on terrain features in the area. Additionally, Sayrac et al. [19] and several others [4, 7, 14] try to reduce the number of drive testing measurements required for coverage evaluation via Baysian kriging, showing how their techniques can be used to detect coverage holes. However, their analysis replies on the spatial correlation between the measurements themselves to detect coverage holes from existing transmission infrastructure. In contrast, our approach aims to analyze geographical features of a region and predict the number of measurements required to obtain an accurate estimate of path loss throughout, including from transmission sources that do not yet exist, by tying the measurement requirements to the terrain itself.

7 CONCLUSION

In this paper, we built the GeoRIPE framework which predicts the minimum number of in-field measurements required to accurately characterize the path loss of a region according to that region's geographical features. To find if such measurements would be sufficient for a given area, we gathered millions of signal strength measurements along with geographical feature ratios in both a downtown and suburban region. Using this data, we correlated several distinct geographical features with different metrics for path loss evaluation complexity. We found that, together, these features are correlated with the number of measurements required to achieve a fixed path loss accuracy. We also evaluated the merit of using area bounded path loss metrics. By abstracting propagation loss parameters away from specific paths and binding them to a specific area, we are able to evaluate path loss for arbitrary paths through the area. We found that the size of the individual path loss evaluation areas should be selected based on the complexity of the terrain features residing in each area. In general, the more complex the area, the smaller the evaluation area should be. Finally, to validate our work, we compared drive testing using our GeoRIPE framework to uniform drive testing in each region. We found that our technique, as opposed to spatially uniform drive testing, required fewer measurements to achieve a similar path loss characterization accuracy.

ACKNOWLEDGMENTS

This work was in part supported by NSF grants: CNS- 1150215, CNS-1526269, and IIP-1600549.

REFERENCES

[1] [n. d.]. Open Street Maps. www.openstreetmap.org. ([n. d.]). License: http://www.openstreetmap.org/copyright.

[2] Mamoru Akimoto, Tatsuya Shimizu, and Masashi Nakatsugawa. 2006. Path loss estimation of 2 GHz and 5 GHz band FWA within 20 km in rural area. *Proc. of ISAP* (2006).

[3] K. Allsebrook and J.D. Parsons. 1977. Mobile radio propagation in British cities at frequencies in the VHF and UHF bands. *Vehicular Technology, IEEE Transactions on* 26, 4 (1977), 313–323.

[4] Hajer Braham, Sana Ben Jemaa, Gersende Fort, Eric Moulines, and Berna Sayrac. 2017. Fixed Rank Kriging for Cellular Coverage Analysis. *IEEE Transactions on Vehicular Technology* 66, 5 (2017), 4212–4222.

[5] Shuo Deng, Ravi Netravali, Anirudh Sivaraman, and Hari Balakrishnan. 2014. WiFi, LTE, or Both?: Measuring Multi-Homed Wireless Internet Performance. In *Proceedings of the 2014 Conference on Internet Measurement Conference*. ACM, 181–194.

[6] Harald T Friis. 1946. A note on a simple transmission formula. *proc. IRE* 34, 5 (1946), 254–256.

[7] Ana Galindo-Serrano, Berna Sayrac, Sana Ben Jemaa, Janne Riihijärvi, and Petri Mähönen. 2013. Automated coverage hole detection for cellular networks using radio environment maps. In *Modeling & Optimization in Mobile, Ad Hoc & Wireless Networks (WiOpt), 2013 11th International Symposium on*. IEEE, 35–40.

[8] S.S. Ghassemzadeh, H.R. Worstell, and R.R. Miller. 2010. Wireless Neighborhood Area Network Path Loss Characterization at 5.7 GHz. In *Proc. of IEEE VTC-Fall*.

[9] Google. 2017. Android API Description. (2017). https://developer.android.com/reference/android/telephony/CellSignalStrength.html

[10] B.Y. Hanci and I.H. Cavdar. 2004. Mobile radio propagation measurements and tuning the path loss model in urban areas at GSM-900 band in Istanbul-Turkey. In *Proc. of IEEE VTC-Fall*.

[11] M. Hata. 1980. Empirical formula for propagation loss in land mobile radio services. *Vehicular Technology, IEEE Transactions on* 29, 3 (1980), 317–325.

[12] Junxian Huang, Feng Qian, Alexandre Gerber, Z Morley Mao, Subhabrata Sen, and Oliver Spatscheck. 2012. A close examination of performance and power characteristics of 4G LTE networks. In *Proceedings of the 10th international conference on Mobile systems, applications, and services*. ACM, 225–238.

[13] William CY Lee. 1985. Estimate of local average power of a mobile radio signal. *Vehicular Technology, IEEE Transactions on* 34, 1 (1985), 22–27.

[14] Han-Wen Liang, Chih-Hsiang Ho, Li-Sheng Chen, Wei-Ho Chung, Shih-Yi Yuan, and Sy-Yen Kuo. 2016. Coverage hole detection in cellular networks with deterministic propagation model. In *Intelligent Green Building and Smart Grid (IGBSG), 2016 2nd International Conference on*. IEEE, 1–6.

[15] Eric Neidhardt, Abdulbaki Uzun, Ulrich Bareth, and Axel Kupper. 2013. Estimating locations and coverage areas of mobile network cells based on crowdsourced data. In *Wireless and Mobile Networking Conference (WMNC), 2013 6th Joint IFIP*. IEEE, 1–8.

[16] Yoshihisa Okumura, Eiji Ohmori, Tomihiko Kawano, and Kaneharu Fukuda. 1968. Field strength and its variability in VHF and UHF land-mobile radio service. *Rev. Elec. Commun. Lab* 16, 9 (1968), 825–73.

[17] Chris Phillips, Douglas Sicker, and Dirk Grunwald. 2013. A survey of wireless path loss prediction and coverage mapping methods. *Communications Surveys & Tutorials, IEEE* 15, 1 (2013), 255–270.

[18] Joshua Robinson, Ram Swaminathan, and Edward W. Knightly. 2008. Assessment of urban-scale wireless networks with a small number of measurements. In *Proc. of ACM MobiCom*.

[19] Berna Sayrac, Janne Riihijärvi, Petri Mähönen, Sana Ben Jemaa, Eric Moulines, and Sébastien Grimoud. 2012. Improving coverage estimation for cellular networks with spatial bayesian prediction based on measurements. In *Proceedings of the 2012 ACM SIGCOMM workshop on Cellular networks: operations, challenges, and future design*. ACM, 43–48.

[20] Hweechul Shin. 2010. *Measurements and models of 802.11 b signal strength variation over small distances*. Ph.D. Dissertation. University of Delaware.

[21] Bernard Sklar. 1997. Rayleigh fading channels in mobile digital communication systems. I. Characterization. *Communications Magazine, IEEE* 35, 7 (1997), 90–100.

INDIGO: Interest-Driven Data Dissemination Framework for Mobile Networks

Kamini Garg
ISIN-DTI-SUPSI - Switzerland
kaminigarg@gmail.com

Silvia Giordano
ISIN-DTI-SUPSI - Switzerland
silvia.giordano@supsi.ch

Mehdi Jazayeri
USI - Switzerland
mehdi.jazayeri@usi.ch

ABSTRACT

In this paper, we present INDIGO, an interest-driven data dissemination framework that enables to predict the performance of data dissemination. INDIGO computes a tight upper bound of data dissemination time under (i) heterogeneous mobility patterns of people and, (ii) interests-driven dissemination strategy. INDIGO automatically learns the interests of people from their browsing history and also captures their heterogeneous mobility patterns.

We model data dissemination with a cut-off point based approach that mimics real-world data process by utilizing the long tail behavior of inter-contact time distribution. We validate INDIGO through our real-world traces and achieve a tight upper bound of data dissemination, within 2-18% of error. We further identify a long tail behavior of users' interest distribution, and use this finding to validate the scalability on large traces with synthetic interest.

INDIGO can empower local businesses or publishers to assess the performance of their localized dissemination based services in advance and with high accuracy.

CCS CONCEPTS

•**Networks** → *Network performance analysis;*

KEYWORDS

data dissemination, interest-driven, upper bound prediction

1 INTRODUCTION

The immense growth of smartphones has enabled to gather various types of information, enhanced by powerful communication and computing resources. The proliferation of these devices has not just altered the way we communicate and interact, but it has also led to a significant innovation of services. It has opened a door to a new set of applications such as location-based advertising or recommendations, and it has also made possible to gather contextual and personalized information. Recent studies have highlighted an enormous rise in location-based search, advertisements and services [9]. People are usually interested in getting and taking advantage of localized information received from their vicinity like local events, shopping offers, local food, etc... Further, local businesses also intend to maximize the reach of their localized offers/advertisements by pushing them to the maximum number of interested people. The scope of such localized information can be augmented by leveraging the capabilities of smartphones through the dissemination of such information to other interested people [19]. The impact of these localized information gathering and dissemination is two-fold: (i) it can help both local businesses (or publishers) to further disseminate their information to other geographical regions and, (ii) it can bring the information close to people who are not aware of it but might be interested in it.

Before deploying any localized offer or advertisement in a given geographical region, some of the key questions that can arise from the publisher point of view could be:

(1) how relevant my localized offer is among people in this region?
(2) how much time is required to disseminate information to a certain fraction of interested people in this region?

For example, if the maximum time to disseminate data to all or fraction of interested people tends to infinity, then the offered service will be useless due to its inability to spread information to people within a reasonable time limit. To answer such questions and enable publishers to assess the performance of their localized service, we need to predict the performance of data dissemination. Mobile networks exhibit heterogeneous contact patterns and the interest of people is a key feature. The importance of interest-driven dissemination is highlighted in [7] [14] [16], as opposed to broadcast scheme. However, these works do not learn interests of people along with their mobility, rather they explicitly ask users for their interests across certain topics.

We introduce INDIGO, an interest-driven data dissemination framework that enables automatic learning of people interests and predicts tighter upper bounds of data dissemination time under heterogeneous mobility, multiple simultaneous contacts and interest-driven data dissemination strategy. INDIGO utilizes a Markov-chain based prediction model from estimated pair-wise contact probabilities and learned web interests of people. We summarize our main contributions as follows:

- An efficient prediction of data dissemination performances: To the best of our knowledge, INDIGO is the first work that predicts tight upper bound of dissemination time by learning real interests of people from web browsing history of their smartphones along with heterogeneous mobility aspects.
- A new data dissemination model: INDIGO employs a cut-off point based approach that segments data dissemination process in two phases, *Fast Growing* and *Long Tail phase* that reflects on the exponential cut-off property of data process.

We first present the different components of INDIGO. Further, we introduce our model for tight data dissemination time bounds in Section 3. In Section 4, we describe our data collection and validate INDIGO with contact traces. We then give an overview of the state of the art, and we conclude the paper along with future directions.

This work is supported by the FP7 CHIST-ERA MACACO project under grant 20CH21_151573, and by the SNSF Sinergia SwissSenseSynergy project, under grant CRSII2_154458.

MSWiM'17, November 21–25, 2017, Miami, FL, USA

ISBN 978-1-4503-5162-1/17/11...$15.00.
DOI: https://doi.org//10.1145/3127540.3127559

2 INDIGO FRAMEWORK

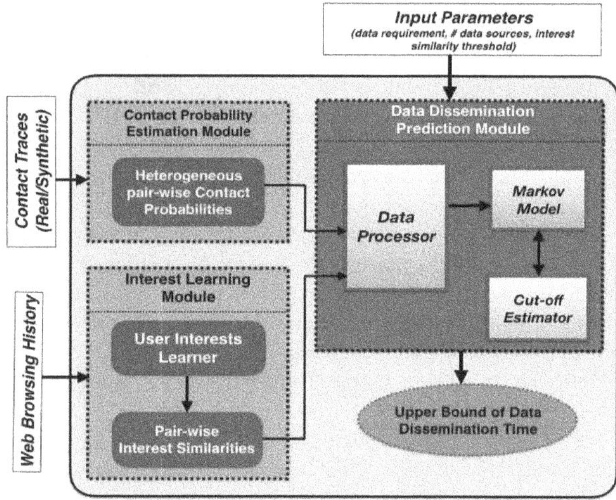

Figure 1: The components of INDIGO used for predicting the upper bound of data dissemination time under interest-driven data dissemination strategy: the *Contact Probability Estimation* module, the *Interest Learning* module, and the *Data Dissemination Prediction* module.

Figure 1 outlines the three components of our interest-driven data dissemination framework INDIGO: the *Contact Probability Estimation* module, the *Interest Learning* module, and the *Data Dissemination Prediction* module. The *Contact Probability Estimation* module estimates pair-wise heterogeneous contact probability of people using real world or synthetic traces. With the help of the *Interest Learning* module, INDIGO learns user interests from their mobile web browsing history and calculates pair-wise interest similarities among them. Finally, the core of INDIGO is the *Data Dissemination Prediction* module that predicts the upper bound of data dissemination time utilizing our Markov chain based model. Table 1 presents the notation used in the rest of the paper.

Table 1: Notation used in INDIGO

Notation	Description
U, D	set of mobile users, set of mobile users selected as data sources
N, M	number of mobile users, number of data sources
u_j, d_i	mobile user $u_j \in U$, data source $d_i \in D$
V	$V = U \cup D$, set of all mobile users and data sources
p^c_{ij}	contact probability between pair $i, j \in V$, $p^c_{ij} \in [0, 1]$
P^C	contact probability matrix of all p^c_{ij}
sim_{ij}	interest cosine similarity between pair $i, j \in V$, $sim_{ij} \in [0, 1]$
I^S	interest similarity matrix of all sim_{ij}
$\mathbb{E}(I^S)$	expected value of I^S
β	interest similarity threshold, $\beta \in [0, 1]$
ut_{ij}	utility value (0 or 1) of data exchange between pair $i, j \in V$
$\mathbb{UT}$	utility matrix of all utility values ut_{ij} to determine data exchange based on interests
α	cut-off point used by Markov model, $\alpha \in [0, 1]$
$\mathbb{D}$	data collection requirement of all mobile users $\mathbb{D} \in [0, 1]$
F	$F = M * N * \mathbb{D}$, final number of messages to collect
msg_i	distinct message associated to data source $d_i \in D$
$MList_{u_j}(t)$	list of data messages received upto time t by mobile user u_j
$D^{ALL}(t)$	list of data messages collected upto time t by all mobile users
$DF(t)$	fraction of data collected till time t, $DF(t) \in [0, F]$
$S(x)$	Markov model state with x messages collected by all mobile users
$S(F)$	Markov model's target state with F messages
$P_{S(x)S(x+k)}$	transition probability to reach $S(x+k)$ from $S(x)$
Δ	time step size of Markov model
T_x	maximum time spent in Markov state $S(x)$
T^{upper}_{dss}	predicted upper bound of data dissemination time
T_{FGP}	maximum time spent Fast Growing Phase
T_{LTP}	maximum time spent Long Tail Phase
T^{meas}_{dss}	measured data dissemination time from real traces under interest-driven data dissemination strategy
t^-, t^+	time before and after time t

2.1 The Contact Probability Estimation Module

This module estimates heterogeneous pair-wise contact probabilities to capture the mobility patterns of people. If people meet each other frequently, then the data dissemination will happen faster and vice versa. Several works in literature have studied the contact probability with respect to data dissemination. However, as discussed in the Related Work section, their assumptions hardly represent the process as it is in real life. In fact, either they consider homogeneous pair-wise contact rate among people [10], or they neglect the multiple simultaneous contacts among people, or the time-varying contact patterns [1] [16].

INDIGO does not assume homogeneous contact probability between all nodes, rather we adopt real world contact patterns [6] [13] [7], i.e. heterogeneous and multiple simultaneous contact probability among users. We use maximum likelihood estimation method from real or synthetic traces to estimate pair-wise contact probability between mobile users or between a user and data source [16]. We construct a contact probability matrix P^C that contains pair-wise heterogeneous contact probability p^c_{ij}.

$$P^C = \{p^c_{ij}\} \ \forall \ i, j \in V \tag{1}$$

2.2 The Interests Learning Module

Usually, people prefer to receive and share information according to their interests (interest-driven) rather than receiving every possible information (broadcast). Our *Interest Learning Module* enables interest-driven data dissemination by learning real web interests of people from their mobile browsing history. The semantic categories of visited websites like social networking, news, shopping etc... reflect user interests. Different works on online advertisement suggest that user profiles built from website categories are an efficient method for user interest profiling [2]. Further, to determine the likelihood to exchange data among people, the module calculates cosine similarity of their interests. Figure 2 presents the working of our *Interests Learning* module that contains two sub-modules: the `User Interests Learner` and the `Pair-wise Interests Similarity`. The `User Interests Learner` investigates web browsing history from user's mobile and finds the hosts

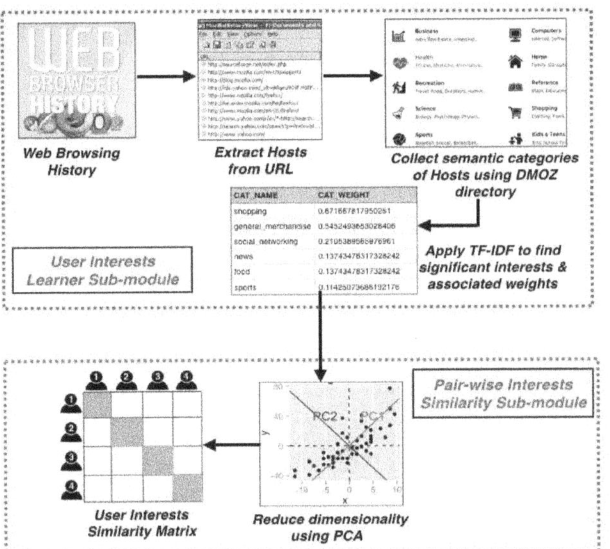

Figure 2: Working of the *Interests Learning Module* using the User Interests Learning and the Pair-wise Interests Similarity sub-modules.

associated with each URL. Later, it queries DMOZ[1], a commonly used open directory of websites, to annotate the destination host names with semantic tags to obtain web categories of each host. The DMOZ directory returns a category of multiple hierarchies for each host, e.g. "Europe/News and Media" for host "bbc.com". We consider all hierarchies categories for user's interests construction.

To learn the interests of a user, we apply the Term Frequency-Inverse Document Frequency (TF-IDF) weighting scheme and create a term vector that contains web categories and their associated weight. TF-IDF emphasizes on categories that distinguish a user from others by considering frequency count of each category (the TF term). The IDF term then decreases the weight of categories that commonly appear across different users like higher hierarchy categories that are abstract.

After we compute the most important web categories for each user, our `Pair-wise Interests Similarities` sub-module creates similarities among each pair of users in two steps:

(1) It applies the Principal Component Analysis (PCA) to reduce the dimensionality of sparse interests term vectors that use singular vector decomposition to create a smaller set of dimensions.
(2) From reduced interest term vectors, it prepares an Interest Similarity Matrix I^S with cosine similarity for all users.

$$I^S = \{sim_{ij}\} \ \forall \ i,j \in V \tag{2}$$

2.3 The Data Dissemination Prediction Module

This module is responsible for predicting the tight upper bound of interest-based data dissemination time. The module consists of three sub-modules: the `Data Processor`, the `Markov Model`, and the `Cut-off Estimator`. The `Data Processor` sub-module pre-processes different inputs required by the `Markov Model` sub-module. The core of this module is the `Markov Model` sub-module that utilizes a cut-off point based approach to provide tight upper bound of data dissemination time. It communicates with the `Cut-off Estimator` to estimate cut-off point α that plays a significant role for tight prediction of T_{dss}^{upper}. This approach incorporates realistic aspects of human mobility (i.e. heterogeneous contact patterns and multiple simultaneous contacts among people) and of data dissemination strategy (i.e. interest-driven data dissemination), as detailed below.

2.3.1 The Data Processor sub-module. This sub-module processes all inputs coming from the *Contact Probability Estimation* and the *Interest Learning* modules and also uses the *Input Parameters.* Out of all users, it randomly assigns M users as data sources and marks the remaining N as mobile users. Further, it calculates[2] the interest similarity threshold β as the expected value of interest similarities matrix I^S. Finally, based on β and I^S, it prepares a Utility matrix $\mathbb{UT}$ as follows:

$$\mathbb{UT} = \{ut_{ij}\} \ \forall \ i,j \in V \tag{3}$$

$$ut_{ij} = \begin{cases} 1 & if \quad sim_{ij} \geq \beta \\ 0 & \text{otherwise} \end{cases}$$

$$\text{Where } \beta = \mathbb{E}(I^S)$$

Both P^C and $\mathbb{UT}$ are then passed as input to `Markov Model` where $\mathbb{UT}$ determines interest-driven data exchange while P^C drives the mobility and heterogeneous contact patterns for the model. It is important to note that data message can only be exchanged if a pair of users has utility value equal to 1. This signifies the importance of interests similarities in real-world data dissemination process.

2.3.2 The Markov Model sub-module. It is a Markov-chain based model that utilizes a cut-off point based approach to mimic real-world data gathering process. Each state $S(x)$ of our Markov-chain based model represents the total number of messages (x) collected by mobile users from different data sources.

To observe the significance of the cut-off point α, we analyze the fraction of data collected over time under interest-driven data dissemination strategy from different real-world traces from diverse environments (conference [17] and university environment [6] during different time periods in Figure 3). We observe that initially the rate of data gathering is faster and after a certain time, it exhibits a long tail cut-off. This happens because after a while the probability of getting new messages from neighboring users reduces as most of them have been already gathered. Therefore, the time taken to gather remaining data increases significantly. In addition, the rate of data gathering depends on the inter-contact time among people that exhibits a long tail cut-off [12]. We utilize this observation in our `Markov Model` and define a cut-off point α as follows:

Definition 1 (Cut-off Point α): It is the data fraction point beyond which the rate of data collection becomes very slow and exhibits a long tail behavior.

To determine α, our `Markov Model` sends to the `Cut-off Estimator` the fraction of data collected in current and previous step, which then compute it as in Equation 4.

Once α is determined, then we estimate T_{dss}^{upper} in 2-phases:

[1] http://www.dmoz.org/

[2] Please note that β can also be enforced as input to the model

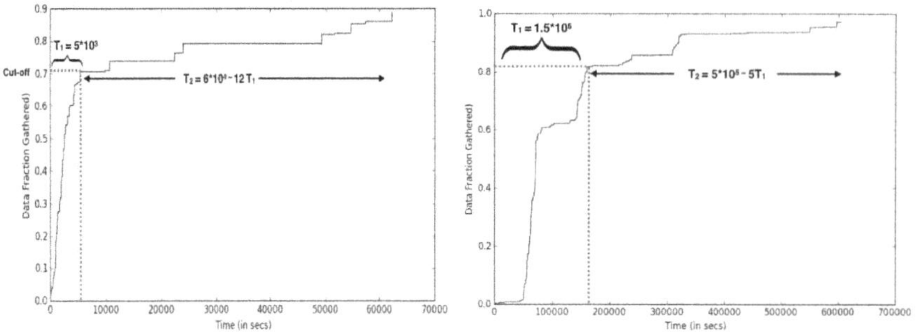

(a) INFOCOM Trace

(b) MIT Trace

Figure 3: Fraction of data gathered with respect to time.

(1) **Fast Growing Phase:** In this phase, we find the expected time required to reach directly to the cut-off state $S(\alpha)$ of our Markov model from initial state $S(0)$. This mimics the initial fast rate of data gathering process.
(2) **Long Tail Phase:** To articulate the long tail of data gathering process, this phase estimates maximum time spent in each state from $S(\alpha)$ to target state $S(F)$.

2.3.3 The Cut-off Estimator sub-module. This sub-module dynamically provides α value to the `Markov Model`. As discussed above, the `Markov Model` communicates the fraction of data collected in one state transition to the `Cut-off Estimator`, which measures the change in data fraction and repeats this process until it reaches to a data fraction α beyond which changes in data fraction becomes smaller than ϵ. The calculated α value is communicated back to `Markov Model`. Given the data fraction $DF(t) \in [0,1]$ and time step size Δ, α is the value for the first time t such that:

$$\alpha : \frac{DF(t+\Delta) - DF(t)}{\Delta} << \epsilon, \epsilon = 10^{-4} \tag{4}$$

Figure 3 presents estimated α for INFOCOM (0.7) and MIT (0.82) traces respectively.

3 TIGHTER PREDICTION OF T_{DSS}^{UPPER} USING THE CUT-OFF POINT BASED APPROACH

3.1 Preliminaries

Let us consider a network with $V = U \cup D$ users where $U = \{u_1, u_2, \ldots.., u_N\}$ represents N mobile users and $D = \{d_1, d_2, \ldots.., d_M\}$ represents M data sources (mobile or static). We assume that every data source $d_i \in D$ has a distinct data message msg_i. Further, the maximum number of messages gathered by a user $u_j \in U$ is determined according to $\mathbb{D}$ obtained as an input parameter. By default, our approach estimates data dissemination bounds for different $\mathbb{D}$ from α to 1 within the interval of 0.05 (α, $\alpha + 0.05$, $\alpha + 0.10$.....1). Please note that $\mathbb{D}$ represents the maximum fraction of data that needs to be collected by all mobile users. Therefore, the maximum number of messages that can be stored in the network are $F = M * N * \mathbb{D}$. [3] The mobility of mobile users, their interests similarities, multiple simultaneous contacts and data sources drives the data dissemination process. The data collection is described by the Contact & Data Gathering process (CDG):

[3]For the sake of tractability we took the assumption of data requirement for entire network similar to other works [16] [15].

Definition 2 (Contact & Data Gathering process): When any two mobile users or any mobile user and data source come in contact with each other they exchange their respective message lists if and only if they share similar interests (i.e utility value is 1).

It is important to note that data sources *do not* exchange any data messages among themselves. Finally, we define multi-contact interest-based data dissemination process as follows:

Definition 3 (Multi-contact Interest-based Data Dissemination): The *CDG* process can happen simultaneously for more than two users or couple user - data source (i.e. more than one message can be disseminated simultaneously).

The data dissemination process continues until the overall data requirement $\mathbb{D}$ is satisfied. Algorithm 1 presents how every mobile user $u_j \in U$ gathers data at time t using *CDG* process. t^- and t^+ represent the time before and after t respectively. Every user u_j maintains a list $MList_{u_j}(t) = \{msg_i, \forall i \in [1,M]\}$ of all messages gathered up to time t.

ALGORITHM 1: Contact & Data Gathering process (CDG)

if Any two users u_j and u_k come in contact at time t with $MList_{u_j}(t^-)$ and $MList_{u_k}(t^-)$ **then**
  if $ut_{u_j u_k} = 1$ **then**
    Users u_j and u_k exchange all of their data messages
    $MList_{u_j}(t^+) = MList_{u_j}(t^-) \cup MList_{u_k}(t^-)$
    $MList_{u_k}(t^+) = MList_{u_j}(t^-) \cup MList_{u_k}(t^-)$
  end if
end if
if Any user u_j with $MList_{u_j}(t^-)$ and any data source d_i with message msg_i come in contact at time t **then**
  if $ut_{u_j d_i} = 1$ **then**
    Users u_j collects data message msg_i from d_i
    $MList_{u_j}(t^+) = MList_{u_j}(t^-) \cup msg_i$
  end if
end if

3.2 Upper Bound of Data Dissemination Time

We define data dissemination time as the time at which all users in the network fulfil data requirement $\mathbb{D}$. Consider a matrix $D^{ALL}(t)$ of size $N \times M$ that represents the list of all data messages collected up to time t by N mobile users.

$$D^{ALL}(t) = \begin{bmatrix} msg_{u_1 d_1} & msg_{u_1 d_2} & \cdots & msg_{u_1 d_M} \\ msg_{u_2 d_1} & msg_{u_2 d_2} & \cdots & msg_{u_2 d_M} \\ \cdot & \cdot & \cdot & \cdot \\ \cdot & \cdot & \cdot & \cdot \\ msg_{u_N d_1} & msg_{u_N d_2} & \cdots & msg_{u_N d_M} \end{bmatrix}_{N \times M}$$

$$msg_{u_j d_i} = \begin{cases} 1 & if \quad msg_i \in MList_{u_j}(t) \\ 0 & \text{otherwise} \end{cases}$$

$$\forall j \in [1,N], \forall i \in [1,M]$$

Definition 4 (The upper bound of data dissemination time T_{dss}^{upper}): is the maximum time slot at which data requirement will be fulfilled and the F elements of matrix $D^{ALL}(t)$ become 1.

It is important to note that since we are using Markov chain based model, the T_{dss}^{upper} will be expressed in event time (number of contact events or ticks) as opposed to standard wall clock time[4].

3.2.1 Cut-off Point Approach. To estimate a tighter T_{dss}^{upper}, our `Markov Model` first sets the target state $S(F)$ according to user data requirement $\mathbb{D}$. Further, it computes the transition probability $P_{S(x),S(x+k)}$ to reach $S(x+k)$ from $S(x)$ using contact probability matrix P^C and utility matrix $\mathbb{UT}$:

$$P_{S(x)S(x+k)} = \sum_{i \in S(x), j \in S(x+k)} p_{ij}^c \times ut_{ij} \qquad (5)$$

$$\text{Where } \forall p_{ij}^c \in P^C, \forall u_{ij} \in \mathbb{UT}$$

Once we reach the target state $S(F)$, the transition probability to remain in the same state will be 1. $S(F)$ is an absorbing state and T_{dss}^{upper} is the sum of maximum time spent in all reachable states before reaching the target state $S(F)$. Due to multiple simultaneous contacts among people, our Markov chain can directly jump from state $S(x)$ to any state $S(x+k)$. To understand how our model considers the impact of multiple simultaneous contacts, let us assume that we are in state $S(2)$, where two users u_1 and u_2 have one unique data message in their respective message list ($MList_{u_1} = \{msg_{d_1}\}$ and $MList_{u_2} = \{msg_{d_2}\}$). When they come in contact, the message lists $MList_{u_1}$ and $MList_{u_2}$ will be exchanged. Further, at the same time users u_{N-1} and u_N also come in contact with two data sources and update their message lists as $MList_{u_{N-1}} = \{msg_{d_M}\}$ and $MList_{u_N} = \{msg_{d_1}\}$ respectively. In this case, we directly jump from state $S(2)$ to state $S(6)$ as the total number of messages in the network becomes 6.

In this case, our model predicts maximum time required to directly reach $S(6)$ from $S(2)$ rather than summing up individual time spent in each transient state $S(3)$, $S(4)$ and $S(5)$. This procedure helps to provide tighter prediction of T_{dss}^{upper} by eliminating the intermediate step. Algorithm 2 presents how we estimate the maximum time ($maxTime$) spent in a state under interest-based data dissemination by utilizing P^C and $\mathbb{UT}$.

Figure 4 presents the process to estimate data dissemination time using the cut-off approach of our `Markov model`. T_{FGP} represents the time spent in the Fast Growing phase (i.e. maximum time required to reach directly to cut-off point state $S(\alpha * F)$ from $S(0)$).

[4]We convert this event time to wall clock time by multiplying it with the beacon interval based on scan interval in contact trace.

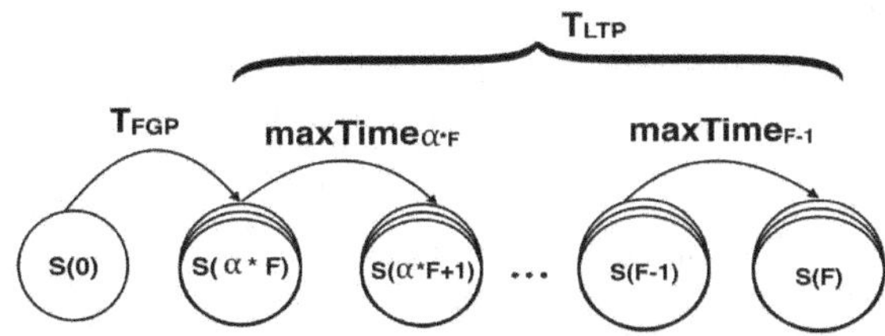

Figure 4: Markov model's cut-off point based approach to predict upper bound of data dissemination time T_{dss}^{upper}.

T_{LTP} is the time spent in the Long Tail Phase (i.e. maximum time spent in each state starting from $S(\alpha * F)$ to $S(F)$). The predicted T_{dss}^{upper} can be defined as follows:

$$T_{dss}^{upper} = T_{FGP} + T_{LTP} \qquad (6)$$

$$\text{Where: } T_{LTP} = \textstyle\sum_{k=\alpha}^{F} T_k$$

The time spent in the long tail phase highly contributes to T_{dss}^{upper}, and its contribution is higher as compared to the time spent in gathering the initial data messages. Therefore, we believe that considering the long tail cut-off, our model provides a much tighter bound of T_{dss}^{upper} and closely resembles the real-world data gathering process.

ALGORITHM 2: getMaxTime: estimate maxTime spent in a state

Require: $startState, endState, D^{ALL}(t), P^C, \mathbb{UT}, NumTrials$
Ensure: $maxTime$

```
for trial = 1 to NumTrials do
    T = ∅
    t = 0
    repeat
        x ← U(0, 1)
        t ← t + 1
        {Assuming CDG process, user-user}
        if x < 0.5 then
            r ← U(0, 1)
            for all pairs of users (i, j) : p^c_{i,j} ≥ r AND u_ij = 1 do
                update D^ALL(t) based on CDG algorithm
            end for
        end if
        {Assuming CDG process, user-data source}
        if x > 0.5 then
            r ← U(0, 1)
            for all user, data-source pair (i, k) : p^c_{i,k} ≥ r, AND u_ik = 1
            do
                update D^ALL(t) based on CDG algorithm
            end for
        end if
        d ← count(D^ALL(t)) {total messages stored in D^ALL(t)}
    until d ≤ endState
    if d = endState then
        T ← T ∪ t
    end if
end for
maxTime ← max(T)
return maxTime
```

Algorithm 3 presents how the Cut-off point approach computes T_{FGP} and T_{LTP} individually to find the tight upper bound for

T_{dss}^{upper}. Once the `Markov Model` determines α through the `Cut-off Estimator`, it segregates the Fast Growing and the Long Tail phases. In the Fast Growing phase, the model sets *startState* as $S(0)$ and *cutoffState* as $S(\alpha * F)$ and predicts (T_{FGP}) to directly reach *cutoffState* for several runs (i.e. the estimation of maximum time spent in a state, *NumRuns*, obtained by using the Algorithm 2). Afterwards, it starts the Long Tail phase by initializing *startState* to $S(\alpha * F)$ and *nextstate* to $S(\alpha * F + 1)$ and predicts maximum time spent in *nextstate* using the Algorithm 2. If the model can reach $S(\alpha * F + 1)$ (i.e $maxTime \neq 0$) then, it sets *startState* as $S(\alpha * F + 1)$ and *nextstate* as $S(\alpha * F + 2)$. If the model cannot reach *nextstate* due to the non-existence of *CDG* process then, *nextstate* will be marked as non-reaching and *maxTime* to reach this state will be set to 0. Our model will restart computing *maxTime* by setting *nextstate* to $S(\alpha * F + 2)$

Likewise, the model repeats the same process until it reaches final state $S(F)$. Finally, the model computes T_{LTP} as the sum of maximum time spent in each reachable state. The *CDG* process presented in the Algorithm 1 is modeled using heterogeneous contact

ALGORITHM 3: Predict T_{dss}^{upper} with cut-off approach

```
Require: P^C, UT, M, N, NumRuns, F, D^ALL(t) = 0_{N×M}
Ensure: T_dss
  startState ← 0
  stopState ← F
  cutoffState ← 0
  T_FGP ← 0, T_LTP ← 0, T_dss^upper ← 0, α ← 0
  T_runs = ∅
  {estimate α from Cut-off Estimator sub-module}
  Set cut-off point α
  cutoffState ← α * F
  {calculate time for Fast Growing phase}
  for i = 0 to NumRuns do
    maxTime ← getMaxTime(startState, cutoffState,
                           D^ALL(t), P^C, UT)
    T_runs ← T_runs ∪ maxTime
  end for
  T_FGP ← max(T_runs)
  T_runs = ∅
  {calculate time for Long Tail phase}
  startState ← cutoffState
  while startState < stopState do
    nextState ← startState + 1
    for i = 0 to NumRuns do
      p ← startState
      randomly set p elements of matrix D^ALL(t) to 1
      maxTime ← getMaxTime(startState, nextState,
                             D^ALL(t), P^C, U)
      T_runs ← T_runs ∪ maxTime
      if maxTime = 0 then
        nextState ← nextState + 1
      else
        startState ← nextState
        nextState ← nextState + 1
      end if
    end for
    T_LTP ← T_LTP + max(T_runs)
  end while
  T_dss^upper ← T_FGP + T_LTP
```

probabilities P^C and utility matrix $\mathbb{UT}$. As described in previous sections, our `Markov Model` predicts T_{dss}^{upper} for different data requirements of the network starting from α to 1, unless $\mathbb{D}$ is provided as an input parameter.

4 PERFORMANCE EVALUATION

We validate INDIGO by predicting upper bounds of data dissemination time T_{dss}^{upper} and comparing this T_{dss}^{pred} with actual data dissemination time T_{dss}^{meas} measured from real-world traces.

4.1 Data Set

To investigate the accuracy of INDIGO, we needed real-world traces that have both contact patterns and web-browsing history of people. To the best of our knowledge, there are no such real-world traces. Therefore, we created our mobile app MACACO[5] to collect such data. Our app periodically scans the Wi-Fi access points connected to smartphones of users with a sampling frequency of 5 minutes. The app also log the information about web browsing history and applications running on user's smartphone. To ensure the privacy of users, our app anonymizes the identity of users and sends collected data to a secure central server. We deployed our app on 27 volunteers residing in two different countries: France (from April 2015 to May 2015) and Brazil (from September 2015 to October 2015).

From the collected data, we create contact traces by using Wi-Fi scan information as in [5] [11]. We create a contact between any two volunteers if they are associated with the same access point within a duration of 30 minutes. Figure 5 presents the contact graphs of volunteers for both countries created in this way. Further,

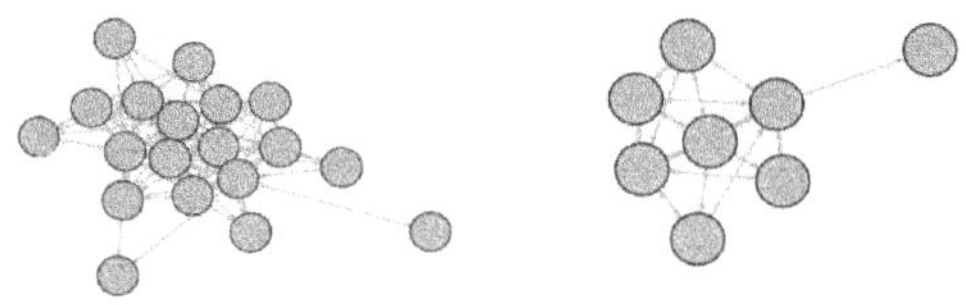

Figure 5: Contact graphs of volunteers in France and Brazil created from their contact traces using Wi-Fi AP data.

from generated contact traces, we consider the month where a maximum number of users make regular and intense use of the wireless network. The most active month for France and Brazil group were May 2015 and October 2015 respectively. Table 2 presents the characteristics of contact traces used in our evaluation. Our *Interests Learning* module generates web interests of volunteers from their

Table 2: Contact traces characteristics.

	France	Brazil
# of Volunteers	19	8
Number of Contacts	559752	72784
Month	May 2015	October 2015
Volunteers Context	Students and staff of different departments	Staff members of same department

[5]The MACACO app is available at Play Store.

Table 3: Simulation settings and T_{dss}^{meas} for maximum data fraction under interest-driven dissemination strategy.

	France		Brazil	
	France-W^H	France-W^L	Brazil-W^H	Brazil-W^L
# Users	15	15	6	6
# Data Sources	4	4	2	2
DF_{max}	0.5714	0.5238	0.50	0.40
T_{dss}^{meas} (in secs)	308020	542396	361425	215638

web browsing history and also creates interest similarities among each pair of users using the `Pair-wise Interests Similarity` sub-module. Some of the web interests categories from our dataset were informatique, science, computer, sports and news etc. Further, in Figure 6, we present the interest similarities among volunteers in France and Brazil respectively. Figure 6 shows that, on average, volunteers in Brazil group have higher interest similarities as compared to the France group.

Finally, to understand the impact of contact patterns variance among different weeks, we further segment one-month data into four weeks and consider the two weeks that exhibit opposite behavior in terms of contact patterns. We take the week having the highest number of contacts and the week having the lowest number of contacts and call them France-W^H, France-W^L, Brazil-W^H and Brazil-W^L for France and Brazil groups respectively.

4.2 Measured data dissemination time T_{dss}^{meas}

We measure data dissemination time T_{dss}^{meas} for France-W^H, France-W^L, Brazil-W^H and Brazil-W^L under interest-driven data dissemination strategy. For each week, we randomly select M users as mobile data sources and remaining N mobile users as those who are interested in gathering data according to different data requirements $\mathbb{D}$. We update the data matrix $D^{ALL}(t)$ based on the contact patterns observed in real contact traces and interest similarities among each pair of users. At each time step, we replay contacts among a pair of users and impose interest-driven data dissemination strategy by comparing their interest similarity. If the interest similarity sim_{ij} between users i and j is above β threshold, then we exchange the message. We stop the simulation when the network data requirement gets fulfilled and record this time as T_{dss}^{meas}. Table 3 presents simulation settings and T_{dss}^{meas} for maximum data fraction DF_{max} collected in all weeks. As compared to broadcast strategy, interest-driven data dissemination strategy restricts the spread of information (max collected data fraction is less than 100%) and arguably the time. We observe a similar behavior for France-W^H and France-W^L (the difference in the fraction of data collected is only slightly higher (5%)), even though France-W^H has much higher contact probabilities among people as compared to France-W^L. Brazil group also produces similar effects as data fraction collected in Brazil-W^H is only 10% higher as compared to Brazil-W^L. Our T_{dss}^{meas} for both groups shows the importance of interest-driven data dissemination strategy on data dissemination time.

To ensure comparable results, we set the maximum fraction of data collected DF_{max} and the measured data dissemination time T_{dss}^{meas} through emulation of real traces as ground truth.

4.3 Predicted upper bound of data dissemination time T_{dss}^{pred}

For each of the selected weeks, INDIGO predicts T_{dss}^{pred} for different data requirements starting from the cut-off point α to the maximum fraction of data collected DF^{max} with 5% step size.

Before predicting upper bounds, the `Data Processor` sets β values to 0.3 and 0.5 using $\mathbb{E}(I^S)$ for France and Brazil respectively. From I^S matrix, we observe that volunteers in France share fewer interests as compared to volunteers in Brazil. This because, in France traces, volunteers range from students to staff of different departments, while in Brazil traces most of the people were researchers from the same group. Finally, based on β, the `Data Processor` builds $\mathbb{UT}$ and provide it as an input to the `Markov Model`.

Figure 7 presents the comparison of predicted T_{dss}^{upper} against T_{dss}^{meas} for France-W^H, France-W^L, Brazil-W^H and Brazil-W^L. For all weeks of both groups, we observe that INDIGO predicts T_{dss}^{upper} within 2-18% error for all data requirements starting from α to DF_{max}. For France-W^H, it gets T_{dss}^{pred} within 2-11% error while for France-W^L, the prediction of upper bounds gets looser with an error of 2-18%. This happens due to lower contact probabilities estimated from INDIGO and its impact on the Long Tail phase of the cut-off point based approach. We also observe a similar trend in Brazil group with 2-15% and 13-18% error in Brazil-W^H and Brazil-W^L weeks respectively.

The importance of interest similarities is also evident in T_{dss}^{pred}: the errors obtained in France and Brazil traces are comparable, even though Brazil traces exhibits much lower contact probabilities, due to higher similarity in Brazil traces. In fact, in the case of France traces, even if there is a high number of contacts among people INDIGO does not exchange many messages because of low interest similarities. This results in an overall increases of T_{dss}^{upper}. As opposite, Brazil traces exhibit lower contacts but a large number of messages are exchanged due to high interest similarities among people. For both traces, our results show highest and lowest error at DF_{max} and α data requirements respectively. This result once again signifies the impact of Long Tail phase on data dissemination time because, in the case of α data requirement, INDIGO only utilizes the Fast Growing Phase while for others, it uses both the Fast Growing and the Long Tail phase.

4.4 Scalability of INDIGO

In order to check the scalability and applicability of INDIGO, we tested it on different sample sizes. Due to lack of dedicated traces that capture both mobility and real interests of people, we artificially created interests of people based on small, medium and weak ties concept of social networks using a power-law distribution of interest. To verify the validity of such power law distribution, we analysed user's real web interests in the MACACO trace for both France and Brazil groups. Figure 8 verifies the suitability of power law distribution for generating the synthetic interests.

The traces we consider for the scalability aspect belong to diverse environments like INFOCOM (conference) [17] and MIT Reality Mining (University) [6] with different sample sizes. For all these traces, INDIGO also provides tight estimates of T_{dss}^{upper} against T_{dss}^{meas}. The values for β for INFOCOM and MIT traces is set to 0.5

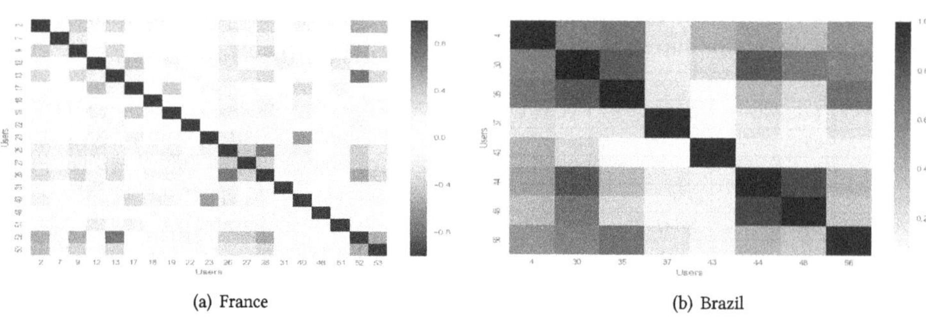

(a) France (b) Brazil

Figure 6: Interests similarities between volunteers of France and Brazil Groups calculated from their web interests profiles.

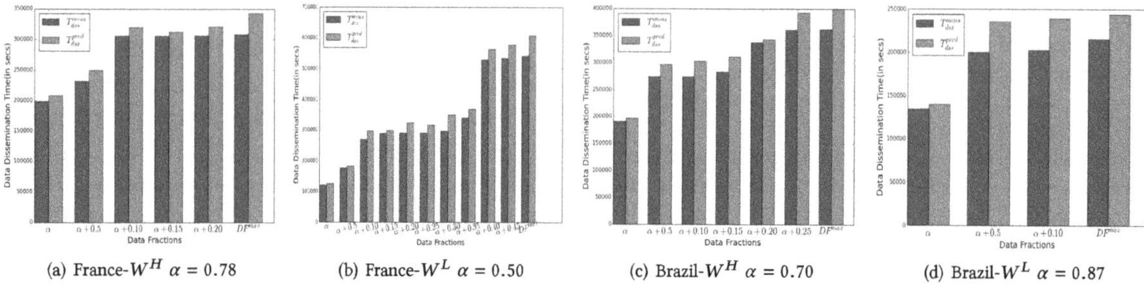

(a) France-W^H $\alpha = 0.78$ (b) France-W^L $\alpha = 0.50$ (c) Brazil-W^H $\alpha = 0.70$ (d) Brazil-W^L $\alpha = 0.87$

Figure 7: Prediction of the upper bound of data dissemination time under interest-driven data dissemination strategy for two different weeks of France and Brazil group, and comparison with ground truth.

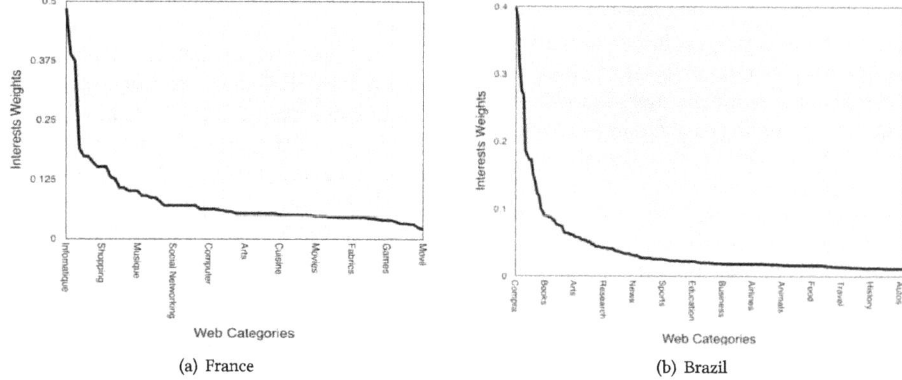

(a) France (b) Brazil

Figure 8: Power low distribution of sample user's web interests for MACACO France and Brazil groups.

and 0.4 respectively. As shown in Figure 9, we observe that the cut-off approach once again provides tight prediction of T_{dss}^{upper} for all contact traces under interest-driven data dissemination strategy.

5 RELATED WORK

The problem of information dissemination in mobile networks has been addressed by existing works mainly using broadcast or epidemic strategies. The epidemic is one of the simplest data dissemination strategies that floods the network with a message [18]. Most of the existing work employ broadcast strategy to model data dissemination time without considering realistic aspects of mobility patterns [20]. They either utilized different mobility random models like Random Mobility, Random Waypoint [4] or homogeneous pair-wise contact rate among people [10]. As a result, these models fail to provide a realistic evaluation of data dissemination time. Recent experimental studies [6] [7] show the existence of considerable heterogeneity in node mobility, thus questions the predictions of existing models.

The works in [1] [16] have considered fixed pair-wise heterogeneous contact rates for the entire duration of time to provide bounds of data dissemination time in opportunistic networks. However, these works also discount the impact of multiple simultaneous contacts among people, time-varying contact patterns, and interest-driven data dissemination strategy. Recent studies highlight the

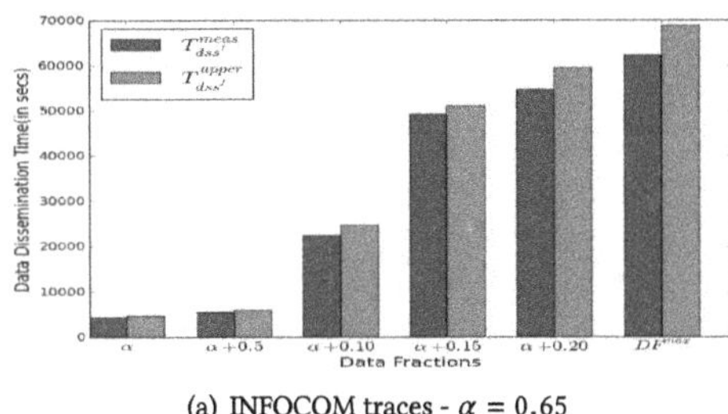

(a) INFOCOM traces - α = 0.65

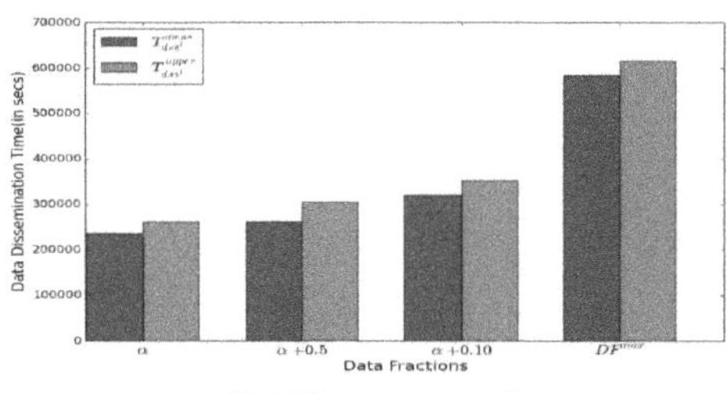

(b) MIT traces - α = 0.68

Figure 9: Comparison of real data dissemination time against the upper bound of data dissemination time predicted using cut-off approaches for INFOCOM and MIT trace under interest-driven dissemination strategy.

importance of mobility [8] and interest-driven strategy aspects in data dissemination modeling [3] [14]. These works do not focus on real interests captured along with user mobility rather they rely on a publish-subscribe scheme where users explicitly show their interests in certain topics. Asking user interests are neither feasible in long term nor scalable because interests change over time. Thus, learning of user interests is a more practical approach to model interest-driven data dissemination.

6 CONCLUSION AND FUTURE WORK

In this paper, we propose INDIGO data dissemination framework that predicts upper bound of data dissemination time by learning real interests of people from web browsing history of their smartphones along with heterogeneous mobility aspects.

We identified some exponential cut-off properties of data gathering process, and we used this finding to predict a tighter upper bound data dissemination time by means of a cut-off based approach that mimics real-world data gathering process through dynamic learning of cut-off point. Further, INDIGO addresses the shortcomings of existing works that do not consider real interests of people along with heterogeneous mobility. Finally, our framework also takes into account the impact of multiple simultaneous contacts and different data requirements on data dissemination time prediction.

Thus, INDIGO allows predicting the performance of data dissemination in a given scenario. For example, it can help local businesses or data publishers to measure the performance of their localized offers among interested people in a given scenario.

We validate INDIGO through our real-world traces collected in France and Brazil and achieve tight upper bounds of data dissemination within 5-18% error. Our simulation results show the applicability of our framework under interest-driven data dissemination strategy. Further, we also confirm the scalability of INDIGO on large state of the art traces (INFOCOM and MIT) by artificially creating interests of people. In future, we plan to improve our framework by incorporating automatic learning of time varying pair-wise contact probabilities along with time-varying interest profiles of people.

REFERENCES

[1] Chiara Boldrini, Marco Conti, and Andrea Passarella. 2014. Performance modelling of opportunistic forwarding under heterogenous mobility. *Computer Communications* 48 (2014), 56–70.

[2] Juan Miguel Carrascosa, Jakub Mikians, Ruben Cuevas, Vijay Erramilli, and Nikolaos Laoutaris. 2014. I Always Feel Like Somebody's Watching Me. Measuring Online Behavioural Advertising. *arXiv preprint arXiv:1411.5281* (2014).

[3] Radu-Ioan Ciobanu, Radu-Corneliu Marin, Ciprian Dobre, and Valentin Cristea. 2015. Interest-awareness in data dissemination for opportunistic networks. *Ad Hoc Networks* 25 (2015), 330–345.

[4] Andrea Clementi, Riccardo Silvestri, and Luca Trevisan. 2012. Information Spreading in Dynamic Graphs. In *Proceedings of the 2012 ACM Symposium on Principles of Distributed Computing (PODC '12)*. ACM, New York, NY, USA, 37–46. https://doi.org/10.1145/2332432.2332439

[5] Vania Conan, Jérémie Leguay, and Timur Friedman. 2006. The heterogeneity of inter-contact time distributions: its importance for routing in delay tolerant networks. (2006).

[6] Nathan Eagle, Alex Sandy Pentland, and David Lazer. 2009. Inferring friendship network structure by using mobile phone data. *Proceedings of the National Academy of Sciences* 106, 36 (2009), 15274–15278.

[7] A. Foerster, K. Garg, H. A. Nguyen, and S. Giordano. 2012. On Context Awareness and Social Distance in Human Mobility Traces. In *3rd International Workshop on Mobile Opportunistic Networks*. ACM.

[8] Kamini Garg and Silvia Giordano. 2015. Towards developing a generalized modeling framework for data dissemination. *ewsn 2015* (2015), 9.

[9] Google. 2015. Understanding Consumer's Local Search Behavior. https://storage.googleapis.com/think-emea/docs/research_study/Report_Google_Local_Search_Behavior_DE_1.pdf. (2015).

[10] Robin Groenevelt, Philippe Nain, and Ger Koole. 2005. The Message Delay in Mobile Ad Hoc Networks. *Perform. Eval.* 62, 1-4 (Oct. 2005), 210–228. https://doi.org/10.1016/j.peva.2005.07.018

[11] W-J Hsu, Thrasyvoulos Spyropoulos, Konstantinos Psounis, and Ahmed Helmy. 2007. Modeling time-variant user mobility in wireless mobile networks. In *IEEE INFOCOM 2007-26th IEEE International Conference on Computer Communications*. IEEE, 758–766.

[12] Thomas Karagiannis, Jean-Yves Le Boudec, and Milan Vojnović. 2007. Power Law and Exponential Decay of Inter Contact Times Between Mobile Devices. In *Proceedings of the 13th Annual ACM International Conference on Mobile Computing and Networking (MobiCom '07)*. ACM, New York, NY, USA, 183–194. https://doi.org/10.1145/1287853.1287875

[13] Vincent Lenders, Jorg Wagner, and Martin May. 2006. Measurements from an 802.11B Mobile Ad Hoc Network. In *Proceedings of the 2006 International Symposium on on World of Wireless, Mobile and Multimedia Networks (WOWMOM '06)*. IEEE Computer Society, Washington, DC, USA, 519–524. https://doi.org/10.1109/WOWMOM.2006.63

[14] Alessandro Mei, Giacomo Morabito, Paolo Santi, and Julinda Stefa. 2011. Social-aware stateless forwarding in pocket switched networks. In *Infocom, 2011 Proceedings Ieee*. IEEE, 251–255.

[15] Damon Mosk-Aoyama and Devavrat Shah. 2008. Fast distributed algorithms for computing separable functions. *Information Theory, IEEE Transactions on* 54, 7 (2008), 2997–3007.

[16] A. Picu, Thrasyvoulos Spyropoulos, and T. Hossmann. 2012. An analysis of the information spreading delay in heterogeneous mobility DTNs. In *World of Wireless, Mobile and Multimedia Networks (WoWMoM), 2012 IEEE International Symposium on a*. 1–10. https://doi.org/10.1109/WoWMoM.2012.6263682

[17] James Scott, Richard Gass, Jon Crowcroft, Pan Hui, Christophe Diot, and Augustin Chaintreau. 2006. CRAWDAD data set cambridge/haggle (v. 2006-01-31). Downloaded from http://crawdad.org/cambridge/haggle/. (Jan. 2006).

[18] Amin Vahdat, David Becker, et al. 2000. Epidemic routing for partially connected ad hoc networks. (2000).

[19] John Whitbeck, Marcelo Amorim, Yoann Lopez, Jeremie Leguay, and Vania Conan. 2011. Relieving the wireless infrastructure: When opportunistic networks meet guaranteed delays. In *World of Wireless, Mobile and Multimedia Networks (WoWMoM), 2011 IEEE International Symposium on a*. IEEE, 1–10.

[20] Eiko Yoneki. 2011. FluPhone Study: Virtual Disease Spread Using Haggle. In *Proceedings of the 6th ACM Workshop on Challenged Networks (CHANTS '11)*. ACM, New York, NY, USA, 65–66. https://doi.org/10.1145/2030652.2030672

Synchronizing Tiny Sensors with SISP: A Convergence Study

Oana Hotescu, Katia Jaffrès-Runser
Institut de Recherche en Informatique de Toulouse
Université de Toulouse, INPT
2 rue Charles Camichel
Toulouse, France 31300
{oana.hotescu,kjr}@enseeiht.fr

Adrien Van Den Bossche, Thierry Val
Institut de Recherche en Informatique de Toulouse
Université de Toulouse, UT2J
BP60073
Blagnac, France 31703
{adrien.van-den-bossche,thierry.val}@irit.fr

ABSTRACT

The SImple Synchronization Protocol (SISP) has been designed for tiny sensors to offer a wireless synchronization service to the network. SISP is completely distributed with a flat architecture. Nodes broadcast a SYNC message periodically that contains the value of their view of a shared clock counter. Every time a SYNC message is received, nodes update their shared clock by averaging it with the clock value embedded in the message. This protocol converges in practice very well, and requires a small amount of energy as SYNC messages can be sent every second only. Moreover, computations are basic, perfectly fitting the tiny sensor platforms needed for the Internet of Things. Its distributed operations enable the network to adjust seamlessly to the appearance or disappearance of other nodes. This paper concentrates on the convergence analysis of this promising protocol. Convergence time and synchronization accuracy are determined analytically, by simulations and by experimenting a real sensor platform. All results show that this protocol offers an accuracy in the order of a few tens of microseconds. Moreover, our analytical derivations capture very well an upper bound on the synchronization accuracy.

CCS CONCEPTS

• **Networks → Protocol testing and verification**; **Sensor networks**; Network performance analysis;

KEYWORDS

Wireless Sensor Network; Synchronization; Convergence analysis

1 INTRODUCTION

The Internet of Things (IoT) is foreseen to be central to future communication technologies. In the next decade, not only humans will exchange information, but machines and objects of different sorts as well. Objects of all kinds, connected wirelessly using various technologies (WiFi, 5G, Ultra Wide Band, LoRa, etc.) will carry data over short or long distances. Different services are envisioned where this data plays a very important role, which may strongly impact the performance of a much larger cyber-physical system. For instance, industry will evolve to a new generation of factories where all processes and humans are monitored to measure the production efficiency, but as well to extract information and metrics that can be leveraged to further improve operations in real-time. Such data can as well warrant the quality of the products by completely tracing the history of all goods and processes.

In such a context, objects (sensors, actuators, robots, smartphones, ...) will coexist in the factory and mostly communicate wirelessly. The density of these systems calls for advanced communication techniques that seamlessly scale. Objects enter or leave the system in an autonomous fashion in this case. As such, network operations have to be designed in a completely distributed manner.

For these objects to efficiently communicate in such a dense context, wireless channel has to be divided among communicating nodes using time or frequency division medium access (or both). Current industry-oriented wireless solutions such as WirelessHart [1] or the TSCH mode of IEEE803.15.4e [2] define an FTDMA medium access layer. This layer offers 10 millisecond time slots to emit a 127 byte frame at 250 kbits/s and receive its acknowledgement. It has been highlighted in [3] that this slot duration is too large and detrimental to overall communication performance. Reducing this duration is only possible if a scalable synchronization protocol can be leveraged to finely synchronize these resource-limited objects.

Synchronizing nodes over a network is not a new problem and lots of solutions exist in the literature. The closest works to this study are related to the synchronization of wireless sensor networks. Representative protocols are RBS [4], TPSN [5], FTSP [6], PulseSync [7], SHARP [8] and SISP [9]. Our aim is to leverage a protocol that provides a seamless synchronization over tiny low-complexity platforms. RBS and TPSN have been created to synchronize a relatively small set of nodes and thus they don't scale well. FTSP and PulseSync, on the contrary, have been designed to flood beacons to rapidly transfer time information to remote sensors. Both algorithms achieve a synchronization accuracy of a few tens of microseconds. FTSP offers a maximum accuracy of $80\mu s$, and PulseSync a maximum accuracy of $38\mu s$ for a line topology of 20 nodes. Both approaches synchronize the network to the time of a selected root node. If this root node dies, another node has to be elected and its time spread in the network, creating a possible cut of synchronization service.

This paper focuses on a different solution that floods beacons as well in the network. These beacons are not forwarded in a multi-hop fashion, but are beamed and exploited by the nodes to agree on a common notion of time called the shared clock. Since this shared clock results from the common decision of all nodes, the departure of one node has little impact on the shared clock value. There is no

MSWiM '17, November 21–25, 2017, Miami, FL, USA

ACM ISBN 978-1-4503-5162-1/17/11...$15.00
https://doi.org/10.1145/3127540.3127564

central entity. This solution is called SISP which stands for *SImple Synchronization Protocol* [9].

SISP is completely distributed with a flat architecture. Nodes broadcast a SYNC message periodically that contains the value of their view of a shared clock counter. Every time a SYNC message is received, nodes update their shared clock by averaging it with the clock value embedded in the message. This protocol converges in practice very well, and requires a small amount of energy as SYNC messages can be sent every second only. Moreover, computations are basic, perfectly fitting the tiny sensor platforms needed for the Internet of Things. Its distributed agreement on a common clock enables the network to adjust seamlessly to the appearance or disappearance of other nodes.

SISP has been evaluated experimentally in the past [9], [8]. It has been shown in [8] that it clearly outperforms RBS on an Arduino Fio embedded platform running a 8MHz micro-controller. RBS reaches only an accuracy of 1509 μs in average while SISP offers a $112\mu s$ accuracy for a 2-node topology (beacons are emitted every 500ms in both protocols). So far, there is no thorough quantification of the SISP convergence properties. The goal of this paper is to fill this gap and exhibit the short convergence of this promising protocol to a stable synchronization with low error. Convergence time and synchronization accuracy are determined analytically, by simulations and though experimentations. All results show that this protocol offers a maximum accuracy in the order of a few tens of microseconds on the investigated hardware. Moreover, our analytical derivations capture very well an upper bound on the synchronization accuracy.

The paper is organized as follows. Section 2 introduces SISP and the model we will leverage for its analysis. The following three sections analyze its convergence properties using three different means: simulations in Section 3, theoretic analysis in Section 4 and experiments in Section 5. Finally, Section 6 concludes this work and draws the main lines of future works.

2 PROTOCOL AND MODEL

2.1 SISP protocol

SISP is a SImple Synchronization Protocol designed for lightweight wireless sensors [9]. SISP is completely distributed, and there is no hierarchy among nodes. Through the exchange of periodic SYNC messages, all nodes adopt a global time reference with a precision of a few tens of microseconds. This global time reference is not the absolute universal time but a time that all nodes agree to follow together. Algorithm 1 presents the actions performed by the `sisp()` function that is called periodically by each node of the network.

SISP defines two integer counters per node: the local clock LCLK and the shared clock SCLK. At onset, both counters are set to zero. Both clocks are incremented by one unit every time the `sisp()` procedure is called. Every P procedure call, a node broadcasts a SYNC message that conveys the SCKL value the sender node measures at emission time. For all other calls, she listens to SYNC messages sent by neighbours. If a SYNC message is received, she reads the embedded clock value, RCLK, and updates her shared clock following:

$$SCLK = \left\lfloor \frac{RCLK + SCLK}{2} \right\rfloor \quad (1)$$

This operation averages both clock values and rounds up the result to the closest inferior integer with $\lfloor\ \rfloor$ operators. SISP is a perfect fit for tiny microprocessors as it requires only one addition plus one division by 2 (i.e. 1 bit right shift).

SYNC frames are not acknowledged, only nodes receiving the frame update their SCLK counter. SISP can be implemented over any type of medium access protocol that offers broadcast communication service. However, its accuracy and convergence duration will be impacted by the number of SYNC messages that collide. Future works will study the impact of SYNC message losses on SISP accuracy and convergence duration. In the following, all derivations, simulations and experiments are made for the ideal case where no SYNC frame collision occurs.

SISP is illustrated in Figure 2 with a sample execution carried out over a 2-node topology. Node $N0$ begins her emissions before node $N1$ by sending SYNC frames every 100 `sisp()` procedure calls. The first three SYNC emissions have no effect on the network since there is no active node. Once $N1$ is turned on, she initialises her SCLK counter to 0. After 20 calls, $N1$ receives the SYNC frame of $N0$ and offsets its SCLK according to Eq. (1). When the LCLK counter of $N1$ reaches 100, $N1$ sends a new SYNC message that causes a change in the SCLK value of $N0$. The execution continues this way, which leads to the gradual convergence of the shared clocks of both nodes after a couple of SYNC broadcasts. The remainder of this paper concentrates on the convergence study of this protocol for simple topologies.

2.2 SISP model

In this paper, we adopt the following model to capture the core elements of SISP for a network composed of N nodes. Each node $Ni, i \in \{0, .., N\}$, has a local hardware clock denoted $LCLK_{Ni}$ and a view of the shared clock denoted $SCLK_{Ni}$. Throughout this study we adopt the notations of Table 1.

The reference clock for all derivations is chosen as the one of node $N0$, naming $LCLK_{N0}$. The local clocks of all other nodes are modeled as linear functions of this reference clock:

$$LCLK_{Ni} = \alpha_{Ni} * LCLK_{N0} + \beta_{Ni} \quad (2)$$

where α_{Ni} and β_{Ni} are respectively the drift and offset of the local clock of Ni with respect to the one of $N0$. Offset and drift can take

```
sisp(){
    lclk = lclk + 1
    sclk = sclk + 1
    if(lclk mod P != 0){
        if msg_received(rclk){
            sclk = (sclk + rclk) / 2
            //if rclk=sclk then nodes share the same SCLK
        }
        else
        {
            broadcast(sclk)
        }
    }
}
```

Figure 1: SISP procedure: LCLK, SCLK and P are global integer variables.

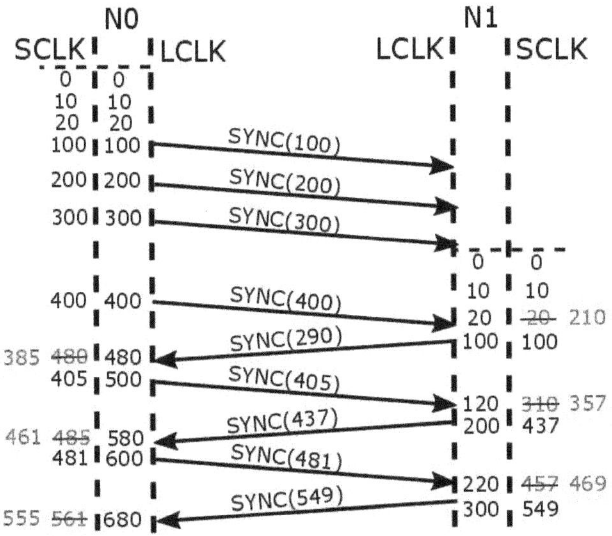

Figure 2: SISP sequence diagram

Table 1: Table of notations

Notation	Definition
α_{Ni}	Node N_i clock drift
$LCLK_{Ni}$	Node N_i local clock
$SCLK_{Ni}$	Node N_i shared clock
t_k	A discrete clock that moves one step forward every time a SYNC message is emitted by a node of the network. Integer k counts the number of SYNC messages emitted since the beginning of the synchronization.
D_k^{Ni}	Duration in seconds that separates t_k and t_{k-1} on node N_i
$d_{NiNj}(t_k)$	Difference between the shared clocks of node N_i and node N_j at t_k
P	SYNC message period in clock tops
a	Synchronization accuracy
t_a	Convergence duration

positive or negative values. A positive (resp. negative) drift implies that Ni runs faster (resp. slower) than $N0$. If α_{Ni} equals one, both clocks run at the same speed. In this case, synchronization is simpler as only offset has to be compensated for by the protocol. Of course, this model is a simplification of reality: drift can change over time because of the variations of the oscillators frequencies of $N0$ and $N1$ with heat, load, etc. The impact of real variations on SISP synchronization will be observed in our experimental study. The linear model will be leveraged in the simulation and analytic studies.

2.3 SISP convergence

This paper aims at measuring and calculating a bound on the convergence time and synchronization accuracy of SISP.

Convergence time. In this protocol, the first SYNC messages mostly compensate for the clock offsets of all nodes. The shared clocks of all nodes converge to a value close to the average of their offsets $\beta_{avg} = 1/N \sum_{i=0}^{i=N-1} \beta_{Ni}$. The time needed for the shared clocks to reach this average offset β_{avg} is defined here as the *convergence time* of SISP. It is denoted by t_a and expressed in seconds.

Synchronization accuracy. Once the shared clocks of all nodes have reached this average offset, all subsequent SYNC emissions permit to combat the drifts by resetting the shared clock periodically. The difference between the shared clocks of two nodes depends on their relative drift and the synchronization period P. For a given P value, the larger the drift between two nodes, the faster their shared clocks diverge before a new SYNC resets their values. The accuracy a of SISP for a set of N nodes is defined as the *maximum shared clock deviation* existing in the network once convergence has occurred. Each pair of node may experience a different shared clock difference. As such, the accuracy a can be formulated as the maximum shared clock difference over all pairs of nodes:

$$a = \max_{(i,j)} d_{NiNj} \tag{3}$$

Convergence time and accuracy will be investigated using (*i*) simulations, (*ii*) analysis and (*iii*) measurements. For the analysis, we will look for an upper bound on accuracy.

2.4 Investigated topologies

Three elementary topologies are investigated in this work that are representative of small deployments:

- the *2-node* topology, where two nodes are in direct view.
- the *3-node ring* topology, where each sensor can communicate with the two other ones. They create a clique.
- the *3-node in line* topology, where nodes are aligned but only the central node can communicate with the two other nodes. Border nodes can not communicate with each other.

All studies have been made by accounting for the technical features of a real sensor platform: the DecaWino sensor [10]. It is an open-source hardware design equipped with the transceiver DWM1000 and an Arduino board, the Teensy 3.2 with ARM Cortex M4 32-bit MCU rated at 64GHz, 64kB RAM and 256kB program memory. The hardware clock of this microprocessor drifts of around 20 ppm (parts per millions). It means that after one million seconds, the oscillator exhibits a deviation of +/- 20 seconds. Our measurements have been made with this sensor platform.

Next and unless specified otherwise, a SYNC message is emitted by a node every second. The `sisp()` procedure is called every microsecond. This setting, for a clock drift of 20 ppm, should limit the time deviation to +/- 20 microseconds.

3 SIMULATION STUDY

Convergence and synchronization accuracy have been investigated first by simulation. An in-house simulator has been designed in Java for this purpose following the SISP and network model introduced earlier. Results for the three topologies of interest are given next. For each of them, convergence and accuracy are given when the drift of all nodes equals 0 ppm or 20 ppm. For 0 ppm, we set all nodes to $\alpha_{Ni} = 1$ and for 20 ppm, we set them to $\alpha_{Ni} = 0,100020$.

3.1 2-node topology

Figure 3 plots the difference of the SCLK counters of both nodes over time. If this difference is zero, both nodes have adopted the same shared clock and are thus perfectly synchronized. The x-axis represents the local clock of $N0$, which represents our reference clock.

Figure 3-(top) gives the shared clock difference when there is no clock drift. Before 10 seconds, the difference of shared clocks is decreasing to compensate for the offset difference of both nodes. After 10 seconds, since no drift exists, clocks stay in tune. For the 20ppm case, represented on Figure 3-(bottom), a similar decay of the SCKL difference is observed, but after 9 seconds, the difference oscillates around a value of $10\mu s$. The accuracy is here of $11\mu s$, given by the maximum shared clock difference. This observation is in line with a SYNC period of 1s. and a 20ppm oscillator.

On Figure 4, we investigate the influence of P on the shared clock difference observed at convergence for different values of clock drift. This figure has been obtained for an oscillator frequency

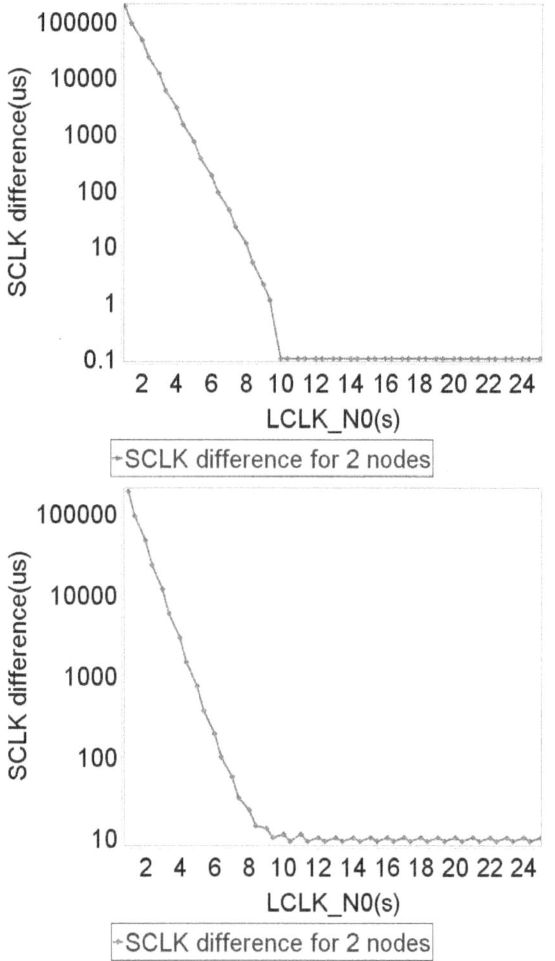

Figure 3: Difference of the shared clocks (in log scale) over time for the 2-node topology, with a 0ppm drift (top) and 20ppm (bottom)

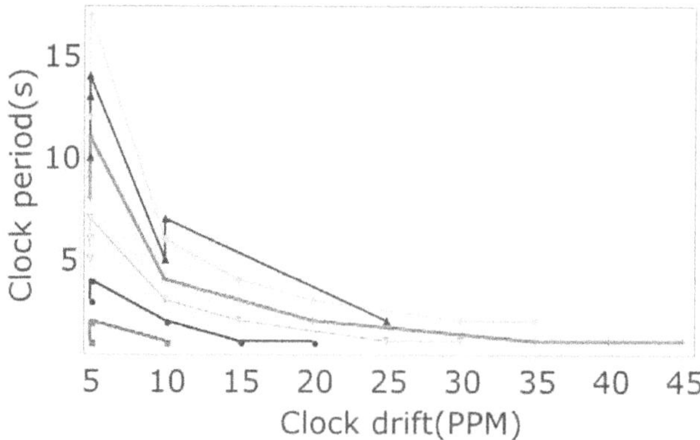

Figure 4: Impact of P on the accuracy for different drifts.

of 1MHz. The x-axis represents the clock drift varying from 0 to 50 ppm while the y-axis represents the period P of SYNC messages in seconds. For instance, for a drift of 20 ppm, the lowest shared clock difference that can be seen here is between 10 and $20\mu s$. This is possible for a SYNC period of 1s. A SYNC period of 3s. offers an accuracy between 30 and $40\mu s$. The general message is that to obtain a better accuracy, shorter SYNC periods have to be chosen.

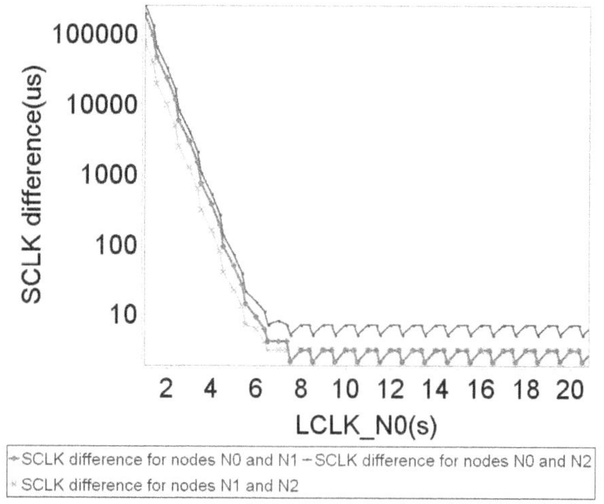

Figure 5: Difference of the shared clocks (in log scale) for a 3-node ring topology. The drift of node $N1$ is 10ppm and the drift of $N2$ is 20ppm.

3.2 3-node topologies

When the drift equals 0ppm for all three nodes, all pairs converge to a difference of shared clocks equal to zero. This result isn't plotted as it will be demonstrated analytically in Section 4. Simulation results for the case where the drifts are non-null are given next.

Figure 5 represents the shared clock difference for a 3-node ring topology, where the local clock of node $N0$ is given as the reference clock. The drift of $N1$ is set to 10ppm and the one of $N2$ to 20ppm. On Figure 5, the three curves represent the shared clock difference observed for the three pairs of nodes. At convergence, the largest difference is observed between nodes $N0$ and $N2$. The shared clock difference is the same between the other 2 pair of nodes, which is correct as they have both a relative drift of 10ppm. As such, the overall synchronization accuracy is given by the pair of nodes experiencing the largest relative drift.

In Figure 6, the pairwise shared clock differences for the 3-node line topology is given. As for the 3-node ring topology, the local clock of $N0$ is the reference clock and the drifts are equal to 10ppm for $N1$ and 20ppm for $N2$. The three differences are periodic as observed for the ring topology, but the convergence duration is twice as long as for the ring topology. This can be easily understood as direct communications between border nodes are impossible: clock updates need two beacons to be accounted for by all nodes. Again, the pair of nodes that experiences the largest relative drift (naming $N2$ and $N0$) is the one showing the largest shared clock difference.

3.3 Simulation results summary

Table 2 shows for each topology the synchronization accuracy and the convergence time observed by simulations. Not surprisingly, it is the 3-node ring topology that offers the shortest convergence time, as 2 nodes can update their shared clock at each SYNC message emission. The longest convergence is observed for the 3-node line topology, as updates have to be 'relayed' by the central node. For the no-drift cases, perfect synchronization is achieved and accuracy is 0. For the 20 ppm drift, an oscillatory behavior is observed after convergence whose maximum value, given by the accuracy, is bounded. Bounds are in the order of a few tens of microseconds, which is in-line with the setting of a one second SYNC emission. In the following, convergence time and synchronization accuracy are investigated analytically.

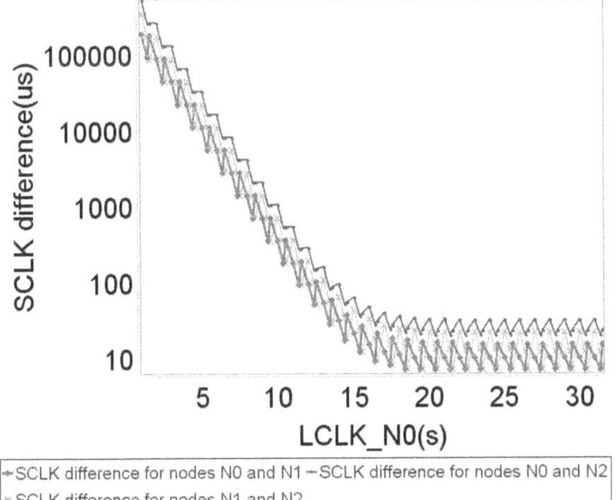

Figure 6: Difference of the shared clocks (in log scale) for a 3-node line topology. The drift of node $N1$ is 10ppm and the drift of $N2$ is 20ppm.

Table 2: Simulation study: synchronization accuracy and convergence time for all topologies.

Topology	Synchronization accuracy (in μs.)	Convergence time (in s.)
2-node ; 0 ppm	0	10
2-node ; 20 ppm	11	9
3-node ring ; 0 ppm	0	8
3-node ring ; 10/20 ppm	7	7.5
3-node line ; 0 ppm	0	21
3-node line ; 10/20 ppm	32	19.5

4 ANALYTIC STUDY

In this section, we conduct an analysis of the convergence of SISP synchronization protocol and we provide a bound on the synchronization accuracy and the minimal number of messages needed to achieve the synchronization state. We begin by describing the methods used to prove the protocol convergence, then we summarize the main results obtained for the considered topologies. A detailed proof for the 2-node topology is given, together with the main proof elements of the 3-node topologies.

4.1 Methodology

Expressions for the convergence time and an upper bound on the synchronization accuracy are derived here for each topology. We study the case where clocks don't drift away (i.e. $\alpha_{Ni} = 1$) and the one where a known drift of $\alpha_{Ni} \neq 1$ is experienced by the nodes. Derivations are made in the latter case for non-homogeneous offsets and drifts as given in the model of Eq.(2). Moreover, offsets and drifts are not a function of time, and thus are assumed to be constant. Propagation delays are neglegted.

Synchronization accuracy is proved by deriving the difference of shared clock values, denoted $d_{NiNj}(t_k)$ and by expressing it as a sequence of real values indexed by t_k. We prove that this difference is a decreasing sequence and that its limit is its infimum using the following Lemma:

LEMMA 4.1. *If a sequence of real numbers is decreasing and bounded below, then its infimum is the limit.*

4.2 Results summary

Bounds obtained analytically are summarized in Table 3. We define $\bar{D} = \frac{P}{1+\alpha_{N1}}$ as the average value of D and $\sigma = \sqrt{\frac{1}{N} * \sum_{k=1}^{N} (D_k^{N0} - \bar{D})^2}$ its standard deviation. Function $LCM(x, y)$ extracts the least common multiple of x and y, with $x > 0$ and $y > 0$.

Synchronization accuracy is proved to be 0 if $\alpha_i = 0, \forall i \in \{0, .., N-1\}$. For the 2-node $\alpha_{Ni} \neq 1$ scenario, we provide an upper bound on the accuracy that is tight. For the 3-node ring and line topologies, we haven't succeeded in deriving analytic bounds for the $\alpha_{Ni} \neq 1$ case so far. However, for the 3-node topologies SISP converges to a perfect synchronization if $\alpha_i = 0$ for all nodes. Thus, we argue that if it is possible to learn and compensate for these drifts over time with an improved version of SISP, we can prove the convergence of this new protocol as it becomes equivalent to the no-drift case. Future works will concentrate on the design of this drift-aware

Table 3: Synchronization accuracy and convergence time expressions. Synchronization accuracy for the 2-node $\alpha_{Ni} \neq 1$ case is an upper bound.

Topology	Synchronization accuracy a	Convergence time t_a
2-node $\alpha_{Ni} = 1$	0	$\log_2 \lvert\beta_{N1}\rvert - 1$
2-node $\alpha_{Ni} \neq 1$	$(1 - \alpha_{N1}) * (\bar{D} + \sigma) + \frac{4}{3}$	$\max(T_{N0N1}, \log_2 \lvert\beta_{N1}\rvert - 1)$ with $T_{N0N1} = LCM(P, P * \alpha_{N1})/\alpha_{N1}$
3-node ring $\alpha_{Ni} = 1$	0	$\log_2(\max_i \lvert\beta_{Ni}\rvert) - 1$
3-node ring $\alpha_{Ni} \neq 1$	-	$\max\left[LCM(T_{N0N1}, T_{N0N2}), \log_2(\max_i \lvert\beta_{Ni}\rvert) - 1\right]$
3-node line $\alpha_{Ni} = 1$	0	$\log_2(\max_i \lvert\beta_{Ni}\rvert) - 1$
3-node line $\alpha_{Ni} \neq 1$	-	$\max\left[LCM(T_{N0N1}, T_{N0N2}), \log_2(\max_i \lvert\beta_{Ni}\rvert) - 1\right]$

SISP protocol. Next, a detailed proof for the 2-node topology convergence time and accuracy is given.

4.3 2-node topology

We illustrate this proof with the sequence of SISP protocol messages given in Figure 7. Assuming the nodes begin sending messages at time t_0, the shared clock values at t_0 for the two nodes can be calculated for the reference clock $LCLK_{N0}$. By recurrence, the shared clock expression at time t_k can be deducted from the shared clock expression at t_{k-1}. Following, the SCLK difference is extracted and interpreted as a sequence. We prove by recurrence that this SCLK difference is a decreasing sequence and deduce its limit. Lemma 4.1 is then leveraged to prove protocol convergence.

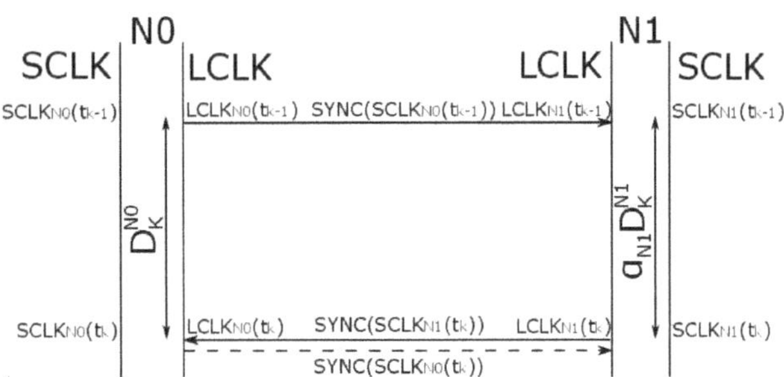

Figure 7: SISP protocol execution for 2-node scenario

4.3.1 No drift case ($\alpha_{Ni} = 1$).

Local clocks of the two nodes run at the same speed. Thus, the duration D_k^{N1} elapsed between the two shared clock updates on node $N1$ is the same as D_k^{N0} on node $N0$.

Synchronization accuracy. The shared clocks values of both nodes are given in Eq. (4) if the first SYNC message is sent by $N0$ and in Eq. (5) if it is sent by $N1$:

$$\begin{aligned} SCLK_{N0}(t_k) &= SCLK_{N0}(t_{k-1}) + D_k^{N0} \\ SCLK_{N1}(t_k) &= \frac{1}{2} * \left[SCLK_{N0}(t_{k-1}) + SCLK_{N1}(t_{k-1}) + 2 * D_k^{N0}\right] \end{aligned} \tag{4}$$

$$\begin{aligned} SCLK_{N1}(t_k) &= SCLK_{N1}(t_{k-1}) + D_k^{N1} \\ SCLK_{N0}(t_k) &= \frac{1}{2} * \left[SCLK_{N0}(t_{k-1}) + SCLK_{N1}(t_{k-1}) + 2 * D_k^{N0}\right] \end{aligned} \tag{5}$$

We are interested in identifying the time t_k where the shared clock values of the two nodes are equal; in this case, the difference between the two shared clocks is 0. We denote this difference $d_{N0N1}(t_k) = SCLK_{N0}(t_k) - SCLK_{N1}(t_k)$. Since only two nodes are considered in this topology, we will drop the index $N0N1$ to simplify notations in all derivations related to the 2-nodes scenario. We substitute in this formulæ the equations of shared clocks given in Eq. (4) or in Eq. (5). For both cases, we obtain after substitution:

$$d(t_k) = \frac{1}{2} * (SCLK_{N0}(t_{k-1}) - SCLK_{N1}(t_{k-1})) = \frac{1}{2} * d(t_{k-1})$$

As such, the difference $d(t_k)$ can be expressed according to the difference at t_0:

$$d(t_k) = \frac{1}{2^k} * d(t_0)$$

The limit of this sequence is 0. It is straightforward to prove by induction that this sequence is decreasing for increasing k. From Lemma 4.1, we can state that the shared clock difference converges to 0. Thus, shared clock values converge to the same value and perfect synchronization is thus achieved.

Convergence time. Convergence time t_a is deduced from the minimum number of messages needed to achieve convergence. It is deduced from setting $\frac{1}{2^k} * d(t_0)$ to 1 and solving it for k:

$$t_a = k = \log_2 d(t_0) = \log_2 \lvert\beta_{N1}\rvert - 1 \tag{6}$$

as $d(t_0) = \beta_{N1}/2$.

4.3.2 Drift case ($\alpha_{N1} \neq 1$).

Clock $LCLK_{N0}$ is still the reference clock, and the local clock of $N1$ drifts away from $LCLK_{N0}$ with rate $\alpha_{N1} \neq 1$. As such, $D_k^{N1} = \alpha_{N1} * D_k^{N0}$.

Convergence time. The simulation results of Section 3 show that the shared clock difference repeats itself periodically after all offsets have been compensated for. The period of the shared clock difference d is given by the least common multiple (LCM) of the SYNC message periods of both nodes: $LCM(P, P * \alpha_{N1})$ (its the hyper-period of the two periodic flows emitted by $N0$ and $N1$). This value has to be converted to the time reference of node $N0$. The period of d is denoted T_{N0N1} and given by:

$$T_{N0N1} = \frac{1}{\alpha_{N1}} * LCM(P, P * \alpha_{N1}) \tag{7}$$

Convergence occurs if all offsets have been compensated for and one hyper-period T_{N0N1} has at least elapsed:

$$t_a = \max(T_{N0N1}, \log_2 |\beta_{N1}| - 1) \tag{8}$$

Synchronization accuracy. As before, we aim at calculating the shared clock difference $d(t_k)$ to prove its convergence and calculate its accuracy. The shared clocks values of both nodes are given in Eq. (9) if the first SYNC message is sent by $N0$ and in Eq. (10) if it is sent by $N1$:

$$\begin{aligned} SCLK_{N0}(t_k) &= SCLK_{N0}(t_{k-1}) + D_k^{N0} \\ SCLK_{N1}(t_k) &= \left\lfloor \frac{1}{2} * [SCLK_{N0}(t_{k-1}) + SCLK_{N1}(t_{k-1}) \right. \\ &\qquad \left. + (\alpha_{N1} + 1) * D_k^{N0}] \right\rfloor \end{aligned} \tag{9}$$

$$\begin{aligned} SCLK_{N1}(t_k) &= SCLK_{N1}(t_{k-1}) + \alpha_{N1} * D_k^{N0} \\ SCLK_{N0}(t_k) &- \left\lfloor \frac{1}{2} * [SCLK_{N0}(t_{k-1}) + SCLK_{N1}(t_{k-1}) \right. \\ &\qquad \left. + (\alpha_{N1} + 1) * D_k^{N0}] \right\rfloor \end{aligned} \tag{10}$$

The difference $d(t_k) = SCLK_{N0}(t_k) - SCLK_{N1}(t_k)$ can be obtained by substituting $SCLK_{N0}(t_k)$ and $SCLK_{N1}(t_k)$ using (9) and (10), respectively. Expressions for the shared clock difference are given in (11) if the first SYNC message is sent by $N0$ and (12) otherwise.

$$d(t_k) = D_k^{N0} - \left\lfloor \frac{1}{2} * \left[-d(t_{k-1}) + (\alpha_{N1} + 1) * D_k^{N0}\right] \right\rfloor \tag{11}$$

$$d(t_k) = \left\lfloor \frac{1}{2} * \left[d(t_{k-1}) + (\alpha_{N1} + 1) * D_k^{N0}\right] \right\rfloor - \alpha_{N1} * D_k^{N0} \tag{12}$$

Using the properties of the integer part it is possible to bound the shared clock difference as shown in inequalities (13) and (14).

$$\begin{aligned} \frac{1}{2} * \left[d(t_{k-1}) + (1 - \alpha_{N1}) * D_k^{N0}\right] &< d(t_k) \\ &< \frac{1}{2} * \left[d(t_{k-1}) + (1 - \alpha_{N1}) * D_k^{N0}\right] + 1 \end{aligned} \tag{13}$$

$$\begin{aligned} \frac{1}{2} * \left[d(t_{k-1}) + (1 - \alpha_{N1}) * D_k^{N0}\right] - 1 &< d(t_k) \\ &< \frac{1}{2} * \left[d(t_{k-1}) + (1 - \alpha_{N1}) * D_k^{N0}\right] \end{aligned} \tag{14}$$

By recurrence, the difference at t_k can be expressed according to the difference at t_0 as in the inequalities (15) and (16).

$$A - \frac{2}{3} < d(t_k) < A + \frac{4}{3} \tag{15}$$

$$A - \frac{4}{3} < d(t_k) < A + \frac{2}{3} \tag{16}$$

where :

$$A = \frac{1}{2^k} * \left[d(t_0) + (1 - \alpha_{N1}) * (D_1^{N0} + 2 * D_2^{N0} + \dots + 2^{k-1} * D_k^{N0})\right].$$

Accuracy upper bound. We recall that D_k^{N0} represents the difference between emission and reception dates of a SYNC message at $N0$. We can assume that in average, it is close to $P/2$, with P the SYNC emission period of SISP. To obtain an estimate of A, and thus an estimate of the bounds on $d(t_k)$, we assume D_k^{N0} is normally distributed: 50% of its values are less than $P/2$ and 50% of the values are greater than $P/2$. The mean of this distribution is equal to $\bar{D} = P/(1 + \alpha_{N1})$ and the standard deviation to $\sigma = \sqrt{\frac{1}{k} * \sum_{i=1}^{k} (D_i^{N0} - \bar{D})^2}$.

With this assumption, we can substitute the durations D_k^{N0} by the mean duration $\bar{D}$ and the standard deviation σ in A. As such, we obtain an approximated value of A :

$$\tilde{A} = \frac{1}{2^k} * \left[d(t_0) + (1 - \alpha_{N1})(2^k - 1)(\bar{D} + \sigma)\right]$$

Calculating the limit of $\tilde{A}$ as k grows to infinity, we get:

$$\tilde{A}_\infty = \lim_{k \to \infty} \tilde{A} = (1 - \alpha_{N1})(\bar{D} + \sigma)$$

Since we may not know which node has started to emit SYNC messages first, we extract from Eq. (15) and (16) an upper bound on $d(t_k)$ which is given by

$$d(t_k) < \tilde{A}_\infty + 4/3 \tag{17}$$

The average value of $d(t_k)$ can as well be computed by setting σ to zero in $\tilde{A}_\infty$. This average value derivation only depends from system parameters and can be computed without any precise information on the protocol execution. To get a more precise estimation of the accuracy, a few values of D_k^{N0} are required to calculate the standard deviation σ. These values can be either obtained by

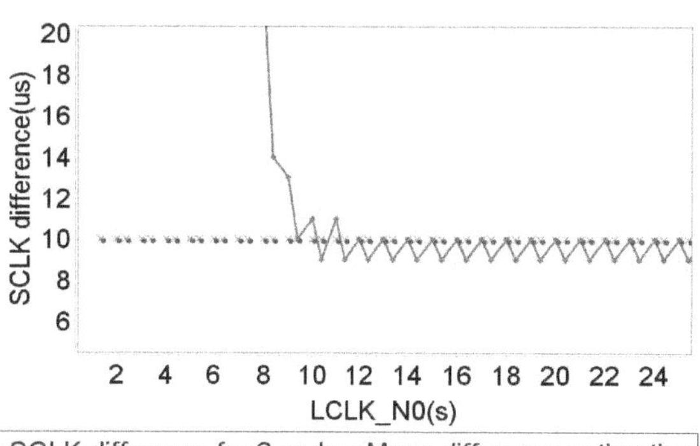

Figure 8: Mean and upper bound estimation of the shared clock difference for the 2-node topology for a 20ppm drift.

the first steps of a simulation or by measurements of the SYNC message emission and reception dates.

Figure 8 illustrates, on top of the simulated shared clock difference of Figure 3, our average and upper bound on $d(t_k)$. The average calculation already provides a meaningful order of magnitude of the accuracy. A more precise estimation, using the upper bound of Eq.(17), is plotted as well. In this example the upper bound on the synchronization accuracy is less than $10\mu s$.

4.4 3-node topology

4.4.1 No drift case ($\alpha_{Ni} = 1$).

This section concentrates on the 3-node topology for the case where no drift exists between the nodes. Derivations are similar to the ones presented earlier for the 2-node topology. Thus, only basic explanations are provided in the following.

Synchronization accuracy. As for the 2-node topology, the difference of SCLK values is computed for each couple of nodes. The protocol is convergent if the three differences converge. By induction we can prove that the sequences of shared clock differences for each pairs are decreasing and that we can calculate their limit which is 0. This derivation holds whether nodes are in a ring setting or in a line setting.

Convergence time. The convergence time is calculated for each pair of nodes as done for the 2-node topology by counting the minimum number of messages to achieve a difference of 1. Convergence time for the whole network is given by the maximum convergence time for the all pairs of nodes. Formally, we have:

$$t_a = \log_2 \max_i(d_{N0Ni}(t_0)) = \log_2(\max_i |\beta_{Ni}|) - 1$$

4.4.2 Drift case ($\alpha_{Ni} \neq 1$).

Convergence time. As for the 2-node case, the simulation results of Section 3 show that the shared clock difference repeats itself periodically after all offsets have been compensated for. The period of the shared clock difference for the two pairs $(N0, N1)$ and $(N0, N2)$ are given by the least common multiple (LCM) of the SYNC message periods of both nodes:

$$T_{N0Ni} = \frac{1}{\alpha_{Ni}} * LCM(P, P * \alpha_{Ni}),\ i = 1, 2 \tag{18}$$

A global period can be computed from T_{N0N1} and T_{N0N2} by computing $T = LCM(T_{N0N1}, T_{N0N2})$. Convergence occurs if all offsets have been compensated for and one global hyper-period T has at least elapsed:

$$t_a = \max(T,\ \log_2(\max_i |\beta_{Ni}|) - 1) \tag{19}$$

Synchronization accuracy. As defined previously, it is given by the maximum shared clock difference observed after convergence over the three pairs of nodes. As observed in the simulations, the maximum shared clock difference is observed for the pair of nodes having the largest difference in drifts. Accounting for all drifts in an analytic derivation of the shared clock difference of all pairs is challenging for both ring and line topologies and have not been derived for this study. However, it is interesting to note that if it is possible to learn and compensate the drifts from the SYNC messages in SISP, calculating the accuracy resumes to the case where no drift exists. In this case, it is possible to prove the convergence and offer a theoretical accuracy of 0. Future works will concentrate on deriving a novel version of SISP that mitigates clock drifts by prediction as proposed in [7].

5 EMPIRICAL STUDY

In order to complete the theoretical and simulation study of the SISP protocol convergence, we have deployed SISP on the DecaWiNo nodes introduced earlier. The implemented protocol uses the same configuration as the one deployed in simulation. The SYNC message period is equal to 1s.

Figure 9 shows the shared clock difference $d(t_k)$ measured for a 2-node topology. The x-axis shows the reference clock $LCLK_{N0}$ and the y-axis the shared clock difference. From this curve, it can be seen that convergence occurs at 13 seconds and that the synchronization accuracy is then around 10 microseconds. The analytic upper bound on the accuracy is plotted in red as well. This bound accounts for the standard deviation derived from the D_k^{N0} values obtained by simulation. Our bound clearly fits very well the measured values.

On Figure 10, the shared clock difference for each couple of nodes has been represented for the 3-node ring topology. The three differences have a similar evolution. They are decreasing until 15s on the reference local clock and then they present regular variations. The synchronization accuracy is of about 8 μs. Similarly, Figure 11 shows the three shared clock differences for the 3-node line topology. Convergence time is clearly longer for the line topology than for the ring topology (26s. versus 15s.). The synchronization accuracy is larger as well (32μs. versus 8μs.). Measurements are close to the values observed by simulations for 2-node and 3-node ring scenarios. For the line scenario, the convergence time

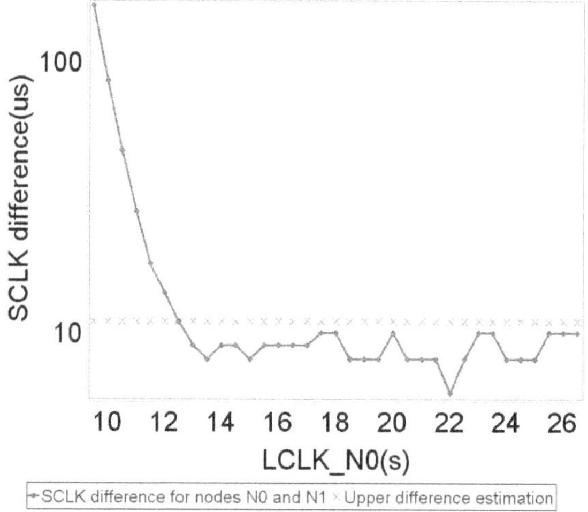

Figure 9: Measured difference of the shared clocks (in log scale) for a 2-node topology.

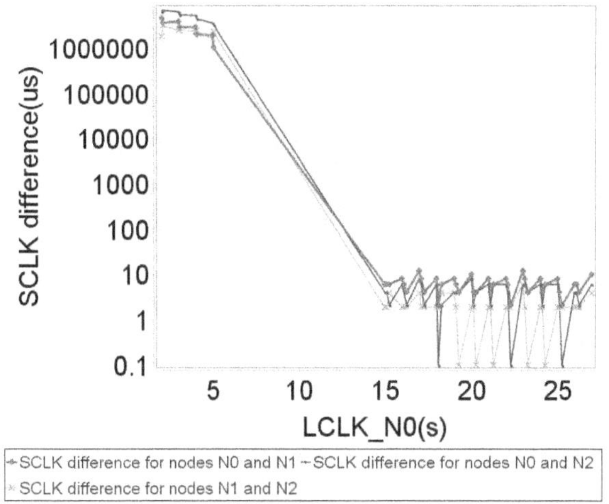

Figure 10: Measured difference of the shared clocks (in log scale) for a 3-node ring topology.

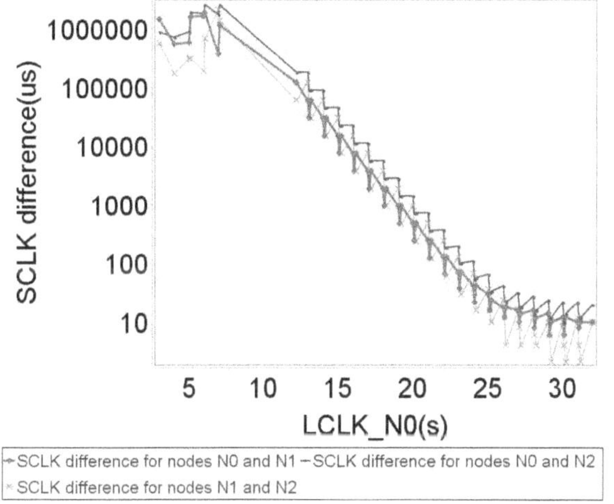

Figure 11: Measured difference of the shared clocks (in log scale) for a 3-node line topology.

Table 4: Measured synchronization accuracy and convergence time. Theoretical values are given in parenthesis if available.

Topology	Synchronization accuracy (μs)	Convergence time (s)
2-node	10 (10)	13 (16)
3-node ring	8	15 (19)
3-node line	32	26 (19)

calculation should be improved to account for the propagation of messages.

Table 4 summarized the synchronization accuracy and the convergence time observed by measurement. Theoretical values are included as well, if available. These results are similar to the simulation results of Table 2. Overall, SISP only needs a few seconds to achieve a stable state. This convergence time depends on the number of nodes and on the network topology. The synchronization accuracy is the order of a few tens of microseconds, which is in line with the protocol design goal.

6 CONCLUSIONS

In this paper we studied the convergence properties of SISP, a lightweight, totally distributed synchronization protocol for wireless sensor networks. Three different approaches have been presented to investigate the protocol behavior. First, simulations have helped us to establish that there is a convergence time before nodes agree on a shared clock. If the clock of nodes drifts apart, the protocol produces periodic variations of the shared clock after initial convergence. Second, we have derived analytic expressions to quantify both convergence time and synchronization accuracy. For the 2-node scenario, we even have been able to calculate a tight upper bound on the accuracy. Last, we present measurements on a real wireless sensor network which are totally in line with simulation and theoretical results.

Future works will now concentrate on extending these results to a larger number of nodes and to the case where SYNC messages collide. Another promising research is the definition of a new version of SISP that compensates for the drift of nodes by learning it over time. This will ensure proper convergence as in this case, the problem reduces to the case where no drifts exist (they are mitigated by the learning step). In other words, we will be able to easily calculate the accuracy and convergence time as the α_{Ni} values will be equal to one.

ACKNOWLEDGEMENTS

This work has been supported by Region Occitanie and European FEDER program under the MHTag GUINESS project.

REFERENCES

[1] *WirelessHART Specification 75, TDMA Data-Link Layer,* HART Communication Foundation Standard hCF SPEC-75, 2008.1.1

[2] *IEEE Standard for Local and Metropolitan Area Networks—Part 15.4 Low-Rate Wireless Personal Area Networks (LR-WPANs) Amendment 1: MAC Sublayer.* IEEE Standard 802.15.4e-2012, Apr. 2012

[3] Q. Wang, K. Jaffrès-Runser, Y. Xu, J.-L. Scharbarg, Z. An and K. Fraboul *TDMA versus CSMA/CA for wireless multi-hop communications: a stochastic worst-case delay analysis,* in IEEE Transactions on Industrial Informatics, vol. 13, no. 2, pp. 877-887, April 2017.

[4] J. Elson, L. Girod, and D. Estrin. *Fine-grained Network Time Synchronization Using Reference Broadcasts.* OSDI '02, 2002. Boston, Massachusetts, USA, pp.147-163.

[5] S. Ganeriwal, R. Kumar, and M. Srivastava. *Timing-sync Protocol for Sensor Networks* SenSys'03, 2003, Los Angeles, California, USA, pp. 138–149,

[6] M. Maróti, B. Kusy, G. Simon, and A. Lédeczi. *The Flooding Time Synchronization Protocol* SenSys '04, 2004, Baltimore, MD, USA, pp. 39–49

[7] C. Lenzen, P. Sommer, and R. Wattenhofer. *PulseSync: an efficient and scalable clock synchronization protocol.* IEEE/ACM Trans. Netw. 23, 3 (June 2015), pp. 717-727.

[8] S. Gonzalez, T. Camp and K. Jaffrès-Runser. *The Sticking Heartbeat Aperture Resynchronization Protocol.* ICCCN'17, Vancouver, Canada, August 2017.

[9] A. van den Bossche, T. Val, and R. Dalce. *SISP: a lightweight Synchronization Protocol for Wireless Sensor Networks.* ETFA WiP, 2011. Toulouse, France, pp. 1–4.

[10] A. van den Bossche. *DecaWiNo ressources.* https://www.irit.fr/ Adrien.Van-Den-Bossche/decaduino/index.html, last accessed April 2017.

REPSYS: A Robust and Distributed Reputation System for Delay-Tolerant Networks

Naercio Magaia, Paulo Pereira, Miguel Correia
INESC-ID, Instituto Superior Técnico, Universidade de Lisboa, Portugal
naercio.magaia@tecnico.ulisboa.pt,prbp@inesc.pt,miguel.p.correia@tecnico.ulisboa.pt

ABSTRACT

Distributed reputation systems can be used to foster cooperation between nodes in decentralized and self-managed systems due to the nonexistence of a central entity. In this paper, a Robust and Distributed Reputation System for Delay-Tolerant Networks (REPSYS) is proposed. REPSYS is robust because despite taking into account first- and second-hand information, it is resilient against false accusations and praise, and distributed, as the decision to interact with another node depends entirely on each node.

Simulation results show that the system is capable, while evaluating each node's participation in the network, to detect on the fly nodes that do not accept messages from other nodes and that disseminate false information even while colluding with others, and while evaluating how honest is each node in the reputation system, to classify correctly nodes in most cases.

CCS CONCEPTS

• **Security and privacy** → *Trust frameworks*; • **Networks** → *Network simulations; Ad hoc networks;*

KEYWORDS

Reputation, Trust, Bayesian, Delay-Tolerant Network

1 INTRODUCTION

Delay-Tolerant Networks (DTNs) [8] are networks in which end-to-end connectivity between a source and target node is not guaranteed due to nodes' mobility or even because nodes can join or leave the network, for example, as a result of devices being turned off or running out of battery. The DTN routing strategy allows messages to be relayed among nodes until the destination is reached, or they are discarded.

To manage and organize decentralized and self-managed systems, *incentive schemes* [11] can be used, hence compensating for the nonexistence of a central or dedicated entity, e.g., for managing reputation and trust. In a *distributed reputation-based incentive scheme* [11], hereafter *reputation scheme*, which is more suitable for DTNs as no central authority is available, nodes' ratings are stored in a distributed fashion and the evaluation of reputation is based on subsets of information (e.g., information provided by neighbor nodes). In such systems, nodes collect reputation information. A reputation system that relies exclusively on first-hand information (direct evidence) may not take advantage of all the available information. However, second-hand information (indirect evidence) should be used with care since negative information, i.e., false accusations or praise, may be used to deceive the system. The collected information is evaluated in order to decide if the node should cooperate or not, based on the other node's reputation. After the nodes' interaction, the degree of cooperation between them is evaluated aiming to reward nodes that presented a good behavior by adequately increasing their reputation. As a result, nodes with bad reputation are isolated henceforward not receiving others' services.

This paper proposes REPSYS, a Robust and Distributed Reputation System for Delay-Tolerant Networks. REPSYS is both robust against false ratings and efficient at detecting nodes' misbehavior. It is based on a Bayesian approach that uses the Beta distribution. REPSYS can be integrated with any DTN routing protocol. It uses special feedback messages taking into account the network density. REPSYS proposed a new approach for obtaining first-hand information based on the attack signature and a modified decision criterion to avoid misclassification that takes into account recent observations.

MSWiM'17, November 21–25, 2017, Miami, FL, USA

ISBN 978-1-4503-5162-1/17/11...$15.00.
DOI: http://dx.doi.org/10.1145/3127540.3127573

2 RELATED WORK

Many reputation schemes have been proposed, but only a few for DTNs. In [3], a cooperative watchdog system to support selfish nodes detection was proposed. Each time a node participated in a contact opportunity, a reputation score was assigned to him. The proposed classification module does not learn as new observations are available. In [9], a Bayesian trust-based framework that can be integrated with single-copy data forwarding protocols was proposed. The proposed special message is not adequate for sparse DTNs. In [12], a Bayesian approach where each node also manages its reputation evidence and demonstrates it whenever necessary was proposed. Second-hand information was not considered in the latter. An iterative trust management and distributed malicious node detection mechanism for DTNs, where only the behavior of the nodes in terms of routing is evaluated, was proposed in [1]. A modified Bayesian approach for reputation and trust representation and update, and for second-hand information integration was proposed in [2]. Despite being similar to REPSYS, it was envisioned for MANET and P2P routing protocols therefore not being suitable for DTNs. Moreover, an offline classifier was used.

3 THE REPSYS SYSTEM

REPSYS is both robust against false ratings and efficient at detecting nodes' misbehavior. REPSYS is robust because despite taking into account all the available information, it is resilient against false accusations and praise, and distributed, as the decision to interact with another node depends entirely on each node. It takes into account all the available information and uses Bayesian decision theory to classify nodes. REPSYS is based on a Bayesian approach that uses the Beta distribution, and can be integrated with any DTN routing protocol. There are three modules in REPSYS: reputation module (reputation collection module, reputation evaluation module), trust module and routing decision module (that uses Bayesian classification).

3.1 Assumptions

There is a network with several nodes, i.e., wireless devices held by people or in vehicles that may be moving. Each node has a Unique IDentifier (UID) that cannot be spoofed. Each node can only monitor its one-hop neighbors, i.e., can only monitor nodes that are directly connected to him. Akin to benign nodes, malicious nodes are also wireless devices. However, they may deviate from the protocol in the following ways: (*i*) *lying attacks (liars),* nodes that not having received a message return wrong confirmation that they have it in their buffer. In addition, these nodes may disseminate false first-hand information; (*ii*) *black-hole attacks,* nodes that do not forward others' messages; and (*iii*) *collusion attacks,* where nodes may forward data to each other to earn reputation. The intensity of individual attacks can be augmented by collusion.

3.2 The modified Bayesian approach

Each node considers that there is a given parameter, θ, known as the state of nature such that another node misbehaves with probability θ, and that the outcome is drawn independently at each observation x. Furthermore, each node considers that there is a different θ for every other node. These parameters are unknown, hence modeled assuming that they are drawn according to a prior distribution, $\pi(\theta)$, which is updated as new observations become available.

The beta probability density function, $Beta(\alpha, \beta)$, is used as the prior as it represents probability distributions of binary events (e.g., good or bad) and the conjugate is also a Beta distribution [5]. The expectation of the Beta density is

$$\mathbb{E}\left[\text{Beta}\left(\theta|\alpha,\beta\right)\right] = \frac{\alpha}{\alpha+\beta} \tag{1}$$

The Bayesian process works as follows. Initially each node has the prior $Beta(1, 1)$, that is, the uniform distribution on $[0, 1]$, for all its neighbors. The $Beta(1, 1)$ prior represents absence of information as there are no observations. When a new observation is made, if a correct behavior is observed then $x = 1$; otherwise $x = 0$. The prior is updated according to $\alpha_{new} = \alpha_{old} + x$ and $\beta_{new} = \beta_{old} + (1 - x)$.

Due to the network dynamics, a node may change its behavior over time in contrast to the standard Bayesian framework that gives the same weight regardless of time of occurrence of the observation. The fading mechanism allows to forget gradually old observations, and it is defined as $y^{\tau}_{\eta} = y^{\tau-1}_{\eta}\eta + y^{\tau}$, where $y \in \{\alpha, \beta\}$ and y^{τ}_{η} is the accumulated rating of a given node at time period τ, y^{τ} is the new rating at time τ and η is the fading factor and $0 < \eta < 1$.

3.3 Information gathering

Each node is equipped with a pseudo-watchdog component that allows it to monitor the behavior of the neighbors with whom it interacts. Specifically, if node i forwards a message to node j, the behavior of j is evaluated in terms of two types of evidence, namely: (*i*) if j accepts messages of i and, (*ii*) if j forwards i's messages of another node, say k. The former evidence is collected through direct communication between two nodes (i.e., through experience), meanwhile the latter, is through *Special Feedback Messages* (SFMs). Therefore, i waits for a SFM. Two types of SFMs, that take into account the network density, are proposed: (*i*) *type-1* that is created by k, which is 2 hops away from node i (which can be the source or forwarder of the message); and (*ii*) *type-2* that is created by the destination of the message. SFM *type-1* and shall suffice for dense networks. Each SFM contains the message identifier, the list of nodes the message traversed and the message digest.

The first-hand information represents the parameters of the Beta distribution assumed by node i in its Bayesian opinion of node j's behavior in the network. Each node keeps two data structures (records): *accept first-hand information* ($\mathcal{F}_{a_{ij}}$) for accepted messages and *forward first-hand information* ($\mathcal{F}_{f_{ij}}$) for forwarded messages. For each record there are two counters: α and β. Accept and forward first-hand information are given by $\mathcal{F}_{\mathfrak{x}_{ij}} = (\alpha_{\mathfrak{x}}, \beta_{\mathfrak{x}}) = (\alpha, \beta)_{\mathfrak{x}}$, where $\mathfrak{x} \in \{a, f\}$, and they are updated to identify *attacks' signature* as follows: (*a*) α is incremented if a good behavior is observed when: (*i*) node j accepts messages of other nodes, e.g., node i. However, nodes that only accept messages may be performing *black-hole attacks*. Therefore, it is also necessary to ensure that node j forwards messages that it receives if the message is not destined to him; or (*ii*) node i receives a SFM from k because of a message i forwarded to j. It is assumed that among all neighbors of j, node k's delivery likelihood to the destination is the highest one; (*b*) β is incremented if a misbehavior is observed when: (*i*) node j not being the destination of a message sent by node i, does not forward the message (no SFM was received neither did the message expire); or (*ii*) node j does not accept messages of other nodes, e.g., node i, may be an indication that j is performing a *lying attack*. Node j can only refuse to accept messages forwarded to him if he already has them in buffer. Moreover, node j must prove to node i that he has the message in buffer as follows: node i sends a message containing the message identifier (MID) and a nonce (N) to node j. If j has the message, it must reply with a digital signature containing the digest of the message with identifier MID and N.

Second-hand information corresponds to first-hand information published by other nodes. For instance, node i can gather node k's first-hand information towards node j. Similarly to first-hand information, each node keeps two records: *accept second-hand information* ($\mathcal{S}_{a_{ij,k}}$) and *forward second-hand information* ($\mathcal{S}_{f_{ij,k}}$). Second- and first-hand information are related according to $\mathcal{S}_{\mathfrak{x}_{ij,k}} = \mathcal{F}_{\mathfrak{x}_{kj}}$.

3.4 Reputation rating

A reputation rating $\mathcal{R}_{ij}$, which is managed by the reputation module, is updated (*i*) when first-hand information is updated, and (*ii*) when received second-hand information is considered valid to be incorporated.

If accept and forward first-hand information that are kept by each node are available, they are combined to form a unique first-hand information, hereafter called first-hand information $\mathcal{F}_{ij} = (\alpha, \beta)_{\mathcal{F}}$, as follows: (*i*) if $\alpha_f > \alpha_a$ then $\alpha_{\mathcal{F}} = \alpha_f$. Otherwise, $\alpha_{\mathcal{F}} = \alpha_a$; (*ii*) $\beta_{\mathcal{F}} = \max(\beta_a, \beta_f)$. For replication-based approaches, an optimizations is proposed to penalize nodes that accept more messages than they forward: if $\alpha_a > \alpha_f$, $\alpha_a = \chi$ and $\alpha_f = 1$, increase $\beta_{\mathcal{F}}$ and decrease α_a. χ represents the number of evidences of accepted messages a node has while not having any evidence of messages that the node forwarded of other nodes.

The first-hand information record, which contains two counters, is never published since it is considered private. What is published is the first-hand information rating that is computed using Eq. 1.

When first-hand information is updated, an exponential weighted moving average (EWMA) is used to allow for reputation fading as follows

$$\mathcal{R}_{ij}^{\tau} = (1-\phi)\mathcal{R}_{ij}^{\tau-1} + \phi\mathcal{F}_{ij}^{\tau} \tag{2}$$

where ϕ is the smoothing factor and $0 < \phi < 1$. Please note that first-hand information is equal to the accept first-hand information on the absence of forward first-hand information.

When received second-hand information is considered valid to be incorporated, linear opinion pooling [4] is used for its integration. Assume two nodes *i* and *k* where *i* has its opinion on how honest node *k* is as an actor in the reputation system (i.e., the trust rating node *i* has on *k*, $\mathcal{T}_{ik}$), and *k* collects first-hand information about node *j*. A *recommendation* then consists in combining *i*'s opinion about *k* with *k*'s opinion about *j* in order for *i* to get its opinion about *j*. It resembles trust transitivity [6]. If *i* considers *k* trustworthy based on $\mathcal{T}_{ik}$, $\mathcal{F}_{kj}$ is used by node *i* for updating $\mathcal{R}_{ij}$ after performing the deviation test (Eq. 4) according to

$$\begin{aligned} \mathcal{R}_{ij}^{\tau} &= w_1\mathcal{R}_{ij}^{\tau-1} + w_2\mathcal{F}_{kj}^{\tau} \\ \omega_2 &= \varsigma\mathcal{T}_{ik},\ 0 < \varsigma < 1 \end{aligned} \tag{3}$$

where w_1 and w_2 are fixed non-negative weights with sum-total 1 and ς is the node's individuality factor. If ς is less than $\frac{1}{2}$, it means that a node trusts more its own experience hence guaranteeing that second-hand information carries less weight than first-hand information.

Moreover, first-hand information received from highly trusted nodes should carry more weight that the one received from nodes with low trust ratings. $\mathcal{T}_{ik}\mathcal{F}_{kj}$ allows to discount the first-hand information received as a function of the trust rating of the node that provided the information.

If *i* considers *k* untrustworthy, the accept and forward deviation tests are performed. The *deviation test* is computed as follows

$$\left| \mathcal{S}_{x_{ij,k}} - \mathcal{F}_{x_{kj}} \right| \geq d \tag{4}$$

where *d* is the deviation threshold. The deviation test allows comparing if nodes *i* and *k* have similar opinions about *j*.

If the results of accept and forward deviation tests are both negative, $\mathcal{F}_{kj}$ is incorporated using Eq. 3. Otherwise, (*i*) if both are positive, $\mathcal{F}_{kj}$ is not incorporated; (*ii*) if at least one of them is positive, $\mathcal{F}_{kj}$ is incorporated at most twice since one of the deviation tests mostly probably failed because of stale recommendations.

Any node *k*'s recommendations towards *j* are synthesized using the same moving average process as in Eq. 2, thus making the system resilient against false praise and accusation. Is it assumed that there is an acceptable number of misbehaving nodes. Second-hand information is integrated using

$$\mathcal{S}_{x_{ij,k}}^{\tau} = (1-\phi)\,\mathcal{S}_{x_{ij,k}}^{\tau-1} + \phi\mathcal{F}_{x_{kj}}^{\tau} \tag{5}$$

3.5 Trust rating

The trust record, which is stored at the trust module, has also the form $\mathcal{T}_{ij} = (\alpha, \beta)_{\mathcal{T}}$. As it was previously mentioned, $(\alpha, \beta)_{\mathcal{T}}$ represents the parameters of the Beta distribution assumed by node *i* in its opinion about how honest node *j* is as an actor in the reputation system. When node *i* receives first-hand information from some node *k* about node *j*, an update is performed.

Prior to incorporating the second-hand information, a deviation test is executed. On the one hand, it is used to update the trust rating node *i* has of *k*, and on the other hand, in addition to the latter, it is also used to decide whether to update the reputation rating node *i* has on *j*. $\alpha_{\mathcal{T}}$ is incremented if both deviation tests are positive. If both deviations tests are negative or if at least one is positive and $\mathcal{F}_{kj}$ was incorporated at most twice, then $\beta_{\mathcal{T}}$ is incremented. The trust rating is computed using Eq. 1.

3.6 Bayesian classification

In classification problems, Θ is discrete and the goal is to estimate θ given an observation *x*. To address the task of finding suitable nodes to forward messages in DTNs, two binary classification problems are considered: the node's behavior ($\mathfrak{P}_1$) and trustworthiness ($\mathfrak{P}_2$) classification problems.

Let $\theta \in \Theta = \{\theta_0, \theta_1\}$ be the unknown state of nature: for $\mathfrak{P}_1$: $\theta = \{\theta_0 = \text{good/normal}, \theta_1 = \text{bad/misbehaving}\}$ and for $\mathfrak{P}_2$: $\theta = \{\theta_0 = \text{trustworthy}, \theta_1 = \text{untrusworthy}\}$. Let $X \in \mathcal{X}$ be a random variable with $\{f(x|\theta),\ x \in X\}$. Let $\pi(0) > 0$ and $\sum_{\theta\in\Theta}\pi(0) - 1$ be the prior probability mass function. Let $a \in \mathcal{A} = \{a_0, a_1\}$ be the allowed decision or action: for $\mathfrak{P}_1$: $a = \{a_0 = \text{FORWARD}, a_1 = \text{DO\_NOT\_FORWARD}\}$ and for $\mathfrak{P}_2$: $a = \{a_0 = \text{TRUST}, \text{a}_1 = \text{DO\_NOT\_TRUST}\}$. Let the "0/1" loss function be used for classification. It assigns zero cost to any correct decision and unit cost to any wrong decision. The optimal Bayesian decision is given by

$$\delta_{\text{Bayes}}(x) = \begin{cases} \theta_0 \leftarrow l(x) \geq t \\ \theta_1 \leftarrow l(x) < t \end{cases} \tag{6}$$

where $l(x) = \frac{f(x|\theta_0)}{f(x|\theta_1)}$ is the likelihood ratio and $t = \frac{\pi(\theta_0)}{\pi(\theta_1)}$ is the decision threshold.

The likelihood function is given by the Bernoulli distribution $f(x|\theta) = \theta^r(1-\theta)^{n-r}$, where $r = \sum_{i=0}^{n} x_i$, and *r* denotes the number of outcomes representing correct behavior.

In the beginning, if the only information available is the conditional probability density function of the observation given the true θ, the maximum likelihood decision criterion (δ_{ML}) [5] is used. δ_{ML} is defined as

$$\delta_{\text{ML}} = \begin{cases} \theta_0 \leftarrow l(x) \geq 1 \\ \theta_1 \leftarrow l(x) < 1 \end{cases} \tag{7}$$

In the *node's behavior classification problem*, after each interaction between two nodes, the sender updates the reputation rating of the other node based on the result of this interaction. Each node clusters the other nodes to whom it interacted in two groups: normal nodes, if $\mathcal{R}_{ij} \geq 1/2$, and misbehaving nodes, if $\mathcal{R}_{ij} < 1/2$. The prior probabilities $\pi(\cdot)$ of these clusters, which allow determining the decision threshold, are coefficients of the convex combination of the number of nodes in these clusters. The optimal Bayesian decision is computed using Eq. 6 given the prior probabilities. However, if a correct behavior is observed and $\pi(\theta_1) > \pi(\theta_0)$, one may incur in false positives, i.e., a misclassification, while using the optimal Bayesian decision criterion, because of the higher weight of the decision threshold in comparison to the likelihood ratio.

A modified optimal Bayesian decision, which is an *online classifier*, is proposed as the workaround. It consists in finding attenuation parameters α and β of the *posterior mean Bayesian estimator* ($\hat{\theta}_{PM}$) [5] and computing an attenuated decision threshold. $\hat{\theta}_{PM}$ is given by

$$\hat{\theta}_{PM} = \frac{\alpha + r}{\alpha + \beta + n} \tag{8}$$

For the minimum possible case, i.e., one correct behavior being observed and two clusters, one with 2 misbehaving nodes and the other with 1 normal node, $l(x)$ is $4/3$. If $\alpha = \beta$, the Bayesian attenuation parameters are given by

$$\alpha \geq 3n - 7r \tag{9}$$

For the case above, $\alpha = 2$ and the decision threshold is equal to the likelihood ratio. If instead the *maximum a posteriori Bayesian estimator* [5] was used, the decision threshold would be greater than the likelihood ratio which would lead to misclassification.

In the *trustworthiness classification problem*, each node also clusters nodes that sent first-hand information to him in two groups: trustworthy, if $\mathcal{T}_{ij} > 1/2$, and untrustworthy, if $\mathcal{T}_{ij} < 1/2$, based on the result of the deviation test. The deviation test is performed after the bootstrapping of the trust module. During bootstrapping, nodes' recommendations are synthesized (Eq. 5). Ideally, the bootstrapping period should not be inferior to the time necessary for the distributed reputation system to converge, i.e., for each node's routing decision module engine to be able to classify correctly all the nodes with which it interacted.

In the same way to the node's behavior classification problem, the modified optimal Bayesian decision is computed (see Eqs. 8 and 9) to avoid misclassifications.

4 SIMULATION MODEL

REPSYS was implemented on the Opportunistic Network Environment (ONE) simulator [7]. The simulation model consisted of a network with 150 pedestrians. A map-based mobility model of the Helsinki City over an area of 4.5 × 3.4 Km was used. The pedestrians were moving in a speed varying between 0.8 to 1.4 m/s. The communication range between nodes was 10 m, and the communication is bidirectional at a constant transmission rate of 2 Mbit/s. Every 1 to 2 minutes, a source node randomly chosen can generate one message to a randomly chosen destination. Nodes do not change their behavior (malicious or not) over time. The TTL attribute of each message was 12 h, and the message size varies from 500 kB to 1 MB. The pedestrians' devices had a buffer size of 20 MB for DTN traffic.The simulation time was 7 days with an update interval of 1.0 s. The deviation threshold was set to 1/6. The individuality factor was set to 2/3, which means that first-hand information weights 2/3, that is, the double of the second-hand information weight, i.e., 1/3. The same goes to the smothing factor. The nodes misbehavior considered for evaluation were liars and black-hole attacks. It was considered that misbehaving nodes were also colluding, i.e., they increased α of misbehaving nodes and β of normal nodes. The effects of nodes' misbehavior was examined on Epidemic similarly to [10]. The percentage of liars and nodes that performed black-hole attacks varied from 20% to 80% with increments of 20%.

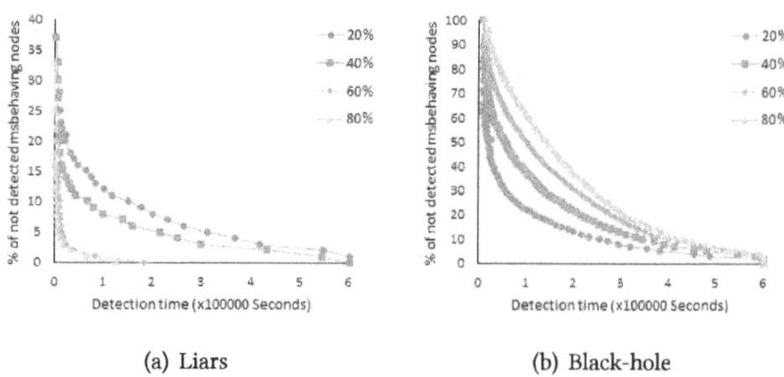

(a) Liars (b) Black-hole

Figure 1: The time necessary to correctly classify misbehaving nodes as DO_NOT_FORWARD for Epidemic with 20, 40, 60 and 80% of liars and black-hole nodes

5 SIMULATION RESULTS

The evaluation of the performance of REPSYS consisted in appraising the reputation and trust modules, similarly to previous work [2]. Additionally, Bayesian classification at the routing decision module was also evaluated. For each setting, i.e., protocol-percentage pair, thirty independent simulations using different seeds were conducted, and the results averaged, for statistical confidence.

The following metrics were considered for the evaluation of REPSYS: *detection time of misbehaving nodes*, which corresponds to the simulation time that took all normal nodes to correctly classify all misbehaving nodes they came in contact with, starting at the detection instant of the first misclassification and *robustness* against false accusations (false negatives) and false praise (false positives), namely Node's Behavior False Positives Ratio (NBFPR), Node's Behavior False Negatives Ratio (NBFNR), Node's Trustworthiness False Positives Ratio (NTFPR) and Node's Trustworthiness False Negatives Ratio (NTFNR).

5.1 Detection time of misbehaving nodes

Figures 1 presents the time necessary for each good node to classify correctly all misbehaving nodes it met as DO_NOT_FORWARD for the Epidemic routing protocol considering four percentages of misbehaving nodes, i.e., 20, 40, 60 and 80%.

The detection time was directly influenced by the routing layer, i.e., the algorithm used to disseminate messages across the network. Ideally, the goal of any reputation system would be to correctly classify all the other nodes with whom a given node interacts (e.g., for

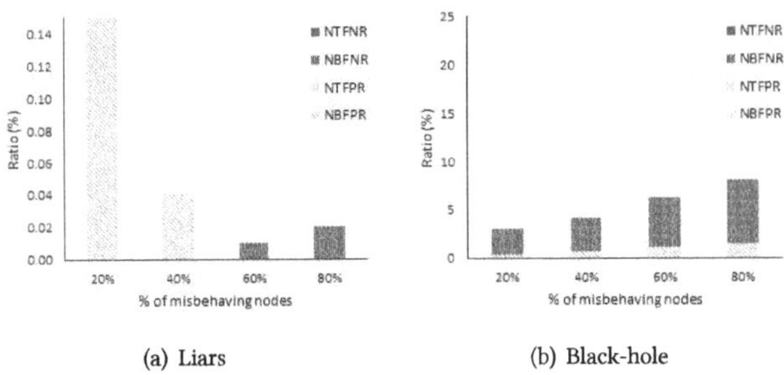

(a) Liars

(b) Black-hole

Figure 2: Node's behavior and Trustworthiness false positives and negatives ratios for Epidemic with 20, 40, 60 and 80% of liars and black-hole nodes

the simplest case, if the node accepted and forwarded the message it received) with the least possible number of contacts. However, overhead causes nodes to interact many times with the same node or group of nodes.

Epidemic's performance was most of the times affected by the overhead of the protocol, therefore increasing the detection time of liars. Nonetheless, the presence of liars improved the performance of Epidemic since less message copies were created, as liars did not accept them and by not accepting they were detected thus reducing the detection time. For the black-hole attack, REPSYS must penalize nodes that only accepted but did not forward messages given that evidence that these messages were not forwarded expired. Even if a small penalization was given, misbehaving nodes performing black-hole attacks would be detected. However, good nodes that behaved similarly to misbehaving nodes would be also isolated from the network, although temporarily, because of the fading mechanism or if they started forwarding messages.

For SFM *type-2*, since an evidence has, by default, the same TTL of a message that originated it, there is a tradeoff between the TTL and the detection time. If the goal is for REPSYS to converge sooner (i.e., to have a small detection time) then the TTL should not be too high. Otherwise, SFMs might not have enough time to be effectively disseminated over the network, which would increase the number of misclassifications as a consequence of a too small TTL. Nevertheless, REPSYS took more time to detect an increasing percentage of nodes performing black-hole attacks in contrast to liars where an increased number of liars took less time to detect, mainly because of forward first-hand information.

5.2 Robustness

In Figure 2, four metrics were considered to measure REPSYS's robustness against false accusations and praise for the lying and black-hole attacks. One can conclude, by analyzing these figures, that there were no misclassified bad nodes for the node's trustworthiness problem. The use of second-hand information may lead to false accusations and praise, but even with the optimal Bayesian decision criterion, it did not have any influence on the metrics considered. There are two reasons for that: (*i*) the bootstrapping of the trust module and (*ii*) the tolerance to nodes that failed the deviation test (Eq. 4). Additionally, there is also a tradeoff between false positives and negatives. By attempting to isolate misbehaving nodes (that is, to reduce the false positives ratio), good nodes that up to a given instant only accepted messages will be misclassified as DO_NOT_FORWARD, therefore increasing the ratio of false negatives.

6 CONCLUSIONS

In this paper, a robust and distributed reputation system for DTNs was proposed. REPSYS takes into account all the available information and uses Bayesian decision theory to classify nodes. The system is robust because despite taking into account all the available information, it is resilient against false accusations and praise, and distributed, as the decision to interact with another node depends entirely on each node.

ACKNOWLEDGMENTS

A warmly thanks to Mário Figueiredo for his numerous inputs. This work was partially supported by Fundação Calouste Gulbenkian and by national funds through Fundação para a Ciência e a Tecnologia (FCT) with reference UID/CEC/50021/2013.

REFERENCES

[1] Erman Ayday and Faramarz Fekri. 2012. An Iterative Algorithm for Trust Management and Adversary Detection for Delay-Tolerant Networks. *IEEE Transactions on Mobile Computing* 11, 9 (sep 2012), 1514–1531. DOI:https://doi.org/10.1109/TMC.2011.160

[2] Sonja Buchegger and Jean-Yves Le Boudec. 2004. A Robust Reputation System for Peer-to-Peer and Mobile Ad-hoc Networks. In *P2PEcon 2004*. http://infoscience.epfl.ch/record/519

[3] J. A. F. F. Dias, J. J. P. C. Rodrigues, F. Xia, and C. X. Mavromoustakis. 2015. A Cooperative Watchdog System to Detect Misbehavior Nodes in Vehicular Delay-Tolerant Networks. *IEEE Transactions on Industrial Electronics* 62, 12 (Dec 2015), 7929–7937. DOI:https://doi.org/10.1109/TIE.2015.2425357

[4] Franz Dietrich and Christian List. 2016. Probabilistic Opinion Pooling. In *The Oxford Handbook of Probability and Philosophy*, Alan Hájek and Christopher Hitchcock (Eds.). Oxford University Press, Chapter 25, 832. https://global.oup.com/academic/product/the-oxford-handbook-of-probability-and-philosophy-9780199607617?cc=pt

[5] Mário A. T. Figueiredo. 2004. *Lecture notes on Bayesian estimation and classification.* Technical Report October. Instituto de Telecomunicações, Instituto Superior Técnico, Lisboa. 172 pages. https://fenix.tecnico.ulisboa.pt/downloadFile/1126518382172510/Bayes

[6] Audun Josang. 1999. Trust-based decision making for electronic transactions. In *Proceedings of the Fourth Nordic Workshop on Secure Computer Systems (NORDSEC'99)*. 496–502.

[7] Ari Keränen, Jörg Ott, and Teemu Kärkkäinen. 2009. The ONE Simulator for DTN Protocol Evaluation. In *Proceedings of the 2nd International Conference on Simulation Tools and Techniques (Simutools '09)*. Article 55, 10 pages. DOI:https://doi.org/10.4108/ICST.SIMUTOOLS2009.5674

[8] Maurice J Khabbaz, Chadi M Assi, and Wissam F Fawaz. 2012. Disruption-Tolerant Networking: A Comprehensive Survey on Recent Developments and Persisting Challenges. *IEEE Communications Surveys & Tutorials* 14, 2 (jan 2012), 607–640. DOI:https://doi.org/10.1109/SURV.2011.041911.00093

[9] Na Li and Sajal K. Das. 2013. A trust-based framework for data forwarding in opportunistic networks. *Ad Hoc Networks* 11, 4 (jun 2013), 1497–1509. DOI:https://doi.org/10.1016/j.adhoc.2011.01.018

[10] Naercio Magaia, Carlos Borrego, Paulo Rogério Pereira, and Miguel Pupo Correia. 2017. PRIVO: A PRIvacy-preserVing Opportunistic routing protocol for Delay Tolerant Networks. In *IFIP Networking*. 1–9. http://dl.ifip.org/db/conf/networking/networking2017/1570333245.pdf

[11] Naercio Magaia, Paulo Rogério Pereira, and Miguel P. Correia. 2015. Security in Delay-Tolerant Mobile Cyber Physical Applications. In *Cyber-Physical Systems: From Theory to Practice*, Danda B. Rawat, Joel J. P. C. Rodrigues, and Ivan Stojmenovic (Eds.). CRC Press, Chapter 15, 373–394. DOI:https://doi.org/10.1201/b19290-22

[12] Lifei Wei, Haojin Zhu, Zhenfu Cao, and Xuemin Shen. 2013. SUCCESS: A secure user-centric and social-aware reputation based incentive scheme for DTNs. *Ad-Hoc and Sensor Wireless Networks* 19, 1-2 (2013), 95–118. DOI:https://doi.org/10.1007/978-3-642-22450-8_14

Cross Fertilization Between Wireless Testbeds and NS-3 Simulation Models

Guillaume Kremer, Philippe Owezarski
CNRS, LAAS,
Université de Toulouse, LAAS

Pascal Berthou
CNRS, LAAS,
Université de Toulouse, LAAS, UPS

ABSTRACT

Network simulators are often used for their simplicity and cost regarding wireless networks. However, their realism is often criticized and their results challenged. The main concern comes from the modeling of the PHY and MAC layers. To assess the performances of these simulators and their models, the results of simulations are often compared with experimental results. However, the comparison methodologies used in these studies may introduce biases. This work focuses on accurately discovering and analyzing the reasons for the calibration problems or implementation bugs in simulators and experimental devices. For this purpose, we leverage the famous Root Cause Analysis (RCA) technique for comparing traces issued from different simulations and real experiments, that includes the study of the root causes of dissimilarities. Throughout the paper, our RCA-based method has been applied to detect and analyze a performance anomaly between NS-3 simulation and our lab wireless testbed when transmitting data over a WIFI 802.11 link. It especially details how low level traffic traces have been generated in both environments for similar scenarios, and how they can accurately be compared and their differences analyzed.

1 INTRODUCTION

Wireless networks are of essential importance nowadays. Users are more and more mobile and access the Internet thanks to mobile devices as laptops, smartphones or tablets. Even when staying at home, users want to get rid of wires. The importance of wireless communication is also aimed at rapidly growing with the emergence of promising upcoming applications involving many kinds of devices constituting the Internet of Things (IoT). However, the wireless networks and their physical layers for media access are technically very complex, and can appear as very fluctuant in terms of behavior, performance, and quality. The wireless networks are more often prone to errors and performance drops than wired networks. Designing wireless networks, compared to wired ones, then requires to accurately and deeply study all communication layers from physical to application, especially focusing on Physical (PHY) and Media Access Control (MAC) ones. It especially has to focus on signal propagation issues as interferences, collisions or distortions in signal propagation.

MSWiM'17, November 21–25, 2017, Miami, FL, USA
 ACM ISBN 978-1-4503-5162-1/17/11...$15.00.
DOI: http://dx.doi.org/10.1145/3127540.3127550

Simulators are very useful tools for first designing and evaluating networks, because they are very simple to use and require less investment than emulation or experimental platforms, in terms of time, and cost. Nevertheless, the results of wireless networks simulators are constantly criticized for their lack of realism, their PHY and MAC layers implementation being largely challenged by simulator users [6]. Therefore, the results of simulations are often compared with experimental results to calibrate simulators, and their PHY and MAC layer behaviors. For instance, OMNET++ performances in terms of throughput and latency estimation are very optimistic due to extreme simplification of MAC algorithms implementation [3]. Issues also appear with the NS-2 simulators that do not consider the operating systems delays [4] as well as at the PHY level with inaccurate signal propagation models in simulators, for instance for the loss models [11]. Tan et al. [5] pointed out anomalies on the measured signal power, due to simulators that are not considering the differences between antennas.

Our objectives focus on accurately discovering and analyzing the reasons for the calibration problems or implementation bugs of both the simulators and experimental devices. For this purpose, we leverage the famous Root Cause Analysis (RCA) technique for comparing traces issued from different simulations and real experiments, that includes the study of the root causes of dissimilarities. Our comparison approach is symmetric, and it can also be used for exhibiting and analyzing deficiency of wireless protocols implementation on the wireless devices. By exhibiting their root causes, it helps network designers to correct either simulator models, or wireless device implementation.

The rest of the paper is as follows: first, the paper describes the platform for wireless communication experiments (section 2), and that is the source of all synchronized traces captured at layers 1, 2, and 3. All together, they constitute an essential database for in deep and efficient wireless network behavior analysis. It especially focuses on studying the 802.11 protocol, and comparing results with the ones of the NS-3 simulator. Section 3 details related experimentation scenarios. Section 4 shows how traces from simulators and real experiments must be paired to avoid biases. Section 5 then presents the RCA method and how it is used for calibrating NS-3 simulation models and experimental devices, as well as for detecting implementation bugs. Finally, section 6 concludes the paper

2 EXPERIMENTAL PLATFORM AND SIMULATOR DESCRIPTION

Our WIFI testbed is designed inside an anechoic room with two WIFI nodes. The nodes are controlled through a wired network to avoid interference with the wireless communication. The nodes are Avila-GW2348-4 gateway platforms and run a Linux OpenWrt

OS. The boxes have an Intel Xscale processor, 64 MB of SDRAM and 16MBytes of Flash memory. The WIFI network controllers are based on the AR5414 chipset from Atheros which uses the ath5k driver. The ath5k driver is open-source and well documented.

The configuration of the wireless interfaces is done in promiscuous mode to capture any packets sensed by their antenna. The packets are captured at the MAC layer using the PCAP library. The packets contain data from link to application layers, such as the 802.11 channel number, the type of frame at the MAC layer, or packet size at the network layer. We modified the ath5k drivers of the OpenWrt OS to permit, when possible, the propagation of packets with frame check sequence (FCS) errors to the upper layers.

Not to overload the WIFI node processors, UDP traffic generation and reception are made on dedicated machines which are connected to the nodes by high performance Ethernet connections. The WIFI nodes are configured as WIFI bridges and are only responsible for MAC and PHY related operations (*i.e.* 802.11 retransmission, FCS checking, ...) as well as for PCAP captures. Tests made on the test bench do not show any impact of this configuration on the accuracy of the data [7].

A WIFI sniffer device (similar to the WIFI bridge devices) is connected to the WIFI bridge 1 antenna by means of a power splitter. The sniffer is set in monitor mode and is totally passive (it does not send any frame and therefore does not perturb communications). In that configuration, the WIFI sniffer is able to capture the frames transmitted by the WIFI bridge 1. All equipment have their clock accurately synchronized by using a NTP server on a dedicated wired connection.

NS-3 is a recent network simulator commonly used to simulate wireless networks. NS-3 has been selected as it is the most recent version of the NS simulator family, a family of generic network simulator widely used in the network research and engineering community. Our configuration is set to use the YANS (Yet Another Network Simulator) models that define the PHY and MAC layer of WIFI nodes [8].

In the NS-3 simulator, nodes can be configured to capture 802.11 and IP traffic into PCAP files that can be analyzed in the same way as traces gathered on the experimental testbed.

However, NS-3 does not consider signal attenuation (cf. figure 1(b)), and thus a method is required to be able to compare NS-3 simulator with experimental testbed results. This involves noise injection capabilities. Similarly as on the experimental platform, this noise must be injected to disturb the receptor of the wireless link. To the best of our knowledge, no solution is available yet to inject noise during frame reception on the NS-3 simulator. Therefore, the YANS module has been modified to add this capability.

2.1 Frame reception in the YANS model

In our configuration, the first steps of 802.11 frames reception are carried by the PHY methods of the YANS module. These steps determine if the frame is received with or without any error. The reception of a frame p begins by the evaluation of the signal strength $S(p, t)$. This value is calculated using the Friis law from the transmission power of the frame and the traveled distance. The signal to noise plus interferences ratio for that frame p, noted $SNIR_A(p, t)$, is then obtained with equation 1. In the SNIR relation, N_f and N_i are respectively the value of the electromagnetic noise floor and the sum of all the signal powers received by the antenna at the time of the frame reception. The N_f value is constant and specific to the simulated circuit.

$$SNIR_A(p, t) = \frac{S_p t}{N_i(p, t) + N_f} \tag{1}$$

This $SNIR_A$ value will then be used by the YANS module to determine if a frame contains any error or not: a frame received with a lower SNR will have a bigger error probability.

2.2 Modifications of the YANS model to support noise injection

According to equation (1), the error probability during packet reception is affected by the strength of the received signal, i.e. the cumulative power of all the interferences and the value of the constant noise floor. To implement the experimental protocol and therefore inject an arbitrary noise power during frame reception, the reception process is modified. Another noise source, N_g, is therefore added to the denominator of the SNIR computation according to equation (2).

$$SNIR_B(p, t) = \frac{S_p t}{N_i(p, t) + N_f + N_g(t)} \tag{2}$$

To generate the N_g values, a new class specialized in generating random noise has been created. This class implements a method *Generate* which is responsible for producing the N_g values. During frame reception, this method is called by another method called *InterferenceHelper::CalculateSnr* which uses *Generate* return value to compute equation 2.

Inside the method *Generate*, N_g values are generated with the Box-Muller algorithm [9] already implemented in NS-3. The Box-Muller algorithm produces normally distributed random numbers. The mean and variance of the distribution are respectively equal to 0 and N_0. The value of N_0 is then defined for each simulation to set the value of the injected noise level.

3 SIMULATION/EXPERIMENT SCENARIOS AND GENERATED TRACES

This section aims at introducing the scenario that serves as the illustrative example in the whole paper. It especially explains how traces are generated to cover the full range of possible situations. It insists on the full set of parameters that are of significant importance for the proposed methodology.

The scenario selected for having all kinds of traffic traces with a very wide range of performance issues consists in sending traffic on an unidirectional 802.11g link, while noise perturbations are generated and injected to the receptor.

The configuration of both environments are identical and detailed in table 1. TCP is used more than UDP but TCP is also a much more complex protocol than UDP. Therefore, not to increase the complexity of these first analyses, the transport protocol used in that study is UDP. For the same reasons, most of the UDP parameters such as the packet size or the throughput are fixed. Moreover, the 802.11 rate control algorithm is disabled and the 54 Mbps mode is used exclusively for the transmission of the data frames. The maximum number of short retries is increased and set to 14 instead of 7 which is the suggested value in the 802.11 standard. Indeed, in the preliminary measurements made to set up our test bed we tested both values and noticed that using 14 would give more interesting results in term of loss at the transmitter (metric referred as DROP).

In both cases, noise power values are selected to achieve a full range of frame error ratio, *i.e.* the ratio of frames received with at least one bit-error varies from approximately 0% to 100% in the experimental and simulation datasets. The experimental and simulation injected noise ranges are linear (*i.e.* the step between two consecutive values is constant). To obtain the specific noise ranges detailed in table 1, we conducted a preliminary set of FER (Frame Error Rate) measures in experimentation and simulation using the same settings and instrumentation. However, in this preliminary set, the noise values used in simulation and experimentation respectively ranged from -75 to -40 dBm and from -75 to -15 dBm. The step between each noise level in this preliminary set was 1 dBm in experimentation and 0.1 dBm in simulation. The measured FER values allowed us to restrict the noise range in our final test set from -67.7 to -65.5 dBm in simulation and from -24.0 to -18.0 dBm in experimentation. The difference observed between these two ranges can be explained by the way noise is injected in the two environments. In the simulation case, the noise is injected directly during frame reception. In the experimentation case however, the noise is transmitted over the air to the receiver by a directive antenna, the value of the experimental noise being the peak amplitude of the noise produced by the signal generator. Therefore, in the experimental case, the noise has to suffer attenuation losses in the different mediums (cable and air) before it can reach the receiving antenna.

4 SIMULATION AND EXPERIMENTAL TRACES PAIRING FOR THE COMPARISON

The simulation and testbed traces used in our comparison methodology have been generated for the same scenario in similar conditions. To avoid biases during the comparison stage, it is essential to pair the two traces in order to make related events in the two traces correspond.

Indeed, data issued from the simulation model and the experimentations could be slightly dissimilar and must be mapped to each other to be compared. Figures 1(a) and 1(b) show the difference of frame error rate between a NS-3 simulation and the related experiment in our testbed. Curves are similar. However, they are not centered on the same noise level value. This difference has been explained in section 3.

To pair each trace of the experimental dataset with one trace selected from the simulation dataset, we propose to apply a combination of easy computable criteria w.r.t. the goals of the study. For instance, this paper focuses on wifi loss behaviour. The pairing will be made according to the frame error ratio and the loss patterns. These two methods are detailed below. While the first pairing method using the FER is well suited in the scenario used in our study, the second method using loss patterns can be more interesting in other more complex situations.

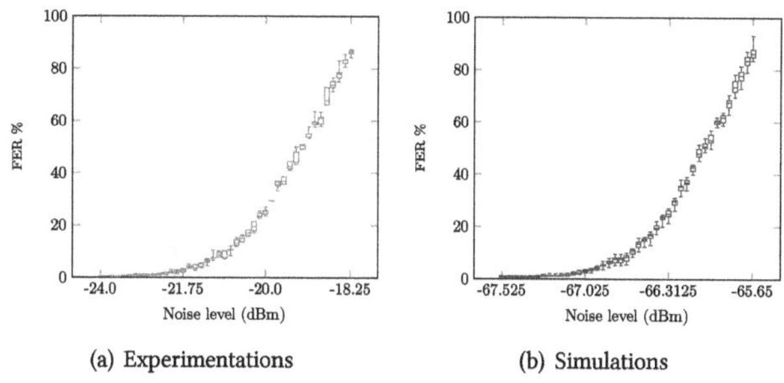

(a) Experimentations (b) Simulations

Figure 1: FER measures regarding the different noise levels in experimentations 1(a) and simulations 1(b). The values are for each trace the 1st and 3rd quartile, as well as the min and max values. The central value displayed is the median.

4.1 FER based traces pairing

Frame errors are artificially generated at the receiver side with signal perturbations to test the wireless protocol behavior. The quantity of frame errors depends on the value of the injected noise. On Figures 1(a) and 1(b) the y-axis represents the medium frame error ratio (FER) experienced for a fixed noise level value. Each point summarizes the loss rate measured in a thousand frames trace.

As shown on table 1, the noise value is different in both environments (simulation, experimentation), however the FER resulting from these values is common across both sets of traces. It ranges from 0 % to 100 %. Consequently, the FER can be used as a common pairing metric. Furthermore, the FER may impact the value of other metrics such as the performance of the link, and therefore comparing traces with different FER may be inefficient since it will result in biases during comparison. Because of this, the median of the FER value is used to pair the experimental and simulation traces. Hence, for each experimental trace, the pairing process associates a specific simulation trace. The selected simulation trace for each experimental trace is the one with the closest measured FER median value.

Therefore, given two traces x and y belonging respectively to the experimental and simulation datasets (respectively named X and Y), given $z = |Median(FER_x) - Median(FER_y)|$, traces x and y are eligible to be paired together if and only if $\forall t \in Y \setminus \{y\}$, $|Median(FER_x) - Median(FER_t)| \geq z$.

If multiple simulation traces are eligible to be paired with one experimental trace, the choice among the simulation traces is made arbitrarily. However, given the diversity measured on the FER values, this case is unlikely to happen. Furthermore, given the configuration of the simulator, two simulation traces sharing the same FER median should be quite similar and should not result in major comparison differences.

4.2 Loss pattern based traces pairing

The pairing process associates traces according to their median FER. However, although the median FER of the two associated traces are similar, their error characteristics and patterns can be different. These differences have an impact on communications. For

Table 1: Detail of the settings used for the experimentations and simulations.

Setting	*Notation*	*Experimentations*	*Simulations*
Transmit power	P_{ptr}	10 dBm	
UDP Throughput	P_{DUDP}	7 Mbps	
Packets size	P_{TP}	1472 B	
Noise power range (linear)	P_{BR}	[-24.00;-18.00] dBm	[-67.7;-65.5] dBm
Corresponding generated FER range		[0%;100%]	
Data frame rate	P_{DT}	fixed to 54 Mbps	
Control frame rate	P_{DC}	fixed to 24 Mbps	
802.11 standard	P_{MAC}	802.11g-DCF-No-QoS-Long Slot (20 μSec)	
Maximum number of consecutive 802.11 retries	P_{RETR}	14	
Distance between sender and receptor	P_{DIST}	2 m (= 6.562 ft)	
Propagation environment	P_{ENV}	Anechoic room	Free space (Friis model)

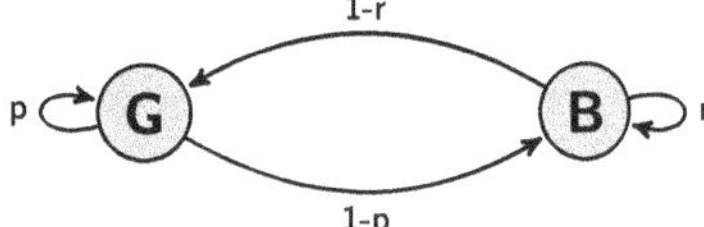

Figure 2: The Gilbert-Eliott model.

example, the BEB (Binary Exponential Backoff) algorithm, which exponentially increases the contention window size between each successive retries, can have significant consequences on a link capacity if this link experiences long bursts.

The Gilbert-Eliott loss model displayed on figure 2 is used to model error patterns over data transmission channels. This model is based on a 2-states Hidden Markov Model. The state labeled G (good) corresponds to the successive reception of error-free packets (also called an *interval*) whereas the state labeled B (bad) corresponds to the successive reception of erroneous packets (also called a *burst*).

p and r are the respective transitions associated with the transition from state B to state G and vice versa. The stationary probabilities associated with state G and B are respectively noted π_G and π_B. The channel memory is defined as the μ parameter.

Hence, additionally to the pairing process which associates traces according to their FER median values, the comparison of the μ, π_B and π_G parameters on the paired traces guarantees that these traces are similar with regards to their error patterns. These two methods limit biases during the following of the comparison process. This is demonstrated in the following section.

4.3 Traces pairing and validation

Figure 3 shows the resulting pairing. The accuracy of the method allows the association of traces that have a median FER with less than 1% difference between each other. The Gilbert-Eliott coefficients π_B, π_G and μ have been calculated for each of these traces.

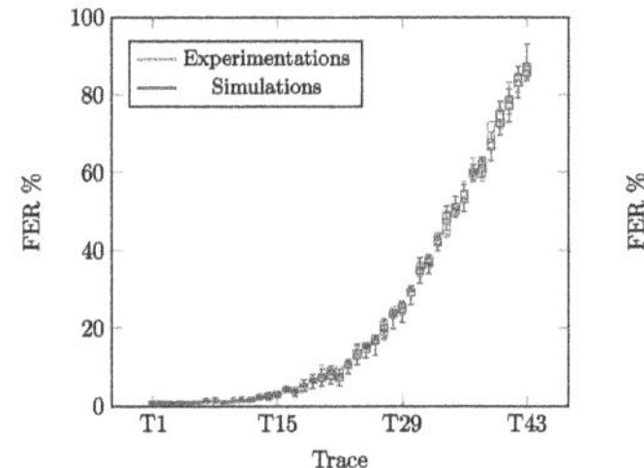

(a) Experimentations and simulations FER after trace pairing

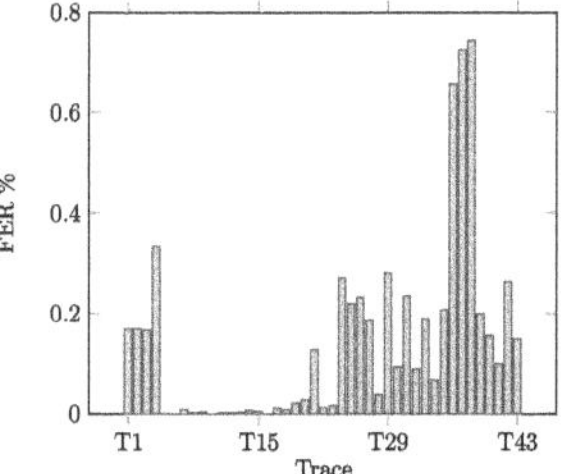

(b) Differences between paired FER

Figure 3: FER values after trace pearing and absolute difference between FER.

There was no difference between the error patterns measured in experimentation and simulations. Moreover, the μ coefficient evolution computed on the traces are similar in both environments and their value is close to 0. This demonstrates the independence of the generated errors.

For a better comprehension, in the rest of the text, the paired traces will now be noted according to table 2 and prefixed by a *T* character.

5 BEHAVIOR DISSIMILARITIES DETECTION AND ANALYSIS BETWEEN SIMULATORS AND EXPERIMENTAL TESTBEDS

Our method for detecting behavior dissimilarities between simulators and/or testbeds, and analyzing their causes takes advantage of the RCA model. RCA is a diagnosis method that identifies root causes of problems and symptoms detected on a monitored system. It specifically relies on the expertise of network administrators and architects. RCA models have been successfully used in [12, 13].

Table 2: Notation of the traces after the pairing process. For commodity reasons, only a small part of the associations are shown.

New notations		$T1$	...	$T15$	...	$T29$	...	$T43$
Respective	experimentations	-24.0	...	-21.75	...	-20.0	...	-18.25
noise level (dBm)	simulations	-67.525	...	-67.025	...	-66.3125	...	-65.65

5.1 The RCA model and its related deduction tree

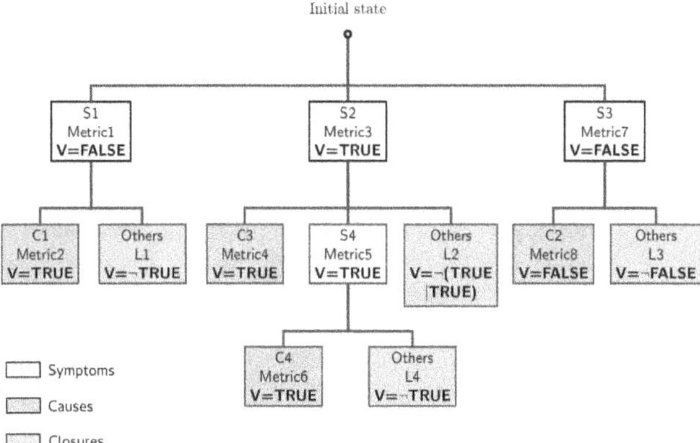

Figure 4: Example of a RCA tree for comparison between traces. V values displayed on the nodes are sample values set arbitrarily and used to present how the analysis process propagates down the RCA tree.

Any RCA model requires a knowledge base which describes the relation between symptoms and causes. A deduction tree [10, 14] can be used for that purpose. Figure 4 presents an example of such tree.

A deduction tree is composed of symptoms and causes nodes which are respectively associated with one or several metrics of the monitored systems. These associations take the form of a logical expression constituted with these metrics. A hierarchical relationship between two nodes represents a causal relationship between the metrics which are respectively associated to the nodes in the modeled system. The symptoms are non terminal nodes since they must be tracked to its or their possible cause(s). At the opposite, cause nodes are terminal nodes. However, a cause can have sibling nodes (symptoms or causes) which are issued from the same parent node.

When the tree is applied on the data of the monitored system, the logical expression associated with each node is evaluated to a boolean value. The application of the tree starts at the initial node and propagates towards terminal nodes. A node is evaluated if and only if its parent is evaluated to *true*. For that reason, high level metrics (e.g. performance metrics or outputs of the monitored system) should be associated with nodes located at the upper levels of the tree since they capture more symptoms than metrics with small radius (e.g indicator metrics or parameters of the system). The goal of such arrangement is to maximize the visibility of the system at the upper levels of the tree and reduce the spectrum of causes while going down the tree levels.

The model of a specific system can be incomplete (either for a lack of knowledge, modeling or measurement capabilities). For that reason, a third type of node is used: closures. Closures allow the inference of the possible cause of a symptom even if all the values of its sibling nodes are evaluated to $false$. The value associated to a closure is therefore automatically set to the following value: if $V = \{V_1, ..., V_n\}$ is the set of logical values of the S symptom siblings, then the value of the associated closure L equals $\neg(V_1 \mid ... \mid V_n)$, where $\mid$ is the exclusive disjunction. At the end of the tree application, if a closure is evaluated to *true*, further analysis may be needed to identify the exact cause of a detected symptom.

For illustration purposes, the propagation of the analysis process in the tree described on figure 4 is the following:

(1) Level 1 nodes $S1$, $S2$ and $S3$ are first evaluated. Only, $S2$ is evaluated to *true*.
(2) Node $S2$ has 3 possible causes: $C3$, $S4$ and $L2$. $L2$ being the closure of $S2$. $C3$ and $S4$ are evaluated to *true*, therefore $L2$ is evaluated to $false$.
(3) The sub-tree issued from $S2$ is evaluated. The value of $S4$ and $C3$ are *true*.
(4) Node $C4$ is evaluated to *true*.

As a conclusion, anomalies have been detected on nodes $S2$, $C3$, $S4$ and $C4$. It follows that the possible root causes are $C3$ and $C4$.

5.2 The RCA deduction tree for comparing the behaviors of our NS-3 and testbed example

The specific RCA model defined for our environments (simulators, testbed) comparison is shown in figure 5. This model has been defined according to our expertise in the wireless domain and our measurement capabilities. The performance metric is the IP throughput of the wireless link. Other metrics are related to timing, errors patterns, or configurations. The 1st node of the tree compares the Bw values computed on the simulation and experimental datasets.

The second level of the tree uses metrics whose variations are known to directly impact the throughput on the link. These metrics are *FER* and *DROP* which are then respectively associated with nodes $S2$ and $S5$. IPERF (the tool used to generate traffic) and packet size parameters have also a direct impact on the measured throughput. Therefore, they need to be checked at that level of the tree.

To find the cause of reception errors dissimilarities, node $S5$ is linked to node $C2$ which compares the values of the Gilbert-Eliott (GE) coefficients in the two datasets. As explained in the

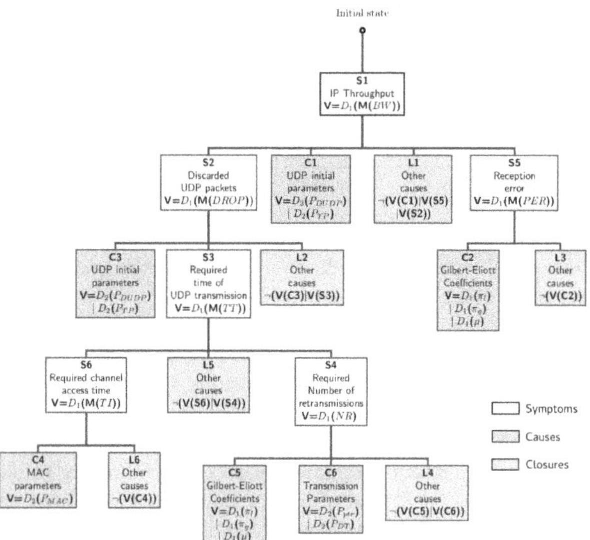

Figure 5: Deduction tree for trace comparison. The M(a) notation used on the nodes is a short notation to express the median of the metric a. For example, M(BW) is the median of the throughput values measured every second on each trace.

previous sections, the GE coefficients can be directly linked with the reception errors.

A large part of the tree is responsible for finding the cause of congestion dissimilarities in the experimental and simulation datasets. This subtree is issued from node $S2$. The causes of congestion are related to limited resources on the wireless link. This resource limitation may be due to longer transmission delays (node $S3$) which may then be caused by longer medium access delays (node $S6$) or harsher medium conditions (node $S4$). For that last node, the number of frame retransmissions may be subordinated to the transmission parameters of the 802.11 frame (e.g. transmission power) and to the GE coefficients. Finally, in our single-link configuration, the channel access time associated with node $S6$ is essentially impacted by the MAC parameters, and hence by the link between nodes $S6$ and $C4$.

5.2.1 Nodes evaluation. The nodes evaluations are made using the boolean functions D_1 and D_2 described below. These functions compare values measured both on the associated traces obtained in simulations and on the testbed. If $Sim(a)$ is the value of a measure a in simulation and $XP(a)$, the value of the same metric obtained experimentally, functions D_1 and D_2 are respectively defined by equations i and ii.

$$\text{(i)} \quad D_1(a) = \begin{cases} true & \text{if } \mid Xp(a) - Sim(a) \mid > t_a \\ false & \text{otherwise} \end{cases}$$

with t_a the threshold associated with metric a

$$\text{(ii)} \quad D_2(a) = \begin{cases} true & \text{if } (Xp(a) \neq Sim(b)) \\ false & \text{otherwise} \end{cases}$$

The $D1$ function requires the definition of a different threshold value for each metric of the tree. The definition of the threshold values have a great importance on the comparisons since they will affect their output and the efficiency of the tree. If the threshold values are too high, all the comparisons will be evaluated to $false$ and no dissimilarities will be found. At the opposite, if the threshold values are to low, the comparison will always be evaluated to $true$. Setting the right values can be difficult and requires some knowledge and experience on the measured environments, the data and the scenario under test. A solution would be to automatically find the best values by doing several consecutive comparisons with different threshold values and select the best configuration, using a dichotomy based method. Because of space limit, the demonstration of such process will not be detailed here. In our configuration and for the example application, we set the thresholds to the following values:

- For node $S1$, the threshold is noted τ_{bw}. It corresponds to a difference of 500 kbps observed on the median of the throughput values measured on the traces. This value has been set to avoid false-positive due to imperfections during the measurement process.
- The threshold τ_{DROP} used by node $S2$ is set to 42 packets/s. Given the packets size, this value corresponds to the 500 kbps limit set for node $S1$.
- The threshold τ_{FER} threshold specifies that the maximum difference allowed for FER is fixed to 1%. This value corresponds to the maximal accuracy available with the pairing algorithm (see part 4.3).
- The threshold value τ_{tt} is an approximation of the time required to send 42 1470-bytes frames in the 54 Mbps PHY datarate. This time corresponds to the sum of the medium access time, the acknowledgement reception and the flying time such as: $42 * DIFS + 42 * SIFS + \frac{42*1470*8}{54*10^6}$. The backoff time is ignored here. With the standard DIFS (DCF Inter-Frame Space) and SIFS (Short InterFrame Space) values set to 28 μs and 10 μs [1], τ_{tt} value is equal to 0.0091s.
- τ_{TI} is the threshold fixed for the interarrival time of packets. It corresponds to the theoretical difference of interarrival packets between flows of throughput respectively equal to 7 Mbps and 6.5 Mbps (according to the 500 kbps threshold), *i.e.* $\tau_{TI} = 0.0002$ s.
- τ_{NR} is the threshold difference used for the number of retransmissions. This value is set to 1, *i.e.* the values are considered different if their median number of retransmissions is greater than 1.

5.3 Application of our RCA model on gathered experimental and simulation data

The tree model shown on figure 5 is applied on gathered traces. The nodes evaluation during this application is presented on table 3.

A first statement concerns the value of the nodes associated with the parameters comparison (UDP parameters, MAC parameters, ...). As described in section 2, the initial experiment and simulation parameters are the same. Consequently, the evaluation of nodes $C1$, $C3$, $C4$ and $C6$ which make the comparisons of these parameters are $false$. Similarly, if nodes $C2$ and $C5$ which compare the GE

Table 3: Nodes evaluation during tree traversal.

Node	*Logical expression*	*Evaluation Result*
S1	$D_1(M(BW))$	*true*
S2	$D_1(M(DROP))$	*true*
C1	$D_2(P_{DUDP}) \vert D_2(P_{TP})$	*false*
L1	¬(V(C1)|V(S5) |V(S2))	*false*
S5	$D_1(M(FER))$	*false*
C2	¬(V(C1)|V(S5)|V(S2))	(not evaluated)
L3	¬(V(C2))	(not evaluated)
C3	$D_2(P_{DUDP}) \mid D_2(P_{TP})$	*false*
L2	¬(V(C3)|V(S3))	*false*
S3	$D_1(M(TT))$	*true*
S6	$D_1(M(TI))$	*true*
L5	¬(V(S6)|V(S4))	*false*
S4	$D_1(NR)$	*false*
C4	¬(V(C1)|V(S5)|V(S2))	(not evaluated)
L4	¬(V(C5)|V(C6))	(not evaluated)
C6	$D_1(\pi_l) \vert D_1(\pi_g) \vert D_1(\mu)$	(not evaluated)
C4	$D_2(P_{MAC})$	*false*
L6	¬(V(C4))	*true*

coefficients are computed, their value is false given the results illustrated in part 4.3. Finally, the value of $S5$ is also *false* given the accuracy of the pairing process which is more important than the τ_{DROP} threshold set to 1%.

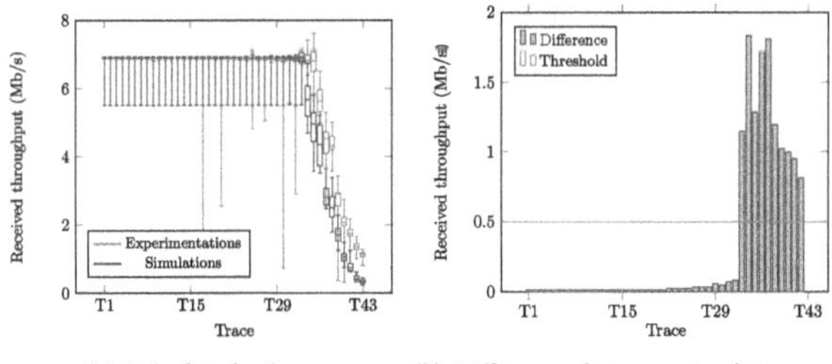

(a) Calculated values

(b) Differences between simulations and experimentations data

Figure 6: Data for BW metric. Graph 6(a) shows the median, the 1st and 3rd quartile, as well as the min and max values for the BW metric measured on the simulation and experimentation traces. Graph 6(b) shows the differences measured for $M(BW)$ between the paired traces of the simulation and the experimental datasets.

Node $S1$, which is the first visited node, compares the measured throughput in both environments. These values and the differences between the paired traces from the experimental and the simulation dataset are respectively shown on figure 6(a) and 6(b). On figure 6(a), a slight difference is observed between the experimental and the simulation values. These values stay stable for the lower noise values and correspond to less than 2,30% of FER (traces $T1$ to $T17$). From trace $T18$, the noise level is high enough to affect the throughput, a slight difference is measured between the experimentation and simulation traces. This difference increases significantly after trace $T33$ (25% of FER) and reaches its maximum value (2 Mbps) for trace $T35$. On figure 6(b), the difference between the traces is greater than the τ_{bw} threshold which is the threshold associated to metric Bw. Therefore node $S1$ is evaluated to *true*.

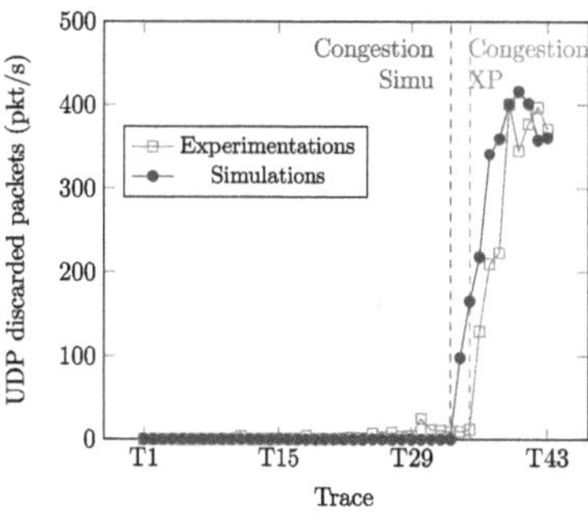

Figure 7: Values of $M(DROP)$ on the paired traces.

At the 2nd comparison level, nodes $S2$, $C2$, $L1$ and $S5$ are visited. Node $S2$ is evaluated to *true*. The values for the associated median metric $M(DROP)$ are presented on figure 7. The loss differences follow the same pattern as the one observed on the throughput values. Data on that figure demonstrates that the congestion caused by the medium saturation happens for lower perturbation in simulation. On both environments, the number of losses per seconds reaches a plateau at 400 packets per second in both environments. When this plateau is reached, the differences calculated between the experimental and simulation traces correspond to 150 lost packets per second; this is similar to the throughput difference of 2 Mbps observed during $S1$ evaluation.

To determine the causes of loss differences observed between the two environments, node $S3$ is evaluated. This node compares the differences between transfer delays in experimentations and simulations. This node is evaluated to *true*. These transport times differences may be caused by the medium access times. This hypothesis is confirmed by the respective evaluation of nodes $S6$ and $S4$ set to true and false. To conclude this root cause detection, the closure node $L6$ is evaluated to *true* since node $C4$ is evaluated to *false*.

Hence, the root cause of these performance differences is traced to channel access times. Since the MAC parameters are the same in both environments, the implementation of the MAC access methods may be responsible of these differences. To accurately demonstrate the implication of these methods further analysis is needed.

5.4 Results analysis

The Binary Exponential Backoff algorithm (BEB) is one of the main factor acting on the channel access time. Before each 802.11 frame transmission, nodes have to randomly pick a transmission slot. The number of slots available to a specific node is limited according to the current number of retransmissions of the frame and managed by the BEB algorithm. The progression of this value, called Cw is given by equation 3. From this equation, Cw follow a geometric progression between the 1st and the 6th level of retransmission of the frame. At the 6th level, Cw has reached its maximum value (1023 slots), and therefore will not be increased during the next level of retransmission. When the frame is successfully transmitted, the Cw values is reset to its initial value Cw_0.

$$Cw_{n+1} = max((CW_n + 1) * 2 - 1, 1023) \quad \text{with } Cw_0 = 15 \tag{3}$$

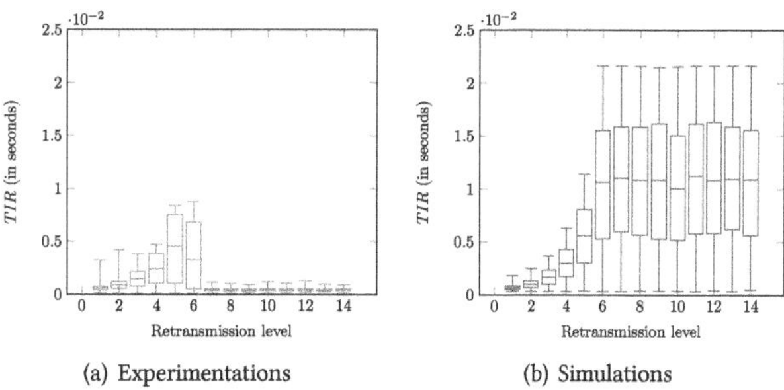

(a) Experimentations (b) Simulations

Figure 8: TIR values measured on the experimentations 8(a) and simulation data 8(b). Values are presented with regards to the level of retransmission. For each trace, the figures depict the min, median and max values as well as the 1st and 3rd quartiles.

The TIR (Retries Inter-arrival Time) metric corresponds to the channel access time measured in experiments and simulations according to the retransmission level of the frames. The experimental and simulation data for this metric are respectively presented on figures 8(a) and 8(b). In the simulation case, the values follow a geometric progression from the 1st to the 5th level of retransmission. From levels 6 to 14, a plateau is reached and the values stay the same, and close to 1.1 ms. At the opposite, in the experimental case, the TIR values increase from the 1st to the 5th retransmission. However between levels 5 and 6, the median of the values decreases. From levels 7 to level 14, the values stay steady and lower than 0.1 ms.

From these statements, only data obtained in simulations seem close to the theoretical results. At the opposite, the experimental implementation of the BEB algorithm in the Atheros chipset seems unexpected for the retry values tested. These results concord with those obtained in [2] which exhibits the unexpected implementations of the backoff mechanism in several WIFI cards. This phenomenon that appears at high levels of retransmission seems to concord with throughput differences observed on figure 6(a). This phenomenon starts at trace $T30$ which corresponds to nearly 20 % of FER.

6 CONCLUSION

This paper presents a full contribution for WIFI network engineering. It includes the evaluation and assessment of WIFI (protocol design, implementation, ...) thanks to the classical NS-3 network simulator, and a lab wireless network testbed. The paper then presents a methodology for comparing the behaviors of NS-3 and a WIFI testbed. This methodology allows the detection of dissimilarities, but also the analysis of their root causes. For that purpose, it takes advantage of the famous RCA method, especially showing how designing and using the RCA comparison tree. To illustrate and validate our detection and analysis methodology, the wireless experimental testbed has been set-up in the framework of an anechoic room. An essential dataset has been built for accurately analyzing the behavior of WIFI networks. This dataset is publicly available.

The paper demonstrates the efficiency of this methodology by analyzing the behavior of our testbed compared to its implementation under the NS-3 simulator.

REFERENCES

[1] *802.11-2012 - IEEE Standard for Information technology–Telecommunications and information exchange between systems Local and metropolitan area networks–Specific requirements Part 11: Wireless LAN Medium Access Control (MAC) and Physical Layer (PHY) Specifications.* Technical Report IEEE Std 802.11™-2012. IEEE-Inst.

[2] G Bianchi, A Di Stefano, C Giaconia, L Scalia, G Terrazzino, and I Tinnirello. 2007. Experimental Assessment of the Backoff Behavior of Commercial IEEE 802.11b Network Cards. In *26th IEEE International Conference on Computer Communications (INFOCOM).*

[3] UM Colesanti, C Crociani, and A Vitaletti. 2007. On the Accuracy of Omnet++ in the Wireless Sensornetworks Domain: Simulation vs. Testbed. In *PE-WASUN'07: Proceedings of the 4th ACM Workshop on Performance Evaluation of Wireless Ad Hoc, Sensor,and Ubiquitous Networks.* ACM, New York, NY, USA, 25–31. http://doi.acm.org/10.1145/1298197.1298203

[4] S Ivanov, A Herms, and G Lukas. 2007. Experimental Validation of the ns-2 Wireless Model using Simulation, Emulation, and Real Network. In *Communication in Distributed Systems (KiVS), 2007 ITG-GI Conference.* 1–12.

[5] T Kefeng, D Wu, A Chan, and P Mohapatra. 2010. Comparing simulation tools and experimental testbeds for wireless mesh networks. In *World of Wireless Mobile and Multimedia Networks (WoWMoM), 2010 IEEE International Symposium on a.* 1–9.

[6] S Khan, B Aziz, S Najeeb, A Ahmed, M Usman, and S Ullah. 2013. Reliability of network simulators and simulation based research. In *IEEE 24th International Symposium on Personal Indoor and Mobile Radio Communications (PIMRC).*

[7] G Kremer, P Owezarski, P Berthou, and G Capdehourat. 2014. Predictive Estimation of Wireless Link Performance from Medium Physical Parameters Using Support Vector Regression and k-Nearest Neighbors. In *TMA'14: Proceedings of the 6th international workshop on Traffic Monitoring and Analysis.*

[8] M Lacage and TR Henderson. 2006. Yet Another Network Simulator. In *WNS2'06: Proceeding from the 2006 Workshop on Ns-2: The IP Network Simulator.*

[9] AM Law and WD Kelton. 2000. *Simulation modeling and analysis.* McGraw-Hill. http://books.google.fr/books?id=QqkZAQAAIAAJ

[10] L Li, M Li, R Fan, and L Li. 2010. A fault diagnosis method based on decision tree for wireless mesh network. In *Communication Technology (ICCT), 2010 12th IEEE International Conference on.* 231–234.

[11] C Phillips, D Sicker, and D Grunwald. 2013. A Survey of Wireless Path Loss Prediction and Coverage Mapping Methods. *Communications Surveys Tutorials, IEEE* 15, 1 (First 2013), 255–270.

[12] M Siekkinen, G Urvoy-Keller, EW Biersack, and D Collange. 2008. A Root Cause Analysis Toolkit for TCP. *Comput. Netw.* 52, 9 (June 2008).

[13] M Siekkinen, G Urvoy-Keller, EW Biersack, and T En-Najjary. 2005. Root Cause Analysis for Long-lived TCP Connections. In *CoNEXT'05: Proceedings of the 2005 ACM Conference on Emerging Network Experiment and Technology.* ACM, New York, NY, USA, 200–210.

[14] X Xiang-Hua, Z Biao, and W Jian. 2009. Tree Topology Based Fault Diagnosis in Wireless Sensor Networks. In *Wireless Networks and Information Systems, 2009. (WNIS). International Conference on.* 65–69.

Tracking You through DNS Traffic: Linking User Sessions by Clustering with Dirichlet Mixture Model

Mingxuan Sun
Louisiana State University
msun@csc.lsu.edu

Guangyue Xu
Louisiana State University
gxu3@lsu.edu

Junjie Zhang
Wright State University
Junjie.Zhang@wright.edu

Dae Wook Kim
Wright State University
kim.107@wright.edu

ABSTRACT

The Domain Name System (DNS), which does not encrypt domain names such as "bank.us" and "dentalcare.com", commonly accurately reflects the specific network services. Therefore, DNS-based behavioral analysis is extremely attractive for many applications such as forensics investigation and online advertisement. Traditionally, a user can be trivially and uniquely identified by the device's IP address if it is static (i.e., a desktop or a laptop). As more and more wireless and mobile devices are deeply ingrained in our lives and the dynamic IP address such as DHCP has been widely applied, it becomes almost impossible to use one IP address to identify a unique user. In this paper, we propose a new tracking method to identify individual users by the way they query DNS regardless of dynamic changing IP addresses and various types of devices. The method is applicable based on two observations. First, even though users may update IP addresses dynamically during different sessions, their query patterns can be stable across these sessions. Secondly, domain name look ups in sessions are different from users to users according to their personal behaviors. Specifically, we propose the constrained Dirichlet multinomial mixture (CDMM) clustering model to cluster DNS queries of different sessions into groups, each of which is considered being generated by a unique user. Compared with traditional supervised and unsupervised models, our model does not acquire any labeled user information that is very hard to obtain in real networks or the specification of the number of clusters, and meanwhile enforces the maximum number of session data in each cluster, which fits the DNS tracking problem nicely. Experimental results on DNS queries collected from real networks demonstrate that our method accomplishes a high clustering accuracy and outperforms the existing methods.

CCS CONCEPTS

• **Security and privacy → Network security**; • **Computing methodologies → Cluster analysis**;

KEYWORDS

DNS behavior tracking; clustering; Dirichlet mixture model

1 INTRODUCTION

The Domain Name System (DNS), which maps between domain names and Internet Protocol (IP) addresses, is involved in almost all network interactions between users and network services such as web browsing, online shopping, instant messaging, and entertainments. DNS, even with security extensions (i.e., DNSSEC), does not encrypt domain names such as "yahoo.com", "bank.us", and "dentalcare.com" that commonly accurately reflect the specific network services offered by their corresponding IPs. As a result, analyzing DNS traffic shows great promise to reveal users' network activities, behaviors, and patterns.

DNS-based behavioral analysis is extremely attractive for many applications such as forensics investigation and online advertisement. Government agencies such as NSA would like to identify users with malicious activities given a collection of DNS query logs, in case adversaries change IP addresses frequently to cover their traces. Secondly, service providers such as Google and OpenDNS may keep track of user visiting behaviors and target personalized ads to each user. Meanwhile, significant privacy concerns are introduced to individual users. If users are aware of the existence of the types of privacy threats through DNS traffic, they can learn to control the amount of information leakage by possibly using different domain name servers or sharing online access with different people in a group.

Despite its promise and privacy concerns, using DNS to infer users' information requires that DNS queries/responses can be correctly attributed to their corresponding originators (i.e., network devices who generate them). This is a trivial task when devices' IP addresses are static (i.e., not changing over time) since we can directly use an IP address to represent a network device (i.e., a desktop or a laptop). Unfortunately, the dynamic IP address such as DHCP has been widely adopted to mitigate the saturation of IPv4 address usage. Specifically, a network device is usually assigned with different IP addresses across multiple days. This makes it impossible to use one IP address to identify a unique network device (or equivalently a user).

It is possible to identify individual users by the way they query DNS regardless of dynamic changing IP addresses and various types of devices based on two observations. First, even though users may update IP addresses dynamically from time to time, their query

MSWiM '17, November 21–25, 2017, Miami, FL, USA

ACM ISBN 978-1-4503-5162-1/17/11...$15.00
https://doi.org/10.1145/3127540.3127567

patterns are likely to be consistent across these periods [8, 10]. As a matter of fact, the online visiting behaviors of each individual user are recurrent and consistent during a short continuous period such as days or weeks. For example, users who have been highly frequent in some services such as "healthcare.com" are likely to remain frequent in the near future. Secondly, domain name look ups in a period are unique from users to users according to their personal behaviors. For example, some always prefer movies and shopping while others focus on stock market news and banking.

A few methods [8, 10] have been proposed to generate DNS-based fingerprints from DNS queries and use the extracted fingerprints to match and attribute DNS queries to their originators. Specifically, Herrmann et al. [8] employed top-visited domains as fingerprints whereas Kim et al. [10] leveraged temporal behaviors of domain queries (e.g., the order in which an arbitrary pair of domains are visited). Both methods follow the supervised learning paradigm, where a large set of DNS queries with labeled users are required to generate fingerprints for each user. Unfortunately, it is extremely challenging to acquire such pre-labeled dataset in real networks, which fundamentally limit the practical application of these types of research methods.

On the other hand, unsupervised learning such as clustering can be used to cluster DNS queries of different sessions into groups, each of which is considered being generated by a unique user. Specifically, we assume that queries issued from the same IP in a session are from the same user, where a session length is a continuous duration such as a day. As illustrated in Figure 1, there are assumed three IP addresses and each issues a set of DNS queries in four consecutive sessions. The goal of clustering is to group DNS query sessions into distinct groups, where sessions in the same group belong to the same user. For example, we believe that sessions labeled in orange belong to the same user since they frequently access particular types of domains such as "Yahoo" and "Learning". Another group linking all sessions labeled in blue tends to be a user who likes particularly shopping and online TV sites, and the last group labeled in green belongs to a user who likes news from "sina.com" and social media actives via "qq.com".

Most existing work such as Kmeans and constrained Kmeans [11] has been proposed under this framework, where top-visited domains are used as features for clustering user sessions. These methods need the number of clusters to bootstrap, which is ideally the number of distinct users in the network. However, due to the bursty nature of human activities, such a design fundamentally undermines the applicability of this method since accurately estimating the number of users is extremely challenging in practice, if not entirely unrealistic. On the other hand, traditional Dirichlet multinomial mixture (DMM) and its variations [2, 7, 22] frequently used in Bayesian nonparametric modeling can automatically adjust the number of clusters. However, each cluster may contain many sessions generated from multiple users, which does not fit into the scenario of DNS tracking since we need to identify pure clusters and each corresponds to a particular user.

As a means towards systematically solving these challenges, we propose the constrained Dirichlet multinomial mixture (CDMM) clustering model, which is a generalization of the traditional Dirichlet multinomial mixture clustering (DMM) model. The key innovation of the proposed model is to sample a session's cluster label only from the qualified candidate clusters whose current sizes are smaller than a threshold, which is the maximum possible number of sessions a user can contribute during the observation period. For example, if session length is defined as a day and all session data is collected in a week, the threshold is 7 assuming each user only contributes one session each day. The constrained model fits the scenarios of DNS clustering better and can potentially improve the clustering performance. To our knowledge, this is the first research about imposing cluster size constraint on nonparametric Bayesian clustering methods. To summarize, we have made the following contributions:

- We have designed a new clustering model without requiring the specification of the number of clusters and meanwhile enforcing the maximum number of sessions in each cluster, which fits the DNS tracking problem nicely.
- Experimental results on DNS queries collected from real networks demonstrate that our method accomplishes a high clustering accuracy and outperforms the existing methods.

2 RELATED WORK

Active research has been conducted to infer users' behaviors through collected network traffic including DNS queries. The focuses of existing methods generally fall into two categories including i) attributing network events to individual network users and ii) inferring users' demographic information. Our method focuses on attributing sessions of DNS queries to their corresponding users (and thus falls into the first category).

A few methods have been proposed to attribute network events to individual users [6, 8–11, 17]. Most of these methods [6, 8–10, 17] first generate behavioral fingerprints for network users and then use these fingerprints to attribute network events whose users are unknown, which requires a significantly large set of events whose users are pre-labeled. This fundamentally limits the practical usage of these systems. In contrast, our method does not require any DNS sessions to be pre-labeled. In addition, methods including [6, 9, 17] generate user fingerprints using data sources (e.g., encrypted wireless traffic, HTTP traffic, and search engine traffic) that offer much finer-grained information compared to DNS traffic. In comparison with our method, Herrmann et al. [8] and Kim et al. [10] generate user fingerprints using the same data source (i.e., DNS queries). However, both methods follow the supervised learning paradigm, where a long period (multiple days) of DNS queries need to be labelled for bootstrapping. The work closest to ours is [11]. Similar to [11], our method uses clustering method to aggregate DNS sessions into clusters, where each cluster is expected to contain sessions generated by one user. In spite of such similarity, the method in [11] mandates the number of clusters. Unfortunately, it is extremely challenging, if not entirely impossible, to specify the number of clusters in practice, fundamentally limiting the application of [11]. In comparison, our method does not require the specification of the number of clusters.

A substantial body of studies [1, 3–5, 12–16, 19–21, 24, 25] have focused on inferring users' application-level activity information

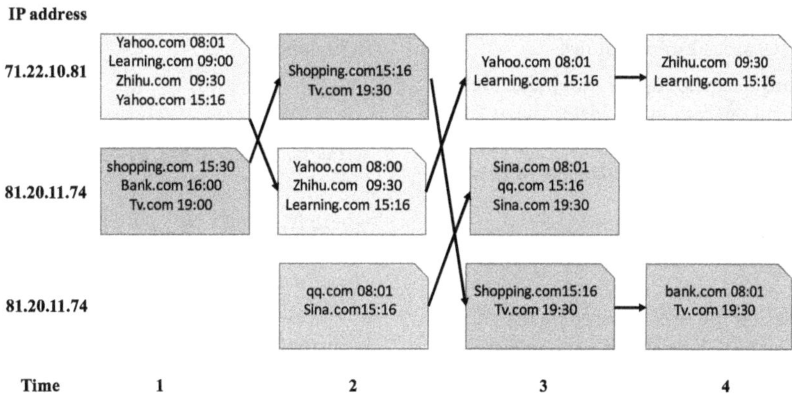

Figure 1: Illustration: Linking user DNS query sessions regardless of changing IP addresses.

from a variety of network resources such as HTTP traffic, search engine traffic, and encrypted skype traffic. For example, Chen et al. [3] used HTTP connection patterns to infer users' browsing activities. In [20, 21], Wright et al. used machine learning methods to reveal spoken language phases from encrypted VoIP traffic. Zhang et al. [23] inferred users' running applications from network-level traffic patterns. Sun et al. [19] also recovered webpages visited by users through encrypted network traffic by adopting carefully designed traffic signatures. Krishnan et al. [12] revealed search engine queries based on domain name correlations. Other types of online activities have also been employed for demographic inference such as friendship on Facebook [15, 24], search queries [1], location check-ins [25], and social network interests [16]. Although these methods have different objectives compared to ours, we expect our method can complement these methods by associating a user with more network events.

3 CONSTRAINED DMM MODEL

In this part, we introduce constrained Dirichlet multinomial mixture clustering (CDMM) model in the context of linking user DNS query activities regardless of dynamically updating IP addresses. A session of a particular IP can be represented as a vector of dimension V, where V is the size of unique domain names and each element of the vector is the query frequency for each domain from the IP during a day. Given a collection of session data $\vec{S} = \{s_i\}_{i=1}^N$, we would like to find the corresponding cluster indicators $\vec{Z} = \{z_i\}_{i=1}^N$, where $z_i \in \{1, 2, \ldots, K\}$ and K is the total number of clusters, e.g., the number of unique users. Since we do not know the actual number of clusters, we can initialize K with a large number, and the clusters will be learned automatically to fit to the data.

Specifically, our model CDMM is a probabilistic generative process, in which each session is generated from a mixture of several components where each component corresponds to a specific user. Session vectors $\{s_i\}_{i=1}^N$ are observed variables and the component indicators $\vec{Z} = \{z_i\}_{i=1}^N$ are latent variables. In addition, our model extends DMM by adding a size constraint to each cluster, that is the number of sessions in each cluster should be less than $maxSize$. In the following sections, we present the details of the probabilistic model, the generative process, and the collapsed Gibbs sampling method for parameter inference for CDMM. The math notations of the model and parameters are listed in Table 1.

Table 1: NOTATIONS

Notation	Description
α, β	concentration parameter for Dir-Mult distribution
$\vec{S}$	all session vectors
$\vec{Z}$	cluster label vectors for corresponding sessions
s_i	i^{th} session vector from $\vec{S}$
z_i	cluster label for i^{th} session
j	j^{th} domain name in dictionary
$\vec{\Phi}_k$	multinomial parameters for cluster k over domain dictionary
$\vec{\theta}$	multinomial parameters for the weights of each cluster
V	the size of domain name dictionary
N	the number of sessions
K	the number of initialized clusters
m_k	the number of sessions in cluster k
N_k	the occurrences of all domains in cluster k
N_k^j	the occurrence of jth domain in cluster k
n_i	the occurrence of all domains in session s_i
n_i^j	the occurrence of jth domain in session s_i
$maxSize$	maximum cluster size
$maxIter$	maximum number of iterations

3.1 Generative Process

The CDMM model is parameterized by two Dirichlet multinomial distributions and corresponding positive scaling parameters α and β. The session vectors $\{s_i\}_{i=1}^N$ are generated with symmetric Dirichlet prior:

$$\theta|\alpha \sim Dir(\alpha|K, ..., \alpha|K), \quad (1)$$

$$z_i|\theta \sim Mult(\theta_1, ..., \theta_k) \quad i = 1, ..., N, \quad (2)$$

$$\Phi_k|\beta \sim Dir(\beta) \quad k = 1, ..., K, \quad (3)$$

$$s_i|z_i, \{\Phi_k\}_{k=1}^K \sim Mult(s_i|\Phi_{z_i}). \quad (4)$$

The process first samples one out of K clusters, e.g., k, based on the multinomial distributions with parameter θ, and then generates session s_i according to the distribution of cluster k parameterized by Φ. In order to enforce size constraint on each cluster, we need to modify the above generative procedure as follows:

- For the current session, constructing the candidate cluster (user) label list, where all the candidate clusters have fewer than *maxSize* DNS queries.
- Sampling the cluster label from the candidate list as in Equation (2).
- Choosing the corresponding multinomial distribution of a candidate cluster from Dirichlet distribution parameterized by β.
- Generating DNS queries for the session based on the chosen cluster label and multinomial distribution parameterized by Φ_{z_i} as defined in Equation (4).

More intuitively, we can use the Chinese Restaurant process (CRP) to illustrate the CDMM model where sessions are customers and users are represented as tables in a Chinese restaurant. Assume there are K fixed tables and N customers. At the very beginning, each user is randomly assigned to a table. If they are not satisfied with the initial assignment, they can change tables dynamically. We assume this reallocating process is guided by the following rules. Firstly, users are more willing to join a table with more people in order to feel comfortable, which means rich clusters gets richer. In addition, users prefer to sit with their friends, that is users like to join a table where they share more similar features with existing table users. Most importantly, different from traditional CRP, we have a size constraint for each table. If the table is full, users has to choose a second preferable table instead.

3.2 Parameter Learning

Given sessions and their initial label assignments, we employ the Gibbs sampling method to infer the hidden cluster for each session. The key concept of Gibbs sampling is to sample the cluster label using the conditional posterior probability $p(z_i|\vec{Z}_{\neg i}, \vec{S})$ as shown in Equation (5):

$$p(z_i = k|\vec{Z}_{\neg i}, \vec{S}, \alpha, \beta) \propto p(z_i = k|\vec{Z}_{\neg i}, \alpha) \cdot p(s_i|z_i = k, \vec{Z}_{\neg i}, \vec{S}_{\neg i}, \beta), \tag{5}$$

where $\vec{Z}_{\neg i}$ is the user assignments for all sessions except for session s_i, The intuition of this formula is that removing the effect of session s_i from the DNS session corpus and using the rest information to infer the user label for session s_i.

The first term on the right side of Equation (5) is the component weight measured by the number of data points in cluster k. The more sessions a user already have, the more likely session s_i is assigned to this user. Our model also imposes size constraint for each cluster in case the cluster becomes increasingly large. The concrete calculation for the component weight is shown in Equation (6):

$$p(z_i = k|\vec{Z}_{\neg i}, \alpha) = \int_\theta p(z_i|\theta)p(\theta|\alpha) = \frac{m_{k,\neg i} + \alpha}{N - 1 + K\alpha}. \tag{6}$$

The second term of Equation (6) in the middle is the likelihood measuring how likely the current cluster generates session s_i. The more features session s_i and the existing sessions of the cluster share, the more likely s_i will fall into this cluster. In CDMM, we adopt multinomial distribution to model each cluster, which can tackle the sparsity problem and is more suitable to our actual session clustering circumstance. And the corresponding formula is shown in Equation (7):

$$p(s_i|z_i = k, \vec{Z}_{\neg i}, \vec{S}_{\neg i}, \beta) \propto \frac{\prod_{j \in s_i} \prod_{l=1}^{n_i^j} (N_{k,\neg i}^j + \beta + l - 1)}{\prod_{t=1}^{n_i} (N_{k,\neg i} + V\beta + t - 1)}, \tag{7}$$

where $N_{k,\neg i}^j$ and $N_{k,\neg i}$ are the cluster-level statistics, with $N_{k,\neg i}^j$ as the total occurrences of domain j in cluster k by removing the effect of session s_i, and $N_{k,\neg i}$ as the number of sessions in cluster k after removing the effect of session s_i. In addition, n_i is the total occurrences of all domains in session s_i, and n_i^j is the occurrences of domain j in session s_i. Since not all domains occur in a specific session s_i, we only take into account the domain names that appear in the session, that is $j \in s_i$, when calculating the probability.

Combining Equations (6) and (7) into Equation (5), we can rewrite the full posterior distribution as follows:

$$p(z_i = k|\vec{Z}_{\neg i}, \vec{S}) \propto \frac{m_{k,\neg i} + \alpha}{N - 1 + K\alpha} \frac{\prod_{j \in s_i} \prod_{l=1}^{n_i^j} (N_{k,\neg i}^j + \beta + l - 1)}{\prod_{t=1}^{n_i} (N_{k,\neg i} + V\beta + t - 1)}. \tag{8}$$

Gibbs sampling works in a similar way as Expectation-Maximization (EM). For each iteration, after determining the cluster label z_i for a session s_i, e.g., $z_i = k$, we need to update the parameters of the kth corresponding cluster. Since we assume each cluster follows a multinomial distribution, the updating rule for each cluster in each iteration is shown in Equation (9):

$$p(\vec{\Phi}_k|\vec{S}, \vec{Z}, \beta) = Dir(\vec{\Phi}_k|\vec{n}_k + \beta) \quad and \quad \Phi_{k,j} = \frac{N_k^j + \beta}{\sum_{j=1}^V N_k^j + V\beta}, \tag{9}$$

where $\vec{n}_k = [N_k^1, N_k^2, \ldots, N_k^V]$ and each entry N_k^j is the occurring number of the jth query in the kth cluster. Different clusters have different weights on the query frequency of domains in the dictionary, meaning users have their own preference when browsing the Internet. The discriminative distribution information can help group the sessions into clusters.

3.3 Hyper-parameters

In CDMM, there are two hyper-parameters, α and β, which balance between the priority knowledge and the observed data. The prior knowledge can be treated as pseudo experimental results before we observe the real data.

The hyper-parameter α controls the component weight. We give α a large value when we are confident about our prior knowledge compared with the real data. A large α means that each cluster has equal probability to generate each session data at the very beginning and these probability needs more observed data to be adjusted. In a similar way, β controls the multinomial distribution of domain name occurrences for each cluster. A small β means that each user has equal preference over all domains, which however can be easily updated by the observed data. In our practice, α with smaller values such as 0.001 and β with smaller values such as 0.05 usually work fine.

3.4 Algorithm

In this part, we list the pseudo code of constrained Gibbs sampling for our CDMM model, as shown in Algorithm 1. It follows the common Gibbs sampling framework: 1) scan session vector iteratively and remove the effect of the current session; 2) construct the qualified cluster list for the session; 3) using rest information to calculate the posterior probability of a session belonging to each qualified cluster and sample cluster label; 4) update multinomial distribution based on the selected cluster label.

Compared with the traditional DMM model, the most significant modification of CDMM is *Step 3*. Before sampling the cluster label for session s_i, we need to construct the qualified cluster list first. The list is dynamic during each iteration and contains clusters who have fewer than $maxSize$ sessions currently. We only sample cluster label from the qualified list because some clusters are already full and cannot take any more sessions.

Algorithm 1: Constrained Dirichlet Multinomial Mixture Model (CDMM)

Input:
- Sessions in the DNS query logs, $\vec{S}$
- Hyper-parameter, α and β
- Estimated initial number of clusters, K
- Maximal size of each cluster size, $maxSize$

Output: Cluster label vector for each session, $\vec{Z}$

begin
- *Step 1*: Set m_k, N_k and N_k^j to zero for each cluster k
- *Step 2*: Randomly assign cluster label for each session and update cluster information based on assignments
- **for** *each session* $i \in [1, N]$: **do**
  - $z_i \leftarrow k \sim Random[1, K]$
  - $m_k \leftarrow m_k + 1$ and $N_k \leftarrow N_k + n_i$
  - **for** *domain* $j \in s_i$ **do**
    - $N_k^j \leftarrow N_k^j + n_i^j$
  - **end**
- **end**
- *Step 3*: Constrained Collapsed Gibbs Sampling
- **for** *iter* $\leftarrow$ *1 to maxIter* **do**
  - **for** *each session* $i \in [1 : N]$ **do**
    - ①save cluster label for the current session: $k = z_i$
    - ②remove session effect
    - $m_k \leftarrow m_k - 1; N_k \leftarrow N_k - n_i$ **for** *each domain name* $j \in s_i$ **do**
      - $N_k^j \leftarrow N_k^j - n_i^j$
    - **end**
    - ③construct qualified cluster list with fewer than $maxSize$ sessions
    - ④sample a cluster k for s_i from the candidate cluster list by Equation (8):
    - $z_i \leftarrow k \sim p(z_i = k|\vec{Z}_{\neg i}, \vec{S})$
    - ⑤recover this session's effect
    - $m_k \leftarrow m_k + 1$ and $N_k \leftarrow N_k + n_i$
    - **for** *each domain name* $j \in s_i$ **do**
      - $N_k^i \leftarrow N_k^i + n_i^j$
    - **end**
  - **end**
- **end**

end

3.5 Complexity Analysis

- **Space complexity**:
  Following Algorithm 1, we need to store all session vectors $\vec{S}$, which essentially is a session-domain matrix of size $N \cdot V$, where N is the number of sessions and V is the size of domain name dictionary. Compared with Dirichlet Process Mixture model, we predefine a fixed number of maximum clusters K. Therefore, for each iteration, we need to store the information about $\vec{Z}$ with size N, m_k and N_k with size K, and N_k^j with size $K \cdot V$. Since the number of clusters is always smaller than the number of data points, the total space complexity of CDMM is $O(N \cdot V)$. In practice, the matrix will be really sparse, thus the actual storage is much less than $O(N \cdot V)$.
- **Time complexity**: The most time-consuming part of CDMM is the collapsed Gibbs sampling procedure. Given the number of iterations and session-Vocabulary matrix, Gibbs sampling alternatively samples user label for each session from the conditional posterior distribution computed with other user labels fixed. For one session, we need to compute K probabilities and each represents the likelihood that the kth cluster generates the session. To compute this probability, we need to go through every domain occurrence in each session. We assume the average number of domains in a session is L. Then given $maxIter$, the complexity of CDMM is $O(maxIter \cdot N \cdot K \cdot L)$.

4 EXPERIMENTS

To evaluate the performance of our proposed CDMM model in clustering DNS sessions, we carry out experiments on real-world dataset and compare results with several state-of-the-art clustering techniques.

4.1 Dataset

Our DNS dataset contains 1M domain queries covering totally 89,009 distinct domain names over 7 days from September 23 to September 31 in 2013. The dataset was collected at a Chinese university where all DNS queries are originated from the student housing network. The log keeps the records of a large number of students with different querying behaviors. For example, each student accesses domains of different types both in their studying and leisure times. Each student is uniquely assigned a static IP address that connects a device in the dorm to the broadband network, so the dataset contains the ground truth that maps between user IP address and DNS queries. The labeled information allows us to evaluate the effectiveness of our proposed clustering algorithms.

We preprocess the raw DNS query log and format it in a matrix as described in the previous section. Empirical studies show that a session time can be a fixed duration of 24 hours since a large number of users do not change IP addresses during a day. The data is sparse. The number of queries per user follows a long tail distribution, where 80% users only query fewer than 50 domains and 20%users query more than 50 domains. Similarly, the number of sessions per domain also follows a long tail distribution. To overcome data sparsity, following the approach in [8], we select the most frequent 200 domains with at least 100 queries from different sessions as the dictionary for feature representation, which largely reduces the dimension without dramatically hurting clustering performance. After feature selection, we construct our testing subset of 4K sessions from 478 distinct users with different activity levels.

4.2 Evaluation Metrics

We evaluate the results against the traditional gold standard using several classic metrics, including adjusted Rand Index (ARI) [18], Normalized Mutual Information (NMI), homogeneity, completeness, and V-score. In addition, we would like to evaluate the clustering performance in the context of tracking individual users with respect to changes of user activity levels, so we also adopt the Traceability metric. We give more information about these metrics below.

ARI: Rand Index (RI) measures the cluster similarity by counting pairs that are assigned correctly or wrong. ARI is an "adjusted for chance" measure which is independent of the number of clusters. We use ARI to compare the clustering performance.

NMI: Mutual Information (MI) measures the information shared between two clusters. The more information they share, the more efficient the clustering algorithm is. NMI is the normalized mutual information by scaling the MI results between 0 and 1, where 0 means sharing no information and 1 means perfect correlation. Given the true labels and the cluster labels, NMI is a symmetric indicator to measure the clustering results.

Homogeneity, Completeness, and V-score: Homogeneity measures the purity of the cluster. If most data points in the cluster have the same label, the homogeneity of this cluster will be high. Otherwise, the cluster is not pure and will have a lower homogeneity. Given ground truth, high completeness means more data points with the same true label fall into the same cluster. V-score measures how well the clustering result satisfies homogeneity and completeness.

Traceability: Adopting the same notation from [11], we define that a user is completely traceable, if all his or her sessions across different days are assigned to a single cluster. It is possible that the session data of completely traceable users are grouped together with other users' session data and the clusters are not necessarily pure. Thus we define a user is perfectly traceable if all his or her sessions are assigned to a single cluster and the cluster is pure without other users' sessions. We would like to measure the percentage of completely linked users and perfectly linked users, respectively.

4.3 Baselines for Comparison

- **Kmeans**: Kmeans is one of the most popular clustering algorithms. Kmeans iteratively clusters N samples into K clusters by assigning samples to the nearest centroid and recomputes the centroid for all clusters. Kmeans quits its iteration when reaching the maximum number of iterations or no cluster reassignment for samples occurs. The drawback of Kmeans clustering is that the number of clusters should be pre-defined. Moreover, measuring similarity by Euclidean distance is not quite appropriate for some clustering problems. And initial centroid will affect the final clustering performance.
- **Constrained Kmeans (c-Kmeans)** [11]: c-Kmeans is an extension to the existing K-means with an additional constraint that the number of points in each cluster should be smaller than a certain threshold. The core idea of this method is to add a reassignment step after the traditional Kmeans method. Given the cluster size constraint, after recomputing the centroid for each cluster, c-Kmeans sorts the data points within a cluster by distance from the centroid. Based on the distance, c-Kmeans removes data points far from the centroid until this cluster satisfies the size constraint. Each removed point will be assigned to the closest cluster with size smaller than the constraint. The method fits our scenario of DNS clustering. C-Kmeans is also sensitive to initialization methods. Moreover, C-Kmeans requires the number of clusters to be pre-defined.
- **Dirichlet Multinomial Mixture Model (DMM)** [22]: In contrast to K-means methods, DMM can dynamically cluster data to k groups where the exact k does not need to be pre-defined. DMM is a generative model and its core idea is to sample the cluster label based on the conditional posterior distribution. The posterior probability of a sample assigning to a cluster is determined by cluster size and the similarity between the sample and the existing cluster samples. The method fits our scenario of DNS clustering, where the number of users changes every day. However, this generative process will make big clusters get bigger and this trend will violate the cluster size constraint.
- **Constrained Dirichlet Multinomial Mixture Model (CDMM)**: With the similar relationship between Kmeans and C-Kmeans, our CDMM model is an extension to DMM with an additional constraint that the number of points in each cluster should be smaller than a certain threshold. The core change of this method to DMM is the cluster sample step. In this step, we do not sample the label from all clusters. We only sample the cluster label from the qualified user list based on the posterior distribution.

4.4 Clustering Results

4.4.1 **Clustering performance using classic metrics:** We first briefly summarize the experimental results and discuss the effects of the maximum number of clusters and the initialization approaches on the clustering accuracy.

To compare the model robustness with respect to the cluster size, we conduct two types of experiments, where the first assumes that the number of users is very close to the ground truth size, and the second assumes that the number of users is 200% of the ground truth to simulate the burstiness in complex online systems.

For each experiment, we further discuss the performance of all four clustering models with two different types of initialization strategies: random initialization (R) and smart initialization (S),

Table 2: Evaluate the clustering performance of eight methods using five classic metrics. Suffix "R" indicates random initialization and suffix "S" indicates smart initialization.

clusterNum	Metrics	Methods							
		Kmeans-R	CKmeans-R	DMM-R	CDMM-R	Kmeans-S	CKmeans-S	DMM-S	CDMM-S
True User Number	ARI	0.3024	0.4802	0.2051	**0.5021**	0.3812	0.6444	0.2744	**0.7539**
	NMI	0.4381	0.5564	0.4089	**0.5610**	0.5206	0.6909	0.5099	**0.7730**
	HOMO	0.8192	**0.8719**	0.7319	0.8654	0.8517	0.9113	0.8063	**0.9320**
	Complete	0.8549	0.8791	**0.8888**	0.8885	0.8773	0.9171	0.9134	**0.9499**
	V-Score	0.8367	0.8755	0.8028	**0.8768**	0.8643	0.9142	0.8565	**0.9409**
200% True User Number	ARI	0.3393	0.4591	0.2197	**0.5082**	0.3793	0.5071	0.2802	**0.7332**
	NMI	0.3931	0.4642	0.4441	**0.5655**	0.4305	0.4993	0.5267	**0.7520**
	HOMO	0.9075	**0.9302**	0.7490	0.8670	0.9138	**0.9417**	0.8111	0.9248
	Complete	0.8418	0.8607	0.9076	**0.8898**	0.8510	0.8700	0.9231	**0.9463**
	V-Score	0.8734	0.8941	0.8207	**0.8782**	0.8813	0.9044	0.8635	**0.9354**

which configure the initial k cluster centroids in different ways. In random initialization, the centroids of each cluster are initialized randomly from one of the session data, which fits the scenario where the algorithm is deployed on a new DNS service with no prior knowledge. In smart initialization, we assume that the ground truth labels are available from k unique users. Specifically, for Kmeans and C-Kmeans, using smart initialization, centroids are initialized as session vectors from k different users as in [8]. For DMM and CDMM, using smart initialization, sessions of the same users are assigned to the same cluster with higher probability, which is an extremely ideal case. After initialization, clustering models will re-assign each point to clusters iteratively to fit to data until the resulting clustering assignments will not change any more.

Table 2 shows the clustering results of Kmeans, C-Kmeans, DMM, and CDMM with both random initialization and smart initialization strategies, a total of 8 methods.

First of all, by comparing two batch experiments, model CDMM-R/S and DMM-R/S are stable even if the maximum number of clusters is very different from the ground truth size, e.g., twice of the ground truth. This is because DMM and CDMM can adjust the number of clusters dynamically to fit the data and the results are less sensitive to the initialized size of clusters. However, Kmeans and C-Kmeans are more sensitive to the initialized size of clusters. For example, the NMI score for Kmeans-R drops from 0.4381 to 0.3931, the NMI score for Kmeans-S drops from 0.5206 to 0.4305, the ARI score for CKmeans-R drops from 0.4802 to 0.4591, and the ARI score of CKmeans-S drops from 0.6444 to 0.5071 when the cluster size doubles.

Furthermore, the performance of clustering methodologies heavily depends on the initial cluster assignments. The results of all four models with smart initialization "-S" are much better than those with random initialization "-R". This indicates that clustering with prior knowledge such as user session patterns from previous days or weeks can largely increase the accuracy.

Finally, our CDMM outperforms all other models consistently with both types of initialization. Specifically, from Table 2, we can see that DMM-R/S have lower metric scores except for homogeneity. From the definition of homogeneity, clusters with large sizes are likely to generate high homogeneity score. However, all session data with different ground truth (e.g., user labels) may fall in the same cluster thus all other metrics are extremely low. Compared with the traditional DMM, our Model CDMM-R/S add the constraint to cluster size, which results in smaller and purer clusters. Similar conclusion can be drawn when comparing C-Kmeans and Kmeans. In summary, due to both advantages of dynamic allocation and size constraints, CDMM achieves better performance compared with other methods.

4.4.2 **Clustering performance in tracking DNS users:** We would like to measure the traceability of users with respect to different activity levels. Specifically, we divide users into two groups: active users who appear more than five days in a week, and less active users otherwise. Figure 2 compares the clustering results of all eight models measured by traceability in different groups. As long as all the sessions of a user is in a cluster, this user is completely traceable. A user is perfectly traceable if all the sessions are in one cluster and the cluster does not have other users' sessions. By definition, perfect traceable rate (displayed on right) is always lower than complete traceable rate (displayed on left).

Generally, the accuracy in terms of traceability is much higher for active users than for less active users. For example, the complete traceability using CDMM-R increases from 26% to 36%, and the perfect traceability increases from 10% to 19% when users are more active.

Further, our CDMM model also gets the best results compared with other models in terms of traceable rate. If users are active on more than 5 days in a week, it is likely that the algorithm can completely identify the users at the rate of 19% with random initialization and 49% with smart initialization.

In summary, our model is very effective to trace active users. From the user perspective, in case to avoid these types of privacy threats through DNS traffic, they may try different domain name servers thus to spread activities in each domain server, or share online access with different people in a group to disguise their unique query patterns.

5 CONCLUSIONS

DNS-based behavioral analysis is extremely attractive for many applications such as forensics investigation and online advertisement. In this paper, we have proposed the constrained Dirichlet multinomial mixture (CDMM) clustering model without requiring the specification of the number of clusters and meanwhile enforcing

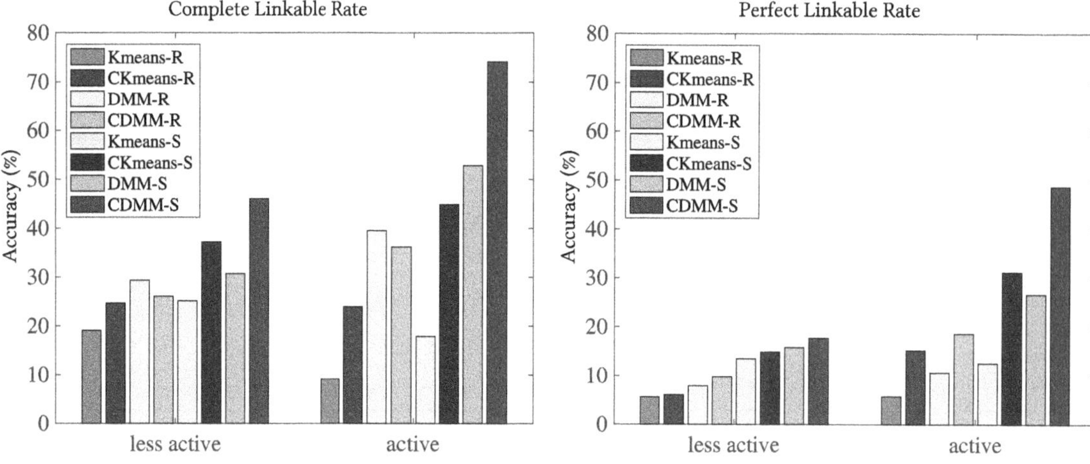

Figure 2: Clustering performance of eight methods measured by complete linkable rate (left) and perfect linkable rate (right) with respect to different user activity groups in the observation period.

the maximum number of data in each cluster, which fits the DNS tracking problems nicely. We have performed extensive evaluation based on DNS queries collected from real networks. Experimental results have demonstrated that our method accomplishes a high clustering accuracy and outperforms the existing methods.

6 ACKNOWLEDGEMENT

This work was supported in part by the Louisiana Board of Regents under Grant LEQSF(2017-20)-RD-A-29 and National Science Foundation under Grant 1560437.

REFERENCES

[1] Bin Bi, Milad Shokouhi, Michal Kosinski, and Thore Graepel. 2013. Inferring the demographics of search users: social data meets search queries. In *Proceedings of the 22nd International Conference on World Wide Web*. 131–140.

[2] Gang Chen, Haiying Zhang, and Caiming Xiong. 2016. Maximum margin Dirichlet process mixtures for clustering. In *Proceedings of the 30th AAAI Conference on Artificial Intelligence*. 1491–1497.

[3] Shuo Chen, Rui Wang, XiaoFeng Wang, and Kehuan Zhang. 2010. Side-channel leaks in web applications: a reality today, a challenge tomorrow. In *Proceedings of the 2010 IEEE Symposium on Security and Privacy*. 191–206.

[4] Mauro Conti, Luigi V Mancini, Riccardo Spolaor, and Nino Vincenzo Verde. 2015. Can't you hear me knocking: identification of user actions on Android apps via traffic analysis. In *Proceedings of the 5th ACM Conference on Data and Application Security and Privacy*. 297–304.

[5] Roberto Gonzalez, Claudio Soriente, and Nikolaos Laoutaris. 2016. User profiling in the time of HTTPS. In *Proceedings of the 2016 ACM Internet Measurement Conference*. 373–379.

[6] Xiaodan Gu, Ming Yang, Jiaxuan Fei, Zhen Ling, and Junzhou Luo. 2015. A novel behavior-based tracking attack for user identification. In *Proceedings of the Third International Conference on Advanced Cloud and Big Data*. 227–233.

[7] Jinjin Guo and Zhiguo Gong. 2016. A nonparametric model for event discovery in the geospatial-temporal space. In *Proceedings of the 25th ACM International Conference on Information and Knowledge Management*. 499–508.

[8] Dominik Herrmann, Christian Banse, and Hannes Federrath. 2013. Behavior-based tracking: exploiting characteristic patterns in DNS traffic. *Computers & Security* 39 (2013), 17–33.

[9] Sakshi Jain, Mobin Javed, and Vern Paxson. 2016. Towards mining latent client identifiers from network traffic. In *Proceedings of Privacy Enhancing Technologies Symposium*. 100–114.

[10] Dae Wook Kim and Junjie Zhang. 2015. You are how you query: deriving behavioral fingerprints from DNS traffic. In *Security and Privacy in Communication Networks*, Bhavani Thuraisingham, Xiaofeng Wang, and Vinod Yegneswaran (Eds.). Springer International Publishing, 348–366.

[11] Matthias Kirchler, Dominik Herrmann, Jens Lindemann, and Marius Kloft. 2016. Tracked without a trace: linking sessions of users by unsupervised learning of patterns in their DNS traffic. In *Proceedings of the 2016 ACM Workshop on Artificial Intelligence and Security*. 23–34.

[12] Srinivas Krishnan and Fabian Monrose. 2010. DNS prefetching and its privacy implications: When good things go bad. In *Proceedings of the Third USENIX Conference on Large-scale Exploits and Emergent Threats: Botnets, Spyware, Worms, and More*. 10–10.

[13] Marc Liberatore and Brian Neil Levine. 2006. Inferring the source of encrypted HTTP connections. In *Proceedings of the 13th ACM Conference on Computer and Communications Security*. 255–263.

[14] Takashi Matsunaka, Akira Yamada, and Ayumu Kubota. 2013. Passive OS fingerprinting by DNS traffic analysis. In *Proceedings of the IEEE 27th International Conference on Advanced Information Networking and Applications*. 243–250.

[15] David Stillwell Michal Kosinski and Thore Graepel. 2013. Private traits and attributes are predictable from digital records of human behavior. *Proceedings of the National Academy of Sciences* 110, 15 (2013), 5802–5805.

[16] Alan Mislove, Bimal Viswanath, Krishna P. Gummadi, and Peter Druschel. 2010. You are who you know: inferring user profiles in online social networks. In *Proceedings of the Third ACM International Conference on Web Search and Data Mining*. 251–260.

[17] Jeffrey Pang, Ben Greenstein, Ramakrishna Gummadi, Srinivasan Seshan, and David Wetherall. 2007. 802.11 user fingerprinting. In *Proceedings of the 13th Annual ACM International Conference on Mobile Computing and Networking*. 99–110.

[18] William M Rand. 1971. Objective criteria for the evaluation of clustering methods. *J. Amer. Statist. Assoc.* 66, 336 (1971), 846–850.

[19] Qixiang Sun, Daniel R. Simon, Yi-Min Wang, Wilf Russell, Venkata N. Padmanabhan, and Lili Qiu. 2002. Statistical identification of encrypted web browsing traffic. In *Proceedings of the 2002 IEEE Symposium on Security and Privacy*. 19–30.

[20] Charles V Wright, Lucas Ballard, Scott E Coull, Fabian Monrose, and Gerald M Masson. 2008. Spot me if you can: uncovering spoken phrases in encrypted VoIP conversations. In *Proceedings of the IEEE Symposium on Security and Privacy*. 35–49.

[21] Charles V Wright, Lucas Ballard, Fabian Monrose, and Gerald M Masson. 2007. Language identification of encrypted VoIP traffic: Alejandra y Roberto or Alice and Bob. In *Proceedings of the 16th USENIX Security Symposium*. 1–12.

[22] Jianhua Yin and Jianyong Wang. 2014. A Dirichlet multinomial mixture model-based approach for short text clustering. In *Proceedings of the 20th ACM SIGKDD International Conference on Knowledge Discovery and Data Mining*. 233–242.

[23] Fan Zhang, Wenbo He, Xue Liu, and Patrick G. Bridges. 2011. Inferring users' online activities through traffic analysis. In *Proceedings of the 4th ACM Conference on Wireless Network Security*.

[24] Elena Zheleva and Lise Getoor. 2009. To join or not to join: the illusion of privacy in social networks with mixed public and private user profiles. In *Proceedings of the 18th International Conference on World Wide Web*. 531–540.

[25] Yuan Zhong, Nicholas Jing Yuan, Wen Zhong, Fuzheng Zhang, and Xing Xie. 2015. You are where you go: inferring demographic attributes from location check-ins. In *Proceedings of the 8th ACM International Conference on Web Search and Data Mining*. 295–304.

CESAR: A Testbed Infrastructure to Evaluate the Efficiency of Wireless Automotive Software Updates

Marco Steger[‡], Carlo A. Boano[†], Kay Römer[†], Michael Karner[‡], Joachim Hillebrand[‡] and Werner Rom[‡]
[‡]Virtual Vehicle Research Center, Graz, Austria
[†]Institute for Technical Informatics, Graz University of Technology, Austria
{marco.steger, michael.karner, joachim.hillebrand, werner.rom}@v2c2.at – {cboano, roemer}@tugraz.at

ABSTRACT

Connected vehicles allow to update the software (SW) running on their integrated electronic control units (ECUs) over-the-air. Such updates are complex procedures that involve several steps, such as the authentication with a remote device, the secure and reliable wireless transfer of the new binary, as well as its installation and verification on the target ECU. Each of these aspects affects the efficiency of the *entire* SW update process, and it is important to evaluate the impact of different solutions on the functionality of a vehicle and to compare their performance on real hardware. In this paper we present CESAR, a configurable testbed infrastructure that allows to evaluate the efficiency of an automotive SW update system in a highly automated way. CESAR allows to specify different update mechanisms, security configurations, wireless protocols used for the data transfer, and to carefully define the scenario of interest (i.e., pin down the number of wireless vehicle interfaces, the network topology, and the target ECU). Furthermore, CESAR can be used to measure the efficiency of a SW update on real hardware, and to derive insights about the weaknesses of a system under test or about the interaction of a specific SW with a given ECU.

KEYWORDS

Automotive Software, IEEE 802.11s, OTA Updates, Testbeds.

1 INTRODUCTION

The ability to wirelessly connect a vehicle to the Internet, to the road infrastructure, or to other vehicles, allows vehicle manufacturers (OEMs) to provide a plethora of new safety functions, comfort features, and services. Among others, automotive OEMs have the possibility to remotely diagnose a vehicle, as well as to install new SW on the ECUs over-the-air, which allows to reduce warranty costs [12]. Besides enabling performance improvements and bug fixes without the need of expensive vehicle recalls, wireless SW updates allow OEMs to upgrade or enable new features remotely.

The use of over-the-air (OTA) SW updates is not only limited to the remote download of up-to-date SW directly by the car owners (e.g., Tesla OTA updates [4]), but can also be exploited in several other stages of a vehicle's lifetime: from the vehicle development and the manufacturing stage on the assembly line, to the maintenance in a service center [13]. In all these scenarios, the vehicle uses its wireless vehicle interface (WVI) to connect to a diagnostic tester (DT) device holding the new SW binary, authorization keys, as well as other information that is required to perform the update. The update procedure itself can be conducted using *automotive diagnostic protocols* such as Unified Diagnostic Services (UDS) [1].

Due to their potential impact, OTA updates have increasingly attracted the attention of several researchers, who started analyzing the vulnerabilities of automotive eco-systems [6], and providing solutions to orchestrate secure SW updates [14]. Among others, the research community has proposed architectures to protect a vehicle from the injection of malicious SW [9, 10], and techniques to ensure reliable (wireless) inter/intra-vehicle communication [15, 17]. Most of the existing works, however, focus only on *single aspects* of an automotive SW update and not on the *entire* update process.

Need to evaluate SW updates in their entirety. The update procedure involves multiple steps ranging from the authentication with the DT and the wireless data transfer, to the installation and verification of the new binary on the target ECU. All of these aspects are interconnected and affect the overall *efficacy* and *efficiency* of a SW update, which should be always studied in its entirety. The latter requires a deep investigation of the main aspects affecting the efficiency of a SW update, such as: i) the *wireless network topology* and the number of involved nodes, ii) the applied *security configuration*, iii) the employed *SW update mechanism*, and iv) the *target ECU* and the properties of the connection to the WVI.

Need for suitable automotive testbeds. All these aspects must be evaluated in a systematic and repeatable way on real hardware (HW) to study their inter-dependency and to show the applicability of the tested SW update system. Towards this goal, it is necessary that the testbed supports not only a number of WVIs, but also their connection to one or more ECUs using automotive standard HW and SW interfaces, as well as means to install and verify the SW running on the ECU by means of diagnostic standards.

Our contributions. In this paper we present CESAR, a Configurable testbed infrastructure that allows to evaluate the effectiveness and Efficiency of wireless automotive Software updates in an Automated and Repeatable way. CESAR allows to investigate the SW update procedure in its entirety, to emulate different SW update scenarios (e.g., SW updates in a service center or in the assembly line), and to evaluate the impact of different network as well as security configurations on the update's efficiency. The proposed testbed infrastructure can be further used to analyze different ECU types, SW update techniques (e.g., the partial transfer of firmware), and wireless communication standards (e.g., multi-hop networks).

MSWiM '17, November 21–25, 2017, Miami, FL, USA

ACM ISBN 978-1-4503-5162-1/17/11...$15.00
https://doi.org/10.1145/3127540.3127580

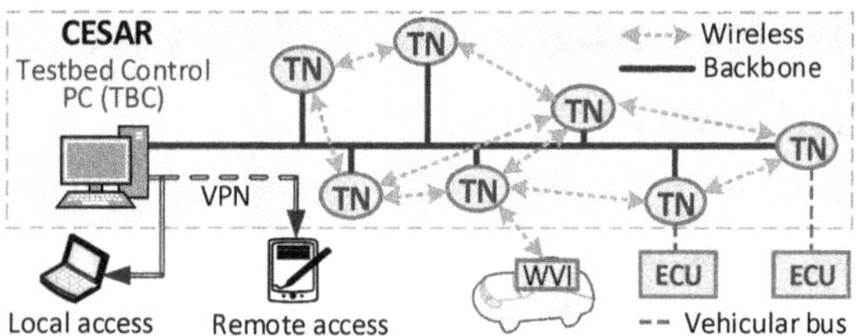

Figure 1: CESAR architecture: TNs interconnected via a backbone network allowing to connect ECUs or vehicles.

CESAR provides configuration profiles containing different node configurations (emulating different real-world scenarios), sets of parameters (e.g., key length, vehicle bus bit-rate), as well as SW update techniques. After describing its design and implementation in the next section, we show in Sect. 3 a series of case studies illustrating how CESAR can be used to evaluate the impact of different security configurations, update techniques, and network protocols on the efficiency of an automotive SW update process.

2 CESAR: DESIGN AND IMPLEMENTATION

We describe next the design and implementation of CESAR, starting from the general requirements of such a testbed infrastructure.

2.1 Testbed Requirements

A proper testbed infrastructure should support the evaluation of the *entire* automotive SW update process and allow to study the impact of different aspects on its efficiency while reducing manual intervention and allowing remote access. The employed testbed nodes must be able to support different roles (i.e., act as WVI, as DT, or as rogue node) and should be connectable to one or more ECUs from different vendors (which requires automotive HW/SW interfaces, as well as diagnostic protocols on top). Furthermore, the testbed should be able to scale up to 100 nodes while providing multiple *configuration profiles* that allow the user to choose between different network topologies and wireless communication stacks (e.g., IEEE 802.11n or 11s). These configuration profiles should include different security configurations and allow the user to choose between different security parameters, such as the authentication scheme or the key length. Ideally, also the installation effort is kept to a minimum by reusing existing network infrastructures.

2.2 Testbed Architecture

The architecture of CESAR is shown in Fig. 1: at the heart of CESAR are several testbed nodes (TNs) connected to each other wirelessly and to a testbed control PC (TBC) through a wired back-channel.

Testbed nodes. Each TN is configurable and can hence assume different roles within the testbed: it can act as a DT, WVI, relay node, or even as rogue node – a node that is compromised by an attacker. Depending on the assigned role, a TN runs a dedicated SW implementation on top of a given HW platform. The latter allows to connect a TN to an ECU using automotive bus systems (e.g., CAN or FlexRay) and easily install a new software.

ECU connection. By using automotive standards, CESAR allows to connect ECUs of different manufacturers and types, hence giving a user the ability to install SW on an ECU and to verify the success of an update procedure. In the simplest case, where different ECU SW versions periodically send CAN frames with different IDs, the verification is done on the TN acting as WVI by monitoring the CAN bus. This simple but efficient mechanism can be used for all target ECUs, even if there is no way to adapt the bootloader or flashing mechanism of the ECU. For more detailed tests, advanced features like computing the hash of the entire memory on the ECU after a SW update can be very beneficial. Therefore, we provide such features on our main target ECU, which allows CESAR to monitor the state of the ECU (via CAN) while a SW update is performed.

Configurability. CESAR provides configuration profiles allowing a simple configuration of the testbed and all its nodes. A configuration profile is a set of configuration files that can contain i) specific security and/or network configurations, ii) a certain node setting allowing to emulate specific real-world SW update scenarios, iii) a set of system parameters such as the vehicle bus bit rate or the employed authentication mechanism, and iv) specific SW update mechanisms. By utilizing the TBC, a developer can easily switch between different experimental settings and redo an experiment later by selecting this configuration profile again.

Remote monitoring. The TBC also allows other devices to access the testbed remotely. We developed a GUI that allows to monitor the state of the TNs, to set basic parameters (e.g., the wireless channel), to individually control TNs (e.g., reset TNs), and to select specific configuration profiles for planned experiments.

Prototype testing. CESAR allows to analyze the performance of different SW versions in a highly automated manner by storing and administrating all developed SW prototypes in a centralized repository. A developer can choose a specific SW version by using a specific configuration profile: prototypes are then automatically distributed to the TNs and locally configured.

SW architecture. The SW architecture of CESAR is shown in Fig. 2, and encompasses the implementations of different testbed features, the SW update system under test, and the interfaces used to interconnect the devices and the implemented prototypes. The testbed-specific SW blocks on the TBC are needed to i) (remotely) control the testbed and the running experiments, ii) retrieve specific versions of the developed DT/WVI prototypes from a GIT repository, and iii) automatically collect, pre-process and store the results of the experiments. On the TNs, testbed-specific SW blocks are required to i) assign the role of the TN, ii) locally configure the TN (e.g., vehicle bus bit-rate when connecting to an ECU), iii) enable/configure local parts of the testbed (e.g., monitoring the vehicle bus or storing debug information w.r.t. the wireless network), and iv) collect the results of an experiment and send it to the TBC.

2.3 Implementation

CESAR currently makes use of twelve TNs deployed on the ceiling of our office building, covering an area of approximately 350 m^2.

Testbed nodes. Each TN consists of a *BeagleBone Black* (BBB) board running Debian Linux and a *TL-WN722 Wi-Fi stick*, connected via USB and enabling wireless connectivity between the TNs (either IEEE 802.11n or 11s). We connect each BBB to a *custom-made PCB board* allowing the TNs to support up to two CAN connections at the same time [14]. UDS is used to perform the actual SW update procedure. Given the popularity of CAN and UDS, CESAR allows to connect a TN to almost any ECU on the market.

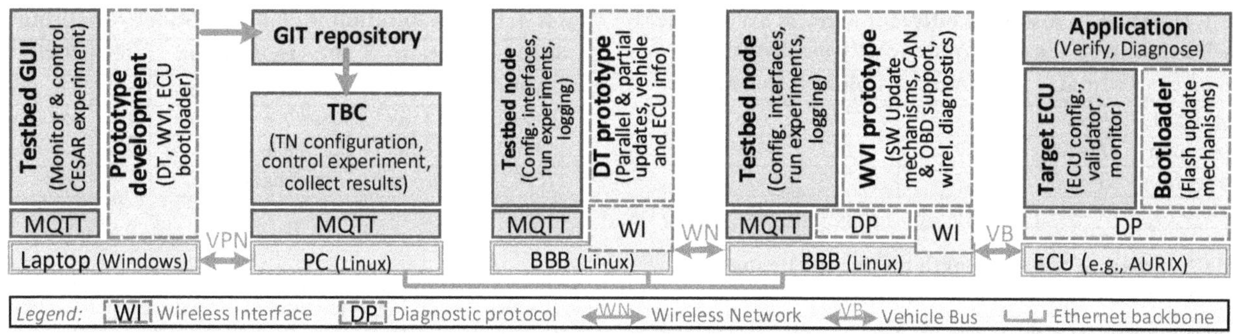

Figure 2: Software architecture. Main blocks of the testbed (green blocks, single solid line) and of the update system under test (orange blocks, dashed line). Interface are shown in blue and the employed devices using a gray block and double solid line.

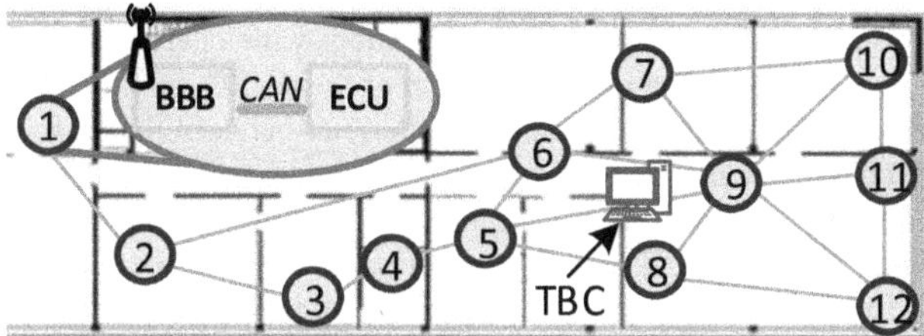

Figure 3: Position of the twelve nodes used in our testbed.

We connected the testbed nodes to two different types of ECU: the *Volvo FlexECU*, a prototype ECU used by Volvo Trucks and other automotive OEMs to test new vehicular features, and the *Infineon AURIX ECU*, a multi-core ECU used in various research and industry projects. In contrast to the Volvo FlexECU, which we had to use as black-box device without the possibility to develop our own ECU application SW, the AURIX comes with a free development tool-chain and can be powered via the I/O pins of the BBB board. This allowed us to easily connect the AURIX to the TN and to have full control on both the ECU application SW and the bootloader.

Backbone network and TBC. Each BBB board is connected to the backbone network using its Ethernet interface. To minimize the cabling effort, we exploit the existing 100 Mb/s LAN infrastructure of our office building. The TNs are decoupled from the rest of the company network infrastructure by using a dedicated subnet supporting up to 250 static IPv4 addresses. Each BBB board uses its Ethernet interface as a back-channel to communicate with the TBC. The latter is a desktop computer running Debian Linux equipped with a dual Ethernet card to connect to both the TNs and the office network infrastructure. This allows the TBC to access the Internet and other company services, such as a GIT server for source code management. To interact with the TNs, the TBC runs a Message Queue Telemetry Transport (MQTT) server. The MQTT publish-subscribe protocol allows to address all TNs at once (e.g., to start a measurement) and to configure a TN individually (e.g., assigning a specific role). Our implementation also allows to access the TBC remotely by using a VPN connection to the company network.

3 CASE STUDIES

We illustrate next a few use cases showing how CESAR can be used to study the efficiency of automotive wireless SW updates and to analyze the impact of different system configurations.

3.1 Impact of different Security Mechanisms

We first use CESAR to analyze the impact of different security mechanisms and key lengths on the duration of a SW update.

Impact of network and application layer security. We select different security configuration profiles at both application and network layer, and let CESAR automatically configure the testbed nodes with the specified security settings, while measuring the update duration and the detailed, per-step latency, using the logging ability of the DTs and the WVIs. We employ security mechanisms on the application layer implemented in SW utilizing the Java Bouncy Castle, whereas we use simultaneous authentication of equals (SAE) to protect the network layer[1]. We use the testbed deployment shown in Fig. 3 and configure node 9 to work as a DT and node 8 to act as WVI with a Volvo FlexECU connected via CAN. We choose this configuration, as it ensures a direct stable link between the DT and the WVI[2]. We perform a wireless SW update of a binary of 445 kB and measure the duration of the following steps ten times: i) Init: including WVI discovery, connection and authentication process between WVI and DT, and SW update initialization and authorization step on the ECU; ii) Upload: wireless data transfer from DT to WVI; iii) Download: data download via CAN and validation of the installed SW on the ECU.

Table 1 shows the measured overall duration and the per-step latency w.r.t. the used security mechanisms and reveals that the data transfer from the WVI to the ECU via CAN takes the largest portion: about 75% of the overall duration with all security features enabled, and up to 87% if these mechanisms are disabled. The results also expose that the security functions have a significant impact on the update duration: plus 18.5% when all mechanisms are enabled.

Impact of the key length on the update duration. We use the aforementioned experimental setup and configure CESAR to disable the security mechanisms on the network layer. Different configuration profiles are then used to evaluate the impact of the key length on the update duration. Specifically, we use different key lengths for both the RSA-based authentication and AES-based data encryption, and perform 10 sequential wireless SW updates using the AURIX ECU for each configuration. Table 2 shows the duration of a SW update depending on the employed key length: varying the key length of the RSA-based authentication has a stronger impact on the update duration than different AES encryption key lengths.

[1]For more details on the utilized security mechanisms, we refer the reader to [13].
[2]CESAR would also allow a more difficult setup with links of intermediate quality.

Table 1: Duration in ms of the different wireless SW update steps depending on the employed security mechanism.

Security	Total	Init&Auth.	Upload	Download
Appl. + Net.	49195.4	4782.3	6585.4	37817.7
Application	47167.1	4859.7	5414.2	36885.3
Network	43745.6	2277.7	3756.0	37703.3
None	41528.6	2277.9	2445.0	36797.5

Table 2: Impact of the key length on the update duration

RSA	AES	Duration	Delta
1024	128	16271.0 ± 323.4 ms	-
1024	256	16375.1 ± 222.3 ms	104.1 ms (+0,6%)
2048	128	18342.7 ± 357.4 ms	2071.7 ms (+12.7%)
2048	256	18359.1 ± 292.3 ms	2088.1 ms (+12.8%)

Table 3: Update duration w.r.t different update mechanisms.

Traditional	Parallel	Partial
20768.8 ± 882.4 ms	25881.8 ± 324.5 ms	3570.7 ± 1189.3 ms

3.2 Impact of different ECU Hardware

We illustrate CESAR's ability to support ECUs of different vendors by connecting a WVI device to both a Volvo FlexECU and an AURIX ECU via CAN (at 500 kb/s). We employ node 9 as DT and node 8 as WVI according to the testbed deployment shown in Fig. 3. As the Volvo FlexECU can only be used as a black-box, we create a dummy application for the AURIX that has the same binary size as the one available for the Volvo FlexECU (i.e., a size of 445 kB). We then run twenty wireless SW updates on each of the two ECUs, and let CESAR measure their average duration a discussed earlier.

The gathered results show that the AURIX ECU can be updated about three times faster than the Volvo FlexECU: the SW update takes indeed 20.77±0.88 and 48.68±0.81 seconds on the AURIX and the FlexECU, respectively. This is due to (i) the higher CPU power and faster storage modules of the AURIX ECU, and (ii) the fact that the FlexECU uses a two-stage update procedure encompassing a secondary bootloader and the application SW itself.

3.3 Impact of different Update Techniques

CESAR can also be used to evaluate the efficiency of different SW update mechanisms: traditional, parallel, and partial updates.

Parallel updates. We first compare the duration of the update process when using traditional SW updates sequentially with the duration of a *parallel* SW update. A parallel SW update is performed on two or more ECUs integrated in two or more vehicles at the same time. For an experiment within CESAR this means that new SW is installed on several (in this particular experiment two) ECUs at the same time by one DT (node 9). Therefore, each ECU is connected to a testbed node acting as WVI (nodes 8 and 11) and the SW update is first done sequentially (first node 8 is updated and then node 11) and then in parallel, meaning on both ECUs at the same time.

Table 3 shows that the overall duration of one parallel SW update (for two ECUs) is increased by about 25% compared to a traditional wireless SW update (for one of the ECUs). This overhead is due to the fact that not all steps of a SW update can be done in parallel. However, carrying out parallel SW updates is significantly faster (approximately 75% quicker) compared to a sequential updates.

Table 4: Update duration w.r.t. different network protocols.

802.11s duration	802.11n duration	TN	RSSI
16590.4 ± 286.1 ms	16545.0 ± 360.8 ms	6	-83 dBm
16943.0 ± 453.1 ms	16504.7 ± 238.4 ms	4	-87 dBm
16918.2 ± 518.4 ms	21274.8 ± 4632.9 ms	2	-90 dBm
17620.1 ± 1696.6 ms	Unreachable	1	>90

Partial updates. A SW update is often only changing specific parameters of an ECU, leaving most of the remaining SW untouched. For this reason, it may be advisable to only update the changed SW portion, instead of the entire binary. We compare next the duration of a traditional SW update with a custom implementation of a *partial* update in which only the portion of code that has changed is installed. We prepare two SW applications with a parameter field stored in a dedicated memory section of the AURIX ECU of size 1 kB: this parameter field is the only difference between the binaries. When utilizing a partial SW update, only this section is transferred to the ECU. Instead, when using a traditional SW update, the entire binary (of size 445 kB) needs to be transferred. The case study was performed using node 9 as DT and node 8 as WVI connected to an AURIX ECU. We performed twenty SW updates using both the traditional and the partial SW update mode.

Table 3 highlights that, as expected, the SW update duration is significantly reduced: the partial update is about six times faster. This decrease in duration of 83% is especially due to the lower amount of data transferred from the WVI to the ECU via CAN.

3.4 Impact of different Network Protocols

In this case study, we evaluate the efficiency of SW updates of two different wireless protocols: IEEE 802.11n and IEEE 802.11s. The key difference between these two protocols is the ability to build mesh networks: IEEE 802.11n is the traditional, access point based Wi-Fi protocol. Instead, IEEE 802.11s allows to form multi-hop networks increasing the reliability and availability of the entire network.

In our experimental setup illustrated in Fig. 3, we select node 11 as DT and different TNs (nodes 1, 2, 4, and 6) connected to an AURIX ECU. For the IEEE 802.11n evaluation, the DT node is also acting as wireless access point. It is important to highlight that, in this configuration, the links between 11 and the other TNs are of different quality. Furthermore, node 1 is the furthest away, and is not in the communication range of node 11. As a result, when employing IEEE 802.11n, no communication can be established between the two nodes. In contrast, when using IEEE 802.11s, the nodes can decide to hop through additional nodes to use only very good links and maximize the reliability of communications.

We then perform ten SW updates for each configuration and let CESAR measure the SW update duration (Table 4). For good links (node 4 and 6), both protocols nearly exhibit the same performance. For node 4, IEEE 802.11n, on average, is about 400 ms faster than IEEE 802.11s. The experimental results show an average path length of 1.06 hops when using IEEE 802.11s. This means that IEEE 802.11s has employed some multi-hop paths during the SW update process (due to lost packets) leading to a slightly increased packet latency. In case of intermediate links (node 2), IEEE 802.11s outperforms IEEE 802.11n by a factor of 25%.

3.5 Connectivity issues of IEEE 802.11s

CESAR can also be used to investigate the connectivity of wireless nodes and thereby, as presented in this case study, to reveal scalability issues. When configuring CESAR to use IEEE 802.11s, we observed that some TNs were not reachable by other nodes, despite being in close proximity. The observed issue is critical as typical SW update scenarios can encompass several vehicles in a dynamic environment frequently joining and leaving the network. To analyze the problem, snapshots of the connectivity in the network (i.e., link and path information) were captured using CESAR. These tests reveal two major problems of the default open11s implementation caused by its limited neighbor table size:

Inefficient network structure. In IEEE 802.11s, peer links are established between two nodes if i) the nodes can *hear* each other and ii) the nodes have a free spot in their neighbor table. Hence, the network topology of 11s is mainly influenced by the sequence of nodes joining the network (and not if a node is close or far away) and thus leads to inefficient links affecting the network performance.

Isolated node. In the worst case the limited neighbor table size (e.g., size=3) can even lead to isolated nodes: a node (e.g., node 5) willing to join an already established network, will fail to connect as the other nodes (e.g., nodes 1 to 4) already have three neighbors stored in their neighbor table. The nodes will decline the join requests and node 5 will be isolated from the network.

We solved this issue by adapting the latest open11s implementation: i) adding new messages to inform the network about isolated nodes, and ii) implementing algorithms to solve the *isolated node problem.* The adapted open11s version can be chosen and configured by CESAR besides the default open11s version.

4 RELATED WORK

In this section, we summarize the body of existing works focusing on wireless automotive SW updates and compare the functionality of existing automotive testbeds to the ones offered by CESAR.

Wireless automotive SW updates. Most of the work on automotive OTA updates has focused on security aspects and proposed security architectures protecting a vehicle from malicious updates [9, 11] or investigated remote SW updates [7, 10]. These works, however, do not consider other scenarios where updates are performed locally (such as within a service center), nor allow testing of advanced update mechanisms such as the parallel transfer of a binary. Solutions are also often evaluated only through simulation [5, 11] or formal methods [9, 10, 13], and very few systems are evaluated on real HW. In this and our previous works [8, 14], automotive ECUs are used to evaluate a SW update framework, verify the update process, and compare different update mechanisms.

Automotive testbeds. Several infrastructures have been proposed to test automotive SW updates. Drolia et al. [3] have designed a testbed consisting of several automotive ECUs interconnected by CAN. Although the testbed provides a basic SW update function, it is not capable of evaluating the entire wireless SW update process. In [16] and [2], authors have proposed Vehicle-to-Vehicle testbeds (either indoor [16] or outdoor [2]) to simulate different V2V scenarios. However, these testbed do not support automotive ECUs and cannot be used to evaluate any aspect w.r.t wireless SW updates.

5 CONCLUSIONS

In this paper we propose CESAR, a testbed infrastructure that allows to investigate the efficiency and dependability of an entire wireless automotive SW update process. After describing the testbed architecture and design, we show through a series of case studies that CESAR allows to derive insights about the impact of different security configurations, update techniques, and network protocols on the efficiency of an automotive SW update process. In the future, we plan to use CESAR to evaluate the reliability of IEEE 802.11s and to run different attacks on the SW update framework presented in [13], in order to evaluate its robustness and expose its weaknesses.

Acknowledgments. This work was partially funded by the SCOTT project. SCOTT (http://www.scott-project.eu) has received funding from the Electronic Component Systems for European Leadership Joint Undertaking under grant agreement No 737422. This joint undertaking receives support from the European Unions Horizon 2020 research and innovation programme and Austria, Spain, Finland, Ireland, Sweden, Germany, Poland, Portugal, Netherlands, Belgium, Norway. SCOTT is also funded by the Austrian Federal Ministry of Transport, Innovation and Technology (BMVIT) under the program "ICT of the Future" between May 2017 and April 2020. More information at https://iktderzukunft.at/en/. The authors also acknowledge the financial support of the COMET K2 Program of the Austrian Federal Ministries BMVIT and BMWFW, the Province of Styria, and the Styrian Business Promotion Agency (SFG).

REFERENCES

[1] ISO 14229:2006(E). 2006. ISO 14229:2006: Road vehicles – Unified diagnostic services (UDS) – Specification and requirements. (2006).
[2] M. Cesana, L. Fratta, M. Gerla, E. Giordano, and G. Pau. 2010. C-VeT the UCLA Campus Vehicular Testbed: Integration of VANET and Mesh Networks. In *Proc. of the European Wireless Conference.*
[3] U. Drolia, Z. Wang, S. Vemuri, M. Behl, and R. Mangharam. 2011. AutoPlug – An automotive test-bed for Electronic Controller Unit Testing and Verification. In *Proc. of the IEEE Intelligent Transportation Systems Conference (ITSC).*
[4] N. Gabe. 2016. Over-the-Air Updates on Varied Paths. *Automotive News* (2016).
[5] I. Hossain, S.M. Mahmud, and M.H. Hwang. 2010. Performance Evaluation of Mobile Multicast Session Initialization Techniques for Remote SW Upload in Vehicle ECUs. In *Proc. of the IEEE Vehicular Technology Conference.*
[6] K. Koscher et al. 2010. Experimental Security Analysis of a Modern Automobile. In *Proc. of the IEEE Symposium on Security and Privacy.*
[7] M. Khurram et al. 2016. Enhancing Connected Car Adoption: Security and OTA Update Framework. In *Proc. of the 3rd World Forum on Internet of Things.*
[8] M. Steger et al. 2017. An Efficient and Secure Automotive Wireless Software Update Framework. *Under submission* (2017).
[9] M.S. Idrees et al. 2011. Secure Automotive On-board Protocols: A Case of Over-the-air Firmware Updates. (2011).
[10] D.K. Nilsson and U.E. Larson. 2008. Secure Firmware Updates Over the Air in Intelligent Vehicles. *IEEE Conference on Communications* (2008).
[11] R. Petri et al. 2016. Evaluation of Lightweight TPMs for Automotive SW Updates over the Air. In *Proc. of the Conference on Embedded Security in Cars.*
[12] Redbend Software. 2011. Updating Car ECUs Over-The-Air (FOTA). (2011).
[13] M. Steger, C.A. Boano, M. Karner, J. Hillebrand, W. Rom, and K. Roemer. 2016. SecUp: Secure and Efficient Wireless Software Updates for Vehicles. In *Proc. of the Conference on Digital System Design (DSD).*
[14] M. Steger, M. Karner, J. Hillebrand, W. Rom, C.A. Boano, and K. Roemer. 2016. Generic Framework Enabling Secure and Efficient Automotive Wireless SW Updates. In *Proc. of the Conf. on Emerging Technologies and Factory Automation.*
[15] I. Studnia, V. Nicomette, E. Alata, Y. Deswarte, M. Kaâniche, and Y. Laarouchi. 2013. Survey on Security Threats and Protection Mechanisms in Embedded Automotive Networks. In *Proc. of the Conf. on Dependable Systems and Networks.*
[16] W. Vandenberghe, I. Moerman, P. Demeester, and H. Cappelle. 2011. Suitability of the wireless testbed w-iLab.t for VANET research. In *Proc. of the 18th Symposium on Communications and Vehicular Technology in the Benelux.*
[17] T.L. Willke, P. Tientrakool, and N.F. Maxemchuk. 2009. A Survey of Inter-Vehicle Communication Protocols and their Applications. *IEEE Communications Surveys & Tutorials* 11, 2 (2009).

Ensuring the Reliability of an Autonomous Vehicle: a Formal Approach based on Component Interaction Protocols

Samir Chouali
FEMTO-St Institute, University of Burgundy Franche-Comté,
Montbéliard, France
schouali@femto-st.fr

Azzedine Boukerche
PARADISE Research Lab, University of Ottawa
Ottawa, Canada
boukerch@site.uottawa.ca

Ahmed Mostefaoui*
FEMTO-St Institute, University of Burgundy Franche-Comté,
Belfort, France
amostefa@femto-st.fr

ABSTRACT

In automotive applications, several components, offering different services, can be composed in order to handle one specific task (autonomous driving for example). Nevertheless, component composition is not straightforward and is subject to the occurrence of bugs resulting from components or services incompatibilities for instance. Hence, bugs detection in component-based systems at the design level is very important, particularly, when the developed system concerns automotive applications supporting critical services. In this paper, we propose a formal approach for modeling and verifying the reliability of an autonomous vehicle system, communicating continuously with off-road infrastructure. We focus on components offering critical services with hard time constraint defining the delay of their availability. We propose to verify whether a set of components, when composed according to the system architecture specified with SysML models, achieve their tasks by respecting their interaction protocols and their time constraints.

CCS CONCEPTS

• **Computer systems organization** → *Embedded software*; *Reliability*; • **Software and its engineering** → *Formal software verification*;

KEYWORDS

Vehicular systems, component assembly, interaction protocols, critical services, time constraints, system architecture.

ACM Reference Format:

Samir Chouali, Azzedine Boukerche, and Ahmed Mostefaoui. 2017. Ensuring the Reliability of an Autonomous Vehicle: a Formal Approach based on Component Interaction Protocols. In *Proceedings of MSWiM '17, Miami, FL, USA, November 21–25, 2017,* 5 pages.
https://doi.org/10.1145/3127540.3127581

1 INTRODUCTION

Modern complex systems often comprise a network of embedded components that interact continuously with each other and with their environment, in order to offer services. These components are generally sensors and actuators, equipped with computing and communication capabilities. Such embedded components appear in diverse areas including automotive, aerospace, health-care, etc. A component is a unit of composition with contractually specified interfaces and explicit dependencies [11]. An interface describes the offered and required services without disclosing the component implementation. It constitutes the only access to the component description. The idea in component-based engineering is to develop applications not from scratch but by assembling various library components, such that the compatibility holds between their interfaces. Indeed, as embedded components are often developed by third party, they were primarily designed to be deployed in different environments. However, in some cases dysfunctions may arise in some environment, caused by incompatibility between interacting components. These dysfunctions may have disastrous consequences in critical applications like automotive ones. Here, the research challenge is to be able to detect such bugs at the design level; i.e., prior to deployment. In most cases, traditional techniques for analyzing systems based on testing and simulation are not adequate and not sufficient to ensure the reliability of the resulted component (i.e., absence of bugs).

In this paper, we propose an approach to model and to ensure formally the reliability of a Component-Based System (CBS) in automotive applications. More precisely, we study an autonomous vehicle, connected with off-road infrastructure, to transport people from one place to another. We study the assembling of both type of components: those embedded in the vehicle as well as those deployed in the infrastructure (i.e., referred to as external components) which communicate directly with the vehicle. In particular, we focus on modeling and verifying the whole system, including critical (i.e., real-time) information exchanged between the autonomous vehicle and the set of stations deployed along the trajectory. We first start with the modeling step which consists in modeling the system with SysML (Systems Modeling Language) [10] diagrams. The SysML language is an UML profile, proposed to graphically specify all aspects of a system consisting of hardware and/or software blocks. In the second step, we propose a formal specification and verification approach to verify component composition based on the SysML models. Our approach exploits and adapts the interface automata formalism to verify components composition. The interface automata based formalism was proposed by L.Alfaro and T.Henzinger [1]. They have specified component interfaces with automata, which are labeled by input, output and internal actions. These automata describe component interaction protocols, that define the order of activating component actions. The verification is based on the composition of interfaces, which is achieved by

*Dr. A. Mostefaoui is a visiting Professor at PARADISE Research Lab.

MSWiM '17, November 21–25, 2017, Miami, FL, USA

ACM ISBN 978-1-4503-5162-1/17/11...$15.00
https://doi.org/10.1145/3127540.3127581

synchronizing shared actions. Inspired from this approach, we propose to adapt the interface automata mechanism in our targeting application. This adaptation is necessary to cope with the particular features of the autonomous vehicle system: within the system, components interact with each others by offering and requiring services. However, a part of these services are critical because of the real-time constraint they exhibit, also called non-functional constraints (NF constraints). To the best of our knowledge, the originality of our proposal in comparison to state-of-art approaches, comes from the integration of critical services within components composition for autonomous vehicle.

2 THE AUTONOMOUS VEHICLE SYSTEM CASE STUDY

To illustrate and show the relevance of our approach, we present in this section the case study of an Autonomous Vehicle (AV). This latter allows to transport people, inside or outside agglomerations, in a fully autonomous manner (inspired from the case study in [12]). The AV is totally controlled by a computer unit, called Traffic Planner (TP), that drives automatically the AV by taking into account the incoming information from its embedded sensors. TP considers also the continuous interactions between the AV and the off-road stations informing the system about constraints that may occur in the vehicle trajectory. Our main concern in this case study is to ensure the reliability of the whole AV system, including the AV sub-system and the components of the off-road stations. We also focus on the embedded components system in the vehicle. So, the whole system is considered as a CBS, composed of two main components: the AV and the station. The AV is also considered as a CBS, composed of many components, that may be developed by third party. In this paper, we focus only on components involved in the autonomous vehicle driving. These components are described in the following. (i) Vehicle Core (VC), this component interacts directly with the physical components of the AV, like the direction system, the brakes, accelerator control, etc. (ii) GPS, the component that calculates the trajectory of the vehicle to reach the requested destination by the users. (iii) Traffic planner (TP), the main component which interacts simultaneously with GPS, VC and the stations. Its main role is to decide how the vehicle navigates in the trajectory generated by the GPS, by taking into account the traffic rules and the current environment of the AV.

The above mentioned components, composing the whole studied system, continuously interact between each others by offering and/or requiring services. The latter are generally resumed to send or receive information between components. These iterations define for each component its interaction protocol that is specifying the scheduling of the service executions in the component. Since components are considered as black box, their protocols are exploited to verify the component compatibility. In This paper, component protocols describe also component NF constraints related to the criticality of some component services. This criticality is about the number of time unit necessary to a component to offer a service. This requirement is important to verify the component compatibility and the whole system reliability.

3 SYSTEM MODELING WITH SYSML

This section presents the system architecture, modeled with SysML diagrams, in order to define system abstract models and consequently analyzing the interaction between components. SysML provides a structural element called a block. A block can represent any type of component of the system: physical, logical, functional or human. Blocks are declared within a Block Definition Diagram (BDD). The role of a BDD is to describe the structure of the system as a hierarchy of blocks. For example, in our case study, with a BDD, we specify that the first block in the hierarchy represents the AV whole system, which is decomposed into sub-blocks autonomous vehicle (AV) and Station, and is linked to them by the composition relationship. We specify also that the component AV is divided into three sub-components which are GPS, VC, and TP. For the lack of space, the BDD is not represented in this paper, however we show the Internal Block Diagram (IBD), of the AV system. The IBD allows the designer to refine the structural aspect of the model. In the IBD, parts are basic elements assembled to define how they collaborate to realize the block structure and/or behavior. Parts represent the physical components of the block while flow ports represent the interfaces of the block, through which it communicates with other blocks. Figure 1 shows the IBDs of the whole system and the AV component. For example, the whole system is composed of the components AV and Station. The IBD illustrates the interactions between these components through the connector *CON1* and the ports *P1* and *P2*. The connectors show the components that will be assembled together. The BDD and IBD diagrams will be exploited in Section 5.2 to define formally the order of composition between the whole system components.

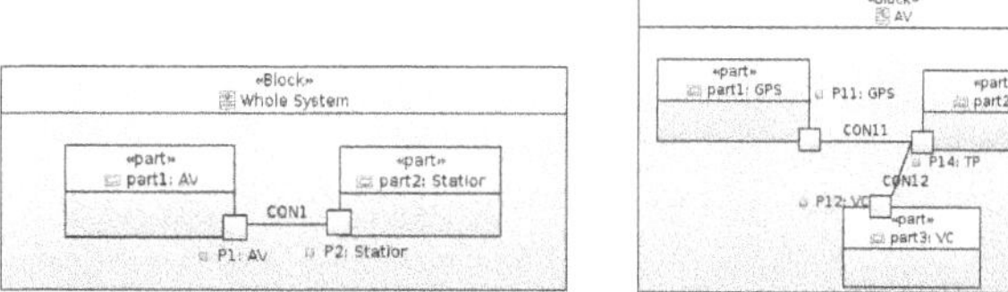

Figure 1: System Internal block diagrams

4 FORMAL MODELING OF COMPONENT INTERACTION PROTOCOLS

In order to specify formally component interaction protocols, we propose to specify each component interface with an interface automaton. This latter is considered as labeled transition system, where the transitions are labeled with the names of actions which are divided into three categories: input (represented by "?"), output (represented by "!") and hidden actions (represented by ";"). As we considered the case study, described in Section 2, we have to define the meaning of the interface automata actions with the component services. So, an input action, *ia*?, specifies a request service from another component; i.e., requesting to receive a message or data from another component. An output action, *oa*!, specifies a provided service by a component, for example by sending messages or data to another component. A hidden action, *ha*;, specifies an internal service in a component; i.e., by activating an internal component operation. We denote by $\Sigma_A^I(s)$, $\Sigma_A^O(s)$, $\Sigma_A^H(s)$ the input, output and hidden actions enabled at the state *s* respectively. As we also considered time constraints in our analysis, we show below how to exploit the interface automata formalism to take them into account; i.e.,

NF requirements of critical component services in the specification of component protocols.

Definition 4.1. (Interface Automata)
An interface automaton, A = $\langle S_A, I_A, \Sigma_A^I, \Sigma_A^O, \Sigma_A^H, \Sigma_A^C, \delta_A, \lambda_A \rangle$ consists of: a finite set S_A of states; a subset of initial states $I_A \subseteq S_A$; three disjoint sets Σ_A^I, Σ_A^O and Σ_A^H of inputs, output, and hidden actions, we denote by $\Sigma_A = \Sigma_A^I \cup \Sigma_A^O \cup \Sigma_A^H$; a set $\delta_A \subseteq S_A \times \Sigma_A \times S_A$ of transitions between states; a set of critical actions $\Sigma_A^C \subset \Sigma_A$, they define critical services which necessitate a limited number of time unit in order to be activated; $\lambda_A : \Sigma_A^C \to \mathbb{N}$ a total function that associates to each critical service the number of time units necessary to its execution, for example to send or to receive data by or from a component.

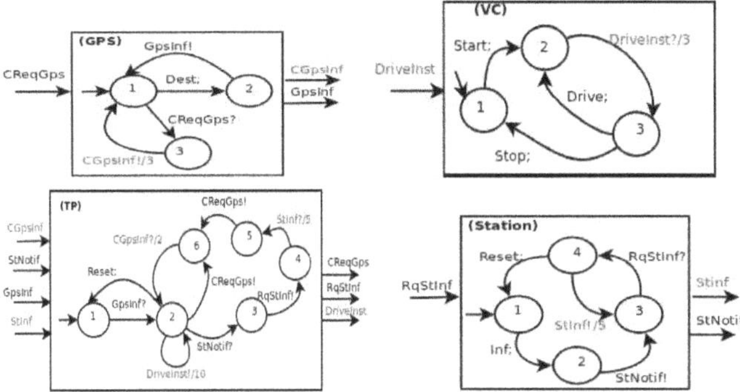

Figure 2: The interface automata of the whole system components

The interaction protocols of our system are specified by the interface automata A_{GPS}, A_{TP}, A_{VC}, and $A_{Station}$, which are described in Figure 2. For example, according to Figure 2, the services in the component VC are described in the following. (i) Required services: The critical service *DriveInst* to indicates that the vehicle is in drive mode. Therefore, the component VC needs drive instructions with the delay that does not exceeds 3 time units. (ii) Internal services: *Start*, waits to receive the internal start message, whereas *Stop* waits to receive the internal stop message. The internal service *Drive* used to send drive instructions to the physical components in the vehicle. The services in the component TP are described in the following. (i) Offered services: *CReqGps* sends a request to GPS for a critical information. *RqStInf* sends a request to Station for information about traffic. *DriveIsnt* sends critical information to give drive instruction to Vehicle Core component. (ii) Required services: *GpsInf* waits to receive information from GPS. *CGpsInf* waits to receive critical information from GPS. *StNotif* waits to receive notification from Station component for the availability of new data about traffic. *StInf* waits to receive critical information from Station component.

5 COMPONENT ASSEMBLY BASED ON COMPONENT INTERACTION PROTOCOLS

In this section, we present our approach to verify the reliability of the autonomous vehicle system. So, we ensure that if there is an incompatibility between the components that compose the whole system, it will be detected at the design level.

5.1 Component Protocols Simulation

Before proceeding with the formal verification step we present the simulation step in order to analyze the component interaction protocols by simulating the interactions of each component, separately, with its environment. So, we ensure that their protocols are consistent with their formalization with the automata and with their informal description. For that, we exploit the model checker SPIN [9], which is a popular open-source software verification tool, used for the simulation and formal verification of distributed systems. In Spin, a formal specification is built using Promela language. A Promela program is composed of a set of processes that interact through channels. So, we propose to specify components protocols with Promela by defining for each component two processes: one for the component and the other for its environment. For example, Figure 3 represents an extract of the result of the random simulation of GPS protocol performed by SPIN. This latter shows the processes GPS and its environment that interact by sending messages in communicating channels that are defined by integers. This simulation shows that the GPS component behaves correctly without any deadlock.

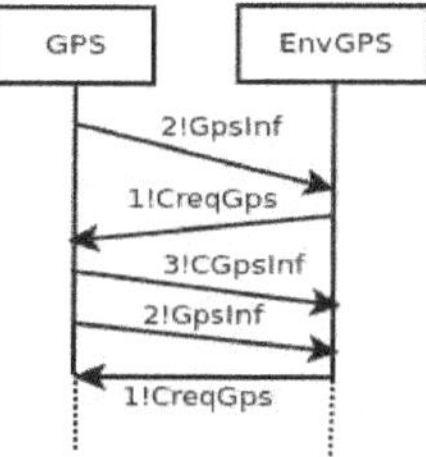

Figure 3: GPS component protocol simulation

5.2 Formal Specification of SysML System Architecture

The compatibility verification is only possible on component that interact directly: communicate through shared services. Hence, to verify the compatibility between all the components composing our system, first we have to analyze the system architecture to find components that are connected by connectors in the BDD and IBD specifications. Therefore, to perform this analysis, we need to specify formally the system architecture from the SysML diagrams, BDD and IBD. So, we propose to specify formally this architecture as a graph, such that its nodes model system blocks and its edges model links between blocks . We consider the symbol || as the composition operator. So, for example, the order of the composition associated to the whole system based on the BDD and IBD described in Figure 1 (in Section 3) is: *(GPS || TP || VC) || (Station)*.

5.3 Verification Approach

We present the formal verification approach to compose components in order to verify their compatibility. With this approach, we verify the compatibility between the component protocols, that compose the AV system, basing on their interface automata. This approach allows to detect deadlock states that might indicate incompatibility between components. Indeed, when we compose two interface automata, the resulting composite automaton, based on the synchronized product of the both automata, might contain *deadlock states* in these following situations. (i) Where one automaton issues an output action that is not acceptable as input in the other one, because this specifies the situation where two components interact and one component sends a requested information and the other component is not ready to receive it. (ii) Where one automaton issues an output action that specifies a critical service, so labeled with number of time units x. This action is acceptable as an input to the other one and labeled with y time units, such that $x > y$. This specifies the situation where two components interact, and one component offers a requested critical service (for example sends critical information) with a time constraint that does not satisfy the time constraint specified by the requested service in the other component. The existence of these deadlock states is not sufficient to decide the incompatibility between interfaces. In fact, the incompatibility holds between two components iff there is no deadlock state in their synchronized product reachable from the initial state by activating internal or output actions [1].

The verification of the compatibility between a component C_1 and another component C_2 is obtained by verifying the compatibility between their interface automata A_1 and A_2. Algorithm 1 shows the verification steps of the compatibility according to the interface automata approach.

Algorithm 1 Verification

```
Require: interface automata A1, A2
Ensure: A1 || A2
  verify that A1 and A2 are composable and compute the synchronized
    product A1 ⊗ A2 by considering critical services;
  compute the set of deadlock states in A1 ⊗ A2;
  compute the composition A1 || A2 by eliminating from the automaton
    A1 ⊗ A2, the deadlock states, and the states from which the deadlock
    states are reachable by enabling only internal and output actions.
  if A1 || A2 is empty then
    A1 and A2 are not compatible;
  else
    A1 and A2 are compatible;
  end if
```

The complexity of this algorithm which calculates the composition of two interface automata $A_1 \parallel A_2$, in order to verify their compatibility, is discussed after Definition 5.1, which defines the synchronized product $A_1 \otimes A_2$ that is necessary to calculate their composition. The composition operation may take effect only if the actions of the two automata are disjoint, except shared input and output actions between them. When we compose them, shared actions are synchronized and all the others are interleaved asynchronously. We note by $Shared(A_1,A_2) = (\Sigma^I_{A_1} \cap \Sigma^O_{A_2}) \cup (\Sigma^I_{A_2} \cap \Sigma^O_{A_1})$ the set of shared actions between A_1 and A_2. These shared actions define the set of services by which the components interact. For example in our case study the component VC (Vehicle Core) requires a service *DriveInst* (Drive Instructions) from the component TP (Traffic planner), so *DriveInst* is a shared service (action).

In the following we present the definition of synchronized product between two interface automata taking into account the time constraints on critical services. The intuition behind the following definition is: two components synchronize on shared services and on critical shared services that have a compatibility in their time constraints.

Definition 5.1. (Synchronized product with critical services) Let A_1 and A_2 be two composable interface automata. The product $A_1 \otimes A_2$ is defined by $\langle S_{A_1 \otimes A_2}, I_{A_1 \otimes A_2}, \Sigma^I_{A_1 \otimes A_2}, \Sigma^O_{A_1 \otimes A_2}, \Sigma^H_{A_1 \otimes A_2}, \Sigma^C_{A_1 \otimes A_2}, \delta_{A_1 \otimes A_2}, \lambda_{A_1 \otimes A_2} \rangle$ such that: $S_{A_1 \otimes A_2} = S_{A_1} \times S_{A_2}$ and $I_{A_1 \otimes A_2} = I_{A_1} \times I_{A_2}$; $\Sigma^I_{A_1 \otimes A_2} = (\Sigma^I_{A_1} \cup \Sigma^I_{A_2}) \setminus Shared(A_1,A_2)$; $\Sigma^O_{A_1 \otimes A_2} = (\Sigma^O_{A_1} \cup \Sigma^O_{A_2}) \setminus Shared(A_1,A_2)$; $\Sigma^H_{A_1 \otimes A_2} = \Sigma^H_{A_1} \cup \Sigma^H_{A_2} \cup Shared(A_1,A_2)$; $\Sigma^C_{A_1 \otimes A_2} = \Sigma^C_{A_1} \cup \Sigma^C_{A_2} \setminus Shared(A_1,A_2)$; $((s_1,s_2),a,(s'_1,s'_2)) \in \delta_{A_1 \otimes A_2}$ iff: (1) $a \notin Shared(A_1,A_2) \wedge (s_1,a,s'_1) \in \delta_{A_1} \wedge s_2 = s'_2$. (2) $a \notin Shared(A_1,A_2) \wedge (s_2,a,s'_2) \in \delta_{A_2} \wedge s_1 = s'_1$. (3) $a \in Shared(A_1,A_2) \wedge (s_1,a,s'_1) \in \delta_{A_1} \wedge (s_2,a,s'_2) \in \delta_{A_2} \wedge((\lambda_{A_1}(a) \geq \lambda_{A_2}(a) \wedge a \in \Sigma^I_{A_1}(s_1) \wedge a \in \Sigma^O_{A_2}(s'_1)) \vee (\lambda_{A_1}(a) \leq \lambda_{A_2}(a) \wedge a \in \Sigma^O_{A_1}(s_1) \wedge a \in \Sigma^I_{A_2}(s'_1)))$. $\lambda_{A_1 \otimes A_2} : \Sigma^C_{A_1 \otimes A_2} \rightarrow \mathbb{N}$, to define $\lambda_{A_1 \otimes A_2}$ we consider the following cases: (i) $\lambda_{A_1 \otimes A_2}(a) = \lambda_{A_1}(a)$ if $a \notin Shared(A_1,A_2) \wedge (a \in \Sigma^I_{A_1} \vee a \in \Sigma^O_{A_1} \vee a \in \Sigma^H_{A_1})$; (ii) $\lambda_{A_1 \otimes A_2}(a) = \lambda_{A_2}(a)$ if $a \notin Shared(A_1,A_2) \wedge (a \in \Sigma^I_{A_2} \vee a \in \Sigma^O_{A_2} \vee a \in \Sigma^H_{A_2})$; (iii) $\lambda_{A_1 \otimes A_2}(a) = min(\lambda_{A_1}(a), \lambda_{A_2}(a))$ if $a \in Shared(A_1,A_2) \wedge ((a \in \Sigma^I_{A_1} \wedge a \in \Sigma^0_{A_2}) \vee (a \in \Sigma^O_{A_1} \wedge a \in \Sigma^I_{A_2}))$ [1].

The complexity for computing the composition $A_1 \parallel A_2$ is in time linear on $|A_1|$ and $|A_2|$.

5.4 Illustration on the Autonomous Vehicle System

To ensure the reliability of our autonomous vehicle system, we have to verify the compatibility between the interaction protocols of its components. And, regarding to the AV system architecture, specified formally in Section 5.2 and to the order of composition obtained from this specification, we have first to verify the compatibility between the interacting components in the composite AV; i.e., verifying the compatibility between VC, TP and GPS (calculate the composition $GPS||TP||VC$). Second, if the compatibility holds in AV, we have to verify the compatibility between AV and the component $Station$. So, first we choose to calculate the composition, $GPS||TP$, then, the obtained result will be composed with VC. To calculate the composition between the components GPS and TP, we follow the steps of the algorithm presented previously. In Figure 4, we show only some paths of the interface automaton corresponding the synchronized product ($GPS \otimes TP$), for the convenience of the presentation. In fact, it is sufficient to analyze only these paths, and presenting the entire automaton which is huge does not bring more interesting details. Hence, Figure 4 shows a path in $GPS \otimes TP$ defined by the transitions: 11 *Dest*; 21, 21 *GpsInf*; 12, 12 *CReqGps*; 36. This path contains a deadlock state, 36, caused by a mismatch between the shared output critical action in GPS, $CGpsInf!/3$ with the number of time unit 3, upper to 2, the number of time units corresponding to the input action in TP, $CGpsInf?/2$. The consequences of this deadlock path is the incompatibility between the components GPS and TP which prevents to built the whole system.

6 RELATED WORKS

In this section, we briefly discuss the relationships between our work and existing works about the modeling and the verification of components-based systems with NF constraints, and also the formal verification in the automotive field.

[1] min is a function which returns a minimum value between two natural numbers.

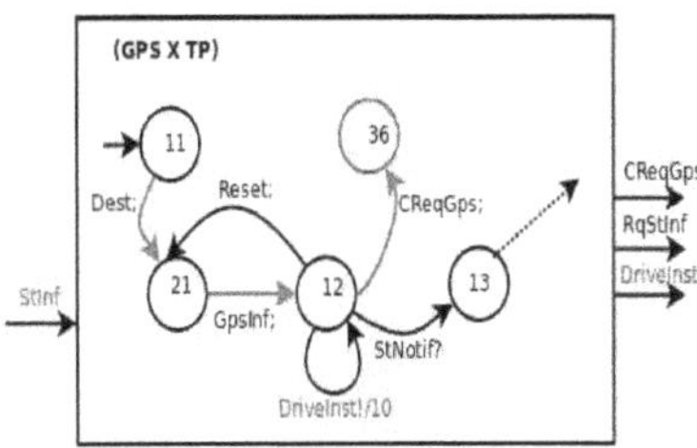

Figure 4: Illustration of the paths in $GPS \otimes TP$

Numerous studies have been conducted around the reliability in the component-based systems, and particularly in the analysis, modeling and management of NF properties in components assembly. In [7], the authors proposed a theory that describes how component developers can design and test their components to produce measurements that are later used by system designers to calculate composite system reliability. The reliability issue is also studied in [2], where the authors proposed an approach, based on a rich definition language, for determining the reliability of component-based software architectures. In [8], the authors proposed assume-guarantee interface algebra for real-time components. In the interface specification, they considered the following properties: an arrival rate function and a latency for each task sequence, and a capacity function for the shared resource. The interface specifies that the component guarantees certain task latencies depending on assumptions about task arrival rates and allocated resource capacities. These properties are considered in the verification of interface compatibility. This approach treats NF properties in component composition but the architecture of the whole system is not considered. In [4], the authors proposed resource interfaces to specify component interfaces with requirements on limited resources. This approach allows verifying if a collection of components when put together exceed the available resources. These interfaces communicate with the environment with input and output variables, which decorate automata states, however in our case the communication is performed only with input and output actions. In [6], the authors proposed an extension of the interface automata approach to capture in addition to component protocols, the timing dimension of component interfaces. Timed interface is encoded as a timed game between input and output players. A verification algorithm for interfaces compatibility was also proposed. A close formalism to timed interfaces was proposed in [5], were the authors define a complete specification framework for real time systems based on timed Input/Output automata formalism. This approach support refinement, consistency checking, and composition. The difference with our approach is, in our case we treat a kind of NF properties that are hard time constraints related to critical services in automotive field, and these constraints necessitate only to exploit lightweight weighted automata (associate a cost to transitions), however in [6], and [5] they exploit complex weighted timed automata: costs associated to transitions and valued states with clock variables in [5], and valued states with clock variables in [6]. Which increases the complexity of the verification of components composition. In our approach we have also to respect SysML diagrams where state variables are not allowed in the description of components, but only the order of actions and their time constraints. Consequently, our formalism is more lightweight and enough expressive for our needs.

In the transport field and particularly in the automotive one, some papers treats the question of the formal verification. In [12], an approach, was proposed, to design and to verify formally properties on an autonomous vehicle system, with the Model-Checking verification approach. In the railway field, the authors in [3] proposed an approach to integrate the verification of RAM (Reliability, Availability, Maintainability) requirements in Model-Driven development of railway applications. The main difference with our proposition is the context of component-based systems which is not considered in the last cited approaches in the transport field.

7 CONCLUSION AND FUTURE WORK

In the context of an automotive application with critical time constraints, we have presented in this paper an approach which combines formal and semi-formal formalism to compose safely components. This approach is based on the component interaction protocols that specify the order of services execution and cope with critical time constraints on a part of component services. So, our approach allows to verify whether a set of components, when composed according to the system architecture, specified with SysML, achieve their tasks by respecting their time constraints related to critical services. It is applied on the case study of an autonomous vehicle system which allows to transport safely people from a place to another. As a future work, we plan to implement the proposed approach in order to evaluate it on a more realistic case study in cooperation with our vehicles manufacturer partners.

REFERENCES

[1] L. Alfaro and T. A. Henzinger. 2001. Interface Automata. In *9th Annual Symposium on Foundations of Software Engineering, FSE*. ACM Press, 109–120.

[2] R. Reussner an H. Schmidt and I. Poernomo. 2003. Reliability Prediction for Component-based Software Architectures. *Journal of Systems and Software* 65, 3 (2003).

[3] S. Bernardi, F. Flammini, S. Marrone, N. Mazzocca, J. Merseguer, R. Nardone, and V. Vittorini. 2013. Enabling the usage of UML in the verification of railway systems: The DAM-rail approach. *Reliability Engineering System Safety* 120 (2013), 112 – 126. https://doi.org/10.1016/j.ress.2013.06.032

[4] Arindam Chakrabarti, Luca de Alfaro, Thomas A. Henzinger, and Mariëlle Stoelinga. 2003. Resource Interfaces. In *EMSOFT*. 117–133.

[5] Alexandre David, Kim G. Larsen, Axel Legay, Ulrik Nyman, and Andrzej Wasowski. 2010. Timed I/O automata: a complete specification theory for real-time systems.. In *HSCC'10*. 91–100.

[6] Luca de Alfaro, Thomas A. Henzinger, and Mariëlle Stoelinga. 2002. Timed Interfaces. In *EMSOFT*. 108–122.

[7] D. Hamlet, D. Mason, and D. Woit. 2001. Theory of Software Reliability Based on Components. In *Proceedings of in ICSE 2001. IEEE Computer, 2001.*

[8] Thomas A. Henzinger. 2006. An interface algebra for real-time components. In *In Proc. of IEEE Real-Time Technology and Applications Symposium*. Society Press, 253–263.

[9] Gerard J. Holzmann. 1997. The Model Checker SPIN. *Software Engineering, IEEE Transactions on* 23 (May 1997), 279–295. Issue 5.

[10] Object Management Group. 2015. *OMG Systems Modeling Language Specification (SysML), version 1.4*. http://www.omg.org/spec/SysML/1.4/.

[11] C. Szyperski. 1999. *Component Software*. ACM Press, Addison-Wesley.

[12] Tichakorn Wongpiromsarn. 2010. *Formal Methods for Design and Verification of Embedded Control Systems: Application to an Autonomous Vehicle*. Ph.D. Dissertation. California Institute of Technology.

Attraction-Area Based Geo-Clustering for LTE Vehicular CrowdSensing Data Offloading

Douglas F. S. Nunes
University of Sao Paulo, Brazil
douglas@usp.br

Edson S. Moreira
University of Sao Paulo, Brazil
edson@icmc.usp.br

Bruno Y. L. Kimura
Federal University of Sao Paulo, Brazil
bruno.kimura@unifesp.br

Nishanth Sastry
King's College London, UK
nishanth.sastry@kcl.ac.uk

Toktam Mahmoodi
King's College London, UK
toktam.mahmoodi@kcl.ac.uk

ABSTRACT

Vehicular CrowdSensing (VCS) is an emerging solution designed to remotely collect data from smart vehicles. It enables a dynamic and large-scale phenomena monitoring just by exploring the variety of technologies which have been embedded in modern cars. However, VCS applications might generate a huge amount of data traffic between vehicles and the remote monitoring center, which tends to overload the LTE networks. In this paper, we describe and analyze a gEo-clUstering approaCh for Lte vehIcular crowDsEnsing dAta offloadiNg (EUCLIDEAN). It takes advantage of opportunistic vehicle-to-vehicle (V2V) communications to support the VCS data upload process, preserving, as much as possible, the cellular network resources. In general, it is shown from the presented results that our proposal is a feasible and an effective scheme to reduce up to 92.98 % of the global demand for LTE transmissions while performing vehicle-based sensing tasks in urban areas. The most encouraging results were perceived mainly under high-density conditions (i.e., above 125 vehicles/km^2), where our solution provides the best benefits in terms of cellular network data offloading.

CCS CONCEPTS

• **Networks → Network protocol design; Mobile networks;**

KEYWORDS

LTE Data Offloading, Vehicular CrowdSensing, VANET

1 INTRODUCTION

The variety of technologies which have been incorporated in modern vehicles is bestowing them the ability to act as amazing Mobile Sensor Platforms (MSP) [14]. Apart from having an increasing number of sensors, these devices are also being equipped with a greater computing power and different wireless communication interfaces. With such features, this generation of connected vehicles is representing a wide dynamic sensing opportunity to build innovative Intelligent Transportation Systems (ITSs) and a fruitful terrain for developing Vehicular CrowdSensing (VCS) solutions towards the Smart City (SC) [11] era. VCS [14] is one of the most emerging and promising schemes designed to remotely collect data (e.g., fuel consumption, GPS position, engine status and speed) from smart vehicles. It allows for the deployment of powerful monitoring systems just by exploring the technologies embedded in MSPs [6].

Using their native wireless communication capabilities, vehicles can make their on-board data available directly to other local vehicles through Vehicle-to-Vehicle (V2V) ad hoc transmissions, or to the Internet via Vehicle-to-Infrastructure (V2I) transmissions. Such an infrastructure might be twofold: (*i*) computational stations placed alongside the roads, namely Road Side Units (RSUs), which are IEEE 802.11p [10] access points envisioned to assist vehicular communication processes; and (*ii*) LTE radio base stations from cellular networks deployed around. When employing local ad hoc transmissions to exchange data, the smart vehicles get into a specific network formation called Vehicular Ad hoc Network (VANET) [15]. Such kind of network is considered a key component to support the building of ITSs and VCS's systems.

Under high-density condition in big cities, the VCS applications might generate a huge amount of traffic between vehicles and monitoring center, tending to overload the network. Once the data upload is usually accomplished via LTE, massive amounts of transmissions can considerably degrade the Quality of Services (QoS) it offers [5]. To deal with this issue, we drew a gEo-clUstering approaCh for Lte vehIcular crowDsEnsing dAta offloadiNg (EUCLIDEAN). EUCLIDEAN is focused on exploring opportunistic V2V communications as a strategy to relieve LTE uplink during VCS data acquisition. The two major contributions of this paper are as follows: (*a*) to evaluate the potential reduction of transmissions over cellular network when V2V is additionally used to support the data upload process; and (*b*) to provide a vehicle geo-clustering formation strategy in order to decrease the overall demand for LTE resources in VCS.

The remainder of this paper is organized as follows: Section 2 reviews the main related works; Section 3 describes our proposal; Section 4 goes into finer details with respect to performed simulations; the experimental results are discussed in Section 5; and, finally, Section 6 provides our conclusions and future works.

2 RELATED WORKS

VCS is a compelling mean to deploy monitoring applications in highly dynamic scenarios. This explains why this paradigm has

MSWiM'17, November 21–25, 2017, Miami, FL, USA

ACM ISBN 978-1-4503-5162-1/17/11...$15.00
https://doi.org/10.1145/3127540.3127576

gained evidence in recent scientific research involving vehicular sensing. In line with our proposal, we segmented some of the ITS and VCS related works in two main groups.

The first one is represented by investigations focused on clustering vehicles in a centralized or decentralized fashion [3, 4, 12]. According to [8] cluster-based networking can be considered an attractive solution to provide spatial reuse of the bandwidth, to reduce network congestion, and to simplify message routing or data fusion methods. The cluster formation process reported by the works belonging to this group usually involves several steps and transmissions of additional packets to (*i*) ensure that the created cluster is the best formation; to (*ii*) ensure that the current cluster formation is consistent and updated; and to (*iii*) guarantee the election and eventual changes of cluster heads. These cluster formation and maintenance messages may incur in an extra and considerable overhead to the VANET, since the vehicles have a high dynamic mobility pattern. To avoid those additional packets, we designed a new geographic clustering approach where the vehicles are able to create clusters and to select their respective cluster heads in a straightforward manner.

The second group brings together studies on provisioning LTE offloading techniques to drain VCS data over alternative networks [5, 12, 13]. The performance results shown by these works demonstrate that the transmissions over cellular radio access system can be drastically reduced when VANET and LTE technologies are combined to support VCS tasks. Our proposal is aligned with the above-mentioned researching, insofar as it integrates some features of those approaches while it extends and creates others for addressing LTE network overload issues. In the majority of the works centered on cellular network offloading, RSUs are fixed on the environment in order to directly collect sensing information from vehicles or/and to forward them to the Internet via a high-speed link. However, deploying these infrastructures in large scale can be infeasible due to its high cost. We are not considering RSUs in our opportunistic LTE offloading scheme. To relieve the cellular network in crowded conditions, with a high volume of VCS data implied, we explore V2V communications to gather *in situ* sensing information and to reduce the number of LTE transmissions needed for uploading those data to the monitoring center.

3 EUCLIDEAN

The following definitions are used throughout this Section to support the explanation of our proposal:

Definition 1 (Region of Interest). *Region of Interest* (ROI) is a well-defined geographical area (e.g., a portion of a city) whose correlated information is relevant to the sensing applications.

Definition 2 (Attraction Area). In this paper, *Attraction Area* is a logical, circular, and stationary geographic region within an ROI whose centroid is the point where it's expected to find an LTE relay.

Definition 3 (Geo-Cluster). A *Geo-Cluster* is a grouping of vehicles created within an *Attraction Area* so that they can cooperate amongst one another and exchange their data.

For an illustrative setting, let's consider an urban-like area and a VCS system which is focused on acquiring data about the road traffic itself, via en route vehicles monitoring. Traffic management authorities, drivers or even passengers are the potential stakeholders. In this scenario, we assume that all vehicles are equipped with an On-Board Unit (OBU), a Global Positioning System (GPS) receiver, an LTE cellular network interface, an IEEE 802.11p short-range wireless communication interface, and some built-in machine information sensors. We also assume that the VCS system encompasses a client application version, named as `VCS_TClientApp`, which is deployed on each OBU, and a corresponding server application version, named as `VCS_TServerApp`, which is hosted on a cloud server environment, here called *monitoring center*.

Before starting a data collection, the acquiring task properties need to be configured by the `VCS_TServerApp`. This process consists of assigning values to parameters, such as *data sample collection frequency, data report frequency, sensing area, kind of data required,* and *target vehicles*. After that, an instance of the task will be sent out to each desired vehicle roaming in the ROI. Once it has been received by a target vehicle, the `VCS_TClientApp` will collect the required on-board data and then, under certain predefined conditions (e.g., a time window or a buffer threshold), it will report (upload) them to the `VCS_TServerApp`. This upload operation is depicted in the Fig. 1, where the data are acquired using only V2I LTE transmissions. This is the main approach adopted by the majority of applications which employ the VCS [13].

When a large number of vehicles is considered to perform VCS tasks (e.g., in big cities), a huge amount of data is expected to require LTE uplink resources in order to traverse the network towards the monitoring center. Since those LTE resources are finite, this condition tends to significantly degrade the QoS that this infrastructure offers. Under exceptional circumstances, the LTE network might even break down. It means that the paradigm illustrated by Fig. 1 does not scale well in very crowded environments. Therefore, in an attempt to reduce this negative impact, we are proposing a strategy to save LTE uplink resources by means of the use of opportunistic V2V communications in addition to the traditional approach presented by Fig. 1. A pictorial representation of our scheme can be seen in Fig. 2. Instead of each vehicle uploading its own data directly to the `VCS_TServerApp`, they will send them to a local subset of vehicles which will be in charge of doing that. The proposed approach, named as EUCLIDEAN, operates over two novel algorithms particularly designed for this purpose: (*i*) Stationary Attraction Areas Allocation's Algorithm; and (*ii*) Attraction Area-based Clustering Protocol.

3.1 Stationary Attraction Areas Allocation Algorithm (S4A)

Finding a subset of vehicles that will be considered LTE relays in VCS systems is not a trivial procedure. Once the sensing is usually performed inside an ROI, defining which vehicles will be selected as LTE relays involves considering where they are located as well. Meeting these two requirements is a challenge, mainly because the VANETs topologies change all the time. Moreover, spreading relays uniformly within the ROI is relevant to guarantee that all vehicles will be able to take advantage of the use of V2V communications to upload their VCS data, thus increasing the potential of saving LTE uplink resources. For this end, we are proposing an effective

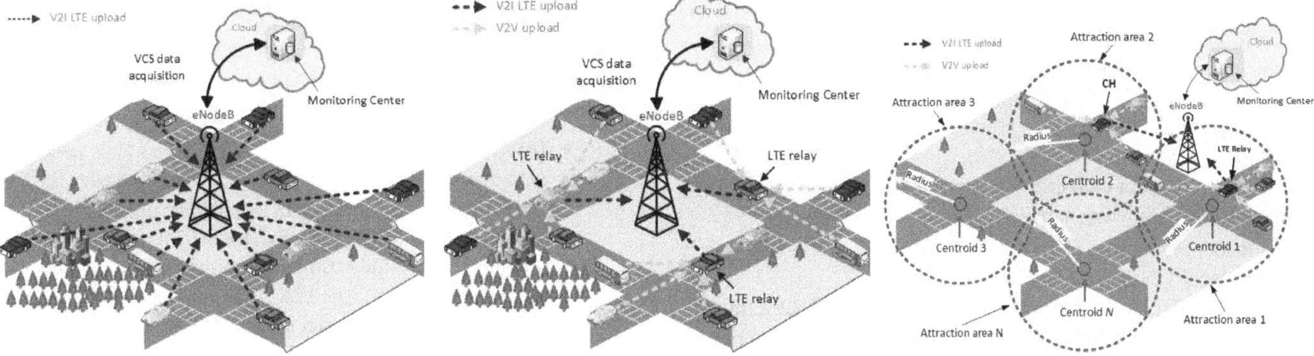

Figure 1: uploading using only V2I. **Figure 2: uploading using V2V and V2I.** **Figure 3: EUCLIDEAN representation.**

method based on the concept of logical *attraction area* (See Definition 2). All vehicles inside an attraction area will send their data to a corresponding LTE relay via V2V transmissions, and then it will report that information to the `VCS_TServerApp` using V2I LTE transmissions, as represented by "Attraction area 1" in Fig. 3.

Whereas a single LTE relay is expected for each attraction area, we defined a *radius* for it with the same value of the V2V wireless transmission technology range used by vehicles (i.e., according to the IEEE 802.11p interface properties). Thus, if an LTE relay is located just above a given centroid, it will be able to communicate with all other vehicles inside that related attraction area. This assumption is relevant because the attraction area amplitude in EUCLIDEAN implies directly in the number of LTE relays selected.

To geo-locate the attraction areas, the S4A first maps all the coordinates of the boundaries of the ROI. Next, it starts to place their centroids side-by-side along the x and y-axis, until the whole ROI is covered. The attraction areas may be totally disjoint among them or they can be distributed in such a way that a given portion of them are overlapped, e.g., they are slightly overlapped in Fig. 3. Therefore, we must provide the allocation algorithm with the bordering coordinates of the ROI and the desired distance amongst the centroids. The S4A was designed to automate the process of determining how much attraction areas will be needed and where they should be placed. It is carried out on the server side, i.e., by the `VCS_TServerApp`, before spreading out the VCS tasks. Performing the S4A on the server side allows the `VCS_TServerApp` to rearrange all the attraction areas at any time. After this step, a list of the attraction area centroid coordinates as well as the assumed *radius* will be sent to the `VCS_TClientApps` along with the VCS tasks themselves. Each vehicle will keep these data stored in its local database, for they are imperative to support the geo-clustering formation.

3.2 Attraction Area-based Clustering Protocol (AACP)

In view of the clustering advantages introduced in Section 2 are relevant to the VCS domain, we considered building ephemeral geo-clusters (See Definition 2) of vehicles in our approach. With this grouping formation, the VCS applications can decrease the number of LTE data transmissions needed to perform their sensing tasks. In the AACP, each geo-cluster has associated with it a set of vehicles named Cluster Members (CMs) and a representative one called Cluster Head (CH). The CH is a vehicle timely selected to be responsible for reporting VCS data to the monitoring center on behalf of its one-hop neighbors. In this sense, only CHs are expected to use LTE resources and not all vehicles inside the ROI. Hereafter, the term CH will be used to refer to LTE relay mentioned in the last subsection.

In order to create a geo-cluster, the vehicles make use of: (i) their GPS coordinates; (ii) the GPS coordinates of their neighbors; (iii) the coordinates of the centroids; and (iv) the *radius* of the attraction areas. The own GPS coordinates are obtained from the onboard GPS receiver, the neighbors' GPS coordinates are known via *beaconing* services[1] used by vehicles, and the last two parameters are provided by the `VCS_TServerApp`, as previously mentioned.

Each vehicle $v_i, \forall v \in \mathcal{V}$, keeps a local database with the list of centroids mapped to that ROI, denoted by C, and an updated table with the ID and the current GPS coordinates of all its neighbors, denoted by $\mathcal{N}$. With those data, a vehicle is able to find its nearest centroid, set the geo-cluster it belongs to, and select its corresponding CH in a distributed and straightforward way. The nearest centroid is discovered by means of the Euclidean distance between the vehicle and centroid,

$$d(v_i, c_j) = \sqrt{(v_{ix} - c_{jx})^2 + (v_{iy} - c_{jy})^2}, \tag{1}$$

where, $\{v_{ix}, v_{iy}\}$ and $\{c_{jx}, c_{jy}\}$ are the GPS coordinates mapped into the Cartesian coordinates of the vehicle v and the centroid c, respectively. The nearest centroid to the vehicle v_i will be that $c_j, \forall c \in C$, with the shortest distance $d_{\min} = \min\{d_1(v_i, c_j), \ldots, d_n(v_i, c_j)\}$. As the AACP assumes that all vehicles roaming up to *radius* meters far from a centroid will belong to the same geo-cluster, by knowing the nearest c_j as well as the current position of its neighbors $\mathcal{N}$, a vehicle v_i becomes conscious of its geo-cluster formation. However, a CH still needs to be defined. A vehicle v_i will be considered a CH of its geo-cluster if it has the shortest distance $d_{\min}$, among its neighbors $\mathcal{N}$, to the corresponding centroid c_j (See *Attraction area* 2 in Fig. 3). When knowing the coordinates and IDs of its neighbors, a vehicle can calculate by itself the distances of each CM to the

[1]We assume that all OBUs periodically broadcast their identity (ID) and GPS location in special packets denoted *beacons*, with the aim of making the vehicles aware of all its neighbors in quasi real time.

nearest centroid. Thus, all vehicles belonging to a geo-cluster are able to identify their respective CH in a distributed way, at any time, without the need to exchange additional messages for this. If CHs move away from their centroids, due to their mobility, new CHs might be selected, once all vehicles inside a geo-cluster are able to become CHs.

During the data collection process, every vehicle periodically performs the following steps:

(s_1) Read the required on-board data samples and insert them into its local `VCS_message_buffer`.

(s_2) Check if it is the current CH. If so, it will send the data samples stored in the `VCS_message_buffer` directly to the remote `VCS_TServerApp`. Otherwise, it will send all data samples to its CH. After receiving an *ack* message from the CH, the vehicle will discard from its buffer those samples that were uploaded via V2V. This latter ad hoc data exchange process employs only single-hop transmissions.

(s_3) Start a timer to the next reading. Once the timer expires (timeout), go back to the step (s_1).

4 SIMULATION DESIGN

4.1 Simulation Setup

In order to evaluate the performance of EUCLIDEAN, we created some experiments using a suite of state-of-art simulation tools. The first one was the OMNeT++ [1], an extensible, modular, and component-based C++ framework to support network simulations. The SUMO [2] was employed to model our urban-like scenario and to model our vehicular transport system. Lastly, we made use of VEINS LTE [9] to couple the network models provided by OMNET++ with the vehicular traffic models provided by SUMO. A summary of the main network and scenario simulation inputs used by our experiments are shown in Table 1 .

Table 1: Simulation Parameters and Values

Parameter	Value
V2V Packet format	WAVE short message
V2V beaconing Frequency	1 Hz
V2V transmission range	500 m
VANET MAC, PHY technology	IEEE 802.11p
802.11p Radio Propagation Model	Simple path loss model
VCS data report Interval	30 s
Simulation duration time	300 s
LTE transport layer Protocol	UDP
LTE MAC Queue size	2 MB
Scenario area	$\approx 4\,\text{km}^2$ (1990 m × 2150 m)
Vehicles densities	[1, 500] vehicles
Maximum vehicles' speed	70 km/h

So that we could reproduce a realistic urban-like scenario, we decided to use a $\approx 4\,\text{km}^2$ portion of the Bologna city [7]. In our experiments, the densities of the vehicles change over time assuming values from 1 to 500; also, the maximum speed reached by them was 70 km/h. The cellular network services are provided by one LTE micro-cell antenna (eNobeB), placed in a central position of the scenario, in such a way it can cover the entire area.

4.2 Performance Metrics

To assist our analysis as well as to demonstrate the potential of our proposal to reduce VCS data transmission over LTE network, we defined the following performance metrics:

- **Total LTE Packets Transmitted (TLPT)**: it is measured by the sum of all VCS data packets transmitted over the LTE network throughout the data acquisition process;
- **Samples per LTE Transmission (SLT)**: this metric is calculated by using the ratio between the number of VCS data samples received by the `VCS_TServerApp` and the number of LTE transmissions used to report those data; and
- **Average Upload Delay (AUD)**: it is measured by the remote `VCS_TServerApp`, computing the average time elapsed between the instant of time when the VCS data were sampled inside the vehicles and the instant of time when they reached the `VCS_TServerApp`.

The simulations were performed using multiple runs, with different seed values. We plotted average results whose confidence intervals were calculated with the significance level of 0.05, i.e., assuming 95 % of confidence level.

4.3 Experimental Methodology

For our experiments, it was considered the illustrative scenario previously presented by Section 3. We implemented an instance of the `VCS_TServerApp` which spreads VCS tasks to acquire and report the current GPS coordinates and the current speed of the vehicles every 30 s (this means that both *data sample collection frequency* and *data report frequency* were set to 30 s). The whole Bologna's scenario was assumed to be the ROI. To assist the geo-cluster formation, all vehicles periodically (by 1 Hz) broadcast a `HELLO` packet, via beaconing service, containing its ID and its current geographical coordinates. Different vehicle densities (1, 10, 50, 100, 300, 500) and three distinct attraction area centroids' distances (500, 700, 1000) were taken into account by simulations: 500 m for heavily overlapped attraction areas; 700 m for slightly overlapped ones; and 1000 m for totally disjoint ones. The labels "V2V and V2I-500", "V2V and V2I-700", and "V2V and V2I-1000" are used in the next figures for referring to the distances of 500 m, 700 m, and 1000 m, respectively, among centroids. The performance of our LTE offloading strategy was evaluated from individuals' perspectives, mostly comparing it with the traditional pure V2I LTE approach.

5 PERFORMANCE ANALYSIS OF SIMULATION RESULTS

5.1 Traffic reduction from the LTE offloading strategy

Firstly, we were interested in knowing the potential reduction in the number of transmissions over cellular network when V2V communications were also considered in the VCS data upload. The results presented in Fig. 4 show a substantial decreasing in higher density conditions and with slightly overlapped geo-clusters. In this setting, our strategy was able to spend only 7.02 % of the total LTE transmissions used by the pure V2I LTE scheme to report all data samples.

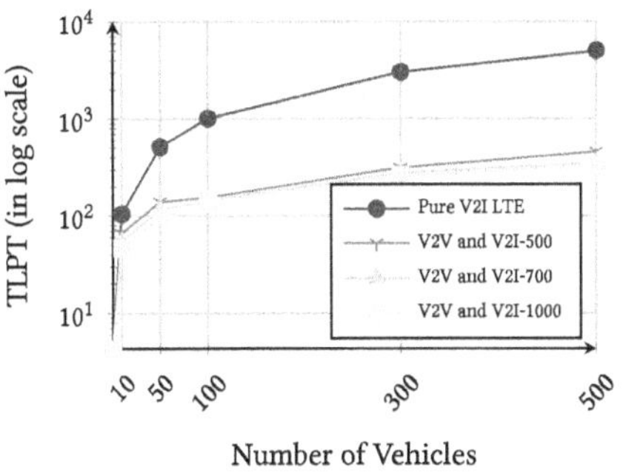

Figure 4: TLPT vs. Number of Vehicles.

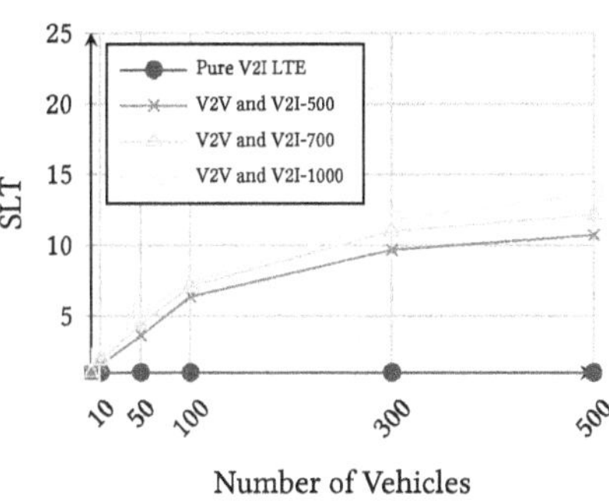

Figure 5: SLT vs. Number of Vehicles.

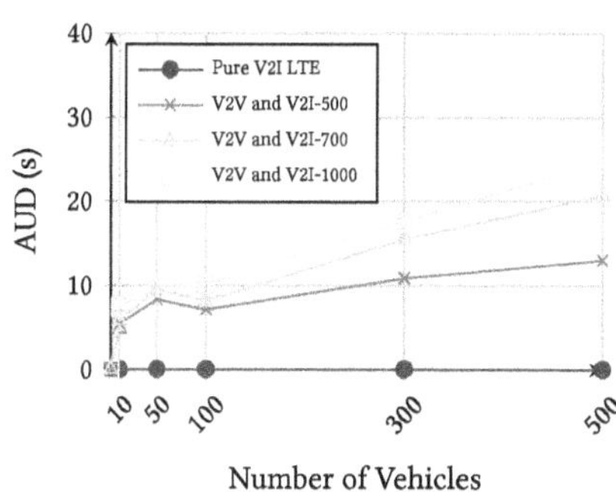

Figure 6: AUD vs. Number of Vehicles.

5.2 The Impact of Cluster Allocation

We were also interested in understanding how the variations in the clusters allocation process would impact in the upload stage. According to the results depicted in Fig. 5, as expected, the ratio of samples sent to the `VCS_TServerApp` per V2I LTE transmission tends to follow the increase of the vehicles' densities. However, the ratio is relatively reduced when the allocation of heavily overlapping geo-clusters is adopted. Since more CHs are present in this setting, the volume of samples carried by each one is smaller. Besides that, the presence of more CHs in the scenario tends to increase the data upload frequency, reducing not only the SLT, but the AUD as well (Fig. 5 and Fig. 6).

From the results of Fig. 5 and Fig. 6, we can observe a close relation between the LTE packet payload length, translated into the SLT metric, and their average upload delays. The higher the SLT, the higher the AUD tends to be. The AUD in the geo-cluster approach is also affected by the time the samples remain stored in the `VCS_message_buffers`. When a sample generated by CMs arrives in the CH just after it reported its buffered messages, this sample will be held by the CH until the next report event is triggered. It is important to point out here that, according to the application requirement, the delays can be reduced by means of mechanisms which periodically check the oldest samples in the buffer. If it exceeds a boundary, the CH may anticipate the data upload process. Comparing the results depicted in Fig. 5 and Fig. 6 we can realize that to obtain smaller end-to-end delays in VCS, it is relevant to consider using EUCLIDEAN with heavily overlapped geo-clusters formation. On the other hand, if the intention is to reduce, as much as possible, the number of LTE transmission, we need to increase the number of samples inside a LTE packet. This requirement can be satisfied by using EUCLIDEAN with slightly overlapped geo-cluster formation or totally disjoint geo-cluster formation, since their results were somewhat similar in higher densities conditions.

6 CONCLUSION

This paper describes and analyzes the EUCLIDEAN: a geo-clustering approach for LTE VCS data offloading. The proposed scheme was designed in such a way that the traffic overhead gets shifted from the cellular network to the ad hoc inter-vehicles level. According to our simulation results, up to 92.98 % of vehicles were able to report their samples without transmitting them directly to the monitoring center. The most encouraging results were perceived mainly under high-density conditions (i.e., above 125 vehicles/km^2. Future steps will consider deepening the research in cellular offloading techniques. This includes: (*i*) incorporating data fusion methods to our approach; and (*ii*) exploiting offloading in LTE downlink as well.

ACKNOWLEDGMENTS

The authors are thankful to the IFSULDEMINAS, ICMC-USP, and São Paulo Research Foundation - FAPESP (grants #2013/07375-0 and #2015/18808-0) for supporting this work.

REFERENCES

[1] 2017. OMNeT++, a Discrete Event Simulator. (apr 2017). https://omnetpp.org/
[2] 2017. SUMO, Simulation of Urban MObility. (apr 2017). http://sumo.dlr.de/
[3] Hamid Reza Arkian, Reza Ebrahimi Atani, Atefe Pourkhalili, and Saman Kamali. 2014. Cluster-based traffic information generalization in Vehicular Ad-hoc Networks. *Vehicular Communications* 1, 4 (2014), 197 – 207.
[4] M. Azizian, S. Cherkaoui, and A. S. Hafid. 2016. A distributed D-hop cluster formation for VANET. In *2016 IEEE Wireless Communications and Networking Conference*. 1–6. https://doi.org/10.1109/WCNC.2016.7564925
[5] A. Bazzi, B. M. Masini, and G. Pasolini. 2012. V2V and V2R for cellular resources saving in vehicular applications. In *2012 IEEE Wireless Communications and Networking Conference (WCNC)*. 3199–3203.
[6] Alessandro Bazzi and Alberto Zanella. 2016. Position Based Routing in Crowd Sensing Vehicular Networks. *Ad Hoc Netw.* 36, P2 (Jan. 2016), 409–424.
[7] Laura Bieker, Daniel Krajzewicz, AntonioPio Morra, Carlo Michelacci, and Fabio Cartolano. 2015. *Traffic Simulation for All: A Real World Traffic Scenario from the City of Bologna*. Springer International Publishing, Cham, 47–60.
[8] Andrea Gorrieri, Marco MartalÃš, Stefano Busanelli, and Gianluigi Ferrari. 2016. Clustering and sensing with decentralized detection in vehicular ad hoc networks. *Ad Hoc Networks* 36, Part 2 (2016), 450 – 464.
[9] Florian Hagenauer, Falko Dressler, and Christoph Sommer. 2014. A Simulator for Heterogeneous Vehicular Networks. In *6th IEEE Vehicular Networking Conference (VNC 2014), Poster Session*. IEEE, Paderborn, Germany, 185–186. https://doi.org/10.1109/VNC.2014.7013339
[10] D. Jiang and L. Delgrossi. 2008. IEEE 802.11p: Towards an International Standard for Wireless Access in Vehicular Environments. In *VTC Spring 2008 - IEEE Vehicular Technology Conference*. 2036–2040.
[11] C. Kyriazopoulou. 2015. Smart city technologies and architectures: A literature review. In *2015 International Conference on Smart Cities and Green ICT Systems (SMARTGREENS)*. 1–12.
[12] P. Salvo, I. Turcanu, F. Cuomo, A. Baiocchi, and I. Rubin. 2016. LTE floating car data application off-loading via VANET driven clustering formation. In *2016 12th Annual Conference on Wireless On-demand Network Systems and Services (WONS)*. 1–8.
[13] R. Stanica, M. Fiore, and F. Malandrino. 2013. Offloading Floating Car Data. In *2013 IEEE 14th International Symposium on "A World of Wireless, Mobile and Multimedia Networks" (WoWMoM)*. 1–9. https://doi.org/10.1109/WoWMoM.2013.6583391
[14] Julian Timpner and Lars Wolf. 2016. Query-response Geocast for Vehicular Crowd Sensing. *Ad Hoc Netw.* 36, P2 (Jan. 2016), 435–449.
[15] Yu Wang and Fan Li. 2009. *Vehicular Ad Hoc Networks*. Springer London, London, 503–525.

Author Index

www.ingramcontent.com/pod-product-compliance
Lightning Source LLC
Chambersburg PA
CBHW080917220326
41598CB00034B/5604

9781450357210